Auditing & Assurance Services

Timothy J. Louwers, PhD, CPA, CISA, CFF

Professor Emeritus
James Madison University

Penelope L. Bagley, PhD, CPA

Department Chair and
Kenneth E. Peacock Distinguished Professor
Appalachian State University

Allen D. Blay, PhD, CPA

Department Chair and
EY Professor of Accounting
Florida State University

Jerry R. Strawser, PhD, CPA

KPMG Chair and Professor of Accounting
Texas A&M University

Jay C. Thibodeau, PhD, CPA

Rae D. Anderson Professor of Accounting
Bentley University

Mc
Graw
Hill

AUDITING & ASSURANCE SERVICES, NINTH EDITION

1 2 3 4 5 6 7 8 9 LWI 28 27 26 25 24 23

ISBN 978-1-266-79685-2 (bound edition)
MHID 1-266-79685-1 (bound edition)
ISBN 978-1-266-84710-3 (loose-leaf edition)
MHID 1-266-84710-3 (loose-leaf edition)

Associate Portfolio Manager: *Stephanie DeRosa*
Product Development Manager: *Michele Janicek*
Product Developer: *Sarah Wood*
Marketing Manager: *Lindsay Wolf Smith*
Content Project Managers: *Mary E. Powers (core), Tammy Juran (assessment)*
Manufacturing Project Manager: *Rachel Hirschfield*
Content Licensing Specialist: *Beth Cray*
Cover Image: *paul kline/E+/Getty Images*
Compositor: *Straive*

Library of Congress Cataloging-in-Publication Data

Names: Louwers, Timothy J., author. | Blay, Allen D., 1970- author. |
 Strawser, Jerry R., author. | Thibodeau, Jay C., author.
Title: Auditing & assurance services / Timothy J. Louwers, Penelope L.
 Bagley, Allen D. Blay, Jerry R. Strawser, Jay C. Thibodeau.
Other titles: Auditing and assurance services
Description: Ninth Edition. | New York: McGraw Hill LLC, [2023] | Revised edition of the authors'
 Auditing & assurance services, 2021. | Summary: "As auditors, we are trained to investigate beyond
 appearances to determine the underlying facts-in other words, to look beneath the surface. From the
 Enron and WorldCom scandals of the early 2000s to the financial crisis of 2007-2008 to present-day
 issues and challenges related to significant estimation uncertainty, understanding the auditor's
 responsibility related to fraud, maintaining a clear perspective, probing for details, and understanding
 the big picture are indispensable to effective auditing. With the availability of greater levels of
 qualitative and quantitative information ("Big Data"), the need for technical skills and challenges facing
 today's auditor is greater than ever. The Louwers, Bagley, Blay, Strawser, and Thibodeau team has
 dedicated years of experience in the auditing field to this new edition of Auditing & Assurance Services,
 supplying the necessary investigative tools for future auditors"– Provided by publisher.
Identifiers: LCCN 2022039639 (print) | LCCN 2022039640 (ebook) |
 ISBN 9781266796852 (hardcover) | ISBN 9781266847929 (ebook)
Subjects: LCSH: Auditing.
Classification: LCC HF5667.A815 2023 (print) | LCC HF5667 (ebook) |
 DDC 657/.45–dc23/eng/20220915
LC record available at https://lccn.loc.gov/2022039639
LC ebook record available at https://lccn.loc.gov/2022039640

mheducation.com/highered

Some people come into our lives and quickly go. Some stay awhile and leave footprints on our hearts and we are never quite the same.

Anonymous

We dedicate this book to the following educators whose footprints we try to follow:

Professor Homer Bates
(University of North Florida)

Professor Stanley Biggs
(University of Connecticut)

Professor Lewis C. Buller
(Indiana State University)

Professor Patrick Delaney
(Northern Illinois University)

Professor William Hillison
(Florida State University)

Professor John Ivancevich
(University of Houston)

Professor Richard Kochanek
(University of Connecticut)

Professor John L. "Jack" Kramer
(University of Florida)

Professor Jack Robertson
(University of Texas at Austin)

Professor Robert Strawser
(Texas A&M University)

Professor Sally Webber
(Northern Illinois University)

Professor "IBM Jim" Whitney
(The Citadel)

Meet the Authors

Courtesy of James Madison
University

Timothy J. Louwers *is Professor Emeritus at James Madison University.*

Professor Louwers received his undergraduate and master's degrees from The Citadel and his PhD from Florida State University. Prior to beginning his academic career, he worked in public accounting with KPMG, specializing in financial, governmental, and information systems auditing. He is a certified public accountant (South Carolina and Virginia) and a certified information systems auditor. He is also certified in financial forensics.

Professor Louwers's research interests include auditors' reporting decisions and ethical issues in the accounting profession. He has authored or coauthored more than 60 publications on a wide range of accounting, auditing, and technology-related topics, including articles in the *Journal of Accounting Research, Accounting Horizons,* the *Journal of Business Ethics, Behavioral Research in Accounting, Decision Sciences,* the *Journal of Forensic Accounting, Issues in Accounting Education,* the *Journal of Accountancy,* the *CPA Journal,* and *Today's CPA.* Some of his published work has been reprinted in Russian and Chinese. He is a respected lecturer on auditing and technology-related issues and has received teaching excellence awards from the University of Houston and Louisiana State University. He has appeared on both local and national television news broadcasts, including MSNBC and CNN news programs.

Courtesy of Appalachian
State University

Penelope L. Bagley *is the Department Chairperson and the Kenneth E. Peacock Distinguished Professor.*

Professor Bagley received her undergraduate and master's degrees from North Carolina State University and her PhD from the University of Georgia. Prior to obtaining her PhD, Professor Bagley worked for a short time in the audit field. She is a certified public accountant in North Carolina. Professor Bagley teaches both undergraduate and graduate auditing courses. She has authored and coauthored publications on accounting and auditing topics in journals such as *Auditing: A Journal of Practice & Theory, Accounting Horizons,* and *Behavioral Research in Accounting.* She has also coauthored auditing cases, published in *Issues in Accounting Education.* Professor Bagley is active in the American Accounting Association and has served on various committees for the Auditing Section. Professor Bagley likes to spend time with her husband Matt and children, Garrett and Julianne. She enjoys exercising in her spare time, she regularly competes in running and triathlon races. Her crowning athletic achievement was qualifying for and running the 2019 Boston Marathon.

Courtesy of Kallen M. Lunt

Allen D. Blay *is the Department Chair and EY Professor of Accounting at Florida State University.*

Professor Blay completed his PhD at the University of Florida in 2000. He teaches auditing at all levels and teaches a seminar in auditing research in the doctoral program. His research interests relate to auditor judgment and decision making. Professor Blay has authored or coauthored publications on a wide range of accounting and auditing topics in journals such as *The Accounting Review, Contemporary Accounting Research, Auditing: A Journal of Practice and Theory, Organizational Behavior and Human Decision Processes,* the *Journal of Business Ethics, Behavioral Research in Accounting, Issues in Accounting Education,* the *International Journal of Auditing,* and the *Journal of Accounting, Auditing, and Finance.* He is currently an editor for *Issues in Accounting Education* and serves on several editorial boards.

Professor Blay has been active in the American Accounting Association and is 2022–23 president of the Auditing Section. He also cochaired the 2020 Auditing Section Mid-year Meeting and served on the steering committee for the Intensive Data and Analytics Summer Workshop each year since its inception, as well as in many other roles over the years. He is also active in the American Institute of CPAs, serving in various volunteer roles relating to the Uniform CPA Exam. Prior to entering academics, Professor Blay worked in public accounting auditing financial institutions. He currently is chair of the accounting department at Florida State University.

Courtesy of Michael Kellett
for Mays Business School

Jerry R. Strawser   *is Associate Dean for Graduate Programs at Mays Business School at Texas A&M University and holds the KPMG Chair in Accounting.*

Prior to his current appointment, Professor Strawser served as executive vice president and chief financial officer at Texas A&M University, dean of Mays Business School at Texas A&M University, interim executive vice president and provost at Texas A&M University, interim dean of the C. T. Bauer College of Business at the University of Houston, and Arthur Andersen & Co. Alumni Professor of Accounting.

Professor Strawser has coauthored three textbooks and more than 60 journal articles. In addition to his academic experience, he had prior public accounting experience at two Big Four accounting firms. He has also developed and delivered numerous executive development programs to organizations such as AT&T, Centerpoint Energy, Continental Airlines, ConocoPhillips, Halliburton, KBR, KPMG, Minute Maid, PricewaterhouseCoopers, McDermott International, Shell, Southwest Bank of Texas, and the Texas Society of Certified Public Accountants. Professor Strawser is a certified public accountant in the state of Texas and earned his BBA and PhD in accounting from Texas A&M University.

Courtesy of Bentley
University

Jay C. Thibodeau   *is the Rae D. Anderson Professor of Accounting and Director of PhD Programs at Bentley University.*

Professor Thibodeau is a former auditor and a CPA. He received his BS degree from the University of Connecticut in 1987 and his PhD from the University of Connecticut in 1996. He has conducted executive education programs for numerous leading firms including Fidelity Investments, KPMG, PricewaterhouseCoopers, Stryker, and Bluecoat Technologies.

He is a coauthor of two books, *Auditing and Assurance Services* and *Auditing and Accounting Cases: Investigating Issues of Fraud and Professional Ethics*. In addition, he has written over 60 articles and book chapters for academics and practitioners and has published in journals such as *Auditing: A Journal of Practice & Theory, Journal of Information Systems, Accounting Horizons* and *Issues in Accounting Education.*

Professor Thibodeau served as the president of the Auditing Section of the American Accounting Association for the 2014/2015 academic year. He has also received national recognition for his work seven times. First, for his thesis, winning the 1996 Outstanding Doctoral Dissertation Award presented by the ABO section of the AAA. Four other times, for curriculum innovation, winning the 2001 Joint AICPA/AAA Collaboration Award, the 2003 Innovation in Assurance Education Award, the 2016 Forensic Accounting Teaching Innovation Award, and the 2019 Innovation in Assurance Education Award. Once, for outstanding service, receiving a Special Service Award from the Auditing Section for his work in helping to create the Center for Audit Quality's Access to Auditors program. And, finally, for research excellence, winning the 2020 Glen McLaughlin Prize for Research in Accounting and Ethics given by the University of Oklahoma.

Look Beneath the Surface. . .

As auditors, we are trained to investigate beyond appearances to determine the underlying facts—in other words, to *look beneath the surface.* Whether evaluating the Enron and World-Com scandals of the early 2000s, the financial crisis of 2007–2008, the Wirecard fraud in 2020 or present-day issues and challenges related to significant estimation uncertainty, understanding the auditor's responsibility related to fraud, maintaining a clear perspective, probing for details, and understanding the big picture are indispensable to effective auditing.

With the availability of greater levels of qualitative and quantitative information ("**Big Data**"), the need for technical skills and challenges facing today's auditor is greater than ever. The Louwers, Bagley, Blay, Strawser, and Thibodeau team has dedicated years of experience in the auditing field to this new edition of *Auditing & Assurance Services,* supplying the necessary investigative tools for future auditors.

Cutting-Edge Coverage

The ninth edition of *Auditing & Assurance Services* continues its tradition as the most up-to-date auditing text on the market. All chapters and modules have been revised to incorporate

- The **latest professional standards, recodifications,** and **proposals** from the **International Auditing and Assurance Standards Board, Auditing Standards Board,** and **Public Company Accounting Oversight Board.**
- A list of the relevant professional standards that are covered in that chapter, including comprehensive coverage of the **new PCAOB standards on auditing estimates.**

Data Analytics

One trend has emerged as a potential sea change in the financial statement auditing process: **the data and analytics challenge.**

We believe students should be prepared to make the best use possible of relevant data using state-of-the-art analytical tools. In fact, the terms big data and data and analytics are frequently being used to describe a growing movement among audit professionals. As the AICPA moves to add data and analytics onto the Uniform CPA Examination, our collective view is that students must be able to not only meet current requirements, but be ahead of the game.

To prepare students, the ninth edition of *Auditing & Assurance Services* has been revised deliberately to help students critically think about the use of **increased data and analytical tools** in the financial statement audit. In addition to changes within the main chapters of the book, we have added

- **A new comprehensive example of data and analytics in auditing included in Module G,** which follows the AICPA Guide to Data Analytics and covers the entire thought process of an auditor.
- **Updated data to Author-Created Cases** and **Exercises** (as part of **Data Analytics Module**) that cover the majority of uses of data analytics in the financial statement audit, along with **extensive solutions** to help instructors implement the materials in their classroom.

It is our belief that students should be trained in the process of data and analytics and learn to think critically about situations they may face in an audit. We believe that the knowledge students attain should be software independent, particularly since software technology changes so rapidly. However, we also believe that it is important for students to become familiar with at least one specific data and analytic software tool, and recent AACSB standards echo this belief. Thus, an important goal of the ninth edition is to provide a clear and implementable method to fully integrate a leading data analysis tool, the **IDEA Data Analysis** software, into the auditing class. *Many of our exercises, however, can be implemented using whatever technology an instructor chooses to use, like Excel or Alteryx.*

We believe that IDEA provides an outstanding platform to illustrate the steps that auditors need to take related to data and data analysis while completing the financial statement audit. Leading auditing professionals have confirmed that using IDEA is an outstanding way for entry-level auditing professionals to begin the journey into the world of big data and data analytics. Simply stated, big data is manifested in the financial statement auditing process through the use of tools like IDEA.

Overall, our revisions related to the big data challenge were designed to provide instructors a set of tools and mechanisms to bring data and analytics into the classroom in a meaningful way. Through the use of these tools, students can be sure they are prepared to enter practice with an appreciation for and knowledge of the increasing importance of data and analytics in the auditing profession.

Perhaps most importantly, the ninth edition of *Auditing & Assurance Services* also continues to be the most up-to-date auditing text on the market. All chapters and modules have been revised to **incorporate the latest updates from the international standards of auditing** (ISAs), the **Auditing Standards Board** (ASB), and the **Public Company Accounting Oversight Board** (PCAOB). With *Auditing & Assurance Services,* ninth edition, students are prepared to take on auditing's latest challenges.

The Louwers author team uses a conversational, yet professional tone—hailed by reviewers as a key strength of the book.

Flexible Organization

Auditing & Assurance Services teaches students auditing concepts by emphasizing real-life contexts when describing the auditing process. The authors use chapters and modules to

> *"The format allows you to integrate the modules into the chapter material in any way you would find useful."*
> —Frank J. Beil, *University of Minnesota*

Chapters	**Modules**
The 12 chapters cover the auditing process extensively with a multitude of cases designed to give students a better understanding of how a best-practice concept developed from real-world situations.	Modules A–I provide instructors additional material that can be used throughout the course. Topics such as fraud, ethics, sampling, technology and the integrated audit are covered in the modules, which are designed to be taught whenever instructors want to introduce the topic in their course.

achieve this goal. Although the chapters follow a logical sequence that we recommend professors consider for their classes, **the modules have been written to be used on a stand-alone basis.** In essence, the modules have been deliberately prepared for entirely flexible implementation of these topics without excessive reliance on chapter sequencing. We encourage you to integrate these modules into your syllabi in a manner that best suits your approach to the auditing course.

An additional feature that provides instructor flexibility is an alternate chapter (with a full complement of supplemental and ancillary materials) that focuses on the PCAOB audit report for issuers. In addition, PCAOB versions of report examples and summary exhibits and end of chapter materials have been prepared to accompany the AICPA reporting chapter. This provides instructors with three options to teach audit reporting:

1. Focus exclusively on the AICPA report (text copy)
2. Focus on the AICPA report while introducing differences between the AICPA report and PCAOB report (text copy and summary materials available on Connect)
3. Focus exclusively on the PCAOB report (alternate chapter available on Connect)

Engage Your Students with Real Examples

An effective accounting textbook integrates real-world scenarios with theoretical discussion. *Auditing & Assurance Services* places the student in the role of a decision maker by illustrating the application of auditing concepts using actual situations experienced by accounting firms and companies such as

- Each chapter or module opens with a "real-world" example that draws upon concepts discussed within that chapter or module.
- A series of mini-cases and Updated Classroom Cases available on the Instructor Resource Center have been developed for use by instructors to further bring text material to life. These resources feature real situations experienced by companies, individuals, or accounting firms and are updated by the authors to include both timeless classics such as Arthur Andersen's failure to detect fraud at Enron to more recent situations such as the Wirecard fraud and PCAOB inspections of audits conducted for Chinese companies listed on U.S. exchanges.

Updated Classroom Cases

The author-prepared *Updated Classroom* Cases provides students and instructors with a brief overview of "real-time" auditing issues, along with references to suggested readings and guidelines for incorporating the content into the classroom. Previous items have featured the KPMG "Steal the Exam" issue related to PCAOB inspections and the 2018 ban of PwC for audits of companies listed on the India Stock Exchange. We have added cases that address recent issues and developments in the accounting and auditing profession, such as the Theranos fraud, Wirecard fraud, Luckin Coffee fraud, and PCAOB inspections of audits conducted for Chinese companies listed on U.S. exchanges. New items are added as events develop and are available in *Connect*.

Fraud Awareness

The fraud coverage in *Auditing & Assurance Services* is extensive and is complemented by real-world examples chosen to engage students through the following tools:

- Auditing Insights integrated throughout the text.
- Mini-cases and Updated Classroom cases that may be assigned to supplement text chapters and modules that expose students to landmark fraud cases including Enron, Satyam Computer Services, and Luckin Coffee.
- Specific discussion of management fraud (Chapter 4), employee fraud (Chapter 6), and the Certified Fraud Examiner Exam (Module D).

Create a State-of-the-Art Learning Environment: Instructor Resources

The author team and McGraw Hill are dedicated to providing instructors with the best teaching resources available. In addition to the solutions manual, test bank, PowerPoint Presentations, and the Apollo Shoe Case, the following resources are also available.

The Updated Auditor

The author team scrutinizes leading business and academic publications for relevant issues and research that sheds light on auditing and the audit process. Recent findings from academic research and discussions from professional literature are drawn from the following publications:

- *Accounting Horizons,*
- Accounting Today,
- Auditing: A Journal of Practice & Theory,
- Behavioral Research in Accounting,
- Bloomberg Businessweek,
- CFO.com,
- CPA Journal,
- Journal of Accountancy,
- Journal of Accounting and Economics,
- The Accounting Review,
- The Wall Street Journal,

These excerpts are highlighted throughout the text as Auditing Insights to allow for easy identification and review by instructors and students.

In addition to the use of Auditing Insights, on a monthly basis, the author team provides an *Updated Auditor* briefing, which summarizes the content of relevant business and academic publications on a chapter-by-chapter basis, to allow students to apply current developments in the profession with material discussed in class. The *Updated Auditor* briefing is available in Connect. With the *Updated Auditor,* instructors will always be at the cutting edge of auditing practice!

Caseware
IDEA

IDEA Software and Workbook

With the availability of unprecedented amounts of quantitative and qualitative information and tools available to access and process that information, it is imperative that students learn and utilize the latest technologies used by auditing professionals. As previously stated, McGraw Hill Education has forged a partnership with Caseware Analytics for the use of the IDEA data analysis tool. Chapters 3 (audit planning), 4 (risk assessment), 5 (internal control), 7–9 (operating cycle chapters), both modules on sampling (Modules E and F), and the new data and analytics module (Module G) have been revised to reference the use of IDEA within the chapter or module.

In addition, the ninth edition includes end-of-chapter exercises utilizing **author-developed databases** exclusively for use with *Auditing & Assurance Services* as well as supplemental materials available in Connect to complement the IDEA workbook and provide hands-on instructions on using the IDEA software. The authors also provide

- Implementation guidance to instructors.
- Robust video walk-throughs.
- Detailed solutions and explanations on this new content.

Overall, the author team has provided significant resources to prepare students for the auditing environment in 2023 and beyond.

Standards Update

The professional standards facing auditors continue to evolve. The author-prepared *Standards Update* provides a summary of current exposure drafts and pronouncements issued subsequent to the publication of the text. This invaluable resource provides students and instructors with an "evergreen" text and summarizes the most current activities of the Auditing Standards Board and Public Company Accounting Oversight Board. The *Standards Update* is updated biannually and is available in *Connect*.

Highlights of *Auditing & Assurance Services,* 9e

In response to feedback and guidance from numerous auditing accounting faculty, the authors have made many important changes to the ninth edition of *Auditing & Assurance Services,* including the following:

- The ninth edition of *Auditing & Assurance Services* features Connect and SmartBook.
- Module G has been updated to include full coverage of the current uses of **Data and Analytics** in auditing, including extensive **Data Analytics Exercises** with **author-created data.**
- Module I is new to the ninth edition. The module is focused on describing the steps and complexities involved in the audit of internal control over financial reporting at an issuer.
- All chapters and modules have been revised to incorporate professional standards adopted through January 2022.
- Updates have been added to the **Apollo Shoes, Inc.** case with **Data Analytics** content. Apollo Shoes, Inc. is an audit case designed to introduce students to the entire audit process. Auto-gradable questions, instructor implementation guide, and videos can be found online in Connect.

- **Auditing Insight boxes** have been added and updated throughout the textbook to place issues discussed within the text into a real-world context. These boxes incorporate numerous examples from business and academic publications as well as actual company annual reports and audit reports.

- Examples using the **Caseware IDEA** software are included in Chapters 3, 4, 5, 7, 8, 9, Module E, Module F, and the new Module G focusing on **Data and Analytics.** In addition, end-of-chapter exercises using **author-developed databases exclusively for use** with *Auditing & Assurance Services* as well as supplemental materials to complement the IDEA workbook are provided.

- Tables in the cycle chapters have been fully standardized to focus on the risk assessment process for each relevant assertion. The chapters provide a consistent focus on how auditors respond to assessed risk of material misstatement, through the incorporation of easy-to-read tables throughout Chapters 6 through 10 to highlight the key issues and risks faced by auditors in the examination of different accounts. These tables take the students through the risk assessment process for each cycle on a step-by-step basis to mirror the methodology used in current audit practice.

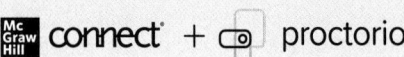

Remote Proctoring and Browser-Locking Capabilities

Remote proctoring and browser-locking capabilities, hosted by Proctorio within Connect, provide control of the assessment environment by enabling security options and verifying the identity of the student.

Seamlessly integrated within Connect, these services allow instructors to control the assessment experience by verifying identification, restricting browser activity, and monitoring student actions.

Instant and detailed reporting gives instructors an at-a-glance view of potential academic integrity concerns, thereby avoiding personal bias and supporting evidence-based claims.

Tegrity: Lectures 24/7

Tegrity in Connect is a tool that makes class time available 24/7 by automatically capturing every lecture. With a simple one-click start-and-stop process, you capture all computer screens and corresponding audio in a format that is easy to search, frame by frame. Students can replay any part of any class with easy-to-use, browser-based viewing on a PC, Mac, iPod, or other mobile device.

Educators know that the more students can see, hear, and experience class resources, the better they learn. In fact, studies prove it. Tegrity's unique search feature helps students efficiently find what they need, when they need it, across an entire semester of class recordings. Help turn your students' study time into learning moments immediately supported by your lecture. With Tegrity, you also increase intent listening and class participation by easing students' concerns about note-taking. Using Tegrity in Connect will make it more likely you will see students' faces, not the tops of their heads.

Test Builder in Connect

Available within Connect, Test Builder is a cloud-based tool that enables instructors to format tests that can be printed or administered within a Learning Management System

(LMS). Test Builder offers a modern, streamlined interface for easy content configuration that matches course needs, without requiring a download.

Test Builder allows you to

- Access all test bank content from a particular title.
- Easily pinpoint the most relevant content through robust filtering options.
- Manipulate the order of questions or scramble questions and/or answers.
- Pin questions to a specific location within a test.
- Determine your preferred treatment of algorithmic questions.
- Choose the layout and spacing.
- Add instructions and configure default settings.

Test Builder provides a secure interface for better protection of content and allows for just-in-time updates to flow directly into assessments.

Association to Advance Collegiate Schools of Business (AACSB) Statement

McGraw Hill Education is a proud corporate member of AACSB International. Understanding the importance and value of AACSB accreditation, *Auditing & Assurance Services,* 9e, recognizes the curricula guidelines detailed in the AACSB standards for business accreditation by connecting selected questions in the text and test bank to the eight general knowledge and skill guidelines in the AACSB standards. The statements contained in *Auditing & Assurance Services,* 9e, are provided only as a guide for the users of this textbook. The AACSB leaves content coverage and assessment within the purview of individual schools, their mission, and their faculty. Although *Auditing & Assurance Services,* 9e, and the teaching package make no claim of any specific AACSB qualification or evaluation, we have within *Auditing & Assurance Services,* 9e, labeled selected questions in Connect according to the eight general knowledge and skills areas.

McGraw Hill Education and UWorld are dedicated to supporting every accounting student along their journey, ultimately helping them achieve career success in the accounting profession.

In partnership with UWorld, a global leader in education technology, we provide students a smooth transition from the accounting classroom to successful completion of the CPA Exam. While many aspiring accountants wait until they have completed their academic studies to begin preparing for the CPA Exam, research shows that those who become familiar with exam content earlier in the process have a stronger chance of successfully passing. Accordingly, students using these McGraw Hill materials will have access to the highest quality CPA Exam multiple-choice questions and task-based simulations from UWorld, with expert-written explanations and solutions. All questions are either directly from the AICPA or are modeled on AICPA questions that appear in the exam. Task-based simulations are delivered via the UWorld platform, which mirrors the look, feel, and functionality of the actual exam. For more information about the full UWorld CPA Review program, exam requirements, and exam content, visit https:// accounting.uworld.com/cpa-review/partner/university/.

New to the Ninth Edition of *Auditing & Assurance Services*

Part I: The Contemporary Auditing Environment

The following breakdown shows the revisions we made on a chapter-by-chapter basis:

CHAPTER 1: Auditing and Assurance Services
- Revised the section on management's financial statement assertions to reflect the changes to the ASB assertion classifications brought on by *SAS 134* (Paragraph A133). The new guidance eliminates the category related to presentation and footnote disclosures and now categorizes those assertions within the events and transactions and the account balances categories. The guidance became effective on December 15, 2021.
- Added new Auditing Insights related to: (1) a new measure of accounting reporting complexity using XBRL; (2) the issue of whether the **Evergrande Group** should have received a going-concern opinion; and (3) the possibility of Big Four firms adding legal services to their professional service offerings.
- Revised the section that introduces assurance, attestation, and audit services. In addition, added two related Auditing Insights that describe the new IFRS International Sustainability Standards Board and Non-Fungible Tokens. Both of these areas represent significant assurance opportunities for CPA firms.

CHAPTER 2: Professional Standards
- Added opening vignette discussing current issues surrounding the PCAOB's inability to inspect audits of Chinese companies listed on U.S. exchanges.
- Added Auditing Insights related to Mattel and independence, updates on the United Kingdom's Financial and Reporting Council requirements for reducing the influence of Big Four firms, and the Wirecard fraud and reliability of audit evidence.
- Updated Auditing Insights on KPMG's advance notification of audits selected for PCAOB inspection, academic research related to PCAOB inspections, and the results of PCAOB inspections for the Big Four firms.

Part II: The Financial Statement Audit

CHAPTER 3: Engagement Planning
- Added new introductory vignette discussing recent large auditor switches and considerations when determining to accept a new audit client.
- Added a new exhibit to better highlight the various parties' responsibilities with regard to communicating with predecessor auditor when making client acceptance decisions.
- Included review checkpoint focusing on independence.
- Added a new Auditing Insight discussing finding from academic study regarding the use of audit specialists in the audit engagement.
- Included a brief discussion of "eating time" in the Time Budget discussion and added a new end of chapter exercise related to eating time.
- Added a new exhibit highlighting relationship of overall materiality to performance materiality, two new review checkpoints, and a new end of chapter question focusing on materiality.
- Updated Assertions, Evidence, and Audit Procedures table for new AICPA assertions, per *SAS No. 134,* Auditor Reporting and Amendments, including Amendments Addressing Disclosures in the Audit of Financial Statements, Paragraph A133.
- Updated Audit Insights and examples throughout the chapter.

CHAPTER 4: The Audit Risk Model and Inherent Risk Assessment
- Consolidated prior Learning Objectives 4-5 and 4-6 into one more comprehensive learning objective.
- Added a new introductory vignette highlighting the impact of the COVID-19 pandemic on audit risk assessment and auditor's planned responses to risk.
- Updated discussion on how the audit risk model is used in practice, moving away from quantitative calculations of risk and instead focusing on qualitative terms (low, moderate, high) and the relationships of the various risks within the model and the implications for audit planning. Updated multiple choice questions at the end of the chapter, moving away from qualitative audit risk model calculations.
- Included review checkpoint focusing on the relationships highlighted throughout the audit risk model.
- Added a new Auditing Insight focusing on how the COVID-19 pandemic has impacted fraud detection and growth.

- Updated Exhibit 4.9 (formally 4.7) to highlight misstatements by assertion, utilizing new AICPA assertions.
- Updated Audit Insights and examples throughout the chapter.

CHAPTER 5: Risk Assessment: Internal Control Evaluation

- Removed all material related to the internal control over financial reporting required for issuers by the Sarbanes–Oxley Act of 2002 and moved such material to a new Module I.
- Focused this chapter entirely on the evaluation of the system of internal control on the financial statement audit. By splitting this chapter, we believe that it will be a better way to present the internal control topic to students.
- Moved the section that described the limitations of an internal control system directly following its definition, allowing for a complete understanding of what is meant by an effective internal control system and its limitations.

CHAPTER 6: Employee Fraud and the Audit of Cash

- Added multiple new and current Auditing Insights.
- Fully updated the audit approach to confirmations to reflect the current electronic confirmation environment.

CHAPTER 7: Revenue and Collection Cycle

- Fully updated Auditing Insight boxes to include several new examples.
- Converted several additional end of chapter exercises to machine-gradable *Connect* versions.
- Provided new PCAOB Inspection Focus boxes to emphasize risk areas in audit inspections.

CHAPTER 8: Acquisition and Expenditure Cycle

- Further revised all tables in the chapter to be identical in format and consistent for all cycle chapters (6-10). This enables instructors to present a common format that matches the current method of auditing, from identification of significant accounts and relevant assertions to substantive procedures to audit residual risks.
- Added multiple new Auditing Insights covering current news related to auditing the expenditure cycle.
- Added new PCAOB Inspection Insight boxes to provide students with specific examples of risk areas in the acquisition and expenditure cycle.

CHAPTER 9: Production Cycle and the Audit of Inventory

- Revised the chapter to continue to remove focus from the production cycle and increase coverage of inventory substantive procedures. The chapter addresses risks of material misstatement in the inventory account for companies ranging from manufacturers to retailers such as Target.
- Revised all tables in the chapter to be identical in format for all cycle chapters (6–10). This enables instructors to present a common format that matches the current method of auditing, from identification of significant accounts and relevant assertions to substantive procedures to audit residual risks.
- Included a discussion of auditing difficulties related to remote auditing of inventory counts.
- New PCAOB Inspection Focus boxes provide a direct link to risk areas in the audit of inventory.

CHAPTER 10: Finance and Investment Cycle

- Significantly expanded the discussion of auditing accounting estimates, including fair values, to address the newly revised PCAOB standards. In addition, added a much more detailed discussion of the general approach to auditing accounting estimates.
- Updated tables throughout the chapter to include examples involving auditing accounting estimates in investment accounts.
- Included new PCAOB Inspection Insight boxes to demonstrate risk areas within the finance and investment cycle.

CHAPTER 11: Completing the Audit

- Added a new introductory vignette featuring Eastman Kodak Company (Kodak) and the going-concern assessment auditors must do when completing the audit.
- Added two new Auditing Insights related to auditing estimates, one discussing the impact of estimates on Amazon Inc.'s financial statements, another discussing the difficulty of auditing estimates.
- Added a new Auditing Insight discussing the difficulty of auditing estimates.
- Updated Audit Insights and examples throughout the chapter.

CHAPTER 12: Reports on Audited Financial Statements

- Added opening vignette illustrating how COVID-19 impacted the going-concern reporting for various companies, including Norwegian Cruise Lines and Carnival Cruise Lines.

- Added or updated Auditing Insights related to scope limitations, component auditors (with data drawn from the PCAOB's Form AP disclosure database), additional disclosures in auditors' reports, going-concern reports (with data drawn from the Audit Analytics database), and comparative reporting for General Motors in light of their change in auditors from Deloitte to EY.
- Added excerpts from actual auditors' reports for consistency (Nike), going concern (PG&E), and supplemental information (General Electric).

- Updated Auditing Insights summarizing the results of recent academic research on going concern reports.
- Included discussion of reporting on financial statements prepared using special purpose frameworks; specified elements, accounts, or items; and compliance with contractual agreements or regulatory requirements.
- Developed alternate reporting chapter and supporting materials that provides instructors with flexibility in covering the AICPA auditors' report, PCAOB auditors' report, or both reports.

Part III: Stand-Alone Modules

MODULE A: Other Public Accounting Services
- Moved material on reporting on financial statements prepared using special purpose frameworks; specified elements, accounts, or items; and compliance with contractual agreements or regulatory requirements to Chapter 12 to focus on engagements other than GAAS/PCAOB audits.
- Incorporated guidance provided by Statement on Standards for Attestation Engagements No. 21 that created two types of examination engagements (assertion-based examination engagements and direct examination engagements).
- Expanded coverage of Service Organization Controls (SOC) engagements, including providing excerpted wording used in Type 1 and Type 2 reports.
- Added Auditing Insights on deficiencies identified in PCAOB inspections for audits involving service organizations and broker-dealer compliance, Phillip Morris' integrated report and examples of assurance provided by auditors on information included in that report, trends in corporate responsibility reporting and academic research examining accountant assurance on this information, and the SEC's 2022 proposal for disclosure of greenhouse-gas emissions and energy consumption and the potential impact of these disclosures on accountant assurance.

MODULE B: Professional Ethics
- Added an Auditing Insight that focuses on recent calls by regulators to investigate possible conflicts of interest at accounting firms, questioning whether consulting services impact their independent financial statement audit.

- Added an Auditing Insight that describes the difficulty in changing auditors. By using the example of KPMG, which had been auditing General Electric since 1909, the insight illuminates that it is not an easy task. As the Insight describes, "in theory making a switch to another auditor sounds simple, the reality is that it is anything but."
- Added an Auditing Insight that describes how two partners at PwC were fined individually, for inadequate audit work on British tech company Redcentric Plc due to a lack of competence in conducting the audit. Also, added an Auditing Insight which illustrates how three Ernst & Young employees violated independence rules when they used contingent fees for billing a client for tax services. Taken together, the insights provide useful examples to students of what can happen if they violate the AICPA rules of conduct.

MODULE C: Legal Liability
- Added a new Auditing Insight featuring the implications of legal liability to junior auditors, highlighting recent filings of UK audit regulator against junior auditors.
- Updated Auditing Insight on Foreign Corrupt Practices Act violations.
- Updated Auditing Insight on class action lawsuits.
- Updated Auditing Insight for recent academic research on factors influencing auditor litigation.

MODULE D: Internal Audits, Governmental Audits, and Fraud Examinations
- Reorganization of Internal Audit section, discussion of Internal Audit Standards now precedes discussion

of Types of Internal Audit Services and Internal Audit Reports.

- Updated Auditing Insights and examples throughout the modules to reflect current events and trends.
- Updated discussion of Benford's Law.

MODULES E and F: Sampling

- Updated Auditing Insights for deficiencies identified in PCAOB inspections related to the application of attributes (Module E) and variables (Module F) sampling.
- Expanded and clarified walk-through examples to illustrate the use of IDEA in attributes and variables sampling.

MODULE G: Data and Analytics in Auditing

- Added a comprehensive example to illustrate the steps that auditors are following in completing **Data and Analytics** in auditing. The example walks through each of the the techniques that should be conducted using the audit of accounts receivable and revenue in a financial statement audit. Importantly, the module follows the approach from the **AICPA Guide to Audit Data Analytics.** Most notably, the example is included within *Connect* to allow for continuous updating and the most current and relevant approach to be employed on a continuous basis.
- Updated data and analytics exercises in the new Module G related to revenue recognition, along with several existing author-created and IDEA workbook exercises, enabling instructors to have many options for integration of data analytics into their courses with new solutions to reduce the availability of answers to students.
- Updated data for all data and analytic exercises included within both this chapter and Module G that focus on issues related to audits of the inventory account. The revised data reduces the likelihood of student access to solutions.
- Updated the section describing the common tools used in Audit Data Analytics based on the author team's cutting-edge understanding of practice.
- The updated end-of-chapter multiple choice, exercises, and problems contain entirely author-created questions and examples, as well as significant assistance for instructors for implementing the exercises in their classrooms.

MODULE H: Auditing and Information Technology

- Included a new introduction to the chapter that describes a relatable example of the different ways that information technology (IT) errors can impact an audit client. The example describes several colleges and universities that mistakenly sent out incorrect scholarship award notifications to students.
- Added several new "PCAOB Inspection Focus" examples which describe recent inspection findings from the PCAOB on issues that are being discussed in the text. For example, one of the examples focuses on a failure to audit information technology general controls (ITGCs) and one of the examples focuses on program change controls.
- Revised the section on important roles in an IT computing environment at an organization to better reflect current practice.
- Added an insight on the SEC's plans regarding the disclosure of cybersecurity risks in regulatory filings.

MODULE I: The Audit of Internal Control for Issuers

- New to this edition, we have added a new Module I that describes the steps and complexities involved in the audit of internal control over financial reporting.
- The new module contains excerpts from the most recent Stanley Black & Decker management report on internal control over financial reporting and excerpts from Deloitte & Touche's most recent opinion on internal control over financial reporting for Fannie Mae, which was an adverse opinion.
- The new module contains a comprehensive section on the benchmarks that auditors use to evaluate internal control effectiveness on the audit of internal control and a robust discussion of the evaluation of internal control design effectiveness and the operating effectiveness of internal control activities.
- The new module also describes the process used by audit teams to evaluate internal control deficiencies, illustrated with an Auditing Insight and examples that illustrate PCAOB Inspection results.
- Of course, the new module includes stand-alone multiple choice questions, along with problems and exercises.

Acknowledgments

OUR SINCEREST THANKS. . .

The American Institute of Certified Public Accountants (AICPA) has generously given permission for liberal quotations from official pronouncements and other AICPA publications, all of which lend authoritative sources to the text. In addition, several publishing houses, professional associations, and accounting firms have granted permission to quote and extract from their copyrighted material. Their cooperation is much appreciated because a great amount of significant auditing thought exists in this wide variety of sources.

A special acknowledgment is due to the Association for Certified Fraud Examiners (ACFE). It has been a generous contributor to the fraud auditing material in this text. The authors also acknowledge the valuable inclusion of the educational version of IDEA software in the eighth edition, which significantly enhances the practical application of the book.

Also, the authors are particularly grateful to Ryan T. Dunn, PhD, CPA (Auburn University), Meghann Cefaratti (Northern Illinois University), Brad Roof (James Madison University), and Yigal Rechtman (Pace University) for their many insightful comments over the past several years. The feedback they contributed while teaching from our text has contributed greatly to the clarity and accuracy of subsequent editions. A special thanks to Michael K. Shaub for his valuable critique of Chapter 5 and to Cristina Alberti, Todd Burns, and Brent Stevens for their input on Module H. In addition, thanks to Steven Dwyer, Suzanne McLaughlin, and Frank Wimer for the example developed to help explain the difference between general and application controls in Module H and to Bill Stearns for the inspiration to include the assurance implications of NFTs in Chapter 1. Thanks to Helen Roybark for her help with the preparation of the instructor PowerPoint presentations and Joleen Kremin for her contribution to the Apollo Shoes, Inc. case.

We are sincerely grateful for the valuable input of all those who helped guide our developmental decisions for the past eight editions of *Auditing & Assurance Services:*

Abdul Qastin
North Carolina A&T State

Adrianne Slaymaker
Metropolitan State University

Alexander K. Buchholz
Brooklyn College of the City University of New York

Amy Bourne,
Oregon State University

Andy Garcia
Bowling Green State University

Anne Albrecht,
Texas Christian University

Aretha Hill
Florida A&M University

Barbara Reider
University of Montana

Barbara Vinciguerra
Moravian College

Beverly Strachan
Troy University at Montgomery

Bharat Merchant
Baruch College

Bobby Waldrup
University of North Florida

Bonita K. Peterson Kramer
Montana State University–Bozeman

Bunney L. Schmidt
Utah Valley State College

Byron Pike
Minnesota State University–Mankato

Carmela Gordon,
Trident Technical College

Carol Shaver
Louisiana Tech University

Charles J. Pendola,
St. Joseph's College-New York

Charles Miller
California Polytech University

Christian Wurst
Temple University

Christine N. Todd
Colorado State University–Pueblo

Clyde Galbraith
West Chester University

David Blum
Moraine Park Technical College

David Gelb
Seton Hall University

Dawn P. Addington
Central New Mexico Community College

Dereck D. Barr
The University of Mississippi

Diana R. Franz
University of Toledo

Dorothy McMullen
Rider University

Douglas Ziegenfuss
Old Dominion University

Dr. Marina Grau,
Houston Community College

Duane Ponko
Indiana University of Pennsylvania

Duane Smith
Brescia University

Dwayne Powell
Arkansas State University

Dwight M. Owsen
Long Island University Brooklyn

Earl Godfrey
Gardner-Webb University

Eddie Metrejean
Georgia Southern University

Emily Elaine Griffith
The University of Georgia

Eric Carlsen
Kean University

Fatima Alali
California State University–Fullerton

Fowler A. Murrell
Lehman College

Frank J. Beil
University of Minnesota

Frank Venezia
State Ryan T. Dunn, PhD, CPA Albany

Gary Peters
University of Arkansas

Heidi H. Meier
Cleveland State University

Hema Rao
SUNY–Oswego

Iris Stuart
California State University

J. Donald Warren Jr.,
Rutgers University

Jack Armitage
University of Nebraska–Omaha

James Hansen
University of Illinois at Chicago

Jason T. Rasso
University of South Florida

Jaysinha Shinde
Eastern Illinois University

Jeffrey J. Archambault
Marshall University

Jennifer McCallen,
University of Georgia

Jerry L. Turner
University of Memphis

John Critchett
Madonna University

John E. Delaney
Southwestern Texas University

John Gabelman
Columbus State Community College

John Rigsby
Mississippi State University

John Trussel
Penn State University–Harrisburg

Joseph Aranyosi,
University of Phoenix

Joseph M. Larkin
St. Joseph's University

Judith G. Grant
Northern Virginia Community College at Annandale

Karl Dahlberg
Rutgers University

Kate Sorensen,
University of Memphis

Kathy Pollock
Indiana University–Purdue University Fort Wayne

Keith Jones
George Mason University

Kristen Kelli Saunders
University of South Carolina

Lin Zheng
Northeastern Illinois University

Linda Quick
University of South Carolina

LuAnn Bean
Florida Institute of Technology

Marcus Mason Doxey
University of Kentucky

Maria Sanchez
Rider University

Marie Blouin
Penn State University–Harrisburg

Marilyn Fisher
Corinthian Colleges

Marshall K. Pitman,
University of Texas at San Antonio

Marshall Pitman
University of Texas–San Antonio

MaryAnne Atkinson
Central Washington University

Maureen Mascha
Marquette University

Meghann Cefaratti
Northern Illinois University

Michael D. Akers
Marquette University

Pamela Legner
College of DuPage

Pamela Roush
University of Central Florida

Patricia Feller
Nashville State Community College

Perry Moore
Lipscomb University

Philip Levine
Berkeley College

R. D. Licastro
Penn State University–University Park

Ramesh Narasimhan
Montclair State University

Raymond Elson
Valdosta State University

Raymond Reisig
Pace University

Richard Hale
Midway College

Rick Warne, Todd Burns, and
Brent Stevens
University of Cincinnati

Rose Layton
University of Southern California

Russell F. Briner
University of Texas at San Antonio

Sara Adams,
Southern Oregon University

Sharon Polansky
Texas A&M University–Corpus Christi

Steven C. Hunt
Western Illinois University

Suzanne M. Busch
California State University–East Bay

Sylvia Anderson
University of Maryland University College

Tammi Schaefer
University of South Carolina

Timothy Andrew Seidel
University of Arkansas

Tom English
Boise State University

Tracy Reed
Appalachian State University

Tu Xu
Georgia State University

Venkataraman Iyer
The University of North Carolina at Greensboro

Vincent Owhoso
Northern Kentucky University

Xu Zhaohui
University of Houston–Clear Lake

Yigal Rechtman
Pace University

In addition, we would like to recognize our outstanding staff at McGraw-Hill: Managing Director, Tim Vertovec; Senior Portfolio Director, Becky Olson; Associate Portfolio Manager, Stephanie DeRosa; Marketing Manager, Lauren Schur; Product Developer, Sarah Wood; Content Project Managers, Mary Powers and Tammy Juran; Buyer, Laura Fuller; and Designer, Matt Diamond. For their encouragement, assistance, and guidance in the production of this book, we are grateful.

Few understand the enormous commitment of time and energy that it takes to put together a textbook. As authors, we are constantly scanning *The Wall Street Journal* and other news outlets for real-world examples to illustrate theoretical discussions, rereading and rewriting each other's work to make sure that key concepts are understandable, and double-checking our solutions to end-of-chapter problems. Among the few who do understand the time and energy commitment are our family members (Matt, Garrett, and Julianne Bagley; Kristin, Jackson, Elijah, Jonah, Ansley, and Laney Grace Blay; Susan and Meghan Strawser; and Ellen, Jenny, Eric, and Jessica Thibodeau) who uncomplainingly endured endless refrains of, "I just need a couple more minutes to finish this section." Words cannot express our gratitude to each of them for their patience and unending support.

A SPECIAL RECOGNITION

As we close, we owe a special debt of gratitude to two former co-authors who contributed mightily to previous editions of this text: Robert Ramsey (who retired from the University of Kentucky) and David Sinason (who retired from the University of Northern Illinois). While they are no longer actively teaching and conducting research, their efforts reflected in this textbook will continue to influence the professional development and lives of future accountants for many years to come.

Tim Louwers
Pennie Bagley
Allen Blay
Jerry Strawser
Jay Thibodeau

Instructors
The Power of Connections

A complete course platform

Connect enables you to build deeper connections with your students through cohesive digital content and tools, creating engaging learning experiences. We are committed to providing you with the right resources and tools to support all your students along their personal learning journeys.

65%
Less Time
Grading

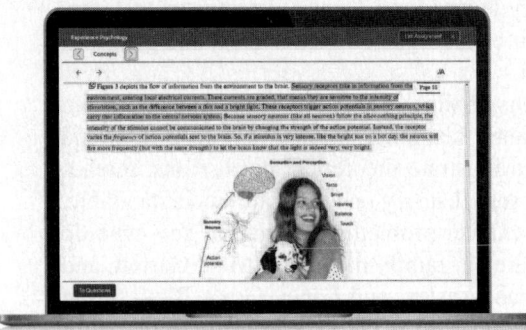

Laptop: Getty Images; Woman/dog: George Doyle/Getty Images

Every learner is unique

In Connect, instructors can assign an adaptive reading experience with SmartBook® 2.0. Rooted in advanced learning science principles, SmartBook 2.0 delivers each student a personalized experience, focusing students on their learning gaps, ensuring that the time they spend studying is time well-spent. **mheducation.com/highered/connect/smartbook**

Affordable solutions, added value

Make technology work for you with LMS integration for single sign-on access, mobile access to the digital textbook, and reports to quickly show you how each of your students is doing. And with our Inclusive Access program, you can provide all these tools at the lowest available market price to your students. Ask your McGraw Hill representative for more information.

Solutions for your challenges

A product isn't a solution. Real solutions are affordable, reliable, and come with training and ongoing support when you need it and how you want it. Visit **supportateverystep.com** for videos and resources both you and your students can use throughout the term.

Students
Get Learning that Fits You

Effective tools for efficient studying

Connect is designed to help you be more productive with simple, flexible, intuitive tools that maximize your study time and meet your individual learning needs. Get learning that works for you with Connect.

Study anytime, anywhere

Download the free ReadAnywhere® app and access your online eBook, SmartBook® 2.0, or Adaptive Learning Assignments when it's convenient, even if you're offline. And since the app automatically syncs with your Connect account, all of your work is available every time you open it. Find out more at **mheducation.com/readanywhere**

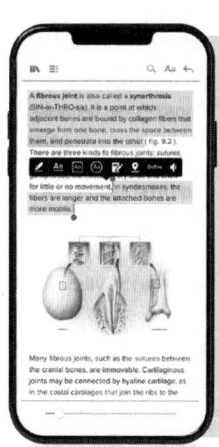

"I really liked this app—it made it easy to study when you don't have your text-book in front of you."

- Jordan Cunningham, Eastern Washington University

iPhone: Getty Images

Everything you need in one place

Your Connect course has everything you need—whether reading your digital eBook or completing assignments for class—Connect makes it easy to get your work done.

Learning for everyone

McGraw Hill works directly with Accessibility Services Departments and faculty to meet the learning needs of all students. Please contact your Accessibility Services Office and ask them to email accessibility@mheducation.com, or visit **mheducation.com/about/accessibility** for more information.

Brief Contents

Contents

PART THREE
STAND-ALONE MODULES

MODULE A

Other Public Accounting Services

MODULE B

Professional Ethics

MODULE C

Legal Liability

Auditing &
Assurance Services

CHAPTER 1

Auditing and Assurance Services

> *Our system of capital formation relies upon the confidence of millions of savers to invest in companies. The auditor's opinion is critical to that trust.*
>
> James R. Doty, Former Chairman, Public Company Accounting Oversight Board

Professional Standards References

Topic	AU-C/ISA Section	AS Section
General Principles and Functions of the Independent Auditor	200	1001 1005 1010 1015
Consideration of Fraud in a Financial Statement Audit	240	2401
Audit Evidence	500	1105
Attestation Standards	AT 101	AT 101
Compliance Auditing Considerations in Audits of Recipients of Governmental Financial Assistance	935	6110

LEARNING OBJECTIVES

You are about to embark on a journey of understanding how auditors work to keep the capital markets safe and secure for the investing public. When an upper management team needs to borrow money or raise capital to fund their business' growth opportunities, creditors and potential investors routinely ask the managers for their historical financial statements before making a final decision about whether to lend or invest in that company. Since those managers have an incentive to present financial statements that potentially overstate their assets or overstate their profitability to try and secure the funds, creditors and investors will often demand that the financial statements be audited by an independent CPA. The audit helps the lenders and investors to feel comfortable that the financial

statements are credible and can be relied upon. In this book, you will be provided with a comprehensive set of materials that will allow you to understand how auditors complete their work and to master the professional standards that they are required to follow. Chapter 1 provides an introduction to the auditing and assurance profession.

Your objectives are to be able to

LO 1-1 Define *information risk* and explain how the financial statement auditing process helps to reduce this risk, thereby reducing the cost of capital for a company.

LO 1-2 Define and contrast *assurance, attestation,* and *financial statement auditing services.*

LO 1-3 Describe and define the assertions that management makes about the recognition, measurement, presentation, and disclosure

LO 1-4 Define *professional skepticism* and explain its key characteristics.

LO 1-5 Describe the organization of public accounting firms and identify the various services that they offer.

of the financial statements and explain why auditors use them as the focal point of the audit.

LO 1-6 Describe the audits and auditors in governmental, internal, and operational auditing.

LO 1-7 List and explain the requirements for becoming a certified public accountant (CPA) and other certifications available to an accounting professional.

USER DEMAND FOR RELIABLE INFORMATION

LO 1-1
Define *information risk* and explain how the financial statement auditing process helps to reduce this risk, thereby reducing the cost of capital for a company.

When seeking capital to grow their business, management has an incentive to present their company's financial statements and future prospects in a manner that will entice potential investors and creditors. Since the possibility exists that management could misrepresent their financial position and results of operations, it is essential that investors and creditors have assurance that they can rely on the information provided by management, which creates demand for the financial statement audit. Stated simply, when an independent auditor completes an audit and then issues a report that states that the financial statements are presented fairly, in all material respects and have been presented in accordance with Generally Accepted Accounting Principles (GAAP), the financial statements can be relied upon by investors and creditors.

Unfortunately, the investors in **Theranos**, a blood-testing startup company, never asked for an independent audit report. In March 2018, the Securities and Exchange Commission (SEC) settled massive fraud charges against Theranos, their CEO Elizabeth Holmes, and their president, Sunny Balwani. The SEC's complaint alleged that the materials provided to potential investors included a company overview, reports of clinical trials, and financial statement information and projections. However, the package did not include an independent audit report. Unfortunately the company, which was valued as high as $9 billion by investors back in 2015, barely had enough cash to pay the bills less than five years later.[1] In January 2022, Elizabeth Holmes was convicted of two counts of wire fraud and two counts of conspiracy to commit wire fraud. She now faces up to 20 years in prison.[2] This example helps to reinforce why it is so important for investors and creditors to review audited financial statements as they consider whether to invest or loan money to a company. Of course, for the audit to have true value to investors and creditors, it must be completed in accordance with professional standards in a high quality manner by independent auditors.

You may be asking, why is audit quality so important? Well, as we have just seen, both investors and creditors depend on reliable financial statement information to make their investment and lending decisions about a company. As a result, the confidence of investors and creditors is shaken whenever audit quality is compromised. To help ensure that audit quality is not compromised, the Sarbanes–Oxley Act of 2002 (hereafter referred to as Sarbanes–Oxley) created the Public Company Accounting Oversight Board (PCAOB) to regulate the audit profession for public companies. In fact, the PCAOB is responsible for setting all audit standards to be followed on audits of public companies. In addition, the PCAOB is required to perform inspections of the audit work completed and the quality control processes employed by audit firms. As a direct result, accounting students should know that if they plan to work as financial statement auditors, they will be entering a world that is focused on audit quality. Consider the following Auditing Insight "Audit Quality."

---

[1]"The investors duped by the Theranos fraud never asked for one important thing," *MarketWatch*, March 19, 2018 (online source).

[2]"Elizabeth Holmes Found Guilty on 4 Counts of Fraud, Conspiracy in Split Verdict," *MarketWatch*, January 3, 2022 (online source).

AUDITING INSIGHT — Audit Quality

In November 2021, Ernst & Young (EY) published its report on audit quality for 2021. In the report, the firm's leaders affirmed their commitment to audit quality through continuous improvement of their audit process and a strong focus on their quality control system. They also firmly embraced their role to serve the public interest and acknowledged their critically important responsibility to the investing public for instilling confidence in the capital markets. The report highlights EY's key areas of focus to drive the firm's audit quality efforts, which include full implementation of their innovative digital audit methodology, an enhanced focus on staff training and project management skills, along with reinforcing the importance of independence and professional skepticism. The report also specifically discussed the enhancement of the firm's use of data and analytics as a way to manage the firm's focus on risks. The report is a clear indication to students that quality matters more than anything else in their future work as auditing professionals.

Source: *Our Commitment to Audit Quality: Information for Audit Committees, Investors and other Stakeholders,* Ernst & Young LLP, November 2021.

Before we think about audit quality any further, we must first explain the vital role that financial statement auditors play in supplying key decision makers with useful, understandable, and timely information. When you have a better understanding of why auditing is so critical to help ensure the liquidity of the world's capital markets, we will then explore in detail the process auditors take to help ensure that audit quality is achieved. Because many of you are likely planning to enter the public accounting profession and work as an auditor, we hope that you will work hard to acquire this knowledge so that you may do your part in playing a key role in maintaining the public's confidence in both the auditing profession and the capital markets.

Information Risk in a Big Data World

All businesses make a countless number of decisions each and every day. Decisions to purchase or sell goods or services, lend money, enter into employment agreements, or buy or sell investments depend in large part on the quality of useful information. These decisions affect **business risk**, which is *the risk that an entity will fail to meet its objectives.* For example, business risk includes the chance a company takes that its own customers will buy from competitors, that product lines will become obsolete, that taxes will increase, that government contracts will be lost, or that employees will go on strike. If the company fails to meet its objectives enough times, the company may ultimately fail. To minimize these risks and take advantage of other opportunities presented in today's competitive business environment, decision makers such as chief executive officers (CEOs) demand *timely, relevant,* and *reliable* information. Similarly, investors and creditors demand high-quality information to make educated investing and lending decisions. Information professionals such as accountants and auditors help satisfy this demand.

In recent years, as a result of ever-increasing computing power, the decision-making environment is rapidly being transformed into one that is characterized by the availability of significant amounts of data and information. Let's face it, the amount of information that organizations are seeking to manage is greater than anyone could have possibly imagined just 10 years ago. You are entering a world where upper management teams are placing more emphasis than ever on how to make sense of this seemingly ever-increasing availability of data and information. To help you prepare for this "big data" challenge as an auditor, we will be drawing upon this theme in multiple chapters throughout this book.

There are at least four environmental conditions in this big data world that increase user demand for relevant and reliable information:

1. *Complexity.* Events and transactions in today's global business environment are numerous and often very complicated. You may have studied derivative securities and hedging activities in other accounting courses, but investors and other decision makers may not have your level of expertise when dealing with these complex transactions. Furthermore, these decision makers are not trained to collect, compile, and summarize

the key operating information themselves. They need the services provided by information professionals to help make the information more understandable for their decision processes.

2. *Remoteness.* Decision makers are usually separated from current and potential business partners not only by a lack of expertise but also by distance and time. Investors may not be able to visit distant locations to check up on their investments. Instead, they need to employ full-time information professionals to do the work they cannot do for themselves.

3. *Time sensitivity.* Today's economic environment requires businesses, investors, and other financial information users to make decisions more rapidly than ever before. The ability to promptly obtain high-quality information is essential to businesses that want to remain competitive in our global business environment.

4. *Consequences.* Decisions can involve a significant investment of resources. The consequences are so important that reliable information, obtained and verified by information professionals, is an absolute necessity. Theranos's aftermath provides a graphic example of how decisions affect individuals' (as well as companies') financial security and well-being. Consider that back in 2015, as a private company, Theranos was valued over $9 billion and employed over 700 people. Yet, by September 2018, Theranos was out of business.[3] The following Auditing Insight "More Consequences" describes another example.

AUDITING INSIGHT   Even More Consequences

Bernard Madoff, a former chairman of the NASDAQ stock market and a respected Wall Street adviser and broker for 50 years, was arrested after his sons turned him in for running "a giant Ponzi scheme," bilking investors out of billions of dollars. Many investors, including actors, investment bankers, politicians, and sports personalities, lost their life savings.

Although some of the world's most knowledgeable investors fell prey to the scam, numerous red flags were present for all who were wise enough to see them. First, Madoff's fund returned 13–16 percent per year, every year, no matter how the markets performed. Second, his stated strategy of buying stocks and related options to hedge downside risk could not have occurred because the number of options necessary for such a strategy did not exist. Third, although his firm claimed to manage billions of dollars, its auditing firm had only three employees, including a secretary and a 78-year-old accountant who lived in Florida.

Sources: "Fund Fraud Hits Big Names," *The Wall Street Journal,* December 13, 2008, pp. A1, A7; "Fees, Even Returns and Auditor All Raised Flags," *The Wall Street Journal,* December 13, 2008, p. A7; "Top Broker Accused of $50 Billion Fraud," *The Wall Street Journal,* December 12, 2008, pp. A1, A14; "Probe Eyes Audit Files, Role of Aide to Madoff," *The Wall Street Journal,* December 23, 2008, pp. A1, A14.

A further complication in effective decision making is the presence of information risk. **Information risk** is *the probability that the information circulated by a company will be false or misleading.* Decision makers usually obtain their information from companies or organizations they want to conduct business with, provide loans to, or engage with in buying or selling the company's stock. Because the primary source of information is the target company itself, an incentive exists for that company's management to make its business or service appear to be better than it actually is, to put its best foot forward. As a result, preparers and issuers of financial information (directors, managers, accountants, and other people employed in a business) might benefit by giving false, misleading, or overly optimistic information. This potential *conflict of interest* between information providers and users, along with financial statement frauds such as the one perpetrated at Theranos, leads to a natural skepticism on the part of users. Thus, they depend on information professionals to serve as independent and objective *intermediaries* who will lend credibility to the information. This *lending of credibility* to information is known as providing **assurance**. When the assurance is provided for specific assertions made by management, we refer to the assurance provided as **attestation**. When the assertions are embodied in a company's

[3] S. Fiegerman and S. O'Brien, "Theranos Employees Struggle to Put Scandal behind Them," CNN, March 14, 2019 (online source).

financial statements, we refer to the attestation as **auditing**. More specifically, when their work is completed, the auditors supply an opinion as to whether the financial statements and related footnotes are presented fairly in all material respects. The actual compilation and creation of the financial statements is completed by the company's accountants.

☑ REVIEW CHECKPOINTS

1.1 What is a *business risk*?

1.2 What four environmental conditions that increase user demand for relevant and reliable information?

1.3 What type of risk creates a demand for independent and objective audit services to decision makers like investors and creditors?

AUDITING, ATTESTATION, AND ASSURANCE SERVICES

LO 1-2
Define and contrast *assurance, attestation,* and *financial statement auditing services.*

Now that you understand why decision makers need independent information professionals to provide assurance on key information, we further define assurance, attestation and financial statement auditing services in this section, and explain their roles in today's information economy.

Assurance Services

The American Institute of Certified Public Accountants (AICPA) defines an **assurance service** as any independent professional service that improves the quality of information, or its context, for decision makers. The definition is intentionally broad to encompass a wide range of services that could be performed by CPAs to add value in today's ever-changing information economy. In fact, given the market opportunities that exist in today's information economy, the AICPA is deliberately seeking to expand the CPA's traditional focus on financial statements to include different types of information, whether it be financial or nonfinancial. Before moving forward, let's take a closer look at the major elements and boundaries of the AICPA's definition for an assurance service which are

- *Independence.* CPAs want to preserve their attestation and audit reputations and competitive advantages by always preserving integrity and objectivity when performing any type of assurance service.
- *Professional services.* Virtually all work performed by CPAs (accounting, auditing, data management, taxation, management, marketing, finance) is defined as a professional service as long as it involves some element of judgment based on education and experience.
- *Improving the quality of information or its context.* CPAs can enhance information quality in a number of different ways. For example, by helping to assure users about the relevance of information being used in a particular decision-making context. Or, the CPA can enhance the quality of information by helping to assure users about the reliability or credibility of the information being used to make decisions. It is important to point out that the emphasis of the definition is on information, which focuses on CPAs' traditional value proposition. Also, remember that when considering assurance services, improving the context of information refers not only to the information itself but to how the information is being used in a decision-making context.

- *For decision makers.* The decision makers are the consumers of assurance services, and they personify the customer focus of different types of professional services being offered by CPAs. Ultimately, the decision makers are the beneficiaries of the assurance services performed, and depending upon the specific nature of the service, decision makers might be a very small, targeted group (e.g., an upper management team of a client, a group of creditors) or a large group (e.g., all potential investors).

The following Auditing Insight "Third Party Assurance" indicates how the quality of information can assist both buyers and sellers in today's market.

AUDITING INSIGHT　　Third Party Assurance

Exhibit 1.1 shows two 1961 **Topps** Mickey Mantle baseball cards. The card on the right was offered on **eBay** with the seller's representation that the card was in Near Mint/Mint condition. This representation is a standard description and is the equivalent of a grade 8 on a standard 10-point scale used in grading the quality of a trading card. The card was purchased on eBay for $205.50.

Within a week, a second 1961 Topps Mickey Mantle baseball card was sold on eBay. Again, this card was offered with the seller's representation that the card was in Near Mint/Mint condition (card on the left). The only difference was that this card had been sent to **Professional Sports Authenticator** (PSA), a company that verifies the authenticity and quality of sports items. Note that PSA does not buy or sell sports merchandise; it acts only as an independent third party expressing a professional opinion regarding the merchandise in question. This card sold for $585.

The only difference between the two transactions was that the buyers of the card on the left had more information concerning the risk inherent in the transaction. Why was the first transaction riskier? What were the buyers' concerns? Were the concerns only from intentional misstatements? How did the grading of the card by PSA reduce these concerns? What are the incentives for PSA to grade the card

EXHIBIT 1.1 Professional Sports Authenticator as Third-Party Assuror

Courtesy of Allen Blay

accurately? How does the business of PSA relate to the profession of auditing?

Examples of Assurance Services

Without a doubt, the most common type of assurance services provided by CPAs are attestation services. In an *attestation service,* the CPA expresses an opinion about information (or an assertion about that information) that is the responsibility of another party. While there are many types of attestation services that can be performed, the financial statement audit is the most common type of attestation service provided by CPAs. When completing an attestation service, the CPA is auditing the information to enhance its reliability or credibility for decision makers. We will discuss attestation services, including the financial statement audit, shortly but before moving forward, just a reminder that assurance services is the most broad categorization of the services typically provided by CPAs. Keeping that in mind, Exhibit 1.2 depicts the relationships among assurance, attestation, and auditing services.

In general, assurance services other than attestation and financial statement auditing services tend to be more customized for use by smaller, targeted groups of decision makers. For example, many companies and organizations have used public accounting firms to conduct a comprehensive assessment of risks that the enterprise faces. This type of enterprise risk assessment can then be used to show stakeholders that the management

EXHIBIT 1.2
The Relationships among Assurance, Attestation, and Audit Engagements

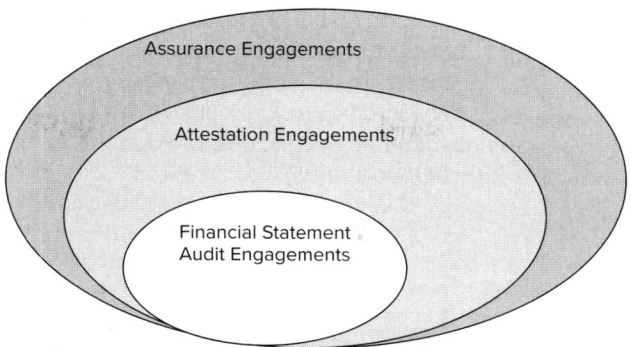

Assurance Engagements

Attestation Engagements

Financial Statement Audit Engagements

team understands and is properly managing the risks that the enterprise faces. We also present a few more examples of assurance services to illustrate the variety of services that fall under the assurance service umbrella. Some will look familiar and others may defy imagination:

- Cybersecurity risk assessment and assurance.
- XBRL (eXtensible Business Reporting Language) reporting.
- Evaluation of investment management policies.
- Internal audit outsourcing
- Fraud and illegal acts prevention and deterrence.

Be aware, that public accounting firms must pick and choose the services that they wish to provide to the market based on the expertise that resides within the firm. Nobody believes or maintains that all public accounting firms will want or be able to provide all types of assurance services. However, as the following Auditing Insight "Can Accounting Complexity Be Measured Using XBRL" illustrates, there may be an emerging benefit of XBRL reporting that has yet to be fully realized.

AUDITING INSIGHT | Can Accounting Complexity Be Measured Using XBRL?

XBRL (also referred to by the SEC as interactive data) is an information format designed specifically for business reporting. Through the "tagging" of specific data items (cash, inventory, sales transactions, etc.), XBRL facilitates the collection, summarization, and reporting of financial information in a medium that users can easily transform for their own decision-making purposes. Recently, researchers have created a measure of reporting complexity for the public companies and foreign private issuers listed with the SEC that are all required to use XBRL for SEC filings.

The researchers proposed a new measure of accounting reporting complexity (ARC) based primarily on the sheer number of items that have an XBRL tag that were disclosed in the company's Form 10-K filings.

It turns out that the disclosure of more XBRL tags is difficult because the accountants need to know more about accounting standards. And if they do not, they found that there is an increased chance of mistakes and outright errors by the company. Their analysis of the data revealed "a greater likelihood of misstatements and material weakness disclosures, longer audit delay, and higher audit fees" for the companies that had more accounting reporting complexity as measured by XBRL.

Sources: R. Hoitash and U. Hoitash, "Measuring Accounting Reporting Complexity with XBRL" *The Accounting Review,* January 2018, pp. 259–287; "Interactive Data to Improve Financial Reporting," AICPA (online source); "XBRL US Center for Data Quality," AICPA (online source).

Before turning our attention to attestation and financial statement auditing services, it is important to point out the difference between assurance services and consulting (or advisory services) performed by public accounting firms. In providing advisory services, CPAs use their professional skills and experiences to provide recommendations to a client's management team for specific outcomes such as information system design and operation; whereas in assurance services, the focus is entirely on the information that decision makers use. However, like advisory services, assurance services do have a "customer focus," and CPAs develop assurance services that add value for customers (i.e., decision makers). Consider the potential market opportunity that may exist related to non-fungible tokens, described in the following Auditing Insight "NFTs, an Emerging Market Opportunity."

AUDITING INSIGHT | NFTs, an Emerging Market Opportunity for CPAs?

Non-Fungible Tokens, or NFTs, are becoming very popular. But what exactly is an NFT? According to Merriam-Webster, an NFT is "a unique digital identifier that cannot be copied, substituted, or sub-divided, that is recorded in a blockchain, and that is used to certify authenticity and ownership (as of a specific digital asset and specific rights relating to it)." Put in simple terms, an NFT is a one-of-a-kind digital asset that allows you to prove that you are the owner of that digital asset. It is non-fungible because there is no asset you can trade equally for it.

An NFT, for now, is anything produced digitally, which is mainly a photo, video, or other type of artwork. However, investors in this market do see the possibility of the deed to your house or even a used ticket to a sporting event as being an NFT. The possibilities appear to be limitless.

So how much money is being spent on NFTs? Prior to 2021, a total of $94.9 million was spent; in 2021 that number jumped to $24.9 billion. What are some of the items purchased for these great sums? Digital art by the artist "Beeple" sold for $6.6 million while the original code for the World Wide Web sold for $5.4 million. The big question to ponder, can information assurers add value to this emerging market?

Sources: The 11 Most Expensive NFTs Sold in 2021 You Need To Know About, Investor Place (online source); NFTs–Definition, Merriam-Webster (online source); What is an NFT? Non-Fungible Tokens Explained, Forbes (online source).

Although attestation engagements and financial statement audits are specific types of assurance engagements and auditors can thus be described more generally as information assurors, hereafter we will use the term *auditor* instead of *information assuror* because of the specific responsibilities that auditors have under generally accepted auditing standards (GAAS) as well as under regulatory bodies such as the SEC and the PCAOB. However, many of the procedures that auditors perform as part of an audit engagement are similar to those performed as part of other information assurance engagements. Throughout this book, we will point out these shared procedures when appropriate. For now, let us turn our attention specifically to attestation engagements.

Attestation Engagements

Many people appreciate the value of auditors' attestations on historical financial statements, and as a result, they have found other types of information to which certified public accountants (CPAs) can attest. The AICPA defines an **attestation engagement** as a service where a practitioner is requested to examine whether management's assertion about some type of subject matter can be relied upon.

Many decision makers have appreciated the value of financial statement auditors' attestations on historical financial statements, and as a result, they have found other types of information to which CPAs can attest to. For example, as more and more companies and organizations seek to demonstrate their efforts related to corporate social responsibility, demand is growing for attestation services related to environmental reporting. When applying the above definition to this context, you will note that a practitioner (i.e., an environmental reporting auditor) is engaged to issue a report on assertions about subject matter (i.e., that the environmental reports are presented in accordance with appropriate laws and regulations) that are the responsibility of another party (i.e., the management team). The following Auditing Insight "An Emerging Growth Opportunity for CPAs", indicates the significance of this emerging market for public accounting firms.

AUDITING INSIGHT | An Emerging Growth Opportunity for CPAs

The International Financial Reporting Standards (IFRS) Foundation has announced a new board to oversee disclosures related to measures of sustainability. The board, which is being called the International Sustainability Standards Board (ISSB) is being asked to develop disclosure standards to help investors obtain relevant and reliable measures of sustainability.

Assurance services related to measures of sustainability is part of a much broader Environmental, Social and Governance (ESG) effort being promoted by institutional investors, mutual funds, private equity, and venture capital funds. It is hoped that a "comprehensive global baseline of high-quality sustainability disclosure standards" will be developed that will help public accounting firms perform assurance services that identify the relevant measures. The key is to identify the set of measures that will meet investors' information needs and maximize the value of the entity. Of course, the standards would also provide a set of criteria that can be used to evaluate the reliability of the measures reported by the entity and allow public accounting firms to complete an attestation service.

Sources: "IFRS Foundation Announces International Sustainability Standards Board, consolidation with CDSB and VRF, and publication of prototype disclosure requirements," IFRS, November 3, 2021 (online source).

Interestingly, in today's global business environment, activist shareholders are increasingly pressuring board of director members and upper management teams regarding issues of social responsibility, the environment, and other matters related to sustainability. As a direct result, more companies than ever are directly integrating their ESG initiatives into their overall business strategy and then seeking to quantify their efforts with measurable outputs. These measurements are often being used to help quantify the company's performance in areas such as the environment, labor, and basic human rights. For example, in the following Auditing Insight "Climate Change Does Matter" students can see one of the world's largest asset managers, has recently toughened their standards related to climate change and environmental risk reporting for the corporations in their investment portfolio.

AUDITING INSIGHT | Climate Change Does Matter

The environment and sustainability matter a great deal. That is the clear message being sent by **BlackRock, Inc**. Indeed, the firm has made clear that it intends to take a much tougher stance against corporations that are unwilling to provide a "full accounting" of the environmental risks that they are facing in their business operations. In taking these steps, BlackRock seeks to show the marketplace that they are doing what they can in relation to climate change. Of course, it is an open question just how much influence BlackRock can have over companies, but their chief executive, Laurence Fink, clearly believes that by doing so, he will position his firm to "win over younger investors and millennials who want to invest money in line with personal values."

Source: "BlackRock Tightens Standards for Firms On Climate Change," *The Wall Street Journal*, January 15, 2020, p. B1.

Of course, whenever a management team makes an assertion about information, there is an opportunity to perform an attestation engagement. And, although sustainability is a prominent example of an emerging attestation engagement completed by CPAs, other examples of attestation engagements completed by CPAs (discussed in more detail in Module A) appear in the following box.

Examples of Attestation Engagements

- **Review Engagements** (AT-C Section 210), such as providing limited assurance about whether the professional becomes aware of any material modifications that need to be made to the subject matter being examined.
- **Agreed-Upon Procedures Engagements** (AT-C Section 215), such as verifying inventory quantities and locations.
- **Prospective Financial Information** (AT-C Section 305), such as analysis of prospective or hypothetical "what-if" financial statements for some time period *in the future.*
- **Reporting on Pro Forma Financial Information** (AT-C Section 310), such as retroactively analyzing the effect of a proposed or consummated transaction on the *historical* financial statements as if that transaction had already occurred.
- **Compliance Attestation** (AT-C Section 315), such as ascertaining a client's compliance with debt covenants.
- **Reporting on Controls at a Service Organization** (AT-C Section 320), such as organizations that provide outsourced processes that are likely to be relevant to the user entities' internal control over financial reporting.
- **Examination of Management's Discussion and Analysis** (AT-C Section 395), prepared pursuant to the rules and regulations of the Securities and Exchange Commission (SEC).

Financial Statement Auditing

The focus of this book is on the financial statement auditing process, which is far and away the most common type of assurance service provided in today's market. Many years ago, the American Accounting Association (AAA) Committee on Basic Auditing Concepts provided a very useful general definition of *auditing* as follows:

> *Auditing* is a systematic process of objectively obtaining and evaluating evidence regarding assertions about economic actions and events to ascertain the degree of correspondence between the assertions and established criteria and communicating the results to interested users.[4]

A closer look at the definition reveals several ideas that are important to an auditing engagement. Auditing is a *systematic process.* It is a purposeful and logical process and is based on the discipline of a structured approach to reaching final decisions. It has a logical starting point, proceeds along established guidelines, and has a logical conclusion. It is not haphazard, unplanned, or unstructured.

The process involves obtaining and evaluating *evidence.* Evidence consists of all types of information that ultimately guide auditors' decisions and relate to *assertions made by management about economic actions and events.* When beginning a financial statement audit engagement, an independent auditor is provided with financial statements and other disclosures by management. In doing so, management essentially makes assertions about the financial statement balances (e.g., that the inventory on the balance sheet really does exist, that revenue transactions recorded on the income statement really did occur, that the list of liabilities on the balance sheet is complete, etc.) as well as assertions that the footnote disclosures are fairly presented. The audit process has been around for a long time as shown in the following Auditing Insight "A Rich History."

 AUDITING INSIGHT   A Rich History

Although most of the largest public accounting firms trace their roots to the turn of the 19th century, auditing in the United States has a rich history. When the Pilgrims had a financial dispute with the English investors who financed their trip, an "auditor" was sent to resolve the difference. George Washington sent his financial records to the comptroller of the treasury to be audited before he could be reimbursed for expenditures he made during the Revolutionary War. One of the first Congress's actions in 1789 was to set up an auditor to review and certify public accounts. Even the "modern" concept of an audit committee is not so modern; the bylaws of the Potomac Company, formed in 1784 to construct locks on the Potomac River to increase commerce, required that three shareholders annually examine the company's records.

Source: D. Flesher, G. Previts, and W. Samson, "Auditing in the United States: A Historical Perspective," *Abacus,* John Wiley & Sons. Inc., 2008, pp. 21–39.

[4]American Accounting Association Committee on Basic Auditing Concepts. *A Statement of Basic Auditing Concepts.* American Accounting Association, 1973.

Financial statement auditors generally begin their work with a focus on assertions (explicit representations) made by management about the financial statement amounts and information disclosed in footnotes, and then they set out to obtain and evaluate evidence to prove or disprove these assertions or representations made by management. The purpose of obtaining and evaluating evidence is to ascertain the degree of correspondence between the assertions made by the information provider and the established criteria. Auditors will ultimately communicate their findings to interested users. To communicate in an efficient and understandable manner, auditors and users must have a common basis or an established criteria for measuring and describing the financial statement information, which is essential for effective communication.

Established criteria may be found in a variety of sources. For independent financial statement auditors, the criterion is whatever the applicable financial reporting framework is, whether it is GAAP in the United States or International Financial Reporting Standards (IFRS) in other jurisdictions. In a financial statement audit, the auditor obtains evidence and evaluates whether the financial statements are being presented fairly based on the evidence obtained. For example, if a company represented that they had $10 million in a cash account, the auditor would have to verify with the bank that the company did in fact have $10 million of cash in the bank. Exhibit 1.3 depicts an overview of financial statement auditing.

The AAA definition already presented is broad and general enough to encompass external, internal, and even governmental auditing. The more specific viewpoint of external auditors in public accounting practice is reflected in the following statement about the financial statement audit made by the AICPA the public accounting community's professional association:

> The purpose of an audit is to provide financial statement users with an opinion by the auditor on whether the financial statements are presented fairly, in all material respects, in accordance with an applicable financial reporting framework, which enhances the degree of confidence that intended users can place in the financial statements. An audit conducted in accordance with GAAS and relevant ethical requirements enables the auditor to form that opinion. (AU-C-100.04)

EXHIBIT 1.3 Overview of Financial Statement Auditing

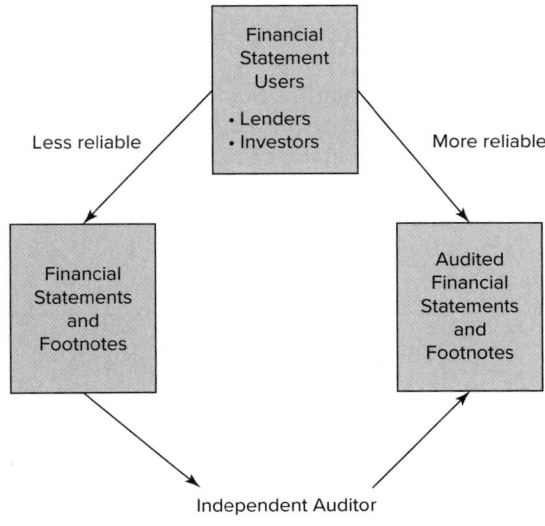

Auditing in a Big Data Environment

In recent years, the auditing environment has been transformed into an environment that is characterized by the availability of significant amounts of data and cutting-edge analytical tools. As a direct result, entry-level professionals joining public accounting firms are being asked to have completed coursework related to the use of data and analytical tools. The following Auditing Insight "Is there really an "APP" for that?" provides compelling market support for this statement.

AUDITING INSIGHT — Is there really an "APP" for that?

It has become clear that the skills needed by entry-level auditing professionals must include proficiency in data analytics and technology.

But the need for a digital mindset is hardly limited to entry-level professionals, and to help in their efforts to upskill all of their professionals, **PwC** introduced an app that is designed to assess an individual's digital fluency. Once the assessment is complete, the app then helps an individual to understand what type of training they need to close any gaps that might exist in their digital fluency.

There are now 60 different subject areas covered on the app, including blockchain, artificial intelligence, cybersecurity, and robotics among other topics. In addition, the Digital Fitness App (DFA) is now available on the App Store and is available for free for anyone to explore key trends in the digital world and to stay in close touch with recent updates.

It is now obvious that the world has changed, and as a result, the set of skills acquired by students must also change to adapt to the new digital world. Most importantly, while PwC is just one firm, our conversations with professionals across firms of varying size are in agreement with the need for a digital mindset to effectively operate in an audit environment characterized by Big Data and advanced analytical tools.

Sources: Digital Fitness Assessment by PricewaterhouseCoopers LLP, AppStore, Apple, (online source); Digital Fitness For The World, PwC (online source).

Among the critical issues for students to consider is how to identify the right set of data to analyze given a set of facts and circumstances. And, of course, how to present the analyses of such data in the most compelling format while documenting the results of their work. In addition, while analytical tools can rely on data sources that are both internal and external to the client, our current understanding is that entry-level audit professionals in today's environment need to first learn how to make the best use of internal data and information produced by the entity, including **system-generated reports** used by the client to execute its internal control activities and produce its financial statements.

Throughout this book, we will be providing examples of how to make the best use of such internal client data, which includes an emphasis on always verifying the completeness and accuracy of the underlying data set being used. There is even an entire module (Module G) of this book that is dedicated to the use of Big Data and advanced analytical tools in the financial statement audit.

✓ REVIEW CHECKPOINTS

1.4 What are the four major elements of the broad definition of assurance services?

1.5 What is an *assurance service engagement*?

1.6 What is an *attestation engagement*?

1.7 In what ways are assurance services similar to attestation services?

1.8 Define and explain financial statement auditing. What would you answer if asked by a communications major on campus, "What do *auditors* do?"

MANAGEMENT'S FINANCIAL STATEMENT ASSERTIONS

LO 1-3
Describe and define the assertions that management makes about the recognition, measurement, presentation, and disclosure of the financial statements and explain why auditors use them as the focal point of the audit.

From your earlier studies, you know that accounting is the process of recording, classifying, and summarizing a company's transactions into financial statements that will create assets, liabilities, equities, revenues, expenses, and related disclosures. It is the means of satisfying users' demands for financial information that arise from the forces of complexity, remoteness, time sensitivity, and consequences.

Auditing does not include the function of producing financial reports. The function of **financial reporting** is to provide statements of financial position (balance sheets), results of operations (income statements, statements of shareholders' equity, and statements of comprehensive income), changes in cash flows (statements of cash flows), and accompanying disclosures to outside decision makers who do not have access to management's internal sources of information. A company's accountants, under the direction of its management team, perform this function. In fact, auditing standards emphasize that the financial statements are the responsibility of a company's management. Thus, the financial statements contain management's assertions about the *transactions and events and related disclosures* that occurred during the period being audited (primarily the income statement, statement of shareholders' equity, statement of comprehensive income, statement of cash flows, and related disclosures), and assertions about the *account balances and related disclosures* at the end of the period (primarily the balance sheet, and related disclosures).

As the Auditing Insight "Sarbanes–Oxley and Management's Responsibility for Financial Reporting" makes clear below, the upper management team at public companies must certify the correctness of the financial statements and the effectiveness of the internal control system for financial reporting. Given the required focus on internal controls, entry-level audit professionals are expected to understand the relationship between a company's internal control activities and the relevant financial statement assertions about the financial statement account balances. We suggest that as a new auditing professional, a detailed understanding of this relationship will provide you with the opportunity to immediately contribute to the audit team. As a result, we are hopeful that this book can provide a foundation of knowledge to help simplify the relationship between internal controls and the financial statements, which is paramount in the post-Sarbanes–Oxley auditing environment.

 AUDITING INSIGHT | Sarbanes–Oxley and Management's Responsibility for Financial Reporting

Congress passed the Sarbanes–Oxley Act in 2002 in an attempt to address a number of weaknesses found in corporate financial reporting as a result of the frauds at companies such as **WorldCom** and Enron. Although the preparation of the financial statements has always been the responsibility of management, Sarbanes–Oxley has enhanced the disclosure provisions to create a heightened sense of accountability. One of its most important provisions (Section 302) states that key company officials must certify the financial statements. Certification means that the company's chief executive officer and chief financial officer must sign a statement indicating:

1. They have read the financial statements.

2. They are not aware of any false or misleading statements (or any key omitted disclosures).

3. They believe that the financial statements present an accurate picture of the company's financial condition.

Management must also make assertions regarding the effectiveness of the company's internal controls over financial reporting. In addition, the auditors are required to issue an attestation report (Section 404) on the system of internal controls to provide assurance that the system of internal controls over financial reporting has been designed and is operating effectively.

Source: U.S. Congress, *Sarbanes–Oxley Act of 2002*, Pub. L. No. 107-204, 116 Stat. 745, 2002.

When planning the audit engagement, auditors use management's assertions to assess external financial reporting risks by determining the different types of misstatements that could occur for each of the relevant management assertions identified and then develop auditing procedures that are appropriate in the circumstances. The auditing procedures are completed to provide the evidence necessary to persuade the auditor that there is no material misstatement related to each of the relevant assertions. Once the auditor is satisfied that the evidence has supported each of the relevant assertions, the auditor issues a report to provide assurance to financial statement users that the financial statements are free of material misstatement in accordance with generally accepted accounting principles. As an auditor, you must keep in mind the importance of understanding management's financial statement assertions and always remember that you are serving the entire public interest, including stakeholders such as bankers, investors, and employees when ultimately reporting that the financial statements are free of material misstatement.

APOLLO SHOES — The Company

Throughout this book, we will use Apollo Shoes, Inc. (the "Company") as a comprehensive case example to help illustrate important auditing concepts. The Company is a distributor of athletic shoes. The Company's products are shipped to large and small retail outlets in a six-state area. The Company operates from a large office, which includes a warehouse in the Shoetown, Maine, area. In this chapter, we will illustrate the financial statement assertions using Apollo Shoes.

When studying and learning about the assertions, a student of auditing must always remember that each assertion gives rise to a question that can be answered with audit evidence. Exhibit 1.4 provides a list of all of management's financial statement assertions and some of the key questions that the audit team must address, with evidence, about each assertion. Note that column 1 in Exhibit 1.4 denotes the assertions currently identified by the PCAOB for public company audits.[5] The PCAOB auditing standards do allow auditors to use different management assertions at their discretion, provided that the assertions cover the pertinent risks in each significant account. In that spirit, the Auditing Standards Board (ASB)[6] provides an additional set of management assertions (columns 2 and 3 in Exhibit 1.4). You will note that the ASB set of assertions, while largely in alignment with the PCAOB assertions, does provide greater detail and clarity for students of auditing to conceptualize. The key questions (column 4) indicate how each of these assertions must be thought about when evaluating specific aspects of management's financial statements and disclosures. Each of the assertions is defined and described in detail in the following sections, organized along the lines of the PCAOB assertions identified in column 1, with the aligned ASB assertion(s) following in parentheses.

Existence or Occurrence (Existence, Occurrence, Cutoff)

The numbers listed on the financial statements have no meaning to financial statement users unless the numbers *faithfully represent* the actual transactions, assets, and liabilities of the company. *Existence* asserts that each of the balance sheet and income statement balances actually exist. *Occurrence* asserts that each of the income statement events and transactions actually did occur in the proper period. As a general rule, the *occurrence* assertion relates to events, transactions, presentations, and footnote disclosures (as indicated in columns 2 of Exhibit 1.4), and the *existence* assertion relates to account balances and footnote disclosures (as indicated in column 3). Therefore, auditors must test whether the balance sheet amounts reported as assets, liabilities, and equities actually *exist*. To test the existence assertion, auditors typically verify cash with banks and count

---

[5]The PCAOB is a nonprofit corporation established by Congress to oversee the audits of public companies. The PCAOB is discussed in more detail in Chapter 2.

[6]The ASB was established by the profession to issue auditing standards. Standards issued by the ASB apply to audits of private companies. The ASB is discussed in more detail in Chapter 2.

EXHIBIT 1.4   Management Assertions

(1) PCAOB Assertions	ASB Assertions		(4) Key Questions
	(2) Assertions about Classes of Transactions and Events, and Related Disclosures	(3) Assertions about Account Balances and Related Disclosures	
Existence or occurrence		Existence	Do the assets listed really exist?
	Occurrence		Did the transactions really occur?
	Cutoff		Did the recorded sales transactions occur in the period?
Completeness		Completeness	Are all accounts recorded on the balance sheet?
	Completeness		Were all transactions recorded on the income statement?
	Cutoff		Are transactions included in the proper period?
Valuation or allocation		Accuracy, valuation, and allocation	Are the balance sheet accounts valued correctly?
	Accuracy		Are the transactions accurately recorded?
Rights and obligations		Rights and obligations	Does the company really own the assets?
	Rights and obligations		Are all legal responsibilities to pay the liabilities identified?
Presentation and disclosure	Classification		Were all transactions recorded in the correct accounts?
		Presentation	Are the disclosures understandable to users?
	Presentation		Are all required footnote disclosures included?

the physical inventory, verify accounts receivables and insurance policies with customers, and perform other procedures to obtain evidence whether management's assertion is in fact supported. Similarly, management asserts that each of the revenue and expense transactions summarized on the income statement or disclosed in the financial statement footnotes really did occur during the period being audited. To test the occurrence and the cutoff assertions, auditors complete procedures to ensure that the reported sales transactions really did occur and were not created to fraudulently inflate the company's profits.

 **APOLLO SHOES**   Existence or Occurrence

On Apollo Shoes, management would assert that their assets or liabilities all exist as of December 31. For example, management asserts that its cash on the balance sheet really does exist. In addition, management asserts that each revenue transaction on the income statement actually did occur.

Completeness (Completeness, Cutoff)

In the financial statements, management asserts that all transactions, events, assets, liabilities, and equities that should have been recorded have been recorded. In addition, management asserts that all disclosures that should have been included in the footnotes have been presented. Thus, auditors' specific objectives include obtaining evidence to determine whether, for example, all inventory is included, all accounts payable are included, all notes payable are included, all expenses are recorded, and so forth. A verbal or written management representation saying that all transactions are included in the accounts is not considered a sufficient basis for deciding whether the completeness assertion is true. Auditors need to obtain persuasive evidence about completeness.

Cutoff is a more detailed expression of the completeness assertion. **Cutoff** refers to accounting for revenue, expense, and other transactions in the *proper period* (neither postponing some recordings to the next period nor accelerating next-period transactions into the current-year accounts). Assuming a calender year-end, simple cutoff errors can occur when (1) a company records late December sales invoices for goods not actually shipped until early January; (2) a company records cash receipts through the end of the week (e.g., Friday, January 4) when the last batch of receipts for the year should have been processed on December 31; (3) a company fails to record accruals for expenses incurred but not yet paid, thus understating both expenses and liabilities; (4) a company fails to record purchases of materials shipped free on board (FOB) shipping point but not yet received and, therefore, not included in the ending inventory, thus understating both inventory and accounts payable; and (5) a company fails to accrue unbilled revenue through the fiscal year-end for customers on a cycle billing system, thus understating both revenue and accounts receivable. In auditor's jargon, the *cutoff date* generally refers to the client's year-end balance sheet date.

APOLLO SHOES   Completeness

On Apollo Shoes, management would assert that their assets or liabilities were complete as of December 31. For example, management asserts that its accounts payable on the balance sheet includes all amounts currently payable. In addition, management would assert that all expenses that should be included on the income statement actually were included.

Valuation and Allocation (Accuracy, Valuation, and Allocation)

In the financial statements, management asserts that the transactions and events have been recorded accurately and that the assets, liabilities, and equities listed on the balance sheet have been valued in accordance with GAAP (or IFRS). The audit objective related to valuation and allocation is to determine whether proper values have been assigned to assets, liabilities, and equities. *Allocation* refers to the appropriate percentage of an asset or liability balance being recorded on the income statement in accordance with GAAP (or IFRS). For example, has the proper depreciation expense been calculated for each fixed asset amount? *Accuracy* refers to the appropriate recording of the transactions at the correct amount. Auditors obtain evidence about specific valuations and mathematical accuracy by comparing vendors' invoices to inventory prices, obtaining lower-of-cost-or-market data, evaluating collectability of receivables, recalculating depreciation schedules, and so forth. Many valuation, accuracy, and allocation decisions amount to reaching conclusions about the proper application of GAAP (or IFRS). For example, due to the complexity in the accounting standards related to fair value (i.e., *ASC Topic 820*), there has been an increased focus on the valuation assertion by auditors.

APOLLO SHOES   Valuation and Allocation

On Apollo Shoes, management would assert that their assets or liabilities were valued in accordance with GAAP as of December 31. For example, management asserts that its accounts receivable balance, net of the allowance for doubtful accounts, was stated at the amount they actually expect to collect. In addition, management would assert that depreciation expense on the income statement reflects the appropriate allocation of fixed assets to the period of benefit under GAAP.

Rights and Obligations (Rights and Obligations)

In the financial statements, management asserts that they have ownership rights for all amounts reported as assets on the company's balance sheet and that the amounts reported as liabilities represent the company's own obligations. In simpler terms, the objective for an auditor is to obtain evidence that the assets are really owned and that the liabilities are really owed by the company being audited. You should be careful about *ownership,* however, because the assertion extends to include assets for which a company may not actually hold title. For example, an auditor will have a specific objective of obtaining evidence about the amounts capitalized for leased property. Likewise, *owing* includes accounting liabilities a company may not yet be legally obligated to pay. For example, an auditor would have to obtain evidence about the estimated liability for product warranties. The auditor also has an obligation to ensure that the details of the company's obligations are properly disclosed in the footnotes to the financial statements.

APOLLO SHOES — Rights and Obligations

On Apollo Shoes, management would assert that they really do own and have the rights to the assets listed on the balance sheet, and that they really are obliged to pay the amount listed on the balance sheet for liabilities as of December 31. For example, management asserts that it really owns its inventory of shoes. In addition, management asserts that it really does owe the amount listed for accrued expenses.

Presentation and Disclosure (Classification, Presentation)

In the financial statements, management asserts that all transactions and events have been presented correctly in accordance with GAAP (or IFRS) and that all relevant information has been disclosed to financial statement users, usually in the footnotes to the financial statements. This assertion embodies several different components. First, disclosures must be relevant, reliable, understandable, and transparent to financial statement users. In addition, auditors will test to make sure that all the proper disclosures have been made in accordance with GAAP (or IFRS). To complete this step, auditors will often use a disclosure checklist that highlights all the disclosures that should be made for a particular entity.

Second, transactions must be classified in the correct accounts (e.g., proper classification of transactions as assets or expenses). To test this assertion, auditors perform audit procedures such as analyzing repair and maintenance expenses to ensure that they should in fact have been expensed rather than capitalized. Similarly, auditors will test from the opposite direction, examining additions to buildings and equipment to ensure that transactions that should have been expensed were not in fact capitalized in error (or fraud).

Third, to be useful to decision makers, information must be understandable. *Statement of Financial Accounting Concepts (SFAC) No. 2,* "Qualitative Characteristics of Accounting Information," defines *understandability* as "the quality of information that enables users to perceive its significance." The responsibility levied on auditors is to make sure that the financial statements are "transparent." In other words, investors should be able to understand how the company is doing by reading its financial statements and footnotes and should not have to rely on financial experts or lawyers to help them figure out what the fine print is saying. Another way to regard this assertion is to ask whether the disclosures have been written in *plain English.*

APOLLO SHOES — Presentation and Disclosure

On Apollo Shoes, management would assert that they have completely and accurately presented and disclosed all of their footnotes. For example, management asserts that its income tax footnote disclosure is complete and accurately shows the breakdown of current and deferred income taxes.

Importance of Assertions

On each audit engagement, the auditor must identify each significant account or disclosure in the financial statements. An account or disclosure is significant if there is a reasonable possibility that the account or disclosure could contain a misstatement that is material. Once the **significant accounts** and disclosures have been identified, the auditor must then consider the relevance of each financial statement assertion, one at a time. An assertion is relevant, if there is a "reasonable possibility" that a material misstatement exists related to that assertion for the significant account being audited. As a result, the relevance of a particular assertion is entirely dependent on the facts and circumstances on the audit engagement. For example, valuation may not be a **relevant assertion** for the cash account unless foreign currency translation is involved; however, the existence of cash is always relevant.

The financial statement assertions are important and at times can be difficult to comprehend. A student of auditing must remember that the key questions that must be answered about each assertion become the *focal points* for the audit procedures to be performed. In other words, audit procedures are the means to answer the key questions posed by management's financial statement assertions. When evidence-gathering audit procedures are specified, you need to be able to relate the evidence produced by each procedure to one or more specific assertions. In essence, the secret to writing and reviewing a list of audit procedures is to ask, "Which assertion(s) does this procedure produce evidence about?" Then ask, "Does the list of procedures (the *audit plan*) cover all the assertions?" Exhibit 1.5 illustrates how the assertions relate to the financial statements.

Although standards-setting bodies such as the PCAOB and ASB try to neatly categorize transactions, balances, and disclosures according to the different assertions, the *real world* is seldom as orderly. For example, although cutoff procedures provide evidence about completeness, they also provide evidence about valuation and occurrence. Prematurely recording sales transactions inflates revenue and/or asset values because the transaction did not *occur* by the income statement date. Similarly, if a cutoff test shows a delay in recording a liability, the liability is not only incomplete but *undervalued* as well. Thus, errors in financial statements may affect multiple management assertions.

> ### ✓ REVIEW CHECKPOINTS
>
> 1.9   What is the difference between financial statement auditing and financial accounting?
>
> 1.10 List and briefly explain each of the Auditing Standards Board's (ASB) management assertions. List at least one key question that auditors must answer with evidence related to each management assertion.
>
> 1.11 Why is the ASB's set of management assertions important to auditors? Do these assertions differ from those included in PCAOB standards? If so, how are they different?

PROFESSIONAL SKEPTICISM

LO 1-4
Define *professional skepticism* and explain its key characteristics.

> ### *Trust, but Verify*
>
> A "signature phrase" used by Ronald Reagan during his term as president of the United States (1980-1988).

Professional skepticism is defined in the professional auditing standards as having an attitude that "includes a questioning mind and a critical assessment of evidence." Essentially,

EXHIBIT 1.5 Management Assertions and Their Relationship to the Financial Statements

STATEMENT OF FINANCIAL CONDITION
APOLLO SHOES INC.
in thousands

As of December 31	2023	2022
Assets		
Cash	$3,245	$3,509
Accounts Receivable (Net of Allowances of $1,263 and 210, respectively) (Note 3)	15,148	2,738
Inventory (Note 4)	15,813	13,823
Prepaid Expenses	951	352
Current Assets	$35,157	$20,422
Property, Plant, and Equipment (Note 5)	1,174	300
Less Accumulated Depreciation	(164)	(31)
	$1,010	$269
Investments (Note 6)	613	613
Other Assets	14	0
Total Assets	$36,794	$21,304
Liabilities and Shareholders' Equity		
Accounts Payable and Accrued Expenses	$4,675	$3,556
Short-Term Liabilities (Note 7)	10,000	0
Current Liabilities	$14,675	3,556
Long-Term Debt (Note 7)	0	0
Total Liabilities	$14,675	3,556
Common Stock	8,105	8,105
Additional Paid-in Capital	7,743	7,743
Retained Earnings	6,271	1,900
Total Shareholders' Equity	$22,119	$17,748
Total Liabilities and Shareholders' Equity	$36,794	$21,304

The accompanying notes are an integral part of the consolidated financial statements.

Existence—Does this cash really exist?

Rights and Obligations—Does the company really own this inventory?

Valuation or Allocation—Are these investments properly valued?

Completeness—Does the accounts payable and accrued expenses balance include all amounts owed?

STATEMENTS OF INCOME
APOLLO SHOES INC.
in thousands (except per share data)

For year ended December 31,	2023	2022
Net Sales (Note 2)	$240,575	$236,299
Cost of Sales	$141,569	$120,880
Gross Profit	$99,006	$115,419
Selling, General and Administrative Expenses	$71,998	$61,949
Interest Expense (Note 7)	$875	0
Other Expense (Income)	($204)	($1,210)
Earnings from Continuing Operations Before Taxes	$26,337	$54,680
Income Tax Expense (Note 10)	$10,271	$21,634
Earnings from Continuing Operations	$16,066	$33,046
Discontinued Operations, Net of tax benefit		($31,301)
Extraordinary Item, Net of tax benefit (Note 11)	($11,695)	
Net Income	$4,371	$1,745
Earnings Per Common Share		
From Continuing Operations	$1.98	$4.08
Other	($1.44)	($3.86)
Net Income	$0.54	$0.22
Weighted shares of common stock outstanding	8,105	8,105

The accompanying notes are an integral part of the consolidated financial statements.

Occurrence—Did these sales transactions really take place?

NOTES TO CONSOLIDATED FINANCIAL STATEMENTS
APOLLO SHOES, INC.

1. Summary of Significant Accounting Policies

Business activity The Company develops and markets technologically superior podiatric athletic products under various trademarks, including *SIREN, SPOTLIGHT,* and *SPEAKERSHOE.*

Marketable Securities Investments are valued using the market value method for investments of less than 20%, and by the equity method for investments greater than 20% but less than 50%.

Cash equivalents Cash equivalents are defined as highly liquid investments with original maturities of three months or less at date of purchase.

Inventory valuation Inventories are stated at the lower of First-in, First-out (FIFO) or market.

Property and equipment and depreciation Property and equipment are stated at cost. The Company uses the straight-line method of depreciation for all additions to property, plant, and equipment.

Intangibles Intangibles are amortized on the straight-line method over periods benefited.

Net Sales Sales for 2023 and 2022 are presented net of sales returns and allowances of $4.5 million, and $0.9 million, respectively, and net of warranty expenses of $1.1 million, and $0.9 million, respectively.

Income taxes Deferred income taxes are provided for the tax effects of timing differences in reporting the results of operations for financial statements and income tax purposes, and relate principally to valuation reserves for accounts receivable and inventory, accelerated depreciation and unearned compensation.

Net income per common share Net income per common share is computed based on the weighted average number of common and common equivalent shares outstanding for the period.

Reclassification Certain amounts have been reclassified to conform to the 2022 presentation.

2. Significant Customers

Approximately 15%, and 11% of sales are to one customer for years ended December 31, 2023 and 2022, respectively.

Presentation and Disclosure—Are these disclosures understandable? Has everything been disclosed that should be?

it is an auditor's responsibility to *not* accept management assertions without corroboration. Stated differently, an auditor must ask management to "prove" each of the relevant assertions with documentary evidence. The possibility of errors and fraud in financial reports highlights the following basic premise, which underlies the importance of professional skepticism: *A potential conflict of interest always exists between the auditors and the management of the company being audited.* This potential conflict arises because management wants to present the company's financial condition in the best possible light whereas auditors must ensure that the information about the company's financial condition is "presented fairly." The following Auditing Insight "Auditors Must Be Skeptical" illustrates why skepticism is needed.

AUDITING INSIGHT | Auditors Must Be Skeptical?

Evergrande Group, the second largest property developer in China with more than 1,300 projects in over 280 cities, received a clean bill of health from its auditors, PricewaterhouseCoopers (PwC),on its 2020 financial statements. But should they have received a going-concern issuance instead? The obvious question is, were the auditors skeptical enough of the issues the company was facing.

Evergrande is a company with significant debt; it has over $300 billion in total liabilities, including $88.5 billion in debt. In fact, in early December of 2021, Evergrande missed its interest payment of $1.2 billion to international investors, causing the ratings company Fitch to declare Evergrande in default. Further, Evergrande is being forced to sell undeveloped land in Hong Kong that is used to secure debt held by a U.S. debt holder. Consider that all of this has occurred in less than a year of PwC's March 31, 2021 audit report. Perhaps a little more skepticism was warranted?

Sources: "Evergrande to push ahead with sale of Hong Kong land after receiver appointment-source," Nasdaq, February 4 2022 (online source); "Evergrande: China property giant misses debt deadline," BBC, December 9, 2021 (online source); "China Evergrande Auditor Gave Clean Bill of Health Despite Debt," Wall Street Journal Online, September 24, 2021 (online source).

With full awareness of this potential conflict of interest, auditors must always remain professionally skeptical in their relationships with management, but not adversarial or confrontational. Nevertheless, knowing that a potential conflict of interest always exists causes auditors to perform procedures to search for errors and frauds that could have a material effect on the financial statements. And even though the vast majority of audits do not contain fraud, auditors have no choice but to exercise professional skepticism at all times and on all audits because of misdeeds perpetrated by just a few people in a few companies. The professional standards emphasize the importance of maintaining and then applying an attitude of professional skepticism throughout the entire audit process.

Auditing firms have long recognized the importance of exercising professional skepticism when making professional judgments. In fact, as illustrated in the following Auditing Insight, "Overcoming Judgment Biases," firms have increasingly stressed the importance of being skeptical when evaluating documentary evidence. You can definitely expect to encounter difficult economic transactions as an auditor. When auditors encounter a difficult transaction, they must take the time to fully understand the economic substance of that transaction and then critically evaluate, with skepticism, the evidence provided by the client to justify its accounting treatment. No shortcuts are allowed. Rather, auditors are required to be unbiased and objective when making their professional judgments.

AUDITING INSIGHT | Overcoming Judgment Biases

Judgment and decision-making researchers in auditing have long known about common biases that can interfere with or obstruct auditors from making excellent professional judgments. One example is the *anchoring bias,* which recognizes the possibility that an auditor might "anchor" on a number provided by a client manager (e.g., an estimate for the allowance for doubtful accounts) and then have difficulty adjusting to the economically correct amount. In its monograph, entitled "Elevating Professional Judgment in Accounting and Auditing," KPMG outlines a professional judgment framework designed to help auditors mitigate professional judgment biases like the anchoring bias. In order to do so, auditors must first be aware of the possibility that these biases might interfere with their professional judgment. Beyond awareness, the monograph argues that auditors must follow a disciplined process that includes (1) clarifying the issues and objectives, (2) considering the possible alternatives, (3) gathering and evaluating the relevant evidence, (4) reaching an audit conclusion, and (5) carefully documenting their rationale for the professional judgment reached. And, perhaps most importantly, the monograph emphasizes the importance of an auditor exercising professional skepticism throughout the entire process.

Source: "Elevating Professional Judgment in Accounting and Auditing: The KPMG Professional Judgment Framework," Montvale, NJ, KMPG, 2011.

Persuading a skeptical auditor is not impossible, just somewhat more difficult than persuading a normal person in an everyday context. Skepticism is a manifestation of objectivity, holding no special concern for preconceived conclusions on any side of an issue. In fact, the auditor should not care about the impact that an economic transaction has on the "bottom line" of a company, only that the accounting rules were followed and were properly applied and that the financial statements are appropriate for the user's needs. Skepticism is not being cynical, hypercritical, or scornful. The properly skeptical auditor asks questions such as the following: (1) What do I need to know? (2) How well do I know it? (3) Does it make sense? and (4) What could go wrong?

Auditors understand that receiving explanations from an entity's management is merely the first step in the professional judgment process, not the last. Auditors must listen to the explanation, and then always test it by examining sufficient competent audit evidence. The familiar phrase "healthy skepticism" should be viewed as a show-me attitude, not a predisposition to accepting unsubstantiated explanations. Auditors must gather the evidence needed, uncover all the implications from the evidence, and then arrive at the most appropriate and supportable conclusion. Time pressure to complete a financial statement audit engagement is no excuse for failing to exercise professional skepticism. Too many auditors have gotten themselves into trouble by accepting a manager's glib explanation and stopping too early in an investigation without seeking corroborating evidence.

AUDITING INSIGHT Professional Skepticism

In its Staff Audit Practice Alert about professional skepticism, the PCAOB expressed serious concern about "whether auditors consistently and diligently apply professional skepticism." The alert recognizes that there are a number of factors that could "impede" the application of professional skepticism but stresses the importance of taking whatever actions are necessary to make sure that professional skepticism is applied in an appropriate manner throughout the audit process.

THE HURTT SKEPTICISM SCALE
How skeptical are you? Answer the following 30 questions to find out. As a benchmark, business students typically fall between 90 to 150 points; auditors score much higher.

Questions	Strongly Disagree					Strongly Agree
1. I often accept other people's explanations without further thought.	1	2	3	4	5	6
2. I feel good about myself.	1	2	3	4	5	6
3. I wait to decide on issues until I can get more information.	1	2	3	4	5	6
4. The prospect of learning excites me.	1	2	3	4	5	6
5. I am interested in what causes people to behave the way that they do.	1	2	3	4	5	6
6. I am confident of my abilities.	1	2	3	4	5	6
7. I often reject statements unless I have proof that they are true.	1	2	3	4	5	6
8. Discovering new information is fun.	1	2	3	4	5	6
9. I take my time when making decisions.	1	2	3	4	5	6
10. I tend to immediately accept what other people tell me.	1	2	3	4	5	6
11. Other people's behavior does not interest me.	1	2	3	4	5	6
12. I am self-assured.	1	2	3	4	5	6
13. My friends tell me that I usually question things that I see or hear.	1	2	3	4	5	6
14. I like to understand the reason for other people's behavior.	1	2	3	4	5	6
15. I think that learning is exciting.	1	2	3	4	5	6
16. I usually accept things I see, read, or hear at face value.	1	2	3	4	5	6
17. I do not feel sure of myself.	1	2	3	4	5	6
18. I usually notice inconsistencies in explanations.	1	2	3	4	5	6

(continued)

AUDITING INSIGHT *(concluded)*

Questions	Strongly Disagree					Strongly Agree
19. Most often I agree with what the others in my group think.	1	2	3	4	5	6
20. I dislike having to make decisions quickly.	1	2	3	4	5	6
21. I have confidence in myself.	1	2	3	4	5	6
22. I do not like to decide until I've looked at all of the readily available information.	1	2	3	4	5	6
23. I like searching for knowledge.	1	2	3	4	5	6
24. I frequently question things that I see or hear.	1	2	3	4	5	6
25. It is easy for other people to convince me.	1	2	3	4	5	6
26. I seldom consider why people behave in a certain way.	1	2	3	4	5	6
27. I like to ensure that I've considered most available information before making a decision.	1	2	3	4	5	6
28. I enjoy trying to determine if what I read or hear is true.	1	2	3	4	5	6
29. I relish learning.	1	2	3	4	5	6
30. The actions people take and the reasons for those actions are fascinating.	1	2	3	4	5	6

Sources: K. Hurtt, "Development of a Scale to Measure Professional Skepticism," *Auditing: A Journal of Practice & Theory,* May 2010, pp. 149–171; *Staff Audit Practice Alert No. 10: Maintaining and Applying Professional Skepticism in Audits,* Washington, DC, PCAOB, 2012.

Although the SEC places constraints on the common practice of auditors' joining public clients that they have previously audited, close relationships often exist between former colleagues now employed by the client and members of the audit team. In these cases, the audit team must guard against being too trusting in accepting representations about the client's financial statements. Of more concern is the fact that former colleagues have inside knowledge of the firm's practices and procedures, knowing where the audit team will probably look (and where they might not look).

To summarize, due care requires an auditor to be professionally skeptical and question all material representations made by management (whether written or oral) during the professional judgment process. Although this attitude must be balanced by maintaining healthy client relationships, auditors should never assume that management is perfectly honest. The key lies in auditors' skeptical attitude toward gathering and evaluating the evidence necessary to reach supportable conclusions.

✅ REVIEW CHECKPOINT

1.12   Why should auditors act as though there is always a potential conflict of interest between the auditor and the management team of the organization being audited?

PUBLIC ACCOUNTING

LO 1-5
Describe the organization of public accounting firms and identify the various services that they offer.

The practice of public accounting is conducted in thousands of practice units ranging in size from sole proprietorships (individuals who "hang out a shingle" in front of their homes) to the largest international firms with thousands of professionals. Furthermore, many public accounting firms no longer designate themselves as *CPA firms.* Many of them describe their businesses and their organizations as *professional services firms* or some variation of this term. While Exhibit 1.6 shows an organization for a typical public

EXHIBIT 1.6
Public Accounting
Firm Organization

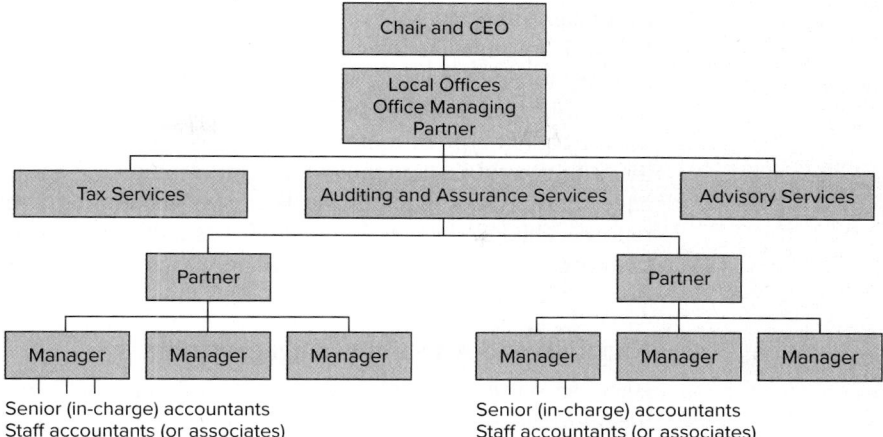

accounting firm, some firms differ in their organization. For example, some have other departments such as small business advisory and forensic accounting. Other firms may be organized by industry (e.g., entertainment, oil and gas, health care, financial institutions) to take advantage of firmwide expertise. And still some other firms have different names for their staff and management positions.

Auditing and Assurance Services

Generally speaking, auditing and assurance services involve adding value (e.g., lending credibility) to information, whether that information is financial or nonfinancial. While financial statement auditing services remain the dominant service area, CPAs have also provided assurance to vote counts (e.g., the Academy Awards), dollar amounts of prizes that sweepstakes have claimed to award, accuracy of advertisements, investment performance statistics, and characteristics claimed for computer software programs. Previously, we talked about the difference between assurance, attestation, and financial statement auditing services. And although assurance services (separate and distinct from auditing and attestation services) currently represent a fairly small part of a normal firm's operating revenues, the AICPA continues to make an effort to market these additional services to the public and businesses. Consider the following Auditing Insight "Baseball Hall of Fame."

 AUDITING INSIGHT   Baseball Hall of Fame

For baseball fans, the annual Hall of Fame vote has always been a source of fun and entertainment which is quite often accompanied by spirited conversation regarding the criteria that a player needs to meet to gain admittance into the Hall.

The Baseball Writers' Association of America is responsible for the voting and only those writers that maintain 10 consecutive years following a team are eligible to vote. But, do you know who verifies that eligible voters are properly registered, has signed a code of conduct,

and verifies the actual count of votes? You may have guessed it, one of the largest audit firms in the world, **EY.** So, although you might disagree with the final outcome from time to time, you can be assured that the appropriate process was followed and an accurate count was conducted each and every year!

Source: "2022 BBWAA Hall of Fame Ballot Features 30 Former Players," Baseball Hall of Fame, November 22, 2021 (online source).

At the present time, public accounting firms will use auditing and assurance services as a revenue category that includes financial statement audit engagements, attestation engagements, and other assurance engagements. We discuss these services as key examples of auditing and assurance services that public accounting firms offer.

Financial Statement Auditing Services

Most of the large, international accounting (Big Four) firms were founded around the turn of the 20th century (late 1800s/early 1900s) during the Industrial Revolution as

European financiers sent representatives (individuals whom we now refer to as *auditors*) to check up on their investments (mostly railroads) in the United States. As such, the primary focus of many large international accounting firms' practice has been traditional accounting and auditing services. Audits of traditional financial statements remain the most frequent type of assurance engagement that public companies (and most large and medium nonpublic companies) demand. Exhibit 1.7 shows the auditing (and other assurance services) revenues of the Big Four accounting firms based on their 2021 annual reports. This level of auditing activity usually drops as the size of the public accounting firm decreases. In other words, smaller firms usually provide more nonaudit and attestation services for their clients.

Nonaudit and Attestation Engagements

Basic accounting and review services are "nonaudit" services, performed frequently for medium and small businesses and not-for-profit organizations. Small public accounting firms perform a great deal of this type of nonaudit work. For example, CPAs can perform a *compilation,* which consists of preparing financial statements from a client's books and records, without performing any evidence-gathering work. They can also perform a *review,* in which limited evidence-gathering work is performed but which is narrower in scope than an audit. CPAs can also attest to the accuracy of management's discussion and analysis (MD&A) that accompanies the financial statements in an annual report, an entity's internal controls, and hypothetical "what-if" projections relating to mergers or acquisitions.

Tax Services

Local, state, national, and international tax laws are often called "accountant and attorney full-employment acts." The laws are complex, and CPAs perform tax planning services and tax return preparation in the areas of income, gift, estate, property, and other taxation. A large proportion of the practice in small public accounting firms is tax related. Tax laws change frequently, and tax practitioners must spend considerable time in continuing education and self-study to keep current. Exhibit 1.7 shows the tax revenues of the Big Four accounting firms based on their 2021 annual reports. Smaller public accounting firms tend to conduct more tax consulting engagements and fewer audit engagements.

Regulatory guidance from the PCAOB and AICPA prohibits an accounting firm from providing auditing services to a public company if the accounting firm provides tax consulting on aggressive interpretations of tax laws or "listed" transactions (those included on the U.S. Treasury Department's list of questionable tax strategies), if contingent fees (i.e., fees depending on a certain outcome) are involved, or if the public accounting firm provides tax services for key company executives. In all three cases, the regulatory guidance suggests that auditor independence would be impaired. Providing normal corporate tax return preparation and advice is permissible as long as the audit committee discusses with the accounting firm the implications of the tax consulting fees on auditor independence and preapproves the relationship in writing. As a result, this remains a common service area for firms to provide to their audit clients, but the firm must always maintain its independence and objectivity.

EXHIBIT 1.7   Revenues for the Big Four CPA Firms

	Deloitte	EY	KPMG	PwC
Total revenues (in billions)	$50.2	$40.0	$32.1	$45.1
Auditing and assurance services revenues	$10.4	$13.6	$11.4	$17.0
(in billions and as a percent of revenue)	21%	34%	36%	38%
Tax revenues	$ 8.9	$10.5	$ 7.1	$11.1
(in billions and as a percent of revenue)	18%	26%	22%	24%
Advisory services revenues	$30.9	$15.9	$13.6	$17.0
(in billions and as a percent of revenue)	61%	40%	42%	38%

Source: "Deloitte 2021 Total Revenue," Deloitte LLP, 2021 (online source); "EY 2021 Total Revenue," Ernst & Young LLP, 2021 (online source); PwC 2021 Total Revenue," PricewaterhouseCoopers LLP, 2021 (online source); KPMG 2021 Total Revenue," KPMG LLP, 2021 (online source).

Advisory Services

Prior to the turn of this century (the 1990s), the largest public accounting firms handled a great deal of advisory services for their auditing clients. In fact, advisory services provided a great new revenue opportunity for firms and the potential for even more business appeared at times to be unlimited. Public accounting firms tried to become "one-stop shopping centers" for clients' auditing, taxation, and advisory services.

The SEC, the governmental agency which is responsible for investor protection, expressed reservations as to whether the performance of nonaudit services (such as advisory) impaired a public accounting firm's ability to conduct an independent audit. The SEC's concern was that the large amount of revenues generated from advisory services might sway the auditor's opinion on the company's financial statements. The public accounting firms, on the other hand, argued that the provision of advisory services allowed them a closer look at the client's operations, providing a synergistic, positive effect on the audit.

In response to the spate of corporate frauds, Congress resolved this difference of opinion, in part, by passing Sarbanes–Oxley which was seen as a broad accounting and corporate governance reform measure. Sarbanes–Oxley prohibits public accounting firms from providing any of the following services to a public audit client: (1) bookkeeping and related services; (2) design or implementation of financial information systems; (3) appraisal or valuation services; (4) actuarial services; (5) internal audit outsourcing; (6) management or human resources services; (7) investment or broker/dealer services; and (8) legal and expert services (unrelated to the audit). As already stated, public accounting firms may provide general corporate tax return preparation and advice and other nonprohibited services to public audit clients if the company's audit committee has approved them in advance.

To briefly summarize these restrictions, Sarbanes–Oxley prohibits public accounting firms from performing any consulting or advisory services in which the auditors may find themselves making managerial decisions or that would result in the firm auditing its own work (e.g., completing a financial information system implementation for its audit client). As a result of Sarbanes–Oxley, most of the large firms now provide consulting only for companies that they do not audit. However, the Big Four firms have still been able to dramatically increase the size of their advisory services in recent years. As shown in Exhibit 1.7, firm advisory revenues ranged between 38 and 61 percent of the Big Four firms' total revenues in 2021. Of course, public accounting firms are not required to follow Sarbanes–Oxley guidelines for their non-SEC clients, and in those situations, firms can provide an array of consulting and advisory services provided they maintain their independence and objectivity when completing the financial statement audit. In fact, the following Auditing Insight "Is There Room for Public Accounting Firms?" shows that public accounting firms may even enter the legal services market.

 AUDITING INSIGHT Is There Room for Public Accounting Firms?

There are some that say it is only a matter of time until the Big 4 public accounting firms become a dominant force in the lucrative corporate legal services marketplace. A recent research study noted that "the Big 4 accounting firms have expanded their legal service arms to historic proportions over the last decade." And, even though "most of the Big 4's revenue from legal services is presently generated outside the U.S.," it appears to be only a matter of time until that changes.

In fact, When the American Bar Association passed a resolution in February 2020 which encouraged state bar associations to look at new ways to access legal services, there are now some states that are considering allowing non-lawyers to own firms that provide legal services, which would appear to open the door for accounting firms to enter the market. Of course, there are very strict regulatory issues to deal with, in particular, in regards to whether a firm can remain independent if they are also performing a financial statement audit of a client. But, this line of service appears to be a promising avenue for growth.

Source: B.E. Brewster, J.H. Grenier D.N. Herda, M.E. Marshall, "Big 4 Firms as Legal Service Providers: Implications for Audit Practice and Future Research Directions," *Accounting Horizons,* September, 2021, pp. 93–112.

OTHER KINDS OF ENGAGEMENTS AND INFORMATION PROFESSIONALS

LO 1-6
Describe the audits and auditors in governmental, internal, and operational auditing.

The AAA and the AICPA definitions of auditing clearly apply to the independent financial statement auditors who work in public accounting firms. The word *audit,* however, is also used in other contexts to describe broader types of work. The variety of engagements performed by different kinds of information assurors causes some problems with terminology. In this textbook, *independent auditor, external auditor,* and *CPA* will refer to people doing financial statement audit work with public accounting firms. In the internal and governmental contexts discussed here, auditors are identified as *operational auditors, internal auditors,* and *governmental auditors.* Although all of these professionals are information assurors (and many are certified public accountants), the term *CPA* in this book will refer to financial statement auditors engaged in public practice. The following sections provide a brief overview of the work completed by these professionals. In Module D, we provide a detailed description for each of these areas.

Internal Auditing

The Board of Directors of the Institute of Internal Auditors (IIA) defines **internal auditing** and states its objective as follows:

> Internal auditing is an independent, objective assurance and consulting activity designed to add value and improve an organization's operations. It helps an organization accomplish its objectives by bringing a systematic, disciplined approach to evaluate and improve the effectiveness of risk management, control, and governance processes.[7]

Internal auditors are employed by organizations such as banks, hospitals, city governments, and industrial companies or work for CPA firms that provide internal auditing services. Internal auditors often perform *operational audits.* **Operational auditing** refers to the study of business operations for the purpose of making recommendations about the efficient and effective use of resources, effective achievement of business objectives, and compliance with company policies. The goal of operational auditing is to help managers discharge their management responsibilities and improve profitability.

Internal auditors also perform audits of financial reports for internal use or limited external distribution (e.g., reports to regulatory agencies) much like external auditors audit financial statements distributed to outside users. Thus, some internal auditing work is similar to the auditing described elsewhere in this textbook. In addition, the services provided by internal auditors include (1) reviews of internal control systems to ensure compliance with company policies, plans, and procedures; (2) compliance with laws and regulations; (3) appraisals of the *economy* and *efficiency* of operations; and (4) reviews of effectiveness in achieving program results in comparison to established objectives and goals.

It should be noted that the AICPA defines operational auditing performed by independent CPA firms as a distinct type of management consulting service whose goal is to help a client improve the use of its capabilities and resources to achieve its objectives. So, internal auditors consider operational auditing integral to internal auditing and external auditors define it as a type of assurance service offered by public accounting firms. In fact, providing these types of internal auditing services continues to be a growing business for

[7] Definition of Internal Audit, The Institute of Internal Auditors. May 17, 2019 (online source).

many large CPA firms. However, both the SEC and the PCAOB prohibit CPA firms from providing internal auditing services to their own public audit clients.

Governmental Auditing

The U.S. Government Accountability Office (GAO) is an accounting, auditing, and investigating agency of the U.S. Congress, headed by the U.S. Comptroller General. In one sense, GAO auditors are the highest level of internal auditors for the federal government. Many states have audit agencies similar to the GAO. These agencies answer to state legislatures and perform the same types of work described in this section for GAO auditors. In another sense, GAO and similar state agencies are really external auditors with respect to government agencies they audit because they are organizationally independent.

Many government agencies have their own internal auditors and inspectors general. Well-managed local governments also have internal audit departments. For example, most federal agencies (Department of Defense, Department of Human Resources, Department of the Interior), state agencies (education, welfare, controller), and local governments (cities, counties, tax districts) have internal audit staffs. Governmental and internal auditors have much in common.

The GAO shares with internal auditors the same elements of *expanded-scope* services. The GAO, however, emphasizes the accountability of public officials for the efficient, economical, and effective use of public funds and other resources. The generally accepted government auditing standards (GAGAS) define and describe three broad types of audits that may be performed. They are financial audits, attestation engagements, and performance audits.

Financial audits include determining whether financial information is presented in accordance with the established and applicable financial reporting framework. There are many types of attestation engagements, including whether the governmental entity's internal control system is suitably designed and implemented to achieve the applicable control objectives.

Attestation engagements would also include a compliance audit function applied with respect to applicable laws and regulations. All government organizations, programs, activities, and functions are created by law, and most are surrounded by regulations that govern the things they can and cannot do. For example, a program established to provide school meals to low-income students must comply with regulations about the eligibility of recipients. A compliance audit of such a program involves a study of schools' policies, procedures, and actual performance in determining eligibility and handing out meal tickets.

Performance audits refer to a wide range of governmental audits that include (1) economy and efficiency audits and (2) program audits. Governments are concerned about accountability for the appropriate use of taxpayers' resources; performance audits are a means of seeking to improve accountability for the efficient and economical use of resources and the achievement of program goals. In addition, the program audit helps determine whether the financial resources being spent are truly helping the government achieve its stated objectives for a particular program. Performance audits, like internal auditors' operational audits, involve studies of the management of government organizations, programs, activities, and functions. Consider the following examples of GAO engagements.

GAO Engagement Examples

- The Capitol Police Need Clearer Emergency Procedures and a Comprehensive Security Risk Assessment Process *(GAO-22-105001, February 17, 2022)*.
- Enhanced Data Capabilities, Analysis, Sharing, and Risk Assessments Needed for Disaster Preparedness *(GAO-22-104289, February 02, 2022)*.
- FY 2021 and FY 2020 Consolidated Financial Statements of the U.S. Government *(GAO-22-105122, February 17, 2022)*.
- Challenges Facing DOD in Strategic Competition with China *(GAO-22-105448, February 15, 2022)*.
- Agencies Need to Assess Adoption of Cybersecurity Guidance *(GAO-22-105103, February 09, 2022)*.

Regulatory Auditors

For the sake of clarity, other kinds of auditors deserve separate mention. The U.S. Internal Revenue Service employs auditors. They take the "economic assertions" of taxable income made by taxpayers on tax returns and determine their correspondence with the standards found in the Internal Revenue Code. They also audit for fraud and tax evasion. Their reports can either certify the correctness of a taxpayer's return, claim that additional taxes are due, or even show that a refund is due to a taxpayer.

State and federal bank examiners audit banks, savings and loan associations, and other financial institutions for evidence of solvency and compliance with banking and other related laws and regulations. As a result of the financial crisis of 2008/2009 and the resulting Dodd-Frank Act of 2010, these examiners have been quite busy for many years to help ensure the safety and security of the U.S. banking system.

☑ REVIEW CHECKPOINTS

1.15   What is *operational* auditing? How does the AICPA view operational auditing?

1.16   What are the three broad types of governmental audits described by the GAGAS issued by the GAO?

1.17   Define what is meant by *compliance* auditing.

1.18   Name some other types of auditors in addition to external, internal, and governmental auditors.

BECOME A PROFESSIONAL AND GET CERTIFIED!

LO 1-7
List and explain the requirements for becoming a certified public accountant (CPA) and other certifications available to an accounting professional.

If you plan to begin your career in accounting (which we hope you do since you are reading this book!), you are on your way to being known as an accounting professional. Congratulations! Being part of a profession implies a higher level of societal responsibility. In order to meet this responsibility, it is absolutely essential that you acquire the knowledge required to do your job; certification indicates that you have acquired that knowledge. In that spirit, being certified as a CPA is generally regarded as the highest mark of distinction and is required to practice as a financial statement auditor in the United States. In Australia, Canada, and the United Kingdom, the chartered accountant (CA) designation is required to practice as a financial statement auditor. For an information technology (IT) audit professional, a certified information systems auditor (CISA) is the key mark of distinction. In fact, depending on your area of professional service within public accounting, a certified fraud examiner (CFE), certified forensic accountant (CFA), certified information systems security professional (CISSP), or even a certified internal auditor (CIA) certification may be just as important. Outside of public accounting, certification as a certified management accountant (CMA) or as a certified information technology professional (CITP) may be the most appropriate. Regardless of your career choice, a certification adds credibility that will assist you throughout your entire career.

Education

While education requirements vary across the different certifying organizations, we focus on the CPA certification in this book because of its importance to financial statement auditors. For the CPA, the specific education requirements vary by state for both having permission to take the CPA examination and for receiving a CPA certificate. As a result, students must visit the website of their own state's board of accountancy and search for the exact regulations that apply in their home state. While you are required to take 150 semester hours of college education before you receive a CPA certificate, many states now allow you to take the CPA examination after only 120 semester hours of college education. Still other certifications (such as the CIA) allow you to take the exam before you have graduated.

In addition to entry-level education requirements, all certifying organizations have regulations about *continuing professional education* (CPE). Indeed, once certified, accounting professionals obtain CPE hours in a variety of ways: continuing education courses, in-house training, and even college courses. These types of courses range in length from one hour to two weeks, depending on the subject. Many CPE providers offer courses online. If in-house training is not an option, many CPAs obtain their CPE by taking part in training sessions offered by their home state's professional accounting organization or other industry conferences.

Examination

When working as a financial statement auditor, CPAs have a critically important role in protecting the public interest when they attest to the reliability of a company's financial statements. As a result, the profession needs to make sure that only qualified individuals can become certified and then licensed as CPAs. To do so, the AICPA creates and then administers the Uniform CPA Examination. When creating the exam, the AICPA works hard to ensure that the knowledge and skills covered on the exam are aligned with those that are needed to protect the public interest in current practice. This is an ongoing process.

In fact, just recently, the AICPA and the National Association of State Boards of Accountancy (NASBA) came together on a joint initiative to redesign the CPA exam to "reflect changes in the profession and technology, focusing newly licensed CPAs on the most relevant and useful knowledge and skills."[8] The proposed changes in the CPA exam are part of the CPA Evolution, a broader initiative to reimagine the CPA licensure model. The new exam is scheduled to debut in 2024 and is expected to include three new sections, Business Analysis & Reporting (BAR), Information Systems and Controls (ISC) and Tax Compliance & Planning (TCP).

Although we encourage you to stay in close touch with changes to the CPA exam as they occur (see www.aicpa.org), at the present time, the CPA exam emphasizes higher-order skills like problem solving, critical thinking, and analytical ability. The exam covers Auditing and Attestation (AUD), Financial Accounting and Reporting (FAR), Regulation (REG), and Business Environment and Concepts (BEC). In the required AUD section, candidates will have four hours to complete 72 multiple-choice questions and eight to nine task-based simulations. The exam score is equally weighted between the multiple-choice questions and task-based simulations. To help candidates prepare for the exam, the AICPA has published detailed blueprints for each of the four sections. Each blueprint is designed to provide clarity about the knowledge content, skills, and types of tasks that might be tested for each exam. The summary blueprint for the AUD section is provided in the accompanying table (with rough approximations of weights given to each content area and skill allocation).[9]

Content Area Allocation	Weight
Ethics, Professional Responsibilities, and General Principles	15–25%
Assessing Risk and Developing a Planned Response	25–35%
Performing Further Procedures and Obtaining Evidence	30–40%
Forming Conclusions and Reporting	10–20%
Skill Allocation	**Weight**
Evaluation	5–15%
Analysis	20–30%
Application	30–40%
Remembering and Understanding	25–35%

Source: https://www.aicpa.org/resources/download/learn-what-is-tested-on-the-cpa-exam. Summary blueprints for REG, FAR, and BEC can also be found at this site.

[8]Ken, Tysiac. "Content for redesigned CPA exam takes shape," *Journal of Accountancy,* AICPA, July 7 2021 (online source).

[9] "Uniform CPA Examination® Auditing and Attestation (AUD)," AICPA, May 31, 2018 (online source).

Generally speaking, each section of the CPA exam consists of multiple-choice questions and task-based simulations (except for BEC, which also includes graded written communication). The task-based simulations are short case studies in which you will be asked to apply your auditing and accounting knowledge. A simulation may involve identifying a potential problem, electronically researching the topic using a database of authoritative standards, and reporting your findings. Each section's exam blueprint is designed specifically for candidates to help prepare for the exam. Throughout this book, you will have many opportunities to acquire the knowledge necessary to pass the AUD section of the exam.

General information about the CPA exam can be obtained from a special site set up by the AICPA (available at www.aicpa.org). Because qualifications for taking the CPA examination vary from state to state, you will need to contact your state board of accountancy for an application or more information. You can find your state board of accountancy website through the NASBA website (www.nasba.org). Exhibit 1.8 lists the requirements for the most commonly recognized professional certifications.

Experience

Although not required to *sit* for a professional exam, experience is required to *become certified.* Most states and territories require a person who has attained the education level and passed the CPA examination to have a period of experience working under a practicing CPA before awarding a CPA certificate. Experience requirements vary across states, but most jurisdictions require one to two years of experience. A few states require that the experience be obtained in a public accounting firm, but most of them accept experience in other organizations (GAO, internal audit, management accounting, Internal Revenue Service, and the like) as long as the applicant performs work requiring accounting judgment and is supervised by a competent accountant, preferably a CPA. Other certifying organizations also have experience requirements.

State Certificate and License

The AICPA does not issue CPA certificates or licenses to practice. Rather, all states and territories have state accountancy laws and state licensing boards to administer them. After satisfying state requirements for education and experience, successful candidates receive their CPA *certificate* from their state board of accountancy. At the same time, new CPAs must pay a fee to obtain a state *license* to practice or work for a CPA firm that is licensed to practice in their state. Thereafter, state boards of accountancy regulate the behavior of CPAs under their jurisdiction (enforcing state codes of ethics) and supervise the continuing education requirements.

After becoming a CPA licensed in one state, a person can obtain a CPA certificate and license in another state by filing the proper application with the second state board of accountancy, meeting that state's requirements, and obtaining another CPA certificate. Many CPAs hold certificates and licenses in several states. From a global perspective, individuals must be licensed in each country. Similar to CPAs in the United States, *chartered accountants (CAs)* practice in Australia, Canada, Great Britain, and India.

Efforts are currently under way through the AICPA and the National Association of State Boards of Accountancy (NASBA) to streamline the licensing process so that CPAs can practice across state lines without having to possess 50 different licenses. Under the concept of **substantial equivalency,** as long as the licensing (home) state requires (1) 150 hours of education, (2) successful completion of the CPA exam, and (3) one year of experience, a CPA can practice (either in person or electronically) in another substantial equivalency state without having to obtain a license in that state.

Skill Sets and Your Education

The requirements to become certified are rather strenuous, but they may not be enough! Let us take you on a brief tour of the core competencies listed by the AICPA, the Association of Certified Fraud Examiners (ACFE), the Institute of Internal Auditors (IIA), the

EXHIBIT 1.8 **Certification Requirements**

	Certified Public Accountant (CPA)	Certified Information Systems Auditor (CISA)	Certified Internal Auditor (CIA)	Certified Fraud Examiner (CFE)	Certified Management Accountant (CMA)
Education Level	Varies by state; Generally 150 hours. However, check with your state board of accountancy	No specific degree requirement	Generally, bachelor's degree or its educational equivalent	Generally, bachelor's degree or its educational equivalent	Bachelor's degree, or pass the CPA, CFA, CIA or CFE examination
Experience	Varies by state; Generally 1-2 years working under a CPA. Check with your state board of accountancy	5 years of professional information system (IS) auditing, control, or security work experience for certification. Some substitutions and waivers are possible.	Generally 2 years of internal auditing experience or its equivalent for certification. May be less with a Master's degree. May be more without a degree.	2 years of professional experience for certification	2 continuous years of professional experience in management accounting and/or financial management
Exam Coverage	1. Auditing and attestation (AUD) 2. Financial accounting and reporting (FAR) 3. Regulation (REG) 4. Business environment and concepts (BEC)	1. The process of auditing information systems 2. Governance and management of IT 3. Information systems acquisition, development, and implementation 4. Information systems operations, and business resilience 5. Protection of information assets	1. Essentials of internal auditing 2. Practice of internal auditing 3. Business knowledge of internal auditing	1. Fraud prevention and deterrence 2. Financial transactions and fraud schemes 3. Investigation 4. Law	1. Financial planning, performance, and analytics 2. Strategic financial management
Test Length	4 parts, 16 hours	1 part, 4 hours (150 mc questions)	3 parts, 6.5 hours (325 mc questions)	4 parts (2 hours each part - 100 questions each); 8 total hours	2 parts (100 mc questions and two 30-minute essays, each) 8 hours
Passing Score	75%	450 (on an 800-point scale)	600 (on a 750-point scale)	75%	360 per part (on a 500-point scale)
Test Dates	On demand	On demand	On demand	Self-administered	On demand during the months of Jan, Feb, May, Jun, Sep, and Oct
Administering Body	American Institute of Certified Public Accountants Board of Examiners	Information Systems Audit and Control Association	Institute of Internal Auditors	Association of Certified Fraud Examiners	Institute of Certified Management Accountants
Website	www.aicpa.org	www.isaca.org	www.theiia.org	www.acfe.com	www.imanet.org

Institute of Management Accountants (IMA), the Information Systems Audit and Control Association (ISACA), and other guidance-providing groups: mathematics, international culture, psychology, economics, statistics, political science, inductive and deductive reasoning, ethics, group dynamic processes, finance, capital markets, managing change, history of accounting, regulation, information systems, taxation, and (oh, yes) accounting and auditing. Add administrative capability, analytical skills, business knowledge, communication skills (writing and speaking), efficiency, intellectual capability, marketing and selling, model building, people development, capacity for putting client needs first, and more.

We hope you are suitably impressed by this recitation of virtually all of the world's knowledge. You will be very old when you accomplish a fraction of the skill development and education suggested. Now the good news: (1) not everyone needs to be completely knowledgeable in all of these areas upon graduation from college, (2) learning and skill development continue over a lifetime, and (3) no one expects you to know everything on the job. In fact, we have observed that audit teams composed of members specializing in some areas with other members specializing in other areas seem to work best in practice. We do, however, stress the need to continue your education even after you leave school. Learning should be a lifelong pursuit, not something that ends when you receive your diploma.

✅ REVIEW CHECKPOINTS

1.19 Why is continuing education required to maintain certification?

1.20 Why do you think experience is required to become certified?

1.21 What are some of the functions of a state board of public accountancy?

1.22 What are some of the limitations to practicing public accounting across state and national boundaries?

Summary

Decision makers need more than just information; they need reliable and credible information that they can rely upon. Internet buyers rely on website information when purchasing online. Financial analysts and investors use financial reports to help make stock investment decisions. Suppliers and lenders use financial reports to decide whether to grant credit and originate loans. Labor organizations use financial reports to help determine a company's ability to pay wages. Government agencies and Congress use financial information in preparing analyses of the economy and in making laws concerning taxes, subsidies, and the like. These various users rely on independent CPAs to reduce information risk. Auditors (and other information assurance providers) assume the role of certifying (or attesting to) published financial information, thereby providing assurance that information risk is low.

This chapter began by defining information risk and explained how auditing and assurance services play a role in minimizing this risk. The financial statements were explained in terms of the primary assertions that management makes in them, and these assertions were identified as the focal points of the auditors' evidence-gathering work. Auditing is practiced in numerous forms by various practice units, including public accounting firms, the Internal Revenue Service, the U.S. Government Accountability Office, internal audit departments in companies, and several other types of regulatory auditors. Fraud examiners, many of whom are internal auditors and inspectors, have also found a niche in auditing-related activities.

The public accounting profession recognizes that, in today's information economy, information risk exists in areas outside of financial transactions. Assurance services is a broad category of information-enhancement services that build on CPAs' auditing, attestation, accounting, and advisory skills to create products useful to a wide range of decision makers (customers). While reliable information helps make capital markets efficient and helps people know the consequences of a wide variety of economic decisions, CPAs practicing the assurance function are not the only information professionals at work in the economy. Bank examiners, IRS auditors, state regulatory agency auditors (e.g., auditors in a state's insurance department), internal auditors employed by a company, and federal government agency auditors all practice information assurance in one form or another.

Most financial statement auditors aspire to become certified public accountants, which involves successfully completing a rigorous examination, obtaining practical experience, and maintaining competence through continuing professional education. Auditors also obtain credentials as certified internal auditors, certified management accountants, certified information systems auditors, and certified fraud examiners. Each of these fields has large professional organizations that govern the professional standards and quality of practice of its members.

Key Terms

assurance: The lending of credibility to information, 4

assurance services: Independent professional services that improve the quality of information, or its context, for decision makers, 5

attestation: A professional service resulting in a report on an assertion (or assertions) about subject matter that is the responsibility of another party, 4

attestation engagement: An engagement where a practitioner is requested to examine whether management's assertions about some type of subject matter can be relied upon, 8

auditing: The systematic process of objectively obtaining and evaluating evidence regarding assertions about economic actions and events to ascertain the degree of correspondence between the assertions and established criteria and communicating the results to interested users, 5

business risk: Those factors, events, and conditions that could prevent the organization from achieving its business objectives, 3

completeness: Management assertion that all of the transactions, events, assets, liabilities, equity interests, and other disclosures that should have been recorded in the financial statements have been recorded, 15

cutoff: Management assertion that refers to accounting for revenue, expense, and other transactions in the proper period. The cutoff date generally refers to the audit client's year-end balance sheet date, 16

existence: Management assertion that all assets, liabilities, and equity interests do actually exist, 15

financial reporting: Process of providing statements of financial position (balance sheets), results of operations (income statements, statements of shareholders' equity, and statements of comprehensive income), changes in cash flows (statements of cash flows), and accompanying disclosures to outside decision makers who do not have access to management's internal sources of information; a company's accountants, under the direction of its management, perform this function, 13

information risk: The probability that the information circulated by an entity will be false or misleading, 4

internal auditing: A professional service provided to a company to assist the company in meeting its corporate goals and objectives in part by evaluating and recommending risk management, control, and governance processes, 26

occurrence: Management assertion that all of the transactions and events that have been recorded are valid, pertain to the entity, and have actually taken place, 15

operational auditing: An examination designed to evaluate the processes and procedures of an organization or an area within an organization to ensure the process or area is operating efficiently and effectively, 26

presentation and disclosure: Management assertion that all transactions and events have been presented correctly and that all relevant information has been disclosed to financial statement users, usually in the footnotes to the financial statements, 15

professional skepticism: A state of mind that is characterized by appropriate questioning and a critical assessment of audit evidence, 18

relevant assertion: A management assertion is relevant if there is a reasonable possibility that a material misstatement exists related to that assertion for the significant account or footnote disclosure being audited, 18

rights and obligations: Management assertion that the entity is entitled to all rights of the assets, the liabilities are the legal responsibility of the entity, and all of the disclosed events and transactions pertain to the entity, 15

significant accounts: A financial statement account or footnote disclosure is considered significant if there is a chance that the account or footnote disclosure could contain a material misstatement. As a result, an auditor will have to conduct some procedures on each significant account or disclosure, 18

system-generated reports: Any report that is generated by the audit client's information system that is used to execute its internal control procedures or produce its financial statements. It is important to test that each system-generated report is complete and accurate if it is being used for either of these purposes, 12

substantial equivalency: The process through which CPAs licensed in one state can practice in another state, 30

valuation or allocation: Management assertion that all assets, liabilities, and equity interests of the entity have been valued in accordance with the relevant financial reporting standards (e.g., GAAP) and are listed in the financial statements at the proper amount, and any resulting valuation adjustments have been appropriately recorded in the financial statements, 15

Multiple-Choice Questions for Practice and Review

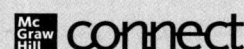 All applicable questions are available with *Connect*.

LO 1-2

1.23 Which of the following would be considered an assurance engagement?
   a. Giving an opinion on a prize promoter's claims about the amount of sweepstakes prizes awarded in the past.
   b. Giving an opinion on the conformity of the financial statements of a university with generally accepted accounting principles.
   c. Giving an opinion on the fair presentation of a newspaper's circulation data.
   d. Giving assurance about the average drive length achieved by golfers with a client's golf balls.
   e. All of the above.

LO 1-4

1.24 It is always a good idea for auditors to begin an audit with the professional skepticism characterized by the assumption that
   a. A potential conflict of interest always exists between the auditor and the management of the enterprise under audit.
   b. In audits of financial statements, the auditor acts exclusively in the capacity of an auditor.
   c. The professional status of the independent auditor imposes commensurate professional obligations.
   d. Financial statements and financial data are verifiable.

LO 1-2

1.25 In an attestation engagement, a CPA practitioner is engaged to
   a. Compile a company's financial forecast based on management's assumptions without expressing any form of assurance.
   b. Prepare a written report containing a conclusion about the reliability of a management assertion.
   c. Prepare a tax return using information the CPA has not audited or reviewed.
   d. Give expert testimony in court on particular facts in a corporate income tax controversy.

LO 1-6

1.26 A determination of cost savings obtained by outsourcing cafeteria services is most likely to be an objective of
   a. Environmental auditing.
   b. Financial auditing.
   c. Compliance auditing.
   d. Operational auditing.

LO 1-6   1.27   The primary difference between operational auditing and financial auditing is that in operational auditing

a. The operational auditor is not concerned with whether the audited activity is generating information in compliance with financial accounting standards.

b. The operational auditor is seeking to help management use resources in the most effective manner possible.

c. The operational auditor starts with the financial statements of an activity being audited and works backward to the basic processes involved in producing them.

d. The operational auditor can use analytical skills and tools that are not necessary in financial auditing.

LO 1-2   1.28   According to the AICPA, the purpose of an audit of financial statements is to

a. Enhance the degree of confidence that intended users can place in the financial statements.

b. Express an opinion on the fairness with which they present financial position, results of operations, and cash flows in conformity with accounting standards promulgated by the Financial Accounting Standards Board.

c. Express an opinion on the fairness with which they present financial position, results of operations, and cash flows in conformity with accounting standards promulgated by the U.S. Securities and Exchange Commission.

d. Obtain systematic and objective evidence about financial assertions and report the results to interested users.

LO 1-1   1.29   Bankers who are processing loan applications from companies seeking large loans will probably ask for financial statements audited by an independent CPA because

a. Financial statements are too complex for the bankers to analyze themselves.

b. They are too far away from company headquarters to perform accounting and auditing themselves.

c. The consequences of making a bad loan are very undesirable.

d. They generally see a potential conflict of interest between company managers who want to get loans and the bank's needs for reliable financial statements.

LO 1-5   1.30   The Sarbanes–Oxley Act of 2002 prohibits public accounting firms from providing which of the following services to an audit client?

a. Bookkeeping services.

b. Internal auditing services.

c. Valuation services.

d. All of the above.

LO 1-1   1.31   Independent auditors of financial statements perform audits that reduce

a. Business risks faced by investors.

b. Information risk faced by investors.

c. Complexity of financial statements.

d. Timeliness of financial statements.

LO 1-6   1.32   The primary objective of compliance auditing is to

a. Give an opinion on financial statements.

b. Develop a basis for a report on internal control.

c. Perform a study of effective and efficient use of resources.

d. Determine whether client personnel are following laws, rules, regulations, and policies.

LO 1-7   1.33   What requirements are *usually* necessary to become licensed as a certified public accountant?

a. Successful completion of the Uniform CPA Examination.

b. Experience in the accounting field.

c. Education.

d. All of the above.

LO 1-6   1.34 The organization primarily responsible for ensuring that public officials are using public funds efficiently, economically, and effectively is the
   a. Governmental Internal Audit Agency (GIAA).
   b. Central Internal Auditors (CIA).
   c. Securities and Exchange Commission (SEC).
   d. Government Accountability Office (GAO).

LO 1-6   1.35 Performance audits usually include [two answers]
   a. Financial audits.
   b. Economy and efficiency audits.
   c. Compliance audits.
   d. Program audits.

LO 1-3   1.36 The objective in an auditor's review of credit ratings of a client's customers is to obtain evidence related to management's assertion about
   a. Completeness.
   b. Existence.
   c. Valuation or allocation.
   d. Rights and obligations.
   e. Occurrence.

LO 1-4   1.37 Jones, CPA, is planning the audit of Rhonda's Company. Rhonda verbally asserts to Jones that all expenses for the year have been recorded in the accounts. Rhonda's representation in this regard
   a. Is sufficient evidence for Jones to conclude that the completeness assertion is supported for expenses.
   b. Can enable Jones to minimize the work on the gathering of evidence to support Rhonda's completeness assertion.
   c. Should be disregarded because it is not in writing.
   d. Is not considered a sufficient basis for Jones to conclude that all expenses have been recorded.

LO 1-1   1.38 The risk to investors that a company's financial statements may be materially misleading is called
   a. Client acceptance risk.
   b. Information risk.
   c. Moral hazard.
   d. Business risk.

LO 1-3   1.39 When auditing merchandise inventory at year-end, the auditor performs audit procedures to ensure that all goods purchased before year-end are received before the physical inventory count. This audit procedure provides assurance about which management assertion?
   a. Cutoff.
   b. Existence.
   c. Valuation or allocation.
   d. Rights and obligations.
   e. Occurrence.

LO 1-3   1.40 When auditing merchandise inventory at year-end, the auditor performs audit procedures to obtain evidence that no goods held on consignment are included in the client's ending inventory balance. This audit procedure provides assurance about which management assertion?
   a. Completeness.
   b. Existence.
   c. Valuation or allocation.
   d. Rights and obligations.
   e. Occurrence.

LO 1-3 1.41 When an auditor reviews additions to the equipment (fixed asset) account to make sure that fixed assets are not overstated, she wants to obtain evidence as to management's assertion regarding

    a. Completeness.

    b. Existence.

    c. Valuation or allocation.

    d. Rights and obligations.

    e. Occurrence.

LO 1-5 1.42 The Sarbanes–Oxley Act of 2002 generally prohibits public accounting firms from

    a. Acting in a managerial decision-making role for an audit client.

    b. Auditing the firm's own work on an audit client.

    c. Providing tax consulting to an audit client without audit committee approval.

    d. All of the above.

LO 1-7 1.43 Substantial equivalency refers to

    a. An auditor's tendency not to believe management's assertions without sufficient corroboration.

    b. Providing consulting work for another firm's audit client in exchange for the other firm's providing consulting services to one of your clients.

    c. The waiving of certification exam parts for an individual holding an equivalent certification from another professional organization.

    d. Permitting a CPA to practice in another state without having to obtain a license in that state.

LO 1-2 1.44 Which of the following best describes the relationship between auditing and attestation engagements?

    a. Auditing is a subset of attestation engagements that focuses on the certification of financial statements.

    b. Attestation is a subset of auditing that provides lower assurance than that provided by an audit engagement.

    c. Auditing is a subset of attestation engagements that focuses on providing clients with advice and decision support.

    d. Attestation is a subset of auditing that improves the quality of information or its context for decision makers.

LO 1-3 1.45 During an audit of a company's cash balance on a company with operations in only one country, the auditor is most concerned with which management assertion?

    a. Existence.

    b. Rights and obligations.

    c. Valuation or allocation.

    d. Occurrence.

LO 1-3 1.46 When auditing an investment in a publicly traded company, an auditor most likely would seek to conduct which audit procedure to help satisfy the valuation assertion?

    a. Inspect the stock certificates evidencing the investment.

    b. Examine the audited financial statements of the investee company.

    c. Review the broker's advice or canceled check for the investment's acquisition.

    d. Obtain market quotations from *The Wall Street Journal* or another independent source.

LO 1-3 1.47 Cutoff tests designed to detect valid sales that occurred before the end of the year but have been recorded in the subsequent year would provide assurance about management's assertion of

    a. Presentation and disclosure.

    b. Completeness.

    c. Rights and obligations.

    d. Existence.

LO 1-3

1.48 Which of the following audit procedures probably would provide the most reliable evidence related to the entity's assertion of rights and obligations for the inventory account?

    a. Trace test counts noted during physical count to the summarization of quantities.

    b. Inspect agreements for evidence of inventory held on consignment.

    c. Select the last few shipping advices used before the physical count and determine whether the shipments were recorded as sales.

    d. Inspect the open purchase order file for significant commitments to consider for disclosure.

LO 1-3

1.49 In auditing the accrued liabilities account on the balance sheet, an auditor's procedures most likely would focus primarily on management's assertion of

    a. Existence or occurrence.

    b. Completeness.

    c. Presentation and disclosure.

    d. Valuation or allocation.

LO 1-2

1.50 Which of the following *best* describes the focus of the following engagements?

Auditing Engagement	Attestation Engagement	Assurance Engagement	Consulting Services Engagement
a. Any information	Financial statements	Advice and decision support	Financial information
b. Financial information	Advice and decision support	Financial statements	Any information
c. Advice and decision support	Any information	Financial information	Financial statements
d. Financial statements, including footnotes	Financial information	Any information	Advice and decision support

LO 1-7

1.51 Which of the following is a reason to obtain professional certification?

    a. Certification provides credibility that an individual is technically competent.

    b. Certification often is a necessary condition for advancement and promotion within a professional services firm.

    c. Obtaining certification is often monetarily rewarded by an individual's employer.

    d. All of the above.

LO 1-3

1.52 During an audit of an entity's stockholders' equity accounts, the auditor determines whether there are restrictions on retained earnings resulting from loans, agreements, or state law. This audit procedure most likely is intended to verify management's assertion of

    a. Existence or occurrence.

    b. Completeness.

    c. Valuation or allocation.

    d. Presentation and disclosure.

LO 1-3

1.53 When auditing the accounts receivable account on the balance sheet, an auditor's procedures most likely would focus primarily on management's assertion of

    a. Existence.

    b. Completeness.

    c. Presentation and disclosure.

    d. Rights and obligations.

LO 1-3

1.54 An auditor selected items for test counts from the client's warehouse during the physical inventory observation. The auditor then traced these test counts into the detailed inventory listing that agreed to the financial statements. This procedure most likely provided evidence concerning management's assertion of

    a. Rights and obligations.

    b. Completeness.

    c. Existence.

    d. Valuation or allocation.

LO 1-3

1.55 An auditor's purpose in auditing the information contained in the pension footnote most likely is to obtain evidence concerning management's assertion about

    a. Rights and obligations.

    b. Existence.

    c. Presentation and disclosure.

    d. Valuation or allocation.

LO 1-5

1.56 Which of the following would best be described as an attest engagement?

    a. An engagement to implement an ERP system.

    b. An engagement to develop a more efficient payroll process.

    c. An engagement to assess the effectiveness of an internal control system.

    d. An engagement to assist the client in an IRS audit.

LO 1-3

1.57 An auditor seeks to test the accuracy of the amount recorded as revenue on a contract with a customer under ASC 606. Which PCAOB assertion is most likely being tested?

    a. Rights and obligations.

    b. Valuation or allocation.

    c. Presentation and disclosure.

    d. Completeness.

LO 1-3

1.58 In testing the goodwill at an audit client in the retail industry, an auditor may seek to determine whether the account balance had been impaired. Such impairment procedures would be designed to test which financial statement assertion?

    a. Existence.

    b. Completeness.

    c. Presentation and disclosure.

    d. Valuation or allocation.

LO 1-3

1.59 In testing inventory at an audit client in the retail industry, you note that some of the inventory is contracted to be held on consignment. As a result, which financial statement assertion is now relevant?

    a. Rights and obligations.

    b. Completeness.

    c. Existence or occurrence.

    d. Valuation or allocation.

Exercises and Problems

 Select Exercises and Problems are available with *Connect*.

LO 1-2

1.60 **Audit, Attestation, and Assurance Services.** Following is a list of various professional services. Identify each by its apparent characteristics as an audit engagement, attestation engagement, or assurance engagement. Because audits are a subset of attestation engagements, which are a subset of assurance engagements, choose the most specific description. In other words, if you believe the engagement is an audit engagement, select only audit engagement rather than checking all three. Similarly, the choice of assurance engagement for an audit, while technically correct, would not be the best choice.

	Audit Engagement	Attestation Engagement	Assurance Engagement
Real estate demand studies			
Certify ballot for awards show			
Utility rates applications			
Newspaper circulation audits			
Third-party reimbursement maximization			
Annual financial report to stockholders			
Rental property operational review			
Examinations of financial forecasts and projections			
Customer satisfaction surveys			
Compliance with contractual requirements			
Benchmarking/best practices			
Evaluation of investment management policies			
Information systems security reviews			
Productivity statistics			
Internal audit strategic review			
Financial statements submitted to a bank loan officer			

LO 1-4

1.61 **Professional Skepticism.** For each of the following scenarios, please evaluate whether you believe that your professional skepticism as an auditor should increase, decrease, or stay the same:

a. The chair of the board of your audit client proposed that the company hire its sales manager as their new financial controller.

b. The financial controller at your client mentions that she has just been on maternity leave for three months and no bank reconciliations were completed during the time she was out of the office.

c. While auditing the accounts receivable account for your audit client, you notice that there is a large amount that is well past due on the aged accounts receivable schedule.

d. While auditing the year-end investment balances, you find that your client's investment balance exactly agrees to the statement from the investment custodian. The custodian is a large bank.

e. The new chair of the board of Adams Corporation decided to fire the entire internal audit department. The chair believed that the work completed by the annual auditor was enough auditing and that they were already paying enough to the external auditors.

f. While auditing the inventory balance at your audit client, you visited the client's warehouse during their inventory count. You observed the count and found that the client made no mistakes during your procedures.

g. The sales manager in charge of the Northeast region retired. She was replaced in the region by the assistant sales manager in the same region.

h. While auditing the interest expense account, you notice that there was no increase in the amount during the current year. However, you noticed that the long-term debt amount doubled during the current year.

i. While auditing the inventory balance at your audit client, you perform test counts at their warehouse. While you are counting, you notice a storage bin of inventory that is covered in dust with damaged products. These items are stored near the garbage dumpsters.

j. You are auditing cash and during your review of the bank statements you notice unusual cash transfers between two bank accounts which are inconsistent with the client's business.

k. While auditing accounts payable, the accounts payable clerk told you that the audit client implemented three new internal control procedures. You tested each new control and found no exceptions in your testing, concluding that the controls are operating effectively.

l. The chair of the board of your audit client decided to double the staff of the internal audit department from 10 professionals to 20 professionals. The chair wanted to have the largest internal audit department in the industry and the increase will let the department complete more internal control audits throughout the year.

LO 1-3

1.62 **Management Assertions.** Complete the following chart indicating the corresponding Auditing Standards Board assertions and whether the assertion relates to transactions or balances.

PCAOB Assertion	Corresponding ASB Assertion (s)	Relates to:
Existence or Occurrence		
Rights and Obligations		
Completeness		
Valuation or Allocation		
Presentation and Disclosure		

LO 1-3

1.63 **Management Assertions.** Your audit manager has asked you to explain the PCAOB assertions by using an account on the balance sheet at your audit client. For the accounts receivable account, please define each of the PCAOB assertions, using the accounts receivable account as a way to illustrate each assertion. You are encouraged to reference Exhibit 1.4 to help you answer this question.

LO 1-6

1.64 **Other Types of Auditing.** Beyond public accounting firms, there are a number of other opportunities to work as an audit professional. Three common examples would be working as an internal auditor, a governmental auditor, or a regulatory auditor.

Required:

For each of the following scenarios, please indicate whether it would be most appropriate to use an internal auditor, a governmental auditor, or a regulatory auditor:

a. The Department of Defense for the United States plans to audit the cost accounting report for a contract signed with a key supplier.

b. Bigdeal Corporation manufactures paper and paper products and is trying to decide whether to purchase Smalltek Company. Bigdeal wants to obtain a report on the operational efficiency and effectiveness of the Smalltek sales, production, and research and development departments.

c. The Federal Deposit Insurance Company (FDIC) plans to audit the collectability of loans at a bank that they insure.

d. The board of directors would like an efficiency audit completed of its manufacturing plant operations.

e. The City of New York would like an audit done of a major construction project to make sure that the taxpayer's funds were used in an efficient manner.

f. A federal bank examiner decides to audit a bank to determine whether it will remain solvent in the upcoming year.

g. The CEO of Franklin Corporation wants to hire an auditor to take responsibility for auditing the company's compliance with environmental laws and regulations.

h. The Internal Revenue Service (IRS) would like to audit the tax returns of a popular restaurant chain.

i. The State of Ohio decided to audit the use of educational grants awarded to cities and towns in the state to make sure the funds were spent in accordance with the grant program.

j. The Department of the Interior for the United States plans to audit the use of funds spent by all National Parks.

LO 1-1, 1-2   1.65 **Auditor as Guarantor.** Your neighbor, Loot Starkin, invited you to lunch yesterday. Sure enough, it was no "free lunch" because Loot wanted to discuss the annual report of Dodge Corporation. He owns Dodge stock and just received the annual report. Loot says, "Our auditors prepared the audited financial statements and gave an unqualified opinion, so my investment must be safe."

Required:

What misconceptions does Loot Starkin seem to have about the auditor's role with respect to Dodge Corporation?

LO 1-6   1.66 **Identification of Audits and Auditors.** Audits may be characterized as (a) financial statement audits, (b) compliance audits, (c) economy and efficiency audits, and (d) program results audits. The work can be done by independent (external) auditors, internal auditors, or governmental auditors (including IRS auditors and federal bank examiners). Following is a list of the purposes or products of various audit engagements:

	Type of Audit	Type of Auditor
1. Analyze proprietary schools' spending to train students for low-demand occupations.		
2. Determine whether an advertising agency's financial statements are fairly presented in conformity with GAAP.		
3. Study the effectiveness of the Department of Defense's expendable launch vehicle program.		
4. Compare costs of municipal garbage pickup services to comparable services subcontracted to a private business.		
5. Investigate financing terms of tax shelter partnerships.		
6. Study a private aircraft manufacturer's test pilot performance in reporting on the results of test flights.		
7. Conduct periodic examinations by the U.S. Comptroller of Currency of a national bank for solvency.		
8. Evaluate the promptness of materials inspection in a manufacturer's receiving department.		
9. Report on the need for the states to consider reporting requirements for chemical use data.		
10. Render a public report on the assumptions and compilation of a revenue forecast by a sports stadium/racetrack complex.		

Required:

For each of the engagements listed, indicate (1) the type of audit (financial statement, compliance, economy and efficiency, or program results) and (2) the type of auditors (external, internal, or govermental) you would expect to be involved.

LO 1-3   1.67 **Financial Assertions and Audit Objectives.** You are engaged to examine the financial statements of Spillane Company for the year ended December 31. Assume that on November 1, Spillane borrowed $500,000 from Second National Bank to finance plant expansion. The long-term note agreement provided for the annual payment of principal and interest over five years. The existing plant was pledged as security for the loan. Due to the unexpected difficulties in acquiring the building site, the plant expansion did not begin on time. To use the borrowed funds, management decided to invest in stocks and bonds and on November 16, invested the $500,000 in publicly traded securities.

Required:

Identify the relevant financial statement assertions for the publicly traded securities account (an asset) based on the PCAOB's five management assertions about the financial statements.

LO 1-3

1.68 **Financial Statement Assertions and Possible Misstatements.** According to the professional standards, a financial statement assertion is relevant if it has a "reasonable possibility of containing a misstatement that would cause the financial statements to be materially misstated." For each of the possible misstatements identified below, please select the appropriate financial statement assertion.

Possible Misstatement/Risk

a. Revenue is overstated because the controller made up fraudulent invoices and recorded them.

b. Revenue is understated because the accountant closed the sales cycle a week early to go on vacation.

c. Accounts receivable is overstated because the accounts receivable clerk forgot to apply available discounts.

d. Accounts receivable is overstated because sales are falsified.

e. Travel expense is overstated because the sales force charged personal expenses on their corporate credit card.

f. Accounts payable is understated because the office manager lost an invoice for supplies received so it was never recorded.

g. The cash balance is understated because funds held in Japan were converted to $USD at the wrong rate.

h. The cash balance recorded on the financial statements is overstated because the treasurer is stealing from the company.

i. Inventory is overstated because it is held on consignment but included in the inventory balance.

j. The cost of goods sold is overstated because time sheets have not been submitted for each job.

k. Long-term debt is overstated due to misclassification by management.

LO 1-3

1.69 **Financial Statement Assertions and Audit Procedures.** According to the professional Standards, a financial statement assertion is relevant if it has a "reasonable possibility of containing a misstatement that would cause the financial statements to be materially misstated." For each audit procedure listed below, please select the appropriate financial statement assertion that would be tested by the procedure (i.e., existence or occurrence, completeness, valuation, rights and obligations, presentation and disclosure) and significant financial statement account:

Audit Procedures

a. The auditor sends a letter to the bank confirming the amount of cash in the bank account.

b. The auditor takes a shipping document and traces it to the sales invoice and sales journal.

c. The auditor selects items from the company's inventory list and observes those items in the warehouse.

d. The auditor compares prices on a vendor invoice to an approved price list from the vendor.

e. The auditor reviews recorded expenses with vendor invoices.

f. The auditor determines whether inventory has been pledged as collateral for a loan.

g. The auditor reads the minutes from the board of directors meeting to make sure that recorded stock options were approved.

h. The auditor reviews new lease agreements to evaluate whether leases have been recorded properly on the balance sheet.

  i. The auditor selects inventory items at a retail store to determine whether any are held on consignment.

  j. The auditor sends letters to customers to confirm amounts owed to the company.

LO 1-7   1.70 **Internet Exercise: Professional Certification.** Each state has unique rules for certification concerning education, work experience, and residency. Visit the website for your state board of accountancy and download a list of the requirements for becoming a CPA in your state. Although not all of the state boards of accountancy have websites, you can find those of most states by accessing the National Association of State Boards of Accountancy at its website.

LO 1-7   1.71 **Internet Exercise: Professional Certification.** Visit the website of the Institute of Internal Auditors, the Institute of Management Accountants, the Association of Certified Fraud Examiners, or the Information Systems Audit and Control Association. Review the information regarding the certifications available. Does the organization explain the benefits of having its certification? What topics are covered on the certification exam? What are the minimum requirements to take the exam? What additional experience is required to receive the certification?

LO 1-5   1.72 **Internet Exercise: Services Offered by the Big Four Public Accounting Firms.** Visit the websites of Deloitte, PwC, EY and KPMG. Review the services offered by each firm. Please identify and briefly describe at least two services offered by each firm to the marketplace.

Apollo Shoes Assume that you are a recently promoted senior (in charge) auditor for Anderson, Olds, and Watershed and have been assigned to the engagement team of a new client, Apollo Shoes Inc. To begin the audit, you need to familiarize yourself with Apollo Shoes. To do so, you will want to review the prior year 10-K, Board of Directors meeting minutes, and CEO letter to the shareholders. Detailed instructions can be found in *Connect*.

gathering sufficient appropriate evidence. Finally, the *reporting* principle provides guidance for "communicating the results" of the audit about whether the financial statements are prepared using "established criteria" (an applicable financial reporting framework, or GAAP).

Based on the fundamental principles, professional standards are established that provide specific objectives and requirements (*Statements on Auditing Standard*s issued by the ASB and *Auditing Standards* issued by the PCAOB). GAAS also includes various *interpretive publications* (such as *Interpretations,* exhibits, *AICPA Audit and Accounting Guides,* and *AICPA Auditing Statements of Position*) which provide guidance on the application of GAAS in specific circumstances, including engagements for entities in certain industries. Although officially considered less authoritative and less binding than the guidance in the *SASs* and *Auditing Standards,* auditors still must justify any departures from these publications. The relationship among these various elements is summarized in the following graphic.

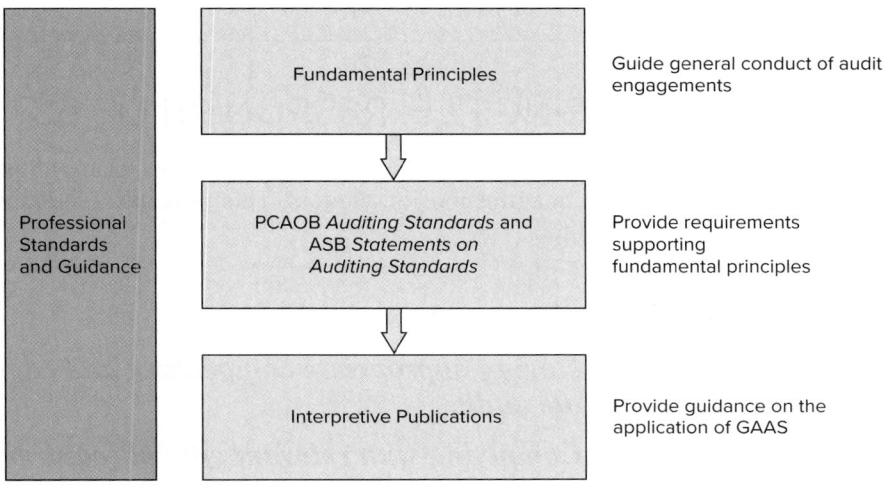

Auditing standards are quite different from *audit procedures.* **Audit procedures** are the particular and specialized actions that auditors take to obtain evidence in a specific audit engagement. **Auditing standards,** on the other hand, are quality guides to the audit that apply to all audits. For example, auditing standards indicate that auditors must determine that recorded accounts receivable are based on actual sales to customers. An audit procedure used to satisfy that standard is to confirm accounts receivable with the company's customers. This difference is the reason auditors' reports refer to an audit "conducted in accordance with *standards* of the PCAOB" [emphasis added] rather than in accordance with audit procedures.

In addition to the standards for U.S. issuers and nonissuers, it is important to note that separate auditing standards have been developed for governmental and foreign entities. A summary of the body charged with establishing standards as well as the standards themselves for various types of audits follows.

	Issuers	Nonissuers	Governmental Entities	Foreign Entities
Rule-making body	Public Company Accounting Oversight Board (PCAOB)	AICPA Auditing Standards Board (ASB)	U.S. Government Accountability Office (GAO)	International Auditing and Assurance Standards Board (IAASB)
Standards	*Auditing Standards (ASs)*	*Statements on Auditing Standards (SASs)*	*Government Auditing Standards* (The Yellow Book)	*International Standards on Auditing (ISAs)*
Website	www.pcaobus.org	www.aicpa.org	www.gao.gov	www.iaasb.org

If an accounting firm audits issuers and nonissuers throughout the world, that firm may be subject to multiple (sometimes conflicting) standards issued by the ASB, PCAOB, and IAASB, among others. For this reason, auditors and regulators have a great interest in *convergence*—that is, making the standards coordinated, if not uniform, throughout the world. The *ISAs* are a first step in the development of one consistent set of guidelines that auditors worldwide can follow. Although the focus in this text will be on audits of

U.S. issuers and nonissuers (and therefore pronouncements of the PCAOB and ASB), it is important that students be aware that additional standards exist related to the audits of governmental and foreign entities.

✅ REVIEW CHECKPOINTS

2.1 Define *generally accepted auditing standards (GAAS)*. What is the purpose of GAAS?

2.2 Who is responsible for developing standards for the audits of issuers? Who is responsible for developing standards for the audits of nonissuers?

2.3 Identify the role of the following bodies in the auditing standards-setting process: (1) the AICPA; (2) the PCAOB; (3) the SEC.

2.4 Identify the three fundamental principles underlying GAAS.

FUNDAMENTAL PRINCIPLE: RESPONSIBILITIES

LO 2-2
Describe the fundamental principle of *responsibilities* and how this principle relates to the characteristics and qualifications of auditors.

The fundamental principle of *responsibilities* relates to the personal integrity and professional qualifications of auditors. This principle addresses the following responsibilities of auditors:

> *Auditors are responsible for*
> - *Having appropriate competence and capabilities to perform the audit.*
> - *Complying with relevant ethical requirements.*
> - *Maintaining professional skepticism and exercising professional judgment throughout the planning and performance of the audit.*

As shown in the following figure, certain issues related to responsibilities are addressed before a firm accepts a prospective client, as the firm considers whether it has the competence and capabilities to perform the engagement and ensures it is independent with respect to the client prior to formal acceptance. However, professional skepticism, professional judgment, and due care must be considered and exercised by the auditor throughout the entire engagement.

STAGES OF AN AUDIT

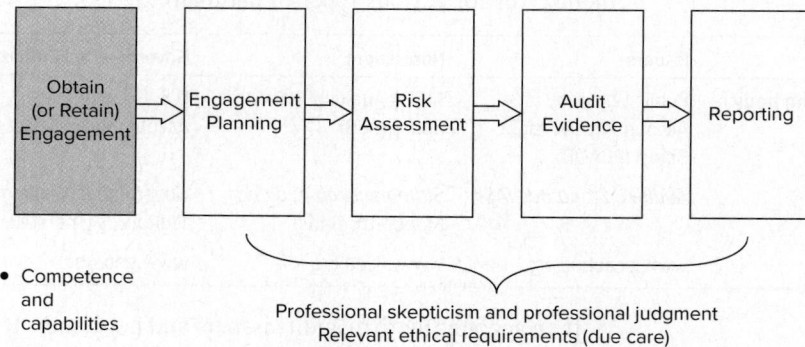

Competence and Capabilities

Competence and *capabilities* begin with education in accounting because auditors hold themselves out as experts in accounting standards, financial reporting, and auditing. In addition to university-level education prior to beginning their careers, auditors are required to participate in continuing professional education throughout their careers to ensure that their knowledge keeps pace with changes in the accounting and auditing profession. In fact, one of the important requirements for maintaining a CPA license is sufficient continuing professional education.

Education is only one element of competence and capabilities. Another important dimension is *experience,* which is gained with hands-on practice and on-the-job training. An important component of this experience is the ability to develop and apply professional judgment in real-world audit situations. These situations include various judgments related to gathering evidence as to the fairness of an entity's financial statements and evaluating whether that evidence indicates that the financial statements are prepared according to generally accepted accounting principles. (Professional judgment is also an important component of the performance principle, which will be discussed later.)

Independence and Due Care

The responsibilities principle requires auditors to comply with appropriate ethical requirements; two important requirements relate to *independence* and *due care.* Auditors must maintain independence in mental attitude; that is, auditors are expected to be unbiased and impartial with respect to the financial statements and other information they audit. This "state of mind" is often referred to as the auditor possessing **independence in fact.** This independence allows auditors to form an opinion on the entity's financial statements without being affected by influences that might compromise that opinion.

It is not only important for auditors to be unbiased; they must also *appear* to be unbiased. **Independence in appearance** relates to others' (particularly financial statement users') perceptions of auditors' independence. For example, imagine that the son or daughter of your professor was enrolled in your class. While your professor may truly be unbiased and evaluate the child fairly, it is unlikely that you and your classmates would believe your professor to be independent. Just as a baseball umpire should not care about the outcome of a game (only that the rules are followed), an auditor should not care about the financial performance of a client (only that its financial statements are prepared according to accounting rules, or GAAP).

Although independence is a complex concept and many different threats to independence exist, two general types of relationships that are believed to jeopardize (or compromise) independence are

1. *Financial relationships,* such as owning shares of stock in a client or having a loan outstanding to or from a client.
2. *Managerial relationships,* such as the ability to act in a decision-making capacity on behalf of a client or to provide advice on systems or information that will subsequently be audited. An example of such an issue is shown in the Auditing Insight "PwC and Mattel."

AUDITING INSIGHT   PwC and Mattel

PwC has served as auditor for **Mattel, Inc.** (a multinational toy manufacturing company whose products and brands include Barbie, Hot Wheels, and Fisher-Price) since 1974. This relationship was recently threatened when Joshua Abrahams, lead audit partner for PwC, provided recommendations for candidates for senior-level positions within Mattel.

In response, PwC placed Abrahams on administrative leave and replaced other members of the Mattel audit team. After a thorough internal investigation, Mattel's audit committee decided to retain PwC as auditor in 2020 and concluded that ". . .the objectivity and impartiality of Mattel's outside auditor has not been impaired. . ."

Sources: *Mattel Completes Internal Investigation of Whistleblower Letter and Announces Remedial Actions,* Mattel, Inc., October 29, 2019 (online source); "Mattel's Finance Chief to Leave," *The Wall Street Journal,* October 30, 2019, p. B5.

Clearly, the relationships just listed would impair perceptions of auditors' independence, but other considerations are necessary. For example, although it seems safe to conclude that an audit team member's spouse should be restricted from the preceding types of relationships for a client for which the team member is providing services, could that spouse have these types of relationships with respect to a client served by a distant office of the team member's firm? Could the audit team member's third cousin have such relationships?

It is difficult to think of a matter more fundamental to the value of an audit than independence. Without independence, third-party users are not able to rely on the auditor's work and opinion on the entity's financial statements. The preceding discussion identifies some of the major factors affecting independence, but the possible relationships involving auditors, entities, and their personnel are endless; the complexities of these relationships have resulted in a number of interpretations and ethics rulings regarding auditor independence. Many individuals fundamentally question whether auditors can be independent given the fee arrangement they have with their clients. (Imagine the situation if you directly paid your professor instead of the university for your tuition!) In addition, the often long-standing relationships between auditors and their clients have resulted in some attempts to require periodic rotation of audit firms to lessen the impact of financial relationships between these two parties and enhance independence.

Issues related to auditor independence may provide some significant challenges in practice. For example, an investigation in the early 2000s of independence violations at PwC revealed that ". . . approximately 86.5 percent of PwC partners and 10.5 percent of all other PwC professionals had independence violations."[6] More recently, PwC violated independence requirements for 15 issuers from 2013 to 2016 by performing prohibited non-audit services (related to the design and implementation of financial reporting software) and failing to appropriately report non-audit services to these issuers' audit committees.[7] The Auditing Insight "Changes in the United Kingdom" summarizes a case that raised concerns about auditor independence.

This section introduced the concept of auditor independence and provided a limited overview of issues that impact auditor independence. A detailed discussion of AICPA and SEC rules related to independence (and various interpretations of those rules) is provided in Module B.

AUDITING INSIGHT — Changes in the United Kingdom

Issues related to the importance of independence have been raised following the collapse of **Carillion**, the second largest United Kingdom (UK) construction company with over 43,000 worldwide employees. Two UK House of Commons committees noted that ". . . conflicts of interest at every turn" resulted in KPMG's failure to challenge questionable accounting practices at Carillion.

In response to this criticism, the UK's Financial and Reporting Council (FRC) is requiring Big Four firms to split their auditing and non-auditing functions into separate operating entities (currently, nonauditing services account for over 75 percent of total firm revenues, and unlike U.S. firms, UK firms can provide significant levels of consulting services to audit clients). Other proposed actions to reduce the influence of the Big Four firms (and increase independence) include requiring firms to utilize a smaller (non-Big Four) firm to conduct part of the audit and capping the number of companies in the FTSE Index a firm could audit.

Sources: "Big Four Auditors Face New U.K. Calls to Break Apart," *The Wall Street Journal Online,* May 16, 2018 (online source); "U.K. Toughens Auditor Rules," *The Wall Street Journal,* December 19, 2018, p. B11; "U.K. Regulator Orders Big Four to Separate Audit Practices by 2024," *The Wall Street Journal Online,* July 6, 2020 (online source); U.K. Mulls Capping Number of Audits Big Four Firms Can Do," *The Wall Street Journal Online,* March 18, 2021 (online source).

[6]*Independent Consultant Finds Widespread Independence Violations at PricewaterhouseCoopers,* SEC Press Release 2000–4, Securities and Exchange Commission, January 6, 2000.

[7] *In the Matter of PricewaterhouseCoopers LLP, Respondent,* SEC Accounting and Enforcement Release No. 4084, Securities and Exchange Commission, September 23, 2019.

A second ethical requirement identified by the responsibilities principle is that of due care. **Due care** (also known as *due professional care*) reflects a level of performance that would be exercised by reasonable auditors in similar circumstances. This standard is often referred to as that of a prudent auditor; auditors are expected to possess the skills and knowledge of others in their profession but are not expected to be infallible. This aspect relates to the competence and capabilities of the auditor to perform the engagement and issue appropriate reports. One specific element of due care noted by the standards is the need for auditors to plan and perform the audit with an appropriate level of professional skepticism as discussed in the following section.

Professional Skepticism and Professional Judgment

Professional skepticism and professional judgment are necessary responsibilities of auditors throughout the entire audit process. **Professional skepticism** (which was introduced in Chapter 1) is a state of mind that is characterized by appropriate questioning and a critical assessment of audit evidence. When exhibiting professional skepticism, auditors do not assume that management is dishonest, nor do they assume that management is unquestionably honest. Rather, auditors evaluate and consider

- Contradictory audit evidence obtained through different procedures.
- The reliability of documentary evidence.
- The reliability of information obtained from management and those charged with governance of the entity (e.g., the audit committee).

Although the preceding discussion suggests that professional skepticism is a relatively straightforward concept, situations occur during the audit that could impede auditors' ability to apply appropriate levels of professional skepticism. A PCAOB *Staff Practice Alert*[8] identified the following conditions that present challenges for auditors maintaining appropriate levels of professional skepticism; these conditions may result in auditors failing to appropriately question, assess, evaluate evidence, and, ultimately, reach the correct conclusion during their engagement:

- Financial incentives and pressures (such as building or maintaining a long-term audit engagement, facing pressures to keep audit fees low, achieving high levels of client satisfaction, and providing other fee-related services to clients).
- Time pressures (such as completing the audit and report prior to deadlines and scheduling and workload demands on partners and other audit team members).
- Personal relationships developed with clients that provide auditors with an inappropriate level of trust or confidence in management.

Professional judgment is the application of relevant training, knowledge, and experience in making informed decisions about appropriate courses of action during the audit engagement. These judgments relate to the evidence obtained during the audit and the conclusions reached based on this evidence. Auditors are required to demonstrate this characteristic throughout the entire audit process as they do professional skepticism. Professional judgment is required as auditors gather evidence, evaluate evidence, and draw conclusions based on evidence. Professional judgment is particularly important in evaluating the reasonableness of various management estimates required in preparing the entity's financial statements.

In addition to demonstrating appropriate levels of professional judgment, auditors are required to carefully document their professional judgment in such a manner that experienced auditors with no previous relationship with the audit can understand the judgments made in reaching conclusions on significant issues. The Auditing Insight "Madoff and the Responsibilities Principle" illustrates some seemingly obvious questions that should have been raised with respect to the professional responsibilities of Madoff's auditor.

---

[8]*Maintaining and Applying Professional Skepticism in Audits,* PCAOB Staff Audit Practice Alert No. 10, PCAOB, December 4, 2012.

AUDITING INSIGHT — Madoff and the Responsibilities Principle

A preliminary investigation of the actions of David Friehling (the individual responsible for the audits of **Bernard L. Madoff Investment Securities LLC**) illustrated the following potential violations of elements of the responsibilities principle:

- Friehling did not verify the existence of assets or securities trades made by Madoff's company, suggesting a lack of professional skepticism and a lack of due care.

- Friehling was the sole auditor at Friehling and Horowitz, raising the question as to whether a "one-man" firm has the capability to effectively audit a company as large as Madoff's.

- Friehling and his family had investment accounts at Madoff's company worth more than $14 million, a conflict of interest that raises questions about his independence.

Source: "Accountant Arrested for Sham Audits," *The Wall Street Journal,* March 19, 2009, p. C1.

 ## REVIEW CHECKPOINTS

2.5 Distinguish between independence in fact and independence in appearance. Can auditors be independent in fact yet not be perceived to be independent in appearance?

2.6 What is *due care?* To what standards are auditors held with respect to due care?

2.7 Define *professional skepticism* and *professional judgment.* During what stages of the audit are auditors required to demonstrate these characteristics?

FUNDAMENTAL PRINCIPLE: PERFORMANCE

LO 2-3
Describe the fundamental principle of *performance* and identify the major activities performed in an audit.

The fundamental principle of *performance* sets forth general quality criteria for conducting an audit. As noted in the preceding section, in addition to the elements of this principle, the performance of the audit is influenced by the need for auditors to exercise *professional skepticism* and *professional judgment* throughout the audit process. The performance principle states that

> *To express an opinion, the auditor obtains reasonable assurance about whether the financial statements as a whole are free from material misstatement, whether due to fraud or error. To obtain reasonable assurance, which is a high but not absolute level of assurance, the auditor*
>
> - *Plans the work and properly supervises any assistants.*
>
> - *Determines and applies appropriate materiality level or levels throughout the audit.*
>
> - *Identifies and assesses risks of material misstatement, whether due to fraud or error, based on an understanding of the entity and its environment, including the entity's internal control.*
>
> - *Obtains sufficient appropriate audit evidence about whether material misstatements exist, through designing and implementing appropriate responses to the assessed risks.*

An important concept underlying the performance principle noted above is that of reasonable assurance. **Reasonable assurance** recognizes that a GAAS audit may not detect all material misstatements and auditors are not "insurers" or "guarantors" regarding the fairness of the entity's financial statements. However, auditors should provide a high level of assurance (or confidence) regarding their work. As the preceding reflects, the performance principle contains four elements: (1) planning and supervision, (2) materiality, (3) risk assessment, and (4) audit evidence. These are discussed in the remainder of this section.

Planning and Supervision

After obtaining or retaining the engagement, the next major stage of the audit is planning, as shown in the following figure. The professional standards contain several considerations for planning and supervising an audit. They are concerned with (1) preparing an audit plan and supervising the audit work, (2) obtaining knowledge of the client's business, and (3) dealing with differences of opinion among the accounting firm's own personnel.

STAGES OF AN AUDIT

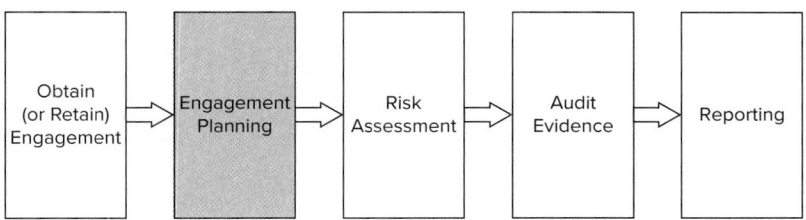

GAAS require the preparation of a written audit plan. An **audit plan** is a list of the audit procedures that auditors need to perform to gather sufficient appropriate evidence on which to base their opinion on the financial statements. The procedures in an audit plan should be stated in enough detail to instruct the assistants about the work to be done. (You will see detailed audit plans later in this textbook.)

Auditors are also required to obtain an understanding of the client's business and industry. This knowledge helps auditors identify areas for special attention (the accounts or classes of transactions where frauds or errors might exist), evaluate the reasonableness of accounting estimates made by management, evaluate management's responses to inquiries, and make judgments about the appropriateness of management's choices among accounting principles. Auditors gain this understanding of a business through a variety of methods, including

- Discussions with management and other client personnel.
- Experience with other entities in the same industry.
- Reviewing AICPA accounting and audit guides, industry publications, other entities' financial statements, business periodicals, and textbooks.

Just as having advance notice of assignments and examinations makes it easier for you (as a student) to perform better on those assignments, timing is important for audit planning. To have time to plan an audit, auditors should be engaged before the client's fiscal year-end. The more advance notice auditors have, the better they are able to provide enough time for planning. The audit team may be able to perform part of the audit at an interim date—a date some weeks or months before year-end—and thereby make the rest of the audit work more efficient. For example, in examining property, plant, and equipment, auditors may evaluate activity in the account balance up to some date during the year (say, September 30) prior to year-end and then evaluate activity occurring between that date and December 31 following year-end (the roll-forward period), as shown in the following graphic. Essentially, at December 31, auditors have evaluated the account balance through the interim date (in this case, September 30) and will evaluate the remainder of the activity following year-end. Doing so permits audit work to be "shifted" from after year-end to prior to year-end and allows the audit to be completed on a more timely basis.

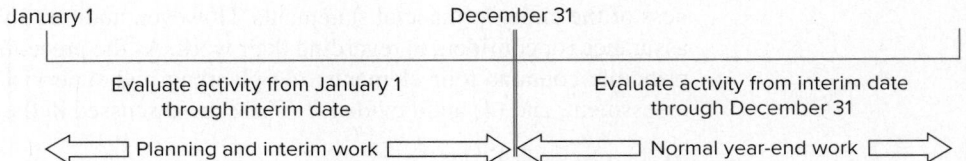

January 1		December 31	
	Evaluate activity from January 1 through interim date		Evaluate activity from interim date through December 31
	⇐ Planning and interim work ⇒	⇐	Normal year-end work ⇒

The Auditing Insight "Too Late" illustrates how late appointment of an auditor may result in the inability to appropriately plan the engagement.

AUDITING INSIGHT Too Late

- In its *Form NT 10-K* filing with the SEC, **Digital Turbine Inc.** disclosed that its multiple acquisitions and growing scale and global profile had resulted in the appointment of a new accounting firm (**Grant Thornton**) in March 2021, just prior to its March 31, 2021, fiscal year-end. Because of the late appointment of Grant Thornton and its inability to plan and perform the audit on a timely basis, the company was unable to meet the deadline for filing its financial statements with the SEC.

- In an academic study, Cassell et al. found that later appointment of auditors leads to a higher likelihood of future financial statement restatements.

Sources: *Digital Turbine Inc. Form NT 10-K* (filed June 2, 2021); C. A. Cassell, J. C. Hansen, L. A. Myers, and T. A. Seidel, "Does the Timing of Auditor Changes Affect Audit Quality," *Journal of Accounting, Auditing, & Finance,* 35(2) 2020, pp. 263-289.

Engagement planning is discussed in greater detail in Chapter 3. In addition, planning activities related to the audit of various accounts and cycles are discussed in Chapters 6, 7, 8, 9, and 10.

Materiality

The concept of **materiality** recognizes that auditors should focus on matters that are important to financial statement users. One common way of viewing materiality is the dollar amount that would influence the lending or investing decisions of financial statement users. Auditors and users do not expect account balances to be accurate to the penny; after all, many entities round their financial statements to the thousands, or even millions, of dollars! For example, **Apple** reported net income of $94.7 billion in 2021; clearly, a misstatement of $1 million (0.001 percent of net income) would not likely affect users' decisions, but a misstatement of $10 billion (10.6 percent of net income) probably would. Materiality is recognized as part of the objective of an audit, which is "to obtain reasonable assurance about whether the financial statements as a whole are free of *material* misstatement" [emphasis added] (AU-C 200.12). Materiality is commonly established based on percentages of key financial statement subtotals, such as net income, sales or revenues, and total assets.

The audit team considers materiality in planning the audit, performing the audit, and evaluating the effect of misstatements on the entity's financial statements. Auditors are responsible only for providing reasonable assurance that misstatements *material* to the entity's financial statements are identified. Stated another way, auditors are not responsible for detecting misstatements that are not material to the financial statements.

Although the concept of materiality appears to be relatively straightforward, implementation of materiality during the audit requires high levels of professional judgment. For example, suppose a small dollar misstatement (in absolute terms) resulted in an entity meeting its earnings expectations or resulted in an entity reporting higher earnings than in the previous year. Certainly, these impacts would likely influence investment decisions, even if the dollar amount is relatively small. Circumstances such as these are referred to as qualitative materiality factors and should also be considered by auditors. The role of materiality in the planning stages of the audit is discussed in more detail in Chapter 3.

Risk Assessment

An important part of the performance principle is for auditors to identify important concerns (or risks) they face in the audit. This process is referred to as *risk assessment*

STAGES OF AN AUDIT

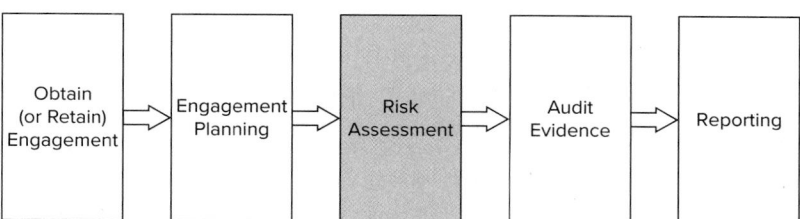

The risk assessment process requires an understanding of the client, its operating environment, and its industry. This includes internal controls operating within the client's accounting information systems that ultimately produce the client's financial statements. **Internal control over financial reporting** (also referred to as internal control) may be defined as the policies and procedures implemented by an entity to prevent or detect material accounting frauds or errors and provide for their correction on a timely basis. Satisfactory internal control reduces the probability of frauds or errors in the accounts. This understanding provides the foundation for the work auditors do in assessing the **risk of material misstatement**, a combination of **inherent risk** (the probability that a material misstatement, either an error or fraud, will occur) and **control risk** (the probability that a material misstatement, either an error or fraud, will not be prevented or detected on a timely basis by the entity's internal controls). One way to think of the risk of material misstatement is the likelihood that an error or fraud will exist in the financial statements prior to considering the auditors' work.

The primary purpose of assessing the risk of material misstatement is to help auditors determine the *nature, timing, and extent of further audit procedures* necessary for gathering evidence about the fairness of the entity's financial statements. The process of risk assessment presumes two necessary relationships:

1. Effective internal control reduces control risk (and decreases the risk of material misstatement), and auditors thus have a reasonable basis for reducing the necessary effectiveness of further audit procedures.
2. Ineffective internal control increases control risk (and increases the risk of material misstatement), and auditors must increase the necessary effectiveness of further audit procedures.

Because these further audit procedures are used to obtain evidence with respect to the fairness of the account balance (i.e., to "substantiate" the account balance), they are referred to as **substantive procedures**. The auditors' substantive procedures are reflected in the determination of detection risk, which is discussed in the next section. A depiction of this relationship follows:

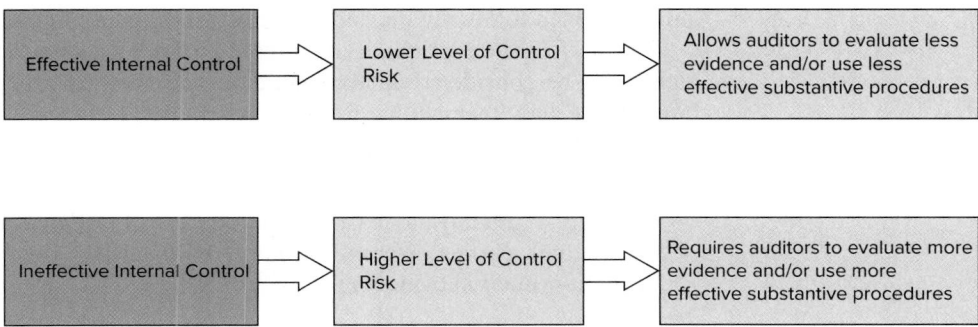

The importance of internal control in the audit examination is evidenced by an increase in auditors' responsibility for internal control in the audit of issuers such that auditors evaluate (through testing the operating effectiveness of specific controls) and report on the effectiveness of an issuer's internal control over financial reporting. This is one example of auditors' responsibility in the audit of an issuer exceeding that for the audit of a nonissuer. Internal control is discussed in more detail in Chapter 5; in addition, important elements of internal control related to the audit of various accounts and cycles are discussed in Chapters 6, 7, 8, 9, and 10.

✔ REVIEW CHECKPOINTS

2.8   Define *reasonable assurance*. How does the audit team provide reasonable assurance in the engagement?

2.9   What is an *audit plan*? During which stage of the audit is an audit plan prepared?

2.10   What is an *interim date*? How do audit procedures conducted prior to an interim date impact the audit examination?

2.11   What is *materiality*? During what stages of the audit do auditors consider materiality?

2.12   For what reasons do auditors obtain an understanding of a client's internal control?

2.13   What is the basic relationship between the effectiveness of the client's internal control and the necessary effectiveness of substantive procedures?

Audit Evidence

The final element of the performance principle requires that the audit team collects and evaluates sufficient appropriate evidence to provide a reasonable basis for their opinion.

STAGES OF AN AUDIT

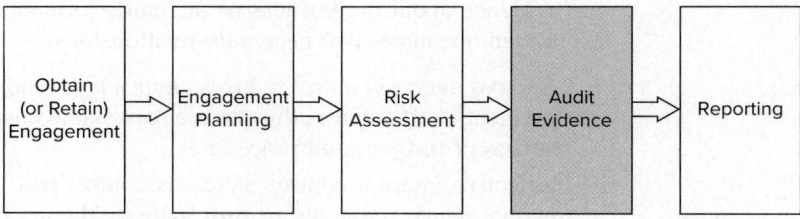

Obtain (or Retain) Engagement → Engagement Planning → Risk Assessment → Audit Evidence → Reporting

Evidence is the information that auditors use in arriving at the conclusions on which to base the audit opinion and includes the underlying accounting data and all available corroborating information. Examples of evidence include minutes of meetings, confirmations with independent third parties, invoices, analyst reports, and all other information that permits auditors to reach valid, logical conclusions. As noted, the methods auditors use to gather and evaluate this evidence are referred to as *substantive procedures,* which are performed following the auditors' risk assessment process.

The performance principle requires auditors to gather "sufficient appropriate" evidence. To be considered **appropriate**, evidence must be trustworthy (*reliable*) and must provide the audit team with information of interest (*relevant*). Professional standards note the following with respect to the reliability of evidence:

- Evidence created by sources external to the entity is more reliable than that created by the entity. From most to least reliable, sources of evidence are auditors (direct personal knowledge), parties external to the entity (external evidence), and parties internal to the entity (internal evidence).

- Evidence created by sources outside the entity is more reliable when received directly from the external source (direct external evidence) than when received from sources internal to the entity (external-internal evidence).
- Evidence obtained from entities with more effective internal controls is more reliable than that obtained from entities with less effective internal controls.
- Evidence obtained from original source documents is more reliable than that obtained from photocopies, facsimiles, or electronic documents. The Auditing Insight "Wirecard's Cash" illustrates an example of the issues that may result from relying on non-original documents.

 AUDITING INSIGHT | Wirecard's Cash

An affiliate of EY (**Ernst & Young GmbH**) relied upon scanned electronic copies of documentation from two Philippine banks to verify the existence of € 1.9 billion ($2.1 billion) of cash in its audit of **Wirecard AG** (a German-based fintech company). A request for subsequent confirmation revealed that the electronic copies were fraudulent and the banks never held any funds on behalf of Wirecard.

Source: "German Regulator Steps Down, EY Changes Leadership Following Wirecard Scandal," *The Wall Street Journal Online,* February 25, 2021 (online source).

Relevance refers to the nature of information provided by the audit evidence; for example, when auditors confirm accounts receivable with customers, this audit procedure provides evidence that the account is legitimate (i.e., the sale actually took place) but does not provide evidence that the account will ultimately be collectible. The nature of information provided by evidence is operationalized through the management assertions identified and discussed in Chapter 1.

Appropriateness relates to evidence *quality,* and **sufficiency** relates to evidence *quantity.* For large entities, auditors do not audit all of the transactions and components but examine a sample of these items in drawing their conclusions. Sufficiency relates to the number of transactions or components evaluated.

The sufficiency and appropriateness of evidence are reflected in the necessary level of detection risk. **Detection risk** represents the risk that the audit team's substantive procedures will fail to detect a material misstatement. As auditors require a higher quality of evidence (lower detection risk), they must gather more relevant and reliable evidence (appropriateness) and evaluate more transactions or components (sufficiency). Evidence-gathering procedures are discussed in more detail in Chapter 3. In addition, specific approaches to gathering evidence in the examination of various accounts and cycles are discussed in Chapters 6, 7, 8, 9, and 10.

Exhibit 2.1 summarizes the key characteristics of evidence just discussed. Note that the desired level of detection risk impacts the necessary sufficiency and appropriateness of audit evidence. Also note that the appropriateness is affected by both the relevance of the evidence and its reliability.

EXHIBIT 2.1 Key Characteristics of Audit Evidence

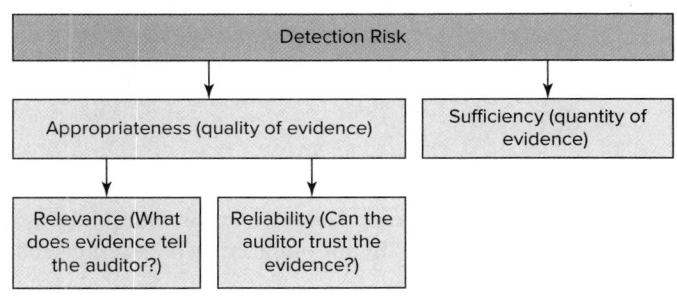

☑ REVIEW CHECKPOINTS

2.14 Define *audit evidence*.

2.15 Define *external, external–internal,* and *internal documentary evidence*.

2.16 Distinguish between relevance and reliability as these concepts relate to audit evidence. How are relevance and reliability associated with the appropriateness of audit evidence?

2.17 How does the source of evidence affect its reliability?

2.18 How are the sufficiency and appropriateness of evidence related to detection risk?

FUNDAMENTAL PRINCIPLE: REPORTING

LO 2-4
Understand the fundamental principle of *reporting* and identify the basic contents of the auditors' report.

The ultimate objective of the audit—the report on the audit—is guided by the fundamental principle of reporting, which states

> *Based on evaluation of the evidence obtained, the auditor expresses in the form of a written report, an opinion in accordance with the auditor's findings, or states that an opinion cannot be expressed. The opinion states whether the financial statements are presented fairly, in all material respects, in accordance with the applicable financial reporting framework.*

As the following graphic shows, reporting is the final stage of an audit and occurs following the gathering of audit evidence.

STAGES OF AN AUDIT

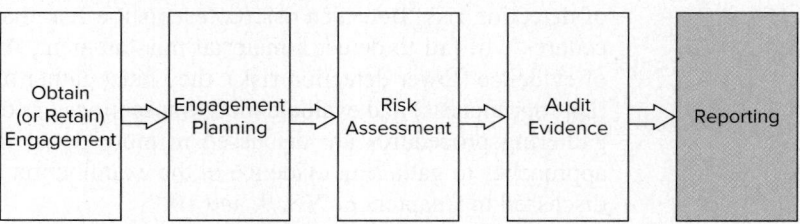

An example of an auditors' report is shown in Exhibit 2.2, and you should review it in relation to the following discussion.

The report in Exhibit 2.2 is the report form used for issuers; differences in wording exist, but the report for nonissuers conveys essentially the same information. You should understand the term *financial statements* to include not only the traditional financial statements, but also all footnote disclosures and additional information (e.g., earnings per share calculations) that are integral elements of the basic financial presentation required by GAAP.

The reporting principle requires the auditor to express an opinion on the entity's financial statements (or indicate that an opinion cannot be expressed). With respect to this requirement, the last sentence in the first paragraph of Deloitte & Touche's report begins with the phrase "In our opinion," which represents the expression of an opinion.

AUDITING INSIGHT \ *(concluded)*

- Abbott and Buslepp found that triennially inspected firms anticipated upcoming PCAOB inspections by expending additional audit effort in inspection years, resulting in higher quality audits.
- Christensen et al. found that firms receiving PCAOB inspection reports with audit deficiencies were more likely to be subject to subsequent litigation, indicating that inspection reports provide negative information about overall audit quality.
- Khurana et al. found that initial PCAOB inspections (beginning in 2003) resulted in the greatest improvement in audit quality for Big 4 firms, followed by triennially inspected non-Big 4 firms, then annually inspected non-Big 4 firms.

Sources: P. T. Lamoreaux, "Does PCAOB Inspection Access Improve Audit Quality? An Examination of Foreign Firms Listed in the United States," *Journal of Accounting and Economics,* April–May 2016, pp. 313–337; D. Aobdia, "The Impact of the PCAOB Individual Engagement Inspection Process–Preliminary Evidence," *The Accounting Review,* July 2018, pp. 53-80; L. J. Abbott and W. L. Buslepp, "The Impact of the PCAOB Triennial Inspection Process on Inspection Year and Non-Inspection Year Audits," *Auditing: A Journal of Practice & Theory,* May 2021, pp. 1-21; B. E. Christensen, N. G. Lundstrom, and N. J. Newton, "Does the Disclosure of PCAOB Inspection Findings Increase Audit Firms' Litigation Exposure?," *The Accounting Review,* May 2021, pp. 191-219; I. K. Khurana, N. G. Lundstrom, and K. K. Raman, "PCAOB Inspection and the Differential Audit Quality Effect for Big 4 and Non-Big 4 US Auditors," *Contemporary Accounting Research,* Spring 2021, pp. 376-411.

 REVIEW CHECKPOINTS

2.21 What is a *system of quality control*? Identify the six elements of a system of quality control.

2.22 What factors should auditors consider in deciding whether to accept or continue the engagement with a particular client? What should firms do if they decide to withdraw from an engagement?

2.23 Provide examples of procedures that firms have used to monitor their quality control policies and procedures.

2.24 What role does the PCAOB play in connection with monitoring and regulating public accounting firms?

2.25 How frequently are firms required to have PCAOB inspections?

Summary

This chapter discussed the professional standards that apply to audit engagements and identified important mechanisms that enable public accounting firms to provide professional services to meet those standards. From an auditing standpoint, generally accepted auditing standards form the basis for professional engagements and the necessary qualifications and characteristics of auditors. These standards are based on three basic principles, which reflect the overall conduct of the audit examination:

1. Responsibilities, which require auditors to possess competence and capabilities, comply with relevant ethical requirements, maintain professional skepticism, and exercise professional judgment.
2. Performance, which involves planning the work and supervising assistants, determining and applying appropriate materiality levels, identifying and assessing the risk of material misstatement, and obtaining sufficient appropriate audit evidence.
3. Reporting, which requires that auditors express an opinion about the fairness of the entity's financial statements.

To provide reasonable assurance of compliance with these standards, firms develop systems of quality control that prescribe policies and procedures related to

- The responsibilities of firm leadership for quality.
- Ethical requirements.
- Acceptance and continuance of client relationships and specific engagements.

- Human resources.
- Engagement performance.
- Monitoring the effectiveness of the system of quality control.

Under Sarbanes–Oxley, firms conducting audits of issuers are required to have inspections of selected engagements and their systems of quality control by the PCAOB. The purpose of these inspections is to identify deficiencies in engagements conducted by the firms and provide suggestions for improvements in their systems of quality control.

Following is a summary of the professional standards and monitoring activities for audits of issuers and nonissuers.

	Professional Standards	**Monitoring Requirements**
Issuer	*Auditing Standards* issued by the PCAOB	Annual or triennial inspections conducted by the PCAOB (frequency depends upon number of audits performed by the firm)
Nonissuer	*Statements on Auditing Standards* issued by the ASB of the AICPA	Triennial peer reviews conducted through the AICPA National Peer Review Committee

Key Terms

American Institute of Certified Public Accountants (AICPA): As related to professional auditing standards, the body charged with establishing auditing standards for the audits of non-issuers through *Statements on Auditing Standards (SASs)* issued by the Auditing Standards Board, 46

appropriate (audit evidence): Characteristics related to the quality (relevance and reliability) of audit evidence, 58

audit plan: A comprehensive list of the specific audit procedures that the audit team needs to perform to gather sufficient appropriate evidence on which to base their opinion on the financial statements, 55

audit procedures: The specialized actions auditors take to obtain evidence in an engagement, 49

auditing standards: The audit quality guides that apply to all audits, 49

control risk: The likelihood that the client's internal control policies and procedures fail to prevent or detect a material misstatement, 57

detection risk: The likelihood that the auditors' substantive procedures will fail to detect a material misstatement that exists within an account balance or class of transactions, 59

due care: A level of performance that would be exercised by reasonable auditors in similar circumstances, 53

engagement quality control review: An internal evaluation of the significant judgments made by the audit team and the conclusions reached in formulating its report on an engagement conducted by that firm, 64

evidence: The information used by auditors in arriving at the conclusion on which the audit opinion is based, which includes the underlying accounting data and all available corroborating information, 58

financial reporting framework: The financial reporting standards (i.e., GAAP, IFRS, etc.) adopted by management and, when appropriate, those charged with governance (audit committee board of directors) in the preparation of the financial statements, 61

generally accepted auditing standards (GAAS): Standards that identify necessary qualifications and characteristics of auditors and guide the conduct of the audit examination, 48

independence in appearance: The extent to which others (particularly financial statement users) perceive auditors to be independent, 51

independence in fact: Auditors' mental attitude and impartiality with respect to the client, 51

inherent risk: The probability that in the absence of internal controls, material errors or frauds could enter the accounting system used to develop financial statements, 57

inspection: An evaluation of an accounting firm's audit engagements and system of quality control conducted by the PCAOB and required for any firms providing auditing services to issuers, 65

internal control over financial reporting: Policies and procedures implemented by an entity to prevent or detect material accounting frauds or errors and provide for their correction on a timely basis, 57

issuer: An entity that offers registered securities, such as stocks and bonds, for sale to the general public (also known as a public entity). Issuers are subject to mandatory audit requirements, 46

materiality: An amount or event that has a substantial likelihood to influence financial statement users' decisions, 56

professional judgment: The application of relevant training, knowledge, and experience in making informed decisions about appropriate courses of action during the audit engagement, 53

professional skepticism: A state of mind that is characterized by appropriate questioning and a critical assessment of audit evidence, 53

Public Company Accounting Oversight Board (PCAOB): As related to professional auditing standards, the body charged with establishing auditing standards for the audits of public entities through the issuance of *Auditing Standards*. The PCAOB is also responsible for inspecting firms that perform audits of issuers, 46

reasonable assurance: The concept that recognizes that the costs of control activities should not exceed the benefits that are expected from the control activities, 55

risk of material misstatement: The combined probability that a material misstatement (error or fraud) will occur and not be prevented or detected on a timely basis by the entity's internal controls. The risk of material misstatement is a combination of inherent and control risk, 57

substantive procedures: The detailed audit and analytical procedures designed to detect material misstatements in account balances and footnote disclosures, 57

sufficiency (audit evidence): The measure of the quantity of audit evidence (the number of transactions or components evaluated), 59

system of quality control: The policies and procedures implemented by a firm to provide with reasonable assurance that the firm and its personnel (1) comply with professional standards and applicable regulatory and legal requirements and (2) issue reports that are appropriate in the circumstances, 63

Multiple-Choice Questions for Practice and Review

 All applicable questions are available with *Connect*.

LO 2-3

2.26 Which of the following categories of principles is most closely related to gathering audit evidence?

    a. Performance

    b. Reasonable assurance

    c. Reporting

    d. Responsibilities

LO 2-2

2.27 Which of the following is *not* related to ethical requirements of auditors?

    a. Due care

    b. Independence in appearance

    c. Independence in fact

    d. Professional judgment

LO 2-5   2.28 One of an accounting firm's basic objectives is to provide professional services that con-
              form to professional standards. Reasonable assurance of achieving this objective can be
              obtained by following
              a. Generally accepted auditing standards.
              b. Standards within a system of quality control.
              c. Generally accepted accounting principles.
              d. International auditing standards.

LO 2-2   2.29 Which of the following best demonstrates the concept of professional skepticism?
              a. Relying more extensively on external evidence rather than internal evidence.
              b. Focusing on items that have a more significant quantitative effect on the entity's finan-
                 cial statements.
              c. Critically assessing verbal evidence received from the entity's management.
              d. Evaluating potential financial interests held by auditors in the client.

LO 2-3   2.30 The primary purpose for obtaining an understanding of the entity's environment (including
              its internal control) in a financial statement audit is
              a. To determine the nature, timing, and extent of substantive procedures to be performed.
              b. To make consulting suggestions to the entity's management.
              c. To obtain sufficient appropriate audit evidence to afford a reasonable basis for an opin-
                 ion on the financial statements.
              d. To determine whether the entity has changed any accounting principles.

LO 2-3   2.31 Ordinarily, what source of evidence should least affect audit conclusions?
              a. External documentary evidence.
              b. Inquiry of management.
              c. Documentation prepared by the audit team.
              d. Inquiry of entity legal counsel.

LO 2-3   2.32 The most reliable evidence regarding the existence of newly acquired computer equipment is
              a. Inquiry of management.
              b. Documentation prepared externally.
              c. Evaluation of the client's procedures.
              d. Physical observation.

LO 2-3   2.33 Which of the following procedures would provide the most reliable audit evidence?
              a. Inquiries of the client's internal audit staff.
              b. Inspection of prenumbered client purchase orders filed in the vouchers payable
                 department.
              c. Inspection of vendor sales invoices received from client personnel.
              d. Inspection of bank statements obtained directly from the client's financial institution.

LO 2-3   2.34 Breaux & Co. CPAs require that all audit documentation indicates the identity of the pre-
              parer and the reviewer. This procedure provides evidence relating to which of the following?
              a. Independence.
              b. Adequate competence and capabilities.
              c. Adequate planning and supervision.
              d. Sufficient appropriate evidence gathered.

LO 2-2   2.35 Which of the following concepts is *least* related to the standard of due care?
              a. Independence in fact
              b. Professional skepticism
              c. Prudent auditor
              d. Reasonable assurance

LO 2-3   2.36 The evidence considered most appropriate by auditors is best described as
              a. Internal documents such as sales invoice copies produced under conditions of strong
                 internal control.
              b. Written representations made by the president of the entity.

c. Documentary evidence obtained directly from independent external sources.

d. Direct personal knowledge obtained through physical observation and mathematical recalculation.

LO 2-3 2.37 Auditors' understanding of the internal control in an entity provides information for

a. Determining whether members of the audit team have the required competence and capabilities to perform the audit.

b. Ascertaining the independence in mental attitude of members of the audit team.

c. Planning the professional development courses the audit staff needs to keep up to date with new auditing standards.

d. Planning the nature, timing, and extent of substantive procedures on an audit.

LO 2-5 2.38 Which of the following elements of a system of quality control is related to firms receiving independence confirmations from its professionals with respect to clients?

a. Acceptance and continuance of client relationships and specific engagements.

b. Engagement performance.

c. Monitoring.

d. Relevant ethical requirements.

LO 2-2 2.39 Which of the following is most closely related to the responsibilities principle?

a. The auditors' responsibility to issue a report as a result of their examination.

b. The requirement that auditors gather sufficient, appropriate evidence upon which to base an opinion on the financial statements.

c. The auditors' compliance with relevant ethical requirements of independence and due care.

d. The auditors' responsibility to plan the audit and properly supervise assistants.

LO 2-2 2.40 Kramer, CPA, consulted an independent appraiser regarding the valuation of fine art for a not-for-profit museum. Consultation with the appraiser in this case would

a. Be considered as exercising proper due care.

b. Be considered a failure to follow generally accepted auditing standards because Kramer should have known how to value fine art before accepting the engagement.

c. Not be considered a violation of generally accepted auditing standards because generally accepted auditing standards does not apply to not-for-profit entities.

d. None of the above.

LO 2-4 2.41 Which of the following topics is *not* addressed in the auditors' report for an issuer?

a. Responsibilities of the auditor and management in the financial reporting process.

b. Absolute assurance regarding the fairness of the entity's financial statements in accordance with GAAP.

c. A description of an audit engagement.

d. A summary of the auditors' opinion on the effectiveness of the entity's internal control over financial reporting.

LO 2-3 2.42 Which of the following recognizes that an audit conducted under generally accepted auditing standards may not detect all material misstatements?

a. Absolute assurance

b. Professional judgment

c. Reliability of audit evidence

d. Reasonable assurance

LO 2-3 2.43 Which of the following combinations would provide the auditor the most reliable evidence?

Source of Evidence	Effectiveness of Internal Control
a. Internal	More effective
b. Internal	Less effective
c. External	More effective
d. External	Less effective

LO 2-3

2.44 Which of the following is most closely related to the relevance of audit evidence?

a. Auditors decide to physically inspect investment securities held by a custodian instead of obtaining confirmations from the custodian.

b. In addition to confirmations of accounts receivable, auditors perform an analysis of the aging of accounts receivable to evaluate the collectability of accounts receivable.

c. In response to less effective internal control, auditors increase the number of customer accounts receivable confirmations mailed compared to that in the prior year.

d. Because of a large number of transactions occurring near year-end, auditors decide to confirm a larger number of receivables following year-end instead of during the interim period.

LO 2-3

2.45 Which of the following statements is *not* true with respect to the performance principle?

a. Auditors are required to prepare a written audit plan during the planning stages of initial audits but are not required to do so in continuing audits.

b. Audit teams consider materiality in planning the audit, performing the audit, and evaluating the effect of misstatements on the entity's financial statements.

c. In assessing the risk of material misstatements, the audit team considers the effectiveness of the entity's internal controls in preventing and detecting misstatements.

d. Auditors are required to consider both the relevance and the reliability of evidence in evaluating whether the evidence they have gathered is appropriate.

LO 2-5

2.46 Which of the following is true with respect to PCAOB inspections of accounting firms?

a. All firms performing audits of issuers are required to have annual inspections conducted by the PCAOB.

b. PCAOB inspections review a sample of audits conducted by firms as well as the firm's systems of quality control.

c. All results of PCAOB inspections are made available to the public following the inspection.

d. Firms performing audits of 100 or fewer issuers may elect to have a peer review conducted through the AICPA in lieu of a PCAOB inspection.

LO 2-1

2.47 The particular and specialized actions that auditors take to obtain evidence during a specific engagement are known as

a. Audit procedures.

b. Audit standards.

c. Interpretive publications.

d. *Statements on Auditing Standards.*

LO 2-1

2.48 Which of the following combinations of standards and types of audits are most closely related to the activities of the Public Company Accounting Oversight Board?

a. Develop *Auditing Standards* for the audits of nonissuers.

b. Develop *Auditing Standards* for the audits of issuers.

c. Develop *Statements on Auditing Standards* for the audits of nonissuers.

d. Develop *Statements on Auditing Standards* for the audits of issuers.

LO 2-4

2.49 Which of the following best describes the general contents of the first paragraph of the "Basis for Opinion" section of the auditors' report?

a. A description of an audit examination, including the fact that the audit was conducted under standards established by the PCAOB.

b. The auditors' conclusion with respect to the fairness of the entity's financial statements.

c. Statements identifying the responsibility of auditors and management in the financial reporting process.

d. The auditors' conclusion with respect to the effectiveness of the entity's internal control over financial reporting.

LO 2-4

2.50 Which of the following opinions would be issued if auditors believed that the entity's financial statements were *not* presented in conformity with GAAP?

a. Adverse opinion

b. Disclaimer of opinion

c. Qualified opinion

d. Unmodified opinion

LO 2-4

2.51 Which of the following principles is most closely associated with the auditors' conclusion as to the fair presentation of the entity's financial statements?

a. Communication principle

b. Performance principle

c. Reporting principle

d. Responsibilities principle

Exercises and Problems

 All applicable questions are available with *Connect.*

LO 2-1, 2-5

2.52 **AICPA and PCAOB Responsibilities.** The creation of the PCAOB by the Sarbanes–Oxley Act has affected both the standards-setting process and the periodic review of the quality of an audit firm's work.

Required:

a. Identify the responsibilities of the AICPA, PCAOB, and SEC in the auditing standards-setting process.

b. Which standard(s) provide guidance for the audits of issuers? Which standard(s) provide guidance for the audits of nonissuers?

c. What role do the AICPA and PCAOB play in the periodic review of the quality of audit firms' work?

LO 2-1

2.53 **Professional Guidance.** A challenge facing auditors is the wide array of professional guidance available to them in the audits of different types of entities.

Required:

For each of the following, identify whether it is most appropriately associated with *Statements on Auditing Standards (SAS), Auditing Standards (AS),* both (B), or neither (N).

a. Issued by the American Institute of Certified Public Accountants.

b. Issued by the Public Company Accounting Oversight Board.

c. Provide guidance for services lesser in scope than an audit engagement.

d. Apply to the audit of nonissuers.

e. Require auditors to gather sufficient, appropriate evidence to support their opinion.

f. Apply to the audit of issuers.

g. Identify necessary qualifications of auditors and guide conduct of the audit examination.

h. Become effective upon approval by the Securities and Exchange Commission.

LO 2-2

2.54 **Independence.** You are meeting with executives of Cooper Cosmetics Corporation to arrange your firm's engagement to audit the corporation's financial statements for the year ending December 31. One executive suggests the audit work be divided among three staff members. One person would examine asset accounts, a second would examine liability accounts, and the third would examine income and expense accounts to minimize audit time, avoid duplication of staff effort, and curtail interference with entity operations.

Advertising is the corporation's largest expense, and the advertising manager suggests that a staff member of your firm whose uncle owns the advertising agency that handles the corporation's advertising be assigned to examine the Advertising Expense account because the staff member has a thorough knowledge of the complex contract between Cooper Cosmetics and the advertising agency.

Required:

a. To what extent should auditors follow the client's suggestions for the conduct of an audit? Discuss.

b. List and discuss the reasons that audit work should not be assigned solely according to asset, liability, and income and expense categories.

c. Should the staff member of your accounting firm whose uncle owns the advertising agency be assigned to examine advertising costs? Discuss.

LO 2-2

2.55 **Independence.** Generally accepted auditing standards require auditors to be independent. Included within this standard are the concepts of independence in fact and independence in appearance.

Required:

a. Define *independence in fact* and *independence in appearance.*

b. What two general types of relationships would normally compromise auditors' independence?

c. For each of the following separate situations, discuss whether you believe the auditors' independence has been compromised.

1. The auditors' firm provides extensive consulting services to the client; these services provide revenues to the firm that exceed revenues received from the audit engagement.

2. The spouse of the partner in charge of the audit engagement occupies an executive-level position within the client.

3. A distant relative of a partner within the firm occupies an entry-level position within a client of the firm. (The audit is conducted by another office of the firm with which the partner has infrequent contact.)

4. A staff member within the firm owns shares of stock of one of that firm's clients. (She is not a member of the engagement team serving that client.)

LO 2-2

2.56 **Professional Skepticism.** An important principle for auditors is the need to maintain an appropriate level of professional skepticism.

Required:

a. Define *professional skepticism.*

b. During which stages of the audit are auditors required to exhibit professional skepticism?

c. How does each of the following independent issues potentially relate to the principle of professional skepticism?

1. The auditor's firm has served the client for a long period of time, and strong friendships have developed between the firm personnel and client's officers.

2. Auditors are anxious to complete the audit shortly because of other workload demands and deadlines related to other engagements.

3. The client has mentioned on a number of occasions its desire to reduce (or limit) the audit fee.

LO 2-2

2.57 **Responsibilities Principle.** Martin is considering submitting a proposal to conduct the audit examination of Phillip Inc., a manufacturer and distributor of automotive parts to large automobile manufacturers. The following are some notes related to Martin's initial consideration of this potential engagement:

a. Martin learned of this client opportunity through one of its staff accountants, who is a cousin of Phillip's chief financial officer.

b. Phillip is a particularly attractive engagement for Martin because it would allow the firm to enter into the manufacturing market (most of Martin's clients are in the services industry and are much smaller than Phillip).

c. Martin inquired with Phillip as to the reason for a change in auditors and was assured that the former auditors decided not to continue auditing Phillip Inc. because they no longer possessed the necessary expertise to audit clients in the automotive parts industry (this explanation was confirmed by the former auditors).

d. Martin is concerned about the numerous locations of Phillip's warehouses and the ability to conduct an appropriate observation of Phillip's year-end inventory balances.

e. When asked about inventory observation, Phillip indicated that its previous auditors observed physical inventory at different warehouses on different days and obtained a written statement from Phillip that transfers between locations did not occur.

f. If Martin obtains the engagement, it will take appropriate actions to ensure that firm personnel are independent in fact and in appearance with respect to Phillip.

Required:

For each of the above, identify the component of the responsibilities principle (competence and capabilities, ethical requirements, or professional skepticism and professional judgment) most closely related to that factor.

LO 2-3

2.58 **Performance Principle: Planning.** Your public accounting practice is located in a city of 15,000 people. The majority of your work, conducted by you and two assistants, consists of compiling clients' monthly statements and preparing income tax returns for individuals from cash data and partnership returns from books and records. You have a small number of audit clients; given the current size of your practice, you generally consider it a challenge to accept new audit clients.

One of your corporate clients is a retail hardware store. Your work for this client has been limited to preparing the corporate income tax return from a trial balance submitted by the bookkeeper.

On December 26, you receive from the president of the corporation a letter containing the following request:

> We have made arrangements with First National Bank to borrow $500,000 to finance the purchase of a complete line of appliances. The bank has asked us to furnish our auditors' certified statement as of December 31, which is the closing date of our accounting year. The trial balance of the general ledger should be ready by January 10, which should allow ample time to prepare your report for submission to the bank by January 20. In view of the importance of this certified report to our financing program, we trust you will arrange to comply with the preceding schedule.

Required:

From a theoretical viewpoint, discuss the difficulties that are caused by such a short notice audit request.

(AICPA adapted)

LO 2-3

2.59 **Performance Principle: Evidence.** Generally accepted auditing standards (the performance principle) require auditors to gather *sufficient appropriate* evidence on which to base an opinion.

Required:

a. Briefly define the characteristics "sufficient" and "appropriate" as they relate to audit evidence.
b. What are *relevance* and *reliability* (as they relate to audit evidence)? How do these concepts relate to the auditors' requirement to gather sufficient appropriate evidence?
c. How does the source of evidence affect its reliability?
d. How does the effectiveness of the entity's internal control affect the sufficiency and appropriateness of evidence gathered by auditors?

LO 2-3

2.60 **Performance Principle.** You have accepted the engagement of auditing the financial statements of the C. Reis Company, a small manufacturing firm that has been your client for several years. Because you were busy writing the report for another engagement, you sent a staff accountant to begin the audit with the suggestion that she start with accounts receivable. Using the prior year's audit documentation as a guide, she prepared a trial balance of the accounts, aged them, prepared and mailed positive confirmation requests, examined underlying support for charges and credits, and performed other work she considered necessary to obtain evidence about the validity and collectability of the receivables. At the conclusion of her work, you reviewed the audit documentation she prepared and found she had carefully followed the prior year's audit documentation.

Required:

The opinion rendered by auditors states that the audit was made in accordance with generally accepted auditing standards. Identify the important components of the performance principle and relate them to the audit of C. Reis Company by indicating how they were fulfilled or, if appropriate, how they were not fulfilled.

(AICPA adapted)

LO 2-3

2.61 **Performance Principle.** Identify how each of the following statements relates to the performance principle by considering which element(s) of the principle are related to that statement. (A statement may be related to more than one element.) Use the following elements in providing your response: reasonable assurance; planning and supervision; materiality; risk assessment; and audit evidence:

- Evaluating the effectiveness of the client's internal control in preventing or detecting misstatements.
- Obtaining an understanding of the client's business and industry.
- Acknowledging that the risk of failing to detect a material misstatement cannot be reduced to zero.
- Obtaining confirmations from the client's customers as to the ending balances in accounts receivable.
- Preparing a written audit plan.
- Designing audit procedures to identify misstatements that would have a significant effect on financial statement users' decisions.
- Considering the likelihood that the account balance contains a material misstatement.
- Limiting overall risks to an acceptably low level.

LO 2-2, 2-3

2.62 **Responsibilities and Performance Principles.** Respond to each of the following comments that you heard related to the audit of Swan Company, an issuer.

a. "We don't need to consider the risk of material misstatement in our work because we really can't do anything to reduce that risk."

b. "Because the client has not implemented effective internal controls, we need to gather more reliable evidence. This means we need to test a greater number of transactions and obtain more reliable forms of evidence."

c. "We will really need to spend a lot of time and effort on this audit. Because this client has just filed for a bond offering, we can't allow for any misstatements in the financial statements. We need to guarantee the accuracy of the client's financial statements."

d. "Because this company has $140 million in revenues, we really shouldn't be concerned about smaller accounts because they are not likely to have a major impact on the financial statements."

e. "I know it will be more time consuming and expensive, but we are required to physically inspect the stock certificates held by the client rather than obtain confirmation from the custodian. After all, our own direct observation is more reliable than receiving a confirmation."

LO 2-4

2.63 **Reporting Principle.** The reporting principle requires auditors to express their opinion through the issuance of a written report.

Required:

a. What is the purpose of the auditors' opinion and report?

b. What are the major sections in the auditors' report on the examination of an issuer? What are the major contents of each of these sections?

c. What are the four types of opinions that auditors can issue?

d. How does the concept of materiality influence the auditors' report?

LO 2-2, 2-3, 2-4

2.64 **Fundamental Principles.** For each of the following related to audit engagements, identify whether the action is most closely related to the responsibilities, performance, or reporting principle.

a. Evaluating the audit firm personnel's independence with respect to a prospective client.

b. Gathering sufficient, appropriate evidence.

c. Exercising an appropriate level of professional skepticism.

d. Issuing a qualified opinion on the financial statements because of a material, yet not pervasive, departure from GAAP.

e. Establishing materiality levels for use in determining the amount of evidence to be gathered.

f. Considering the susceptibility of the account balance to misstatement to assess the risk of material misstatement.

g. Possessing the appropriate competence and capabilities to perform the audit.

h. Considering whether a scope limitation precludes sufficient evidence to allow an opinion to be expressed on the entity's financial statements.

i. Planning the audit to provide reasonable assurance that the financial statements are free of material misstatement.

j. Evaluating the potential relationships between the auditor and family who are employed by the entity.

LO 2-2, 2-3, 2-4   2.65 **Comprehensive Principles Case Study.** Ray, the owner of a small entity, asked Holmes, CPA, to conduct an audit of the entity's records. Ray told Holmes that the audit was to be completed in time to submit audited financial statements to a bank as part of a loan application. Holmes immediately accepted the engagement and agreed to provide an auditors' report within three weeks. Ray agreed to pay Holmes a fixed fee plus a bonus if the loan was granted.

Holmes hired two accounting students to conduct the audit and spent several hours telling them exactly what to do. Holmes told the students not to spend time reviewing the controls but instead to concentrate on proving the mathematical accuracy of the ledger accounts and on summarizing the data in the accounting records that support Ray's financial statements. The students followed Holmes's instructions and, after two weeks, gave Holmes the financial statements, which did not include footnotes. Holmes studied the statements and prepared an unmodified auditors' report. The report, however, did not refer to generally accepted accounting principles or to the fact that Ray had changed to the accounting standard for capitalizing interest.

Required:

Briefly describe each of the principles and indicate how the action(s) of Holmes resulted in a failure to comply with these principles.

(AICPA adapted)

LO 2-2, 2-3, 2-4   2.66 **Fundamental Principles (Comprehensive).** In each of the following, identify which of the elements of the fundamental principles (responsibilities, performance, or reporting) is most applicable. In addition, discuss what action(s) (if any) you believe auditors should take with respect to these issues.

a. An entity has contacted you about performing its audit engagement. You have not previously served a client in the entity's industry, which has many industry-specific accounting issues that are both technical and complex.

b. An entity has entered into a number of lease agreements. Based on the requirements of GAAP, you believe that these obligations have not been properly classified in the financial statements; however, the entity has provided full and complete disclosure of this treatment in the footnotes to the financial statements.

c. Because of a disagreement with its current auditors, an entity has contacted you about conducting its current-year audit. However, because the previous auditors have just recently resigned from the engagement, you have some questions as to whether an audit can be completed in time to meet the entity's deadlines for providing audited financial statements to a lender.

d. Based on the effectiveness of the entity's internal control, you have assessed control risk at low levels and decided that a smaller number of customer accounts need to be confirmed.

e. An entity has contacted you about performing its audit engagement. This entity became aware of your firm because the husband of one of your partners is currently serving as the entity's chief financial officer.

f. One of your clients is currently a potential defendant in several cases because of the damage caused by one of its products. Because this entity does not believe that it is likely to receive an unfavorable outcome from this litigation, it did not disclose the potential litigation in the footnotes accompanying their financial statements.

g. You are performing tests of the client's controls over the processing of revenue transactions to determine whether these controls are operating effectively and can be relied upon to prevent or detect misstatements.

h. One of your supervisors has requested a number of clarifications based on her review of your work on an audit engagement. A subsequent meeting with her has resolved these clarifications, and you both have concluded that your work supports the opinion on the client's financial statements.

LO 2-2, 2-3, 2-4

2.67 **Fundamental Principles (Comprehensive).** Identify which of the major fundamental principles (responsibilities, performance, or reporting) is most closely related to each of the following:

a. The need for auditors to consider their financial relationships with prospective clients.

b. An auditor has raised some questions with respect to management's response to various inquiries concerning pending litigation facing the client.

c. The auditors' consideration of the effectiveness of the entity's internal control on the nature, timing, and extent of substantive procedures.

d. The auditors' evaluation of the magnitude of a misstatement that would impact perceptions of the entity's profitability.

e. The auditors' issuance of a disclaimer of opinion because of a significant scope limitation.

f. Relevant education and experience requirements for CPA licensure.

g. The inability of an audit examination to provide absolute assurance with respect to detecting all material misstatements.

h. The requirement that auditors possess the skills and knowledge of others in their profession.

i. The preparation of a written audit plan that guides the conduct of the audit engagement.

j. The auditors' issuance of a qualified opinion because of a departure from GAAP.

LO 2-2, 2-3, 2-4

2.68 **Fundamental Principles (Comprehensive).** Comment on each of the following statements you heard in a conversation between two newly hired staff auditors.

a. "Of course, I'm qualified to be assigned to this engagement. I have an accounting degree from a top university and was an honors graduate. I know some of the accounting rules have changed since I graduated, but I'll be able to figure that out as we go through the audit."

b. "It doesn't really matter what others think. . . . I'm completely independent of Acme Industries and should be a member of the audit team. While I own some stock, it's a small amount and I'm holding it for the long term, anyway."

c. "You really have to question everything the client tells you. That's what professional skepticism is all about. It's a shame you can't believe a word they say."

d. "The evidence is lower in quality, but we typically use internal evidence when we audit property, plant, and equipment. It just takes too much time and costs too much to get more reliable evidence."

e. "On that last job, we really planned the audit well. We were able to finish everything by November 1 and didn't need to do any work after year-end."

f. "We're not too worried about internal control. We always do the same substantive procedures anyway, so why take the time to look at the client's controls?"

g. "Because the client isn't accounting for its leases properly, we need to issue either a qualified opinion or a disclaimer of opinion. Just how large a dollar impact does this have on the financial statements?"

h. "When we evaluate items for materiality, the only thing we need to worry about is the absolute dollar amount. There really isn't anything else we need to consider."

LO 2-5

2.69 **System of Quality Control.** Each of the following quality control policies and procedures is typical of ones that can be found in public accounting firms' systems of quality control. Identify each of them with one of the six elements of quality control.

a. Assign management responsibilities in such a manner that commercial considerations do not override the quality of work performed.

b. Establish policies and procedures for resolving differences of opinion among firm personnel that arise during professional engagements.

c. Develop policies and procedures to ensure that professionals are provided appropriate professional development opportunities.

d. Review engagement documentation, reports, and the client's financial statements.

e. Develop effective performance evaluation, compensation, and advancement procedures.

f. Identify circumstances and relationships that create threats to independence and take appropriate action to eliminate those threats or reduce them to an acceptable level.

g. Identify whether the firm possesses the competency, capability, and resources to appropriately serve a specific client.

h. Devote sufficient resources to develop, communicate, and support the firm's quality control procedures.

i. Retain engagement documentation for a sufficient period of time to satisfy the needs of the firm, professional standards, laws, and regulations.

LO 2-5

2.70 **Evaluating Quality Control.** Firms auditing issuers are required to have periodic inspections conducted by the PCAOB.

Required:

a. What are the major characteristics of PCAOB inspections?

b. What types of firms typically have PCAOB inspections? How frequently are these evaluations conducted?

LO 2-5

2.71 **Internet Exercise: Public Company Accounting Oversight Board Inspection Reports.** Refer to the website of the Public Company Accounting Oversight Board (PCAOB) (www.pcaobus.org), review the information under "Inspections," and select the most current inspection report for one of the Big Four firms (Deloitte, EY, KPMG, and PwC).

Required:

a. What information is contained in the "public" version of the PCAOB's inspection reports? Is there any additional information that you would like to see?

b. For the firm you selected, how many practice offices had audits inspected by the PCAOB?

c. For the firm you selected, for how many audits (issuers) did the PCAOB find deficiencies?

d. Identify five deficiencies that were cited in the PCAOB's inspection report. For each deficiency, to which of the elements of the principles does it most closely relate? (If the firm had fewer than five deficiencies, evaluate all of the deficiencies identified in the report.)

e. Briefly summarize the firm's response (if any) to the PCAOB's inspection report.

Appendix 2A

Referencing Professional Standards

Shown here is a comparison of the categories of standards issued by the PCAOB and Auditing Standards Board (ASB). (Section numbers are shown in parentheses for each category.) These general categories parallel the majors stages of an audit engagement and serve as an appropriate starting point when researching the professional auditing literature with respect to an issue that may be encountered during the audit examination.

ASB	PCAOB
General Principles and Responsibilities (200–299)	General Auditing Standards (1001–1305)
Risk Assessment and Response to Assessed Risks (300–499)	Audit Procedures (2101–2905)
Audit Evidence (500–599)	Audit Procedures (2101–2905)
Using the Work of Others (600–699)	Incorporated in General Auditing Standards and Audit Procedures
Audit Conclusions and Reporting (700–799)	Auditor Reporting (3101–3320)
Special Considerations (800–899)	Other Matters Associated with Audits (6101–6115)
Special Considerations in the United States (900–999)	Other Matters Associated with Audits (6101–6115) Matters Related to Filings Under Federal Securities Laws (4101–4105)

EXAMPLE: AUDITING REPORTING

Assume that you were seeking guidance on the contents of the portion of the auditors' report related to the opinion on the financial statements. For issuers, "Auditor Reporting" is covered under AS sections 3101–3320. Reviewing AS 3101 (*The Auditor's Report on an Audit of Financial Statements When the Auditor Expresses an Unqualified Opinion*), paragraph 8 provides a detailed summary of both the contents of the section of the report related to the financial statement opinion and the actual wording of the section. This section is shown in Appendix B of AS 3101). In documenting your reference to the professional standards, you would cite AS 3101.08 or AS 3101 (Appendix B) as the appropriate source of professional guidance.

For nonissuers, "Audit Conclusions and Reporting" are covered under AU-C sections 700–799. AU-C section 700 (*Forming an Opinion and Reporting on Financial Statements*) specifically relates to the content of auditors' reports. When you access AU-C section 700, you will see the source identified as SAS Nos. 134, 137, 138, and 141. If future pronouncements issued by the ASB affect audit reporting, AU-C section 700 will be updated to include those pronouncements. In this way, auditors can find all of the appropriate professional guidance for an area under one AU-C section rather than needing to reference several individual pronouncements.

Each AU-C section includes a number of paragraphs that address various matters related to that topic. AU-C section 700 has 61 paragraphs outlining the professional guidance for reporting and 81 other paragraphs (referred to as Application and Other Explanatory Material) to provide more specific guidance for applications of the standard. Paragraphs 24 through 27 provide the content related to the opinion on the financial statements; paragraph A81 (the "A" refers to application material) provides the actual wording of the report. In documenting your reference to the professional standards, you could refer to either *SAS No. 134* (the primary guidance for audit report content), AU-C 700.24-700.27, or AU-C 700.A81.

EXAMPLE: AUDIT CONFIRMATIONS

You are seeking guidance for the use of confirmations in the audit of an issuer; specifically, you want to know what alternative procedures should be performed for nonresponses to confirmations. Reviewing the categories of standards, "Audit Procedures" (AS sections 2101–2905) appears to be most applicable; a review of standards within this category allows you to identify AS 2310, *The Confirmation Process.* Reviewing this standard, paragraphs 31 and 32 describe the auditors' responsibility for performing alternative procedures if replies to confirmations are not received. In documenting your reference to the professional standards, you would cite AS 2310.31-32.

For the audits of nonissuers, audit evidence is covered under AU-C sections 500–599. AU-C section 505 (*External Confirmations*) specifically relates to the use of external confirmations. When you access section 505, you will see the source identified as *SAS No. 122.* Paragraphs A24–A26 provide guidance for auditors' responsibility for nonresponses to confirmations. In documenting your response, you could cite either *SAS No. 122* or AU-C 505.A24–A26.

CHAPTER 3

Engagement Planning and Audit Evidence

> *He who fails to plan is planning to fail.*
>
> *Sir Winston Churchill*

Professional Standards References

Topic	AU-C/ISA Section	AS Section
Overall Objectives of the Independent Auditor	200	1001, 1005, 1010, 1015
Terms of Engagement	210	1301
Communication between Predecessor and Successor Auditors	210	2610
Supervision of the Audit Engagement	220, 300	1201
Audit Documentation	230	1215
Audit Planning	300	2101
Materiality	320	2105
Audit Evidence	500	1105
Substantive Analytical Procedures	520	2305
Consideration of the Internal Audit Function in a Financial Statement Audit	610	2605
Using the Work of an Auditor-Engaged Specialist	620	1210

LEARNING OBJECTIVES

During the planning phase of an engagement, the professional standards emphasize that risk assessment underlies the entire audit process. Motivated by the importance of risk assessment, standards setters at both the PCAOB and ASB have each adopted a suite of standards related to the auditor's assessment of, and response to, risk in a financial statement audit. Collectively, the standards also include guidance pertaining to audit planning, supervision, materiality, and other related topics. In this chapter, we cover engagement planning, beginning with pre-engagement activities, supervision, and materiality. Next, we cover the types of audit procedures that can be completed and audit documentation. In Chapter 4, we provide a comprehensive explanation of an auditor's assessment of risk.

Your objectives are to be able to

LO 3-1　List and describe the required pre-engagement activities that auditors undertake before beginning an audit engagement.

INTRODUCTION

Deciding whether to accept a new client is arguably one of the most important decisions an audit firm can make and it is not one that is taken lightly. Audit firms must consider several issues when making client acceptance decisions, including whether they have the industry knowledge needed to audit the client, if there are independence issues, whether the new client is too risky, and also if they have the capacity and man-power to perform the audit in question. Capacity and man-power would have definitely been a big consideration for both the **General Motors (GM)** and the **General Electric (GE)** recent auditor changes.

In 2017, **GM** announced **EY** would be their new auditor, beginning with the 2018 audit.[1] **Deloitte** had been **GM**'s auditor for the 100 years prior to the change. In June 2020, **GE** announced that after the 2020 audit, they would switch auditors from **KPMG** to **Deloitte. KPMG** had been **GE**'s auditor since 1909.[2] To put these changes into perspective, in 2020 **GM** paid $21 million dollars for their external audit, and an additional $4 million in audit-related fees.[3] In 2020, **GE** paid $61.6 million dollars for their external audit, and an additional $14.6 million in audit-related fees.[4] Deciding whether to accept **GM** or **GE** as a new audit client is definitely not a decision for an audit firm to take lightly! Can you imagine the amount of resources (personnel, time, knowledge, etc.) needed for a firm to perform a $21 million dollar audit, let alone a $61 million audit? It would be substantial, to say the least! And, as this chapter discusses further, sheer capacity to perform the audit would only be a small part of the considerations a firm would need to make prior to accepting a new audit client.

This chapter is devoted to the audit planning process, beginning first with the pre-engagement activities of client acceptance and continuance. Audit Standards require auditors to perform due diligence prior to accepting or continuing with a client, in part to help minimize the risk of an audit failure.

Once a client acceptance or a continuance decision is made, the auditor must develop a detailed audit plan documenting the audit testing procedures to be performed. The testing procedures, outlined later in this chapter, are designed in response to the risk of material misstatement for each of the relevant financial statement assertions in significant accounts. In this chapter we discuss how materiality is calculated, further discussion of the risk of material misstatement is included in Chapter 4. The audit plan and any work done related to the plan must be documented, as further discussed at the end of the chapter.

---

[1] "General Motors Appoints Ernst & Young As Auditor for Fiscal 2018," *GM Authority,* September 26, 2017 (gmauthority.com).
[2] "GE Names New Auditor for First Time in Over a Century," *Forbes,* June 22, 2020 (forbes.com).
[3] *General Motors Company Proxy Statement and Notice of 2021 Annual Meeting of Shareholders,* June 14, 2021 (investor.gm.com).
[4] *GE 2021 Notice of Annual Meeting and Proxy Statement,* https://www.ge.com/sites/default/files/ge_proxy2021.pdf

PRE-ENGAGEMENT ACTIVITIES

LO 3-1
List and describe the required pre-engagement activities that auditors undertake before beginning an audit engagement.

Public accounting firms try to reduce their own business risks by carefully managing their audit engagements. To do so, public accounting firms undertake several activities before beginning any audit engagement. In general, these activities can be called *risk management activities.* Risk in an audit engagement generally refers to the probability that the firm could issue a clean, unmodified audit opinion when in fact a material misstatement *does* exist in the financial statements and the opinion should have been modified. Because of the importance of these activities, professional standards state that the auditor should engage in the following activities: (1) perform procedures regarding the acceptance or continuance of the audit client relationship, (2) determine compliance with independence and ethics requirements, and (3) reach a contractual understanding with the client for the terms and conditions of the audit engagement. Exhibit 3.1 outlines the major stages of the audit. These pre-engagement activities occur in the Obtain (or Retain) Engagement phase highlighted. Each of these three activities is further discussed below.

Client Acceptance or Continuance

An important element of a public accounting firm's quality control policies and procedures is a system for deciding whether to accept a new client and, on a continuing basis, whether to continue providing services to existing clients. Public accounting firms are not obligated to accept undesirable clients, nor are they obligated to continue to serve clients when relationships deteriorate or when the management comes under a cloud of suspicion. The process activities are clearly focused on understanding and managing risk to the audit firm. In fact, to mitigate their business risk, public accounting firms devote substantial time to make sure that the audit clients that they serve do not become the focus of the next big accounting scandal.

Auditing a client that has integrity generally results in a problem-free engagement. Conversely, despite conducting an audit in accordance with generally accepted auditing standards, it is difficult for a public accounting firm to avoid appearing "guilty by association" with a client that lacks integrity. When a firm recognizes such a lack in a client, they may choose to withdraw from an engagement.

In addition, companies are free to, and often do, change auditors periodically, sometimes as a result of corporate policy to rotate auditors, sometimes because of fee considerations, and sometimes because of arguments about the scope of the audit or the acceptability of accounting principles. It is possible that a change in auditors occurred for the purpose of procuring new auditors who will agree with management's treatment of questionable accounting practices. Not surprisingly, these types of disagreements between auditors and management would be of interest to investors and future auditors.

The public accounting firm that has been terminated or has voluntarily withdrawn from the engagement (whether the audit has been completed or not) is known as the **predecessor auditor**. To reduce the risk of accepting a problem client, auditing standards require a prospective auditor to initiate contact with and *attempt* to obtain basic information directly from the predecessor regarding issues that reflect directly on the *integrity of management.* The audit client must grant its approval before the communication can occur between the prospective auditor and the predecessor auditor. Once approval is obtained, the prospective auditor should ask the predecessor auditor for information on management's

EXHIBIT 3.1
Stages of an Audit:
Obtain (or Retain)
Engagement

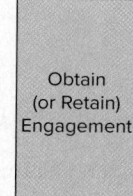

| Obtain (or Retain) Engagement | Engagement Planning | Risk Assessment | Substantive Procedures | Reporting |

integrity; on disagreements with management about accounting principles, audit procedures, or similar matters; and the reasons for a change of auditors.

The following Auditing Insight provides some insight into how often auditor changes among larger companies actually occur.

AUDITING INSIGHT — How often do companies switch auditors?

Not as often as you would think, and especially not for big clients. Overall, the average audit tenure for public companies is 15 years, however, there is a definite positive relationship between the audit tenure and the size of the client. The average auditor tenure for public companies in the first quartile of revenues (average revenue of $17 million) is 8 years, as opposed to 25.3 years for companies in the fourth quartile of revenues (average revenue of $19,779 million). When looking specifically at the S&P 500, whose average revenues are $26,060 million, the average auditor tenure is 32.7 years. While that might seem like a long time, that is nothing compared to companies like these:

- Sherman Williams, who have been audited by EY since 1908
- Proctor & Gamble, who have been audited by Deloitte since 1890
- Goodyear Tire & Rubber, who have been audited by PwC since 1898!

Source: "Audit Tenure by Revenue," *Audit Analytics,* August 20. 2020 (blog. auditanalytics.com).

When a public company changes auditors, the company must file a *Form 8-K* report with the SEC and disclose that the board of directors approved the change. **Form 8-K**, the "special events report," is required whenever certain significant events such as changes in control and legal proceedings occur. Public companies also must report any disagreements with the former auditors concerning matters of accounting principles, financial statement disclosures, or auditing procedures. At the same time, the former auditor must submit a letter stating whether the auditors agree with the explanation and, if not, provide particulars. These documents are available to the public through the SEC's Electronic Data Gathering, Analysis, and Retrieval (EDGAR) system, available on the SEC's website (www.sec.gov). The purpose of these public disclosures is to make information available about client–auditor conflicts that have occurred.

If you read closely, professional standards require only that the auditors *attempt* to communicate with the predecessor auditors. The AICPA Code of Professional Conduct does not permit the predecessor auditor to provide information obtained during any audit engagements without the explicit consent of the client. Confidentiality remains even when the auditor–client relationship ends. Therefore, auditing standards require the prospective auditor to ask that the consent be given to permit the predecessor auditor to respond fully to their inquiries. If this consent is refused, the refusal should be regarded as a *red flag,* and the prospective auditor should be cautious about accepting the engagement. Exhibit 3.2 summarizes the responsibilities of the prospective auditor, client, and the predecessor auditor in the communication process.

EXHIBIT 3.2 Party Responsibilities for Required Communication with Predecessor Auditor

Prospective Auditor	• Request client to authorize predecessor auditor to fully respond to inquiries
	  ▪ If management refuses to authorize predecessor to respond or limits response, auditor should inquire as to the reason and consider the implications for refusal in deciding whether to accept the engagement.
	• Initiate contact with predecessor auditor
	• Inquire with predecessor auditor about
	  ▪ management integrity
	  ▪ disagreements with management
	  ▪ reason for auditor change

Client	• Authorize predecessor auditor to respond fully to prospective auditor inquiries
Predecessor Auditor	• Upon permission from client, respond fully (or limited depending on client authorization) to prospective auditor inquiries

Source: *AU-C Section 210 Terms of the Engagement,* AICPA, 2021.

In addition to communication with the predecessor auditor, client acceptance and continuance policies and procedures generally include

- Obtaining and reviewing financial information about the prospective client: annual reports, interim statements, registration statements, Form 10-Ks, and reports to regulatory agencies.
- Acquiring detailed criminal background checks of all senior managers.
- Requesting the prospective client's bankers, legal counsel, underwriters, analysts, or other persons who do business with the entity to provide information about it and its management.
- Considering whether the engagement would require special attention or involve unusual risks to the public accounting firm.
- Evaluating the public accounting firm's independence with regard to the prospective client.
- Considering the need for individuals possessing special skills or knowledge to complete the audit (e.g., information technology auditor, valuation specialist, industry specialist).

The firms also search for news articles, lawsuits, and bankruptcy court outcomes naming the entity, the chairman of the board, the CEO, the CFO, and other high-ranking officers. In fact, the firms often engage private investigators to conduct additional searches for information when the prospective clients are financial institutions, companies accused of fraud, companies under SEC or other regulatory investigation, companies that have changed auditors frequently, and companies showing recent losses. These characteristics are red flags of potential problems, and public accounting firms want to know as much as they can about the companies and their officers before entering into a relationship with them. Without a doubt, management integrity (or lack thereof) is the primary reason for accepting (or not accepting) an audit engagement.

Client continuance decisions are similar to acceptance decisions except that the firm will have more firsthand experience with the entity. These types of client retention reviews are typically done annually and also with the occurrence of major events such as changes in management, directors, ownership, legal counsel, financial condition, litigation status, nature of the client's business, or scope of the audit engagement. In general, conditions that would have caused a public accounting firm to reject a prospective client can develop and lead to a decision to discontinue the engagement. For example, a client company could expand and diversify on an international scale so that a small public accounting firm might not have the resources to continue the audit. In addition, it would not be unusual to see newspaper stories about public accounting firms dropping clients after directors or officers admit to falsification of financial statements, theft and misuse of corporate assets, or other improprieties. The following Auditing Insight provides an example of **KPMG** dropping a client for exactly that reason.

 AUDITING INSIGHT | KPMG Severs Relationship with Liberty Tax

In December of 2017, **KPMG** announced their decision to resign as **Liberty Tax**'s auditor, three months after the firing of CEO John Hewitt. Hewitt was fired for having romantic relationships with female employees and giving them preferential treatment, yet remained the chairman of the board due to his status as controlling shareholder of the company. When announcing the decision, KPMG cited concerns around internal controls over financial reporting, more specifically related to management integrity and the tone at the top. Ultimately

Hewitt did agree to resign as chairman of the board and sell his ownership shares in the company in July 2018, following delayed earnings reports and violation warnings of listing requirements from the NASDAQ exchange.

Sources: M. Cohn, "KPMG Resigns from Auditing Liberty Tax," *Accounting Today,* December 11, 2017, A. Melin, "Liberty Tax Soars After Founder Involved in Sex Scandal Agrees to Leave Firm," *Accounting Today*, July 24, 2018.

Compliance with Independence and Ethical Requirements

If you recall from Chapter 2, the *responsibilities principle* requires auditors to comply with appropriate ethical requirements for each audit engagement; two important requirements relate to *independence* and *due care*. Auditors must maintain independence *in mental attitude;* that is, auditors are expected to be unbiased and impartial with respect to the financial statements and other information they audit. This "state of mind" is often referred to as the auditor possessing **independence in fact**. This independence allows auditors to form an opinion on the entity's financial statements without being affected by influences that might compromise that opinion. Not only is it important for auditors to *be* unbiased, but they must also *appear* to be unbiased. **Independence in appearance** relates to others' (particularly financial statement users') perceptions of auditors' independence.

In fact, if the auditor is not independent, the financial statements are considered unaudited for all practical purposes. A lack of independence can result in disciplinary action by regulators and/or professional organizations and litigation by those who relied on the financial statements (e.g., clients and investors). The profession as a whole depends on the value of independence in that the auditor's opinion on the financial statements loses its value if the auditor is not considered to be independent from the management of the firm. As a result of the importance placed on independence, public accounting firms must have a process in place to ensure that they are independent of the company being audited.

Because public accounting firms are subject to strict independence rules, they actively monitor the key relationships and the investment portfolios of their individual partners. These processes are in place to help ensure that the firm is independent of any relationship that might impact the firm's professionals from maintaining objectivity when making professional judgments on each audit. In fact, even after an audit client has passed the client acceptance process, independence rules must continue to be rigorously maintained. The importance of this process is exemplified by the way that **KPMG** handled a recent situation involving a rogue partner, described in the following Auditing Insight.

 AUDITING INSIGHT   Compromised Independence?

KPMG LLP was forced to resign from two large audit clients, **Herbalife Ltd.** and **Skechers USA Inc.**, because Scott London, the partner assigned to each client, admitted to providing stock tips about the two audit clients to a friend in exchange for cash and gifts. The friend is believed to have made more than $1 million from trading on the insider information. By providing confidential insider information, London directly violated the AICPA Code of Professional Conduct regarding confidential client information. As a result, the firm immediately fired him and resigned as the external auditor for the two clients.

The resignation was necessary because London "violated the firm's rigorous policies and protections, betrayed the trust of clients as well as colleagues, and acted with deliberate disregard for KPMG's long-standing culture of professionalism and integrity." There was a fear that the firm's independence and objectivity toward the clients would potentially be compromised as a result of this partner's actions.

In addition to resigning from the two audits, KPMG decided to withdraw its audit report on the financial statements of Herbalife for the three previous years and for Skechers for the previous two years. In doing so, KPMG stated that it did not believe there were any errors in the financial statements. However, because of London's actions, the firm believed doing so was appropriate. London pleaded guilty to a federal insider-trading charge on July 1, 2013, publicly admitting that he did reveal confidential information about his clients to a friend. The friend used the information to make over $1 million. London was sentenced to serve 14 months in a federal prison in April 2014.

Sources: "Trading Case Embroils KPMG," The Wall Street Journal, April 10, 2013, p. A1; "FBI Probes Trading as KPMG Quits Herbalife, Skechers Audits." Reuters.com, April 9, 2013, "Former KPMG Partner Scott London Pleads Guilty to Insider Trading." *Los Angeles Times*, July 1, 2013; "Former KPMG Partner Sentenced for Insider." *Los Angeles Times*, April 24, 2014; "FBI Probes Trading as KPMG Quits Herbalife, Skechers Audits," *Reuters*, April 9, 2013.

Engagement Letters

Professional standards require auditors to reach a mutual understanding with clients concerning engagement requirements and expectations and to document this understanding, usually in the form of a written letter. When a new client is accepted or when an audit engagement continues from year to year, an **engagement letter** should be prepared. This letter sets forth the understanding with the client, including in particular (1) the objectives of the engagement,

(2) management's responsibilities, (3) the auditors' responsibilities, and (4) any limitations of the engagement. Other matters of understanding, such as the ones shown in Exhibit 3.3, also may be included in the letter. For example, the additional internal control considerations required by the Public Company Accounting Oversight Board are specifically mentioned in the example engagement letter. In fact, a close review of this exhibit reveals the importance of an auditor being quite detailed when completing the engagement letter.

In effect, the engagement letter acts as a contract. Thus, it serves as a means for reducing the risk of misunderstandings with the client and as a means of avoiding legal liability for claims that the auditors did not perform the work promised.

Many public accounting firms also have policies about sending a **termination letter** to former clients. Such a letter is a good idea because it provides an opportunity to deal with the subject of future services, in particular, (1) access to audit documentation by successor auditors, (2) reissuance of the auditors' report when required for SEC reporting or comparative financial reporting, and (3) fee arrangements for such future services. The termination letter also may include a report of the auditors' understanding of the

EXHIBIT 3.3   Engagement Letter

September 15, 2023

Mr. Matt Lancaster Chair,
Audit Committee
Dunder-Mifflin Inc.
P.O. Box 349 Scranton,
Pennsylvania 18503

Dear Mr. Lancaster:

This letter will confirm our understanding of the arrangement for our audit of the financial statements of Dunder-Mifflin Inc. for the year ending December 31, 2023.

We will audit the Company's balance sheet at December 31, 2023, and the related statements of income, comprehensive income, stockholders' equity, and cash flows for the year then ended, for the purpose of expressing an opinion on them. We will also audit whether Dunder-Mifflin Inc. maintained effective internal control over financial reporting as of December 31, 2023, based on criteria established in Internal Control—Integrated Framework issued by the Committee of Sponsoring Organizations of the Treadway Commission (COSO criteria). Dunder-Mifflin Inc.'s management is responsible for these financial statements and for maintaining effective internal control over financial reporting. Management is also responsible for making financial records and related information available for audit and for identifying and ensuring that the company complies with the laws and regulations that apply to its activities. Our responsibility is to express an opinion on these financial statements and an opinion on the effectiveness of the company's internal control over financial reporting based on our audits. If, for any reason, we are unable to complete the audit or are unable to form or have not formed an opinion, we may decline to express an opinion or decline to issue a report as a result of the engagement.

We will conduct our audits in accordance with the standards of the Public Company Accounting Oversight Board (United States). Those standards require that we plan and perform the audit to obtain reasonable assurance about whether the financial statements are free of material misstatement and whether effective internal control over financial reporting was maintained in all material respects. Our audit of the financial statements includes examining, on a test basis, evidence supporting the amounts and disclosures in the financial statements, assessing the accounting principles used and significant estimates made by management, and evaluating the overall financial statement presentation. Our audit of internal control over financial reporting includes obtaining an understanding of internal control over financial reporting, testing and evaluating the design and operating effectiveness of internal control, and performing such other procedures as we considered necessary in the circumstances. We believe that our audits provide a reasonable basis for our opinions.

Our fee for these services will be at our regular hourly rates, plus travel and other out-of-pocket costs. Invoices will be rendered on a monthly basis and are payable on presentation. If this letter correctly expresses your understanding, please sign the enclosed copy where indicated and return it to us.

Very truly yours,

Michael Scarn, LLP

DUNDER-MIFFLIN Inc.

By _____

Date _____

circumstances of termination (e.g., disagreements about accounting principles and audit procedures, fees, or other conflicts). These matters can be of great interest to prospective auditors who should always remember to ask for a copy of the termination letter.

☑ REVIEW CHECKPOINTS

3.1 What sources of information can auditors use in connection with deciding whether to accept a new client?

3.2 Why do predecessor auditors need to obtain the client's consent to give information to prospective auditors? What information should prospective auditors try to obtain from predecessor auditors?

3.3 What does it mean for an auditor to be independent in fact? What does it mean for an auditor to be independent in appearance?

3.4 What benefits are obtained by having an *engagement letter?* What is a *termination letter?*

AUDIT PLAN

LO 3-2
Understand the importance of planning the audit engagement so that it is conducted in accordance with professional standards.

An **audit plan** is a comprehensive list of the specific audit procedures that the audit team needs to perform to gather sufficient appropriate evidence on which to base their opinion on the financial statements. The professional standards require that the auditor plan each audit engagement, including the establishment of an overall strategy for each audit engagement. Specifically, when planning the engagement, the auditor needs to develop and document a plan that describes the nature, timing, and extent of further audit procedures to be performed to assess the risk of material misstatement at the financial statement and the assertion level. Next, the auditor must carefully plan the nature, timing, and extent of control tests and substantive tests that are designed to mitigate these risks to an acceptable level. This planning process is required to be led by the assigned engagement partner.

The professional standards are absolutely clear that the nature and extent of work completed during engagement planning will depend on the company's size, complexity, and industry. In addition, the auditor's prior experience with the company, including any major changes from prior years, will have an impact on the nature and extent of planning activity. Furthermore, the client's information technology system used to process accounting transactions will also have an impact on planning activities. As a result, audit firms spend a considerable amount of time on risk assessment at both the financial statement level and the management assertion level for the client being audited.

Importantly, this process begins with a detailed understanding of the client's business, industry, and strategy to achieve a competitive advantage in its marketplace. During this process, the auditor should obtain an understanding of important events that have affected the client, its operations, and its accounting information system. When understanding the accounting information system, the auditor should pay particular attention to

- The complexity of the computer operations used by the entity (e.g., batch processing, online processing, outside service centers).
- The organizational structure of the computerized processing activities.
- The availability of data for the auditor.
- The need for specialized skills.

Relatedly, the auditor should obtain an overall understanding of the financial statements, and ultimately the management assertions. This understanding provides the base of knowledge necessary to assess audit risk, providing the underlying basis to construct the audit plan.

For example, the evaluation of the risk of material misstatement is likely to vary for different financial statement accounts and may even vary for different classes of significant transactions related to the same financial statement account. Ultimately, the audit plan will need to identify each of the relevant financial statement assertions (i.e., *existence, occurrence, completeness, cutoff, rights and obligations, valuation and allocation, accuracy, classification,* and *understandability*) for each of the significant financial statement accounts and disclosures identified at an audit client.

The risk assessment process provides the basis to determine the nature, timing, and extent of internal control tests and substantive tests of account balances and disclosures at an audit client. That is, for each relevant assertion, the auditor must determine the combination of control and substantive tests that will be necessary to gather enough evidence to persuade the auditor that no material misstatement exists for the relevant assertion being audited. When the tests have been completed, audit team members will often indicate the date that the procedure was performed and where the evidence is documented in the audit plan. Thus, audit plans are used not only for quality control and supervision but also as documentation to show that the audit engagement was planned and supervised in accordance with professional standards.

Risk assessment is absolutely critical in the audit planning process. Although Exhibit 3.4 below implies that risk assessment occurs after the engagement planning phase, in reality, the two phases are both part of the overall process of planning an audit. Remember that the professional standards require that when planning, the auditor should establish the overall audit strategy for the company being audited, which includes the risk assessment procedures that will be performed. Therefore some engagement planning must occur prior to risk assessment. However, following risk assessment, the auditor must develop a plan to respond to each of the assessed risks of material misstatement with specific auditing procedures. Because of the importance of risk assessment to the financial statement audit process, we devote exclusive attention to this subject in Chapter 4. The remainder of this chapter will focus on all other aspects of engagement planning, which occur in the audit stage highlighted in Exhibit 3.4. Essentially, there are three goals of audit planning:

1. To make sure that the firm has the requisite staff to conduct the audit in accordance with professional standards in a timely and profitable manner.
2. To determine materiality.
3. To outline the specific audit procedures, including tests of control and substantive tests that need to be executed properly in order to mitigate assessed risks of material misstatement and be in compliance with professional standards.

EXHIBIT 3.4 Stages of an Audit: Engagement Planning

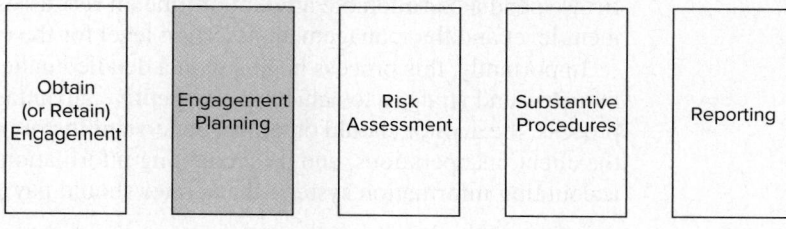

Staffing the Audit Engagement

When a new client is obtained, most public accounting firms assign a full-service team to the engagement. For a typical audit engagement, this team usually consists of the **audit engagement partner** (the person with final responsibility for the audit, usually an industry specialist), an audit manager, an information technology (IT) auditor, a tax specialist, a **quality assurance partner** (the second audit partner who reviews the audit team's work in critical audit areas), and audit staff. The assignment of staff depends on the riskiness of the engagement. For new clients, companies with complex significant transactions, and public companies, more experienced staff members are typically assigned. The following Auditing Insight underscores the importance of proper engagement staffing on audit quality.

AUDITING INSIGHT Plan for Quality

The Center for Audit Quality (CAQ) is a nonprofit organization that is dedicated to promoting "high quality performance by public company auditors," which helps to ensure the highest level of "investor confidence" in the capital markets. In providing the financial support for the CAQ, the public company auditing firms recognize the importance of working together to achieve audit quality.

The importance of planning was recently elevated by the CAQ when it released its own set of Audit Quality Indicators. In fact, one of the four key themes of audit quality outlined by the CAQ was the "engagement team knowledge, experience, and workload." Among other issues, the report stressed that "The knowledge, experience,

and workload of the audit engagement partner and certain other members of the engagement team are important elements in the execution of an audit. It is the responsibility of the engagement partner to determine that, collectively, the engagement team has the appropriate experience and competencies, and that specialists are engaged, as needed. The level of detail that may be provided on changes in the composition of the engagement team is dependent on the audit committee's needs and expectations, size of the engagement team, and other considerations."*

Sources: *Center for Audit Quality, "CAQ Approach to Audit Quality Indicators," Accessed June 24, 2019, www.thecaq.org.

No matter the type of engagement, planning meetings should include all team members and focus on the financial statement accounts that represent the highest risk of material misstatement. These planning meetings help to ensure that the engagement is properly planned and that the audit team (especially new) members are properly supervised. The meetings also are intended to be brainstorming sessions to (1) ensure that all audit team members are informed about potential risks in the engagement and (2) increase team members' awareness for potential fraud. This required brainstorming session is discussed in more detail in Chapter 4.

In the sections below are further discussions of specific engagement staffing issues, including the role of IT auditors on the engagement team, relying on the work of internal auditors, and the use of audit specialists.

Use of IT Auditors

When planning the engagement, the audit team members should consider their training and experience relative to the methods of information processing. A review of the client's computer hardware could show the extent of complexity involved. Whenever a complex computing environment exists, specialized information technology skills are needed to evaluate the effect of computerized processing on the audit process. IT auditors are members of the audit team who are specially trained to evaluate computerized controls and processes. The audit team could need their specialized skills relating to various methods of data processing and extraction, programming languages, software packages, or computer-assisted audit techniques. For audits of large companies in today's environment, IT auditors will be required and included on the engagement team. Module H further discusses the role of IT systems in the financial statement audit.

If the client *outsources* significant accounting applications (e.g., payroll), the audit team might need to coordinate audit procedures with service auditors at the processing center. This topic is covered in more detail in Module A.

Considering the Work of Internal Auditors

External auditors must obtain an understanding of a client's internal audit department and its work as part of the understanding of the client's internal control system. Internal auditors were discussed briefly in Chapter 1 and will be discussed in more detail in Module D, but here we talk about the working relationship between internal and external auditors. Audit efficiency can be realized when the two groups work together. However, prior to relying on the work of internal auditors, external auditors should consider internal auditors' *objectivity* and *competence:*

- *Objectivity.* Internal auditors can never be considered *independent* in the same sense that external auditors are because internal auditors are either directly employed or paid as contractors by the client; however, they can (and should) be *objective.*[5] Internal auditors' objectivity is investigated by learning about their organizational status and lines of communication in the company. Objectivity is enhanced when the internal auditors report directly to the audit committee of the board of directors. Objectivity is questioned when

  - Internal auditors report to divisional management, line managers, or other persons with a stake in the outcome of their findings.
  - Managers have some power over the pay or job tenure of the internal auditors.
  - Individual internal auditors have relatives in audit-sensitive areas or are scheduled to be promoted to positions in the activities under internal audit review.

- *Competence.* Internal auditors' competence is investigated by obtaining evidence about their educational and experience qualifications, their certifications (CPA, CIA, CISA, etc.) and continuing education status, the department's policies and procedures for work quality and for making personnel assignments, the supervision and review activities, and the quality of reports and audit documentation. This evidence enables the external auditors to evaluate internal auditors' performance.

Favorable conclusions about competence and objectivity enable external auditors to rely on the work completed by the internal audit department related to gaining an understanding of and testing of a company's internal control system. Internal auditors also can assist (under the supervision of the independent audit team) with performing some substantive testing of balances on the audit, reducing the external auditors' work, and avoiding duplication of effort. As an example, internal auditors can conduct observations and make test counts during physical inventory counts thereby allowing auditors to be able to reduce the nature, timing, or extent of their own procedures for these accounts. This utilization of internal auditors' work, however, cannot be a complete substitute for the external auditors' own procedures, as it is the work of the external auditors that must always provide the basis for the auditors' opinion.

The external auditors can never delegate responsibility for audit decisions to the internal auditors. Rather, they must supervise, review, evaluate, and perform independent testing of all the work performed by internal auditors. Internal auditors should never be delegated tasks that require the external auditors' *professional judgment.* Following is an illustration of how an accounting firm could address the use of internal auditors on its engagements. Note that internal auditors' work can be utilized more extensively without reperforming a percentage of the work when the account balance involves low professional judgment and risk, and internal auditors are considered to be more competent and objective.

Reliance on Internal Auditors

	Objectivity and Competence	
	Low	**High**
High judgment/risk	Auditor should not rely on internal auditors' work	Auditor should not rely on internal auditors' work
Low judgment/risk	Auditor can rely on internal auditors' work but should reperform some of the work	Auditor can rely on internal auditors' work and may want to reperform some of the work

[5]Internal auditors refer to their level of objectivity as *independence.* This concept is discussed further in Module D.

Using the Work of an Auditor-Employed or Auditor-Engaged Specialist

Gaining an understanding of the business can often lead to acquiring information that reveals the need to employ *audit specialists* on the audit. Audit **specialists** are persons skilled in fields other than accounting and auditing—actuaries, appraisers, attorneys, environmental engineers, and geologists—who are not members of the audit team. Auditors are not expected to be experts in all fields of knowledge that can contribute information to the financial statements. Audit specialists can be employed by the auditor's firm (i.e., auditor-employed specialists) or engaged from an outside provider, referred to simply as an auditor-engaged specialist. Specialists should typically be involved in planning meetings and supervised as other team members in accordance with professional standards. When an auditor-engaged specialist is used, the audit engagement partner should assess the specialist's knowledge, skill, and ability in that particular area. This includes gaining knowledge about his or her professional qualifications, experience, and reputation.

The engagement team must also assess the objectivity of the auditor-engaged specialist. An auditor-engaged specialist should be unrelated to the company under audit if possible. Regardless of whether the specialist is auditor-employed or auditor-engaged, the engagement partner and team should clearly inform the audit specialist of the work to be performed and of any matters that may affect his or her work. The engagement partner and audit team must also evaluate the work of the specialist. The extent of the evaluation is contingent upon the reliance on the specialist's work, the risk of material misstatement in the area, the experience and skill of the specialist, and the objectivity of the specialists. Provided that some additional auditing work is done on the data that the audit specialist uses in reaching his or her conclusions, auditors may rely on the work of an audit specialist in connection with audit decisions. Normally, audit specialists are not referred to in the auditor's report unless they are involved in addressing a critical audit matter disclosed in the audit report or unless their findings (e.g., a difference in an estimate from that of management) cause the auditors' report to be modified (e.g., because of a GAAP departure). In these cases, references to the findings of the audit specialists may facilitate a better understanding of the nature of the GAAP departure.

Using the Work of a Company's Specialist

Auditors may also use the work of a company's specialist as audit evidence. Much like when using the work of internal auditors, external auditors must consider the objectivity and competence, specifically the knowledge, skill, and ability, of the company specialist. As with the auditor-engaged specialist, the auditor must evaluate the work of the company specialist, including evaluating any data, methods, or assumptions made by the specialist. Similarly, the extent of the evaluation is contingent upon the risk of material misstatement in the area, the significance of the company specialist's work to the auditor's conclusion, the knowledge, skill, and ability of the specialist, and the objectivity of the specialist's judgment.

The Auditing Insight below provides a glimpse into how auditors in practice use the work of specialists.

 AUDITING INSIGHT   How do auditors really use specialists?

Determining the fair value of an asset or liability is difficult and subjective. Auditing assets and liabilities reported at fair value is even more difficult and is one area where auditors are increasingly engaging specialists for help. But are auditors really using specialists the way they should? Turns out, not really. In a recently published academic paper, the author interviews auditors and valuation specialists and finds that auditors don't fully value the work done by valuation specialists. Auditors use specialists to feel more secure in the performance of the audit, however, they tend to not fully trust the results of the specialists. In short, auditors use the work of specialists for comfort, not

insight. Through interviews, the author discovers instances of auditors editing and finalizing, deleting select information, and even ignoring issues raised by valuation specialists. Auditors tend to make the work of the specialists conform to their view, thus somewhat defeating the purpose of using a specialist altogether. Based on these insights, it appears that auditors have some work to do when it comes to the proper use of specialists.

Source: E. Griffith, "Auditors, Specialists, and the Professional Jurisdiction in Audits of Fair Values," *Contemporary Accounting Research*, Spring 2020, Vol. 37(1), pp. 245–276.

Time Budget

The timing of the work and the number of hours that each segment of the engagement is expected to take are detailed in a preliminary time budget. *Time budgets* are used to maintain control of the audit by identifying problem areas early in the engagement, thereby ensuring that the engagement is completed on a timely basis. Time budgets are usually based on the prior-year's performance for continuing clients while considering changes in the client's business. In a first-time audit, the budget may be based on a predecessor auditor's experience or on general experience with similar companies. Extra time also may be assigned to those accounts containing the highest amount of audit risk. A simple time budget for an audit engagement follows.

	Audit Time Budget (Hours)	
	Interim	Year-End (Final)
Gain an understanding of business	15	
Evaluate internal audit function	10	
Understand internal control system	30	10
Prepare audit plan	25	
Investigate related party transactions	5	15
Meet with client personnel	10	18
Complete cash substantive testing	10	15
Complete accounts receivable substantive testing	15	5
Complete inventory substantive testing	35	20
Complete accounts payable substantive testing	5	35
Evaluate legal letters		20
Review financial statement		25
Prepare audit report		12

This time budget is illustrative—actual time budgets are much more detailed and complex. Most budgets specify the expected time according to the level of staff people on the team (partner, manager, in-charge accountant, staff assistant, IT specialist, tax specialist). The illustration shows time at *interim* and at *year-end*. **Interim audit work** refers to procedures performed several weeks or months before the date of the financial statements. (Account balances audited during interim are later *rolled forward* at year-end.) **Year-end audit work** refers to procedures performed shortly before and after the date of the financial statements. Public accounting firms typically spread the workload during the year by scheduling interim audit work so they will have enough time and people available when several audits have year-ends on the same date. (December 31 is quite common.) For many public accounting firms, the auditing "busy season" runs from September through March of the following year. The interim work typically consists of risk assessment work, internal control testing, and substantive testing of balances as they exist at the interim date.

Everyone who works on the audit engagement is typically required to report the time taken to perform procedures for each phase of the audit. These time reports are recorded by budget categories for the purposes of (1) evaluating the efficiency of the audit team members, (2) compiling a record for billing the client, and (3) compiling a record for planning the next audit. Although the purposes of a time budget are straightforward, these budgets create job pressures. Staff members are under pressure to meet the budget, and beginning auditors often experience frustration over learning how to complete their audit work in an efficient manner. As a result, staff members may be tempted to "eat" time, that is, underreport the actual number of hours spent to perform the audit work. Eating time is considered unethical behavior. Many accounting firms have policies and procedures prohibiting auditors from underreporting their time. Despite this, eating time is still a common occurrence. However, for proper client billing and audit planning for future audits, it is essential for auditors to truthfully report their time.

MATERIALITY

LO 3-3
Define *materiality* and explain its importance in the audit planning process.

As you know, financial statement measurements and information in some footnote disclosures are not flawlessly accurate. Management has the choice, for example, of depreciation method, inventory valuation method, and classification of marketable securities, all of which affect final financial statement numbers. Furthermore, many financial measurements are based on estimates such as the estimated depreciable lives of fixed assets or the estimated amount of uncollectible accounts receivable. Thus, net income is not necessarily the one "true" figure but one possibility in a range of potential net income figures allowable under the relevant reporting framework (e.g., GAAP or International Financial Reporting Standards [IFRS]).

Given this range permitted, some amount of inaccuracy is allowed in financial statements. This is because (1) unimportant inaccuracies do not affect users' decisions and hence are not material, (2) the cost of finding and correcting small misstatements is too high, and (3) the time taken to find them would delay issuance of the financial statements. Although not absolutely accurate, accountants and auditors do want to maintain that financial reports are materially accurate and do not contain material misstatements.

As a result, to plan the nature, timing, and extent of further audit procedures to be performed, professional standards require an auditor to consider earnings and other factors and determine an appropriate **materiality** level for the financial statements. Information is considered material if it is likely to influence financial statement users' decisions. When referring to materiality, the standards rely on the definition as established by the Supreme Court, that a fact is material if there is "a substantial likelihood that the . . . fact would have been viewed by the reasonable investor as having significantly altered the 'total mix' of information made available." The emphasis in this definition is on the financial statement users' point of view, not on the auditors' or managers' point of view. Although financial statement users are expected to have a basic knowledge of business and financial statements as well as an understanding of the limitations of the audit process, auditors remain conservative when setting the materiality level.[6]

Given this, the engagement partner needs to think carefully about the appropriate level of materiality during the planning process. By doing so, the auditor helps to avoid unnecessary surprises on the audit engagement. Suppose that near the end of an audit, the partner decided that all misstatements of more than $50,000 should be considered material but then realized that the nature, timing, and extent of substantive procedures had been completed assuming a materiality level of $250,000! As a result, the nature, timing, and extent of further audit procedures would have to be modified significantly, which would likely be an unpleasant surprise for the engagement team.

The professional standards also require the auditor to evaluate the facts and circumstances of each engagement carefully to determine whether there are particular accounts or disclosures where amounts lower than established materiality might influence the

---

[6]PCAOB Release No. 2010-004, "AS 2105: Consideration of Materiality in Planning and Performing and Audit," August 5, 2010.

judgment of a reasonable financial statement user. If that is the case, the auditor must determine an amount that would be considered a tolerable misstatement for that account or disclosure when completing risk assessment procedures and further planning and performing the necessary audit procedures in that area.[7]

Therefore, auditors use *performance materiality* (an amount less than materiality for the financial statements as a whole) to make sure that the aggregate of uncorrected and undetected immaterial misstatements does not exceed materiality for the financial statements as a whole. For example, auditors may use different amounts (smaller than overall financial statement materiality) when auditing particular classes of significant transactions, account balances, or disclosures. The audit team cannot look at every significant transaction, so the concept of performance materiality takes this risk into account. When auditors use sampling, performance materiality is referred to as *tolerable misstatement.*

The extent to which performance materiality is based on the overall materiality is a matter of professional judgment and, as a result, the amount may vary from auditor to auditor, as could the methods for assigning performance materiality to accounts. The auditing standards do not even require that the overall materiality amount be assigned to individual accounts in dollar amounts. While there may be many different processes for determining performance materiality, most auditors start with a top-down approach: judging an overall material amount for the financial statements and then determining performance materiality to particular accounts to help determine the amount of work to be done in each area. Such a top-down approach is considered theoretically preferable because this method requires the audit team to think first about the financial statements taken as a whole.

Exhibit 3.5 below highlights the top-down approach and the relationship between overall materiality and performance materiality. As seen in the Exhibit, performance materiality may be impacted by the risk associated with the account. Auditors may choose to set a higher performance materiality when risk is low versus when there is a high risk of material misstatement. It should also be noted that overall materiality is not "allocated" among the various audit areas. In other words, if one were to add all of the performance materiality amounts assigned to the various areas of the audit, that sum would exceed overall materiality.

Materiality Calculation

Although some accountants wish that standard setters could issue definitive, quantitative materiality guidelines, many fear the rigidity that such guidelines would impose. Therefore, in the end, materiality is a matter of professional judgment that the engagement partner must decide on each audit engagement. However, on each audit engagement, the

EXHIBIT 3.5
Top-Down Approach to Overall Materiality and Performance Materiality Judgments

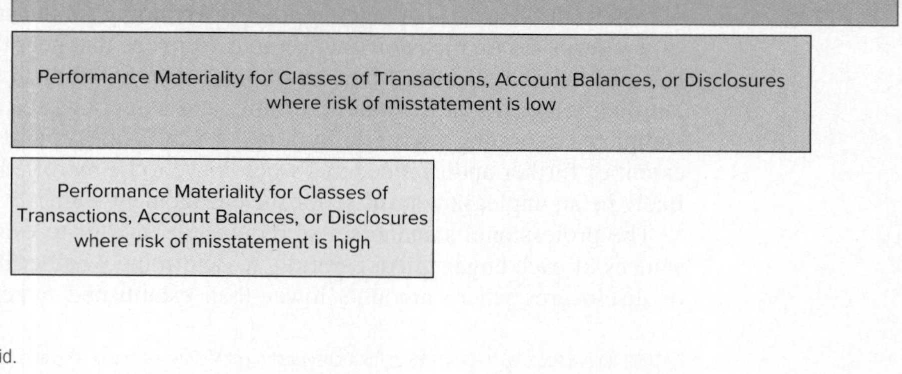

Overall Materiality

Performance Materiality for Classes of Transactions, Account Balances, or Disclosures where risk of misstatement is low

Performance Materiality for Classes of Transactions, Account Balances, or Disclosures where risk of misstatement is high

[7]Ibid.

planning process begins with a calculation of a preliminary materiality amount that is based on a relevant benchmark and a rule of thumb percentage applied to that benchmark.

The choice of appropriate benchmark relates directly back to what is most important for the financial statement users and the industry in which the client operates. Auditors most commonly use profit before tax (PBT), total net assets, or total revenues as the benchmark for their initial determination of materiality, depending on the client industry. Some examples of commonly used benchmarks per industry are

- Asset based entities – total net assets.
- Profit based companies, such as manufacturing – PBT.
- High technology start-up companies – total revenue.
- Nonprofit entities – gross revenue or total contributions.

The rule of thumb percentages applied to the benchmarks often range from 3–5 percent of PBT or 1/2–1 percent of revenue or total assets.

As noted, the percentages and benchmarks per industry are only rules of thumb and will not be appropriate for all clients. If, for example, the PBT for a profit-based company fluctuates widely, an average PBT over recent years may be a more appropriate benchmark for materiality. Alternatively, if a profit-based company experienced a net loss, an alternative benchmark may be more appropriate to use to determine materiality. **Amazon,** the internet retail giant, provides an example of both of these scenarios. For the fiscal year 2020, Amazon reported $24.2 billion in income before taxes (i.e., profit before tax). For the years ended 2019 and 2018, Amazon reported $14.0 and $11.3 billion PBT, respectively. Using the rule of thumb of 3 percent of PBT, the overall materiality set for the 2020 Amazon audit would be approximately $725 million dollars. That amount is closer to 6 percent of Amazon's PBT in each of the prior years, in other words, twice the amount of materiality from the prior two audits! In a situation like this, auditors may decide to use the average PBT of the prior years to determine materiality. Although hard to believe today, in 2002, Amazon reported a net loss of $149 million and net sales of $3.9 billion. In a loss scenario such as this, auditors may decide using a percentage of sales or total assets is a more appropriate benchmark for materiality. Of course, in the end, materiality is a matter of professional judgment, keeping in mind what matters most to the financial statement users.

Although standards require materiality to be expressed as a quantitative amount, auditors must consider qualitative factors as well. The SEC cautions auditors about overreliance on certain quantitative benchmarks to assess materiality, noting that "misstatements are not immaterial simply because they fall beneath a numerical threshold."[8] Thus, auditors must examine both quantitative and qualitative factors when assessing materiality. Some of the more common qualitative factors that auditors use in making materiality judgments are the nature of the item or issue, engagement circumstances, and possible cumulative effects—all discussed in the following paragraphs.

Other Issues that Impact Materiality

Nature of the Item or Issue

An important qualitative factor is the descriptive nature of the item or issue. An illegal payment is important primarily because of its nature as well as because of its absolute or relative amount. In addition, the auditor would consider any type of fraud committed by a member of management material regardless of the amount. Finally, generally speaking, potential errors in the more liquid assets (cash, receivables, and inventory) are considered more important than potential errors in other accounts (such as fixed assets and deferred charges).

[8]SEC, *Staff Accounting Bulletin No. 99,* "Materiality," August 12, 1999.

Engagement Circumstances

An auditor's legal liability is always a relevant consideration when determining materiality. That is, auditors generally place extra emphasis on the detection of misstatements in financial statements that will be widely used (such as those of public companies) or used by important outsiders (such as bank loan officers). In addition, troublesome political events in foreign countries can cause auditors to try to be more accurate with measurements and disclosures. Other circumstances that affect quantitative materiality involve amounts that could turn a net loss into a profit or allow a company to meet earnings expectations. In these circumstances, when management can exercise discretion over an accounting treatment, auditors tend to exercise more care and use a more stringent quantitative materiality criterion. Finally, matters surrounded by uncertainty about the outcome of future events usually come under more stringent quantitative materiality considerations.

Possible Cumulative Effects

At the end of each audit engagement, auditors must also evaluate the aggregate sum of known or potential misstatements. For example, consider an audit for which overall materiality is set at $50,000. If the audit test work revealed five individual $15,000 misstatements, they would each, on their own, be considered immaterial. However, what if all five misstatements each had the effect of increasing net income? In that situation, the auditor must factor in the probability that the aggregate of uncorrected and undetected misstatements could exceed overall materiality for the financial statements. The following Auditing Insight demonstrates the potential costly effect of cumulative errors.

AUDITING INSIGHT   Costly Cumulative Effects

In early 2019, Hertz, the rental car company giant, agreed to pay a $16 million penalty to the SEC over accounting errors that lead to material misstatements in the audited financial statements for 2012 and 2013, as well as portions of the unaudited 2011 financial statements. Hertz identified 17 areas with material accounting errors across several business units, including one misstatement valued at $48 million. The cumulative effect of the misstatements resulted not only in the hefty SEC fine, but a reduction in previously reported pre-tax income of $235 million.

Source: "SEC Penalizes Hertz $16M for Accounting Violations," *Accounting Today,* January 12, 2019.

How Auditors Use Materiality

Although we have presented a number of different factors affecting overall materiality, decisions about materiality ultimately remain a function of auditors' professional judgment. Many experienced auditors will state that these judgments are among the most difficult they make. Materiality is one of the most important audit concepts you will learn about because of its pervasive effect on the audit engagement. To summarize, on an audit engagement, the audit team uses materiality three ways:

1. As a guide to *planning substantive testing procedures*—directing attention and audit work to those items or accounts that are important, uncertain, or susceptible to material misstatements.

2. As a guide for determining *performance materiality* to help make sure that the aggregate of uncorrected and undetected immaterial misstatements does not exceed the materiality level for the financial statements as a whole. For example, auditors may use an amount smaller than overall financial statement materiality when auditing particular classes of significant transactions, account balances, or disclosures.

3. As a guide for making *decisions about the audit report.* An account such as inventory can be material in an audit context because of its size or its place in the financial statements.

☑ REVIEW CHECKPOINTS

3.8 What is meant by material information in accounting and auditing?

3.9 What is the difference between overall materiality and performance materiality?

3.10 What qualitative factors can impact materiality?

3.11 How does an audit team use materiality on an audit engagement?

AUDIT PROCEDURES FOR OBTAINING AUDIT EVIDENCE

LO 3-4

List and describe the eight general types of audit procedures for gathering evidence.

Auditors use audit procedures for three purposes. First, they use audit procedures to gain an understanding of the client and the risks associated with the client (*risk assessment procedures*). These procedures are covered in detail in Chapter 4. Second, auditors use audit procedures to test the operating effectiveness of client internal control activities (*tests of controls*) discussed in Chapter 5. Finally, auditors use audit procedures to produce evidence about management's assertions (i.e., relating to *existence, occurrence, completeness, cutoff, rights and obligations, valuation and allocation, accuracy, presentation,* and *classification*) related to the amounts and disclosures in a client's financial statements. Exhibit 3.6 shows the relationship among the assertions, the types of evidence available to the auditor, and the procedures most closely related to each.

EXHIBIT 3.6   Assertions, Evidence, and Audit Procedures

PCAOB Assertions	ASB Assertions	What Could Go Wrong?	Examples of Evidence Available	Representative Audit Procedures
Existence or occurrence	Existence	Do the assets recorded really exist?	The physical presence of the assets	Inspection of tangible assets
	Occurrence	Did the recorded sales transactions really occur?	Client shipping documents	Inspection of records or documents (vouching)
Rights and obligations	Rights and obligations	Does the entity really own the assets? Are related legal responsibilities identified?	Statements by independent parties	Confirmation
Completeness	Completeness	Are the financial statements (including footnotes) complete?	Documents prepared by the client	Inspection of records or documents (tracing)
	Cutoff	Were all transactions recorded in the proper period?	Client receiving, shipping reports	Inspection of records or documents (tracing or vouching)
Valuation and allocation	Valuation or allocation	Are the accounts valued correctly?	Client-prepared accounts receivable aging schedule	Reperformance
	Accuracy	Were transactions recorded accurately?	Vendor invoices	Inspection of records or documents (tracing or vouching)
Presentation and disclosure	Presentation	Are transactions and events appropriately presented and clearly described?	Management-prepared financial statements and footnotes	Inquiry
	Classification	Were all transactions recorded in the proper accounts?	Comparisons of current-year amounts with those from the prior year	Analytical procedures

EXHIBIT 3.7A
Dunder-Mifflin Trial Balance, December 31, 2023

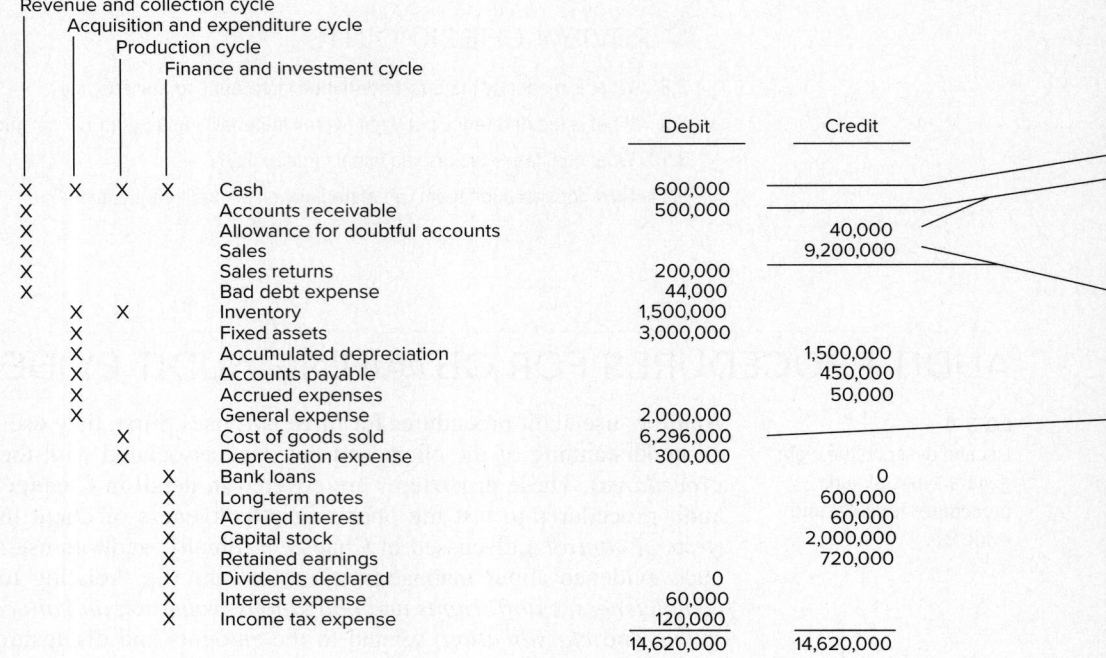

					Debit	Credit
Revenue and collection cycle						
	Acquisition and expenditure cycle					
		Production cycle				
			Finance and investment cycle			
X	X	X	X	Cash	600,000	
X				Accounts receivable	500,000	
X				Allowance for doubtful accounts		40,000
X				Sales		9,200,000
X				Sales returns	200,000	
X				Bad debt expense	44,000	
	X	X		Inventory	1,500,000	
		X		Fixed assets	3,000,000	
		X		Accumulated depreciation		1,500,000
		X		Accounts payable		450,000
		X		Accrued expenses		50,000
		X		General expense	2,000,000	
		X		Cost of goods sold	6,296,000	
		X		Depreciation expense	300,000	
			X	Bank loans	0	
			X	Long-term notes		600,000
			X	Accrued interest		60,000
			X	Capital stock		2,000,000
			X	Retained earnings		720,000
			X	Dividends declared	0	
			X	Interest expense	60,000	
			X	Income tax expense	120,000	
					14,620,000	14,620,000

Once the risk assessment procedures have been completed and the relevant financial statement assertions have been identified, an auditor then considers whether specific control activities are in place to prevent or detect a misstatement related to each of the relevant financial statement assertions. Ultimately, the audit plan needs to specify a list of procedures that must be completed to gather sufficient and appropriate evidence directed toward achieving particular audit objectives. For example, an **internal control audit plan** would contain the specific procedures needed to obtain an understanding of the client's internal control system and test that understanding for those controls that relate to the relevant financial statement assertions. If the auditor decides to rely on specific internal control activities, the plan would also identify the specific types of tests of controls that would need to be completed to validate the operating effectiveness of the internal control activities.

A **substantive audit plan** would contain a list of audit procedures for gathering evidence related to the relevant assertions identified for an audit client's significant financial statement accounts and disclosures. The substantive audit plan (i.e., the *nature, timing, and extent* of further procedures) depends almost exclusively upon the assessment of risk at an audit client. As an example, consider the nature of procedures. There are two ways to conduct substantive tests: (1) substantive analytical procedures and (2) tests of details.

When completing analytical procedures to gather evidence, the auditor must develop an independent expectation of what he or she thinks the account balance should be. Once this is developed, the expectation is compared to the recorded amount. Any significant differences must be investigated and then corroborated with evidence. When applying substantive test of details, the auditor must seek to understand the account balance and/or economic transaction to ensure, based on valid and reliable evidence, that the amount was recorded in accordance with the applicable financial reporting framework. In general, analytical procedures are considered more efficient while a test of details is considered more effective. Thus, an auditor must take great care in determining the nature of the testing procedure (i.e., substantive analytical procedure or test of detail) to specify in the audit plan.

To simplify the audit plan, auditors typically group the accounts into *cycles* (see Exhibit 3.7A). A *cycle* is a set of accounts that are logically grouped in the internal control system, which has been designed to produce the financial statements and notes (see Exhibit 3.7B). Most audit firms recognize four cycles, and each of these cycles is featured

EXHIBIT 3.7B   Dunder-Mifflin Unaudited Financial Statements

FINANCIAL POSITION

Cash	$ 600,000		
Accounts receivable	460,000	Accounts payable	$ 450,000
Inventory	1,500,000	Accrued expenses	110,000
Current Assets	$2,560,000	Current Liabilities	$ 560,000
Fixed assets (net)	$3,000,000	Long-term debt	$ 600,000
Accum. depreciation	(1,500,000)	Capital stock	2,000,000
Fixed Assets (net)	$1,500,000	Retained earnings	900,000
		Total Liabilities	
Total Assets	$4,060,000	and Stockholder Equity	$4,060,000

RESULTS OF OPERATIONS

Sales (net)	$9,000,000
Cost of goods sold	6,296,000
Gross Profit	$2,704,000
General expenses	$2,000,000
Bad debt expense	$ 44,000
Depreciation expense	300,000
Interest expense	60,000
Operating income before taxes	$ 300,000
Income tax expense	120,000
Net Income	$ 180,000

CASH FLOWS

Operations:	
Net income	$ 180,000
Depreciation	300,000
Increase in accounts receivable	(141,500)
Decrease in inventory	50,000
Decrease in accounts payable	(25,000)
Decrease in accrued expenses	(15,000)
Decrease in accrued interest	(20,500)
Cash Flow from Operations	$ 328,000
Investing Activities:	
Purchase Fixed Assets	$ 0
Financing Activities:	
Repay bank loan	$(275,000)
Repay notes payable	(200,000)
Financing Activities	$(475,000)
Increase (decrease) in cash	$(146,500)
Beginning balance	746,500
Ending Balance	$ 600,000

NOTES TO FINANCIAL STATEMENTS

1. Accounting Policies
2. Inventories
3. Plant and Equipment
4. Long-Term Debt
5. Stock Options
6. Income Taxes
7. Contingencies
Etc.

in a chapter of this book: (1) the revenue and collection cycle (Chapter 7), (2) the acquisition and expenditure cycle (Chapter 8), (3) the production cycle (Chapter 9), and (4) the finance and investment cycle (Chapter 10). Using the revenue and collection cycle as an example, the idea of the cycle organization is to group accounts (sales, accounts receivable, cash) related to one another by the transactions that normally affect them all. This cycle starts with a sale to a customer along with recording an account receivable, which is later collected in cash or provided for in the allowance for doubtful accounts.

☑ REVIEW CHECKPOINTS

3.12 What are the two primary ways to conduct substantive tests? Explain how the tests are different.

3.13 Identify the four cycles featured in Dunder-Mifflin's accounting system featured in Exhibit 3.7A. Next, list the financial statement accounts that can be identified within each of the cycles identified as featured in Exhibit 3.7B.

As a rule, auditors use eight general audit procedures to gather evidence: (1) inspection of records and documents (*vouching, tracing, scanning*), (2) inspection of tangible assets,

(3) observation, (4) inquiry, (5) confirmation, (6) recalculation, (7) reperformance, and (8) analytical procedures. Many of these procedures are performed or aided by the use of computer-assisted audit techniques (CAATs) such as the IDEA or ACL programs. In this book, we have integrated the IDEA software package, a CAAT program used by many audit professionals, to help students understand how these procedures are performed in practice. The "Using IDEA in the Audit" excerpt following the discussion of the various audit procedures is designed to help you get started in IDEA.

In the following sections, we discuss each of the eight aforementioned audit procedures in more detail.

1. Inspection of Records and Documents

Much auditing work involves gathering evidence by examining authoritative documents, either in paper form or, more increasingly, in electronic form, prepared by independent parties and by the client. Auditors frequently inspect such documents to ensure they contain the correct information and/or authorization. Such documents can provide "evidence of varying degrees of reliability, depending on their nature and source," regarding many of management's financial statement assertions.

Documents Prepared by Independent Outside Parties

The most reliable form of documentary evidence is external, which means that the document was received directly from an independent outside third party (e.g., a bank). External documents can be either formal or informal. Formal documents are less susceptible to alteration, if electronic they have controls in place to make them difficult to alter or change, if paper they may have seals or other distinctive attributes. Formal documents, therefore, are more reliable than informal external documents. Examples of formal external documents include bank statements, title papers, and insurance policies, whereas informal external documents include vendor invoices, simple contracts, and written correspondence. Regardless, when either type of document is received directly from an independent outside party, the evidence is considered reliable.

In addition, a great deal of documentary evidence is considered external-internal, which means that the documents were initially prepared by an external third party but they were received by the client first and then given to the auditor. Since the client had possession of the documents, there is always a possibility that the client altered the documents. As a result, external-internal documents are not as reliable as external documents.

Documents Prepared and Processed by the Client

Documentation of this type is referred to as internal evidence. Some of these documents may be quite informal and not very authoritative or reliable. When such documents are prepared by the client but are mailed to third parties, they become slightly more reliable. However, as a general proposition, the reliability of these documents depends on the quality of internal control under which they were produced and processed. Because the client produces the evidence, an auditor must perform additional testing on this type of information before placing any reliance at all on the internal evidence. Some of the most common of these documents are

1. Sales invoice copies	7. Shipping documents
2. Sales summary reports	8. Receiving reports
3. Cost distribution reports	9. Requisition slips
4. Loan approval memos	10. Purchase orders
5. Budgets and performance reports	11. Credit memos
6. Documentation of significant transactions with subsidiaries	12. Transaction logs

Vouching—Examination of Documents

When testing the existence or the occurrence assertion, the auditor will take the vouching direction when examining documents. The important point about *vouching* is that the auditor begins the search for evidence by focusing on transactions that have already been recorded in the financial statements. In **vouching**, an auditor selects an item in the financial records, usually from a journal or ledger, and follows its path back through the processing steps to its origin (i.e., the *source documentation* that supports the item selected from the ledger). Consider a revenue entry made in the financial statements. For that entry, the auditor will find the journal entry, the sales summary, the sales invoice copy, the shipping documents, and, finally, the sales order from the customer. Vouching of documents can help auditors decide whether all recorded significant transactions are adequately supported (the *existence* and *occurrence* assertions), but vouching does not provide evidence to show whether all significant transactions were actually recorded (the *completeness* assertion). However, if the auditors verify amounts during their testing, evidence regarding *valuation and allocation* also may be obtained while vouching documents.

Tracing—Examination of Documents

When testing the completeness assertion, the auditor will take the tracing direction when examining documents. When taking the **tracing** direction, the auditor selects a basic source document and follows its processing path *forward* to find its final recording in a summary journal or ledger and ultimately the financial statements. For example, samples of shipping documents can be obtained from the warehouse and then traced to sales invoices, the sales journal, and ultimately their recording in the financial statements as revenue earned.

Using tracing, an auditor can decide whether all significant transactions and events that should have been recorded actually were recorded (the *completeness* assertion). In doing so, the auditor complements the evidence obtained by vouching. This implies that an auditor must always be alert to events that were not entered into the accounting system. For example, the search for unrecorded liabilities for raw materials purchases must include examination of invoices received in the period following the fiscal year-end and examination of receiving reports dated near the year-end. In practice, it is important to remember that the direction of the examination of documents is critical in relation to the assertion being tested.

Vouching
(Would be used to test the existence or occurrence assertion. The audit test would be designed to answer the following question: Did all recorded sales occur?)

Summary Listing
(Sales Journal)

Tracing
(Would be used to test the completeness assertion. The audit test would be designed to answer the following question: Were all shipments made to customers actually recorded as sales?)

Source Documents
(Shipping Documents)

Scanning—Examination of Documents

Scanning is the way auditors exercise their general alertness to unusual items and events in clients' documentation. A typical scanning directive in an audit plan is "Scan the expense accounts for credit entries; vouch any to source documents."

In general, scanning is an "eyes-open" approach of looking for anything unusual. The scanning procedure usually does not produce direct evidence itself, but it can raise questions related to other evidence that must be obtained. Scanning can be accomplished on digital records by using CAATs to select records that are exceptions to the auditors' criteria. For example, CAATs can easily scan client's data for (1) accounts receivable balances for amounts over the credit limit, (2) inventory quantities for negative balances or unreasonably large balances, (3) payroll files for terminated employees, (4) loan files for loans with negative balances, (5) debits in revenue accounts, and (6) credits in expense accounts, to name a few. Scanning can contribute some evidence related to the existence of assets and the completeness of accounting records, including the proper cutoff of significant transactions.

2. Inspection of Tangible Assets

Inspection of tangible assets includes examining property, plant, and equipment; inventory; and securities certificates. Physical inspection of tangible assets provides compelling evidence of *existence* and may provide tentative evidence of *valuation*. For example, audit team members can verify the existence of specific pieces of equipment listed on the client's fixed asset register by locating them and noting their condition (*valuation*). However, inspection does not necessarily provide evidence that the entity owns the assets (*rights*). For example, fixed assets on the client's premises may be leased under operating lease agreements, and inventory inspected by auditors may be held on consignment. The following Auditing Insight discusses innovative ways firms are using technology to help improve the inspection of inventory and tangible assets.

AUDITING INSIGHT Fly-by Audit Procedures?

Technology is changing the look of the traditional inventory observations and asset inspections for the better. The Big 4 audit firms have recently begun using drone technology to help make the audit more efficient and effective. One-way drones are being used is to get a better view of hard to count inventory items, such as crops, livestock, and coal reserves. Inventory observations that would have taken auditors hours to perform now take a fraction of the time with more reliable results. This allows auditors to focus their attention on identifying and responding to areas of risk.

Sources. "EY Scaling the use of Drones in the Audit Process", EY.com, June 13, 2017; "PwC uses drone in audit for first time" Economia, January 2, 2019; "How Drones are Being Used in Audit", Discoveraudit.org, Dec 14, 2017.

3. Observation

Although inventory observation often refers to the physical inspection of inventory (i.e., tangible assets), auditors use *observation* when they view the client's physical facilities and personnel on an inspection tour, when they watch personnel carry out accounting and control activities (such as observing client inventory counts), and when they participate in a surprise payroll distribution. Observation also can produce a general awareness of events in the client's offices. In this sense, observation is commonly used as a test of controls.

4. Inquiry

Inquiry is a procedure that generally involves the collection of verbal evidence from independent parties and management (commonly referred to as *written representations* or *management representations*). Important inquiries and responses should be documented by the auditor in the workpapers. Auditors typically use inquiry procedures during the early planning stages of the engagement. Evidence gathered by formal and informal inquiry generally cannot stand alone as convincing, and auditors must corroborate responses with independent findings based on other procedures. In fact, the professional standards state that "inquiry alone" is never enough to reach an audit conclusion. An exception to this general rule might be a negative statement in which someone volunteers adverse information such as an admission of theft, fraud, or use of an accounting policy that is misleading. However, even in such a situation, an auditor would most likely follow up to obtain documentary evidence to support the negative statement.

AUDITING INSIGHT   Verbal Inquiry = Interview

Auditors conduct interviews almost every day. Sometimes these seem more like casual conversations than "interviews." Nevertheless, the following guidelines for the inquiry/interview procedure can help you obtain good information and maintain good relations with client personnel.

1. *Prepare.* Think about the information you want to obtain, the questions to ask, and the best person to interview.

2. *Make an appointment.* Call in advance for a time or at least ask permission to interrupt: "Do you have time to talk with me about [subject]?" Introduce yourself and make enough conversation to warm up the person without wasting time.

3. *Be conversational.* Try to get the person to describe the accounting, the controls, or whatever the subject in his or her own words. You will get more information. Just firing off questions makes the meeting an interrogation. Most auditors find it difficult to think of all of the right questions ahead of time anyway. Don't exhibit a questionnaire or checklist; doing so makes the interview too mechanical. You can take informal notes to remember the substance of the interview.

4. *Ask questions.* Fill in the gaps in the person's description or explanation by asking prompting questions to elicit additional descriptions and explanations. Start with broad, open-ended questions and use specific questions to obtain more detail.

5. *Listen carefully.* Repeat items you don't completely understand.

6. *Be noncommittal.* Refrain from expressing your own value judgments or criticisms while you talk with the client personnel. Don't reveal any audit-sensitive information.

7. *Close gracefully.* Thank the person for the time and information. Ask permission to return later for "anything I forgot."

8. *Document the interview.* Write a memorandum for the audit documentation. Now you can get out the questionnaire or checklist, complete it, and see whether you overlooked anything important.

5. Confirmation

Confirmation by direct correspondence with independent parties is a procedure widely used in auditing. It can produce evidence of *existence* and *rights and obligations* and sometimes of *valuation* and *cutoff*. Auditors typically limit their use of confirmation to significant transactions and balances about which outside parties could be expected to provide information. A selection of confirmation applications includes the following:

- Banks—cash and loan balances.
- Customers—receivables balances.
- Borrowers—note terms and balances.
- Agents—inventory on consignment or in warehouses.
- Lenders—note terms and balances.
- Policyholders—life insurance contracts.
- Vendors—accounts payable balances.
- Registrar—number of shares of stock outstanding.
- Attorneys—litigation in progress.
- Trustees—securities held, terms of agreements.
- Lessors—lease terms.

Several points about confirmations are important to remember. First, confirmation letters are typically printed on the client's letterhead and signed by a client officer; third parties usually do not release information without client permission. Second, confirmation requests should seek information the recipient can supply, such as the amount of a balance or the amounts of specified invoices or notes. Third, the audit firm should control confirmations rather than giving them to client personnel for mailing. The audit team should be very careful that the recipient's address is reliable and not subject to alteration by the client in such a way as to misdirect the confirmation. Fourth, responses should be returned directly to the audit firm, not to the client. And last, auditors are increasingly using technology to aid and improve the confirmation process.

Auditors are using technology in both the confirmation selection and execution process. Auditors can use CAATs to program statistical or judgmental criteria for selecting customers' accounts receivable, loans, and other receivables for confirmation. In addition, the use of electronic confirmations by auditors (e.g., confirmation.com) has led to improvements in both the effectiveness and the efficiency of the confirmation process. The use of electronic confirmations is covered in detail in Chapter 6.

6. Recalculation

Auditor recalculation of computations previously performed by client personnel produces compelling evidence. A client calculation must always be mathematically accurate. Client calculations performed by computer programs can be recalculated using CAATs with differences printed out for further audit investigation. Mathematical evidence can serve the objectives of *existence* and *valuation* for financial statement amounts that exist principally as calculations, for example, depreciation, interest expense, pension liabilities, actuarial reserves, bad debt reserves, and product guarantee liabilities. Recalculation, in combination with other procedures, is also used to provide evidence of *valuation* for all other financial data.

7. Reperformance

Although similar to recalculation, reperformance is much broader in approach. As discussed in Chapter 4, reperformance is commonly used by auditors while completing walkthroughs when gaining an understanding of a client's internal control system. In fact, reperformance can generally be completed for any client control procedure such as matching vendor invoices with supporting purchase orders and receiving reports. Reperformance may be done either manually or with the assistance of CAATs. An auditor, for example, can verify that an accounts receivable aging schedule was prepared properly by sorting accounts receivable by due date.

8. Analytical Procedures

Auditors can evaluate financial statement accounts by developing expectations about what an account balance should be based on an analysis of relevant financial and nonfinancial data. When an auditor compares the expectation to a recorded balance, **analytical procedures** are being performed. Auditors are required to use them when planning the audit and when performing the review of the financial statements near the end of the audit before the audit report is issued. In addition, auditors use analytical procedures to provide evidence about management's financial statement assertions during the testing phase of the audit.

Analytical procedures take the five general forms shown in the following table. Auditors need to be careful to use independent, reliable information for analyses. The sources of information shown for the analytical procedures are very important, and auditors must gain comfort over the information that is used to develop expectations during analytical procedures. CAATs are useful when developing expectations as they can match data in separate files to help extract the data necessary to make comparisons between financial and nonfinancial information. In addition, CAATs can be used to extract the data necessary to make comparisons to other companies in the same industry.

Analytical Procedures	Sources of Information
1. Comparison of current-year account balances to balances of one or more comparable periods	Financial account information for comparable period(s) *Example: Current-year cost of goods sold compared to last year's balance*
2. Comparison of current-year account balances to anticipated results found in the company's budgets and forecasts	Company budgets and forecasts *Example: Current-year cost of goods sold compared to the company's budgeted amount*
3. Evaluation of the relationships of current-year account balances to other current-year balances for conformity with predictable patterns based on the company's experience	Financial relationships among accounts in the current period *Example: Relationship between inventory and cost of goods sold*
4. Comparison of current-year account balances and financial relationships (e.g., ratios) with similar information for the industry in which the company operates	Industry statistics *Example: Comparing inventory and cost of goods sold levels to comparable companies in the industry*
5. Study of the relationships of current-year account balances with relevant nonfinancial information (e.g., physical production statistics)	Nonfinancial information such as physical production statistics *Example: Comparing the number of unfilled orders to inventory and cost of goods sold levels*

Because of their effectiveness in directing attention to high-risk areas, professional standards require that analytical procedures be used during *planning* and during *final evaluation* phases of the audit. Although not required to be used during the *substantive testing* phase of the engagement, auditors must consider the value of using substantive analytical procedures, especially because they are usually less costly than more detailed, document-oriented procedures. The professional standards clearly indicate that a well-planned analytical procedure conducted during the substantive testing phase can be quite effective if executed properly. The increased use of data and analytics in the audit, discussed further in Module G, has improved both the execution and frequency of use of substantive analytical procedures. Consequently, analytical procedures often take a prominent place in the *audit plan.* When applying substantive analytical procedures to gather evidence in this manner, it is important to remember that any significant differences must be investigated and corroborated with evidence.

 AUDITING INSIGHT   Accessing Client Data

The first step in using a CAAT like IDEA is to gain access to the client's data. The data may be available in multiple forms, depending on the audit client's unique computing environment. However, IDEA is designed to be flexible enough to handle multiple computing environments. Your instructor will provide you with access to the IDEA software and the latest electronic version of the IDEA Data Analysis Workbook. Your instructor will also provide you with access to the data files for the audit procedures to be completed for Accounts Receivable, Accounts Payable, and Inventory.

For each set of files, your first step is to import the client's data into the IDEA software. We suggest that you complete this step for each of the areas that have been assigned by your instructor. To proceed, please refer to the IDEA workbook provided by your instructor for step-by-step instructions on how to properly import each file.

✅ REVIEW CHECKPOINTS

3.14 What is meant by (a) vouching, (b) tracing, and (c) scanning? What is the difference between vouching and tracing?

3.15 Identify and then briefly explain the eight general audit procedures used to gather evidence. Next, please provide an example for each of the eight procedures.

3.16 What are the five types of general analytical procedures? List five sources of information for analytical procedures.

3.17 When are analytical procedures required during an audit engagement?

AUDIT DOCUMENTATION

LO 3-5
Define what is meant by the proper form and content of audit documentation.

An engagement is not complete without preparation of proper documentation. PCAOB AS 1215 defines **audit documentation** as

> The written record of the basis for the auditor's conclusions that provides the support for the auditor's representations, whether those representations are contained in the auditor's report or otherwise.[9]

In other words, audit documentation provides the auditors' record of compliance with generally accepted auditing standards. The documentation (often referred to as *workpapers* despite that it is typically in electronic format)* should contain support for the decisions regarding planning and performing the audit, procedures performed, evidence

[9]PCAOB Release No. 2004-006, "AS 1215: Audit Documentation," June 9, 2004.

obtained, and overall conclusions reached near the end of the audit. Even though the auditors legally own the audit documentation, professional ethics require that the files not be transferred without the client's consent because of the confidential information recorded in them.

Audit documentation can be classified in two categories: (1) *permanent files* (which contain information that is relevant to ongoing client relationships) and (2) *current files* (which relate to just one year of the client relationship). The following sections describe the information contained in each file in more detail.

Permanent Files

The **continuing audit files (or permanent files)** contain information of *continuing audit significance* over many years' audits of the same client. The audit team may use this file year after year, but each year's current audit documentation is stored after the files have served their purpose. Documents of permanent interest and applicability include

1. Copies or excerpts of the corporate or association charter, bylaws, or partnership agreement.
2. Copies or excerpts of continuing contracts such as leases, bond indentures, and royalty agreements.
3. A history of the company, its products, markets, and background.
4. Copies or excerpts of minutes of meetings of stockholders and/or directors on matters of lasting interest.
5. Continuing schedules of accounts with balances that are carried forward for several years, such as owners' equity, retained earnings, partnership capital, and the like.
6. Copies of prior-years' financial statements and audit reports.
7. Client organization chart.

Copies of financial statements and auditors' reports from prior years also may be included. Public accounting firms collect articles and other information regarding a client and key personnel throughout the year. This information is often placed in the permanent file to facilitate a review of the client prior to continuing the relationship. Because of the importance of the documents contained and summarized in this one place, the permanent file is a ready source of information for familiarization with the client by new personnel on the engagement.

Current Files

The current files include all client acceptance or continuance documentation along with planning documentation for the year under audit. They usually include the engagement letter, staff assignment notes, conclusions related to understanding the client's business, results of preliminary analytical procedures, assessments of audit risks, and determination of audit materiality. Many public accounting firms follow the practice of summarizing these data in a **planning memorandum** with specific directions about the impact on the audit.

Basically, the planning memorandum summarizes all important overall planning information and documents that the audit team is following generally accepted auditing standards. All planning becomes a basis for preparing the audit plan, which is a list of the audit procedures to be performed by the audit team to gather sufficient appropriate evidence on which to base the opinion on the financial statements. Auditing standards require a documented audit plan for each relevant assertion on the audit.

The planning documentation must include a listing of each significant account and disclosure in the client's financial statements. According to the professional standards, if there is a chance the account could contain a misstatement that is material, it should be identified as significant. The documentation also must include a listing of each relevant financial statement assertion related to the significant accounts and disclosures. According to the professional standards, if the assertion has "a reasonable possibility of containing a misstatement that would cause the financial statements to be materially misstated,"[10] it must be categorized as relevant. Documentation of the significant accounts and disclosures, along with the relevant assertions, forms the basis of the current file documentation.

Audit documentation should be prepared in sufficient detail to provide a clear understanding of its purpose, its source, and the overall conclusions reached near the end of the audit. The audit documentation communicates the quality of the audit, so it must be clear, concise, complete, neat, well indexed, and informative. Each workpaper must be complete in the sense that it can be removed from the audit documentation file and considered on its own with proper cross-references available to show how the document coordinates with other audit documentation. In other words, the documentation must be sufficient to enable an experienced auditor, having no previous connection with the engagement, to understand (1) the nature, timing, extent, and results of procedures; (2) the overall conclusions reached with respect to the area covered by the audit documentation; and (3) the audit team member performing the work, the date of work, the audit team member reviewing the work, and the date of review. The audit documentation should also be sufficient to allow another auditor to reperform the work if necessary.

The most important facet of the current audit evidence documentation files is the requirement that they show the auditors' conclusions. The documentation must record the management assertions that were audited, the evidence gathered about them, and final conclusions. Professional audit standards require the audit documentation to show that (1) the client's accounting records agree or reconcile with the financial statements, (2) the work was adequately planned and supervised, (3) a sufficient understanding of the client's internal control was obtained, and (4) sufficient appropriate audit evidence was obtained as a reasonable basis for an audit opinion. Common sense also dictates that the audit documentation be sufficient to show that the financial statements conform to the relevant accounting framework and that the disclosures are adequate. The audit documentation also should explain how exceptions, unusual accounting questions, and findings contradictory to the audit team's final conclusions were resolved or treated. In addition, the resolution of any differences among audit team members must be documented. Taken altogether, these features should demonstrate that all auditing standards were observed and executed.

Audit Documentation Arrangement and Indexing

Each public accounting firm has a different method of arranging and indexing audit documentation files. In general, however, the documentation is electronically hyperlinked and numbered in order behind the trial balance according to balance-sheet and income-statement captions. Usually, the current assets are numbered (or *indexed*) first, followed by fixed assets, other assets, liabilities, equities, income, and expense accounts. A **lead schedule** is a summary of the accounts or components in an account group. For cash, the lead schedule includes all of the company's cash accounts. For inventory, the lead schedule may include inventory amounts by product line, cost of goods sold, and reserves for obsolescence. The amounts on the lead schedule should agree with prior-year numbers, the current-year general ledger amounts, and, after any adjustments, the audited financial statements. To help better visualize, the typical arrangement is shown in writing in Exhibit 3.8.[11]

Several audit documentation preparation techniques are quite important for the quality of the finished product. The points explained here are illustrated in Exhibit 3.9.

---

[10]PCAOB Release No. 2007-005A, "AS 2201: An Audit of Internal Control Over Financial Reporting That Is Integrated with An Audit of Financial Statements," June 12, 2007.

[11]Apollo Shoes, the comprehensive audit case accompanying this text, utilizes electronic workpapers. The Apollo Shoes mini-cases provide good examples to students of how electronic workpapers appear and are organized, which is similar to that shown in Exhibit 3.8.

EXHIBIT 3.8 Current Audit Documentation File

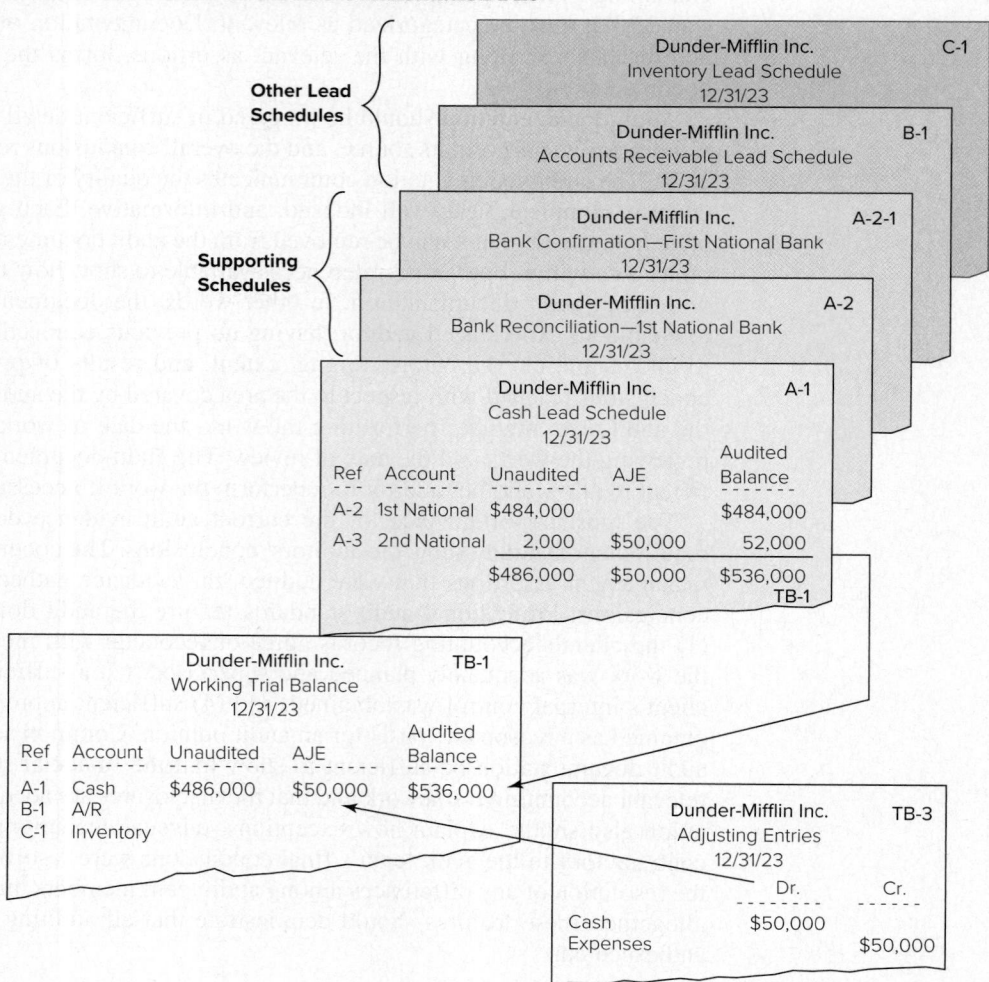

- *Indexing.* Each document (e.g., each worksheet an Excel workbook) is given an index number, like a book page number, so it can be found, removed, and replaced without loss.
- *Cross-referencing.* Numbers or memoranda related to other documents carry the index of the other documents so the connections can be followed. Electronic documents will include hyperlinks to documents cross-referenced.
- *Heading.* Each document is titled with the name of the company, the balance-sheet date, and a descriptive title of the document's contents.
- *Signatures and initials.* The auditor who performs the work and the supervisor who reviews it must sign the audit documentation so personnel can be identified.
- *Dates of audit work.* The dates of performance and review are recorded on the documents so reviewers of the documentation can tell when the work was performed.
- *Audit marks and explanations.* Audit marks (or "tick marks") are the auditor's shorthand for abbreviating comments about work performed. Audit marks always must be accompanied by a full explanation of the auditing work. (Notice in Exhibit 3.9 the auditor's confirmation of the disputed account payable liability.) On electronic

EXHIBIT 3.9   Illustrative Audit Documentation

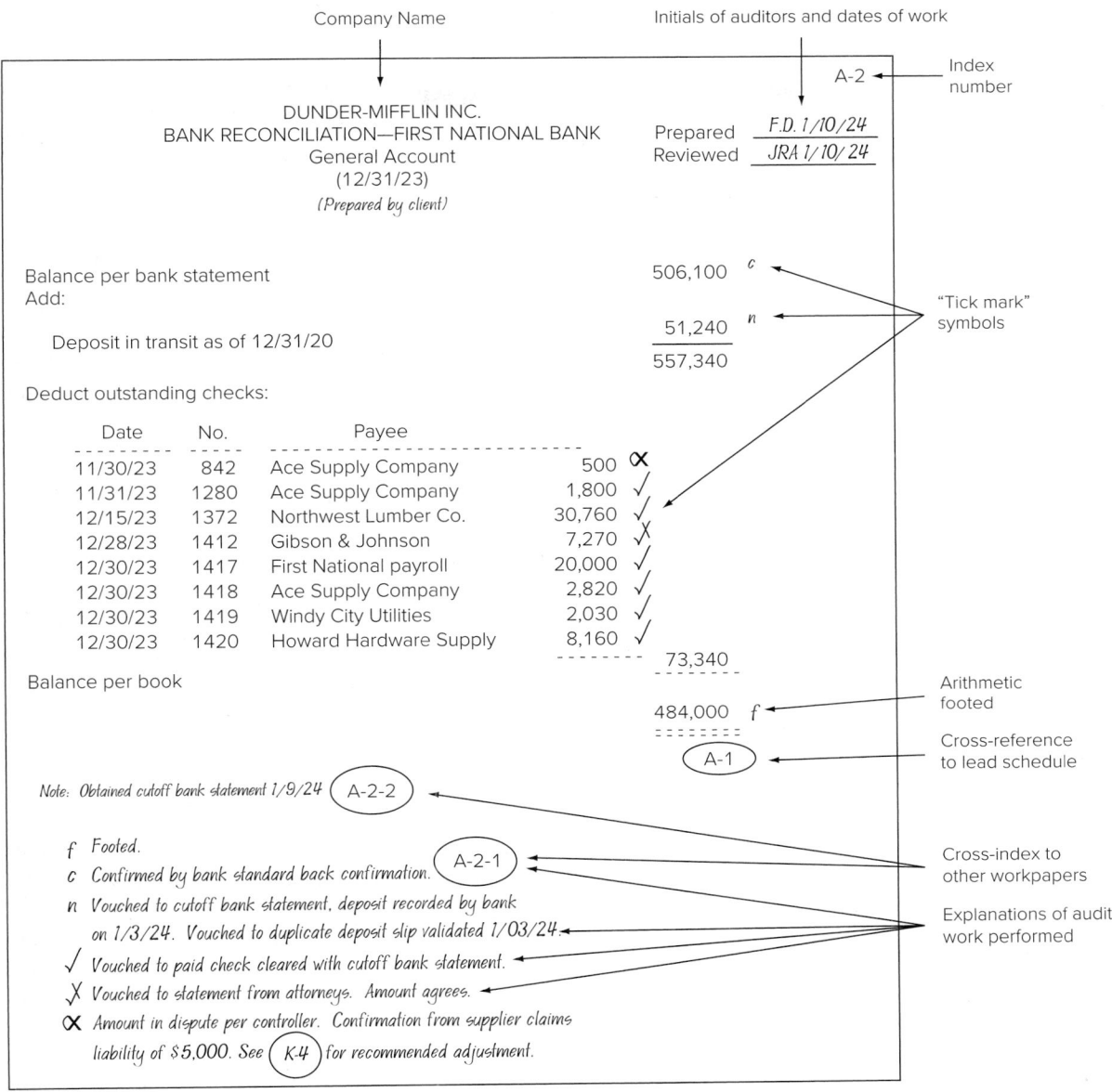

Company Name

Initials of auditors and dates of work

A-2 — Index number

DUNDER-MIFFLIN INC.
BANK RECONCILIATION—FIRST NATIONAL BANK
General Account
(12/31/23)
(Prepared by client)

Prepared   *F.D. 1/10/24*
Reviewed   *JRA 1/10/24*

Balance per bank statement   506,100   *c*
Add:

  Deposit in transit as of 12/31/20   51,240   *n*
                                                     557,340

"Tick mark" symbols

Deduct outstanding checks:

Date	No.	Payee		
11/30/23	842	Ace Supply Company	500	⋈
11/31/23	1280	Ace Supply Company	1,800	√
12/15/23	1372	Northwest Lumber Co.	30,760	√
12/28/23	1412	Gibson & Johnson	7,270	√
12/30/23	1417	First National payroll	20,000	√
12/30/23	1418	Ace Supply Company	2,820	√
12/30/23	1419	Windy City Utilities	2,030	√
12/30/23	1420	Howard Hardware Supply	8,160	√
			73,340	

Balance per book

                                                     484,000   *f*

Arithmetic footed

A-1

Cross-reference to lead schedule

Note: Obtained cutoff bank statement 1/9/24   A-2-2

f   Footed.
c   Confirmed by bank standard back confirmation.   A-2-1
n   Vouched to cutoff bank statement, deposit recorded by bank
    on 1/3/24. Vouched to duplicate deposit slip validated 1/03/24.
√   Vouched to paid check cleared with cutoff bank statement.
X   Vouched to statement from attorneys. Amount agrees.
⋈   Amount in dispute per controller. Confirmation from supplier claims
    liability of $5,000. See K-4 *for recommended adjustment.*

Cross-index to other workpapers

Explanations of audit work performed

documents, comments can be hyperlinked so that reviewers can find additional explanations of audit procedures performed.

Professional standards require that audit documentation, including workpapers and other documents that form the basis of the engagement, be retained for a minimum of five years following the conclusion of the engagement for nonpublic company clients and seven years for public clients. Standards also stress that audit documentation to be retained include those workpapers that document any discussions and subsequent resolution of differences in professional judgment among the audit team members. Standards require that all documentation be finalized within 60 days of the audit report's release date for nonpublic companies and within 45 days for public companies. Although the documentation requirements differ for public versus nonpublic clients, for simplicity, most public accounting firms use the documentation requirements for public company engagements for nonpublic clients as well.

✅ REVIEW CHECKPOINTS

3.18   What is the purpose of a planning memorandum?

3.19   What information would you expect to find in a permanent audit file?

3.20   What information would you expect to find in a current audit file?

3.21   What are the documentation retention requirements for nonpublic and public clients?

Summary

This chapter contains a description of the specific set of planning activities that auditors undertake when completing an engagement. *Pre-engagement activities* start with the work of deciding whether to accept a new client and, on an annual basis, whether to continue the engagement for existing clients. Public accounting firms are not obligated to provide audit services to every company or organization that requests them, and they regularly exercise discretion when deciding which they choose to undertake. For audit engagements, the investigation may involve the cooperative task of communicating with the organization's former (predecessor) auditors. In addition, firms need to make sure that they are in compliance with both independence and ethical requirements before deciding whether to accept a new client or continue with an existing client.

The *audit plan* is a comprehensive list of the specific audit procedures that the audit team needs to perform to gather sufficient appropriate evidence on which to base its opinion on the financial statements. Although risk assessment (discussed in Chapter 4) provides the basis to determine the nature, timing, and extent of procedures to be performed at an audit client, many other aspects of audit planning are also discussed in this chapter. Other planning issues include properly staffing the audit, including using IT auditors, considering the work of audit specialists and using the work of internal auditors, and creating the time budget.

Because financial statement measurements and footnote disclosure information are not flawlessly accurate, auditors need to ultimately ensure that the financial statements are materially accurate and do not contain material misstatements. Information is material if it is likely to influence financial statement users' decisions. As a result, the engagement team needs to think carefully about the appropriate level of materiality during the planning process. The auditor will then use this materiality as a guide to (1) plan and execute substantive testing procedures, (2) evaluate audit evidence, and (3) make final decisions about the auditor's report.

Auditors then use a variety of procedures to gather evidence about management's assertions related to the amounts and disclosures in a client's financial statements. In general, auditors use eight different types of audit procedures to gather evidence: (1) inspection of records and documents (*vouching, tracing, scanning*), (2) inspection of tangible assets, (3) observation, (4) inquiry, (5) confirmation, (6) recalculation, (7) reperformance, and (8) analytical procedures. One or more of these procedures may be used no matter what account balance, control procedure, class of transactions, or other information is under audit. Auditors must consider a number of factors when planning based on the audit client's computing environment. And of course, the selection of procedures to be completed must always be tailored to the exacting nuances of the client's computing environment. Finally, CAATs can improve both engagement effectiveness and efficiency and are used by auditors on most engagements.

The closing topic in this chapter is a brief overview of audit documentation with some basic pointers about their form, content, and overall purpose. At this stage in the audit process, we have accepted (or retained) the client, considered the types of audit procedures that might be performed to gather evidence, and thought about the impact of a client's technological environment. The next step in the audit process is the assessment of inherent risk in both the financial statement account balances and footnote disclosures, which serves as the focus of the next chapter.

Key Terms

analytical procedures: Procedures that allow auditors to evaluate financial information by studying relationships among both financial and nonfinancial data. When used near the end of the audit, analytical procedures allow auditors to assess the conclusions reached during the audit and evaluate the overall financial statement presentation, 106

audit documentation: The written basis for the auditor's conclusions that provides the necessary support for the auditor's assertions and representations made in the auditor's report, 107

audit engagement partner: The person with the final responsibility for the audit, usually an industry specialist, 90

audit plan: A comprehensive list of the specific audit procedures that the audit team needs to perform to gather sufficient appropriate evidence on which to base their opinion on the financial statements, 89

continuing audit files (or **permanent files**)**:** The audit documentation containing information of *continuing audit significance* for current and past audits of the same client, 108

engagement letter: This letter sets forth the understanding with the client, including in particular (1) the objectives of the engagement, (2) management's responsibilities, (3) the auditors' responsibilities, and (4) any limitations of the engagement, 87

Form 8-K: The "current events" report filed periodically at the occurrence of major events, such as earnings releases, major asset sales, acquisitions, and auditor changes, 85

independence in appearance: The extent to which others (particularly financial statement users) perceive auditors to be independent, 87

independence in fact: Auditors' mental attitude and impartiality with respect to the client, 87

interim audit work: The procedures performed several weeks or months before the balance-sheet date, 94

internal control audit plan: A plan that would contain a list of the specific procedures needed to obtain an understanding of the client's internal control system and test that understanding for those controls that relate to the relevant financial statement assertions, 100

lead schedule: A summary of the accounts in or components of an account group, 109

materiality: An amount or event that has a substantial likelihood to influence financial statement users' decisions. Thus, *material information* is a synonym for *important information.* The emphasis is on the financial statement users' point of view, not on the auditors' or managers' points of view, 95

planning memorandum: The document summarizing the preliminary analytical procedures and the materiality assessment with specific directions about the effect on the audit, 108

predecessor auditor: The public accounting firm that has been terminated or has voluntarily withdrawn from an audit engagement (whether the audit has been completed or not), 84

quality assurance partner: The second audit partner on the audit team as required for audits of financial statements filed with the SEC who reviews the audit team's work in critical audit areas (those areas with the highest potential audit risk), 90

specialists: The persons skilled in fields other than accounting and auditing—actuaries, appraisers, attorneys, engineers, and geologists—who are not members of the public accounting firm, 93

substantive audit plan: Document that contains a list of audit procedures for gathering evidence related to the relevant assertions identified for the significant financial statement accounts and disclosures on an audit client, 100

termination letter: The documentation provided to former clients dealing with the subject of future services, in particular (1) access to audit documentation by new auditors, (2) reissuance of the auditors' report when required for SEC reporting or comparative financial reporting, and (3) fee arrangements for such future services. The termination letter also can contain a report of the auditor's understanding of the circumstances of termination (e.g., disagreements about accounting principles and audit procedures, fees, or other conflicts), 88

tracing: An audit procedure in which the auditor selects a basic source document and follows its processing path *forward* to find its final recording in a summary journal or ledger. In practice, however, the term *tracing* may be used to describe following the path in either direction, 103

vouching: An audit procedure in which an auditor selects an item of financial information, usually from a journal or ledger, and follows its path back through the processing steps to its origin (i.e., the *source documentation* that supports the item selected), 103

year-end audit work: The procedures performed shortly before and after the balance-sheet date, 94

Multiple-Choice Questions for Practice and Review

Mc Graw Hill connect All applicable questions are available with *Connect*.

LO 3-1

3.22 When initiating communications with predecessor auditors, prospective auditors should expect

a. To take responsibility for obtaining the client's consent for the predecessor to give information about prior audits.

b. To conduct interviews with the partner and manager in charge of the predecessor public accounting firm's engagement.

c. To obtain copies of some or all of the predecessor auditors' audit documentation.

d. All of the above.

LO 3-2

3.23 Generally accepted auditing standards require that auditors always prepare and use

a. A written planning memorandum explaining the auditors' understanding of the client's business.

b. A written client consent to discuss audit matters with prospective auditors.

c. A written audit plan.

d. The written time budgets and schedules for performing each audit.

LO 3-2

3.24 When planning an audit, which of the following is *not* a factor that affects auditors' decisions about the quantity, type, and content of audit documentation?

a. The auditors' need to document compliance with generally accepted auditing standards.

b. The auditors' need to verify the existence of new sales contracts important for the client's business.

c. The auditors' judgment about their independence with regard to the client.

d. The auditors' judgments about materiality.

LO 3-5

3.25 Audit documentation that shows the detailed evidence and procedures regarding the balance in the accumulated depreciation account for the year under audit will be found in the

a. Current file audit documentation.

b. Permanent file audit documentation.

c. Administrative audit documentation in the current file.

d. Planning memorandum in the current file.

LO 3-5

3.26 An auditor's permanent file audit documentation most likely will contain

a. Internal control analysis for the current year.

b. The most recent engagement letter.

c. Memoranda of conference with management.

d. Excerpts of the corporate charter and bylaws.

LO 3-3

3.27 Which of the following is *not* a benefit claimed for the practice of determining materiality in the initial planning stage of an audit?

a. Being able to fine-tune the audit work for effectiveness and efficiency.

b. Avoiding the problem of doing more work than necessary (overauditing).

c. Being able to decide early what type of audit opinion to issue.

d. Avoiding the problem of doing too little work (underauditing).

LO 3-4

3.28 Which of the following is an advantage of computer-assisted audit techniques (CAATs)?

a. All the CAATs programs are written in one computer language.

b. The software can be used for audits of clients that use differing computer equipment and file formats.

c. The use of CAATs has reduced the need for the auditor to study input controls for computer-related procedures.

d. The use of CAATs can be substituted for a relatively large part of the required testing.

LO 3-2   3.29   An audit engagement letter should normally include which of the following matters of agreement between the auditor and the client?

     a. Schedules and analyses to be prepared by the client's employees.

     b. Methods of statistical sampling the auditor will use.

     c. Specification of litigation in progress against the client.

     d. Client representations about availability of all minutes of meetings of the board of directors.

LO 3-2   3.30   When auditing Vandalay Jewelry, Costanza, CPA, was not familiar with the quality and cut of the company's precious jewel inventory. To address this shortcoming, Costanza hired Benes, an expert in jewel valuation, to assist as an audit specialist for the inventory valuation. Should Costanza refer to Benes's work in the audit report?

     a. Yes, the auditors' report should mention the fact that an audit specialist was used.

     b. The auditors' report should mention the use of the audit specialist only when the audit specialist's findings affect the auditors' conclusions.

     c. The use of an audit specialist need not be mentioned if the auditors decide not to take responsibility for the audit specialist's findings.

     d. The auditors' report should mention the audit specialist only if Vandalay agrees with the audit specialist's findings.

LO 3-2   3.31   Which of the following engagement planning procedures would most likely assist the auditor in identifying related-party transactions before the balance-sheet date?

     a. Interviewing internal auditors about their reporting responsibilities.

     b. Reviewing accounting records for recurring transactions occurring near year-end.

     c. Inspecting communications with the client's legal counsel regarding recorded contingent liabilities.

     d. Scanning the minutes for significant transactions with members of the board of directors.

LO 3-2   3.32   Which of the following communications is most likely to be written before the balance-sheet date?

     a. A report to the audit committee on the results of testing of internal control over cash receipts.

     b. Confirmation letters to vendors confirming the amounts they owe to the client.

     c. An attorney's letter regarding contingent liabilities.

     d. An engagement letter.

LO 3-2   3.33   Which of the following procedures would most likely be performed during planning?

     a. Surprise counting of the client's petty cash fund.

     b. Reporting internal control deficiencies to the audit committee.

     c. Performing a search for unrecorded liabilities.

     d. Identifying related parties.

LO 3-1   3.34   Prior to accepting a new audit engagement, a public accounting firm should

     a. Attempt to contact the predecessor auditors.

     b. Evaluate the integrity of management.

     c. Assess the firm's resources to ensure that they are sufficient to permit the firm to accept the engagement.

     d. All of the above.

LO 3-2   3.35   An audit plan contains

     a. Specifications of audit standards relevant to the financial statements being audited.

     b. Specifications of procedures the auditors believe appropriate for the financial statements under audit.

     c. Documentation of the assertions under audit, the evidence obtained, and the conclusions reached.

     d. Reconciliation of the account balances in the financial statements with the account balances in the client's general ledger.

LO 3-4

3.36 The revenue cycle of a company generally includes which accounts?
   a. Inventory, accounts payable, and general expenses.
   b. Inventory, general expenses, and payroll.
   c. Cash, accounts receivable, and sales.
   d. Cash, notes payable, and capital stock.

LO 3-4

3.37 When auditing the existence assertion for an asset, auditors proceed from the
   a. Financial statement amounts back to the potentially unrecorded items.
   b. Potentially unrecorded items forward to the financial statement amounts.
   c. General ledger back to the supporting original transaction documents.
   d. Supporting original transaction documents to the general ledger.

LO 3-4

3.38 Confirmations of accounts receivable provide evidence primarily about which two assertions?
   a. Completeness and valuation.
   b. Valuation and rights and obligations.
   c. Existence and rights and obligations.
   d. Existence and completeness.

LO 3-3

3.39 With respect to the concept of materiality, which of the following statements is correct?
   a. Materiality depends only on the dollar amount of an item relative to other items in the financial statements.
   b. Materiality depends on the nature of a transaction rather than the dollar amount of the transaction.
   c. Materiality is determined by reference to AICPA guidelines.
   d. Materiality is a matter of professional judgment.

LO 3-4

3.40 When evaluating whether accounting estimates made by management are reasonable, the audit team would be most concerned about which of the following?
   a. Key factors that are consistent with prior periods.
   b. Assumptions that are similar to industry guidelines.
   c. Measurements that are objective and not susceptible to bias.
   d. Evidence of a conservative systematic bias.

LO 3-4

3.41 Which of the following would be considered an analytical procedure?
   a. Testing purchasing, shipping, and receiving cutoff activities.
   b. Comparing inventory balances to recent sales activities.
   c. Projecting the deviation rate of a statistical sample to the population.
   d. Reconciling physical counts to perpetual records and general ledger balances.

(AICPA adapted)

LO 3-2

3.42 Which of the following procedures would a CPA most likely perform in planning a financial statement audit?
   a. Make inquiries of the client's lawyer concerning pending litigation.
   b. Perform cutoff tests of cash receipts and disbursements.
   c. Compare financial information with nonfinancial operating data.
   d. Recalculate the prior-years' accruals and deferrals.

(AICPA adapted)

LO 3-4

3.43 Which of the following statements is correct concerning analytical procedures used in planning an audit engagement?
   a. They often replace the tests of controls that are performed to assess control risk.
   b. They typically use financial and nonfinancial data aggregated at a high level.
   c. They usually involve the comparison of assertions developed by management to ratios calculated by an auditor.
   d. They are often used to develop an auditor's preliminary judgment about materiality.

(AICPA adapted)

LO 3-2

3.44   The company being audited has an internal auditor who is both competent and objective. The independent auditor wants to assign tasks for the internal auditor to perform. Under these circumstances, the independent auditor may

    a. Allow the internal auditor to perform certain tests of internal controls.

    b. Allow the internal auditor to audit a major subsidiary of the company.

    c. Not assign any task to the internal auditor because of the internal auditor's lack of independence.

    d. Allow the internal auditor to perform analytical procedures but not be involved with any tests of details.

(AICPA adapted)

LO 3-1

3.45   Which of the following conditions most likely would pose the greatest risk in accepting a new audit engagement?

    a. Staff will need to be rescheduled to cover this new client.

    b. There will be a client-imposed scope limitation.

    c. The firm will have to hire a specialist in one audit area.

    d. The client's financial reporting system has been in place for 10 years.

(AICPA adapted)

Exercises and Problems

 All applicable Exercises and Problems are available with *Connect*.

LO 3-4

3.46   **General Audit Procedures and Financial Statement Assertions.** The eight general audit procedures produce evidence about the principal management assertions in financial statements. However, some procedures are useful for producing evidence about certain assertions, and other procedures are useful for producing evidence about other assertions. The assertion being audited can influence the auditors' choice of procedures.

Required:

Opposite each general audit procedure, write the management assertions best tested by using each procedure.

Audit Procedures	PCAOB Assertions	ASB Assertions
a. Inspection of records or documents (vouching)		
b. Inspection of records or documents (tracing)		
c. Inspection of records or documents (scanning)		
d. Inspection of tangible assets		
e. Observation		
f. Confirmation		
g. Inquiry		
h. Recalculation		
i. Reperformance		
j. Analytical procedures		

LO 3-4

3.47   **Audit Procedures.** Auditors use different types of audit procedures to gather the evidence necessary to conclude that the risk of material misstatement for each relevant assertion has been reduced to an acceptably low level. List eight different types of procedures auditors can use during an audit of financial statements and give an example of each.

LO 3-4

3.48   **Confirmation Procedure.** A CPA accumulates various types of evidence on which to base the opinion on financial statements. Among this evidence is confirmations from third parties.

Required:

    a. What is an audit confirmation?

    b. What characteristics of the confirmation process and the recipient are important if a CPA is to consider the confirmation evidence appropriate?

LO 3-4

3.49 **Potential Audit Procedure Failures.** For each of the general audit procedures of (a) recalculation, (b) observation, (c) confirmation (accounts receivable, securities, or other assets), (d) inquiry, (e) inspection of internal documents, (f) recalculation, (g) reperformance, and (h) analytical procedures, discuss one way the procedure could be misapplied or the auditors could be misled in such a way as to render the work (audit evidence) misleading or irrelevant. Give examples that are different from the examples in the chapter.

LO 3-5

3.50 **Audit Documentation.** The preparation of audit documentation is an integral part of an auditor's examination of financial statements. On a recurring engagement, auditors review the audit plans and audit documentation from the prior audit while planning the current audit to determine their usefulness for the current-year work.

Required:

    a. (1) What are the purposes or functions of audit documentation?

       (2) What records may be included in audit documentation?

    b. What factors affect the auditors' judgment of the type and content of the audit documentation for a particular engagement?

    c. What should be included in audit documentation to support auditors' compliance with generally accepted auditing standards?

    d. How can auditors make the most effective use of the prior-year audit plans in a recurring audit?

(AICPA adapted)

LO 3-1

3.51 **Communications between Predecessor and Successor Auditors.** Assume that Smith & Smith, CPAs, audited Apollo Shoes Inc., last year. Now CEO Larry Lancaster wishes to engage Anderson, Olds, and Watershed, CPAs (AOW) to audit its annual financial statements. Lancaster is generally pleased with the services provided by Smith & Smith, but he thinks the audit work was too detailed and interfered excessively with normal office routines. AOW has asked Lancaster to inform Smith & Smith of the decision to change auditors, but he does not wish to do so.

Required:

List and discuss the steps AOW should follow with regard to dealing with a predecessor auditor and a new client before accepting the engagement.

LO 3-1

3.52 **Predecessor and Successor Auditors.** The president of Allpurpose Loan Company had a genuine dislike for external auditors. Almost any conflict generated a towering rage. Consequently, the company changed auditors often.

The firm of Wells & Ratley (W&R), CPAs, was recently hired to audit the 2023 financial statements. W&R succeeded the firm of Canby & Company (C&C), which had obtained the audit after Albrecht & Hubbard (A&H) had been fired. A&H audited the 2022 financial statements and rendered a report that contained an additional paragraph explaining an uncertainty about Allpurpose Loan Company's loan loss reserve. Goodbye A&H! The president then hired C&C to audit the 2023 financial statements, and Chris Canby started the work, but before the audit could be completed, Canby was fired and W&R was hired to complete the audit. C&C did not issue an audit report because the audit was not finished.

Required:

Does the Wells & Ratley firm need to initiate communications with Canby & Company? With Albrecht & Hubbard? With both? Explain your response in terms of the purposes of communications between predecessor and successor auditors.

LO 3-1

3.53 **Client Selection.** You are a CPA in a regional public accounting firm that has 10 offices in three states. Mr. Shine has approached you with a request for an audit. He is president of Hitech Software and Games Inc., a five-year-old company that has recently grown to $500 million in sales and $200 million in total assets. Shine is thinking about going public with a $25 million issue of common stock, of which $10 million would be a secondary issue of shares he holds. You are very happy about this opportunity because you know Shine is the new president of the Symphony Society board and has made quite a civic impression since he came to your medium-size city seven years ago. Hitech is one of the growing employers in the city.

Required:

a. Discuss the sources of information and the types of inquiries that you and the firm's partners may make in connection with accepting Hitech as a new client.

b. Do professional audit standards require any investigation of prospective clients?

c. Suppose Shine also told you that 10 years ago his closely held hamburger franchise business went bankrupt, and on investigation, you learn from its former auditors (your own firm in another city) that Shine was fraudulent in its application of franchise-fee income recognition rules and presented such difficulties that your firm resigned from the audit (before the bankruptcy). Do you think the partner in charge of the audit practice should accept Hitech as a new client?

LO 3-2

3.54 **Using the Work of Internal Auditors.** North, CPA, is planning an independent audit of the financial statements of General Company. In determining the nature, timing, and extent of the audit procedures, North is considering General's internal audit function, which is staffed by Tyler.

Required:

a. In what ways can the internal auditor's work be relevant to North, the independent auditor?

b. What factors should North consider, and what inquiries should North make in deciding whether to use Tyler's internal audit work?

(AICPA adapted)

LO 3-4

3.55 **Using the Computer to Discover Intentional Financial Misstatements in Transactions and Account Balances.** AMI International is a large office products company. Headquarters management imposed pressure on operating division managers to meet profit forecasts. The division managers met these profit goals using several accounting manipulations involving the record-keeping system that maintained all transactions and account balances on computer files. Employees who operated the computer accounting system were aware of the modifications of policy the managers ordered to accomplish the financial statement manipulations. The management and employees carried out these activities:

1. Deferred inventory write-downs for obsolete and damaged goods.

2. Kept open the sales entry system after the quarterly and annual cutoff dates, recording sales of goods shipped after the cutoff dates.

3. Recorded leases of office equipment as sales transactions.

4. Recorded shipments to branch offices as sales.

5. Postponed recording vendors' invoices for parts and services until later, but the actual invoice date was faithfully entered according to accounting policy.

Required:

Describe one or more procedures that could be performed with CAATs to detect signs of each of these transaction manipulations. Limit your answer to the actual work accomplished by the computer software.

LO 3-4

3.56 **Inspection of Documents and Records.** A large portion of audit evidence is gathered through inspection of documents and records. External documents, documents that are generated outside of the organization, provide more reliable evidence than documents generated and maintained at the client.

Required:

a. For each of the documents below, indicate if the document is a strictly external document (obtained from an external party), an external-internal document (generated outside of the organization but given to the auditor by the client), or an internal document (generated and maintained by client).

1. Receiving report.

2. Customer purchase order.

3. Bank statements received directly from the bank.

4. Copies of sales invoices.

5. Utility bill.

6. Departmental budget.

7. Insurance policy.

8. Remittance advice.

b. Why are external documents considered more reliable evidence than internal documents? What aspects of internal documents would help to increase their reliability?

LO 3-5

3.57 **Audit Documentation -Permanent or Current Year Files.** Audit documentation can be classified in two categories: (1) permanent files (which contain information that is relevant for many years' audits for the client) and (2) current files (which contain information that is relevant to supporting the current year's audit).

Required:

For each of the documents listed below, indicate whether they would appear in the permanent or current year files.

1. Audit planning memorandum

2. Client organizational chart

3. Prior-years' financial statements and audit reports

4. Engagement letter

5. Bank confirmations

6. Schedule for current-year depreciation calculation

7. Royalty agreements

LO 3-1

3.58 **Pre-engagement activities.** Client acceptance policies and procedures generally include obtaining and reviewing financial information from prospective clients.

Required:

Your firm is considering accepting **Apple Inc.** as a new audit client. You are helping to perform client acceptance procedures by reviewing prior financial information. Go to the sec. gov website and search for Apple Inc.'s most recent 10-K filing. Read through the Item 1, Business, and Item 1A, Risk Factors, sections. What characteristics are red flags for potential problems? What characteristics would make Apple a desirable client?

LO 3-3

3.59 **Materiality calculations.** Materiality is ultimately a matter of professional judgment. However, during the planning process auditors make a calculation of preliminary materiality based on a benchmark or rule of thumb.

Required:

FastFix is an online retail company that sells a variety of products including groceries, clothing, toys, and home decor and promises delivery within 5 days. The table below has select financial data from 2022, 2023, and 2024. Using this information, calculate overall preliminary materiality using the following rules of thumb:

- 5% of profit before tax
- 1/2% of revenues
- 1% of total assets

FastFix Select Financial Data (in millions)

	2022	2023	2024
Net revenues	121,776	160,223	285,052
Profit before taxes	1,682	3,548	12,754
Total assets	98,325	101,524	157,221

Which of these do you think is most appropriate to use for FastFix for 2022, 2023, and 2024, and why?

LO 3-2

3.60 **Time budget.** Miguel is a first year staff at Anderson, Olds, and Watershed, CPAS. He has been working on the accounts receivable substantive testing at FastFix, which has an audit time budget of five hours. Through no fault of his own, the accounts receivable testing has been much more difficult than anticipated. It has taken Miguel eight hours to complete his testing. Miguel is considering "eating time" and indicating the testing has only taken five hours on his time sheet.

Required:

a. What are the purposes for reporting time?

b. What are the pros and cons of Miguel reporting five hours to complete the work, versus the eight hours it actually has taken? What would you do if you were Miguel?

Apollo Shoes

Audit Planning Part Two

You are a recently promoted senior (in charge) auditor for Anderson, Olds, and Watershed and have been assigned to the engagement team of a new client, Apollo Shoes Inc. You have been asked to begin the planning process for the audit. This includes making decisions about the use of audit resources and further familiarizing yourself with the engagement and the client. Detailed instructions regarding the information needed, as well as other procedures you need to perform in this planning phase of the audit, can be found in *Connect*.

CHAPTER 4

The Audit Risk Model and Inherent Risk Assessment

Don't be fearful of risks. Understand them, and manage and minimize them to an acceptable level.

Navid Abdali

Professional Standards References

Topic	AU-C/ISA Section	AS Section
Consideration of Fraud in a Financial Statement Audit	240	2401
Consideration of Laws and Regulations	250	2405
Communications with Audit Committees	260	1301
Audit Planning	300	2101
Identifying and Assessing the Risks of Material Misstatement	315	2110
Materiality	320	2105
Auditors' Responses to Risks of Material Misstatement	330	2301
Audit Evidence	500	1105
Substantive Analytical Procedures	520	2305
Related Parties	550	2410

LEARNING OBJECTIVES

The professional standards emphasize the importance of an auditor's identification and assessment of the risks of material misstatement that exist related to an audit client. Once each of the risks is identified and assessed, the auditor needs to plan an appropriate response. Given the importance of risk assessment, it is not surprising that the professional standards state that the risk assessment process underlies the entire audit process. In Chapter 3, we covered the engagement planning process, beginning with pre-engagement activities, supervision, and materiality. In this chapter, we provide comprehensive coverage of an auditor's risk assessment and its impact on the audit process.

Your objectives are to be able to

LO 4-1 Define *audit risk* and describe how it can be broken down into the three separate components of the audit risk model to help assess and respond to such risks during the audit planning process.

LO 4-2 Explain auditors' responsibility for fraud risk assessment and define and explain the differences among several types of fraud and errors that might occur in an organization.

LO 4-3 Explain auditors' responsibility to assess inherent risk, including a description of the type of risk assessment procedures that should be performed when assessing inherent risk on an audit engagement.

LO 4-4 Understand the different sources of information and the audit procedures used by auditors when assessing risks, including analytical procedures, brainstorming, and inquiries.

LO 4-5 Explain how auditors complete and document the overall assessment of inherent risk and the special considerations given to fraud risks and noncompliance with laws and regulations.

LO 4-6 Describe the content and purpose of an audit strategy memorandum.

INTRODUCTION

When the COVID-19 pandemic hit in March 2020, many businesses faced uncertainty: some wondering when they would see a return of customers, when employees would return to the office, and how they would survive for the unknown length of time until things returned to some form of normalcy. These uncertainties made the auditor's job more challenging too, in particular the job of identifying and assessing risks.

Risk assessment is the foundation of the audit process. It is the auditor's assessment of risk that should drive what audit procedures to perform in order for the auditor to obtain reasonable assurance that financial statements are free from material misstatement. COVID-19 brought about new or different risks to companies, including risks related to liquidity and debt compliance, the ability to continue as a going concern, cybersecurity risks related to remote working, risks related to business interruption, and even a potential increase in risk due to fraud.[1]

For the 2020 and 2021 audits in particular, auditors had to consider how those COVID-19-related business risks impacted their assessment of risk of material misstatement and then develop an appropriate response with audit procedures that would limit the risk of audit failure. What made this all the more difficult was that auditors had to re-envision their approach to performing the audit procedures. Limitations on travel, the lack of the ability to be "on-site" at the client, and the lack of in-person interactions with both clients and audit team members that were a side effect of COVID-19 meant the auditors had to consider new and/or alternative methods for performing audit procedures.[2]

This chapter focuses on the risk assessment phase of the audit, specifically discussing typical procedures and information auditors use to help identify and assess risks. As highlighted in Exhibit 4.1 below, risk assessment is critical in order to properly plan and perform the appropriate substantive procedures to continue the audit.

AUDIT RISK

LO 4-1
Define *audit risk* and describe how it can be broken down into the three separate components of the audit risk model to help assess and respond to such risks during the audit planning process.

Audit Risk

Audit risk is the probability that an audit team will express an inappropriate audit opinion when the financial statements are materially misstated (i.e., give an unmodified opinion on financial statements that are misleading because of material misstatements that the auditors failed to discover). Such a risk always exists, even when audits are well planned

---

[1]*A CAQ COVID-19 Resource: Focus on the Auditor's Risk Assessment,* CAQ, June 2020.
[2]*COVID-19: Reminders for Audits Nearing Completion,* PCAOB Staff Spotlight, 2020.

EXHIBIT 4.1
Stages of an Audit:
Risk Assessment

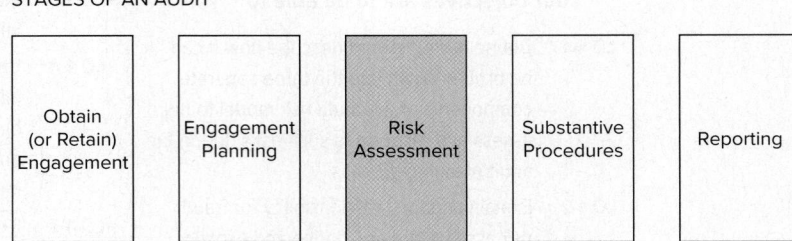

STAGES OF AN AUDIT

| Obtain (or Retain) Engagement | Engagement Planning | Risk Assessment | Substantive Procedures | Reporting |

and carefully performed. Of course, the risk is much higher in poorly planned and carelessly performed audits. The auditing profession has no official standard for an acceptable level of overall audit risk except that it should be "appropriately" low. In practice, audit risk is evaluated at both the overall financial statement level (as a whole) and for each *significant account and disclosure* through a focus on the *relevant assertions* identified.

A **significant account or disclosure** is an account or disclosure that has a reasonable possibility of containing a material misstatement regardless of the effect of internal controls. A **relevant assertion** is a management assertion that has a reasonable possibility of containing a material misstatement without regard to the effect of internal controls. The concern an auditor has regarding any particular assertion depends on the significant account that the auditor is testing (or to which the assertion relates). For example, an auditor may deem the occurrence assertion to present more risk when testing revenue than the completeness assertion presents. Most companies want to report a healthy stream of revenue, so it is unlikely that they will omit sales that would violate the completeness assertion. It is more likely that a company reports sales that did not occur to present more revenue, which would violate the occurrence assertion.

To help better understand and ultimately mitigate audit risk, the professional standards break down overall audit risk (see Exhibit 4.2) into the risks (1) that a material misstatement will even occur (*inherent risk*), (2) that it would not be prevented or detected by client internal controls (*control risk*), and (3) that it is not detected by the auditor's own procedures (*detection risk*). Because inherent risk and control risk are related to the company and its overall environment, these two components are combined into the **risk of material misstatement (RMM)**, which is the risk a material misstatement exists in the financial statements before auditors apply their own procedures. Each of these components is now discussed in detail.

EXHIBIT 4.2
Inherent, Control, and Detection Risk

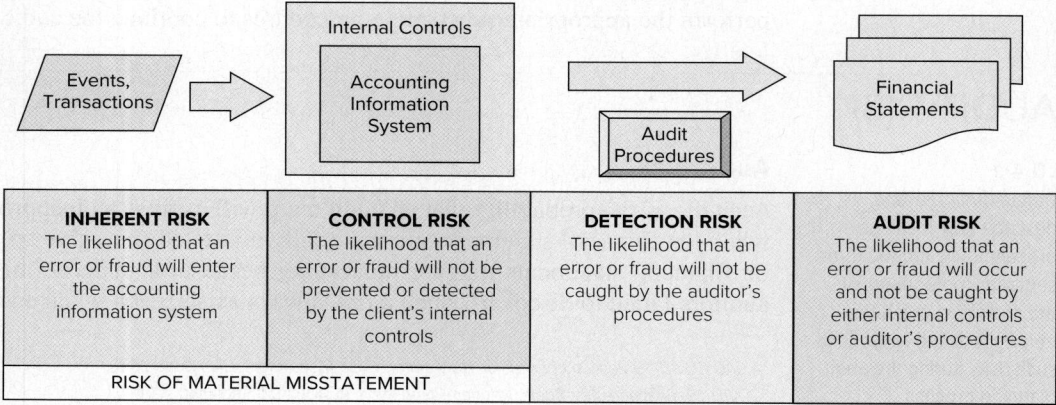

INHERENT RISK	CONTROL RISK	DETECTION RISK	AUDIT RISK
The likelihood that an error or fraud will enter the accounting information system	The likelihood that an error or fraud will not be prevented or detected by the client's internal controls	The likelihood that an error or fraud will not be caught by the auditor's procedures	The likelihood that an error or fraud will occur and not be caught by either internal controls or auditor's procedures

RISK OF MATERIAL MISSTATEMENT

Inherent Risk

Inherent risk is the probability that, in the absence of internal controls, material errors or frauds could enter the accounting system used to develop financial statements. You can think of inherent risk as the *susceptibility* of the account to misstatement. Inherent risk is a function of the nature of the client's business and strategy to achieve competitive advantage, the major types of transactions, and the effectiveness and integrity of its managers and accountants. It is important to understand that for different accounts, various *assertions* are riskier than others. For cash, *existence* is riskier than *completeness* because it is more likely that a client would try to include more cash than it really had on its balance sheet rather than less; and for accounts payable, *completeness* is riskier than *existence* because it is more likely that a client would try to understate what it really owed rather than overstate the amount. As a result, auditors focus their attention on *relevant assertions*. Finally, it is important for students to remember that auditors do not create or control inherent risk. They can only try to assess its magnitude in an appropriate manner. This will be discussed in more detail later in the chapter.

Control Risk

Control risk is the probability that the client's internal control activities will *fail* to prevent or detect material misstatements provided that such misstatements enter or would have entered the accounting system in the first place. So, for misstatements that could occur, what is the audit client doing about such occurrences? Does it have the proper systems, processes, and controls in place to either prevent or detect misstatements? Recall from our discussion of auditing standards in Chapter 2 that one of the major purposes of an internal control system is to ensure appropriate processing and recording of transactions for the production of reliable financial statements. Similar to inherent risk, auditors do not create or manage control risk. They can only evaluate an entity's internal control system and assess its magnitude in an appropriate manner.

External auditors' task of control risk assessment begins with learning about an entity's internal controls that are designed to prevent and detect material misstatements related to each relevant assertion for each significant account and disclosure. The auditors then perform tests of controls if appropriate to determine whether they are operating effectively. This process is discussed in detail in Chapter 5.

Detection Risk

Detection risk is the probability that the auditor's own procedures will *fail* to detect material misstatements provided that any have entered the accounting system in the first place and have not been prevented or detected and corrected by the client's internal controls. In contrast to inherent risk and control risk, auditors *are* responsible for performing the evidence-gathering procedures that manage and establish detection risk. These audit procedures represent the auditors' opportunity to detect material misstatements that may exist in the financial statements. In other words, unlike inherent risk and control risk, auditors can and do influence the level of detection risk.

In Chapter 3, you learned about substantive procedures, the procedures used to detect material misstatements that may exist in the significant account balances and disclosures presented in the financial statements and footnotes. The two categories of *substantive procedures* are (1) tests of details of transactions and balances, which provide specific evidence directly supporting assertions; and (2) substantive analytical procedures, which study plausible relationships among financial and nonfinancial data. Auditors are able to reduce detection risk by completing more and stronger substantive tests. Generally speaking, in response to a higher assessed risk of material misstatement for a relevant assertion being audited, auditors must reduce detection risk to an appropriate level by planning appropriate substantive procedures. This relationship is now further illustrated with a discussion of the audit risk model.

Audit Risk Model

The three components of audit risk can be expressed in a conceptual model that is designed to help auditors understand how the assessment of each component affects the overall audit risk being faced on the engagement. It is also important to point out that the audit risk model assumes that each of the elements is *independent*. Thus, the risks can be expressed in a model form as follows:

$$\text{Audit risk (AR)} = \text{Inherent risk (IR)} \times \text{Control risk (CR)} \times \text{Detection risk (DR)}$$

In practice, the model is used in the following way. Suppose an audit team was auditing the valuation assertion related to inventory. The team would initially *set* the desired level of AR to low. Auditors would then gather information and perform procedures to *assess* the susceptibility of misstatement (IR) related to the valuation of inventory. Let's say that there is a high risk of misstatement, therefore IR is assessed at a high level. Auditors would also evaluate whether the client has internal controls in place to help mitigate that risk. Assuming the client does not have very effective internal controls, auditors would then *assess* CR at a moderate or high level. Thus, the overall RMM (IR X CR) would be high. The auditors would then *solve for* the DR. In order to maintain an overall audit risk at a low level, the DR would be low or very low. A low or very low DR means the auditors are taking very low risk that their audit procedures will fail to detect a misstatement. Thus, the auditors would need to design audit procedures that would provide more appropriate and sufficient evidence that a misstatement *does not* exist related to the valuation of inventory. Given that IR is high and that controls over the valuation of inventory are not effective, it makes sense that the audit procedures would need to be more appropriate and sufficient in order to keep the overall AR low. Exhibit 4.3 illustrates the process described in the example.

Notice that the assessment of inherent risk (IR) and control risk (CR) led to a determination of detection risk (DR). As a result, detection risk depends on and is planned for based on the assessment of the other risk factors. DR is calculated and derived from the others by solving the risk model equation. It is not an independent judgment. Hence,

$$\text{DR} = \text{AR}/(\text{IR} \times \text{CR})$$

Exhibit 4.4 provides a visual display of the steps in the audit risk process.

EXHIBIT 4.3

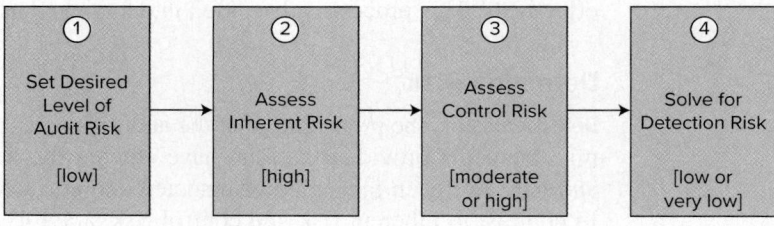

EXHIBIT 4.4
Audit Risk Model

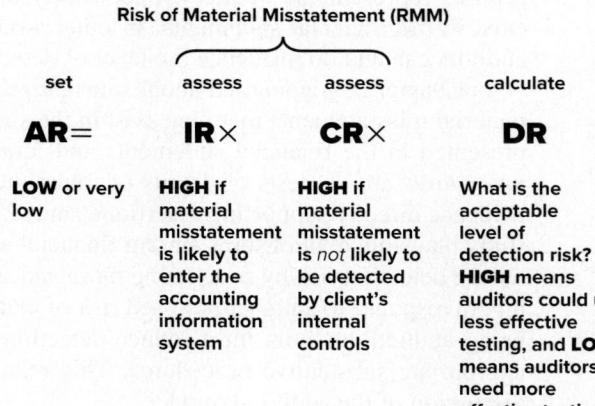

Based on the allowable or planned level of detection risk (which is always based on the assessment of IR and CR), auditors modify the *nature,* the *timing,* and the *extent* of further audit procedures. The *nature* of an audit procedure refers to the type of procedure (e.g., observation, recalculation, inquiry). When determining the nature of the audit procedure, the auditor is considering *what* to do. When doing so, the auditor considers the overall effectiveness of different types of audit procedures in detecting misstatements. While inquiry of management about whether accounts receivable listed on the balance sheet really exist is an audit procedure, it would not be an *effective* one. A much more effective procedure would be to confirm accounts receivable directly with the client's customers.

Timing refers to *when* the audit procedures will be completed. To do so, the auditor typically considers whether to complete the procedures at an interim date or at the balance sheet date. While confirmation of accounts receivable may be performed at an interim date, auditors are expressing an opinion on year-end balances. The closer the procedures are performed to year-end (the balance sheet date), the more effective they are because there is less chance of a material misstatement occurring between the interim confirmation date and year-end.

Finally, *extent* refers to the number of tests performed. Clearly, the larger the number of accounts receivable confirmations that are mailed to customers, the greater the chance of finding errors and fraud, and therefore, the lower the detection risk. Exhibit 4.5 summarizes the impact of detection risk on the nature, timing, and extent of audit procedures.

Note that there is an inverse relationship between RMM (i.e., inherent risk and control risk) and detection risk. In other words, the greater the risk of material misstatement, the lower the detection risk that auditors could allow in order to maintain the level of audit risk with which they feel comfortable. This makes sense. If the relevant assertion is risky or the related controls are poor, auditors would want to reduce detection risk by employing more appropriate and sufficient substantive procedures to increase their effectiveness. On the other hand, if the account is not risky and controls are strong, the auditor could employ less appropriate and sufficient (and presumably less costly) substantive audit procedures.

Also note that, although the audit risk model implies a numerical calculation, the example and discussion of how auditors use the audit risk model is in *qualitative* measures such as "low," "moderate," and "high." In practice, firms use qualitative measures of risk when using the audit risk model. Firms cannot know *exact* IR and CR, therefore auditors cannot calculate the *exact* level of DR. The model represents more of a way to think about audit risks than a way to calculate them.

The conceptual model does allow for some additional key insights, including these:

1. Auditors cannot estimate inherent risk to be none or zero and omit other evidence-gathering procedures.
2. Auditors cannot place complete reliance on internal controls (that is, CR of none or zero) to the exclusion of other audit procedures.
3. Auditors would not seem to exhibit due professional care if the level of audit risk was too high.
4. Although permissible, audit teams rarely choose to rely exclusively on evidence produced by substantive procedures. Even if they think that control risk is high, auditors often perform some tests of controls to make sure the controls are in place.

Given that firms measure risks qualitatively, firms typically use a matrix approach similar to the one shown in Exhibit 4.6. A matrix such as this relies on the relationships within the audit risk model for determining detection risk. Auditors find the appropriate detection risk by reading the cell at the intersection of the assessed levels of inherent risk and control risk.

EXHIBIT 4.5
The Impact of Detection Risk Allowed on the Nature, Timing, and Extent of Further Audit Procedures

	Lower Detection Risk Allowed	Higher Detection Risk Allowed
Nature	More effective tests	Less effective tests
Timing	Testing performed at year-end	Testing can be performed at interim
Extent	More tests	Fewer tests

EXHIBIT 4.6
Matrix Approach to Detection Risk (DR) Determination

		Control Risk (CR)		
		Low	Moderate	High
Inherent Risk (IR)	Low	DR—High	DR—Moderate to High	DR—Moderate
	Moderate	DR—Moderate to High	DR—Moderate	DR—Low to Moderate
	High	DR—Moderate	DR—Low to Moderate	DR—Low

✅ REVIEW CHECKPOINTS

4.1 Define *audit risk*.

4.2 What are the components of the risk of material misstatement (RMM)? What are the components of the audit risk model?

4.3 How is the audit risk model used to plan the audit?

4.4 What is meant by the terms *nature, timing,* and *extent* of further audit procedures?

4.5 When detection risk is determined to be low, as shown in the lower right corner of Exhibit 4.6, what impact does that have on planned substantive audit procedures, as opposed to when detection risk is determined to be high, as shown in the upper left corner of Exhibit 4.6?

FRAUD RISK

LO 4-2
Explain auditors' responsibility for fraud risk assessment and define and explain the differences among several types of fraud and errors that might occur in an organization.

In the next section we will discuss the process auditors use to assess inherent risk. Prior to assessing inherent risk, it is important to consider the risk of fraud and the role it plays in the assessment of risk of material misstatement. **Fraud** is the act of knowingly making material misrepresentations of fact with the intent of inducing someone to believe the falsehood and act on it and, thus, suffer a loss or damage. In our previous discussion of the audit risk model, there is no specific mention of fraud risk. While fraud risk is not a stated part of the audit risk model, fraud risk can never be ignored and impacts the risk of material misstatement (i.e., inherent risk and control risk) assessments. Auditors are required to consider fraud risk on each audit engagement for each relevant assertion related to each significant account and disclosure identified for an audit client. In effect, fraud risk is a special case of risk of material misstatement related to those situations where management intended to mislead the marketplace by issuing fraudulent financial statements.

When applying the audit risk model and assessing the risk of material misstatement, the auditor must always remember that a misstatement in the financial statements may be caused by an error or a fraud. What makes fraud different from errors is *intent*. Specifically, did a manager at the client intend to defraud? Or, was the misstatement simply due to an error made by an employee? Because of the damage to the capital markets caused by fraudsters who have intentionally misstated their financial statements, and the difficulty of discovering misstatements that management is actively trying to hide, auditors must give separate and careful attention to fraud risk on every audit engagement. The following Auditing Insight identifies a number of infamous fraudsters.

AUDITING INSIGHT When Upper Management Goes Bad

Perpetrator (age at trial)	Company	Verdict	Punishment
Bernie Ebbers (63)	**WorldCom**	Found guilty on fraud and conspiracy charges related to an $11 billion accounting scandal.	Sentenced to 25 years in federal prison, served 13 and was released due to health issues in December 2019. Died February 2020.
Dennis Kozlowski (59)	**Tyco International**	Found guilty of stealing $600 million from the company.	Served a total of 6.5 years in a New York state prison. Released in 2015.
Jeffrey Skilling (52)	**Enron**	Found guilty of securities fraud and related charges.	Originally sentenced to 24 years in prison; after many challenges to the punishment, in 2013 the sentence was reduced to 14 years. Released in August 2018 after serving 11 years.
Sanjay Kumar (44)	**Computer Associates 28 International Inc. (CA)**	Pleaded guilty to obstruction of justice and securities fraud charges related to CA's $3.3 billion accounting scandal.	Fined $8 million, sentenced to 12 years in prison, and ordered to pay $798.6 million in restitution. Released in 2017 after serving nearly 10 years.
Bernie Madoff (71)	**Madoff Investment Securities**	Pleaded guilty to securities fraud, money laundering, filing false statements with the SEC, wire fraud, mail fraud, and several other charges.	Sentenced to 150 years in prison. Died in prison in April 2021.
Nathan Hardwick IV (53)	**LandCastle Title**	Found guilty on 21 counts of wire fraud, one count of conspiracy to commit wire fraud, and one count of making false statements to a federally insured financial institution.	Sentenced to 15 years in prison.
Elizabeth Holmes (34)	**Theranos**	Settled fraud charges with the SEC. Found guilty of fraud and conspiracy to defraud investors.	Settled charges with the SEC for $500,000 and $18.9 million shares of stock. Awaiting sentencing in October 2022.
Billie McFarland (26)	**Fyre Media (Fyre Festival)**	Pleaded guilty to wire fraud charges related to Fyre Festival and to various fraud charges from a separate ticket-selling scheme.	Sentenced to 6 years in prison and ordered to pay $26 million.
Jan Marselek (40)	**Wirecard**	Currently on the run. One of Interpol's most wanted for role in $2 billion fraud.	
Jeffrey Hastings (62)	**SAExploration**	Pleaded guilty for conspiracy to commit securities fraud and wire fraud.	Sentenced to 3 years in prison.

Sources: "Ebbers Is Sentenced to 25 Years for $11 Billion WorldCom Fraud," *The Wall Street Journal,* July 14, 2005, p. A1; "Dennis Kozlowski, former Tyco CEO who went to prison, back in M&A business," *South Florida SunSentinel,* January 11, 2017, www.sun-sentinel.com; "Skilling Gets 24 Years in Prison," *The Wall Street Journal,* October 24, 2006, p. C1; "Ex-Enron CEO Skilling Has 10 Years Lopped off Sentence," CNN.com, June 21, 2013, "Ex-leader of Computer Associates gets 12 year Sentence and Fine," *The New York Times,* November 3, 2006, www.nytimes.com; "Sanjay Kumar, Former Software Executive, Released from Prison," *Newsday,* March 17, 2017, www.newsday.com; "Ponzi Schemer Bernie Madoff Dies in Prison at 82," *Associated Press,* April 14, 2021, www.apnews.com; "Theranos' Holmes to be Sentenced in September for Fraud Conviction," *US News and World Report,* January 12, 2022, www.usnews.com; "Theranos Founder Elizabeth Holmes Settles with SEC in Alleged 'elaborate, years-long fraud'," *Abcnews.go.com,* March 15, 2018; "The Fyre Festival was a total disaster. Its founder is going to prison for wire fraud." *The Washington Post,* October 11, 2018, "Fyre Festival Organizer Billy McFarland Sentenced to 6 years on Fraud Charges," *NBC News,* October 11, 2018, "Former LandCastle Title CEO Nat Hardwick found guilty of embezzling $26 million," *Housingwire.com,* February 13, 2019, "Former Enron CEO Jeff Skilling Released From Prison," *Fortune,* August 31, 2018; "Ex-Wirecard COO Fled to Belarus with Help from Austrian Officials - Bloomberg," *S&P Global Market Intelligence,* January 26, 2021, www.spglobal.com. "Former SEAX CEO Pleads Guilty to Accounting Fraud Scheme," *Accounting Today,* August 13, 2021, www.accountingtoday.com; "SAExploration's Ex-CEO Gets Three Years in Accounting Fraud Case," *Bloomberg Tax,* November 15, 2021, news.bloombergtax.com.

Given the damage that can occur to the capital markets as a result of fraud, auditors are required by professional standards to hold a brainstorming session to consider the risk of fraud in every audit engagement. The required brainstorming session will be discussed later in the chapter in the context of gathering information for risk assessment. It is important for students to recognize that the nature, timing, and extent of audit work should change as a result of the auditor's ultimate fraud risk assessment. In general, the lower the risk of material misstatement due to fraud, the less persuasive the audit evidence needs to be. It therefore follows that when fraud risk factors are identified, the auditor generally must obtain more persuasive audit evidence. Most importantly, once fraud risk factors are identified, the auditor should clearly identify the fraud risks and then design and perform procedures that respond directly to fraud risks. The next several paragraphs provide some basic definitions and examples of fraud and fraud risk factors to help further your understanding.

Fraud

Through both fraud and aggressive financial reporting, some companies have caused financial statements to be misstated, usually by (1) overstating revenues and assets, (2) understating expenses and liabilities, and (3) giving disclosures that are misstated or that omit important information.[3] Fraud that affects financial (or other) information and causes financial statements to be materially misstated often arises from the perceived need to get through a difficult period. The difficult period may be characterized by cash shortage, increased competition, cost overruns, and similar events that cause financial difficulty. Managers usually view these conditions as temporary, believing that getting a new loan, selling stock, or otherwise buying time to recover can overcome them. In the meantime, falsified financial statements are used to benefit the company. Generally, fraudulent financial statements show financial performance and ratios that are more favorable than current industry experience or than the company's own history. Exhibit 4.7 illustrates three categories of factors that might indicate increased risk of fraudulent financial reporting.

EXHIBIT 4.7   Fraud Risk Factors

Management's Characteristics and Influence	Industry Conditions	Operating Characteristics and Financial Stability
• Management has a motivation (bonus compensation, stock options, etc.) to engage in fraudulent reporting.	• Company profits lag those of its industry.	• A weak internal control environment prevails.
• Management decisions are dominated by an individual or a small group.	• New requirements are passed that could impair stability or profitability.	• The company is not able to generate sufficient cash flows to ensure that it is a going concern.
• Management fails to display an appropriate attitude about internal control and financial reporting.	• The company's market is saturated due to fierce competition.	• There is pressure to obtain capital.
• Managers' attitudes are very aggressive toward financial reporting.	• The company's industry is declining.	• The company operates in a tax haven jurisdiction.
• Managers place too much emphasis on earnings projections.	• The company's industry is changing rapidly.	• The company has many difficult accounting measurement and presentation issues.
• Management participates excessively in the selection of accounting principles or the determination of estimates.		• The company has significant transactions or balances that contain estimates that are difficult to audit.
• The company has a high turnover of senior management.		• The company has significant and unusual related-party transactions.
• The company has a known history of violations.		• Company accounting personnel are lax or inexperienced in their duties.
• Managers and employees tend to be evasive when responding to auditors' inquiries.		
• Managers engage in frequent disputes with auditors.		

[3]An academic study (see M. Nelson, J. Elliott, and R. Tarpley, "How Are Earnings Managed? Examples from Auditors," *Accounting Horizons,* November 2002) examined more than 500 attempts to manage earnings that were detected by auditors. The majority (more than 50 percent) of the attempts involved improper expense reductions, approximately 20 percent involved improper revenue increases, and the remainder involved business combinations and other accounting artifices.

A very common reason cited for falsifying financial statements is so a company can meet its earnings projections either provided by management or set by financial analysts. Simply stated, when a company fails to meet earnings projections, its stock price usually falls and the managers of the company face great scrutiny. As a result, managers work very hard to meet expectations set by analysts. In fact, sometimes a company's performance will exactly meet the earnings targets announced by management months earlier. To avoid the negative outcomes that typically accompany a failure to meet expectations, managers sometimes commit fraud. The accompanying Auditing Insight illustrates an example that occurred at Bankrate.

AUDITING INSIGHT | Meeting Analyst Expectations at Bankrate

While reviewing the preliminary financial results for the second quarter of 2012, the chief financial officer, VP of finance, and director of accounting at **Bankrate Inc.** concluded that their quarterly performance was going to fall dramatically short of analyst expectations. In order to avoid possible repercussions from Wall Street, the managers directed two different divisions to record additional revenue totaling $800,000, without supporting documentation or analysis. Eventually,

the company's auditors, **Grant Thornton**, discovered and flagged the unsupported revenue. In July 2015, Bankrate restated its financial statements for the second quarter of 2012. In addition, in September 2015, Bankrate was fined $15 million to settle the accounting fraud charges.

Sources: *SEC* Accounting and Auditing Enforcement Release No. 3683, September 8, 2015. "Bankrate to Pay $15 Million to Settle Accounting Fraud Charges," *Accounting Today*, September 8, 2015.

While not as common, there are times when management may find it beneficial to commit fraud by understating assets and revenues and overstating expenses and liabilities. This is likely to occur during times when profits are high and management wants to put reserves in a "cookie jar"[4] that can be used to increase profits in future years and "smooth earnings" at the discretion of the management team. Understating profits also can be desirable if the company is under scrutiny by governmental bodies, taxing authorities, labor unions, or competitors. Therefore, auditors must be aware of the potential for fraudulent activity in both directions, depending on the relevant facts and circumstances.

When assessing the risk of fraud, auditors need to know about the *red flags,* those telltale signs and indications that have accompanied many frauds that have occurred in the past. Because of the double-entry bookkeeping system, fraudulent accounting entries always affect at least two accounts and two places in financial statements. Because many frauds involve improper recognition of assets, there is a theory of the "dangling debit," which is an asset amount that can be investigated and found to be false or questionable. Frauds may involve the omission of liabilities, but the matter of finding and investigating the dangling credit is normally very difficult. It "dangles" off the books. In other words, the "dangling credit" is a credit that was never recorded to a liability account, resulting in an omission of a liability that should have been recorded. (Consider the implications for the completeness assertion in this scenario.) Misstated disclosures also present difficulty, mainly because they involve words and messages instead of numbers. Omissions may be difficult to notice, and misleading inferences may be very subtle. Exhibit 4.7 presents some of the other risk factors that have characterized situations in which frauds have occurred. Among the fraud risk factors identified, a company's difficult accounting issues or balances that contain difficult estimates to audit can be very challenging for auditors.

Types of Fraud

Remember, financial statements may be materially misstated as a result of *errors* or *fraud.* While accounting errors are usually unintentional, fraud consists of knowingly making material misrepresentations of fact with the *intent* of inducing someone to believe the

---

[4]*Cookie jar* reserves are overaccruals created by a company (credit accrual, debit expense). In times when the company struggles, it reverses the overaccrual (debit accrual, credit expense) to inflate profits. Once the "cookie jar" reserve has been established, auditors are in a bind because it may be difficult to object to the company correcting the overaccrual.

falsehood and act on it and, thus, suffer a loss or damage. This definition encompasses all means by which people can lie, cheat, steal, and dupe other people. There are, in essence, two different types of fraud: Fraudulent financial reporting and misappropriation of assets.

Fraudulent financial reporting is defined in AU-C 240.A2 as "intentional misstatements, including omissions of amounts or disclosures in financial statements to deceive financial statement users. It can be caused by the efforts of management to manage earnings in order to deceive financial statement users by influencing their perceptions about the entity's performance and profitability."[5] Given this definition, fraudulent financial reporting is often referred to as management fraud. **Management fraud** is deliberate fraud committed by management that injures investors and creditors through materially misstated information.

Misappropriation of assets is defined in AU-C 240.A7 as involving "the theft of an entity's assets and is often perpetrated by employees in relatively small or immaterial amounts."[6] Therefore, misappropriation of assets is often referred to as employee fraud. **Employee fraud** is the use of fraudulent means to misappropriate funds or other property from an employer. It usually involves falsifications of some kind: using false documents, lying, exceeding authority, or violating an employer's policies. It consists of three phases: (1) the fraudulent act, (2) the conversion of the funds or property to the fraudster's use, and (3) the cover-up. Employee fraud can be classified as either embezzlement or larceny. This type of fraud is discussed in detail in Chapter 6. Other definitions related to misappropriation of assets are

- **Embezzlement** is a type of fraud involving employees or nonemployees wrongfully misappropriating funds or property entrusted to their care, custody, and control, often accompanied by false accounting entries and other forms of deception and cover-up.
- **Larceny** is simple theft; for example, an employee's misappropriation of an employer's funds or property that has not been entrusted to the custody of the employee.
- **Defalcation** is another name for employee fraud, embezzlement, and larceny.

Misstatements due to fraudulent financial reporting or misappropriation of assets are distinctly different than errors. **Errors** are unintentional misstatements or omissions of amounts or disclosures in financial statements. Errors are not considered fraud because they occur unintentionally.

Exhibit 4.8 shows some acts and devices that are often involved in financial frauds. Notice that these actions may be perpetrated *by* the organization or may be perpetrated *upon* the organization. Collectively, these are known as **white-collar crimes**—the misdeeds of people who wear ties to work and steal with a pencil or a computer terminal. White-collar crime produces ink stains instead of bloodstains.

Auditing standards require that auditors specifically assess the risk of material misstatement due to fraud for each engagement. Fraud risk factors relate to both misstatements arising from *fraudulent financial reporting* and misstatements arising from *misappropriations of assets* (usually as a result of employee theft and the related attempt to conceal this theft through erroneous journal entries). Furthermore, auditors should consider these risk factors when determining what audit procedures to perform. With regard to the audit risk model, fraud risk is always considered a key factor when an auditor assesses inherent risk. A complete discussion of inherent risk assessment follows in the next section. The following Auditing Insight provides an example of how current world events can impact and change fraud risk factors.

---

[5]American Institute of Certified Public Accountants. "*Consideration of Fraud in a Financial Statement Audit.*" Accessed June 24, 2019.
[6]Ibid.

One last note regarding our responsibility for fraud: audit teams are concerned with fraud *only as it affects the financial statements.* Of those frauds, audit teams are responsible to detect cases where fraudulent activity results in *materially* misstated financial statements. For example, if a warehouse employee is misappropriating inventory but that embezzlement does not result in materially misstated financial statements, auditors do not necessarily have a responsibility to detect this type of fraud. However, if management is materially misstating revenues in order to meet earnings expectations, auditors *are* responsible for detecting this misstatement. That is not to say that auditors would ignore immaterial fraud (indeed, any instance of fraud would cause auditors to re-evaluate their assessment of management's integrity), but only that auditors' primary responsibility is to design procedures to provide *reasonable assurance* that *material* frauds that might misstate the financial statements are detected. The fraudulent acts highlighted in Figure 4.8 above are more likely to have a material impact on the financial statements and thus be of more concern to the auditor.

EXHIBIT 4.8
Overview of Types of Frauds

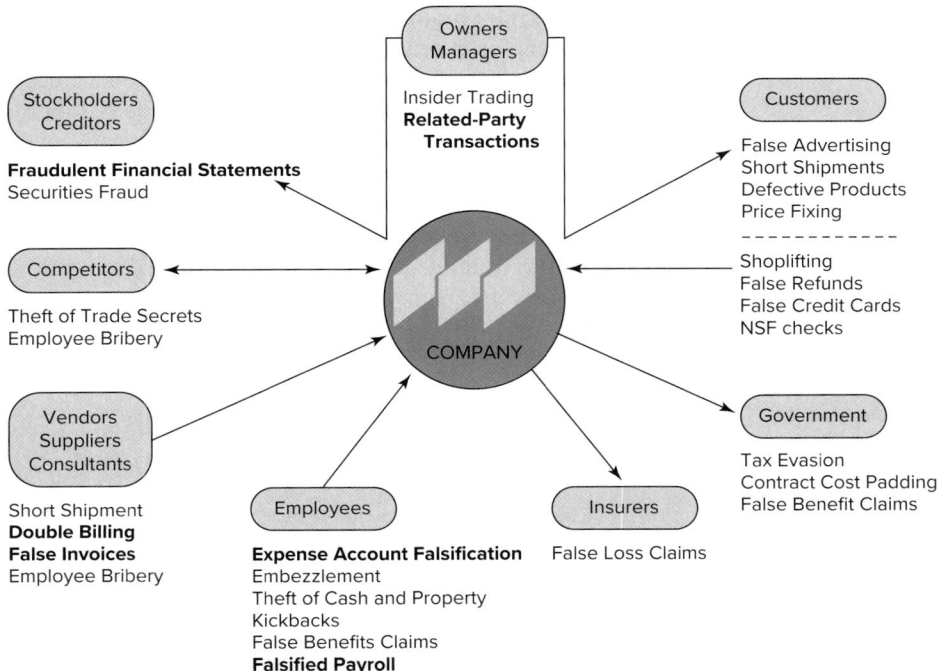

☑ REVIEW CHECKPOINTS

4.6 What is the primary difference between a material misstatement due to fraud and one due to error?

4.7 What is the auditor's responsibility regarding fraud risk?

4.8 What are the defining characteristics of (a) white-collar crime, (b) employee fraud, (c) embezzlement, (d) larceny, (e) defalcation, (f) management fraud, and (g) errors?

4.9 Identify three different categories of fraud risk factors. Next, for each category, what are some of the conditions that can help contribute to a higher likelihood of financial statement fraud?

INHERENT RISK ASSESSMENT—"WHAT COULD GO WRONG?"

LO 4-3

Explain auditors' responsibility to assess inherent risk, including a description of the type of risk assessment procedures that should be performed when assessing inherent risk on an audit engagement.

The professional standards make clear that risk assessment underlies the entire audit process. As a result, it is absolutely essential that auditors take great care to appropriately assess the risks of material misstatement, either due to error or fraud that exists on an audit engagement. When performing risk assessment procedures to accomplish this objective, the first step taken by auditors is often to assess inherent risk for each relevant assertion related to each of the significant accounts and disclosures identified on an audit engagement.

Recall that inherent risk is the probability that, in the absence of internal controls, material errors or frauds could enter the accounting system used to develop financial statements. Inherent risks can arise from a variety of different sources, and an auditor's basis for assessing a client's inherent risk is often found in his or her familiarity with the types of misstatements that could occur for each assertion in any account balance or class of transactions. Exhibit 4.9 shows the type of misstatement that can exist within transactions and the assertion that is violated.

A detailed understanding of an audit client's business model, including its products and services, is an essential part of an auditor's inherent risk assessment process at both the financial statement and the financial statement assertion levels. Inherent risk assessment helps to guide the auditor in allocating more and stronger resources to test specific accounts and disclosures that present a higher likelihood of material misstatement and therefore present a higher level of inherent risk. In effect, inherent risk assessment provides the basis for executing an appropriate response to the risks identified. Remember that the assessment of inherent risk can be based on a variety of types of information.

At a preliminary level, the best indicator of the risk of a material misstatement in the year under audit is a material misstatement that was discovered during the previous audit. Also, changes in transaction types, technology, personnel, or accounting principles may increase the risk of material misstatement. The nature of the client's business can produce complicated transactions and calculations that are subject to information processing and accounting treatment error. For example, real estate, franchising, and oil and gas transactions are frequently complicated and subject to accounting error. Some types of

**EXHIBIT 4.9
Misstatements by
Assertion**

Misstatement Type	Assertion Violated
1. Invalid transactions are recorded.	Occurrence
2. Valid transactions or disclosures are omitted from the financial statements.	Completeness
3. Transaction or disclosure amounts are inaccurate.	Accuracy
4. Transactions are classified in the wrong accounts.	Classification
5. Transactions are inappropriately aggregated or disaggregated and are not clearly described.	Presentation
6. Transactions are recorded in the wrong period.	Cutoff

inventories are more difficult than others to count, value, and keep accurately in perpetual records. The following factors have been suggested as being related to the susceptibility of accounts to misstatement or fraud:

- *Dollar size of the account.* The higher the account balance, the greater the chance of having errors or fraud in the account.
- *Liquidity.* The greater the account's liquidity (ability to be easily converted to cash), the more susceptible the account is to fraud. For example, cash is more susceptible to theft than, say, a building.
- *Volume of transactions.* The higher the volume of transactions, the higher the chance of error or fraud occurring in the transactions.
- *Complexity of the transactions.* Very complex transactions (e.g., those involving derivative securities or hedging transactions) tend to have a higher percentage of errors than simple transactions.
- *Subjective estimates.* Subjective measurements (e.g., estimating the allowance for doubtful accounts) tend to have more errors and fraud than objective measurements (e.g., counting petty cash). Simply stated, the more subjective the measurement, the easier it is to manipulate.

Understanding the Client's Business and Its Environment

As previously noted, understanding the client's business and its environment is essential in order to properly assess inherent risk. Auditing standards require auditors to obtain a thorough grasp of the business in order to properly plan and perform the audit. Understanding the following elements of the client's business is essential:

- Relevant industry, regulatory, and other external factors.
- The nature of the company and related parties.
- The effect of client computerized processing.
- The company's selection and application of accounting principles, including related disclosures.
- The company's objectives and strategies and those related business risks that might reasonably be expected to result in risks of material misstatement.
- The company's measurement and analysis of its financial performance.

Each of these areas are discussed further below.

Industry, Regulatory, and Other External Factors

Auditors must obtain an understanding of relevant industry, regulatory, and other external factors that encompass the client's competitive environment. This includes a detailed understanding of the regulatory environment, including the applicable financial reporting framework (e.g., U.S. GAAP or IFRS). Auditors must also understand the broad economic environment in which the client operates, including such things as the effects of national economic policies (e.g., price regulations and import/export restrictions), the geographic location and its economy (e.g., northeastern states versus sunbelt states), and developments in taxation and regulatory areas (e.g., industry regulation, approval processes for products in the drug and chemical industries).

Industry characteristics are also important. There is a great deal of difference in the production and marketing activities of banks, insurance companies, mutual funds, supermarkets, hotels, oil and gas industries, agriculture organizations, manufacturers, and so forth. Likewise, there can be a great deal of difference in where difficult and complex accounting transactions occur among the industries. Therefore knowledge of the industry, including the competition and market in which the client operates, is essential in helping to identify areas of increased risk of misstatement. In addition, auditors should be aware of the effects of world events, such as the recent COVID-19 pandemic, that impact the economy and the subsequent impact on the industry and their clients in particular.

The Nature of the Company and Related Parties

Obtaining an understanding of the nature of the company includes understanding

- *The company's organizational structure and management personnel.* Is the client centralized or decentralized? Are senior managers familiar with accounting and reporting requirements? Do they value the importance of good controls? Are any officers, employees, or shareholders involved in related-party transactions?
- *The sources of funding of the company's operations and investment activities.* Is the company funded by debt or equity? Are there restrictions placed by lenders that management must meet (e.g., debt covenants)? Does it have the financing in place to meet future cash requirements? Are any lenders or shareholders involved in related-party transactions?
- *The company's significant investments.* Is the company invested in other companies for strategic purposes? What is the company's investment policy? Do overseas investments present a risk of nationalization? Are any subsidiaries involved in related-party transactions? Is the company planning to acquire another company? As the nearby Auditing Insight reveals, there are additional risks for auditors if their client is either about to be acquired by or planning to acquire another company.
- *The company's operating characteristics, including its size and complexity.* Does the company operate internationally? Do subsidiaries operate in diverse industries?
- *The sources of the company's earnings, including the relative profitability of key products and services, and key supplier and customer relationships.* Are there any threats to loss of revenue from losing suppliers or customers? Could key products be overtaken by competitors' products? Could advances in technology make the client's products obsolete? Are any customers or suppliers *related parties?*

 AUDITING INSIGHT How Hewlett-Packard Overpaid for Autonomy

When **Hewlett-Packard** (HP) admitted that it overpaid when it acquired **Autonomy** for $11.1 billion in October 2011, the management team did not accept responsibility for the blunder. Rather, an investigation completed by HP concluded that there were serious "accounting improprieties" and "outright misrepresentations" found on Autonomy's financial statements. According to HP CEO Meg Whitman, "There appears to have been a willful sustained effort" to inflate Autonomy's revenue and profitability. "This was designed to be hidden." As a result, HP wrote down $8.8 billion of Autonomy's value just one year after the acquisition. To help recoup some of their losses, in 2015 HP filed a lawsuit against former Autonomy CEO Mike Lynch for $5 billion. In 2022, after years in the UK court system, HP won their lawsuit, although the amount due is yet to be determined and will likely be "considerably less" than $5 billion. In the meantime, in April 2018 the U.S. Department of Justice convicted Autonomy CFO Sushovan Hussain of falsifying financial statements and exaggerating the company's value and sentenced him to five years in prison. Criminal charges have also been filed in the U.S. against Mike Lynch, his extradition to the U.S. to face those charges was approved in January 2022.

For its part, **Deloitte UK** defends its audit work completed at the company. In fact, a spokesman for Deloitte UK "categorically denies that it had any knowledge of any accounting improprieties or any misrepresentations in Autonomy's financial statements, or that it was complicit in any accounting improprieties or misrepresentations." The Financial Reporting Council (FRC), the auditing regulator in the UK, disagrees. In 2020, the FRC hit Deloitte with a record 15 million pounds fine ($19.4 million) for conducting audit work that, in their view, "fell significantly short of the standards expected of an audit firm."

Source: "HP Says It Was Duped, Takes $8.8 Billion Charge," *The Wall Street Journal,* November 21, 2012, p. A1; "US Charges Autonomy Founder With Fraud Over Hewlett Packard Deal," *The Wall Street Journal,* November 30, 2018, "Deloitte and Former Autonomy Chiefs Face Action," *BBC News,* May 31, 2018; Gareth Corfield, "HPE wants British ex-CFO to testify in UK Autonomy lawsuit before Uncle Sam sentences him," *The Register,* February 18, 2019. "Deloitte Hit with Record 15 Million Pound Fine for Autonomy Audit," *Reuters,* September 17, 2020. "HP Wins Fraud Case Against Autonomy's Mike Lynch," *Wired,* January 28, 2022.

You may have noticed that many of the questions typically asked to gain an understanding of the nature of the company referenced related parties and related-party transactions. **Related parties** are those individuals or organizations that can influence or be influenced by decisions of the company, possibly through family ties or investment relationships. According to the professional standards, an auditor's primary objective in regard to

Finally, auditors who have industry expertise often have more than one client in that industry, so they can transfer general knowledge of risks encountered in other clients while maintaining confidentiality standards required by the profession.

What's in the Minutes of Meetings?

Boards of directors are responsible for monitoring their companies' businesses. The minutes of their meetings and the meetings of their committees (e.g., executive committee, finance committee, compensation committee, and audit committee) frequently contain information of vital interest to the independent auditors. Some information examples follow:

- Amount of dividends declared.
- Elections of officers and authorization of officers' salaries.
- Authorization of stock options and other incentive compensation arrangements.
- Acceptance of contracts, agreements, and lawsuit settlements.
- Approval of major purchases of property and investments.
- Discussions of possible mergers and divestitures.

- Authorization of financing by stock issuance, long-term debt issuance, and leases.
- Approval to pledge assets as security for debts.
- Discussion of negotiations on bank loans and payment waivers.
- Approval of accounting policies and accounting for significant and unusual transactions.
- Authorizations of individuals to sign bank checks.

Auditors take notes or make copies of important parts of these minutes and compare them to information in the accounts and disclosures (e.g., compare the amount of dividends declared to the amount paid, compare officers' authorized salaries to amounts paid, compare agreements to pledge assets to proper disclosure in the notes to financial statements).

Preliminary Analytical Procedures

Professional standards mandate that auditors complete analytical procedures at the beginning of an audit—preliminary analytical procedures—and at the end of an audit when the partners in charge review the overall quality of the work and look for apparent problems. Analytical procedures can also be used as a substantive testing procedure to gather evidence about the relevant assertion being tested. When completing analytical procedures at any time during the audit, auditors are required to develop an expectation about what an account balance should be and then compare that expectation to the recorded balance. When performing preliminary analytical procedures, as discussed in this section, auditors typically use the prior-year balances as the starting point for their expectation for each account balance. At this stage, **analytical procedures** are *reasonableness tests;* auditors compare their expectation for each of the account balances with those recorded by management. During this critical point of the engagement, auditors use analytical procedures to identify potential problem areas so that subsequent audit work can be designed to reduce the risk of missing something important. Analytical procedures during the preliminary stages also provide an organized approach—a standard starting place—for becoming familiar with the client's business and identifying areas of risk. Auditors need to remember that preliminary analytical procedures are based on unaudited data, so they should consider the effectiveness of controls over their reliability when deciding how much weight to place on the results.

Auditors should perform five steps when completing analytical procedures:

1. *Develop an expectation.* A variety of sources can provide evidence for auditors' expectations of the balance in a particular account:
   - Balances for one or more comparable periods (e.g., vertical and horizontal analyses).
   - Anticipated results found in the company's budgets and forecasts.
   - Leveraging predictable patterns among account balances based on the company's experience.
   - Relevant information from third-party sources for the industry in which the company operates.
   - Relevant nonfinancial information (e.g., physical production statistics, sales orders).

2. *Define a significant difference.* Basically, the question is, "What percentage (or dollar) difference from your expectation can still be considered reasonable?" It is important

that this decision be made *before* making the comparison to prevent auditors from rationalizing differences and failing to follow up.

3. *Compare expectation with the recorded amount.* Many auditors start with comparative financial statements and calculate year-to-year changes in balance-sheet and income-statement accounts (**horizontal analysis**). They next calculate common-size statements (**vertical analysis**) in which financial statement amounts are expressed as percentages of a base, such as sales for the income-statement accounts or total assets for the balance-sheet accounts. Although vertical and horizontal analyses are fairly basic, other analytical procedures—including mathematical time series and regression calculations, comparisons of multiyear data, and trend analyses—can be more complex.

4. *Investigate significant differences.* Auditors typically look for relationships that do not make sense as indicators of problems in the accounts, and they use such indicators to plan additional audit work. In the planning stage, analytical procedures are used to identify potential problem areas so that subsequent audit work can be designed to reduce the risk of missing something important. The application demonstrated here can be described as *attention directing:* pointing out accounts that could contain errors and frauds. The insights derived from *preliminary* analytical procedures do not provide direct evidence about the numbers in the financial statements. Although the insights derived from preliminary analytical procedures provide only limited evidence about the numbers in the financial statements, they do help auditors identify risks as an aid in preparing the audit plan.

5. *Document each of the preceding steps.* Auditors should document each step in completing their analytical procedures.

As an example, let's walk through the steps for completing preliminary analytical procedures for Dunder-Mifflin Inc. Exhibit 4.10 contains financial balances for the Dunder-Mifflin Inc.'s prior year (consider them audited) and the current year (consider them unaudited at this stage). Let's assume there have been no significant changes in operations or the industry, therefore current-year recorded amounts should be fairly similar to those of the prior year (step 1). Because changes are not expected, auditors can identify any changes that are more than 10 percent and $100,000 as deserving additional attention (step 2). Note that the threshold is *both* 10 percent *and* $100,000 instead of just one trigger or the other. A change in an account balance from $100 to $200 is a 100 percent change, but the change is clearly immaterial. Similarly, an increase in sales from $9.9 million to $10 million meets the $100,000 threshold but does not appear unreasonable in percentage terms. In step 3, auditors compare expectations with the recorded balances. Along with financial balances, Exhibit 4.10 also shows common-size statements (vertical analysis) for both the prior and current year and the dollar amount and percentage change (horizontal analysis) between the two years.

The investigation of significant differences (step 4) is probably the most critical step in the analytical procedures process. After generating basic financial data and relationships, the next step is to determine whether the financial changes and relationships actually describe what is going on within the company. According to the current-year unaudited financial statements in Exhibit 4.10, the company increased net income by increasing sales 10 percent, reducing cost of goods sold as a proportion of sales, and controlling other expenses. At least some of the sales growth appears to have been prompted by easier access to credit (accounts receivable increased by 80 percent) and more service (more equipment in use). The company also appears to have used most of its cash and borrowed more to purchase equipment, make payments on long-term debt, and pay dividends. Inventory and cost of goods sold, on the other hand, remained fairly consistent compared to the previous year, with both accounts increasing by only 6.7 percent.

The next step is to ask, "What could be wrong?" and "What errors and frauds, as well as legitimate explanations, could account for these financial results?" As an example of how analytical procedures are used, we limit our attention to the Accounts Receivable and Inventory accounts. At this point, some other ratios can help support the analysis.

EXHIBIT 4.10   Dunder-Mifflin Inc.—Preliminary Analytical Procedures Data

	Prior Year		Current Year		Change	
	Balance	Common Size	Balance	Common Size	Amount	Percent Change
Income						
Sales (net)	$9,000,000	100.00%	$9,900,000	100.00%	$ 900,000	10.00%
Cost of goods sold	6,750,000	75.00	7,200,000	72.73	450,000	6.67
Gross margin	2,250,000	25.00	2,700,000	27.27	450,000	20.00
General expense	1,590,000	17.67	1,734,000	17.52	144,000	9.06
Depreciation	300,000	3.33	300,000	3.03	0	0.00
Operating income	360,000	4.00	666,000	6.46	306,000	85.00
Interest expense	60,000	0.67	40,000	0.40	(20,000)	−33.33
Income taxes (40%)	120,000	1.33	256,000	2.59	136,000	113.33
Net income	$ 180,000	2.00%	$ 370,000	3.74%	$ 190,000	105.56%
Assets						
Cash	$ 600,000	14.78%	$ 200,000	4.12%	($400,000)	−66.67%
Accounts receivable	500,000	12.32	900,000	18.56	400,000	80.00
Allowance for doubtful accounts	(40,000)	−0.99	(50,000)	−1.03	(10,000)	25.00
Inventory	1,500,000	36.95	1,600,000	32.99	100,000	6.67
Total current assets	2,560,000	63.05	2,650,000	54.63	90,000	3.52
Equipment	3,000,000	73.89	4,000,000	82.47	1,000,000	33.33
Accumulated depreciation	(1,500,000)	−36.95	(1,800,000)	−37.11	(300,000)	20.00
Total assets	$4,060,000	100.00%	$4,850,000	100.00%	$ 790,000	19.46%
Liabilities and Equity						
Accounts payable	$ 500,000	12.32%	$ 400,000	8.25%	($100,000)	−20.00%
Bank loans, 11%	0	0.00	750,000	15.46	750,000	
Accrued interest	60,000	1.48	40,000	0.82	(20,000)	−33.33
Total current liabilities	560,000	13.79	1,190,000	24.53	630,000	112.50
Long-term debt, 10%	600,000	14.78	400,000	8.25	(200,000)	−33.33
Total liabilities	1,160,000	28.57	1,590,000	32.78	430,000	37.07
Capital stock	2,000,000	49.26	2,000,000	41.24	0	0.00
Retained earnings	900,000	22.17	1,260,000	25.98	360,000	40.00
Total liabilities and equity	$4,060,000	100.00%	$4,850,000	100.00%	$ 790,000	19.46%

Exhibit 4.11 contains several familiar ratios. (Appendix 4A at the end of this chapter contains these ratios and their formulas.)

- *Question:* Are the accounts receivable collectible? (*Alternative:* Is the allowance for doubtful accounts large enough?) Easier credit can lead to more bad debts. The company has a much larger amount of receivables, the days' sales in receivables has increased significantly, the receivables turnover has decreased, and the allowance for doubtful accounts is smaller in proportion to the receivables. If the prior-year allowance for bad debts at 8 percent of receivables was appropriate and conditions have not become worse, it could be that the allowance should be closer to $72,000 than $50,000. The auditors should work carefully on the evidence related to accounts receivable valuation.

EXHIBIT 4.11
Dunder-Mifflin Inc.—
Selected Financial
Ratios

	Prior Year	Current Year	Percent Change
Balance-Sheet Ratios			
Current ratio	4.57	2.23	− 51.29%
Days' sales in receivables	18.40	30.91	67.98
Doubtful accounts ratio	0.08	0.06	− 30.56
Days' sales in inventory	80.00	80.00	0.00
Debt/equity ratio	0.40	0.49	21.93
Operations Ratios			
Receivables turnover	19.57	11.65	− 40.47
Inventory turnover	4.50	4.50	0.00
Cost of goods sold/Sales	75.00%	72.73%	− 3.03
Gross margin percentage	25.00%	27.27%	9.09
Return on beginning equity	6.62%	12.76%	92.80
Financial Distress Ratios (Altman)			
Working capital/Total assets	0.49	0.30	− 38.89
Retained earnings/Total assets	0.22	0.26	17.20
EBIT/Total assets	0.09	0.14	54.87
Market value of equity/Total debt	2.59	1.89	− 27.04
Net sales/Total assets	2.22	2.04	− 7.92
Discriminant Z-score	4.96	4.35	− 12.32

- *Question:* Could the inventory be overstated? (*Alternative:* Could the cost of the goods sold be understated?) Overstatement of the ending inventory would cause the cost of goods sold to be understated. The percentage of cost of goods sold to sales shows a decrease. If 75 percent of the prior year represents a more accurate cost of goods sold amount, then the income before taxes could be overstated by $225,000 (75 percent of $9.9 million minus $7.2 million unaudited cost of goods sold). The days' sales in inventory and the inventory turnover remained the same, but you could expect them to change in light of the larger volume of sales. Careful work on the physical count and valuation of inventory appears to be needed.

Investigating significant differences and generating hypotheses of the cause of difference (i.e., "what can go wrong") are important for maintaining professional skepticism and properly assessing risk. However, as the following Auditing Insight discusses, while generating hypotheses is important, auditors need not come up with an exhaustive list.

AUDITING INSIGHT   Too Much of a Good Thing?

The fourth step in the process of performing analytical procedures is investigating significant differences between what is expected and what is recorded. Coming up with more explanations for why a significant difference exists seems like it would be a good thing, as the auditor would be more likely to discover the true reason for the difference. Well, it seems in this case that too much of a good thing can actually be bad. A recent experimental study examines auditors tendency to rely on client explanations after generating their own ideas for why a difference exists between expected and recorded amounts. Auditors that were asked to generate more ideas (6) were more likely to anchor on the client's explanation than auditors that were only asked to generate two ideas. This phenomenon occurred even when auditors were given information indicating that control risk was high, a situation that generally warrants higher levels of professional skepticism. Overall these results indicate that the difficulty of generating more ideas can actually cause auditors to let their guard down and get "lazy" when it comes to professional skepticism.

Source: A.M. Rose, J.M. Rose, I. Suh, and J. Thibodeau, "Analytical Procedures: Are More Good Ideas Always Better for Audit Quality?," *Accounting Horizons,* Spring 2020, pp. 37-49.

Other questions can be asked and other relationships derived when industry statistics are available. Industry statistics can be obtained from such services as Yahoo! Finance, Google Finance, Dun & Bradstreet, and Standard & Poor's. These statistics include industry averages for important financial benchmarks such as gross profit margin, return on sales, current ratio, debt/net worth, and various others. A comparison with client data can reveal out-of-line statistics, indicating a relatively strong feature of the company, a weak financial position, or possibly an error or misstatement in the client's financial statements. However, care must be taken with industry statistics. A particular company could or could not be well represented by industry averages.

Comparing reported financial results with internal budgets and forecasts also can be useful. If the budget or forecast represents management's estimate of probable future outcomes, planning questions can arise for items that fall short of or exceed the budget. If a company that expected to sell 10,000 units of a product sold only 5,000 units, the auditors would want to plan a careful analysis of the inventory of unsold units for obsolescence (*valuation*). If 15,000 were sold, an auditor would want to audit for sales validity (*occurrence*). Budget comparisons can be tricky, however. Some companies use budgets and forecasts as goals rather than as expressions of probable outcomes. Also, meeting the budget with little or no shortfall or excess can result from managers' manipulating the numbers to "meet the budget." Auditors must be careful to know something about an entity's business conditions from sources other than the internal records when analyzing comparisons with budgets and forecasts to determine inherent risk.

As previously stated, professional standards require auditors to perform analytical procedures during the planning stages of the audit "with the objective of identifying unusual or unexpected relationships" involving significant financial accounts "that might indicate a material misstatement, including material misstatement due to fraud." When doing so, the auditor should consider all types of relevant data to help improve their understanding of risk on the audit. Importantly, professional standards allow the use of "data that is preliminary or data that is aggregated at a high level" when completing analytical procedures at the planning stages. As a result, the increased use of big data and analytical tools has the potential to improve the effectiveness of this type of risk assessment procedure.[8]

Indeed, auditors now have the opportunity to use new types of analyses that utilize third-party data to supplement their "traditional" analytical procedures. The additional data can help auditors refine their expectations and improve the results of preliminary analytical procedures, which form initial beliefs about the nature, timing, and extent of audit evidence to be gathered from an audit client. While this type of access to increased volumes of data on the client has the potential to improve audit effectiveness, it also can have an initial negative impact on audit efficiency if audit professionals are unable to efficiently execute such additional procedures.

While the availability of even more third-party data offers considerable promise for auditors when completing preliminary analytical procedures, audit professionals in today's environment also need to learn how to make the best use of internal client data when completing such procedures. For example, when completing preliminary analytical procedures, the availability of largely all of the client's internal data can allow for a more robust trend analysis (i.e., year over year) on a multitude of financial and nonfinancial data. Auditors are encouraged to consider the facts and circumstances of each audit engagement and utilize computer-assisted audited techniques to facilitate the most useful trend analyses for the financial statement audit. The following insert provides guidance on how IDEA can be used to improve the efficiency of analytical procedures.

---

[8]See PCAOB Release 2010-04. "Identifying and Assessing Risks of Material Misstatement." August 5, 2010.

USING IDEA IN THE AUDIT — Analytical Procedures

The IDEA software package can be helpful when summarizing internal client data for purposes of analytical procedures used during the planning process. For example, in the IDEA Analysis Workbook, it is stated that "IDEA can help with the preparation of figures for an analytical review. In particular, IDEA can generate analyses that would not otherwise be available. The **Stratification** task (from the **Analysis** tab on the IDEA Ribbon) generates a profile of the population in value bands, groups of codes, or dates. This is particularly useful when auditing assets such as accounts receivable, inventories, or loans or

for a breakdown of transactions. Additionally, the information can be summarized by particular codes or subcodes. Figures can also be compared against previous years to determine trends. A chart can be produced if required."

At the end of this chapter, problems 4.68, 4.69 and 4.70 can be completed to illustrate the use of IDEA during preliminary analytical procedures. To be most useful, each of these analyses would have to be completed for multiple years so comparisons could be made and meaningful expectations could be developed.

Audit Team Brainstorming Discussions

On every audit engagement, the risk assessment process includes *required* audit team brainstorming sessions in which critical audit areas are discussed. These sessions update audit team members on important aspects of the audit and heighten team members' awareness of the potential for fraud and errors in the engagement. Items typically discussed include previous experiences with the client, how a fraud might be perpetrated and concealed by the client, and procedures that might detect fraud. When studying a business operation, auditors' ability to think like a criminal and devise ways to steal can help in creating procedures to determine whether fraud has happened. Often, imaginative extended procedures can be employed to unearth evidence of fraudulent activity.

A secondary objective of the discussions is to set a proper tone for the engagement. These sessions address not only fraud risk, but also other client business and audit-related risk assessments. While these brainstorming sessions typically begin during the planning stage of engagements, they should be held on a continual basis through the conclusion of the engagement.

Many firms have fraud specialists that assist audit teams throughout the risk assessment process. If an auditor's specialists are assigned to the audit, their involvement during brainstorming sessions is particularly important because, as a result of their experience, they are particularly adept at identifying critical audit areas and how these areas influence the risk of misstatement due to fraud.

AUDITING INSIGHT — Some Best Practices in Brainstorming

- An engagement partner or an auditor's forensic specialist is the best choice to lead the brainstorming session, but the use of group decision software (which protects individuals' identities) allows each engagement team member to participate freely without fear of intimidation or repercussion. Managers and partners should be active participants.

- Audit team members should be reminded of the purpose of the brainstorming session and stress the importance of professional skepticism.

- A good strategy is to discuss material misstatements found in previous audits and/or frauds found on similar engagements.

- When checklists are used, fully discuss each item on the list and don't limit discussions solely to items on the checklist. In other words, consider what might have been left off the checklist.

- The idea-generation phase should be separated from the idea-evaluation phase. Considering each threat as it is

brought up may cause individuals to feel slighted and may inhibit further idea generation. Engagement team members should be encouraged to discuss why they feel an identified risk is important.

- An information technology audit specialist should attend.

- The session should be held during preplanning or early in the planning stage.

- It should include discussion of how management might perpetrate fraud and audit responses to fraud risk.

- Time should be set aside at the end of the session to indicate how the audit plan should be modified as a result of the discussions.

Sources: M. Landis, S. Jerris, and M. Braswell, "Better Brainstorming," *Journal of Accountancy,* October 2008, pp. 70–73; J. F. Brazel, T. D. Carpenter, and J. G. Jenkins, "Auditors' Use of Brainstorming in the Consideration of Fraud: Reports from the Field," *The Accounting Review* 85, no. 4 (July 2010), pp. 1273–1301.

Inquiry of Audit Committee, Management, and Others within the Company

Interviewing the entity's management, internal auditors, directors, the audit committee, and other employees is a required audit process that can bring auditors up to date on changes in the business and the industry. Such inquiries of client personnel have the multiple purposes of building personal working relationships, observing the competence and integrity of client personnel, obtaining a general understanding of the client or company, and probing for problem areas that could harbor financial misstatements. Issues to discuss include selection of accounting principles; susceptibility to errors and fraud, including known or suspected fraud; and how management controls and monitors fraud risks. Other company employees to question might include operations or marketing managers or those involved in significant and unusual transactions.

Another source of information is company discussion boards, apps, or websites, such as that highlighted in the Auditing Insight that follows, where anonymous whistleblowers can post information that management may not wish to disclose to auditors.

AUDITING INSIGHT What do Apps Like "Blind" Mean for Auditors?

Blind is an app launched originally in the U.S. in 2015 that allows employees to anonymously post about compensation, workplace harassment, company policies, and more. Employees use company email addresses to create an account with Blind, after which the employee is verified and added to a specific company board that is only visible by employees of that firm. Despite using a work email address to sign up, Blind claims on their website to have a "patented infrastructure" to guarantee the anonymity of posts. Blind has recently begun accepting public domain names such as Gmail and Yahoo, although accounts created with public domains will have limited access to only topics channels, which include HR Issues, office life, and so on. Blind is not the first app of its kind; it follows apps such as

Secret and Whisper, although it is unique in that it is more focused on sharing "workplace" secrets.

In the past few years, Blind received a lot of press for exposing sexual harassment issues and inappropriate accessing of customer data within organizations. As auditors, what kind of information could Blind tell us about management integrity at the client? Could accounting fraud be the next big trending topic on Blind? Auditors may want to consider thinking out of the box and looking inside the apps as another source of information about their clients.

Source: Sara O'Brien, "App lets workers talk about their companies anonymously," *CNN Business,* February 12, 2018.

 REVIEW CHECKPOINTS

4.14 What are some types of knowledge and understanding about a client's business and industry that an auditor is expected to obtain? What are some of the methods and sources of information for understanding a client's business and industry?

4.15 What is the purpose of performing preliminary analytical procedures in audit planning?

4.16 What are the five steps involved with the use of preliminary analytical procedures?

4.17 What are some of the ratios that can be used in preliminary analytical procedures?

4.18 When are analytical procedures required, and when are they optional?

OVERALL ASSESSMENT AND DOCUMENTATION OF INHERENT RISK ASSESSMENT

LO 4-5
Explain how auditors complete and document the overall assessment of inherent risk and the special considerations given to fraud risks and noncompliance with laws and regulations.

The overall goal of the risk assessment process that has been described in this chapter is to identify and then properly assess the risks of material misstatement that exist at an audit client. Once the risk assessment process is complete, auditors have a basis to plan and then implement an appropriate testing response for each of the assessed risks. This process must be completed in a very detailed manner for each relevant assertion related to each significant financial statement account and disclosure. In a sense, auditors need to think about how all of the risks identified at the company and the financial statement level could affect risks of material misstatement at the relevant assertion level.

If you recall from our discussion of the audit risk model, the overall risk of material misstatement includes both inherent risk and control risk. We will discuss the assessment of control risk and the effect of tests of control in Chapter 5. For now, we will focus on the assessment of inherent risk, which needs to be evaluated without regard to the system of internal controls.

The assessment of inherent risk needs to occur for each significant financial statement account and disclosure. An account or disclosure is significant if there is a chance that it could contain a material misstatement. When making this determination, the auditor should evaluate both the quantitative and the qualitative risk factors associated with the financial statement account or disclosure. When doing so, clearly the overall materiality level is a critically important factor. However, it is possible that an account or disclosure could be significant even though its balance is below materiality. For example, an account balance may be understated or a disclosure could be omitted, among a host of other factors. Once each of the significant accounts and disclosures have been identified, the auditor then needs to identify the relevant financial statement assertions.

Relevant Assertions

According to the professional standards (AS 2201.28), a financial statement assertion is relevant if it has a "reasonable possibility of containing a misstatement that would cause the financial statements to be materially misstated." Therefore, based on all of the risk assessment procedures performed, auditors must identify those assertions that have a meaningful bearing on whether the account is fairly stated. For example, the valuation assertion would only be relevant to the cash account if the audit client had cash accounts that were denominated in a foreign currency. However, due to the nature of cash, it is likely that the existence assertion would always be relevant.

Once each relevant assertion is identified for each significant account and disclosure, the auditor must then identify the likely sources of misstatements that could cause the financial statements to be materially misstated. It is important that this step is completed at a detailed and almost granular level. To do so, the professional standards suggest that an auditor should consider "what could go wrong" when thinking about each of the relevant financial statement assertions. The comprehensive identification of "what could go wrong" for each relevant financial statement assertion is the foundation for the risk assessment process and ultimately the audit plan. Exhibit 4.12 provides a summary of this process.

Once the likely sources of misstatements that could cause the financial statements to be materially misstated have been identified, the auditors' next task is to assess the types of risk present, the likelihood that material misstatement has occurred, the magnitude of the risk, and the pervasiveness of the potential for misstatement. This lays the groundwork for the identification of internal controls that the client should have in place

EXHIBIT 4.12
What Could Go Wrong?

Significant Account	Relevant Assertions	What Could Go Wrong?
Cash	Existence	The cash balance may not exist in the company's bank accounts.
	Valuation	The cash balance that is held in foreign countries may not have been translated properly.
	Presentation and disclosure	There may be restrictions on the cash balance that were not properly disclosed.
Accounts Receivable	Existence	Accounts receivable balances are inflated and don't really exist.
	Completeness	Not all accounts receivable have been recorded.
	Valuation	Receivables are not included in financial statements at the appropriate amount, and valuation adjustments are not recorded properly.

assertions are relevant to those accounts, the auditor should establish an overall audit strategy that sets the scope, timing, and direction for auditing each relevant assertion. The strategy is a result of the audit risk model. If auditors believe they can rely on company controls to mitigate risks, they test the controls as described in Chapter 5. Depending on the results of such tests, the auditors determine the nature, timing, and extent of substantive procedures. If the auditors identified fraud risk or other significant risks or noncompliance with laws and regulations, they specifically address them in the strategy, including the possibility of adding fraud specialists to the team or by expanding testing.

In establishing the overall audit strategy, the auditor should take into account (1) the reporting objectives of the engagement and the nature of the communications required by auditing standards, (2) the factors that are significant in directing the activities of the engagement team, and (3) the results of preliminary engagement activities and the auditor's evaluation risk assessment. Also, various laws or regulations may require other matters to be communicated. The strategy should outline the nature, timing, and extent of *resources* necessary to perform the engagement. Planned tests of controls, substantive procedures, and other planned audit procedures required to be performed so that the engagement complies with auditing standards should be documented with specific directions about the effect on the audit.

The audit strategy memorandum becomes the basis for preparing the audit plan that lists the audit procedures to be completed for each relevant assertion related to each significant account and disclosure identified on the audit engagement. Since the audit procedures to be performed by the auditors are designed to gather sufficient appropriate evidence on which to base their audit opinion on the financial statements, the professional auditing standards require a *written* audit plan that documents the audit strategy on each engagement. An example of an audit strategy memorandum is presented in Appendix 4B.

☑ REVIEW CHECKPOINT

4.22   What is the purpose of an audit strategy memorandum? What information should it contain?

Summary

According to AS 1101.03, "To form an appropriate basis for expressing an opinion on the financial statements, the auditor must plan and perform the audit to obtain reasonable assurance about whether the financial statements are free of material misstatement due to error or fraud. Reasonable assurance is obtained by reducing audit risk to an appropriately low level through applying due professional care, including obtaining sufficient appropriate audit evidence."[10] In order to accomplish this objective, the auditor must take the time to carefully assess audit risk on each audit engagement.

Audit risk is the risk assumed by the auditors that they could express an incorrect opinion on financial statements that are materially misstated as a result of errors or fraud. The audit risk model breaks down audit risk into three components: *inherent risk, control risk,* and *detection risk.* Inherent risk involves the susceptibility of accounts to misstatement (assuming that no controls are present). Control risk addresses the effectiveness (or lack thereof) of the controls in preventing or detecting misstatements. Inherent and control risk are often combined and referred to as the *risk of material misstatement.* Detection risk involves the effectiveness of the auditors' procedures in detecting fraud or misstatement. Solving for detection risk in the audit risk model yields guidance for the preparation of the audit plan and the nature, timing, and extent of further audit procedures to be performed.

Risk assessment starts with knowledge of the types of errors and frauds that can be perpetrated. It involves understanding the company, its industry, and its environment. Auditors assess risk by obtaining public and internal information, holding team brainstorming

---

[10]PCAOB Release 2010-004. "Auditing Standard No. 14: Evaluating Audit Results." August 5, 2010.

discussions, performing analytical procedures, and inquiring of management, directors, and key employees. The culmination of the auditor's risk assessment process is the identification of the risk of material misstatement for each relevant assertion for each significant account and disclosure on each audit engagement. During the engagement, auditors respond to identified risks by increasing the effectiveness of their procedures and employing specialists and experienced personnel when necessary. Audit strategies are the auditors' summaries of their assessments and how they will respond to identified risks, particularly significant risks, which include the risk of fraud. Audit strategies are documented in the audit plan.

Key Terms

accounting estimates: The approximations of financial statement amounts often included in financial statements, 138

analytical procedures: Procedures that allow auditors to evaluate financial information by studying relationships among both financial and nonfinancial data. When used near the end of the audit, analytical procedures allow auditors to assess the conclusions reached during the audit and evaluate the overall financial statement presentation, 141

audit committee: A subcommittee of the board of directors that is generally composed of three to six "outside" members of the organization's board of directors, 150

audit risk: The risk that the auditor will express an inappropriate audit opinion when the financial statements are materially misstated (e.g., giving an unmodified opinion on financial statements that are misleading because of material misstatements the auditors failed to discover), 123

audit strategy memorandum: The scope, timing, and direction for auditing each relevant assertion based on the results of the audit risk model, 152

business risks: Those factors, events, and conditions that could prevent the organization from achieving its business objectives, 138

control risk: The likelihood that the client's internal control policies and procedures fail to prevent or detect a material misstatement, 125

defalcation: Another name for employee fraud and embezzlement, 132

detection risk: The likelihood that the auditors' substantive procedures will fail to detect a material misstatement that exists within an account balance or class of transactions, 125

direct-effect noncompliance: The violations of laws or government regulations by the entity or its management or employees that produce direct and material effects on dollar amounts in financial statements, 151

embezzlement: A type of fraud involving employees or nonemployees wrongfully taking money or property entrusted to their care, custody, and control, often accompanied by false accounting entries and other forms of lying and cover-up, 132

employee fraud: The use of fraudulent means to take money or other property from an employer. It consists of three phases: (1) the fraudulent act, (2) the conversion of the money or property to the fraudster's use, and (3) the cover-up, 132

errors: The unintentional misstatements or omissions of amounts or disclosures in financial statements, 132

extended procedures: The audit procedures used in response to heightened fraud awareness as the result of the identification of significant risks, 149

fraud: The misrepresentation of facts that the individual knows to be false with the intention to deceive, 128

fraudulent financial reporting: Intentional misstatements, including omissions of amounts or disclosures in financial statements intended to deceive financial statement users, 132

horizontal analysis: The comparative analysis of year-to-year changes in balance-sheet and income-statement accounts, 142

indirect-effect noncompliance: The violation of laws and regulations that does not directly affect specific financial statement accounts or disclosures (e.g., violations relating to insider securities trading, occupational health and safety, food and drug administration regulations, environmental protection, and equal employment opportunity), 151

inherent risk: The probability that in the absence of internal controls, material errors or frauds could enter the accounting system used to develop financial statements, 125

larceny: The simple theft of an employer's property that is not entrusted to an employee's care, custody, or control, 132

management fraud: The deliberate fraud committed by management that injures investors and creditors through materially misleading information, 132

misappropriation of assets: Asset theft from an entity. It is often perpetrated by employees in small amounts and is sometimes referred to as employee fraud, 132

related parties: Those individuals or organizations that are closely tied to the audit client, possibly through family ties or investment relationships, 136

relevant assertion: A financial statement assertion that has a reasonable possibility of containing a misstatement or misstatements that would cause the financial statements to be materially misstated, 124

risk of material misstatement (RMM): The combined inherent and control risk; in other words, the likelihood that material misstatements may have entered the accounting system and not been detected and corrected by the client's internal control, 124

significant account or disclosure: An account or disclosure that has a reasonable possibility of containing a material misstatement individually or when aggregated with others regardless of the effect of controls, 124

significant risk: A risk of material misstatement that requires special audit consideration. Fraud risk is always considered significant risk, 149

vertical analysis: The common-size analysis of financial statement amounts created by expressing amounts as proportions of a common base such as sales for the income-statement accounts or total assets for the balance-sheet accounts, 142

white-collar crime: Fraud perpetrated by people who work in offices and steal with a pencil or a computer terminal. The contrast is with violent street crime, 132

Multiple-Choice Questions for Practice and Review

 All applicable questions are available with *Connect*.

LO 4-2

4.23 Auditing standards do not require auditors of financial statements to
   a. Understand the nature of errors and frauds.
   b. Assess the risk of occurrence of errors and frauds.
   c. Design audits to provide reasonable assurance of detecting errors and frauds.
   d. Report all errors and frauds found to police authorities.

LO 4-2

4.24 If sales were overstated by recording a false credit sale at the end of the year, where could you find the false "dangling debit"?
   a. Inventory.
   b. Cost of goods sold.
   c. Bad debt expense.
   d. Accounts receivable.

LO 4-2

4.25 One of the typical characteristics of management fraud is
   a. Falsification of documents in order to misappropriate funds from an employer.
   b. Victimization of investors through the use of materially misleading financial statements.
   c. Illegal acts committed by management to evade laws and regulations.
   d. Conversion of stolen inventory to cash deposited in a falsified bank account.

LO 4-2

4.26 Which of the following circumstances would most likely cause an audit team to perform extended procedures?
   a. Supporting documents are produced when requested.
   b. The client made several large adjustments at or near year-end.
   c. The company has recently hired a new chief financial officer after the previous one retired.
   d. The company maintains several different petty cash funds.

LO 4-3

4.27   The likelihood that material misstatements may have entered the accounting system and not been detected and corrected by the client's internal control is referred to as
   a. Inherent risk.
   b. Control risk.
   c. Detection risk.
   d. Risk of material misstatement.

LO 4-1

4.28   The risk of material misstatement is composed of which audit risk components?
   a. Inherent risk and control risk.
   b. Control risk and detection risk.
   c. Inherent risk and detection risk.
   d. Inherent risk, control risk, and detection risk.

LO 4-1

4.29   The risk that the auditors' own testing procedures will lead to the decision that material misstatements do not exist in the financial statements when in fact such misstatements do exist is
   a. Audit risk.
   b. Inherent risk.
   c. Control risk.
   d. Detection risk.

LO 4-1

4.30   If tests of controls induce the audit team to change the assessed level of control risk for fixed assets from low to high and audit risk and inherent risk remain constant, the acceptable level of detection risk is most likely to
   a. Change from moderate to high.
   b. Change from low to moderate.
   c. Change from high to moderate.
   d. Be unchanged.

LO 4-2

4.31   Which of the following is a specific audit procedure that would be completed in response to a particular fraud risk in an account balance or class of transactions?
   a. Exercising more professional skepticism.
   b. Carefully avoiding conducting interviews with people in areas that are most susceptible to fraud.
   c. Performing procedures such as inventory observation and cash counts on a surprise or unannounced basis.
   d. Studying management's selection and application of accounting principles more carefully.

LO 4-4

4.32   Analytical procedures are generally used to produce evidence from
   a. Confirmations mailed directly to the auditors by client customers.
   b. Physical observation of inventories.
   c. Relationships among current financial balances and prior balances, forecasts, and nonfinancial data.
   d. Detailed examination of external, external-internal, and internal documents.

LO 4-4

4.33   Which of the following relationships between types of analytical procedures and sources of information are most logical?

Type of Analytical Procedure	Source of Information
a. Comparison of current account balances with prior periods	Physical production statistics
b. Comparison of current account balances with expected balances	Company's budgets and forecasts
c. Evaluation of current account balances with relation to predictable historical patterns	Published industry ratios
d. Evaluation of current account balances in relation to nonfinancial information	Company's own comparative financial statements

LO 4-4   4.34 Analytical procedures can be used in which of the following ways?

       a. As a means of overall review near the end of the audit.

       b. As "attention-directing" methods when planning an audit at the beginning.

       c. As substantive audit procedures to obtain evidence during an audit.

       d. All of the above.

LO 4-4   4.35 Analytical procedures used when planning an audit should concentrate on

       a. Weaknesses in the company's internal control activities.

       b. Predictability of account balances based on individual significant transactions.

       c. Management assertions in financial statements.

       d. Accounts and relationships that can represent specific potential problems and risks in the financial statements.

LO 4-4   4.36 When a company that sells its products with a positive gross profit increases its sales by 15 percent and its cost of goods sold by 7 percent, the cost of goods sold ratio will

       a. Increase.

       b. Decrease.

       c. Remain unchanged.

       d. Not be able to be determined with the information provided.

LO 4-3   4.37 Auditors are not responsible for accounting estimates with respect to

       a. Making the estimates.

       b. Determining the reasonableness of estimates.

       c. Determining that estimates are presented in conformity with GAAP.

       d. Determining that estimates are adequately disclosed in the financial statements.

LO 4-6   4.38 An audit strategy memorandum contains

       a. Specifications of auditing standards relevant to the financial statements being audited.

       b. Specifications of procedures the auditors believe appropriate for the financial statements under audit.

       c. Documentation of the assertions under audit, the evidence obtained, and the conclusions reached.

       d. Reconciliation of the account balances in the financial statements with the account balances in the client's general ledger.

LO 4-1   4.39 It is acceptable under generally accepted auditing standards for an audit team to

       a. Assess risk of material misstatement at high and achieve an acceptably low audit risk by performing extensive substantive tests.

       b. Assess control risk at zero and perform a minimum of substantive testing.

       c. Assess inherent risk at zero and perform a minimum of substantive testing.

       d. Decide that audit risk can be high.

LO 4-5   4.40 Under the Private Securities Litigation Reform Act (the act), independent auditors are required to first

       a. Report in writing all instances of noncompliance with the act to the client's board of directors.

       b. Report to the SEC all instances of noncompliance with the act they believe have a material effect on financial statements if the board of directors does not first report to the SEC.

       c. Report clearly inconsequential noncompliance with the act to the audit committee of the client's board of directors.

       d. Resign from the audit engagement and report the instances of noncompliance with the act to the SEC.

LO 4-3   4.41 When evaluating whether accounting estimates made by management are reasonable, auditors would be most interested in which of the following?

       a. Key factors that are consistent with prior periods.

       b. Assumptions that are similar to industry guidelines.

    c. Measurements that are objective and not susceptible to bias.

    d. Evidence of a conservative systematic bias.

LO 4-3

4.42 An audit committee is

    a. Composed of internal auditors.

    b. Composed of members of the audit team.

    c. Composed of members of a company's board of directors who are not involved in the day-to-day operations of the company.

    d. A committee composed of persons not associating in any way with the client or the board of directors.

LO 4-5

4.43 When auditors become aware of noncompliance with a law or regulation committed by client personnel, the primary reason that the auditors should obtain a better understanding of the nature of the act is to

    a. Recommend remedial actions to the audit committee.

    b. Evaluate the effect of the noncompliance on the financial statements.

    c. Determine whether to contact law enforcement officials.

    d. Determine whether other similar acts could have occurred.

LO 4-5

4.44 Which of the following statements best describes auditors' responsibility for detecting a client's noncompliance with a law or regulation?

    a. The responsibility for detecting noncompliance exactly parallels the responsibility for errors and fraud.

    b. Auditors must design tests to detect all material noncompliance that indirectly affect the financial statements.

    c. Auditors must design tests to obtain reasonable assurance that all noncompliance with direct material financial statement effects is detected.

    d. Auditors must design tests to detect all noncompliance that directly affects the financial statements.

LO 4-4

4.45 Auditors perform analytical procedures in the planning stage of an audit for the purpose of

    a. Deciding the matters to cover in an engagement letter.

    b. Identifying unusual conditions that deserve more auditing effort.

    c. Determining which of the financial statement assertions are the most important for the client's financial statements.

    d. Determining the nature, timing, and extent of further audit procedures for auditing the inventory.

LO 4-4

4.46 A primary objective of analytical procedures used in the final review stage of an audit is to

    a. Identify account balances that represent specific risks relevant to the audit.

    b. Gather evidence from tests of details to corroborate financial statement assertions.

    c. Detect fraud that may cause the financial statements to be misstated.

    d. Assist the auditor in evaluating the overall financial statement presentation.

(AICPA adapted)

LO 4-4

4.47 An auditor's analytical procedures indicate a lower than expected return on an equity method investment. This situation most likely could have been caused by

    a. An error in recording amortization of the excess of the investor's cost over the investment's underlying book value.

    b. The investee's decision to reduce cash dividends declared per share of its common stock.

    c. An error in recording the unrealized gain from an increase in the fair value of available-for sale securities in the income account for trading securities.

    d. A substantial fluctuation in the price of the investee's common stock on a national stock exchange.

(AICPA adapted)

LO 4-4
4.48 Which of the following risk types increase when an auditor performs substantive analytical audit procedures for financial statement accounts at an interim date?
    a. Inherent
    b. Control
    c. Detection
    d. Sampling

                       (AICPA adapted)

LO 4-3
4.49 Which of the following matters relating to an entity's operations would an auditor most likely consider as an inherent risk factor in planning an audit?
    a. The entity's fiscal year ends on June 30.
    b. The entity enters into significant derivative transactions as hedges.
    c. The entity's financial statements are generated at an outside service center.
    d. The entity's financial data is available only in computer-readable form.

                       (AICPA adapted)

LO 4-2
4.50 What is the primary objective of the fraud brainstorming session?
    a. Determine audit risk and materiality.
    b. Identify whether analytical procedures should be applied to the revenue accounts.
    c. Assess the potential for material misstatement due to fraud.
    d. Determine whether the planned procedures in the audit plan will satisfy the general audit objectives.

                       (AICPA adapted)

Exercises and Problems

 All applicable Exercises and Problems are available with *Connect*.

LO 4-4
4.51 **Analytical Procedures and Interest Expense.** Weyman Z. Wannamaker is the chief financial officer of Cogburn Company. He prides himself on being able to manage the company's cash resources to minimize the interest expense. Consequently, on the second business day of each month, Weyman pays down or draws cash on Cogburn's revolving line of credit at First National Bank in accordance with his cash requirements forecast.

    You are the auditor. You find the information on this line of credit in the following table. You inquired at First National Bank and learned that Cogburn Company's line of credit agreement specifies payment on the first day of each month for the interest due on the previous month's outstanding balance at the rate of "prime plus 1.5 percent." The bank gave you a report that showed the prime rate of interest was 8.5 percent for the first six months of the year and 8.0 percent for the last six months.

Cogburn Company Line of Credit Balance	
Date	Balance
Jan 1	$150,000
Feb 1	200,000
Mar 1	200,000
Apr 1	225,000
May 1	285,000
Jun 1	375,000
Jul 1	375,000
Aug 1	430,000
Sep 1	290,000
Oct 1	210,000
Nov 1	172,000
Dec 1	95,000

Required:

a. Prepare an audit estimate of the amount of interest expense you expect to find as the balance of the interest expense account related to these notes payable.

b. Which of the types of analytical procedures did you use to determine this estimate?

c. Suppose that you find that the interest expense account shows expense of $23,650 related to these notes. What could account for this difference?

d. Suppose that you find that the interest expense account shows expense of $24,400 related to these notes. What could account for this difference?

e. Suppose that you find that the interest expense account shows expense of $25,200 related to these notes. What could account for this difference?

LO 4-3 4.52 **Appropriateness of Evidence and Related Parties.** Johnson & Company, CPAs, audited Guaranteed Savings & Loan Company. M. Johnson had the assignment of evaluating the collectability of real estate loans. Johnson was working on two particular loans: (1) a $4 million loan secured by Smith Street Apartments and (2) a $5.5 million construction loan on Baker Street Apartments now being built. The appraisals performed by Guaranteed Appraisal Partners Inc. showed values in excess of the loan amounts. On inquiry, Bumpus, the S&L vice president for loan acquisition, stated, "I know the Smith Street loan is good because I myself own 40 percent of the partnership that owns the property and is obligated on the loan."

Johnson then wrote in the audit documentation: (1) the Smith Street loan appears collectible as Bumpus personally attested to knowledge of the collectability as a major owner in the partnership obligated on the loan; (2) the Baker Street loan is assumed to be collectible because it is new and construction is still in progress; and (3) the appraised values all exceed the loan amounts.

Required:

a. Do you perceive any problems with related-party involvement in the evidence used by Johnson? Explain.

b. Do you perceive any problems with Johnson's reasoning or the appropriateness of evidence used in that reasoning?

LO 4-3 4.53 **Risk of Misstatement in Various Accounts.** An auditor must identify the relevant assertions about each significant financial statement account and disclosure and then gather evidence to conclude whether a material misstatement exists for each assertion. The nature of each financial statement account and disclosure contributes to the likelihood that a material misstatement exists.

a. In general, which accounts are most susceptible to overstatement? To understatement?

b. Why do you think a company could permit asset accounts to be understated?

c. Why do you think a company could permit liability accounts to be overstated?

d. Which direction of misstatement is most likely: income overstatement or income understatement?

LO 4-3 4.54 **Analysis of Accounting Estimates.** Oak Industries, a manufacturer of radio and cable TV equipment and an operator of subscription TV systems, had a multitude of problems. Subscription services in a market area, for which $12 million of cost had been deferred, were being terminated, and the customers were not paying on time ($4 million receivables in doubt). The chances are 50-50 that the business will survive another two years.

An electronic part turned out to have defects that needed correction. Warranty expenses are estimated to range from $2 million to $6 million. The inventory of this part ($10 million) is obsolete, but $1 million can be recovered in salvage, or the parts in inventory can be rebuilt at a cost of $2 million. (The selling price of the inventory on hand would then be $8 million, with 20 percent of the selling price required to market and ship the products, and the normal profit is expected to be 5 percent of the selling price.) If the inventory were scrapped, the company would manufacture a replacement inventory at a cost of $6 million, excluding marketing and shipping costs and normal profit.

The company has defaulted on completion of a military contract, and the government is claiming a $2 million refund. Company attorneys think the dispute might be settled for as little as $1 million.

The auditors had previously determined that an overstatement of income before taxes of $7 million would be material to the financial statements. These items were the only ones left for audit decisions about possible adjustment. Management has presented the following analysis for the determination of loss recognition:

Write off deferred subscription costs	$ 3,000,000
Provide allowance for bad debts	4,000,000
Provide for expected warranty expense	2,000,000
Lower-of-cost-or-market inventory write-down	2,000,000
Loss on government contract refund	????????

Required:

Prepare your own analysis of the amount of adjustment to the financial statements. Assume that none of these estimates have been recorded yet, and give the adjusting entry you would recommend. Give any supplementary explanations you believe necessary to support your recommendation.

LO 4-4

4.55 **Horizontal and Vertical Analysis.** *Horizontal analysis* refers to changes of financial statement numbers and ratios across two or more years. *Vertical analysis* refers to financial statement amounts expressed each year as proportions of a base such as sales for the income-statement accounts and total assets for the balance-sheet accounts. Exhibit 4.55.1 contains Retail Company's prior-year (audited) and current-year (unaudited) financial statements, along with amounts and percentages of change from year to year (horizontal analysis) and common-size percentages (vertical analysis). Exhibit 4.55.2 contains selected financial ratios based on these financial statements. Analysis of these data can enable auditors to discern relationships that raise questions about misleading financial statements.

EXHIBIT 4.55.1 Retail Company

	Prior Year (Audited)		Current Year (Unaudited)		Change	
	Balance	Common Size	Balance	Common Size	Amount	Percent
Assets:						
Cash	$ 600,000	14.78%	$ 484,000	9.69%	$ (116,000)	−19.33%
Accounts receivable	500,000	12.32	400,000	8.01	(100,000)	−20.00
Allowance doubt. accts.	(40,000)	−0.99	(30,000)	−0.60	10,000	−25.00
Inventory	1,500,000	36.95	1,940,000	38.85	440,000	29.33
Total current assets	2,560,000	63.05	2,794,000	55.95	234,000	9.14
Fixed assets	3,000,000	73.89	4,000,000	80.10	1,000,000	33.33
Accum. depreciation	(1,500,000)	−36.95	(1,800,000)	−36.04	(300,000)	20.00
Total assets	$4,060,000	100.00%	$4,994,000	100.00%	$ 934,000	23.00%
Liabilities and equity:						
Accounts payable	$ 450,000	11.08%	$ 600,000	12.01%	$ 150,000	33.33%
Bank loans, 11%	0	0.00	750,000	15.02	750,000	NA
Accrued interest	50,000	1.23	40,000	0.80	(10,000)	−20.00
Accruals and other	60,000	1.48	10,000	0.20	(50,000)	−83.33
Total current liab.	560,000	13.79	1,400,000	28.03	840,000	150.00
Long-term debt, 10%	500,000	12.32	400,000	8.01	(100,000)	−20.00
Total liabilities	1,060,000	26.11	1,800,000	36.04	740,000	69.81
Capital stock	2,000,000	49.26	2,000,000	40.05	0	0
Retained earnings	1,000,000	24.63	1,194,000	23.91	194,000	19.40
Total liabilities and equity	$4,060,000	100.00%	$4,994,000	100.00%	934,000	23.00%
Statement of operations:						
Sales (net)	$9,000,000	100.00%	$8,100,000	100.00%	$ (900,000)	−10.00%
Cost of goods sold	6,296,000	69.96	5,265,000	65.00	(1,031,000)	−16.38
Gross margin	2,704,000	30.04	2,835,000	35.00	131,000	4.84
General expense	2,044,000	22.7	2,005,000	24.75	(39,000)	−1.91
Depreciation	300,000	3.33	300,000	3.70	0	0
Operating income	360,000	4.00	530,000	6.54	170,000	47.22
Interest expense	50,000	0.56	40,000	0.49	(10,000)	−20.00
Income taxes (40%)	124,000	1.38	196,000	2.42	72,000	58.06
Net income	$ 186,000	2.07%	$ 294,000	3.63%	$ 108,000	58.06%

"NA" means not applicable.

EXHIBIT 4.55.2
Retail Company

	Prior Year (audited)	Current Year (unaudited)	Percent Change
Balance-sheet ratios:			
Current ratio	4.57	2.0	−56.34%
Days' sales in receivables	18.40	16.44	−10.63
Doubtful accounts ratio	0.08	0.08	−6.25
Days' sales in inventory	85.77	132.65	54.66
Debt/equity ratio	0.35	0.56	40.89
Operations ratios:			
Receivables turnover	19.57	21.89	11.89
Inventory turnover	4.20	2.71	−35.34
Cost of goods sold/sales	69.96%	65.00%	−7.08
Gross margin %	30.04%	35.00%	16.49
Return on equity	6.61%	9.80%	48.26

Required:

Study the data in Exhibits 4.55.1 and 4.55.2. Write a memorandum identifying and explaining potential problem areas where misstatements in the current-year financial statements could exist. Additional information about Retail Company is as follows:

- The new bank loan, obtained on July 1 of the current year, requires maintenance of a 2:1 current ratio.
- Principal of $100,000 plus interest on the 10 percent long-term note obtained several years ago in the original amount of $800,000 is due each January 1.
- The company has never paid dividends on its common stock and has no plans for a dividend.

LO 4-3

4.56 **Analysis and Judgment.** As part of your regular year-end audit of a public client, you must estimate the probability of success of its proposed new product line. The client has experienced financial difficulty during the last few years and, in your judgment, a successful introduction of the new product line is necessary for the client to remain a going concern.

Five elements are necessary for the successful introduction of the product: (1) successful labor negotiations before the strike deadline between the construction firms contracted to build the necessary addition to the present plant and the building trades unions, (2) successful defense of patent rights, (3) product approval by the Food and Drug Administration (FDA), (4) successful negotiation of a long-term raw material contract with a foreign supplier, and (5) successful conclusion of distribution contract talks with a large national retail distributor.

In view of the circumstances, you contact experts who have provided your public accounting firm with reliable estimates in the past. The labor relations expert estimates that there is an 80 percent chance of successfully concluding labor negotiations. Legal counsel advises that there is a 90 percent chance of successfully defending patent rights. The expert on FDA product approvals estimates a 95 percent chance of new product approval. The experts in the remaining two areas estimate the probability of successfully resolving (1) the raw materials contract and (2) the distribution contract talks to be 90 percent in each case. Assume that these estimates are reliable.

Required:

What is your assessment of the probability of successful product introduction? (*Hint:* You can assume that each of the five elements is independent of the others.)

LO 4-4

4.57 **Analytical Procedures.** Kelly Griffin, an audit manager, had begun preliminary analytical procedures of selected statistics related to the Majestic Hotel. Her objective was to obtain an understanding of the hotel's business in order to draft a preliminary audit plan. She wanted to see whether she could detect any troublesome areas or questionable accounts that could require special audit attention. Unfortunately, Griffin caught the flu and was hospitalized. From her sickbed, she sent you the schedule she had prepared (Exhibit 4.57.1) and has asked you to write a memorandum identifying areas of potential misstatement or other matters that the preliminary audit plan should cover.

EXHIBIT 4.57.1
Analytical Procedure Documentation

	Majestic (percent)	Industry (percent)
Sales:		
Rooms	60.4%	63.9%
Food and beverage	35.7	32.2
Other	3.9	3.9
Costs:		
Rooms department	15.2	17.3
Food and beverage	34.0	27.2
Administrative and general	8.0	8.9
Management fee	3.3	1.1
Advertising	2.7	3.2
Real estate taxes	3.5	3.2
Utilities, repairs, maintenance	15.9	13.7
Profit per sales dollar	17.4	25.4
Rooms dept. ratios to room sales dollars:		
Salaries and wages	18.9	15.7
Laundry	1.1	3.7
Other	5.3	7.6
Profit per rooms sales dollar	74.8	73.0
Food/beverage (F/B) ratios to F/B sales dollars:		
Cost of food sold	42.1	37.0
Food gross profit	57.9	63.0
Cost of beverages sold	43.6	29.5
Beverages gross profit	56.4	70.5
Combined gross profit	57.7	64.6
Salaries and wages	39.6	32.8
Music and entertainment	—	2.7
Other	13.4	13.8
Profit per F/B sales dollar	4.7	15.3
Average annual percent of rooms occupied	62.6	68.1
Average room rate per day	$160	$120
Number of rooms available per day	200	148

Required:
Write a memorandum describing Majestic's operating characteristics compared to the industry average insofar as you can tell from the statistics. Do these analytical procedures identify any areas that could represent potential misstatements in the audit?

LO 4-4

4.58 **Preliminary Analytical Procedures.** Dunder-Mifflin Inc. wanted to expand its manufacturing and sales facilities. The company applied for a loan from First Bank, presenting the prior-year audited financial statements and the forecast for the current year shown in Exhibit 4.58.1. (Dunder-Mifflin Inc.'s fiscal year-end is December 31.) The bank was impressed with the business prospects and granted a $1,750,000 loan at 8 percent interest to finance working capital and the new facilities that were placed in service July 1 of the current year. Because Dunder-Mifflin Inc. planned to issue stock for permanent financing, the bank made the loan due on December 31 of the following year. Interest is payable each calendar quarter on October 1 of the current year and January 1, April 1, July 1, October 1 of the following year.

**EXHIBIT 4.58.1
Dunder-Mifflin Inc.**

	Prior Year (audited)	Forecast	Current Year (unaudited)
Revenue and Expense:			
Sales (net)	$9,000,000	$9,900,000	$ 9,720,000
Cost of goods sold	6,296,000	6,926,000	7,000,000
Gross margin	2,704,000	2,974,000	2,720,000
General expense	2,044,000	2,000,000	2,003,000
Depreciation	300,000	334,000	334,000
Operating income	360,000	640,000	383,000
Interest expense	60,000	110,000	75,000
Income taxes (40%)	120,000	212,000	123,200
Net income	180,000	318,000	184,800
Assets:			
Cash	600,000	880,000	690,800
Accounts receivable	500,000	600,000	900,000
Allowance for doubtful accounts	(40,000)	(48,000)	(90,000)
Inventory	1,500,000	1,500,000	1,350,000
Total current assets	2,560,000	2,932,000	2,850,800
Fixed assets	3,000,000	4,700,000	4,500,000
Accumulated depreciation	(1,500,000)	(1,834,000)	(1,834,000)
Total assets	$ 4,060,000	$ 5,798,000	$ 5,516,800
Liabilities and Equity:			
Accounts payable	$ 450,000	$ 450,000	$ 330,000
Bank loans, 8%	0	1,750,000	1,750,000
Accrued interest	60,000	40,000	40,000
Accruals and other	50,000	60,000	32,000
Total current liabilities	$ 560,000	$ 2,300,000	$ 2,152,000
Long-term debt, 10%	600,000	400,000	400,000
Total liabilities	$ 1,160,000	$ 2,700,000	$ 2,552,000
Capital stock	2,000,000	2,000,000	2,000,000
Retained earnings	900,000	1,098,000	964,800
Total liabilities and equity	$ 4,060,000	$ 5,798,000	$ 5,516,800

The auditors' interviews with Dunder-Mifflin Inc. management near the end of the current year produced the following information: The facilities did not cost as much as previously anticipated. However, sales were slow and the company granted more liberal return privilege terms than in the prior year. Officers wanted to generate significant income to impress First Bank and to preserve the company dividend ($120,000 paid in the prior year). The production managers had targeted inventory levels for a 4.0 turnover ratio and were largely successful even though prices of materials and supplies had risen about 2 percent relative to sales dollar volume. The new facilities were depreciated using a 25-year life from the date of opening.

Dunder-Mifflin Inc. has now produced the current-year financial statements (Exhibit 4.58.1, Current Year column) for the auditors' work on the current audit.

Required:

Perform preliminary analytical procedures on the current-year unaudited financial statements for the purpose of identifying accounts that could contain errors or frauds. Use your knowledge of Dunder-Mifflin Inc. and the forecast in Exhibit 4.58.1. Calculate comparative and common-size financial statements as well as relevant ratios. (Assume that the market value of the equity for the company is $3 million.) Once your calculations are complete, identify the accounts that could be misstated.

LO 4-1

4.59 **Audit Risk Model.** Audit risks for particular accounts and disclosures can be conceptualized in the model: Audit risk (AR) = Inherent risk (IR) × Control risk (CR) × Detection risk (DR). Use this model as a framework for considering the following situations and deciding whether the auditor's conclusion is appropriate.

a. Paul, CPA, has participated in the audit of Tordik Cheese Company for five years, first as an assistant accountant and the last two years as the senior accountant. Paul has never seen an accounting adjustment recommended and believes the inherent risk must be zero.

b. Hill, CPA, has just (November 30) completed an exhaustive study and evaluation of the internal controls of Edward Foods Inc. (fiscal year ending December 31). Hill believes the control risk must be zero because no material errors could possibly slip through the many error-checking procedures and review layers that Edward used.

c. Fields, CPA, is lazy and does not like audit jobs in Philadelphia. On the audit of Philly Manufacturing Company, Fields decided to use substantive procedures to audit the year-end balances very thoroughly to the extent that the risk of failing to detect material errors and irregularities should be very low. Fields gave no thought to inherent risk and conducted only a very limited review of Philly's internal control system.

d. Shad, CPA, is nearing the end of a "dirty" audit of Allnight Protection Company. All of Allnight's accounting personnel resigned during the year and were replaced by inexperienced people. The comptroller resigned last month in disgust. The journals and ledgers were a mess because the one computer specialist was hospitalized for three months during the year. "Thankfully," Shad thought, "I've been able to do this audit in less time than last year when everything was operating smoothly."

(AICPA adapted)

LO 4-3

4.60 **Auditing an Accounting Estimate.** Suppose management estimated the market valuation of some obsolete inventory at $99,000; this inventory was recorded at $120,000, which resulted in recognizing a loss of $21,000. The auditors obtained the following information: The inventory in question could be sold for an amount between $78,000 and $92,000. The costs of advertising and shipping could range from $5,000 to $7,000.

Required:

a. Would you propose an audit adjustment to the management estimate? Prepare the appropriate accounting entry.

b. If management's estimate of inventory market (lower than cost) had been $80,000, would you propose an audit adjustment? Prepare the appropriate accounting entry.

LO 4-1

4.61 **Risk Assessment.** This question consists of a number of items pertaining to an auditor's risk analysis for a company. Your task is to tell how each item affects overall audit risk—that is, the probability of issuing an unmodified audit report on materially misleading financial statements.

Bond, CPA, is considering audit risk at the financial statement level in planning the audit of Toxic Waste Disposal (TWD) Company's financial statements for the year ended December 31, 2023. TWD is a privately owned company that contracts with municipal governments to remove environmental wastes. Audit risk at the overall financial statement level is influenced by the risk of material misstatements, which may be indicated by a combination of factors related to management, the industry, and the company.

Required:

Based only on the following information, indicate whether each of the following factors (items 1 through 15) would most likely increase overall audit risk, decrease overall audit risk, or have no effect on overall audit risk. Discuss your reasoning.

Company Profile

1. This was the first year TWD operated at a profit since 2020 because the municipalities received increased federal and state funding for environmental purposes.
2. TWD's board of directors is controlled by Mead, the majority stockholder, who also acts as the chief executive officer.
3. The internal auditor reports to the controller, and the controller reports to Mead.
4. The accounting department has experienced a high rate of turnover of key personnel.
5. TWD's bank has a loan officer who meets regularly with TWD's CEO and controller to monitor TWD's financial performance.
6. TWD's employees are paid biweekly.
7. Bond has audited TWD for five years.

Recent Developments

8. During 2023, TWD changed the method of preparing its financial statements from the cash basis to the accrual basis under generally accepted accounting principles.
9. During 2023, TWD sold one-half of its controlling interest in United Equipment Leasing (UEL) Co. TWD retained significant interest in UEL.
10. During 2023, the state dropped litigation filed against TWD in 2019 alleging that the company discharged pollutants into state waterways. Loss contingency disclosures that TWD included in prior-years' financial statements are being removed for the 2023 financial statements.
11. During December 2023, TWD signed a contract to lease disposal equipment from an entity owned by Mead's parents. This related-party transaction is not disclosed in TWD's notes to its 2023 financial statements.
12. During December 2023, TWD completed a barter transaction with a municipality. TWD removed waste from a municipally owned site and acquired title to another contaminated site at below-market price. TWD intends to service this new site in 2024.
13. During December 2023, TWD increased its casualty insurance coverage on several pieces of sophisticated machinery from historical cost to replacement cost.
14. Inquiries about the substantial increase in revenue that TWD recorded in the fourth quarter of 2023 disclosed a new policy. TWD guaranteed several municipalities that it would refund the federal and state funding paid to it if any municipality fails federal or state site cleanup inspection in 2024.
15. An initial public offering of TWD's stock is planned for late 2024.

LO 4-2

4.62 **Auditing Standards Review.** Management fraud (fraudulent financial reporting) is not the expected norm, but it happens from time to time. In the United States, several cases have been widely publicized. They happen when motives and opportunities overwhelm managerial integrity.

a. What distinguishes management fraud from a defalcation?
b. What are an auditor's responsibilities under auditing standards to detect management fraud?
c. What are some characteristics of management fraud that an audit team should consider to fulfill the responsibilities under auditing standards?
d. What factors might an audit team notice that should heighten the concern about the existence of management fraud?
e. Under what circumstances might an audit team have a duty to disclose management's frauds to parties other than the company's management and its board of directors?

(AICPA adapted)

LO 4-4

4.63 **Analytical Procedures: Ratio Relationships.** The following situations represent errors and frauds that could occur in financial statements.

Required:

State how the ratio in question would compare (higher, equal, or lower) to what the ratio should have been had the error or fraud not occurred.

a. The company recorded fictitious sales with credits to sales revenue accounts and debits to accounts receivable. Inventory was reduced, and cost of goods sold was increased for the profitable "sales." Is the current ratio higher than, equal to, or lower than what it should have been?

b. The company recorded cash disbursements by paying trade accounts payable but held the checks past the year-end date, meaning that the "disbursements" should not have been shown as credits to cash and debits to accounts payable. Is the current ratio higher than, equal to, or lower than what it should have been? Consider cases in which the current ratio before the improper "disbursement" recording was (1) higher than 1:1, (2) equal to 1:1, and (3) lower than 1:1.

c. The company uses a periodic inventory system for determining the balance-sheet amount of inventory at year-end. Very near the year-end, merchandise was received, placed in the stockroom, and counted, but the purchase transaction was neither recorded nor paid until the next month. What was the effect of this on inventory, cost of goods sold, gross profit, and net income? How were these ratios affected compared to what they would have been without the error: current ratio [remember three possible cases from part (b)], gross margin ratio, cost of goods sold ratio, inventory turnover, and receivables turnover?

d. The company is hesitant to write off customer accounts receivable even though the financial vice president makes entirely adequate provision for uncollectible amounts in the allowance for bad debts. The gross receivables and the allowance both contain amounts that should have been written off long ago. How are these ratios affected compared to what they would have been if the receivables had been properly written off: current ratio, days' sales in receivables, doubtful account ratio, receivables turnover, return on beginning equity, and working capital/total assets?

e. Since last year, the company has reorganized its lines of business and placed more emphasis on its traditional products while selling off some marginal businesses merged by the previous management. Total assets are 10 percent less than they were last year, but working capital has increased. Retained earnings remained the same because the disposals created no gains, and the net income after taxes is still near zero, which is the same as last year. Earnings before interest and taxes (EBIT) remained the same, a small positive EBIT. The total market value of the company's equity has not increased, but that is better than the declines of the past several years. Proceeds from the disposals have been used to retire long-term debt. Net sales have decreased 5 percent because the sales' decrease resulting from the disposals has not been overcome by increased sales of the traditional products. Is the discriminant Z-score of the current year higher or lower than the one of the prior year? (See Appendix 4A for the Z-score formula.)

LO 4-6

4.64 **Audit Strategy Memorandum.** The auditor should establish an overall audit strategy that sets the scope, timing, and direction of the audit and guides the development of the audit plan. In establishing the overall audit strategy, the auditor should develop and document an audit plan that includes a description of (a) the planned nature, timing, and extent of the risk assessment procedures, (b) the planned nature, timing, and extent of tests of controls and substantive procedures, and (c) other planned audit procedures that must be performed so that the engagement complies with auditing standards.

Required:

Select a public company and determine a significant risk that could affect its financial statements. (*Hint:* Go to the EDGAR database at www.sec.gov and select the company's form 10-K. The 10-K will have a list of risk factors the company faces.) Describe the risk and how it could affect the financial statements, including what assertions might be misstated. Prepare an audit strategy memorandum for the risk describing what controls the company might use to mitigate the risk, how you could test the controls, and what substantive procedures you might use to determine whether there is a misstatement. Because this is early in your auditing class, do not worry about specific procedures; just be creative and think about a general strategy an auditor might use.

LO 4-2

4.65 **Errors and Frauds.** Give an example of an error or fraud that would misstate financial statements to affect the accounts as follows, taking each case independently. (*Note:* "Overstate" means the account has a higher value than would be appropriate under GAAP and "understate" means it has a lower value.)

a. Overstate one asset; understate another asset.

b. Overstate an asset; overstate stockholders' equity.

c. Overstate an asset; overstate revenue.

d. Overstate an asset; understate an expense.

e. Overstate a liability; overstate an expense.

f. Understate an asset; overstate an expense.

g. Understate a liability; understate an expense.

LO 4-5

4.66 **Compliance with Laws and Regulations.** Audit standards distinguish auditors' responsibility for planning procedures for detecting noncompliance with laws and regulations having a direct effect on financial statements versus planning procedures for detecting noncompliance with laws and regulations that do not have a direct effect on financial statements.

Required:

a. What are the requirements for auditors to plan procedures to detect direct-effect compliance versus indirect-effect compliance?

b. For each of the following instances of noncompliance, explain why they are either direct-effect (D) or indirect-effect (I) noncompliance:

1. A manufacturer inflates expenses on its corporate tax return.

2. A retailer pays men more than women for performing the same job.

3. A coal mining company fails to place proper ventilation in its mines.

4. A military contractor inflates the overhead applied to a combat vehicle.

5. An insurance company fails to maintain required reserves for losses.

6. An exporter pays a bribe to a foreign government official so that government will buy its products.

7. A company backdates its executive stock options to lower the exercise price.

8. A company fails to fund its pension plan in accordance with ERISA.

LO 4-5

4.67 **Identifying Significant Accounts –** Auditors gather information from a variety of sources, including 10-K reports, to help assess risk and identify significant accounts and relevant assertions.

Required:

You are performing risk assessment procedures for Apple Inc. One source of information you will use to help assess risk and identify significant accounts is Apple's most recent 10-K filing. Go to the sec.gov website and search for Apple Inc.'s most recent 10-K filing. Read through the Item 1, Business, and Item 1A, Risk Factors, sections. Based off this discussion, what accounts do you believe might be susceptible to misstatement and why?

LO 4-4

4.68 **Preparing and Analyzing an Aging Schedule — Using IDEA.** For this exercise, your client, Bright IDEAs Inc., has provided you with a listing of sales invoices. To test whether the client appears to have a receivables collectability problem, the auditor must complete a series of related steps:

1. Import the client's database of sales invoices. You may have already completed this step in Chapter 3.

2. Perform an aging analysis by following the instructions in the IDEA Workbook.

Required Data and additional instructions available on *McGraw-Hill Connect.*

Required:

Complete the preceding steps and answer the following questions:

a. What percentage of customers have accounts that are aged greater than 90 days?

b. What percentage of customer balances are aged greater than 90 days?

c. What effects would the findings in parts (a) and (b) have on the auditor's assessment of the risk of material misstatement? What accounts and assertions are most likely influenced by these findings?

LO 4-4

4.69   **Summarizing Obsolete Inventory — Using IDEA.** For this exercise, your client, Bright IDEAs Inc., has provided you with a listing of inventory as of year end. To analyze the amount of obsolete inventory, as reported by the client, the auditor must complete a series of related steps:

1. Import the client's database of inventory on hand. You may have already completed this step in Chapter 3.

2. Summarize items identified as obsolete by the client by following the instructions in the IDEA Workbook.

Required Data and additional instructions available on *McGraw-Hill Connect*.

Complete the preceding steps and answer the following questions:

a. What percentage of the dollar amount of the client's inventory has been identified as obsolete?

b. What effects would the findings in part (a) have on the auditor's assessment of the risk of material misstatement? What accounts and assertions are most likely influenced by these findings?

LO 4-4

4.70   **Analyzing Profit Margins — Using IDEA.** For this exercise, your client, Bright IDEAs Inc., has provided you with a listing of inventory as of year end, which includes current selling prices. To test whether profit margins appear adequate to justify the inventory valuation provision, the auditor must complete a series of related steps:

1. Import the client's database of inventory on hand. You may have already completed this step in Chapter 3 or Exercise 4.69.

2. Create an analysis of selling price changes by following the instructions in the IDEA Workbook.

3. Create an analysis of profit margins by following the instructions in the IDEA Workbook.

Required Data and additional instructions available on *McGraw-Hill Connect*.

Required:

Complete the preceding steps and answer the following questions:

a. What percentage of inventory items have price movements in excess of 50%? How many of these items experienced price increases? How many experienced price decreases? Which direction of change would be most concerning to the auditor?

b. What percentage of items have negative profit margins?

c. What effects would the findings in part (a) and (b) have on the auditor's assessment of the risk of material misstatement? What accounts and assertions are most likely influenced by these findings?

Apollo Shoes

Preliminary Analytical Procedures

You are a recently promoted senior (in charge) auditor for Anderson, Olds, and Watershed and have been assigned to the engagement team of a new audit client, Apollo Shoes Inc. You have been asked to perform preliminary analytical procedures in an effort to help identify significant accounts and relevant assertions and assess risk of material misstatement. Detailed instructions for performing the preliminary analytical procedures, as well as working papers, can be found in *Connect*.

Apollo Shoes

Audit Risk Model

You are a recently promoted senior (in charge) auditor for Anderson, Olds, and Watershed and have been assigned to the engagement team of a new audit client, Apollo Shoes Inc. You have been asked to evaluate a set of facts to determine the relationship of each with inherent or control risk, in an effort to determine the impact on detection risk. Detailed instructions for performing the audit risk case, as well as working papers, can be found in *Connect*.

Appendix 4A

Selected Financial Ratios

Balance-Sheet Ratios	Formula*
Current ratio	$$\frac{\text{Current assets}}{\text{Current liabilities}}$$
Days' sales in receivables	$$\frac{\text{Ending net receivables}}{\text{Credit sales}/360}$$
Doubtful account ratio	$$\frac{\text{Allowance for doubtful accounts}}{\text{Ending gross receivables}}$$
Days' sales in inventory	$$\frac{\text{Ending inventory}}{\text{Cost of goods sold}/360}$$
Debt-to-equity ratio	$$\frac{\text{Current liabilities and long-term debt}}{\text{Stockholder equity}}$$

Operations Ratios	
Receivables turnover	$$\frac{\text{Credit sales}}{\text{Ending net receivables}}$$
Inventory turnover	$$\frac{\text{Cost of goods sold}}{\text{Ending inventory}}$$
Cost of goods sold ratio	$$\frac{\text{Cost of goods sold}}{\text{Net sales}}$$
Gross margin ratio	$$\frac{\text{Net sales} - \text{Cost of goods sold}}{\text{Net sales}}$$
Return on stockholder equity	$$\frac{\text{Net income}}{\text{Stockholder equity (beginning balance)}}$$

Financial Distress Ratios (Altman)

The discriminant Z-score is an index of a company's financial health. The higher the score, the healthier the company. The lower the score, the closer financial failure approaches. The score that predicts financial failure is a matter of dispute. Research suggests that companies with scores above 3.0 never go bankrupt. Generally, companies with scores below 1.0 experience financial difficulty of some kind. The score can be a negative number.

(X_1) Working capital/Total assets	$$\frac{\text{Current assets} - \text{Current liabilities}}{\text{Total assets}}$$
(X_2) Retained earnings/Total assets	$$\frac{\text{Retained earnings (ending)}}{\text{Total assets}}$$
(X_3) Earnings before interest and taxes/Total assets	$$\frac{\text{Net income} + \text{Interest expense} + \text{Income tax expense}}{\text{Total assets}}$$
(X_4) Market value of equity/Total debt	$$\frac{\text{Market value of common and preferred stock}}{\text{Current liabilities and long-term debt}}$$
(X_5) Net sales/Total assets	$$\frac{\text{Net sales}}{\text{Total assets}}$$
Discriminant Z-score (Altman)	$1.2 * X_1 + 1.4 * X_2 + 3.3 * X_3 + 0.6 * X_4 + 1.0 * X_5$

*These ratios are shown to be calculating using year-end rather than year-average numbers for balances such as accounts receivable and inventory. Other accounting and finance reference books could contain formulas using year-average numbers. As long as no dramatic changes have occurred during the year, the year-end numbers can have much audit relevance because they reflect the most current balance data. For comparative purposes, the ratios should be calculated on the same basis for all years being compared.

Appendix 4B

Sample Audit Memorandum

**INTEGRATED CARE HEALTH INSURANCE INC AUDIT
MEMORANDUM (ABRIDGED)**

OVERVIEW

Integrated Care Health Insurance Inc. (Integrated) offers a variety of valuable products and services ranging from medical, dental, and behavioral health coverage to life insurance and disability plans as well as management services for Medicaid plans. Purchasing health coverage ensures future security with respect to high and unexpected costs of health care for individuals, families, and businesses. Benefits offered by Integrated include not only coverage for medical expenses but access to a wide network of doctors, hospitals, and specialists.

PRODUCT PRICING

Integrated uses a special process to calculate premiums charged for services offered. The method involves pooling customers with similar characteristics into a single risk group based on age, gender, medical history, lifestyle, and other factors such as benefits desired, administration costs, and tax obligations. After Integrated pools customers into their respective risk groups, Integrated has the responsibility to balance projected future costs with premiums charged. The most important factor in determining financial success for Integrated is its ability to predict trends and future medical costs. Therefore, faulty forecasts can lead to huge risks and downfalls for Integrated if expectations fall short of actual results. Competing in an industry where new technology and medical breakthroughs are discovered almost daily means that sustaining profitability is an increasing concern.

GOVERNMENT INFLUENCES

Along with a great deal of risk being inherent in its business, Integrated operations are impacted by the U.S. economy and unemployment rate. Additionally, the health care reform legislation passed in 2023 has caused significant changes to many facets of the industry's operation. Given that the new legislation requires coverage for those who are currently uninsured, the insurance companies acquired millions of new customers virtually overnight. Health care reform is a constant source of debate in the government, therefore it is uncertain how future legislation will impact the industry.

CUSTOMERS, SUPPLIERS, AND COMPETITORS

Integrated's customers include employer groups, self-employed individuals, part-time and hourly workers, governmental organizations, labor groups, and immigrants. Although there are a considerable number of companies competing, experts have noted a trend that competition is virtually disappearing due to the domination of markets by only a few providers. In a study published by the American MedicalAssociation, 24 of 43 states have one or two insurers constituting a market share of a staggering 70 percent.[11] These statistics may suggest that there is essentially no competition in the market. However, 1,300 companies are competing in the health insurance industry, and Integrated faces significant competition in highly concentrated markets. In addition to the competition and governmental influences already present, Integrated is also facing competition from hospitals that play a pertinent role in determining the amounts billed for services provided.

[11]D. W. Emmons, J. R. Guardado, C. K. Kane, "Competition in Health Insurance: A Comprehensive Study of U.S. Markets, 2010 Update," American Medical Association.

RISK ASSESSMENT

The following analysis provides an overview of the identified risks and expected controls for Integrated for one accounting cycle.

REVENUE AND COLLECTION CYCLE

Risks

Due to the contract nature of the insurance industry, revenue recognition is not a high-risk area when compared to other industries. Integrated has set contracts with commercial organizations, individuals, and the government. Therefore, large fluctuations throughout the year do not typically occur. However, one area of significant risk involves the Medicare risk adjustment. The Centers for Medicare & Medicaid Services (CMS) determines Medicare and Medicaid premium payments employing a risk-based formula using coding provided by the insurance companies based on data from the diagnosis. Members with Medicare and Medicaid benefits associated with the health insurance entity are given a risk category based on their health conditions. However, because these contracts are preset for a year, patients' risk categories might fluctuate, causing an increase in needed payment from the CMS. Integrated must ensure that revenue is recognized properly by recording a risk adjustment for the difference between what CMS paid and what should have been paid based on the appropriate risk categories. CMS also performs audits known as *Risk Adjusted Data Validation (RADV) audits* to ensure CMS remits premium payments to insurance organizations appropriately.

Another area of significant risk around revenue recognition involves the Medicare Part D risk-sharing provision. With Medicare Part D, insurance entities contract with CMS for set premiums on an annual basis. The ultimate payment of total premiums, however, depends on certain thresholds that might require additional payment by CMS or reimbursement to CMS. A reconciliation (true-up) is performed after year-end to account for these differences. However, because this true-up process might occur six to nine months after year-end, Integrated must account for this process by recording receivables or payables that estimate these differences. Significant estimates are used to develop these adjustments and require the company to plan the audit procedures to provide reasonable assurance that these estimates do not include material misstatements.

Controls

The difficulty in predicting revenue adjustment amounts from these two programs concerns Integrated management's assertions of completeness, accuracy, valuation of financial statement accounts, and proper disclosure of required revenue recognition elements. To meet disclosure assertions, Integrated established a disclosure committee to determine what revenue-related disclosures should be made regarding Medicare and Medicaid. This committee meets prior to the release of each quarter's financial statements or as often as management requires. Valuation and accuracy assertions are met by requiring that qualified personnel utilize acceptable models commonly used in industry practice when estimating the amounts for the varying revenues. Appropriate supervisors review all estimates for accuracy and verify that estimates conform to the company's operational objectives.

AUDIT APPROACH

Due to the high-risk nature of the unique business and audit risks detailed here, an audit plan for Integrated must include both test of controls and substantive procedures to provide for the appropriate level of detection risk. As mentioned, significant estimates are included in the financial statements for almost every accounting cycle within the health insurance industry. The amount of management judgment needed to determine these estimates requires the use of extensive substantive testing to provide reasonable assurance that material misstatements do not exist within the financial statements. The following detailed audit plan provides guidance on the types of control testing and substantive testing that would provide reasonable assurance that material misstatements do not exist in relation to the risks outlined within this report.

AUDIT STRATEGY MEMORANDUM
Integrated Care Health Insurance Inc.

Overview

This audit strategy is intended to provide our responses to the risks identified for Integrated and generally detail the associated tests of controls and substantive procedures that will be required during the audit.

Risks

Revenue recognition related to participation in Medicare and Medicaid programs (Revenue and Collection Cycle)

Assertions	Tests of Controls	Substantive Procedures
Valuation or allocation	Test information technology and manual controls relative to calculation of revenues from Medicare and Medicaid contracts.	Reperform revenue calculations for a sampling of Medicare- and Medicaid-issued contracts.
	Confirm that management estimates for risk-sharing and risk-adjustment provisions (reviews include determining whether qualified personnel perform the estimates, making estimates conform to industry practices, and verifying that estimates are accurate).	Reperform estimates for risk-sharing and risk-adjustment provisions.
	Confirm that assumptions and methodologies for estimates of risk-sharing and risk-adjustment provisions are documented and approved by management.	Produce independent estimates for risk-sharing and risk-adjustment provisions.
	Obtain an understanding of assumptions and methodology of estimates for risk-sharing and risk-adjustment provisions.	
Presentation and disclosure	Confirm that a disclosure committee has been established.	Review disclosure committee meeting minutes
	Confirm that comparisons of actual and budgeted Medicare and Medicaid revenues are conducted by management and significant variances are monitored.	Review board of directors meeting minutes, agreements, budgets, and plans for Medicare and Medicaid revenues that should be included in financial statements.
		Test whether disclosures and classifications conform to accounting principles.

Source: Mark Fedewa, Emily O'Bryan, Amela Pajazetovic, and Susan Schmidt, "An Analysis of Business and Audit Risk for a Health Insurance Provider," unpublished working paper, University of Kentucky. February 28, 2011.

CHAPTER 5

Risk Assessment: Internal Control Evaluation

Adequate internal controls are the first line of defense in detecting and preventing material errors or fraud in financial reporting . . . when internal control deficiencies are left unaddressed, financial reporting quality can suffer.

As stated on January 29, 2019, by SEC Chief Accountant Wesley Bricker when commenting on the issuance of separate "cease and desist" orders against four public companies for failure to maintain proper internal controls. SEC (online source).

Professional Standards References

Topic	AU-C/ISA Section	AS Section
General Principles and Responsibilities of the Independent Auditor	200	1001, 1005, 1010, 1015
Audit Documentation	230	1215
Consideration of Fraud in a Financial Statement Audit	240	2401
Communications with Audit Committees	260	1301
Communications about Control Deficiencies in an Audit of Financial Statements	265	1305
Reporting on Whether a Previously Reported Material Weakness Continues to Exist	265	6115
Audit Planning	300	2101
Identifying and Assessing Risks of Material Misstatement	315	2110
Consideration of Materiality in Planning and Performing an Audit	320	2105
The Auditors' Responses to the Risks of Material Misstatement	330	2301
Audit Evidence	500	1105
Consideration of the Internal Audit Function	610	2605
Compliance Auditing Considerations in Audits of Recipients of Governmental Financial Assistance	935	6110

LEARNING OBJECTIVES

An important objective of the internal control system is to help ensure that the financial statement information being presented by an organization is credible and can be relied upon. Therefore, it is essential that an auditor take the time to understand whether an entity's internal control system has been designed and is operating effectively. In fact, the fundamental principles of auditing state that, to fulfill auditors' responsibility "[t]o obtain reasonable assurance . . . the auditor *identifies and assesses risks of material misstatement, whether due to fraud or error, based on an understanding of the entity and its environment, including the entity's internal control*" [emphasis added].

Beyond its importance in the production of reliable financial statement information, the establishment of an internal control system is an important management function to help ensure the effectiveness and efficiency of operations and the entity's compliance with laws and regulations. As a result, understanding the elements of internal control and how to evaluate their effectiveness is an important skill that every accountant should have. Even if you do not work as an auditor, you probably will have responsibility for internal controls at some point in your accounting career.

This chapter presents a general introduction to the theory and definitions you will find useful for internal control evaluation and control risk assessment. The chapter uses the payroll cycle to provide specific examples of internal control activities and related audit procedures.

Your objectives are to be able to

LO 5-1   Define and describe what is meant by *internal control*.

LO 5-2   Distinguish between the responsibilities of management and auditors regarding an entity's internal control.

LO 5-3   Define and describe the five basic components of internal control and specify some of their characteristics.

LO 5-4   Explain the process the audit team uses to assess control risk; understand its impact on the risk of material misstatement; and, ultimately, know how it affects the nature, timing, and extent of further audit procedures to be performed on the audit.

LO 5-5   Explain the communication of internal control deficiencies to those charged with governance, such as the audit committee and other key management personnel.

INTRODUCTION

On January 29, 2019, the SEC issued "cease and desist" orders against four issuers: **Lifeway Foods Inc., Digital Turbine Inc., CytoDyn Inc.,** and **Grupo Simec S.A.B de C.V.** According to the SEC's orders, each company had acknowledged that their internal control systems had material weaknesses. However, after providing each of these companies with as many as 10 years to address their problems, the SEC finally had enough and decided to take action.

As stated in their "cease and desist" orders, "disclosure of material weaknesses is not enough without meaningful remediation. We are committed to holding corporations accountable for failing to timely remediate material weaknesses."[1] It seems clear that the substantial penalties levied by the SEC send a message to all issuers that if your internal control system has a material weakness, the management team had better take remedial action to fix any problems that exist. Because, if they do not, the SEC will take action.

Why the emphasis on internal controls by the SEC? To start, maintaining a system of internal controls for the accounting system is required under the law by the Securities and Exchange Act of 1934 for public entities, also known as **issuers**. In addition, Section 404 of the Sarbanes-Oxley Act of 2002 requires the management team of issuers to assess the effectiveness of its own system of internal control and then have an independent CPA firm assess the effectiveness of its internal control system during its annual audit.

By holding both management and the auditor responsible for evaluating the effectiveness of the internal control system, the Act appears to have imposed the necessary oversight

---

[1]*"SEC Charges Four Public Companies With Longstanding ICFR Failures,"* Release No. 2019-6, SEC, January 29, 2019.

to improve the accuracy and reliability of the financial statements reported by the entity. Indeed, the Act places an emphasis on the internal control system as an important mechanism to prevent or detect material misstatements in the financial statements due to fraud. Simply stated, the intense scrutiny on both the design and operating effectiveness of internal control systems over financial reporting improves the reliability of the financial statements which clearly benefits the capital markets, as shown in the following auditing insight.

AUDITING INSIGHT Was The Tweet Worth $20 Million?

Elon Musk, the billionaire co-founder of **Tesla Inc.,** will pay a $20 million fine to the SEC for a tweet made on August 7, 2018, which indicated that he had secured financing to take the company private, causing an increase of over six percent in the company's stock price.

The SEC's complaint against Tesla relates to the lack of controls or procedures in place as to whether Musk's tweets contained information required in SEC disclosures. The SEC also contends that Tesla did not have sufficient processes in place to determine whether the tweets were accurate or complete.

Source: "Elon Musk Settles *SEC* Fraud Charges; Tesla Charged With and Resolves Securities Law Charge," Release No. 2018-226, SEC, September 29, 2018.

In this chapter, we explore the process followed by auditors to gain an understanding of and then evaluate the internal control system on audits of issuers and nonissuers. There are a number of additional considerations and steps that need to be taken by auditors when completing an audit of the internal control system for issuers as required by Section 404 of the Sarbanes-Oxley Act of 2002. These matters are covered in detail in Module I.

DEFINITION OF INTERNAL CONTROL

LO 5-1
Define and describe what is meant by *internal control*.

For purposes of the financial statement auditing process, as you will soon learn in this chapter, if the system of internal control is properly designed and is also operating effectively, it should be producing reliable financial statements. The most important goal of the system should be to produce reliable financial statements, and as long as the system is operating effectively, auditors should be able to rely on the internal control system to reduce substantive testing procedures. Of course, audit professionals need to follow a required process in order to reach this conclusion, which we cover in this chapter.

Internal Control Effectiveness

The *Committee of Sponsoring Organizations* (COSO) is responsible for defining what is meant by internal control effectiveness. COSO is comprised of leaders in the auditing profession from the Financial Executives Institute, the American Accounting Association, the Institute of Internal Auditors, the Institute of Management Accountants, and the American Institute of Certified Public Accountants. It publishes an integrated framework which is used by management teams and auditors as the benchmark to assess internal control effectiveness.[2] The resulting report, known as the COSO framework, was last updated in 2013 and defined **internal control** as follows:

> Internal control is a process, effected by an entity's board of directors, management and other personnel, designed to provide reasonable assurance regarding the achievement of objectives in the following three categories:
> - Reliability of financial reporting.
> - Effectiveness and efficiency of operations.
> - Compliance with applicable laws and regulations.

Stated differently, internal control is a set of policies and procedures designed to achieve *management objectives* in three different categories. In the *financial reporting category,*

[2]COSO, "Enterprise Risk Management—Integrated Framework Executive Summary," September 2004, New York: AICPA, p. 2.: COSO. "Enterprise Risk Management—Integrating with Strategy and Performance," June 2017, New York: AICPA.

the management objectives are related to producing reliable financial reports and safeguarding assets. In the *operations category,* some examples of management objectives are maintaining a good business reputation, ensuring a positive return on investment, increasing market share, promoting new product innovation, and using assets effectively and efficiently. In the *compliance category,* the broad management objective is to comply with laws and regulations that affect the entity. It is important to point out that external auditors are *primarily* concerned with a client's internal control system as it relates to the financial reporting category.

The updated framework acknowledges the widespread use of the COSO framework and provides enhancements that were specifically designed to make it easier to be used as a benchmark for evaluating internal control effectiveness by auditors across the world. We believe that the framework can be very helpful as students learn about the underlying concepts and principles of an effective internal control system. As a result of its importance, throughout this chapter we will highlight how the COSO framework has impacted the auditor's role in evaluating a client's internal control system during the audit.

Limitations of Internal Control

Internal control provides *reasonable* assurance, not *absolute* assurance, that management's objectives will be achieved. Because people operate the controls, breakdowns can occur. Internal control can help prevent and detect many errors, but it cannot guarantee that they will never happen. In that spirit, several limitations to internal control systems prevent management from obtaining complete assurance that controls are absolutely effective:

- *Human error* due to mistakes in judgment, fatigue, and carelessness can still occur.
- Although controls are implemented to prevent and detect errors, *deliberate circumvention* by people in the system can still occur. Consider the following:
  - Because most internal controls are directed at lower-level employees, *management override* can occur. For example, it is often possible for management to override controls by force of authority (i.e., if the CEO says to do something, most employees will).
  - Although separation of duties can be extremely effective in an internal control system, *collusion* among people who are supposed to act independently can lead to a failure in the achievement of relevant internal control objectives.

In addition, one other limitation deserves special consideration. That is, an internal control system is always subject to cost–benefit considerations. Internal control could be made perfect, or nearly so, but at great expense. For example, at the lowest level of control, a company's inventory could be left completely unlocked and unguarded (i.e., with no controls at all); next, a fence could be used; locks could be installed; lighting could be used all night; television monitors could be put in place; or at the highest level of control, armed guards could be hired. Each of these successive safeguards costs additional money (as does extensive supervision of clerical personnel in an office). At some point, the cost of protecting the inventory from theft (or the cost of supervisors catching every clerical error) exceeds the benefit of the internal control activity. In the professional auditing standards, the concept of **reasonable assurance** recognizes that the costs of controls should not exceed the benefits that are expected from the controls. Hence, an entity can decide that certain controls are too costly considering the risk of loss that can occur.

Finally, it is important for students to remember that internal control is a *process,* a means for management to achieve its objectives, not an end in itself. It is also dynamic, operating every day within an entity's operating structure, which can and does evolve as the entity and its operating environment change over time.

✓ REVIEW CHECKPOINTS

5.1 What is the *Committee of Sponsoring Organizations* (COSO)? Briefly describe the purpose of the COSO framework of internal control effectiveness.

5.2 What are the three management objectives of an internal control system according to the COSO report? Which of the three is most important to auditors?

5.3 What is the concept of reasonable assurance as it relates to an internal control system? What are the key limitations of an internal control system?

MANAGEMENT VERSUS AUDITORS' RESPONSIBILITY FOR INTERNAL CONTROL

LO 5-2
Distinguish between the responsibilities of management and auditors regarding an entity's internal control.

Management's Internal Control Responsibilities

The management team is responsible for establishing and maintaining an internal control system. To accomplish this objective, management is responsible for assessing the full range of risks it would like to control, including financial reporting risks. Such a risk assessment process generally leads to the establishment of important objectives for the internal control system. For example, management must make sure that transactions are properly authorized, and that the accounting records and other system-generated reports are complete and accurate. In addition, management must ensure the security of their assets, including their data. It is also important that an appropriate control environment is established which allows for the implementation of appropriate internal control activities, appropriate information and communication channels, and proper monitoring of the operation of all internal control activities.

Management is also responsible for maintaining documentation that is sufficient to provide evidence that the system of internal control has been designed and is operating effectively. For example, such documentation needs to provide evidence regarding how important internal control decisions were considered and ultimately how the final decisions were reached for key professional judgments. Finally, the documentation must be robust enough to allow auditors to gain an understanding of the internal control system and to determine whether the client's internal control system can be relied upon when conducting their overall financial statement audit.

Auditors' Internal Control Responsibilities

Auditors are required to gain an understanding of the client's internal control system on each audit. They are also required to document that understanding in the audit documentation. When gaining an understanding of the client's internal control system, auditors will typically preliminarily assess the risk of material misstatement (RMM) for each relevant assertion. The assessment of RMM at the assertion level is completed for all financial statement audits in order to give the audit team a basis for planning the audit and determining the *nature, timing,* and *extent* of further audit procedures to be conducted for the financial statement audit. RMM is composed of *inherent risk* and *control risk.* The assessment of inherent risk, the susceptibility of an account to misstatement, was the focus of Chapter 4; this chapter focuses on control risk assessment.

Recall that **control risk** is the probability that an entity's controls will fail to prevent or detect material misstatements due to errors or frauds that would otherwise have entered the system. The audit team assesses control risk to complete the preliminary determination of RMM for each relevant assertion identified in the audit plan; the higher the assessment of control risk, the higher the assessment of RMM. Most audit teams express their control risk assessment decision with descriptive terminology (e.g., high, moderate, low), which recognizes the imprecise nature of evaluating risk.

An audit team's assessment of control risk as high implies that the controls are not effective at preventing or detecting material misstatements and could not be relied upon by the audit team. In this situation, the audit team would likely use substantive tests of details designed to obtain evidence (*nature*) at or near the entity's fiscal year-end (*timing*) with large sample sizes (*extent*).

On the other hand, an audit team's assessment of control risk as low implies that the controls are effective at preventing or detecting material misstatements and could possibly be relied upon by the audit team. In this situation, the audit team might be able to use less time-consuming substantive analytical procedures to obtain evidence (*nature*) at an interim date before the entity's fiscal year-end (*timing*) with much smaller sample sizes (*extent*).

Of course, an audit team might assess control risk as moderate (between low and high) and adjust the substantive procedures accordingly in order to obtain enough evidence to mitigate the risk of material misstatement to a low level for the relevant assertion being tested. Ultimately, the final decision about nature, timing, and extent of testing is a matter of professional judgment for the audit team. Exhibit 5.1 illustrates the trade-off between testing and relying on internal controls and how it impacts the nature, timing, and extent of further audit procedures to be performed.

In addition, for each fraud risk that is identified during the planning stage (see Chapter 4), the audit team should evaluate whether the client has implemented control activities that are specifically designed to address the risk of fraud that has been identified. These might include control activities that are designed to address fraud risks for specific financial statement accounts or, more generally, control activities that are designed to promote a culture of honest and ethical behavior. For example, the audit team evaluates the controls related to the use of period-end journal entries on each audit engagement due to their frequent use in the past to commit frauds at companies such as **WorldCom, Waste Management,** and **Dell Inc.**

EXHIBIT 5.1
Relationship between Internal Control Reliance and Audit Procedures

	Less Reliance on Internal Control (higher control risk; higher RMM; lower detection risk)	More Reliance on Internal Control (lower control risk; lower RMM; higher detection risk)
Nature	More effective tests (for example, use of substantive tests of detail)	Less effective tests (for example, use of substantive analytical procedures)
Timing	Testing performed at year-end	Testing can be performed at interim
Extent	Higher sample size	Lower sample size

✔ REVIEW CHECKPOINTS

5.4 What are management's and auditors' respective responsibilities regarding internal control?

5.5 Define *control risk* and explain the role of control risk assessment in audit planning.

5.6 What is the primary reason for conducting an evaluation of an audit client's internal control on a financial statement audit?

5.7 How does control risk affect the nature, timing, and extent of further audit procedures?

COMPONENTS OF INTERNAL CONTROL

LO 5-3
Define and describe the five basic components of internal control and specify some of their characteristics.

According to the COSO framework, an internal control system that is designed and operating effectively will have met three overarching goals within an organization (Exhibit 5.2). First, the system will allow for effective and efficient operations. Second, it will allow for reliable financial reporting. And third, the system will allow the organization to comply with laws and regulations.

To achieve the specific objectives for each of these three goals, the COSO framework defines five interrelated components of a properly designed internal control system: (1) control environment, (2) risk assessment, (3) control activities, (4) monitoring, and (5) information and communication. It is important to point out that the five components should not operate independently of each other. Instead, they should be considered as working in an integrated manner to support the internal control system's overall effectiveness. Each of these components is now discussed in detail.

Control Environment

The control environment sets the tone of the organization. It is the foundation for all other components of internal control. It provides discipline and structure to all participants and stakeholders. Control environment factors include the integrity, ethical values, and competence of the entity's people. According to the COSO framework, a well-functioning internal control environment is characterized by philosophies such as the following:

- *Integrity and ethical values.* Sound integrity and ethical values, particularly of top management, are developed and understood and set the standard of conduct for financial reporting.
- *Board of directors.* The board of directors understands and exercises oversight responsibility related to financial reporting and related internal control.
- *Management's philosophy and operating style.* Management's philosophy and operating style support achieving effective internal control over financial reporting.

EXHIBIT 5.2
Internal Control—
Integrated Framework
(COSO)

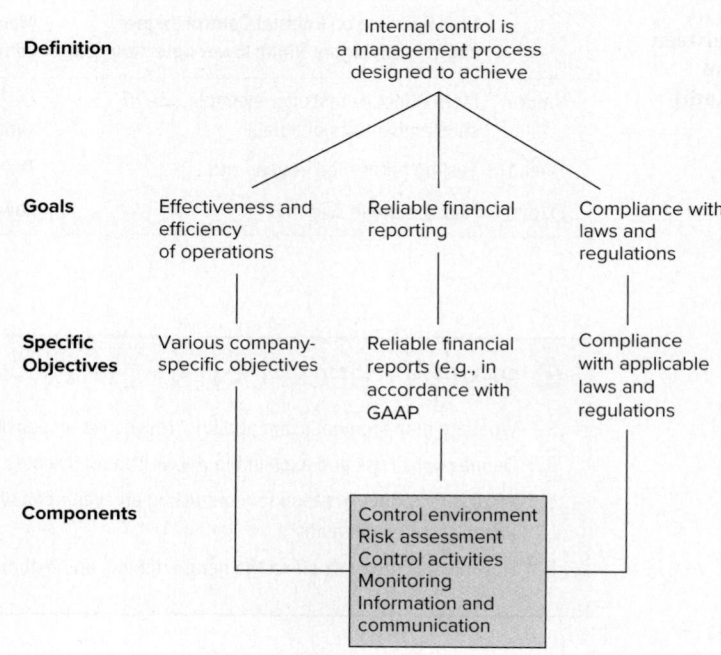

Definition		Internal control is a management process designed to achieve	
Goals	Effectiveness and efficiency of operations	Reliable financial reporting	Compliance with laws and regulations
Specific Objectives	Various company-specific objectives	Reliable financial reports (e.g., in accordance with GAAP)	Compliance with applicable laws and regulations
Components		Control environment Risk assessment Control activities Monitoring Information and communication	

- *Organizational structure.* The company's organizational structure supports effective internal control over financial reporting by establishing clear and unambiguous reporting lines.
- *Financial reporting competencies.* The company retains individuals who are competent in financial reporting and related oversight roles.
- *Authority and responsibility.* Management and employees are assigned appropriate levels of authority and responsibility to facilitate effective internal control over financial reporting.
- *Human resources.* Human resource policies and practices are designed and implemented to facilitate effective internal control over financial reporting.

Most importantly, the effectiveness of the control environment is influenced heavily by a company's management team and is strongly and unquestionably related to the "tone at the top" set by management. The key is for management to be deliberate in trying to impact the attitudes toward internal controls throughout the organization by setting the proper example for the organization to follow. It has been said that the control environment has a "pervasive" effect on the reliability of financial reporting because it affects *all* other components of an organization's internal control system.

AUDITING INSIGHT — Tone at the Top – How Hertz Got It Wrong

In February 2019, **Hertz Global Holdings Inc.** agreed to pay the SEC $16 million to settle accounting fraud charges. Feeling the pressure to meet internal budgets, business plans and earnings estimates, executives at Hertz overstated pre-tax income by $235 million from 2012 to 2014. The managers used improper accounting methodologies that were inconsistent with GAAP in order to meet expectations.

However, Hertz isn't taking this lying down. The company has sued its former CEO, CFO, general counsel, and others in an effort to clawback $70 million in incentive compensation that was tied to the fraudulent financials. According to Hertz's board,

the former CEO "created a pressure-cooker work environment in which he leaned on subordinates to make "inappropriate accounting decisions" so the firm could hit its financial targets" sometimes "berating subordinates who did not come up with 'non-traditional' accounting approaches to fill the gaps between Hertz's actual and expected performance."

Sources: "*SEC* Charges Hertz with Inaccurate Financial Reporting and Other Failures," Administrative Proceeding File No. 3-18965, SEC, February 1, 2019; "Hertz seeks $70 Million in Clawbacks Tied to Accounting Scandal," Bloomberg, April 1 2019, (online source).

Because the control environment sets the overall foundation for internal control, professional auditing standards require an auditor to obtain an understanding of the control environment on all engagements. As part of this understanding, auditors also have to take the time to consider the functioning of the client's board of directors and, in particular, the impact of its audit committee on the client's control environment. The **audit committee** is a subcommittee of the board of directors that is generally composed of three to six independent members (those not involved in the entity's day-to-day management) of the organization's board of directors. Each member must be *financially literate,* and one member must be a *financial expert.* The purpose of including independent members is to provide a buffer between the audit team and the operating management team of the company. The buffer allows the audit team (and the corporate internal audit department) to report any controversial findings to members of the board of directors without fear of reprisal.

For example, should the internal auditors find wrongdoing in the CEO's office, it would do no good to report the matter to the CEO. Similarly, if management does not have control over appointing auditors, management is prevented from threatening to dismiss the auditors if they do not agree with an inappropriate accounting practice. Some of the more important duties of the audit committee are:

- Appointment, compensation, and oversight of the public accounting firm conducting the entity's audit.

- Resolution of disagreements between management and the audit team.
- Oversight of the entity's internal audit function.
- Approval of nonaudit services provided by the public accounting firm performing the audit engagement.
- Oversight of the anonymous fraud hotline that is designed to provide employees a confidential and effective manner in which to report possible financial reporting issues.
- Authority to engage legal counsel in the event of management fraud.

Small and midsize entities may implement the control environment factors differently than larger entities. For example, smaller entities might not have a written code of conduct but instead develop a culture that emphasizes the importance of integrity and ethical behavior through oral communication and by management example. Similarly, a smaller entity may not have an independent or outside member on its board of directors. Regardless of the size of the entity, the COSO framework establishes principles which, if applied properly, should result in an effective control environment component.

Risk Assessment

In recent years, entities of all sizes have increasingly recognized the need for a formalized process to identify, properly assess, and ultimately manage the full range of **business risks** that they face: factors, events, and conditions that can prevent organizations from achieving their business objectives. One way managers address these concerns is to employ an **enterprise risk management (ERM)** framework such as the one developed by COSO to facilitate the assessment and mitigation of business risks that the entity faces. COSO defines ERM as "a process, effected by an entity's board of directors, management and other personnel, applied in a strategy setting and across the enterprise, designed to identify potential events that may affect the entity, and manage risks to be within its risk appetite, to provide reasonable assurance regarding the achievement of entity objectives."[3] In other words, management, boards, and employees have to be constantly thinking about what could go wrong with the business and how they can prevent it.

Although not all entities will employ a robust ERM framework, at a minimum, an effective internal control system will include some type of process where management takes the steps necessary to identify risks, estimate their significance and likelihood, and consider how to manage the risks. By setting management objectives, management can identify critical success factors and institute policies and procedures to ensure that they are met. (*Note:* The risk assessment element of the COSO framework is *management's* responsibility and is *not related* to an auditor's assessment of inherent risk, control risk, and the overall risk of material misstatement at the assertion level.) Although an audit client's risk assessment process should relate to all its objectives, the professional standards require the auditor to specifically gain an understanding of the process as it relates to financial reporting risks, including fraud risk. When gaining such an understanding, the auditor should determine whether management is actually assessing the likelihood of fraud risks and how it is managing such risks.

In completing their work, the audit team members seek to understand whether management is specifying financial reporting objectives with sufficient clarity and criteria to enable the identification of risks of material misstatement in financial reporting, in particular due to fraud. Once identified, the audit team also would like to see that management has a basis for determining how to manage the identified risks. For smaller entities, the risk assessment process is likely to be less formal and less structured. Although all entities should have established financial reporting management objectives, they may be recognized implicitly rather than explicitly in smaller entities. Regardless of the size of the entity, the COSO framework establishes principles that, if applied properly, should result in an effective risk assessment component when evaluating the system of internal control.

---

[3]COSO, "Enterprise Risk Management —Integrated Framework Executive Summary," September 2004, New York: AICPA.

Control Activities

In a well-functioning internal control system, once the risks to management's objectives have been identified, internal control activities are established to eliminate, mitigate, or compensate for the risks. **Control activities** are specific actions that a client's management and employees take to help ensure that management's directives are carried out. The professional standards require the audit team members to document their understanding of the internal control system on each audit, which includes their understanding of whether management has implemented control activities that are sufficient to address the risks of material misstatement for each relevant assertion related to each significant account or disclosure.

To answer this important question, the audit team members usually begin the process by considering what they learned about the internal control system as they were gaining an understanding of the other components of the COSO framework—in particular, the control environment and risk assessment components described earlier. The next step in the process requires the audit team members to document their understanding of the extent to which each of the client's control activities has been designed to sufficiently address a relevant financial statement assertion. To do so, an auditor first considers "what could go wrong" for each of the identified relevant assertions. That is, an auditor must consider how a material misstatement could occur for each relevant assertion. Once each "what could go wrong" is identified, an auditor must then determine if management has implemented a control activity that is designed to mitigate the risk of material misstatement identified for that assertion. This step will be covered in more depth later in the chapter. However, for now, see Exhibit 5.3 for several examples of this process that might occur for several relevant assertions related to the revenue account.

Importantly, when documenting their understanding of the internal control system, the audit team should keep in mind the following questions related to control activities:

- *Information technology.* Has the audit client taken full advantage of their existing technological platform (e.g., SAP) by using entirely automated control activities whenever it is efficient and effective?

- *Level of integration with their risk assessment process.* Has the audit client's management team taken the actions necessary to sufficiently address the identified risks of material misstatement for each relevant assertion?

EXHIBIT 5.3
Relevant Assertions, What Could Go Wrong and Control Activities for the Revenue Account

Relevant Assertion	What Could Go Wrong?	Control Activity
Occurrence	Sales revenue is recorded when the goods have not been shipped to the customers.	All sales invoices are matched to shipping documents before recording them in the general ledger.
Valuation	Goods will be shipped to a new customer who is unable to pay for the goods.	The credit department performs a detailed credit check for all new customers.
Completeness	Goods will be shipped to a customer, and the revenue is not recorded.	All shipping documents are matched to sales invoices that have been recorded in the general ledger.

Source: The Committee of Sponsoring Organizations of the Treadway Commission. *COSO Internal Control—Integrated Framework Principles.* Accessed June 25, 2019 (online source).

- *Selection and development of control activities.* Has the audit client's management team designed and implemented control activities with full consideration of their cost and their potential effectiveness in mitigating the risks of material misstatement identified?
- *Policies and procedures.* Have the policies related to reliable financial reporting been documented and communicated throughout the company by the audit client's management team?

In addition, regardless of the size of the entity, the COSO framework establishes principles that, if applied properly, should result in an effective evaluation of the control activities component.

Not surprisingly, there are a number of different types of controls in today's financial statement audit environment. Ultimately, financial reporting control activities are imposed on the accounting system for the purpose of *preventing, detecting,* and *correcting* errors and frauds that could enter and flow through to the financial statements. Clearly, **preventive controls**, procedures that prevent misstatements before they occur (those that ensure hiring competent people, limiting access, requiring approval, separating duties, etc.), are preferable to **detective controls**, procedures that detect misstatements after they occur. In some sense, all control activities can be thought of as *preventive controls* because the possibility of being caught by a *detective control* might prevent someone from committing an error or a fraud. Control activities also include management review controls, information processing controls, physical security controls, and controls that allow for proper separation of duties. Each of these additional categories is now discussed in turn.

Management Review Controls

An audit client's management team has primary responsibility for ensuring that the organization's objectives are being met. As a result, management review controls are an important way for a management team to actively participate in the supervision of operations. For example, management's study of budget variances with follow-up action is an example of a management review control. In general, a management team that performs more frequent reviews has more opportunities to detect errors in the records than management that does not perform frequent reviews. The frequency, of course, is governed by the costs and benefits. In addition, subsequent action to investigate or correct differences is critically important to demonstrate that the control is truly operating in an effective manner. Without a doubt, periodic management reviews and subsequent follow-up action to correct identified errors tends to lower the risk that material misstatements exist in the financial statement accounts.

Information Processing Control Activities

Information processing control activities are essential to the effectiveness of an internal control system. Generally speaking, all organizations employ computerized information processing on a routine basis. When entities use computerized information processing, the professional standards make clear that information technology (IT) poses specific risks to an entity's internal control system. And, although the focus of this chapter is on providing a broad understanding of internal control, you should be aware that the use of computerized information processing requires entities to implement specific control activities to enable it to support the relevant financial statement assertions.

For staff auditors in today's financial statement audit environment, the most important information processing control activities are the ones that are designed to ensure the completeness and accuracy of system-generated reports. Recall from Chapter 1 that a **system-generated report** is a report generated by the audit client's information system that is used to execute its internal control procedures or produce its financial statements. If such a report is used by the audit client's management for either of these purposes, the client must have control activities in place to ensure that each report is complete and accurate. See Exhibit 5.4 for several examples of system-generated reports and the related control activity where the report is needed for its proper execution.

**EXHIBIT 5.4
System-Generated
Reports and Internal
Control Activities**

System-Generated Reports	Internal Control Activities
Accounts Receivable Aging Report	The accounts receivable aging report is generated on a monthly basis by the information system. The report is reviewed by the chief financial officer to evaluate the adequacy of the allowance for doubtful accounts.
Three-Way Match Exception Report	In an accounts payable process, the three-way match refers to the process where a vendor invoice is compared to an approved purchase order and a receiving report to make sure that a payable is valid before payment is made. The three-way match exception report is generated on a weekly basis by the information system to determine if any exceptions exist. The report is reviewed by the accounts payable clerk and all exceptions are followed up on and resolved by the clerk.
New-Hires Report	The new-hires report is generated on a quarterly basis by the information system. The report is reviewed by the payroll clerk to ensure that all new employees are reflected in payroll expense.

Source: The Committee of Sponsoring Organizations of the Treadway Commission. *COSO Internal Control - Integrated Framework Principles*. Accessed June 25, 2019 (online source).

The full range of auditing considerations that are relevant to an audit client's computerized information processing environment are discussed in detail in Module H. However, before moving on, it is important to realize that even "spreadsheet goofs" can pose risks to an entity's internal control system. As an example, consider that **Fannie Mae** had to restate its unrealized gains account by $1.2 *billion* for errors in "mark-to-market" calculations that were the result of "honest mistakes" that were made in a spreadsheet that was used to implement a new accounting standard.[4] In addition, although almost all organizations employ computerized information processing, manual controls over certain information processing activities remain important in many systems. For example, important manual control activities over the purchasing and cash disbursement cycle include using purchase orders to ensure proper authorization (the *occurrence* assertion), matching vendor invoices with receiving reports and purchase orders to ensure that the quantity billed agrees with the quantity ordered and received at previously agreed-upon prices (the *accuracy* assertion), and using *and accounting for* prenumbered documents (checks, purchase orders, and receiving reports) to ensure that all transactions have been recorded (the *completeness* assertion). The specific control activities for each cycle are discussed in more detail in Chapters 6 through 10.

Physical Security Controls

Physical access to assets, data and important records, documents, and blank forms should be limited to authorized personnel only. Assets such as inventory and securities should not be available to persons who have no need to handle them. Likewise, access to records should be denied to people who do not have a record-keeping responsibility for them. Some blank forms are very important for accounting and certain control activities, and their availability should also be restricted.

In addition, given the importance of the computerized information processing system, physical security of computer equipment and restricting access to the organization's data and computer application files are important to achieving effective internal control. Access controls help prevent the improper use or manipulation of data files, unauthorized use of computer programs, and improper use of the computer equipment. Overall, in today's environment, it is essential that organizations have a robust set of cyber security control activities in place and operating effectively. As illustrated in the following Auditing Insight, sometimes a weakness in cyber security control activities can lead to the loss of assets.

[4]"Fannie Mae Corrects Mistakes in Results," *New York Times*, October 30, 2003, P. C1.

AUDITING INSIGHT Did They Really Lose $100 million?

In late 2018, the SEC reported that nine public companies, from a variety of industries including technology, real estate, financial and consumer goods, energy, and more, lost nearly $100 million to cyber criminals. The companies were defrauded by two different schemes, emails from fake executives and emails from fake vendors.

According to the report, the spoofed emails from fake executives "were not sophisticated frauds in general design or the use of technology. In fact, from a technological perspective they only required creating an email address to mimic the executive's address."

The emails actually included spelling mistakes! However, the fake vendor emails were more sophisticated and were generally not discovered as fraud until the real vendor contacted the company for payment for its past due invoices. In each case, company personnel wired money to the fraudulent accounts costing each of the nine companies anywhere from $1 million to $45 million dollars that will not be recovered.

Sources: SEC (online sources).

Also, locked doors, security passes, passwords, and check-in logs can be used to limit access to the computer system hardware. One way to detect inappropriate computer usage is by specifying a planned schedule for running large-scale computerized applications. A schedule can help detect unauthorized access because most software can produce usage reports that can be compared to the planned schedule. Applications that are being run at unauthorized times can then be investigated for inappropriate use of computer resources.

Separation of Duties

A very important characteristic of an effective internal control system is that an appropriate separation of duties (or functional responsibilities) plan is in place . Four types of functional responsibilities should be performed by different departments (see Exhibit 5.5), or at least by different persons on the entity's accounting staff:

1. *Authorization to execute transactions.* This duty belongs to people who have the authority and the responsibility for initiating or approving transactions. Authorization may be general, referring to a class of transactions (e.g., all purchases up to $100,000), or it may be specific (e.g., sale of a major asset).

2. *Recording transactions.* This duty refers to the accounting and record-keeping function, which is typically accomplished through the deliberate assignment of access rights to employees in a computerized information system. People who control computerized processing are the record keepers.

3. *Custody of assets involved in the transactions.* This duty refers to the actual physical possession or effective physical control of property.

4. *Periodic reconciliation of existing assets to recorded amounts.* This duty refers to making comparisons at regular intervals and taking appropriate action with respect to any differences.

Incompatible responsibilities are combinations of responsibilities that place a person alone in a position to create and conceal misstatements due to errors or frauds in her or his normal job. Duties should be divided so that no one person can control more than one of these responsibilities. If different departments or persons are forced to deal with these different facets of transactions, frauds are more difficult to commit because they would then require collusion of two or more persons, and most people hesitate to seek the help

EXHIBIT 5.5
Separation of Duties

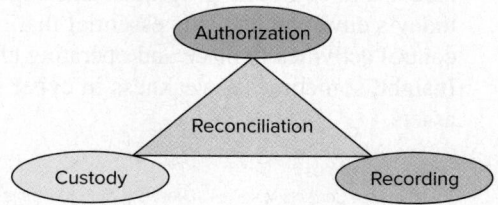

of others in order to conduct wrongful acts. A second benefit of separating duties is that by acting in a coordinated manner (handling different aspects of the same transaction), innocent errors are more likely to be found and corrected. The old saying "Two heads are better than one" is often proven to be true.

In most computerized information processing environments, employees who have access to an application (such as payroll) might be in a position to perform incompatible functions. As a result, to achieve proper separation of duties, it is essential for an organization to have a well-thought-out plan that limits employees' access to the computerized information processing system (e.g., SAP, Oracle) to only those applications that are necessary for such employees to complete their jobs. In effect, companies must design internal control activities that will effectively limit opportunities for any one individual to both perpetrate and conceal vmisstatements or losses due to errors or fraud. In most situations, these often include password access controls that are designed to align the computer access rights to transactions, data, key documents, and assets with only those employees who require such access to complete their clearly defined role within the internal control system. In a sense, proper separation of duties is accomplished through appropriate system access controls.

Control Activities: Other Considerations

When gaining an understanding of an internal control system, it is important for the auditor to consider the level of automation used to execute each control activity. In general, control activities are categorized by auditors as purely manual controls, manual controls that rely on a system-generated report, and entirely automated controls.

Manual controls are control activities that operate in a manner that is fully dependent on a person. An example of this control would be a three-way match control in the purchases cycle where the accounts payable clerk was responsible for physically matching the details of a purchase order, receiving report, and a vendor invoice before authorizing the amount for payment. Since the control is operated manually without the use of the computer information system, there is no reliance on the computer information system for it to operate effectively.

Like purely manual controls, manual controls that rely on a system-generated report also depend on a person. However, the difference is that the person operating the control must rely on a report that is generated by the computer information system. An example would be a control, executed by the controller, that was designed to evaluate the accounts receivable aging report to determine the reasonableness of the allowance for doubtful accounts. Importantly, the proper execution of the control is dependent on the completeness and accuracy of the accounts receivable aging report.

Entirely automated control activities operate completely within the computer information system. An example of this would be an automated credit approval control that is used by a bank to ensure that it does not extend credit beyond each customer's credit limit. The proper execution of the control is entirely automated. Thus, when a customer attempts to use the credit card, the amount of the sale is added to that customer's existing balance and the amount is compared to the credit limit for that customer. If you have ever been denied when attempting to pay for dinner or purchase clothes, you certainly know about this automated control.

☑ REVIEW CHECKPOINTS

5.12 What is a *control activity*?

5.13 What is the difference between *preventive controls* and *detective controls*? Give an example of each.

5.14 What is a *management review control*? Please provide an example.

5.15 What is a *system generated report*? Please provide an example.

5.16 What is a *physical security control*? Why is it important in an internal control system?

5.17 What kinds of functional responsibilities should be performed by different departments or persons in a control system with good separation of duties?

Information and Communication

When evaluating the information and communication component of internal control, the "auditor should obtain an understanding of the **information system** including the related business processes, relevant to financial reporting. As part of that process, the auditor must seek to understand the nature of the underlying accounting records, supporting information and the accounts that are used to fully execute a transaction." The auditor should also understand "how the information system captures events and conditions, other than transactions, that are significant to the financial statements."[5] Clearly, the size of the entity will have an impact on this component. However, regardless of the entity's size. the COSO framework establishes principles that, if applied properly, should result in an effective evaluation of the information and communication component.

The professional standards recognize that to make effective decisions, managers must have access to *timely, reliable,* and *relevant* information. As a result, an entity's information system should be designed to identify data from reliable external sources such as suppliers, customers, economic databases, and so on, as well as internal sources. Having superior information systems can be a part of an entity's strategy and competitive advantage (e.g., **Amazon.com**). Management evaluates the quality of information by determining whether the content is appropriate and the information is timely, accurate, and accessible. Note that these are sometimes contradictory. For example, waiting to ensure that information is *accurate* can cause it not to be *timely*.

Communication includes report production and distribution. The account balances are summarized in internal management reports and external financial statements. The internal reports are management's feedback for monitoring operations. The external reports are the financial information for outside investors, creditors, and others. Communication also involves expectations, responsibilities of individuals and groups, and other important matters. Specific duties must be made clear, and people need to know how their activities relate to the work of others. People also need to know what behavior is expected. In addition, personnel need a means of communicating significant information upstream in an organization. Outsiders also should know that fraudulent and unethical behavior by entity personnel is unacceptable and should be reported to management.

The information system produces a trail of activities (often referred to as an *audit trail*) from data identification to reports. You can visualize that the audit trail begins with the *source documents* (purchase orders, sales orders, etc.) and proceeds through to the financial reports. Auditors often follow this trail frontward and backward, identifying and testing relevant control activities along the way (Exhibit 5.6). They follow it backward from the financial reports to the source documents to determine whether everything in the financial reports is supported by appropriate source documents (the *occurrence* assertion). They follow it forward from source documents to reports to determine whether everything that happened (i.e., transactions) was recorded in the accounts and reported in the financial statements (the *completeness* assertion).

EXHIBIT 5.6
Occurrence and Completeness of a Sales Transaction

Source: The Committee of Sponsoring Organizations of the Treadway Commission. *COSO Internal Control - Integrated Framework Principles.* Accessed June 25, 2019 (online source).

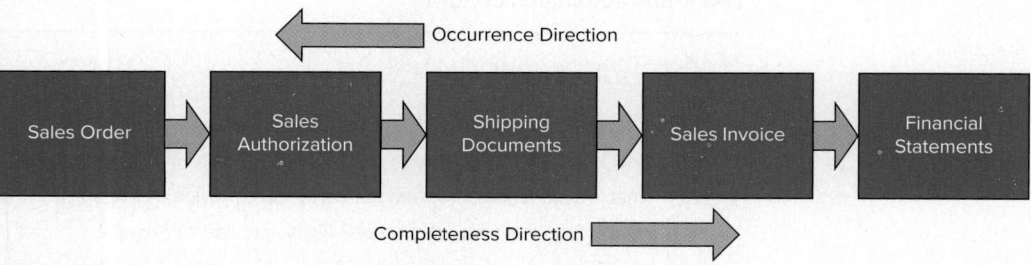

Occurrence Direction

Sales Order → Sales Authorization → Shipping Documents → Sales Invoice → Financial Statements

Completeness Direction

[5]PCAOB Auditing Standard 2110, "*Identifying and Assessing Risks of Material Misstatement.*"

Information systems in small or midsize organizations are likely to be less formal than in larger organizations, but their role is just as significant. Smaller entities with active management involvement may not need extensive descriptions of accounting procedures, sophisticated accounting records, or written policies. Communication may be less formal and easier to achieve in a small or midsize company than in a larger enterprise because the smaller organization has fewer levels, and management has more visibility and availability.

One final and very important consideration made by the audit team when gaining an understanding of this component relates to the use of information produced by the company during the audit (like system-generated reports discussed previously). The professional standards are clear that an auditor cannot ever rely on information produced by the company's information system without investigation. Instead, the audit team is required to perform audit procedures that are designed either to test the controls that have been designed to ensure that the information is complete and accurate, or to test the completeness and accuracy of the information using substantive testing procedures. This is most definitely an area of PCAOB Inspection Focus, which we now illustrate.

 PCAOB INSPECTION FOCUS | **PCAOB Identifies Deficiencies Related to System-Generated Data**

In a recent public report about its inspections program, the PCAOB specifically discussed a recurring finding related to information that is produced by the entity being audited. Specifically, the PCAOB noted that its "inspections staff has continued to observe instances in which auditors selected controls for testing but did not sufficiently test the controls over completeness and accuracy of system-generated data or reports used in the operation of those controls." For example, "management used reports that were generated by the issuer's information system to perform its review control; however, the engagement team did not test controls over the accuracy and completeness of these reports. In addition, the engagement team did not test the reports to verify the completeness and accuracy of the individual variance calculations to determine whether the investigation of other variances was necessary." Because an entity's use of IT affects the fundamental manner in which information is produced, it is essential that an auditor is comfortable with the completeness and accuracy of all information used by management to execute control activities that are deemed important to the auditor.

Sources: *PCAOB Staff Inspection Brief - Preview of Observations from 2016 Inspections of Auditors of Issuers.* Volume 2017/4. November 2017; *PCAOB Observations from 2010 Inspections of Domestic Annually Inspected Firms Regarding Deficiencies in Audits of Internal Control over Financial Reporting.* PCAOB Release No. 2012-006. December 10, 2012 (both from online sources).

Monitoring

The COSO framework recognizes that in order to allow for continuous improvements and consider changes in the entity's operating environment, management needs to monitor its internal control systems. According to COSO, a well-functioning monitoring system is characterized by philosophies such as the following:

- *Ongoing and separate evaluations.* Ongoing evaluations of controls that are separate from other types of evaluations (e.g., operational) enable management to determine whether the other components of internal control continue to function over time.
- *Reporting deficiencies.* Internal control deficiencies are identified and communicated in a timely manner to those parties responsible for taking corrective action and to management and the board as appropriate.

It is important to note that monitoring does not include regular management and supervisory control activities and other actions that employees take in performing their everyday duties. Effective monitoring involves ongoing evaluation of the controls. Some common monitoring controls include:

- Periodic evaluation of controls by the internal audit department.
- Analysis of and appropriate follow-up of operating reports or metrics that might identify anomalies indicative of a control failure.

- Supervisory review of controls, such as reconciliation reviews as a normal part of processing.
- Self-assessments by boards and management regarding the tone they set in the organization and the effectiveness of their oversight functions.
- Audit committee inquiries of internal and external auditors.
- Quality assurance reviews of the internal audit department.

As you can see, some of the control activities explained earlier in this chapter also serve as monitoring activities. For example, analyzing customer complaints for follow-up is a control activity, but analyzing them to determine whether the complaints result from a weakness in other controls (e.g., a failure to compare shipping documents to customer orders) is a monitoring activity.

Although the preceding procedures provide management with daily monitoring opportunities, the oversight provided to the entity by the board of directors (and, more specifically, the audit committee) provides the highest level of monitoring. In addition, management's close involvement in operations often will identify significant variances from expectations and inaccuracies in financial data. Finally, ongoing monitoring activities of small and midsize entities are more likely to be informal and are typically performed as a part of the overall management of the entity's operations. However, regardless of the entity's size, the COSO framework establishes principles that, if applied properly, should result in an effective evaluation of the monitoring component.

✅ REVIEW CHECKPOINTS

5.18 What is meant by the information and communications component of an effective internal control system? How can an auditor evaluate whether a client's internal control system is functioning properly for this component?

5.19 Give some examples of everyday activities that an entity's management can use to enact the monitoring component of internal control. When are such activities control activities, and when are they monitoring activities?

INTERNAL CONTROL EVALUATION

LO 5-4
Explain the process the audit team uses to assess control risk; understand its impact on the risk of material misstatement; and, ultimately, know how it affects the nature, timing, and extent of further audit procedures to be performed on the audit.

To this point, we have defined internal control and noted its limitations, identified both management's and the audit team's responsibility for the internal control system, and then described the five components of internal control defined by COSO in detail. The five components of the COSO framework are considered to be essential criteria for evaluating an entity's internal control over financial reporting for purposes of assessing the risk of material misstatement (RMM) at both the financial statement and the relevant assertion level. An essential component of assessing RMM at the relevant assertion level is the assessment of control risk (along with the assessment of inherent risk which was covered in Chapter 4) for each relevant assertion about each significant financial statement account or disclosure.

In this chapter, we explain how to assess control risk for each of the relevant assertions identified in the planning stage of the audit. In assessing control risk, audit teams typically use a three-phase procedure: (1) understand and document the client's internal control system at the relevant financial statement level; (2) assess the control risk for each relevant assertion identified; and (3) identify controls to test and perform tests of control. The three-phase procedure is also illustrated by the figure below:

Understand and Document the Client's Internal Control
Assessment of Control Risk
Identify Controls to Test and Perform Tests of Control

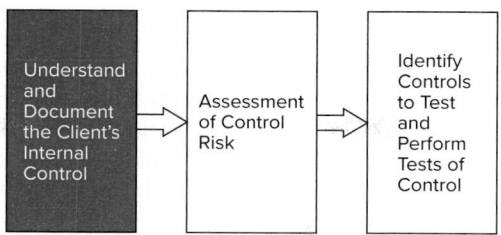

It is important to emphasize that these three phases must be completed for each relevant financial statement assertion identified during the planning stage whenever the auditor plans to rely on a control activity to modify the nature, timing, and extent of substantive audit procedures. We now describe each phase in detail, which is illustrated in Exhibit 5.7.

EXHIBIT 5.7
Phases of Internal Control Evaluation

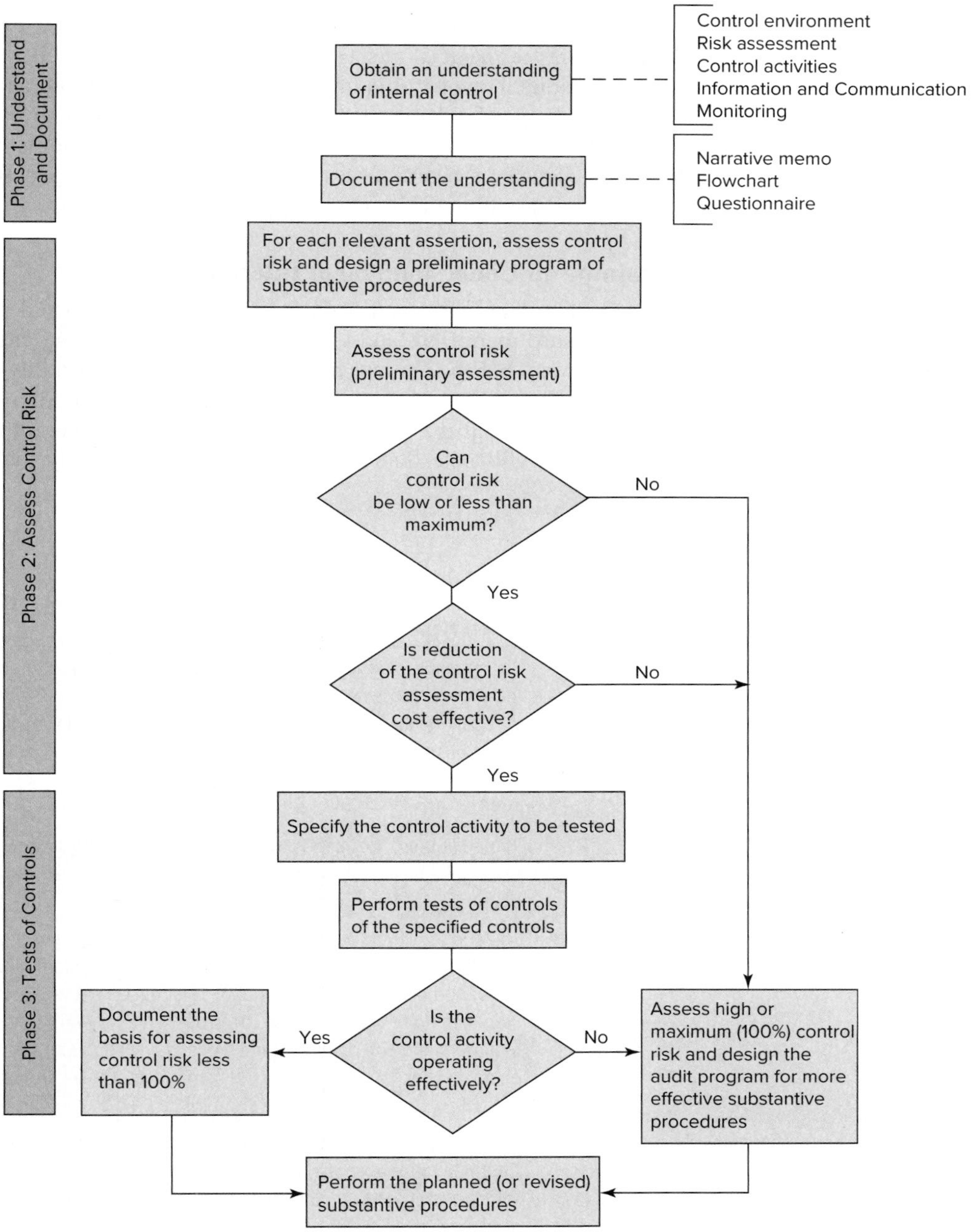

Phase 1: Understand and Document
Phase 2: Assess Control Risk
Phase 3: Tests of Controls
Obtain an understanding of internal control
Control environment
Risk assessment
Control activities
Information and Communication
Monitoring
Document the understanding
Narrative memo
Flowchart
Questionnaire
For each relevant assertion, assess control risk and design a preliminary program of substantive procedures
Assess control risk (preliminary assessment)
Can control risk be low or less than maximum?
No
Yes
Is reduction of the control risk assessment cost effective?
No
Yes
Specify the control activity to be tested
Perform tests of controls of the specified controls
Is the control activity operating effectively?
Yes
No
Document the basis for assessing control risk less than 100%
Assess high or maximum (100%) control risk and design the audit program for more effective substantive procedures
Perform the planned (or revised) substantive procedures

Phase 1: Understand and Document the Client's Internal Control System

The process of obtaining an understanding of the client's internal control system and then documenting that understanding should occur during the early stages of an audit engagement. On every audit engagement, the audit team should evaluate the design of the internal control system and determine whether control activities have been implemented over each relevant assertion related to each of the identified significant accounts and financial statement disclosures. The initial procedures used to gain an understanding of internal controls need to provide the audit team with an understanding of the control environment and management's risk assessment, the flow of transactions through the accounting system, and the design of some client control activities.

Gaining an understanding of internal controls should be performed in a "top-down" risk-based manner that first identifies *significant accounts* and disclosures and their *relevant assertions.* This was discussed in Chapter 4. Recall that an account's *significance* is based in large part on its *inherent risk* (i.e., the likelihood of containing a material misstatement before the consideration of internal control). Thus, audit teams focus on likely sources of material misstatements. This determination is not based on quantitative measures alone, however it is unlikely that a large, material account balance would ever be omitted from consideration at this stage of the audit. *Relevant assertions* are those that represent the reasonable possibility of a material misstatement. Thus, an assertion that does not represent a meaningful risk of misstatement (e.g., completeness of cash) is not relevant and should not be considered by the audit team.

Obtaining an Understanding of Internal Control

As previously stated, for each of the relevant assertions related to each significant account and disclosure identified, audit teams begin by examining **entity-level controls**, controls that are pervasive to the internal control system and the reliability of the financial statements taken as a whole. See Exhibit 5.8 for a list of entity-level controls as identified in professional standards and the audit team's methods used to obtain an understanding of such controls. You will note that the standard setters explicitly include parts of each of the

EXHIBIT 5.8   Entity-Level Controls and Their Assessment

Types of Entity-Level Controls	Assessment
• Controls related to the control environment • Controls related to management override • Centralized processing and controls including shared service environments • Controls to monitor results of operations • Controls to monitor other controls.	The primary evidence to test these controls is gathered through observation and inquiry and some document examination. Ultimately, the auditor needs to determine whether management's integrity, values, and operating style promote effective control consciousness throughout the entity.
• Management's risk assessment	The audit team next needs to gain an understanding of how the client assesses and responds to risk. If the client already uses enterprise risk management, inquiring and obtaining documentation of such processes is usually enough.
• Period-end financial reporting process	The auditor should assess the processes that are used to produce its annual and quarterly financial statements, including the extent to which information technology is involved in the period-end process. The auditor must document who is actually participating from the management team and where the process actually takes place. Finally, the auditor needs to understand and document the types of adjusting entries that have occurred and the extent of process oversight by the management team, the board, and the audit committee.
• Policies that address significant business control and risk management practices	An entity's internal auditors and systems staff often review and evaluate this documentation. Independent auditors may review and study their work instead of doing the same tasks over again. Other sources of information include (1) previous experience with the entity as found in the prior-year audit, (2) responses to inquiries directed to client personnel, and (3) examination of documents and records.

components of the COSO framework. This is deliberate. If the audit team decides that an entity-level control sufficiently reduces a specific risk of material misstatement for a relevant assertion, it may not need to delve further into transaction-level controls (discussed next) related to that risk. For example, if a chief financial officer who is very familiar with the company's payroll process performs reviews of weekly payroll reports and investigates discrepancies thoroughly, this may provide a control that is sufficient to meet the internal control objectives for payroll reporting (i.e., address or mitigate the risk of material misstatement for each of the relevant assertions for payroll expense).

In addition to entity-level controls, the audit team also identifies **transaction-level controls**, controls that pertain to specific classes of transactions, account balances, and disclosures. The most effective method used by auditors to gain an understanding of the internal control system is to perform a **walkthrough** of a single transaction through the entire accounting system. During the walkthrough, the auditor is able to learn by observing the activities that occur and the documents that are used within an internal control process. When doing so, the professional standards state that auditors should seek to understand (1) the flow of transactions; (2) the points in the process where a material misstatement could occur; and (3) the controls that management has put in place to mitigate each risk of material misstatement that is identified. The auditor must gain this understanding of internal control in order to evaluate *design effectiveness.*

Design effectiveness determines whether the internal controls over financial reporting, *if operating effectively,* would be expected to prevent or detect errors or fraud that could result in a material misstatement in the financial statements. The techniques used by auditors during a walkthrough include inquiry of personnel, observation of the client's operations, and examining documents while tracing a single transaction through the entire audit trail from the beginning or the initiation of the transaction to its final inclusion in the financial statements. Each client employee involved is asked to demonstrate the procedures that he or she follows in processing the transaction. This aspect of the walkthrough is quite important because, often, the information that is contained in procedure manuals and understood by supervisors may not be the same as the procedures that are actually being performed. People can change procedures to make them more efficient, they can forget to perform procedures, they may go on vacation, they may even intentionally fail to perform required procedures, or the procedures may not be well understood by the employee.

Once the walkthroughs are completed, the audit team has gained an understanding of the *design* of internal controls (or at least how those internal controls are intended to function). However, this does not necessarily inform the audit team about the *operating effectiveness* of internal controls (unless there were automated controls testing or reperformance tests completed during the walkthrough). **Operating effectiveness** refers to whether the control is *operating as designed* and whether the person performing the control possesses the necessary authority and qualifications to perform the control effectively. Obtaining evidence to test the operating effectiveness of identified internal controls will be discussed in a subsequent phase of the audit team's evaluation of the internal control system.

Document the Internal Control Understanding

Once the audit team has completed the walkthrough and learned about the nature of the control activities implemented and the design of the entity's internal control system, they must document that understanding. The understanding can be summarized and documented effectively in the form of narratives, flowcharts, and even questionnaires. Each of these is now discussed.

The most common way for documenting the audit team's understanding of internal control is to write a **narrative description** of each significant process within the internal control system. Such a narrative is designed to describe all environmental elements, the process flow of transactions through the accounting system, and all of the control activities that have implemented. The narrative description can be quite useful for all audits. However, for larger complex entities which operate in multiple industries around the world, it can be difficult to identify all of the process risk points, which are the points in each process where a material misstatement might occur. As a result, auditors will often augment the narrative description with a **flowchart**.

Indeed, an accounting process flowchart is another commonly used method for documenting the auditors' understanding of an entity's internal control system. And, perhaps most importantly, most companies have their own flowcharts that the audit team may use as a starting point instead of constructing their own from scratch. The advantages of flowcharts can be summarized by an old adage: "A picture is worth a thousand words." Flowcharts tend to help the audit team better assess the points in the process where a material misstatement can occur which helps to reveal key points in the process where a control activity is needed. This of course can be quite beneficial in helping audit teams identify missing control activities in the process.

Construction of a flowchart can be time-consuming because an auditor must take the time to learn about the operating personnel involved in the system and gather samples of relevant documents. Thus, the information for the flowchart, like the narrative description, involves much effort and observation. When the flowchart is complete, however, the result is an easily evaluated, informative description of the system that shows the various duties performed by individuals and provides graphic evidence of any conflicting responsibilities (i.e., lack of separation of duties). Further, once a flowchart is complete, subsequent audits can easily access the flowchart and update it for changes that have been made in the process since the prior year. In recent years, flowcharting has become even more popular as a way to document an auditor's understanding of the internal control system, primarily because of its effectiveness in evaluating internal control design. In addition, advances in technological tools have also made the construction of a flowchart much more efficient.

Refer to Exhibit 5.9 for a partial flowchart representation of the beginning stages of a payroll processing system. The connectors shown by the circled numbers indicate continuation on the flowchart. Ultimately, the flowchart ends showing entries in accounting journals and ledgers. In Exhibit 5.9, you can see some characteristics of both flowchart

EXHIBIT 5.9 Payroll System Flowchart

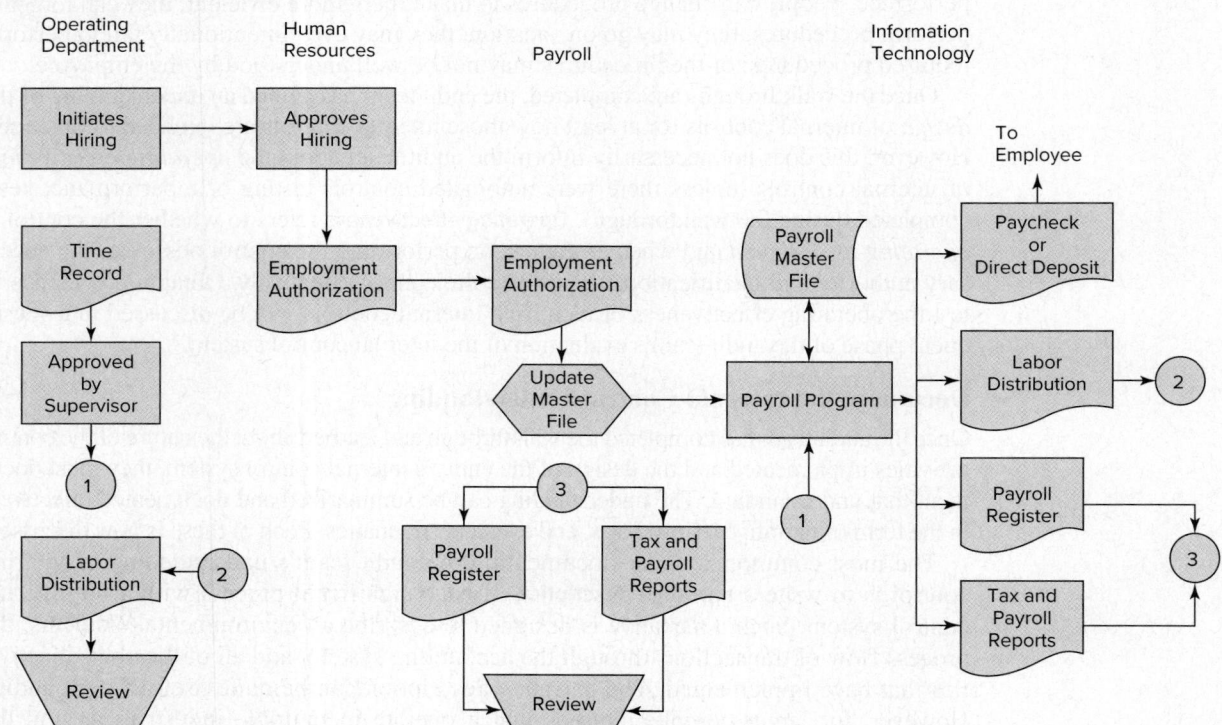

Source: The Committee of Sponsoring Organizations of the Treadway Commission. *COSO Internal Control - Integrated Framework Principles*. Accessed June 25, 2019 (online source).

construction and this specific accounting system. By reading down the columns for each department, you can see that transaction-initiation authority and custody of checks are separated (i.e., separation of duties).

Most importantly, for any flowcharting application, the chart must be understandable to an audit supervisor. Flowcharts are created with audit-specific flowcharting software but also can be created rather easily in Excel or PowerPoint. The flowchart should communicate all relevant information and evidence about separation of duties, authorization, and accounting and control activities in an understandable, visual form. The starting point in the system, if possible, should be placed at the upper-left-hand corner. The flow of procedures and documents should be from left to right and from top to bottom as much as possible. The shapes of the symbols are commonly understood and fairly obvious. For example, rectangles are processes, circles are connectors, quadrilaterals are manual processes, and so on. Narrative explanations should be written on the face of the chart as annotations or in a readily available reference key.

A third way to document the auditor's understanding of an internal control system is to conduct a formal interview with knowledgeable managers using an **internal control questionnaire** illustrated in Exhibit 5.10. Such a questionnaire is typically organized under headings that identify questions related to relevant themes like the control environment and relevant management assertions. Not all questionnaires are organized like this, so audit teams need to know the general objectives in order to know whether the questionnaire is complete. Likewise, if you are assigned to prepare an internal control questionnaire, you will need to be careful to include questions about each relevant assertion.

Internal control questionnaires are designed to help the audit team obtain evidence about the control environment and the accounting and control activities that are considered appropriate for normal circumstances. All organizations have unique features, and answers to the questions should not be taken as final and definitive evidence about how well controls actually function. Evidence obtained through the interview process is categorized as inquiry-level information that is not sufficient to demonstrate the operating effectiveness of a control activity. The person being interviewed could always give answers that reflect what the system should be rather than what it really is. The person can be unaware of informal ways in which duties have been changed or can be innocently ignorant of the system details. Nevertheless, interviews and questionnaires can be useful for detecting internal control weaknesses.

As we move forward to the next step of assessing control risk for each relevant assertion, it is important to point out that, in practice, audit teams typically use a combination of methods to document their understanding of a client's internal control system.

✓ REVIEW CHECKPOINTS

5.20 What is an *entity-level control* and why is it important to the evaluation of internal controls?

5.21 What is a *transaction-level-control*?

5.22 What are the three different ways an auditor can document their understanding of a client's internal control system?

5.23 What are the advantages and disadvantages of documenting internal control by using (1) an internal control questionnaire, (2) a narrative memorandum, and (3) a flowchart?

EXHIBIT 5.10 **Internal Control Questionnaire—Payroll Processing**

	Yes/No	Comments

Control Environment

1. Are all employees paid by check or direct deposit?

2. Is a special payroll bank account used?

3. Are payroll checks signed by persons who do not prepare checks or keep cash funds or accounting records?

4. If a check-signing machine is used, are the signature plates controlled?

5. Is the payroll bank account reconciled by someone who does not prepare, sign, or deliver paychecks?

6. Are payroll department personnel rotated in their duties? Required to take vacations? Bonded?

7. Is there a timekeeping department (function) independent of the payroll department?

8. Are authorizations for deductions signed by the employees on file?

Occurrence

9. Are time cards or piecework reports prepared by the employee approved by her or his supervisor?

10. Is a time clock or other electromechanical or computerized system used?

11. Is the payroll register sheet signed by the employee preparing it and approved prior to payment?

12. Are names of terminated employees reported in writing to the payroll department?

13. Is the payroll periodically compared to personnel files?

14. Are checks distributed by someone other than the employee's immediate supervisor?

15. Are unclaimed wages deposited in a special bank account or otherwise controlled by a responsible officer?

Completeness

16. Are names of newly hired employees reported in writing to the payroll department?

17. Are blank payroll checks prenumbered and the numerical sequence checked for missing documents?

Accuracy

18. Are all wage rates determined by contract or approved by a personnel officer?

19. Are timekeeping and cost accounting records (such as hours, dollars) reconciled with payroll department calculations of hours and wages?

20. Are payrolls audited periodically by internal auditors?

21. Are individual payroll records reconciled with quarterly tax reports?

Classification

22. Do payroll accounting personnel have instructions for classifying payroll debit entries?

Cutoff

23. Are monthly, quarterly, and annual wage accruals reviewed by an accounting officer?

Phase 2: Assessment of Control Risk

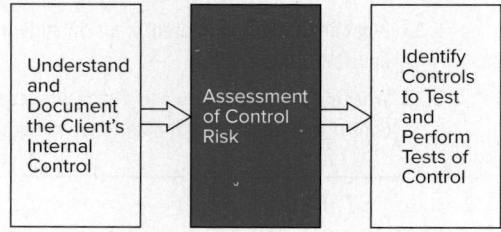

After completing the first phase of understanding and documenting internal control, the audit team should be able to make a preliminary assessment of control risk for each relevant assertion identified during the planning stage. At this preliminary stage, the audit team is assessing the internal control design to determine if it might be possible to rely upon the internal control system during the financial statement audit. At this point in the process, the audit team may also use their internal control findings from the previous year's audit to help inform this preliminary assessment. When doing so, auditors seek to identify internal control activities that are explicitly designed to support reliable financial statement reporting for the relevant financial statement assertion identified about each significant account and disclosure. In a sense, the audit team must ask whether the client has put internal control activities in place that are designed to prevent or detect material misstatements for the relevant assertions. For an integrated audit at an issuer, the auditor ***must*** test controls for all relevant assertions for each significant account and disclosure. This will be discussed in detail in Module I. However, for audits of nonissuers, after the audit team members have documented their understanding of the entity's internal control, an important decision needs to be made: Should the audit team perform tests of the operating effectiveness of those controls?

Deciding Whether to Perform Tests of Controls

When making the important decision of whether to perform test controls or not, it is important to remember that audit teams may choose *not* to perform tests of controls for one of two reasons:

1. The audit team may conclude that the internal control system is ineffective.
2. The costs of testing the operating effectiveness exceed the cost of substantive testing.

Each of these reasons is now discussed in greater detail. Related to the first reason, after gaining an understanding of the internal control system, the audit team may conclude that the internal control system is too ineffective in preventing or detecting misstatements to rely upon and justify reductions of subsequent substantive audit procedures for the relevant assertions identified during the planning stages. This conclusion is equivalent to assessing control risk at the highest level and planning more extensive substantive testing procedures. In such a situation, since the audit team would not likely be able to rely upon the internal control system, they would have no choice but to conduct significant substantive testing to make sure that the audit is conducted in an effective manner.

The second reason that audit teams might not test controls would be the team's decision that it would take more time to test the operating effectiveness of the control activities than it would take to perform the substantive tests that would be necessary to obtain enough comfort for a relevant assertion. In order to make such a decision, audit teams typically will have to design a preliminary program of substantive procedures that would have to be completed in order to obtain enough comfort if tests of controls were performed and the controls were operating effectively and compare that result to the substantive procedures that would have to be completed if tests of controls were not performed. In a sense, this is purely a decision made by the audit team that relates to the profitability of the audit engagement and reflects the reality that the cost of obtaining a low control risk assessment can be high (because of the time needed to conduct tests of *operating effectiveness* of control activities.

For either reason, however, the result is the same if the audit teams makes the decision to not perform tests of controls: control risk is assessed at the maximum level and more extensive substantive procedures are required to be completed in order to reduce the risk of material misstatement for a relevant assertion to an acceptably low level. For example, suppose that completion time for tests of controls for the accuracy of payroll expense is estimated as 40 hours. Also suppose that, if the tests of controls provided evidence that the controls were in fact operating effectively, the substantive testing needed for the accuracy assertion for payroll expense (e.g., confirmation sent to employees) could be reduced by 30 hours. In this scenario, the additional work needed to perform the tests of controls would not be economical. The decision to stop work on control risk assessment in this case is a matter of audit *efficiency*—it doesn't make sense to spend 40 hours testing controls to reduce substantive tests by 30 hours. Of course, the auditors' rationale for their final decision must be carefully documented. Before moving on, remember that this

EXHIBIT 5.11 **What Could Go Wrong and Control Activities**

Significant Account	Relevant Assertions	What Could Go Wrong?	Internal Control Activity
Cash	Existence	The cash balance may not exist in the company's bank accounts.	The CFO performs a detailed review of the bank reconciliation on a monthly basis.
	Valuation	The cash balance that is held in foreign countries may not have been translated properly.	The treasurer reviews the cash translation adjustment calculation monthly and independently checks that the appropriate spot rate has been used for each foreign currency.
	Presentation and disclosure	There may be restrictions on the cash balance that were not properly disclosed.	The corporate secretary reviews the cash footnote disclosure on a quarterly basis to ensure that all legal restrictions on the cash balance have been properly disclosed.
Accounts Receivable	Existence	Accounts receivable balances are inflated and don't really exist.	Check sales order and shipping document to make sure sales were earned and a customer owes a balance.
	Completeness	Not all accounts receivable have been recorded.	Check invoices with shipping document to A/R ledger.
	Valuation	Receivables are not included in financial statements at the appropriate amount, and valuation adjustments are not recorded properly.	Management evaluates the collectability of delinquent receivables on a timely basis.

Source: The Committee of Sponsoring Organizations of the Treadway Commission. *COSO Internal Control - Integrated Framework Principles*. Accessed June 25, 2019 (online source).

decision is appropriate only for **nonissuers**; (i.e., nonpublic entities) audit teams must perform tests of controls over financial reporting for issuers, which is covered in Module I.

Remember, at this stage of the process, auditors are trying to identify the control activities that may be relied upon as part of the overall audit process. To do so, auditors need to identify the controls that they believe will mitigate the risks of material misstatement that have already been identified for each of the relevant assertions when gaining an understanding of the internal control system. In a well-designed internal control system, the key internal control activities will be clearly linked to the relevant financial statement assertions being supported by the control. Exhibit 5.11 provides an illustration of this step by extending the exhibit that was developed in Chapter 4 (Exhibit 4.12) with a fourth column.

When identifying these control activities, auditors will often categorize controls as either preventive or detective, automated or manual, and will also note how often the control is performed (e.g., daily, weekly, monthly, etc.). The categorization process helps an auditor to better understand each control which facilitates internal control testing. Indeed, it is important to remember that any control that may be relied upon would have to be tested before the audit team could rely on them to reduce substantive testing. However, it is important to point out that audit teams should not perform tests of controls for those controls that will not be relied upon because there is no need to prove that they are operating effectively. Doing so would be inefficient. Instead, the audit team would have to perform additional substantive procedures to compensate for the lack of internal controls that could be relied upon to obtain sufficient appropriate evidence that would allow the auditor to reach a conclusion for each of the related relevant assertions.

Tests of controls must be performed to obtain evidence as to whether control activities that are candidates to be relied upon actually operate as described. The test of controls audit plan consists of procedures designed to produce evidence of how effectively the controls actually operate in practice. If they are determined to be operating effectively after testing, control risk can be assessed below the maximum. If they do not operate with the required level of effectiveness, the final conclusion is to assess a high control risk, revise the audit plan to consider the control weakness, and then proceed with additional substantive audit procedures.

The distinction between the understanding and documenting phase and assessing the control risk is useful for understanding the audit team's study and evaluation of internal control. However, the audit team may very well perform these phases together, and not necessarily as separate and distinct audit tasks. For nonissuers, the audit team can halt the control evaluation process for efficiency or effectiveness reasons. However, if the audit team wants to justify a low assessment of control risk that will reduce the substantive audit procedures for a particular relevant assertion, the evaluation must be continued in phase 3, the testing phase.

To summarize, then, at this stage, the audit team members have now assessed control risk for each relevant assertion based on its understanding and documentation of internal control. If this assessment is lower than the maximum level (i.e., the audit team members have decided to rely on internal controls to reduce the extent of substantive testing), the auditors must next perform tests of controls. This final phase is discussed in the next section.

Phase 3: Identify Controls to Test and Perform Tests of Controls

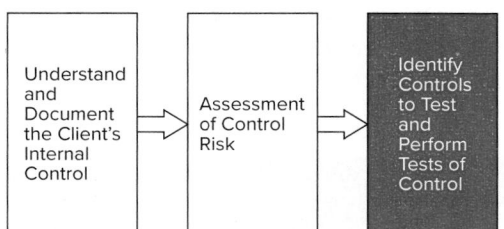

As stated above, the process of identifying controls to test begins when auditors have determined that a control, if operating effectively, will reduce the risk of material misstatement for an identified relevant assertion and that it makes sense to test those control activities. These represent controls that have been assessed as low control risk and are often referred to as *controls on which the audit team intends to rely upon* as part of the financial statement audit process. To support the reduced control risk assessment and the reduction of related substantive procedures for each relevant assertion, audit teams must test the control activities to determine whether they are operating effectively throughout the period. The required level of effectiveness is a matter of professional judgment. Audit teams know that operating effectiveness cannot realistically be expected to be perfect. The auditors could decide, for example, that evidence such as 98 percent of recorded payroll being supported by validated time cards may be sufficient to assess a "low" control risk for the occurrence assertion. Most public accounting firms have internal guidelines to determine the acceptable rate of compliance for an internal control activity to be considered effective. Generally, if a control is judged to be more important and would result in a more significant reduction in substantive testing, the level of compliance must be higher. Factors to consider in determining appropriate levels of compliance are discussed in more detail in Module E.

Performing Tests of Control

The professional standards make clear that when designing tests of controls, the auditor needs to consider the means of selecting items for testing. For tests of internal controls, there are two approaches that are commonly used: (1) testing all items in a population and (2) testing a sample from a population. The decision of which approach to use depends on the nature of the control that is being tested, along with the availability of data. For example, a control activity that is entirely automated might best be tested by an automated audit procedure that can be efficiently and effectively applied to the entire population of occurrences of that control activity. However, for a manual control activity, the auditor is likely to take a sample from the population of occurrences of that control activity. In addition, it should be noted that some manual controls (such as locking a door to safeguard assets) may have little documentation and may require other means of testing (e.g., observation and inquiry). Not surprisingly, the increased use of computers by both the client and the auditor has dramatically increased the number of tests of control that can be effectively applied to the *entire* population of control occurrences in an efficient manner.

For example, one way to subject all items in a population of occurrences for a particular control activity is to use exception testing. Exception testing is designed to identify a violation of a particular control activity through the use of an automated test procedure designed to test all items in a population. For example, consider an entirely automated control activity that is designed to compare a customer's credit limit to the sum of (1) a potential sales transaction and (2) that customer's outstanding credit balance before approval of that sales transaction. If the control activity operated effectively throughout the year, a customer's outstanding credit balance would not exceed its credit limit.

Given the nature of the control activity, one way to test the operating effectiveness would be through the use of exception testing. That is, an auditor could obtain evidence about the control's operating effectiveness by using a procedure that compares each customer's credit limit to that customer's outstanding credit balance at the end of each day for the year under audit. Such a testing strategy would not have been possible (at least economically) historically. However, due to advances in information technology, such testing is now possible. As a direct result, entry-level audit professionals are now expected to consider the full extent of client data available for testing purposes, before they move forward with audit tests.

USING IDEA IN THE AUDIT   Internal Control Testing

IDEA can be helpful to audit professionals when completing exception tests and conducting audit sampling. Ultimately, exception tests provide evidence about the operating effectiveness of internal control activities by testing all items in a population and can be a highly efficient manner to complete testing. For sampling, module E provides a detailed illustration of how auditors use the sampling features of IDEA to select a representative sample from a complete population of control occurrences for a control activity to be tested.

At the end of this chapter, problems 5.63 and 5.64 can be completed to illustrate the use of IDEA during internal control testing.

Of course, there are many control activities that do not lend themselves to automated audit testing. In such situations, auditors are likely to take a sample from the population of occurrences for the control activity being tested. Most importantly, in such situations, the population being sampled must include all occurrences of the relevant control activity for the entire period of reliance, and the sample must be representative of that population to be considered appropriate audit evidence.

Tests of controls, when performed, should be applied to samples of transactions and control activities executed *throughout the period* under audit. The reason for this requirement is that the conclusions about controls will be generalized to the whole period under audit. If the auditor obtains audit evidence about the operating effectiveness of controls during an interim period, additional audit evidence should be obtained for the remaining period. There are certain situations when audit teams can rely on tests from previous periods if they have evidence that the procedure has not changed and the auditor does not believe there is a significant risk of material misstatement. However, in an annual audit, the auditor may not rely on audit evidence about the operating effectiveness of controls obtained in prior audits, for controls that have changed since they were last tested or for controls that mitigate a significant risk. Audit sampling is discussed in detail in Module E.

Methods Used to Perform Tests of Controls

Once the items have been selected for testing, the four methods of testing controls are: inquiry, observation, document examination, and reperformance. Generally, audit teams use *inquiry* about the existence of control activities and then corroborate the oral evidence by observing that the client-described control activities are actually being performed. *Observation* occurs when auditors have eyewitness observation of employees at their jobs performing control activities. Observation is typically used when certain control activities, such as separation of employees' duties, leave no documentary evidence for subsequent examination. Observation also can produce evidence of access controls such as the use of password-secured access to the computerized information system, locked doors, and security guards. The limitation of observation is that this test of control is performed as of one point in time (usually near year-end), and what is observed at that point in time may not be representative of prior time periods.

Some tests of controls depend on documentary evidence such as a payroll entry supported by a time card. In these cases, *document examination* for evidence of signatures, initials, checklists, reconciliations, and the like provides better evidence than procedures that leave no documentary tracks. Document examination might be enough; the audit team may look to see whether the documents were marked with an initial, signature, or stamp to indicate they had been checked. For example, audit teams could examine canceled checks for authorized signatures, inspect voucher packets for the initials of the employee who matched vendor invoices with supporting purchase orders and receiving reports, or examine bank reconciliations to make sure that they have been performed on a timely basis.

Generally, the most effective test of controls is reperformance. *Reperformance* can involve any client internal control activity, such as the detailed review of the monthly bank reconciliation by the entity's controller. For this control, the auditor would follow up on each reconciling item reviewed by the controller and then reperform each of the mathematical calculations. The key difference between document examination and reperformance is that with the former, audit teams inspect documents for evidence that employees have performed the control activity; reperformance provides direct evidence that the control activity was (or was not) done correctly. Exhibit 5.12 puts control testing within the perspective of the payroll function with examples of specific assertions being supported. Appendix 5A illustrates a sample audit plan for these tests.

Overall, the audit team's choice of which method to use in order to perform a test of controls to use depends on the nature and importance of the control activity being tested. Not surprisingly, certain types of tests produce more persuasive evidence about the operating effectiveness of a control activity than others. The following hierarchy lists the type of control tests from the least persuasive (inquiry) to the most persuasive (reperformance) type of evidence:

- Inquiry of client personnel.
- Observation of the control activity being performed.
- Inspection of relevant documentation.
- Reperformance of the control activity.

Importantly, if the control activity has high risk, the audit team needs more persuasive evidence about its operating effectiveness than it would for a lower risk control in order to determine if it is operating effectively. Since gathering more persuasive evidence is typically associated with a higher cost than gathering less persuasive evidence, if the audit team wants to achieve a lower control risk assessment, it will be more costly. This is why it may be more efficient for the auditor to choose not to rely on controls and instead rely on substantive testing procedures to gain assurance for certain significant accounts.

Of course, the level of automation of the control activity will also have a big impact on the nature of the tests of control being performed. That is, for manual controls that rely on a system-generated report, the audit team would have to separately test whether the report is being generated by the system in a complete and accurate manner. In addition, for automated control activities that operate entirely within the entity's computer information system, the audit team would have to perform tests on the system to make sure that the control is operating effectively. The auditing considerations that are relevant to testing the completeness and accuracy of system-generated reports and testing the operating effectiveness of purely automated controls are discussed in detail in Module H.

Direction of the Tests of Controls

The tests of controls in Exhibit 5.12 are designed to test the payroll accounting cycle in two directions. One is the tracing/completeness direction, whereby the audit team is interested in ensuring that all valid hours are included in the entity's payroll records; as a result, time logs (which represent valid hours worked) are traced to payroll department files and the payroll register (which represents hours included in the payroll records). Exhibit 5.13 shows that the sample for this direction is taken from the population of time logs (including listings of electronic clock-ins).

For the vouching/occurrence direction, the purpose of the test is to ensure that all labor hours included in the payroll (represented by the payroll register) were actually worked (represented by time logs). As a result, entries would be selected from the payroll register and vouched back to the time logs by the auditor. Because payroll provides access to cash, this cycle is highly susceptible to fraudulent activity on the part of an organization's employees. If a fictitious employee were created and added to the payroll, his or her pay could be deposited into another person's account. Of course, this is relatively difficult to detect given that most paychecks are direct deposited.

Reassess the Assessment of Control Risk

The audit team should evaluate the evidence obtained from an understanding of the client's internal control and from the related tests of control activities. If control risk (and the related RMM) is assessed very low, the substantive procedures on the relevant

EXHIBIT 5.12   Relevant Assertions about Payroll Cycle Transactions

Relevant Assertion	Control to Mitigate the Risk of Material Misstatement	Tests of Controls
Occurrence. Payroll and related events that have been recorded have occurred and pertain to the entity.	1. Payroll accounting is separated from personnel and supervision. 2. Labor usage reports are compared to job time tickets or lists of amount of time clocked. 3. Payroll supervisor approved labor usage.	1. Observe separation of duties. 2a. Vouch labor costs to labor reports. 2b. Vouch labor reports to time tickets authorized by management. 3. Examine documentary evidence of supervisor approval.
Completeness. All payroll events that occurred should have been recorded.	1. All documents are prenumbered and numerical sequence reviewed. 2. Labor costs were reviewed by supervisors and compared to budgets. 3. The personnel department notified the payroll department of new hires to include in payroll.	1. Inspect numerical sequence of selected job cost tickets and paychecks. 2. Examine documentary evidence of supervisor review of labor costs. 3. Trace a sample of employees in the personnel file to payroll time logs and the payroll register.
Accuracy. Payroll amounts and related data have been recorded accurately.	1. Payroll entries are reviewed by a person independent of preparation. 2. Budgeted payroll expenses by department are compared to actual expenses.	1. Examine evidence of review and ensure that a party independent of preparation conducted the review. 2. Examine documentary evidence of budget comparison.
Classification. Payroll-related events are recorded in the proper accounts.	1. Job cost sheets are posted weekly and summary journal entries of work-in-process and of work completed prepared monthly. 2. Payroll supervisor is required to approve distribution of payroll expense accounts and to compare payroll costs to budget.	1. Observe that payroll account distribution and job cost sheets agree. 2. Examine supervisor signature on payroll reports. Note evidence of comparison to budget.
Cutoff. Payroll-related events have been recorded in the correct accounting period.	1. Payroll reports are prepared weekly and transmitted to cost accounting.	1. Observe that the date of payroll reports agrees with dates in weekly journal entries.

EXHIBIT 5.13
Dual-Direction Test of
Payroll Controls

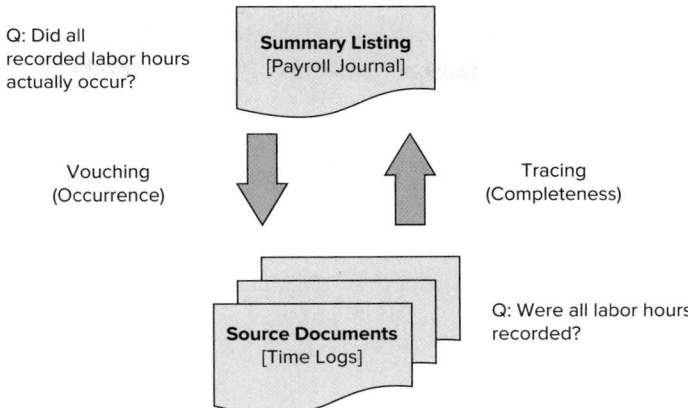

Vouching/Tracing (Payroll Cycle)

Q: Did all recorded labor hours actually occur?

Summary Listing [Payroll Journal]

Vouching (Occurrence)

Tracing (Completeness)

Source Documents [Time Logs]

Q: Were all labor hours recorded?

assertions for significant account balances can be limited, as previously discussed. For example, detailed vouching of recorded labor costs as a substantive test might be considered unnecessary or the audit team might decide it is appropriate to place considerable reliance on control activities in the payroll system. On the other hand, if tests of control activities reveal that the controls are not operating effectively, the RMM would be assessed at higher levels and substantive procedures would need to be increased in order to mitigate the risk of material misstatement for the relevant assertion related to the significant account (i.e., payroll expense) in the financial statements.

Perhaps not surprisingly, the final assessment of control risk (and consequently, the RMM) can be a difficult professional judgment. In the relevant sampling module (Module E), you will find explanations of sampling methods for performing tests of controls of the type illustrated in Exhibit 5.12. Further discussion of reaching a final assessment of control risk (and RMM) is covered in that module. However, remember that, in a sense, the overall evaluation of an entity's internal control system is based on the assessment of the control risk related to each relevant assertion for the identified significant accounts and disclosures. These assessments are the auditors' expression of the effectiveness of control activities for preventing, detecting, and correcting specific errors and frauds in management's relevant financial statement assertions.

An assessment of control risk should be coordinated with the final audit plan, which includes the list of **substantive procedures** to detect material misstatements in account balances and financial statement disclosures for each relevant assertion. Note that the reassessment of control risk typically can go only one direction: upward. If the controls are not functioning as described, they cannot be relied upon. On the other hand, even if weak controls are functioning, they are still weak and do not reduce the risk of material misstatement. There is one exception and that would be if the audit team finds that they were in error during the understanding of internal controls phase and the auditor becomes aware of additional controls about which they were previously unaware of. In that case, lowering control risk might be considered.

Thus far, our discussion of tests of control activities and substantive procedures has assumed that these are easily distinguishable. Be advised, however, that general audit procedures can at times be used as **dual-purpose tests**. That is, a single audit test can produce both control and substantive testing evidence and, thus, serve both purposes. For example, a selection of recorded payroll entries could be used to (1) vouch payroll to time cards and (2) calculate the correct dollar amount of payroll. The first procedure provides relevant information about an important control activity. The second provides dollar value information that can help offer substantive evidence to support the account balance in the financial statements.

☑ REVIEW CHECKPOINTS

5.24 What are *tests of control activities*?

5.25 What are the two reasons that an auditor may use to decide not to test controls on a financial statement audit of a nonissuer?

5.26 What are the four methods used to perform tests of control?

5.27 What is the difference between document examination and reperformance when conducting tests of controls?

5.28 What purposes are served by a dual-purpose test?

INTERNAL CONTROL COMMUNICATIONS

LO 5-5

Explain the communication of internal control deficiencies to those charged with governance, such as the audit committee and other key management personnel.

During the financial statement audit, there are times when the audit team determines that the internal control system has not been designed in a manner that will prevent or detect material misstatements. Also, there are times when the audit team determines that an internal control activity is not operating effectively. An **internal control deficiency** exists when either the internal control design or the operation of the control activity under consideration does not allow the entity's management or employees to detect or prevent misstatements in a timely fashion. A *design deficiency* is a problem relating to either a control activity that is missing, or an existing control activity that is so poorly designed that it fails to satisfy the control's objective. An *operating deficiency,* on the other hand, occurs when a control does not operate as it was designed to or when the person responsible for completing the control does not possess the authority or the competence to perform the control in an effective manner (possibly because employees are poorly trained). More serious internal control deficiencies can be categorized into one of two groups—material weaknesses or significant deficiencies—depending on their severity.

- A **material weakness** in internal control is defined as a deficiency, or combination of deficiencies, that results in a *reasonable possibility* that a *material misstatement* would not be prevented or detected on a timely basis.

- A **significant deficiency** is a deficiency or a combination of deficiencies in internal control that is less severe than a material weakness yet important enough to merit attention by those charged with governance.

The primary difference between a significant deficiency and a material weakness involves the *magnitude* of the potential misstatement that could occur and would not be detected on a timely basis. As the potential misstatement reaches overall materiality, an auditor may conclude that a material weakness exists. The final determination is always a matter of professional judgment.

For each financial statement audit engagement, the audit team must communicate significant deficiencies and material weaknesses in internal control that come to their attention during the performance of the audit. Auditors' communications of significant deficiencies and material weaknesses are intended to help management carry out its responsibilities for internal control monitoring and change. However, external auditors' observations and recommendations are usually limited to external financial reporting matters.

The auditors' internal control communication must be in writing and presented to those in charge of governance (usually the audit committee). The communication is to be addressed to management, the board of directors, or the audit committee. See Exhibit 5.14 for an illustration of such a communication, in the form of a letter. In addition, all deficiencies noted must be communicated in writing to management.

EXHIBIT 5.14
Internal Control
Communication

Michael Scarn, LLP
Scranton, PA

March 7, 2024

Board of Directors
Adams Company

In planning and performing our audit of the financial statements of Adams Company for the year ended December 31, 2023, we considered its internal control in order to determine our audit procedures for the purpose of expressing our opinion on the financial statements as well as the effectiveness of the company's internal control over financial reporting. Our consideration of internal control would not necessarily disclose all deficiencies in internal control that might be significant deficiencies. However, we noted a certain matter involving the internal control and its operation that we consider to be a significant deficiency under generally accepted auditing standards.

The matter noted is that shipping personnel have both transaction-initiation and alteration authority as well as custody of inventory assets. If invoice/shipping copy documents are altered to show a shipment of smaller quantities than actually shipped, customers or accomplices can receive your products without charge. The sales revenue and accounts receivable could be understated, and the inventory could be overstated. This deficiency caused us to spend more time auditing your inventory quantities.

A material weakness in internal control is defined as a deficiency, or combination of deficiencies, that results in a reasonable possibility that a material misstatement would not be prevented or detected on a timely basis. We do not believe that the significant deficiency described above is a material weakness.

This report is intended solely for the information and use of the board of directors and its audit committee, and is not intended to be, and should not be, used by anyone other than these specified parties.

Respectfully yours,

Michael Scarn, LLP

Audit teams often issue another type of report to management called a *management letter*. This letter may contain commentary and suggestions on a variety of matters in addition to internal control matters. Examples include issues identified during the audit related to operational and administrative efficiency, business strategy, and profit-making possibilities. Auditing standards do not require management letters, but they represent a type of value-added management advice rendered as part of an audit.

☑ REVIEW CHECKPOINT

5.29 What is meant by an internal control deficiency?

5.30 What is a material weakness?

5.31 What is a significant deficiency?

5.32 What is the nature of communications about internal control that an audit team would provide to an entity's management, board of directors, or audit committee?

Summary

The purposes of the audit team's evaluation of internal control are to assess the control risk (as part of the overall assessment of the RMM) in order to make the substantive audit plan and to report control deficiencies to management and the board of directors.

Internal control consists of five components: control environment, risk assessment, information and communication system, control activities, and monitoring of the control system. The auditor is required to gain an understanding of each of these components and to document this understanding in the audit files. The control environment and management's risk assessment are explained in terms of understanding the client's business. Elements of the accounting system are explained in conjunction with control activities designed to prevent, detect, and correct misstatements that occur in transactions. Documentation of an entity's internal control system is accomplished through the use of questionnaires, flowcharts, and narratives.

Internal control is assessed in a top-down manner by which audit teams first identify accounts that may contain significant risks of material misstatement. Audit teams then identify which relevant assertions may be misstated. After determining "what could go wrong," audit teams examine entity-level controls that might mitigate the risk of material misstatement. Finally, audit teams identify transaction level controls that would mitigate any residual risks. If the audit team relies on controls, it must test the controls to ensure they are operating effectively. Where controls are not in place to reduce the risk, or if testing the controls would not be cost effective, substantive tests are designed to identify any material misstatements.

It is important to distinguish the "client's control activities" from the "audit team's tests of controls." Control activities are part of the internal control designed and operated by the entity. The audit team's procedures are the audit team's own evidence-gathering work performed to obtain evidence about the client's control activities.

Key Terms

audit committee: A subcommittee of the board of directors that is generally composed of three to six "outside" members of the organization's board of directors, 181

business risks: Those factors, events, and conditions that could prevent the organization from achieving its business objectives, 182

control activities: The specific actions taken by a client's management and employees to help ensure that management directives are carried out, 183

control risk: The likelihood that the client's internal control policies and procedures fail to prevent or detect a material misstatement, 178

design effectiveness: A condition expressing whether controls would be expected to prevent or detect errors or fraud that could result in a material misstatement in the financial statements, 193

detective controls: The activities that detect misstatements after they occur, 184

dual-purpose test: An audit procedure used as both a test of controls and a substantive test, 203

enterprise risk management (ERM): A process effected by an entity's board of directors, management, and other personnel applied in strategy setting and across the enterprise that is designed to identify potential events that may affect the entity and to manage risks to be within its risk appetite to provide reasonable assurance regarding the achievement of entity objectives, 182

entity-level controls: The controls that are pervasive to the financial statements taken as a whole, 192

flowchart: The audit documentation that provides a visual display of the accounting system and control activities in an entity's internal control system, 193

information system: An entity's system, usually built on some type of technological platform that has been designed to produce the information necessary for the entity to operate and control its business operations, 188

internal control: Policies and procedures implemented by an entity to prevent or detect material accounting frauds or errors and provide for their correction on a timely basis, 176

internal control deficiency: A condition that exists when the design or operation of a control does not allow the entity's management or employees to detect or prevent misstatements in a timely fashion, 204

internal control questionnaire: The audit documentation that uses a checklist of internal control–related questions to gain and document an understanding of the client's internal control, 195

issuer: An entity that offers registered securities, such as stocks and bonds, for sale to the general public (also known as a public entity). Issuers are subject to mandatory audit requirements, 175

material weakness: A deficiency or combination of deficiencies that results in a reasonable possibility that a material misstatement would not be prevented or detected on a timely basis, 204

nonissuer: An entity that does not offer registered securities, such as stocks and bonds, for sale to the general public (also known as a nonpublic entity). Nonissuers are not subject to mandatory audit requirements, 197

narrative description: The audit documentation that describes the environmental elements, the accounting system, and the control activities in an entity's internal control, 193

operating effectiveness: Description of a condition expressing whether a control is operating as designed and whether the person performing the control possesses the necessary authority and qualifications to perform the control effectively. When a control is operating effectively, it is helping to prevent or detect misstatements. 193

preventive controls: The activities that prevent misstatements before they occur, 184

reasonable assurance: The concept that recognizes that the costs of control activities should not exceed the benefits that are expected from the control activities, 177

significant deficiency: A deficiency or a combination of deficiencies in internal control that is less severe than a material weakness yet important enough to merit attention by those charged with governance, 204

system-generated report: Any report that is generated by the audit client's information system that is used to execute its internal control procedures or produce its financial statements. It is important to test that each system-generated report is complete and accurate if it is being used for either of these purposes, 184

substantive procedures: The detailed audit and analytical procedures designed to detect material misstatements in account balances and footnote disclosures, 203

transaction-level controls: The controls that relate to specific classes of transactions, account balances, and disclosures, 193

walkthrough: The tracing of one or more transactions through the audit trail from initiation of the transaction to its inclusion in the financial statements, 193

Multiple-Choice Questions for Practice and Review

 All applicable Exercises and Problems are available with *Connect*

LO 5-3

5.33 The most important foundational component of an entity's internal control system is
 a. Effectiveness and efficiency of operations.
 b. The control environment.
 c. Reliability of financial reporting.
 d. Compliance with applicable laws and regulations.

LO 5-4

5.34 The primary purpose for obtaining an understanding of internal control during the audit of a nonissuer is to
 a. Provide a basis for making constructive suggestions in a management letter.
 b. Determine the nature, timing, and extent of further audit tests to be performed.
 c. Provide the rationale for the inherent risk assessment at the financial statement assertion level.
 d. Provide information for a communication of internal control–related matters to management.

LO 5-4

5.35 Effectiveness of audit procedures would be reduced by
 a. Selecting larger sample sizes for audit.
 b. Performing audit procedures at the fiscal year-end date as opposed to the interim period.
 c. Deciding to obtain external evidence instead of internal evidence.
 d. Performing procedures during the interim period as opposed to at the fiscal year-end date.

LO 5-4

5.36 To test the operating effectiveness of a control, an audit team might use a combination of each of the following tests *except* for
 a. Inquiry of client personnel.
 b. Observation of company operations.
 c. Confirmation of balances.
 d. Inspection of documentation.

LO 5-4

5.37 Which of the following is a preventive control?
 a. Reconciliation of a bank account.
 b. Recalculation of a sample of payroll entries by internal auditors.
 c. Separation of duties between the payroll and personnel departments.
 d. Detailed fluctuation analysis completed by the CFO for revenue.

LO 5-4

5.38 In most audits of large entities, control risk assessment contributes to audit efficiency, which means that
   a. The cost of substantive procedures will exceed the cost of control evaluation work.
   b. Auditors will be able to reduce the cost of substantive procedures by an amount more than the control evaluation costs.
   c. The cost of control evaluation work will exceed the cost of substantive procedures.
   d. Auditors will be able to reduce the cost of substantive procedures by an amount less than the cost of tests of controls.

LO 5-4

5.39 Which of the following is a device designed to help the audit team obtain evidence about the accounting and control activities of an audit client?
   a. A narrative memorandum describing the control system.
   b. An internal control questionnaire.
   c. A flowchart of the documents and procedures used by the company.
   d. All of the above.

LO 5-4

5.40 Tests of controls in a GAAS audit are used for
   a. Obtaining evidence about the financial statement assertions.
   b. Accomplishing control over the occurrence of recorded transactions.
   c. Applying analytical procedures to financial statement balances.
   d. Obtaining evidence about the operating effectiveness of client control activities.

LO 5-4

5.41 A transaction-level internal control activity is best described as
   a. An action taken by auditors to obtain evidence.
   b. An action taken by client personnel for the purpose of preventing, detecting, and correcting errors and frauds in transactions to eliminate or mitigate risks identified by the company.
   c. A method for recording, summarizing, and reporting financial information.
   d. The functioning of the board of directors in support of its audit committee.

LO 5-4

5.42 The purpose of separating the duties of hiring personnel and distributing payroll checks is to separate the
   a. Authorization of transactions from the custody of related assets.
   b. Operational responsibility from the record-keeping responsibility.
   c. Human resources function from the controllership function.
   d. Administrative controls from the internal accounting controls.

                                                                      (AICPA adapted)

LO 5-4

5.43 If the auditor plans to assess control risk at less than the maximum and rely on controls, and the nature, timing, and extent of further audit procedures are based on that lower assessment, the auditor must
   a. Obtain evidence that the controls selected for testing are designed effectively and operated effectively during the entire period of reliance.
   b. Assess control risk at less than the maximum for all relevant assertions.
   c. Perform only substantive procedures.
   d. Provide additional examples of responses to assessed fraud risks relating to fraudulent financial reporting.

LO 5-4

5.44 If they decide to rely on internal controls, the audit team should assess control risk for relevant assertions by considering the evidence obtained from all sources, including
   a. The auditor's testing of internal controls from the prior year.
   b. Misstatements detected during the financial statement audit.
   c. Any control deficiencies identified during the audit.
   d. All of these.

LO 5-4

5.45 When assessing control risk on a preliminary basis during a financial statement audit, a key objective of evaluating the design of an internal control system is to
   a. Determine that the company's employees are executing the control activities in accordance with the operating manuals at the client.

    b. Determine whether the company's internal control activities mitigate the risk of material misstatement for the relevant assertions if they operate effectively.

    c. Determine that the data being relied upon by the client's controller is complete and accurate.

    d. Determine whether the company's internal controls are operating effectively.

LO 5-1

5.46 According to the COSO Framework, internal control is a process that is designed to achieve objectives in three different categories. Which of the following responses is ***not*** one of the categories identified in the COSO Framework?

    a. Effective and efficient operations.

    b. Compliance with laws and regulations.

    c. Relevant financial reports.

    d. All these responses are categories in the COSO framework.

LO 5-5

5.47 A material weakness is a situation in which

    a. It is probable that an immaterial financial statement misstatement would not be prevented or detected and corrected on a timely basis.

    b. There is a remote likelihood that a material misstatement would not be prevented or detected and corrected on a timely basis.

    c. It is reasonably possible that a material misstatement would not be prevented or detected and corrected on a timely basis.

    d. It is reasonably possible that an immaterial misstatement would not be prevented or detected and corrected on a timely basis.

LO 5-5

5.48 When evaluating an internal control deficiency as part of a financial statement audit, the primary difference between a significant deficiency and a material weakness depends on

    a. Whether there is a reasonable possibility that the company's internal control system will fail to prevent or detect and correct a misstatement of an account balance or disclosure.

    b. Whether a misstatement has actually occurred as a result of the deficiency or the deficiencies.

    c. The magnitude of the potential misstatement resulting from the deficiency or the deficiencies.

    d. All of these are correct.

LO 5-1

5.49 Which of the following is an example of a limitation of an internal control system?

    a. Collusion among employees.

    b. Human error.

    c. Management override of controls.

    d. None of these items are limitations.

    e. All of the above are limitations.

LO 5-2

5.50 Both management and auditors have responsibilities related to the audit client's internal control system. What is an example of management's responsibility related to internal control system?

    a. Management must assess financial reporting risk.

    b. Management must establish an appropriate control environment.

    c. Management must ensure the security of the company's assets, including data.

    d. Only b and c are the responsibility of management.

    e. All of these are the responsibility of management.

LO 5-2

5.51 When considering auditor's responsibilities for the client's internal control system, much depends on whether the audit team believes it can rely on the client's internal control system in order to modify substantive testing on the financial statement audit. If the audit team is able to rely on the internal control system, which impact on substantive testing would you expect to see

    a. An increase in sample size from 60 to 90 selections.

    b. The use of a more effective substantive testing procedure.

    c. The timing of the substantive testing might occur at the interim testing date.

    d. No impact on substantive testing would be expected.

LO 5-4

5.52 Which of the following methods would be the most effective technique for an auditor to perform when testing the operating effectiveness of an internal control activity?

    a. Inquiry of appropriate personnel.

    b. Reading over the company's code of conduct.

    c. Reperformance of the control activity.

    d. Examination of appropriate documents for proper signatures.

LO 5-3

5.53 Which of the following items is *not* one of the five components of an internal control system, according to the COSO framework?

    a. Control environment.

    b. Risk assessment.

    c. Information and communication.

    d. Control activities.

    e. Completeness and accuracy.

LO 5-3

5.54 Which of the following controls is not an example of a monitoring control that is used to fulfill the monitoring component of the COSO framework?

    a. Audit committee inquiries of internal and external auditors.

    b. Three-Way match of purchase order, receiving report and vendor invoice.

    c. Supervisory review of controls, such as reconciliation reviews as a normal part of processing.

    d. Periodic evaluation of controls by the internal audit department.

Exercises and Problems

 All applicable Exercises and Problems are available with *Connect*.

LO 5-4

5.55 **Internal Control Audit Standards.** Auditors are required to obtain a sufficient understanding of each component of a client's internal control. This understanding is used to assess control risk and plan the audit of the client's financial statements.

Required:

    a. For what purposes should an auditor's understanding of the internal control components be used in planning an audit?

    b. What is required for an audit team to assess control risk below the maximum level?

    c. What should an audit team consider when seeking to reduce the planned assessed level of control risk below the maximum?

    d. What are the documentation requirements concerning a client's internal control components and the assessed level of control risk?

(AICPA adapted)

LO 5-3

5.56 **Separation of Duties.** Your small business client, Phillip's Computer Repair Shop, is experiencing financial difficulties and has to lay off one of its four employees in the accounting area. Phillip has asked you to determine what duties should be assigned to the three remaining employees—Abigail, Bryan, and Chris—to maintain the best separation of duties.

Required:

Assign the following 10 duties to each of the three employees.

    a. Reconcile bank statement.

    b. Open mail and list checks.

    c. Prepare checks for Phillip's signature.

    d. Prepare payroll checks.

    e. Maintain personnel records.

    f. Prepare deposit and take to bank.

    g. Maintain petty cash.

    h. Maintain accounts receivable records.

    i. Maintain general ledger.

    j. Reconcile accounts receivable records to general ledger account.

LO 5-4

5.57 **Types of Audit Tests.** Indicate whether each of the following audit procedures is primarily a test of controls or a substantive test. Please note that many of these tests could be used as a dual-purpose test. However, for purposes of this exercise, please indicate whether it would primarily be used as a test of controls or substantive test. Next, indicate the financial statement assertion most closely related to each audit procedure.

Required:

a. Vouch recorded sales invoices to supporting shipping documents.

b. Inspect recorded sales invoices for credit approval.

c. Vouch recorded sales invoices prices to the approved price list.

d. Send confirmations to all customers regarding accounts receivable.

e. Recalculate the arithmetic accuracy of the recorded sales invoices.

f. Compare the shipment date of recorded sales invoices with the invoice record date.

g. Trace recorded sales invoices to posting in the general ledger control account and in the correct customer's account.

h. Select a sample of shipping documents from the shipping department file and trace shipments to recorded sales invoices.

i. Scan recorded sales invoices and shipping documents for missing numbers in sequence.

j. Vouch sales invoices and shipping documents.

k. Evaluate the adequacy of the allowance for doubtful accounts.

l. Obtain financial statements or credit reports on large past due accounts and inquire of the credit manager about collections.

m. Calculate an estimate of the allowance for doubtful accounts using prior relations of write-offs and sales.

LO 5-4

5.58 **Internal Control Questionnaire Items: Assertions, Tests of Controls, and Possible Errors or Frauds.** The following is a selection of items from the internal control questionnaire on a payroll system in Exhibit 5.10.

1. Are names of terminated employees reported in writing to the payroll department?

2. Are authorizations for deductions signed by the employees on file?

3. Is there a timekeeping department (function) independent of the payroll department?

4. Are timekeeping and cost accounting records (such as hours, dollars) reconciled with payroll department calculations of hours and wages?

Required:

For each of the four preceding questions

a. Identify the assertion to which the question applies.

b. Specify one test of controls an auditor could use to determine whether the control was operating effectively.

c. Provide an example of an error or fraud that could occur if the control were absent or ineffective.

d. Identify a substantive auditing procedure that could detect errors or frauds that could result from the absence or ineffectiveness of the control items.

LO 5-4

5.59 **Obtaining a "Sufficient" Understanding of Internal Control.** The 12 partners of a regional public accounting firm met in special session to discuss audit engagement efficiency. Jones spoke up, saying, "We all certainly appreciate the firmwide policies set up by Martin and Smith, especially in connection with the audits of the large clients that have come our way recently. Their experience with a large public accounting firm has helped build our practice. But I think the standard policy of conducting tests of internal control on all audits is raising our costs too much. We can't charge our smaller clients fees for all of the time the staff spends on this work. I would like to propose that we give engagement partners discretion to decide whether to do a lot of work on assessing control risk. I may be old-fashioned, but I think I can finish a competent audit without it." Discussion on the subject continued but ended when Martin said, with some emotion, "But we can't disregard generally accepted auditing standards like Jones proposes!"

Required:

What do you think of Jones's proposal and Martin's view of the issue? Discuss.

LO 5-4

5.60 **Fraud Opportunities.** Simon Blank Construction Company has two divisions. The president (Chris Simon) manages the roofing division. Simon delegated authority and responsibility for management of the modular manufacturing division to John Gault. The company has a competent accounting staff and a full-time internal auditor. Unlike Simon's procedures, however, Gault and his secretary handle all bids for manufacturing jobs, purchase all materials without competitive bids, control the physical inventory of materials, contract for shipping by truck, supervise the construction activity, bill the customer when the job is finished, approve all bid changes, and collect the payment from the customer. With Simon's tacit approval, Gault has asked the internal auditor not to interfere with his busy schedule.

Required:
Discuss this situation in terms of internal control and identify frauds that could occur.

LO 5-4

5.61 **Internal Control Questionnaire Items: Errors That Could Occur from Control Weaknesses.** Refer to the internal control questionnaire on a payroll system (Exhibit 5.10).

a. Assume that the answer to each question is no. Prepare a table matching the questions to errors or frauds that could occur because of the absence of the control. Your column headings should be

Question	Possible Error or Fraud Due to Weakness

b. Which controls are preventive controls and which are detective?

LO 5-3

5.62 **Role of a Board of Directors in Internal Control.** Assume that the local newspaper just ran the following headline and article: *"Audit Results: Airport executives from Kentucky racked up $500K in lavish expenses, concert tickets, and even gentlemen's club tabs"*

LEXINGTON, Ky. (AP)—A small commercial airport in Kentucky—and the taxpayers who support it—picked up top executives' tabs in recent years for Hannah Montana concert tickets, Nintendo Wii video game bundles and even a $4,400 gentlemen's club check, according to a state auditor's report.

The report released Wednesday outlines indulgences ranging from pricey electronics and exercise equipment to lavish meals and champagne. In three years, officials tallied more than $500,000 in questionable personal expenses. [Author's note: General fund expenses were approximately $10,000,000 annually.]

Kentucky Auditor Crit Luallen said the former executive director at Lexington's **Blue Grass Airport** created a culture of wasteful spending so vast, employees sometimes were paid twice for the same expense and used airport credit cards as if they were personal checkbooks.

"I don't think we have ever seen an audit where so many different individuals involved in the management of a public agency abused the trust with such arrogance and lack of ethical standards," she said.

Luallen says she has forwarded the case to the Kentucky attorney general, the U.S. attorney's office, and the FBI.

Although the audit only covered the past three years, it does refer to one of the more glaring examples reported by the *Herald-Leader:* a $4,400 charge Michael Gobb and two other directors incurred at a Dallas strip club in 2004.

The charge, which appeared on the credit card statement of the airport's director of planning, was listed as going to Millennium Restaurant. The word "marketing" was handwritten next to the amount. The Associated Press obtained that receipt and others through an open records request.

The audit found that airport employees also used the coffers for tuxedos and other expensive clothing; more than 400 DVDs—many of them currently missing—for the internal airport library; $14,000 in holiday hams given out as gifts; and $7,400 for a NASCAR driving experience excursion for staff described as "team building."

More than 92 percent of the things Gobb charged to his airport card lacked proper documentation, Luallen said.

While Luallen acknowledged that Gobb was responsible for the free-spending culture, she said the board and its public accounting firm should have supervised the airport more closely.*

Source: Reprinted with permission from the February 26, 2009, online edition of the Daily Report 2009 (ALM Media Properties, LLC). All Rights reserved.

Required:

    a. Discuss the role of the board of directors in monitoring the behavior of a chief executive officer.

    b. If the chief executive officer has subordinates incur expenses that he or she approves, how can the board prevent abuse?

    c. Should external auditors be expected to detect abuses such as these?

    d. How should the use of credit cards be controlled?

LO 5-4

5.63 **Authorization of Credit Tests of Controls — Using IDEA** For this exercise, your client, Bright IDEAs Inc., has provided you with data for two related files, a listing of sales invoices, and a listing of customers with credit limits. To test whether credit authorization controls are in place, the auditor must complete a series of related steps:

    1. Import the client's database of sales invoices.

    2. Summarize the Accounts Receivable balance by customer.

    3. Import the client's customer credit limit data into IDEA.

    4. Join the Accounts Receivable balances by customer with the credit limit data.

    5. Extract customers with exceeded credit limits.

Required Data and IDEA workbook page references for current version available on *Connect*

Required:

Complete the preceding steps and answer the following questions:

    a. How many customers were granted credit with no indication that they had any credit limit assigned to them?

    b. How many customers exceeded their credit limit?

    c. What effects would the findings in parts (a) and (b) have on the auditor's assessment of the risk of material misstatement? What accounts and assertions are most likely influenced by these findings?

LO 5-4

IDEA
Data Analysis Software

5.64 **Identifying Payments to Unauthorized Suppliers — Using IDEA** For this exercise, your client, Bright IDEAs Inc., has provided you with data for two related files: an accounts payable history file and a supplier master file. To test the authorization of purchases to only legitimate suppliers, the auditor must complete a series of related steps:

    • Import the client's database of accounts payable.

    • Import the client's authorized supplier list.

    • Merge the accounts payable and supplier databases.

    • Identify payments to unauthorized suppliers.

Required Data and IDEA workbook page references for current version available on *Connect*

Required:

Complete the preceding steps and answer the following questions:

    • How many different unauthorized suppliers were paid during the year?

    • What was the total dollar amount of the payments to unauthorized suppliers?

    • What effects would the findings in parts (a) and (b) have on the auditor's assessment of the risk of material misstatement? What accounts and assertions are most likely influenced by these findings?

Apollo Shoes

Internal Control Testing

You are a recently promoted senior (in charge) auditor for Anderson, Olds, and Watershed and have been assigned to the engagement team of a new audit client, Apollo Shoes Inc. You have been asked to perform certain procedures related to the internal control system for Apollo Shoes. A detailed audit program for performing the procedures related to the internal control system, as well as working papers and supporting documentation, can be found on *Connect*.

Appendix 5A

Audit Plan

DUNDER-MIFFLIN INC. Audit Plan for Tests of Controls in the Payroll Cycle 12/31/23		
	Performed By	**Ref.**
1. Observe the separation of duties between the personnel, timekeeping, and payroll departments.		
2. Select a sample of payments from the payroll distribution for the year.		
a. Vouch labor costs to labor reports.		
b. Vouch labor reports to time tickets or computerized listing.		
c. Examine documentary evidence of supervisor review of labor costs.		
d. Examine documentary evidence of supervisor approval.		
3. Account for numerical sequence of selected job cost tickets and paychecks. Trace a sample of employees in the personnel file to payroll department files and the payroll register.		
4. Examine documentary evidence of budget comparison.		
5. Reconcile the payroll account distribution report and the job cost sheets.		
6. Examine supervisor's signature on payroll reports. Note evidence of comparison to budget.		

CHAPTER 6

Employee Fraud and the Audit of Cash

Rather fail with honor than succeed by fraud.

Sophocles, Greek playwright and scholar (496–406 BC)

Professional Standards References

Topic	AU-C/ISA Section	AS Reference
Consideration of Fraud in a Financial Statement Audit	240	2401
Consideration of Laws and Regulations	250	2405
Audit Planning	300	2101
Consideration of Internal Control in an Integrated Audit	265	2201
Identifying and Assessing the Risks of Material Misstatement	315	2110
Auditors' Responses to Risks of Material Misstatement	330	2301
Audit Considerations Relating to an Entity Using a Service Organization	402	2601
Audit Evidence	500	1105
External Confirmations	505	2310
Using the Work of an Audit Specialist	620	1210

LEARNING OBJECTIVES

In Chapter 5, we emphasized the important role of the internal control system in helping to ensure that the financial statement information being presented by an organization is credible and can be relied upon. Beyond its critical nature in the production of reliable financial statement information, the establishment of an internal control system is also important to help protect an organization's assets from being stolen. In this chapter, we focus on the auditor's role in helping clients prevent and/or detect the misappropriation (or theft) of assets in their organization.

Recall that in Chapter 4 we focused on the auditor's responsibilities related to fraudulent financial reporting, that is when an organization intentionally issues false or misleading financial statements to the investing marketplace. The professional standards make clear that auditors are also responsible for considering the possibility of misstatements that arise from the misappropriation of assets, otherwise known as employee theft. As a result, this chapter begins with a comprehensive discussion of this type of fraud.

Next, because cash is often the primary target of employee theft, the chapter logically transitions to a discussion of how the cash balance is audited. This discussion includes a description of the most common relevant financial statement assertions, along with a focus on the control and substantive testing procedures that are typically performed during the audit of cash balances. Importantly, our discussion of controls includes specific examples of additional internal control activities that can be put in place to help prevent or detect employee theft, also known as a misappropriation of assets fraud.

Your objectives are to be able to:

LO 6-1 Define and explain the differences among several kinds of employee frauds that might occur at an audit client.

LO 6-2 Identify and explain the three conditions (i.e., the fraud triangle) that often exist when a fraud occurs.

LO 6-3 Describe techniques that can be used to prevent employee fraud.

LO 6-4 Identify the relevant assertions and risks of material misstatement that are typically related to the cash balance.

LO 6-5 Identify important internal control activities present in a properly designed system to mitigate the risk of material misstatements for each relevant assertion related to cash and to help prevent or detect employee fraud.

LO 6-6 Give examples of substantive procedures used to test cash and relate them to the relevant assertions.

LO 6-7 Describe some extended procedures for detecting employee fraud schemes involving cash.

INTRODUCTION

LO 6-1
Define and explain the differences among several kinds of employee frauds that might occur at an audit client.

Rita Crundwell served as Comptroller and Treasurer of the city of Dixon, Illinois, for nearly three decades. Outside of work, she was a respected and well-known breeder of quarter horses. In fact, her horses won 52 world championships and she was honored as the leading owner by the American Quarter Horse Association for eight consecutive years. Ms. Crundwell was also highly respected at work, and she was regularly praised for her stewardship of taxpayer dollars. However, behind the scenes, Rita Crundwell was building her horse empire using taxpayer dollars! Using a secret bank account, she created false invoices and wrote checks payable to the harmless-sounding "Treasurer," which she deposited into an official-sounding account that was, in reality, her own. For nearly two decades, her scheme remained undetected, and by the time it was discovered in 2012, Rita Crundwell had stolen over $53 million from the city of Dixon. The fraud is considered to be the largest municipal fraud in American history, and became the subject of an award-winning 2017 film, *All the Queen's Horses.* Following her arrest, a fraud examination discovered the extent of the theft, and Ms. Crundwell was sentenced to a long jail term. However, she was released to home confinement in 2021 following 8 1/2 years in prison.[1]

Fraud examinations can be very exciting for auditors. A fraud examination has the aura of detective work—finding things that people want to keep hidden. However, such examinations are not easy and are not activities to be pursued without special training, experience, and care. While Module D presents a more detailed discussion of fraud examinations, this chapter presents a general introduction to the theory and definitions related specifically to misappropriation of assets-type fraud. In addition, you will learn how auditors evaluate the design and operating effectiveness of internal controls that are designed to mitigate the risk of this type of employee fraud. Importantly, because cash is often the primary target of fraudsters in these schemes, we illustrate internal controls as they relate to cash. Next, we present a discussion of the audit of the cash account on the balance sheet, with specific examples of internal control activities and related control tests and substantive audit procedures.

---

[1]"Former Dixon, IL Comptroller, Rita Crundwell, Sentenced to 19 1/2 years in Prison," *Forbes,* February 3, 2013.; "Rita Crundwell, who embezzled nearly $54 million from Dixon, released from federal prison," *Chicago Sun-Times,* August 5, 2021.

The Need for Skepticism in Audits of Cash

It is essential that auditors maintain their professional skepticism at all times throughout the engagement. In fact, professional standards require that when auditors brainstorm about the potential for all types of fraud in an engagement, the activity should "occur with an attitude that includes a questioning mind, and the key engagement team members should set aside any prior beliefs they might have that management is honest and has integrity."[2] Why is it so important that auditors maintain such a high degree of skepticism? Because a fraud is often committed by a person that an auditor least expects. Consider a Little League coach ripping off the league to buy expensive jewelry by using a routing number from a league payroll check.[3] Or consider an executive assistant at a large public accounting firm who wrote more than $1 million in checks to herself that were drawn on a client's bank account.[4] You just never know from where the next fraud might originate, as discussed in the following Auditing Insight!

AUDITING INSIGHT \ Let's Go for a Hike on the Appalachian Trail . . . for Life

This is exactly the plan that was put into action by James Hammes after stealing $8.7 million from his employer, a **Pepsi-Cola** bottler based in Ohio. Amazingly, his plan almost worked as he eluded capture by hiking and then living on the Appalachian Trail using an assumed name.

Hammes committed the crime while working as a controller at the company from 1998 to 2009. Because he had access to both the cash and the accounting records, he was able to divert company cash into a personal bank account and then cover up his crime by manipulating the accounting records. When the FBI started to ask him questions about the missing cash, Hammes decided to take a hike. Eventually, another hiker became aware of his story and tipped off the authorities. Hammes was sentenced to eight years in prison and must repay the money stolen.

Source: "Accountant Who Hid on Appalachian Trail Jailed for Embezzling Millions from Pepsi Bottler," *Accounting Today,* June 23, 2016.

Not surprisingly, whenever a fraud risk exists, the professional standards require that auditors gain an understanding of the internal controls that are in place to mitigate the assessed fraud risk. At a minimum, auditors are required to document that understanding in the audit documentation. In fact, auditors are also likely to evaluate the design, implementation, and operating effectiveness of identified internal control activities related to fraud risks that exist. Importantly, an entity's internal control cannot thwart or detect all fraud schemes. Inherent limitations in internal control (such as *collusion* among employees) prevent complete assurance that every fraud scheme will be detected before a loss is incurred. For this reason, the entity's auditors, accountants, and security personnel must be acquainted with the basics of fraud awareness. Although the professional auditing standards concentrate on fraudulent financial reporting—the production of materially false and misleading financial statements—the standards also require auditors to pay particular attention to employee fraud perpetrated against a client for several reasons. First, it is possible that employee fraud can result in a material financial statement misstatement to the extent that a crime was covered up using the financial statements. Second, employee fraud can be indicative of control deficiencies which can influence the auditor's assessment of control risk. Finally, audit clients always want to know if they are being robbed by their employees, regardless of the amount being stolen!

Employee Fraud Overview

Fraud consists of knowingly making material misrepresentations of fact with the intent of inducing someone to believe the falsehood and act upon it and, thus, suffer a loss or damage. This definition encompasses all ways by which people can lie, cheat, steal, and

[2]*PCAOB Auditing Standard No. 2110,* "Identifying and Assessing Risks of Material Misstatement."
[3]"Little League Coach Accused of Fraud," *St. Petersburg Times,* p. 3B, July 4, 2009.
[4]"Aide Gets 2 Years in Fraud Case," *San Francisco Chronicle,* p. D2, October 28, 2010.

Other Definitions Related to Fraud and Illegal Acts

Management fraud is an intentional deception that is orchestrated by management and is designed to injure investors and creditors by providing materially misleading information.

Errors are unintentional misstatements or omissions of amounts or disclosures in financial statements.

Direct-effect illegal acts are violations of laws or government regulations by the company, or its management or employees, that produce direct and material effects on dollar amounts in financial statements.

Embezzlement is a type of fraud that typically involves an employee wrongfully stealing assets that were entrusted to his or her care, custody, or control. In many situations, embezzlement is accompanied by false accounting entries or lying to try to cover up the crime.

deceive other people. **Employee fraud** (often referred to as **misappropriation of assets**) is the use of fraudulent means to take money or other property from an employer. It usually involves falsifications of some kind—false documents, lying, exceeding authority, or violating an employer's policies. Employee frauds generally consist of (1) the fraudulent act itself, (2) the conversion of assets to the fraudster's use (very easy if cash is involved), and (3) the cover-up. Catching people in the fraudulent act is difficult to accomplish. The act of conversion is equally difficult to observe because it typically takes place in secret away from the entity's offices (e.g., selling stolen inventory). By noticing signs and signals of fraud and then following the trail of missing, mutilated, or false documents that are part of the accounting records cover-up, alert auditors uncover many frauds. Being able to notice red flags, oddities, and unusual events takes some experience, but this chapter provides you with some ideas about where and when to look.

Employee Fraud Red Flags

Employee fraud can involve all types of employees from high-level executives to hourly employees in the warehouse. Even partners in accounting firms can be responsible as discussed in the next Auditing Insight. For most people, committing a fraudulent act is stressful. Observation of changes in a person's habits and lifestyle may reveal some red flags.[5] Fraudsters often exhibit these behaviors:

- Experience sleeplessness.
- Drink too much.
- Take drugs.
- Become irritable easily.
- Can't relax.
- Get defensive, argumentative.
- Can't look people in the eye.
- Sweat excessively.
- Go to confession (e.g., priest, psychiatrist).
- Find excuses and scapegoats for mistakes.
- Work standing up.
- Work alone.
- Work late frequently.
- Don't take vacations.

[5]Long lists of red flags can be found in G. J. Bologna and R. J. Lindquist, *Fraud Auditing and Forensic Accounting* (New York: John Wiley & Sons, 1995), pp. 49–56; W. S. Albrecht et al., in R. K. Elliott and J. J. Willingham, *Management Fraud: Detection and Deterrence* (New York: Petrocelli Books Inc., 1980), pp. 223–226; *Statement on Auditing Standards No. 99* (New York: AICPA, 2002); Auditing for Fraud courses of the Association of Certified Fraud Examiners; and courses offered by other organizations such as the AICPA and The Institute of Internal Auditors.

Personality red flags are difficult because (1) honest people often show them as well, (2) they often are hidden from view, and (3) auditors are not in a good position to notice these characteristics. Managers are in the best position to notice changes, especially when a person varies his or her lifestyle or spends more money than his or her salary seems to justify—for example, on homes, furniture, jewelry, clothes, boats, autos, vacations, and the like. Therefore, it is imperative that the auditor make specific inquiries of management regarding changes in an employee's demeanor and lifestyle.

AUDITING INSIGHT   Are You Kidding Me?

In February 2013, investigators arrested Craig Haber, a partner in tax and advisory services in the New York City office of **Grant Thornton** for stealing payments made by clients to the firm. Allegedly, his crimes began in July 2004 and continued through July 2012. In total, he is alleged to have stolen approximately $4 million from Grant Thornton. Apparently, Haber provided instructions to his clients to send checks or wire transfers directly to him in New York instead of sending the payments to Grant Thornton's headquarters in Chicago. He then took the checks and deposited them in a bank account that was opened "in the name of a sham business that was very similar to Grant Thornton's name." Haber then would transfer the funds from this account to his personal account.

Source: "Former Grant Thornton Partner Arrested for Stealing $4 Million in Client Payments," *Accounting Today,* February 7, 2013.

Characteristics of Fraudsters

White-collar criminals are not like typical bank robbers who are often described as "young and dumb." Bank robbers and other strong-arm criminals often make comical mistakes such as writing their holdup note on the back of a probation identification card, leaving the getaway car keys on the convenience store counter, using a zucchini as a holdup weapon, going through a fast-food restaurant's drive-through window backward, and timing the holdup to get stuck in rush hour traffic. Then there's the classic story about the robber who ran into his own mother at the bank. (She turned him in!)

Burglars and robbers average about $400–$500 for each hit. Employee frauds often range from $20,000 up to $500,000 or even millions if a computer is used. Yet employee frauds are not usually the intricate, well-disguised ploys you find in espionage novels. Who are these thieves wearing ties? What do they look like? Unfortunately, they look like most everybody else, including you and me. A typical white-collar criminal

- Has education beyond high school.
- Is likely to be married.
- Is a member of a church, mosque, or temple.
- Ranges in age from teens to over 60.
- Is socially conforming.
- Has an employment tenure from 1 to 20 years (although the scale of the fraud typically increases with tenure as the employee becomes more trusted).
- Has no arrest record.
- Usually acts alone (70 percent or more of incidents).

White-collar criminals do not make themselves obvious, although they may leave telltale signs or red flags. Older individuals (usually over 50) who hold high executive positions, have long tenure, and are respected and trusted employees have often gained the trust and confidence of others and, therefore, are in a position to commit the largest frauds. After all, these are the people who have access to the largest amounts of money and have the power to give orders and override controls. When managers minimize the significance of a weak or missing control by rationalizing that the employee involved is a "long-time trusted employee," most experienced auditors will actually escalate their level of fraud risk awareness. You should as well, as demonstrated by the following Auditing Insight.

AUDITING INSIGHT   Trusted Employees?

- A small business owner hired his best friend to work as his accountant. The friend was given full, unlimited access to all aspects of the business and was completely responsible for the accounting. Five years later, the owner finally terminated the friend's employment because the business was not profitable. Upon taking over the accounting responsibilities, the owner's wife found that cash receipts from customers were twice the amounts formerly recorded by the accountant "friend." An investigation revealed that the friend had stolen $450,000 in cash sales receipts from the business while the owner had never made more than $16,000 a year. (The friend had even used the stolen money to make loans to the owner to keep the business going!)

- An electrical supply company employed only one bookkeeper. She wrote the checks and reconciled the bank account. In the cash disbursements journal, she coded some checks as inventory, but she wrote the checks to herself, using her own name. When the checks

were returned with the bank statement, she simply destroyed them. Confronting continuous guilt over doing something she knew was wrong, she contacted a lawyer and turned herself in but not before she had stolen $416,000 over a five-year period. Because of the lack of separation of duties and her trusted status in the company, the fraud might have continued indefinitely (or at least until she bankrupted the company).

- Alex W. was a 47-year-old treasurer of a credit union. Over a seven-year period, he stole $160,000 from it. He was a good husband and father of six children, and he was a highly regarded credit union official. His crime came as a stunning surprise to his associates. Why did he do it? He owed significant amounts on his home, cars, college for two children, two side investments, and five credit cards. His monthly payments significantly exceeded his take-home pay.

Source: Association of Certified Fraud Examiners (ACFE), "Auditing for Fraud."

 REVIEW CHECKPOINTS

6.1 What are the defining characteristics of employee fraud? Embezzlement?

6.2 What does a fraud perpetrator look like? How does one act?

THE FRAUD TRIANGLE

LO 6-2
Identify and explain the three conditions (i.e., the fraud triangle) that often exist when a fraud occurs.

The three conditions that are likely to be present when a fraud occurs (Exhibit 6.1) are commonly referred to as the *fraud triangle*. The first condition (incentive/pressure) recognizes that an employee or manager of a company is likely to either have incentives in place (e.g., bonus compensation) or be under significant pressure to meet specific estimates, forecasts, or expectations about net income. The second condition (opportunity) recognizes that in order for a fraud to be perpetrated, there must either be a weakness in the system of internal control or an ability to circumvent the system. Finally, the third condition (attitude/rationalization) recognizes that for an employee or a manager of a company to perpetrate a fraud, the individual must possess an "attitude" that allows her or him to rationalize why he or she is knowingly committing a crime. Each of these conditions is now discussed.[6]

Incentive/Pressure

Incentive or pressure gives rise to a motive to commit fraud. A **motive**, in the fraud context, is essentially a reason for a person to take a fraudulent action that is believed to be unshareable with friends and confidants. Psychotic motivation is relatively rare, but it is characterized by the habitual criminal who steals simply for the sake of stealing. In

[6]For further reference, see D. R. Cressey, "Management Fraud, Accounting Controls, and Criminological Theory," pp. 117–147, and Albrecht et al., "Auditor Involvement in the Detection of Fraud," pp. 207–261, both in R. K. Elliott and J. J. Willingham, *Management Fraud: Detection and Deterrence* (New York: Petrocelli Books Inc., 1980); J. K. Loebbecke, M. M. Eining, and J. J. Willingham, "Auditors' Experience with Material Irregularities: Frequency, Nature, and Detectability," *Auditing: A Journal of Practice and Theory,* Fall 1989, pp. 1–28.

As noted previously in Chapter 5, an important feature of an effective internal control system is the separation of duties and responsibilities for (1) transaction authorization, (2) record keeping, (3) custody of or access to assets, and (4) reconciliation of actual assets to the accounting records. In general, a person acting alone or in a conspiracy who can perform two or more of these functions can commit a fraud by taking assets, converting them, and then covering up the crime. Proper separation of duties and responsibilities can prevent such fraudulent actions. For example, as it relates to cash disbursements, effective internal control begins with different people and different departments handling the cash disbursement *authorization; custody* of blank documents (checks); *record keeping* for payments; and bank *reconciliation.* Auditing with fraud awareness often involves the combination of observing client control activities that were put in place and trying to "think like a crook" and imagine ways that theft could occur. When controls are missing, the ways and means for theft may be obvious. Otherwise, it might take significant planning and collusion to figure out how to steal from an employer. An auditor often tries to assess fraud risk by considering the factors in the following Auditing Insight.

AUDITING INSIGHT   When Assessing Fraud Risk, Answer These Questions

According to fraud experts Joseph Wells and John Gill of the Association of Certified Fraud Examiners, when assessing fraud risk, answering a set of 15 questions is a good starting point for sizing up a company's vulnerability to fraud and creating an action plan for lessening the risks. Their key questions are

1. Is the company dominated by one or two key employees?

2. Do any key employees appear to have a close association with vendors?

3. Do any key employees have outside business interests that might conflict with their job duties?

4. Does the organization conduct pre-employment background checks to identify previous dishonest or unethical behavior?

5. Does the organization educate employees about the importance of ethics and antifraud programs?

6. Does the organization have antifraud policies and provide an anonymous way to report suspected violations of ethics?

7. Is job or assignment rotation mandatory for employees who handle cash receipts and accounting duties?

8. Has the company established positive pay controls with its bank by supplying the bank with a daily list of checks issued and authorized for payment?

9. Are refunds, voids, and discounts evaluated on a routine basis to identify patterns of activity among employees, departments, shifts, or merchandise?

10. Are purchasing and receiving functions separate from invoice processing, accounts payable, and general ledger functions?

11. Is the employee payroll list periodically reviewed for duplicate or missing Social Security numbers?

12. Are there policies and procedures that address the identification, classification, and handling of proprietary information?

13. Do employees who have access to proprietary information sign nondisclosure agreements?

14. Is there a company policy that addresses the receipt of gifts, discounts, and services offered by a supplier or customer?

15. Are the organization's financial goals and objectives realistic?

Source: Joseph T. Wells and John D. Gill, "Assessing Fraud Risk," *Journal of Accountancy,* October 2007, pp. 63–65.

When collecting corroborating evidence to support the financial statements, the audit team must remain vigilant against the potential for fraud. Discrepancies in the accounting records, conflicting evidence, and missing documentation are all symptomatic of financial statement fraud. When the audit team identifies such instances, members must follow up with management to identify the source of the problems. Management's response is a key source of evidence; vague, implausible, or inconsistent responses to inquiries can be a key indicator of the pervasiveness of the fraud. Similarly, problematic or unusual relationships between the audit team and management are often present in financial statement frauds.

Module D presents a comprehensive discussion of fraud examinations and how they differ from financial statement audits. However, an example to illustrate the difference between the engagements relates to evidence. The collection of evidence in a fraud examination (which can lead to prosecution and court scrutiny) is fundamentally different from the collection of evidence to support the auditor's opinion. If the auditors do come across questionable documents or any other evidence that may indicate fraud, they should immediately work to preserve the chain of custody of evidence. The *chain of custody* is the crucial link of the evidence to the criminal suspect that bears directly on the *relevance of evidence* often referred to by attorneys and judges. If documents are lost, mutilated, coffee stained, or otherwise compromised (so a defense attorney can argue that they were altered to frame the suspect), they lose their effectiveness for the prosecution. When completing a fraud examination, auditors should learn to mark the evidence, writing an identification of the location, condition, date, time, and circumstances as soon as it appears to be a signal of fraud. This marking should be on a separate tag or page; the original document should be put in a protective (plastic) envelope for preservation and locked away for protection. Then audit work should proceed with copies of the documents instead of originals. A record should be made of the safekeeping and of all persons who use the original. Any eyewitness observations should be recorded in a timely manner in a memorandum or on tape (audio or video) with corroboration of colleagues, if possible.

Similarly, an auditor may be involved in collecting evidence that is found in computers or stored in a digital manner. This type of computer forensic work must be completed with great care, and the goal is to examine the evidence in a manner that would be appropriate in reaching the goal of "identifying, preserving, recovering, analyzing, and presenting facts and opinions about the information." Generally, the evidence that is gathered from a computer forensic investigation is subject to the same rules of evidence as manual data in the eyes of law enforcement. This brief example underscores the importance of an auditor being properly trained to conduct a fraud examination.

Tone at the Top

Establishing the right tone at the top is an essential step toward building a strong fraud prevention program. This tone is established by upper management, in large part, to demonstrate a commitment to integrity and high ethical standards in the completion of all activities throughout the organization. The upper management team is responsible for setting the tone at the top. To send the right message from the top, many organizations publish codes of conduct for employees. Some of these codes are simple, and some are very elaborate. Government agencies and defense contractors typically have the most elaborate rules for employee conduct. Sometimes these codes are effective; sometimes they are not. However, a code can be effective only if the control environment and tone at the top support it. When the chairman of the board and the president make themselves visible and living examples of the code of conduct, other people will then believe it is real. Subordinates tend to follow the boss's lead.

Hiring and termination policies are important. Background checks on prospective employees are advisable and very good business practice. A new employee who has been a fraudster in some other organization's accounting department has a higher probability of being a fraudster in a new organization. As a result, organizations have even been known to hire private investigators to make background checks. Fraudsters should be fired and, in most cases, prosecuted. Experience has shown that they have a low rate of repeat offenses if they are prosecuted, but they have a high rate if not. Prosecution has the added benefit of sending the message that management does not believe that fraudulent activity is acceptable.

Unfortunately, the accompanying Auditing Insight, while incredibly disappointing, is far more common than it should be. As a result, auditors must always be vigilant and remain skeptical about the possibility of discovering employee fraud at their audit clients. This is why we have just provided so much coverage of the topic to begin this chapter. We now turn our attention to the account that is most frequently targeted by employee thieves—cash.

AUDITING INSIGHT   Hope He Doesn't Need Medical Care...

Ralph Puglisi embezzled at least $12.8 million over a six-year period from the University Medial Services Association, which pays for the operation of the University of South Florida's medical system. The association lacked appropriate segregation of duties, enabling Puglisi to use company credit cards, which he managed, to funnel the money through accounts on an adult website. Puglisi would charge large amounts on the site and pay a 40% fee to the recipients and

receive the difference. An investigation into the fraud began in 2021. Puglisi was able to accomplish the fraud because he had full authority to open up new credit card accounts, set the spending limits, and manage card access. This incident further demonstrates the importance of segregating duties when cash is involved.

Source: "An Employee Embezzled $12.9 Million from a Medical School's Non-profit. He spent most of it at one adult site," *The Washington Post.* August 17, 2021.

 REVIEW CHECKPOINT

6.7   What are some red flags that may indicate a cover-up or concealment of a fraud?

6.8   Is there anything odd about these two situations? (a) A check to Larson Electric Supply was endorsed with "Larson Electric" above the signature of "Eloise Garfunkle." (b) Numerous electronic payments were made and dated December 25, January 1, and July 4.

THE AUDIT OF CASH

LO 6-4
Identify the relevant assertions and risks of material misstatement that are typically related to the cash balance.

This section of the chapter is focused on the procedures that are completed as part of the financial statement audit for cash. However, our discussion of controls also includes examples of internal control activities that are specifically put in place to help prevent or detect employee fraud. In addition, because cash is relevant to each of an audit client's accounting cycles, we also discuss cash when describing the audits of the different cycles in the following chapters. For example, the basic activities in the revenue and collection cycle (Chapter 7) are (1) receiving and processing customer orders, including credit granting; (2) delivering goods and services to customers; (3) billing customers and accounting for accounts receivable; (4) collecting and depositing cash received from customers; and (5) reconciling bank statements. The basic acquisition and expenditure activities (Chapter 8) are (1) purchasing goods and services and (2) paying the bills. Similarly, the production and conversion cycle (Chapter 9) and the investing and financing cycle (Chapter 10) also feature the collection or expenditure of cash.

Management Reports and Data Files in an Audit of Cash

There are a number of different management reports, documents, and data files that are typically used by auditors when completing work on the cash account. These include the cash receipts journal, the cash disbursements journal, bank reconciliations, canceled checks, and bank statements.

Cash Receipts Journal

The cash receipts journal contains all of the detailed entries for all receipts of cash by the entity (debits to the cash account), including cash deposits. It contains the population of credit entries that should be reflected in the credits to accounts receivable for customer payments. It also contains the adjusting and correcting entries that can result from the bank account reconciliation. These entries are important because they may signal the types of accounting errors or manipulations that occur in the cash receipts accounting.

Cash Disbursements Journal

The cash disbursements journal is the company's detailed record of entries for checks written and electronic payments made during the period being audited (cash disbursements). Because all cash disbursements (other than those from a petty cash or payroll account) should be made via check or electronic transfer, the cash disbursements journal contains the cash credit entries that provide a population for testing cash disbursements. It also contains the adjusting and correcting entries that can result from the bank account reconciliation. These entries are important because they may signal the types of accounting errors or manipulations that occur in the cash disbursements accounting. The cash disbursements journal is usually inspected for suspect items such as checks made out to "cash" or "bearer" or electronic payments made to unauthorized vendors. In addition, company procedures should require that "voided" checks be retained and auditors should review these checks to ensure they were in fact actually voided and have not been recorded in bank statements.

Bank Reconciliations

The company's bank reconciliation is the primary document used to test the cash balance in the financial statements. The amount of cash in the bank is almost always different from the amount in the general ledger (financial statements), and the reconciliation is designed to explain the difference between these two amounts. In addition, a bank account reconciliation that compares the book cash balance to the bank cash balance provides management with an opportunity to monitor the separation of duties for cash receipts and cash disbursements. The timely preparation of bank reconciliations is, therefore, an important element of a company's internal control activities over cash.

Detecting Fraudulent Checks

Exhibit 6.2 describes the information found on the front of a typical check. Although companies do not receive the actual check back, a scanned image obtained of the check front is

EXHIBIT 6.2   How to Read the Front of a Check

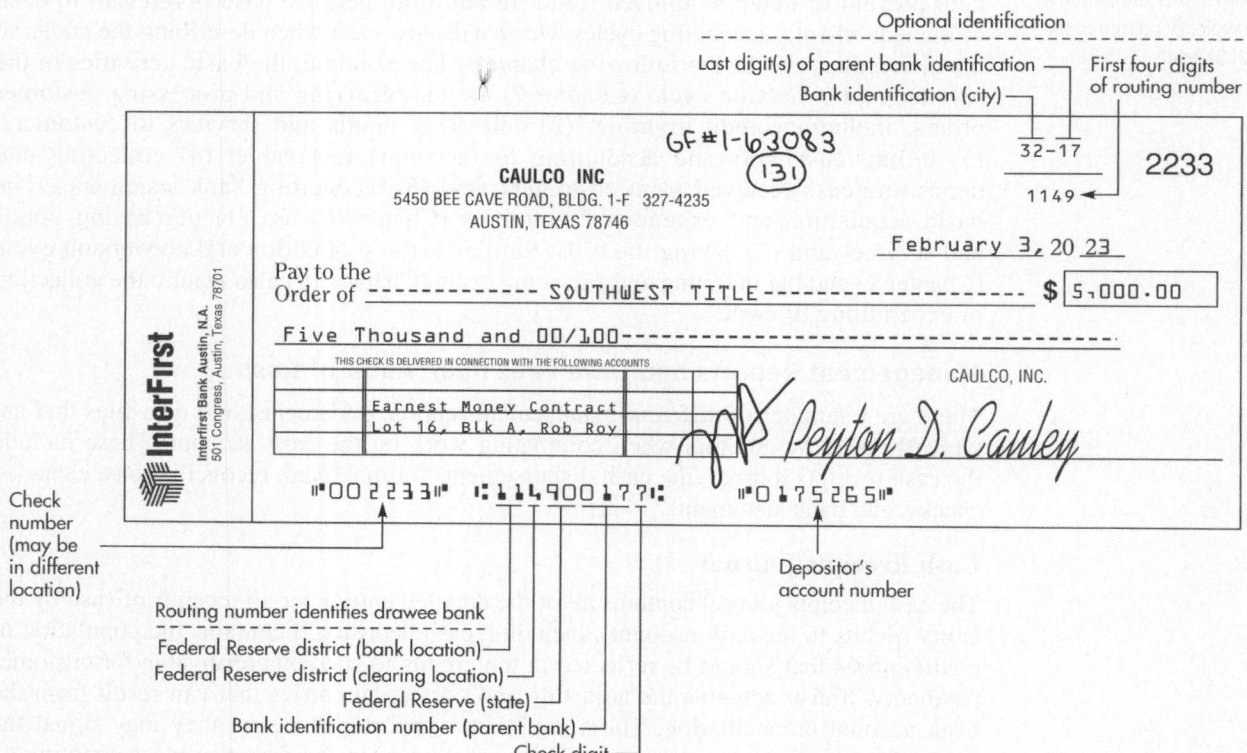

generally included with most bank statements and can be used to test for payees, amounts, or dates that do not match the cash disbursements journal. Further, check fronts obtained directly from a bank statement can be used to verify appropriate use of certain important internal controls, such as dual signatures for expenditures greater than a certain amount. It is important to understand characteristics of legitimate checks, not only for auditing purposes, but also for protecting yourself from fraud. Fake check scams have increased over 65% since 2015 and targeted victims are often not the elderly, as with most scams, perhaps because the elderly have more experience with checks. The recent target population—college students and the 20-something population, as described in the next Auditing Insight.

AUDITING INSIGHT   Secret Shopper? More Like Secret Scammer

Mika Benkert thought she had taken on a new job as a secret shopper. To test the system for her job, she was given a check for $3,450 and asked to wire $1,000 each to three separate people and keep the rest. Within days, the $3,450 check bounced and Mika was out $3,000— money she counted on to pay her rent and buy food. Unfortunately, Mika's story is not unique. Over 27,000 victims were reported in 2019 alone, and the number appears to be increasing each year with an average loss of $2,000. Why do smart, educated young victims fall for this so regularly? A likely explanation is lack of familiarity with checks. With the emergence of Venmo, Apple Pay, and other instant payment systems, younger victims expect that once they see the money in their account, it is theirs. Most college students are well aware of the risk of fraud with Apple Pay or Venmo. However,

checks are somewhat of a mystery for many. They can take *weeks* to actually clear and represent valid cash, even after it shows up in your account and the bank says it is cleared. The Federal Trade Commission warns that you should never wire or otherwise transfer money to a stranger, including through gift cards. In addition, they recommend ignoring any offers that ask you to pay for a prize, and never accept a check for more than the selling price. If you ever suspect that you have been approached or victimized by a scammer, report it to the Federal Trade Commission, your state attorney general, or the U.S. Postal Inspection Service.

Sources: "Millennials Targeted in New Scams Using Fake Checks," *NBC Nightly News,* February 7, 2020; "How to Spot, Avoid, and Report Fake Check Scams," Federal Trade Commission.

Historically, individuals engaging in fraudulent schemes involving cash often try to conceal their crimes by removing canceled checks they made payable to themselves or endorsed on the back with their own names. However, banks no longer return the canceled checks to their customers. Instead, copies of the front of the checks are included with the bank statement, often received electronically. This information is sufficient for reconciling an account, but it does not provide the information that may assist a company or auditor in detecting or investigating possible frauds. Other banks retain images of checks (generally only the front) on their websites. Given the reduction in ability to detect fraud through canceled check documentation, auditors, controllers, and CFOs should strongly recommend that their client or company pay close attention to the information that is available, and an increased emphasis on internal controls over checks is warranted.

Bank Statements

Most of the information shown on the bank statement in Exhibit 6.3 is self-explanatory. However, auditors should not overlook the usefulness of some of the information: The number and dollar amount of deposits and checks can be compared to the detail data on the bank statement; the account holder's federal business identification number is on the statement, and this can be used in other databases; and the statement itself can be studied for alterations.

✅ REVIEW CHECKPOINTS

6.9 Since checks are not returned to clients, how can an auditor tell whether the amount on a check was altered prior to payment by a bank?

6.10 Take a closer look at Exhibit 6.3. Is there anything wrong with the bank statement? What are some ways to tell whether any of the amounts have been altered?

EXHIBIT 6.3
Small Business Bank Statement

```
                                                                    27
      First RepublicBank

      FIRST REPUBLICBANK AUSTIN, N.A.                        ACCOUNT
      P.O. BOX 908                         ---          604017-526-5
      AUSTIN, TEXAS  78781                 ---    ---
                                           ---                  PAGE
                                           ---                     1

      CAULCO INC                                          SSN/TAX ID
      BLDG 1 OFFICE F                                     74-2076251
      5450 BEE CAVE RD
      AUSTIN,  TX                                        CYC MC FREQ
      78746                                              01 01 M0000

      **  YOUR CHECKING ACCOUNT       01-29-23 THRU 02-29-23  **

      TO YOUR PREVIOUS BALANCE OF - - - - - - - -        7,559.06
      YOU ADDED          1 DEPOSITS FOR  - - - - -        5,654.16
      YOU SUBTRACTED   26 WITHDRAWALS FOR - - - - -      10,838.29
      GIVING YOU A CURRENT BALANCE OF - - - - - -         7,374.93

      NUMBER OF DAYS USED FOR AVERAGES  - - - - -               31
      YOUR AVERAGE LEDGER BALANCE - - - - - - - -         4,014.67
      YOUR LOW BALANCE OCCURRED ON 02-22 AND WAS  -       2,374.93

                         THANK YOU


      ----------------------------------------------------------------
      ----------------------------------------------------------------
                    DEPOSITS AND OTHER ADDITIONS

         DATE    AMOUNT
         0204    5654.16
      ----------------------------------------------------------------
                    CHECKS AND OTHER WITHDRAWALS

      CHECK DATE    AMOUNT CHECK DATE    AMOUNT CHECK DATE    AMOUNT
       2201 0211     57.83  2214 0203    403.92  2225 0217    182.77
       **                   2215 0203    135.59  **
       2205 0222     16.72  2216 0216      6.16  2231 0205    254.37
       2206 0203    533.28  2217 0217    138.43  2232 0210     60.61
       2207 0203   1312.15  2218 0217    131.92
       **                   2219 0217     82.97  2234 0217     64.69
       2209 0203    247.10  2220 0217     87.49  2235 0218    279.97
       2210 0203    249.98  2221 0217     85.68  **
       2211 0203    255.26  2222 0217     84.69  2238 0219     90.00
       2212 0203    242.09  **
       2213 0203    384.91  2224 0217    449.71
```

Significant Accounts and Relevant Assertions

According to the professional standards, an account or disclosure is significant if there is a reasonable chance that it could contain a material misstatement. The auditor identifies significant accounts and relevant assertions by applying the audit risk model.

Chapter 4 introduced the audit risk model. As noted there, this model allows auditors to reduce audit risk to desired levels. *Audit risk* is defined as the risk that auditors will issue an unmodified opinion on financial statements that contain a material misstatement. Audit risk is manifested when a material misstatement enters the financial reporting process (inherent risk) that the client's internal controls do not prevent or detect (control risk) and that the auditors' substantive procedures do not detect (detection risk). Recall the basic three-step approach for using the audit risk model to plan an engagement:

1. Set audit risk at desired levels (normally, low).

2. Assess risk of material misstatement, which incorporates inherent risk based on the nature of the account balance or class of significant transactions and control risk based on gaining an understanding of internal control.

3. Determine detection risk at the significant account and assertion level based on the level of audit risk and risk of material misstatement.

The components of the audit risk model are assessed for each significant account and relevant assertion. This assessment recognizes that certain accounts and assertions assume an increased level of importance and are of more interest to auditors than others. For cash, existence is always a relevant assertion in the audit plan. Other assertions may also be relevant, depending on the facts and circumstances of the engagement. For example, if an audit client has worldwide operations, valuation may be relevant because certain cash balances may be denominated in foreign currencies, necessitating a translation adjustment.

Once all of the significant accounts and disclosures have been identified, the auditor then needs to identify the relevant assertions. According to the professional standards, a financial statement assertion is relevant if it has a reasonable possibility of containing a misstatement that would cause the financial statements to be materially misstated. Exhibit 6.4 identifies the assertions that are typically most relevant for cash. Although different companies may have other risks, in general the most significant risks relate to the existence of cash and the presentation and disclosure of cash. As previously stated, depending on the nature of the audit client's operations, valuation may also be a relevant assertion for cash. Although we will focus our discussion on these assertions, other assertions may be relevant depending on the facts and circumstances at the audit client.

Risk of Material Misstatement

As part of the planning process, the auditor must determine the source of a misstatement that could cause the financial statements to be materially misstated. One way to assess the risk of material misstatement is to use the "what could go wrong?" (WCGW) approach when thinking of each financial statement assertion. WCGW is a part of each audit firm's process and enables a thorough assessment of the risk of material misstatement.

When considering WCGW for cash, auditors consider three primary concerns: (1) Does the reported cash balance really exist? (2) Is the cash balance valued properly? (3) Is the reported cash balance presented properly and have the appropriate disclosures been made? Exhibit 6.5 summarizes the WCGW analysis for cash.

EXHIBIT 6.4
Significant Accounts and Relevant Assertions

Significant Account	Relevant Assertions
Cash	Existence
	Valuation
	Presentation and disclosure

EXHIBIT 6.5
What Could Go Wrong?

Significant Account	Relevant Assertions	What Could Go Wrong?
Cash	Existence	The cash balance may not exist in the company's bank accounts.
	Valuation	The cash balance that is held in foreign countries may not have been translated properly.
	Presentation and disclosure	There may be restrictions on the cash balance that were not properly disclosed.

Evaluating the Design and Operating Effectiveness of Internal Controls

When evaluating the design of internal controls related to cash, an auditor must always consider whether the controls have been designed to mitigate the risk of material misstatement for each relevant assertion identified for the cash balance. In addition, because cash is so frequently a favorite target of employee thieves, controls over cash must be unusually strong and include special considerations related to employee fraud. As a consequence, when evaluating the design of internal controls related to cash, an auditor must also consider whether the controls have been designed to mitigate the risk of employee fraud. Clearly, there is overlap between these two goals (i.e., mitigating the risk of material misstatement *and* preventing employee fraud), meaning that certain control activities may help to achieve objectives at an audit client. However, to help improve your understanding of both objectives, we now consider these topics separately.

Internal Control Evaluation for Mitigating the Risk of Material Misstatement

Recall from the audit risk model that the auditor assesses inherent risk to determine where in the financial statements it is reasonably possible that a material misstatement could enter the process *before the consideration of any internal controls.* However, risk of material misstatement is the combination of both inherent risk and control risk.

Professional standards require auditors to first gain an understanding of the internal controls that have been designed to mitigate the risk of material misstatement for each relevant assertion identified by the auditor. In a well-designed system, the internal control activity should be explicitly designed to be aligned with this relevant assertion that was identified in a WCGW analysis.

In effect, the question an auditor should ask is, "Has the audit client designed and implemented a control that, *if operating effectively,* would mitigate the identified risk of material misstatement? Would it prevent or detect the material misstatement?" Importantly, we have already discussed how auditors would gain an understanding of the internal controls related to cash earlier in this chapter, including the control environment and tone at the top. This discussion remains relevant when auditing the cash balance.

However, when auditing the cash balance, for each WCGW identified, the auditor seeks to identify a control activity that has been placed in operation to mitigate the identified risk of material misstatement. For example, as shown in Exhibit 6.6, for the WCGW scenario related to the existence of cash (i.e., the cash does not exist in the company's bank account), the auditor must consider what management can do to prevent this misstatement from entering the financial statements or from going undetected. One control that the auditor would expect management to implement involves periodic reconciliation of the bank balance to the book balance. If an employee regularly completes the reconciliation and a supervisor reviews the reconciliation, the control should mitigate the risk that a material misstatement can proceed through the accounting system undetected.

In order to rely on the design of the client's internal controls and support a reduction in control risk, the auditor must determine if each identified control is operating as designed and whether the person operating the control has the authority and competence to do so. The auditor's ultimate responsibility is to document enough support to conclude whether the control activity was operating effectively to mitigate the risk of material misstatement for the relevant assertion identified.

Auditors can perform tests of controls to determine whether company personnel are properly performing controls that are said to be in place. In general, the procedures used in tests of controls are inquiry, observation, inspection, and reperformance. Understand that if a control is missing or ineffective, the risk of a material misstatement increases, but an error or fraud may or may not exist. Thus, if controls are not in place or personnel in the organization are not performing their control activities effectively, auditors need to design substantive procedures to try to detect whether control failures have produced material misstatements in the financial statements. Exhibit 6.6 includes a column that identifies

- *Custody.* Blank documents such as blank checks should be kept secure at all times. If unauthorized persons can obtain a blank check, they can be in another country before an embezzlement is detected.
- *Authorization.* Cash disbursements are typically authorized by an accounts payable department's assembly of purchase orders, vendor invoices, and internal receiving reports to demonstrate a valid obligation to pay. This assembly of supporting documents is called a *voucher* and will be discussed in more detail in Chapter 8. (Accounts payable obligations usually are recorded when the purchaser receives the goods or services ordered.) A person authorized by management signs the checks. A company may have a policy to require two signatures on checks over a certain amount (e.g., $50,000). Vouchers should be marked "PAID" or otherwise stamped to show that they have been processed completely so they cannot be paid a second time.
- *Recording.* When checks are prepared, entries are made to debit accounts payable and credit cash. Someone without access to the check-writing function should always perform the recording function.
- *Reconciliation.* Monitoring of the internal control over cash can be provided by timely bank reconciliations made by individuals outside of the normal cash operations.

If combinations of two or more of these responsibilities are completed by one person or within the same office, there may be an opportunity for a fraudster to commit a crime. In addition, and almost more important in today's environment, is the fact that the computerized information-processing system must also provide for proper separation of duties. In practice, this is often accomplished by assigning the proper functional "permissions" to the appropriate employees through their password access credentials. Simply stated, in a computerized environment, proper separation of duties is dependent on proper password access controls. This is discussed in more detail in Module H.

Tests of Controls over Cash Disbursements   An entity should have detailed control activities in place and operating to prevent, detect, and correct accounting errors. Auditors can perform tests of controls to determine whether the internal control activities related to the correct handling of cash disbursements are operating effectively. If the internal control activities are not operating effectively (e.g., because personnel in the organization are not performing the cash control activities very well), auditors need to expand substantive audit procedures to ensure that the cash balance is not materially misstated and to identify possible fraudulent acts related to cash.

Exhibit 6.9 identifies common internal control activities that are designed to prevent or detect the misappropriation of cash and the typical test of control that would be used by auditors. As you will note, many of these procedures can be characterized as steps taken to make it difficult for a fraudster to steal cash. However, there are also controls designed to detect fraudulent activity if it occurs. The control tests are designed to enable the audit team to obtain objective evidence about the *operating effectiveness* of control

EXHIBIT 6.9
Tests of Controls over Cash Disbursements

Internal Control	Test of Control
• Checks are not printed until voucher packets are prepared. • An employee compares amounts on printed checks with voucher packets prior to submission for signature. • Only authorized signers are permitted to sign checks.	1. For a sample of recorded cash disbursements from the cash disbursements journal, inspect supporting documentation for evidence of mathematical accuracy, correct classification, proper approval, authorized signature and then compare the date on the check with the date recorded in the disbursements journal.
• Checks are prenumbered and accounted for.	2. Scan checks for sequence. Look for gaps in sequence and duplicate numbers.
• Bank reconciliations are prepared on a timely basis.	3. Review bank reconciliations to ensure that they were prepared on a timely basis.

activities. Many businesses rarely write paper checks. The controls required for electronic payments requires the same system of separation of duties. However, the majority of the access and authorization controls are accomplished through passwords and restrictions of access to data and accounting information systems.

☑ REVIEW CHECKPOINTS

6.11 What is the basic sequence of activities in the cash collection process?

6.12 Why should a list of cash remittances be made and sent to the accounting department? Wouldn't it be easier to send the cash and checks to the accountants so they can enter the credits to customers' accounts accurately?

6.13 What is *lapping*? What procedures can auditors employ to detect lapping?

6.14 What feature of the acquisition and expenditure control would be expected to prevent an employee from embezzling cash by creating fictitious vouchers?

LO 6-6
Give examples of substantive procedures used to test cash and relate them to the relevant assertions.

Substantive Procedures

As you have learned previously while studying audit risk, the primary reason for evaluating the internal control system at an audit client is to reach an overall assessment of risk of material misstatement for each relevant assertion. In fact, the assessment of risk of material misstatement is completed to help form the basis for determining the nature, timing, and extent of substantive testing. Risk of material misstatement at the assertion level is composed of both inherent risk and control risk for each relevant assertion.

If inherent risk has already been assessed as high, this means that there is high susceptibility for this account to be misstated. Recall that control risk is the probability that an entity's controls will fail to prevent or detect material misstatements due to errors or frauds. Due to the nature of cash, the majority of audit clients have strong controls over cash, and tests of controls often support a reduction in control risk. This reduction in control risk reduces the auditor's assessment of the risk of material misstatement over cash. However, regardless of the final assessment of the risk of material misstatement, as with any significant account, the auditor will perform at least some substantive procedures over cash.

As stated previously, there are two types of substantive tests: analytical procedures and tests of detail and balances. As you may recall, a substantive analytical procedure is one where the auditor substantiates an account or disclosure by developing an independent estimate of the amount and then comparing the recorded balance to the estimate. Due to the lack of predictability of the cash balance, auditors rarely, if ever, use substantive analytical procedures to test cash. Rather, auditors typically rely exclusively on tests of detail. For example, auditors will generally test the bank reconciliations in detail, including sending confirmations to all banks in order to substantiate the existence of cash. Exhibit 6.10 presents the substantive tests that are likely to be completed to address remaining risks of material misstatement related to cash.

Without question, the most important test of detail completed on cash is to test the details of the entity-prepared and reviewed bank reconciliation for each significant banking relationship, including confirmation of the balance with the financial institution. For that reason, our discussion of substantive procedures will focus almost exclusively on testing the bank reconciliation in detail. In effect, the auditor needs to obtain the bank reconciliation for each significant account and audit the details contained on each of them. In a well-functioning control environment, auditors should never have to perform the company's internal control activity of preparing the bank reconciliation. Always remember that the timely completion of the bank reconciliation is the responsibility of the client and is a critical element of internal control over cash.

EXHIBIT 6.10   Substantive Tests

Significant Account	Relevant Assertions	Internal Control Activity	Tests of Internal Control	Possible Substantive Tests of Detail
Cash	Existence	The CFO perfoms a detailed review of the bank reconciliation on a monthly basis.	For a sample of bank reconciliations, reperform the reconciliation. Trace several reconciling items to the appropriate supporting documentation.	Test the bank reconciliation details for each significant cash account being held. Confirm the bank balance with each financial institution.
	Valuation	The treasurer reviews the cash translation adjustment calculation monthly and independently checks that the appropriate spot rate has been used for each foreign currency.	Inspect the monthly cash translation adjustment calculation for evidence of the treasurer's review.	For a sample of monthly cash translation adjustment calculations, trace each foreign currency spot rate to a third-party pricing service.
	Presentation and disclosure	The corporate secretary reviews the cash footnote disclosure on a quarterly basis to ensure that all legal restrictions on the cash balance have been properly disclosed.	For a sample of cash accounts, reperfom the work completed by the corporate secretary to ensure that all cash restrictions have been properly disclosed.	For a sample of cash accounts, examine the legal agreements with each financial institution. Based on the examination, determine whether the audit client has properly disclosed any legal restrictions in their footnotes.

Bank Reconciliation

A client-prepared bank reconciliation is shown in Exhibit 6.11. When auditing the bank reconciliation, the auditor should begin by confirming the account balance listed as the "balance per bank" on the top of the bank reconciliation for each bank account from each bank that the client utilizes in the business. The auditor is required to send a confirmation request, and each bank should respond directly to the public accounting firm's office. This procedure is important because the auditor needs to make sure that the confirmation request was actually completed by an independent professional at a third-party bank. In fact, despite suspicions about unusual cash arrangements, **Ernst & Young GmbH** signed off on the audit opinion for three years for **Wirecard,** a fintech company based in Germany, before recognizing material fraudulent financial reporting. A description is found in the nearby Auditing Insight.

 AUDITING INSIGHT   The Dangers of Bank Confirmations

Wirecard AG was a "shining star" of the European tech scene. The company processed payments for a wide variety of online businesses and recorded huge amounts of revenue from its operations. However, much of it was a sham. Approximately $2.1 billion of the company's cash did not exist. The auditors, **Ernst & Young GmbH,** verified the amounts through confirmation. However, the scanned electronic copies of the confirmations from two Philippine banks proved to be fraudulent. When the auditors requested additional support in March 2020, it was discovered that the banks in question never held *any* cash for Wirecard. Unlike many revenue fraud schemes that involve fictitious accounts receivable, CEO Markus Braun inflated cash and confused the auditors with multiple offshore bank accounts. This incident further demonstrates an advantage of electronic confirmations received directly through a secure portal from known and registered banks.

Source: "Wirecard Scandal Puts Spotlight on Auditor Ernst & Young," *The Wall Street Journal,* June 27, 2020.

The Auditing Insight "The Dangers of Bank Confirmations" demonstrates the difficulties auditors can have with authenticating the source of confirmations. The use of third-party electronic information intermediaries, such as Confirmation (formerly called Confirmation. com), has changed the process of cash confirmation greatly over the past decade, but it has not reduced the auditor's responsibility to authenticate the source of the information.

EXHIBIT 6.11
Bank Reconciliation

C-2

| Prepared By | SSS, III | Date | 1/24/2024 |
| Reviewed By | SSS, Jr. | Date | 1/28/2024 |

Dunder-Mifflin Inc.
Bank Reconciliation
12/31/2023

Prepared by Client

Balance per bank statement			$343,055.04 ᵉ
Add:			
Deposits in transit, 12/31/23			$6,000.00 ᶜᴿᴶ, ˣ
			$349,055.04
Deduct O/S Checks			
3086	12/27/23	8,533.12 ˣ ᶜᴰᴶ	
3087	12/27/23	4,741.30 ˣ ᶜᴰᴶ	
3088	12/27/23	14,122.85 ˣ ᶜᴰᴶ	
3089	12/28/23	6,707.05 ˣ ᶜᴰᴶ	
3090	12/28/23	10,587.77 ˣ ᶜᴰᴶ	
3091	12/28/23	7,566.07 ˣ ᶜᴰᴶ	
3092	12/28/23	5,684.08 ˣ ᶜᴰᴶ	
3093	12/28/23	18,421.90 ˣ ᶜᴰᴶ	
3094	12/28/23	12,741.49 ˣ ᶜᴰᴶ	
3095	12/28/23	988.55 ˣ ᶜᴰᴶ	
3096	12/28/23	10,014.94 ˣ ᶜᴰᴶ	
3097	12/28/23	15,746.44 ˣ ᶜᴰᴶ	
3098	12/28/23	16,472.00 ˣ ᶜᴰᴶ	
3099	12/28/23	12,610.96 ˣ ᶜᴰᴶ	(144,938.52) ᶠ
			$204,116.52 ᵀ/ᴮ⁻¹
General Ledger Cash Balance			ᶠ

ᶠ Footed

ˣ Traced from cuttoff bank statement on page *C-2-2*

ᵉ Confirmed by bank, confirmation on page *C-2-1*

ᶜᴿᴶ Agreed to cash receipts journal

ᶜᴰᴶ Agreed to cash disbursements journal

It is rare for a bank to respond to a paper request for confirmation, and thus nearly all audit firms confirm bank balances through a third-party intermediary, often Confirmation. A standard confirmation request to a bank will also confirm outstanding loan balances, which will provide substantive evidence to test the existence and completeness assertions for liabilities. We will discuss substantive tests of loan balances in more detail in Chapter 10.

As discussed above with the Satyam case, the key issue with confirmations of any kind is the reliability of the response. The use of electronic confirmation through an intermediary such as Confirmation provides many benefits to the auditor. It allows information to be transmitted in a safe and secure manner, and most importantly, it allows for validation of the authenticity of the bank employee responding to the confirmation request, an issue which was previously a major concern for auditors. Before an auditor can rely on an electronic confirmation, the auditor must obtain an understanding of the intermediary's internal control system. In most situations, the auditor relies upon a report provided by another auditor who audited the design and operating effectiveness of the intermediary under SSAE 16, and provided a Service Organization Controls (SOC) report, most commonly a SOC1 report. SOC reports are discussed in more detail in Module A.

The confirmation process through an online intermediary generally requires the registration of the auditor, the client, and the financial institution, although in some situations, the intermediary will make paper confirmation requests on behalf of an auditor. Clients must provide electronic authorization in order for the auditor to request confirmation. Upon authorization, the auditor will initiate a confirmation request. Unlike traditional paper confirmations which often take multiple weeks for completion, electronic confirmation requests are often completed in a matter of days.

Exhibit 6.12 provides an example of a standard electronic bank confirmation performed through Confirmation. You will note in Exhibit 6.12 that the auditor can also confirm outstanding loan balances listed on the balance sheet. As shown, the auditors would be gathering evidence to test the completeness assertion for liabilities because the auditor would trace the information provided by the bank to loan balances listed on the balance sheet. We will discuss substantive tests of the loan balance in more detail in Chapter 10.

A word of caution is in order. Although financial institutions may note exceptions to the information requested in a confirmation and may confirm items omitted from it, the AICPA warns auditors that sole reliance on a confirmation to satisfy the completeness assertion for cash and liabilities is inappropriate. Employees of financial institutions cannot be expected to search their information systems for balances and loans that may not be immediately evident as the client company's assets and liabilities—in fact the electronic response shown here specifically notes that.

Once the "balance in the bank" has been confirmed and cross-referenced to the balance in the bank reconciliation, the following additional procedures are typically used in auditing the bank reconciliation:

- Test the mathematical accuracy of the reconciliation, including the listing of outstanding checks and deposits in transit.
- Examine reconciling items to ensure they are appropriately classified (e.g., that they were legitimate outstanding checks that were written but not paid by the bank at the statement date).
- Reconcile the book balance to the trial balance, which has been traced to the general ledger.

The auditors' information source for validating the bank reconciliation items is typically a **cutoff bank statement**, which is normally a complete bank statement for the month following the date of the financial statements. The cutoff bank statement is important because it (1) is received directly by the auditors (which qualifies as *external evidence*) and (2) documents important bank transactions occurring early in the subsequent period. These transactions subsequent to the date of the financial statements are important for testing the completeness of the client's outstanding check list as well as the existence of any deposits in transit. The bank cutoff statement can also be used in a *search for unrecorded liabilities* discussed in more detail in Chapter 8.

Deposits in transit should be *vouched* from the bank reconciliation to the bank cutoff statement (*existence*) and should have been recorded by the bank in the first business days of the cutoff period. If recorded later, the inference is that the deposit may have been composed of receipts of the period after the date of the financial statements.

When auditing reconciling items that decrease cash (i.e., outstanding checks) listed on the bank reconciliation and because the audit team is most concerned about the existence of cash (i.e., overstatement) rather than the completeness of cash (i.e., understatement), the completeness of the outstanding checks listing is more critical than to support the existence of such checks. Comparably, when auditing reconciling items that increase cash (i.e., deposits in transit) listed on the bank reconciliation, the *existence* of the deposits-in-transit on the reconciliation is more critical than their *completeness* because the audit team is most concerned about the existence of cash (i.e., overstatement) rather than the

EXHIBIT 6.12
Bank Confirmation

C-2-1

Report Name Completed Confirmation Report - Detail
Client Name : Dunder Mifflin, Inc.
As of Date : 12/31/2023

| Prepared By | SSS, III | Date | 1/24/2024 |
| Reviewed By | SSS, Jr. | Date | 1/28/2024 |

Client's Statement

We have provided to our accountants the following information as of the close of business on the Request Date below regarding our deposit and loan balances. Please confirm the accuracy of the information, noting any exceptions to the information provided. If the balances have been left blank, please complete this form by furnishing the balance in the appropriate space below.† Although we do not request nor expect you to conduct a comprehensive, detailed search of your records, if during the process of completing this confirmation additional information about other deposit and loan accounts we may have with you comes to your attention, please include such information below.

At the close of business on the Request Date below, our records indicated the below deposit balances, and that we were also directly liable to the financial institution for loans at the close of business on the stated Request Date as indicated below.

† Ordinarily, balances are intentionally left blank if they are not available at the time the form is prepared.

Client's Company Information

Dunder Mifflin, Inc.
1725 Slough Avenue
-
Scranton, PA - 18501
United States

Engagement Number
21379380

Requestor Information

Michael Scarn, LLP
123 Vine St -
Scranton, PA - 18501
United States

Lead
Michael Scarn
580-555-1212
mscarn@scarnllp.com
Office: Michael Scarn, LLP

Authorized Signers

| **Name** | **Job Title** | **Phone** | **Email** |
| Michael Scott | General Manager | 570-555-5635 | mscott@dundermifflin.com |

Responder Information

Twenty-First National Bank-Demo
P.O. Box 1
-
Scranton, PA - 18503
United States

Contact
-
I.M. Rich
******
******

Client's Account Information

| **Type/Form** | **Account ID** | **Account Name** |
| Financial/Asset | 604-17-526-5 | Checking |

Confirmation Request

| **Status** | **As of Date** | **Currency** | **Request ID** | **Delivery Method** |
| ✓ Completed | 12/31/2023 *(mm/dd/yyyy)* | USD* | m06va2g36v5s7x | ☑ In-Network |

Balance: $ 343,055.04   C-2
Interest:

* USD - United States of America, Dollars

Questions / Comments

(01/22/2024 10:46 AM) I.M. Rich said - Balance as of 12/31/2023

Responder Statements

The information presented is in agreement with our records. Although we have not conducted a comprehensive, detailed search of our records, no other deposit or loan accounts have come to our attention except as noted.

Request ID:m06va2g36v5s7x

Requestor

Michael Scarn, LLP
123 Vine St -
Scranton, PA - 18501
United States

Contact: Michael Scarn
580-555-1212
mscarn@scarnllp.com
Date/Time: 01/20/2024 10:44 AM
IP: 50.59.221.154

Responder

Responder: Twenty-First National Bank-Demo
Address: P.O. Box 1
-
Scranton, PA-18503
United States

Contact: I.M. Rich
Title: -
Email: ******
Phone: ******
Date/Time: 01/22/2024 10:46 AM
IP:

Client Electronic Signature

Company: Dunder Mifflin, Inc.
Address: 1725 Slough Avenue
-
Scranton, PA-18501
United States

Contact: Michael Scott
Title: General Manager
Email: mscott@dundermifflin.com
Phone: 570-555-5635

Date/Time: 01/07/2024 09:43 AM
IP: 50.59.221.154

Michael Scott

Activity Log

Date/Time	Name	Email	IP	Description
01/05/2024 10:41 AM	Michael Scarn	mscarn@scarnllp.com	50.59.221.154	Requested Client Authorization - Michael Scott
01/07/2024 09:43 AM	Michael Scott	mscott@dundermifflin.com	50.61.221.154	Client Signature Submitted
01/20/2024 10:44 AM	Michael Scarn	mscarn@scarnllp.com	50.59.221.154	Confirmation Initiated
01/22/2024 10:46 AM	I.M. Rich	********	61.79.221.154	Confirmation Completed

Note: System dates and text are displayed according to your user profile settings. Manually entered text and dates will display as entered by the user.

completeness of cash (i.e., understatement). As a result, the audit team *traces* outstanding checks that cleared on the cutoff bank statement (and were either returned with that statement or identified in that statement) to the client's list of outstanding checks for evidence that all checks that were written prior to the reconciliation date were included on the list of outstanding checks. Additionally, canceled checks should be traced to the cash disbursements listing (journal). For large outstanding checks not clearing in the cutoff period, other documentation supporting the disbursement may be used. These procedures are key and described by tick marks in Exhibit 6.11. As the next Auditing Insight suggests, it is important to pay close attention to possible errors in the bank reconciliation.

AUDITING INSIGHT \ The Darn Stuff Is So Easy to Count

Through the use of discretionary estimates, **HealthSouth,** one of the largest health care providers in the United States, inflated its assets by $1.5 billion. In an even more bizarre twist, the company overstated its cash by more than $300 million, according to prosecutors. Because auditors use standardized forms to confirm cash balances with financial institutions, how the auditors missed the cash overstatement is

a mystery. "I'm shocked that cash is manipulated and overstated, because the darn stuff is so easy to count," stated one audit expert. Nevertheless, auditors must never take the cash balance for granted when conducting the audit.

Source: "Did HealthSouth Auditor Ernst Miss Key Clues to Fraud Risks?" *The Wall Street Journal,* April 10, 2003.

 REVIEW CHECKPOINT

6.15 What is a bank reconciliation? Who should prepare it and how do auditors use it?

"EXTENDED PROCEDURES" TO DETECT FRAUD

LO 6-7
Describe some extended procedures for detecting employee fraud schemes involving cash.

The auditing literature often refers to "extended procedures," which are "specific responses to fraud risk factors." Although the professional standards list a few of these procedures, an exhaustive list would be very lengthy. Moreover, authorities fear that a definitive list might limit the range of such procedures, so extended procedures are generally identified as whatever is necessary in the circumstances. This section describes some of the extended procedures and warns that (1) some auditors may consider them ordinary and (2) other auditors may consider them unnecessary in any circumstances. They are useful detective procedures in either event. Consider the following procedures.

Schedule of Interbank Transfers

Due to the nature of the cash balance, auditors also will sometimes, although rarely because of decreased float times, prepare a **schedule of interbank transfers** to determine whether transfers of cash from one bank to another were recorded properly (correct amount and correct date). The audit team should also be alert to the possibility of a company's practice of illegal "kiting." **Check kiting** is the deliberate floating of funds between two or more bank accounts in order to make it appear that more cash is present than is really the case. When a check is deposited in one bank, the cash receipts journal immediately includes that deposit. At the same time, the check, drawn on a different bank account, does not appear in the cash disbursements journal for several days. By this method, an entity can use the time required for checks to clear to inflate the cash amount on the entity's books. Advances in information technology and increased bank scrutiny have reduced the incidences of check kiting dramatically in recent years. However, auditors must still be aware of the possibility; and the schedule of interbank transfers is a technique designed to detect the practice.

These are some characteristic signs of check-kiting schemes:

- Frequent deposits and checks in rounded and the same amounts.
- Frequent deposits with checks written on the same (other) banks.
- Short time lags between deposits and withdrawals.
- Frequent ATM account balance inquiries.
- Many large deposits made on Friday to take advantage of the weekend.
- Large periodic balances in individual accounts with no apparent business explanation.
- Low average balance compared to high level of deposits.
- Many checks made payable to other banks.
- Banks' willingness to pay against uncollected funds.
- "Cash" withdrawals with deposit checks drawn on another bank.
- Checks drawn on foreign banks with lax banking laws and regulations.

Today, banks have implemented the Check Clearing for the 21st Century Act, referred to as "Check 21." In this system, checks are converted to digital images, allowing for a dramatic increase in speed in check clearing. The benefit is that the "float" on the check is virtually eliminated, and kiting becomes difficult to perform and conceal. However, in the Check 21 system, the paper check is usually destroyed, a hard copy of the check is never returned to the customer or its bank, and consequently, the nature of the audit trail is significantly different. In investigating possible fraud, the audit team is able to obtain only an electronic copy of the front of the check and the controls over the safeguarding of the imaging files will be of great importance.

Proof of Cash

Auditors can use another method to discover unrecorded cash transactions. It is called a *proof of cash*. The **proof of cash** is a reconciliation in which the bank balance, the bank report of cash deposited, and the bank report of cash paid are all reconciled to the corresponding records maintained in the entity's general ledger, cash receipts journal, and cash disbursements journal.

The proof of cash attempts to reconcile the deposits and payments reported by the bank to the deposits and payments recorded in the cash receipts and cash disbursements journals, respectively, as well as the final general ledger totals. The proof of cash is a very effective procedure to verify cash transactions but is usually used only when controls over cash are weak, which is rarely the case. Thus, a proof of cash is not always performed in an audit of cash.

Count and Recount Cash on the Same Day

If a client maintains a significant amount of cash on hand, such as a financial institution or some retailers, a second cash count is unexpected. Auditors might catch an embezzling employee who incorrectly believes that "the auditors are gone, so now it's safe!" Auditors should always make sure a client employee is present during the count and that the employee signs for the returned cash so the auditor cannot be blamed for any shortages. Another "trick of the trade" is to make sure that the auditor's pockets are empty (leave wallets locked up safely elsewhere) when counting client cash on hand. This is especially important when counting cash at a financial services client such as a bank or credit union. All cash should be counted simultaneously to prevent embezzling employees from substituting cash from other places. If this is not possible (e.g., the employee claims that he or she does not have the safe combination), there is audit tape (similar to police tape) to seal the safe until it can be opened with the auditor present. If the seal is broken, the auditor's suspicions should be raised.

AUDITING INSIGHT Free Givenchy, Anyone?

Identity theft and hacking have become a major headache for both businesses and consumers. But sometimes, identity theft can be low tech. Five sales associates for **Saks Fifth Avenue** used stolen customer personal information to purchase hundreds of thousands of dollars of high-end handbags and shoes from the retailer's famous Manhattan location. A ringleader stole the information and recruited associates and customers to assist with the scheme. The associates would use fake customers to make the purchases, then sell the items on the black market or return them to the store.

Source: "5 Indicted in Alleged Saks Fifth Avenue ID Theft Shopping Spree," ABC News, October 6, 2014.

Retrieve Customers' Checks

If an employee has diverted customer payments for his or her own use, the canceled checks and deposits to a bank where the company has no account are not available because they are returned to the issuing customer. Ask the customer to give copies of the front of the check or provide access for examination.

Use Marked Coins and Currency

Plant marked money in locations where cash collections should be gathered and turned over for deposit.

Analyze the Mix of Cash and Checks in Deposits

This procedure is most effective for retail operations in which cashiers receive significant amounts of both cash and checks. Unless there is a marked change in consumer behavior, one should expect the mix of cash and checks to be relatively consistent over time. A decrease in the proportion of cash in the mix is often a sign that employees may be stealing cash.

Measure Deposit Lag Time

Compare the date of the deposit slip to the date recorded as a debit in the general ledger to the date the deposit was credited in the account by the bank. Someone who takes cash and then holds the deposit for the next cash receipt to make up the difference causes a delay between the date of recording and the bank's date of deposit.

Document Examination

When performing this procedure, auditors will look for erasures, alterations, and photocopies where originals should be filed, telltale lines from a copier when a document has been pieced together, handwriting, and other oddities. Auditors should always insist on seeing original documents instead of photocopies. Importantly, while professional document examination is a technical activity that requires special training (e.g., training by the IRS, FBI), crude alterations may still be observed by the auditor when performing procedures, which should lead to a consultation with a professional document examiner when deemed necessary.

Inquiry

Be careful not to discuss fraud possibilities with the managers who might be involved. It gives them a chance to cover up their fraud or even resign from the organization prior to detecting the fraud. Described as a nonaccusatory method of asking key questions of personnel during a regular audit, *fraud audit questioning* provides employees an opportunity to furnish information about possible misdeeds. Fraud possibilities are addressed in a direct manner, so this approach must have the support of management. Example questions are: "Do you think fraud is a problem for business in general?" "Do you think this company has any particular problem with fraud?" "In your department, who is beyond suspicion?" "Is there any information you would like to furnish regarding possible fraud within this organization?"[8]

Covert Surveillance

When performing this procedure, auditors will observe activities while not being seen. For example, audit team members might watch employees as they punch in to a work shift, observing whether they use only one time card. Casino auditors actually get paid to gamble so they can observe cash-handling procedures. Traveling hotel auditors may check in unannounced, use the restaurant and entertainment facilities, and observe employees to determine if they are stealing cash receipts or tickets. (Trailing people on streets, undercover surveillance, and maintaining a "stake-out" should be left to trained investigators.)

 **AUDITING INSIGHT** · The Case of the Extra Checkout

The district manager of the grocery store could not understand why receipts and profitability had fallen and inventory was hard to manage at one of the largest stores in her area. She hired an investigator who covertly observed the checkout clerks and reported that no one had shown suspicious behavior at any of the nine checkout counters.

"Nine? That store only has eight," she exclaimed! As it turns out, the local store manager had installed another checkout aisle not connected to the cash receipts and inventory maintenance central computer and was pocketing all the receipts from that register.

Source: Association of Certified Fraud Examiners (ACFE), "Auditing for Fraud."

Horizontal and Vertical Analyses

Horizontal and vertical ratio analysis procedures are very similar to preliminary analytical procedures explained in earlier chapters. *Horizontal analysis* refers to changes of financial statement numbers and ratios across several years. *Vertical analysis* refers to financial statement amounts expressed each year as proportions of a base such as sales for the income statement accounts and total assets for the balance sheet accounts. Auditors look for relationships that do not appear logical as indicators of potential large misstatement and fraud.

Net Worth Analysis

This analysis is used when fraud has been discovered or strongly suspected and the information to calculate a suspect's net worth can be obtained (e.g., asset and liability records, bank accounts). The method involves calculating the suspect's net worth (known assets minus known liabilities) at the beginning and end of a period (months or years) and then trying to account for the difference as (1) known income less living expenses and (2) unidentified difference. The unidentified difference may be the best available approximation of the amount of a theft.

Expenditure Analysis

This analysis is similar to net worth analysis except the data are the suspect's spending for all purposes compared to known income. If spending exceeds legitimate and explainable income, the difference may be the amount of a theft.

Reasonableness Tests

Often, auditors become so involved in ticking and tying numbers that they forget to ask themselves the simplest questions: Where is the cash going? For what purpose? Is this reasonable? The answers to these questions often motivate the auditor to ask more penetrating questions of management and to dig for more evidence.

---

[8] Joseph T. Wells, "From the Chairman: Fraud Audit Questioning," *The White Paper,* National Association of Certified Fraud Examiners, May–June 1991, p. 2. This technique must be used with extreme care and practice.

✔ REVIEW CHECKPOINTS

6.16   Why would an auditor prepare a *proof of cash*?

6.17   What is the difference between a *normal* procedure and an *extended* procedure?

6.18   What can an auditor find using net worth analysis? Expenditure analysis?

Summary

Although auditing standards concentrate on management fraud—the production of materially false and misleading financial statements (i.e., fraudulent financial reporting)—professional standards also require auditors to consider employee fraud perpetrated against an entity. Attention to employee fraud is important in the context that the cover-up may create financial statement misstatements (e.g., overstating inventory to disguise unauthorized removal of valuable products). The three conditions that are likely to be present when a fraud occurs (Exhibit 6.1) are commonly referred to as the "fraud triangle." The first condition (incentive/pressure) recognizes that an employee or a manager of a company is likely to either have incentives in place (e.g., bonus compensation) or be under significant pressure to meet specific estimates, forecasts, or expectations about net income. The second condition (opportunity) recognizes that in order for a fraud to be perpetrated, there must be a weakness in the system of internal control to allow the fraud to occur. Finally, the third condition (attitude/rationalization) recognizes that for an employee or a manager of a company to perpetrate a fraud, the individual must possess an "attitude" that allows her or him to rationalize that she or he is knowingly committing a crime.

Audit team members need to know about the red flags, those telltale signs and indications that have accompanied many frauds. When studying a business operation, members' ability to "think like a crook" to devise ways to steal can help in planning procedures designed to determine whether fraud has happened. Often, imaginative "extended procedures" can be employed to unearth evidence of fraudulent activity. Audit team members must always exercise technical and personal care, however, because accusations of fraud are taken very seriously. For this reason, after preliminary findings indicate fraud possibilities, the audit team should enlist the cooperation of management and assist fraud examination professionals when bringing an investigation to a conclusion.

Once the relevant assertions have been identified for cash (e.g., existence) and the tests of control activities are complete, the auditor must evaluate the evidence obtained from risk assessment activities and control tests to determine the risk of material misstatement for each relevant assertion. Cash is highly liquid, very portable, and not easily identifiable. For these reasons, cash is often the primary target of fraudulent activities and must be carefully controlled and monitored. Accordingly, controls over cash receipts and disbursements must be strong. With respect to auditing the cash balance, the detailed procedures performed on the bank reconciliation provide evidence about the existence of cash.

Additional procedures can be performed to try to detect attempts at lapping accounts receivable collections. These procedures include comparing the details of customer payments listed in bank deposits to the details of customer payment postings (remittance lists).

Key Terms

check kiting: The practice of building up balances in one or more bank accounts based on uncollected (floating) checks drawn against similar accounts in other banks, 243

cutoff bank statement: A client bank statement (usually sent directly to the auditor) that includes all paid checks and deposits made through a certain date, usually the end of the month following the financial statement date, 241

direct-effect illegal acts: The violations of laws or government regulations by a company or its management or employees that produce direct and material effects on dollar amounts in financial statements, 218

embezzlement: A type of fraud involving employees or nonemployees wrongfully taking money or property entrusted to their care, custody, and control, often accompanied by false accounting entries and other forms of lying and cover-up, 218

employee fraud (also called **misappropriation of assets**): The use of fraudulent means to take money or other property from an employer. It consists of three phases: (1) the fraudulent act, (2) the conversion of the money or property to the fraudster's use, and (3) the cover-up, 218

errors: The unintentional misstatements or omissions of amounts or disclosures in financial statements, 218

fidelity bond: An insurance policy that covers most kinds of cash embezzlement losses, 235

fraud: The misrepresentation of facts that the individual knows to be false with the intention to deceive, 217

lapping: The theft of a payment and the application of subsequent payments to cover the theft, 235

lockbox: An arrangement in which a fiduciary (e.g., a bank) receives the payments, lists the receipts, deposits the money, and sends the remittance advices (stubs showing the amount received from each customer) to the company, 234

management fraud: The deliberate fraud committed by management that injures investors and creditors through materially misleading information, 218

misappropriation of assets: See employee fraud, 218

motive: In the fraud context, essentially a reason for a person to take a fraudulent action that is believed to be unshareable with friends and confidants, 220

proof of cash: A reconciliation in which the bank balance, the bank report of cash deposited, and the bank report of cash paid are all reconciled to the company's general ledger and cash receipts and disbursements journals, 244

schedule of interbank transfers: A document prepared for use in analyzing whether transfers of cash from one bank to another were recorded properly (correct amount and correct date), 243

Multiple-Choice Questions for Practice and Review

 All applicable Exercises and Problems are available with *Connect*.

LO 6-2

6.19 When auditing with "fraud awareness," auditors should especially notice and follow up employee activities under which of these conditions?

a. The company always estimates the inventory but never takes a complete physical count.

b. The petty cash box is always locked in the desk of the custodian.

c. Management has published a company code of ethics and sends frequent communication newsletters about it.

d. The board of directors reviews and approves all investment transactions.

LO 6-3

6.20 The best way to enact a broad fraud prevention program is to

a. Install airtight control systems of checks and supervision.

b. Name an "ethics officer" who is responsible for receiving and acting on fraud tips.

c. Place dedicated hotline telephones on walls around the workplace with direct communication to the company ethics officer.

d. Practice management "of the people and for the people" to help them share personal and professional problems.

LO 6-3

6.21 A good fraud prevention program should address employees' motivation to steal from the company. The best method for doing this is to

a. Establish employee assistance programs.

b. Require a fidelity bond on all employees.

c. Require reconciliations of all accounts to be reviewed by a supervisor.

d. Ensure that all accounts with high inherent risk of fraud are audited.

LO 6-3

6.22 A code of ethics is an important element of a fraud prevention program. Which of the following would diminish the effectiveness of a company's code of conduct?

a. The establishment of a chief ethics officer.

b. The establishment of a hotline for reporting unethical behavior.

c. The violation of the code of ethics by senior management.

d. The posting of the code of ethics in the company workplace.

LO 6-2

6.23 Which of the following is *least* indicative of fraudulent activity?

a. Numerous cash refunds have been made to different people at the same post office box address.

b. Internal auditors cannot locate several credit memos to support reductions of customers' balances.

c. Bank reconciliation has no outstanding checks or deposits older than 15 days.

d. Three people were absent the day the auditors handed out the paychecks and have not picked them up four weeks later.

LO 6-6

6.24 When performing confirmation of cash balances with a bank, the auditor is primarily gathering evidence related to which financial statement assertion?

a. Existence

b. Completeness

c. Valuation

d. Presentation and Disclosure

LO 6-6

6.25 Which of the following is true about electronic cash confirmations obtained through **Confirmation** (Confirmation.com)?

a. Responses to electronic confirmations are often delayed compared with manual confirmations.

b. Electronic cash confirmations provide more convincing evidence for the completeness assertion than manual confirmations.

c. Auditors must obtain evidence supporting the reliability of controls surrounding the **Confirmation** (Confirmation.com) process.

d. It is more difficult to determine the authenticity of an electronic confirmation obtained through **Confirmation** compared with confirmations mailed to the auditors.

LO 6-5

6.26 Allison Everhart, an employee in accounts payable, believes she can run a fictitious invoice through the accounts payable system and collect the money. She knows payments are subject to an audit. Which account would be the best place to hide the fraud?

a. Inventory

b. Wage expense

c. Consulting service expense

d. Property tax expense

LO 6-1

6.27 Which of these arrangements of duties could most likely lead to an embezzlement or theft?

a. The inventory warehouse manager has responsibility for making the physical inventory observation and reconciling discrepancies to the perpetual inventory records.

b. The cashier prepared the bank deposit, endorsed the checks with a company stamp, and delivered the cash and checks to the bank for deposit (no other bookkeeping duties).

c. The accounts receivable clerk received a list of payments received by the cashier so he could make entries in the customers' accounts receivable subsidiary accounts.

d. The financial vice president received checks made out to suppliers and the supporting invoices, signed the checks, and mailed the checks.

LO 6-5

6.28 Which of the following would the auditor consider to be an incompatible operation if the cashier receives remittances?

a. The cashier prepares the daily deposit.

b. The cashier makes the daily deposit at a local bank.

c. The cashier posts the receipts to the accounts receivable subsidiary ledger cards.

d. The cashier endorses the checks.

LO 6-5

6.29 Which of the following is an effective audit procedure that an auditor might use to detect kiting between intercompany banks?

a. Review the composition of authenticated deposit slips.

b. Review subsequent bank statements.

c. Prepare a schedule of the bank transfers.

d. Prepare a year-end bank reconciliation.

LO 6-5

6.30 Immediately upon receipt of cash, a responsible employee should
    a. Record the amount in the cash receipts journal.
    b. Prepare a remittance listing.
    c. Update the subsidiary accounts receivable records.
    d. Prepare a deposit slip in triplicate.

(AICPA adapted)

LO 6-4

6.31 Each morning the controller gets the prior day's list of remittances, a copy of the payment report, and a copy of the deposit slip returned from the bank. When comparing these items, the controller would be able to determine that
    a. No checks were returned for insufficient funds.
    b. The cash received and remittance advice received were maintained in a single batch.
    c. The accounts receivable system has controls over unauthorized access.
    d. The assistant controller does not also reconcile the subsidiary accounts payable.

LO 6-4

6.32 Upon receipt of customers' checks in the mail room, a responsible employee should prepare a remittance list that is forwarded to the cashier. A copy of the list should be sent to the
    a. Internal auditor to investigate the list for unusual transactions.
    b. Treasurer to compare the list with the monthly bank statement.
    c. Accounts receivable bookkeeper to update the subsidiary accounts receivable records.
    d. Entity's bank to compare the list with the cashier's deposit slip.

(AICPA adapted)

LO 6-4

6.33 Cash receipts from sales on account have been misappropriated. Which of the following acts would conceal this defalcation and be least likely to be detected by an auditor?
    a. Understating the sales journal.
    b. Overstating the accounts receivable control account.
    c. Overstating the accounts receivable subsidiary ledger.
    d. Overstating the sales journal.

LO 6-1

6.34 Embezzlement is a type of fraud that involves
    a. An employee's misappropriating an employer's money or property not entrusted to him or her.
    b. A manager's falsification of financial statements for the purpose of misleading investors and creditors.
    c. An employee's mistaken representation of opinion that causes incorrect accounting entries.
    d. An employee misappropriating an employer's money or property entrusted to the employee's control in the employee's normal job.

LO 6-5

6.35 Which of the following control activities would best protect against the preparation of improper or inaccurate cash disbursements?
    a. All checks must be signed by an officer designated by the board of directors.
    b. All signed checks must be reviewed and compared with supporting documentation by the treasurer before mailing.
    c. All checks must be sequentially numbered and accounted for by internal auditors.
    d. All checks must be perforated or otherwise effectively canceled when they are returned with the bank statement.

LO 6-4

6.36 During an audit of cash, the auditor is most concerned with the management assertion of
    a. Existence.
    b. Rights and obligations.
    c. Valuation or allocation.
    d. Occurrence.

LO 6-6

6.37 In preparing for the audit of cash, the auditors perform analytical procedures concerning cash balances. Which of the following would be the best source of information for use in the estimate of cash?
    a. Prior-years' balances.
    b. Management inquiry.

    c. Cash budgets.

    d. Aged accounts receivable reports.

LO 6-5

6.38 Which of the following control activities could prevent a paid disbursement voucher from being presented for payment a second time?

    a. Vouchers should be prepared by individuals who are responsible for signing disbursement checks.

    b. Disbursement vouchers should be approved by at least two responsible management officials.

    c. The date on a disbursement voucher should be within a few days of the date the voucher is presented for payment.

    d. The official signing the check should compare it with the voucher and should stamp "paid" on the voucher documents.

LO 6-2

6.39 Fraud risk factors are events or conditions that indicate which of the following?

    a. An opportunity to carry out a fraud.

    b. An attitude or rationalization that justifies a fraudulent action.

    c. An incentive or pressure to perpetrate fraud.

    d. All of these are correct.

LO 6-7

6.40 If the auditor believes that a misstatement is or might be intentional and the effect on the financial statements could be material or cannot be readily determined, the auditor should do which of the following?

    a. Inquire of management as to the possibility of fraud.

    b. Discuss with the audit committee what should be done to prevent possible future misstatements.

    c. Perform procedures to obtain additional audit evidence to determine whether fraud has occurred or is likely to have occurred.

    d. Both (a) and (b) are correct.

    e. None of these is correct.

LO 6-7

6.41 In what way can audit procedures be modified to address assessed fraud risks?

    a. Obtain more reliable information.

    b. Perform procedures close to year-end.

    c. Apply computer-assisted techniques to all items.

    d. All of these are valid modifications.

LO 6-7

6.42 Incorporating elements of unpredictability in the selection of audit procedures to be performed by auditors include all of the following *except*

    a. Varying the timing of the audit procedures.

    b. Selecting items for testing that have lower amounts or are otherwise outside customary selection parameters.

    c. Performing audit procedures on an unannounced basis.

    d. Sending attorney letters to every attorney listed under the legal expense account.

    e. None of these is correct.

LO 6-2

6.43 Fraud risk factors are events or conditions that indicate

    I. An incentive or pressure to perpetrate fraud.

    II. An opportunity to carry out the fraud.

    III. An attitude or rationalization that justifies the fraudulent action.

    Which of the following statements is true?

    a. I is a fraud risk factor.

    b. I and II are fraud risk factors.

    c. II and III are fraud risk factors.

    d. None of these is a fraud risk factor.

    e. I, II, and III are fraud risk factors.

Exercises and
Problems

Mc Graw Hill connect All applicable Exercises and Problems are available with *Connect*.

LO 6-5

6.44 **Tests of Controls over Cash Disbursements.** The Runge Controls Corporation manufactures and markets electrical control systems: temperature controls, machine controls, burglar alarms, and the like. The company acquires electrical and semiconductor parts from outside vendors and assembles systems in its own plant. The company incurs other administrative and operating expenditures. Liabilities for goods and services purchased are entered in a vouchers payable journal, at which time the debits are classified to the asset and expense accounts to which they apply.

The company has specified control activities for approving vendor invoices for payment, for signing checks, for keeping records, and for reconciling the checking accounts. The procedures appear to be well specified and in operation.

You are the senior auditor on the Runge engagement and need to specify a list of test of control procedures to evaluate the effectiveness of the controls over cash disbursements.

Required:

Using management's assertions over transactions as a guide, specify two or more tests of control procedures to audit the effectiveness of typical control activities. (*Hint:* From one sample of recorded cash disbursements, you can specify procedures related to several objectives. See Exhibit 6.9 for examples of test of control procedures over cash disbursements.) Organize your list according to the following example for the "completeness" assertion.

Completeness Assertion	Test of Controls
All valid cash disbursements are recorded and none are omitted.	Determine the numerical sequence of checks issued during the period and scan the sequence for missing numbers.

(AICPA adapted)

LO 6-5

6.45 **Internal Control Questionnaire for Book Buy-Back Cash Fund.** Taylor, a CPA, has been engaged to audit the financial statements of University Books, Incorporated. University Books maintains a large cash fund exclusively for the purpose of buying used books from students for cash. The cash fund is active all year because the nearby university offers a large variety of courses with varying starting and completion dates throughout the year.

Receipts are prepared for each purchase. Reimbursement vouchers periodically are submitted to replenish the fund.

Required:

Construct an internal control questionnaire to be used in evaluating the internal control over University Books' repurchasing process using the revolving cash fund. The internal control questionnaire should elicit a yes or no response to each question. *Do not discuss the internal controls over books that are purchased from publishers.*

(AICPA adapted)

LO 6-5

6.46 **Test of Controls over Cash Receipts.** You are the in-charge auditor examining the financial statements of the Gutzler Company for the year ended December 31. During late October, with the help of Gutzler's controller, you completed an internal control questionnaire and prepared the appropriate memoranda describing Gutzler's accounting procedures. Your comments relative to cash receipts are as follows:

- All cash receipts are sent directly to the accounts receivable clerk with no processing by the mail department. The accounts receivable clerk keeps the cash receipts journal, prepares the bank deposit slip in duplicate, posts from the deposit slip to the subsidiary accounts receivable ledger, and mails the deposit to the bank.

- The controller receives the validated deposit slips directly (unopened) from the bank. She also receives the monthly bank statement directly (unopened) from the bank and promptly reconciles it.

- At the end of each month, the accounts receivable clerk notifies the general ledger clerk by journal voucher of the monthly totals of the cash receipts journal for posting to the general ledger.
- With regard to the general ledger cash account, the general ledger clerk makes an entry each month to record the total debits to cash from the cash receipts journal. In addition, the general ledger clerk, on occasion, makes debit entries in the general ledger cash account from sources other than the cash receipts journal, for example, funds borrowed from the bank. In the audit of cash receipts, you have already performed certain standard audit procedures:
- All columns in the cash receipts journal have been totaled and cross-totaled.
- Postings from the cash receipts journal have been traced to the general ledger.
- Remittance advices and related correspondence have been traced to entries in the cash receipts journal.

Required:

Considering Gutzler's internal control over cash receipts and the standard audit procedures already performed, list all other audit procedures that should be performed to obtain sufficient appropriate audit evidence regarding controls over cash and give the reasons for each procedure. Do not discuss the procedures for cash disbursements and cash balances. Also, do not discuss the extent to which any of the procedures are to be performed. Assume that adequate controls exist to ensure that all sales transactions are recorded. Organize your answer sheet as follows:

(AICPA adapted)

Other Audit Procedure	Reason for Other Audit Procedures

LO 6-3

6.47 **Internal Control over Sales Returns.** You are the auditor for Konerko's Office Supply Store, which is opening for business next week. The store owner has established all the controls you have recommended for ensuring that sales are recorded properly and cash is accounted for. The owner has heard from other small business owners that employees often used returned goods as means of skimming money from the register.

Required:

a. How might an employee use returned goods to skim money from the register?

b. What controls would you recommend to prevent or detect fraudulent returns?

c. What audit procedures might you perform to detect fraudulent returns?

LO 6-6

6.48 **Procedures for Auditing a Client's Bank Reconciliation.** Auditors typically will find the items lettered A–F in a client-prepared bank reconciliation.

GENERAL COMPANY
Bank Reconciliation: 1st National Bank
September 30

A.	Balance per bank		$28,375
B.	Deposits in transit		
	Sept 29	$4,500	
	Sept 30	1,525	6,025
			34,400
C.	Outstanding checks:		
	988 Aug 31	$2,200	
	1281 Sept 26	675	
	1285 Sept 27	850	
	1289 Sept 29	2,500	
	1292 Sept 30	7,255	(11,450)
			20,950
D.	Customer note collected by the bank:		(3,000)
E.	Error: Check #1282, written on Sept. 26 for $270, was erroneously charged by bank as $720; bank was notified Oct. 2		450
F.	Balance per books		$20,400

Required:

Assume these facts: On October 11, the auditor received a cutoff bank statement dated October 7. The September 30 deposit in transit; the outstanding checks 1281, 1285, 1289, and 1292; and the correction of the bank error regarding check 1282 appeared on the cutoff bank statement.

a. For each of the preceding lettered items A–F, select one or more of the following procedures 1–10 that you believe the auditor should perform to obtain evidence about the item. These procedures may be selected once, more than once, or not at all. Be prepared to explain the reasons for your choices.

1. Trace to cash receipts journal.
2. Trace to cash disbursements journal.
3. Compare to the September 30 general ledger.
4. Confirm directly with the bank.
5. Inspect bank credit memo.
6. Inspect bank debit memo.
7. Ascertain reason for unusual delay, if any.
8. Inspect supporting documents for reconciling items that do not appear on the cutoff bank statement.
9. Trace items on the bank reconciliation to the cutoff bank statement.
10. Trace items on the cutoff bank statement to the bank reconciliation.

b. Auditors ordinarily foot a client-prepared bank reconciliation. If the auditors had performed this recalculation on the preceding bank reconciliation, what might they have found? Be prepared to discuss any findings.

(AICPA adapted)

LO 6-6

6.49 **Manipulated Bank Reconciliation.** You can use the computer-based *Electronic Workpapers* on the textbook website to prepare the bank reconciliation solution.

Caulco Inc. is the audit client. The February bank statement is shown in Exhibit 6.3 in the text. You have obtained the client-prepared bank reconciliation as of February 28 (see the following).

Required:

Check 2231 was the first check written in February. All earlier checks cleared the bank, some during January and some during February. Assume that the only February-dated canceled checks returned in the March bank statement are 2239 and 2240 showing the amounts listed in the February bank reconciliation. They cleared the bank on March 3 and March 2, respectively. The first deposit on the March bank statement was $1,097.69 credited on March 3. Assume also that all checks entered in Caulco's cash disbursements journal through February 29 have either cleared the bank or are listed as outstanding checks in the February bank reconciliation.

Determine whether any errors exist in the following bank reconciliation. If errors exist, prepare a corrected reconciliation and explain the problem.

CAULCO INC.
Bank Reconciliation
February 28

Balance per bank			$7,374.93
Deposit in transit			1,097.69

Outstanding Checks

Number	Date	Payee	Amount
2239	Feb 26	Alpha Supply	500.00
2240	Feb 28	L.C. Stateman	254.37
Total outstanding			(754.37)
General ledger balance Feb. 28			$7,718.25

LO 6-7

6.50 **Investigating a Fraud.** Suppose you are auditing cash disbursements and discover several payments to a company you are unfamiliar with and cannot find information about this company on the Internet or in the local telephone directory. The invoices from this company have numbers very close to each other in the sequence, there is no phone number on the invoice, and each bill is for a dollar amount just under the amount that would require additional approvals before payment. Based on this information, you now suspect this may be a fraud.

Required:

Based on your suspicions, how would you change the audit procedures you would perform, and how might you change the evidence you gather?

LO 6-5

6.51 **Fraud in Purchasing.** Consider the following scenario:

Adam worked for the local hardware store as an outside sales representative. His job was to visit local companies and contractors in an attempt to identify their needs for tools and materials and provide a bid to supply those items. When a local contractor accepted a new job, Adam would get its material requirements, come back to the store, and prepare and submit a proposal for the items. After some initial success with Big Builder, a large contractor, the number of jobs awarded to Adam had decreased dramatically.

One day, Adam was back at the store after losing a bid to Big Builder when he noticed someone in the store purchasing the exact items and quantities that were in the specification for that bid. The combination of items was unusual, and it would be an unlikely coincidence for someone else to want such a combination in that exact quantity. The customer paid the retail price for the merchandise and left.

Adam decided to contact Big Builder, but he knew he could not do so and make any accusations. Adam set up a meeting with the president of Big Builder and inquired as to how Adam might "increase his business and better meet the needs of Big Builder." Eventually, the recent bid entered the conversation. Adam showed his copy of the bid to the president. The president retrieved a copy of the purchase order and recognized that the amount on it was more than the bid Adam had submitted. The company that submitted the bid was K. A. Supplies Inc. Adam had never heard of K. A. Supplies and noted its address on the purchase order. The president of Big Builder promised to investigate the bidding process.

Adam drove to the address of K. A. Supplies and found a packaging and shipping store at that address. Furthermore, Adam went to the county courthouse and inquired about K. A. Supplies. The company was listed in the county records, and one of the purchasing agents for Big Builder was listed as an officer.

Required:

a. Given the information that Adam knows, what do you believe is occurring at Big Builder?

b. What other information would you want to obtain, and how might you retrieve that information?

c. What controls might be instituted at Big Builder to prevent improprieties in the bidding and purchasing process?

LO 6-1

6.52 **The Perfect Crime?** Consider the following story of an actual embezzlement:

This was the ingenious embezzler's scheme: (a) He hired a print shop to print a private stock of Ajax Company checks in the company's numerical sequence. (b) In his job as an accounts payable clerk at Ajax, he intercepted legitimate checks written by the accounts payable department and signed by the Ajax treasurer and destroyed them. (c) He substituted the same numbered check from the private stock, payable to himself in the same amount as the legitimate check, and he "signed" it with a rubber stamp that looked enough like the Ajax Company treasurer's signature to fool the paying bank. (d) He deposited the money in his own bank account. The bank statement reconciler (a different person) was able to agree the check numbers and amounts listed in the cleared items in the bank statement to the recorded cash disbursement (check number and amount) and thus did not notice the embezzler's scheme. The embezzler was able to process the vendor's "past due" notice and the next month's statement with complete documentation, enabling the Ajax treasurer to sign another check the next month paying both the past due balance and current charges. The embezzler was careful to scatter the double-expense payments among numerous accounts (telephone, office supplies, inventory, etc.) so the double-paid expenses did not distort any accounts very much. As time passed, the embezzler was able to recommend budget amounts that allowed a large enough budget so his double-paid expenses in various categories did not often pop up as large variances from the budget.

Required:

List and explain the ways and means you believe someone might detect the embezzlement. Think first about the ordinary everyday control activities. Then think about extensive detection efforts assuming a tip or indication of a possible fraud has been received. Is this a "perfect crime"?

LO 6-7

6.53 **Select Effective Extended Procedures.** The following are some "suspicions." You have been requested to select some effective extended procedures designed to confirm or deny the suspicions.

Required:

Write the suggested procedures for each case in definite terms so another person can know what to do.

a. The custodian of the petty cash fund may be removing cash on Friday afternoon to pay for weekend activities.

b. A manager noticed that eight new vendors were added to the purchasing department's approved vendor list after the assistant purchasing agent was promoted to chief agent three weeks ago. She suspects all or some of them might be fictitious companies set up by the new chief purchasing agent.

c. The payroll supervisor may be stealing unclaimed paychecks of employees who resigned and did not collect their last check.

d. Although no customers have complained, cash collections on accounts receivable have decreased, and the counter clerks may have stolen customers' payments.

e. The cashier may have "borrowed" cash receipts, covering this by holding each day's deposit until cash from the next day(s) collection is enough to make up the shortage from an earlier day and then sending the deposit to the bank.

LO 6-7

6.54 **Forensic Accounting: Assurance Engagement 1: Expenditure Analysis.** Expenditure analysis is used when fraud has been discovered or strongly suspected and the information to calculate a suspect's income and expenditures can be obtained (e.g., asset and liability records, bank accounts). Expenditure analysis consists of establishing the suspect's known expenditures for all purposes for the relevant period, subtracting all known sources of funds (e.g., wages, gifts, inheritances, bank balances), and identifying the difference as "expenditures financed by unknown sources of income."

The law firm of Gleckel and Morris has hired you. The lawyers have been retained by Blade Manufacturing Company in a case involving a suspected kickback by a purchasing employee, E. J. Cunningham. Cunningham is suspected of taking kickbacks from Mason Varner, a salesman for Tanco Metals. Cunningham has denied the charges, but Lanier Gleckel, the lawyer in charge of the case, is convinced the kickbacks have occurred.

Gleckel filed a civil action and subpoenaed Cunningham's financial records, including last year's bank statements. The beginning bank balance January 1 was $3,463, and the ending bank balance December 31 was $2,050. Over the intervening 12 months, Cunningham's per-month gross salary was $3,600 with a net of $2,950. His house payments were $1,377 per month. In addition, he paid $2,361 per month on a new Mercedes 500 SEL and a total of $9,444 last year toward a new Nissan Maxima (including $5,000 down payment). He also purchased new state-of-the-art audio and video equipment for $18,763 with no down payment and made total payments of $5,532 on the equipment last year. A reasonable estimate of his household expenses during the period is $900 per month ($400 for food, $200 for utilities, and $300 for other items).

Required:

Using expenditure analysis, calculate the amount of income, if any, from "unknown sources."

LO 6-7

6.55 **Forensic Accounting: Assurance Engagement 2: Net Worth Analysis.** You can use the computer-based *Electronic Workpapers* on the textbook website to prepare the net worth analysis required in this problem.

Net worth analysis is performed when fraud has been discovered or is strongly suspected and the information to calculate a suspect's net worth can be obtained (e.g., asset and liability records, bank accounts). The procedure used is to calculate the person's change in net worth (excluding changes in market values of assets) and to identify the known sources of funds to finance the changes. Any difference between the change in net worth and the known sources of funds is called *funds from unknown sources,* which might include ill-gotten gains.

Nero has worked for Bonne Consulting Group (BCG) as the executive secretary for administration for nearly 10 years. Her dedication has earned her a reputation as an outstanding employee and has resulted in increasing responsibilities. Nero is also a suspect in a fraud.

During Nero's first five years of employment, BCG subcontracted all of its feasibility and marketing studies through Jackson & Company. This relationship was terminated because Jackson & Company merged with a larger, more expensive consulting group. At the time of termination, Nero and her supervisor were forced to select a new firm to conduct BCG's market research. However, Nero never informed the accounting department that the Jackson & Company account had been closed.

Because her supervisor allowed Nero to sign the payment voucher for services rendered, she was able to continue to process checks made payable to Jackson's account. Nero was trusted to be the only signature required to authorize payments less than $10,000. The accounting department continued to write the checks and Nero took responsibility for delivering the checks. She opened a bank account in a nearby city under the name of Jackson & Company, where she made the deposits.

Nero's financial records have been obtained by subpoena. The following table provides a summary of the data obtained from her records:

Nero's Subpoenaed Records

	Year 1	Year 2	Year 3
Assets:			
Residence	$100,000	$100,000	$100,000
Stocks and bonds	30,000	30,000	42,000
Automobiles	20,000	20,000	40,000
Certificate of deposit	50,000	50,000	50,000
Cash	6,000	12,000	14,000
Liabilities:			
Mortgage balance	90,000	50,000	—
Auto loan	10,000	—	—
Income:			
Salary		34,000	36,000
Other		6,000	6,000
Expenses:			
Scheduled mortgage payments		6,000	6,000
Auto loan payments		4,800	—
Other living expenses		20,000	22,000

Required:

You have been hired to estimate the amount of loss by estimating Nero's "funds from unknown sources" that financed her comfortable life style. (*Hint:* Set up a working paper like the following:)

	End Year 1	End Year 2	End Year 3
Assets (list)			
Liabilities (list)			
Net worth (difference)			
Change in net worth			
Add total expenses			
= Change plus expenses			
Subtract known income			
= Funds from unknown sources			

LO 6-1

6.56 **Employee Embezzlement via Cash Receipts and Payment of Personal Expenses.** Assume you have received a message from an informant regarding the following case. Your assignment is to write the "audit approach" portion of the case.

 a. Write a brief explanation of desirable controls, missing controls, and especially the kinds of "deviations" that might arise from the situation described in the case. (Refer to controls explained in Chapter 5.)

 b. Develop some procedures for obtaining evidence about existing controls, especially procedures that could discover deviations from controls. If there are no controls to test, then there are no procedures to perform. Then just move on to part (c). (Refer to test of controls procedures explained in this chapter.) An audit "procedure" should instruct someone about the source(s) of evidence to obtain and the work to perform.

 c. Write some procedures for gathering evidence in this case.

 d. Write a short statement about the discovery you expect to accomplish with your procedures.

The Extra Bank Account

The Ourtown Independent School District, like all others, had formal, often bureaucratic, procedures regarding school board approval of cash disbursements. To get around the rules and to make possible timely payment of selected bills, the superintendent of schools had a school bank account that was used in the manner of a petty cash fund. The board knew about it and had given blanket approval in advance for its use to make timely payment of minor school expenses. The board, however, never reviewed the activity in this account. The business manager had sole responsibility for the account subject to the annual audit. The account received money from transfers from other school accounts and from deposit of cafeteria cash receipts. The superintendent did not like to be bothered with details and often signed blank checks so the business manager would not need to obtain a signature all the time. The business manager sometimes paid her personal American Express credit card bills, charged personal items to the school's Visa account, and pocketed some cafeteria cash receipts before deposit.

An informant called the state education audit agency and told the story that this business manager had used school funds to buy hosiery. When told of this story, the superintendent told the auditor to place no credibility in the informant, who was "out to get us." The business manager had, in fact, used the account to write unauthorized checks to "cash," put her own American Express bills in the school files (the school district had a Visa card, not American Express), and signed on the school card for gasoline and auto repairs during periods of vacation and summer when school was not in session. (As for the hosiery, she purchased $700 worth with school funds one year.) The superintendent was genuinely unaware of the misuse of funds. The business manager had been employed for six years, was trusted, and embezzled an estimated $25,000.

LO 6-6

6.57 **Electronic Confirmations.** As stated in the text, most banks require auditors to use electronic audit confirmation requests, and as a result, nearly all audit firms now use them. At present, **Confirmation** is the market-leading technological platform for electronic audit confirmations. To obtain a greater understanding of the process used to confirm accounts with electronic confirmation requests, watch the introduction video to **Confirmation's** process at https://vimeo.com/301903513.

Required:

 a. Based on the video, describe the process of using **Confirmation** for sending bank confirmations.

 b. Discuss advantages and disadvantages of electronic confirmation. Do electronic confirmations provide stronger audit evidence than mailed confirmations? Why or why not?

LO 6-7

6.58 **Case of the Missing Petty Cash** The case below tells the actual story of a cash embezzlement scheme. The case has two major parts: (1) problem and (2) audit approach. For the case, please consider how the auditor may have discovered the cash embezzlement scheme.

Problem

The petty cash custodian (1) brought postage receipts from home and paid them from the fund, (2) persuaded the supervisor to sign blank authorization slips the custodian could use when the supervisor was away and used them to pay for fictitious meals and minor supplies, and (3) took cash to get through the weekend, replacing it the next week. Postage receipts were from a distant post office station the company did not use. The blank authorization slips were dated on days the supervisor was absent. The fund was cash short during the weekend and for a few days the following week. The fund was small ($500), but the custodian replenished it about every two working days, stealing about $50 each time. With about 260 working days per year and 130 reimbursements, the custodian was stealing about $6,500 per year. The custodian was looking forward to getting promoted to general cashier and bigger and better things!

Audit Approach

The audit team should discuss petty cash procedures with the custodian and supervisor, especially those that relate to situations in which the custodian or supervisor is not available to provide needed petty cash. Next, a sample of petty cash reimbursement check copies with receipts and authorization slips attached should be studied for evidence of authorization and validity. On Friday, an audit team member should count the petty cash and receipts to see that they total $500. Then the fund should be recounted later in the afternoon. (The second count should be a surprise.) The custodian or supervisor should be present at all times so that the auditor will not be accused of theft.

Required:

Based on the audit approach discussed, how would the auditor have caught this fraudulent scheme?

LO 6-2

6.59 **The Laundry Money Skim** The case below tells the actual story of a cash embezzlement scheme. The case has two major parts: (1) problem and (2) audit approach. For the case, please consider how the auditor may have discovered the cash embezzlement scheme.

Problem

Albert owned and operated 40 coin laundries around town. As the business grew, he could no longer visit each one, empty the cash boxes, and deposit the receipts. Each location grossed about $140 to $160 per day, operating 365 days per year—gross receipts of about $2 million per year. Each of four part-time employees visited 10 locations, collecting the cash boxes and delivering them to Albert's office where he would count the coins and currency (from the change machine) and prepare a bank deposit. One of the employees skimmed $5 to $10 from each location visited each day.

The daily theft does not seem like much, but at an average of $7.50 per day from each of 10 locations, totaled about $27,000 per year. If all four of the employees had stolen the same amount, the loss could have been over $100,000 per year.

Audit Approach

Controls over the part-time employees were nonexistent. There was no overt or covert surprise observation and no times when two people went to collect cash (thereby needing to agree, in collusion, to steal). There was no rotation of locations or other indications to the employees that Albert was concerned about control. With no controls, there is no test of control activities. Obviously, however, "thinking like a crook" leads to the conclusion that the employees could simply pocket money.

Assuming that some employees are honest, periodically rotating the stores assigned to each employee and performing revenue comparisons (analytical procedures) on a store-by-store basis may be helpful. If revenues consistently decline for stores assigned to a specific employee, further investigation may be warranted.

Required:

Based on the audit approach discussed, how might an auditor devise a procedure to catch this fraudulent scheme?

Apollo Shoes Audit of the Cash Account

You are a recently promoted senior (in charge) auditor for Anderson, Olds, and Watershed and have been assigned to the engagement team of a new audit client, Apollo Shoes Inc. You have been asked to perform certain procedures for the audit of the cash account. A detailed audit program for performing the audit of cash, as well as bank reconciliations and supporting documentation, can be found in *Connect*.

Appendix 6A

Internal Control Questionnaires

EXHIBIT 6A.1   Internal Control Questionnaire—Cash Receipts Processing

	Yes	No	Comments
1. Are cash receipts deposited daily, intact, and without delay?			
2. Does someone other than the cashier or accounts receivable bookkeeper take the deposits to the bank?			
3. Are the duties of the cashier entirely separate from record keeping for notes and accounts receivable? From general ledger record keeping?			
4. Is the cashier denied access to receivables records or monthly statements?			
5. Is a bank reconciliation performed monthly by someone who does not have cash custody or record-keeping responsibility?			
6. Are the cash receipts journal entries compared to the remittance lists and deposit slips regularly?			
7. Does the person who opens the mail make a list of cash received (a remittance list)?			
8. Are currency receipts controlled by mechanical devices? Are machine totals checked by the internal auditor?			
9. Are prenumbered cash receipts listings used? Is the numerical sequence checked for missing documents?			
10. Does the accounting manual contain instructions for dating cash receipts entries the same day as the date of receipt?			
11. Is a duplicate deposit slip retained by someone other than the employee preparing the deposit?			
12. Is the remittance list compared to the deposit by someone other than the cashier?			
13. Does the accounting manual contain instructions for classifying cash receipts credits?			
14. Does someone reconcile the accounts receivable subsidiary to the control account regularly (to determine whether all entries were made to customers' accounts)?			
15. Is the duty of processing credit card payments separated from the process of processing voids?			
16. If the company processes credit cards, does it maintain documentation that it is PCI (Payment Card Industry) compliant?			

EXHIBIT 6A.2   Internal Control Questionnaire—Cash Disbursements Processing

	Yes	No	Comments
1. Are persons with cash custody or check-signing authority denied access to accounting journals, ledgers, and bank reconciliations?			
2. Is access to blank checks denied to unauthorized persons?			
3. Are all disbursements except petty cash made by check?			
4. Are check signers prohibited from drawing checks to cash?			
5. Is signing blank checks prohibited?			
6. Are voided checks mutilated and retained for inspection?			
7. Are invoices, receiving reports, and purchase orders reviewed by the check signer?			
8. Are the supporting documents stamped "paid" (to prevent duplicate payment) before being returned to accounts payable for filing?			
9. Are checks mailed directly by the signer and not returned to the accounts payable department for mailing?			
10. Do checks require two signatures? Is there dual control over machine signature plates?			
11. Are blank checks prenumbered and the numerical sequence checked for missing documents?			
12. Are checks dated in the cash disbursements journal with the date of the check?			
13. Are bank accounts reconciled by personnel independent of cash custody or record keeping?			
14. Do internal auditors periodically conduct a surprise audit of bank reconciliations?			
15. Do the chart of accounts and accounting manual give instructions for determining debit classifications of disbursements not charged to accounts payable?			

(continued)

	Yes	No	Comments
16. Is the distribution of charges checked periodically by an official? Is the budget used to check on gross misclassification errors?			
17. Are special disbursements (e.g., payroll and dividends) made from separate bank accounts?			
18. Is the bank reconciliation reviewed by an accounting official with no conflicting cash receipts, cash disbursements, or record-keeping responsibilities?			
19. Are electronic banking access rights maintained on a timely basis and do not contain employees who have left the company?			
20. Is dual authorization required to process electronic payments?			
21. For accounts with highly significant amounts of cash, is a third individual required to process electronic transfers or payments?			

Appendix 6B

Audit Plans

EXHIBIT 6B.1   **Audit Plan—Tests of Controls—Cash Receipts**

	Documentation Reference	Performed By

1. Inquire of management concerning employees who
   a. Receive remittances from customers.
   b. Record collections in accounts receivable.
   c. Prepare and deliver deposits to the bank.
2. Observe the opening of the mail and ensure that
   a. Two employees are opening the mail.
   b. Checks are restrictively endorsed.
   c. A listing of all checks is being prepared.
3. Observe the flow of checks and remittance advices and ensure that
   a. Checks are delivered directly to the cashier.
   b. Remittance advices are delivered to the accounting department.
4. Examine reconciliations of cash listings, accounts receivable payments, and bank deposits.
5. Examine reconciliations of bank statements for
   a. Initials of proper review.
   b. Investigation of all outstanding items reviewed for propriety.
6. Inspect evidence of payment card industry (PCI) compliance for acceptance of credit card payments.		

EXHIBIT 6B.2   **Audit Plan—Selected Substantive Procedures—Cash**

	Documentation Reference	Performed By

1. Obtain confirmations from banks (standard bank confirmation).
2. Obtain reconciliations of all bank accounts.
   a. Trace the bank balance on the reconciliation to the bank confirmation.
   b. Trace the reconciled book balance to the general ledger.
   c. Recompute the bank reconciliation for mathematical accuracy.
3. Examine the bank confirmation for evidence of loans and collateral.
4. Inquire of the client to request a cutoff bank statement for each account, to be mailed directly to the audit firm.
   a. Vouch deposits in transit on the reconciliation to the bank cutoff statement.
   b. Trace the outstanding checks that have cleared the cutoff statement back to the list of outstanding checks on the bank reconciliation.
5. Prepare a schedule of interbank transfers for a period of 10 business days before and after the year-end date. Document dates of book entry transfer and correspondence with bank entries and reconciliation items, if any.
6. Count cash funds in the presence of a client representative.
7. Obtain management representations concerning compensating balance agreements.		

CHAPTER 7

Revenue and Collection Cycle

I call it the Rule of Three. If you read a company's financial statements three times, and you still can't figure out how they make their money, that's usually for a reason.

James Chanos, American investment manager known for short-selling stocks

Professional Standards References

Topic	AU-C/ISA Section	PCAOB Reference
Audit Documentation	230	AS 1215
Consideration of Fraud in a Financial Statement Audit	240	AS 2401
Audit Planning	300	AS 2101
Identifying and Assessing the Risks of Material Misstatement	315	AS 2110
The Auditor's Responses to Risks of Material Misstatement	330	AS 2301
Audit Evidence	500	AS 1105
External Confirmations	505	AS 2310
Substantive Analytical Procedures	520	AS 2305
Auditing Accounting Estimates	540	AS 2501

LEARNING OBJECTIVES

This is the first of four "cycle chapters" in which you will go through the process of evaluating the audit risks present in a specific cycle and learn how to apply the auditing standards to the identified risks. First, we give a general overview of the typical activities in the revenue and collection cycle. Next, we discuss the significant accounts and relevant assertions in the revenue cycle. After that, we discuss the risk of material misstatement in the revenue cycle. Many recent frauds have consisted of improper revenue recognition, which also results in an overstatement of assets, usually receivables. Next, we examine the appropriate design of controls normally included in the cycle and how the auditor evaluates the operating effectiveness of these controls. Finally, we discuss substantive procedures, including common analytical procedures. You will note that accounts receivable confirmations are a central part of accounts receivable auditing and are required by GAAS. You will see examples of confirmations and a discussion of procedures auditors perform when sending those confirmations. We conclude with an application of what you have learned to a specific audit issue within the revenue and collection cycle.

Your objectives are to be able to

LO 7-1 Describe the revenue and collection cycle, including typical source documents.

LO 7-2 Identify significant accounts and relevant assertions related to the revenue and collection cycle.

LO 7-3 Discuss the risk of material misstatement in the revenue and collection cycle, with a specific focus on improper revenue recognition.

LO 7-4 Identify important internal control activities present in a properly designed system to mitigate the risk of material misstatements for each relevant assertion in the revenue and collection cycle.

LO 7-5 Give examples of tests of controls to test the operating effectiveness of internal controls in the revenue and collection cycle.

LO 7-6 Give examples of substantive procedures in the revenue and collection cycle and relate them to assertions about significant account balances at the end of the period.

LO 7-7 Apply your knowledge to perform audit procedures in the revenue and collection cycle and evaluate the findings of your tests.

INTRODUCTION

In January 2018, **Carillion** was the second largest construction firm in the United Kingdom (UK). Less than a month later, the name Carillion was associated far less with construction and much more with being the company whose fraud led to calls in the UK to break up the Big Four accounting firms for failing to report Carillion's "accounting tricks," as was discussed in a May 2018 Parliamentary report:

"Richard Adam, as Finance Director between 2007 and 2016, was the architect of Carillion's aggressive accounting policies. He, more than anyone else, would have been aware of the unsustainability of the company's approach. His voluntary departure at the end of 2016 was, for him, perfectly timed. He then sold all his Carillion shares for £776,000 just before the wheels began very publicly coming off and their value plummeted. These were the actions of a man who knew exactly where the company was heading once it was no longer propped up by his accounting tricks."[1]

In the construction industry, a common method of estimating revenues is to recognize the percentage of revenue earned to date based on the percentage of expected costs already incurred. Carillion used this type of accounting estimate as the primary tool to manipulate its earnings. Specifically, by underestimating the total expected costs, the company was able to materially overstate revenues, and show profits when losses existed. The company accomplished this by using management estimates of costs and ignoring independent peer reviews which indicated far higher expected costs and project losses, which should have been recognized immediately. One large project resulted in the recognition of an expected profit margin of 4.9 percent, when independent estimates indicated a loss of 12.7 percent.

In the U.S., the estimation of revenue is often a significant audit risk under the accounting standard for revenue from contracts with customers (under *ASC 606*), which will be discussed in detail in this chapter. High degrees of estimation uncertainty and the need for experts in estimating revenue almost always result in the occurrence of contract revenue being evaluated as both a fraud risk and a significant risk of material misstatement. In fact, the PCAOB has placed special emphasis on audits of estimates and the use of specialists in many of their recent standard-setting activities. These standards will be covered in greater detail in Chapter 10, but as the Carillion example shows, are equally relevant in auditing revenue.

---

[1]House of Commons, Business, Energy and Industrial Strategy and Work and Pensions Committees, May 16, 2018.

REVENUE AND COLLECTION CYCLE: TYPICAL ACTIVITIES

LO 7-1
Describe the revenue and collection cycle, including typical source documents.

There is no such thing as a typical *revenue and collection cycle*. Companies come in all shapes and sizes, and the actual revenue generation process can vary greatly among industries. For example, banks and other financial services firms do not sell tangible goods. Restaurants typically do not grant credit to customers. Further, many companies accept all payments electronically. For the purposes of our discussions in the four-cycle chapters, we assume a typical manufacturing company that sells products of some kind to customers—often other businesses—on credit. The basic activities in the revenue and collection cycle for a company like this are (1) receiving and processing customer orders, including credit approval; (2) delivering goods and services to customers; (3) billing customers and accounting for accounts receivable; and (4) collecting and depositing cash received from customers. See Exhibit 7.1 for the activities and transactions involved in a revenue and collection cycle. Note that collecting and depositing cash received from customers was covered in Chapter 6. As you follow the discussion in the text, you can track some of the highlighted elements of the cycle. The numbers listed next to the headings correspond to the numbers in Exhibit 7.1. We will discuss how different companies may vary from this "typical" cycle.

EXHIBIT 7.1   Revenue and Collection Cycle

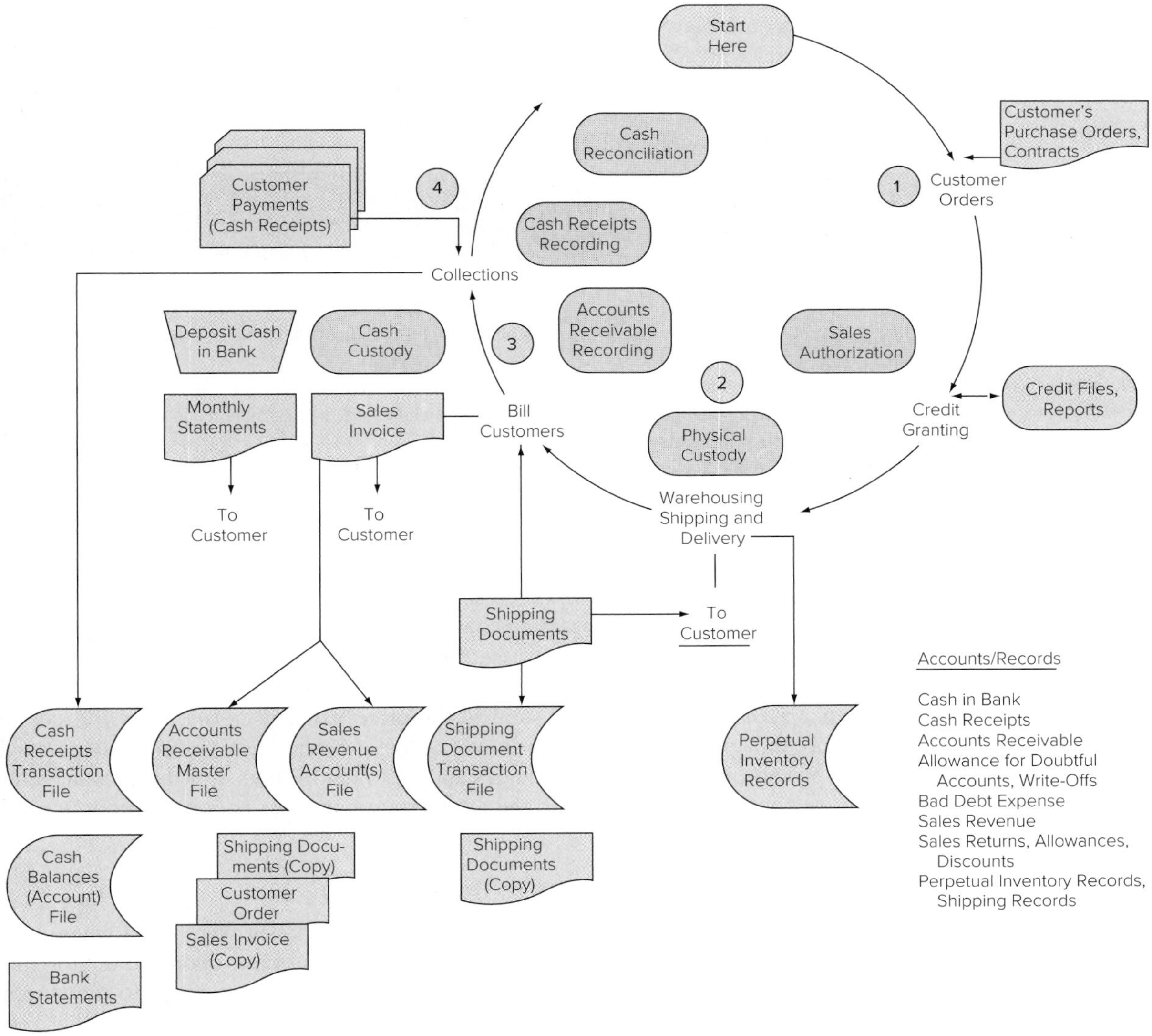

Receiving and Processing Customer Orders, Including Credit Granting ①

Customers initiate sales orders in a variety of ways. They can mail purchase orders, call or fax orders, e-mail orders, place orders on a website, or simply come to the company's place of business and buy their goods. In some cases, companies are directly linked to production schedules in their customers' computer files (via electronic data interchange, EDI), so they can ship goods automatically as the customer needs them. Electronic or Internet sales orders require special software controls that protect against unauthorized orders and protect customer information.

If a company sells its goods or services for something other than cash, it is important that someone authorizes credit sales to ensure that the customer will be able to pay for the goods or services. Because various authorizations are embedded in a computerized system, access to the customer master file for additions, deletions, and other changes must be limited to employees directly responsible for these tasks. If these controls fail, orders might be processed for fictitious customers, credit might be approved for bad credit risks, and shipping documents might be created for goods that do not exist in the inventory.

Although many companies directly grant credit to customers, others rely on third-party credit, such as accepting credit cards from Visa or American Express. When a retailer accepts a third-party credit card, the authorization function is performed electronically, and the risk of nonpayment generally shifts to the third party in exchange for a processing fee. Sales such as this are considered cash sales to the retailer. Although authorization controls are minimized in this situation, data security becomes a significant issue. Retailers who accept third-party credit cards must maintain compliance with Payment Card Industry Data Security Standard requirements (PCI DSS). When companies fail to adequately protect information, they can become liable for losses to customers, as discussed in the following Auditing Insight.

AUDITING INSIGHT A Designer Theft

Giant high-end retailer **Neiman Marcus** had its customers' credit card and debit card data breached in May 2020. Perhaps most concerning, the breach was not detected until September 2021, allowing the crooks plenty of time to take advantage of the theft. Neiman Marcus estimates that approximately 5 million customers had their personal credit or debit card information stolen, including other personal information. Neiman Marcus filed for bankruptcy in 2021, and some pundits speculated they waited to disclose the credit card breach until after the filing. Sadly, this was not the first time the company had been a victim to a data breach. Neiman Marcus agreed to a settlement in 2019 worth $1.5 million with 43 states after a similar 2014 incident.

Note how important it is to protect information received during the revenue cycle.

Source: *"Neiman Marcus says May 2020 breach includes millions of payment card numbers and expiration dates,"* ZDNet, October 1, 2021.

Customer orders, shipping documents, and invoices should all be assigned sequential numbers and should be in prenumbered sequence so the system can check the sequence and determine whether any transactions have not been recorded (*completeness* assertion) or have been duplicated (*occurrence* assertion). Prenumbered documents are an example of an internal control (i.e., control activity).

Another authorization in the system is the price list master file. This file contains the product unit prices for billing customers. Persons who have power to alter this file have the power to authorize price changes and customer billings. For this reason, general controls surrounding system access and authorization are tremendously important in the revenue cycle.

Delivering Goods and Services to Customers ②

Physical custody of inventory goods starts in the storeroom or warehouse where inventory is kept. Custody is transferred to the shipping department upon the authorization of the shipping order that permits the inventory clerk to release goods to the shipping department. Proper authorization is important: Employees performing each of these steps should document the inventory transfers so they are held accountable. This control procedure prevents employees from misappropriating the goods or shipping product to friends without billing them. A **bill of lading** is a form that the carrier signs to verify that the goods are shipped. A **packing slip,** which describes the goods being shipped, and the quantity of goods shipped, is often included with the shipment. If you have ever shipped goods through a **UPS** store, you have seen a smaller version of this process in action. When you drop off your package, UPS scans it, which assigns a tracking number, and they also provide you with a receipt. If you were a company selling goods, the carrier would likely pick it up from you, along with all your other shipments, and they would acknowledge receipt of the goods through your company's bill of lading, as well as a receipt with all the tracking information. As you probably have noted from making purchases online, nearly all of this documentation is electronic.

Billing Customers and Accounting for Accounts Receivable ③

When a delivery or shipment is complete, the transaction is completed by filing a shipment record and preparing a final invoice for the customer (which is recorded as sales revenue and accounts receivable). A **sales invoice** is the bill sent to the customer that indicates the amount due and the payment terms. Any person who has the power to alter these transactions or to change the invoice before it is mailed to the customer should not have any custody of goods or cash, nor any recording responsibilities.

Access to accounts receivable records implies the power to alter them directly or enter transactions (e.g., returns and allowance credits, write-offs) to alter them. Personnel with this power have a combination of authorization and recording responsibility. Another important facet of control is physical protection of the files. If the files are lost or destroyed, it is unlikely the accounts will be collected, so the records are truly assets. Limited access, frequent backup, and disaster recovery plans are important general controls to ensure the availability of information. In addition, and quite importantly, customer and employee information must be protected.

The most frequent reconciliation is the comparison of the sum of customers' unpaid balances (customer database or subsidiary ledger maintained in the accounts receivable department) with the accounts receivable control account total (maintained in corporate accounting). This reconciliation is accomplished by preparing a trial balance of the accounts receivable subsidiary ledger and comparing its total with the control account balance in the general ledger. Internal auditors can perform periodic reviews of the customers' balances by sending confirmations to the customers. Auditors will also test controls surrounding collection of cash from customers, shown as ④ in Exhibit 7.1. The cash collection process was discussed in Chapter 6.

System-Generated Reports and Data Files in the Revenue and Collection Cycle

Because revenue and cash receipts transactions are generally processed using electronic systems, management is able to generate reports and data sets that can provide important information not just for management, but also for audits. Exhibit 7.2 represents a typical system for processing customer orders and accounts receivable. In this section, we discuss the system-generated reports that are typically produced in this system that will be used to evaluate the risk of material misstatement and perform audit tests.

Pending Order and Back Order Master File

Sales transactions that were initiated but are not yet completed, and thus not yet recorded as sales, are kept in the *pending order master file.* A *back order master* file contains orders for products that are out of stock currently. Long-standing orders may represent unfilled sales to a customer, which may result in low customer satisfaction and loss of potential revenue. They also may represent shipments that actually were made but for some reason were not recorded in the sales journal or could not be matched to a customer order.

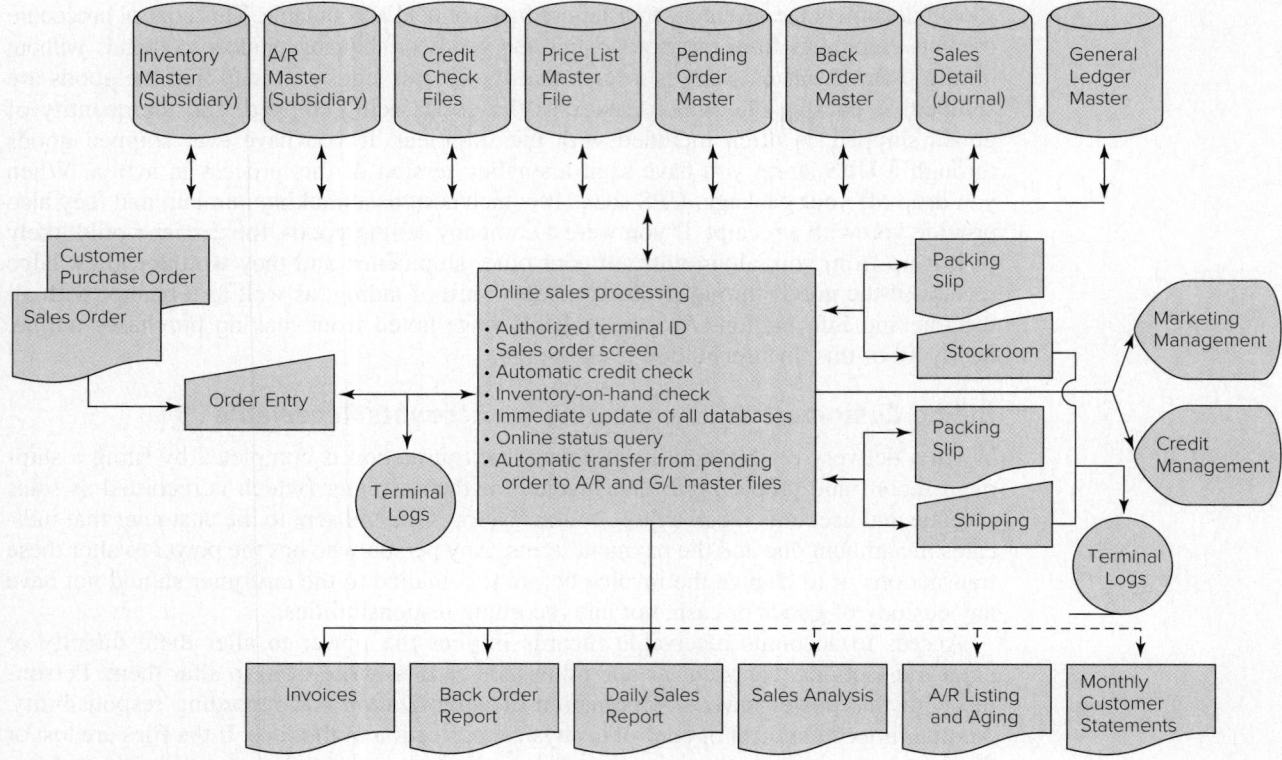

EXHIBIT 7.2 **Sales and Accounts Receivable Processing**

Typically, a pending or back order report will be reviewed by the company at least weekly, and exceptions should be reviewed. Auditors will test controls surrounding this process and may review items in the pending orders file for evidence of the *completeness* of recorded sales and accounts receivable.

Customer Master File

The system may make automatic credit checks, but up-to-date maintenance of customer information is very important. Credit checks based on dated or incomplete information are not good business practice. A sample of the *customer master file* can be tested for current status, including up-to-date credit limit information. Alternatively, the company's data change controls will likely be tested to ensure the files are accurately maintained. The company should regularly review credit limits to ensure appropriate limits are placed on customers, and auditors will often perform exception testing on credit checks. (See Application in the Field example later in this chapter.)

Price List Master File

The system may produce customer invoices automatically, but if the *price list master file* is incorrect, the billings will be incorrect. The pricing file can be compared to an official price source for accuracy. Generally, the official pricing should be generated by management within the sales department. The company should perform this comparison every time it changes its prices. Remember that prices can change throughout the year. Therefore, when vouching invoices and sales journal entries to price lists, the auditor must be sure to have the price list that was in effect at the time of the customer's order.

Sales Detail (Journal) File

The detailed sales entries, which should correspond with the issuance of invoices to customers and should include the shipping references and dates, should be in the *sales detail file*.

The file can be scanned using computer-assisted auditing techniques (CAATs) checking for entries without shipping references (fictitious sales?) and for matching recording dates with shipment dates (sales recorded before shipment?). The company should always compare daily credit sales totals in the sales journal to the total debits posted to accounts receivable.

Sales Analysis Reports

A variety of *sales analysis reports* can be produced. Sales that are classified by product lines provide required information for the business segment disclosures. Sales classified by sales employee or region can show unusually high or low volume that might bear further investigation if an error or fraud is suspected. Analytical procedures, such as trend analysis or comparison among sales units, can be a great help to the auditor as illustrated by the following Auditing Insight.

AUDITING INSIGHT   Peaks and Valleys

During the year-end audit of a national manufacturer, the independent auditors imported the weekly sales volume reports classified by region into Tableau, a data visualization software used in many audits. By creating graphical workbooks, the auditors noticed that sales volume was very high in Region 2 in the last two weeks of March, June, September, and December. The volume was unusually low in the first two weeks of April, July, October, and January. In fact, the peaks far exceeded the volume in all the other six regions. The analysis of the sales volume reports enabled the auditors to identify and focus their efforts on a potential overstatement of revenue in a specific region, increasing the effectiveness and efficiency of the audit. Further investigation revealed that the manager in Region 2 was holding open the sales journal at the end of each quarterly reporting period (i.e., including sales from the next period) in an attempt to make the quarterly reports look good. This is an example of an analytical procedure made possible by the ability to analyze all of the client's data.

Accounts Receivable Listing and Aging

The *accounts receivable listing* of customers' balances contains the actual amounts specifically identified with individual customers. If the control account total is higher than the sum of the customers' balances (trial balance), it will have to be adjusted after the difference is thoroughly investigated. Remember, a receivable amount that cannot be identified with a customer cannot be collected! The trial balance is used as the starting point for selecting accounts for confirmation. The *accounts receivable aging* information is used in connection with assessing the allowance for doubtful accounts. Auditors must ensure that the calculation of the aging is accurate to verify that customer accounts are not listed as current when they are in fact past due. An example of this listing, also called an **aged trial balance**, is presented in Exhibit 7.10, which is shown later in this chapter. Most audit software, including IDEA, can create an aged trial balance simply by defining delinquency groups (e.g., <30 days, 30–59 days, etc.). This enables the auditor to assess the adequacy of the client's allowance for doubtful accounts.

Cash Receipts Listing

The cash receipts journal contains all the detailed entries for cash deposits and credits to various accounts. It contains the population of entries that should be reflected in the credits to accounts receivable for customer payments. It also contains adjusting and correcting entries that can result from the bank account reconciliation. These entries are important because they might signal the types of accounting errors or manipulations that occur in the *cash receipts listing.*

Customer Statements

Probably the best control over whether cash is received and recorded is the customer. Therefore, sending *customer statements* of what has been billed, what has been paid, and ending balances on a monthly basis enables customers to spot discrepancies and notify the company. Statements should be sent if there is *any* activity in the account, even if the ending balances are zero.

✅ REVIEW CHECKPOINTS

7.1 What is the basic sequence of activities and accounting in a revenue and collection cycle?

7.2 What purpose is served by prenumbering sales orders, shipping documents, and sales invoices?

7.3 What controls should be implemented to safeguard accounts receivable files?

7.4 What system-generated reports might auditors examine to find evidence of unrecorded sales? Of inadequate credit checks? Of incorrect product unit prices?

7.5 Suppose that you selected a sample of customers' accounts receivable and wanted to find supporting evidence for the entries in the accounts. Where would you go to vouch the debit entries to accounts receivable? What would you expect to find? Where would you go to vouch the credit entries? What would you expect to find?

SIGNIFICANT ACCOUNTS AND RELEVANT ASSERTIONS

LO 7-2

Identify significant accounts and relevant assertions related to the revenue and collection cycle

According to the professional standards, an account or disclosure is significant if there is a reasonable chance that it could contain a material misstatement. The auditor identifies significant accounts and relevant assertions by applying the audit risk model.

Chapter 4 introduced the audit risk model. As noted there, this model allows auditors to control audit risk to desired levels. *Audit risk* is defined as the risk that auditors will issue an unqualified opinion on financial statements that contain a material misstatement. Audit risk is manifested when a material misstatement enters the financial reporting process (inherent risk) that the client's internal controls do not prevent or detect (control risk) and that the auditors' substantive procedures do not detect (detection risk). Recall the basic three-step approach for using the audit risk model to plan an engagement:

1. Set audit risk at desired levels (normally, low).
2. Assess risk of material misstatement, which incorporates inherent risk, based on the nature of the account balance or class of significant transactions, and control risk, based on gaining an understanding of internal control. Remember that AS 2110 indicates that the auditor should presume that there is a fraud risk involving improper revenue recognition.
3. Set detection risk at the significant account and assertion level based on the level of audit risk and risk of material misstatement.

The components of the audit risk model are assessed for each significant account and relevant assertion. This assessment recognizes that certain accounts and assertions assume an increased level of importance and are of more interest to auditors than other accounts and assertions. For example, because of the tendency to use fictitious sales to overstate assets and revenues, the *existence* assertion is extremely important in the audit of accounts receivable, and *occurrence* is important for sales. In addition, because material errors happen, auditors need to examine revenue and accounts receivable for completeness. However, the auditor generally presumes that management has an incentive to overstate revenues. Thus, auditors may assess inherent risk for the *existence* assertion to be higher than for the *completeness* assertion for these accounts, all other things being equal.

Once all of the significant accounts and disclosures have been identified, the auditor then needs to identify the relevant assertions. According to AS 2201.A9, a financial statement assertion is relevant if it has a "reasonable possibility of containing a misstatement or misstatements that would cause the financial statements to be materially misstated."

Exhibit 7.3 identifies the significant accounts and relevant assertions in the revenue cycle. Although different companies may have other risks, in general, the most significant risks relate to the occurrence of revenues and the existence and valuation of accounts receivable. Because of the risk of unrecorded revenue, the completeness of revenue and accounts

EXHIBIT 7.3
Significant Accounts and Relevant Assertions in the Revenue and Collection Cycle

Significant Account	Relevant Assertions
Revenue	Occurrence
	Completeness
	Cutoff
Accounts Receivable	Existence
	Completeness
	Valuation

☑ REVIEW CHECKPOINTS

7.6 What makes an account significant or an assertion relevant?

7.7 Why do auditors focus on revenue as a significant account and the occurrence of revenue as a relevant assertion in the revenue cycle?

7.8 Why is inherent risk for the existence assertion for accounts receivable often set higher than inherent risk for the completeness assertion?

receivable is also considered a significant risk in the revenue and collection cycle. Although we will focus our discussion on revenue and accounts receivable, we will also discuss other accounts and assertions that may require consideration in the revenue cycle.

RISK OF MATERIAL MISSTATEMENT

LO 7-3
Discuss the risk of material misstatement in the revenue and collection cycle, with a specific focus on improper revenue recognition.

As part of the planning process, the auditor must determine the source of a misstatement that could cause the financial statements to be materially misstated. One way to assess the risk of material misstatement is to use the "what could go wrong?" (WCGW) approach when thinking of each financial statement assertion. The WCGW approach is a part of each audit firm's process and enables a thorough assessment of the risk of material misstatement.

When considering WCGW in the revenue and collection cycle, auditors consider three primary concerns: (1) Is revenue recognized when appropriate? (2) Is there a possibility of customers returning the goods? (3) Are the accounts receivable collectible? Exhibit 7.4 summarizes the WCGW analysis for the revenue and collection cycle.

Revenue Recognition

The Carillion example at the beginning of this chapter is an extreme example of the violation of accounting standards related to **revenue recognition** (recording revenues in the entity's books). FASB defines revenues as, "inflows or other enhancements of assets

EXHIBIT 7.4
What Could Go Wrong in the Revenue and Collection Cycle?

Significant Account	Relevant Assertions	What Could Go Wrong?
Revenue	Occurrence	Management may overstate sales by adding fictitious transactions or inflating actual sales.
		Management may fail to recognize the possibility of customer returns.
	Completeness	Not all sales are recorded.
	Cutoff	Sales have been recorded in incorrect periods.
Accounts Receivable	Existence	Accounts receivable are overstated and do not represent amounts owed from actual sales.
	Completeness	Not all accounts receivable have been recorded.
	Valuation	Receivables are not included in financial statements at the appropriate amount, and the uncollectible portion of the balance is not properly estimated.

of an entity or settlements of its liabilities (or a combination of both) from delivering or producing goods, rendering services, or other activities that constitute the entity's ongoing major or central operations." The core revenue recognition principle is that revenue should be recognized when goods or services are transferred to customers for the amount the company expects to be entitled to receive in exchange for those goods or services.[2]

An entity's revenue-earning activities involve delivering or producing goods, rendering services, or performing other activities that constitute its ongoing major or central operations. Revenues are considered to have been earned when the entity has substantially accomplished what it must do to be entitled to the benefits represented by the revenues.

Similarly, the SEC believes that revenue generally is realized or realizable and earned when *all* of the following criteria are met:

- Persuasive evidence of an arrangement exists.
- Delivery has occurred or services have been rendered.
- The seller's price to the buyer is fixed or determinable.
- Collectability is reasonably ensured.[3]

The SEC and the popular press have expressed concern about appropriate recognition of revenue in financial statements. A study by research firm Audit Analytics indicated that approximately 17.3 percent of all restatements in 2020 were related to revenue recognition. Since 2001, the percentage of restatements related to revenue recognition has varied from a low of 10.2 percent of all restatements in 2010 to a high of 21.3 percent of all restatements in 2003.[4] Some recent restatements are listed in Exhibit 7.5. The fact that the financial statements were restated means that the auditors missed the original misstatement or went along with the company's accounting treatment. In some cases, predecessor auditors accepted the accounting treatment, but the current auditors demanded the restatement. The SEC has increased enforcement actions related to revenue recognition, as discussed in the following Auditing Insight.

AUDITING INSIGHT · Watchful Eyes

SEC Chair Mary Jo White indicated in 2014 that the SEC had increased enforcement actions on revenue recognition by more than 20 percent as a result of the new FASB revenue recognition standard. The SEC's director of enforcements, Andrew Ceresney, called revenue recognition "the New Frontier" in enforcements. The increased focus has certainly had an effect as the SEC increased independent enforcement actions overall from 341 in 2013 to a high of 548 in 2016. However, as companies have become more comfortable with the revenue standard, independent enforcement actions decreased to 434 in 2021.

Sources: *"Revenue Recognition Changes Could Spur SEC Fraud Probes,"* CFO, December 12, 2019; *"SEC Announces Enforcement Results for FY 2021,"* SEC, November 18, 2021.

The PCAOB has also noted the difficulties with auditing revenue. In its Staff Preview of 2018 inspection results, the PCAOB noted that, "We observed frequent deficiencies related to the design and performance of audit procedures that address the assessed risk of material misstatement, particularly when auditing revenue."[5] These difficulties with revenue have always been present, but have perhaps become more challenging with the issuance of *FASB ASC 606 (ASU 2014-09)*. The standard requires a five-step process to achieve the core principle of revenue recognition:

1. Identify the contract(s) with a customer.
2. Identify the performance obligations in the contract.
3. Determine the transaction price.
4. Allocate the transaction price to the performance obligations in the contract.
5. Recognize revenue when (or as) the entity satisfies a performance obligation.

[2]Accounting Standards Update 2014-09, "Revenue from Contracts with Customers (Topic 606)."
[3]Securities and Exchange Commission, *Staff Accounting Bulletin No. 104.* December 17, 2003.
[4]Audit Analytics, *2020 Financial Restatements: A Twenty Year Review* November 2021.
[5]Public Company Accounting Oversight Board, "Staff Preview of 2018 Inspection Observations," May 6, 2019.

EXHIBIT 7.6 **Internal Control Activities in the Revenue and Collection Cycle**

Significant Account	Relevant Assertions	What Could Go Wrong?	Internal Control Activity
Revenue	Occurrence	Management may overstate sales by adding fictitious transactions or inflating actual sales.	Invoices are supported by customer purchase orders. Bill of lading or other shipping documents exist for all invoices, and recorded sales in the Sales Revenue account file are supported by invoices.
		Management may fail to recognize the possibility of customer returns.	Management analyzes sales returns regularly and estimates an allowance for returns.
	Completeness	Not all sales are recorded.	Invoices, shipping documents, and sales orders are prenumbered, and the numerical sequence is checked.
	Cutoff	Sales have been recorded in incorrect periods.	The date of shipping document is compared to the invoice date. Management evaluates all new contracts to ensure revenue recognition compliance with *ASC 606*.
Accounts Receivable	Existence	Accounts receivable are overstated and do not represent amounts from actual sales.	Management reviews the sales order and shipping document to verify that sales were earned and a customer owes a balance.
	Completeness	Not all accounts receivable have been recorded.	Management compares invoices with the shipping document and the A/R ledger.
	Valuation	Receivables are not included in financial statements at the appropriate amount, and the uncollectible portion of the balance is not properly estimated.	Authorize and record discounts when customers take them. Management evaluates the collectability of delinquent receivables on a timely basis.

Exhibit 7.6 above describes some of the important control factors that an auditor would consider when evaluating the design effectiveness of internal control in the revenue and collection cycle.

Perhaps the most important controls in the revenue and collection cycle for many companies involve ensuring that revenues are only recorded when the revenue generation process is complete, and ensuring that all revenues that are earned are recorded once and only once. These controls primarily involve the significant accounts of revenue and accounts receivable, and the relevant assertions of occurrence (existence), completeness, and cutoff.

AUDITING INSIGHT | System-Generated Reports in the Revenue Cycle

System-generated reports are commonly used by audit clients in the revenue cycle to help ensure the appropriate timing for revenue to be recognized. For example, the three-way match internal control activity described below is nearly always entirely automated. In **SAP,** a widely used financial accounting and reporting software, a weekly exception report is produced by the system for any exceptions for the three-way match that may exist. In a sense, the actual control activity implemented by the client is the *follow-up* to the weekly system-generated report. Management evaluates all exceptions to the three-way match and then verifies that the appropriate amount of revenue has been recorded.

A primary control in the revenue cycle is ensuring that revenue is only recorded when a complete set of matched sales documents is present. A three-way match of a customer sales order, evidence of shipment, and a customer invoice provides strong evidence that a sale has been completed and a revenue has been earned. By requiring all three documents to be present before recording a revenue, a company reduces the risk of overstating revenues and accounts receivable, providing assurance related to the existence of accounts receivable, and the occurrence of revenue.

Similarly, by ensuring that all three of these primary sales documents are prenumbered, and the numerical sequence is checked, the company can ensure the completeness of recorded revenue and accounts receivable. Verifying the dates on the documents helps reduce risk of misstatement related to the cutoff assertion of revenue.

The valuation assertion of accounts receivable is also a relevant assertion in the revenue cycle. Because collectability problems can be addressed prior to making a sale, companies should have controls in place to ensure that all credit sales are authorized based on a credit limit in the customer master file. Further, collectability of delinquent receivables should be considered on a regular basis, and management should regularly evaluate the adequacy of allowances for sales returns and discounts.

In addition to the critical controls discussed previously and in Exhibit 7.6, the following control activities should generally be in place to prevent and detect errors or fraud:

- Access to inventory and the shipping area should be restricted to authorized personnel.
- Access to billing terminals and blank invoice forms should be restricted to authorized personnel.
- Care should be taken to record sales and receivables as of the date the goods were shipped and the cash receipts on the date the payments were received.
- Customer invoices should be compared with bills of lading and customer orders to determine that the customer is sent the goods ordered at the proper location for the proper prices and that the quantity being billed is the same as the quantity shipped.
- Pending order files should be reviewed frequently to avoid failure to bill and record shipments.

Finally, procedures must be in place to ensure that errors noted by these steps are properly corrected. An error control log monitored by the information systems supervisor ensures that this is done. Such a log may aid in the identification of patterns that indicate either control weaknesses or possible fraudulent activities. This documentation and subsequent action is part of the information and communications aspect of internal controls.

Information about a company's controls often is gathered by completing an internal control questionnaire. Questionnaires for both manual controls and computerized controls over the revenue and collection cycle are in Appendix 7A. You can study these questionnaires for details of desirable control activities. They are organized under headings that address the assertions regarding classes of transactions. Auditors should also perform a *walkthrough* to verify that they understand each of the process activities. The revenue and collection cycle walkthrough involves following a sale from the initial customer order through credit approval, billing, and delivery of goods to the entry in the sales journal and subsidiary accounts receivable records and then its subsequent collection and cash deposit to ensure that the sale and related transactions are accurately reflected in the financial statements.

✅ REVIEW CHECKPOINTS

7.12 What are the primary control procedures to ensure completeness of recorded revenues?

7.13 The primary control procedure to ensure the occurrence of revenues requires which three documents to be matched prior to recording sales revenue?

7.14 What effect do entity-level controls have on the control risk assessments of an auditor?

TESTS OF OPERATING EFFECTIVENESS OF INTERNAL CONTROL

LO 7-5
Give examples of tests of controls to verify the operating effectiveness of internal controls in the revenue and collection cycle.

In order to rely on the design of the client's internal controls and support a reduction in control risk, the auditor must determine if the control is operating as designed and whether the person operating the control has the authority and competence to do so. The auditor's ultimate responsibility is to document enough support to conclude whether the control activity was operating effectively to mitigate the risk of material misstatement for the assertion.

Auditors can perform tests of controls to determine whether company personnel are properly performing controls that are said to be in place. In general, the procedures used in tests of controls are client inquiry, observation, inspection of documents and records, reperformance, and walkthroughs. Understand that if a control is missing or ineffective, the risk of a material misstatement increases, but an error or fraud is by no means certain. For example, a person with both recordkeeping and custody of inventory has incompatible duties, but if that person is diligent and honest, no errors or frauds may exist. If controls are not in place or personnel in the organization are not performing their control activities effectively, auditors need to design substantive procedures to try to detect whether control failures have produced material misstatements in the financial statements.

To be effective, auditor tests of control in the revenue cycle must be performed using dual-direction tests of controls. Exhibit 7.7 demonstrates how an auditor performs tests of control to assess control risk for both the occurrence assertion and the completeness assertion.

EXHIBIT 7.7

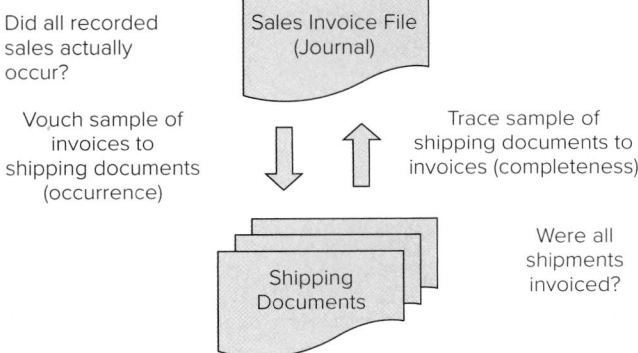

Exhibit 7.8 begins with the internal control activities related to the significant accounts and relevant assertions in the revenue cycle and suggests auditor tests of controls that may be performed to support a reduction in control risk.

To verify that the client's required three-way match is in effect and operating appropriately to ensure the occurrence assertion, the auditor will select a sample of recorded sales from the sales journal and vouch the sales to supporting customer invoices, shipping documents, and customer purchase orders. The availability of electronic client data and audit software sometimes enables auditors to perform exception testing on the entire population of sales and identify any instances where the three-way match did not occur. The auditor can then directly address the specific situations where exceptions occurred and make a more accurate assessment of control risk.

To complete the dual-direction test, the auditor performs tests of control in the completeness direction. Because shipment of goods is the event that generally leads to earned revenue, the auditor will select a sample of shipping documents and trace the documents to sales invoices and postings in the sales journal. This assures the auditor that goods shipped were invoiced and posted. The auditor will also scan data files for numerical sequence and will observe the client checking numerical sequence of shipping documents and invoices. Note, if the auditor can obtain the sales journal in electronic form, audit software (e.g., IDEA) can be employed to check the numerical sequence and duplication of invoice numbers.

EXHIBIT 7.8 **Tests of Controls in Revenue and Collection Cycle**

Significant Account	Relevant Assertions	What Could Go Wrong/ Risk of Material Misstatement	Internal Control Activity (Mitigate Risk)	Test of Internal Control
Revenue	Occurrence	Management may overstate sales by adding fictitious transactions or inflating actual sales.	Invoices are supported by customer purchase orders. Bill of lading or other shipping documents exist for all invoices, and recorded sales in the Sales Revenue account file are supported by invoices.	Vouch sales in sales detail file to invoices, supporting shipping documents, and customer purchase orders for customer name, product description, terms, dates, and quantities.
		Management may fail to recognize the possibility of customer returns.	Management analyzes sales returns regularly and estimates an allowance for returns.	Inspect documents for evidence that management evaluates the allowance for returns regularly.
	Completeness	Not all sales are recorded.	Invoices, shipping documents, and sales orders are prenumbered, and the numerical sequence is checked.	Scan documents for numerical sequence, observe client-checking sequence, and trace shipping document to recording in sales detail file.
	Cutoff	Sales have been recorded in incorrect periods.	Date of shipping document is compared to invoice date. Management evaluates all new contracts to ensure revenue recognition compliance with *ASC 606*.	Trace shipping date on shipping documents with sales invoice date, and check FOB terms. Inspect documents for evidence that management evaluates the timing of revenue recognition from contracts.
Accounts Receivable	Existence	Accounts receivable are overstated and do not represent actual sales.	Management reviews sales order and shipping documents to verify that sales were earned and a customer owes a balance.	When payments are received, vouch checks listed on sample deposit slips to the customer credits listed on the day's posting to customer accounts receivable.
	Completeness	Not all accounts receivable have been recorded.	Management compares invoices with the shipping document and the A/R ledger.	Inspect documents for evidence that the billing department supervisor matches prenumbered shipping documents with entries in the sales journal.
	Valuation	Receivables are not included in financial statements at the appropriate amount, and the uncollectible portion of the balance is not properly estimated.	Authorize and record discounts when customers take them.	Inspect documentation for evidence that subsequent cash receipts from the customer are reviewed. Inquire of the credit manager procedures regarding unpaid accounts. Inspect credit files for most recent review of customer creditworthiness.
			Management evaluates the collectability of delinquent receivables on a timely basis.	Inspect documentation for evidence that management evaluates the collectability of receivables.

One thing you may note is that these tests of controls described above also are gathering evidence on the assertions in the account balances. The audit processes to gather evidence on the assertions in account balances are called *substantive procedures*. Substantive procedures differ from tests of controls in their basic purpose. Substantive procedures are designed to obtain direct evidence about the assertions related to specific transactions or details of account balances, while tests of controls are designed to obtain evidence about the company's performance of its own control activities. Sometimes an audit procedure can be used for both purposes, and when it is, it is called a **dual-purpose procedure**. When the auditor tests the controls surrounding three-way matches of customer orders, shipping documents, and invoices, the items directly tested provide both evidence on controls and on the relevant assertions. Thus, these tests related to controls surrounding occurrence and completeness of revenues can be used as dual-purpose procedures.

To test the client's controls related to the valuation assertion, the auditor will discuss procedures with the credit manager and examine credit file documentation for evidence of regular evaluation of credit limits and follow-up on delinquent accounts. The auditor will also examine evidence of credit approval prior to shipment for a sample of sales.

It is important to note that online business models bring significant changes to the required controls surrounding revenue recognition and sales returns. The traditional three-way match controls take on significantly different forms, and authorization of transactions is very different compared with a storefront retailer or a manufacturer. When auditing an online business, auditors often focus heavily on application controls within the relevant processes and general IT controls surrounding the system overall. When those controls are lacking, misstatements and employee fraud can occur. Consider the following Auditing Insight for an example of how poor process controls can enable creative employees to commit fraud in the revenue cycle.

AUDITING INSIGHT   It's Amazon-ing That He Pulled This Off!

Vu Anh Nguyen was employed by Amazon as a Selling Support Associate. His job included assisting with the creation and management of employee-controlled accounts that enabled management of seller listings for third-party seller accounts. When an employee uses these accounts, they are able to assist sellers by manually authorizing refunds. Lack of controls surrounding this process enabled Nguyen to both authorize the accounts and have custody of them. Taking advantage of this internal control deficiency, he fraudulently accessed an employee account to issue nearly $100,000 in refunds to himself and others.

However, the purchased items were never returned to Amazon. It turns out, Nguyen is an expert at fraud schemes. He is separately under investigation for a securities fraud known as "free-riding," profiting over $1 million at the expense of eight brokerage firms. In November, 2021, Nguyen was sentenced to 30 months for securities fraud.

Source: *"Feds Arrest Former Amazon Employee After Company Reported Him to FBI for Fraud,"* Techcrunch.com, *October 5, 2020; "Chandler Man Sentenced to 30 Months for Securities Fraud and Embezzlement," United States Attorney's Office District of Arizona, November 12, 2021.*

In addition to the critical controls discussed previously and in Exhibit 7.6, the auditor might also perform other tests of controls related to assertions in the revenue cycle, such as

- *Completeness of revenue and accounts receivable*—Examine evidence of client review and follow-up of sales data related to specific classes of products or locations.
- *Accuracy of revenue and accounts receivable*—Vouch prices to approved price listing.
- *Accuracy of revenue*—Observe client comparing shipping quantities to quantities recorded as sold. Examine evidence of client making the comparison.
- *Cutoff of revenue*—Trace shipping date on shipping documents to sales invoice date. Check FOB terms.
- *Classification of accounts receivable*—Trace posting of intercompany sales, sales returns, etc., to sales.

When a business receives many cash or check payments from customers on an account, a detailed audit should include a comparison of the checks listed on a sample of deposit slips to the customer credits listed on the day's posting to customer accounts receivable (daily remittance list or other record of detail postings). This procedure is a test for a type of accounts receivable fraud—also known as *lapping* (see Chapter 6). Auditors look for credits given to customers from whom no payments were received on the day in question.

See Appendix Exhibit 7B.1 for a test of controls audit plan. These steps are designed to direct the audit team in obtaining sufficient appropriate evidence about the effectiveness of controls and about the reliability of accounting records. Thus, the tests of controls produce evidence that helps auditors determine whether the specific control was properly designed and is operating effectively.

The PCAOB considers the auditor's testing of the operating effectiveness of internal controls to be critical, as evidenced by the following PCAOB Inspection Focus.

PCAOB INSPECTION FOCUS
Revenue Cycle Controls

The PCAOB is required to perform detailed inspections of the audit process employed by each firm auditing publicly traded corporations. A formal inspection report is issued by the PCAOB for each firm inspected. In a recent inspection report, the PCAOB highlighted the importance of testing the operating effectiveness of controls over the revenue cycle:

"The issuer recorded certain revenue based on information about the quantities sold and delivery dates that was provided by a third-party administrator. The following deficiencies were identified":

- "The firm did not identify and test any controls over the accuracy and completeness of the information provided by the third-party administrator. (AS 2201.39)"

- "The firm used the quantities sold and delivery date information in its substantive testing of this revenue but did not perform any substantive procedures to test or, in the alternative, identify and test any controls over (as discussed above), the accuracy and completeness of this information. (AS 1105.10)"

- "The sample size the firm used in certain of its substantive procedures to test this revenue was too small to provide sufficient appropriate audit evidence because these procedures were designed based on a level of control reliance that was not supported due to the deficiency in the firm's control testing discussed above. (AS 2301.16, .18, and .37; AS 2315.19, .23, and .23A)"

Source: *Report on 2020 Inspection of KPMG LLP.,* PCAOB, September 30, 2021.

Summary: Control Risk Assessment

Auditors must evaluate the evidence obtained from their understanding of internal control and from tests of controls. The initial process of obtaining an understanding of the company's controls and the later process of obtaining evidence from actual tests of controls are two of the phases of control risk assessment. If the control risk is assessed to be very low, the substantive procedures on the account balances can be reduced, resulting in audit efficiencies. For example, the accounts receivable confirmations can be sent on a date prior to the year-end, and the sample size can be small.

On the other hand, if tests of controls reveal weaknesses (such as posting sales without shipping documents, charging customers the wrong prices, or recording credits to customers without supporting documentation), the substantive procedures need to be designed to lower the risk of failing to detect material misstatement in the account balances (detection risk). For example, the confirmation procedure may need to be scheduled on the year-end date with a large sample of customer accounts.

 REVIEW CHECKPOINTS

7.15 What specific control procedures (in addition to separation of duties and responsibilities) should be in place and operating in internal controls governing revenue recognition?

7.16 What is a *walkthrough* of a sales transaction? How can the walkthrough work complement the use of an internal control questionnaire?

7.17 What types of audit procedures are typically performed in testing operating effectiveness of controls over the revenue and collection cycle?

7.18 What is *dual-direction* test of controls sampling in the revenue and collection cycle?

SUBSTANTIVE ANALYTICAL PROCEDURES AND TESTS OF DETAILS

LO 7-6
Give examples of substantive procedures in the revenue and collection cycle and relate them to assertions about significant account balances at the end of the period.

As you have learned previously while studying audit risk, the primary reason for evaluating the internal control system at an audit client is to reach an overall assessment of the risk of material misstatement for each relevant assertion. In fact, the assessment of the risk of material misstatement is completed to help form the basis for determining the nature, timing, and extent of substantive testing. Risk of material misstatement at the assertion level comprises both inherent risk and control risk for each relevant assertion.

If inherent risk has already been assessed as high, this means there is high susceptibility for this account to be misstated. Recall that control risk is the "probability that an entity's controls will fail to prevent or detect material misstatements due to errors or frauds." Because the revenue cycle consists of routine transactions, the majority of audit clients have strong controls in the revenue cycle, and thus tests of controls often support a reduction in control risk. This reduction in control risk reduces the auditor's assessment of the risk of material misstatement in the revenue cycle.

However, auditing standards also indicate that there is a presumptive risk of fraud in the revenue cycle. Further, according to professional standards, for significant risks, the auditor should perform substantive procedures, including tests of details, that are specifically responsive to the assessed risks. Because revenue is a presumptive high-fraud risk and an overall significant risk, the auditor always performs *substantive procedures* in the revenue cycle. These procedures are classified as substantive analytical procedures and substantive tests of details.

A substantive analytical procedure is one in which the auditor substantiates an account or disclosure by developing an independent estimate of the amount and then comparing the recorded balance to the estimate. As we will discuss later in this chapter, the evaluation of the accounting estimate for the allowance for doubtful accounts generally involves an analytical review of the adequacy of the provision for bad debt expense.

A substantive test of details is one in which the auditor substantiates an account or disclosure by directly testing the transactions that make up the account or the items that constitute the balance of the account. For example, auditors will generally send confirmations to customers to substantiate the existence and rights and obligations assertions of accounts receivable.

Exhibit 7.9 presents common substantive tests that are performed to address remaining risks of material misstatement related to the significant accounts and relevant assertions in the revenue cycle.

When considering relevant assertions and obtaining evidence about accounts receivable and other assets, auditors must emphasize the *existence* assertion. This emphasis on existence is appropriate because a large number of restatements of reports on financial statements involve overstated assets and revenues. When credit sales are recorded too early or fictitious sales are posted, this results in overstated accounts receivable and overstated sales revenue.

Discerning the population of assets to audit for existence is easy because the company has asserted its existence by putting them on the balance sheet. Despite the general presence of strong controls, obtaining substantive evidence supporting the existence of accounts receivable is required in audits where receivables are material. The auditor typically obtains evidence about the existence of accounts receivable through a combination of analytical procedures and confirmations.

AUDITING INSIGHT It Takes a Long Time to Catch It. . .

Revenue restatements can often take a long time to detect. In fact, sometimes restatements that resulted from errors and misapplications, as opposed to fraud, can persist for a long period of time. Consider the case of **Alphabet Inc.**, the parent company of Google. During 2015, Alphabet discovered that they had inappropriately accounted for revenues related to transactions between "legal entities" since 2008! The net result of the error was an increased income tax expense of $711 million.

According to Audit Analytics, Alphabet's restatement was the largest restatement of the year. However, Alphabet determined that the amount was "immaterial" and did not separately disclose the restatement outside of their annual report. Nevertheless, the $711 million restatement was 0.9% of total revenues and 4.3% of net income, an amount auditors would often consider material.

Sources: *Alphabet Inc. 2015 Annual Report, p. 21; Audit Analytics, 2017 Financial Restatements: A Seventeen Year Comparison,* May 2018.

Analytical Procedures

During an audit, a variety of analytical procedures might be employed, depending on the circumstances and the nature of the business. Comparisons of asset and revenue balances with recent history might help detect overstatements. Such relationships as receivables turnover, days' sales in receivables, amount of past due receivables, gross margin ratio, and sales/asset ratios can be compared to historical data and industry statistics for evidence

EXHIBIT 7.9 **Substantive Procedures in the Revenue and Collection Cycle**

Significant Account	Relevant Assertions	What Could Go Wrong?	Internal Control Activity	Test of Internal Control	Possible Substantive Analytical Procedures	Possible Substantive Tests of Detail
Revenue	Occurrence	Management may overstate sales by adding fictitious transactions or inflating actual sales.	Invoices are supported by customer purchase orders. Bill of lading or other shipping documents exist for all invoices, and recorded sales in the Sales Revenue account file are supported by invoices.	Vouch sales in sales detail file to invoices, supporting shipping documents, and customer purchase orders for customer name, product description, terms, dates, and quantities.	Compare asset and revenue balances with recent history to help detect overstatements. Sales ratios can be compared to historical data and industry statistics for evidence of overall reasonableness.	Vouch journal entry, sales summary, sales invoice copy, shipping documents, and, finally, the customer's purchase order.
		Management may fail to recognize the possibility of customer returns.	Management analyzes sales returns regularly and estimates an allowance for returns.	Inspect documents for evidence that management evaluates the allowance for returns regularly.	Obtain a summary of sales returns subsequent to year-end, and evaluate the adequacy of the allowance.	Select a sample of sales returns subsequent to year-end, and trace to proper charging against the allowance account.
	Completeness	Not all sales are recorded.	Invoices, shipping documents, and sales orders are prenumbered, and the numerical sequence is checked.	Scan documents for numerical sequence, observe client-checking sequence, and trace shipping document to recording in sales detail file.	Compare current year's sales to last year's sales by geographic location.	Select samples of shipping documents, and trace to sales invoice and the sales journal.
	Cutoff	Sales have been recorded in incorrect periods.	The date of shipping document is compared to the invoice date.	Trace shipping date on shipping documents to sales invoice date, and check FOB terms.	Compare prior year's sales in same month to current year's sales in same month.	Trace shipping documents before and after year-end to the sales journal to ensure the sale was recorded in the proper period, credit memos for returns after year-end are vouched to receiving reports, and any goods returned after year-end that were sold during the year being audited have been deducted from sales.
			Management evaluates all new contracts to ensure revenue recognition compliance with ASC 606.	Inspect documents for evidence that management evaluates the timing of revenue recognition from contracts.		Inspect licensing contracts and prepare documentation memo evaluating revenue recognition in accordance with ASC 606

EXHIBIT 7.9 **Substantive Procedures in the Revenue and Collection Cycle** *(Concluded)*

Significant Account	Relevant Assertions	What Could Go Wrong?	Internal Control Activity	Test of Internal Control	Possible Substantive Analytical Procedures	Possible Substantive Tests of Detail
Accounts Receivable	Existence	Accounts receivable are overstated and do not represent actual sales.	Management verifies sales order and shipping document to verify that sales were earned and a customer owes a balance.	When payments are received, vouch checks listed on sample deposit slips to the customer credits listed on the day's posting to customer accounts receivable.	Compare prior year's A/R balance in relation to sales with current year's A/R balance in relation to sales.	Confirm accounts receivable.
	Completeness	Not all accounts receivable have been recorded.	Management compares invoices with the shipping document and the A/R ledger.	Inspect documents for evidence that the billing department supervisor matches prenumbered shipping documents with entries in the sales journal.	Compare A/R relationship with sales to COGS relationship with inventory.	Select a sample of remittance worksheets (or bank deposits), vouch details to bank deposit slips (trace details to remittance worksheets if the sample is bank deposits), and trace to complete accounting posting in customer accounts receivable.
	Valuation	Receivables are not included in financial statements at the appropriate amount, and valuation adjustments are not recorded properly.	Authorize and record discounts when customers take them.	Inspect documentation for evidence that subsequent cash receipts from the customer are reviewed. Inquire of the credit manager procedures regarding unpaid accounts. Inspect credit files for most recent review of customer creditworthiness.	Accounts receivable write-offs should be compared with estimates of doubtful accounts. Recalculate customer discounts to make sure they are accurate.	Inspect aged trial balance, compare current year's write-off experience with prior year's allowance for bad debts.
			Management evaluates the collectability of delinquent receivables on a timely basis.	Inspect documentation for evidence that management evaluates the collectability of receivables.		

of overall reasonableness. Account interrelationships also can be used in analytical procedures. For example, sales returns and allowances and sales commissions generally vary directly with dollar sales volume, bad debt expense usually varies directly with credit sales, and freight expense varies with the physical sales volume. Accounts receivable write-offs may also be compared with estimates of doubtful accounts. An example of a common substantive analytical procedure is discussed in the following Auditing Insight.

AUDITING INSIGHT Simple Analytical Comparison

Days Sales Outstanding (DSO) represents the average number of days it takes a company to collect accounts receivable after a sale. It is the inverse of the receivables turnover ratio and is commonly used by management to assess the collections process. Auditors also can use the DSO to provide assurance related to the valuation of accounts receivable. To provide substantive evidence, the analytical procedures need to be at a sufficient level of detail to enable the auditor to assess whether the allowance for doubtful accounts is sufficient.

Often, the auditor will examine DSO at the location and product class level to identify trends that do not match with trends in allowance for doubtful accounts. When the auditor recognizes that DSO is increasing without a comparable increase in allowance, the auditor can follow up with additional detail testing. However, if the DSO and allowance accounts appear reasonable and correlated, the substantive analytical procedure may provide sufficient appropriate evidence for the valuation of accounts receivable.

Confirmation of Accounts and Notes Receivable

In general, the use of confirmations for accounts receivable is considered a required audit procedure by audit standards. If auditors decide not to use them, the burden of proof is on the auditors to justify their position. Auditors should document justifications for the decision not to use confirmations for accounts receivable in a particular audit. Justifications might include (1) receivables are not material; (2) confirmations would be ineffective, based on prior-years' experience or knowledge that responses could be unreliable; and (3) analytical procedures and other substantive procedures provide sufficient, competent evidence. The following Auditing Insight provides an example of one such situation.

AUDITING INSIGHT A Decision Not to Use Accounts Receivable Confirmations

Sureparts Manufacturing Company sold all its production to three auto manufacturers and six aftermarket distributors. All nine of these customers typically paid their accounts in full by the 10th of each following month. The auditors were able to vouch the cash receipts for the full amount of the accounts receivable

in the bank statements and cash receipts records in the month following the Sureparts year-end. Confirmation evidence was not necessary in these circumstances because direct evidence of payment provided full verification of the existence and valuation of the receivables.

Confirmations provide evidence of *existence* as well as *rights and obligations* of accounts and notes receivable. However, they do not provide strong evidence on the *valuation* of accounts receivable. Remember that just because a customer owes an amount does not mean they will pay that amount. Customers in bankruptcy routinely confirm amounts owed, although the receivable's value may be only a small fraction of that amount. The accounts to be confirmed are often documented with an aged trial balance. (An aged trial balance annotated to show the auditors' work is shown in Exhibit 7.10.) Accounts for confirmation can be selected at random or in accordance with another sampling method consistent with the audit objectives. Statistical methods may be useful for determining the sample size. Audit software such as IDEA is often used to access receivables files, select, and even print the confirmations.

Unlike cash confirmations, which as described in Chapter 6 are almost always electronic, accounts receivable confirmations are still largely manual. The primary reason is that most confirmation intermediaries, such as Confirmation, require the registration and authentication of respondents. Unlike banks, which respond to confirmations for

EXHIBIT 7.10 Accounts Receivable Aged Trial Balance

C-2
Prepared *DHS 2/14/2021*
Review *ADB 2/16/2021*

DUNDER-MIFFLIN INC
Accounts Receivable Aged Trial Balance
For Year Ended 12/31/2023
(Prepared by Client)

	2023 Total Balance	Conf. No.	Date Mailed	Date Rec'd	Current < 30 Days	30–60 Days	Past Due 60–90 Days	>90 Days
Pay More Paper	$ 173,406.37					$173,406.37		
Nuke Me Office Supplies	11,630.14				$ 11,630.14			
Bet Your Life Printing	718,986.45	1 C	1/15	1/22	718,986.45			
Paper Shack	242,568.88				242,568.88			
Shreadables	461.09						$ 461.09	
Mall-Wart	6,822,725.10	2 C	1/15	1/27	γ 5,765,081.85			$ 1,057,643.25
House of Paper	3,181.49						3,181.49	
Sunshine Office Supplies	1,644.41				1,644.41			
Imelda's Printing	32,023.89	3 E	1/15	1/21	32,023.89			
Hip Hop Invitations	230,932.95					230,932.95		
The Paper Federation	405,846.10				405,846.10			
Office Least	15,026.57	4 E	1/15	1/25	γ(1,388.75)	γ16,415.32		
Lamour Glamor Printing	127,907.18β	5 NR	1/15	n/a			127,907.18	
Bullseye	1,013,239.57	6 E	1/15	2/2	1,013,239.57			
Peyton's Paper	879.43				879.43			
Total	$9,800,459.62CF				$ 8,190,511.97	$420,754.64	$131,549.76	$1,057,643.25
	u TB				u	u	u	u

C Confirmation received without exception.
γ Tested calculation of aging.
E Confirmation received with exception. See C-2.1 for follow-up.
β Examined related invoices and shipping documents.
NR Confirmation not returned. See C-3 for application of subsequent cash receipts.
CF Crossfooted.
u Footed.
TB Agreed to trial balance.

the majority of their larger business customers, other companies and individuals do not receive many, if any, confirmation requests. As a result, the customers of most audit clients would not have the ability to securely authenticate and respond to electronic confirmations without a great deal of effort—which they may choose not to exert.

There are two primary methods of confirming accounts receivable: positive confirmations and negative confirmations. A **positive confirmation** asks the customer to respond as to whether the balance is correct or incorrect. See Exhibit 7.11 for an example of a positive confirmation. A variation of the positive confirmation is the *blank form.* A blank confirmation does not contain the balance; customers are asked to fill it in themselves. The blank positive confirmation may produce better evidence because the recipients need to get the information directly from their own records instead of just signing the form and returning it with no exceptions noted. (However, the effort involved on the part of the recipient may cause a lower response rate.) As illustrated in several of the exhibits below, the auditors must follow up on all exceptions. For example, they may choose to examine the bank deposit that includes a check mentioned by the customer. The reason for any discrepancy will have to be investigated by the client, and the audit team will examine corroborative evidence of the client's resolution.

EXHIBIT 7.11
Positive Confirmation Form

Dunder-Mifflin Inc.
Scranton, PA

Bullseye
1359 Central Boulevard
Derma, MS 39530
Attn: Accounts Payable Dept.

Our auditor, Michael Scarn, LLP, is making his regular audit of our financial statements. Part of this audit includes direct verification of customer balances.

PLEASE EXAMINE THE DATA BELOW CAREFULLY AND EITHER CONFIRM ITS ACCURACY OR REPORT ANY DIFFERENCES DIRECTLY TO OUR AUDITORS USING THE ENCLOSED REPLY ENVELOPE.

This is not a request for payment. Please do not send your remittance to our auditors.

Your prompt attention to this request will be appreciated.

Samuel Carboy

Samuel Carboy, Controller

The balance due Dunder-Mifflin Inc. as of December 31, 2023, is
$1,013,239.57 C-2

This balance is correct except as noted below:

Our records indicate that we wrote a check to Dunder-Mifflin on 12/28 for this amount. ✓

Date: *1/21/24*   By: *Rudy Robinson*

Title: *Accounts Payable*

✓ *Check Received 1/3/24 RJR*

See Exhibit 7.12 for the **negative confirmation** for the same request in Exhibit 7.11. The positive form asks for a response. The negative form asks for a response *only if something is wrong with the balance;* thus, lack of response to negative confirmations is considered evidence that the account is fairly stated.

The positive form is by far the more common and is used when individual balances are relatively large or when accounts are in dispute. Positive confirmations generally ask for information about the entire account balance as of a specific date. However, when customers are less likely to be able to respond to entire account balances, auditors may confirm specific invoices. The negative form is used mostly when the risk of material misstatement is considered low, when a large number of small balances is involved, and when the client's customers can be expected to consider the confirmations properly. Auditors must use negative confirmations with great care. Occasionally, they use both forms by sending positive confirmations on some (large) customers' accounts and negative confirmations on others (usually smaller account balances).

**EXHIBIT 7.12
Negative Confirmation
Form**

Dunder-Mifflin Inc.
Scranton, PA

Bullseye
1359 Central Boulevard
Derma, MS 39530
Attn: Accounts Payable Dept.

Our auditor, Michael Scarn, LLP, is making his regular audit of our financial statements. Part of this audit includes direct verification of customer balances.

PLEASE EXAMINE THE DATA BELOW CAREFULLY AND COMPARE THEM TO YOUR RECORDS OF YOUR ACCOUNT WITH US. IF THE INFORMATION IS NOT IN AGREEMENT WITH YOUR RECORDS, PLEASE STATE ANY DIFFERENCES BELOW AND RETURN DIRECTLY TO OUR AUDITORS IN THE RETURN ENVELOPE PROVIDED. **IF THE INFORMATION IS CORRECT, NO REPLY IS NECESSARY.**

This is not a request for payment. Please do not send your remittance to our auditors.

Your prompt attention to this request will be appreciated.

Samuel Carboy
Samuel Carboy, Controller

The balance due Dunder-Mifflin Inc. as of December 31, 2023, is
$1,013,239.57 C-2

This balance is correct except as noted below:

Our records indicate that we wrote a check to Dunder-Mifflin on 12/28 for this amount. ✓

Date: *1/21/24*   By: *Rudy Robinson*
                             Title: *Accounts Payable*

✓ *Check Received 1/3/24 RJR*

Getting confirmations delivered to the intended recipient requires auditors' careful attention. Auditors need to control the mailing of the confirmations, including the addresses to which they are sent, and the confirmations should be returned directly to the auditors. The confirmations should normally be addressed to the customer's accounts payable department. There have been cases in which confirmations were mailed to company accomplices, who provided false responses. The auditors should carefully consider features of the reply, such as postmarks, fax and telephone responses, letterhead, e-mail, or other characteristics that may indicate a false response. Auditors should follow up on electronic and telephone responses to determine their origin (e.g., returning the telephone call to a known number, looking up telephone numbers to determine addresses, or using a directory to determine the location of a respondent). On the other hand, an electronic confirmation process (e.g., confirmation.com) that creates a secure confirmation environment may mitigate the risks of human intervention and misdirection. For example, encryption, electronic digital signatures, and procedures to verify website authenticity may improve the security of the electronic confirmation process. Second and third requests should be sent to motivate responses to positive confirmations, and auditors should audit nonresponding customers by alternative procedures. Furthermore, the lack of response to a negative confirmation is no guarantee that the intended recipient received it or read it. Exhibit 7.13 illustrates some common confirmation responses and the appropriate follow-up action.

If an exception cannot be resolved or it appears to indicate a misstatement, auditors should (1) determine the cause of the misstatement, (2) extrapolate the misstatements over the population, and (3) consider whether fraud may have occurred. If similar misstatements could exist, additional procedures are generally necessary to determine the extent of misstatements. In the case of fraud, an extensive investigation may be necessary.[6]

Confirmation of receivables may be performed at a date other than the year-end. When confirmation is done at an interim date, the audit firm is able to spread work throughout the year and avoid the pressures of overtime that typically occur during "busy season." In addition, the audit can be completed sooner after the year-end date if confirmations have been done earlier. The primary consideration when planning confirmation of receivables before the balance sheet date is the client's internal control over transactions affecting receivables. When confirmation is performed at an interim date, the following additional procedures should be considered:

1. Obtain a summary of receivables transactions from the interim date to the year-end date, and review them for unusual items.
2. Vouch a selected sample of transactions for the period.
3. Obtain a year-end trial balance of receivables, compare it to the interim trial balance, and obtain evidence and explanations for large variations.
4. Consider the necessity for additional confirmations as of the balance sheet date if balances have significantly increased.

EXHIBIT 7.13
Responses to Positive Confirmations (as of December 31)

Response	Follow-Up Action
"This amount was paid on December 28."	This account is probably valid because the check was likely received after year-end. However, it should be treated as an exception and the date of the receipt should be verified.
"We are unable to confirm this amount."	This is treated the same way as a nonresponse, and alternative procedures should be performed.
"We returned these items."	This is an exception that should be discussed with the client. The auditor should verify that there are no other returns included in receivables.
"We received these goods on January 3."	This is also probably valid because the shipment was likely made in late December. However, this should also be treated as an exception and the shipment should be verified. The auditor should also make sure the goods were removed from the year-end inventory.

[6]AICPA Practice Alert 03-1, "Audit Confirmations," June 2007.

The PCAOB considers revenue to be an area of high risk. As a result, PCAOB inspections often focus on revenue, and deficiencies are sometimes identified in accounts receivable audits, as shown in the following PCAOB Inspection Focus.

PCAOB INSPECTION FOCUS — Accounts Receivable

The PCAOB is required to perform detailed inspections of the audit process employed by each firm auditing publicly traded corporations. A formal inspection report is issued by the PCAOB for each firm inspected. In a recent inspection report, the PCAOB highlighted the importance of substantively testing the client's accounts receivable:

- "The firm's substantive procedures to test accounts receivable as of an interim date consisted of performing confirmation pro-

cedures for a sample of invoices. The firm did not perform sufficient procedures to extend its conclusions from the interim date to year end because its procedures were limited to performing confirmation procedures for a small sample of invoices recorded as accounts receivable at year end. (AS 2301.45)"

Source: *Report of 2020 Inspection of Deloitte & Touche LLP.*, PCAOB, September 30, 2021.

Alternative Procedures

Often, the client's customers are not willing or able to return the confirmation. They may not be able if, for example, they are on a voucher system that lists payables by invoice instead of by vendor account. The U.S. government is notorious for not returning confirmations because records may be kept at various agencies. In these cases, auditors must perform alternative procedures to ensure existence. These include examining (1) subsequent cash receipts; (2) sales orders, invoices, and shipping documents; and (3) correspondence files for past-due accounts. Examining subsequent cash receipts is a particularly effective test because if the customer paid the account, it provides strong evidence that the receivable existed. This examination is often performed even when the customer has confirmed the account, because subsequent collection of cash is the strongest evidence supporting the valuation assertion of accounts receivable. The cash receipt should be traced to the remittance advice and the deposit into the client's cash account.

Additional Notes about Confirmations

Because of the importance of confirmations for verifying the validity of accounts receivable, the auditor should take special care to consider the sufficiency of evidence obtained. Some other considerations that auditors should make when sending confirmations follow:

- Confirmations returned by the postal service as "undeliverable" are always a red flag. The address should be double-checked and evidence that the company actually exists obtained.

- Confirmations of accounts, loans, and notes receivable may not produce sufficient evidence of ownership by the client (rights assertion). Debtors may not be aware that the client sold the accounts, notes, or loans receivable to financial institutions or to the public (collateralized securities). Auditors should also consider whether their clients ever factor, or sell, receivables to third parties. Auditors need to perform additional inquiries and detailed procedures to get evidence of the ownership of the receivables and the appropriateness of disclosures related to financing transactions secured by receivables.

- Although confirmations are most often used for account balances, experienced auditors recognize that confirming a specific transaction, especially a large one, may be more effective. This is especially true if the balance consists primarily of a few large transactions. In your own life, you probably do not know what your current balance is on your credit cards, but you likely remember a recent large purchase (e.g., for textbooks).

- It is also possible for an auditor to receive an oral response to a confirmation. Such a response does not meet the definition of an external confirmation because there is no *direct written response* to the auditor. The auditor should request a written response, and if one is not forthcoming, the auditor should determine whether alternative audit procedures are warranted.

Dual-Purpose Nature of Accounts Receivable Confirmations

Accounts receivable confirmation is a substantive procedure designed to obtain evidence—primarily of the existence and, secondarily, rights and obligations of customers' balances—directly from the customer. However, if such confirmations show numerous exceptions, auditors are concerned with the controls over the details of sales and cash receipts transactions even if previous control evaluations seemed to show little control risk.

The goal in performing substantive procedures is to detect evidence of any material misstatement due to errors or fraud. If there is a risk of material misstatement involving revenue recognition, auditors should consider confirming contract terms and investigate the presence of side agreements with customers. Items to be considered would be acceptance criteria, delivery and payment terms, future or continuing vendor obligations, rights of return, guaranteed resale, and cancellation or refund provisions.

Review for Collectability

Even if the customer confirms that the account exists, this does not necessarily mean that the customer can or will pay it! Therefore, the primary evidence gained from confirmations relates to existence. However, the audit team must review accounts for collectability and determine the adequacy of the allowance for doubtful accounts in support of the *valuation* assertion. To do this, auditors review subsequent cash receipts from the customer, discuss unpaid accounts with the credit manager, and examine the credit files. In addition, a discussion of the bankruptcy of a large customer may appear in the minutes of the board of directors meetings, the audit committee meetings, or a meeting of an executive committee. Credit files should contain the customer's financial statements, credit reports, and correspondence between the client and the customer. Based on this evidence, the audit team estimates the likely amount of nonpayment for the customer, which is included in the estimate of the allowance for doubtful accounts. In addition, an allowance should be estimated for all other customers, perhaps as a percentage of the current accounts with a higher percentage of past due accounts. The auditors then compare their estimate to the recorded balance in the allowance account and propose an adjusting entry for the difference if needed.

Cutoff and Sales Returns

The *cutoff* assertion is particularly relevant in the revenue cycle because of the significance of revenue as a benchmark for users of the financial statements. This high significance of revenues makes it highly appealing to managers for earnings management and fraud. Many questionable adjustments to revenues occur very close to year-end. As a result, auditors must make sure that sales are recorded in the proper period. To do this, they employ **sales cutoff tests**. Procedures include tracing shipping documents before and after year-end to the sales journal to ensure the sale was recorded in the proper period. Credit memos for returns after year-end are vouched to receiving reports. Any goods returned after year-end that were sold during the year being audited should be deducted from net sales.

Adjusting entries for cutoff errors (i.e., sales recorded in the current period for next month's shipments) must be considered carefully because not only are accounts receivable and sales overstated, but also inventory is understated and cost of goods sold (COGS) is overstated.

In addition to the substantive tests discussed earlier and in Exhibit 7.9, the auditor often performs other substantive tests related to assertions in the revenue cycle:

- *Completeness of revenue and accounts receivable*—Include a sample of zero-balance accounts in the confirmation process.
- *Rights and obligations of accounts receivable*—Inquire whether any receivables have been sold or factored.

- *Rights and obligations of accounts receivable*—Inspect the bank confirmations, loan agreements, and minutes of the board for indications of pledged, discounted, or assigned receivables.

Companies may sell or **factor** their accounts receivable to a financial institution to obtain cash immediately. It is difficult to determine whether receivables have been sold because the customers usually do not know that someone else actually owns their account. The cash goes to the original seller, who passes it on to the financial institution. Inquiring of management and examining support for large cash receipts is the best way to detect these transactions.

- *Classification of accounts receivable*—Scan receivables ledger for negative balances for reclassification to accounts payable.
- *Presentation and disclosure of accounts receivable and revenues*—Complete a disclosure checklist and ensure completeness and accuracy of required disclosures.

When auditors are satisfied that controls have been examined and transactions and balances have been appropriately tested, the job is not over. The accounts in the revenue cycle require certain disclosures. Revenue recognition policies and the amount of the allowance for doubtful accounts are some of the items requiring specific presentation and disclosures. These disclosures must ensure that the disclosures are complete, accurate, and understandable. To ensure this, the auditor will often complete the audit of the revenue cycle with a disclosure checklist.

The bottom line with auditing revenues is that the risk of revenue misstatement is nearly always present in the office, and the auditor should never take anything for granted, as shown by the following Auditing Insight

AUDITING INSIGHT   Not Luckin' Out

Ernst & Young Hua Ming LLP identified a fraud involving fictitious revenue recorded by Luckin Coffee Inc., a Chinese rival to Starbucks Corp. The fraud involved 2.2 billion yuan ($310 million) recognized as revenue but not earned. Employees within the company used individual customer accounts and those of smaller companies to record huge bulk purchases of vouchers that could be redeemed for coffee products. Many of the companies had ties to Luckin's chairman, Charles Lu. The difficulty with auditing revenues in some jurisdictions

is highlighted by this case. Up until that time, the Chinese government had prevented the inspection of audits, even when the companies were issuers in the United States. In response to the Luckin fraud, in 2021 Congress passed the Holding Foreign Companies Accountable Act, which requires the ability to inspect an audit within three years.

Source: "SEC Investigates China's Luckin Coffee," *The Wall Street Journal*, April 30, 2020, p. B6.; "U.S. Seeks to Audit Chinese Firms in Latest Shot in Nations' Rivalry," *The Wall Street Journal*, May 27, 2020, p. A1, A6.

☑ REVIEW CHECKPOINTS

7.19 Why is it important to emphasize the *existence* assertion when auditing accounts receivable?

7.20 Which audit procedures are usually the most useful for auditing the existence assertion?

7.21 What analytical procedures might be informative regarding the existence assertion?

7.22 Distinguish between positive and negative confirmations. Under what conditions would you expect each type of confirmation to be appropriate?

7.23 What are some justifications for not using confirmations of accounts receivable on a particular audit?

7.24 What special care should be taken with regard to examining the sources (e.g., emailed copy) of accounts receivable confirmation responses?

7.25 What alternative procedures should be applied to accounts that do not return confirmations?

7.26 What procedures should be performed to determine the adequacy of the allowance for doubtful accounts?

AUDIT RISK MODEL APPLIED

Now that the inherent and control risk elements for the revenue and collection cycle along with some of the important substantive procedures have been presented, let's examine how an audit team might apply the audit risk model for the *existence* assertion.

Healthy Delights Ice Cream Inc.

Healthy Delights is a publicly held company that sells health-based ice cream to grocery store chains in the United States. Annual sales have steadily remained at around $100 million. Marsha Fields has been assigned as the senior auditor. Her firm's policy is always to set overall audit risk as low. She knows previous years' errors were few and the food industry is sound. The company is generally profitable; management's compensation is based on long-term performance, not short-term goals; and the overall economy was strong during the year under audit, so she assesses inherent risk as low to moderate. Controls have been historically strong, including hiring of competent people; maximum use of computer technology, which is reviewed by internal auditors; and careful reviews of detailed sales analyses by management. Testing of controls in accordance with *AS 2201* found no design or operating deficiencies. Thus, Fields assesses the risk of material misstatement as low. In this situation, she can be comfortable setting detection risk at a moderate to high level. This will allow her to limit her sample of accounts for positive confirmations to the largest accounts with a small random sample for negative confirmations on smaller accounts. The confirmations will be sent at an interim date. She also can rely heavily on analytical procedures. In addition, a smaller sample of transactions will be selected for detail testing. This combination of low risk of material misstatement and moderate to high detection risk should lead Fields to an acceptably low overall audit risk.

APPLICATION IN THE FIELD

LO 7-7
Apply your knowledge to perform audit procedures in the revenue and collection cycle and evaluate the findings of your tests.

Historically, auditors testing the revenue cycle would select samples of items to test significant assertions and the controls that help ensure the accurate and complete processing of transactions. With an increase in the ability to handle larger amounts of data, auditors can now test all instances of some controls and transactions instead of selecting a sample.

One way to subject all items in a population of occurrences for a particular control activity in the revenue cycle is to use *exception testing*. Exception testing is designed to identify a violation of a particular control activity through the use of an automated test procedure designed to test all items in a population. For example, companies often design an automated control activity to compare a customer's credit limit to the sum of (1) a potential sales transaction and (2) that customer's outstanding credit balance before approval of that sales transaction. If the control activity operated effectively throughout the year, a customer's outstanding credit balance would not exceed its credit limit.

Given the nature of the control activity, one way for an auditor to test the operating effectiveness of this control would be through the use of exception testing. An auditor could obtain evidence about the control's operating effectiveness by using a procedure that compares each customer's credit limit to that customer's outstanding credit balance at the end of each day for the year under audit. Such a testing strategy would not have been possible (at least economically) previously. However, due to advances in information technology, such testing is now possible. Using IDEA or other audit software, the computer can make these comparisons and provide a listing of exceptions, as outlined in the following example. As a direct result, entry-level audit professionals are now expected to consider the full extent of client data available for testing purposes before proceeding with audit tests.

Of course, auditors prefer to rely on their client's controls, and testing credit authorization controls is always part of an audit when a client issues substantial credit to customers. As part of testing the control, auditors will evaluate the effectiveness of the design of the control and also the operating effectiveness of the control. Part of testing the operating effectiveness of the control may involve analyzing client data, as described in the Using IDEA in the Audit example that follows.

USING IDEA IN THE AUDIT \ Credit Authorization Controls

One opportunity for auditors to take advantage of the availability of improved data analytic tools is to perform exception testing on granting credit to customers. For example, an auditor may want to test whether any customers were granted credit when they either had no approved credit limit or had exceeded their credit limit.

To accomplish this, the auditor will most likely join two related client data files—an Accounts Receivable subsidiary ledger and a customer master list with credit authorizations—based on customer identification. In IDEA, this can be accomplished using the **Join** command from within the **Analysis** tab.

After joining the data, the auditor can perform a direct extraction using the **Direct** command from the **Extract** group in the **Analysis** tab and create a new database of any transactions that caused a customer to exceed the credit limit. This enables the auditor to identify exceptions to authorization controls, leading to more accurate assessments of control risk and more efficient selection of substantive tests.

At the end of this chapter, you can perform this exception test in Exercise 7.78.

AUDIT CASES: EXTENDED AUDIT PROCEDURES

This part of the chapter uses a set of cases that provide specific examples of tests of controls and substantive procedures (recalculation, observation, confirmation, inquiry, vouching, tracing, scanning, and analytical procedures). The case stories are better than listing schemes and detection procedures in the abstract.

The cases follow a standard format that first tells about an error or fraud situation in terms of the problem, the audit approach, and the discovery. The first part of each case gives you the "inside story" that auditors seldom know before they perform the audit work. The next part is an audit approach section, which discusses the audit objective (assertion), controls, tests of controls, and substantive procedures that could be considered in approaching the situation. The audit approach section presumes that the auditors do not know everything about the situation.

At the end of the chapter, some similar discussion cases are presented, and you can write the audit approach to test your ability to design audit procedures for detecting errors and frauds. Appendix 7B provides a substantive audit plan for reference.

Case 7.1

The Canny Cashier

PROBLEM

D. Bakel was the assistant controller of Sports Equipment Inc. (SEI), an equipment retailer. SEI maintained accounts receivable for school districts in the region; otherwise, customers received credit by using their own credit cards.

As the company cashier, Bakel received all incoming mail payments on school accounts, credit card accounts, and cash and checks taken over the counter. He prepared the bank deposit, listing all checks and currency, and prepared a remittance worksheet (daily cash report) that showed amounts received, discounts allowed on school accounts, and amounts to credit to the accounts receivable. Another accountant used the remittance worksheet to post credits to the accounts receivable. Bakel delivered the deposit to the bank and reconciled the bank statement. No one else reviewed the deposits or the bank statements except the independent auditors.

Bakel opened a bank account in the name of Sport Equipment Company (SEC) after properly incorporating the company in the secretary of state's office. Over-the-counter cash, checks, and school district payments were taken from the SEI receipts and deposited in the SEC account. (None of the customers noticed the difference between the rubber stamp endorsements for the two similarly named corporations, and neither did the bank.) SEC kept the money a while, earning interest, and then Bakel wrote SEC checks to SEI to replace the "borrowed" funds, in the meantime taking new SEI receipts for deposit to SEC.

Bakel also stole payments made by the school districts, depositing them to SEC. Later he deposited SEC checks in SEI, giving the schools credit, but approved an additional 2 percent discount in the process. Thus, the schools received proper credit later, and SEC paid less by the amount of the extra discount.

SEI's bank deposits systematically showed small currency deposits. Bakel was nervous about taking too many checks, so he preferred cash. The deposit slips had to include the SEC checks because bank tellers compare the deposit slip listing to the checks submitted. The remittance worksheet showed different details: Instead of showing SEC checks, it showed receipts from school districts and currency but not many over-the-counter checks from customers.

The transactions became complicated enough that Bakel had to use the office computer to keep track of the school districts that needed to receive credit. There were no vacations for this hard-working cashier because a substitute might notice the discrepancies, and Bakel needed to give the districts credit later.

Over a six-year period, Bakel built up a $150,000 average balance in the Sport Equipment Company (SEC) account that earned a total of $67,500 interest that Sports Equipment Inc. (SEI) should have earned. By approving the "extra" discounts, Bakel skimmed 2 percent of $1 million in annual sales, for a total of $120,000. Because SEI would have had net income before taxes of about $1.6 million over these six years (about 9 percent of sales), Bakel's embezzlement took about 12.5 percent of the income.

AUDIT APPROACH

Authorization related to cash receipts, custody of cash, recording cash transactions, and bank statement reconciliation should be separate duties designed to prevent errors and frauds. Some supervision and detail review of one or more of these duties should be performed as a next-level control designed to detect errors and frauds, if they have occurred. For example, someone else should prepare the remittance worksheet, or at least the controller should approve the discounts; someone else should prepare the bank reconciliation.

Bakel performed incompatible duties. (While he did not actually perform the recording, Bakel provided the source document—the remittance worksheet—the other accountant used to make the cash and accounts receivable entries.) According to the company president, the "control" was the diligence of "our long-time, trusted, hard-working assistant controller." (*Note:* A vigilant auditor who "thought like a crook" might have been able to imagine ways Bakel could have committed fraud and thus prevented or detected this cash embezzlement and accounts receivable lapping scheme.)

Because the "control" purports to be Bakel's honest and diligent performance of the accounting and control activities that might have been performed by two or more people, the test of controls is an audit of cash receipts transactions as they relate to accounts receivable credit. The dual-direction samples and procedures are these:

Occurrence direction. The auditors selected a sample of customer accounts receivable and vouched payment credits to remittance worksheets and bank deposits, including recalculation of discounts allowed in comparison to sales terms (2 percent), classification (customer name) identification, and correspondence of receipt date to recording date.

Completeness direction. The auditors selected a sample of remittance worksheets (or bank deposits), vouched details to bank deposit slips (traced details to remittance worksheets if the sample is bank deposits), and traced to complete accounting posting in customer accounts receivable.

Because there was a control risk of incorrect accounting, accounts receivable were confirmed as of year-end using positive confirmations. The sample included all school district accounts.

When prompted by notice of an oddity (noted in the following discovery summary), the audit team used the Internet, chamber of commerce directory, local crisscross directory, and a visit to the secretary of state's office to determine the location and identity of Sport Equipment Company.

DISCOVERY SUMMARY

The test of controls samples showed four cases of discrepancy, one of which is discussed here.

The auditors sent positive confirmations on all 72 school district accounts. Three of the responses stated the districts had paid the balances before the confirmation date. Follow-up procedures on their accounts receivable credit in the next period showed they had received credit in remittance reports and the bank deposits had shown no checks from the districts but had contained a check from Sports Equipment Company.

Investigation of SEC revealed the connection of Bakel, who was confronted and then confessed.

Bank Deposit Slip		Cash Remittance Report				
		Name	Amount	Discount	AR	Sales
Jones	25	Jones	25	0	0	25
Smith	35	Smith	35	0	0	35
Hill District	980	Hill District	980	20	1,000	0
Sport Equipment	1,563	Marlin District	480	20	500	0
Currency	540	Waco District	768	32	800	0
Deposit	3,143	Currency	855	0	0	855
		Totals	3,143	72	2,300	915

Case 7.2

The Taxman Always Rings Twice

PROBLEM

J. Shelstad was the tax assessor-collector in the Ridge School District, serving a large metropolitan area. The staff processed tax notices on a computerized system and generated 450,000 tax notices each October. An office copy was printed and used to check off "paid" when payments were received. Payments were processed by computer, and a master file of "accounts receivable" records (tax assessments, payments) was kept on the computer hard drive.

Shelstad was a good personnel manager and often took over the front desk at lunchtime so the teller staff could enjoy lunch together. During these times, she took payments over the counter, gave the taxpayers a counter receipt, and pocketed some of the money, which was never entered in the computerized system.

Shelstad resigned when she was elected to the Ridge school board. The district's assessor-collector office was eliminated upon the creation of a new countywide tax agency.

The computerized records showed balances due from many taxpayers who had actually paid their taxes. The book of printed notices was not marked "paid" for many taxpayers who had received counter receipts. These records and the daily cash receipts reports (cash receipts journal) were available when the independent auditors had performed the most recent annual audit in April. When Shelstad resigned in August, a power surge permanently destroyed the hard drive receivables file, and the cash receipts journals could not be found.

The new county agency managers noticed that the total of delinquent taxes disclosed in the audited financial statements was much larger than the total turned over to the county attorney for collection and foreclosure.

Shelstad had been the assessor-collector for 15 years. The "good personnel manager" pocketed 100–150 counter payments each year in amounts of $500–$2,500, stealing about $200,000 a year for a total of approximately $2.5 million. The district had assessed about $800–$900 million per year, so the annual theft was less than 1 percent. Nevertheless, the taxpayers got mad.

AUDIT APPROACH

The school district had a respectable system for establishing the initial amounts of taxes receivable. The professional staff of appraisers and the independent appraisal review board established the tax base for each property. The school board set the price (tax rate). The computerized system authorization for billing was validated on these two inputs.

The cash receipts system was well designed, calling for preparation of a daily cash receipts report (cash receipts journal that served as a source input for computerized entry). The "boss,"

Shelstad, always reviewed this report.

Unfortunately, Shelstad had the opportunity and power to override the controls and become both cash handler and supervisor. She made the decisions about sending delinquent taxes to the county attorney for collection and withheld the ones known to have been paid but stolen.

The auditors performed dual-direction sampling to test the processing of cash receipts:

Occurrence direction. The auditors selected a sample of receivables from the computer hard disk and vouched (1) charges to the appraisal record, recalculating the amount using the authorized tax rate and (2) payments, if any, to the cash receipts journal and bank deposits. (The auditors found no exceptions.)

Completeness direction. The auditors selected a sample of properties from the appraisal rolls and determined that tax notices had been sent and tax receivables (charges) recorded in the computer file. They next selected a sample of cash receipts reports, vouched them to bank deposits of the same amount and date, and traced the payments forward to credits to taxpayers' accounts. They also selected a sample of bank deposits and traced them to cash receipts reports of the same amount and date. Finally, they compared the details on bank deposits to the details on the cash receipts reports to determine whether the same taxpayers appeared on both documents. (The auditors found no exceptions.)

The auditors confirmed a sample of unpaid tax balances with taxpayers. In such cases, response rates may not be high, follow-up procedures determining the ownership (county title files) may need to be performed, and new confirmations may need to be sent.

DISCOVERY SUMMARY

Shelstad persuaded the auditors that the true receivables were the delinquencies turned over to the county attorney. The confirmation sample and other work were based on this population. Thus, confirmations were not sent to the "unpaid" balances that Shelstad knew had been paid, therefore, the auditors never had the opportunity to receive "I paid" complaints from taxpayers.

Shelstad did not influence the new managers of the countywide tax district. They questioned the discrepancy between the delinquent taxes in the audit report and the lower amount turned over for collection. Because the computer file was not usable, the managers had to use the printed book of tax notices in which paid accounts had been marked "paid." (Shelstad had not marked the stolen ones "paid," so the printed book would agree with the computer file.) Tax due notices were sent to the taxpayers with unpaid balances, and they began to show up bringing their counter receipts and loud complaints.

Acting overzealously in their documentation, the independent auditors had earlier photocopied the entire set of cash receipts reports (cash journal) and were then able to determine that the counter receipts (all signed by Shelstad) had not been deposited or entered. Shelstad was prosecuted and sentenced to a jail term.

Case 7.3

Bill Often, Bill Early

PROBLEM

McGossage Company experienced profit pressures for two years in a row. Actual profits were squeezed in a recessionary economy, but the company reported net income decreases that were not as severe as other companies' in the industry.

Sales for orders that had been prepared for shipment but not actually shipped until later were recorded in the grocery products division. Employees backdated the shipping documents. Gross profit on these "sales" was about 30 percent. Customers took discounts on payments, but the company did not record them, leaving the debit balances in the customers' accounts receivable instead of charging them to the sales discounts and allowances account. Company accountants were instructed to wait 60 days before recording discounts taken.

The division vice president and general manager knew about these accounting practices, as did a significant number of the 2,500 employees in the division. The division managers were under orders from headquarters to achieve profit objectives they considered unrealistic.

The customers' accounts receivable balances contained amounts due for discounts the customers already had taken. The cash receipts records showed payments received without credit for discounts. Discounts were entered monthly by a special journal entry.

The unshipped goods were on the shipping dock at year-end with papers showing earlier shipping dates.

As misstatements go, some of these were on the materiality borderline. Sales were overstated 0.3 percent and 0.5 percent in the prior and current years, respectively. Accounts receivable were overstated 4 percent and 8 percent, respectively. The combined effect was to overstate the division's net income by 6 percent and 17 percent. Selected data follow:

	One Year Ago*		Current Year*	
	Reported	**Actual**	**Reported**	**Actual**
Sales	$330.0	$329.0	$350.0	$348.0
Discounts expense	1.7	1.8	1.8	2.0
Net income	6.7	6.3	5.4	4.6

*Dollars in millions.

AUDIT APPROACH

The accounting manual should provide instructions to record sales on the date of shipment (or when title passes, if later). Management subverted this control procedure by having shipping employees date the shipping papers incorrectly.

Cash receipts procedures should provide for authorizing and recording discounts when customers take them. Management overrode this control instruction by giving instructions to delay the recording.

Questionnaires and inquiries should be used to determine the company's accounting policies. It is possible that employees and managers would lie to the auditors to conceal the policies. It is also possible that pointed questions about revenue recognition and discount recording policies would elicit answers to reveal the practices.

For detail procedures, the auditors select a sample of cash receipts, examine them for authorization, recalculate the customer discounts, and trace them to accounts receivable input for recording the proper amount on the proper date. They select a sample of shipping documents, vouch them to customer orders, and then trace them to invoices and to the accounts receivable account with proper amounts on the proper date. These tests follow the tracing direction—starting with data that represent the beginning of transactions (cash receipts, shipping) and tracing them through the company's accounting process.

The audit team should confirm a sample of customer accounts and use analytical procedures to determine relationships of past years' discount expense to a relevant base (sales, sales volume) to calculate an overall test of the discounts expense.

DISCOVERY SUMMARY

The managers lied to the auditors about their revenue and expense timing policies. The sample of shipping documents showed no dating discrepancies because the employees had inserted incorrect dates. The analytical procedures on discounts did not show the misstatement because the historical relationships were too erratic to show a deficient number. However, the sample of cash receipts transactions showed that discounts had not been calculated and recorded at time of receipt. Additional inquiry led to the discovery of the special journal entries and knowledge of the recording delay. Two customers in the sample of 65 confirmations responded with exceptions that turned out to be unrecorded discounts.

Two other customers in the confirmation sample complained that they did not owe for late invoices on December 31. Follow-up showed that the shipments were noticed on the shipping dock. Auditors taking the physical inventory noticed the goods on the shipping dock during the December 31 inventory taking. Inspection revealed the shipping documents dated December 26. When the auditors traced these shipments to the sales recording, they found them recorded as **bill and hold** sales on December 29. (These procedures were performed and the results obtained by a new audit firm in the third year!)

Case 7.4

Thank Goodness It's Friday

PROBLEM

Alpha Brewery Corporation generally has good controls related to authorization of transactions for accounting entry, and the accounting manual has instructions for recording sales transactions in the proper accounting period. The company regularly closes the accounting process each Friday at 5 p.m. to prepare weekly management reports. The year-end date (cutoff date) is December 31, and this year, December 31 was a Monday. However, the accounting was performed through Friday as usual and the accounts were closed for the year on January 4.

AUDIT TRAIL

All entries were properly dated after December 31, including the sales invoices, cash receipts, and shipping documents. However, the trial balance from which the financial statements were prepared was dated December 31 (this year). Nobody noticed the slip of a few days because the Friday closing was normal.

Alpha recorded sales of $672,000 and gross profit of $268,800 over the January 1–4 period. Cash collections on customers' accounts were recorded in the amount of $800,000.

AUDIT APPROACH

The company had in place the proper instructions for people to date transactions on the actual date on which they occurred, to enter sales and cost of goods sold on the day of shipment, and to enter cash receipts on the day received in the company offices. An accounting supervisor should have checked the entries through Friday to make sure the dates corresponded with the actual events and that the accounts for the year were closed with Monday's transactions.

In this case, the auditors need to be aware of the company's weekly routine closing and the possibility that the December 31 date might cause a problem. Asking the question: "Did you cut off the accounting on Monday night this week?" might elicit the "Oh, we forgot!" response. Otherwise, it is normal to sample transactions around the year-end date to determine whether they were recorded in the proper accounting period.

Select transactions 7–10 days before and after the year-end date and inspect the dates on supporting documentation for evidence of accounting in the proper period.

The audit for sales overstatement is partly accomplished by auditing the cash and accounts receivable at December 31 for overstatement. Confirm a sample of accounts receivable. If the accounts are too large, the auditors expect the debtors to say so, thus leading to detection of sales overstatements.

Cash overstatement is audited by auditing the bank reconciliation to see whether deposits in transit (the deposits sent late in December) actually cleared the bank early in January. Obviously, the January 4 cash collections could not reach the bank until at least Monday, January 7. That is too long for a December 31 deposit to be in transit to a local bank.

The completeness of sales recordings is audited by selecting a sample of sales transactions (and supporting shipping documents) in the early part of the next accounting period (January next year). One way this year's sales could be incomplete would be to postpone recording December shipments until January, and this procedure will detect those deferred sales if the shipping documents are dated properly.

The completeness of cash collections (and accounts receivable credits) is examined by auditing the cash deposits early in January to see whether there is any sign of holding cash without entry until January.

In this case, the existence objective is more significant for discovery of the problem than the completeness objective. After all, the January 1–4 sales, shipments, and cash collections did not "exist" in December this year.

DISCOVERY SUMMARY

The test of controls sample from the days before and after December 31 quickly revealed the problem. Company accounting personnel were embarrassed, but there had been no effort to misstate the financial statements. This was a simple error. The company readily made the following adjustment:

	Debit	Credit
Sales	$672,000	
Inventory	403,200	
Accounts receivable	800,000	
Accounts receivable		$672,000
Cost of goods sold		403,200
Cash		800,000

✅ REVIEW CHECKPOINTS

7.27 What are the goals of dual-direction testing regarding an audit of the accounts receivable and cash collection system?

7.28 In the case of The Canny Cashier, name one control that could have revealed signs of the embezzlement.

7.29 What feature(s) could SEI have installed in its cash receipts internal controls that would have been expected to prevent the cash receipts journal and recorded cash sales from reflecting more than the amount shown on the daily deposit slips?

7.30 In the case of The Taxman Always Rings Twice, what information could have been obtained from confirmations directed to the real population of delinquent accounts?

7.31 In the case of Bill Often, Bill Early, what information might have been obtained from inquiries? From tests of controls? From observations? From confirmations?

7.32 With reference to the case of Thank Goodness It's Friday, what contribution could an understanding of the business and the management reporting system have made to discovery of the open cash receipts journal cutoff error?

Summary

The revenue and collection cycle consists of customer order processing, credit checking, shipping goods, billing customers, accounting for accounts receivable, and collecting and accounting for cash receipts. Companies reduce control risk by having a suitable separation of authorization, custody, recording, and periodic reconciliation duties. Error-checking activities of comparing customer orders and shipping documents are important for billing customers the correct prices for the delivered quantities. Otherwise, many things could go wrong—ranging from making sales to fictitious customers or customers with bad credit to erroneous billings for the wrong quantities at the wrong prices at the wrong time.

Confirmation is the primary substantive audit procedure accompanied by analytical procedures, application of subsequent cash receipts, and other alternative procedures. Confirmations of loans, accounts receivable, and notes receivable are required unless auditors can justify substituting other procedures in the circumstances of a particular audit. Confirmations for accounts and notes receivable can be in positive or negative form, and the positive form may be a blank confirmation. Confirmations yield evidence about *existence* and gross *valuation*. Other procedures must be undertaken to audit the collectability of the accounts. Nevertheless, confirmations can give some clues about collectability when customers tell about balances in dispute. Confirmations of accounts, notes, and loans receivable should not be used as the only evidence of the ownership (*rights* assertions) of these financial assets.

Although these procedures may seem to be common sense, auditing the revenue and collection cycle is not straightforward. Note that revenue recognition issues can involve more than a slap on the wrist and added staff training. In December 2007, the PCAOB fined Deloitte & Touche $1 million for failing to exercise due professional care and obtain sufficient evidential matter regarding revenues in the audit of **Ligand Pharmaceuticals.**

Key Terms

aged trial balance: A schedule that lists each receivable and indicates whether it is current or past due and if past due, for how long; the total should equal the accounts receivable general ledger balance, 269

bill and hold: A fraudulent financial reporting activity by which a company recognizes a sale even though it does not ship the merchandise to the customer,* but holds it in its own warehouse, 299

bill of lading: A contract between the shipper and the carrier; includes shipping information such as ship dates and origination, purchase order number, and signatures for receipt of merchandise, 267

dual-purpose procedure: An audit procedure that simultaneously serves the substantive purpose (obtain direct evidence about the dollar amounts in account balances) and the test of controls purpose (obtain evidence about the company's performance of its own control activities), 280

factor: The action to sell accounts receivable to another party (the factor) at a discount from face value, 293

negative confirmation: A form sent to a customer by auditors requesting that the customer respond only if the balance shown on it is incorrect, 289

packing slip: A document included with a shipment that shows the description and quantity of the goods being shipped, 267

positive confirmation: A letter sent to a customer by auditors requesting that the customer respond as to whether the balance shown on it is correct or not, 288

revenue recognition: The recording of revenues in the general ledger, often done fraudulently by schemes such as bill and hold, 272

sales cutoff tests: The tests that ensure that sales are recorded in the proper period—generally, when they are shipped—and that the cost of sales is recorded and removed from inventory, 292

sales invoice: A bill sent to customers for payment showing the amount due and payment terms, 267

Multiple-Choice Questions for Practice and Review

 All applicable questions are available with *Connect*.

LO 7-1

7.33 Revenues are normally considered to have been earned when
  a. All possibility of return has expired.
  b. The company has substantially accomplished what it must to be entitled to the benefits.
  c. The cash is collected.
  d. Goods have been shipped.

LO 7-3

7.34 Sales are normally recorded on the date of the
  a. Customer purchase order.
  b. Bill of lading.
  c. Sales invoice.
  d. Payment check.

LO 7-6

7.35 When auditing the revenue and collection cycle, auditors normally select balances to confirm from the
  a. Sales journal.
  b. Accounts receivable listing.
  c. General ledger.
  d. Cash receipts listing.

LO 7-2

7.36 Which of the following accounts is *not* normally part of the revenue and collection cycle?

    a. Sales

    b. Accounts Receivable

    c. Cash

    d. Purchases Returns and Allowances

LO 7-4

7.37 The control procedure "credit sales approved by credit department" is directed toward which transaction assertion?

    a. Occurrence

    b. Completeness

    c. Accuracy

    d. Cutoff

LO 7-4

7.38 Which of the following would be the best protection for a company that wishes to prevent the "lapping" of trade accounts receivable?

    a. Separate duties so that the bookkeeper in charge of the general ledger has no access to incoming mail.

    b. Separate duties so that no employee has access to both checks from customers and currency from daily cash receipts.

    c. Have customers send payments directly to the company's depository bank.

    d. Request that customer's payment checks be made payable to the company and addressed to the treasurer.

LO 7-4

7.39 Which of the following internal control activities will most likely prevent the concealment of a cash shortage by improperly writing off a trade account receivable?

    a. Write-offs must be approved by a responsible officer after review of credit department recommendations and supporting evidence.

    b. Write-offs must be supported by an aging schedule showing that only receivables overdue several months have been written off.

    c. Write-offs must be approved by the cashier who is in a position to know whether the receivables have, in fact, been collected.

    d. Write-offs must be authorized by company field sales employees who are in a position to determine customers' financial standing.

LO 7-3

7.40 Auditors sometimes use comparisons of ratios as audit evidence. An unexplained decrease in the ratio of gross profit to sales may suggest which of the following possibilities?

    a. Unrecorded purchases.

    b. Unrecorded sales.

    c. Merchandise purchases being charged to selling and general expense.

    d. Fictitious sales.

LO 7-6

7.41 An audit team is auditing sales transactions. One step is to vouch a sample of debit entries from the accounts receivable subsidiary ledger back to the supporting sales invoices. The purpose of this audit procedure is to establish that

    a. Sales invoices represent bona fide sales.

    b. All sales have been recorded.

    c. All sales invoices have been properly posted to customer accounts.

    d. Entries in the accounts receivable subsidiary ledger were properly invoiced.

Use the following information to answer questions 7.42 and 7.43:

An auditor noted that client sales increased 10 percent for the year. At the same time, Cost of Goods Sold as a percentage of sales had decreased from 45 percent to 40 percent and year-end accounts receivable had increased by 8 percent.

LO 7-3

7.42 Based on this information, the auditor is most likely concerned about

    a. Unrecorded costs.

    b. Improper credit approvals.

    c. Improper sales cutoff.

    d. Fictitious sales.

LO 7-6

7.43 Based on this information, the auditor interviewed the sales manager, who stated that the increase in sales without a corresponding increase in cost of goods sold was due to a price increase enacted by the company during the year. How would the auditor test the sales manager's representation?

a. Perform additional inquiries with sales personnel.

b. Obtain copies of all price lists in use during the year and vouch the prices to sales invoices.

c. Send confirmations asking customers about unit prices paid for product.

d. Vouch vender invoices to payments made after year-end.

LO 7-3

7.44 To conceal a theft involving receivables, a dishonest bookkeeper might charge which of the following accounts?

a. Miscellaneous income

b. Petty cash

c. Miscellaneous expense

d. Sales returns

LO 7-6

7.45 Which of the following responses to an accounts receivable confirmation at December 31 would cause an audit team the most concern?

a. "This amount was paid on December 30."

b. "We received this shipment on January 2."

c. "These goods were returned for credit on November 15."

d. "The balance does not reflect our sales discount for paying by January 5."

LO 7-6

7.46 A client has a separate sales group for its largest "preferred" customers, a select group of customers who normally make purchases in excess of $250,000 and often have accounts receivable balances in excess of $1 million. Which of the following audit procedures would the auditor most likely perform?

a. Prepare a schedule of purchases and payments for these customers.

b. Send out negative confirmations on a large sample of these customers.

c. Inquire of the sales manager regarding the accounts receivable terms.

d. Send out positive confirmations on a large sample of these customers.

LO 7-6

7.47 Audit documentation often includes a client-prepared, aged trial balance of accounts receivable as of the balance sheet date. The audit team uses this aging primarily to

a. Evaluate internal control over credit sales.

b. Test the accuracy of recorded charge sales.

c. Estimate credit losses.

d. Verify the existence of the recorded receivables.

LO 7-6

7.48 Which of the following might be detected by auditors' cutoff review and examination of sales journal entries for several days prior to the balance sheet date?

a. Lapping year-end accounts receivable.

b. Inflating sales for the year.

c. Kiting bank balances.

d. Misappropriating merchandise.

LO 7-6

7.49 Confirmation of individual accounts receivable balances directly with debtors will, of itself, normally provide the strongest evidence concerning the

a. Collectability of the balances confirmed.

b. Ownership of the balances confirmed.

c. Existence of the balances confirmed.

d. Internal control over balances confirmed.

LO 7-4

7.50 Which of the following is the best reason for prenumbering in numerical sequence documents such as sales orders, shipping documents, and sales invoices?

a. Enables company personnel to determine the accuracy of each document.

b. Enables personnel to determine the proper period recording of sales revenue and receivables.

c. Enables personnel to check the numerical sequence for missing documents and unrecorded transactions.

d. Enables personnel to determine the validity of recorded transactions.

LO 7-2

7.51 When a sample of customer accounts receivable is selected for vouching debits, auditors will vouch them to
   a. Sales invoices with shipping documents and customer sales invoices.
   b. Records of accounts receivable write-offs.
   c. Cash remittance lists and bank deposit slips.
   d. Credit files and reports.

LO 7-4

7.52 In the audit of accounts receivable, the most important emphasis should be on the
   a. Completeness assertion.
   b. Existence assertion.
   c. Rights and obligations assertion.
   d. Presentation and disclosure assertion.

LO 7-6

7.53 When accounts receivable are confirmed at an interim date, auditors need not be concerned with
   a. Obtaining a summary of receivables transactions from the interim date to the year-end date.
   b. Obtaining a year-end trial balance of receivables, comparing it to the interim trial balance, and obtaining evidence and explanations for large variations.
   c. Sending negative confirmations to all customers as of the year-end date.
   d. Considering the necessity for some additional confirmations as of the balance sheet date if balances have increased materially.

LO 7-6

7.54 The negative request form of accounts receivable confirmation is useful particularly when the

Assessed Level of Risk of Material Misstatement Relating to Receivables Is	Number of Small Balances Is	Proper Consideration by the Recipient Is
a. Low	Many	Likely
b. Low	Few	Unlikely
c. High	Few	Likely
d. High	Many	Likely

(AICPA adapted)

LO 7-5

7.55 When an audit team traces a sample of shipping documents to the related sales invoice copies, they are trying to find relevant evidence that
   a. Shipments to customers were invoiced.
   b. Shipments to customers were recorded as sales.
   c. Recorded sales were shipped.
   d. Invoiced sales were shipped.

(AICPA adapted)

LO 7-4

7.56 Write-offs of doubtful accounts should be approved by
   a. The salesperson.
   b. The credit manager.
   c. The treasurer.
   d. The cashier.

LO 7-6

7.57 When an audit team does not receive a response on a positive accounts receivable confirmation, auditors should do all of the following *except*
   a. Send a second request.
   b. Do nothing for immaterial balances.
   c. Examine shipping documents.
   d. Examine client correspondence files.

LO 7-3

7.58 Cash receipts from sales on account have been misappropriated. Which of the following acts would conceal this defalcation and be *least likely* to be detected by an auditor?

    a. Understating the sales journal.

    b. Overstating the accounts receivable control account.

    c. Overstating the accounts receivable subsidiary ledger.

    d. Understating the cash receipts journal.

(AICPA adapted)

LO 7-4

7.59 Which of the following internal control activities most likely would deter lapping of collections from customers?

    a. Independent internal verification of dates of entry in the cash receipts journal with dates of daily cash summaries.

    b. Authorization of write-offs of uncollectable accounts by a supervisor independent of credit approval.

    c. Separation of duties between receiving cash and posting the accounts receivable ledger.

    d. Supervisory comparison of the daily cash summary with the sum of the cash receipts journal entries.

(AICPA adapted)

LO 7-6

7.60 The financial records of the Movitz Company show that R. Dennis owes $4,100 on an account receivable. An independent audit is being carried out, and the auditors send a positive confirmation to R. Dennis. What is the most likely reason as to why a positive confirmation rather than a negative confirmation was used here?

    a. Control risk was particularly low for accounts receivable.

    b. Inherent risk was particularly high for accounts receivable.

    c. Dennis's account was not yet due.

    d. Dennis's account was not with a related party.

LO 7-3

7.61 An audit client sells 15 to 20 units of product annually. A large portion of the annual sales occur in the last month of the fiscal year. Annual sales have not materially changed over the past five years. Which of the following approaches would be most effective concerning the timing of audit procedures for revenue?

    a. The auditor should perform analytical procedures at an interim date and discuss any changes in the level of sales with senior management.

    b. The auditor should inspect transactions occurring in the last month of the fiscal year and review the related sale contracts to determine that revenue was posted in the proper period.

    c. The auditor should perform tests of controls at an interim date to obtain audit evidence about the operational effectiveness of internal controls over sales.

    d. The auditor should review period-end compensation to determine whether bonuses were paid to meet earnings goals.

(AICPA adapted)

LO 7-3

7.62 An auditor is required to confirm accounts receivable if the accounts receivable balances are

    a. Older than the prior year.

    b. Material to the financial statements.

    c. Smaller than expected.

    d. Subject to valuation estimates.

(AICPA adapted)

LO 7-6

7.63 During the confirmation of accounts receivable, an auditor receives a confirmation via the client's fax machine. Which of the following actions should the auditor take?

    a. Not accept the confirmation and select another customer's balance to confirm.

    b. Not accept the confirmation and treat it as an exception.

    c. Accept the confirmation and file it in the working papers.

    d. Accept the confirmation but verify the source and content through a telephone call to the respondent.

(AICPA adapted)

Exercises and Problems

LO 7-4

7.64   **Control Objectives and Procedures Associations.** The following exhibit contains an arrangement of examples of transaction errors (lettered a–g) and a set of client control procedures and devices (numbered 1–15). Make a copy of the exhibit page and complete the following requirements.

EXHIBIT

a.	Sales recorded, goods not shipped
b.	Goods shipped, sales not recorded
c.	Goods shipped to a bad credit risk customer
d.	Sales billed at the wrong price or wrong quantity
e.	Product line A sales recorded as Product line B
f.	Failure to post charges to customers for sales
g.	January sales recorded in December

CONTROL PROCEDURES

1. Sales order approved for credit
2. Prenumbered shipping doc prepared, sequence checked
3. Shipping document quantity compared to sales invoice
4. Prenumbered sales invoices, sequence checked
5. Sales invoice checked to sales order
6. Invoiced prices compared to approved price list
7. General ledger code checked for sales product lines
8. Sales dollar batch totals compared to sales journal
9. Periodic sales total compared to same period accounts receivable postings
10. Accountants have instructions to date sales on the date of shipment
11. Sales entry date compared to shipping doc date
12. Accounts receivable subsidiary totaled and reconciled to accounts receivable control account
13. Intercompany accounts reconciled with subsidiary company records
14. Credit files updated for customer payment history
15. Overdue customer accounts investigated for collection

Required

a. Opposite the examples of transaction errors lettered a–g, write the name of the transaction assertion clients wish to achieve to prevent, detect, or correct the error.

b. Opposite each numbered control procedure, place an "X" in the column that identifies the error(s) the procedure is likely to control by prevention, detection, or correction.

LO 7-4

7.65   **Assertion Associations.** The exhibit in Exercise 7.64 contains an arrangement of examples of transaction errors (lettered a–g) and a set of client control procedures and devices (numbered 1–15).

Required:

For each error/control objective, identify the assertion about classes of transactions and events most benefited by the control.

LO 7-5

7.66   **Client Control Procedures and Audit Tests of Controls.** The exhibit in Exercise 7.64 contains an arrangement of examples of transaction errors (lettered a–g) and a set of client control procedures and devices (numbered 1–15).

Required:

For each client control procedure numbered 1–15, write a test of controls that could produce evidence on the question of whether the client's control procedure has been implemented and is in operation.

7.67 **Confirmation of Trade Accounts Receivable.** L. King, CPA, is auditing the financial statements of Cycle Company, a client that has receivables from customers arising from the sale of goods in the normal course of business. King is aware that the confirmation of accounts receivable is a generally accepted auditing procedure.

Required:

a. Under what circumstances could King justify omitting the confirmation of Cycle's accounts receivable?

b. In designing confirmation requests, what factors are likely to affect King's assessment of the reliability of confirmations that King sends?

c. What alternative procedures could King consider performing when replies to positive confirmation requests are not received?

(AICPA adapted)

7.68 **Audit Objectives and Procedures for Accounts Receivable.** In the audit of accounts receivable, auditors develop specific audit assertions related to the receivables. They then design specific substantive procedures to obtain evidence about each of these assertions.

Required:

For each of the following assertions, select the following audit procedure (numbered 1–7) that is best suited for the audit plan. Select only one procedure for each audit objective. A procedure may be selected once, not at all, or more than once.

Assertions:

a. Accounts receivable represent all amounts owed to the client company at the balance sheet date.

b. The client company has a legal right to all accounts receivable at the balance sheet date.

c. Accounts receivable are stated at net realizable value.

d. Accounts receivable are properly described and presented in the financial statements.

Procedures:

1. Analyze the relationship of accounts receivable and sales and compare with relationships for preceding periods.

2. Perform sales cutoff tests to obtain assurance that sales transactions and corresponding entries for inventories and cost of goods sold are recorded in the same and proper period.

3. Review the aged trial balance for significant past due accounts.

4. Obtain an understanding of the business purpose of transactions that resulted in accounts receivable balances.

5. Review loan agreements for indications of whether accounts receivable have been factored or pledged.

6. Review the accounts receivable trial balance for amounts due from officers and employees.

7. Analyze unusual relationships between monthly accounts receivable and monthly accounts payable balances.

7.69 **Overstated Sales and Accounts Receivable.** This case is designed like the ones in the chapter. Your assignment is to write the "audit approach" portion of the case, organized around these sections:

Objective. Express the objective in terms of the facts supposedly asserted in financial records, accounts, and statements.

Control. Write a brief explanation of desirable controls, missing controls, and especially the kinds of "deviations" that might arise from the situation described in the case.

Tests of controls. Write some procedures for getting evidence about existing controls, especially procedures that could discover deviations from those controls. If there are no controls to test, then there are no procedures to perform; go then to the next section. A "procedure" should instruct someone about the source(s) of evidence to tap and the work to do.

Audit of balance. Write some procedures for getting evidence about the existence, completeness, valuation, ownership, or disclosure assertions identified in the objective section you wrote.

Discovery summary. Write a short statement about the discovery you expect to accomplish with your procedures.

Ring around the Revenue

Mattel toy manufacturing company had experienced several years of good business. Income had increased steadily, and the common stock was a favorite among investors. Management had confidently predicted continued growth and prosperity. However, business turned worse instead of better. Competition became fierce.

In earlier years, Mattel had accommodated a few large retail customers with the practice of field warehousing coupled with a "bill and hold" accounting procedure. These large retail customers executed noncancelable written agreements, asserting their purchase of toys and their obligation to pay. The toys were not actually shipped because the customers did not have available warehouse space. The toys were set aside in segregated areas on the Mattel premises and identified as the customers' property. Mattel would later ship the toys to various retail locations upon instructions from the customers. The "field warehousing" was explained as Mattel's serving as a temporary warehouse and storage location for the customers' toys. In the related bill and hold accounting procedure, Mattel prepared invoices billing the customers, mailed the invoices to the customers, and recorded the sales and accounts receivable.

When business took a downturn, Mattel expanded its field warehousing and its bill and hold accounting practices. Invoices were recorded for customers who did not execute the written agreements used in previous arrangements. Some customers signed the noncancelable written agreements with clauses permitting subsequent inspection, acceptance, and determination of discounted prices. The toys were not always set aside in separate areas, and this failure later gave shipping employees problems with identifying shipments of toys that had been "sold" earlier and those that had not.

Mattel also engaged in overbilling. Customers who ordered closeout toys at discounted prices were billed at regular prices, even though the customers' orders showed the discounted prices to which Mattel sales representatives had agreed.

In a few cases, the bill and hold invoices and the closeout sales were billed and recorded in duplicate. In most cases, the customers' invoices were addressed and mailed to specific individuals in the customers' management instead of the routine mailing to the customers' accounts payable departments.

Audit trail. The field warehousing arrangements were well known and acknowledged in the Mattel accounting manual. Related invoices were stamped "bill and hold." Customer orders and agreements were attached in a document file. Sales of closeout toys also were stamped "closeout," indicating the regular prices (basis for salespersons' commissions) and the invoice prices. Otherwise, the accounting for sales and accounts receivable was unexceptional. Efforts to record these sales in January (last month of the fiscal year) caused the month's sales revenue to be 35 percent higher than the January of the previous year.

In the early years of the practice, inventory sold under the field warehousing arrangements (both regular and closeout toys) was segregated and identified. The shipping orders for these toys left the "carrier name" and "shipping date" blank, even though they were signed and dated by a company employee in the spaces for the company representative and the carrier representative signatures.

The lack of inventory segregation caused problems for the company. After the fiscal year-end, Mattel solved the problem by reversing $6.9 million of the $14 million bill and hold sales. This caused another problem because the reversal was larger than the month's sales, causing the sales revenue for the first month of the next year to be a negative number!

Amount. Company officials gave persuasive reasons for the validity of recognizing sales revenue and receivables on the bill and hold procedure and field warehousing. After considering the facts and circumstances, the company's auditors agreed that the accounting practices appropriately accounted for revenue and receivables.

Mattel's abuse of the practices caused financial statements to be materially misstated. In January of the year in question, the company overstated sales by about $14 million, or 5 percent of the sales that should have been recorded. The gross profit of $7 million on these sales caused the income to be overstated by about 40 percent.

LO 7-6

7.70 **Systems Application—Receivables Confirmation.** You are using computer audit software to prepare accounts receivable confirmations during the annual audit of the Eastern Sunrise Services Club. The company has the following data files:

Master file—debtor credit record.

Master file—debtor name and address.

Master file—account detail:

Ledger number.

Sales code.

Customer account number.

Date of last billing.

Balance (gross).

Discount available to customer (memo account only).

Date of last purchase.

The discount field represents the amount of discount available to the customer if the customer pays within 30 days of the invoicing date. The discount field is cleared for expired amounts during the daily updating. You have determined that this is properly executed.

Required:

From the data files shown, list the information that you would include on the confirmation requests. Identify the file from which the information can be obtained.

LO 7-5

7.71 **Rock Island Quarry—Evidence Collection in an Online System.** Your firm has audited the Rock Island Quarry Company for several years. Rock Island's main revenue comes from selling crushed rock to construction companies from several quarries owned by the company in Illinois and Iowa. The rock is priced by weight, quality, and crushed size.

Past procedure. Trucks owned by purchasing contractors or by Rock Island needed to display a current certified empty weight receipt or be weighed in. The quarry yard weigh master recorded the empty weight on a handwritten "scale ticket" along with the purchasing company name, the truck number, and the date. After the truck was loaded, it was required to leave via the scale where the loaded weight and rock grade were recorded on the scale tickets. The scale tickets were sorted weekly by grade and manually recorded on a summary sheet that was forwarded to the home office. Scale tickets were prenumbered and an accountant in the home office checked the sequence for missing numbers.

Audit procedures for revenue (and receivables) involved evaluating the controls at selected quarries (rotated each year) and vouching a statistical sample of scale tickets to weekly summaries. Weekly summaries were traced through pricing and invoicing to the general ledger on a sample basis, and general ledger entries were vouched back to weekly summaries on a sample basis. Few material discrepancies were found.

New procedures. At the beginning of the current year, Rock Island converted to a local area network of personal computers to gather the information formerly entered manually on the scale ticket. This conversion was done with your knowledge but without your advice or input. Now all entering trucks must weigh in. The yard weigh master enters "NEW" on the terminal keyboard and a form appears on the screen that is similar to the old scale ticket except that the quarry number, transaction number, date, and incoming empty weight are automatically entered. Customer and truck numbers are keyed in. After the weigh-in, the weigh master enters "HOLD" through the terminal. The weight ticket record is stored in the computer until weigh-out.

When a truck is loaded and stops on the scale, the weigh master enters "OLD" and a directory of all open transactions appears on the screen. The weigh master selects the proper one and enters "OUT." The truck out-weighs and the rock weights are computed and entered automatically. The weigh master must enter the proper number for the rock grade but cannot change any automatically entered field. When satisfied that the screen weight ticket is correct, the weigh master enters "SOLD," and the transaction is automatically transmitted to the home office computer, and the appropriate accounting database elements are updated. One copy of a scale ticket is printed and given to the truck driver. Rock Island keeps no written evidence of the sale.

Required:

It is now midyear for Rock Island, and you are planning for this year's audit.

a. What control procedures (manual and computerized) should you expect to find in this system for recording quarry sales?

b. The computer programs that process the rock sales and perform the accounting reside at the home office and at the quarries. What implication does this have for your planned audit procedures?

c. What are you going to do to gather substantive audit evidence now that there are no written scale tickets?

LO 7-3

7.72 **Organizing a Risk Analysis.** You are the director of internal auditing of a large municipal hospital. You receive monthly financial reports prepared by the accounting department and your review of them has shown that total accounts receivable from patients have steadily and rapidly increased over the past eight months.

Other information in the reports shows the following conditions:

a. The number of available hospital beds has not changed.

b. The bed occupancy rate has not changed.

c. Hospital billing rates have not changed significantly.

d. The hospitalization insurance contracts have not changed since the last modification 12 months ago.

Your internal audit department audited the accounts receivable 10 months ago. The audit file for that assignment contains financial information, a record of the risk analysis, documentation of the study and evaluation of management and internal risk mitigation controls, documentation of the evidence-gathering procedures used to produce evidence about the existence and collectability of the accounts, and a copy of your report, which commented favorably on the controls and collectability of the receivables.

However, the current increase in receivables has alerted you to a need for another audit so that things will not get out of hand. You remember news stories last year about the manager of the city water system who got into big trouble because his accounting department double-billed all the residential customers for three months.

Required:

You plan to perform a risk analysis to get a handle on the problem if one indeed exists. Write a memo to your senior auditor listing at least eight questions to use to guide and direct the risk analysis. (*Hint:* The questions used last year were organized under these headings: (1) Who does the accounts receivable accounting? (2) What information processing procedures and policies are in effect? and (3) How is the accounts receivable accounting done? This time, you will add a fourth category: What financial or economic events have occurred in the past 10 months?)

(AICPA adapted)

LO 7-4

7.73 **Study and Evaluation of Management Control.** The study and evaluation of management risk mitigation control is not easy. First, auditors must determine the risks and the controls subject to audit. Then they must find a standard by which performance of the control can be evaluated. Next, they must specify procedures to obtain the evidence on which an evaluation can be based. Insofar as possible, the standards and related evidence must be quantified. The following description gives certain information (in italics) that internal auditors would know about or be able to determine on their own. Fulfilling the requirement thus amounts to taking some information from the scenario and figuring out other things by using accountants' and auditors' common sense.

The Scenario

Ace Corporation ships building materials to more than a thousand wholesale and retail customers in a five-state region. The company's normal credit terms are n/30, and no cash discounts are offered. Fred Clark is the chief financial officer, and he is concerned about risks related to maintaining control over customer credit. In particular, he has stated two management control principles for this purpose:

1. Sales are to be billed to customers accurately and promptly. *Clark knows that errors will occur but thinks company personnel ought to be able to hold quantity, unit price, and arithmetic errors down to 3 percent of the sales invoices. He considers an invoice error of $1 or less not to matter.* He believes prompt billing is important because customers are expected to pay within 30 days. *Clark is very strict in thinking that a bill should be sent to the customer one day after shipment.* He believes he has staffed the billing department well enough to be able to handle this workload. The relevant company records consist of an accounts receivable control account; a subsidiary ledger that enters customers' accounts by billing (invoice) date and credits and by date of payment receipts; a sales journal that lists invoices in chronological order; and a file of shipping documents cross-referenced by the number on the related sales invoice copy kept on file in numerical order.

2. Accounts receivable are to be aged and followed up to ensure prompt collection. *Clark has told the accounts receivable department to classify all customer accounts in*

categories of (a) current, (b) 31–59 days overdue, (c) 60–90 days overdue, and (d) more than 90 days overdue. He wants this trial balance to be complete and to be transmitted to the credit department within five days after each month-end. In the credit department, prompt follow-up means sending a different (stronger) collection letter to each category, cutting off credit to customers over 60 days past due (putting them on cash basis), and giving the over-90-days accounts to an outside collection agency. These actions are supposed to be taken within five days after receipt of the aged trial balance. The relevant company records, in addition to the others listed, consist of the aged trial balance, copies of the letters sent to customers, copies of notices of credit cutoff, copies of correspondence with the outside collection agent, and reports of results—statistics of subsequent collections.

Required:

Take the role of a senior internal auditor and write a memo to the internal audit staff to inform them about comparison standards for the study and evaluation of these two management control policies. You also need to specify two or three procedures for gathering evidence about performance of the controls. The body of your memo should be structured as follows:

1. Control: Sales are billed to customers accurately and promptly.
   a. Accuracy.
      (1) Policy standard . . .
      (2) Audit procedures . . .
   b. Promptness.
      (1) Policy standard . . .
      (2) Audit procedures . . .
2. Control: Accounts receivable are aged and followed up to ensure prompt collection.
   a. Accounts receivable aging.
      (1) Policy standard . . .
      (2) Audit procedures . . .
   b. Follow-up prompt collection.
      (1) Policy standard . . .
      (2) Audit procedures . . .

LO 7-3

7.74 **Cash Receipts and Billing Control.** The following narrative description of a company's cash receipts and billing system is in the auditors' audit files:

Rural Building Supplies Inc. is a single-store retailer that sells a variety of tools, garden supplies, lumber, small appliances, and electrical fixtures. About half of the sales are to walk-in customers and about half to construction contractors. Rural employs 12 salaried sales associates, a credit manager, 3 full-time clerical workers, and several part-time cash register clerks and assistant bookkeepers. The full-time clerical workers are the cashier who handles the cash and the bank deposits, the accounts receivable supervisor who prepares invoices and does the accounts receivable work, and the bookkeeper who keeps journals and ledgers and sends customer statements. Their work is described more fully in the narrative.

Control Narrative

Rural's retail customers pay for merchandise by cash or credit card at cash registers when they purchase merchandise. A building contractor can purchase merchandise on account if approved by the credit manager. The credit manager bases approvals on general knowledge of the contractor's reputation. After credit is approved, the sales associate files a prenumbered charge form with the accounts receivable (A/R) supervisor to set up the contractor's account receivable.

The A/R supervisor independently verifies the pricing and other details on the charge form by reference to a management-authorized price list, corrects any errors, prepares the sales invoice, and supervises a part-time employee who mails the invoice to the contractor. The A/R supervisor electronically posts the details of the invoice in a customer database, and the computerized system simultaneously transmits the transaction details to the bookkeeper. The A/R supervisor also prepares (1) a monthly computer-generated A/R subsidiary ledger without reconciliation to the A/R control account and (2) a monthly report of overdue accounts.

The cashier performs the cash receipts functions, including supervising the cash register clerks. The cashier opens the mail, compares each check with the enclosed remittance advice, stamps each check "for deposit only," and lists the checks on the deposit slip. The cashier then gives the remittance advices to the bookkeeper for recording. The cashier deposits the checks each day and prepares a separate deposit of the cash from the cash registers. The cashier retains the verified bank deposit slips (stamped and dated at the bank) to use in reconciling the monthly bank statements. The cashier sends to the bookkeeper a copy of the daily cash register summary. The cashier does not have access to the bookkeeper's journals or ledgers.

The bookkeeper receives information for journalizing and posting to the general ledger from the A/R supervisor (details of credit transactions) and from the cashier (cash reports). After recording the remittance advices received from the cashier, the bookkeeper electronically transmits the information to the A/R supervisor for subsidiary ledger updating. Upon receipt of the A/R supervisor's report of overdue balances, the bookkeeper sends monthly statements of account to contractors with unpaid balances. The bookkeeper authorizes the A/R supervisor to write-off accounts as uncollectable six months after sending the first overdue notice. At this time, the bookkeeper notifies the credit manager not to approve additional credit to that contractor.

Required:

Take the role of the supervising auditor on the Rural engagement. Your assistants prepared the narrative description. Now you must analyze it and identify the internal control weaknesses. Organize them under the heading of employee job functions: credit manager, accounts receivable supervisor, cashier, and bookkeeper. (Do not give advice about correcting the weaknesses.)

Optional Requirement:

Discuss the possibilities for fraud you notice in this control system.

LO 7-5

7.75 **Tests of Controls and Errors/Frauds.** The following four questions are taken from an internal control questionnaire.

Required:

For each question, state (1) one test of controls procedure you could use to find out whether the control technique was really functioning and (2) what error or fraud could occur if the question were answered "no" or if you found the control was not effective.

a. Are blank sales invoices available only to authorized personnel?

b. Are sales invoices prenumbered and are all numbers accounted for?

c. Are sales invoices checked for the accuracy of quantities billed? Prices used? Mathematical calculations?

d. Are the duties of the accounts receivable bookkeeper separate from all cash functions?

e. Are customer accounts regularly balanced with the control account?

f. Do customers receive a monthly statement even when the ending balance on the account is zero?

LO 7-1

7.76 **Revenue Recognition and Ethics.** The following article was published in *Newsday* on February 9, 2009:

Call for Probe of Ticket Sales

Bruce Springsteen fans were victims of a "classic bait and switch" scam by the nation's largest concert ticket seller, Senator Charles Schumer said yesterday, as he called for a federal investigation into the company, Ticketmaster. Schumer wants the Federal Trade Commission to look into whether the Ticketmaster website withheld the best tickets from the public and then shuttled fans to TicketsNow, a fully owned subsidiary. TicketsNow had the best seats available immediately— at sky-high prices—after Springsteen tickets went on sales at 10 a.m. on February 2.

A federal investigation would look into whether Ticketmaster was instantly scalping the tickets, never giving fans a chance to buy them at face value, Schumer said. Customers who tried to buy tickets originally priced at $95 on Ticketmaster's website were directed to TicketsNow where they were priced at more than $2,000

Since buying TicketsNow in February, Ticketmaster has faced similar criticism for its handling of Elton John tickets in Canada and numerous U.S. concert tours, including Radiohead. Law enforcement agencies in Connecticut and New Jersey have also launched investigations.

Required:

a. During the course of an audit, do you believe that the auditor should look into how revenues are being generated? Do you think the auditors should have looked at the business practices of Ticketmaster?

b. Assume that Ticketmaster had properly accounted for the revenue it received from the Springsteen concert. Should the auditors have asked Ticketmaster to make adjustments or disclosures regarding its sales practices?

c. Should Ticketmaster disclose the investigations being conducted in Connecticut and New Jersey?

Source: Joseph Mallia, "Bruce Springsteen Fans Victim of 'Bait and Switch,' Schumer Says." *Newsday,* February 8, 2009.

LO 7-7

7.77 Substantive Analytical Procedures

You have been selected to audit football ticket revenues for the 2023 Championship State University (CSU) football season. Because CSU handles its own tickets, you cannot rely on internal counts of sold tickets to estimate ticket revenue. However, you do know all of the following facts:

- For the 2023 Football Season, unaudited ticket revenues are reported as $26,600,000.
- For the 2022 Football Season, total ticket sales were $18,900,000. Ticket prices for 2022 were $54 per ticket. During the 2022 season, there were 5 home games, 4 of which were in-conference games (average attendance 75,000) and 1 nonconference game against a smaller school opponent (attendance 50,000). CSU's Stadium has a capacity of 88,300.

Your supervisor believes that this amount absolutely must be overstated due to the large increase, and he asks you to audit ticket revenues. Tolerable misstatement is set at $500,000 for this procedure. You realize that doing detailed tests of ticket sales would be cost prohibitive. You decide to perform analytical procedures on the reported revenues as a substantive procedure. You gather the following information:

- During the 2023 season, CSU had seven home football games. two of these games were nonconference games against a smaller school opponent, four were in-conference games, and the final game was against the school's biggest rival, which always sells out. You anticipate that average attendance at other games will be similar to comparable games from 2022.
- Ticket prices were increased to $56 for the 2023 season.

Required:

a. Estimate 2023 season ticket revenue for Championship State University football.

b. Based on your estimate, do you believe that ticket revenues are fairly stated in all material respects? Why or why not? What further substantive procedures, if any, would you suggest your firm should perform?

c. The facts stated that you chose to use this analytical procedure as substantive audit evidence. Do Generally Accepted Auditing Standards allow you to use analytical procedures as substantive evidence?

Note: See Exercises G.36–G.41 for a similar scenario with Data and Analytics applications of this exercise.

LO 7-7

7.78 Authorization of Credit Tests of Controls—Using IDEA. For this exercise, your client, Bright IDEAs Inc., has provided you with data for two related files, a listing of sales invoices, and a listing of customers with credit limits. To test whether credit authorization controls are in place, the auditor must complete a series of related steps:

1. Import the client's database of sales invoices.

2. Summarize the Accounts Receivable balance by customer.

3. Import the client's customer credit limit data into IDEA.

4. Join the Accounts Receivable balances by customer with the credit limit data.

5. Extract customers with exceeded credit limits.

Required Data and IDEA workbook page references for current version are available on *Connect*

Required:

Complete the preceding steps and answer the following questions:

a. How many customers were granted credit with no indication that they had any credit limit assigned to them?

b. How many customers exceeded their credit limit?

c. What effects would the findings in parts (a) and (b) have on the auditor's assessment of the risk of material misstatement? What accounts and assertions are most likely influenced by these findings?

Source: C1202 IDEA Data Analysis Workbook: IDEA Version Ten. 2016. CaseWare IDEA, Inc. Toronto, CA.

Applying IDEA to the Revenue Cycle—Elm Manufacturing Company

Exercises 7.79, 7.80, and 7.81 require the application of IDEA in the revenue cycle audit. Elm Manufacturing Company (ELM) is a small manufacturer of backpacks located in Rochelle, Illinois. You have access to ELM's electronic records on *Connect.* The appropriate file for these exercises is the Sales 2023—4th Q dataset. Detailed information about ELM, instructions for accessing datasets, and a data directory for data sets can be found on *Connect.*

LO 7-5, 7-7

7.79 **Tests of Control Exceptions with IDEA.** You have identified relevant controls for several assertions within the revenue cycle, and you must use IDEA to perform several tests of controls.

Required:

a. ELM has a policy of using prenumbered customer order forms to help control for the completeness assertion. Inquiry of the client determined that order forms 17001–17405 were used during the quarter. Using IDEA, create a schedule of missing customer order forms. How many missing order forms were there?

b. Each customer order should be entered into the system once and only once. Using IDEA, search for duplicate customer order forms. What is the total dollar amount of duplicate orders?

c. To assist with the collectability of accounts receivable, ELM has a policy that all customer orders must be approved and marked as approved in the order system. Create a schedule of exceptions to this policy. How many exceptions are there?

d. To ensure the posting of sales in a timely manner and increase the collectability of accounts receivable, ELM has a policy to always invoice customers within two days of shipping. Create a schedule of exceptions to the invoicing policy. How many exceptions are there?

e. Draft a memo outlining the findings of your tests of controls. Address not only your findings, but also the effects of your findings on your assessment of control risk related to specific financial statement assertions.

LO 7-5, 7-7

7.80 **Tests of Controls with IDEA—Payment Receipts.** Use the information related to ELM's payment and discount policy (referenced earlier) to analyze the company's discount program and late payments. All dates for payments are based off the date the customer is invoiced.

Required:

a. Are there any companies that made their payments after the stated due date? How many companies, and what is the total dollar amount of the payments? (*Hint:* Each company has a two-day grace period beyond the stated due date.)

b. Refer to ELM's discount policy. Are any companies receiving discounts when the invoice terms indicate they should never be eligible for discounts? What is the total dollar amount of the discounts taken by these companies? (*Hint:* This refers to the terms of the invoices, not whether these companies paid too late to receive discounts.)

c. Refer to ELM's discount policy. Are there any companies receiving discount percentages greater than the amount accounting to the policy?

d. Are any companies taking the discount even if they are not paying within the 10-day period? How many companies have done this? (*Hint:* Each company has a two-day grace period beyond the stated discount period. Also note that companies can partially pay an invoice—payments less than invoice are not necessarily discounts. Only companies eligible for discounts should be considered in this question.)

LO 7-5, 7-7

7.81 **Testing the Valuation Assertion with IDEA—Aging Accounts Receivable.** You have been instructed to create an aging schedule for ELM's accounts receivable using IDEA. For the purposes of this exercise, assume the aging begins on the date that the customer is invoiced and should only include valid accounts receivable (e.g., amounts not yet fully paid by the customer). You can assume that rounding differences on discounts taken by customers are considered to be fully paid. Your senior has instructed you to create a schedule with the following tranches: Current, 0–30 days delinquent, 31–60 days delinquent, 60+ days delinquent.

Required:

a. Create an aged accounts receivable according to your senior's instructions. Assume there are no receivables still outstanding from prior to January 1, 2023. Note that the data set includes all orders received between January 1, 2023, and March 31, 2023. This includes orders that have already been paid for, orders received at the end of March that were shipped but have not been invoiced, and orders that have been received that have not shipped. These orders would not be considered a receivable as of March 31; therefore, these items need to be excluded from the data for this schedule and in other requirements within this assignment.

b. What is the total amount of accounts receivable as of March 31, 2023?

c. What is the total amount of accounts receivable that are past due less than 30 days? Recall that invoices are due n/30, thus they become past due 30 days after invoice date.

d. What is the total amount of accounts receivable that are more than 30 days past due?

Apollo Shoes

Accounts Receivable Audit

You are a recently promoted senior (in charge) auditor for Anderson, Olds, and Watershed and have been assigned to the engagement team of a new audit client, Apollo Shoes Inc. You have been asked to perform certain procedures for the audit of the accounts receivable. Detailed instructions for performing the accounts receivable audit, as well as working papers and supporting documents, can be found in *Connect*.

Appendix 7A

Internal Control Questionnaires

EXHIBIT 7A.1   Internal Control Questionnaire—Revenue and Collection Cycle

	Yes/No	Comments
Occurrence		
1. Is the customer database maintained by someone who does *not* have access to cash?		
2. Is access to sales invoice blanks restricted?		
3. Are prenumbered bills of lading or other shipping documents prepared or completed in the shipping department?		
4. Are customers' statements mailed monthly by the accounts receivable department?		
5. Are direct confirmations of accounts and notes obtained periodically by the internal auditor?		
6. Are differences reported by customers routed to someone outside the accounts receivable department for investigations?		
7. Are returned goods checked against receiving reports?		
8. Are returned sales credits and other credits supported by documentation as to receipt, condition, and quantity and approved by a responsible officer?		
9. Are write-offs, returns, and discounts allowed after discount date subject to approval by a responsible officer?		
10. Are large loans or advances to related parties approved by the directors?		
Completeness		
11. Are sales invoice forms prenumbered?		
12. Is the sequence checked for missing invoices?		
13. Is the numerical sequence for shipping documents checked for missing bills of lading numbers?		
14. Are credit memo documents prenumbered and the sequence checked for missing documents?		
Accuracy		
15. Is customer credit approved before orders are shipped?		
16. Are delinquent accounts listed periodically for review by someone other than the credit manager?		
17. Is the credit department separated from the sales department?		
18. Are sales prices and terms based on approved standards?		
19. Are shipped quantities compared to invoice quantities?		
20. Are sales invoices checked for error in quantities, prices, extensions and footings, and freight allowances and checked with customers' orders?		
21. Do the internal auditors confirm customer accounts periodically to determine accuracy?		
22. Does someone reconcile the accounts receivable subsidiary to the control account regularly?		
Cutoff		
23. Does the accounting manual contain instructions to date sales invoices on the shipment date?		
Classification		
24. Does the accounting manual contain instructions for classifying sales?		
25. Are summary journal entries approved before posting?		
26. Are sales of the following types controlled by the same procedures described: sale to employees, cash-on-delivery sales, disposals of property, cash sales, and scrap sales?		
27. Are receivables from officers, directors, and affiliates identified separately in the accounts receivable records?		

EXHIBIT 7A.2   Internal Control Questionnaire—Sales and Accounts Receivable System Controls

	Yes/No	Comments
1. Does each terminal perform only designated functions? For example, the terminal at the shipping dock cannot be used to enter initial sales information or to access the payroll database.		
2. Are an identification number and password (issued on an individual person basis) required to enter the sale and each command that a subsequent action has been completed? Unauthorized entry attempts are logged and immediately investigated. Furthermore, certain passwords have "read-only" (cannot change any data) authorization. For example, the credit manager can determine the outstanding balance of any account or view online "reports" summarizing overdue accounts receivable but cannot enter credit memos to change the balances.		
3. Is all input information immediately logged to provide restart processing should any terminal become inoperative during the processing?		
4. Does a transaction code call up on the terminals a full-screen "form" that appears to the operator in the same format as the original paper documents? Each clerk must enter the information correctly or the computer will not accept the transaction. This is called *online input validation* and utilizes validation checks such as missing data, check digit, and limit tests.		
5. Are all documents prepared by the system numbered with the number stored as part of the sales record in the accounts receivable database?		
6. Is a daily search of the pending order database made by the system with sales orders outstanding more than seven days listed on the terminal in marketing management?		

Appendix 7B

Audit Plan

EXHIBIT 7B.1

	Performed By	Ref.
DUNDER-MIFFLIN INC. **Audit Plan for Tests of Controls in the Revenues and Collection Cycle** **12/31/23**		

Sales

1. Select a sample of recorded sales from the sales journal.
   - *a.* Vouch to supporting shipping documents.
   - *b.* Vouch to supporting sales order.
   - *c.* Inspect sales orders for credit approval.
   - *d.* Vouch prices to the approved price list.
   - *e.* Vouch the quantity billed to the quantity shipped. Recalculate the invoice arithmetic.
   - *g.* Compare the shipment date with the sales journal record date.
   - *h.* Trace the invoice to posting in the general ledger control account and in the correct customer's account.
   - *i.* Inspect for proper revenue account classification.
2. Select a sample of shipping documents from the shipping department file and trace shipments to entries in the sales journal.
3. Scan recorded sales invoices and shipping documents for missing numbers in sequence.

Accounts Receivable

1. Select a sample of customers' accounts from the accounts receivable database.
   - *a.* Vouch recorded sales to supporting sales invoices.
   - *b.* Vouch recorded payments to supporting cash receipts documents
2. Select a sample of credit memos.
   - *a.* Inspect for proper approval.
   - *b.* Trace to posting in customers' accounts.
3. Scan the accounts receivable control for postings from sources other than the sales and cash receipts journals (e.g., general journal adjusting entries, credit memos). Vouch a sample of such entries to supporting documents.

EXHIBIT 7B.2

	Performed By	Ref.
DUNDER-MIFFLIN INC. **Audit Plan for Accounts and Notes Receivable and Revenue** **12/31/23**		

	Performed By	Ref.
A. Accounts and Notes Receivable		
1. Obtain an aged trial balance of individual customer accounts. Recalculate the total and trace to the general ledger control account.		
2. Review the aging for large and unusual items.		
3. Send confirmations to all accounts over $X.* Select a random sample of all remaining accounts for confirmation.		
a. Investigate exceptions reported by customers.		
b. Investigate any confirmations returned by the post office as undeliverable.		
c. Perform alternative procedures on accounts that do not respond to positive confirmation requests.		
(1) Vouch cash receipts after the confirmation date for subsequent payment.		
(2) Vouch sales invoices and shipping documents.		
4. Review the adequacy of the allowance for doubtful accounts.		
a. Inquire of management regarding assumptions used in calculating the allowance for doubtful accounts.		
b. Vouch a sample of current amounts in the aged trial balance to sales invoices to determine whether amounts aged current should be aged past due.		
c. Compare the current-year write-off experience to the prior-year allowance.		
d. Vouch cash receipts after the balance sheet date for collections on past due accounts.		
e. Obtain financial statements or credit reports and inquire of the credit manager about collections on large past due accounts.		
f. Calculate an allowance estimate using prior relations of write-offs and sales, taking under consideration current economic events.		
5. Inspect the bank confirmations, loan agreements, and minutes of the board for indications of pledged, discounted, or assigned receivables.		
6. Inspect or obtain confirmation of notes receivable.		
7. Recalculate interest income and trace to the income account.		
8. Obtain management representations regarding pledge, discount, or assignment of receivables, and about receivables from officers, directors, affiliates, or other related parties.		
9. Review the adequacy of control over recording all charges to customers (completeness) audited in the sales transaction test of controls audit plan.		
B. Revenue		
1. Select a sample of sales recorded in the sales journal and vouch to underlying shipping documents.		
2. Select a sample of shipping documents and trace to sales invoices.		
3. Obtain production records of physical quantities sold and calculate an estimate of sales dollars based on average sale prices.		
4. Compare revenue dollars and physical quantities with prior-year data and industry economic statistics.		
5. Select a sample of sales invoices prepared a few days before and after the balance sheet date and vouch to supporting documents for evidence of proper cutoff.		

*The auditor will determine a threshold for large accounts based on performance materiality

CHAPTER 8

Acquisition and Expenditure Cycle

Show those numbers to the damn auditors and I'll throw you out the $%# @ window.*

> —Buddy Yates, director of WorldCom Inc. general accounting, to an employee asking for an explanation of a large accounting discrepancy related to the expenditure cycle

Professional Standards Reference

Topic	AU-C/ISA Section	PCAOB Reference
Consideration of Internal Controls in an Integrated Audit	265	AS 2201
Audit Documentation	230	AS 1215
Auditors' Responses to Risks of Material Misstatement	240	AS 2301
Audit Planning	300	AS 2101
Identifying and Assessing the Risks of Material Misstatement	315	AS 2110
Materiality	320	AS 2105
Audit Considerations Relating to an Entity Using a Service Organization	402	AS 2601
Audit Evidence	500	AS 1105
External Confirmations	505	AS 2310
Substantive Analytical Procedures	520	AS 2305
Auditing Accounting Estimates	540	AS 2501
Written Representations	580	AS 2805

LEARNING OBJECTIVES

This chapter contains an overview of the cycle for the acquisition of goods and services as well as the expenditure of cash in connection with paying for purchases and acquisitions. This cycle affects more general ledger accounts than any other cycle. Major accounts discussed include accounts payable, expenses, and long-term assets. For accounts payable, the focus shifts to the *completeness* assertion. A series of short cases is used to show the application of audit procedures when errors or fraud might be discovered. Payroll is a sub-cycle related to the acquisition and expenditure cycle and to the production cycle. A discussion of payroll controls and audit tests is included in Appendix 8C.

Your objectives are to be able to

LO 8-1   Describe the acquisition and expenditure cycle, including typical source documents.

LO 8-2   Identify significant accounts and relevant assertions related to the acquisition and expenditure cycle.

LO 8-3   Discuss the risk of material misstatement in the acquisition and expenditure cycle.

LO 8-4   Identify important internal control activities present in a properly designed system to mitigate the risk of material misstatements for each relevant assertion in the acquisition and expenditure cycle.

LO 8-5   Give examples of tests of controls to verify the operating effectiveness of internal controls in the acquisition and expenditure cycle.

LO 8-6   Give examples of substantive procedures in the acquisition and expenditure cycle and relate them to assertions about significant account balances at the end of the period.

LO 8-7   Apply your knowledge to perform audit procedures in the acquisition and expenditure cycle and evaluate the findings of your tests.

LO 8-8   Describe the payroll cycle including risks, source documents, and controls (Appendix 8C).

INTRODUCTION

In July 2015, **The Kraft Heinz Company (KHC)** was formed from the merger of Kraft Foods Group Inc., an issuer, with H.J. Heinz Co., a private company. The combined company trades on the NASDAQ stock exchange. As with most public companies, executive officers and employees often face significant pressure to appear highly profitable for the purposes of both investors and for internal performance-based compensation targets. KHC executives made promises to investors that the combined entity would reduce operational costs through synergies and elimination of redundancies. This new strategy was touted heavily by the company and was the focus of stock market analysts. To implement this strategy, KHC tied employee compensation in the purchasing division to reductions in costs achieved through negotiations with suppliers, presumably a result of the company's increased purchasing power.

From the fourth quarter of 2015 until the end of 2018, KHC's employees in the purchasing area materially misstated cost of goods sold (COGS) through manipulation of credits and discounts negotiated with suppliers using a variety of techniques:

- Prebate Transactions: The company agreed to extend contracts and make purchases in the future in exchange for credits by suppliers. However, employees fraudulently documented these transactions as rebates for past or same-year purchases.
- Clawback Transactions: The company took discounts and upfront payments subject to future price increases and volume commitments, but failed to document or report the future repayment obligations.
- Price-Phasing Transactions: Suppliers reduced prices in exchange for a directly offsetting price increase in the future but failed to document this arrangement for accounting employees.

U.S. GAAP requires the recognition of rebates, refunds, and price agreements on a systematic and rational allocation over the period of benefit. However, KHC recognized the entire reduction in COGS in the period of the initial benefit. The large majority of the 59 COGS-related transactions identified by the U.S. SEC occurred between 2017 and 2018 when market pressures grew to document increased cost savings.

In June 2019, KHC restated its financial statements from 2015–2018 for a total of $208 million, of which $50 million was understated COGS. In September 2021, KHC and Chief Operating Officer Eduardo Pelleissone agreed to sanctions imposed by the SEC. KHC agreed to pay fines of $62 million and Pelleissone agreed to personal penalties in excess of $300,000.[1]

As you can see from the KHC example, manipulating expense accounts and payments can lead to significant misstatements and frauds. GAAP prescribes that expenses be

---

[1] *The Kraft Heinz Co. and Eduardo Pelleissone,* SEC Accounting and Auditing Enforcement Release No. 4248, September 3, 2021.

charged to income to reflect the consumption of economic benefits. The FASB *Statement of Concepts* discusses three ways to recognize expenses:

1. When they can be matched with related revenues (e.g., cost of goods sold with sales) and those revenues are recognized.
2. In the period in which they are incurred.
3. When they are allocated to the future periods benefited by a "systematic and rational" process (e.g., depreciation).[2]

It is imperative that the auditor understands the concept of expense recognition and ascertain that the client is correctly applying the appropriate concept to the expense at hand and is properly valuing the expense.

ACQUISITION AND EXPENDITURE CYCLE: TYPICAL ACTIVITIES

LO 8-1

Describe the acquisition and expenditure cycle, including typical source documents.

The basic acquisition and expenditure activities include (1) purchasing goods and services, (2) receiving the good or service, (3) recording the asset or expense and related liability, and (4) paying the vendor. (Note that paying the vendor was covered in Chapter 6.) See Exhibit 8.1 for the activities and transactions involved in an acquisition and expenditure cycle. The numbers listed in the headings correspond with Exhibit 8.1. The exhibit also lists the accounts and records typically found in this cycle. As you follow the exhibit, you can track the elements of internal control described in the following sections.

EXHIBIT 8.1 **Acquisition and Expenditure Cycle**

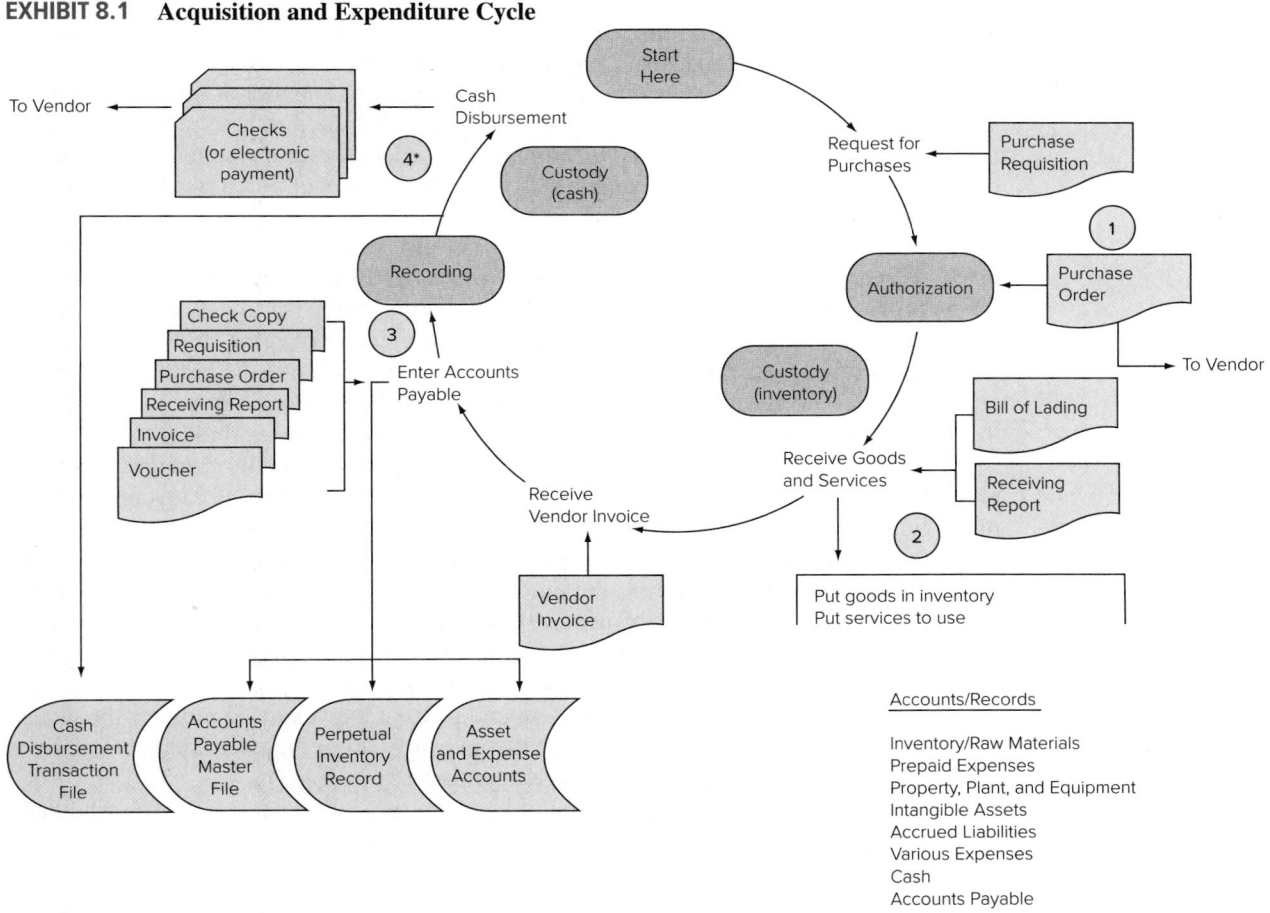

Accounts/Records

Inventory/Raw Materials
Prepaid Expenses
Property, Plant, and Equipment
Intangible Assets
Accrued Liabilities
Various Expenses
Cash
Accounts Payable

*Paying the vendor is discussed in the "Cash Disbursements" section of Chapter 6.

[2]*SFAC No. 5,* "Recognition and Measurement in Finance Statements."

Purchasing Goods and Services ⓵

The expenditure cycle begins when an individual or department needs supplies, materials, equipment, or services. The individual or department requests these items by sending a **purchase requisition**, often electronically, to the purchasing department. The purchase requisition will include the name of the department asking for the items, a listing of the items being requested, an account number where the cost of the material is to be charged when received, and an authorization signature from someone with the authority to commit the department to that amount of expense. The requisition may also include a recommended vendor.

The purchasing department reviews the purchase requisition and, if everything is in order, seeks to order the items where the best price, quality, and appropriate delivery can be obtained. Generally, the vendor must be on the approved vendor list. The **approved vendor list** includes only vendors that have been inspected by the organization and are authorized for purchases. It often requires several departments to approve a vendor. Purchasing usually approves the vendor for appropriate pricing, payment terms, and delivery; quality control may approve a vendor for both the quality of the product it makes and its system of quality control used during the vendor's manufacturing process; and production (or engineering) may approve the items as appropriate for its purposes on the purchasing company's production line. There have been several frauds where only one person approved a vendor for inclusion on the approved vendor list. The individual was able to add to the list fictitious companies or disreputable firms willing to provide kickbacks to the individual.

There may be instances where material must be purchased from a vendor, not on the approved vendor list. For example, the current vendors cannot deliver the needed material or a new part is required that cannot be manufactured by existing approved vendors. In this instance, there should be a process where multiple individuals and departments approve the purchase and steps must be taken to approve the vendor as soon as possible.

Once purchasing identifies the appropriate vendor for the purchase, a **purchase order** is sent to the selected vendor. Note that a purchase order represents the formal authorization of a purchase. In most companies, if a purchase or series of purchases from a vendor exceeds a certain dollar amount, there is a requirement to receive bids from several vendors (usually at least three). The bidding process ensures that the company gets the best price, delivery, and payment terms. However, because of the large amounts at stake in this process (often multimillion-dollar orders), vendors may wish to get "an edge" in the process. To control for kickbacks, information leaks, and corruption, bids should come to someone other than the purchasing agent and be secured until the bidding process is complete. As a manager (or auditor), what would you think if one company was always the last bidder and its bids were always just below the second lowest bidder?

Often inventory is automatically ordered from approved vendors through automatic replenishment systems. When production plans indicate a need for the inventory, automatic links to the vendor result in a system-generated purchase order. Sometimes purchasing writes a *blanket purchase order.* For example, purchasing gives the vendor an order for 1 million parts; however, the purchase order tells the vendor to deliver 100,000 on the 10th of each month for the next 10 months. The company may get a discount for ordering a million parts, and the vendor has the flexibility to make the parts during slow times in its production schedule. Further, the company could give the vendor access to the inventory record for that particular item and instruct the vendor to monitor the inventory with the instructions that "every time the inventory drops below 10,000 parts deliver 100,000 parts as soon as possible but no longer than two weeks."

The purchasing department is an area of high-fraud risk because employees who have the authority to purchase assets and services for the company are in a unique position to take advantage of their authority to enrich themselves or their friends. The abuse can simply be giving business to vendors that do not supply the best quality or price to the company. This may occur because of a conflict of interest. An employee might have an ownership interest in a supplier, might receive a kickback (the vendor provides the purchasing agent a gift or payment), or the employee might set up a "shell" company (a company created by the employee to provide fictitious invoices and receipt of payment). The abuse can extend to misdirecting purchases for the employee's personal benefit. These abuses are difficult to detect because vendors are often reluctant to lose favor with purchasing decision makers. Although expense fraud can add up, detecting the fraud can be difficult, as discussed in the following Auditing Insight "Is it Worth the Time to Detect It?".

AUDITING INSIGHT | Is It Worth the Time to Detect It?

Although expense fraud is often listed as one of the most common types of employee fraud in terms of number of incidents, many companies do not put in much effort to detect it. Why? On average, employees who commit expense fraud admit to stealing $100–$499 annually, an amount that may not justify detection costs and is much smaller than other types of employee frauds. As artificial intelligence (AI) systems improve, detection and flagging of unusual expenses become easier. Further, expense frauds are nearly always less than materiality and are not a significant focus for auditors. Nonetheless, an interesting aspect of expense fraud is that it happens at all. As one CEO, Alan Rich of **Chrome River**, says, "The fascinating human element of this is that usually the amount of money that people are stealing through expense fraud is small, but the risk they are taking for their personal lives and career is very large."

Source: "Why Companies Aren't That Worried About Expense Fraud," *Skift Research*, October 4, 2018.

Receiving the Goods or Services ②

When goods arrive at a company, the supplier will have a **bill of lading** that should include the purchase order number of the company receiving the delivery. It is imperative that the bill of lading be matched to the purchase order upon receipt. If a company obtains a reputation for receiving any goods that show up at its receiving department, any "undeliverable" item on a truck may find its way to the company's receiving docks. After the delivery is verified as the company's purchase, the receiving department inspects the goods received for quantity and quality and prepares a **receiving report**. The items are sent to the area designated by the department that originally requisitioned the material (e.g., engineering may order a piece of equipment but want it delivered to the production facility). A receiving report is completed to indicate the quantity and description of the item. Receiving departments should receive a "blind" purchase order that has all purchase information except the quantity, which is left blank for the receiving department to fill in after an independent inspection and count. Services are not "received" in this manner, but responsible persons indicate that the service was satisfactorily performed by signing the invoice or some other form that can be used like a receiving report to verify that the service was completed.

Recording the Asset or Expense and Related Liability ③

Accounts payable usually are recorded when the purchaser receives the goods or services ordered. The accounts payable department attaches a **voucher** to the purchase order, a **vendor's invoice**, and a receiving report. The combined documents are often called the **voucher package**. The voucher shows the accounts that are debited and indicates who checked the invoice for proper date, price, math, and reconciled the purchase order, receiving report, and vendor invoice. After the voucher package has been completed, accountants enter the accounts (or vouchers) payable with debits to proper inventory, fixed asset, or expense accounts with a corresponding credit to accounts payable. Technology allows companies to automate large portions of the acquisition and expenditure cycle. This can lead to significantly reduced risk in the audit, as long as controls are in place. Automation is discussed in the following Auditing Insight "Robotic Process Automation for Procurement".

AUDITING INSIGHT   Robotic Process Automation for Procurement

Historically, the process of acquisition and expenditure has followed processes similar to what is described above in the text. However, many larger companies have been investing in robotic process automation (RPA) as a way to optimize procurement and data aggregation, enabling employees to focus on efficiency and make data-driven decisions.

As discussed more in Module G, RPA is a software process that handles repetitive, transactional, rules-based tasks that require little or no human intervention. Software such as **UiPath** and **Automation Anywhere** interact with a wide variety of other software programs and systems to perform routine or highly manual tasks. An example of a common RPA application in the acquisition and expenditure cycle is ordering of materials and services for a manufacturing process.

Research claims that a fully optimized RPA process can save the equivalent of 59 employees per $1 billion of purchases! Interestingly, research has also shown diminishing returns to RPA, and possibly reversal. Although causality is difficult to demonstrate, similar organizations with more than 20 RPA bots process fewer purchase orders per employee than organizations with 6–20 RPA bots.

Auditors need to evaluate the controls surrounding RPA bots, as well as understand and often walk through the process managed by the bots. A well-designed RPA bot can significantly reduce the risk of accounting errors in the acquisition and expenditure cycle, but an improperly controlled one can magnify the risk.

Source: "Robotic Process Automation for Procurement," *Supply & Demand Chain Executive,* March 8, 2021.

REVIEW CHECKPOINTS

8.1 What is a *voucher?* What is a *voucher package?*

8.2 How can purchasing managers use their position to defraud the company? What can be done to prevent it?

8.3 Why is a "blind" purchase order used as a receiving report document?

SIGNIFICANT ACCOUNTS AND RELEVANT ASSERTIONS

LO 8-2

Identify significant accounts and relevant assertions related to the acquisition and expenditure cycle.

STAGES OF AN AUDIT

Obtain (or Retain) Engagement	Engagement Planning	Risk Assessment	Audit Evidence	Reporting

Remember that an account or disclosure is significant if there is a reasonable chance that it could contain a material misstatement. The auditor identifies significant accounts and relevant assertions by applying the audit risk model.

We introduced the audit risk model in Chapter 4 and reviewed it in Chapter 7. Therefore, this chapter and subsequent chapters will not review the components of the model again. Instead, these chapters will focus on the use of the audit risk model in assessing risk and planning the engagement in the specific areas addressed in these chapters.

Exhibit 8.2 identifies the significant accounts and assertions in the expenditure cycle. In this cycle, the most significant risks usually relate to the completeness of expenditures and the valuation of acquisitions. It is also possible that individuals will attempt to run personal expenses through accounts payable and receive reimbursement for the purchase of these items. Therefore, the validity of expenses is also a significant risk in the expenditure cycle.

Accounts Payable

In many ways, the purchasing process, including accounts payable, is the most important to the organization. If purchasing is not done well, manufacturers may need to cease production because of raw material shortages, retailers may have insufficient inventory for

EXHIBIT 8.2
Significant Accounts and Assertions in the Expenditure and Acquisition Cycle

Significant Account	Relevant Assertions
Accounts Payable	Completeness
	Cutoff
	Existence
	Presentation
	Valuation
Expenses	Completeness
	Cutoff
	Accuracy
	Classification

customer needs, and needed services may not be obtained. Purchasing and the subsequent receipt of goods and services give rise to accounts payable—the obligation to pay the vendor for the goods and services acquired. If accounts payable are not paid on time and for the proper amount, vendors may raise the price charged to that client to cover the cost of capital in the delayed payment, ask for orders to be paid in advance, or cease to provide products or services to the organization. We have already learned that audit firms will not do business with clients if the relationship is improper. Vendors may also decide not to do business with a customer who does not appropriately honor their obligations or may require advance payment, as described in the following Auditing Insight, "Give Me All Your Money".

AUDITING INSIGHT   Give Me All Your Money

Aeropostale, a large fashion retailer, filed for Chapter 11 bankruptcy protection in a New York court and quickly closed 113 of its 739 U.S. stores and all 41 of its Canada stores. The bankruptcy filing comes after a dispute with one of its largest suppliers, MGF Sourcing, which demanded cash on delivery (C.O.D.).

Source: "Aeropostale Files for Chapter 11 Bankruptcy," *USA Today,* May 5, 2016.

There are three primary relevant assertions for accounts payable: completeness, cutoff, and valuation. Completeness and cutoff go hand-in-hand because management may desire to present a more favorable financial condition by not recording an obligation in the correct period. An incomplete listing of accounts payable at the end of the period lowers current liabilities (and corresponding expenses). Because vendors do need to be paid eventually, management may accomplish this by delaying the recording of accounts payable until the subsequent period—in other words, by closing the accounting records early so end-of-period obligations become the obligations of the subsequent period. Accounts payable may also be understated. Obligations may not reflect the total cost of the purchase such as freight, tariff, and taxes. On large purchases, this may be substantial and may be the result of an error or an intentional act to reduce the accounts payable liability.

Auditors should be cautious not to discount other assertions. While management would not intentionally create a fictitious accounts payable, the item may not reflect an obligation of the company. A vendor account may have been paid, but the payment has not been recorded in the proper account. The liability remains on the books but no longer reflects an obligation. Individuals may try to run personal expenses through the payable system. This is especially true in companies where the duties of authorization and custody are not segregated. If this is the case, the payable does not represent an obligation of the firm and may be fictitious or an obligation of an employee.

Expenses

The corresponding entry to the accounts payable is often to an expense account. Because expenses affect the income statement, the misstatement of expenses is often the objective of misstating a purchase or payable. Again, not recording expenses in the current period or delaying the recognition of expenses to the subsequent period is often the method for financial

AUDITING INSIGHT   Would You Like Me to Pay Your Credit Card Bill?

Nathan Mueller's wife was pregnant, and his $80,000 salary was not allowing him to pay all his bills. He believed if he could just catch up with the bills, then everything would be all right.

Mueller had the authority to approve checks up to $250,000 for his company **ING**. He had the ability to log onto the accounts payable system as someone else and issue checks made out to *Universal*. ING did business with an insurance company that had *Universal* as part of its name, and Mueller's credit card company had *Universal* as part of its name. In June 2003, he ran a check for $1,100 to pay his credit card bill in order to "test his scheme." Once that check went through and his credit card was paid, he transferred all his outstanding debt to that credit card and, over several months, paid $88,000 in credit card debt.

According to Mueller, "in our small accounting department, we knew everyone else's system passwords. This was a practical workaround for when we needed to get something done when someone was out of the office. We logged in as someone else to get the job done." Eventually, Mueller logged on to the system as someone else and requested a check for *Ace Business Consulting*. (Remember, service expenses are easier for fraudsters.) The check request was routed to Mueller for approval. He received his first check for $27,000 a few days later and deposited it in a bank account he opened in the name of *Ace Business Consulting*. Using this method, he stole approximately $8 million from 2004 to 2007. According to Mueller, after getting his $88,000 "bonus" he couldn't help himself. "I wanted to do it again, even though I didn't really need the money like before."

Source: "Lessons from an $8 Million Fraud: What the Criminal Was Thinking and What Can Be Done to Prevent or Uncover Similar Crimes," *Journal of Accountancy,* August 2014, pp. 32–37.

statement fraud. Closing the accounting records early for expenses (say, December 22 for December 31 year-end clients) forces ensuing expenses into the next period. Further, an unethical controller might lock in their desk several large bills received near year-end and place them into the payables system after year-end, thereby violating the cutoff assertion.

Another issue for expenses is classification. There may be many reasons to classify expenses in the wrong account. **WorldCom Inc.** is an example of a company that simply placed ordinary expenses in capital accounts, thus lowering expenses and increasing assets by billions of dollars. While capitalizing expenses increase net income in the year in which they should have been completely expensed, the expenses do not go away. (Amounts would be expensed over a number of years as depreciation or amortization expense.) When forced to restate these expenses, WorldCom recorded nearly $5 billion in immediate recognition of expenses. WorldCom is just one of many companies that used expenses to improve the appearance of their financial statements. It isn't any wonder that some officers and directors were not happy when the auditors were looking closely at their financial records, as demonstrated by the opening quote at the beginning of this chapter. Exhibit 8.3 shows some of the more egregious misstatements in recent years.

EXHIBIT 8.3   Cost and Expense Capers

Company	Alleged Fraud Strategy	Restatement Amount
MCI (WorldCom)	The telecommunications company improperly capitalized expense items.	$11 billion
Waste Management Inc.	The waste disposal giant used "top-level adjustments" to improperly eliminate and defer current-period expenses and avoided depreciation on garbage trucks by assigning unsupported, inflated, and arbitrary salvage values and extending the useful lives.	$1.1 billion
Kraft Heinz Corporation	The food giant improperly recorded discounts from suppliers.	$208.0 million
Orbital Sciences Corporation	The satellite manufacturer improperly capitalized costs.	$124.0 million
Aurora Food, Inc.	The food company did not record trade-marketing expenses (e.g., case discounts to induce grocery stores to stock its goods).	$81.5 million
Dixon, Illinois	The treasurer/controller created a fictitious account that she used to pay her personal expenses.	$53.0 million
Collins and Aikman	The automotive supply company booked rebates as lump sums that should have been spread out over time.	$16.0 million

Other reasons may exist for improper classification of expenses. For example, some projects are performed under cost-plus contracts. These are often large construction projects, such as military ship building, where changes to the contract specifications are expected during construction. Here, the construction company submits bills for material and labor and is reimbursed for all expenses and paid a set percentage over the costs (say, an 8 percent profit). There may be little incentive for a disreputable contractor to restrain costs and few restrictions for a dishonest contractor to place costs from one project to another. Investors also focus on "core earnings," which are typically defined as earnings before interest, taxes, depreciation, and amortization (EBITDA). EBITDA also excludes special items. Thus, to look good to investors, management may have an incentive to shift expenses out of core earnings as in the following Auditing Insight, "Rotten to the 'Core'".

AUDITING INSIGHT   Rotten to the "Core"

Analysts and investors often focus on a company's "core earnings," the income earned from the primary business the company conducts. Thus, if a company wants to look strong to investors, there is an incentive to misclassify a period expense as a special item that does not affect core earnings. Importantly, classification shifts do not influence net income but do influence the core earnings metrics used by investors and analysts. One such time when a company may have a very strong incentive is when they are issuing stock publicly for the first time, known as an Initial Public Offering (IPO).

Recently, academic researchers investigated whether there is systematic evidence that companies misclassify expenses when conducting an IPO and whether investors are fooled by this misclassification.

The researchers discovered that yes, on average expense misclassification does occur prior to IPOs and yes, investors are fooled. The researchers found that companies that misclassify core expenses as special items obtain higher IPO price revisions but, importantly, have lower stock returns after the IPO when core earnings return to appropriate levels.

This demonstrates the importance of the classification assertion for expenses. Even though net income is not affected, the location of the expense does matter.

Source: X. Liu and B. Wu, "Do IPO Firms Misclassify Expenses? Implications for IPO Price Formation and Post-IPO Stock Performance," *Management Science,* July 2021, pp. 4505–31.

 ## REVIEW CHECKPOINTS

8.4 Why do auditors focus on completeness of expenditures as a significant account and relevant assertion in the expenditure cycle?

8.5 Why is inherent risk for the existence of inventory an issue in the expenditure cycle audit?

8.6 Why is a service expense a good account for recording a fictitious expense?

RISK OF MATERIAL MISSTATEMENT

LO 8-3
Discuss the risk of material misstatement in the acquisition and expenditure cycle.

Audit Analytics reported that, for 2020, there were 42 financial statement restatements for expenses (including general and administrative expenses, payroll, and related liabilities). This accounted for 11 percent of all restatements and ranked as fifth on the list of reasons for financial statement restatements. The *Audit Analytics* report indicates that restatements as a whole have declined since 2007 (a finding attributed to the PCAOB rigorous inspections), with expense recognition errors continuing to decrease over time (54 in 2018; 104 in 2014; 236 in 2007).[3]

In many accounting systems, liabilities are not recorded until receiving reports have been matched to purchase orders and invoices. This is often referred to as a "three-way match," and is perhaps the most important control in the purchasing cycle. Often, when there is a problem in matching the documents, the recording of the liability is delayed or not recorded, thus understating costs and overstating profits. Further, in an attempt to make the financial

[3]*2020 Financial Restatements: A 20-Year Review,* Audit Analytics, November 2021.

statements appear stronger, management may decide to delay the recording of expenses and related liabilities until after the fiscal year-end. Additionally, noncancelable purchase agreements may exist where goods are ordered for future delivery (as with blanket purchase orders). If market forces or technology causes a permanent decline in the value of those goods, the company must recognize any related losses immediately, even though no liability or expense exists because the goods have not been received. Therefore, risks in the acquisition and expenditure cycle include *unrecorded liabilities* and *noncancelable purchase agreements.*

Remember from Chapter 7 that as part of the planning process, the auditor must determine the source of a misstatement that could cause the financial statements to be materially misstated. We established the idea of assessing the risk of material misstatement by using the "what could go wrong?" approach when thinking of each financial statement assertion. The WCGW is a part of each audit firm's process and enables a thorough assessment of the risk of material misstatement.

When considering WCGW in the expenditure and acquisition cycle, auditors consider five primary concerns:

1. Have liabilities and corresponding expenses or assets been recorded (completeness)?
2. Have liabilities and corresponding expenses or assets been recorded in the proper period (cutoff)?
3. Do liabilities reflect the actual needs and obligations of the company (occurrence and obligation)?
4. Have liabilities and corresponding expenses or assets been recorded at their proper amount (valuation)?
5. Have expenses been recorded in the proper account (classification)?

Exhibit 8.4 summarizes the WCGW analysis for the expenditure and acquisition cycle.

We have seen in several of the Auditing Insights large accounts payable schemes perpetrated to enhance the financial statements or for an employee's benefit. Clearly, these frauds can result in material misstatements. Remember, while large dollar frauds and errors that occur in well-known companies are widely reported in the financial news, most frauds are perpetrated in smaller companies where $100,000 may be the difference between success and bankruptcy.

EXHIBIT 8.4
Assertions and What Could Go Wrong

Significant Account	Relevant Assertions	What Could Go Wrong?
Accounts Payable	Completeness	Liabilities are not recorded.
	Cutoff	Liabilities are recorded in the incorrect period.
	Existence	Liabilities may not represent actual obligations of the company.
	Presentation	Liabilities are not recorded in the proper accounts and properly disclosed in the footnotes.
	Valuation	Payables are recorded at an incorrect amount.
Various Expenses	Completeness	Not all expenses are recorded.
	Cutoff	Expenses have been recorded in the incorrect period.
	Accuracy	Expenses are recorded at an incorrect amount.
	Classification	Expenses have been improperly recorded in the wrong account.

✓ REVIEW CHECKPOINTS

8.7 What are the short-term and the long-term effects of improperly capitalizing expenditures on the financial statements?

8.8 If an account payable is omitted from the end of the period balance, what are the possible other accounts that may be misstated?

INTERNAL CONTROL ACTIVITIES AND DESIGN EVALUATION

LO 8-4
Identify important internal control activities present in a properly designed system to mitigate the risk of material misstatements for each relevant assertion in the acquisition and expenditure cycle.

Control risk assessment is important because it governs the nature, timing, and extent of substantive procedures that will be applied in the audit of account balances in the acquisition and expenditure cycle. The primary accounts discussed in this chapter are accounts payable and expenses, and the assertions and significant internal control activities are summarized in Exhibit 8.5. However, you should not lose sight of the fact that many other accounts are affected by activities in this cycle. These accounts include the following:

- Prepaid expenses
- Fixed assets
- Inventory
- Accrued liabilities
- Supplies

Entity-Level Controls

It is important that auditors consider entity-level controls in all processes and procedures. In the expenditure process, management should have a process for continually reviewing expenses and comparing them to budgets and forecasts. Proper authorization for all expenditures should be established and included in company policy and procedures. Corporate values and ethics that have been established should be communicated to suppliers

EXHIBIT 8.5 **Internal Control Activities in the Expenditure and Acquisition Cycle**

Significant Account	Relevant Assertion	What Could Go Wrong?	Internal Control Activity
Accounts Payable	Completeness	Liabilities are not recorded	Receiving reports should be prenumbered and used in order. All receiving reports completed by the end of the period should be accounted for in that period.
	Cutoff	Liabilities are recorded in the incorrect period.	Payables recorded in the first weeks of a period should be compared to receiving reports and invoices for the recording period.
	Existence	Liabilities may not represent actual obligations of the company.	Voucher packages for payments to vendors should include purchase orders and receiving reports. Vendors should be on the approved vendor list. A three-way match should be performed for purchase orders, receiving reports, and vendor invoices.
	Presentation	Liabilities are not recorded in the proper accounts and properly disclosed in the footnotes	Chart of accounts used for classifying purchase transactions.
	Valuation	Payables recorded at an incorrect amount.	Prices on vendor invoices are agreed to approved price list. Vendor invoices are tested for mathematical accuracy.
Various Expenses	Completeness	Not all expenses are recorded.	Use of prenumbered vouchers, receiving reports, purchase orders, and checks; and the numerical sequence is verified.
	Cutoff	Expenses have been recorded in the incorrect period.	Comparison by managers of actual expenses with budgeted amounts.
	Accuracy	Expenses are recorded at an incorrect amount.	Expenses should be matched with vendor invoices or work orders for the proper cost of items or service performed.
	Classification	Expenses have been improperly recorded in the wrong account.	Expenses should be reviewed to determine that they have been recorded in the proper account.

and other partners of the entity along with a place where inappropriate behavior (such as the solicitation of a bribe or kickback) may be reported. The security of items such as blank purchase orders and blank receiving reports is an important control, as are the proper delivery and safeguarding of all material received by the entity.

Control Considerations

Control activities for proper separation of responsibilities should be in place and operating. By referring to Exhibit 8.1, you can see that proper separation involves different people and different departments performing the purchasing, receiving, and cash disbursement authorization; custody of inventory, fixed assets, and cash; record keeping for purchases and payments; and reconciliation of assets, cash, and accounts payable. Combinations of two or more of these responsibilities in one person, one office, or one computerized system can open the door for errors and frauds. Specifically, the persons authorizing purchases should not be responsible for recording them. Persons who actually handle the receipt and storage of goods should neither authorize nor account for them. The persons who sign checks should not prepare the vouchers, nor should they mail the checks.

In addition, the internal controls should provide for detailed control-checking activities. For example, purchase requisitions and purchase orders should be signed or initialed by authorized personnel. System-generated purchase orders should come from a system where master file specifications for reordering and vendor identification are restricted to changes by authorized persons.

Improper recording of expenses may occur intentionally, or may be due to a mistake in judgment or merely entering a transaction, as illustrated by the following Auditing Insight, "That must have been a LONG drive!". Many accounting systems use automated processes for the recording of expenses. A three-way match control is a common automated control to ensure the proper recording of expenses. When an approved purchase order, vendor invoice, and receiving report are all present in the system, an expense should be recorded automatically. The system generates exception reports which enable management to detect errors. For example, a listing of unmatched receiving reports should be produced by the system and evaluated by management to detect received items that may have incorrectly not been recorded. Similarly, a listing of unmatched vendor invoices can help prevent payment for fraudulent billings and also can detect missing receiving reports leading to unrecorded liabilities.

 AUDITING INSIGHT   That must have been a LONG drive!

Because of personnel limitations related to COVID-19, the **City of Chattanooga** changed its policies related to employee reimbursements. Instead of issuing separate checks for reimbursements, the company added reimbursements into the employees' paychecks, adding an extra manual step in the process. When a reimbursement was approved, the amount would be manually keyed into the payroll system for reimbursement.

While out on family leave, Eulena Davis received a paycheck of over $44,000—when her paycheck should have been approximately $400! The cause of the mistake—a mis-keyed mileage reimbursement. When finally discovered by the city nearly seven months later,

the employee denied noticing and refused to share her bank information. The city is suing the employee for recovery of the funds.

According to City Auditor Stan Sewell, the mistake occurred because "internal control procedures were relaxed (primarily) due to the COVID-19 pandemic." Whenever human input is involved, the opportunity for error increases. A second Payroll Division staff member was required to complete a control check to identify errors, but that control was ineffective.

Source: "Overpaid: Chattanooga sues employee who mistakenly got $44K for mileage reimbursement," *WTVC newschannel 9,* October 12, 2021.

Custody

Access to inventory and other physical assets must be restricted by placing them in locked areas when possible. Responsibility must be established by having someone sign for receipt of the assets when they are moved. Cash "custody" rests largely in the hands of the person or persons authorized to sign checks.

Another aspect of custody involves access to blank documents such as purchase orders, receiving reports, and checks. If unauthorized persons can obtain blank copies of these internal business documents, they can forge a false purchase order to a fictitious vendor, forge a false receiving report, send a false invoice from a fictitious supplier, and receive a company check, thereby accomplishing embezzlement. In addition, a blank purchase order can be used to order merchandise, material, or services for personal use. If this material can be diverted and if sound controls are not in place, the company may end up paying for an employee's home improvement project.

Periodic Reconciliation

A periodic comparison or reconciliation of existing assets to recorded amounts is not shown in Exhibit 8.1, but it occurs in several ways, including the following:

- Preparing an accounts payable trial balance and comparing it to the accounts payable control account.
- Comparing accounts payable records to vendors' monthly statements.
- Reviewing unmatched purchase orders, receiving reports, and invoices.
- Taking a physical inventory and comparing it to inventory records.
- Inspecting fixed assets and comparing them to detailed fixed asset records.

Information about the control system is often gathered by completing an *internal control questionnaire*. Appendix 8A provides examples of questionnaires for both manual controls and system controls. These questionnaires can be studied for details of desirable control activities. They are organized under headings that identify the management assertions.

✅ REVIEW CHECKPOINTS

8.9   What primary functions should be separated in the acquisition and expenditure cycle?

8.10 What feature of the acquisition and expenditure control would be expected to prevent an employee's embezzling cash through creation of fictitious vouchers?

TESTING OF OPERATING EFFECTIVENESS OF INTERNAL CONTROL

LO 8-5

Give examples of tests of controls to verify the operating effectiveness of internal controls in the acquisition and expenditure cycle.

Tests of Controls

An organization should have controls in place and operating to prevent, detect, and correct accounting errors. Arguably, the most risks in the expenditure cycle are in the purchasing activity. Purchasing itself is not an account (except in government accounting), but it does affect the occurrence and valuation of other accounts. Exhibit 8.6 continues with the example of some of the most important considerations in the expenditure and acquisition cycle and relates the test of controls to what could go wrong.

Auditors can perform tests of controls to determine whether company controls actually are in place and operating effectively. Tests of controls consist of identification of (1) the control that will be relied on to reduce assessed control risk and (2) the data population from which a sample of items will be selected for audit. In general, the actions in tests of controls involve inspecting, inquiry, observing, scanning, matching, and recalculating.

An auditor might select a sample of voucher packages and inspect the documents for indications that reconciliations and approvals for payment are evident. If personnel in the organization are not performing control activities effectively, auditors need to design substantive procedures to try to detect whether control failures have produced materially

EXHIBIT 8.6 **Tests of Controls in the Expenditure and Acquisition Cycle**

Significant Account	Relevant Assertion	What Could Go Wrong?	Internal Control Activity	Tests of Internal Control
Accounts Payable	Completeness	Liabilities are not recorded.	Receiving reports should be prenumbered and used in order. All receiving reports completed by the end of the period should be accounted for in that period.	Verify use and sequence of prenumbered receiving reports. Inspect evidence of management review of system-generated unmatched receiving reports.
	Cutoff	Liabilities are recorded in the incorrect period.	Payables recorded in the first weeks of a period should be compared to receiving reports and invoices for the recording period.	Trace receiving reports and invoices occurring near year end to recording in appropriate period.
	Existence	Liabilities may not represent actual obligations of the company.	Voucher packages for payments to vendors should include purchase orders and receiving reports. Vendors should be on the approved vendor list. A three-way match should be performed for purchase orders, receiving reports, and vendor invoices.	Vouch a sample of payments to vendors to complete three-way match. Trace vendors to approve vendor list. Test automated system for accurate performance of three-way match procedure and managerial review of exception reports.
	Presentation	Liabilities are not recorded in the proper accounts and properly disclosed in the footnotes.	Chart of accounts used for classifying purchase transactions.	Observe that client reporting software includes a pre-populated chart of accounts.
	Valuation	Payables recorded at an incorrect amount.	Prices on vendor invoices are agreed to approve price list. Vendor invoices are tested for mathematical accuracy.	Inspect evidence of client comparing prices to approved price listing. Observe client testing invoices for mathematical accuracy.
Various Expenses	Completeness	Not all expenses are recorded.	Use of prenumbered vouchers, receiving reports, purchase orders, and checks; and the numerical sequence is verified.	Inspect evidence of client verifying numerical sequence.
	Cutoff	Expenses have been recorded in the incorrect period.	Comparison by managers of actual expenses with budgeted amounts.	Examine evidence that managers review actual versus budget and follow up on unusual amounts
	Accuracy	Expenses are recorded at an incorrect amount.	Expenses should be matched with vendor invoices or work orders for the proper cost of items or service performed.	Inspect evidence of comparison between recorded expenses and vendor invoices.
	Classification	Expenses have been improperly recorded in the wrong account.	Expenses should be reviewed to determine that they have been recorded in the proper account.	Inspect evidence of journal entry review procedures.

incorrect account balances. Procedures such as matching, recalculating, and scanning for unusual items often can be performed electronically using computer-assisted audit techniques (CAATs). For example, CAATs can scan the accounts payable balances for debit balances. Exhibit 8.7 shows some additional control considerations in the purchasing cycle.

Tests of controls over occurrence involve tests of the additions to the expense accounts. The chart in Exhibit 8.8 shows the direction of the test for tests of controls in the acquisition and expenditure cycle. Selecting a sample of closed purchase orders, receiving reports, or vendor invoices and tracing them to the accounts payable journal provides evidence of completeness.

EXHIBIT 8.7 Purchasing Transactions and Events: Acquisition and Expenditure Cycle—Additional Control Activities and Tests of Controls

What Could Go Wrong?	Internal Control Activity	Tests of Internal Control
Completeness—Purchases received have not been properly recorded.	• Separation of duties between purchasing, receiving, and accounting • Use of prenumbered vouchers, receiving reports, purchase orders, and checks; and the numerical sequence checked • Purchase orders supported by authorized requisitions. • Purchases received are matched with receiving report and vendor invoices • Purchases from approved vendors listed on an approved vendor list • Overall comparisons of purchases by a statistical or product line analysis made periodically • Comparison by managers of actual expenses with budgeted amounts	• Observe separation of duties. • Trace receiving reports to recording in purchases journal. • Scan purchases journal for numerical sequence of purchase orders and receiving reports. • Scan cash disbursements journal for client checking sequence. • Vouch purchase orders to requisitions and review requisitions for authorizations. • Review and reconcile voucher packages for three-way match of purchase order, receiving reports, and invoice. • Vouch purchase order to the approved vendor list, and review the purchase order for correct customer name, address, product description, terms, dates, and quantities. • Examine evidence that managers review statistical analyses, and follow up on unusual relationships. • Examine evidence that managers review actual versus budget, and follow up on unusual items.
Accuracy—Purchase amounts and other data related to significant purchase transactions and events have not been recorded properly.	• Purchase contracts authorized at the appropriate level • Comparison of invoice quantities and prices with purchase orders and receiving reports • Vendor statements reviewed and approved by appropriate personnel • Prices and mathematical accuracy independently checked before approving voucher for payment • Journal entries reviewed at the appropriate level • Individual accounts payable reconciled to general ledger	• Examine contracts for authorization. Inquire how accounting is notified of pending contracts. • Observe client comparing receiving quantities, and inspect documentary evidence of comparison. • Inspect evidence of client review of vendor statements. • Inspect evidence of recalculation of price extensions and discounts. • Inspect evidence of approval for payment. • Inspect evidence of managerial review of journal entries • Review reconciliation and support for reconciling items.
Cutoff—Purchases have been recorded in the incorrect period.	• Date of receiving report compared with invoice date	• Trace the date of receipt to date recorded in voucher journal. • Inspect evidence of client comparison of dates. • Inspect purchases occurring near year-end for recording in appropriate period.
Classification — Purchases have not been recorded in the proper accounts.	• Purchases from subsidiaries and affiliates classified as intercompany purchases and payables • Purchase returns and allowances properly classified	• Observe correct account classification for intercompany transactions. • Inspect sample of purchase returns for appropriate accounting

At the same time, the auditor can inspect these documents for proper authorization and agreement to an approved vendor list. Taking a sample of payments to vendors and vouching those payments to the receiving report and purchase order provides evidence that the delivery occurred and the purchase existed. Further, vouching payments to receiving reports and purchase orders may find fictitious vendors (there is usually no receiving report because fictitious vendors don't deliver product) or payments for employee personal use (often, the purchase order is missing or lacks the proper approval). Auditors can also use CAAT such as IDEA to assist in performing tests of controls, as discussed in the following Auditing Insight, "Using IDEA in the Audit: Approved Vendor List".

EXHIBIT 8.8
Direction of Tests

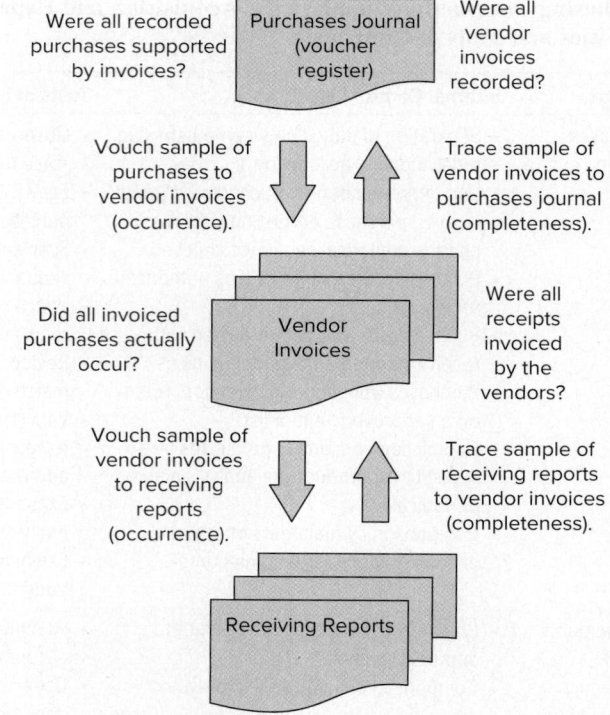

 AUDITING INSIGHT   Using IDEA in the Audit: Approved Vendor List

Significant issues in accounts payable occur when vendors that are not on the approved vendor list are paid. Auditors can take advantage of CAATs by comparing all vendor payments to the approved vendor list. In the past, such a complete test was virtually impossible, and the best the auditors could do was to test a sample of payments. In addition, auditors can search for duplicate payments to vendors. Only a few vendor payments should reoccur each month for the exact amount (e.g., loan payments, insurance payments, rents). A vendor being paid for goods or services repeatedly for the exact amount of money may indicate a fraud.

To gather evidence in these situations, an auditor will most likely join the approved vendor list with the cash disbursements list or purchase journal. In addition, the auditor can request the program to provide a listing of identical payments to the same vendor. The resulting reports should be carefully reviewed by the auditor and evidence gathered as to the propriety of the items. At the end of this chapter, you can perform this exception test in Exercise 8.63.

Summary: Control Risk Assessment

The auditor should evaluate the evidence obtained from understanding internal controls and from the tests of controls. This evaluation of control risk along with the auditor's understanding of the inherent risk leads to the auditor's determination of the risk of material misstatement (RMM). If the control risk is assessed below the maximum, the substantive procedures can be reduced in cost-saving ways. For example, if *completeness* controls are strong, only large items in purchases, accounts payable, cash disbursements, and fixed assets need to be examined in the search for unrecorded liabilities in accounts payable, and if *occurrence* controls are strong, vouching of expenses can be limited to significant items. On the other hand, if the tests of controls reveal weaknesses, the substantive procedures need to be designed to lower the detection risk for the account balances. For example, if *completeness* controls are weak, the auditor might send confirmation letters to vendors with small or zero balances. If *occurrence* controls are weak, the auditor may have to perform substantive tests of significant transactions by recalculating and testing a sample of payments for the period for monetary errors rather than just evidence of control effectiveness. Other substantive procedures that can be affected include vouching of debits to assets and expenses.

✅ REVIEW CHECKPOINTS

8.11 How should an auditor test for proper authorization in the expenditure cycle?

8.12 Where would an auditor find the proper authorization that indicates it is okay to pay a vendor?

SUBSTANTIVE PROCEDURES

LO 8-6
Give examples of substantive procedures in the acquisition and expenditure cycle and relate them to assertions about significant account balances at the end of the period.

STAGES OF AN AUDIT

Obtain (or Retain) Engagement	Engagement Planning	Risk Assessment	Audit Evidence	Reporting

Recall that management can always override controls. For this reason, the high fraud risk in the Revenue and Collection cycle leads to a strong need for substantive procedures. Although employee expenditure fraud is fairly common in the expense cycle, financial reporting fraud is considered to be a lower risk in the expense cycle compared with the revenue cycle. The primary reason for this is that purchasing activities are not considered as important a metric to many outside users, thus management incentives to manipulate purchases are lower. In some ways, however, it is easier for errors to occur in the purchasing cycle because many different vendors, billing processes, and departments within the company are involved in purchasing goods and services. Thus, the audit approach in the purchasing cycle is one that relies almost entirely on testing controls within the system, and far less on procedures. For this reason, we do not present a table of substantive procedures as we did for the sales cycle. In fact, much of the substantive evidence obtained in the purchasing cycle is obtained through testing three-way match controls and system-generated exception reports, described in the following Auditing Insight, "Automated Three-Way Match Controls". These procedures can sometimes result in testing 100% of purchase transactions.

 AUDITING INSIGHT | Automated Three-Way Match Controls

When a client has a well-defined purchasing process, the auditor may obtain a majority of its substantive evidence through testing exceptions to the process. Consider an organization that follows a standard process of obtaining a purchase order, and requiring a receiving report and vendor invoice matched to the purchase order to record the purchase. This process by the client is typically automated—the client's system identifies exceptions to the policy, which enables both the client and auditor to identify exceptions and verify appropriate recording. The auditor tests the process and validates the completeness and accuracy of the system data. By testing the system, the auditor has gained assurance related to the large majority of transactions that follow the standard process, sometimes over 95% of all purchasing transactions. The auditor can then evaluate and test the exceptions to understand why some transactions do not follow the standard process. The auditor's additional substantive testing will focus on those items that did not follow the standard process.

Accounts Payable and the Completeness Assertion

When considering assertions and obtaining evidence about accounts payable and other liabilities, auditors must emphasize the *completeness* assertion. (Remember from Chapter 7 that the emphasis is on the *existence* assertion for asset and occurrence for revenue accounts.) This emphasis on completeness is rightly placed because financial statement users are typically more concerned if a company understates expenses and liabilities than if management overstates those accounts.

Evidence is much more difficult to obtain to support the *completeness* assertion than the *existence* assertion. Auditors cannot rely entirely on a management assertion of *completeness,* even in combination with a favorable assessment of the risk of material misstatement. The **search for unrecorded liabilities** is the set of procedures designed to yield audit evidence of liabilities that were not recorded in the reporting period. Such a search normally should be performed from the audit client's balance sheet date to the date of the auditors' report.

The following is a list of procedures useful in the *search for unrecorded liabilities.* The audit objective is to search all places where evidence of liabilities could exist:

- Inquire of client personnel about their procedures for ensuring that all liabilities are recorded.
- Scan the open purchase order file at year-end for indications of material purchase commitments at fixed prices. Obtain current prices and determine whether any adjustments for loss and liability for purchase commitments are needed.
- Examine the unmatched vendor invoices and determine when the goods were received, focusing on the unmatched receiving reports and receiving reports prepared around year-end. Determine which invoices, if any, should be recorded by tracing them to the payables listing.
- Review the unmatched receiving reports and determine whether entries are recorded in the proper accounting period.
- Select a sample of cash disbursements from the accounting period following the balance sheet date. Vouch them to supporting documents (invoice, receiving report) to determine whether the related liabilities were recorded in the proper accounting period.
- Confirm accounts payable with vendors, especially those most likely to be understated (regular suppliers showing small or zero balances in the year-end accounts payable ledger). Unlike accounts receivable confirmations, accounts payable confirmations are not required by auditing standards. Such confirmations are not commonly used because they are primarily directed at the *existence* assertion, and the main concern regarding liabilities is *completeness.* However, accounts payable confirmations might be used under the following circumstances:
  - Internal controls are weak.
  - The company is in a tight cash position, and bill paying is slow.
  - Physical inventories exceed general ledger inventory balances by significant amounts.
  - Certain vendors do not send statements.
  - Vendor accounts are pledged by assets.
  - Vendor accounts include unusual transactions.
- Perform analytical procedures appropriate in the circumstances. In general, accounts payable volume and period-end balances should increase when the company experiences increases in physical production volume or engages in inventory stockpiling. Some liabilities can be functionally related to other activities; for example, sales taxes are functionally related to sales dollar totals, payroll taxes to payroll totals, excise taxes to sales dollars or volume, and income taxes to income.
- Purchase cutoff must be tested both at year-end and in conjunction with the observation of the physical inventory count. Receiving reports issued and unissued at the end of the period are examined and listed. Later, auditors check to ensure that the goods received on the issued reports are included in inventory and payables and to ensure that no goods are recorded for the unissued receiving reports.

A valuable source of testing for unrecorded liabilities involves testing open purchase orders and other unmatched receiving reports and vendor invoices, as described in the following sections.

Open Purchase Orders

Purchase orders are "open" from the time they are issued until all goods and services have been received. They are held in an *open purchase order file*. Generally, no liability exists until the transactions have been completed (i.e., the merchandise or services are received). However, auditors can find evidence of losses on purchase commitments in this file if market prices have fallen below the purchase price shown in purchase orders, as discussed in the following Auditing Insight, "Thinking Ahead".

AUDITING INSIGHT \ Thinking Ahead

Lone Moon Brewing purchased bulk aluminum sheets and manufactured its own cans. To ensure a source of raw materials supply, the company entered into a long-term purchase agreement for 6 million pounds of aluminum sheeting at 40 cents per pound. At the end of the year, it had purchased and used 1.5 million pounds, but the market price had fallen to 32 cents per pound. Lone Moon was on the hook for a $360,000 (4.5 million pounds at 8 cents) purchase commitment in excess of current market prices that should be recognized as a loss in the period.

Unmatched Receiving Reports

Liabilities should be recorded on the date the goods and services are received and accepted by the receiving department or by another responsible person. Sometimes, however, vendor invoices arrive later. In the meantime, the accounts payable department holds the purchase order and receiving reports *unmatched* with invoices, awaiting enough information to record an accounting entry. Auditors can inspect the unmatched receiving report file to determine whether the company has material unrecorded liabilities on the financial statement date for goods that were received but not matched to invoices.

Unmatched Vendor Invoices

Sometimes vendor invoices arrive in the accounts payable department before the receiving activity is complete. Such invoices are held *unmatched* with receiving reports, awaiting information that the goods and services were actually received and accepted. Auditors can inspect the *unmatched invoice file* and compare it with the *unmatched receiving report file* to determine whether liabilities that have been incurred are unrecorded. Systems failures and human coding errors can cause unmatched invoices and related unmatched receiving reports to sit around unnoticed when all of the information for recording a liability is actually in hand. Sometimes, however, unmatched invoices are indicators of fraudsters looking for an easy score, as noted in the following Auditing Insight, "Paying for Nothing".

AUDITING INSIGHT \ Paying for Nothing

A Toronto man received more than $7 million by mailing thousands of phony invoices to companies around the world. Emanuel Medeiros mailed fake "renewal notices" in the amount of $297.83 and received payments from more than 25,000 companies. Medeiros hired a commercial mailing company in New York to send out 200 to 400 bills stamped "RENEWAL" in large, bold letters every two weeks. The bills were sent in the name of two companies, Bradstreet International and Boom Global Media. One company tried to contact Boom to cancel the service. When the next bill arrived for twice the amount and threatened that the account would be turned over for collection, the company immediately sent a check for $595.66.

After receiving complaints, the U.S. Postal Service stopped the mailing, and after some communications, Medeiros agreed to come to New York. He pleaded guilty to fraud, agreed to pay $300,000, and was sentenced to 46 months in prison. In addition, the U.S. Attorney's Office in New York notified victim companies who may file for restitution.

Source: "Fake Invoices Net $7M and Four Years," *National Post,* January 29, 2009.

In addition to unmatched purchasing documents, several other client records provide the auditor with additional substantive evidence.

Accounts (Vouchers) Payable Trial Balance

This trial balance is a list of payable amounts by vendor, and the total should agree with the accounts payable control account. (Some organizations keep records by individual vouchers instead of vendor names, so the trial balance is a list of unpaid vouchers. The total still should agree with the control account balance.) The best type of trial balance for audit purposes is one that contains the names of all vendors with whom the organization has done business, even those whose balances are zero. The search for unrecorded liabilities should emphasize accounts with small and zero balances, especially for regular vendors, because these accounts can be the places where unrecorded liabilities may exist.

Purchases Journal

A list of all purchases may or may not be printed. It may exist only in a computer transaction file. In either event, it provides information for (1) the analysis of purchasing patterns that can exhibit characteristics of errors and frauds and (2) the sample selection of transactions for tests of controls. (A company could have already performed analyses of purchases that auditors can use for analytical procedures, provided the analyses are produced under reliable control activities.)

Fixed Asset Reports

Many large purchases are for fixed assets. Auditors should trace large purchases to the fixed asset reports and ensure that the details of fixed assets in control accounts are consistent with purchase orders. Furthermore, additions to fixed assets should be vouched to the purchasing documents to ensure that items were acquired in accordance with policy and procedure.

Additional procedures are included in a sample audit plan in Appendix 8B.

☑ REVIEW CHECKPOINTS

8.13 Where could an auditor look to find evidence of (a) losses on purchase commitments or (b) unrecorded liabilities to vendors?

8.14 List the management reports and computer files that can be used for audit evidence. What information in them can be useful to auditors?

8.15 How would substantive procedures for accounts payable be affected by (a) a low risk of material misstatement or (b) a high risk of material misstatement?

8.16 Describe the purpose and give examples of audit procedures in the search for unrecorded liabilities.

8.17 In substantive procedures, why is the emphasis on the *completeness* assertion for liabilities instead of on the *existence* assertion as in the audit of assets?

Other Expenditure Cycle Accounts

There are other accounts affected by the expenditure and acquisition cycle that the auditor needs to review. We have not covered inventory in this chapter because inventory is the main focus of Chapter 9.

Prepaid Expenses and Accrued Liabilities

Some of the other accounts affected by the acquisition and expenditure cycle are listed in Exhibit 8.1. Performing substantive procedures for cash and inventory accounts is

EXHIBIT 8.9 **Account Analysis for Prepaid Expenses**

		DUNDER-MIFFLIN INC. Prepaid Expenses For Year Ended 12/31/2023 Prepared by Client			E-1	
					Prepared by RJR	1/16/24
					Reviewed by TJL	1/18/24

Acct #	Account Title	(Audited) Balance 12/31/2022	Additions	Amortization/ Disposals	Unaudited Balance 12/31/2023
14100	Prepaid insurance	$706,148.66 PY	$941,531.55 v	$904,365.83 C X-10	$743,314.38
14200	Prepaid rent	190,000.00 PY	760,000.00 v	750,000.00 C X-11	200,000.00
14300	Office supplies	7,036.48 PY	26,025.00 v	25,654.66 C X-12	7,406.82
		$903,185.14 F	$1,727,556.55 F	$1,680,020.49 F	$950,721.20 CF F TB

PY = Agreed to prior-year documentation.
v = Vouched to policies or agreements and vendor invoice.
C = Calculated.
CF = Crossfooted.
F = Footed.
TB = Carried forward to the Trial Balance.

discussed in other chapters. Many accounts, particularly expense accounts, can be tested using analytical procedures, such as horizontal and vertical analyses. Other accounts such as prepaid expenses can be analyzed by a schedule similar to Exhibit 8.9. In addition to vouching payments, related expense accounts are cross-referenced to expense workpapers (X-10, 11, 12 in Exhibit 8.9). A sample audit plan for prepaid, deferred, and accrued expenses is shown in Appendix Exhibit 8B.2.

Accrued Income Taxes

Income taxes are a special audit area because the accounting and underlying federal tax laws are so complex. State and local tax differences add to the complexity. Approximately one-third of the first round of adverse opinions on internal controls under Sarbanes–Oxley requirements cited tax accounting control weaknesses.[4] In addition, income tax expense is one of the largest items on the income statement. *Accounting Standard Codification 740 (ASC 740)* requires companies to estimate deferred income tax assets and liabilities, both of which are very subjective. An important aspect of *ASC 740* requires a higher standard for tax benefits before they can be recognized in a company's financial statements. Public accounting firms normally include tax specialists on the audit team to assess tax liabilities and estimates. The procedures for auditing estimates (discussed in detail in Chapter 10) are generally followed, including evaluating controls over management's procedures for determining assumptions and calculating the amounts. Basic audit procedures are similar to those discussed for accrued liabilities: Auditors vouch payments, test the expense, and recalculate the liability. All tax returns and government communications are carefully reviewed. Income taxes can sometimes lead to material misstatements and PCAOB inspection deficiencies, as shown in the following PCAOB Inspection Focus.

[4]"Too Taxing" *CFO Magazine,* November 7, 2005.

PCAOB INSPECTION FOCUS — Accounting for Income Taxes

The PCAOB is required to perform detailed inspections of the audit process employed by each firm auditing publicly traded corporations. A formal inspection report is issued by the PCAOB for each firm inspected. In a recent inspection report, the PCAOB highlighted the importance of testing a client's accounting for income taxes:

- "The firm selected for testing a control that consisted of the issuer's review of the provision for income taxes, including the valuation of deferred tax assets. The firm did not evaluate the specific review procedures that the control owner performed to evaluate the reasonableness of the valuation of deferred tax assets. (AS 2201.42 and .44)"

- "The issuer recorded a partial valuation allowance against recorded deferred tax assets based on an estimate of forecasted taxable income that included the expected sale of a certain asset. The firm did not evaluate whether the issuer considered all available evidence, both positive and negative, and the reasonableness of the issuer's weighting of that evidence as it related to the valuation of the asset held for sale. (AS 2501.11)"

- "Unrelated to our review, the issuer reevaluated its accounting for the income tax provision and concluded that a material misstatement existed that had not been previously identified. The issuer subsequently restated its financial statements to correct this and other material misstatements, and the firm revised and reissued its report on the financial statements. The issuer also reevaluated its controls over the income tax provision and concluded that a material weakness existed that had not been previously identified. The issuer subsequently revised its report on ICFR to reflect this material weakness and the other material weaknesses discussed herein, and the firm modified its opinion on the effectiveness of the issuer's ICFR to express an adverse opinion and reissued its report."

Source: *Report on 2019 Inspection of Grant Thornton LLP.,* PCAOB, December 17, 2020.

Property, Plant, and Equipment and Intangible Assets

Management makes assertions about *existence, completeness, rights and obligations,* and *valuation and allocation.* Typical specific assertions relating to property, plant, and equipment (PP&E) and intangible assets include these:

- Recorded PP&E exist.
- All PP&E are recorded (completeness).
- PP&E are owned (rights).
- Freight-in is included as part of purchase and added to equipment costs (valuation).
- Purchased goodwill is properly valued (valuation).
- Goodwill is not impaired (valuation).
- Capitalized intangible costs relate to intangibles acquired in exchange transactions (existence).
- Amortization and depreciation expenses are properly allocated (valuation).
- Costs are appropriately distributed between Repair and maintenance expenses and capitalized PP&E (classification).
- Items listed in PP&E are used in operations (classification).

The two primary means of gathering evidence supporting management's assertions with respect to PP&E are physical inspection and vouching. The principal goal of the physical inspection of PP&E is to determine actual *existence* and condition of the property (*valuation*). The auditor should compare the inspection of equipment to the detailed PP&E records. Unlike current assets, most of the items in PP&E were also in the account in the previous year. Therefore, if the company was audited last year, the audit team can trace existing items to the previous-year audit documentation. The newly acquired PP&E can be vouched to invoices, purchase documents, or physically inspected (*existence, valuation*), and title documents (for items such as land, buildings) may be inspected (*rights and obligations*). Disposals of items that were on last year's list should also be traced to cash receipts records if they were sold or to other documentation if they were traded in, donated, or abandoned. Auditors also should prepare or obtain a schedule of casualty insurance on buildings and equipment and determine the adequacy of insurance in relation to asset market values. Auditors should always keep their eyes open for buildings or equipment not in use. Equipment not in use with no intention of being used in the future (e.g., held for disposal or sale) should not be included in PP&E.

EXHIBIT 8.10   Sample PP&E and Depreciation

<table>
<tr><td colspan="9">DUNDER-MIFFLIN INC.
Building and Land Improvements
For Year Ended 12/31/2023
Prepared By Client</td><td>F-1</td></tr>
</table>

	Prepared by RJR	2/18/24
	Reviewed by TJL	2/20/24

Description	Asset Cost ($)				Accumulated Depreciation ($)			
	Beginning Balance 12/31/2022	Added	Sold	Ending Balance 12/31/2023	Beginning Balance 12/31/2022	Depreciation Expense	Sold	Ending Balance
Building 1	$218,367 PY	$ 0	$ 0	$218,367	$54,591 PY	$10,918 C	$ 0	$65,509
Building 2	0	155,976 v	0	155,976	0	1,050 C	0	1,050
Building 1 improvements	149,737 PY	109,825 v	10,000 E	249,562	37,434 PY	10,232 C	2,500 C	45,166
Total buildings and improvements	$368,104	$265,801	$10,000	$623,905	$92,025	$22,200	$2,500	$111,725
	F	F	F	F/CF	F	F	F	F/CF

PY = Agreed to prior-year documentation.
C = Recalculated.
v = Vouched to purchase contract.
E = Examined sales agreement and related cash receipts.
F = Footed.
CF = Crossfooted.

The depreciation schedule is audited by recalculating the depreciation expense (*valuation or allocation*), using the company's methods, estimates of useful life, and estimates of residual value. Auditors also must evaluate the useful lives and residual values assigned by the client for reasonableness. Industry groups often publish tables of useful lives of assets commonly found in the industry. The asset acquisition and disposition information in the schedule gives auditors some key information for auditing the asset additions and disposals. When the schedule covers a large number of assets and numerous additions and disposals, auditors can use (1) CAATs to recalculate the depreciation expense and (2) sampling to choose additions and disposals for tests of controls and substantive procedures. See Exhibit 8.10 for an abbreviated illustration of audit documentation for PP&E and depreciation. Note that the ending balances of PP&E, accumulated depreciation, and depreciation expense are carried forward to the trial balance.

Although property, plant, and equipment are not usually considered as a high-risk audit areas, the PCAOB occasionally identifies deficiencies in the audits of long-lived assets, as shown in the following PCAOB Inspection Focus.

PCAOB INSPECTION FOCUS — Property, Plant and Equipment

The PCAOB is required to perform detailed inspections of the audit process employed by each firm auditing publicly traded corporations. A formal inspection report is issued by the PCAOB for each firm inspected. In a recent inspection report, the PCAOB highlighted the importance of testing property, plant, and equipment:

- "The firm selected for testing a control that included the issuer's review of possible impairment indicators for property, plant, and equipment at one of the issuer's subsidiaries. The firm did not evaluate (1) whether the control was appropriately designed to identify the impairment indicators that were present and (2) the review procedures that the control owner performed, including

the procedures to identify items for follow up and the procedures to determine whether those items were appropriately resolved. (AS 2201.42 and .44)"

- "In performing its substantive procedures related to the issuer's assessment of the possible impairment of this property, plant, and equipment, the firm did not evaluate the issuer's determination that there were no indicators of potential impairment beyond inquiring of management. (AS 2301.08)"

Source: *Report on 2019 Inspection of Grant Thornton LLP.*, PCAOB, December 17, 2020.

With respect to intangible assets, official documents of patents, copyrights, and trademark rights can be inspected to see that they are recorded in the client's name. Goodwill is of special interest to companies and auditors. The client must review goodwill for impairment, and the auditors must review and evaluate management's calculations and decisions to ensure that goodwill is correctly valued and impairments are properly recorded. These impairments are often extremely large as discussed in the following Auditing Insight, "How Good is Goodwill?". Amortization of other intangibles should be recalculated. Similar to depreciation expense, this expense owes its existence to a calculation, and recalculation based on audited costs and rates is sufficient appropriate audit evidence.

AUDITING INSIGHT · How Good Is Goodwill?

GAAP requires companies to consider whether Goodwill or specifically identifiable intangible assets have been impaired. Goodwill and intangible asset impairments can sometimes reach extremely large levels. According to Audit Analytics, during the 2020 and 2021 fiscal years, issuers recorded 58 Goodwill and intangible asset charges of over $1 billion! Among the companies taking intangible asset, impairment charges greater than $10 billion were **AT&T, Baker Hughes Co., Viatris, and Berkshire Hathaway, Inc.** These charges were material to the company and the audit. On average, these 58 impairment charges were equal to 35.5% of the total revenues recognized by the companies!

Source: Audit Analytics.

Auditors inquire of company counsel about knowledge of any lawsuits or defects relating to patents, copyrights, trademarks, or trade names. Questions about lawsuits challenging patents, copyrights, or trade names can produce early knowledge of problem areas for further investigation. Likewise, discussions and questions about research and development successes and failures can alert the audit team to problems of valuation of intangible assets and related amortization expenses. Responses to questions about licensing of patents can be used in the audit of related royalty revenue accounts. Auditors can confirm royalty income from patent licenses received from a single licensee and review licensing and royalty contracts. However, such income amounts usually are audited by vouching the licensee's reports and the related cash receipt.

Vouching may be extensive in the areas of research and development (R&D) and deferred software development costs. The principal evidence problem is to determine whether costs are properly classified as assets or as R&D expenses. Recorded amounts generally are selected on a sample basis and the purchase orders, receiving reports, payroll records, authorization notices, and management reports are compared with them. Some R&D costs can resemble non-R&D costs (such as supplies, payroll costs), so auditors must be very careful in the vouching to be alert for costs that appear to relate to other operations.

Merger and acquisition transactions should be reviewed in terms of the appraisals, judgments, and allocations used to assign portions of the purchase price to tangible assets, intangible assets, liabilities, and goodwill. In the final analysis, nothing really substitutes for the inspection of transaction documentation, but verbal inquiries can help auditors to understand the circumstances of a merger. An illustrative plan of substantive procedures for PP&E and related accounts can be found in Appendix Exhibit 8B.3.

Other Expenses

As mentioned earlier, most expense accounts can be tested in conjunction with tests of related assets and liabilities (e.g., depreciation) or through analytical procedures. However, if risk of material misstatement is high, expenses can be tested by **tests of details**, by which a sample of significant transactions is tested much like a test of controls except that auditors look for evidence that the significant transactions are properly recorded rather than that controls are operating. Payroll expense is usually audited by testing controls or using substantive tests of transactions and performing analytical procedures (see Appendix 8C). Some expenses should be examined separately because of their unique nature.

For example, the client should list legal and professional expenses, and significant amounts should be vouched so the auditors can determine what legal and professional services the client is using. Miscellaneous expenses likewise should be listed and examined for significant unusual items. Finally, maintenance and repairs should be examined to determine whether any items should be capitalized.

Presentation and Disclosure

Once auditors are satisfied that controls have been examined and significant transactions and balances have been appropriately tested, the job is not over. The accounts in the acquisition and expenditure cycle require many disclosures. Depreciation methods, asset impairments, leases, and details about income taxes are only a few of the essential items with specific presentation and disclosure requirements. These disclosures must ensure that the presentation and disclosure assertions of *occurrence and rights and obligations, completeness, classification and understandability,* and *accuracy and valuation* are all met.

☑ REVIEW CHECKPOINTS

8.18 How do audit procedures for prepaid expenses and accrued liabilities also provide audit evidence about related expense accounts?

8.19 What assertions found in PP&E, investments, and intangibles accounts are of interest to an auditor during the examination of the expenditure and acquisition cycle?

8.20 What columns in a client's PP&E and depreciation schedule are the most common focus of audit procedures?

8.21 What methods are used to audit other expense accounts?

AUDIT RISK MODEL APPLIED

LO 8-7
Apply your knowledge to perform audit procedures in the acquisition and expenditure cycle and evaluate the findings of your tests.

Now that the elements of risk of material misstatement for the acquisition and expenditure cycle as well as some of the important substantive procedures have been presented, let's examine how auditors might apply the audit risk model for the completeness and classification assertions.

Chi-Chi's Clothing Stores Inc. Example

Chi-Chi's Clothing Stores Inc. is a chain of women's clothing stores that sells upscale fashions, mostly in the northeastern United States. Chi-Chi's is a public company with annual sales increasing at a rate of almost 30 percent per year. David Escobar has been assigned as the senior auditor. The policy of his firm is to always set overall audit risk as low. Chi-Chi's accounting department and systems have not kept up with the rapid growth. As a result, numerous audit adjustments have been required every year, and the company received an adverse report on internal controls in the previous year. One problem has been that invoices do not come from the stores on a timely basis. The company has been very profitable, causing enormous increases in management stock options, which are a significant part of management compensation. Although the economy has taken a downturn, management and analyst forecasts still project a 30 percent growth rate. Escobar is concerned that management could be biased toward understating costs and liabilities and therefore sets inherent risk at high.

As mentioned, controls have not kept pace with company growth. Chi-Chi's has been working to improve the systems, but the accounting department and internal audit department are overworked. Their staff members have not had time to sufficiently test new systems or train new personnel. Thus, Escobar assesses control risk as high and plans to test only year-end controls sufficiently to comply with professional standards.

In this situation, Escobar believes he must set risk of material misstatement as high and set detection risk at low. He will perform an extensive search for unrecorded liabilities, examining a large sample of disbursements after the balance sheet date, and he will send confirmations to vendors that historically have had activity but have small or zero year-end balances. Escobar also will vouch a sample of additions to PP&E accounts to ensure they are not items that should be expensed. The combination of high inherent risk, high control risk, and low detection risk should lead Escobar to an acceptably low overall audit risk.

Finding Fraud Signs in Accounts Payable

In addition to errors that can occur as a result of weak controls, fraudsters can also have a field day generating false payments through a company's acquisition and expenditure systems. A common scheme is to send false invoices on the letterhead of a fictitious vendor to the company and have an insider manipulate supporting documents or controls to make payments. Sometimes, a company's own employees engage in unauthorized "business" as suppliers to their employers. In these cases, the perpetrators receive company payments from these "vendors" for personal use.

These frauds can proceed undetected for a long time as long as auditors and managers do not identify the signs and signals the perpetrators leave behind. If the review for fraud risk indicates that a potential significant risk of fraud exists in the acquisition and expenditure cycle, auditors can try several types of searches and matches in the company's records. These searches and matches are often performed using CAATs.

- *Inspect the invoices in the files for photocopies.* Fraudsters alter real invoices for false or duplicate payments and make photocopies to hide whiteout and cut-and-paste changes.
- *Inspect vendor's invoices submitted in numerical order.* False vendors sometimes use the same pad of prenumbered invoices (easily purchased at an office supply store) to send bills to the company. Either the company is the vendor's only customer, or the company is a victim of a false billing scheme.
- *Inspect vendor's invoices for invoices that always are in round numbers.* Prices, shipping charges, and taxes too often come in penny amounts, making a vendor's invoice in even dollars an unusual occurrence.
- *Scan vendor's invoices for invoices that are always slightly lower than a review threshold.* Insiders know that a company gives special attention and approval to invoices over a specified dollar amount (e.g., $10,000). Therefore, the fraudster always avoids invoices for more than that amount.
- *Scan vendor files for vendors with only post office box addresses.* Although many businesses use post office box addresses for receiving payments, files also should show a street address location.
- *Scan vendor invoices for invoices with no listed telephone number.* Legitimate businesses normally do not hide behind unlisted telephone numbers. In addition, cheap fraudsters sometimes do not buy a phone line for their false companies.
- *Match vendor and employee addresses and telephone numbers.* Many companies have policies that their employees cannot also be vendors. Insiders (employees) often know how to circumvent controls when their business with the employer could be suspicious.
- *Scan multiple vendors at the same address and telephone number.* Many invoices from the same location, especially invoices for different kinds of products and services, could simply come from a front organization conducting a false invoice scheme. However, legitimate suppliers often operate under several company names and conduct business from the same location and office parks with multiple offices at the same street address exist. This procedure can be done quickly with CAATs and is a red flag that should be investigated.
- *Vouch a sample of vendor invoices to the approved vendor list.* All vendors should be approved. If a company is doing business with a vendor not on the approved vendor

list, this relationship should be investigated. Look for names that are similar, but not the same. For example, the company may be doing business with Dan's Hardware Supply and a fraudster may submit invoices for Don's Hardware Service (an account the fraudster has established at a bank).

- *Review invoices for addresses of the local mail drops (e.g., shipping and packaging stores that accept client mail).* These stores provide a street address for fraudulent companies, adding false legitimacy to their fraudulent invoices. However, legitimate companies use these services as well. The use of such a mail drop is a red flag that needs further investigation.

☑ REVIEW CHECKPOINTS

8.22 What items could indicate a significant risk of fraud in the acquisition and expenditure cycle (i.e., be red flags)?

8.23 Describe the purpose and give examples of specific fraud detection procedures in the acquisition and expenditure cycle.

8.24 Are these specific fraud detection procedures designed to detect fraudulent financial reporting or misappropriation of assets? Explain.

FRAUD CASES: EXTENDED AUDIT PROCEDURES

The audit of account balances consists of making procedural efforts to detect errors and frauds that could exist in the balances, thus making them misleading in financial statements.

Case 8.1

Printing (Copying) Money

PROBLEM

Argus Productions Inc., a motion picture and commercial production company, assigned M. Welby the authority and responsibility for obtaining copies of scripts used in production. Established procedures permitted Welby to arrange for outside script-copying services, receive the copies, and approve the bills for payment. In effect, Welby was the "purchasing department" and the "receiving department" for this particular service. To a certain extent, he was also the "accounting department" by virtue of approving bills for payment and coding them for assignment to projects. Welby did not make the actual accounting entries or sign the checks.

Welby set up a fictitious company under the registered name **Quickprint Company** with himself as the incorporator and stockholder complete with a post office box number, letterhead stationery, and nicely printed invoices but no printing equipment. Legitimate copy services were "subcontracted" by Quickprint to perform the actual printing and then billed Quickprint. Welby then prepared Quickprint invoices billing Argus, usually at the legitimate shop's rate, but for a few extra copies each time. Welby also submitted Quickprint bills to Argus for fictitious copying jobs on scripts for movies and commercials that never went into production. As the owner of Quickprint, Welby endorsed Argus's checks with a rubber stamp and deposited the money in the business bank account, paid the legitimate printing bills, and took the rest for personal use.

Argus's production cost files contained all of the Quickprint bills sorted under the names of the movie and commercial production projects. Welby even created files for proposed films that never went into full production and thus should not have had script-copying costs. There were no copying service bills from any shop other than Quickprint Company.

Welby conducted this fraud for five years, embezzling $475,000 in false and inflated billings. (Argus's net income was overstated a modest amount because copying costs were capitalized as part of production cost and then amortized over a two- to three-year period.)

AUDIT APPROACH

Management should assign the authority to request copies and the purchasing authority to different responsible employees. Other persons also should perform the accounting, including coding cost assignments to projects. Managerial review of production results could result in notice of excess costs.

The request for the quantity (number) of copies of a script should come from a person involved in production who knows the number needed. This person also should sign off for the receipt (or approve the bill) for this requested number of copies, thus acting as the "receiving department." This procedure could prevent waste (excess cost), especially if the requesting person also were held responsible for the profitability of the project. A company agent always performs actual purchasing, and in this case, the agent was Welby. Purchasing agents generally have latitude to seek the best service at the best price with or without bids from competitors. A requirement to obtain bids is usually a good idea, but much legitimate purchasing is done without bid. However, an approval process should be employed before vendors are placed on the approved vendor list.

Someone in the accounting department should be responsible for coding invoices for charges to authorized projects, thus making it possible to detect costs charged to projects not actually in production. Someone with managerial responsibility should review project costs and the purchasing practices. However, this is an expensive use of executive time. It was not spent in the Argus case.

In gaining an understanding of the internal controls, auditors could learn of the trust and responsibility vested in Welby. Because the embezzlement was about $95,000 per year, the total copying cost under Welby's control must have been around $1 million or more. (It might attract unwanted attention to inflate a cost more than 10 percent.)

Controls were very weak, especially in the combination of duties performed by Welby and in the lack of managerial review. For all practical purposes, there were no controls to test other than to see whether Welby had approved the copying cost bills and coded them to active projects. This provides an opportunity because proper classification is a control objective.

The auditors should select a sample of project files and vouch costs charged to them to support source documents (*occurrence* direction of the test). Select a sample of expenditures and trace them to the project cost records shown coded on the expenditures (*completeness* direction of the test).

Substantive procedures are directed at obtaining evidence about the *existence* of film projects, *completeness* of the costs charged to them, *valuation* of the capitalized project costs, *rights* in copyright and ownership, and proper *disclosure* of amortization methods. The most important procedures are the same as the tests of control activities; thus, when performed at the year-end date on the capitalized cost balances, they are dual-purpose audit procedures. Either of the procedures described earlier as tests of controls should show evidence of projects that had never gone into production. (Auditors should be careful to obtain a list of actual projects before they begin the procedures.) Chances are good that the discovery of bad project codes with copying cost will reveal a pattern of Quickprint bills.

Knowing that controls over copying cost are weak, auditors could be tipped off to the possibility of a Welby–Quickprint connection. Efforts to locate Quickprint should be taken (telephone book, chamber of commerce, other directories). Inquiry with the secretary of state for names of the Quickprint incorporators should reveal Welby's connection. The audit findings can then be turned over to a trained investigator to arrange an interview and confrontation with Welby.

DISCOVERY SUMMARY

In this case, internal auditors performed a review of project costs at the request of the manager of production, who was worried about profitability. The auditors performed the procedures described earlier, noticed the dummy projects and the Quickprint bills, investigated the ownership of Quickprint, and discovered Welby's association. They had first tried to locate Quickprint's shop but could not find it in the telephone, chamber of commerce, or other city directories. They were careful not to direct any mail to the post office box for fear of alerting the then-unknown parties involved. A sly internal auditor already had used a ruse at the post office and learned that Welby rented the box, but the auditors did not know whether anyone else was involved. Alerted, the internal auditors gathered all Quickprint bills and determined the total charged for nonexistent projects. Carefully, under the covert observation of a representative of the local district attorney's office, Welby was interviewed and readily confessed.

Case 8.2

Real Cash Paid to Phony Doctors

PROBLEM

As manager of the medical claims processing department, Martha Lee was considered one of Beta Magnetic's best employees. She had never missed a day of work in 10 years, and her department had one of the company's best efficiency ratings. Controls were considered good, including the verification by a claims processor that (1) the patient was a Beta employee, (2) medical treatments were covered in the plan, (3) the charges were within approved guidelines, (4) the cumulative claims for the employee did not exceed $50,000 (paid all claims less than $50,000 but submitted claims more than $50,000 to an insurance company), and (5) the calculation for payment was correct. After verification processing, claims were sent to the claims payment department to pay the doctor directly. No payments ever went directly to employees.

Lee prepared false claims on real employees, forging the signatures of various claims processors, adding her own review approval, and naming bogus doctors who would be paid by the payment department. The payments were mailed to various post office box addresses and to her husband's business address.

Nobody ever verified claims information with the employees. The employees received no reports of medical benefits paid on their behalf. Although the department had performance reports by claims processors, these reports did not show claim-by-claim details. No one verified the credentials of the doctors. As noted, Martha never missed a day of work for vacation or sickness. She was considered an ideal employee.

The falsified claim forms were in Beta's files, containing all fictitious data on employee names, processor signatures, doctors' bills, and phony doctors and addresses. The canceled checks were returned by the bank and were kept in Beta's files, containing "endorsements" by the doctors. Lee and her husband were clever: They deposited the checks in various banks in accounts opened in the names of the "doctors."

Lee did not stumble on the audit trail. She drew the attention of an auditor who saw her take her 24 claims processing employees out to an annual staff appreciation luncheon in a fleet of stretch limousines.

Over the seven years, Lee and her husband had stolen $3.5 million, and until the last, no one noticed anything unusual about the total amount of claims paid.

AUDIT APPROACH

The controls were good as far as they went. The claims processors used internal data in their work: employee files for identification, treatment descriptions submitted by doctors with comparisons with plan provisions, and mathematical calculations. This work amounted to all approval necessary for the claims payment department to prepare a check. No controls connected the claims data with outside sources such as employee acknowledgment or doctor investigation. Employees certainly should be notified of any payments made on their behalf.

By never taking a day off, Lee was able to make sure she saw all documents related to her scheme. The company needed an enforced vacation and employee rotation policy.

The processing and control work in the claims payment department can be audited for deviations from controls. The auditors should select a sample of paid claims and reperform the claims processing procedures to verify the employee status, coverage of treatment, proper guideline charges, cumulative amount of less than $50,000, and accurate calculation. However, this procedure would not help answer the question, "Does Martha Lee steal the money to pay for the limousines?"

"Thinking like a crook" points out the holes in the controls. Nobody seeks to verify data with external sources. However, the audit team must be careful in an investigation not to cast aspersions on a manager by letting rumors start when interviewing employees to find out whether they actually had the medical attention whose claim is paid on their behalf. If money is being taken, the company check must be intercepted in some manner.

The balance under audit is the sum of the charges in the employee medical benefits expense account, and the objective relates to the valid existence of the payments.

The first procedure can be as follows: Obtain a list of doctors paid by the company and look them up in the state medical society directory. Look up their business addresses and determine whether they are valid. You could try comparing claims processors' signatures on various forms, but this is difficult and requires training. An extended procedure would be as follows: Compare the doctors' addresses to addresses known to be associated with Lee and other claims processing employees.

DISCOVERY SUMMARY

The comparison of doctors to the medical society directory showed eight "doctors" who were not licensed in the current period. Five of these eight had post office box addresses, and discrete inquiries and surveillance showed that Lee rented them. The other three had the same mailing address as her husband's business. Further investigation involving the district attorney and police was necessary to obtain personal financial records and reconstruct the thefts from prior years.

☑ REVIEW CHECKPOINTS

8.25 What key control concept was missing at Argus Productions?

8.26 What evidence could the *verbal inquiry* audit procedure provide in "Printing (Copying) Money"?

8.27 If Lee had not been seen taking employees out in a limousine, how else could she have been caught?

8.28 How would a policy of mandatory vacations have helped discover the Beta fraud?

Summary

The acquisition and expenditure cycle consists of purchase requisitioning, purchase ordering, receiving goods and services, recording vendors' invoices, recording accounts payable, and making cash disbursements. Companies reduce control risk by having a suitable separation of authorization, custody, recording, and periodic reconciliation duties. Error-checking procedures requiring the comparison of purchase orders, receiving reports, and vendor invoices are important for recording proper amounts of accounts payable liabilities. Having a separation of duties between preparing cash disbursement checks and actually signing them provides supervisory control. Otherwise, many things—ranging from processing false or fictitious purchase orders to failing to record liabilities for goods and services received—could go wrong.

Purchases are executed for a myriad of items, including inventory; property, plant, and equipment; supplies; and all other items necessary for a business to operate. Large purchases for capital equipment may be significant items requiring the auditors' inspection and review. Reviewing the accruals for income taxes may be complex, especially if the organization is operating in multiple tax jurisdictions. The use of a tax specialist may be appropriate in auditing income tax expense.

The *completeness* assertion is important in the audit of liabilities because misleading financial statements often have involved unrecorded liabilities and expenses. The search for unrecorded liabilities is an important set of audit procedures.

Key Terms

approved vendor list: A record of vendors that have been vetted to ensure that they meet company policy and procedure in terms of price, quality, delivery, and so on. This control activity provides evidence of vendor existence to auditors, 324

bill of lading: A contract between the shipper and the carrier; includes shipping information such as ship dates and origination, purchase order number, and signatures for receipt of merchandise, 325

clearing accounts [Appendix 8C]: The temporary storage places for transactions awaiting final accounting that should eventually have zero balances, 372

ghost employees [Appendix 8C]: The fictitious or separated employees fraudulently maintained on the payroll to obtain checks, 371

imprest bank account [Appendix 8C]: An account used for special purposes such as payroll or branch banking that is maintained at a zero or fixed balance in the general ledger. Checks written on the account are offset by deposits of the same amount, 372

purchase order: A formal contractual document (may be a computer document) between a buyer and seller issued by the buyer establishing price, delivery point, delivery dates, and other information pertinent to the purchase, 324

purchase requisition: An internal document initialed by a department or person within the entity asking the purchasing department to buy specific goods or services, 324

receiving report: The documentation completed by the receiving department that includes receiving date and time, purchase order number, condition of material received, and amount of material received; provides evidence regarding the receipt of materials by the entity, 325

search for unrecorded liabilities: A substantive procedure to test the completeness assertion for liability accounts, 338

tests of details: The tests of a sample of transactions during the period for monetary errors, 344

vendor's invoice: A bill sent from the vendor to the entity purchasing the goods or services, 325

voucher/voucher package: A document used as a source for recording payables. It shows approvals, accounts, and amounts to be recorded, usually attached to the supporting purchase order, receiving report, and vendor invoice, 325

W-2 [Appendix 8C]: The annual report of gross salaries and wages and the income, Social Security, and Medicare taxes withheld, 373

Multiple-Choice Questions for Practice and Review

All applicable Exercises and Problems are available with *Connect*.

LO 8-1

8.29   Which of the following accounts does *not* appear in the acquisition and expenditure cycle?

   a. Cash.

   b. Purchases returns.

   c. Sales returns.

   d. Prepaid insurance.

LO 8-1

8.30   For which of the following accounts would the matching concept be the most appropriate?

   a. Cost of goods sold.

   b. Research and development.

   c. Depreciation expense.

   d. Sales.

LO 8-1

8.31   An audit team was testing source documents in the purchasing cycle and identified the following circumstances. Which of the following would be the most indicative of source document fraud?

   a. The same purchase order number appears on two invoices from the same vendor.

   b. The same item code appears on different invoices from the same vendor.

   c. The same invoice number appears on different invoices from the same vendor.

   d. The same invoice date appears on different invoices from the same vendor.

LO 8-1

8.32   Which of the following would *not* overstate current-period net income?

   a. Capitalizing an expenditure that should be expensed.

   b. Failing to record a liability as an expense.

   c. Failing to record a check paying an item in Vouchers Payable.

   d. All of the above would overstate net income.

LO 8-2   8.33 A client's purchasing system ends with the recording of a liability and its eventual payment. Which of the following best describes the control objective that auditors are most interested in when performing tests of liabilities?

a. Accounts payable are not materially understated.

b. Authority to incur liabilities is restricted to one designated person.

c. Acquisition of materials is not made from one vendor or one group of vendors.

d. Commitments for all purchases are made only after established competitive bidding procedures are followed.

LO 8-3   8.34 An audit firm is testing controls within the purchasing cycle. In which of the following procedures would the firm most likely apply sampling techniques?

a. Risk assessment procedures performed to obtain an understanding of internal control in the purchasing cycle.

b. Tests of automated application controls involving check amount limits when effective information technology general controls are present.

c. Analyses of controls to determine the appropriate segregation of duties in the purchasing cycle.

d. Testing of operating effectiveness of controls over authorization of purchase orders.

LO 8-3   8.35 Which of the following results of analytical procedures would most likely indicate possible unrecorded liabilities?

a. Current ratio of 3:1 as compared to 6:1 for the prior period.

b. Percentage of accounts payable to total liabilities 30% during the current year compared with 40% in the prior year.

c. Accounts payable turnover of 4, compared to 8 for the prior period.

d. Accounts payable balance increase greater than 10 percent over the prior period.

(AICPA adapted)

LO 8-4   8.36 Which of the following is an internal control activity that could prevent a paid disbursement voucher from being presented for payment a second time?

a. Vouchers should be prepared by individuals who are responsible for signing disbursement checks.

b. Disbursement vouchers should be approved by at least two responsible management officials.

c. The date on a disbursement voucher should be within a few days of the date the voucher is presented for payment.

d. The official who signs the check should compare the check with the voucher and should stamp "PAID" on the voucher documents.

LO 8-4   8.37 Budd, the purchasing agent of Lake Hardware Wholesalers, has a relative who owns a retail hardware store. Budd arranged for hardware to be delivered by manufacturers to the retail store on a cash-on-delivery (C.O.D.) basis, thereby enabling his relative to buy at Lake's wholesale prices. Budd was probably able to accomplish this because of Lake's poor internal control over

a. Purchase requisitions.

b. Cash receipts.

c. Perpetual inventory records.

d. Purchase orders.

LO 8-6   8.38 Which of the following is the *best* audit procedure for determining the existence of unrecorded liabilities?

a. Examine confirmation requests returned by creditors whose accounts are on a subsidiary trial balance of accounts payable.

b. Examine a sample of cash disbursements in the period subsequent to year-end.

c. Examine a sample of invoices a few days prior to and subsequent to the year-end to ascertain whether they have been properly recorded.

d. Examine unusual relationships between monthly accounts payable and recorded purchases.

LO 8-6 8.39 Which of the following procedures is *least* likely to be performed before the balance-sheet date?

    a. Observation of inventory.

    b. Review of internal control over cash disbursements.

    c. Search for unrecorded liabilities.

    d. Confirmation of receivables.

LO 8-6 8.40 To determine whether accounts payable are complete, auditors perform a test to verify that all merchandise received has been recorded. The population for this test consists of all

    a. Vendors' invoices.

    b. Purchase orders.

    c. Receiving reports.

    d. Canceled checks.

(AICPA adapted)

LO 8-6 8.41 When verifying debits to the perpetual inventory records of a nonmanufacturing company, auditors would be most interested in examining a sample of purchase

    a. Approvals.

    b. Requisitions.

    c. Invoices.

    d. Orders.

LO 8-4 8.42 A furniture company ordered 84 tables from a supplier. The supplier accidentally sent only 48 tables, but the receiving department at the furniture company accepted the tables. The invoice was eventually received but was for the original 84 tables. The furniture company paid the entire amount. Which of the following controls would have been *least* likely to have prevented this erroneous payment?

    a. The copy of the purchase order sent to the furniture company's receiving department should not have shown an expected quantity.

    b. Personnel in the furniture company's accounts payable department should compare the receiving report to the purchase invoice before creation of the voucher.

    c. Personnel in the furniture company's cash disbursements department should compare the check that is prepared to all of the backup documentation.

    d. Personnel in the furniture company's purchasing department should compare the purchase requisition with the purchase order.

LO 8-4 8.43 Curtis, a maintenance supervisor, submitted maintenance invoices from a phony repair company and received the checks at a post office box. This should have been prevented by

    a. Comparison of the company name to the approved vendor list by the check signer.

    b. Recognition of the excess maintenance costs by Curtis's supervisor.

    c. Refusal by the purchasing department to approve the vendor.

    d. All of the above.

LO 8-6 8.44 An audit team would most likely examine the detail support for charges to which of the following accounts?

    a. Payroll expense.

    b. Cost of goods sold.

    c. Supplies expense.

    d. Legal expense.

LO 8-6 8.45 Which of the following accounts would most likely be audited in connection with a related balance-sheet account?

    a. Property tax expense.

    b. Payroll expense.

    c. Research and development.

    d. Legal expense.

LO 8-6

8.46 When auditing account balances of liabilities, auditors are most concerned with management's assertion about

    a. Existence.

    b. Rights and obligations.

    c. Completeness.

    d. Valuation and allocation.

LO 8-5

8.47 In a test of controls, auditors may trace receiving reports to vouchers recorded in the voucher register. This is a test for

    a. Occurrence.

    b. Completeness.

    c. Classification.

    d. Cutoff.

LO 8-4

8.48 A company employs three accounts payable clerks and one treasurer. Their responsibilities are as follows:

Employee	Responsibility
Clerk 1	Reviews vendor invoices for proper signature approval.
Clerk 2	Enters vendor invoices into the accounting system and verifies payment terms.
Clerk 3	Posts entered vendor invoices to the accounts payable ledger for payment and mails checks.
Treasurer	Reviews the vendor invoices and signs each check.

Which of the following would indicate a weakness in the company's internal control?

    a. Clerk 1 opens all of the incoming mail.

    b. Clerk 2 reconciles the accounts payable ledger with the general ledger monthly.

    c. Clerk 3 mails the checks and remittances after they have been signed.

    d. The treasurer uses a stamp for signing checks.

                                                                (AICPA adapted)

LO 8-6

8.49 Which of the following tests of details most likely would help an auditor determine whether accounts payable have been misstated?

    a. Examining reported purchase returns that appear too low.

    b. Examining vendor statements for amounts not reported as purchases.

    c. Searching for customer-returned goods that were not reported as returns.

    d. Reviewing bank transfers recorded as cash received from customers.

                                                                 (AICPA adapted)

Exercises and Problems

 All applicable questions are available with *Connect*

LO 8-1, LO 8-2, LO 8-5

8.50 **Payable ICQ Items: Assertions, Tests of Controls, and Possible Errors or Frauds.** Following is a selection of items from internal control questionnaires.

    1. Are purchase orders above a certain level approved by an officer?

    2. Are the quantity and quality of goods received determined at the time of receipt by receiving personnel independent of the purchasing department?

    3. Are vendors' invoices matched against purchase orders and receiving reports before a liability is recorded?

    4. Are journal entries authorized at appropriate levels?

Required:

For each preceding item

    a. Identify the management assertion to which it applies.

b. Specify one test of controls auditors could use to determine whether the control was operating effectively.

c. Give an example of an error or fraud that could occur if the control were absent or ineffective.

d. Specify a substantive procedure that could find errors or frauds that could result from the absence or ineffectiveness of the control items.

LO 8-6

8.51 **Unrecorded Liabilities Procedures.** You are in the final stages of your audit of the financial statements of Ozine Corporation for the year ended December 31, 2023, when the corporation's president consults you. The president believes there is no point to your examining the 2024 voucher register and testing data in support of 2024 entries. She stated that any bills pertaining to 2023 that were received too late to be included in the December voucher register were recorded by a year-end journal entry and the internal auditor tested for unrecorded liabilities after the year-end. The president will provide you a letter certifying that there are no unrecorded liabilities.

Required:

a. Should your procedures for unrecorded liabilities be affected by the fact that the client made a journal entry to record 2023 bills that were received later? Explain.

b. Should your test for unrecorded liabilities be affected by the fact that a letter is obtained in which a responsible management official certifies that, to the best of that person's knowledge, all liabilities have been recorded? Explain.

c. Should your test for unrecorded liabilities be eliminated or reduced because of the internal audit work? Explain.

d. What sources, in addition to the 2024 voucher register, should you consider for locating possible unrecorded liabilities?

(AICPA adapted)

LO 8-3, LO 8-6

8.52 **Accounts Payable Confirmations.** Partners Clark and Kent, both CPAs, are preparing their audit plan for the audit of accounts payable on Marlboro Corporation's annual audit. Saturday afternoon they reviewed the thick file of last year's documentation, and they both remembered too well the six days they spent last year on accounts payable.

Last year, Clark had suggested that they mail confirmations to 100 of Marlboro's suppliers. The company regularly purchases from about 1,000 suppliers, and these account payable balances fluctuate widely, depending on the volume of purchase and the terms Marlboro's purchasing agent is able to negotiate. Clark's sample of 100 was designed to include accounts with large balances. In fact, the 100 accounts confirmed last year covered 80 percent of the total dollars in accounts payable. Both Clark and Kent had spent many hours tracking down minor differences reported in confirmation responses. Nonresponding accounts were investigated by comparing Marlboro's balance with monthly statements received from suppliers.

Required:

a. Identify the accounts payable audit objectives that auditors must consider in determining the audit procedures to be performed.

b. Identify situations when auditors should use accounts payable confirmations, and discuss whether they are required to use them.

c. Discuss why the use of large dollar balances as the basis for selecting accounts payable for confirmation is not the most effective approach, and indicate a more effective sample selection procedure that could be followed when choosing accounts payable for confirmation.

LO 8-6

8.53 **Search for Unrecorded Liabilities.** C. Marsh, CPA, is the independent auditor for Compufast Corporation, which sells personal computers, peripheral equipment (printers, data storage), and a wide variety of programs for business and games. From experience on Compufast's previous audits, Marsh knew that the company's accountants were very much concerned with timely recording of revenues and receivables and somewhat less concerned with keeping up-to-date records of accounts payable and other liabilities. Marsh knew that the control environment was strong in the asset area and weak in the liability area.

Required:

List substantive procedures that Marsh and the audit staff can perform to obtain reasonable assurance that Compufast's unrecorded liabilities are discovered and adjusted in the financial statements currently under audit.

LO 8-4, LO 8-5, LO 8-6

8.54 **Fictitious Vendors, Theft, and Embezzlement.** The following case is designed like the ones in the chapter. Your assignment is to write the audit approach portion of the cases organized around these sections:

Objective. Express the objective in terms of the facts supposedly asserted in financial records, accounts, and statements.

Control. Write a brief explanation of desirable controls, missing controls, and especially the kinds of "deviations" that could arise from the situation described in the case.

Tests of controls. Write some procedures for getting evidence about existing controls, especially procedures that could discover deviations from controls. If there are no controls to test, then there are no procedures to perform; go to the next section. A "procedure" should instruct someone about the source(s) of evidence to tap and the work to do.

Audit of balance. Write some procedures for getting evidence about the existence, completeness, valuation or allocation, or rights and obligations assertions identified in your objective section.

Discovery summary. Write a short statement about the discovery you expect to accomplish with your procedures.

Bailey Books Inc. is a retail distributor of upscale books, periodicals, and magazines. Bailey has 431 retail stores throughout the southeastern states. Three full-time purchasing agents work at corporate headquarters. They are responsible for purchasing all inventory at the best prices available from wholesale suppliers. They can purchase with or without obtaining competitive bids. The three purchasing agents are R. McGuire in charge of purchasing books, M. Garza in charge of purchasing magazines and periodicals, and L. Collins (manager of purchasing) in charge of ordering miscellaneous items such as paper products and store supplies.

One of the purchasing agents is suspected of taking kickbacks from vendors. In return, Bailey is thought to be paying inflated prices, which first are recorded in inventory and then in cost of goods sold and other expense accounts as the assets are sold or used.

The duties of Collins, the manager in charge, do not include audit or inspection of the performance of the other two purchasing agents. No one audits or reviews Collins's performance.

The purchasing system is computerized and detail records are retained. An extract from these records is in the exhibit on the next page.

This kickback scheme has been going on for two or three years. Bailey Books could have overpaid by several hundred thousand dollars.

(ACFE adapted)

LO 8-1, LO 8-4

8.55 **Bidding Process.** Maine Construction builds office buildings. The buildings generally cost between $5 million and $8 million to build, and the plumbing can cost between $300,000 and $600,000 depending on the building requirements. Therefore, Maine always sends the plumbing work out for bid before deciding on whom to use as a subcontractor. The company has had 21 projects over the past five years with $10 million dollars in plumbing contracts being sent out for bids.

Over the past five years, Maine has asked for bids from three contractors: Beltran Plumbing, Delgado Plumbing Services, and Wright Contracting–Plumbing Specialists. Each vendor has been reviewed by Maine and is on Maine's approved vendor list.

Required:

For each of the following situations (each situation is independent), determine whether the auditor should be concerned about the controls over the bidding process. If yes, what control would you recommend to Maine to ensure a fair and honest bidding process?

a. Of the 21 projects sent out for bid, Wright had the winning bid on 12 of the projects.

b. Of the 21 projects sent out for bid, Wright had the winning bid on 12 of the projects. In each of these bidding processes, Wright's bid was the last bid received.

c. Of the 21 projects sent out for bid, each vendor had the winning bid on 7 of the projects.

d. Of the 21 projects sent out for bid, Delgado was awarded 5 contracts even though he did not have the lowest bid.

BAILEY BOOKS, INC

Selected Purchases 2021–2023

Vendor	Items Purchased	2021	2022	2023	Date of Last Bid	Percent of Purchases Bid (3-yr. period)
Armour	Books	$ 83,409	$402,929	$ 810,103	12/01/16	87%
Burdick	Sundries	62,443	70,949	76,722	—	—
Canon	Magazines	1,404,360	1,947,601	2,361,149	11/03/18	94
DeBois, Inc.	Paper	321,644	218,404	121,986	06/08/18	57
Elton Books	Books	874,893	781,602	649,188	07/21/18	91
Fergeson	Books	921,666	1,021,440	1,567,811	09/08/18	88
Guyford	Magazines	2,377,821	2,868,988	3,262,490	10/08/18	81
Hyman, Inc.	Supplies	31,640	40,022	46,911	10/22/18	—
Intertec	Books	821,904	898,683	949,604	11/18/18	86
Jerrico	Paper	186,401	111,923	93,499	10/04/18	72
Julian-Borg	Magazines	431,470	589,182	371,920	02/07/18	44
King Features	Magazines	436,820	492,687	504,360	11/18/18	89
Lycorp	Sundries	16,280	17,404	21,410	—	—
Medallian	Books	—	61,227	410,163	12/15/18	99
Northwood	Books	861,382	992,121	—	12/07/17	—
Orion Corp.	Paper	86,904	416,777	803,493	11/02/17	15
Peterson	Supplies	114,623	—	—	N/A	N/A
Quick	Supplies	—	96,732	110,441	11/03/18	86
Robertson	Books	2,361,912	3,040,319	3,516,811	12/01/18	96
Steele	Magazines	621,490	823,707	482,082	11/03/18	90
Telecom	Sundries	81,406	101,193	146,316	—	—
Union Bay	Books	4,322,639	4,971,682	5,368,114	12/03/18	97
Victory	Magazines	123,844	141,909	143,286	06/09/18	89
Williams	Sundries	31,629	35,111	42,686	—	—

LO 8-7

8.56 **Grounds for Dismissal.** This case is designed like the ones in the chapter. Your assignment is to write the "audit approach" portion of the case organized around these sections:

Objective. Express the objective in terms of the facts supposedly asserted in financial records, accounts, and statements.

Control. Write a brief explanation of desirable controls, missing controls, and especially the types of "deviations" that might arise from the situation described in the case.

Tests of controls. Write some audit procedures for getting evidence about existing controls, especially procedures that could discover deviations from controls. If there are no controls to test, then there are no procedures to perform; go to the next section. A "procedure" should instruct someone about the source(s) of evidence to tap and the work to do.

Audit of balance. Write some procedures for getting evidence about the existence, completeness, valuation or allocation, or rights and obligations assertions identified in your objective section.

Discovery summary. Write a short statement about the discovery you expect to accomplish with your procedures.

A. Doe, IT application manager for The Coffee Company, signed a consulting services agreement with Fictitious Consulting Company (FCC). Doe was required to obtain written approval of the contract from a supervisor but forged the supervisor's signature. More than 100 invoices came in, which were approved with Doe's initials. Even though Doe's approval authority was only $5,000, many of the invoices were for more than $40,000.

FCC was not registered in the state or listed in telephone directories. The phone number was for a cell phone registered to Doe, and the mailing address was a post office box. When Doe's supervisor asked to meet the FCC consultants, Doe was evasive, saying they "had just left" or "they were working away from the office." Ultimately, Doe told her supervisor that she had dismissed FCC, but she simply moved the charges to capital accounts that the supervisor did not monitor.

The Coffee Co. paid more than $3.7 million to FCC between December 1999 and August 2000. (*Source:* M. Atkinson and M. Biliske, "Grounds for Dismissal," *Internal Auditor,* February 2005.)

LO 8-6, LO 8-7

8.57 **Audit the PP&E and Depreciation Schedule.** Bart's Company has prepared the PP&E and depreciation schedule shown at the bottom of this page.

The following information is available. Assume the beginning balance has been audited

- The land was purchased eight years ago when building 1 was erected. The location was then remote but now is bordered by a major freeway. The appraised value of the land is $35 million.
- Building 1 has an estimated useful life of 35 years and no residual value.
- Building 2 was built by a local contractor this year. It also has an estimated useful life of 35 years and no residual value. The company occupied it on May 1 this year.
- Computer A system was purchased on January 1 six years ago when the estimated useful life was eight years with no residual value. It was sold on May 1 for $500,000.
- Computer B system was placed in operation as soon as Computer A system was sold. It is estimated to be in use for six years with no residual value at the end.
- The company estimated the useful life of the press at 20 years with no residual value.
- Auto 1 was sold during the year for $1,000.
- Auto 2 was purchased on July 1. The company expects to use it for five years and then sell it for $2,000.
- All depreciation is calculated on the straight-line method using months of service.

Required:

a. Verify the depreciation calculations. Are there any errors? Put the errors in the form of an adjusting journal entry, assuming that 90 percent of the depreciation on the buildings and the press has been charged to Cost of Goods Sold and 10 percent is still capitalized in the inventory, and the other depreciation expense is classified as General and Administrative Expense (i.e., building and press depreciation is considered a product cost; inventory on hand includes 10 percent of the depreciation expense for buildings and the press: $180,700; Cost of Goods Sold contains the other 90 percent: $1,626,300).

b. List two audit procedures for auditing the additions to PP&E.

c. What will auditors expect to find in the Gain and Loss on Sale of Assets account? What amount of cash flow from investing activities will be in the statement of cash flows?

PP&E and Depreciation

| Description | Asset Cost (000s) | | | | Accumulated Depreciation (000s) | | | |
	Beginning Balance	Added	Sold	Ending Balance	Beginning Balance	Added	Sold	Ending Balance
Land	$10,000			$10,000				
Building 1	30,000			30,000	$ 6,857	$ 857		$7,714
Building 2		42,000		42,000		800		800
Computer A	5,000		5,000	0	3,750	208	3,958	0
Computer B		3,500		3,500		583		583
Press	1,500		1,500		300	150		450
Auto 1	15		15	0	15		15	0
Auto 2		22		22		2		2
Total	$46,515	$45,522	$5,015	$87,022	$10,922	$2,600	$3,973	$9,549

LO 8-2, LO 8-6

8.58   **PP&E Assertions and Substantive Procedures.** This question contains three items that are management assertions about property and equipment. Following them are several substantive procedures for obtaining evidence about management's assertions.

Assertions

1. The entity has legal right to property and equipment acquired during the year.
2. Recorded property and equipment represent assets that actually exist at the balance-sheet date.
3. Net property and equipment are properly valued at the balance-sheet date.

Substantive Procedures

a. Trace opening balances in the summary schedules to the prior-year audit documentation.
b. Review the provision for depreciation expense and determine whether depreciable lives and methods used in the current year are consistent with those used in the prior year.
c. Determine whether the responsibility for maintaining the property and equipment records is separated from the responsibility for custody of property and equipment.
d. Examine deeds and title insurance certificates.
e. Perform cutoff tests to verify that property and equipment additions are recorded in the proper period.
f. Determine whether property and equipment are adequately insured.
g. Physically examine all major property and equipment additions.

Required:

For each of the three assertions (1, 2, and 3), select the one best substantive audit procedure (a–g) for obtaining competent evidence. A procedure may be selected only once or not at all.

(AICPA adapted)

LO 8-2, LO 8-6

8.59   **Assertions and Substantive Procedures for Property, Plant, and Equipment (PP&E).** Following are the four assertions about account balances that can be applied to the audit of a company's PP&E, including assets the company has constructed itself: existence, rights and obligations, completeness, and valuation and allocation.

Required:

For each of the following substantive procedures, (1) cite one assertion most closely related to the evidence the procedure will produce (the primary assertion) and (2) when appropriate, cite one or more other assertions that also are related to the evidence the procedure will produce—the secondary assertion(s).

a. For major amounts charged to PP&E and a sample of smaller charges, examine supporting documentation for expenditure amounts, budgetary approvals, and capital work orders.
b. For a sample of capitalized PP&E, examine construction work orders in detail.
c. For a sample of construction work orders, vouch time and material charges to supporting payroll and material usage records. Review the reasonableness of the hours worked, the work description, and the material used.
d. Evaluate the policy and procedures for allocating overhead to the work orders, and recalculate their application.
e. Determine whether corresponding retirements of replaced PP&E have occurred and have been properly entered in the detail records.
f. Select major additions for the year and a random sample of other additions, and inspect the physical assets.
g. Vouch a sample of charges in the Repairs account, and determine whether they are proper repairs, not capital items.
h. Review the useful lives, depreciation methods, and salvage values for reasonableness. Recalculate depreciation.
i. Study loan documents for terms and security of loans obtained for purchase of PP&E.
j. Inspect title documents for automotive and real estate assets.
k. Analyze the productive economic use of PP&E to determine whether any other-than-temporary impairment is evident.

(AICPA adapted)

LO 8-6

8.60 **CAATs Application—PP&E.** You are supervising the audit fieldwork of Sparta Springs Company and need certain information from Sparta's equipment records, which are maintained on a computer file. The particular information is (1) net book value of assets so that your assistant can reconcile the subsidiary ledger to the general ledger control accounts (the general ledger contains an account for each asset type at each plant location) and (2) sufficient data to enable your assistant to find and inspect selected assets. The record layout of the master file follows:

Asset number.

Description.

Asset type.

Location code.

Year acquired.

Cost.

Accumulated depreciation, end of year (includes accumulated depreciation at the beginning of the year plus depreciation for year to date).

Depreciation for the year to date.

Useful life.

Required

From the data file described earlier,

a. List the information needed to verify correspondence of the subsidiary detail records with the general ledger accounts. Does this work complete the audit of PP&E?

b. What additional data are needed to enable your assistant to inspect the assets?

LO 8-7

8.61 **Search for Unrecorded Liabilities.** The list of vouchers payable for Potter's Magic Shoppe at December 31 follows:

Vendor	Invoice Date	Amount
Hagrid Cleaning Services	11/15	$ 4,322.43
Hermione's Hats	12/02	2,167.76
Lockhart Magic Books	12/31	6,489.11
Malfoy Financial Consultants	12/28	23,752.63
McGonagall Veterinary Supplies	12/23	4,590.60
Moaning Myrtle's Mystical Capes	10/14	11,529.88
Nicholas Fancy Headwear	12/29	51,268.62
Snape's Snakes	12/28	36,152.45
Weasley's Wands	12/28	6,400.55
Hogwart's Rentals	12/15	53,000.00
Total vouchers payable		$199,674.03

Checks written in the following January are

Check Number	Payee	Description	Invoice Date	Amount
1842	Malfoy Financial Consultants	Professional services	12/28	$23,752.63
1843	Hagrid Cleaning Services	October monthly cleaning	11/15	4,322.43
1844	Hogwart's Rentals	January rent	12/15	53,000.00
1845	Lockhart Magic Books	Inventory	12/31	6,489.11
1846	Dudley Pastries	Catering for office Christmas party	1/15	6,300.00
1847	Weasley's Wands	Inventory	12/28	6,400.55
1848	Rowlin' Enterprises	Trademark	1/1	10,000.00
1849	McGonagall Veterinary Supplies	Inventory	12/23	4,590.60
1850	Nicholas Fancy Headwear	Inventory	12/29	51,268.62
1851	Weasley's Wands	Inventory	12/31	6,400.55
1852	Hermione's Hats	Inventory	12/02	2,167.76
1853	Lockhart Magic Books	Inventory	12/31	5,932.89
1854	Hagrid Cleaning Service	November monthly cleaning	12/15	4,322.43
1855	Malfoy Financial Consultants	Professional services	1/28	13,888.56

Required

a. Prepare an audit plan for the audit of unrecorded liabilities for Potter's Magic Shoppe.

b. Prepare an adjusting journal entry to correct accounts payable. Potter's maintains perpetual inventory records, and the inventory was counted and adjusted on December 31.

LO 8-2, 8-4, 8-6

8.62 **Identifying Assertions, Control Activities, and Substantive Procedures Related to Misstatements.** During your audit of the December 31, 2023, financial statements of Bramble Thornburg, Inc., a wholesaler of "pointy objects," you conduct your testing on the inventory and purchasing cycle. There are several misstatements in the company's inventory and accounts payable, but of course you don't know that before the audit begins. For each of the misstatements, **write the letter in the box** for (1) the management assertion violated, (2) a specific *internal control* procedure the company could implement to prevent this misstatement from occurring in the future, and (3) a specific *substantive audit* procedure the auditor would most likely perform to detect the misstatement. Any selection may be used once, more than once, or not at all. Each box can have only one letter written in it. It is possible that there may be multiple correct responses for some questions.

Assertion	Control Activity/Procedure	Substantive Audit Procedure
a. Existence of Inventory	a. Segregate authorization from record keeping and custody.	a. Perform an inventory count.
b. Completeness of Inventory	b. Three-way match of POs, receiving reports, and vendor invoices.	b. Confirm Accounts Payable with vendors.
c. Valuation of Inventory	c. Pre-numbered receiving reports with daily reconciliation of sequence.	c. Perform purchase cutoff tests.
d. Classification of Inventory	d. All purchases require authorization.	d. Agree purchases to board of directors minutes.
e. Existence of Accounts Payable	e. Regular comparisons to budgets are made by management.	e. Vouch recorded purchases to vendor invoices.
f. Completeness of Accounts Payable	f. Daily reconciliations from recorded postings to supporting documents.	f. Obtain management representation letter.
g. Classification of Accounts Payable	g. Pre-numbered checks with daily reconciliation of sequence.	g. Perform substantive analytical procedures.

a. Payments to suppliers made on December 31, 2023, were not recorded until January 3, 2024.

Assertion:	Control Activity:	Substantive Procedure:

b. Invoices for purchases were posted to incorrect vendor accounts.

Assertion:	Control Activity:	Substantive Procedure:

c. Inventory is being stolen upon receipt prior to being placed in the company warehouse.

Assertion:	Control Activity:	Substantive Procedure:

d. Inventory costing $1,254,721 was shipped to customers on January 3, 2024, and was recorded as COGS on December 31, 2023.

Assertion:	Control Activity:	Substantive Procedure:

e. Some purchase transactions were not recorded.

Assertion:	Control Activity:	Substantive Procedure:

LO 8-7

8.63 **Identifying Payments to Unauthorized Suppliers.** For this exercise, your client, Bright-IDEAs Inc., has provided you with data for two related files, an accounts payable history file and a supplier master file. To test the authorization of purchases to only legitimate suppliers, the auditor must complete a series of related steps:

1. Import the client's database of accounts payable.
2. Import the client's authorized supplier list.
3. Merge the accounts payable and supplier databases.
4. Identify payments to unauthorized suppliers.

Required:

Produce a listing of payments to unauthorized suppliers.

Required Data and IDEA Workbook page references are available on *Connect*.

Applying IDEA to the Purchasing Cycle—Elm Manufacturing Company

Exercises 8.64, 8.65, and 8.66 require the application of IDEA in the purchasing cycle audit. Elm Manufacturing Company (ELM) is a small manufacturer of backpacks located in Rochelle, Illinois. You have access to ELM's electronic records in *Connect*. The appropriate files for these exercises are the Purchases 2023–4th Q dataset, as well as the Cash Disbursements 2023–4th Q dataset. You will also require the Approved Vendors dataset to complete these assignments. Detailed information about ELM, instructions for accessing datasets, and a data directory for data sets can be found in *Connect*.

LO 8-7

8.64 **Summarizing Purchasing Data with IDEA.** You have been assigned the task of understanding the client's purchasing habits, including their use of authorized vendors and payment time frames, and you must use IDEA to gather this information.

Required:

a. Determine the total dollar amount ordered from each vendor. What companies are the three largest vendors by dollar amount? How would this information assist an auditor in planning the audit?

b. Determine what products are ordered most often. What item is ordered most often? How might this information affect the audit?

c. Determine the accounts payable amount for each vendor as of March 31. What companies have the three largest accounts payable balances? How would this information assist an auditor in planning the audit?

d. Were any orders made to vendors not on the approved vendor list? How would this information assist an auditor in planning the audit?

e. Were there any discounts available that were not taken? Why is this important to the auditor?

f. Were there any vendors paid late? Why is this important to the auditor?

g. Were there any items that did not pass inspection? Why is this information important to the auditor?

LO 8-7

8.65 **Tests of Controls in the Purchasing Cycle with IDEA.** You have identified relevant controls for several assertions within the purchasing cycle, and you must use IDEA to perform several tests of controls.

Required:

a. Are all checks accounted for? If there are checks that are not accounted for, how would this affect the audit?

b. Are there any duplicate check numbers? If there are duplicate checks, how would this affect the audit?

c. Are there any payments to vendors not on the approved vendor list? If there are checks to such vendors, how would this affect the audit?

d. Were any checks voided? Were any checks written to at cash or bearer? How would this affect the audit?

LO 8-7

8.66 **Testing for Unmatched Invoices.** A concern in all audits is the risk that payments are made that do not represent valid expenses. One common test is to match payments to valid invoices, and you must use IDEA to perform this test.

Required:

Match the paid invoice numbers in the purchases data set with the invoice numbers in the cash disbursements data set. Are there unmatched invoices from the purchase data? Are there any disbursements with invoices that do not match to the purchase data? What are the possible causes for discrepancies between these data sets? How would the auditor address these discrepancies?

Apollo Shoes

Audit of Liabilities

You are a recently promoted senior (in charge) auditor for Anderson, Olds, and Watershed and have been assigned to the engagement team of a new audit client, Apollo Shoes Inc. You have been asked to audit Apollo's liability accounts, which includes evaluating documents such as debt confirmations, vendor invoices, etc. Detailed instructions, supporting documents, and audit documentation needed to complete the audit of liabilities can be found in *Connect*.

Appendix 8A

Internal Control Questionnaires

APPENDIX EXHIBIT 8A.1   **Internal Control Questionnaire—Acquisitions and Expenditures**

	Yes/No	Comments
Occurrence		
1. Are the purchasing department, accounting department, receiving department, and shipping department independent of each other?		
2. Are receiving reports prepared for each item received and copies transmitted to inventory custodians? To purchasing? To the accounting department?		
3. Are purchases made by employees authorized through standard purchase procedures?		
4. Are quantity and quality of goods received determined at the time of receipt by receiving personnel independent of the purchasing department?		
5. Are vendors' invoices reconciled against purchase orders and receiving reports before a liability is recorded?		
6. Do managers compare actual expenses to budget?		
7. Are all documents in the vouchers package canceled with a PAID stamp when paid?		
8. Are shipping documents authorized and prepared for goods returned to vendors?		
9. Are invoices approved for payment by a responsible officer?		
Completeness		
1. Are the purchase order forms prenumbered and the numerical sequence checked for missing documents?		
2. Are receiving report forms prenumbered and the numerical sequence checked for missing documents?		
3. Is the accounts payable department notified of goods returned to vendors?		
4. Are vendors' invoices recorded immediately on receipt?		
5. Are unmatched receiving reports reviewed frequently and investigated for proper recording?		
6. Is statistical analysis used to examine overall purchasing levels?		
7. Are vendors' monthly statements reconciled with individual accounts payable accounts?		
Accuracy		
1. Are competitive bids received and reviewed for certain items?		
2. Are all purchases made only on the basis of approved purchase requisitions?		
3. Are all purchases, whether for inventory or expense, routed through the purchasing department for approval?		
4. Does the accounts payable department check invoices against purchase orders and receiving reports for dates, quantities, prices, and terms?		
5. Does the accounting department check invoices for mathematical accuracy?		
6. Is the accounts payable listing balanced periodically with the general ledger control account?		
7. Are purchase prices approved by a responsible purchasing officer?		
8. Is accounts payable reconciled to the general ledger every period?		
9. Are monthly statements reviewed by senior officials?		
Classification		
1. Do the chart of accounts and the accounting manual give instructions for classifying debit entries when purchases are recorded?		
2. Are journal entries authorized at appropriate levels?		
Cutoff		
1. Does the accounting manual give instructions to date purchase/payable entries on the date of receipt of goods?		

APPENDIX EXHIBIT 8A.2   Selected System Questionnaire Items—General and Application Controls[*]

	Yes/No	Comments
General Controls		
1. Are computer operators and programmers excluded from participating in the input and output control functions?		
2. Are programmers excluded from entering transactions or performing other routine computer operations?		
3. Is there a database administrator who is independent of computer operations, systems, programming, and users?		
4. Are computer personnel restricted from initiating, or authorizing, transactions or adjustments to the general ledger master database or the subsidiary ledger master database?		
5. Is access to the computer room restricted to authorized personnel?		
6. Is online access to data and programs controlled with the use of department account codes, personal ID numbers, and passwords?		
7. Are systems, programs, and documentation stored in a fireproof area?		
8. Can current files, particularly master files, be reconstructed from files stored in an offsite location?		
Application Controls		
1. Are process manuals for purchasing and accounts payable current?		
2. Are process documents (e.g., purchase requisitions, purchase orders, bills of lading) signed as evidence of review and authorization?		
3. Are all data fields subject to input validation tests—missing data tests, limit and range tests, check digits, valid codes, and so forth?		
4. Are input error reports generated daily? Are they returned to the accounting department for correction of errors?		
5. Is an accounting department person assigned the responsibility for promptly correcting input errors and reentering the data for inclusion with the next report?		
6. Are controls used to reconcile computerized output to input control data?		
7. Are reports reviewed for reasonableness, accuracy, and legibility by the responsible department personnel?		

APPENDIX EXHIBIT 8A.3   Acquisitions and Expenditures Questionnaire—System Controls[*]

	Yes/No	Comments
1. Is each terminal restricted to designated functions? For example, the receiving clerk's terminal cannot accept a purchase order entry.		
2. Are identification numbers and passwords required to enter purchase orders, vendors' invoices, and the receiving report information?		
3. Are certain personnel authorized to determine the status of various records, such as an open voucher, but not authorized to enter data? Do these personnel have "read only" authorization?		
4. Is all input immediately logged to provide restart processing should any terminal become inoperative during the processing?		
5. Do transaction codes call up a full screen "form" on the terminals that appears to the operators in the same format as the original paper documents?		
6. Does the system reject incomplete or incorrect information (online input validation)?		
7. Are all printed documents computer numbered, and are the numbers stored as part of the record?		
8. Do all records in the open databases have the vendor's number as the primary search and matching field key?		
9. Can status searches be made by another field? For example, the inventory number can be the search key to determine the status of a purchase of an item in short supply.		
10. Is a daily search of the open databases made—for example, open purchase orders more than 10 days past the delivery date?		
11. Is the check signature printed using a signature plate that is installed on the computer printer only when checks are printed?		
12. Does a designated person in the treasurer's office maintain custody of this signature plate and take it to the computer room to be installed when checks are printed?		
13. Is this person restricted from access to blank check stock?		
14. Are the printed checks taken immediately from the computer room for mailing?		

[*]General and Application Control and System Controls are covered in Module H.

APPENDIX EXHIBIT 8A.4 **Acquisitions and Expenditures Questionnaire—Property and Equipment Controls**

	Yes/No	Comments
Existence/Occurrence		
1. Is the accounting department notified of actions of disposal, dismantling, or idling a productive asset? For terminating a lease or rental?		
2. Are assets inspected periodically and physically counted?		
Completeness		
1. Are detailed property records maintained for the various assets included in PP&E?		
2. Are property tax assessments periodically analyzed? When was the last analysis?		
3. Are purchase contracts for major assets provided to the accounting department?		
Valuation/Accuracy		
1. Are capital expenditure and leasing proposals prepared for review and approval by the board of directors or by responsible officers?		
2. When actual expenditures exceed authorized amounts, is the excess approved?		
3. Is there a uniform policy for assigning depreciation rates, useful lives, and salvage values?		
4. Are depreciation calculations checked by internal auditors or other officials?		
5. Are subsidiary records periodically reconciled to the general ledger accounts?		
Classification		
1. Does the accounting manual contain policies for capitalization of assets and expensing repair and maintenance?		
2. Are memorandum records of leased assets maintained?		
Cutoff		
1. Does the accounting manual give instructions for recording PP&E additions on a proper date of acquisition?		

Appendix 8B

Audit Plans

APPENDIX EXHIBIT 8B.1

DUNDER-MIFFLIN, INC. Audit Plan for Accounts Payable 12/31/23		
	Performed by	**Ref.**

1. Obtain a trial balance of recorded accounts payable as of year-end.
   a. Foot and trace the total to the general ledger account.
   b. Vouch a sample of balances to vendors' statements. Review the trial balance for related-party payables.
2. Send confirmations to creditors, especially those with small or zero balances and those with which the company has done significant business.
3. Inquire of client personnel about their procedures for ensuring that all liabilities are recorded.
4. Scan the open purchase order file at year-end for indications of material purchase commitments at fixed prices. Obtain current prices and determine whether any adjustments for loss are needed.
5. Obtain a list of unmatched vendor invoices and review receiving reports for receipt of goods.
6. For goods received before year-end, trace the unmatched receiving reports to accounts payable and determine whether items recorded in the next accounting period need to be adjusted.
7. Select a sample of cash disbursements from the accounting period following the balance-sheet date. Vouch them to supporting documents (invoice, receiving report) to determine whether the related liabilities were recorded in the proper accounting period.		

APPENDIX EXHIBIT 8B.2

DUNDER-MIFFLIN, INC. Audit Plan for Prepaid Expenses, Accrued Expenses, Deferred Costs 12/31/23		
	Performed by	**Ref.**

1. Obtain a schedule of all prepaid expenses, deferred costs, and accrued expenses.
2. Review documentation to determine whether each item is properly allocated to the current or future accounting periods.
3. Select significant additions to deferred and accrued amounts and vouch them to supporting invoices, contracts, or calculations.
4. Examine documentation for the basis for deferral and accrual and recalculate the recorded amounts.
5. Review the nature of each item, inquire of management, and determine whether the remaining balance will be recovered from future operations.
6. Scan income and expense items for items that should be considered prepaid, deferred, or accrued and allocated to current or future accounting periods.
7. Scan the expense accounts in the trial balance and compare to prior year.
   a. Investigate an unusual difference that could indicate failure to account for a prepaid or accrual item.
   b. Review each item to determine the proper current or noncurrent balance sheet classification.		

APPENDIX EXHIBIT 8B.3

	Performed by	Ref.
DUNDER-MIFFLIN, INC. **Audit Plan for Long-Lived Assets** **12/31/23**		

Property, Plant, and Equipment

1. Summarize and foot detailed asset subsidiary records, and reconcile to general ledger control account(s).
2. Select a sample of detailed asset subsidiary records:
   a. Perform a physical observation (inspection) of the assets recorded.
   b. Inspect title documents, if any, to ensure ownership by the client.
3. Prepare, or have client prepare, a schedule of asset additions and disposals for the period:
   a. Vouch to documents indicating proper approval.
   b. Vouch costs to invoices, contracts, or other supporting documents.
   c. Review all costs of shipment, installation, testing, and other appropriate costs for proper capitalization.
   d. Vouch proceeds (on dispositions) to cash receipts or other asset records.
   e. Recalculate gain or loss on dispositions.
   f. Trace amounts to detailed asset records and general ledger control account(s).
4. Observe the taking of a physical inventory of the assets and compare with detailed asset records.
5. Obtain written representations from management regarding pledge of assets as security for loans and leased assets.
6. Select a sample of repair and maintenance expense entries and vouch them to supporting invoices for evidence of property that should be capitalized.

Depreciation

1. Review depreciation expense for overall reasonableness with reference to costs of assets and average depreciation rates.
2. Prepare, or have client prepare, a schedule of accumulated depreciation showing beginning balance, current depreciation, disposals, and ending balance.
   a. Review the schedule for appropriate asset costs, useful life, and salvage value.
3. Trace equipment listed to depreciation expense and asset disposition analyses.
4. Recalculate depreciation expense and trace to general ledger account(s).
5. Trace amounts to general ledger account(s).

Other Accounts

1. Review prepaid insurance for proper recording and adequacy of coverage.
2. Review accrued property taxes to determine whether taxes due on assets have been paid or accrued.
3. Recalculate prepaid and/or accrued insurance and tax expenses.
4. Select a sample of rental expense entries and vouch to rent/lease contracts to determine whether any leases qualify for capitalization.

Intangibles and Related Expenses

1. Review merger documents for proper calculation of purchased goodwill.
2. Inquire of management about legal status of patents, leases, copyrights, and other intangibles.
3. Review documentation of new patents, copyrights, leaseholds, and franchise agreements.
4. Select a sample of recorded research and development expenses. Vouch to supporting documents for evidence of proper classification.
5. Recalculate amortization of goodwill, patents, and other intangibles.
6. Perform tests for goodwill impairment.

Appendix 8C

The Payroll Cycle

LO 8-8
Describe the payroll cycle, including typical source documents and controls.

Martin Bodner, the former finance chief of **Tommy Hilfiger Group Handbags and Small Leather Goods Inc.,** pleaded guilty to mail fraud and wire fraud for allegedly stealing more than $19 million, according to Michael Garcia, U.S. Attorney for the Southern District of New York. According to Garcia, Bodner began working at the Hilfiger licensee in March 2000, eventually rising to CFO. Among his responsibilities was to supervise the company's payroll. Beginning in 2000, Bodner began stealing money from his employer by secretly increasing the amount of money that he was to be paid in salary and bonus and arranging to be reimbursed by the handbag and leather goods unit for phony expenses he purportedly had incurred. In addition, during 2004 and 2005, Bodner added one of his sons, who did not work for the company, to the company's payroll. He arranged for his son to be paid about $225,500 during those years. Bodner was fired on December 21, 2007.

Bodner entered into a plea deal in which he agreed to forfeit a home in Sands Point, New York, along with a Manhattan apartment, three cars, and various other properties. Bodner also was accused of causing hundreds of checks to be issued to various recipients for the purpose of paying off his personal credit card bills; purchasing a luxury automobile for himself; paying for insurance for a home, apartments, and automobiles owned by Bodner; and paying for decorating services.[5]

Every company has payroll. It can include manufacturing labor, research scientists, administrative personnel, or all of these. Payroll may take different forms. Personnel management and the payroll accounting cycle not only include transactions that affect the wage and salary accounts, but also the transactions that affect pension benefits, deferred compensation contracts, compensatory stock option plans, employee benefits (such as health insurance), payroll taxes, and related liabilities for these costs. An important aspect of the payroll cycle is that it is self-policing. If employees are not paid, they will complain. If someone commits fraud by overpaying an employee and then diverts the difference, the employee will complain because his or her W-2 will be overstated and the employee will owe too much tax. As a result, company employees report many misstatements (both intentional and unintentional).

Typically, balance sheet accounts such as accrued payroll and accrued taxes are not material to companies' financial position. In addition, because of the self-policing nature of the accounts and the regulatory restrictions of the Internal Revenue Service and the Department of Labor, controls over payroll are normally stronger than over other areas. Therefore, most audit procedures related to payroll consist of evaluation of internal control and analytical procedures.

THE PAYROLL CYCLE: TYPICAL ACTIVITIES

Appendix Exhibit 8C.1 shows a payroll cycle. The numbers after the headings below refer to the numbers in the exhibit. It starts with hiring (and firing) people and determining their wage rates and deductions, proceeds to attendance and work (timekeeping), and ends with payment followed by preparation of governmental (tax) and internal reports.

The elements that follow are part of the payroll internal control system.

Personnel ①

A human resources department that is independent of the other functions should have authority to add new employees to the payroll, delete terminated employees, obtain authorizations for deductions, and transmit authority for pay rate changes to the payroll department. A process should exist to ensure that terminated employees are removed

[5]"Hilfiger Unit Ex-CFO Pleads Guilty to $19M Fraud," CFO.com, September 16, 2008.

EXHIBIT 8C.1 **Typical Activities in the Payroll Cycle**

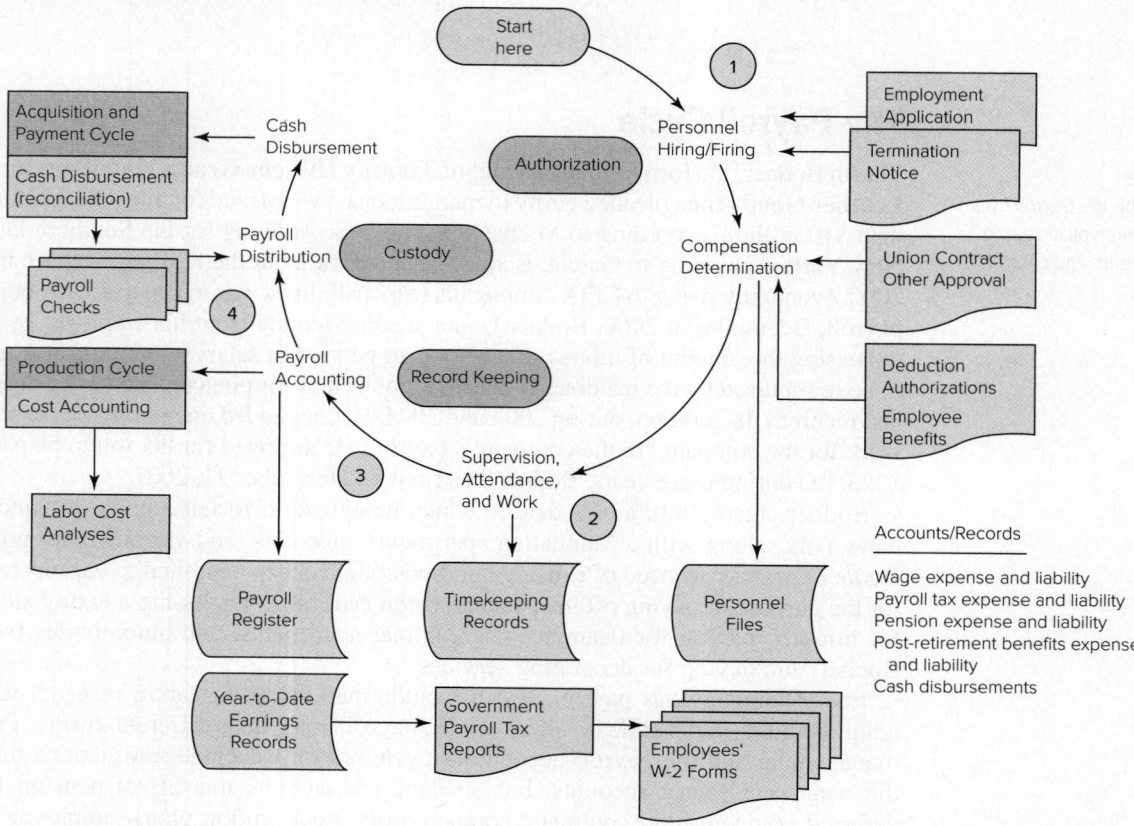

from the payroll. This is often done in conjunction with an exit interview performed by human resources. Final checks and W-2s should be mailed to the employee's home.

Supervision ②

Supervisors assign the employees to their jobs and approve any overtime. The immediate supervisor should approve all employee activity data (number of hours worked, job number, absences, time off allowed for emergencies, and the like). Finally, supervisors compare production plans and budget reports to actual employee costs for discrepancies.

Timekeeping ③

Employees paid by the hour or on various incentive systems require records of time, production, piecework, or other measures of the basis for their pay. (Salaried employees do not require such detailed records.) Timekeeping or similar records are collected in a variety of ways. The traditional time clock is still used in many organizations. More sophisticated computerized systems perform the same function without the paper time card. Production employees may clock in for various jobs or production processes in the system for assigning labor cost to various stages of production.

Supervisors should approve timekeeping records. In computerized systems, this approval may be automatic by virtue of the supervisory passwords used to input data into a computerized payroll system.

Record Keeping ④

The payroll accounting function should prepare individual paychecks and pay envelopes or make electronic transfers using rate and deduction information supplied by the personnel function and data supplied by the timekeeping–supervision functions. Persons in charge of the hiring, supervision, and timekeeping functions should not also prepare the payroll. They could be tempted to get checks for fictitious or terminated employees. Payroll accounting maintains individual year-to-date earnings records and prepares the state and federal tax reports. The payroll tax returns and the annual W-2 report to employees are useful records for audit recalculation and analytical procedures.

The main feature of custody in the payroll cycle is the possession of the paychecks, cash, or electronic transfer codes for direct payments. A payroll distribution function should control the delivery of pay to employees so that unclaimed checks, cash, or incomplete electronic transfers are not returned to persons involved in any of the other functions. The functional duties and responsibilities just described relate primarily to nonsalaried (hourly) employees. For salaried employees, the system is simplified by not having to collect timekeeping data. In nonmanufacturing businesses, the cost accounting operations can be very simple or even nonexistent.

Direct deposit is an excellent control for payroll distribution. Employees on vacation, ill, or otherwise not at the facility will still have their check delivered, and unclaimed paychecks are almost nonexistent. Further, there is no opportunity for employees to alter a paycheck in any manner. Be aware that some individuals do not have (and do not want) a bank account. Also, the client cannot require an employee to have a bank account. Therefore, even if the client has a direct deposit system, the auditor should make inquiries as to those employees paid by check.

The relative importance of each of these four areas should be determined for each engagement in light of the nature and organization of the company's operations. However, one thing auditors should always remember is that an inherent limitation of internal controls is that they can always be circumvented by management, as discussed in the following Auditing Insight.

AUDITING INSIGHT   Why Am I Underpaid?

Leonid Fridman, 60, owned and operated **Millennium Commercial Corp.,** a Brooklyn-based company that performed tile work for the Port Authority of New York and New Jersey. The defendant and his company performed tile restoration work as a subcontractor on the renovation of the TWA Flight Center at John F. Kennedy Airport in 2009 and 2010. Under the Port Authority contract for the project and labor law, the defendant was required to pay his laborers and mason tenders more than $50 per hour and more than $70 per hour for tile setters.

According to court records, Fridman was aware that he was required to pay the prevailing wages but still paid his workers only $10 to $30 per hour. To avoid detection, Fridman filed false certified payroll reports stating he paid his workers the prevailing wages and issued paychecks to the workers that matched those payroll reports. Fridman then made his workers cash the checks at his bank and kick back, or return, a majority of the cash to him, according to the New York Attorney General's office.

Prosecutors say that Fridman then hid more than $100,000 of the money he stole by moving it into the account of a Florida corporation, Green Investments Inc., that he controlled.

Source: "NYC Contractor Charged with Payroll Fraud, Larceny, and Laundering," CPA Practice Advisor, February 6, 2013.

✔ REVIEW CHECKPOINTS

8C.1 What functional responsibilities are associated with the payroll cycle?

8C.2 Which duties should be separated in the payroll cycle?

8C.3 How does a company ensure that terminated employees are removed from the payroll?

8C.4 Describe a walkthrough of the payroll transaction flow from hiring authorization to payroll check disbursement. (a) What document copies would be collected? (b) What controls should be noted?

Significant Accounts and Relevant Assertions

The major risks in the payroll cycle include

- Paying **ghost employees**, employees who do not exist (invalid transactions).
- Paying terminated employees (who have not been removed from payroll) whose paychecks are then endorsed with forged signatures by their supervisors.
- Overpaying for time or production (inaccurate transactions, improper valuation).
- Accounting incorrectly for costs and expenses (incorrect classification, improper or inconsistent presentation and disclosure).
- Not ensuring that related taxes and third parties (e.g., insurance providers) are appropriately paid.

Because of these risks, and the desire of employees to obtain more money, the valuation of payroll is the most relevant assertion. This is illustrated in the next Auditing Insight. The potential for ghost employees makes existence a key assertion as well. Management may also gain from misclassifying payroll so the auditor must consider the classification assertion a risk. Certainly, if an employee was left off the payroll, the employee would make that known to the organization, therefore, completeness is a very low risk.

AUDITING INSIGHT   A Dedicated Employee

Prosecutors told the Winchester Crown Court in southern England that Jaswinder Bains, 45, was "blatantly dishonest" on the time cards for his job as a social worker on at least 24 occasions. In one instance, Bains allegedly claimed he worked 23 hours in one day on 29 case files, even though his credit card records show he was on a shopping spree in Paris that day. Bains testified that he did not falsify his work hour records. "I was working very long hours without sleep," he said. "I do not need a lot of sleep." He did not explain what was behind his records on another day, when he claimed he worked 28 hours.

Source: "Social Worker 'Claimed for 28-Hour Day,'" *The Guardian,* May 9, 2005.

Payroll systems produce numerous reports. Some are internal reports and bookkeeping records. Others are government tax reports.

Personnel Files

The personnel, human relations, or labor relations department keeps individual employee files. The files usually include an employment application, a background investigation report, a notice of hiring, a job classification with pay rate authorization, and employee authorizations for deductions. When employees retire, resign, or are otherwise dismissed, appropriate notices of termination are filed.

A personnel file should establish a person's existence and employment. The background investigation report is important for employees in such sensitive areas as accounting, finance, and asset custody positions. News reports are rich with reports of errors and frauds perpetrated by people who falsified their credentials.

Payroll Register

The *payroll register* is a special journal. It typically contains a row for each employee with columns for the gross regular pay, gross overtime pay, income tax withheld, Social Security and Medicare tax withheld, other deductions, and net pay. The net pay amount usually is transferred from the general bank account to a special **imprest bank account** that maintains a zero or fixed balance.

Payroll department records contain the canceled checks (or a similar computerized deposit record). The checks have the employees' endorsements on the back.

Labor Cost Analysis

One of the internal reports in the payroll cycle is a report of labor cost to the cost accounting department, thus linking the payroll cycle with cost accounting in the production cycle. The cost accounting department can receive its information in more than one way. Some companies have systems that independently report time and production work data from the production floor directly to the cost accounting department. Other companies let their cost accounting department receive labor cost data from the payroll department. When the data are received independently, they can be reconciled with a report from the payroll department.

The cost accounting department (or a similar accounting function) is responsible for labor distribution. This is the most important part of the classification assertion with respect to payroll. Labor distribution is an assignment of payroll to the accounts where it belongs for internal and external reporting.

Payroll data flow from the hiring process, through the timekeeping function, into the payroll department, then to the cost accounting department, and finally to the accounting entries that record the payroll for inventory cost determination and financial statement presentation. The same data are used for various governmental and tax reports.

Beware the "Clearing Account"

Clearing accounts are temporary storage places for transactions awaiting final accounting. All clearing accounts should have zero balances after the accounting is completed. A balance in a clearing account means that some amounts have not been classified properly in the accounting records. When the dollars in the clearing account are material, auditors usually investigate the nature of the account with a great deal of skepticism.

Governmental and Tax Reports

One of the main objectives of a payroll system is to calculate the payments due to third parties, including insurance fees, union dues, retirement funds, and so on. Of most importance is the calculation of payroll taxes due to the federal, state, and local governments. Large fines, mounting interest, or business closure is a possible ramification if these taxes are not paid timely and accurately. These issues cause payroll systems to be complicated and change almost every year as tax law and tax rates change. The payroll system produces several reports. Auditors can use these reports in tests of controls and substantive procedures produced by accumulating numerous payroll transactions.

Companies in financial difficulty have been known to try to postpone payment of employee taxes withheld. However, the consequences can be serious. The IRS can and will padlock the business and seize its assets for nonpayment.

Year-to-Date Earnings Records

The year-to-date (YTD) earnings records are the cumulative subsidiary records of each employee's gross pay, deductions, and net pay. Each time a periodic payroll is produced, the YTD earnings records are updated for the new information. The YTD earnings records are a subsidiary ledger of the wages and salaries cost and expense in the financial statements. Like any subsidiary and control account relationship, their sum (i.e., the gross pay amounts) should be equal to the costs and expenses in the financial statements. These YTD records provide the data for periodic governmental tax forms. They can be reconciled to the tax reports. Details can be compared to the company's YTD earnings records.

Employee W-2 Reports

The **W-2** is the annual report of gross salaries and wages and the income, Social Security, and Medicare taxes withheld. Copies are filed with the Social Security Administration and the IRS, and copies are sent to employees for use in preparing their income tax returns. The W-2s contain the annual YTD accumulations for each employee. Auditors can use the name, address, Social Security number, and dollar amounts in certain procedures to obtain evidence about the existence of the employees. The W-2s can be reconciled to the payroll tax reports.

W-2s should be mailed directly to employees' homes so if someone has been collecting additional pay in an employee's name (e.g., if an employee leaves and the supervisor continues to send in a time card), the employee can spot the added income.

The assessment of payroll-cycle control risk normally takes on added importance because most companies have fairly elaborate and well-controlled personnel and payroll functions. The significant transactions in this cycle are numerous during the year yet result in small amounts in balance-sheet accounts at year-end. Therefore, in most audit engagements, the review of controls, tests of controls, and substantive tests of transactions constitute the major portion of the evidence gathered for these accounts. On most audits, the substantive procedures devoted to auditing the payroll-related account balances are limited.

INTERNAL CONTROL ACTIVITIES AND EVALUATION

In the payroll function, auditors pay special attention to the controls that have been put in place. In a large company, tens of thousands of payroll checks or direct deposit payments may be made during the year. While auditors may test the detail of some transactions, it is the evaluation of internal controls that is deemed most important.

Control activities for proper separation of responsibilities should be in place and operating. By referring to Exhibit 8C.1, you can see that proper separation involves authorization (personnel department hiring and termination, pay rate, and deduction authorizations) by persons who do not have payroll preparation, paycheck distribution, or reconciliation duties. Payroll distribution (custody) is in the hands of persons who do not authorize employees' pay rates or time or prepare the payroll checks. Record keeping is performed by payroll and cost accounting personnel who do not make authorizations or distribute pay. Combinations of two or more of the duties of authorization, payroll preparation and record keeping, and payroll distribution in one person, one office, or one computerized system can open the door for errors and frauds.

In addition, the internal controls should provide for detailed control checking procedures. Examples of these controls are

- Periodic comparison of the payroll register to the personnel department files to check hiring authorizations and any terminated employees who have not been deleted.
- Periodic rechecking of wage rate and deduction authorizations.
- Reconciliation of time and production material to cost accounting calculations.
- Quarterly reconciliation of YTD earnings records with tax returns.
- Payroll bank account reconciliation.

Some companies send each supervisor a copy of the payroll register, showing the employees paid under the supervisor's authority and responsibility. The supervisor has a chance to reapprove the payroll after it has been completed. Managers also should receive a comparison of actual labor costs to standards to review any unusual differences. The payroll report sent to cost accounting can be reconciled to the labor records used to charge labor cost to production. The cost accounting function should determine whether the labor paid is the same as the labor cost used in the cost accounting calculations. Finally, the payroll bank account can be reconciled like any other bank account.

Information about the payroll cycle control often is gathered initially by completing an internal control questionnaire (ICQ). An example of an ICQ for payroll controls is in Exhibit 5.10. You can study this questionnaire for details of desirable controls. It is organized with headings that identify the important assertions.

Computerized Payroll

Complex computerized systems that gather payroll data, calculate payroll amounts, print checks, and transfer computerized deposits are found in many companies. Even though the technology is complex, the basic management and control functions of ensuring a flow of data to the payroll department should be in place. Various paper records and approval signatures may not exist. They may be embedded in computerized payroll systems. Companies often use service organizations to process their payroll because it is a specialized function that can be performed effectively and efficiently by an organization whose specialty is to keep up with and apply changes in tax laws and rates. Auditors should refer to the requirements related to service organizations in addressing this function.

Service Organizations

Service organizations are widely used for payroll preparation. This process can range from the calculation of payroll including the amounts due to third parties and to the actual payment of the payroll to individuals and third parties. Even when service bureaus are used to process payroll, the client is still responsible for payroll. For example, if the calculation for federal taxes is incorrect, the IRS will be auditing the client, not the service organization payroll provider. Therefore, the auditor must review the payroll controls both at the client and the service organization for processing payroll. This would include getting a report on controls from the service organization's auditor and ensuring that controls at the client are in place. The client should verify that the number of checks issued by the service organization equals the number of employees eligible for compensation during the period. The client should review reports from the third party such as a payroll register (a listing of changes made to the payroll file), and a report of payments due to third parties should be reviewed by the client. The auditor should ensure that payroll numbers are reasonable given the activity level at the client. Analytical procedures can be a powerful test in these situations. Service organizations can pose a risk in the audit, as shown in the following Auditing Insight, "When Your Payroll Processor is Paying Himself". Service organization reports are discussed in more detail in Module A.

 AUDITING INSIGHT When Your Payroll Processor Is Paying Himself

MyPayrollHR is a large service organization that processes payroll records and payments for other companies. Companies remit the money to MyPayrollHR, which processes the payroll and pays employees for its customers. CEO Michael Mann devised a fraud that used bank loans to embezzle $101 million from the company for personal use in business acquisitions and other expenditures. To keep the loan balances down, Mann used his customers' payroll remittances to pay down loan balances.

Upon discovery and conviction in 2021, Mann was sentenced to 12 years in prison. However, many victims have not recovered from the fraud. In the course of the trial and sentencing, the judge received 165 letters, mostly from small businesses, explaining how they were harmed and in many cases have not recovered, with some employees out many paychecks. The case is so complex that many victims have still not been identified.

MyPayrollHR filed for bankruptcy as a result of the fraud. This example shows the importance of service organizations in audits of payroll and the risks that can arise if proper controls are not present at service organizations.

Source: "Feds Still Need to Identify Who Gets $20 Million in Payroll Fraud Case," *Albany Times Union,* August 15, 2021.

Substantive Analytical Procedures and Tests of Details

As stated, for the payroll process, auditors rely heavily on tests of controls. However, there are substantive tests that can be performed. If the workforce is stable, payroll from one period to the next will be relatively consistent. If a weekly payroll significantly declines or increases, the auditor should inquire of management about the inconsistency. Layoffs, overtime, or seasonality may explain the discrepancy, and the auditor can review the payroll register for that period to corroborate the change in the number of paychecks or the increase in overtime.

There are times when the auditor is concerned about payroll controls or inexplicable changes in payroll expenses. In these cases, the auditor may select a sample of items from the payroll register (remember completeness is low risk so the register should include all employees) and vouch the information to the time cards (hours worked), payroll master file (wage), and the personnel file for authorizations for deductions (insurance, withholding, pension) and wage rate. Personnel files are excellent sources of information when ghost employees are expected. Few ghost employees have life or health insurance. Auditors may scan the payroll register looking for employees with no voluntary deductions from their paycheck and vouch the employee information to the personnel files in human resources.

 REVIEW CHECKPOINTS

8C.5 What documents should be included in an employee's personnel file?

8C.6 What features of a payroll system could be expected to prevent or detect the (a) payment of a fictitious employee and (b) omission of payment to an employee?

8C.7 What are the most common errors and frauds in the personnel and payroll cycle? Which control characteristics are auditors looking for to prevent or detect these errors and frauds?

FRAUD CASE: EXTENDED AUDIT PROCEDURES

Case 8C.1

Time Card Forgeries

PROBLEM

A personnel agency that leased employees to hospitals assigned Nurse Jane Kent to work at **County Hospital**. She claimed payroll hours on agency time cards that showed approval signatures of a hospital nursing shift supervisor. The hospital had terminated the shift supervisor several months prior to the periods covered by the time cards in question. Kent worked one or two days per week but submitted time cards for a full 40-hour workweek. The personnel agency paid Kent and then billed County Hospital for the wages and benefits. Supporting documents were submitted with the personnel agency's bills.

Each hospital workstation keeps ward shift logs, which are sign-in sheets showing nurses on duty at all times. Nurses sign in and sign out when going on and going off duty. County Hospital maintains personnel records showing, among other things, the period of employment of its own nurses, supervisors, and other employees.

Kent's wages and benefits were billed to the hospital at $22 per hour. False time cards overcharging about 24 extra hours per week cost the hospital $528 per week. Kent was assigned to County Hospital for 15 weeks during the year, so she caused overcharges of about $7,900. However, she told three of her friends about the procedure, and they overcharged the hospital another $24,000.

AUDIT APPROACH

Control activities should include a hiring authorization to put employees on the payroll. When temporary employees are used, this authorization includes contracts for nursing time, conditions of employment, and terms including the contract reimbursement rate. Control records of attendance and work should be kept (ward shift log). Supervisors should approve time cards or other records used by the payroll department to prepare paychecks. In this case, the contract with the personnel agency provided that approved time cards had to be submitted as supporting documentation for the agency billings.

Although the activities and documents for control were in place, the controls did not operate because no one at the hospital ever compared the ward shift logs to time cards, and no one examined the supervisory approval signatures for their validity. The fraud was easy in the personnel agency situation because the nurses submitted their own time cards to the agency for payment. The same fraud could be operated by the hospital's own employees if they, too, could write their time cards and submit them to the payroll department.

Auditors should make inquiries (e.g., internal control questionnaire) about the error-checking activities performed by hospital accounting personnel. Tests of controls are designed to determine whether control activities are followed properly by the organization. Because the comparison and checking activities were not performed, there is nothing to test.

Select a sample of personnel agency billings and their supporting documentation (time cards). Vouch rates billed by the agency to the contract for agreement to proper rate. Vouch time claimed to hospital work attendance records (ward shift logs). Obtain handwriting examples of supervisors' signatures and compare them to the approval signatures on time cards. Use personnel records to determine whether supervisors were actually employed by the hospital at the time they approved the time cards. Use available work attendance records to determine whether supervisors were actually on duty at the time they approved the time cards.

DISCOVERY SUMMARY

The auditors quickly found that Kent (and others) had not signed in on ward shift logs for days they claimed to have worked. Further investigation showed that the supervisors who supposedly signed the time cards were not even employed by the hospital at the time their signatures were used for approvals. Handwriting comparison showed that the signatures were not those of the supervisors.

The personnel agency was informed and refunded the $31,900 overpayment that the auditors had proved. The auditors continued to comb the records for more!

Source: Adapted from vignette published in *Internal Auditor.*

Multiple-Choice Questions for Practice and Review

 All applicable Exercises and Problems are available with *Connect*.

LO 8-8

8C.8 An audit team most likely would assess control risk at the maximum if the payroll department supervisor is responsible for

a. Examining authorization forms for new employees.

b. Comparing payroll registers with original batch transmittal data.

c. Authorizing payroll rate changes for all employees.

d. Hiring all subordinate payroll department employees.

(AICPA adapted)

LO 8-8

8C.9 Which of the following departments most likely would approve changes in pay rates and deductions from employee salaries?

a. Personnel.

b. Treasurer.

c. Controller.

d. Payroll.

(AICPA adapted)

LO 8-8

8C.10 Matthew Corp. has changed from a system of recording time worked on clock cards to a computerized payroll system in which employees record time in and out with magnetic cards. The computerized system automatically updates all payroll records. Because of this change

a. A generalized computer audit plan must be used.

b. Part of the audit trail is altered.

c. The potential for payroll-related fraud is diminished.

d. Transactions must be processed in batches.

(AICPA adapted)

LO 8-8   8C.11 Effective control over the cash payroll function would mandate which of the following?

a. The payroll clerk should fill the envelopes with cash and a computation of the net wages.

b. Unclaimed payroll envelopes should be retained by the paymaster.

c. Each employee should be asked to sign a receipt.

d. A separate checking account for payroll should be maintained.

LO 8-8   8C.12 A large retail enterprise has established a policy that requires the paymaster to deliver all unclaimed payroll checks to the internal audit department at the end of each payroll distribution day. This policy was most likely adopted to

a. Ensure that employees who were absent on a payroll distribution day are not paid for that day.

b. Prevent the paymaster from cashing checks that are unclaimed for several weeks.

c. Prevent a bona fide employee's check from being claimed by another employee.

d. Detect any fictitious employee who may have been placed on the payroll.

(AICPA adapted)

LO 8-8   8C.13 Auditors ordinarily ascertain whether payroll checks are properly endorsed during the audit of

a. Clock cards.

b. The voucher system.

c. Cash in bank.

d. Accrued payroll.

(AICPA adapted)

LO 8-8   8C.14 In determining the effectiveness of an entity's policies and procedures relating to the occurrence assertion for payroll transactions, auditors most likely would inquire about and

a. Observe the separation of duties concerning personnel responsibilities and payroll disbursement.

b. Inspect evidence of accounting for prenumbered payroll checks.

c. Recompute the payroll deductions for employee benefits.

d. Verify the preparation of the monthly payroll account bank reconciliation.

(AICPA adapted)

LO 8-8   8C.15 Which of the following activities most likely would be considered a weakness in an entity's internal control over payroll?

a. A voucher for the amount of the payroll is prepared in the general accounting department based on the payroll department's payroll summary.

b. Payroll checks are prepared by the accounts payable department and signed by the treasurer.

c. The employee who distributes payroll check returns unclaimed payroll checks to the payroll department.

d. The personnel department sends employees' termination notices to the payroll department.

LO 8-8   8C.16 Which of the following payroll control activities would most effectively ensure that payment is made only for work performed?

a. Require all employees to record arrival and departure by using the time clock.

b. Have a payroll clerk recalculate all time cards.

c. Require all employees to sign their time cards.

d. Require employees to have their direct supervisors approve their time cards.

(AICPA adapted)

LO 8-8   8C.17 Which of the following activities performed by a department supervisor most likely would help to prevent or detect a payroll fraud?

a. Distributing paychecks directly to department employees.

b. Setting the pay rate for departmental employees.

c. Hiring employees and authorizing them to be added to payroll.

d. Approving a summary of hours each employee worked during the pay period.

(AICPA adapted)

Exercises and Problems

Exercises and
Problems

McGraw Hill **connect**   All applicable Exercises and Problems are available with
Connect.

LO 8-8

8C.18 Major Risks in Payroll Cycle. Prepare a schedule of the major risks in the payroll cycle. Identify the financial statement assertions related to each. Create a two-column schedule like this:

Payroll Cycle Risk	Assertion

LO 8-8

8C.19 Payroll Authorization in a Computerized System. Two accountants were discussing control activities and tests of controls for payroll systems. The senior accountant in charge of the engagement said: "It is impossible to determine who authorizes transactions when the payroll account is computerized."

Required:

Evaluate the senior accountant's statement about control in a computerized payroll system. List the points in the flow of payroll information where authorization takes place.

LO 8-8

8C.20 Payroll Processed by a Service Organization. Assume that you are the audit senior conducting a review of a new client's payroll system. In the process of interviewing the payroll department manager, she makes the following statement: "We don't need many controls because our payroll is done outside the company by Automated Information Processing, a service organization."

Required:

Evaluate the payroll department manager's statement and describe how a service organization affects an auditor's review of controls.

LO 8-8

8C.21 Payroll Audit Procedures, Computers, and Sampling. You are the senior auditor in charge of the annual audit of Onward Manufacturing Corporation for the year ending December 31. The company is of medium size with only 300 employees. All 300 employees are union members paid by the hour at rates set forth in a union contract, a copy of which is furnished to you. Job and pay rate classifications are determined by a joint union–management conference, and a formal memorandum is placed in each employee's personnel file.

Every week, clock cards prepared and approved in the shop are collected and transmitted to the payroll department. The total of labor hours is summed on a calculator and entered on each clock card. Batch and hash totals are obtained for the following: (1) labor hours and (2) last four digits of Social Security numbers. These data are input into a disk file, batch balanced, and batch processed. The clock cards (with cost classification data) are sent to the cost accounting department.

The payroll system is computerized. As each person's payroll record is processed, the Social Security number is matched to a table (in a separate master file) to obtain job classification and pay rate data, then the pay rate is multiplied by the number of hours, and the check is printed. (Ignore payroll deductions for the following requirements.)

Required:

a. What audit procedures would you recommend to obtain evidence that payroll data are accurately totaled and transformed into machine-readable records? What deviation rate might you expect? What tolerable deviation rate would you set? What "items" would you sample? What factors should you consider in setting the size of your sample?

b. What audit procedures would you recommend to obtain evidence that the pay rates are appropriately assigned and used in figuring gross pay? In what way, if any, would these procedures be different if the gross pay were calculated by hand instead of on a computer?

LO 8-8

8C.22 Payroll Tests of Controls. The following diagram describes several payroll tests of controls. It shows the direction of the tests, leading from samples of clock cards, payrolls, and cumulative year-to-date earnings records to blank squares.

Required:

For each blank square in the diagram, write a payroll test of controls procedure and describe the evidence it can produce. (*Hint:* Refer to Exhibit 5.9.)

**Diagram of Payroll
Tests of Controls**

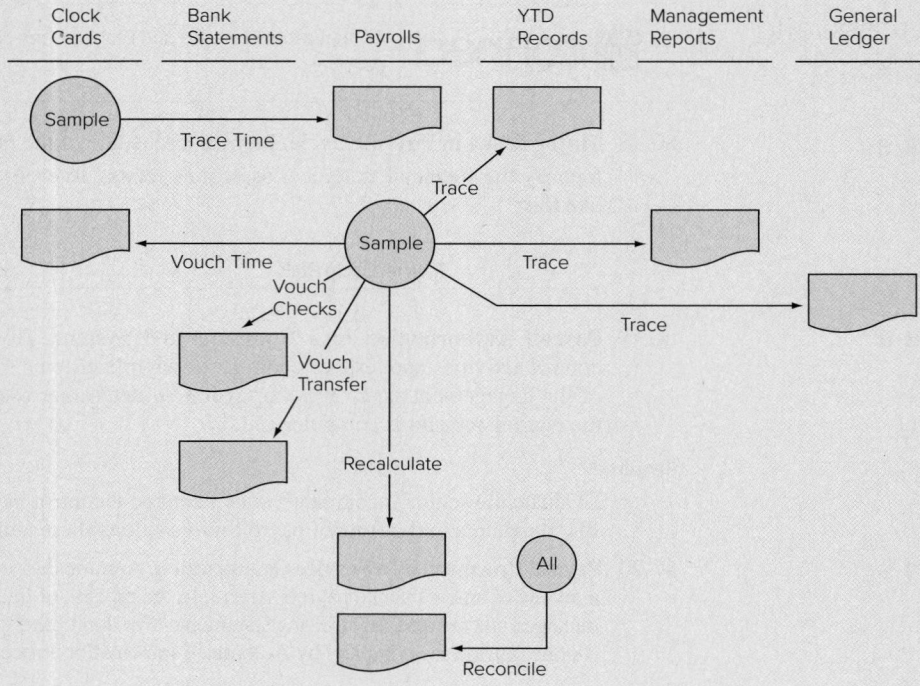

Apollo Shoes

Payroll Audit

You are a recently promoted senior (in charge) auditor for Anderson, Olds, and Watershed and have been assigned to the engagement team of a new audit client, Apollo Shoes Inc. You have been asked to perform certain procedures for the audit of the payroll process. A detailed audit program for payroll and supporting documentation, including audit documentation, can be found in *Connect*.

CHAPTER 9

The Production Cycle and Auditing Inventory

> *There is one rule for industrialists and that is: Make the best-quality of goods possible at the lowest cost possible, paying the highest wages possible.*
>
> *Henry Ford*

Professional Standards References

Topic	AU-C/ISA Section	PCAOB Reference*
Audit Documentation	230	AS 1215
Auditors' Responses to the Risks of Material Misstatements	240	AS 2301
Audit Planning	300	AS 2101
Identifying and Assessing the Risks of Material Misstatement	315	AS 2110
Materiality	320	AS 2105
Audit Evidence	500/501	AS 1105
Substantive Analytical Procedures	520	AS 2305
Auditing Accounting Estimates	540	AU 2501
Using the Work of an Audit Specialist	620	AU 1210

LEARNING OBJECTIVES

For most nonfinancial service companies, inventory is a material and risky area of the audit. For nonmanufacturing companies, inventory is purchased in the purchasing cycle, as described in Chapter 8. However, manufacturers have an additional cycle. In the production cycle, materials, labor, and overhead are converted into finished goods (inventory) and services. This chapter introduces the production cycle but focuses on the audit of inventory in general, especially determining the existence and valuation of a client's inventory, as well as cost of goods sold. Observation of the client's physical inventory count is such an important audit procedure that auditing standards require it. This chapter discusses procedures to be followed in observing the physical inventory count. It also discusses procedures for auditing the accumulation and pricing of inventory and recording it in the financial statements.

This chapter includes several short cases to illustrate the application of audit procedures in situations in which errors and frauds can be discovered.

Your objectives are to be able to

LO 9-1 Describe the production cycle, including typical source documents.

LO 9-2 Identify significant accounts and relevant assertions related to the audit of inventory.

LO 9-3 Discuss the risk of material misstatement in the audit of inventory.

LO 9-4 Identify important internal control activities present in a properly designed system to mitigate the risk of material misstatements for each relevant assertion in inventory management.

LO 9-5 Give examples of tests of controls to test the operating effectiveness of internal controls in managing inventory.

LO 9-6 Give examples of substantive procedures in audits of inventory and relate them to assertions about significant account balances at the end of the period.

LO 9-7 Apply your knowledge to perform audit procedures in the audit of inventory and evaluate the findings of your tests.

KEEPING COUNT

Nearly every auditor who has audited a nonfinancial services company has participated in an inventory count and has stories to tell. From the young, professionally dressed staff auditor climbing a grain silo while every employee from the client cheers, to celebrating New Year's Eve in a warehouse, inventory observation is a procedure that provides critical and required evidence in an audit. Inventory is considered so important that the procedures for evaluating the existence and condition of material amounts of inventory are specifically outlined in the auditing standards.

Similar to practice, auditing courses often spend considerable time discussing the difficulties of specific interesting inventory count issues. For example, the issues associated with free-range livestock can be challenging. Counts often entail moving cows, sheep, or other animals through a gate, while having two people keep a count. Because the animals are uncontrollable and the farms often have issues with dust flying everywhere, obtaining an accurate count can be challenging, tedious, and definitely not much fun. Similarly, controlling the movement of raw materials in a production increase, or goods in retail stores can involve shutting down production or sales, and the increased possibility of human error.

Advances in technology are beginning to change the landscape of inventory counts. Advanced, programmable drones have the capability to count an entire warehouse and even detect any movement of items during the count. Another application of drone technology is in the counting of livestock. Consider the example mentioned in the last paragraph—a farm with thousands of free-range sheep. As an alternative to the tedious, messy, and error-prone process of counting the sheep manually as they charge through a gate often four or five at a time, a professionally trained drone pilot, licensed through the Federal Aviation Administration, flies a drone over the farm. The pilot takes one or more high-resolution photographs capturing the sheep in real time. The images are then pulled into automated counting software, such as **CountThings** and a preliminary count is obtained. The auditor then uses a magnified digital image of the count to identify errors the software made in counting, where perhaps an oddly colored sheep is missed or two sheep close together are counted as one, or perhaps a sheep-like bush is counted. By using the drone technology, the process is far less messy and tedious. Further, the audit documentation is superior because photo records of the count exist and can be verified.

However, the advancement of technology does not take away the need for auditor skepticism and judgment. How does the auditor know the condition or health of the sheep in a drone photo? How does the auditor know that the boxes counted in a warehouse by a drone have the correct product in them? Are the 5,000,000 microchips counted in an instant salable and as described? Because of the importance of auditor judgment, no amount of technology can take away the need for professionally trained auditors, and if anything, the importance of high-quality judgment is more important now than ever. The process may just be less smelly and dusty, and fewer auditors will experience the joy of being a celebrity for a day, climbing up the side of a grain silo.

This chapter will begin with a description of a production cycle in a manufacturing environment because although nearly all auditing students have shopped at a retailer or have driven past a farm, many likely do not know the issues involved with producing goods. However, the chapter will focus on the significant accounts and relevant assertions for auditing inventory in a variety of industries.

INVENTORY MANAGEMENT: TYPICAL ACTIVITIES

LO 9-1
Describe the production cycle, including typical source documents.

Many companies, including retailers such as **Target,** sell goods produced by other parties. In Chapter 8 you learned about the purchasing cycle, where companies purchase goods for both use in the business and for sale. There you learned about important controls surrounding the purchasing and handling of goods, as well as substantive tests that are performed in the purchasing process. Chapter 8 did not discuss how auditors obtain assurance regarding the goods held by the client at year-end, or how an auditor gains assurance related to the costing of goods produced by an entity. For any company with a material amount of inventory, auditors are concerned about the existence as well as the pricing of that inventory. For a retailer like Target, auditors focus on verifying the quantity of goods on hand, the company's system for inventory cost flow assumptions, and whether all goods on hand are salable at an amount greater or equal to cost. However, many other companies, such as **Ford Motor Company,** manufacture the goods that they sell. When auditing a manufacturer, whether it is a small entity producing specialty goods or one of the world's largest automakers, it is paramount that an auditor understand all stages involved with converting raw materials into finished goods. If this process is not properly controlled, not only are financial statement misstatements likely, but also mismanagement of inventory can quickly put a company out of business when companies either are not able to manufacture enough goods or are faced with large overstocks that are obsolete and overvalued.

The production cycle links the acquisition cycle, in which goods and services are purchased, to the revenue cycle, in which the inventory is sold (see Exhibit 9.1). These cycles, along with the payroll cycle, account for all additions and reductions of inventory items. Thus, the production cycle (Exhibit 9.2) is mostly concerned with accounting for inventory as it moves through the production stages from raw materials to work-in-process to finished goods and for accumulating accurate costs of the inventory items. Because the production cycle is critical for manufacturers, this chapter begins with a discussion of the typical activities for companies that produce the goods they sell.

EXHIBIT 9.1
Relationship of Business Cycles

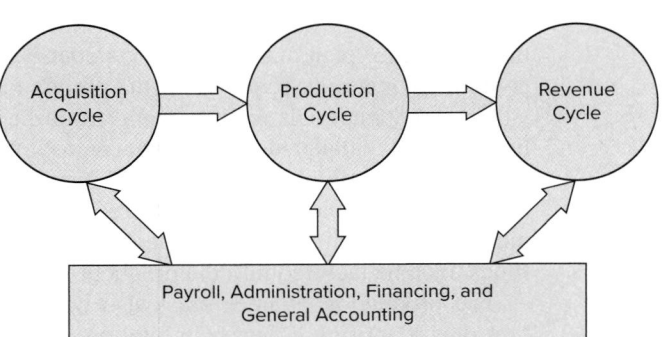

EXHIBIT 9.2
Production Cycle

Stage	Activities
Production Planning	• Prepare **Sale Forecast** • Prepare **Production Plan** • Identify necessary materials **(Bill of Materials)** • Acquire materials (see Acquisition Cycle)
Production	• Prepare **Production Order** • Transfer materials to production **(Materials Requisition)** • Complete production (allocate direct labor and overhead costs)
Cost Accounting	• Account for differences between standard and actual costs • Allocate costs between inventory and cost of goods sold

Sales Forecasts and Production Planning

Production activities start with a sales forecast, a marketing projection of product sales, based on past performance and marketing initiatives. Based on this forecast and other pertinent factors (e.g., production setup costs, scheduled equipment maintenance, finished goods inventories, and raw material inventories), the production planner can determine both the type and the quantity of products that need to be produced to meet anticipated demand and can schedule the products in a production plan. The sales forecast is one of the most important documents in any organization. If it is incorrect and underestimates the company's production requirements, hundreds of thousands of dollars of potential profits may be unattainable. However, if it is incorrect and overstates the product demand, millions of dollars of raw material and finished goods inventory may needlessly utilize corporate assets and warehouse space.

The goal of production planning is to provide a schedule for manufacturing, called the production plan, so that quality products will be available at the appropriate time for the lowest cost. For example, production planners must balance the finished goods warehousing costs associated with making large (high-quantity) production runs with the changeover costs of making several smaller (low-quantity) production runs. In addition, production planners must integrate corporate strategies such as long-range plans and just-in-time (JIT) inventory management.

The physical output of a production cycle is inventory (starting with raw materials, proceeding to work-in-process, and then moving through to finished goods). The finished goods link the production process to the revenue and collection cycle in terms of orders and deliveries. Most of the transactions in a production cycle are cost accounting allocations, unit cost determinations, and standard cost calculations. These are internal transactions produced entirely within the company's accounting system. Therefore, accounting in the production cycle also includes the elements of depreciation cost calculation, cost of goods sold determination, and production cost analysis as examples of these transactions.

The job of the production planner is one of the most critical in any manufacturing operation and can be thought of as the authorization function. The production planner should never have custody of the materials, nor should the planner be involved in record keeping or reconciliation. The production planner not only creates a production plan but also must identify the total quantity of raw materials necessary for production based on the production plan and the bill of materials (a specification of the type and quantity of component materials required for the production).

Once raw materials requirements (from the bill of materials) are known, the planner uses the raw material inventory status report to determine whether enough raw materials are in stock to complete production. If insufficient raw materials exist, additional materials must be purchased, and if required, the planner must send a purchase requisition to purchasing (which begins the expenditure cycle as discussed in Chapter 8). Purchase lead times must be factored into the production plan.

The production planner must also be aware of labor requirements. If the production plan identifies a change in total production, human resources must be aware of the impact on the labor force. When the labor force is an issue, major problems can occur in the production process, as discussed in the following Auditing Insight, "Production Problems Galore".

AUDITING INSIGHT   Production Problems Galore

The COVID-19 pandemic lead to a substantial disruption in production and supplies in a large number of areas. Toilet paper and hand sanitizer became unavailable. Used cars went up in price substantially as new cars became unavailable. Manufactured items were reported to be of lower quality. Furthermore, some companies canceled inventory counts and others would not allow auditors to be present at their factories. Nearly every major audit regulator and CPA society issued reports providing guidance to auditors on how to deal with scope restrictions related to inventory. Some auditors adopted advanced video technology that enabled them to be present at counts from a remote location. Others found alternative ways to substantiate production counts and inventory balances. The pandemic represents just one of many events that can disrupt a production process, which is why auditors should always be familiar with the production process for their clients.

Source: *Coronavirus (Covid-19): Considerations for Inventory Audit Testing,* The Institute of Chartered Accountants in England and Wales, 2022.

Production

Once the production plan has been finalized, it is generally shared with managers in the sales/marketing department, production department, and possibly human resources who may be required to "sign off" as evidence of their approval of the plan. Managers may request adjustments to the schedule or may need to adjust personnel, maintenance schedules, even overtime, to ensure that production operates efficiently. As you can see, an error in the production plan may mean insufficient raw materials and personnel, excessive warehousing of finished goods, an oversupply of raw materials, unnecessary personnel, or insufficient finished goods to meet demand. All of these conditions represent real, substantial costs to the entity.

As the time for production nears, the production planner issues a **production order** to the appropriate production personnel including inventory control and production managers. The employees who handle materials and finished goods within the production department make up the custody function. They should never authorize production, nor should they have direct authority for recordkeeping or reconciliation. Inventory control will receive a **materials requisition**, or **materials transfer ticket**, that authorizes inventory to release raw materials and supplies to production. These documents are the inventory record-keepers' authorizations to update the raw materials inventory files by recording the reductions of the raw materials inventory.

Cost Accounting

When production is completed, production orders and the related records of materials and labor used are sent to the cost accounting department. Labor is reported by various means from time sheets to computerized clocks. Employees designate what job or product they worked on, or the labor is automatically assigned based on the department or machinery to which the employee is assigned. Because these accounting documents may come from the production workers, it may require an independent verification of hours worked from other sources (e.g., notifications of materials from the inventory custodian or labor costs assigned from the payroll department). The accounting for the costs of production should never be done by individuals with access to the inventory or with the ability to authorize production.

Cost accounting generally records finished goods at **standard costs**. Developing standard costs is a difficult, time-consuming process, even for relatively simple products. All materials, supplies, labor, and overhead that go into the product must be measured based on the bill of materials and accumulated into the production cost. Differences between standard costs and actual costs are recorded in variance accounts and reviewed by supervisors. (*Note:* GAAP recognizes specific-item; first-in, first-out [FIFO]; last-in, first-out [LIFO]; and weighted-average costing but does not recognize standard costs per se.

The auditor must ensure that standard costs are not materially different from the GAAP method that the client has adopted.)

The cost accounting department produces analyses of actual cost per unit, standard cost, and variances. Cost accounting also may determine the **overhead allocation** to production in general, to production orders, and to finished units. Depending on the design of the company's cost accounting system, these costs are used to value inventory and ultimately to determine the cost of goods sold. In addition, production reports are authorization for the finished goods inventory custodian to place the units in the finished goods inventory. The reports also authorize the inventory record-keepers to update the finished goods inventory.

It would be wrong to think of some elements of the production cycle as only applying to manufacturing companies. Clearly, Target has a sales forecast, and its product managers (their equivalent of a production manager) need to determine what products are available in stores and in the warehouses and compare that with the forecasted needs. Purchase requisitions are issued to buy additional product and have it available at the appropriate time. In a sense, production for a retailer may be viewed as the process of getting items from the warehouse to the store and into the appropriate retail space for sale.

 REVIEW CHECKPOINTS

9.1 What functions are normally associated with the production cycle?

9.2 What inventory costing methods does GAAP recognize?

9.3 Describe a walkthrough of a production transaction from receiving production orders to making an entry in the finished goods perpetual inventory records. What document copies would be collected? What controls noted? What duties separated?

9.4 How might an auditor use a client's sales forecast for general familiarity with the production cycle or for evaluation of slow-moving inventory?

SIGNIFICANT ACCOUNTS AND RELEVANT ASSERTIONS

LO 9-2

Identify significant accounts and relevant assertions related to the audit of inventory.

STAGES OF AN AUDIT

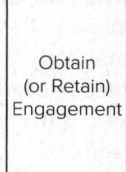 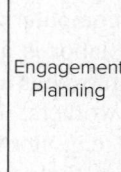 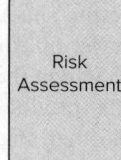 

Obtain (or Retain) Engagement | Engagement Planning | Risk Assessment | Audit Evidence | Reporting

Exhibit 9.3 identifies the significant accounts and assertions in the audit of inventory. In this portion of the audit, the most significant risks usually relate to the existence and valuation of inventory. In addition, because whenever inventory is sold a cost for the inventory must be recognized, cost of goods sold also has significant risk. If management wants to inflate sales by creating fictitious sales or inflating sales amounts, there must be a corresponding debit. Expenses can be used for this purpose as explained in Chapter 8. However, inventory has also been a favorite place to hide fraud for many infamous frauds (e.g., **Phar-Mor, Crazy Eddie's**).

EXHIBIT 9.3
Significant Accounts and Assertions in the Production Cycle

Significant Account	Relevant Assertions
Inventory	Existence
	Completeness
	Cutoff
	Valuation & Allocation
	Rights
	Presentation & Disclosure
Cost of goods sold	Completeness
	Accuracy

Unethical managers might prefer to manipulate inventory instead of other expenses because of the double effect on the financial statements. When ending inventory is overstated, assets are overstated and cost of goods sold is understated, thereby increasing both total assets and income. Analysts often look at a company's profit margins to determine how well it is managing costs and to determine whether the company can maintain sufficient markup to cover other operating and nonoperating costs and be competitive.

Another reason that inventory is an inviting target for manipulation is the complexity and subjectivity involved in accounting for it. Because there are many large purchases of inventory, many fraudsters believe that fictitious or overstated transactions may be hard to catch or the audit of inventory can be controlled to the extent that such inflated inventory numbers can be obscured from the auditors. Further, even if the inventory account is correct, the manipulation of the cost by only a few cents on many items can result in a multimillion dollar misstatement. Therefore, the audit of inventory is especially important to ensure that the financial statements are not materially misstated.

Even a relatively simple inventory process can be manipulated and misstated. Many corporate frauds such as those at **Crazy Eddie's, Leslie Fay,** and **Health Management** were concealed by creating nonexistent or overvalued inventory. Inventory is often the largest current asset on a company's balance sheet, and it is likely to be a complex account. Imagine trying to value the cars at **General Motors,** the $33 billion of product held by **Amazon.com, Inc.,** or the oil reserves at **ExxonMobil.** How about the $1.2 billion in livestock listed as inventory by **Tyson Foods**? That's a lot of animals to count and value! Even inventories of simple commodities present issues of measurement and valuation. Inventories of more complex items such as biochemicals or genetically modified crops can require the use of specialists by the auditors.

Items should be added to inventory when the company has title to them and included in cost of goods sold when the related revenue is recognized.[2] In addition, when a manufacturer has work-in-process inventory, this may be especially difficult because each item has different amounts of materials and labor incorporated into the product at the inventory date. These multiple and often subjective evaluations make inventory a high-risk area that is susceptible to errors. Also, management can use inventory manipulation to overstate assets and income.

A number of problems can arise in accounting for inventory. Some inventories are very susceptible to theft. Others require complex cost build-ups (especially if they are valued at LIFO). GAAP requires inventory to be stated at the lower of cost or **net realizable value (NRV)**. Cost is the total price paid, including freight-in, or estimates of actual costs using LIFO, FIFO, or an average. Net realizable value is the selling price of the goods less all costs to complete and to sell the goods (e.g., sales commissions). In some volatile industries, inventory valuation impairments can be extremely large as discussed in the following Auditing Insight, "What's the Film Worth Today?".

[2]FASB, "Revenue Recognition," *ASC 606,* May 2014.

AUDITING INSIGHT | What's the Film Worth Today?

It's hard to imagine the costs of production of films and television series as inventory, but for many companies in film production, the capitalized costs are considered to be inventory. **AT&T, Inc.** is one such company that capitalizes the production costs of television episodes and films. With the onset of the COVID-19 pandemic, film production companies suffered significant declines in value to their digital inventory assets. Because of continuous closings of theaters during the pandemic and a decision by the company to release some completed films directly to streaming services, the company assessed a change in estimate and recognized a $524 million impairment to total inventories. This impairment was part of a larger $18.8 billion impairment charge recognized by the company. Ernst & Young, AT&T's auditors, recognized the impairment charges as a critical audit matter in the company's February 25, 2021, auditors' report. The auditors stated that auditing the impairment evaluations was "complex because the determination of expected cash flows ... involve subjective management assumptions.: Critical audit matters are further discussed in Chapter 12.

Source: *AT&T*, Inc. 2020 Annual Financial Review

Because of the multiple and complex risks for inventory, there are several relevant risks of material misstatement, as discussed in the next section.

 REVIEW CHECKPOINTS

9.5 If the actual sales for the year are substantially lower than the sales forecasted at the beginning of the year, what potential valuation problems could arise in the production cycle accounts?

9.6 The balance sheet of a company lists $25 million of inventory. What assertions is management making regarding inventory?

RISK OF MATERIAL MISSTATEMENT

LO 9-3
Discuss the risk of material misstatement in the audit of inventory.

When considering what could go wrong (WCGW) related to a client's inventory, auditors consider seven primary concerns:

1. Items included in inventory were in inventory on the balance sheet date (existence and cutoff).
2. All inventory items have been included (completeness).
3. Inventory has been properly accounted for and properly valued using an acceptable GAAP accounting method (valuation).
4. Items included in inventory were the property of the client (rights).
5. Proper presentation and disclosures have been provided for inventory (presentation and disclosure).
6. Cost of goods sold includes all costs of the inventory items sold during the year (completeness)
7. The amount of cost of goods sold has been properly accounted for using an acceptable GAAP accounting method (accuracy).

Exhibit 9.4 summarizes the WCGW analysis for inventory.

As previously discussed in this chapter, inventory is a significant account, with a pervasive effect on the financial statements, and combined with its volume and its complexity, a misstatement may be probable if sufficient internal controls are not in place. In order for inventory to be properly disclosed, all items constituting inventory must be included and correctly valued. Consider the balance sheet except and inventory footnote for Target's 2021 fiscal year (January 29, 2022) shown in Exhibit 9.5. Note that Target asserts that it has $13.9 billion in inventory, which represents 64 percent of its current assets and 26 percent of its total assets. Other than buildings and improvements, it is the largest single asset that

EXHIBIT 9.4
Assertions and What Could Go Wrong in the Audit of Inventory

Significant Account	Relevant Assertions	What Could Go Wrong?
Inventory	Existence	Items included in inventory records are not actual items in inventory.
	Completeness	Some items are not included in inventory.
	Cutoff	Inventory transactions occurring near year end are recorded in the incorrect period.
	Valuation	Inventory cost flow assumptions (e.g. FIFO) have been applied incorrectly Proper costs of direct materials, direct labor, and overhead are not allocated to produced inventory. Inventory is damaged or obsolete and has declined in value.
	Rights	Items held on consignment for others are included in inventory.
	Presentation & Disclosure	Inventory pledged as collateral is not disclosed. Cost flow assumptions are not disclosed. Inventory is misclassified among raw materials, work in process and finished goods.
Cost of goods sold	Completeness	Labor or material may be omitted from production costs.
	Accuracy	Costs of direct material, labor, and overhead have not been properly calculated.

EXHIBIT 9.5
Excerpts from Target Corporation's 10-K
Panel A Consolidated Statements of Financial Position (millions, except footnotes)

	January 29, 2022	January 30, 2021
Assets		
Cash and cash equivalents	$5,911	$8,511
Inventory	13,902	10,653
Other current assets	1,760	1,592
Total current assets	21,573	20,756
Property and equipment		
Land	6,164	6,141
Buildings and improvements	32,985	31,557
Fixtures and equipment	6,407	5,914
Computer hardware and software	2,505	2,765
Construction-in-progress	1,257	780
Accumulated depreciation	(21,137)	(20,278)
Property and equipment, net	28,181	26,879
Operating lease assets	2,556	2,227
Other noncurrent assets	1,501	1,386
Total assets	$53,811	$51,248

Panel B Inventory Footnote

12. Inventory

The vast majority of our inventory is accounted for under the retail inventory accounting method (RIM) using the last-in, first-out (LIFO) method. Inventory is stated at the lower of LIFO cost or market. Inventory cost includes the amount we pay to our suppliers to acquire inventory, freight costs incurred to deliver product to our distribution centers and stores, and import costs, reduced by vendor income and cash discounts. Distribution center operating costs, including compensation and benefits, are expensed in the period incurred. Inventory is also reduced for estimated losses related to shrink and markdowns. The LIFO provision is calculated based on inventory levels, markup rates, and internally measured retail price indices.

Under RIM, inventory cost and the resulting gross margins are calculated by applying a cost-to-retail ratio to the inventory retail value. RIM is an averaging method that has been widely used in the retail industry due to its practicality. **The use of RIM will result in inventory being valued at the lower of cost or market because permanent markdowns are taken as a reduction of the retail value of inventory.**

Source: *Target Form 10-K,* March 9, 2022.

Target owns. Further, consider the difficulties in establishing this number in its 1,926 stores and 48 distribution centers in the United States. Consider that if Target has 1,000 pairs of socks in each store and 10,000 in each warehouse and the cost was misstated by 10 cents, the balance sheet error would be more than $240,000. While this is not a material amount to an inventory of $13.9 billion, it illustrates how a small error or misstatement can result in a large inventory valuation error. Target's auditors, Ernst & Young, also considered inventory to be one of two critical audit matters specifically addressed in the audit report.

An additional review of Target's inventory footnote reveals other important information. As noted in the footnote (emphasized in bold), the footnote speaks of using a retail inventory accounting method to value inventory and discusses that some items have been marked down in value. Without good internal controls, a small error in the application of the cost estimation could produce a substantial inventory misstatement. Clearly, Target must take great care in establishing the value of its inventory in its entire system, and auditors must take care that the accumulation of inventory misstatements does not lead to a material misstatement in its financial statements.

Now let's look at how an inventory misstatement might affect the overall financial statements. The following table provides numbers for inventory, sales, cost of sales, earnings from continuing operations, and net income reported by Target in its January 29, 2022, 10-K report (all amounts in millions of dollars). While Target does an excellent job of preparing financial statements and we have no reason to suspect that the numbers presented are inaccurate in any way, for our purposes, let's suppose that 5 percent of Target's reported inventory, or $695 million, is overstated. The third column shows how this hypothetical misstatement affects each of the accounts presented. Ignoring tax effects, this 5 percent inventory misstatement would result in a 11 percent overstatement of true net income. When auditors identify inventory as a pervasive issue, they are referring to this cascading effect of the error—it affects many areas of the financial statements.

Account	Actual Amount as Reported for Target Jan 29, 2022	Actual if a 5% Inventory Overstatement Error Exists
Inventory	$ 13,902	$13,207
Sales	104,611	104,611
Cost of sales	74,963	75,658
Net Income	6,946	6,251

✅ REVIEW CHECKPOINTS

9.7 What are the different types of cost included in cost of goods sold for a production operation? What are the significant risks that would make this calculation inaccurate?

9.8 What makes the recording of inventory at its proper amount difficult on the financial statements?

9.9 Why do auditors consider inventory errors pervasive?

INTERNAL CONTROL ACTIVITIES AND DESIGN EVALUATION

LO 9-4
Identify important internal control activities present in a properly designed system to mitigate the risk of material misstatements for each relevant assertion in inventory management.

In order to properly assess control risk, the auditor must understand the internal control system, assess the design of the controls, and assess whether the controls are in operation. Control risk assessment is important because it governs the *nature, timing,* and *extent* of substantive procedures that will be performed in the audit of inventory. For many retailers and wholesalers, the inventory balance consists of the costs of acquiring the inventory from third parties. However, for a manufacturer, the inventory account balances take into account that goods may be at multiple stages of the production cycle. Thus, multiple inventory account balances include

- Raw materials inventory.
- Work-in-process inventory.
- Finished goods inventory.

With respect to inventory valuation, this leads to significantly more risk in determining the cost basis of inventory. Controls surrounding the purchase of inventory by a retailer are similar to the controls for the purchase of any item, and were discussed in Chapter 8. Thus, this chapter focuses on the cost accounting function and its role in determining the cost valuation of manufactured finished goods, as well as controls surrounding inventory held in stock.

Entity-Level Controls

It is important that auditors consider entity-level controls in all processes and procedures. In the production cycle, controls over access to the production facility, including inventory, are essential. The prevention of theft of inventory and equipment begins with a facility that requires escorts for visitors and ensures that only authorized personnel have access to inventory and production areas. Furthermore, adequate security must be enforced when the facility is not in operation. Finally, production reports should be adequate to ensure that only authorized operations are performed and that performance statistics are reviewed on a timely basis and anomalies are investigated promptly.

Control Considerations

Control activities for proper separation of duties should be in place and operating. Proper separation involves authorization (production planning, inventory planning, and purchase requisitions) by persons who do not have custody, record-keeping, cost accounting, or reconciliation duties. Custody of inventories (raw materials, work-in-process, and finished goods) is in the hands of persons who do not authorize the amount or timing of production or the purchase of materials and labor, perform the cost accounting record keeping, or prepare cost analyses (reconciliations). Persons who do not authorize production or have custody of assets in the production process perform cost accounting (a recording function). Combinations of two or more of the duties of authorization, custody, and accounting in one person, one office, or one computerized system could open the door for errors and frauds.

In addition, the internal control system should provide for detailed authorization, information processing, and management review control activities, for example

- Production orders should contain a list of materials and their quantities, and they should be approved by a production planner/scheduler.
- Material should not be issued to the production floor without an authorized material requisition.
- Material requisitions should be compared in the cost accounting department with the list of materials on the production orders, and the production operator and the materials inventory storekeeper should sign the materials requisitions.
- All material requisitions should be accounted for. Material requisitioned is used in production, is unusable (scrap), or excess material returned to raw material inventory.
- Documentation for material returned to raw material inventory should accompany the returned items with a copy going to inventory control for use in adjusting the perpetual raw material inventory.
- Production supervisors should sign (or review if the time is kept electronically) labor time records on jobs, and the cost accounting department should reconcile these cost amounts with the labor report from the payroll department.

- The production supervisor and finished goods inventory custodian should review production reports of finished units and then forward them to cost accounting.
- Inventory should be periodically counted with the counts agreed to perpetual inventory records.

These control activities track the raw materials and labor from the beginning of production to completion of the production process. With each internal transaction, the responsibility and accountability for assets are passed from one person or location to another.

Many entities have complex computer systems to manage production and materials flow. Even though the technology is complex, the basic management and control functions of ensuring the flow of labor and materials to production and the control of waste should be in place. Manual signatures, paper production orders, and paper requisitions often do not exist, but electronic equivalents should be in place.

Custody

Supervisors and production workers have physical custody of materials and labor documents (time cards, job tickets, etc.) while the production work is being performed. Authorized employees can requisition materials from the raw materials inventory, assign people to jobs, and control the pace of work. In a sense, they have custody of a "moving inventory." The work-in-process (WIP) is literally "moving" and changing form in the process of being transformed from raw materials into finished goods.

Inventory warehouses and fixed asset locations should be under adequate physical security (storerooms, fences, locks, and the like). However, control over goods in process is more difficult than control over a warehouse of raw materials or finished goods where unauthorized individuals cannot gain access. Control over WIP can be exercised by holding supervisors and workers accountable for the use of materials specified in the production orders, for the timely completion of production, and for the quality of the finished goods. This accountability can be achieved with effective cost accounting, cost analysis, performance reviews, and quality control testing. Accountability may be evident by ensuring that supervisors and management are analyzing the costs of production orders, comparing the costs to prior experience or to standard costs, and determining lower-of-cost-or-NRV valuations. When costs of material or labor, scrap rates for materials, or production numbers do not meet expectations, management should require a documented assessment by cost accounting or internal audit to determine the cause and corrective action required.

AUDITING INSIGHT ⟩ Temp or Perm?

The Securities and Exchange Commission charged the Jacksonville, Florida-based retail chain **Stein Mart Inc.** with materially misstating its pretax income due to improper valuation of inventory subject to price discounts and for having inadequate internal accounting controls.

An SEC investigation found the retailer often offered its merchandise to customers at retail price reductions referred to as "Perm POS markdowns" and that merchandise subject to such a markdown never reverted back to its original retail price. Stein Mart reduced the value of inventory subject to these markdowns at the time the item was sold rather than immediately at the time the markdown was applied.

As a result, according to the SEC, Stein Mart materially misstated its pretax income in certain quarterly public filings with the SEC, including an overstatement of almost 30 percent in the first quarter of 2012.

"Inventory is one of the most significant assets for retail companies, and as a result, it is critical that companies have effective internal accounting controls to ensure that inventory is valued properly," said

Michael Maloney, chief accountant of the SEC's Enforcement Division, in a statement. "Stein Mart failed in this regard as its internal accounting controls to ensure proper inventory valuations were inadequate in various ways."

According to the SEC's order instituting a settled administrative proceeding, Stein Mart's internal accounting controls over Perm POS markdowns were inadequate. For example, until at least the middle of 2011, the retailer's decision to characterize a markdown as Perm POS resided solely with Stein Mart's merchandising department, which did not understand the impact that Stein Mart's markdowns could have on inventory valuation accounting, according to the SEC.

In the fall of 2012, Stein Mart raised its accounting treatment of Perm POS markdowns with its external auditor, and the external auditor informed Stein Mart that its accounting for Perm POS markdowns was not acceptable under GAAP. In May 2013, Stein Mart restated its financial results for the first quarter of 2012, all reporting periods in

EXHIBIT 9.8   Additional Risks and Controls Specific to the Production Cycle

What Could Go Wrong?	Internal Control Activity	Tests of Internal Control
Occurrence—Production and related events that have been recorded have not actually occurred.	• Cost accounting is separated from production, payroll, and inventory control. • Material usage reports are reconciled with raw material stores' issue slips, scrap reports, and documentation of unused material returned to inventory.	• Observe separation of cost accounting function from production, payroll, and inventory control. • Inspect evidence of reconciliations.
Completeness—Some production documents have not been recorded.	• All documents are prenumbered and numerical sequence reviewed. • Periodic count of raw materials and WIP inventory is compared to perpetual records. • Open production cost reports are reconciled to the WIP inventory cost report. • Receiving reports and material usage are posted to perpetual inventory records. • Job cost sheets are posted weekly, and summary journal entries of work-in-process and work completed are prepared monthly.	• Inspect evidence of review of numerical sequence. Select a sample of documents and examine numerical sequence. • Inspect evidence that inventory counts are compared to perpetual records. • Inspect reconciliation of production cost reports to WIP inventory control report. • Trace receiving reports to perpetual inventory. Trace materials used reports to production cost reports. • Inspect journal entries and agree with approved cost sheets. Compare costs to standard cost listing.
Accuracy—Production information, including costs, has been improperly calculated and recorded.	• Labor usage reports are compared to job time tickets. • Material usage and labor usage reports are prepared by floor supervisor and approved by production supervisor. • Periodic count of inventory is compared to perpetual records. • Receiving reports are posted to perpetual inventory on a timely basis.	• Inspect evidence of comparison by client. • Inspect evidence of approval of material and labor usage reports. • Inspect evidence that client reconciled inventory counts with perpetual records. • Trace dates on receiving reports to date posted in perpetual inventory records.
Cutoff—Production events have not been recorded in the correct accounting period.	• Receiving reports are posted to perpetual inventory in the proper period. • Finished goods are recorded in the proper period. • Production reports of material and labor are prepared weekly and transmitted to cost accounting.	• Vouch the dates of inventory records to receiving reports. • Inspect production data and agree with finished goods inventory status reports. • Inspect production reports and agree dates with dates in weekly journal entries.
Classification—Production material has been not been recorded in the proper accounts.	• Production supervisor is required to account for all material and labor as direct or indirect and to identify appropriate job classifications.	• Observe supervisor allocation. • Test allocation. • Examine supervisor signature.

general and application controls over the production reporting system in order to have some assurance that reports can be relied on for testing.

Direction of Tests of Controls

The tests of controls in Exhibit 9.8 are designed to test production accounting in two directions. One is the *completeness* direction, in which the auditors are interested in determining that all production that was started was recorded. Exhibit 9.9 shows that the sample for this direction is taken from the population of production orders found in the production-planning department. The procedures trace the cost accumulation forward to the production cost reports in the cost accounting department.

Testing the other direction relates to the *occurrence* of production. The auditors are interested in determining that items composing WIP and finished goods inventories recorded in the inventory accounts were produced. Exhibit 9.10 shows that the sample for this test is from the inventory accounts. This sample is vouched to the production

EXHIBIT 9.9
Test of Production Cost Controls: Completeness Direction

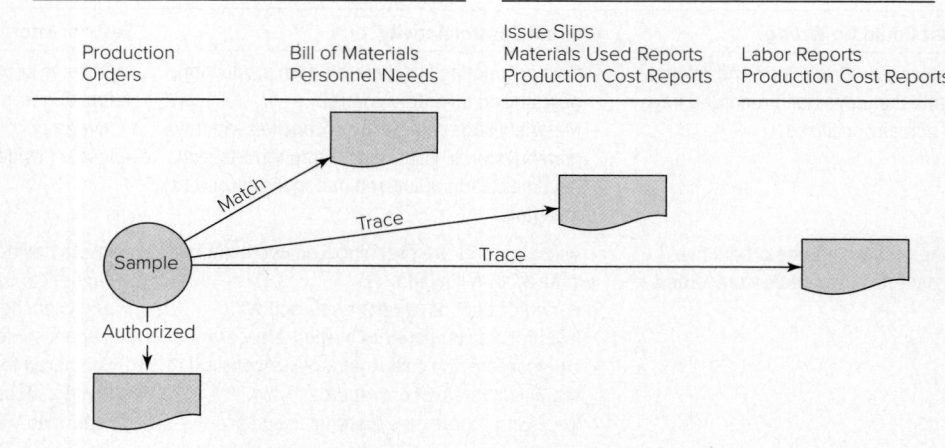

EXHIBIT 9.10
Test of Production Cost Controls: Occurrence Direction

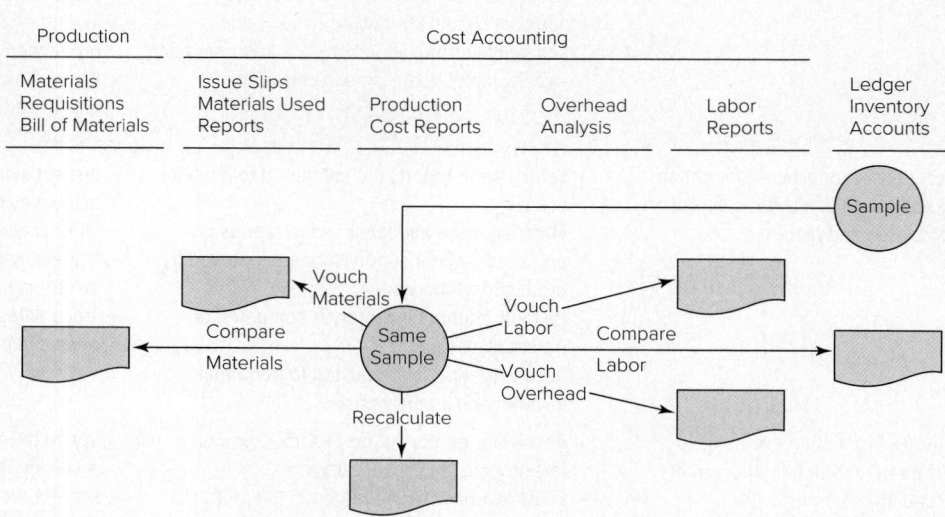

reports (quantity and cost) recorded in the inventory accounts. Additional testing may include vouching from the production reports to the recorded material, labor, and payroll reports. Potential findings include errors in the *accuracy* of the recorded inventory cost. Of course, CAATs could be used to perform a 100 percent match that would accomplish both goals.

Summary: Control Risk Assessment

The audit team should evaluate the evidence obtained from an understanding of the internal controls and from the tests of controls. The evaluation of control risk with the assessment of inherent risk provides the auditors an assessment of the risk of material misstatement. If the risk of material misstatement is relatively low, the substantive procedures on the account balances can be reduced. For example, if inventory observation test counts are performed on a date prior to the year-end, fewer counts would be made, and the inventory valuation procedures could be reduced in scope (i.e., smaller sample size). Furthermore, substantive analytical procedures could be used with more confidence in detecting material misstatements not otherwise evident in the accounting details.

On the other hand, if tests of controls reveal weaknesses and the risk of material misstatement is higher, the substantive procedures need to be designed to lower detection risk in the inventory and cost of goods sold account balances. For example, a large number of inventory production reports may be selected for valuation calculations, and the inventory observation may be scheduled nearer the year-end date with the audit team making a large number of test counts. Descriptions of significant deficiencies, control weaknesses, and inefficiencies may be incorporated in a letter to the client and must be communicated to the audit committee.

☑ REVIEW CHECKPOINTS

9.13   What population of documents would an auditor examine to determine whether (a) all authorized production was completed and placed in inventory or recorded as scrap and (b) finished goods inventory was actually produced and the costs were accounted for properly?

9.14   Why should receiving reports be prenumbered? What assertion would an auditor test using the receiving reports, and how would the auditor do this?

SUBSTANTIVE ANALYTICAL PROCEDURES AND TESTS OF DETAILS

LO 9-6
Give examples of substantive procedures in audits of inventory and relate them to assertions about significant account balances at the end of the period.

See Exhibit 9.11 for a continuation of the linking of assertions to sample risks and tests of controls, including a listing of primary substantive procedures used in an audit of inventory. When inventory is significant, GAAS requires auditors to be present to observe the client's physical inventory count. After the inventory has been counted, the client summarizes the count by item number and then applies a chosen costing method to determine the total amount of inventory owned on that date, which is compared with the amount in the general ledger. For example, recall from earlier in the chapter that Target uses a retail inventory accounting method.

EXHIBIT 9.11   Substantive Procedures in the Audit of Inventory

Significant Account	Relevant Assertions	What Could Go Wrong?	Internal Control Activity	Test of Internal Control	Possible Substantive Analytical Procedures	Possible Substantive Tests of Detail
Inventory	Existence	Items included in inventory records are not actual items in inventory.	Inventory areas should be secure.	Observe locked inventory areas and functioning cameras.	Compare inventory turnover ratio to budget and previous periods.	Observe client's physical inventory count.
			Any transfer of inventory must be authorized.	Inspect documentation of appropriate authorization of inventory transfers.	Compare gross profit percentage to budget and previous periods.	Confirm inventory held by others on consignment.
			Periodic physical inventory counts with reconciliation to records are performed.	Inspect documentation of periodic inventory counts and reconciliation.		Vouch items on inventory listing to inventory count tags.
	Completeness	Some items are not included in inventory.	Material requisitions are prenumbered, used in sequence, and reconciled daily.	Inspect requisition forms for numerical sequence and evidence of reconciliation.		Observe client's physical inventory count and ensure all items were counted.
						Trace inventory test counts to inventory listing.

(continued)

EXHIBIT 9.11 Substantive Procedures in the Audit of Inventory *(continued)*

Significant Account	Relevant Assertions	What Could Go Wrong?	Internal Control Activity	Test of Internal Control	Possible Substantive Analytical Procedures	Possible Substantive Tests of Detail
	Cutoff	Inventory transactions occurring near year end are recorded in the incorrect period.	Receiving reports are prenumbered, used in sequence, and reconciled daily.	Inspect receiving reports for sequential numbering and reconciliation.		Perform sales and purchase cutoff tests.
	Valuation	Inventory cost flow assumptions (e.g. FIFO) have been applied incorrectly.	Inventory costing records are reviewed by management.	Inspect documentation of management review.	Compare average unit costs of inventory with prior periods and purchase records.	Test mathematical accuracy of management's application of cost flow assumptions.
		Proper costs of direct materials, direct labor, and overhead are not allocated to produced inventory.	Cost sheets are reviewed for all projects and production runs.	Inspect job cost sheets for evidence of managerial review. Vouch costs from cost sheets to supporting documentation.		Vouch inventory costs to standard costs and recalculate standard costs.
		Inventory is damaged or obsolete and has declined in value.	Inventory items are reviewed periodically for salability.	Inspect documentation of review procedures and observe evaluation.	Compare inventory turnover ratio at the product level to previous periods or budget.	Inquire whether any inventory is obsolete or unsalable. Perform lower-of-cost-or-NRV tests.
	Rights	Items held on consignment for others are included in inventory.	A separate account number is used to track inventory on consignment.	Inspect documentation of procedures for consigned inventory and observe use of separate account numbers.		Inquire of management whether any inventory is held on consignment for others.
	Presentation & Disclosure	Inventory pledged as collateral is not disclosed.	Disclosure checklist is completed prior to issuance of financial statements.	Inspect disclosure checklist for reasonableness.		Inquire whether inventory has been pledged as collateral or security. Perform bank and loan confirmations. Inspect lending agreements and other contracts for the use of inventory as collateral.
		Cost flow assumptions are not disclosed.	Management reviews all financial statement disclosures.	Inspect documentation of management review of disclosure checklist.		Review inventory calculation for proper classification among raw materials, work-in-process, and finished goods.

(continued)

Inventory Counts —A Ripe Field for Fraud

Although auditing standards do not expect the auditor to assume high fraud risk in inventory, as they do with revenue, there are nonetheless many examples of inventory frauds:

- Auditors were fooled as a result of taking a small sample for test counting, thus missing important information.
- Entities included inventory they pretended to have ordered.
- Entities stacked inventory on pallets in such a manner that "empty spaces" were not visible to auditors, resulting in overstatements of inventory.
- Auditors permitted company officials to follow them and note their counts. Then the managers falsified counts for inventory the auditors did not count.
- Shipments between plants (transfers) were reported as inventory at both plant locations.
- Auditors spotted a barrel whose contents management had valued at thousands of dollars, but it was filled with sawdust. The auditors required management to exclude the value from the inventory, but it never occurred to them that they had found just one instance in an intentional and pervasive overstatement fraud.
- Auditors observed inventory at five store locations and told the management in advance of the specific stores. Management took care not to make fraudulent entries in these five stores but, instead, made fraudulent adjustments in many of the other 236 stores.
- After counting an inventory of computer chips, the auditors received a call from the client's controller: "Just hours after you left the plant, 2,500 chips arrived in a shipment in transit." The auditors included them in inventory but never checked to see whether the chips were actually received.[3]

Accounting Firm Tips

To help detect inventory fraud, **Grant Thornton,** a large national accounting firm, advises its audit personnel:

- Focus test counts on high-value items and sample lower-value items. Test count a sufficient dollar amount of the inventory.
- If all locations will not be observed, do not follow an easily predictable pattern. Advise client personnel as late as possible of the locations to be visited.
- Be skeptical of large and unusual test count differences or of client personnel making notes or displaying particular interest in procedures and test counts.
- Be alert for inventory not used for some time; stored in unusual locations; or showing signs of damage, obsolescence, or excess quantities.

Pricing and Compilation

The physical observation procedures are designed to audit for *existence* and *completeness* (physical quantities). The **pricing and compilation** tests examine *valuation* (recalculation of appropriate FIFO, LIFO, or other pricing at cost, and lower of cost or NRV, and write-down of obsolete or worn inventory).

The compilation and pricing stage starts by listing all inventory items counted. The auditor foots[4] the list and tests the mathematical accuracy by multiplying the quantities and the price to get the total value for each item. Test counts taken by the auditor during the physical count are traced to the list, and other items from the list are vouched back to inventory count tags. The unit price is vouched to the vendor invoices for the purchase

---

[3]Examples cited in this list have been taken from *The Wall Street Journal.*
[4]*Foot* is an accounting term meaning to add up a column.

price for raw materials and to standard cost for in-process and finished goods. Many of these tests can be performed automatically using CAATs.

Lower-of-cost-or-NRV testing is an important step toward the *valuation* assertion. NRV can be obtained by examining the client's catalog and actual sales in the subsequent period and reviewing the costs associated with product sales. Items that are slow moving or obsolete can be spotted during the inventory observation if they demonstrate evidence of unsalability (e.g., old inventory tags, dust, and rust). Exhibit 9B.2 in Appendix 9B illustrates an audit plan for inventory pricing and compilation tests.

Presentation and Disclosure Assertions

When the auditor is satisfied that controls have been examined and transactions and balances are fairly presented according to GAAP, the job is not over. The aspects of production, especially inventory, require many disclosures. The components of inventory (raw materials, work-in-process, finished goods), inventory valuation method, lower of cost or NRV, and allocation of fixed costs are only a few of the essential items with specific presentation and disclosure requirements. These disclosures must ensure that the presentation and disclosure assertions of *occurrence, rights and obligations, completeness, classification and understandability,* and *accuracy and valuation* are all met. See Exhibit 9.13 for excerpts from the footnote contained in **Boeing Corporation's** 2021 financial statements.

✓ REVIEW CHECKPOINTS

9.19 Why is it important to obtain shipping and receiving cutoff information during the inventory observation?

9.20 What procedures do auditors employ to audit inventory when the physical inventory is taken on a cycle basis or on a statistical plan but never a complete count on a single date?

9.21 What could be happening when a client's managers take notes of auditors' test counts while an inventory is being counted?

9.22 What analytical procedures might reveal obsolete or slow-moving inventory?

EXHIBIT 9.13 Excerpts from Inventory Footnote in Boeing Aircraft 2021 Annual Report

Disclosure Assertion	Excerpt from Boeing Footnote
Completeness	Inventoried costs on commercial aircraft programs and long-term contracts include direct engineering, production and tooling and other non-recurring costs, and applicable overhead, which includes fringe benefits, production related indirect and plant management salaries and plant services, not in excess of estimated net realizable value.
Classification of items included in inventory costs	To the extent a material amount of such costs are related to an abnormal event or are fixed costs not appropriately attributable to our programs or contracts, they are expensed in the current period rather than inventoried. Inventoried costs include amounts relating to programs and contracts with long-term production cycles, a portion of which is not expected to be realized within one year. Included in inventory for federal government contracts is an allocation of allowable costs related to manufacturing process reengineering.
Accuracy and valuation of inventoried parts	We review our commercial spare parts and general stock materials quarterly to identify impaired inventory, including excess or obsolete inventory, based on historical sales trends, expected production usage, and the size and age of the aircraft fleet using the part. Impaired inventories are charged to Cost of products in the period the impairment occurs.
Presentation	Early issue sales consideration is recognized as a reduction to revenue when the delivery of the aircraft under contract occurs.

AUDIT RISK MODEL APPLIED

LO 9-7

Apply your knowledge to perform audit procedures in the audit of inventory and evaluate the findings of your tests.

Now that the control and inherent risk elements for the production cycle and some of the important substantive procedures have been presented, let's examine how an auditor might apply the audit risk model for the account balance assertion of existence. First, we show a table relating levels of detection risk to the extent of substantive procedures; note that the level of detection risk influences the nature (use of analytical procedures), timing (year-end counts versus interim counts versus cycle counts), and extent (number of inventory purchases vouched) of substantive tests. Then we provide an example of how they might be employed in practice. It is important to note that similar examples could be provided for the remaining material financial statement assertions related to inventory.

Extent of Substantive Inventory Procedures for Balance Assertion of Existence	
Low detection risk	Observe physical inventory count at year-end. Take substantial number of test counts and use large sample for vouching inventory purchases. Perform analytical procedures during planning and at audit completion.
Moderate detection risk	Observe inventory count at interim date. Test roll-forward to year-end. Use moderate vouching of purchases. Perform analytical procedures during planning and at audit completion.
High detection risk	Rely heavily on analytical procedures. Observe cycle counts of inventory. Rely on roll-forward procedures with minimal testing.

World Electronics LLC

Martin Phelps has been assigned as audit manager for **World Electronics LLC,** a medium-size publicly held manufacturer of semiconductors used in the computer industry. It has four manufacturing facilities located in Lexington, Kentucky; Dublin, Ireland; Barcelona, Spain; and Bangkok, Thailand. World uses just-in-time inventory management at all plants so that when a plant receives a customer order, it electronically forwards a purchase order for the materials to vendors. The company takes cycle counts of its inventory so it will not disrupt production. When World receives goods, the receiving clerk enters the receipt into the system, which automatically updates the perpetual inventory. Likewise, as semiconductors are completed, they are scanned and automatically moved from in-process to finished goods. The computerized controls were reviewed and tested by the audit firm's computer audit specialist, who noted no exceptions. Therefore, Phelps has set control risk as low. Control risk also has been set as low in the acquisition cycle and the revenue cycle.

The company is a leader in the industry, and management has a very good reputation. The semiconductor industry is experiencing strong growth, and the company is consistently profitable. There have been only minor audit adjustments in previous years, and the company has moved quickly to correct the cause of the adjustments. Consequently, Phelps also has set inherent risk as low. Therefore, considering these factors and the assessment of control risk, the risk of material misstatement is assessed as low and detection risk has been set as high. As a result, Phelps can select a sample of the cycle counts to observe on a surprise basis. He can record limited test counts and rely on limited testing of the computer records that roll forward the perpetual inventory until year-end. Because risk of material misstatement is low in the acquisition cycle, Phelps can limit vouching of invoices to test the prices of raw materials. Finally, Phelps can rely heavily on analytical procedures, particularly gross margin percentages, to ensure that no serious errors or frauds have occurred. The combination of a low risk of material misstatement and a high detection risk combine to give Phelps an acceptably low audit risk.

Fraud Case: Extended Audit Procedures

This case refers to a former discount retail store, **Phar-Mor**. "The Problem" section describes the "inside story," which auditors seldom know before they perform the audit procedures. The second part of the case under the heading "Audit Approach" tells a structured story about the audit objective, controls, tests of controls, substantive procedures, and discovery summary. Exercises 9.63–9.65 present some similar cases and you can prepare the audit approach to test your ability to design audit procedures for the detection of errors and frauds.

Case 9.1

We Will Not be Undersold!⁵

PROBLEM

Mickey Monus, the CEO of Phar-Mor, stated on many occasions that he would "not let Walmart undersell Phar-Mor." To that end, Phar-Mor would actually sell many products at a loss resulting in corporate net losses. Phar-Mor dumped these losses in a "bucket account" and spread them over the individual stores by increasing inventory amounts. When company personnel found out which stores the auditors would be visiting for inventory observation, they simply moved goods from the stores that were not visited to make up for shortages. Phar-Mor used an outside service for inventory counting, but after receiving the results, Phar-Mor personnel would inflate the amounts during the pricing and compilation process. In some cases, the compilations were altered after the auditors tested them. When Phar-Mor rolled forward the inventory from the count date, the inventory showed large increases right at year-end. These increases were due to the "blow-out" entries allocating the losses in the bucket account to stores' inventory. One entry was as high as $139 million. Finally, Phar-Mor did not have perpetual records but used the retail inventory method instead. Employees used distorted margin percentages to increase the estimated cost of the inventory on hand.

Phar-Mor issued fictitious invoices for purchases, made fictitious journal entries to increase inventory and decrease cost of sales, recognized purchases but failed to record the liabilities, and overcounted the merchandise.

The fraud lasted over a 10-year period, resulting in a financial statement fraud of more than $1 billion.

AUDIT APPROACH

The primary control should have been an environment that discouraged false accounting. However, this clearly was not the case. Other controls that should have prevented or detected these misstatements include a review of nonstandard journal entries, comparison of inventory records to actual periodic counts, and management analysis of gross margins and cash flows. Senior management can easily override any controls. Doing so requires only employees who can be bribed, threatened, or intimidated into going along.

How does one test the control environment? In the client acceptance/continuation stage of planning, the auditors should obtain evidence about management's reputation for integrity. In this case, many vendors were complaining because they were "squeezed" by Phar-Mor to provide rebates and promotion allowances, and some were threatening to cut the company off for nonpayment of bills. Many employees, including the controller, were very concerned about the company's practices and might have been persuaded to come clean had the auditors approached the audit with skepticism. However, because the client's chief financial officer was a former partner of the audit firm, the auditors appeared to lack skepticism.

It is not practical to observe inventory at all stores. However, because the auditors had identified inventory valuation as a high-risk area, they probably should have visited more than four stores! Moreover, the actual stores that the auditors visited for inventory observation should have been kept secret until the day of the count and randomized from one year to the next.

---

⁵Additional data taken from, "Finding Auditors Liable for Fraud: What the Jury Heard in the Phar-Mor Case," *CPA Journal,* July 1997, pp.14–21.

The auditors performed only a reasonableness test of the margins used in the retail method. They selected a sample of items in a "haphazard" method that turned out not to be representative. When the sample margins differed from the company's margins, the auditors explained the difference away without expanding their sample. In vouching the costs of inventory, the auditors should have been alert to phony documentation. Finally, large nonstandard journal entries at the end of the year should have been thoroughly scrutinized.

DISCOVERY SUMMARY

When a travel agent noticed that a bill for the World Basketball League (WBL), a league started by Monus, was paid with a Phar-Mor check, she asked a neighbor, who was a major shareholder, why Phar-Mor would pay the WBL's expenses. The neighbor phoned a board member, who initiated the investigation that uncovered the fraud.

 AUDITING INSIGHT \ Using IDEA in the Audit

INVENTORY TESTING

Significant issues in inventory occur when amounts in the physical inventory do not match the amounts in the accounting records. Auditors are aware of the beginning inventory for the year, (the audited value for ending inventory form the previous year) and using computer software can calculate inventory received from receiving reports and inventory used from production reports. Using these numbers, the auditor can obtain an approximation of inventory that should be in this year's ending inventory, as follows:

Beginning inventory + inventory purchases − inventory usage = ending inventory.

If we adjust the ending inventory for scrap, the number is even more accurate.

The recorded ending inventory and the inventory account should not be materially misstated from the preceding calculation. Major discrepancies should be investigated and may be the result of poor record keeping or theft of inventory. Further, audit software like IDEA can compare physical counts with actual inventory. The use of such a program is extremely important when inventory includes tens of thousands of items. (*Note:* A typical Walmart store has approximately 140,000 SKUs.)

Further, inventory valuation is critical to reaching an audit conclusion about inventory, and audit software can assist the auditor in identifying unusual and potentially obsolete inventory items.

At the end of this chapter, you can perform testing related to the valuation assertion in Exercise 9.69, and tests related to inventory summarization in Exercises 9.70–9.73.

☑ REVIEW CHECKPOINTS

9.23 What steps should auditors take if the client has multiple locations being counted?

9.24 What is an inventory roll-forward? What roll-forward tests should be performed?

Summary

Audits of inventory vary greatly from client to client. An audit of a retailer's inventory is almost completely different from an audit of a manufacturer, yet the same auditing standards apply.

Audits of companies who purchase their inventory are characterized by strong external evidence regarding the timing and cost of inventory acquisition. An audit of the revenue cycle provides substantial evidence surrounding the sales of the inventory.

The production cycle for manufacturers, on the other hand, is characterized by having mostly internal documentation as evidence and having relatively little external documentary evidence; therefore, the systems that produce these documents must be evaluated to ensure the validity of the information.

Companies reduce control risk by having a suitable separation of authorization, custody, recording, and periodic reconciliation duties within the inventory cycle. Error-checking procedures, including analyzing production orders, purchase orders, sales orders, and finished production cost reports, are important for the proper determination of inventory values and proper valuation of cost of goods sold. Otherwise, many things could go wrong, ranging from overvaluing the inventory to understating costs of production by deferring costs that should be expensed.

Cost accounting is a central feature of a production cycle for manufacturers. The illustrative case in the chapter tells the stories of financial reporting manipulations and the audit procedures that will detect them. The physical inventory observation audit work was discussed because actual contact with inventories provides auditors direct eyewitness evidence of important tangible assets.

Many frauds have been hidden in the inventory accounts. Therefore, the auditors should pay attention to the inventory balance assertions of *existence* and *valuation and allocation.* The audit of inventory requires professional judgment, professional skepticism, and due professional care.

Key Terms

bill of materials: A list of raw materials and supplies used to build a product that is used to develop standard costs, 384

consignment (consigned-out) goods: The goods that are given by one party, the consignor, to another party, the consignee, to sell; however, the consignee retains title until the goods are sold, 407

cycle counts: A method of physically counting different areas of inventory throughout the year, 406

inventory roll-forward: An accounting process from date of physical inventory count to the end of the period; includes additions for purchases and production and reductions for sales, scrap, and so on, 406

materials requisition (materials transfer ticket): A form used to obtain raw materials and supplies from inventory custodian, 385

net realizable value (NRV): The selling price less costs to sell (e.g., sales commissions), 387

overhead allocation: An accounting procedure used to assign indirect costs to various products, 386

physical inventory count: The client's procedure for determining actual amount of inventory on hand, 403

physical inventory observation: The auditor's procedures during client's physical inventory count; includes observing inventory procedures and performing test counts on selected inventory items, 403

pricing and compilation: The procedure for translating units counted in the physical inventory count to amounts recorded in the accounting records, including gains or losses for shortages or overages; involves mathematically accumulating counts and applying standard costs, 409

production order: A document that communicates to production personnel the specific product, product quantity, and date a product is to be produced, 385

production plan: A schedule of goods to be produced for a period based on sales forecasts, 384

raw material inventory status report: A periodic report (usually daily or weekly) that includes a list of all raw materials and the inventoried quantity of each material, 384

sales forecast: A report, usually prepared by marketing, predicting future sales of product, 384

standard costs: The estimates of cost to produce a product; used for transferring products between departments and to finished goods and to record cost of goods sold; compared to actual costs to obtain variances, 385

Multiple-Choice Questions for Practice and Review

 All applicable Exercises and Problems are available with *Connect.*

LO 9-1

9.25 Which cycle is *not* directly linked to the production cycle?

a. Acquisition and expenditure cycle.

b. Payroll cycle.

c. Revenue and collection cycle.

d. Finance and investment cycle.

LO 9-1

9.26 To determine the client's planned amount and timing of production of a product, the auditor reviews the

a. Sales forecast.

b. Inventory reports.

c. Production plan.

d. Purchases journal.

LO 9-1

9.27   An auditor reviews job cost sheets to test which *transaction assertion*?

    a. Occurrence

    b. Completeness

    c. Accuracy

    d. Classification

LO 9-4

9.28   Which of the following is an internal control weakness for a company whose inventory of supplies consists of a large number of individual items?

    a. Supplies of relatively little value are expensed when purchased.

    b. The cycle basis is used for physical counts.

    c. The warehouse manager is responsible for maintenance of perpetual inventory records.

    d. Perpetual inventory records are maintained only for items of significant value.

LO 9-2

9.29   To make a year-to-year comparison of inventory turnover *most* meaningful, the auditor performs the analysis

    a. For the company as a whole.

    b. By division.

    c. By product.

    d. All of the above.

LO 9-4

9.30   Which of the following procedures would best prevent or detect the theft of valuable items from an inventory that consists of hundreds of different items selling for $1 to $10 and a few items selling for hundreds of dollars?

    a. Maintain a perpetual inventory of only the more valuable items with frequent periodic verification of the accuracy of the perpetual inventory record.

    b. Have an independent accounting firm prepare an internal control report on the effectiveness of the controls over inventory.

    c. Have separate warehouse space for the more valuable items with frequent periodic physical counts and comparison to perpetual inventory records.

    d. Require a manager's signature for the removal of any inventory item with a value of more than $50.

LO 9-6

9.31   An auditor usually traces the details of the test counts made during the observation of physical inventory counts to a final inventory compilation. This audit procedure is undertaken to provide evidence that items physically present and observed by the auditor at the time of the physical inventory count are

    a. Owned by the client.

    b. Not obsolete.

    c. Physically present at the time of the preparation of the final inventory schedule.

    d. Included in the final inventory schedule.

LO 9-3

9.32   A retailer's physical count of inventory was higher than that shown by the perpetual records. Which of the following could explain the difference?

    a. Inventory items had been counted, but the tags placed on the items had not been taken off and added to the inventory accumulation sheets.

    b. Credit memos for several items returned by customers had not been recorded.

    c. No journal entry had been made on the retailer's books for several items returned to its suppliers.

    d. An item purchased FOB shipping point had not arrived at the date of the inventory count and had not been reflected in the perpetual records.

(AICPA adapted)

LO 9-6

9.33   From the auditors' point of view, inventory counts are more acceptable prior to the year-end when

    a. Internal control is weak.

    b. Accurate perpetual inventory records are maintained.

    c. Inventory is slow moving.

    d. Significant amounts of inventory are held on a consignment basis.

LO 9-4

9.34 Which of the following internal control activities most likely addresses the completeness assertion for inventory?

a. The work-in-process account is periodically reconciled with subsidiary inventory records.

b. Employees responsible for custody of finished goods do not perform the receiving function.

c. Receiving reports are prenumbered, and the numbering sequence is checked periodically.

d. There is a separation of duties between the payroll department and inventory accounting personnel.

LO 9-6

9.35 When auditing inventories, an auditor would *least* likely verify that

a. All inventory owned by the client is on hand at the time of the count.

b. The client has used proper inventory pricing.

c. The financial statement presentation of inventories is appropriate.

d. Damaged goods and obsolete items have been properly accounted for.

(AICPA adapted)

LO 9-6

9.36 A client maintains perpetual inventory records in quantities and in dollars. If the assessed control risk is high, an auditor would probably

a. Apply gross profit tests to ascertain the reasonableness of the physical counts.

b. Increase the extent of tests of controls relevant to the inventory cycle.

c. Request the client to schedule the physical inventory count at the end of the year.

d. Insist that the client perform physical counts of inventory items several times during the year.

(AICPA adapted)

LO 9-6

9.37 An auditor selected items for test counts while observing a client's physical inventory. The auditor then traced the test counts to the client's inventory listing. This procedure *most likely* obtained evidence concerning management's balance assertion of

a. Rights and Obligations.

b. Completeness.

c. Existence.

d. Valuation.

(AICPA adapted)

LO 9-6

9.38 Which of the following auditing procedures probably would provide the most reliable evidence concerning the entity's assertion of rights and obligations related to inventories?

a. Trace test counts noted during the entity's physical count to the entity's summarization of quantities.

b. Inspect agreements to determine whether any inventory is pledged as collateral or subject to any liens.

c. Select the last few shipping documents used before the physical count and determine whether the shipments were recorded as sales.

d. Inspect the open purchase order file for significant commitments that should be considered for disclosure.

(AICPA adapted)

LO 9-6

9.39 An auditor *most* likely would analyze inventory turnover rates to obtain evidence concerning management's balance assertions about

a. Existence.

b. Rights and obligations.

c. Completeness.

d. Valuation.

LO 9-2

9.40 An auditor would vouch inventory on the inventory status report to the vendor's invoice to obtain evidence concerning management's balance assertions about

a. Existence.

b. Rights and Obligations.

c. Completeness.

d. Valuation.

LO 9-5   9.41 When evaluating inventory controls, an auditor would be *least* likely to

a. Inspect documents.

b. Make inquiries.

c. Observe procedures.

d. Consider policy and procedure manuals.

LO 9-5   9.42 When testing a company's cost accounting system, the auditor uses procedures that are primarily designed to determine that

a. Quantities on hand have been computed based on acceptable cost accounting techniques that reasonably approximate actual quantities on hand.

b. Physical inventories agree substantially with book inventories.

c. The system is in accordance with generally accepted accounting principles and is functioning as planned.

d. Costs have been properly assigned to finished goods, work-in-process, and cost of goods sold.

LO 9-6   9.43 The auditor tests the quantity of materials charged to work-in-process by vouching these quantities to

a. Cost ledgers.

b. Perpetual inventory records.

c. Receiving reports.

d. Material requisitions.

LO 9-6   9.44 Your client counts inventory three months before the end of the fiscal year because controls over inventory are excellent. Which procedure is *not* necessary for the roll-forward?

a. Check that shipping documents for the last three months agree with perpetual records.

b. Trace receiving reports for the last three months to perpetual records.

c. Compare gross margin percentages for the last three months.

d. Request the client to recount inventory at the end of the year.

LO 9-5   9.45 An auditor is examining a nonissuer's inventory procurement system and has decided to perform tests of controls. Under which of the following conditions do GAAS require tests of controls be performed by an auditor?

a. Significant weaknesses were found in the company's internal control.

b. The auditor hopes to reduce the amount of work to be done in assessing inherent risk.

c. The auditor believes that testing the controls could lead to a reduction in overall audit time and cost.

d. Tests of controls are always performed when the auditor begins to assess control risk.

LO 9-6   9.46 Which of the following management assertions is an auditor *most* likely testing if the audit objective states that all inventory on hand is reflected in the ending inventory balance?

a. The entity has rights to the inventory.

b. Inventory is properly valued.

c. Inventory is properly presented in the financial statements.

d. Inventory is complete.

(AICPA adapted)

LO 9-6   9.47 A portion of a client's inventory is in public warehouses. Evidence of the existence of this merchandise can most efficiently be acquired through which of the following methods?

a. Observation.

b. Confirmation.

c. Calculation.

d. Inspection.

(AICPA adapted)

LO 9-6

9.48 The purpose of tracing a sample of inventory tags to a client's computerized listing of inventory items is to determine whether the inventory items

    a. Represented by tags were included on the listing.

    b. Included on the listing were properly counted.

    c. Represented by tags were reduced to the lower of cost or market.

    d. Included in the listing were properly valued.

LO 9-3

9.49 Which of the following results of analytical procedures would most likely indicate possible unrecorded inventory?

    a. Current ratio of 3:1 as compared to 5:1 for the prior period.

    b. Inventory turnover of 3.25 during the current year compared to 3.75 during the prior year.

    c. Inventory balance increase of 10% during the current period.

    d. Accounts payable turnover of 6 as compared with 8 for the prior period.

LO 9-5

9.50 An auditor is testing internal controls in the manufacturing of a client's inventory. Which of the following audit procedures, if used, should be combined with other audit procedures when testing the operating effectiveness of controls?

    a. Observation.

    b. Inspection of documents.

    c. Inquiry.

    d. Reperformance.

Exercises and Problems

 All applicable Exercises and Problems are available with *Connect.*

LO 9-4

9.51 **Internal Control Questionnaire Items: Possible Error or Fraud Due to Weakness.** Refer to the internal control questionnaire for the production cycle (Exhibit 9A.1) and assume that the answer to each question is "no." Prepare a table matching questions to errors or frauds that could occur because of the absence of the control. Your column headings should be as follows:

Question	Possible Error or Fraud Due to Weakness

LO 9-5

9.52 **Tests of Controls Related to Controls and Assertions.** Each of the following tests of controls could be performed during the audit of the controls in the production cycle.

Required:

For each procedure, identify (a) the internal control activity (strength) being tested and (b) the assertion(s) being addressed.

    1. Balance and reconcile detailed production cost sheets to the work-in-process inventory control account.

    2. Scan closed production cost sheets for missing numbers in the sequence.

    3. Vouch a sample of open and closed production cost sheet entries to (a) labor reports and (b) issue forms and materials used reports.

    4. Locate the material issue forms and determine whether they are (a) prenumbered, (b) kept in a secure location, and (c) available to unauthorized persons.

    5. Select several summary journal entries in the work-in-process inventory and (a) vouch them to weekly labor and material reports and to production cost sheets and (b) trace them to the control account.

    6. Select a sample of the material issue forms in the production department file. Examine them for

        a. Issue date and materials used report date.

        b. Production order number.

        c. Floor supervisor's signature or initials.

    d. Name and number of material.

    e. Raw material stores clerk's signature or initials.

    f. Material requisition in raw material stores file, noting the date of requisition

  7. Determine by inquiry and inspection whether cost clerks review dates on reports of units completed for accounting in the proper period.

LO 9-4

9.53 Cost Accounting Tests of Controls. The diagram that follows describes several cost accounting tests of controls. It shows the direction of the tests, leading from samples of cost accounting analyses, management reports, and the general ledger to blank squares.

Required:

For each blank square in the diagram, write a cost accounting test of controls procedure and describe the evidence it can produce. (*Hint:* Refer to Exhibit 9.6.)

Diagram of Cost Accounting Tests of Controls

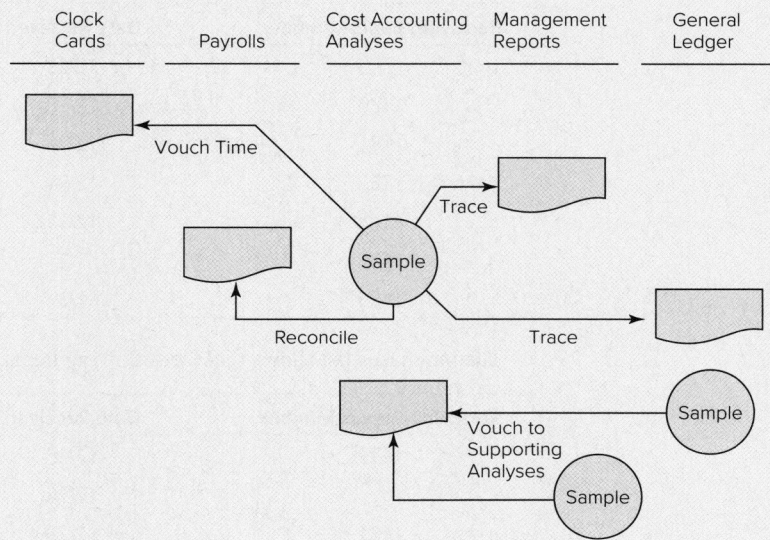

LO 9-6

9.54 Inventory Count Observation: Planning and Substantive Procedures. Sammy Smith is the partner in charge of the audit of Blue Distributing Corporation, a wholesaler that owns one warehouse containing 80 percent of its inventory. Smith is reviewing the audit documentation that was prepared to support the firm's opinion on Blue's financial statements and wants to be certain that essential audit procedures are well documented.

Required:

What evidence should Smith expect to find indicating that the observation of the client's physical count of inventory was well planned and that assistants were properly supervised?

What substantive procedures should Smith find in the audit documentation of management's balance assertions about existence and completeness of inventory quantities at the end of the year? (Refer to Appendix 9B for the audit plan's procedures.)

(AICPA adapted)

LO 9-6

9.55 Sales/Inventory Cutoff. Your client took a complete physical inventory count under your observation as of December 15 and adjusted the inventory control account (perpetual inventory method) to agree with the physical inventory. After considering the count adjustments as of December 15 and after reviewing the transactions recorded from December 16 to December 31, you are almost ready to accept the inventory balance as fairly stated. However, your review of the sales cutoff as of December 15 and December 31 disclosed the following items not previously considered:

Sales		Date		
Cost	Price	Shipped	Billed	Credited to Inventory Control
$28,400	$36,900	12/14	12/16	12/16
39,100	50,200	12/10	12/19	12/10
18,900	21,300	1/2	12/31	12/31

Required:

What adjusting journal entries, if any, would you make for each of these items? Explain why each adjustment is necessary.

(AICPA adapted)

LO 9-6

9.56 **Purchasing Cutoff.** When tracing using the cutoff information from the December 31 inventory count of Thermo-Tempur Mattresses, you note the following information:

Receiving Report Number	Date Received	Total Cost
	12/28	$12,433.61
1180	12/28	8,923.34
1181	12/29	15,448.22
1182	12/31	14,109.33
1183	12/31	11,482.57
1184	1/2	17,852.56
1185	1/3	8,753.95

The purchases list shows that the following items were recorded in December:

Receiving Report Number	Date Received	Total Cost
1179	12/28	$12,433.61
	12/28	8,923.34
1181	12/29	15,448.22
1182	12/31	14,109.33
1184	1/2	17,852.56

The documentation indicates that the last receiving report included in the inventory count was Receiving Report 1182. Receiving Reports 1183 and 1184 were for goods received on the company's truck but not unloaded. Receiving report 1185 was for goods received on January 3.

Required:

Prepare a correcting journal entry assuming that Thermo-Tempur uses (a) a periodic inventory system and (b) a perpetual inventory system that was updated for the inventory count.

LO 9-6

9.57 **Statistical Sampling Used to Estimate Inventory.** ACE Corporation does not conduct a complete annual physical count of purchased parts and supplies in its principal warehouse but uses statistical sampling to estimate the year-end inventory. ACE maintains a perpetual inventory record of parts and supplies. Management believes that statistical sampling is highly effective in determining inventory values and is sufficiently reliable, making a physical count of each item of inventory unnecessary.

Required:

a. List at least 10 normal audit procedures that should be performed to verify physical quantities whenever a client conducts a periodic physical count of all or part of its inventory. (See Exhibit 9B.1 for procedures.)

b. Identify the audit procedures you should use that change or are in addition to normal required audit procedures [in addition to those listed in your solution to part (a)] when a

LO 9-7

9.65 **Chips Ahoy.** Follow the instructions preceding Problem 9.63. Write the audit approach section following the case in the chapter.

The following is an excerpt from an article, "Memory Chip Trader Gets 14 Years for Bank Fraud," *The Straits Times* (Singapore), February 13, 2009:

Through most of the 1990s, entrepreneur Kelvin Ang Ah Peng rode the crest of a wave as his company traded in memory chips and recycled used ones for sale at a good price. His story, which follows the ebb and flow of the integrated circuit (IC) chip business, started at **EC–Asia International (ECI)** in 1993. Computer chips were expensive, so his business did well. A major earthquake in Taiwan in 1999 totaled the computer chip factories there. Production halted and the market price of computer chips soared even higher. The bubble burst the following year, when the Taiwan factories recovered and several computer chip businesses folded. In 2001, as ECI struggled to keep afloat, Ang started abusing its credit facilities. Between that year and early 2007, he bought and sold worthless memory chips and created fake orders and invoices to receive payment from banks.

He was charged in October 2008 on 687 charges involving US$290 million; last month, he pleaded guilty to 30 charges—28 for cheating and 2 for money laundering and falsifying revenues in ECI's initial public offering (IPO) prospectus. Deputy Public Prosecutor David Chew Siong Tai said that, to secure credit in the absence of incoming orders, Ang fashioned an elaborate scheme with the help of Hong Kong firms. He got ECI's partners to issue the necessary trade documents and to circulate computer chips and money between Hong Kong and Singapore. Chips were actually shipped in these sham transactions as if they were bona fide trades. In reality these were worthless, defective chips due for scrapping by ECI. In November 2006 when asked about ECI's unusually large inventory in Hong Kong and the huge debts owed by the firm's Hong Kong "customers," Ang confessed to an ECI subsidiary's director that 90 percent of the inventory did not exist and that its billings were all faked.

Yesterday [February 12, 2009], Ang, 44, was jailed for 14 years for having swindled banks of US$23 million (US$35 million) and laundering these proceeds through Hong Kong. The Australian-listed ECI is now being liquidated, and Ang was declared bankrupt last year.

LO 9-7

9.66 **Detection of Errors and Fraud.** For each of the following independent events, indicate the (1) effect of the error or fraud on the financial statements and (2) what auditing procedures could have detected the misstatement resulting from error or fraud.

a. The physical inventory count of J. Payne Enterprises, which has a December 31 year-end, was conducted on August 31 without incident. In September, the perpetual inventory was not reduced for the cost of sales.

b. Holmes Drug Stores counted its inventory on December 31, which is its fiscal year-end. The auditors observed the count at 20 of Holmes's 86 locations. The company falsified the inventory at 20 of the locations not visited by the auditors by including fictitious goods in the counts.

c. Pope Automotive inadvertently included in its inventory automobiles that it was holding on consignment for other dealers.

d. Peffer Electronics Inc. overstated its inventory by pricing wiring at $200 per hundred feet instead of $200 per thousand feet.

e. Goldman Sporting Goods counted boxes of baseballs as having one dozen baseballs per box when they had only six per box.

LO 9-2, 9.4, 9.6

9.67 **Inventory Fraud and Detection Issues.** You are auditing the financial statements of Holly's Happenin' Hula Hoops Club (4H Club). Unbeknownst to you as the auditor, there is a fraud being committed related to the inventory account. For the fraud described below, specifically list (a) the assertion about the inventory account that is violated, (b) a control procedure the client should have had in place that could have potentially prevented the fraud, and (c) an audit procedure that you would likely perform during the audit of inventory that would detect the fraud.

Each month, an employee in the receiving department submits a fictitious receiving report to accounting. A few days later, he sends the 4H Club an invoice for the quantity of goods ordered from a small company he owns and operates. The invoice is always paid when the accounts payable clerk matches the receiving report with the vendor's invoice.

Required:

a. Describe the Inventory assertion violated.

b. Describe the Control procedure to prevent this misstatement.

c. Suggest an Audit procedure to detect this misstatement.

9.68 **Substantive Testing of Inventory Variances.** An auditor observed Bizarre Costume Shop's physical inventory count on the last day of the client's fiscal year, October 31, 2023. In addition to being somewhat disturbed by the costumes, the auditors identified several variances in the test counts relative to the client's recorded inventory. Through inquiry, the auditors obtained explanations from the client's management.

Required:

For each variance listed and client explanation in the table below, select the audit response the auditor would most likely make from the list of possible responses. Each response may be used once, more than once, or not at all. Write only the letter of the response in the space provided.

Possible audit responses:

a. Inspect supporting documents and agree quantities received to purchase order.

b. Inspect supporting purchase documents for proper shipping terms and receiving information to verify exclusion from inventory count.

c. Inspect supporting purchase documents for proper shipping terms and receiving information to verify inclusion in inventory count.

d. Inspect supporting sale and shipment documentation for proper shipping terms for exclusion in inventory count.

e. Inspect supporting sale and shipment documentation for proper shipping terms for inclusion in inventory count.

f. Request that client make appropriate correction to record additional inventory.

g. Request that client make appropriate correction to reduce inventory.

Test Count number	Inventory Item	Recorded Inventory Quantity	Auditor's Test Count	Variance	Client Explanation	Auditor Response (letter)
1	SpiderHorse	175	125	(50)	Inventory in transit shipped f.o.b. shipping point; received 11/2/2023	
2	Unibrow Man	850	715	(135)	Inventory sold to customer f.o.b. destination; not received by customer until 11/2/2023	
3	Werewolf Wonder Woman	200	225	25	Sale recorded based on customer request to hold items. Customer has not paid or picked items up yet.	
4	Hairy Potter	455	500	45	Inventory received 10/30/2023; vendor shipment receipt not recorded.	
5	Rainbow Unicorn	650	550	(100)	Inventory was separated for an 11/1/2023 sale; held on dock for customer pickup.	

LO 9-7

9.69 **Identifying Obsolete Inventory and Proposing Provisions.** For this exercise, your client, BrightIDEAs Inc., has provided you with a listing of inventory on hand as of the end of the year. You have been assigned the task of performing procedures to identify unusual or potentially obsolete inventory items and propose a valuation allowance.

Required Data and IDEA workbook page references available on *Connect*

Required:

    a. Import the client's database of inventory and reconcile it to the general ledger.

    b. Use data extraction techniques to identify client-identified obsolete inventory items in the client's inventory listing or items showing negative amounts or quantities.

    c. Calculate inventory usage ratios to identify inventory items not flagged by the client that may nonetheless be obsolete.

    d. Use your calculations from the above steps to estimate a provision for obsolete inventory.

    e. Do you consider the difference between what the client proposed and your proposed provision to be a material difference?

Applying IDEA to the Production Cycle—Elm Manufacturing Company

Exercises 9.70–9.73 require the application of IDEA in the production cycle audit in summarizing client data and recalculating inventory balances using client records. Elm Manufacturing Company (ELM) is a small manufacturer of backpacks located in Rochelle, Illinois. You have access to ELM's electronic records on Connect. The appropriate files for these exercises are the Sales 2023 4th Q data set, the Purchases 2023-4th Q data set, the Inventory Count data set, the Ending Inventory Balances 2023-3rd Q data set, the Finished Goods Production 2023-4th Q data set, the Production Bill of Raw Materials data set, and the Combined Materials and Supplies Vendor Price List data set. You will also require the 2023 ELM Production Cycle Supplementary Information document. Detailed information about ELM, instructions for accessing data sets, and a data directory for data sets can be found on *Connect*.

LO 9-7

9.70 **Summarizing Direct Materials Production Costs Using IDEA.** ELM reports that the following is the total cost for each product:

Product	Direct material	Direct Labor	Overhead*	Total Cost
SP001	$ 5.91	$ 1.99	$ 0.16	$ 8.06
HB005	$ 13.40	$ 4.96	$ 0.40	$ 18.76
CB008	$ 56.39	$ 8.11	$ 0.65	$ 65.15

*Overhead is allocated at 8% of direct labor costs (rounded)

Required:

Assume that the cost of Direct Labor and Overhead has been separately verified. Use the bill of materials and the materials unit cost sheet to recalculate the direct materials cost per unit for the three products. Do you find any differences in calculated materials costs?

LO 9-7

9.71 **Summarizing Finished Goods Quantities Using IDEA.** You have been assigned the task of recalculating the client's finished goods ending inventory quantity based on sales and manufacturing records and comparing it to the year-end inventory count. You may assume there is no work-in-process inventory as of year-end.

Required:

    a. Perform an inventory roll-forward and calculate the total year-end quantity for each of the three items in finished goods inventory (Hints: Beginning balance + Finished goods manufactured – Sales = Ending balance. Don't forget that you should only consider sales that have shipped during the quarter and that the company sells products in cases of 12. You may assume there were no shipments of outstanding orders from prior quarters.).

    b. Compare the ending inventory balances from *(a)* to the quantity based on the year-end inventory count. Are there any significant discrepancies between the calculated ending inventory and the inventory counts?

    c. What are some of the reasons that could cause these discrepancies? How would you resolve these issues?

    d. What would you propose as the final inventory quantity?

LO 9-7

9.72 **Summarizing Raw Materials Quantities Using IDEA.** You have been assigned the task of recalculating the client's raw materials ending inventory quantity based on purchase and manufacturing records and comparing it to the year-end inventory count. You may assume there is no work-in-process inventory as of year-end.

Required:

a. Calculate the total year end quantity for raw materials inventory (Hint: Beginning balance + Purchases – Used in production = Ending balance. Don't forget that you should only include purchases that have been received in calculating purchases. Column "TYPE" in 3rd q inventory database will be helpful for extracting relevant records.)

b. Are there any significant discrepancies between the calculated ending inventory and the inventory counts? Identify possible reasons for such discrepancies.

c. How would you proceed to resolve these issues?

d. What would you propose as the final raw materials inventory quantity?

LO 9-7

9.73 **Testing Supplies Inventory and Expense Using IDEA.** You have been assigned the task of testing the client's Supplies Expense based on purchase records and the year-end inventory count. ELM's unaudited trial balance shows a recorded amount of $33,650 for supplies expense during the 4th quarter. Per the client, supplies expense consists of the all supplies indirectly used in the factory, but which do not get included in the cost of the manufacturing process. These products are all inventory units with stock numbers beginning with E, Q, or J. Assume that the cost of supplies remained constant throughout the quarter.

Required:

a. Using the information given about beginning balances, purchases, ending counts, and the vendor price list, recalculate supplies expense. For the purposes of this exercise, ignore any taxes or shipping charges and base costs solely on the price list.

b. Does ELM's recorded supplies expense appear reasonable? Would the auditor perform any further detail testing on supplies expense? Explain your reasoning.

Apollo Shoes

Inventory Audit

You are a recently promoted senior (in charge) auditor for Anderson, Olds, and Watershed and have been assigned to the engagement team of a new audit client, Apollo Shoes Inc. You have been asked to perform substantive procedures related to the audit of inventory. As part of your audit you will evaluate documents such as inventory observation memos, count sheets, and purchase invoices. Detailed instructions, as well as the audit documentation and supporting documents, can be found in *Connect*.

Appendix 9A

Internal Control Questionnaires

EXHIBIT 9A.1 **Production Cycle**

	Yes/No	Comment
Occurrence		
1. Is cost accounting separate from production, payroll, and inventory control?		
2. Is access to blank production order forms restricted to authorized persons?		
3. Is access to blank bills of materials and labor needs forms restricted to authorized persons?		
4. Is access to blank material requisition forms restricted to authorized persons?		
5. Are production orders prepared by authorized persons?		
6. Are bills of materials and labor needs prepared by authorized persons?		
7. Are material usage reports compared to raw material stores issue forms?		
8. Are labor usage reports compared to job time tickets?		
9. Are material requisitions and job time tickets reviewed by the production supervisor after the floor supervisor prepares them?		
10. Are the weekly direct labor and materials used reports reviewed by the production supervisor after preparation by the floor supervisor?		
Completeness		
1. Are production orders prenumbered and the numerical sequence checked for missing documents?		
2. Are bills of materials and labor needs forms prenumbered and the numerical sequence checked for missing documents?		
3. Are material requisitions and job time tickets prenumbered and the numerical sequence checked for missing documents?		
4. Are inventory issue forms prenumbered and the numerical sequence checked for missing documents?		
5. Is accounting notified of terms on purchase agreements?		
6. Is accounting notified of orders received on consignment?		
Accuracy		
1. Are differences between inventory issue forms and materials used reports recorded and reported to the cost accounting supervisor?		
2. Are differences between job time tickets and the labor report recorded and reported to the cost accounting supervisor?		
3. Are standard costs used? If so, are they reviewed and revised periodically?		
4. Are reports for materials issued to production reconciled with finished goods reports?		
Cutoff		
1. Does the accounting manual give instructions to date cost entries on the date of use?		
2. Does an accounting supervisor review monthly, quarterly, and year-end cost accruals?		
Classification		
1. Are summary entries reviewed and approved by the cost accounting supervisor?		
2. Does the accounting manual give instructions for proper classification of cost accounting transactions?		

EXHIBIT 9A.2 **Inventory Transaction Processing**

	Yes/No	Comment
Occurrence		
1. Are perpetual inventory records kept for raw materials? Supplies? Work-in-process? Finished goods?		
2. Is merchandise or materials held on consignment (not the property of the company) physically segregated from goods owned by the company?		
3. Are additions to inventory quantity records made only on receipt of a receiving report copy?		
4. Do inventory custodians notify inventory record keepers of reductions of inventory?		
Completeness		
1. Are reductions of inventory record quantities made only on receipt of inventory issuance documents?		
2. Do inventory custodians notify the records department of additions to inventory?		
3. Are separate records maintained for consignment inventory?		
Accuracy		
1. Are perpetual records reconciled to general ledger control accounts?		
2. Do the perpetual records show both quantities and prices?		
3. Are inventory records maintained by someone other than the inventory stores custodian?		
4. Are the inventory records compared to physical counts?		
5. Are production reports of material and labor prepared weekly and transmitted to cost accounting?		
6. Are job cost sheets posted weekly and summary journal entries of work-in-process and work completed prepared monthly?		
7. Are job cost sheet entries reviewed by a person independent of the preparer?		
8. If standard costs have been used for inventory pricing, have they been reviewed for reasonableness and current applicability?		
9. Is there a periodic review for overstocked, slow-moving, or obsolete inventory? Have any adjustments been made during the year?		
10. Are periodic counts of physical inventory made to correct errors in the individual perpetual records?		
Cutoff		
1. Does the accounting manual give instructions to record inventory additions on the date of the receiving report?		
2. Does the accounting manual give instructions to record inventory issues on the issuance date?		
Classification		
1. Are perpetual inventory records kept in dollars periodically reconciled to general ledger control accounts?		

Appendix 9B

Audit Plans

EXHIBIT 9B.1

	Performed by	Ref.
DUNDER-MIFFLIN, INC **Audit Plan for Physical Inventory Observation** **December 31, 2023**		
1. Obtain client's inventory-counting instructions and review for completeness.		
2. Tour facility before the inventory count looking for out-of-the-way items, obsolete items, and patterns of inventory flow.		
3. Observe client personnel taking inventory counts for compliance with instructions.		
4. Test count a selection of items throughout the facility, and record a sample of your test counts. Note description, stage of completion, counting unit, and condition.		
5. Obtain and record tag numbers used and ensure all tag numbers are accounted for.		
6. Select sample of used tags and trace them to the items on the floor.		
7. Record the last five receiving reports and last five shipping documents and the numbers of next five unused items in sequence. Vouch the recorded items to inventory count to determine that the item was appropriately included (or excluded) from the inventory count.		
8. Tour facilities to ensure all items have been counted.		

EXHIBIT 9B.2

DUNDER-MIFFLIN, INC Audit Plan for Inventory Observation and Cost of Goods Sold December 31, 2023	Performed by	Ref.
Inventory		
1. Obtain client's inventory list, recalculate, and check it against the general ledger.		
2. Trace test counts from inventory observation to the final inventory compilation.		

3. Select a sample of inventory items.
   a. Vouch unit prices to vendors' invoices or other cost records.
   b. Recalculate the inventory valuation for sampled items.		

4. Scan the inventory compilation for items added from sources other than the physical count and items that appear to be large round numbers or systematic fictitious additions.		
5. Recalculate the extensions and footings of the final inventory compilation for mathematical accuracy. Reconcile the total to the adjusted trial balance.		
6. For selected inventory items and categories, determine the replacement cost and the applicability of lower-of-cost-or-NRV valuation.		
7. Inspect inventory for evidence of obsolete or damaged goods. Trace identified obsolete or damaged goods to inventory records for write-down.		
8. Inquire about obsolete, damaged, slow-moving, and overstocked inventory.		
9. Scan the perpetual records for slow-moving items.		
10. During the physical observation, be alert to notice damaged or scrap inventory.		
11. Compare the list of obsolete, slow-moving, damaged, or unsalable inventory from last-year's audit to the current inventory compilation.		
12. At year-end, identify the numbers of the last shipping and receiving documents for the year. Compare these to the sales, inventory/cost of sales, and accounts payable entries for proper cutoff.		
13. Read bank confirmations, debt agreements, and minutes of the board and make inquiries about pledge or assignment of inventory to secure debt.		
14. Inquire about inventory held by third parties on consignment and inventory on hand on consignment from vendors.		
15. Confirm or inspect inventories held in public warehouses.		
16. Recalculate the amount of intercompany profit to be eliminated in consolidation.		
17. Obtain management representations concerning pledging of inventory as collateral, intercompany sales, and other related-party transactions.		
Cost of Sales		
1. Select a sample of recorded cost of sales entries and vouch to supporting documentation.		
2. Select a sample of basic transaction documents (such as sales invoices, production reports) and determine whether the related cost of goods sold was calculated and recorded properly.		
3. Review the accounting costing method used by the client (such as FIFO, LIFO, standard cost) for proper application.		
4. Compute the gross margin ratio and compare to prior years.		
5. Compute the ratio of cost elements (such as labor, material) to total cost of goods sold and compare this ratio to that for prior years.		

CHAPTER 10

Finance and Investment Cycle

Credit has done a thousand times more to enrich mankind than all the goldmines in the world. It has exalted labor, stimulated manufacture, and pushed commerce over every sea.

Daniel Webster, American statesman, lawyer, and orator (1782–1852)

Professional Standards References

Topic	AU-C/ISA Section	PCAOB Reference
Audit Evidence—Specific Consideration for Selected Items	501	
External Confirmations	505	AS 2310
Analytical Procedures	520	AS 2305
Auditing Accounting Estimates, including Fair Value Measurements	540	AS 2501
Related Parties	550	AS2410
Using the Work of an Audit Specialist	620	AS 1210

LEARNING OBJECTIVES

The finance and investment cycle consists of planning for capital requirements and raising the required money by borrowing, selling stock, and entering into acquisitions and joint ventures. The finance part of the cycle involves obtaining money through stock or debt issues. The investment portion of the cycle encompasses using the funds for investments in property, plant, and equipment (covered in the acquisition and expenditure cycle in Chapter 8); marketable securities; joint ventures and partnerships; and subsidiaries. The transactions discussed in this chapter generally involve large dollar amounts and occur relatively infrequently. They can involve complex accounting issues and generally receive significant attention from management, the board of directors, and the auditors. The audit approach often differs significantly compared with auditing the operating cycle.

Your objectives are to be able to

LO 10-1 Describe the finance and investment cycle, including typical source documents.

LO 10-2 Identify significant accounts and relevant assertions related to the finance and investment cycle.

LO 10-3 Discuss the risk of material misstatement in the finance and investment cycle, with a specific focus on improper valuation and disclosure.

LO 10-4 Identify important internal control activities present in a properly designed system to mitigate the risk of material misstatements for each relevant assertion in the finance and investment cycle.

INTRODUCTION

On August 15, 2019, Harry Markopolos, a fraud investigator best known as the whistle-blower in Bernie Madoff's $65 billion Ponzi scheme, issued a 175-page report accusing **General Electric (GE)** of committing a $38 billion fraud in its financial statements. GE stock plummeted by nearly $8 billion. Nearly all of Markopolos's accusations involved accounting for estimates, many involving reserves for long-term insurance contracts. Markopolos referred to "discovery of an Enronesque business approach that has left GE on the verge of insolvency." GE's executives responded immediately that Markopolos was wrong, putting their money on their company—investing heavily in the declining stock. Surely, KPMG, the auditors for GE, took notice of the accusations because valuation of financial assets and liabilities is an area ripe with risk. Even several years later, it is still unclear whether GE did anything wrong. However, the immediate reactions by the executives and stock markets demonstrated two clear points relevant to auditors: (1) Accounting for estimates and fair values are often material and risky and (2) No one wants to hear their name and a comparison to **Enron** in the same sentence.

Enron used hundreds of off-the-book arrangements known as **special-purpose entities (SPEs)** ostensibly to create joint ventures for new businesses such as energy trading and on-demand movies. (The company created so many SPEs that officers named them after *Star Wars* characters [Chewco and Jedi], animals [raptors and bobcats], and even officers' children.) In fact, however, they were used to enrich company officers and hide more than $1 billion of debt from the company's creditors, investors, and auditors. Rather than vehicles to fund expansion into new innovative markets, the SPEs essentially hid the problems facing the company. Many of the SPEs were financed by pledges of Enron stock as collateral, and their viability depended on the company's stock price. When the company's stock started to fall, the SPEs collapsed. When the firm's stock price dropped from $80 to less than $1 in under a year, millions of investors suffered losses, and thousands of current and former company employees had their retirement plans wiped out. The restatement of the company's financial statements totaled $586 million. Although **Andersen**'s obstruction of justice conviction for shredding Enron audit documentation was later overturned by the U.S. Supreme Court, the 86,000-employee accounting firm had been ruined.

Enron appeared to be a spectacular, greatly successful business; therefore, the audit failure captured the attention of the country, and when you hear the name you probably immediately think "failure." However, hidden behind all of the headlines was the enormous difficulty the auditors faced in unraveling Enron's complex financing arrangements. Enron management had paid millions of dollars to Wall Street firms to design the SPEs so that they could be kept off the balance sheet. Early knowledge of the extent of Enron's deception might have caused its auditors to insist on consolidating the SPEs on Enron's books and, thereby, might have saved Andersen.

It is very likely that KPMG already considered the issues brought up in the GE Markopolos report. Perhaps the auditors collected sufficient, appropriate evidence to support the GAAP valuation presented in the financial statements. Because of the inherent uncertainty and measurement error in estimates of this type, it may be very hard to tell ex-post.

However, these two examples illustrate the potential size and complexity of transactions in the finance and investment cycle. Transactions in this cycle are much less frequent than in the other cycles; however, they tend to be large and complex. Thus, the focus of control activities is on the authorization of transactions and making sure that the client has competent accounting personnel who can understand the transactions and related accounting standards. Further, because management is so closely involved in these transactions, it is critical that the audit committee, the board of directors, and often third parties are involved to maintain control over management. In addition, many assets in this cycle, such as leases, hedges, and investments, are difficult to value. Use of professional judgment in determining the fair market value (FMV) of these items is difficult and inherently risky for the auditor. Auditors must examine with professional skepticism all aspects of the transactions in the finance and investment cycle. However, the focus of substantive procedures is gaining an understanding of the significant transactions, verifying the amounts and calculations, determining FMV on certain assets, and ensuring proper presentation and disclosure. Finance and investment cycle transactions have become a leading cause of recent financial statement restatements, and many of these issues have led to the creation of both new auditing standards on auditing fair values and new accounting standards on derivative securities, leases, and insurance contracts. Some of the largest financing and investment cycle restatements are described in Exhibit 10.1.

EXHIBIT 10.1   Finance and Investment Shenanigans

Company	Cause of Misstatement	Amount
Bernard Madoff Investments	Extensive Ponzi scheme used to defraud thousands of investors, including individuals, charities, and pension funds.	$65.0 billion
Lehman Brothers	The company overstated fair values, and also created improper "repo" transactions, which enabled them to keep debt off the books and appear financially stronger than competition.	$50+ billion
Freddie Mac	The mortgage lending giant used improper accounting techniques and financial transactions structured to push unwanted earnings into the future and hide gains that senior management thought would make the entity appear too volatile.	$4.5 billion
AIG	The insurance giant hid deferred compensation that some executives received through an investment entity, **Starr International Co.,** with long ties to AIG. AIG disclosed the amounts in prior filings but did not run the cost through its financial statements, as it now admits it should have. In addition, the company had problems with accounting for investments by AIG's subsidiaries in synthetic-fuel production facilities. These facilities wrongly booked tax credits from the investments as net investment income or other revenue when it should have used them to reduce tax expenses and accounted for syndication transactions from low-cost housing as sales, boosting net income by $209 million over five years.	$2.7 billion
El Paso	The energy company used improper hedges of anticipated natural gas production.	$2.4 billion
Tyco	Most of the substantive accounting changes centered on $50.6 million in pretax credits that it took to reverse merger reserves set up in prior periods but never used. The SEC said the reserves either should never have been set up or should have been reversed earlier. Additionally, a subsidiary, **ADT,** improperly carried canceled alarm accounts on its books. Other issues were included in the final total.	$1.15 billion
Goodyear Tire Company	The company changed the way it accounted for income taxes and the costs of retirees' health and life insurance benefits.	$1.03 billion
General Electric	The company misapplied a rule on how to account for certain derivative deals.	$460 million
Millennium Chemicals	The company changed the accounting treatment on a five-year agreement for its requirements for gold used for production of acetyls that should have been accounted for as a secured financing lease rather than as an operating lease, underestimated the obligation due to its largest domestic pension plan, and understated deferred taxes.	$400 million
Sequential Brands Group, Inc.	The company failed to record a goodwill impairment.	$304.1 million
Xerox	Over a period of years, several senior managers in Mexico collaborated to circumvent Xerox's accounting policies and administrative procedures. The restatement related to uncollectible long-term receivables; a failure to record liabilities for amounts due to concessionaires; and, to a lesser extent, for contracts that did not fully meet the requirements to be recorded as sales-type leases.	$207 million

(continued)

EXHIBIT 10.1 **Finance and Investment Shenanigans** *(concluded)*

Company	Cause of Misstatement	Amount
Gap Inc.	The popular clothier used improper lease accounting related to accounting for rent holidays and tenant allowances.	$200 million
Provident Financial Group	Auto leases were reported off the company's balance sheet as sale and leasebacks of operating leases, but after a review, the company determined that none of the transactions should have been recorded that way. Instead, they should have been recorded as financing leases with all assets and liabilities appearing on the company's balance sheet.	$114.7 million

FINANCE AND INVESTMENT CYCLE: TYPICAL ACTIVITIES

LO 10-1
Describe the finance and investment cycle, including typical source documents.

The finance and investment cycle contains a large number of accounts and records ranging across tangible (e.g., property, plant, and equipment [PP&E], investment securities) and intangible assets (e.g., goodwill, patents), long-term liabilities, deferred credits, stockholders' equity, gains and losses, expenses, and income taxes. See Exhibit 10.2 for a list of the major accounts and records. These include some of the more complicated topics in accounting: equity method accounting for investments, consolidation accounting, goodwill, income taxes, and derivatives, to name a few. The purpose of this chapter is to focus on the auditing issues associated with each of these accounting topics, not to explain how to account for these balances and transactions. Further, we will focus on the more general characteristics of assets, liabilities, and equity accounts in this cycle.

You may recall that an entity's operations and accounting records consist of routine transactions, nonroutine transactions, and accounting estimates. Auditors typically approach audits of routine transactions with a reliance approach—evaluate internal controls and rely on the operation of controls found to be in place. In contrast, audits of

EXHIBIT 10.2
Finance and Investment Cycle

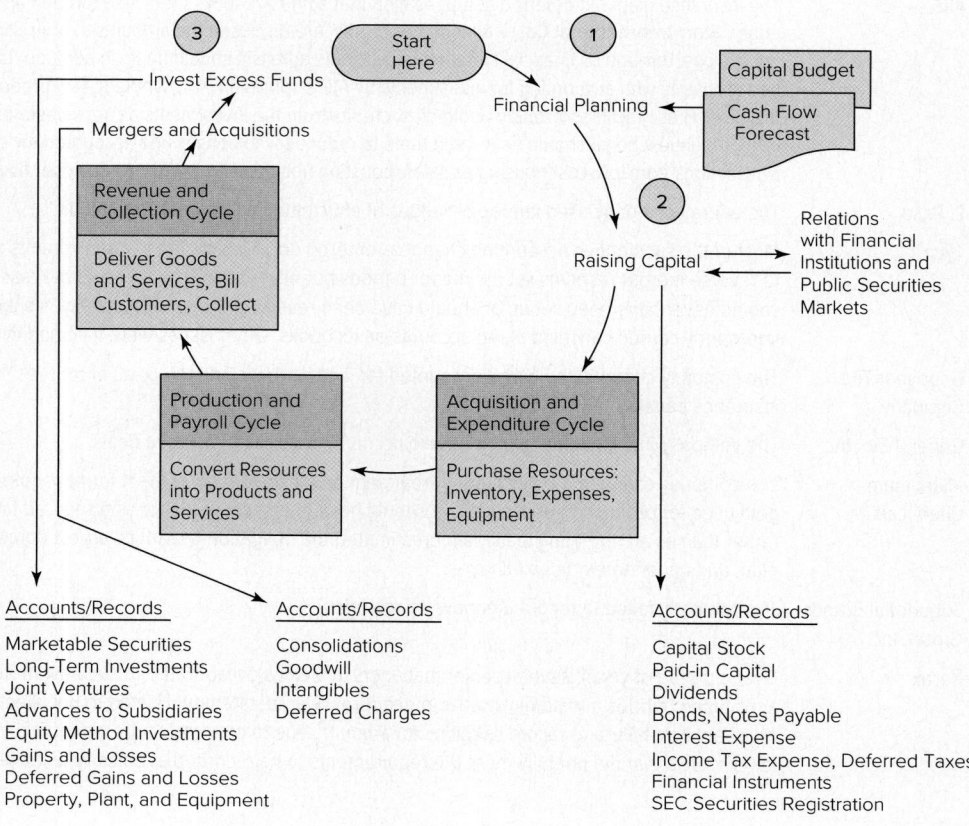

Accounts/Records

Marketable Securities
Long-Term Investments
Joint Ventures
Advances to Subsidiaries
Equity Method Investments
Gains and Losses
Deferred Gains and Losses
Property, Plant, and Equipment

Accounts/Records

Consolidations
Goodwill
Intangibles
Deferred Charges

Accounts/Records

Capital Stock
Paid-in Capital
Dividends
Bonds, Notes Payable
Interest Expense
Income Tax Expense, Deferred Taxes
Financial Instruments
SEC Securities Registration

nonroutine transactions generally take a substantive approach. In the large majority of audits that do not require an audit of internal controls, auditors may do very few tests of controls related to nonroutine transactions and rely on substantive tests. Similarly, auditors apply a more substantive approach with accounting estimates. Because the financing and investment cycle generally involves large, infrequent, significant transactions—often with some degree of estimation—auditors usually employ more substantive testing procedures in this cycle and rely less on tests of controls.

Exhibit 10.2 is an illustration of the finance and investment cycle, which interacts with all of the other cycles. Its major functions are financial planning, raising capital, and entering into mergers, acquisitions, and other investments. As you follow the exhibit, you can use the numbers after the headings to track the elements of internal control described in the following sections.

Financing the Entity Through Debt and Stockholder Equity

Transactions in debt and stockholder equity are normally few in number but large in monetary amount, and with a high level of management involvement. The highest levels of corporate governance authorize and execute these transactions. The control-related duties and responsibilities reflect this high-level attention.

Financial Planning ①

The purpose of financial planning is to ensure that the entity has enough cash to operate the business. Entities can fund capital needs through their operations, but any additional needs must be fulfilled through financing activities. Financial planning starts with the cash flow forecast by the chief financial officer (CFO). This forecast informs the board of directors and management of the business plans, the prospects for cash inflows, and the total needs for cash outflows. The cash flow forecast usually is integrated with the capital budget, which contains the plans for asset purchases and business acquisitions. A **capital budget** approved by the board of directors constitutes the authorization for major capital asset acquisitions (acquisition cycle) and investments. Cash flow planning and capital budgeting are important controls over major management decisions.

Raising Capital ②

The board of directors usually authorizes sales of capital stock and debt-financing transactions. All directors must sign registration documents for public securities offerings. However, authority normally is delegated to the CFO or treasurer to complete other significant transactions (e.g., periodic renewals of notes payable and other ordinary types of significant financing transactions without specific board approval of each transaction). Auditors should expect to find the authorizing signatures of the CEO, CFO, treasurer, chair of the board of directors, and perhaps other high-ranking officers on financing documents. Because financing transactions are typically authorized and executed by top management and directors, it is much more difficult to rely on segregation of duties to ensure that these transactions flow properly through the accounting system using only internal employees. As a result, most entities rely on external parties to process debt and equity transactions involving multiple investors.

Company bonds and stocks are normally handled by an intermediary called a **transfer agent**, generally a bank or trust company. The transfer agent tracks securities' owners for payment of interest or dividends. The certificate records are kept by a **registrar** who updates the records based on information from the transfer agent. Often, the registrar and transfer agent are the same company.

In the past, many financing transactions have been off the balance sheet. Companies entered into obligations and commitments that did not require entries in the accounting system. Examples of transactions that did not necessitate reporting on the balance sheet include operating leases and endorsements on discounted notes or on other companies' obligations, letters of credit, guarantees, repurchase or remarketing agreements, commitments to purchase at fixed prices, commitments to sell at fixed prices, and certain kinds of stock options. As noted previously, the Enron debacle was a case of using SPEs to keep certain large transactions off the company's balance sheet. Off-balance-sheet transactions often cause problems in financial reporting and disclosure. Although new accounting standards will reduce the number of off-balance-sheet transactions (e.g., new rules make it harder to create SPEs and have mandated more disclosure), auditors must still be aware of their existence and ensure their proper use and adequate disclosure. Because of the complexity of the transactions, often the most difficult task for the auditor is discovery and understanding of the transactions.

Record Keeping for Long-Term Liabilities

The accounting department and the CFO or controller maintain records of notes and bonds payable. The record-keeping procedures should be similar to those used to account for vendor accounts payable: comparing payment notices from lenders to the accounting records, monitoring due dates, setting up interest in vouchers for payment, and making accruals for unpaid interest on financial reporting dates. If the company has only a few bonds and notes outstanding, it usually does not keep subsidiary records of them. All information is in the general ledger accounts. However, many large companies, especially in industries such as utilities, have large numbers of bonds and notes and may keep control and subsidiary accounts as is done for accounts payable. Exhibit 10.3 shows selected debentures of **Consolidated Edison Inc.** as disclosed in its 2021 financial statements.

EXHIBIT 10.3
Consolidated Edison Inc. 2021 Financial Statements

Consolidated Edison, Inc. Consolidated Statement of Capitalization				
LONG-TERM DEBT (Millions of Dollars)			At December 31,	
Maturity	**Interest Rate**	**Series**	**2021**	**2020**
DEBENTURES:				
2021	0.60	2018C	-	640
2024	3.30	2014B	250	250
2026	2.90	2016B	250	250
2027	3.125	2017B	350	350
2028	3.80	2018A	300	300
28 Additional Debentures*	Various		16,975	14,725
TOTAL DEBENTURES			18,125	16,515
TAX-EXEMPT DEBT—Notes issued to New York State Energy Research and Development Authority for Facilities Revenue Bonds†:				
2036	0.10	2010A	225	225
2039	0.10	2004C	99	99
2039	0.09	2005A	126	126
TOTAL TAX-EXEMPT DEBT			450	1,086
Unamortized debt expense			(145)	(130)
Unamortized debt discount			(48)	(46)
TOTAL			18,382	16,789
Less: Long-term debt due within one year			-	640
TOTAL LONG-TERM DEBT			18,382	16,149
TOTAL CAPITALIZATION			$34,694	$30,998

* Excluded for brevity. These debentures are listed in the Consolidated Edison Annual Report.
† Rates are to be reset weekly; December 31, 2021, rates shown.
The accompanying notes are an integral part of these financial statements.

With 36 debentures and other long-term debt totaling $18 billion as of the end of 2021, record keeping and auditing records represent a formidable task. Also, when all or parts of the notes become due within the next year, the CFO and controller must have the necessary information for properly classifying current and long-term amounts. As shown in Exhibit 10.3, long-term debt accounts for over half of Consolidated Edison Inc.'s total capitalization, making this a significant audit issue.

Another class of credit balances for which the functions of authorization, custody, and reconciliation are not easy to describe are the "calculated liabilities and credits": lease obligations, deferred income taxes, pension and postretirement benefit liabilities, and foreign currency translation gains and losses, to name a few. These are accounting transactions calculated according to accounting rules using basic data from company plans and operations. Management usually has considerable discretion in structuring leases, tax strategies, pension plan and employee benefit terms, foreign holdings, and the like. These accounting calculations often involve significant accounting estimates made by management. Company accountants try to capture the economic reality of these calculated liabilities by following generally accepted accounting principles, which are often complex and difficult to understand. Auditors need to discuss these transactions at length and ensure that the fundamental economic and business assumptions underlying significant transactions are reasonable.

Periodic Reconciliation

Most public entities use registrars and transfer agents to issue certificates and track stock ownership. Reports can be obtained from registrars and transfer agents to verify that the company's record of the number of shares outstanding agrees with the registrar's number. (Without this reconciliation, counterfeit shares handled by the transfer agent and recorded by the registrar might go unnoticed.) A **trustee** having duties and responsibilities similar to those of registrars and transfer agents can handle ownership of bonds. Confirmations and reports from bond trustees can be used to reconcile the trustee's records to the company's records.

Some small, especially closely held, corporations may issue stock certificates themselves. These companies utilize a stock certificate book to issue certificates as authorized by the board of directors. A responsible independent person should periodically inspect the stock certificate book to determine whether all certificates are recorded and in the possession of bona fide owners. If necessary, officials in very small companies can confirm the ownership of shares with the holders of record.

Investing Transactions: Investments and Intangibles ③

Company investments can take many shapes. Management invests company resources through the purchase or lease of PP&E, which was discussed in Chapter 8. Investments in intangible assets may be in the form of purchased assets (e.g., patents, trademarks) or accounting allocations (e.g., goodwill, deferred charges). Finally, a company can have a variety of types of investments in marketable securities. The following sections are phrased in the context of a manufacturing or service company; however, financial institutions (banks, thrifts), investment companies (mutual funds, small business investment companies), and insurance companies have more elaborate systems for managing their investments and intangibles.

Authorization

Those in the entity charged with governance (e.g., board of directors or investment committee) should approve all investment policies. It is not unusual to find board or executive committee approval required for major investment transactions. However, auditors should expect to find a great deal of variation across companies about the nature and amount of transactions that must have specific high-level approval. It is imperative that auditors understand the approval process and vouch major acquisitions to the appropriate documented approval.

Custody

Negotiable certificates such as stocks and bonds may be kept in a brokerage account. Other negotiable certificates (such as titles to real estate) may be in the actual possession of the client. If the company keeps them, they should be in a safe or a bank safe deposit box. Only high-ranking officers (e.g., CFO, CEO, president, and chairman of the board) should have access, which should require two people (**dual control**) to access these documents. This may require two signatures to access a safe deposit box or ensure that no one person knows the complete combination to the safe. When it is not possible for one person to access a safe, cabinet, or drawer, as in two locks and no one has both keys, or no one knows the entire combination, a strict form of dual custody, known as **joint custody**, is implemented as a control.

Patents, trademarks, copyrights, and similar legal intangible rights can be evidenced in legal documents and contracts. These seldom are negotiable, and they usually are kept in ordinary company files. However, these intangible assets are highly valued, and entities make every effort to protect these assets as indicated in the following Auditing Insight.

AUDITING INSIGHT   Don't Use Our Logo

The University of Texas at Austin has trademark rights over the "longhorn" symbol and a particular school color (burnt orange). The university actively prohibits businesses from using these symbols without permission. For example, a local cleaning business and a trash-hauling business were informed that they must cease and desist using the longhorn head logo on their buildings, signs, and trucks. The businesses complied by repainting and finding other ways to promote their business.

The **Coalition to Advance the Protection of Sports Logos** (CAPS), whose members are colleges and the professional leagues (NFL, NBA,

MLB, and NHL), uses a national network of investigators to scour flea markets, customs ports, and parking lots on game days to ferret out unlicensed T-shirts, caps, and other gear. Since 1993, CAPS, working with local law enforcement, has seized more than 9 million illegal products valued at more than $329 million.

Source: "Stopping Knockoffs an Elusive Goal for Flyers," *The Philadelphia Inquirer,* May 15, 2008, p. C01.

Record Keeping for Investments

Unauthorized transactions can be a major risk for investments and intangibles. The board of directors or other responsible officials should authorize large transactions. These authorizations provide the approval for initializing the purchase of the investment. The procedures for purchase of investments vary greatly depending on the type of investment involved. For example, in a more manual system, the voucher system previously described in Chapter 8 may be used. The authorization from the board provides the purchasing department the go-ahead to acquire the assets and the accounting department the approval to prepare the voucher and the check. The treasurer or CFO signs the check to purchase the investment. Alternatively, many investment transactions are performed electronically. For these transactions, multifactor authentication, transaction limits, and other automated controls become critical.

The record keeping for many types of investments and intangibles can be complicated. The complications arise not so much from the original recording of transactions, but from the maintenance of the accounts over time. This is where complex accounting standards for marketable securities, equity method accounting, consolidations, goodwill, intangibles' amortization and valuation, depreciation, deferred charges, deferred taxes, pension and postretirement benefit liabilities, and various financial instruments enter the picture. High-level accountants who prepare financial statements are involved with the accounting rules and the management estimates required to account for such investments and intangibles. Management plans and estimates of future events and interpretations of the accounting standards often become elements of the accounting maintenance of these balances. These decisions are ripe areas for overstatement of assets, understatement of liabilities, and understatement of expenses.

Periodic Reconciliation

Investment accounts may be overstated by recording marketable securities that the entity does not own (this represents a violation of the rights assertion). When a brokerage firm holds the securities, the inspection is accomplished with a written confirmation, which is the most typical situation. However, when a company physically holds marketable securities in its possession, a reconciliation performed through inspection and count of negotiable securities certificates is a critical control. This reconciliation is similar to a physical inventory count consisting of an inspection of certificates on hand and comparison with the information recorded in the accounts.

A securities count is not a mere handling of bits of paper. A securities count should include a record of the name of the company represented by the certificate, the interest rate for bonds, the dividend rate for preferred stocks, the due date for bonds, the serial numbers on the certificates (known as the *CUSIP number*), the number of stock shares or face amount of bonds, and notes on the name of the owner shown on the face of the certificate or on the endorsements on the back (should be the client company). Companies should perform this reconciliation reasonably often and not wait for an annual visit by the independent auditors. A securities count in a financial institution that holds thousands of shares in multibillion-dollar asset accounts is a major undertaking. A surprise count by the auditors may be done during the interim testing. As with other assets, the auditor should insist that client personnel are present during the entire count.

✓ REVIEW CHECKPOINTS

10.1 Who is normally responsible for the authorization of investment activities? Why is the authorization normally performed at this level?

10.2 What constitutes the authorization for notes payable? What documentary evidence could auditors examine to confirm this authorization?

10.3 What documents would a company need to correctly account for its investment securities, and what information would they obtain from these documents?

10.4 Describe the activities a company should perform to ensure the accuracy of an investment listing of marketable securities.

SIGNIFICANT ACCOUNTS AND RELEVANT ASSERTIONS

LO 10-2
Identify significant accounts and relevant assertions related to the finance and investment cycle.

Exhibit 10.4 identifies significant accounts and assertions in the finance and investment cycle. It is nearly impossible to describe a "typical" finance and investment cycle. Depending on the company and the industry, audit clients may be almost entirely equity financed or largely debt financed. In addition, some companies have simple investment activities consisting of purchasing plant assets and occasionally investing excess cash in highly liquid securities with publicly available valuations. The type of investment can have a huge influence on the effort required by the auditor. For example, Microsoft Corporation reported approximately $116 billion of investment securities in its 2021 annual report. However, the large majority of these securities are government debentures that are relatively simple to audit because of their short-term nature and publicly available valuations. However, Microsoft also reported approximately $66 billion of equity method investments and intangible assets—much more difficult to audit, as we will discuss later when addressing audits of estimates, including fair value measurements. Thus, although Exhibit 10.4 simply lists "Investments" as a significant account, the type of investment has a huge effect on the most relevant assertions and the amount of work done. As discussed in the following Auditing Insight, some of these acquisitions can be extremely large. In subsequent sections of this chapter, we will discuss how the activities within the accounts can vary and how the auditor approaches these varying risks.

EXHIBIT 10.4

Significant Account	Relevant Assertions
Investments	Existence/occurrence
	Completeness
	Valuation
	Presentation and disclosure
Long-Term Debt	Existence/occurrence
	Completeness
	Valuation
	Presentation and disclosure
Capital Stock	Completeness
	Presentation and disclosure
Retained Earnings	Completeness

AUDITING INSIGHT   It's Just a Small Purchase . . .

Mergers and acquisitions are very common ways for companies to invest their assets and grow their businesses. Some companies compete via acquisition. As a result, investments often represent a significant activity for large companies. **Verizon,** the giant telecommunications company, announced on July 25, 2016, its intent to purchase **Yahoo!** for $4.8 billion in an effort to compete with **Google** and **Facebook** for advertising revenue. With this purchase, Verizon acquired not only the tangible assets and liabilities of Yahoo!, but also intangible assets—some which can be specifically identified—as well as goodwill. The valuation and distinction between specifically identifiable intangible assets and goodwill is critical from an audit perspective. Specifically identifiable assets are

amortized, but under ASC 350, goodwill is only subject to impairment tests. Although Yahoo! is a very large and well-known company, it is only the fourth-largest acquisition made by Verizon in the past 10 years. Verizon has also purchased **Verizon Wireless** ($130.1 billion), **Alltel** ($28.1 billion), and **MCI** ($10.3 billion), in addition to **AOL** ($4.3 billion) and in November 2021 **Tracfone** ($3.1 billion). The Verizon Wireless acquisition was the largest acquisition ever when it occurred in 2013. As discussed later in this chapter, the valuation of assets in acquisitions can represent a significant risk of material misstatement.

Source: Verizon Company History and Timeline, *Verizon,* 2022.

RISK OF MATERIAL MISSTATEMENT

LO 10-3
Discuss the risk of material misstatement in the finance and investment cycle, with a specific focus on improper valuation and disclosure.

As previously mentioned, the transactions in the financing and investing cycle do not occur in most firms on a daily, or even weekly, basis and are often for large amounts. Therefore, there is a premium on ensuring that transactions are properly authorized. In addition, there is significant risk and professional judgment in determining the fair market value (FMV) of certain assets, and accounting standards require significant detailed disclosure regarding the FMV of these items. Therefore, presentation and disclosure have increased risk in the finance and investment cycle. Refer to Exhibit 10.5 for a summary of some of the things that can go wrong in a typical corporation that lead to a risk of material misstatement in the finance and investment cycle.

A quick analysis of Exhibit 10.5 shows that many of the common problems in the finance and investment cycle involve failure to record and disclose transactions and failure to appropriately adjust asset valuations for either changes in fair value on marketable securities or impairments. These problems can occur for a variety of reasons: (1) complex transactions make the accounting and disclosure rules difficult; (2) the infrequent transactions do not lend themselves to routine control procedures, making errors and omissions more frequent; and (3) because of higher amounts of estimation and judgment, top management may intentionally misstate financial statements. In this section, we will discuss some of the more difficult issues that can occur in the finance and investment cycle from a perspective of why there is a higher risk of material misstatement.

EXHIBIT 10.5

Significant Account	Relevant Assertions	What Could Go Wrong?
Investments	Existence/occurrence	Management may sell company-owned securities for their own benefit.
		Investment securities held by the entity may be stolen.
		Management may record fictitious interest income.
	Completeness	Investment transactions from the current period may be recorded in the subsequent period.
	Valuation	Management fails to mark marketable equity securities to fair market value.
		Equity method investments are not accurately adjusted for investee income and dividends.
		Impairments to investment securities are not properly recorded.
	Presentation and disclosure	Management fails to appropriately account for derivative transactions that do not qualify for hedge treatment.
		Available for sale debt securities are misclassified as held to maturity.
Long-Term Debt	Existence/occurrence	Fully paid notes are not properly removed from schedule of long-term debt.
	Completeness	Management fails to record capital lease obligations.
	Valuation	Amortization of long-term debt is calculated incorrectly.
	Presentation and disclosure	Management fails to reclassify current portions of long-term debt.
		Management fails to disclose future minimum required debt payments.
		Violations of restrictive loan covenants are not properly disclosed.
Capital Stock	Completeness	Some issued stock is not recorded.
		Treasury stock repurchases are not recorded.
	Presentation and disclosure	Exercises of stock options are not allocated correctly between capital stock accounts.
Retained Earnings	Completeness	Declared dividends are not recorded.
		Prior-period error corrections are not recorded appropriately.

Complex Transactions

In the past, clients have worked with investment bankers to create investing and financing transactions that are structured to get around GAAP rules. Management may want to keep risky ventures off the financial statements to make the company look better. The Enron example from earlier in the chapter is one example of this, as is the example in the following Auditing Insight. However, many transactions are complex, and even ones that reach the balance sheet can be challenging. For example, complex instruments that contain characteristics of both debt and equity can be difficult to classify and value the components. Merger and acquisition transactions also have large amounts of estimation, which can lead to large differences in judgments. These transactions are usually complex, are difficult to audit, and can be used as vehicles to hide fraud—all of which lead to higher risks of material misstatement.

 AUDITING INSIGHT | Don't Just Look at the Balance Sheet

For some companies, off-balance-sheet risk exposure can significantly influence the amount of risk present. For example, an important risk measure for banks is the Basel III Supplementary Leverage ratio. This ratio measures the core strength of a bank from a regulatory perspective by comparing the amount of tier 1 capital, primarily common stock and retained earnings, to the bank's total leverage exposure, which measures both the on- and off-balance-sheet assets of a bank. A higher ratio indicates less risk from a regulatory perspective. Because of the importance of the ratio to regulators, a key user of the financial statements, auditors must pay close attention not only to the on-balance-sheet assets, but also the off-balance-sheet assets of a bank. These off-balance-sheet exposures can be complex contracts such as derivatives, cancelable commitments, and guarantees. For the year ended December 31, 2018, **Citigroup,** one of the largest multinational financial institutions, reported off-balance-sheet risk exposures related to guarantees of $606 billion. To put this number in perspective, Citigroup's off-balance-sheet guarantee exposures are equal to more than 2.6 percent of the 2021 U.S. GDP!

Source: Citigroup Form 10-K, December 31, 2021.

Fair Market Value

Judgment, as defined by **KPMG,** is "the process of reaching a decision or drawing a conclusion where there are a number of possible alternative solutions."[1] Judgment is made in an environment of uncertainty and risk. As the uncertainty and risk increase, the need for greater skepticism and increased experience or expertise is required to ensure that sound audit judgment is applied.

The investment cycle covers a number of difficult-to-value assets such as

- Investments in debt and equity securities or unique assets.
- Derivative instruments.
- Certain financial instruments.
- Intangible assets, including goodwill.
- Loans and other receivables that are possibly impaired.
- Pension and other postretirement assets and liabilities.

Each of these and other assets and liabilities require the auditor to exercise professional judgment in an area of high risk. Management will value most of these assets using assumptions they have made about the financial markets, commodity prices, and short- and long-term economic activity. The auditor will evaluate the assumptions that management has made regarding all assets for which FMV is a concern, but even the most diligent audit cannot remove the inherent risk of the changing economic and financial markets that affect the FMV of these assets and liabilities, leading to high risk of material misstatement. This issue of estimation uncertainty is covered in the following Auditing Insight.

AUDITING INSIGHT | Small Changes in Assumptions, Huge Changes in Estimates

Estimate calculations in the investment area very often involve complex, level 3 fair value estimates. Level 3 fair value estimates involve unobservable variables, such as expected growth rates or discount rates. A recent study on estimation uncertainty within public companies revealed that, often, very small changes in underlying assumptions, well within a margin for error, could lead to changes in valuation estimates many times materiality levels. Consider the example of a company acquiring another company. After considering tangible assets, the purchasing company has $3 billion to allocate between corporate trademarks, which are limited life intangibles and must be amortized, and goodwill, which is not subject to

amortization. Assume the trademark has 10 or more years of useful life remaining. It is likely that a 0.5 percent change in the assumed discount range may lead to a fluctuation in the estimated value of the trademark many times materiality. Because a company may have the incentive to recognize more goodwill (because it is not amortized), the auditor must be vigilant in evaluating whether the discount rate used in the fair value estimate is overstated, which would reduce the computed FV of the trademark.

Source: B. E. Christensen, S. M. Glover, and D. A. Wood, "Extreme Estimation Uncertainty in Fair Value Estimates: Implications for *Audit Assurance,*" *Auditing: A Journal of Practice & Theory* 31, no. 1 (2012): 127–146.

Related-Party Transactions

Related-party transactions occur frequently in companies. For example, **Caterpillar Inc.** has a division that builds construction equipment and a division that builds engines. Because engines are sold from the engine division to the construction division and because the corporation's management could influence the nature of these transactions, such a sale qualifies as a related-party transaction. The issue for the auditor is determining that the engine division sold engines to the construction division under the same terms as sales made by the engine division to outside customers. In other words, these sales should be the equivalent of an *arm's-length transaction.*

Many of the examples of fraud in this chapter occurred through related-party transactions. Essentially, a **related party** is one that can exert significant influence over another party. Related parties are frequently used in fraudulent activity because they can conceal

[1]KPMG, "Evaluating Professional Judgment in Auditing and Accounting," www.scribd.com/doc/105344428/KPMG-monograph.

activities that the auditors would normally be aware of if the activity occurred between unrelated parties. The auditing standards specifically list significant transactions with related parties not in the ordinary course of business as risk factors relating to fraudulent financial reporting. The objective of the auditor is to obtain sufficient appropriate audit evidence to determine whether related parties and relationships and transactions with related parties have been properly identified, accounted for, and disclosed in the financial statements.

Lease Accounting

A company can make an investment by purchasing property, plant, or equipment. These transactions were discussed in the acquisition and expense cycle in Chapter 8. Often, companies do not want to purchase assets because of cash considerations or the flexibility in changing assets as the business changes. Leases may offer businesses a better cash flow situation or the ability to easily terminate or modify an asset. However, the accounting for leases is more complex than a direct purchase of an asset. Historically, the classification of leases as either operating or capitalized was based on a series of assumptions that could be easily manipulated by management. For example, if the present value of lease payments is 90 percent or more of the property's value, the lease is capitalized; if it is only 89.9 percent of the value, the lease is classified as operating and is not reported as a liability on the balance sheet. This ability to structure lease transactions produced less transparent information and allowed certain leases not to be capitalized. The SEC estimated that as of 2005, SEC registrants alone had $1.25 trillion of off-balance-sheet operating lease commitments.[2] To improve financial reporting about lease transactions, on February 25, 2016, the FASB issued *ASU No. 2016-02* (Topic 842). According to the new standard, all leases greater than 12 months must be recognized as assets with their matching liabilities. In addition, the standard increased the quantity of disclosures required for leasing transactions. Thus, although the new standard reduced the ability of management to structure lease transactions, in many ways it increased the risk to the auditor by requiring all leases to be accounted for using imputed present value estimations. The new standard was effective for public companies beginning with fiscal year 2019 and for nonpublic companies for fiscal year 2020. These assets are often material. For example, Microsoft reported over $11 billion of operating lease right-of-use assets in its June 30, 2021, balance sheet, which is approximately three percent of assets. Previously, these operating lease assets would not have been shown on the balance sheet.

Loan Covenants

To protect themselves, banks usually insert clauses in loan agreements intended to keep the borrower's financial position at a level that will ensure repayment of the loan. These **loan covenants** may restrict payment of dividends, additional borrowings, or use of assets for collateral on other debt. They often require the borrower to maintain certain ratio levels (e.g., a current ratio of no less than 2:1). If borrowers violate these restrictions, the debt can be called (payment demanded) immediately. If the borrower cannot pay the debt when called, the lender can force the borrower into bankruptcy. Auditors must check to see that their clients are not in violation of their loan covenants. An additional risk is that companies' managements will misstate their other accounts to meet the covenant requirements. A loan covenant violation can also trigger other difficult decisions for the auditor. For example, if a company is in violation of a loan covenant and has not reached a resolution with the lender, this will often trigger an assessment of substantial doubt related to going-concern uncertainty. This assessment may lead to a modification of the standard auditor's report.

---

[2] 2005 SEC report on off-balance-sheet activities.

Impairments

When auditing large investment balances and purchase-related intangible assets, auditors must be aware of the risk of material misstatement related to the valuation assertion. GAAP require that impairments to asset values should normally be taken as losses when they occur. Valuing investments and determining possible impairment of related goodwill is very complex. Moreover, companies have been accused of taking a "big bath," which means writing off assets and building up reserves to reduce expenses in future years. This is more likely to happen when a company is experiencing a bad year or when it hires a new CEO (like a football coach going 1–11 his first year and blaming it on his predecessor's players). Thus, auditors must always consider whether assets are overstated due to a possible impairment or whether impairment write-offs have been delayed, both of which can lead to material misstatements.

Presentation and Disclosure

As previously mentioned, failure to appropriately disclose complex transactions and estimates can lead to confusion and the inability for both auditors and investors to understand exactly what a company is doing. For that reason, presentation and disclosure assertions take on added importance in the finance and investment cycle. In Exhibit 10.5, we listed several examples of potential hazards facing auditors. With investment securities, classification of marketable securities and derivative instruments are critical. The classification of a security as trading or available for sale affects whether changes in value influence net income. Even more critically, marketable debt security investments classified as held-to-maturity are not subject to mark-to-market accounting on the face of the financial statements. Similarly, the classification of a derivative instrument as a hedge influences the presentation and characterization of fluctuations in value. On the financing side, disclosures related to pensions, leases, and stock options are complex and extensive, and the completeness and accuracy of the disclosures represent high risks of material misstatement. The SEC takes disclosure very seriously, and the following Auditing Insight represents just one example where lack of disclosure was considered to be a material omission.

AUDITING INSIGHT Not Disclosing Information Can Hurt

According to the SEC, five former **San Diego** city officials knew that the city had been intentionally underfunding its pension obligations so that it could increase pension benefits but defer the costs. They were aware that the city would face severe difficulty funding its future pension and retiree health care obligations unless new revenues were obtained, pension and health care benefits were reduced, or city services were cut. They specifically knew that the city's unfunded liability to its pension plan was projected to dramatically increase from $284 million at the beginning of fiscal year 2002 to an estimated $2 billion by 2009 and that the city's liability for retiree health care was another estimated $1.1 billion. But the officials failed to disclose these and other material facts to rating agencies or to investors in bond-offering documents and continuing disclosures.

Specifically, the SEC alleges that the city manager signed the closing letter for one of the bond offerings, falsely certifying that it was accurate and did not contain misleading statements. The city auditor and comptroller signed letters falsely representing that the city's audited financial statements included in the securities offerings were accurate. The deputy city manager of finance regularly reviewed and revised the false and misleading disclosure documents and signed the

closing letter for two of the five bond offerings. She falsely certified that the disclosures were accurate and did not contain misleading statements, and she reviewed and made presentations to the rating agencies. The assistant auditor and comptroller reviewed the city's financial statements that contained some of the false and misleading disclosures, and the city treasurer participated in drafting the city's false and misleading disclosures. Additionally, the city treasurer and the assistant auditor and comptroller knew that in 2003, the rating agencies had concerns about the city's growing pension obligations and that those obligations could negatively affect the city's credit rating. Nevertheless, they withheld material facts from the rating agencies.

In October 2010, four of the accused officials agreed to pay a total of $80,000 to settle the fraud charges with the Securities and Exchange Commission. Regulators have pointed to this case as an indication that they intend to pursue individuals engaged in perceived abuses in the $2.8 billion municipal bond market.

Source: *"SEC Charges Five Former San Diego Officials with Securities Fraud,"* SEC Press Release 2008-57, April 7, 2008; *"Ex-San Diego Officials Fined in Fraud Case,"* www.ft.com, October 28, 2010.

INTERNAL CONTROL ACTIVITIES AND DESIGN EVALUATION

LO 10-4
Identify important internal control activities present in a properly designed system to mitigate the risk of material misstatements for each relevant assertion in the finance and investment cycle.

In the finance and investment cycle, auditors look for control activities such as authorization, appropriate custody, record keeping, and periodic reconciliation. They especially look for information about the level of management that is involved in these functions. Tests of controls generally begin with inquiries and observations related to these features. Inspection of documents, primarily looking for proper authorizations, and a walkthrough of controls over the determination of the fair value of assets should also be performed.

Because finance and investment transactions are often individually material, each transaction usually is audited using substantive procedures. Auditors do not normally examine samples of significant transactions for tests of controls as they do in the other cycles because reliance on controls does not normally reduce the extent of substantive procedures on finance and investment cycle accounts. However, lack of controls can lead to performance of significant extended procedures. Of particular importance are the entitywide controls that restrict access to systems, documents, and assets—many of which are key in the performance of investment cycle activities. Establishing appropriate procedures, including adequate controls, for determining the fair market value of investments, derivatives, hedges, and other investment instruments is imperative in accessing the overall control structure for any company that maintains a material amount of such instruments. Of course, for public companies in which the auditors must issue a report on the effectiveness of controls over the financial reporting process, evaluation of controls over these transactions is essential. However, for the majority of nonpublic clients, tests of controls may be limited to entity level in the finance and investment cycle. Exhibit 10.6 outlines some of the primary control considerations in the finance and investment cycle that entities use to mitigate risk.

EXHIBIT 10.6

Significant Account	Relevant Assertions	What Could Go Wrong?	Internal Control Activity
Investments	Existence/ occurrence	Management may sell company-owned securities for their own benefit.	Broker transaction confirmations should be periodically reviewed by the investment committee of the board of directors (BOD).
			Investment purchases and sales should be approved by the BOD.
		Investment securities held by the entity may be stolen.	Securities should be held in lockboxes, and responsibility for custody should be separated from responsibility for record keeping.
		Management may record fictitious interest income.	The investment committee of the BOD should regularly compare investment performance to expectations.
	Completeness	Investment transactions from the current period may be recorded in the subsequent period.	The responsibility for authorization of purchases of securities should be separated from recording purchases in the securities ledger.
	Valuation	Management fails to mark marketable equity securities to fair market value.	Qualified staff is responsible for end-of-period fair value estimates.
		Equity method investments are not accurately adjusted for investee income and dividends.	Ensure accurate financial statements for investees are obtained on a timely basis.
		Impairments to investment securities are not properly recorded.	Management reviews investment securities for evidence of other than temporary declines in value.
			Separate the duty of investment acquisition from the duty of investment valuation.
	Presentation and disclosure	Management fails to appropriately account for derivative transactions that do not qualify for hedge treatment.	Properly trained employees supervise the estimation process for derivative securities.

(continued)

EXHIBIT 10.6 *(concluded)*

Significant Account	Relevant Assertions	What Could Go Wrong?	Internal Control Activity
		Available for Sale Debt securities are misclassified as Held to Maturity.	Ensure the investment committee of the BOD has a written policy on investment classification.
Long-Term Debt	Existence/ occurrence	Fully paid notes are not properly removed from schedule of long-term debt.	The BOD authorizes all issuances of long-term notes and bonds.
	Completeness	Management fails to record capital lease obligations.	Separate the duties of authorization of lease agreements from accounting for lease agreements.
	Valuation	Amortization of long-term debt is calculated incorrectly.	Hire qualified personnel and review their work.
	Presentation and disclosure	Management fails to reclassify current portions of long-term debt.	Ensure active oversight by independent financial experts from the audit committee.
		Management fails to disclose future minimum required debt payments.	Ensure active oversight by independent financial experts from the audit committee.
		Violations of restrictive loan covenants are not properly disclosed.	Ensure active oversight by independent financial experts from the audit committee.
Capital Stock	Completeness	Some issued stock is not recorded.	Management regularly obtains register of issued stock from third-party registrar and compares with recorded capital stock.
		Treasury stock repurchases are not recorded.	Require authorization of BOD for treasury stock repurchases.
	Presentation and disclosure	Exercises of stock options are not allocated correctly between capital stock accounts.	Hire qualified accounting staff and review their work.
Retained Earnings	Completeness	Declared dividends are not recorded.	Management should periodically review equity accounts.
		Prior-period error corrections are not recorded appropriately.	Hire qualified personnel and review their work.

Control Considerations

Control activities for suitable handling of responsibilities should be in place and operating. By referring to the discussion accompanying Exhibit 10.2, you may notice that these responsibilities are primarily in the hands of senior management officials. You also can surmise that different companies may have widely different policies and activities.

It is difficult to have a strict separation of functional responsibilities when the principal officers of a company authorize, execute, and control finance and investment activities. It is not realistic to have the CEO authorize investments but not have access to stockholder records, securities certificates, and the like. Real separation of duties can be found in middle management and lower ranks, but it is difficult to create and enforce among upper managers.

Because of this control problem, a company should have *compensating control activities.* A **compensating control** is a control activity used because a specific standard control activity is not in place. The compensating control reduces the risk due to the missing control. For example, the board of directors may authorize the purchase of an investment and delegate the execution of investment purchases to the CFO. The CFO would call the company's broker to execute the authorized transaction. Because the CFO is authorized to instruct the broker to buy and sell securities, the CFO is in a position to sell company securities for personal use. A compensating control might be an agreement with the broker to mail transaction confirmations to other company personnel or to use electronic transfer directly into the company's account for all proceeds from the sale of investments. In the area of finance and investment, the compensating control feature often involves two or more persons in each area of important functional responsibility.

If involvement by multiple persons is not specified, an oversight or review can be substituted. For example, the board of directors can authorize the purchase of securities or the creation of a partnership. The CFO or CEO can carry out the transactions, have custody of certificates and agreements, manage the partnership or the portfolio of securities, oversee the record keeping, and make the decisions about valuations and accounting (authorizing the journal entries). These are normal management activities, and they combine several responsibilities. The compensating control can exist in the form of periodic reports to the board of directors, oversight by the investment committee of the board, and internal audit involvement in making a periodic reconciliation of securities certificates in a portfolio with the amounts and descriptions recorded in the accounts.

Auditors considering the design of internal controls in the finance and investment cycle typically perform a walkthrough, which involves starting with an inquiry of management about how the processes are completed. For example, the auditor may ask management who initiates an investment transaction, how the transaction is approved, and how the transaction is executed. The auditor may then inspect and document a sample investment transaction to obtain a clear understanding of the design of the controls put into action. Based on the understanding, the auditor will then often discuss the resulting flowchart or narrative with management and document a preliminary risk assessment related to the purchase or sale of an investment transaction. A similar process can be repeated for other significant accounts and assertions within the finance and investment cycle.

TESTS OF OPERATING EFFECTIVENESS OF INTERNAL CONTROL

LO 10-5
Give examples of tests of controls to verify the operating effectiveness of internal controls in the finance and investment cycle.

Following an assessment of the design effectiveness of internal controls in the finance and investment cycle, the auditor may consider testing the operating effectiveness of internal control. Of course, recall that auditors performing an integrated audit must always test the operating effectiveness of internal controls. Exhibit 10.7 outlines some of the tests of controls that an auditor may perform in the finance and investment cycle. A scan of the exhibit likely shows you that tests of controls in this cycle are very different from the ones covered in the other cycle chapters. Auditors do not typically vouch or trace transactions as control tests in this cycle. The primary reason is that there are often so few transactions, and they are likely material, so the auditor tests the transactions as substantive tests, not tests of controls for the purpose of assessing control risk. In fact, tests of controls in the finance and investment cycle primarily deal with determining whether there is sufficient board oversight in practice, proper authorization and review of transactions, and sufficient documentation of finance and investment policies. In this section, you will learn about some of the more difficult

EXHIBIT 10.7

Significant Account	Relevant Assertions	What Could Go Wrong?	Internal Control Activity	Tests of Internal Control
Investments	Existence/ occurrence	Management may sell company-owned securities for their own benefit.	Broker transaction confirmations should be periodically reviewed by the investment committee of the board of directors (BOD).	Inspect documents for evidence of periodic board review of purchase transactions.
		Investment securities held by the entity may be stolen.	Investment purchases and sales should be approved by the BOD. Securities should be held in lockboxes, and responsibility for custody should be separated from responsibility for record keeping.	Review BOD minutes for evidence of authorization of investment purchases. Inquire about proper segregation of duties and about lockbox security procedures.
		Management may overstate current-period interest income.	The investment committee of the BOD should regularly compare investment performance to expectations.	Inspect documents for evidence of periodic board review of investment performance.
	Completeness	Investment transactions from the current period may be recorded in the subsequent period.	The responsibility for authorization of purchases of securities should be separated from recording purchases in the securities ledger.	Inquire about proper segregation of duties.

(continued)

EXHIBIT 10.7 *(concluded)*

Significant Account	Relevant Assertions	What Could Go Wrong?	Internal Control Activity	Tests of Internal Control
	Valuation	Management fails to mark marketable equity securities to fair market value.	Qualified staff is responsible for end-of-period fair value estimates.	Inquire about the estimation process, and observe evidence that process is being followed.
		Equity method investments are not accurately adjusted for investee income.	Ensure accurate financial statements for investees are obtained on a timely basis.	Inquire about the process of obtaining investee financial statement information, and inspect evidence of timeliness.
		Impairments to investment securities are not properly recorded.	Management reviews investment securities for evidence of other than temporary declines in value.	Inspect documentation for evidence of management review of investment valuation.
			Separate the duty of investment acquisition from the duty of investment valuation.	Inquire of personnel about impairment process, and observe separation of duties.
	Presentation and disclosure	Management fails to appropriately account for derivative transactions that do not qualify for hedge treatment.	Properly trained employees supervise the estimation process for derivative securities.	Inquire about the client's policies and procedures for determining hedge treatment of derivative securities.
		Available for Sale Debt securities are misclassified as held to maturity.	Ensure the investment committee of the BOD has a written policy on investment classification.	Review entity's investment classification policy.
Long-Term Debt	Existence/occurrence	Fully paid notes are not properly removed from schedule of long-term debt.	The BOD authorizes all issuances of long-term notes and bonds.	Inspect BOD meeting minutes for evidence of approval of debt.
	Completeness	Management fails to record capital lease obligations.	Separate the duties of authorization of lease agreements from accounting for lease agreements.	Inquire of personnel about lease contracting process, and observe separation of duties.
	Valuation	Amortization of long-term debt is calculated incorrectly.	Hire qualified personnel and review their work.	Inspect documents for evidence of management review of debt schedules.
	Presentation and disclosure	Management fails to reclassify current portions of long-term debt.	Ensure active oversight by independent financial experts from the audit committee.	Obtain minutes of audit committee meetings, and inspect for evidence of appropriate oversight.
		Management fails to disclose future minimum required debt payments.	Ensure active oversight by independent financial experts from the audit committee.	Obtain minutes of audit committee meetings, and inspect for evidence of appropriate oversight.
		Violations of restrictive loan covenants are not properly disclosed.	Ensure active oversight by independent financial experts from the audit committee.	Obtain minutes of audit committee meetings, and inspect for evidence of appropriate oversight.
Capital Stock	Completeness	Some issued stock is not recorded.	Management regularly obtains register of issued stock from third-party registrar and compares with recorded capital stock.	Inspect documents for evidence that management periodically reviews stock registers.
		Treasury stock repurchases are not recorded.	Require authorization of board of directors for treasury stock repurchases.	Inspect BOD meeting minutes for evidence of approval of treasury stock repurchases.
	Presentation and disclosure	Exercises of stock options are not allocated correctly between capital stock accounts.	Hire qualified accounting staff and review their work.	Inquire about hiring process, and inspect evidence of management review of capital stock transactions.
Retained Earnings	Completeness	Declared dividends are not recorded.	Management should periodically review equity accounts.	Inquire of management about process for ensuring accuracy and completeness of equity accounts.
		Prior-period error corrections are not recorded appropriately.	Hire qualified accounting staff and review their work.	Inquire about hiring process, and inspect evidence of management review of error corrections.

evaluations auditors must make in assessing control risk in the finance and investment cycle. First, you will learn about tests of controls surrounding accounting estimates and then about tests of controls surrounding authorization, record keeping, and custody.

Control over Accounting Estimates

An **accounting estimate** is a measurement or recognition in the financial statements of (or a decision to not recognize) an account, disclosure, transaction, or event that generally involves subjective assumptions and measurement uncertainty. Estimates often are included in basic financial statements because the measurement of some amount is uncertain, perhaps depending on the outcome of future events, or relevant data cannot be accumulated on a timely, cost-effective basis. Some examples of accounting estimates in the finance and investment cycle include the following:

- *Plant and equipment depreciation.* Useful lives, salvage values.
- *Financial instruments.* Valuation of securities, including fair values assigned to debt and equity securities; classification into held-to-maturity, available-for-sale, and trading securities investment portfolios; probability of a correlated hedge; sales of securities with puts and calls; investment model assumptions; and impairments. The issue of valuation may be especially difficult if the investment was received in a noncash transaction and is not readily marketable. Appraisals, financial modeling, or other methods may be necessary to estimate the investment's value.
- *Accruals.* Compensation in stock option plans, actuarial assumptions in pension costs.
- *Leases.* Initial direct costs, useful lives, and residual values; rate of interest implicit in the lease.
- *Rates.* Imputed interest rates on long-term receivables and payables.
- *Other.* Losses and net realizable value on segment disposal and business restructuring, fair values in nonmonetary exchanges, and impairment of goodwill.

A client's management is responsible for making estimates and should have processes and controls designed to reduce the likelihood of material misstatements in them. Specific relevant aspects of such controls include the following:

- Management communication of the need for proper accounting estimates.
- Accumulation of relevant, sufficient, and reliable data for estimates.
- Preparation of estimates by qualified personnel.
- Adequate review and approval by appropriate levels of authority.
- Comparison of prior estimates with subsequent results to assess the reliability of the process used to develop estimates.
- Consideration by management of whether particular accounting estimates are consistent with the company's operational plans.

Although accounting estimates are primarily tested substantively, the quality of the client's internal controls affects the nature of the substantive tests. We will discuss this later in the chapter. Auditors' tests of controls over the estimation process include making inquiries and observations. Inquiries would include such questions as: Who prepares estimates? When are they prepared? What data are used? Who reviews and approves the estimates? Have prior estimates been compared with subsequent actual events? The auditor also will assess the involvement of the audit committee of the board of directors in evaluating the estimation process. If the audit committee is more heavily involved in risk assessment and process evaluation, control risk may be reduced for relevant assertions in the finance and investment cycle. Observations in tests of controls over accounting estimates include study of data documentation, study of comparisons of prior estimates with subsequent actual experience, and study of intercompany correspondence concerning estimates and operational plans. The audit of a valuation estimate starts with the tests of controls, many of which have a bearing on the quality of the estimation process and of the estimate itself. Audits of valuation estimates are challenging and can sometimes lead to identification by the PCAOB of audit deficiencies in internal control testing, as shown in the following PCAOB Inspection Focus.

PCAOB INSPECTION FOCUS

Investment Valuation

The PCAOB is required to perform detailed inspections of the audit process employed by each firm auditing publicly traded corporations. A formal inspection report is issued by the PCAOB for each firm inspected. In a recent inspection report, the PCAOB highlighted the importance of testing controls surrounding the client's valuation process:

- "The firm selected for testing a control that consisted of the issuer's review and approval of its annual budget. The issuer used this budget in its qualitative assessment of goodwill for possible impairment. The firm did not evaluate the review procedures that the control owners performed, including the procedures to identify items for follow up and the procedures to determine whether those items were appropriately resolved. (AS 2201.42 and .44)"

- "The firm selected for testing a control that consisted of the issuer's review of possible impairment indicators for its finite-lived intangible assets. The firm did not evaluate the review procedures that the control owner performed, including the procedures to identify items for follow up and the procedures to determine whether those items were appropriately resolved. (AS 2201.42 and .44)"

Source: *Report on 2020 Inspection of KPMG LLP.*, PCAOB, September 30, 2021; *Report on 2019 Inspection of Grant Thornton LLP.*, PCAOB, December 17, 2020.

Authorization

Most of the transactions in the financing and investing cycle involve large amounts of cash or other assets. Therefore, authorization is a critical issue when examining these transactions. The issuance, sale, or purchase of company stock and bonds, the obtaining of large bank loans, and the purchase or sale of large assets generally are discussed at the highest levels of the organization. Auditors must review minutes of the board of directors meetings, finance committee meetings, or other appropriate committee meetings for the authorization of significant transactions, including dividends, treasury stock repurchases, issuance of stock options, and acquisitions, among many others. In addition, the authorization for the purchase of large assets may reside in the capital budget, which should have been approved by senior management and the board. If no tangible evidence of the authorization of significant transactions exists, the auditor should make inquiries at the highest levels to ensure that these major transactions have been approved.

Record Keeping

Transactions that occur on a daily basis are usually recorded in a journal designed especially for those transactions (e.g., sales journals, purchase journals, payroll journals). Usually, the transactions in this cycle occur infrequently and are recorded in the general journal. In addition, because the transactions are infrequent, vary greatly in type, and are for large dollar amounts, controls over the proper recording of the transaction must be implemented. The competency of the individuals making these journal entries and the review and reconciliation of the general ledger are essential controls that the auditor should test. Assessing the competency of client employees can be difficult but should begin with inquiry of management regarding the qualifications of employees responsible for record keeping in the finance and investment cycle. Auditors will also often evaluate the hiring process of employees in an audit of the company's human resources and payroll accounts. The auditor also can use evidence obtained from prior audits as an indication of the competency/lack thereof of a company's employees. For this reason, employee turnover is deemed a significant risk factor when considering controls over complex transactions.

Custody

In large companies, custody of **stock certificate books** is not a significant management problem because of the use of registrars and transfer agents. Small companies often keep their own stockholder records. A stock certificate book looks like a checkbook. It has perforated stubs for recording the number of shares, the owner's name and other identification, and the date of issue. Actual unissued share certificates are attached to the stubs, like blank checks in a checkbook. The company should have a record of certificates that are outstanding in the possession of owners. Custody of the stock certificate book is important because the unissued certificates are like money or collateral. If improperly removed, they can be sold to buyers who think they are genuinely issued or can be used as collateral with unsuspecting lenders. Auditors should test controls surrounding the physical security of stock certificate books and should test the process for issuance of stock certificates.

Lenders have custody of debt instruments (e.g., leases, bonds, and notes payable). However, when a company repurchases its bonds or pays off its debt, the debt instruments are returned to the company. These documents could be misused by improperly reselling them to unsuspecting investors. Auditors should inspect documentation indicating the extinguishment of debt and should inspect returned bonds or notes for appropriate cancellation or evidence of destruction to avoid issues like the one discussed in the subsequent Auditing Insight.

AUDITING INSIGHT   A New Meaning for "Recycling"

Something strange must have happened on the way to the dump. Hundreds of long-term bonds were redeemed early and presented to **Citibank** in New York, which acted as the agent for the issues. Many of the bonds still had not reached the maturity date marked on them. Citibank sent about $1 billion of the canceled U.S. corporate bonds to a landfill dump in New Jersey, but some of them turned up at banks in Europe and the United States. Although the bonds are worthless, they still might look genuine to a layperson or even to some bankers. The FBI traced the canceled bonds to a defunct company in New Jersey that had a contract to destroy the bonds. (*Note:* Companies obtain a destruction certificate when bonds and stock certificates are canceled. The certificates obtained by Citibank apparently were fraudulent.)

Source: Securities Exchange Act Release No. 31612, December 17, 1992.

Summary: Control Risk Assessment

From the preceding discussion, you can tell that tests of controls take a variety of forms: inquiries, observations, inspection of documentation, comparisons with related data, and detail audits of some significant transactions. However, because of the nature of finance and investment transactions (i.e., few in number and high in dollar amount), auditors often focus on substantive tests rather than tests of controls. For example, a company may have only 10 significant security investment transactions during the year. The most efficient use of audit time may be to review all 10 significant transactions for all relevant assertions. Conversely, some companies may have numerous debt-financing transactions and a more detailed evaluation of control risk may be pertinent, including the selection of a sample of significant transactions for control risk assessment evidence.

See Appendix 10A for internal control questionnaires for the finance and investment cycle. They illustrate typical questions about the assertions. These inquiries give auditors insights into the client's specifications for review and approval of major investing and financing transactions, the system of accounting for them, and the provision for error-checking review activities.

The audit team should evaluate the evidence obtained from an understanding of the design of internal control and from tests of the operating effectiveness of controls. These tests can take many forms because management systems for finance and investment accounts can vary a great deal among clients. The involvement of senior officials in a relatively small number of high-dollar transactions makes control risk assessment a process tailored specifically to the company's situation. Some companies enter into complicated financing and investment transactions while others keep to the simple transactions. One type of investment, that isn't accounted for the same way as most investments, is becoming more common among companies as a result of new types of payment methods—Cryptocurrency. The following Auditing Insight provides a discussion of this issue.

AUDITING INSIGHT Blockwhat?

Many companies, particularly companies that have significant inter-national and online businesses, are beginning to accept payments in Bitcoin, a digital asset and payment system first introduced by Satoshi Nakamoto in 2008. As of 2022, hundreds of thousands of merchants were accepting Bitcoins or other types of cryptocurrency as payment, including large corporations such as **Microsoft, Expedia, Wikipedia, and Overstock.** Bitcoin transactions are peer-to-peer and do not require an intermediary, thus reducing transaction costs con-siderably. In addition, Bitcoin transactions are permanently recorded in blockchain, a distributed database of transactions that cannot be tampered with or revised. Blockchain technology has the potential to lead to better electronic audit trails. However, from an auditing stand-point, Bitcoins present potential issues both for valuation and for con-trols. Because they are not a currency, they are not treated as cash. Unlike investment securities, however, Bitcoins are not backed by any asset. Further, they are maintained in digital wallets, and anyone

with access to the wallet can immediately steal the Bitcoins. Further, the SEC has required custodians of Bitcoins to disclose that there are no guarantees owners would recover the assets in a bankruptcy pro-ceeding. As a result, Bitcoins are treated under GAAP as an intangible asset, although there is no formal standard currently and some com-panies attempt to claim them as mark-to-market investments. Thus, existence, valuation, classification, and rights and obligations of Bit-coins represent significant risks of material misstatement, and tests of controls must be performed on clients with material bitcoin assets or transactions. Further, verifying rights to Bitcoin is challenging and often requires the client to execute a small Bitcoin transaction from a digital wallet to demonstrate they control the private key, and hence own the Bitcoin.

Sources: "Bitcoin Now Accepted by 100,000 Merchants Worldwide," *Interna-tional Business Times* February 4, 2015; "Continued EY investments in block-chain market to support increased demand," EY Press Release, May 17, 2021.

 REVIEW CHECKPOINTS

10.5 What is a compensating control? Give some examples for finance and investment cycle accounts.

10.6 What are some of the specific relevant aspects of management's control over the estimation process? What are some inquiries auditors can make?

10.7 What are some specific transactions that an auditor would expect to be approved by the board of directors? How would it affect the audit if these transactions were not required to be approved by the board?

10.8 What documentation should an auditor inspect when a client has paid off a bank note? How could an employee defraud the company if the bank note has no indication of being paid?

SUBSTANTIVE ANALYTICAL PROCEDURES AND TESTS OF DETAILS

LO 10-6
Give examples of substantive procedures in the finance and investment cycle and relate them to assertions about significant account balances at the end of the period.

As discussed earlier, the finance and investment cycle is primarily audited with a sub-stantive approach. When the auditor uses a reliance approach in the operating cycle, reductions in control risk enable the use of less detailed substantive testing. For example, an auditor may choose to use analytical procedures to assess the reasonableness of certain current liabilities without testing the transactions or balances in detail. However, because the finance and investment cycle consists of infrequent and significant transactions, the auditor relies less on tests of controls and more on direct substantive tests of details. This section addresses the typical types of substantive tests an auditor uses to obtain sufficient, appropriate evidence in the finance and investment cycle. As in previous chapters, the section concludes with some cases illustrating errors and frauds to describe useful audit approaches.

Exhibit 10.8 completes the audit approach for the finance and investment cycle. In the exhibit, substantive analytical procedures and substantive tests of details that are often used to obtain evidence about significant accounts and relevant assertions are presented.

Some of the more significant issues associated with these accounts are discussed in the remainder of this section.

EXHIBIT 10.8

Significant Account	Relevant Assertions	What Could Go Wrong?	Internal Control Activity	Tests of Internal Control	Possible Substantive Analytical Procedures	Possible Substantive Tests of Details
Investments	Existence/ occurrence	Management may sell company-owned securities for their own benefit.	Broker transaction confirmations should be periodically reviewed by the investment committee of the board of directors (BOD).	Inspect documents for evidence of periodic board review of purchase transactions.		Confirm investments with brokerage.
			Investment purchases and sales should be approved by the BOD.	Review BOD minutes for evidence of authorization of investment purchases.		Vouch purchases and sales of securities to broker's advices.
		Investment securities held by the entity may be stolen.	Securities should be held in lockboxes, and responsibility for custody should be separated from responsibility for record keeping.	Inquire about proper segregation of duties and about lockbox security procedures.		Physically inspect all investment securities held by entity.
		Management may overstate current-period interest income.	The investment committee of the BOD should regularly compare investment performance to expectations.	Inspect documents for evidence of periodic board review of investment performance.	Recalculate interest income on debt securities based on principal balances and interest rates.	Vouch recorded interest income to cash receipts journal and premium/discount amortization.
	Completeness	Investment transactions from the current period may be recorded in the subsequent period.	The responsibility for authorization of purchases of securities should be separated from recording purchases in the securities ledger.	Inquire about proper segregation of duties.	Compare current-year investment account balances with expected balances based on prior-year balances and current-year operating and financing activities.	Scan cash disbursements ledger for large purchases surrounding year-end.
	Valuation	Management fails to mark marketable equity securities to fair market value.	Qualified staff is responsible for end-of-period fair value estimates.	Inquire about the estimation process, and observe evidence that process is being followed.	Inspect client budgets, and compare with actual investment returns.	Vouch market values of marketable investment securities to *The Wall Street Journal*.
		Equity method investments are not accurately adjusted for investee income.	Ensure accurate financial statements for investees are obtained on a timely basis.	Inquire about the process of obtaining investee financial statement information, and inspect evidence of timeliness.		Obtain financial statements of investments accounted for by the equity method, and recalculate recorded amounts.
		Impairments to investment securities are not properly recorded.	Ensure management reviews investment securities for evidence of other than temporary declines in value.	Inspect documentation for evidence of management review of investment valuation.		Test the company's process used to develop the impairment estimate.

(continued)

EXHIBIT 10.8 *(continued)*

Significant Account	Relevant Assertions	What Could Go Wrong?	Internal Control Activity	Tests of Internal Control	Possible Substantive Analytical Procedures	Possible Substantive Tests of Details
			Separate the duty of investment acquisition from the duty of investment valuation.	Inquire of personnel about impairment process, and observe separation of duties.		
	Presentation and disclosure	Management fails to appropriately account for derivative transactions that do not qualify for hedge treatment.	Properly trained employees supervise the estimation process for derivative securities.	Inquire about the client's policies and procedures for determining hedge treatment of derivative securities.		Inspect documentation supporting client classification of derivative securities.
		Available for Sale Debt securities are misclassified as held to maturity.	The investment committee of the BOD has a written policy on investment classification.	Review entity's investment classification policy.		Obtain representations from management regarding intent of debt investments.
Long-Term Debt	Existence/ occurrence	Fully paid notes are not properly removed from schedule of long-term debt.	The BOD authorizes all issuances of long-term notes and bonds.	Inspect BOD meeting minutes for evidence of approval of debt.	Compare expected debt balances to actual debt balances based on understanding of client's financing needs and prior-year balances.	Confirm long-term debt with debtors, including terms and interest rates.
	Completeness	Management fails to record capital lease obligations.	Separate the duties of authorization of lease agreements from accounting for lease agreements.	Inquire of personnel about lease contracting process, and observe separation of duties.		Inspect lease agreements, and evaluate appropriate accounting treatment.
	Valuation	Amortization of long-term debt is calculated incorrectly.	Hire qualified personnel and review their work.	Inspect documents for evidence of management review of debt schedules.		Obtain debt amortization schedules, and recalculate balances.
	Presentation and disclosure	Management fails to reclassify current portions of long-term debt.	Ensure active oversight by independent financial experts from the audit committee.	Obtain minutes of audit committee meetings, and inspect for evidence of appropriate oversight.		Inspect schedule of long-term debt, and evaluate appropriate classification of debt.
		Management fails to disclose future minimum required debt payments.	Ensure active oversight by independent financial experts from the audit committee.	Obtain minutes of audit committee meetings, and inspect for evidence of appropriate oversight.		Complete disclosure checklist, and agree footnote disclosures to debt instruments.
		Violations of restrictive loan covenants are not properly disclosed.	Ensure active oversight by independent financial experts from the audit committee.	Obtain minutes of audit committee meetings, and inspect for evidence of appropriate oversight.		Inspect debt agreements, and recalculate ratios for compliance with debt covenants.

EXHIBIT 10.8 *(continued)*

Significant Account	Relevant Assertions	What Could Go Wrong?	Internal Control Activity	Tests of Internal Control	Possible Substantive Analytical Procedures	Possible Substantive Tests of Details
Capital Stock	Completeness	Some issued stock is not recorded.	Management regularly obtains register of issued stock from third-party registrar and compares with recorded capital stock.	Inspect documents for evidence that management periodically reviews stock registers.	Compare current-year capital stock accounts with expectations based on review of board minutes and prior-year balances.	Confirm capital stock with third-party registrar.
						Inspect cash receipts ledger for presence of equity transactions surrounding year-end.
		Treasury stock repurchases are not recorded.	Require authorization of BOD for treasury stock repurchases.	Inspect BOD meeting minutes for evidence of approval of treasury stock repurchases.		Inspect schedule of treasury stock repurchases, and trace to general ledger.
	Presentation and disclosure	Exercises of stock options are not allocated correctly between capital stock accounts.	Hire qualified accounting staff and review their work.	Inquire about hiring process, and inspect evidence of management review of capital stock transactions.		Inspect BOD minutes for approval of stock options.
						Obtain schedule of stock options, and test for accuracy. Trace to capital stock ledger and general ledger.
Retained Earnings	Completeness	Declared dividends are not recorded.	Management should periodically review equity accounts.	Inquire of management about process for ensuring accuracy and completeness of equity accounts.		Inspect BOD minutes for evidence of dividend declarations, and trace to general ledger.
		Prior-period error corrections are not recorded appropriately.	Hire qualified accounting staff and review their work.	Inquire about hiring process, and inspect evidence of management review of error corrections.		Trace schedule of known prior period adjustments to retained earnings.

Investment Securities

In general, substantive procedures on finance and investment accounts are extensive. Nevertheless, control deficiencies and unusual or complicated transactions can cause auditors to adjust the nature and timing of audit procedures. For example, if separation of duties is lacking in the execution of investment transactions, the auditor may move most testing of investment securities and related accounts to year-end. Complicated financial instruments, pension plans, exotic equity securities, related-party transactions, and nonmonetary exchanges of investment assets call for procedures designed to find evidence of errors and frauds in the finance and investment accounts.

As shown in Exhibit 10.8, the auditor's primary concerns surrounding typical marketable investment securities mostly involve the existence of the securities and the valuation of the securities. For this reason, auditors typically rely on either positive external confirmation with a broker or direct physical examination of security certificates to ensure the existence of the investments, and they verify ownership through confirmation or inspection to determine that the client is listed as the owner. Similarly, the auditor relies on vouching the reported market value of securities to a public source such as *The Wall Street Journal*. Auditors also evaluate disclosures and recalculate both realized and unrealized gains and losses on marketable investment securities, as well as consider the reasonableness of management's classification of the securities within the relevant financial accounting standard. However, companies can have a wide variety of investments and relationships with affiliates. Investment accounting may be on the market value method, cost method, equity method, or full consolidation, depending on the nature, size, and influence represented by the investment. Consolidations usually create problems of accounting for the fair value of acquired assets and the related goodwill. Auditors must identify the appropriate accounting method for each investment and ensure that investments are properly valued. The next section discusses some of the more complex issues auditors may face in auditing investment securities. The section concludes with two specific valuation and classification issues: auditing fair value measurements and derivative securities.

To some, it might appear that the audit of investments and intangibles presented in this chapter is straightforward. After all, in many instances, we have stated that the auditor can test most, if not all, of the significant transactions in these areas; finding documentation for authorization is the key control. Some of the complex issues in the audit of investments and intangibles follow:

- Valuation of investments at cost or market; or impairment that is other than temporary.
- Determination of significant influence relationship for equity method investments.
- Impairment of goodwill.
- Capitalization and continuing valuation of intangibles and deferred charges.
- Propriety, effectiveness, and risk disclosure of derivative securities used as hedges of exposure to changes in fair value (fair value hedge), variability in cash flows (cash flow hedge), or fluctuations in foreign currency.
- Determination of the fair value of derivatives and securities, including valuation models and the reasonableness of key assumptions.
- Realistic distinctions of research, feasibility, and production milestones for capitalization of software development costs.
- Adequate disclosure of restrictions, pledges, or liens related to investment assets.

Investment costs should be vouched to brokers' confirmations, monthly statements, or other documentary evidence of cost. At the same time, the amounts of investment sales should be traced to gain or loss accounts, and the amounts of sales prices and proceeds should be vouched to the brokers' statements and the cash receipts journal. Auditors should determine what method of cost-out assignment was used (i.e., FIFO, specific identification, or average cost) and whether it is consistent with prior-years' transactions.

Market valuation of securities is required for securities classified in trading portfolios and available-for-sale portfolios. Although management may assert that an investment valuation is not impaired, the subsequent sale at a loss before the end of audit fieldwork will indicate otherwise. Auditors should review significant investment transactions subsequent to the balance-sheet date for this kind of evidence about value impairment.

Classification of marketable securities is another management judgment that auditors must evaluate. If management classifies securities as trading securities, net income includes unrealized gains. When the market is doing well, these gains can provide significant additions to the bottom line. When the market is down, management can classify the securities as available for sale, which removes the losses from net income. However, management is required to make transfers between trading and available-for-sale securities at fair value, thus the auditor must verify consistent classification of securities. Similar management judgments can move securities from noncurrent to current, thus affecting current ratios. Auditors must use their professional judgment to ensure that management is basing its classifications on sound business judgments, not their financial statement effect. However, there is often little tangible evidence in support of management responses to these audit inquiries. By consulting quoted market values for securities, auditors can calculate market values and determine whether investments should be written down in value. If quoted market values are not available, financial statements related to investments must be obtained and analyzed for evidence of basic value. If such financial statements are unaudited, they provide extremely weak evidence.

Income amounts can be verified by consulting published or online dividend records for quotations of dividends actually declared and paid during a period (e.g., Moody's and Standard & Poor's dividend records). Because auditors know the holding period of securities, dividend income can be calculated and compared to the amount in the account. Any difference could indicate a cutoff error, misclassification, defalcation, or failure to record a dividend receivable. In a similar manner, application of interest rates to bond or note investments produces a calculated interest income figure (considering amortization of premium or discount if applicable).

Inquiries should deal with the nature of investments and the reasons for holding them, especially derivative securities used for hedging activities. The classification affects the accounting treatment of market values and the unrealized gains and losses on investments. Due to the complexity of *ASC 815,* "Derivatives and Hedging," auditors may need special skills or knowledge to understand clients' hedging transactions, to ensure that effective controls are in place to monitor them, and to audit the significant transactions.

When equity method accounting is used for investments, auditors need to obtain financial statements of the investee company. These should be audited statements. The inability to obtain financial statements from a closely held investee could indicate that the client investor does not have the significant controlling influence required by *APB Opinion No. 18.* When available, these statements are used as the basis for recalculating the amount of the client's share of income to recognize in the accounts. In addition, these statements can be used to audit the disclosure of investees' assets, liabilities, and income presented in footnotes, a disclosure recommended when investments accounted for by the equity method are material.

Auditing Accounting Estimates, Including Fair Value Measurements

As described in the earlier discussion of internal controls in the finance and investment cycle, an accounting estimate generally involves subjectivity and measurement uncertainty. Because of the subjectivity involved in the calculation of an estimate, the auditor is especially concerned about management bias in the process. This potential for bias, and the inherent measurement uncertainty, often leads to the auditor assessing the risk of material misstatement at an elevated level for accounting estimates. Although the auditor considers and tests the client's internal controls over accounting estimates, auditing standards require that as the risk of material misstatement increases, the evidence from substantive procedures should also increase.

When performing substantive procedures to test accounting estimates, auditing standards provide the auditor with three approaches to choose from, including a combination of any of the three:

1. Test the company's process used to develop the accounting estimate.
2. Develop an independent expectation for comparison to the company's estimate.
3. Evaluate audit evidence from events or transactions occurring after the measurement date related to the accounting estimate for comparison to the company's estimate.

Although developing an independent expectation would potentially lead to the most unbiased testing of accounting estimates, auditors most commonly test the company's process.[3] Researchers have documented that when choosing this approach, auditors sometimes fail to sufficiently test the underlying data, missing inconsistencies among assumptions, and other internal and external data. As a result, it is critical that auditors exercise professional skepticism and make high-quality professional judgments in audits of complex accounting estimates. A key part of this exercise of professional judgment is a required brainstorming discussion among key engagement personnel about how the financial statements could be manipulated through management bias in accounting estimates in significant accounts and disclosures. This discussion is including during the auditor's brainstorming about the potential for fraud in the financial statements.

Two areas of significant measurement uncertainty that are critical to the audit of the finance and investment cycle are audits of fair value estimates and derivative securities. GAAP pronouncements increasingly require the use of fair value for measurement of transactions and disclosure amounts. In addition, recent FASB pronouncements have required more stringent determination and more complete disclosures for investments, derivatives, and other assets and liabilities that are measured at fair value on a recurring basis. A fair value hierarchy has been established at three different levels as explained in Exhibit 10.9.

Disclosure is required not only as to the level for assets and liabilities, but also as to specific information if an item is moved between levels. For level 3 assets and liabilities, a reconciliation of the beginning and ending balances is required. These additional disclosure requirements increase the risk for assets and liabilities measured at fair value.

As part of performing substantive procedures for auditing fair value accounting estimates, auditors follow the same standards for any accounting estimate. Specifically, an auditor should determine whether (1) the valuation principles are acceptable under the financial reporting framework, (2) the valuation principles are consistently applied, (3) the valuation principles are supported by the underlying documentation, and (4) the method of estimation and the significant assumptions are properly disclosed according to GAAP.

As with other estimates, management has primary responsibility for determining fair value in accordance with GAAP. Observable market-based values are generally preferred (level 1). However, if market prices are not readily available, clients should incorporate assumptions that would have been used by the marketplace (level 2). If information about the assumptions is not readily available, management can use their own assumptions. Thus, auditors first must determine whether a market-based value is available; if not, they must evaluate whether clients' assumptions would have been used by the marketplace or there are data contrary to what the client used—very murky waters, indeed. The auditor must take considerable care when auditing fair value calculations for level 3. These calculations use a considerable amount of judgment and estimates resulting in an increased risk of improper valuation. Exhibit 10B.1 in Appendix 10B provides an example of an audit plan for the fair market value of assets and liabilities.

The failure of auditors to appropriately substantively test the fair value of a client's assets, particularly goodwill, has been a focus of the PCAOB inspectors, as shown in the following PCAOB Inspection Focus.

Derivative instruments are those that take their value from another asset or index. For example, an option to buy Disney stock is a derivative instrument. Interest rate swaps,

EXHIBIT 10.9
Fair Market Value Measurement Hierarchy

The Financial Accounting Standards Board (FASB) and International Accounting Standards Board (IASB) have established a three-level hierarchy in dealing with the problem of fair values that do not result from market prices:

Level 1: Fair values are derived from quoted market prices for identical assets or liabilities from an active market to which an entity has immediate access.

Level 2: Market prices are available for similar (as opposed to identical) assets or liabilities.

Level 3: If values for levels 1 or 2 are not available, fair value is estimated using valuation techniques. Level 3 fair values involve at least one unobservable value.

[3]E. E. Griffith, J. S. Hammersley, and K. Kadous, "Audits of Complex Estimates as Verification of Management Numbers: How Institutional Pressures Shape Practice." *Contemporary Accounting Research,* 2015.

PCAOB INSPECTION FOCUS

Business Combinations and Goodwill

The PCAOB is required to perform detailed inspections of the audit process employed by each firm auditing publicly traded corporations. A formal inspection report is issued by the PCAOB for each firm inspected. In a recent inspection report, the PCAOB highlighted the importance of substantively testing the client's accounting for business combinations and goodwill:

- "During the year, the issuer acquired multiple businesses. The firm performed certain substantive procedures but did not obtain sufficient appropriate audit evidence regarding the reasonableness of the projected financial information used by the issuer to determine the fair value of certain acquired intangible assets and contingent consideration. (AS 2502.26, .28, .31, and .36)"

- "During the year, the issuer created a subsidiary to purchase certain assets from a counterparty. The firm did not evaluate whether, due to the terms in the agreement, the subsidiary was a variable interest entity under FASB ASC Topic 810, Consolidation. (AS 2810.30)"

- "The firm did not identify, and evaluate the significance to the financial statements of, omissions from a required disclosure

under FASB ASC Topic 805, Business Combinations. (AS 2810.30 and .31)"

- "The forecasts the issuer used in its analyses to assess goodwill for possible impairment for this one reporting unit assumed significant revenue growth for certain years and improved gross margin percentages. The firm concluded that the forecasted revenue growth rates were reasonable without performing any substantive procedures to evaluate the issuer's ability to carry out certain of its planned strategies to achieve the forecasts, beyond inquiring of management. The firm's procedures to test the forecasted gross margin percentages were not sufficient because they were limited to inquiring of management about the issuer's planned strategies and comparing the forecasted gross margin percentages to the actual gross margin percentages of another reporting unit. (AS 2502.26, .28, .31, and .36)"

Source: *Report on 2020 Inspection of BDO USA LLP.*, PCAOB, September 30, 2021; *Report on 2020 Inspection of Ernst & Young LLP.*, PCAOB, September 30, 2021.

options, futures contracts, and foreign currency options are also derivatives. Derivatives can be used as **hedging instruments** to protect companies from uncertainties in the marketplace. For example, a clothing manufacturer could buy futures contracts on cotton to lock the price of its main raw material so that it can predict the future cost of goods sold. Likewise, companies selling overseas use currency futures to lock in the exchange rate for their sales. Accounting for derivatives is extremely complex, and new ones are constantly being developed. There are even derivatives to protect against bad weather!

Depending on why a company engages in derivative activities, the company may have only a few derivatives (e.g., foreign currency hedges to protect a few large contracts where foreign currency is the method of payment) or a large number of derivatives (commodity options to protect the company from price swings in essential raw materials). In the latter case, the auditor may need to focus on control activities and adjust the substantive testing based on the control risk assessment. When derivative activity is characterized by few significant transactions, the auditor likely focuses on the transaction authorization and performs substantive tests on most or all of the significant transactions. Auditors must ensure that derivatives are recorded at their fair market value at the balance-sheet date and should review derivative activities after the balance-sheet date in a search for unrecorded derivatives. Because of the risk of misclassifying derivative securities, auditors must also test

AUDITING INSIGHT

Trimming the Hedge?

J.M. Smucker Company, the maker of Smucker's jams and Jif peanut butter, saw a strong first quarter on higher volumes in its key brands and expects the momentum to continue into the second quarter, helped by its hedging activities taken in response to increasing coffee prices. The company said it has protected itself against exposure to coffee price fluctuations for the second quarter very well. Indeed, Smucker, whose coffee brands include Folgers and Dunkin' Donuts,

said the coffee segment, which accounts for about 38 percent of its revenue, surpassed its expectations with a 7 percent increase in sales for the quarter, but the margin took a beating due to higher green coffee costs. Coffee futures had rallied about 40 percent since the beginning of March.

Source: "JM Smucker Sees Strong Q2 on Coffee Price Hedging," *Reuters,* August 20, 2010.

management's evaluation of the successfulness of the hedges. Some of the issues that auditors face with derivative securities are discussed in the following Auditing Insight.

An illustrative audit plan of substantive procedures for investments and related accounts is presented in appendix Exhibit 10B.2. Part B of this audit plan covers portfolio classification, fair value determination, and evidence about impairment.

☑ REVIEW CHECKPOINTS

10.9   What are some of the important assertions found in investment accounts?

10.10 What are some of the typical areas of concern to auditors involving investment accounts?

10.11 How can confirmations be used in auditing investments in stocks?

10.12 How can auditors gain assurance about estimates in the investment cycle?

Long-Term Liabilities and Related Accounts

Exhibit 10.8 also presents substantive procedures for audits of long-term debt. The primary audit concerns with the verification of long-term liabilities is that all of them are recorded, that the interest expense is properly paid or accrued, and that they are classified and disclosed appropriately. Therefore, the balance-sheet assertions of *completeness* and *presentation and disclosure* are paramount. Alertness to the possibility of unrecorded liabilities during the performance of procedures in other areas frequently uncovers liabilities that have not been recorded. For example, when PP&E are acquired during the year under audit, auditors should inquire about the source of funds to finance the new assets. Auditors also should be alert for large cash disbursements and maintenance expenses for upgrades of electrical, plumbing, and air-conditioning systems. Often, all of these are indicators of the purchase and installation of equipment.

When auditing long-term liabilities, auditors usually obtain independent written confirmations for notes and bonds payable. In the case of notes payable to banks, the standard bank confirmation may be used and should include a request to list any banking relationships not listed on the confirmation request. The amount and terms of bonds payable, mortgages payable, and other formal debt instruments can be verified by reading the bond **indenture**, the written agreement with the bondholders, and confirmed by requests to bondholders or the bond trustee. The confirmation request should include questions not only of amount, interest rate, and due date, but also of collateral, restrictive covenants, and other items of agreement between lender and borrower. Confirmation requests should be sent to lenders with whom the company has done business in the recent past, even if no liability balance is shown at the confirmation date. Such extra coverage is a part of the search for unrecorded liabilities. An illustration of typical audit documentation for auditing long-term debt and interest expense is in Exhibit 10.10. Note that the interest expense consists of additions to the accrual account as well as amortization of premiums or discounts on long-term debt. An illustrative audit plan of substantive procedures for notes payable and long-term debt is in appendix Exhibit 10B.3.

Confirmation and inquiry procedures may be used to obtain responses on a class of items loosely termed *off-balance-sheet information.* Within this category are terms of loan agreements, leases, endorsements, guarantees, and insurance policies (whether issued by a client insurance company or owned by the client). Among these items is the difficult-to-define set of commitments and contingencies that often pose evidence-gathering problems. See Exhibit 10.11 for some common types of commitments.

Footnote disclosure should be considered for the types of commitments shown in Exhibit 10.11. Some of them can be estimated and valued and, thus, can be recorded in the accounts and shown in the financial statements themselves (such as losses on fixed-price purchase commitments and losses on fixed-price sales commitments). Interest expense generally is related item by item to interest-bearing liabilities. Based on the evidence of long-term liability transactions (including those that have been

EXHIBIT 10.10   Audit Documentation—Long-Term Debt and Interest Expense

| | | **DUNDER-MIFFLIN INC.**
Long-Term Debt, Accrued Interest Payable, and Interest Expense
For Year Ended 12/31/2023
Prepared by Client | | | | Prepared by | RJR
3/10/2024 |
| | | | | | | Reviewed by | DHS
3/12/2024 |

		Long-Term Debt				**Accrued Interest Payable**			
	Date Due	**Balance 12/31/2022**	**Additions**	**Amortization/ Payments**	**Balance 12/31/2023**	**Balance 12/31/2022**	**Interest Expense**	**Payments**	**Balance 12/31/2023**
5.25% senior subordinated debt	6/30/27	$2,500,000 ^{PY}	0	$250,000 ^v	$2,250,000 ^{CF/} TB	$66,750	$ 131,437 ^C	$143,750 ^v	$54,437 ^{CF}
4% note payable— Bank One	9/30/25	0	$500,000 ^u	0	$ 500,000 ^{CF/} TB	$ –	$ 20,000 ^c	$ 15,000 ^v	$ 5,000 ^{CF}
Premium on long-term debt		$ 354,128 ^{PY}	0	$ 18,266 ^c	$ 335,862 ^{CF/} TB				
						$66,750 F PY	$151,437 F/TB	$158,750 F	$59,437 ^{CF} F/TB

EXHIBIT 10.11   Off-Balance-Sheet Commitments

Type of Commitment	Typical Audit Procedures
Repurchase or remarketing agreements	Vouching of contracts, confirmation by customer, and inquiry of client management
Commitments to purchase at fixed prices	Vouching of open purchase orders, inquiry of purchasing personnel, and confirmation by supplier
Commitments to sell at fixed prices	Vouching of sales contracts, inquiry of sales personnel, and confirmation by customer
Guaranteed obligations of unconsolidated subsidiaries	Vouching of contracts, confirmation with debtors, and inquiry of client management
Loan commitments (as in a savings and loan association)	Vouching of open commitment file, inquiry of loan officers
Lease commitments	Vouching of lease agreement, confirmation with lessor or lessee

retired during the year), the related interest expense amounts can be recalculated. The amount of debt, the interest rate, and the time period are used to determine whether the interest expense and accrued interest are properly recorded. Interest expense also may be estimated by the analytical procedure of multiplying average debt outstanding by the average interest rate.

Stockholders' Equity

Stockholders' equity transactions usually are well documented in the minutes of the meetings of the board of directors, proxy statements, and securities offering registration statements. For publicly traded companies, stock transactions usually require a filing with the SEC (e.g., an offering of stock to raise capital). Transaction authorization can be vouched to these documents, and the cash proceeds can be traced to the bank accounts. Capital stock may be subject to confirmation when independent registrars and transfer agents are employed. Such agents are responsible for knowing the number of shares authorized and issued and for keeping lists of stockholders' names. The basic information about capital stock—such as number of shares, classes of stock, preferred dividend rates, conversion terms, dividend payments, shares held in the company name, expiration dates, and terms of warrants and stock dividends and splits—can be confirmed with the independent agents. The audit team's own inspection and reading of stock certificates, charter authorizations, directors' minutes, and registration statements can corroborate many of these items. However, when the client company does not use independent agents, most audit evidence is gathered by inspecting and vouching stock record documents (such as certificate book stubs). When circumstances call for extended procedures, information on outstanding stock in very small corporations having only a few stockholders may be confirmed directly with the holders.

ASC 718 requires that employee stock-based compensation must be recorded using a fair value–based method at the date the award is granted and must be credited to paid-in-capital and expensed over the compensation period. The definition of fair value accounting in *ASC 718* is different from the general definition of fair value in *ASC 820* and often requires the application of complex option-pricing models. As a result, auditing stock-based compensation can be a risky area. There are many types of employee stock-based compensation, and some, such as employee stock options, require appropriate allocation between common stock and paid-in-capital accounts upon exercise.

When auditing employee share options, auditors must follow the standards for auditing accounting estimates as discussed earlier. However, because employee share options are complex financial instruments, and no market value is available, companies typically use option-pricing models, which have assumptions that can be difficult to evaluate. Some of these assumptions include a stock price volatility rate and a risk-free interest rate that are assumed to be constant. In auditing employee share option plans, auditors focus on valuation of the options as well as presentation and disclosure of the options. The auditor should obtain copies of any employee stock-based compensation plans and vouch to approval by the board of directors. In addition, auditors should test the accounting for the valuation estimates and recalculate compensation expense. The PCAOB has specifically addressed auditing of employee share options and focuses on auditors' understanding of the process used by management for valuing and accounting for share options.[4]

With the exception of stock-based compensation plans, audits of stockholders' equity are considered to be low risk. See appendix Exhibit 10B.4 for an illustrative audit plan of substantive procedures for stockholders' equity.

✅ REVIEW CHECKPOINTS

10.13 What are some of the important assertions found in stockholders' equity account balances and disclosures?

10.14 What are some of the important assertions found in the long-term liability accounts?

10.15 How can confirmations be used in auditing (a) stockholder capital accounts and (b) notes and bonds payable?

10.16 What information about capital stock could be confirmed with outside parties? How could the auditors corroborate this information?

10.17 Define and give examples of off-balance-sheet information. Why should auditors be concerned with such items?

10.18 Define the three levels of fair values. Which one is the most difficult to audit? Why? Audits of which asset accounts are most likely affected by these most difficult fair values?

[4]PCAOB, Staff Questions and Answers, Auditing the Fair Value of Share Options Granted to Employees, October 17, 2006.

FRAUD CASES: EXTENDED AUDIT PROCEDURES

LO 10-7

Apply your knowledge to perform audit procedures in the revenue cycle and evaluate the findings of your tests.

These cases first set the stage with a story about an accounting error or fraud. The problem section of each case gives you the "inside story," which auditors seldom know before they perform this audit work. The second part of the case is the audit approach, which tells a structured story about the audit objective, desirable controls, test of control activities, and audit of balance procedures. The third part wraps up the case with a discovery summary. You will have an opportunity to develop your own audit approach for similar cases in Exercises 10-60 through 10-62 at the end of this chapter.

Case 10.1

Unregistered Sale of Securities

PROBLEM

A.T. Bliss & Company (Bliss) salespeople contacted potential investors and sold limited partnership interests in the company. The setup deal called for these limited partnerships to purchase solar hot-water heating systems for residential and commercial use from Bliss. All partnerships entered into arrangements to lease the equipment to Nationwide Corporation, which then rented the equipment to end users. The limited partnerships were, in effect, financing conduits for obtaining investors' money to pay for Bliss's equipment. The investors depended on Nationwide's business success and ability to pay under the lease terms for their return of capital and profit.

Bliss published false and misleading financial statements, which used a non-GAAP revenue recognition method and failed to disclose cost of goods sold. Bliss overstated Nationwide's record of equipment installation and failed to disclose that Nationwide had little cash flow from end users (resulting from rent-free periods and other inducements). Bliss knew—and failed to disclose to prospective investors—the fact that numerous previous investors had filed petitions with the U.S. tax court to contest the disallowance by the IRS of all their tax credits and benefits claimed in connection with their investments in Bliss's tax-sheltered equipment lease partnerships.

All of the money put up by the limited partnership investors was at risk but was not disclosed to investors.

AUDIT APPROACH

Management should employ experts—attorneys, underwriters, and accountants—who can determine whether securities and investment contract sales require registration. Auditors should learn the business backgrounds and securities industry expertise of the client's senior managers. They should study the minutes of board of directors meetings for authorization of the fund-raising method, obtain and study opinions rendered by attorneys and underwriters about the legality of the fund-raising methods, and inquire about management's interaction with the SEC in any presale clearance. (The SEC gives advice about the necessity for registration.)

Auditors should study the offering documents and literature used in the sale of securities to determine whether financial information is being used properly. In this case, the close relationship with Nationwide and the experience of earlier partnerships give reasons for extended procedures to obtain evidence about the representations concerning Nationwide's business success (in this case, lack of success).

DISCOVERY SUMMARY

The auditors gave unmodified reports on Bliss's materially misstated financial statements. The auditors apparently did not question the legality of the sales of the limited partnership interests as a means of raising capital. They apparently did not perform procedures to verify representations made in offering literature reflecting Bliss or Nationwide finances. Two partners in the audit firm were enjoined because of violations of the securities laws. The partners resigned from practice before the SEC and were ordered not to perform any attest services for companies making filings with the SEC. According to *SEC Litigation Release 10274, AAER 20,* and *AAER 21,* they later were expelled from the AICPA as reported in *The CPA Letter,* for failure to cooperate with the Professional Ethics Division in its investigation of alleged professional ethics violations.

Case 10.2

Off-Balance-Sheet Inventory Financing

PROBLEM

Verity Distillery Company's president incorporated the Veritas Corporation, making him and two other Verity officers the sole stockholders. The president arranged to sell $40 million of Verity's inventory of whiskey in the aging process to Veritas, showing no gain or loss on the transaction. The officers negotiated a 36-month loan with a major bank to get the money Veritas used for the purchase, pledging the inventory as collateral. Verity pledged to repurchase the inventory for $54.4 million, which amounted to the original $40 million plus 12 percent interest for three years.

The contract of sale was in the files, specifying the name of the purchasing company, the $40 million amount, and the cash consideration. Nothing mentioned the relationship of Veritas to the officers. Nothing mentioned the repurchase obligation. However, the sale amount was unusually large for a company the size of Verity.

The $40 million amount was 40 percent of the normal inventory. Veritas's cash balance increased 50 percent. The current asset total was not changed, but the inventory ratios (e.g., inventory turnover, days' sales in inventory) and quick ratio were materially altered. Long-term liabilities were understated by not recording the liability. The ploy was actually a secured loan with inventory pledged as collateral, but this reality was neither recorded nor disclosed. The total effect would be to keep debt off the books, to avoid recording interest expense, and later to record inventory at a higher cost. Subsequent sale of the whiskey at market prices would not affect the ultimate income results, but the unrecorded interest expense would be buried in the cost of goods sold. The net income in the first year when the "sale" was made was not changed, but the normal relationship of gross margin to sales was distorted by the zero-profit transaction.

	Before Transaction ($ in millions)	Recorded Transaction ($ in millions)	Pro Forma ($ in millions)
Assets	$530	$530	$570
Liabilities	$390	$390	$430
Stockholder equity	$140	$140	$140
Debt/equity ratio	2.79	2.79	3.07

AUDIT APPROACH

The relevant control in this case would rest with the integrity and accounting knowledge of the senior officials who arranged the transaction. Remember, competent individuals in key positions is an element of the control environment at the entity level. Authorization in the board minutes might detail the arrangements, but, if the officials wanted to hide it from the auditors, they also would suppress the telltale information in the board minutes.

Inquiries should be made about large and unusual financing transactions. This might not elicit a response because the event is a sales transaction according to Veritas. Other audit work on controls in the revenue and collection cycle might reveal the large sale. Fortunately, this one sticks out as a large one.

Analytical procedures to compare monthly or seasonal sales probably will identify the sale as large and unusual. This identification should lead to an examination of the sales contract. Auditors should discuss the business purpose of the transaction with knowledgeable officials. If being this close to discovery does not result in an admission of the loan and repurchase arrangement, the auditors nevertheless should investigate further. Even if the "customer" names were not a give-away, a quick inquiry of the corporation records office at the secretary of state will show the names of the officers, and the auditors will know the related-party nature of the deal. A request for the financial statements of Veritas should, therefore, be made.

DISCOVERY SUMMARY

The auditors found the related-party relationship between the officers and Veritas. Confronted, the president admitted the attempt to make the cash position and the debt/equity ratio look better than they were. The financial statements were adjusted to reflect the pro forma set of figures shown earlier.

Case 10.3

Go for the Gold

PROBLEM

In 2009, Alta Gold Company was a public shell corporation that was purchased for $1,000 by the Blues brothers. Operating under the corporate names of Silver King and Pacific Gold, the brothers purchased numerous mining claims in auctions conducted by the U.S. Department of the Interior. They invested a total of $40,000 in 300 claims. Silver King sold limited partnership interests in its 175 Nevada silver claims to local investors, raising $20 million to begin mining production. Pacific Gold then traded its 125 Montana gold mining claims for all of the Silver King assets and partnership interests, valuing the silver claims at $20 million. (Silver King valued the gold claims received at $20 million as the fair value in the exchange.) The brothers then put $3 million obtained from dividends into Alta Gold and, with the aid of a bank loan, purchased half of the Silver King gold claims for $18 million. The Blues brothers then obtained another bank loan of $38 million to merge the remainder of Silver King's assets and all of Pacific Gold's mining claims by purchase. They paid off the limited partners. At the end of 2009, Alta Gold had cash of $16 million, mining assets valued at $58 million, and liabilities on bank loans of $53 million.

Alta Gold had in its files the partnership-offering documents, receipts, and other papers showing partners' investment of $20 million in the Silver King limited partnerships. The company also had Pacific Gold and Silver King contracts for the exchange of mining claims. The $20 million value of the exchange was justified in light of the limited partners' investments.

Appraisals in the files showed one appraiser's report that there was no basis for valuing the exchange of Silver King claims other than the price limited partner investors had been willing to pay. The second appraiser reported a probable value of $20 million for the exchange based on proved production elsewhere, but no geological data on the actual claims had been obtained. The $18 million paid by Alta to Silver King also had similar appraisal reports.

The transactions occurred over a period of 10 months. The Blues brothers had $37 million of cash in Silver King and Pacific Gold as well as the $16 million in Alta (all of which was the gullible bank's money, which the bank had loaned to Alta with the mining claims and production as security). The mining claims that had cost $40,000 were now in Alta's balance sheet at $58 million, the $37 million was about to flee, and the bank was about to be left holding the bag containing 300 mining claim papers.

AUDIT APPROACH

Alta Gold, Pacific Gold, and Silver King had no internal controls. The Blues brothers engineered all transactions and hired friendly appraisers. The only control that might have been effective was at the bank in a more diligent loan process.

The most likely control would have been the engagement of competent, independent appraisers. Because the auditors need to use (or try to use) the appraisers' reports, the procedures involve investigating the reputation, engagement terms, experience, and independence of the appraisers. The auditors can use local business references, local financial institutions that keep lists of approved appraisers, membership directories of the professional appraisal associations, and interviews with the appraisers themselves *(AU-C 620)*.

The procedures for auditing the asset values include analyses of each of the transactions through all of the complications, including obtaining knowledge of the owners and managers of the several companies and the identities of the limited partner investors. If the Blues brothers did not disclose their connection with the other companies (and perhaps with the limited partners), the auditors need to inquire at the secretary of state's offices where Pacific Gold and Silver King are incorporated and try to discover the identities of the players in this flip game. Numerous complicated premerger transactions in small corporations and shells often signal manipulated valuations.

Loan applications and supporting papers should be examined to determine the representations Alta made in connection with obtaining the bank loans. These papers may reveal some contradictory or exaggerated information.

Ownership of the mining claims might be confirmed with the Department of Interior auctioneers or be found in the local county deed records (spread all over Nevada and Montana).

DISCOVERY SUMMARY

The inexperienced audit staff was unable to unravel the Byzantine exchanges and never questioned the relation of Alta Gold to Silver King and Pacific Gold. They never discovered the Blues brothers' involvement in the other side of the exchange, purchase, and merger transactions. They accepted the appraisers' reports because they had never worked with appraisers before and thought all appraisers were competent and independent. The bank lost $37 million. The Blues brothers changed their names.

Case 10.4

No Treasure in This Treasure Planet[5]

PROBLEM

In 2002, **Disney** had to take a last-minute write-down of motion picture production costs for the movie *Treasure Planet*. The set-in-space version of Robert Louis Stevenson's *Treasure Island* cost $140 million to make, but opening five-day revenues were only $16.7 million, compared to relatively successful *Lilo & Stitch,* which grossed $35.3 million in its first weekend.

Revenue forecasts are based on many factors, including facts and assumptions about number of theaters, ticket prices, receipt-sharing agreements, domestic and foreign reviews, and moviegoer tastes. Several publications track the box-office records of movies. You can find them in newspaper entertainment sections and in industry trade publications. Of course, the production companies themselves are the major source of the information. However, company records also show the revenue realized from each movie. Revenue forecasts can be checked against actual experience, and the company's history of forecasting accuracy can be determined by comparing actual to forecast over many films and many years.

The write-down in 2002 was $74 million.

AUDIT APPROACH

Revenue forecasts should be prepared in a controlled process that documents the facts and underlying assumptions built into the forecast. Forecasts should break down the revenue estimate by years, and the accounting system should produce comparable actual revenue data so that forecast accuracy can be assessed after the fact. Forecast revisions should be prepared in as much detail and documentation as original forecasts.

The general procedures and methods used by personnel responsible for revenue forecasts should be studied (inquiries and review of documentation), including their sources of information, both internal and external. Procedures for review of mechanical aspects (arithmetic) should be tested. Select a sample of finished forecasts and recalculate the final estimate.

Specific procedures for forecast revision also should be studied in the same manner. A review of the accuracy of forecasts for other movies with hindsight on actual revenues helps in a circumstantial way, but past accuracy on different film experiences does not directly influence the forecasts on a new, unique product.

The audit of motion picture development costs concentrates on the content of the forecast itself. The preparation of forecasts used in the impairment calculation should be studied

[5]Ahrens, "Is Disney Losing Its Boy Appeal?" *The Washington Post,* December 19, 2002.

to distinguish underlying reasonable expectations from hypothetical assumptions. A hypothetical assumption is a statement of a condition that is not necessarily expected to occur but nonetheless is used to prepare an estimate. For example, a hypothetical assumption is like an "if-then" statement: "If *Treasure Planet* sells 15 million tickets in the first 12 months of release, then domestic revenue and product sales will be $40 million, and foreign revenue can eventually reach $10 million." Auditors need to assess the reasonableness of the basic 15-million-ticket assumption. It helps to have some early actual data from the film's release in hand before the financial statements need to be finished and distributed. For actual data, auditors should review industry publications and pay special attention to competing films and critics' reviews (yes, movie reviews!).

DISCOVERY SUMMARY

The company was too optimistic in its revenue forecasts, and management did not weigh unfavorable actual/forecast history comparisons heavily enough. Apparently, management let itself be convinced that the movie was comparable to recent animated hits from other studios such as *Shrek* and *A Bug's Life*. One of the possible problems was the long development time—17 years from conception. The audit of forecasts and estimates used in accounting determinations is very difficult, especially when company personnel have incentives to hype the numbers, seemingly with conviction about the artistic and commercial merit of their productions. The high production costs finally came home to roost in big write-offs when the film was released.

☑ REVIEW CHECKPOINTS

10.19   What unfortunate lesson did the auditors learn from the situation in the Unregistered Sale of Securities case? What should auditors do when a violation of U.S. securities laws is suspected?

10.20   How could auditors have discovered the off-balance-sheet financing described in the Off-Balance-Sheet Inventory Financing case?

10.21   What effect can related-party transactions have in some cases of asset valuation? (Refer to the Go for the Gold case.)

10.22   How should an audit team assess the reasonableness of a film studio's estimate of film revenues? (Refer to the No Treasure in This Treasure Planet case.)

Summary

The finance and investment cycle contains a wide variety of accounts: capital stock, dividends, long-term debt, interest expense, income tax expense and deferred taxes, financial instruments, marketable securities, equity method investments, related gains and losses, consolidated subsidiaries, goodwill, and other intangibles. These accounts involve some of the most technically complex accounting standards. They create many of the difficult judgments for financial reporting.

Senior officials generally authorize these transactions and maintain control of them in these accounts. Therefore, internal control is centered on the integrity and accounting knowledge of these officials. The procedural controls over details of transactions are not very effective because senior managers can override them and order their own desired accounting presentations. As a consequence, auditors' work on the assessment of control risk is directed toward the senior managers and the board of directors, focusing on authorization and design of finance and investment activities. Because of the threat of management override and the high-dollar value of many of these transactions, auditors ensure the occurrence and valuation of transactions as well as the existence and valuation of year-end balances. Many accounts consist of relatively few high-dollar transactions; therefore, the auditor often relies on substantive testing of most, if not all, of the transactions that occurred during the audit period.

Key Terms

accounting estimate A measurement or recognition in the financial statements of (or a decision to not recognize) an account, disclosure, transaction, or event that generally involves subjective assumptions and measurement uncertainty, 451

capital budget A listing of the proposed expenditures for property, plant, and equipment or other capital items for a period of time (usually annually). The capital budget is submitted to senior management with corporate governance responsibilities for approval; is often a part of the annual budget, 437

compensating control A control activity instituted by a company to offset the risk imposed by *a weakness* in another activity, 448

derivative instrument A financial instrument whose value is based on an index or value of another financial instrument, 460

dual control Having two people perform a task (e.g., open the mail) as a control over the process, 440

hedging instrument An investment made to reduce the risk of adverse price movements in a security or future transaction by taking an offsetting position in a related security such as an option or a short sale, 461

indenture A written agreement between the issuers of bonds and the bondholders, usually specifying interest rate, maturity date, convertibility, and other terms, 462

joint custody The safeguarding of assets by placing them in a secured area that requires two people to access (e.g., a cabinet with two locks to which no individual has both keys), 440

loan covenant A provision in a loan agreement that requires the borrower to undertake or refrain from specified actions and to maintain specified financial levels and ratios, 445

registrar A financial institution appointed to record issue and ownership of company securities, 437

related party A relationship between two businesses that have a personal or other association that might destroy the self-interest of one of the parties to an extent that one of them might be prevented from fully pursuing its own separate interests, 444

special-purpose entity (SPE) A partnership formed by a company to pursue particular lines of business, often used to keep risky enterprises off the company's books. QSPE (qualified special-purpose entity) is the newer term used by the FASB, 434

stock certificate book A book (similar to a checkbook) with prenumbered stock certificates. These certificates are issued to investors with the custodian of the book recording the number of shares, the owner's name, the date of issue, and other identification information; basically used only by small companies that are not traded publicly, 452

transfer agent A bank or other company employed by a corporation to maintain shareholder records, including purchases, sales, and account balances, 437

trustee Agent of a bond issuer who handles the administrative aspects of a loan and ensures that the borrower complies with the terms of the bond indenture, 439

Multiple-Choice Questions for Practice and Review

 All applicable Exercises and Problems are available with *Connect*

LO 10-1

10.23 Which of the following approaches is most suitable for auditing the finance and investment cycle?

a. Perform extensive tests of controls and limit substantive procedures to analytical procedures.

b. Ignore internal controls and perform extensive substantive procedures.

c. Gain an understanding of internal controls and perform extensive substantive procedures.

d. Ignore internal controls and limit substantive procedures to analytical procedures.

LO 10-1

10.24 Loan covenants are used for which of the following reasons?

a. To protect the lender from the borrower's substantially weakening financial position.

b. To protect the borrower from the lender's calling the loan early.

c. To protect the auditors from false information by the borrower.

d. To protect shareholders from management taking on too much debt.

LO 10-1

10.25 A related party is a person or entity that

    a. Has a family tie to a management member.

    b. Does business with the company.

    c. Can exert significant influence over or be influenced by the company.

    d. Is a member of the company's management team or board of directors.

LO 10-6

10.26 Jones was engaged to examine the financial statements of Gamma Corporation for the year ended June 30. Having completed an examination of the investment securities, which of the following is the *best* method of verifying the accuracy of recorded dividend income?

    a. Tracing recorded dividend income to cash receipts records and validated deposit slips.

    b. Performing analytical procedures and statistical sampling.

    c. Comparing recorded dividends with amounts appearing on federal information Form 1099.

    d. Comparing recorded dividends with a standard financial reporting service's record of dividends.

LO 10-4

10.27 When the client holds a large amount of negotiable securities, auditors need to plan to guard against

    a. Unauthorized negotiation of the securities before they are counted.

    b. Unrecorded sales of securities after they are counted.

    c. Substitution of securities already counted for other securities that should be on hand but are not.

    d. Substitution of authentic securities with counterfeit securities.

LO 10-3

10.28 Which of the following internal control activities would most likely justify reducing the assessment of the risks of material misstatement for long-term notes payable?

    a. The use of prenumbered purchase orders to prevent unrecorded notes.

    b. All direct borrowings on notes payable are authorized by the board of directors.

    c. Any use of assets for collateral on long-term notes payable are analyzed for criticality to operations.

    d. Proceeds from long-term notes payable are included in regular review of budgets to ensure adequacy of cash flow availability.

LO 10-2

10.29 Which of the following assertions is most likely to have the highest risk of material misstatement for the goodwill account?

    a. Existence

    b. Completeness

    c. Valuation

    d. Rights & Obligations

LO 10-6

10.30 In connection with the audit of an issue of long-term bonds payable, the audit team should

    a. Determine whether bondholders are persons other than owners, directors, or officers of the company issuing the bond.

    b. Calculate the effective interest rate to see whether it is substantially the same as the rates charged for similar issues.

    c. Decide whether the bond issue was made without violating state or local laws or regulations.

    d. Ascertain that the client has obtained the opinion of counsel on the legality of the issue.

LO 10-3

10.31 Which of the following is the most important audit consideration when examining the stockholders' equity section of a client's balance sheet?

    a. Changes in the capital stock account are verified by an independent stock transfer agent.

    b. Stock dividends and stock splits during the year under audit were approved by the stockholders.

    c. Stock dividends are capitalized at par or stated value on the dividend declaration date.

    d. Entries in the capital stock account can be traced to resolutions in the minutes of meetings of the board of directors.

LO 10-3 10.32 If the auditors discover that the carrying amount of a client's investments is overstated because of a loss in value that is other than a temporary decline in market value, they should insist that

a. The approximate market value of the investments be shown in parentheses on the face of the balance sheet.

b. The investments be classified as long term for balance-sheet purposes with full disclosure in the footnotes.

c. The loss in value be recognized in the financial statements.

d. The equity section of the balance sheet separately shows a charge equal to the amount of the loss.

LO 10-6 10.33 The primary reason for preparing a reconciliation between interest-bearing obligations outstanding during the year and interest expense in the financial statements is to

a. Evaluate internal control over securities.

b. Determine the validity of prepaid interest expense.

c. Ascertain the reasonableness of imputed interest.

d. Detect unrecorded liabilities.

LO 10-6 10.34 The auditors should insist that a representative of the client be present during the inspection and count of securities to

a. Lend authority to the auditors' directives.

b. Detect forged securities.

c. Coordinate the return of all securities to proper locations.

d. Acknowledge the receipt of securities returned.

LO 10-4 10.35 When independent stock transfer agents are not employed and the corporation issues its own stock and maintains stock records, canceled stock certificates should

a. Be defaced to prevent reissuance and attached to their corresponding stubs.

b. Not be defaced but be segregated from other stock certificates and retained in a canceled certificates file.

c. Be destroyed to prevent fraudulent reissuance.

d. Be defaced and sent to the secretary of state.

LO 10-6 10.36 When a client company does not maintain its own capital stock records, the auditors should obtain written confirmation from the transfer agent and registrar concerning

a. Restrictions on the payment of dividends.

b. The number of shares issued and outstanding.

c. Guarantees of preferred stock liquidation value.

d. The number of shares subject to agreements to repurchase.

(AICPA adapted)

LO 10-6 10.37 All corporate capital stock transactions should ultimately be traced to the

a. Minutes of the meetings of the board of directors.

b. Cash receipts journal.

c. Cash disbursements journal.

d. Numbered stock certificates.

LO 10-6 10.38 An audit plan for the examination of the retained earnings account should include a step that requires verification of the (choose *two* steps)

a. Market value used to charge retained earnings to account for a 2-for-1 stock split.

b. Approval of the adjustment to the beginning balance as a result of a write-down of account receivables.

c. Authorization for both cash and stock dividends declared and paid.

d. Gain or loss resulting from disposition of treasury shares.

LO 10-4

10.39 When an entity uses a trust company as custodian of its marketable securities, the possibility of concealing fraud *most likely* would be reduced if the

    a. Trust company has no direct contact with the entity employees responsible for maintaining investment accounting records.

    b. Securities are registered in the name of the trust company rather than the entity itself.

    c. Interest and dividend checks are mailed directly to an entity employee who is authorized to sell securities.

    d. The trust company places the securities in a bank safe deposit vault under the custodian's exclusive control.

                                                                (AICPA adapted)

LO 10-6

10.40 An audit team would *most likely* verify the interest earned on bond investments by

    a. Vouching the receipt and deposit of interest checks.

    b. Confirming the bond interest rate with the issuer of the bonds.

    c. Recomputing the interest earned on the basis of face amount, interest rate, and period held.

    d. Testing internal controls relevant to cash receipts.

                                                                (AICPA adapted)

LO 10-6

10.41 A client has a large and active investment portfolio that is kept in a bank safe deposit box. If the auditors are unable to count securities at the balance sheet date, they *most likely* will

    a. Request the bank to confirm to the auditors the contents of the safe deposit box at the balance-sheet date.

    b. Examine supporting evidence for transactions occurring during the year.

    c. Count the securities at a subsequent date and confirm with the bank whether securities were added or removed since the balance-sheet date.

    d. Request the client to have the bank seal the safe deposit box until the auditors can count the securities at a subsequent date.

                                                                 (AICPA adapted)

LO 10-6

10.42 An audit team testing long-term investments would ordinarily use analytical procedures to ascertain the reasonableness of the

    a. Existence of unrealized gains or losses.

    b. Completeness of recorded investment income.

    c. Classification as available-for-sale or trading securities.

    d. Valuation of trading securities.

                                                                 (AICPA adapted)

LO 10-6

10.43 In auditing for unrecorded long-term bonds payable, an audit team *most likely* will

    a. Perform analytical procedures on the bond premium and discount accounts.

    b. Examine documentation of assets purchased with bond proceeds for liens.

    c. Compare interest expense with the bond payable amount for reasonableness.

    d. Confirm the existence of individual bondholders at year-end.

                                                                 (AICPA adapted)

LO 10-6

10.44 An audit plan to examine long-term debt *most likely* would include steps that require

    a. Comparing the carrying amount of held-to-maturity securities with their year-end market values.

    b. Correlating interest expense recorded for the period with outstanding debt.

    c. Verifying the existence of the holders of the debt by direct confirmation.

    d. Inspecting the accounts payable subsidiary ledger for unrecorded long-term debt.

                                                                 (AICPA adapted)

LO 10-4

10.45 Which of the following questions would auditors *most likely* include on an internal control questionnaire for notes payable?

    a. Are assets that collateralize notes payable critically needed for the entity's continued existence?

    b. Are two or more authorized signatures required on checks that repay notes payable?

c. Are the proceeds from notes payable used to purchase noncurrent assets?

d. Are direct borrowings on notes payable authorized by the board of directors?

(AICPA adapted)

LO 10-6

10.46 An audit team's purpose in reviewing the documentation concerning the renewal of a note payable shortly after the balance-sheet date *most likely* is to obtain evidence concerning management's assertions about

a. Existence.

b. Valuation.

c. Completeness.

d. Classification.

(AICPA adapted)

LO 10-6

10.47 Which of the following audit procedures would *not* likely be performed for audits of investments?

a. Read board of directors' minutes for authorization of investment strategies.

b. Confirm investments with registrar.

c. Confirm investments with broker or trustee.

d. Compare valuation to published market prices.

LO 10-6

10.48 Which of the following audit procedures would *not* likely be performed for audits of shareholders' equity?

a. Read board of directors' minutes for authorization of equity transactions.

b. Confirm outstanding common and preferred stock with stock registrar.

c. Compare valuation of stock to published market prices.

d. Obtain management representation about number of shares issued and outstanding.

LO 10-6

10.49 ABC Company has 100 shares of IBM stock that it holds as an investment. The stock was purchased three years ago and has been in the client's safe deposit box along with other investment securities. During an inspection of securities held by the client, the auditor noted the 100 shares of IBM stock had a different CUSIP number than the number listed when purchased and the number verified during the previous audit. Which of the following would be the auditor's main concern about this discovery?

a. The certificates in the safe deposit box were forgeries.

b. There had been unauthorized buying and selling of investment securities.

c. The securities may be misclassified on the balance sheet.

d. ABC Company no longer owns the securities.

Exercises and Problems

 All applicable questions are available with *Connect*

LO 10-4

10.50 **Internal Control Questionnaire for Equity Investments.** Cassandra Corporation, a manufacturing company, periodically invests large sums in marketable equity securities. The investment committee of the board of directors established the investment policy. The treasurer is responsible for carrying out the investment committee's directives. All securities are stored in a bank safe deposit vault. Your internal control questionnaire with respect to Cassandra's investments in equity securities contains the following three questions:

1. Is investment policy established by the investment committee of the board of directors?

2. Is the treasurer solely responsible for carrying out the investment committee's directive?

3. Are all securities stored in a bank safe deposit vault?

Required:

In addition to these three questions, what questions should your internal control questionnaire include with respect to the company's investment in marketable equity securities? (*Hint:* Prepare questions to cover management's transaction assertions of *occurrence, completeness, cutoff, accuracy,* and *classification.*)

(AICPA adapted)

LO 10-6, 10-7

10.51 **Investment Securities.** You are engaged in the audit of the financial statements of Bass Corporation for the year ended December 31 and you are about to begin an audit of the investment securities. Bass's records indicate that the company owns various bearer bonds as well as 25 percent of the outstanding common stock of Commercial Industrial Inc. All securities in Bass's portfolio are actively traded in a broad market. You are satisfied with evidence that supports the presumption of significant influence over Commercial Industrial Inc. The various securities are at two locations as follows:

1. Recently acquired securities are in the company's safe in the custody of the treasurer.
2. All other securities are in the company's bank safe deposit box.

Required:

a. Assuming that the internal controls over securities are satisfactory, what are the objectives (specific assertions) for the audit of the held-to-maturity securities?

b. What audit procedures should you undertake with respect to obtaining audit evidence for the existence and cost valuation of Bass's securities in the held-to-maturity classification?

c. What audit procedures should you undertake with respect to obtaining audit evidence against Bass's investment in Commercial Industrial Inc.?

d. What audit procedures should you undertake with respect to obtaining audit evidence about the classification of held-to-maturity securities in the Bass portfolio? (*Hint:* Review the audit plan in Appendix Exhibit 10B.1.)

e. Suppose that the held-to-maturity portfolio (excluding the investment in Commercial Industrial Inc.) is carried at cost in the amount of $3,450,000. What audit procedures should you undertake with respect to obtaining audit evidence about the fair market value of this portfolio?

f. Suppose that the auditors determine that the held-to-maturity portfolio (excluding the investment in Commercial Industrial Inc.) has an aggregate fair market value of $2,970,000. What audit procedures should they undertake with respect to obtaining audit evidence regarding a value impairment that might be "other than temporary"? (*Hint:* Review the audit plan in appendix Exhibit 10B.1.)

(AICPA adapted)

LO 10-6, LO 10-7

10.52 **Lease Accounting. Union Pacific Corp.** opened its new 19-story, $260 million headquarters in Omaha, Nebraska. The railroad operator is the owner of the city's largest building, the Union Pacific Center. Under an initial operating lease, Union Pacific guaranteed 89.9 percent of all construction costs through the building's completion date. After completing the building, the company signed a new operating lease, which guarantees 85 percent of the building's costs. Both were "synthetic" leases, which allow the company to take income tax deductions for interest and depreciation while maintaining complete operational control (Jonathan Weil, "Open Secrets: How Leases Play a Shadowy Role in Accounting," *The Wall Street Journal,* September 22, 2004).

Required:

a. Explain why Union Pacific would want to structure the lease to be an operating lease.

b. What audit evidence would you require for testing the appropriate accounting for this lease?

LO 10-6, 10-7

10.53 **Securities Examination and Count.** You are in charge of the audit of the financial statements of Demot Corporation for the year ended December 31. The corporation has a policy of investing its surplus funds in marketable securities. Its stock and bond certificates are kept in a safe deposit box in a local bank. Only the president and the treasurer of the corporation have access to the box. You were unable to obtain access to the safe deposit box on December 31 because neither the president nor the treasurer was available. Arrangements were made for your assistant to accompany the treasurer to the bank on January 11 to examine the securities. Your assistant should be able to inspect all securities on hand in an hour. Your assistant has never examined securities in the safe deposit box and requires instructions.

Required:

a. List the instructions that you should give to your assistant regarding the examination of the stock and bond certificates kept in the safe deposit box. Include in your instructions the details of the securities to be examined and the reasons for examining these details.

b. After returning from the bank, your assistant reports that the treasurer had entered the box on January 4 to remove an old photograph of the corporation's original building. The photograph was loaned to the local chamber of commerce for display purposes. List the additional audit procedures that are required because of the treasurer's action.

(AICPA adapted)

LO 10-6, LO 10-7

10.54 **Audit Objectives and Procedures for Investments.** In the audit of investment securities, auditors develop specific audit assertions related to the investments. They then design specific substantive procedures to obtain evidence about each of these assertions. Following is a selection of investment securities assertions:

1. Investments are properly described and classified in the financial statements.
2. Recorded investments represent investments actually owned at the balance-sheet date.
3. Investments are properly valued at the balance-sheet date.

Required:

For each of the above assertions, select the following audit procedure that is best suited for the audit plan. Select only one procedure for each assertion. A procedure may be selected once or not at all.

a. Trace opening balances in the general ledger to prior-year audit documentation.
b. Determine whether employees who are authorized to sell investments have access to cash.
c. Examine supporting documents for a sample of investment transactions to verify that prenumbered documents are used.
d. Determine whether any other-than-temporary impairments in the carrying value of investments have been properly recorded.
e. Verify that transfers from the trading portfolio to the held-to-maturity investment portfolio have been properly recorded.
f. Obtain positive confirmations as of the balance sheet date of investments held by independent custodians.
g. Trace investment transactions to minutes of the board of directors meetings to determine that transactions were properly authorized.

(AICPA adapted)

LO 10-6, 10-7

10.55 **Intangibles.** Sorenson Manufacturing Corporation was incorporated on January 3, 2022. The corporation's financial statements for its first year's operations were not examined by a CPA. You have been engaged to audit the financial statements for the year ended December 31, 2023, and your work is substantially completed. A partial trial balance of the company's accounts follows:

SORENSON MANUFACTURING CORPORATION
Trial Balance
At December 31, 2023

	Debit	Credit
Cash	$11,000	
Accounts receivable	42,500	
Allowance for doubtful accounts		$ 500
Inventories	38,500	
Machinery	75,000	
Equipment	29,000	
Accumulated depreciation		10,000
Patents	85,000	
Leasehold improvements	26,000	
Prepaid expenses	10,500	
Organization expenses	29,000	
Goodwill	24,000	
Licensing Agreement No. 1*	50,000	
Licensing Agreement No. 2*	49,000	

*An intangible asset representing the right to use a patent.

The following information relates to accounts that may yet require adjustment:

1. Patents for Sorenson's manufacturing process were purchased January 2, 2023, at a cost of $68,000. An additional $17,000 was spent in December 2023 to improve machinery covered by the patents and charged to the Patents account. The patents had a remaining legal term of 17 years.

2. On January 3, 2022, Sorenson purchased two licensing agreements; at that time they were believed to have unlimited useful lives. The balance in the Licensing Agreement No. 1 account included its purchase price of $48,000 and $2,000 in acquisition expenses. Licensing Agreement No. 2 also was purchased on January 3, 2022, for $50,000, but it has been reduced by a credit of $1,000 for the advance collection of revenue from the agreement.

3. In December 2022, an explosion caused a permanent 60 percent reduction in the expected revenue-producing value of Licensing Agreement No. 1, and in January 2023, a flood caused additional damage, which rendered the agreement worthless.

4. A study of Licensing Agreement No. 2 made by Sorenson in January 2023 revealed that its estimated remaining life expectancy was only 10 years as of January 1, 2023.

5. The balance in the Goodwill account includes $24,000 paid December 30, 2022, for an advertising program, which it is estimated will assist in increasing Sorenson's sales over a period of four years following the disbursement.

6. The Leasehold Improvement account includes (a) the $15,000 cost of improvements with a total estimated useful life of 12 years, which Sorenson, as tenant, made to leased premises in January 2022; (b) movable assembly-line equipment costing $8,500, which was installed in the leased premises in December 2023; and (c) real estate taxes of $2,500 paid by Sorenson, which, under the terms of the lease, should have been paid by the landlord. Sorenson paid its rent in full during 2023. A 10-year nonrenewable lease was signed January 3, 2022, for the leased building that Sorenson used in manufacturing operations.

7. The balance in the Organization Expenses account includes preoperating costs incurred during the organizational period.

Required:

For each of the items 1–7

a. Prepare adjusting entries as necessary.

b. Identify the substantive audit procedures you would perform to test the transactions.

(AICPA adapted)

LO 10-1, 10-6

10.56 **Loan Covenants.** A *loan covenant* is a condition requiring the borrower to comply with the terms of a loan agreement. If the borrower does not act in accordance with the covenants, the loan can be considered in default and the lender has the right to demand payment (usually in full).

Required:

a. Why do banks add covenants to loan agreements?

b. The following is a list of common loan covenants. For each covenant, indicate what the bank is trying to accomplish by requiring it.

(1) Maintain hazard insurance/content insurance.

(2) Maintain key-person life insurance.

(3) Make all payments of taxes/fees/licenses.

(4) Provide financial information on borrower and guarantor.

(5) Maintain a certain level in key financial ratios such as

(a) Minimum quick and current ratios (liquidity).

(b) Minimum return on assets and return on equity (profitability).

(c) Minimum equity and minimum working capital.

(d) Maximum debt to worth (leverage).

(6) Make no change of management or merger without prior approval.

(7) Obtain no more loans without prior approval.

(8) Make no dividends/withdrawals or limited dividend withdrawals.

c. For each item 1–8, indicate where the auditor would be *most likely* to find evidence of the company's adherence with the covenant.

d. Why is it important for an auditor to review the covenants and review documents related to each item listed in *(b)*?

LO 10-6

10.57 **Long-Term Financing Agreement.** You have been engaged to audit the financial statements of Broadwall Corporation for the year ended December 31, 2023. During the year, Broadwall obtained a long-term loan from a local bank pursuant to a financing agreement, which provided the following:

1. The loan is to be secured by the company's inventory and accounts receivable.
2. The company is to maintain a debt:equity ratio not to exceed 2:1.
3. The company is not to pay dividends without permission from the bank.
4. Monthly installment payments are to commence July 1, 2023. In addition, during the year, the company also borrowed, on a short-term basis, substantial amounts just prior to the year-end from the president of the company.

Required:

a. For the purposes of your audit of the Broadwall Corporation's financial statements, what procedures should you employ in examining the described loans? Do not discuss internal control.

b. What are the financial statement disclosures that you should expect to find with respect to the loan from the president?

LO 10-6

10.58 **Bond Indenture Covenants.** The following covenants are extracted from the indenture of a bond issue. The indenture provides that failure to comply with its terms in any respect automatically advances the due date of the loan to the date of noncompliance (the stated date is 20 years hence). Give any audit steps or reporting requirements you believe should be taken or recognized in connection with each of the following:

1. "The debtor company shall endeavor to maintain a working capital ratio of 2:1 at all times and, in any fiscal year following a failure to maintain said ratio, the company shall restrict compensation of officers to a total of $500,000. Officers for this purpose shall include the board chair, president, all vice presidents, secretary, and treasurer."

2. "The debtor company shall keep all property that is security for this debt insured against loss by fire to the extent of 100 percent of its actual value. Policies of insurance comprising this protection shall be filed with the trustee."

3. "The debtor company shall pay all taxes legally assessed against property that is security for this debt within the time provided by law for payment without penalty and shall deposit receipted tax bills or equally acceptable evidence of payment of same with the trustee."

(AICPA adapted)

LO 10-6

10.59 **Common Stock and Treasury Stock: Substantive Audit Procedures.** You are the continuing auditor of Sussex Inc. and are beginning the audit of the common stock and treasury stock accounts. You have decided to design substantive procedures with reliance on internal controls.

Sussex has no-par, no-stated-value common stock and acts as its own registrar and transfer agent. During the past year, Sussex both issued and reacquired shares of its own common stock, some of which the company still owned at year-end. Additional common stock transactions occurred among the shareholders during the year.

Common stock transactions can be traced to individual shareholders' accounts in a subsidiary ledger and to a stock certificate book. The company has not paid any cash or stock dividends. There are no other classes of stock, stock rights, warrants, or option plans.

Required:

What substantive procedures should you apply in examining the common stock and treasury stock accounts? Organize your answer as a list of audit procedures organized by the financial statement assertions. (See appendix Exhibit 10B.4 for examples of substantive procedures for stockholders' equity.)

(AICPA adapted)

LO 10-6

10.60 **Stockholders' Equity.** You are a CPA engaged in an audit of the financial statements of Pate Corporation for the year ended December 31. The financial statements and records of Pate Corporation have not been audited by a CPA in prior years. The stockholders' equity section of Pate Corporation's balance sheet at December 31 follows:

Pate Corporation was founded in 1985. The corporation has 10 stockholders and serves as its own registrar and transfer agent. No capital stock subscription contracts are in effect.

Required:

a. Prepare the detailed audit plan for the examination of the three accounts composing the stockholders' equity section of Pate Corporation's balance sheet. Organize the audit plan under broad financial statement assertions. (Do not include in the audit plan the audit of the results of the current-year operations.)

b. After every other figure on the balance sheet has been audited, it might appear that the retained earnings figure is a balancing figure and requires no further audit work. Why do auditors audit retained earnings as they do the other figures on the balance sheet? Discuss.

(AICPA adapted)

LO 10-6

10.61 **Intercompany and Interpersonal Investment Relations.** You have been engaged to audit the financial statements of Hardy Hardware Distributors Inc., as of December 31. In your review of the corporate nonfinancial records, you have found that Hardy Hardware owns 15 percent of the outstanding voting common stock of Hardy Products Corporation. Upon further investigation, you learn that Hardy Products Corporation manufactures a line of hardware goods, 90 percent of which is sold to Hardy Hardware.

James L. Hardy, president of Hardy Hardware, has supplied you objective evidence that he personally owns 30 percent of the Hardy Products voting stock and the remaining 70 percent is owned by Juana Hardy Lewis, his sister and president of Hardy Products. Hardy also owns 20 percent of the voting common stock of Hardy Hardware Distributors, another 20 percent is held by an estate of which Hardy and Lewis are beneficiaries, and the remaining 60 percent is publicly held. The stock is listed on the American Stock Exchange.

Hardy Hardware consistently has reported operating profits higher than the industry average. Hardy Products Corporation, however, has a net return on sales of only 1 percent. The Hardy Products investment always has been reported at cost, and no dividends have been paid by the company. During the course of your conversations with the Hardy siblings, you learn that you were appointed as auditor because they had a heated disagreement with the former auditors over the issues of accounting for the Hardy Products investment and the prices at which goods have been sold to Hardy Hardware.

Required:

Discuss the following:

a. Identify the issues in this situation as they relate to (1) conflicts of interest and (2) controlling influences among individuals and corporations.

b. Should the investment in Hardy Products Corporation be accounted for using the equity method?

c. What evidence should the auditor seek with regard to the prices paid by Hardy Hardware for products purchased from Hardy Products Corporation?

d. What information would you consider necessary for adequate disclosure in the financial statements of Hardy Hardware Distributors?

Instructions for Discussion Cases 10.62–10.64

These cases are designed to be similar to the ones in the chapter. They give the problem, and your assignment is to write the audit approach portion of the case organized around these sections:

- *Objectives.* Express the objective in terms of the facts supposedly asserted in financial records, accounts, and statements.

- *Control.* Write a brief explanation of control considerations, especially the kinds of manipulations that could arise from the situation described in the case.

- *Tests of controls.* Write some procedures for getting evidence about existing controls, especially procedures that could discover management manipulations. If there are no controls to test, there are no procedures to perform; go on then to the next section. A *procedure* should instruct someone about the source(s) of evidence to tap and the work to do.

- *Audit of balance.* Write some procedures for getting evidence about the *existence, completeness, valuation, rights,* and *disclosure* assertions identified in your objectives section.

- *Discovery summary.* Write a short statement about the discovery you expect to accomplish with your procedures.

LO 10-1, 10-6, 10-7

10.62 **Related-Party Transaction "Goodwill."** Write the audit approach section like the cases in the chapter.

Hide the Loss under the Goodwill

Gulwest Industries, a public company, decided to discontinue its unprofitable line of business of manufacturing sporting ammunition. Gulwest had capitalized the startup cost of the business, and with its discontinuance, the $7 million deferred cost should have been written off. Instead, Gulwest formed a new corporation, Amron, and transferred the sporting ammunition assets (including the $7 million deferred cost) to it in exchange for all Amron stock. In the Gulwest accounts, the Amron investment was carried at $12.4 million, which was the book value of the assets transferred (including the $7 million deferred cost).

Gulwest and a different public company (Big Industrial) created another company (BigShot Ammunition). Gulwest transferred all Amron assets to BigShot in exchange for (1) common and preferred stock of Big Industrial valued at $2 million and (2) a note from BigShot in the amount of $3.4 million. Big Industrial thus acquired 100 percent of the stock of BigShot. Gulwest management reasoned that it had "given" Amron stock valued at $12.4 million to receive stock and notes valued at $5.4 million, so the difference must be goodwill. Thus, the Gulwest accounts carried amounts for Big Industrial Stock ($2 million), BigShot's note receivable ($3.4 million), and Goodwill ($7 million).

Gulwest directors included an analysis of the sporting ammunition business's lack of profitability in the minutes of board meetings. The minutes showed approval of a plan to dispose of the business, but they did not use the words *discontinue the business*. The minutes also showed approval of the creation of Amron, the deal with Big Industrial, the formation of BigShot, and the acceptance of Big's stock and BigShot's note in connection with the final exchange and merger.

LO 10-1, 10-6, 10-7

10.63 **Related-Party Transaction Valuation.** Follow the instructions preceding the case in problem 10.62. Write the audit approach section like the cases in the chapter.

In Plane View

Whiz Corporation owned 160,000 shares of Wing Company stock, carried on the books as an investment in the amount of $6,250,000. Whiz bought a used airplane from Wing, giving in exchange (1) $480,000 cash and (2) the 160,000 Wing shares. Even though the quoted market value of the Wing stock was $2,520,000, Whiz valued the airplane received at $3,750,000, indicating a stock valuation of $3,270,000. Thus, Whiz recognized a loss on disposition of the Wing stock in the amount of $2,980,000.

Whiz justified the airplane valuation with another transaction. On the same day it was purchased, Whiz sold the airplane to the Mexican subsidiary of one of its subsidiary companies (two layers down, but Whiz owned 100 percent of the first subsidiary, which in turn owned 100 percent of the Mexican subsidiary). The Mexican subsidiary paid Whiz with US$25,000 cash and a promissory note for US$3,725,000 (market rate of interest).

The transaction was within the authority of the chief executive officer, and company policy did not require a separate approval by the board of directors. A contract of sale and correspondence with Wing detailing the terms of the transaction were in the files. Likewise, a contract of sale to the Mexican subsidiary, a copy of the deposit slip, and a memorandum of the promissory note were on file. The note itself was kept in the company vault. None of the Wing papers cited a specific price for the airplane.

Whiz overvalued the Wing stock and justified it with a related-party transaction with its own subsidiary company. The loss on the disposition of the Wing stock was understated by $750,000.

LO 10-6, 10-7

10.64 **Lack of Controls over Investments.** Follow the instructions preceding the case in problem 10.62. Write the audit approach section like the cases in the chapter.

Rogue Trader

In February 1989, 22-year-old Nicholas Leeson joined **Barings Investment Bank.** In 1993, he began trading on behalf of the Barings group as a "proprietary trader" on the Singapore International Monetary Exchange (SIMEX). By 1995, he had wiped out the 233-year-old bank, which had counted Queen Elizabeth as a client. He left behind liabilities totaling $1.3 billion. As a proprietary trader, Leeson was to arbitrage or take advantage of differences between the prices quoted for identical contracts on SIMEX and on other exchanges. This was supposed to be achieved by entering into matching purchase and sale contracts simultaneously to capture favorable price differences. Unfortunately, Leeson entered into very large contracts that were not matched with offsetting contracts, exposing the bank to enormous potential losses from even small market movements. These trades were hidden in a separate account: 88888. Transactions were transferred from other Barings accounts into account 88888 to artificially generate a profit for the other accounts.

During the period, Barings was reorganizing and Leeson reported to local managers in Singapore and product managers in London. Neither set of managers checked Leeson's activities. An internal audit report had criticized the reporting structure, but its recommendations were never implemented. Funds to finance Leeson's trades were requested from him to ostensibly fund client positions and were recorded as receivables from clients. The credit-control group never reviewed the creditworthiness of the clients because they said they were never informed of the remittances.

Leeson's managers accepted reports of his profitability with admiration. They did not question the unusually large profits from his trading that would have been unlikely from an arbitrage operation.

Appendix 10A

Internal Control Questionnaires

EXHIBIT 10A.1   Internal Control Questionnaire: Investments

	Yes/No	Comments
Environment		
1. Does the board of directors authorize investment strategies?		
2. Are investment structures based on legitimate business goals?		
3. Are trading guidelines and limits established by company policy?		
4. Are derivatives used for legitimate company objectives?		
5. Are brokerage relationships reviewed for potential conflicts of interests?		
6. Are personnel recording investments competent and appropriately trained to ensure the accuracy and appropriateness of journal entries?		
Existence/Occurrence		
7. Are brokerage statements reconciled to the general ledger monthly?		
Completeness		
8. Are company traders monitored in their discussions with brokers?		
Valuation		
9. Does accounting review all significant transactions?		
10. Are purchases and sales of investments listed on brokerage statements compared to changes in the investment account?		
11. Are purchases and sales of investments listed on brokerage statements compared to receipts and disbursements?		
12. Are changes in investments accounted for on the equity method monitored and recorded in the financial statements?		
13. Are accounting personnel trained in standards for hedge accounting?		
Cutoff		
14. Are purchases and sales of investments listed on brokerage statements compared to changes in the investment account to ensure they were recorded in the proper period?		
Presentation and disclosure		
15. Are investment classifications based on legitimate management intentions?		
16. Are disclosures reviewed by senior management?		

EXHIBIT 10A.2   Internal Control Questionnaire: Long-Term Debt

	Yes/No	Comments
Environment		
1. Are notes payable records kept by someone who cannot sign notes or checks?		
2. Are direct borrowings on notes payable authorized by the directors? By the treasurer or by the chief financial officer?		
3. Are two or more authorized signatures required on notes?		
Existence/Occurrence		
4. Are paid notes canceled, stamped PAID, and filed?		
Completeness		
5. Is all borrowing authorized by the directors checked to determine whether all notes payable are recorded?		
Valuation		
6. Are loan documents forwarded to accounting for review?		
7. Are bank due notices compared with records of unpaid liabilities?		
8. Is the subsidiary ledger of notes payable periodically reconciled with the general ledger control account(s)? Are interest payments and accruals monitored for due dates and financial statement dates?		
Cutoff		
9. Are new notes recorded in the appropriate period?		
Presentation and disclosure		
10. Is sufficient information available in the accounts to enable financial statement preparers to classify current and long-term debt properly?		
11. Are loan documents evaluated for debt covenants?		

Appendix 10B

Substantive Audit Plans

EXHIBIT 10B.1

	Performed By	Ref.
DUNDER-MIFFLIN INC. **Audit Plan for Fair Market Value of Assets and Liabilities** **December 31, 2023**		
A. Review Details of Management's Valuation Approach		
1. Assess the completeness of management assumptions (i.e., whether management has considered all relevant issues).		

2. Determine the reasonableness of significant assumptions, including whether these assumptions reflect
  a. The general economic environment.
  b. The specific industry's economic and regulatory environment.
  c. Other market information.
  d. Assumptions made in prior periods.
  e. Past experience with the entity.
  f. The potential variability in the amount and timing of cash flows and related effect on the discount rate.
  g. Results of other audit procedures.		

3. Obtain data used in reaching these assumptions including
  a. Recency of data.
  b. Source of data.
  c. Consistency of data (i.e., assumptions used in one calculation are consistent with assumptions used in other calculations).		

4. Reperform computations.		
5. Trace data to source documents for accuracy.		
6. Identify possible bias or misapplication of assumptions.		
B. Reperform the Valuation Process to Provide an Auditor's Estimate of the Value Estimate and Compare That Value to Management's Estimate		
C. Review Transactions That Have Occurred since Year-End That Provide Evidence		
1. Determine whether the assumptions underlying management's valuation supports (or refutes) that valuation.		
2. Review the valuation itself.		
D. Document All Management Assumptions and Audit Procedures Used to Substantiate Those Assumptions		

EXHIBIT 10B.2

	Performed By	Ref.
DUNDER-MIFFLIN INC. **Audit Plan for Investments and Related Accounts** **December 31, 2023**		
A. Investments and Related Accounts		
1. Obtain a schedule of all investments, including purchase and disposition information for the period. Reconcile with investment accounts in the general ledger.		
2. Inspect or confirm with a trustee or broker the name, number, identification, interest rate, and face amount (if applicable) of securities held as investments.		
3. Vouch the cost of recorded investments to brokers' reports, contracts, canceled checks, and other supporting documentation.		
4. Vouch recorded sales to brokers' reports and bank deposit slips and recalculate gain or loss on disposition.		
5. Recalculate interest income and verify dividend income from a dividend-reporting service (such as Moody's or Standard & Poor's annual dividend record).		
6. Obtain market values of investments and determine whether any write-down or write-off is necessary. Scan transactions soon after the client's year-end to see whether any investments were sold at a loss. Recalculate the unrealized gains and losses required for fair value securities accounting.		
(continued)		

EXHIBIT 10B.2 *(concluded)*

DUNDER-MIFFLIN INC. Audit Plan for Investments and Related Accounts December 31, 2023	Performed By	Ref.
7. Read loan agreements and minutes of the board of directors and inquire of management about pledges of investments as security for loans.		
8. Obtain audited financial statements of joint ventures, investee companies (equity method of accounting), subsidiary companies, and other entities in which an investment interest is held. Evaluate indications of significant controlling influence. Inspect documents for proper balance sheet classification and conformity with accounting principles.		
9. Obtain management representations concerning pledge of investment assets as collateral.		
B. Investments in Debt and Equity Securities		

1. Review the proper classification of securities in the categories of held-to-maturity, available-for-sale, and trading securities.
  a. Inquire about management's intent regarding classifications.
  b. Inspect written records of investment strategies.
  c. Inspect documentation for investment activities and transactions.
  d. Review instructions to portfolio managers.
  e. Inspect minutes of the investment committee of the board of directors.		

2. Review whether facts support management's intent to hold securities to maturity.
  a. Inquire of management concerning the company's financial position, working capital requirements, results of operations, debt agreements, guarantees, and applicable laws and regulations.
  b. Inspect documentation and review for compliance with working capital requirements, debt agreements, guarantees, and applicable laws and regulations.
  c. Inspect the company's cash flow forecasts.
  d. Obtain management representations confirming proper classification with regard to intent and ability.		

3. Review the value of debt and equity securities by performing the following:
  a. Obtain published market quotations.
  b. Obtain market prices from broker-dealers who are market makers in particular securities.
  c. Obtain valuations from expert specialists.
  d. Inspect documentation and review proprietary market valuation models for reasonableness and evaluate the data and assumptions in them are appropriate.		

4. Review whether value impairments are "other than temporary," considering evidence of the following:
  a. Fair market is materially below cost.
  b. The value decline is due to specific adverse conditions.
  c. The value decline is industry or geographically specific.
  d. Management does not have both the intent and the ability to hold the security long enough for a reasonable hope of value recovery.
  e. The fair value decline has existed for a long time.
  f. A debt security has been downgraded by a rating agency.
  g. The financial condition of the issuer has deteriorated.
  h. Dividends of interest payments have been reduced or eliminated.		

EXHIBIT 10B.3

DUNDER-MIFFLIN INC. Audit Plan for Notes Payable and Long-Term Debt December 31, 2023		
	Performed By	**Ref.**
1. Obtain a schedule of notes payable and other long-term debt (including capitalized lease obligations) showing beginning balances, new notes/issuances, repayment, and ending balances. Trace to general ledger accounts.		
2. Confirm liabilities with creditor: amount, interest rate, due date, collateral, and other terms. Some of these confirmations may be standard bank confirmations.		
3. Review the standard bank confirmation for evidence of assets pledged as collateral and for unrecorded obligations.		
4. Review loan agreements for terms and conditions that need to be disclosed and for pledge of assets as collateral.		
5. Recalculate the portion of long-term debt classified as a current liability and trace to the trial balance.		
6. Inspect lease agreements for indications of need to capitalize leases. Recalculate the capital and operating lease amounts for required disclosures.		
7. Recalculate interest expense on debts and trace to the interest expense and accrued interest accounts.		
8. Obtain written representations from management concerning notes payable, collateral agreements, and restrictive covenants.		

EXHIBIT 10B.4

DUNDER-MIFFLIN INC. Audit Plan for Stockholders' Equity December 31, 2023		
	Performed By	**Ref.**

1. Obtain an analysis of stockholders' equity transactions. Trace additions and reductions to the general ledger.
  a. Vouch additions to directors' minutes and cash receipts.
  b. Vouch reductions to directors' minutes and other supporting documents.		

2. Read the directors' minutes for stockholders' equity authorization. Trace to entries in the accounts. Review related disclosures for completeness and accuracy.		
3. Confirm outstanding common and preferred stock with stock registrar.		
4. Vouch stock option and profit-sharing plan disclosures to contracts and plan documents.		
5. Vouch treasury stock transactions to cash receipts and cash disbursement records and to directors' authorization. Inspect treasury stock certificates.		

6. When the company keeps its own stock records:
  a. Inspect the stock record stubs for certificate numbers and number of shares.
  b. Inspect the unissued certificates.		

7. Obtain written representations about the number of shares issued and outstanding.		

Completing the Audit

> *It ain't over till it's over.*
>
> *"Yogi" Berra, former American Major League Baseball
> catcher, coach, and manager*

Topic	AU-C/ISA Section	AS Section
Quality Control for an Audit Engagement	220	1220
Communication with Those Charged with Governance	260	1301
Communicating Internal Control-Related Matters Identified in an Audit	265	1305
Evaluation of Misstatements	450	2810
Inquiry of a Client's Lawyer	501	2505
Analytical Procedures	520	2305
Accounting Estimates	540	2501
Subsequent Events and Subsequently Discovered Facts	560	2801, 2905
Going Concern	570	2415
Written Representations	580	2805
Omitted Procedures	585	2901

LEARNING OBJECTIVES

This chapter discusses the completion of the audit examination and identifies major events and auditors' responsibilities in the completion stage of the audit.

Your objectives are to be able to

LO 11-1 Identify major activities performed by auditors in completing the substantive procedures following the date of the financial statements.

LO 11-2 Understand the role of attorney letters in evaluating litigation, claims, and assessments.

LO 11-3 Explain why auditors obtain written representations and identify the key components of written representations.

LO 11-4 Identify the final steps in the completion of an audit.

LO 11-5 Understand auditors' responsibility for subsequent events and subsequently discovered facts.

LO 11-6 Identify important activities and communications following the completion of the audit and audit report release date.

INTRODUCTION

Evaluating a company's ability to continue as a going concern, that is, their ability to remain a viable company for the next year, is a difficult task, yet one auditors are required to do in the final steps of the audit. If, based on all of the evidence gathered throughout the audit, auditors believe a company's viability is uncertain, they would next need to evaluate management's plans to stay afloat and the likelihood that plan would work. After evaluating that plan, if the auditors are still uncertain, they must indicate so in the audit report, by issuing what is typically referred to as a going-concern opinion.

That evaluation is hard, subjective, and certainly not always a predictor of what will happen to the company. Take **Eastman Kodak Company (Kodak),** for example. Kodak filed for bankruptcy in 2012, reported a net loss of $1,379 million, and had negative operating cash flows for the year. **PwC,** their auditor at the time, would have considered this, as well as other information including debt structure, revenue trends, and much more, to determine whether to give Kodak a going-concern opinion. Based on their assessment, they did have substantial doubt and decided to give a going-concern opinion in 2012. Clearly, Kodak survived the next year, as in 2013, they emerged from bankruptcy a much smaller organization and did not receive a going-concern opinion. Nor did they receive a going-concern opinion in 2014, 2015, 2016, or 2017, despite having had negative operating cash flows and continuing net losses each year. In 2018, however, based on the combination of maturing debt, negative cash flows, and operating losses, PwC once again doubted Kodak's ability to continue as a going concern enough to issue a going-concern opinion. Yet again, Kodak survived another year and for year-end 2019, once again, PwC evaluated the evidence gathered, reviewed management's plan, and issued another going-concern opinion. In 2020, despite showing net losses for yet another year, **EY,** Kodak's new auditor, evaluated the evidence gathered and management's plan and decided there was not a need to issue a going-concern opinion.[1]

The above vignette underscores the difficulty and numerous factors involved in evaluating a company's ability to continue as a going concern, one of the many difficult decisions an auditor needs to make when wrapping up the audit. This chapter focuses on the completion of the audit, in particular, the final procedures (including assessing a company's ability to continue as a going concern) and responsibilities of the auditor when finishing the audit. The chapter also discusses the responsibilities of an auditor after the audit is completed.

AUDIT TIMELINE

During the completion of the audit (or wrap-up), many important issues arise, and many other issues that have served as the focus of the auditors' work need to be documented. To provide an overview of the general time frame of the audit and the potential emergence of issues and matters for the auditors' consideration, consider the following broad time line:

Beginning of Year January 1, 2023	Year-End Date (date of the financial statements) December 31, 2023	Date of the Auditor's Report (audit completion date) February 15, 2024	Audit Report Release Date February 17, 2024
Interim testing • Test of controls • Substantive procedures	Completing substantive procedures Attorneys' letters Written representations Going-concern assessment Adjusting journal entries Audit documentation review Subsequent events	Subsequently discovered facts	Subsequently discovered facts Omitted audit procedures Management letter Communications with those charged with governance

[1]Sources: Eastman Kodak Company Form 10-Ks for years ending 2012–2020.

The preceding time line suggests four important periods, beginning with the period under audit. Auditors often do a significant amount of tests of controls and substantive procedures prior to year-end to "spread" the audit work over a more extended period. This *interim testing* occurs between the beginning of the year (January 1, 2023) and the year-end date under audit (December 31, 2023), also referred to as the **date of the financial statements**.

The second period of interest begins on the date of the financial statements (December 31, 2023) and runs through the completion of the audit (February 15, 2024). Although a significant amount of audit evidence is typically gathered prior to the date of the financial statements, auditors will continue to perform other procedures and gather evidence following this date. At some point, auditors will have gathered sufficient, appropriate evidence on which to base their opinions on the financial statements and internal control over financial reporting; this includes the review of audit documentation, preparation of the financial statements and related disclosures, and management's assertion that they take responsibility for the financial statements and disclosures. We refer to this as the **date of the auditor's report**, which is the date auditors use for their reports on the client's financial statements and internal control over financial reporting. (This date is also referred to as the *audit completion date* and, in our example, would be February 15, 2024.) Recall that the auditor's report on the entity's financial statements covers all events that occur up to this date, and, as a result, auditors need to continue to be alert for developments affecting the client.

In some instances, auditors become aware of a development affecting the client *after* the date of the auditor's report (in our example, February 15, 2024) but *prior* to the **audit report release date** (date on which auditors allow the client to use the auditor's reports in conjunction with the financial statements, in our example, February 17, 2024).[2] This is the third period of interest to the auditor. Although this period normally is fairly short, events occurring between the date of the auditor's report and audit report release date present significant challenges to auditors; they are no longer actively obtaining audit evidence however their reports have yet to be issued. The auditors' dilemma is simple: how to report on the new development without increasing the responsibility for other (unknown) developments. As discussed later in this chapter, auditors may consider dual dating the report on the financial statements to limit responsibility to specifically identified developments.

Finally, some issues can come to the auditor's attention after the audit report release date and the issuance of the client's financial statements (in our example, February 17, 2024); this is the fourth period of interest.[3] Although the auditor's reports have been released, information may come to the auditor's attention that could cause the auditor to take steps to ensure that third parties do not inappropriately rely on an auditor's reports that are no longer reliable. In addition, following the audit report release date, the auditor makes other communications to the client and individuals charged with governance based on observations during the audit examination.

This chapter focuses on a number of the topics addressed in the preceding time line. Regarding auditors' responsibility for various matters, it is important to consider the timing of these topics in the time line discussed.

 REVIEW CHECKPOINT

11.1 Identify four primary periods in an audit examination and the tasks and activities that occur in each.

---

[2]These reports include opinions on the financial statements and the effectiveness of internal control over financial reporting. As noted in Chapter 12, both auditors' reports are dated on the audit completion date and included with the 10-K filed with the U.S. Securities and Exchange Commission (SEC).

[3]Larger public entities must file annual reports with the SEC within 60 days after the date of the financial statements. Thus, audit fieldwork must be completed and auditors' reports for these companies must be dated earlier than 60 days after the date of the financial statements.

PROCEDURES PERFORMED DURING FIELDWORK

LO 11-1
Identify major activities performed by auditors in completing the substantive procedures following the date of the financial statements.

Completing Substantive Procedures

Roll-Forward Procedures

From earlier chapters, you know that auditors often test account balances at an interim point for efficiency reasons. For example, if relevant internal controls are effective, accounts receivable can be confirmed at November 30 for a December 31 year-end client. Similarly, although most inventory observations occur near year-end, they actually can be performed at an earlier time. In such cases, auditors use **roll-forward procedures** to *roll* the conclusions *forward* to the year-end date under audit. Common roll-forward procedures include examining material account transactions that occur between the interim testing date and the date of the financial statements.

Analytical Procedures and Review of Accounts

Throughout the text, we have discussed the use of **analytical procedures**, which allow auditors to evaluate financial information by studying relationships among both financial and nonfinancial data. Professional standards state that analytical procedures can be used throughout the audit:

1. During planning to assist auditors in planning the nature, timing, and extent of other auditing procedures (*required*).
2. As part of substantive testing, to obtain audit evidence about particular assertions related to account balances or classes of transactions (*optional*).
3. Near the end of the audit as an overall review of the financial information to assess the conclusions reached and evaluate the overall financial statement presentation (*required*).

This latter use of analytical procedures is of interest to auditors in completing the audit. In this use, auditors review the financial statements and footnotes to the financial statements to evaluate (1) the adequacy of evidence gathered in response to unexpected account balances or relationships among account balances identified during the audit and (2) unusual or unexpected account balances or relationships among account balances that were not previously identified in other parts of the audit. In this way, analytical procedures near the end of the audit act as a final "catch all." If there are unusual or unexpected balances not previously identified, it is not too late to investigate them before the audit report is issued!

In addition to the preceding, auditors should be alert for "miscellaneous," "other," and "clearing" accounts classified as revenues or expenses, particularly when they result from adjustments made at the end of the year or quarter. These items can be identified by scanning accounts for large and unusual entries. In many cases, these items reflect adjustments made to meet analysts' earnings expectations (known as *earnings management*) and should be more appropriately classified as *deferred items, assets, liabilities, contra-assets,* or *contra-liabilities.* If items of this nature are identified, auditors should examine related documentation and inquire of the client to verify that classification as a revenue or expense is appropriate.

Review of Accounting Estimates

Chapters 6 through 10 discuss auditing procedures performed in the examination of various cycles. As noted in these chapters, the entity's account balances and financial statements are affected by many significant estimates that must be made by management. For example, **Amazon** identifies the following as some of the estimates necessary in preparing its financial statements where actual results could be materially different than estimated amounts:

- Income taxes.
- Equipment useful lives for depreciation calculations.
- Commitments and contingencies.
- Valuation of acquired intangibles and goodwill.

- Stock-based compensation and forfeiture rates.
- Receivables collections.
- Vendor funding.
- Inventory valuation.
- Valuation and impairment of estimates.[4]

As highlighted in the Auditing Insight below, simple changes in estimates can have a material impact on the financial statements.

AUDITING INSIGHT   A Small Change with a Big Impact

In the fourth quarter of 2021, Amazon finished up a useful-life study of their servers and networking equipment and determined that they needed to increase their estimate of the useful lives of the servers and equipment by one year. That may not seem like much, but that one "small" estimate change is expected to have a $3.1 billion impact on operating income for 2022!

Source: Amazon.com Inc. Form 10-K (filed February 4, 2022).

Because estimates, by their very nature, reflect uncertainty and future outcomes, auditors cannot "audit," "corroborate," or "verify" accounting estimates. However, auditors should consider whether estimates are *reasonable* in the circumstances. For example, it is not likely that assigning computer equipment a 20-year useful life for purposes of depreciation would be considered reasonable. Although the reasonableness of accounting estimates is assessed to some extent on an account-by-account basis throughout the audit, auditors will evaluate management's process for developing estimates as well as the overall *reasonableness* of management's estimates near the end of the audit. With respect to reasonableness, auditors should ensure that estimates are consistent with one another, historical data, and industry data.

In addition, auditors should consider how events occurring after the date of the financial statements may affect the reasonableness of accounting estimates. For example, a significant economic downturn may suggest that previous estimates related to uncollectible accounts are insufficient and a higher percentage of uncollectible accounts should be estimated. In a sense, this overall review of the reasonableness of accounting estimates is similar in nature and purpose to the role of analytical procedures conducted near the end of the audit.

Determining the reasonableness of accounting estimates is difficult, and an area where auditors struggle, as discussed further in the nearby PCAOB Inspection Focus.

PCAOB INSPECTION FOCUS   Estimation Issues

The PCAOB identified the accounting estimates as a common area of auditor deficiencies during their 2020 inspections. In a summary report issued in late 2021, the PCAOB, while acknowledging that auditors had improved in auditing estimates, noted the following common deficiencies:

- Auditors failed to evaluate evidence supporting certain assumption changes (or lack thereof) from prior year when evaluating the reasonableness of assumptions.
- Auditors failed to obtain sufficient appropriate evidence to support assumptions used or to perform procedures to resolve known contradictory evidence when evaluating the reasonableness of financial statement forecasts used to determine certain estimates.
- Auditors failed to evaluate the appropriateness of valuation models and the reasonableness of assumptions used when determining certain estimates.
- Auditors failed to perform sufficient procedures to resolve known contradictory evidence when evaluating the recoverability of long-lived assets.

Source: *Spotlight: Staff Update and Preview of 2020 Inspection Observations,* PCAOB, October 2021.

---

[4]*Amazon.com, Inc. Form 10-K* (filed February 4, 2022).

REVIEW CHECKPOINTS

11.2   What are roll-forward procedures? Provide some examples.

11.3   How are analytical procedures used near the end of the audit?

11.4   What additional issues are involved with miscellaneous, other, and clearing accounts?

11.5   What are auditors' responsibilities with respect to accounting estimates made by management?

LO 11-2
Understand the role of attorney letters in evaluating litigation, claims, and assessments.

Attorney Letters

For financial statements to be presented according to an applicable financial reporting framework (such as GAAP), all material contingencies (contingent gains or losses) must be properly accounted for and disclosed in the financial statements. According to *Accounting Standards Codification 450 (*ASC 450*)*, a **contingency** is

> an existing condition, situation, or set of circumstances involving uncertainty as to possible gain or loss to an enterprise that will ultimately be resolved when one or more future events occur or fail to occur.

Examples of contingent liabilities include potential payments related to warranties for products and services sold by the entity, income taxes in dispute with the Internal Revenue Service, and guarantees of debt on behalf of another party. With respect to contingencies, auditors should ensure that (1) all contingencies have been appropriately identified and (2) any client disclosure of contingencies reflects the most current information and all recent developments, both favorable and unfavorable to the client. These contingencies are normally evaluated as part of the audit of the related account balances and classes of transactions and have been discussed in previous chapters of this text. Contingencies can be quite impactful, as illustrated in the following Auditing Insight.

 AUDITING INSIGHT   Costly Contingencies for Volkswagen

In their 2020 financial statements, Volkswagen disclosed 4.2 billion euros (approximately $3.7 billion U.S. dollars at the time) for contingent liabilities related to a diesel emissions cheating scandal that was uncovered five years earlier.

In 2015, the Environmental Protection Agency announced that several Volkswagen models sold in the United States were equipped with software that would detect when emissions were being tested and change the performance accordingly to improve the emission testing results. Initially, Volkswagen recorded approximately $7.3 billion dollars in charges to earnings to cover anticipated fines, litigation, and various other payouts. That estimation was way off. As of October 2020, the total charges to earnings related to the scandal were $35 billion U.S. dollars!

Source: Edward Taylor, "Volkswagen sets aside 5.5 billion euros in contingent liabilities for diesel scandal," *Reuters Business News,* May 2, 2019; Russle Hotten, "Volkswagen: The scandal explained," *BBC News,* December 10, 2015. Geoff Colvin, "5 years in, damages from the VW emissions cheating scandal are still rolling in," *Fortune,* October 6, 2020 (www.fortune.com). *Volkeswagon Annual Report 2020,* March 16, 2021 (www.volkswagenag.com).

A contingent liability that requires special consideration by auditors is the uncertain outcome of litigation, claims, and assessments pending against the entity. From the auditors' standpoint, two important issues relating to pending litigation, claims, and assessments are ensuring that all pending litigation, claims, and assessments (1) have been disclosed to auditors and (2) are properly presented and disclosed in the client's financial statements. Because the client's attorneys are most familiar with the existence and classification of pending litigation, claims, and assessments, they play a very important role in auditors' evaluation of these matters.

Auditors should inquire of management and discuss potential litigation, claims, and assessments. Once this inquiry has identified litigation, claims, and assessments, auditors perform the following procedures:

- Obtain from management a description and evaluation of litigation, claims, and assessments.
- Examine documents in the client's possession concerning litigation, claims, and assessments, including correspondence and invoices from attorneys.
- Obtain assurance from management that it has disclosed all material unasserted claims the attorney has advised them are likely to be litigated.
- Read minutes of meetings of stockholders, directors, and appropriate committees.
- Read contracts, loan agreements, leases, and correspondence from taxing or other governmental agencies.
- Obtain information concerning guarantees from bank confirmations.
- Review the legal expense account, cash disbursements records, and invoices related to legal services.

The client's responsibility is to respond to auditors' inquiries and provide auditors with a description and evaluation of litigation, claims, and assessments. When auditors assess a risk of material misstatement from pending litigation, claims, and assessments, they will request that the client send an **attorney letter** (or letter of inquiry) to all attorneys who worked for the client during the period under audit. It is important to note that the client should make this request because it informs the attorney that the client is waiving the attorney–client privilege and is authorizing the attorney to provide information to auditors. The attorney letter should contain the following information (prepared from the client's perspective):

- A list of pending or threatened litigation, claims, or assessments.
- A description of each item, including the nature of the case and management responses or intended responses to the case.
- An evaluation of the likelihood of an unfavorable outcome.
- An estimate of the range of potential loss.

Review the flow of correspondence related to the attorney letter outlined in Exhibit 11.1. The process begins when auditors request the client to *prepare* a letter to its attorney(s) (step 1).

EXHIBIT 11.1
Attorney Letter Flow of Correspondence

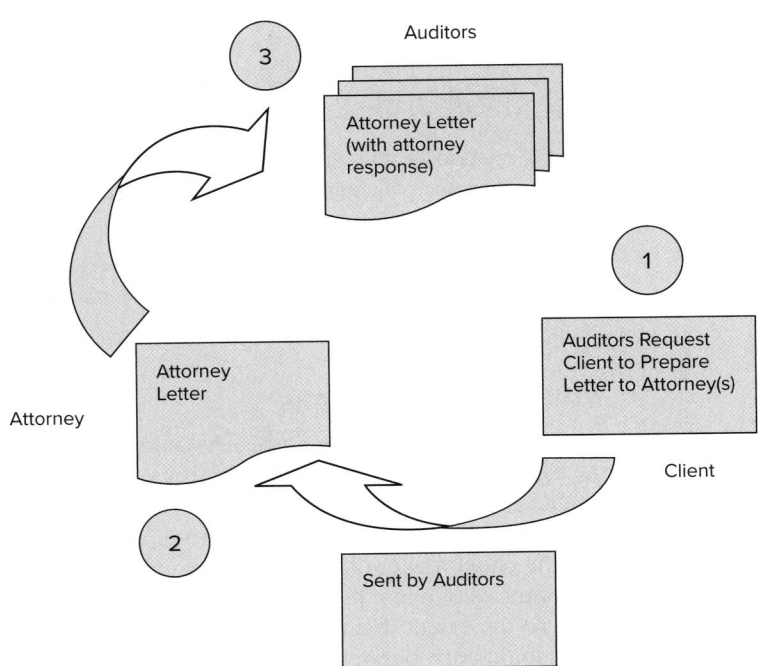

EXHIBIT 11.2
Role of Various Parties in Audit of Litigation, Claims, and Assessments

Party	Responsibilities
Auditors	• Inquire of client regarding the existence of litigation, claims, and assessments. • Perform various procedures regarding litigation, claims, and assessments. • Initiate request to the client for attorney letter. • Mail attorney letter prepared by client.
Client	• Respond to auditors' inquiries regarding litigation, claims, and assessments. • Provide auditors a list, description, and evaluation of litigation, claims, and assessments. • Prepare letter to attorney (attorney letter) that includes information related to litigation, claims, and assessments.
Attorney	• Respond to auditors regarding client's description of litigation, claims, and assessments contained in the attorney letter.

In step 2, the attorney receives the letter *mailed by the auditor* asking the attorney to respond to the letter (step 3). The *attorney's response* should be provided *directly* to auditors for purposes of control and should explain any matters noted in the attorney letter in which the attorney's view differs from the information in the letter. For example, the client may indicate that the likelihood of an unfavorable outcome is "remote," but the attorney may believe that it is higher than "remote." In addition, the attorney may inform auditors of pending litigation, claims, or assessments not included in the attorney letter.

The general roles of the client, auditors, and attorney(s) in this process are summarized in Exhibit 11.2.

Unasserted claims raise additional issues for attorney letters. An **unasserted claim** represents that no formal lawsuit or claim has been filed or threatened on behalf of others but that circumstances such as a catastrophe, accident, or other physical occurrence could result in a suit or claim being filed in the future. Because unasserted claims have not been filed, the issue of client disclosure of these matters to auditors is less clear. Attorneys should encourage their clients to disclose this information to auditors when the assertion of a claim is at least *probable*. However, the American Bar Association's guidelines to attorneys do not require them to disclose unasserted claims to auditors unless the client specifically lists them in the attorney letter. Thus, auditors must rely on the attorney to inform the client (not the auditors) if an unasserted claim must be disclosed. The attorney letter explicitly asks that this understanding be communicated to the client's auditors through the attorney's response.

✅ REVIEW CHECKPOINTS

11.6 What are the responsibilities of (a) client management, (b) auditors, and (c) the client's attorneys with respect to obtaining evidence regarding litigation, claims, and assessments?

11.7 What is the typical content of attorney letters?

11.8 In addition to obtaining responses to attorney letters, what other procedures can be used to gather audit evidence regarding litigation, claims, and assessments?

LO 11-3
Explain why auditors obtain written representations, and identify the key components of written representations.

Written Representations

Under Section 302 of the Sarbanes–Oxley Act of 2002, all 10-Q and 10-K filings with the SEC are required to include certifications from the chief executive officer and chief financial officer related to the fairness of the financial statements and effectiveness of the internal control over financial reporting. However, these are only some representations that the client makes. As noted in previous chapters, important sources of audit evidence are inquiries of client personnel. Many of the responses to these inquiries are very important. To the extent that additional evidence is obtainable through other procedures, auditors should corroborate these representations.

Professional standards require that auditors obtain **written representations** (also known as *management representations* or *client representations*) to confirm certain matters and support other evidence obtained during the audit.[5] The representations take the form of a letter on the client's letterhead addressed to auditors and signed by responsible officers of the client (normally the chief executive officer [CEO], chief financial officer [CFO], and other appropriate officers). The letter is dated as of the date of the auditor's reports, which is when the audit is completed (in fact, the audit is not complete until the auditor's receipt of assertions from management regarding its responsibility for the fairness of the financial statements and related disclosures through written representations). Thus, written representations cover events and representations running beyond the date of the financial statements up to the audit report date.

It is important to note that written representations are not substitutes for corroborating evidence obtained by applying other substantive procedures. That is, as emphasized in the following Auditing Insight, auditors cannot substitute client inquiry (and representations regarding that inquiry) for substantive procedures. For example, the representation that "management told us that the inventory costing method was FIFO and adequate allowance for obsolescence was provided" is not a good excuse for failing to obtain the evidence from the records and other sources.

AUDITING INSIGHT   Can You Trust Management Representations?

In an address made in September 2016, Andrew Ceresney, the director of the Division of Enforcement at the Securities and Exchange Commission (SEC) at the time, highlighted enforcement actions that showed a "variety of professional failures" on the part of the auditor, including a lack of due professional care and professional skepticism. One particular area of weakness he noted was auditors' "failure to exercise sufficient professional skepticism in evaluating management representations." Mr. Ceresney referenced two separate audit failures due, in part, to auditor overreliance on management representations

and the failure to gather sufficient appropriate related evidence. As a result, two engagement partners and one senior manager were charged for their respective roles in the audit failures and subsequently suspended from working on SEC engagements.

Source: Andrew Ceresney, "The SEC Enforcement Division's Focus on Auditors and Auditing," Keynote Address: American Law Institute Conference on Accountants' Liability 2016: Confronting Enforcement and Litigation Risks, September 22, 2016, https://www.sec.gov/news/speech/ceresney-enforcement-focus-on-auditors-and-auditing.xhtml.

In some cases, however, written representations are the only available evidence about important matters of management intent. For example, the following representations (written by the client's management) provide auditors important audit evidence regarding presentation and disclosure matters:

- "We will discontinue the parachute manufacturing business, wind down the operations, and sell the remaining assets" (classification of the parachute manufacturing business as a discontinued operation).
- "We will exercise our option to refinance the maturing debt on a long-term basis" (classification of the maturing debt as long-term debt).

Within the letter, management representations are organized into three sections that discuss:

1. The entity's financial statements, including
   - Management's responsibilities for the financial statements and internal control over financial reporting.
   - The appropriate disclosure, presentation, and reasonableness of certain items (accounting estimates, related parties, subsequent events, and litigation and claims).

---

[5]Auditing standards for nonpublic entities (i.e., nonissuers) refer to these representations as written representations, whereas auditing standards for public entities (i.e., issuers) refer to them as management representations.

- A statement that uncorrected misstatements are immaterial to the financial statements taken as a whole.

2. Types and completeness of information provided to the auditors, both in general and related to sensitive areas (fraud, noncompliance with laws and regulations, litigation, and related-party transactions).

3. Representations made related to internal control over financial reporting (for audits of issuers).

Although representations should be limited to matters that are material, professional standards note that materiality guidelines do not apply for representations not related to amounts included in the financial statements (such as management's responsibility for the financial statements) or for management's acknowledgment regarding its responsibility for designing, implementing, and maintaining internal control to prevent and detect fraud.

Clearly, written representations provide an important part of auditors' overall ability to support the opinion on the financial statements. As a result, management's refusal to furnish representations constitutes a scope limitation, which typically results in a withdrawal from the engagement or a disclaimer of an opinion. However, contingent upon the nature of the representations not obtained or the reasons for refusal, auditors can opt to qualify the opinion. Regardless, auditors should be very skeptical of any situation in which the client's management refuses to furnish representations.

In addition to those discussed, auditors may obtain representations related to specific transactions or activities, particularly if they have a material effect on the companies' financial statements.[6]

✅ REVIEW CHECKPOINTS

11.9 What are the major categories of information contained in written representations?

11.10 Why are written representation and attorney letters obtained near the end of the evidence-gathering process and dated on the date of the auditor's report?

11.11 How should auditors respond if the client refuses to furnish written representations?

LO 11-4
Identify the final steps in the completion of an audit.

Ability to Continue as a Going Concern

As auditors gather evidence throughout the engagement, they may encounter information that raises questions as to the client's ability to continue as a going concern, such as

- Negative trends, including recurring operating losses, working capital deficiencies, and negative cash flow from operations.

- Indications of financial difficulties, including default on loans, denial of trade credit from suppliers, restructuring of debts, or dividends in arrears.

- Internal matters, including work stoppages or substantial dependence on the success of a particular project or activity.

- External matters, including legal proceedings; loss of a key franchise, license, or patent; or loss of a major customer or supplier.

Auditors are not expected to design and perform procedures solely for the purpose of identifying conditions that indicate going-concern uncertainties. However, procedures performed during the normal course of the audit might reveal such situations. For

---

[6]See AU-C 580.A35 for an example of a Representation Letter for nonissuers and AS 2805.16 for an example of a Management Representation Letter for issuers.

Chapter 11 *Completing the Audit* **499**

EXHIBIT 11.3
Proposed Adjusting Journal Entries (Score Sheet)

	Income Statement	Balance Sheet		
	Increase (Decrease) Net Income	Increase (Decrease) Assets	Increase (Decrease) Liabilities	Increase (Decrease) Equity
(1) Unrecorded cash disbursements				
Accounts payable			($42,000)	
Cash		($42,000)		
(2) Improper sales cutoff				
Sales	($13,000)			($13,000)
Inventory		7,800		
Cost of goods sold	7,800			7,800
Accounts receivable		(13,000)		
(3) Unrecorded liabilities				
Utilities expense	(700)			(700)
Commissions expense	(3,000)			(3,000)
Wage expense	(2,500)			(2,500)
Accounts payable			700	
Accrued expenses payable			5,500	
Net effect before taxes	($11,400)	($47,200)	($35,800)	($11,400)
(4) Reduction in income taxes ($11,400 X 0.21)				
Income tax expense	2,394			2,394
Income taxes payable			(2,394)	
Current-year effects	($9,006)	($47,200)	($38,194)	($9,006)
Uncorrected misstatements from prior audits	($18,000)			($18,000)
Cumulative effect of uncorrected misstatements	($27,006)			($27,006)

Conclusion: Uncorrected misstatements from previous audits had a net debit effect of $18,000 on the income statement (decrease in net income) and a net credit effect on the balance sheet (decrease in net assets, or equity). When considered with the $9,006 effect noted in the current year, the cumulative uncorrected misstatements ($27,006) are less than performance materiality ($100,000). As a result, no adjustment to the financial statements is considered necessary.

However, assuming this obligation has not been paid, at least in part, by the end of year 4, the cumulative effect on the entity's balance sheet would become material ($100,000).

Auditors may use either of two methods to evaluate the materiality of uncorrected misstatements. The **rollover method** considers only the current-period income effect(s); when using the rollover method as in the example shown in Exhibit 11.3, auditors would consider the misstatement to be $9,006. In contrast, the **iron curtain method** considers the aggregate effect of the misstatements on the entity's balance sheet; when using the iron curtain method, auditors would consider the misstatement to be $27,006 (the $9,006 of current-year adjustments and the $18,000 of uncorrected prior-year adjustments). Auditors are required by the Securities and Exchange Commission's *Staff Accounting Bulletin No. 108* to evaluate misstatements using both methods and propose an adjustment if either method indicates that the misstatement is material. Because neither the amount of the current-year uncorrected misstatement in Exhibit 11.3 ($9,006) nor the cumulative effect of uncorrected misstatements ($27,006) exceeds performance materiality of

$100,000, the auditors would conclude that the financial statements are not materially misstated (see conclusion in Exhibit 11.3). Although auditors could recommend the client adjust its financial statements for all known adjustments, no adjustment is required in this situation. In the Auditing Insight that follows, academic research provides a glimpse at how the recommendations (referred to as "negotiations") for adjustments often work.

AUDITING INSIGHT Academic Insights into Auditor Negotiations

A significant amount of academic research has evaluated the process through which auditors and clients "negotiate" with respect to adjustments identified during the audit examination. These studies demonstrate that this process is prevalent; Gibbins, Salterio, and Webb found that 67 percent of audit partners entered into some level of negotiation with more than one-half of their clients and that all partners have negotiated with at least one client. Some interesting conclusions in these studies include

- Gibbins, McCraken, and Salterio found that while approximately one-third of surveyed chief financial officers (CFOs) and audit partners indicated they "won" the negotiation (34 percent for CFOs and 32 percent for auditors), both groups indicated that negotiations resulted in a compromise (26 percent for CFOs and 41 percent for auditors) or a new solution generated during the negotiation (17 percent for CFOs and 16 percent for auditors). Each group was asked to recall an auditor–client negotiation and was not necessarily considering the same negotiation.

- Gibbins, McCracken, and Salterio also found that factors considered as important by CFOs in the outcome of the negotiation include accounting and disclosure standards, the prior relationship with the audit partner, the organization's (client's) accounting expertise, and the audit firm's accounting expertise; auditors primarily considered accounting and disclosure standards and the audit firm's accounting expertise as important in influencing the outcome of the negotiation.

- Hatfield et al. found that (income-decreasing) adjustments proposed by auditors are smaller in cases in which the magnitude of the audit difference is higher and when the client has previously conceded with respect to an audit issue.

- Brown-Liburd et al. found that auditors are less influenced by management's need to meet or beat analysts' expectations when negotiating misstatements in a post-Sarbanes–Oxley environment than in prior.

- Schmidt and Cross found experimental evidence indicates that negotiations with management are less contentious and management is more accommodating when negotiating with a newly rotated audit partner.

Sources: M. Gibbins, S. Salterio, and A. Webb, "Evidence about Auditor-Client Management Negotiation Concerning Client's Financial Reporting," *Journal of Accounting Research,* December 2001, pp. 535–563; M. Gibbins, S. McCracken, and S. Salterio, "Negotiations over Accounting Issues: The Congruency of Audit Partner and Chief Financial Officer Recalls," *Auditing: A Journal of Practice & Theory, Supplement 2005,* pp. 171–193; R. C. Hatfield, R. W. Houston, C. M. Stefaniak, and S. Usrey, "The Effect of Magnitude of Audit Differences and Prior Client Concessions on Negotiations of Proposed Adjustments," *The Accounting Review,* September 2010, pp. 1647–1668; H. Brown-Liburd, J. Cohen, and G. Trompeter, "Effects of Earnings Forecasts and Heightened Professional Skepticism on the Outcomes of Client-Auditor Negotiation," *Journal of Business Ethics, August 2013, pp. 311–325;* R. Schmidt and B. Cross, "The Effects of Auditor Rotation on Client Management's Negotiation Strategies," *Managerial Auditing Journal,* 2014, pp. 110–130.

Auditors are required to communicate all nontrivial misstatements detected during the audit to the client's audit committee (or other individuals charged with governance). These should be communicated regardless of whether they have a material effect on the financial statements. Auditors' identification of material misstatements is normally considered to be a "strong indicator" of a material weakness in internal control over financial reporting even if these misstatements are ultimately adjusted by the client.

✓ REVIEW CHECKPOINTS

11.15 Why are adjusting entries and note disclosures labeled "proposed"?

11.16 What is an uncorrected misstatement? What is the auditors' responsibility for communicating misstatements detected during the audit?

11.17 Identify the two methods of evaluating the performance materiality of uncorrected misstatements. What are the requirements of *Staff Accounting Bulletin No. 108* for evaluating the performance materiality of these misstatements?

Audit Documentation Review

During fieldwork, the audit supervisor—and sometimes the audit manager—reviews the audit documentation soon after the audit staff completes it. The general purpose of this review is to ensure that all appropriate steps in the audit plan were performed, the referencing among audit documentation is clear, and the explanations contained in the audit documentation are understandable. In general, the supervisor is attempting to determine that the work was performed with due care and that, if necessary, the work can be reperformed or verified by another party. A common outcome of this review is a set of "review notes" prepared by the audit supervisor that are to be completed or addressed by the audit staff; these notes address the procedures performed, the referencing among audit documentation, and the appropriateness of the audit staff member's conclusions based upon the procedures performed. This review process provides evidence of compliance with the performance principle, which requires proper planning and supervision.

When this initial review has been completed, the audit manager and audit partner review the audit documentation. This review focuses more on the overall scope of the audit and whether the overall conclusions in the audit documentation are sufficient to provide support for the opinion on the financial statements.

Current GAAS require the audit documentation to be reviewed by an additional person (normally, a partner or equivalent with the firm) who has not been involved with the audit (known as an *engagement quality reviewer*). This review focuses on the significant judgments made by the engagement team and the conclusions reached by the engagement team in preparing the auditor's report. Professional standards note that this **engagement quality review** (formally known as a *second-partner review* or *concurring-partner review*) is undertaken to ensure that the quality of audit work and reporting is in keeping with the public accounting firm's quality standards. In addition, the engagement quality review provides a very high-level review of whether the evidence obtained during the audit is sufficient to support the opinion on the client's financial statements. The use of electronic audit documentation and the accompanying search capabilities has enhanced the efficiency and effectiveness of audit documentation review. Audit documentation review provides a number of benefits to the firm, including these:

- Because audit documentation is the primary evidence of the audit procedures performed and conclusions reached by auditors, the review ensures that the audit is conducted in accordance with GAAS.

- Audit documentation review provides the firm an opportunity to evaluate the overall quality of the firm's audit practices as a method of quality control.

- Audit documentation review often serves as an important component of the training and evaluation of audit staff members.

- Audit documentation review allows the firm to adhere to the performance principle, which requires that auditors adequately plan the work and properly supervise any assistants.

✅ REVIEW CHECKPOINTS

11.18 Describe the audit documentation review process in a public accounting firm.

11.19 What is an engagement quality review?

11.20 What are some of the benefits of audit documentation review to a public accounting firm?

SUBSEQUENT EVENTS AND SUBSEQUENTLY DISCOVERED FACTS

LO 11-5
Understand auditors' responsibility for subsequent events and subsequently discovered facts.

What is the auditors' responsibility for events occurring after the date of the financial statements but before the audit report is released? On February 5, 2022, after the company's fiscal year-end, **Frontier Airlines** entered into an agreement to merge with **Spirit Airlines, Inc.**[7] On one hand, because this agreement happened *after* December 31, 2021 (the date of Frontier's financial statements), it did not affect the financial position or results of operations as of December 31, 2021. However, it would clearly be misleading for Frontier to fail to disclose this proposed merger transaction if it was known prior to the issuance of its financial statements. As a result, auditors not only should evaluate the fairness of the entity's financial statements based on facts and circumstances that exist as of the date of the financial statements but also should consider the impact of events occurring after the date of the financial statements.

Subsequent Events

Events occurring between the date of the financial statements and the date of the auditor's report are referred to as **subsequent events**. The auditors' primary objective with respect to subsequent events is to ensure that any material events that affect the fairness of the client's financial statements and disclosures are properly identified and disclosed in the client's financial statements. Professional standards identify the following two types of subsequent events:

1. Events that provide additional evidence of conditions that existed *at the date of the financial statements* (e.g., the deteriorating financial condition of the client's customer that had a large accounts receivable balance at the date of the financial statements).

2. Events that provide evidence of conditions that arose *following the date of the financial statements* (e.g., a major acquisition occurring after the date of the financial statements).

Examples of subsequent event disclosures from recent SEC filings are shown in the accompanying Auditing Insight.

 AUDITING INSIGHT The Real World of Subsequent Events

The following are examples of subsequent events disclosed by companies in their footnotes to the financial statements:

- In February 2022, **Overstock.com** entered into a purchase agreement along with several other companies for Series B Preferred stock of **tZero.** Their $15 million contribution, along with the contributions of other investors, reduced their direct equity interest in tZero. They were unable to estimate how this transaction would impact the valuation of their currently owned shares of common stock in tZero.

- In February 2022, one month after their fiscal year-end, **Walmart** announced dividends declared of $2.24 per share to be paid out in 4 quarterly installments over the next fiscal year.

- In February 2022, airline company **Frontier Airlines** entered into a merger agreement with **Spirit Airlines.** The disclosure references the agreement terms, in which each share of Spirit Airlines' common stock will be converted into the right to receive 1.9126 shares of common stock of Frontier and $2.13 per share in cash.

- In February 2022, **Harley-Davidson** issued $500 million of medium-term notes maturing in Febraury 2027 and paying annual interest of 3.05 percent.

Sources: Overstock.com, Walmart, Frontier Airlines, and Harley-Davidson Inc. 10-K filings.

Auditors may learn of subsequent events through audit procedures performed in obtaining evidence related to account balances or classes of transactions. For example, the deterioration of a customer's financial condition may be identified through accounts receivable confirmations obtained after the date of the financial statements. Other procedures performed during the completion stage of the audit (such as attorney letters and written representations) may provide auditors information about the existence of

[7]In late July 2022, Spirit Airlines, Inc. terminated the merger agreement Frontier Airlines. (https://www.cnbc.com/2022/07/27/spirit-airlines-frontier-terminate-deal-that-was-marred-by-jetblues-rival-bid.html).

subsequent events. Professional standards identify the following procedures that should be performed specifically to determine whether material subsequent events exist:

- Obtain an understanding of procedures management performed to identify material subsequent events.
- Inquire of management and those charged with governance as to the existence of subsequent events. (This inquiry should subsequently be corroborated through written representations.)
- Read minutes of meetings of owners, management, or those charged with governance held after the date of the financial statements.
- Review the entity's latest interim financial statements, if applicable.

When material subsequent events are identified, auditors are required to ensure that the financial statement disclosure of these events reflects all current information and is according to GAAP. This might require adjustment to the financial statements to reflect new information (for conditions existing at the date of the financial statements) or disclosure of the information in the financial statements or footnotes accompanying the financial statements (for conditions that arose after the date of the financial statements).

Subsequently Discovered Facts

In the preceding discussion, we assumed that auditors identified material subsequent events prior to the date of the auditor's report. This assumption is noteworthy because the auditors are still conducting fieldwork and can obtain evidence regarding the appropriate presentation and disclosure of the subsequent events. However, in some situations, auditors learn of events or facts following the date of the auditor's report. The dilemma for auditors in these situations is that the fieldwork is complete, and in some cases, the financial statements and auditor's report may have been issued. Facts that become known to auditors after the date of the auditor's report that, had they been known at that time, may have caused the auditors to revise their report, are known as **subsequently discovered facts**.

The auditors' response to subsequently discovered facts depends on when the facts are identified. In some circumstances, auditors could learn of these facts *after the date of the auditor's report* but *prior to the audit report release date.* The issue this raises for the auditors is that auditing procedures have been performed only through the date of the auditor's report, yet the facts are discovered prior to the release of the financial statements and auditor's report. As a result, the financial statements, or auditor's report, or both could still be revised prior to issuance. If these facts require revision of the financial statements or footnote disclosures, auditors should perform additional procedures and evaluate the appropriateness of the disclosure of these events. One option would be to do so and change the date on the auditor's report to reflect the new (later) date. However, a disadvantage of this approach is that the auditors' responsibility for *all events* is now extended to this later date.

When facts are discovered following the date of the auditor's report but prior to the audit report release date, auditors normally choose to **dual date** the report (i.e., to give it two dates). For example, **KPMG** completed the fieldwork for the 2018 audit of **Papa Johns International** on March 8, 2019. Following the end of fieldwork date, a material weakness in internal controls over financial reporting was discovered. Therefore the date used by KPMG in the 2018 auditor's report of Papa Johns was as follows:

> March 8, 2019, except for the restatement as to the effectiveness of internal control over financial reporting for the material weaknesses related to variable interest entity and consolidation matters, as to which the date is May 7, 2019.

As this report dating noted, KPMG has taken full responsibility for all material subsequent events through March 8, 2019, except for the material weakness in internal controls. KPMG has responsibility for this event through May 7, 2019. While not the case in the KPMG example above, often times the report dating will refer to a financial statement note where more information about the dual dated event can be found.

Dual dating serves two important functions. First, it provides a way to modify the financial statements and disclosures for information discovered by auditors after the date of the auditor's report. This gives financial statement users the most complete and current set of information about the entity. Second, it limits auditors' liability for events after the date of the auditor's report to the event(s) specifically identified in the report date. In some cases (particularly if facts become known immediately before a filing deadline), auditors may choose not to evaluate the effect of subsequently discovered facts on the financial statements. In that scenario, the event should be disclosed in the footnotes to the financial statements and marked as "unaudited."

AUDITING INSIGHT   How Long Does It Take?

For S&P 500 companies fiscal 2020 year-end, the average lag between the date of the financial statements and the date of the auditor's report was 49.4 days and from the date of the auditor's report to the filing of the 10-K with the SEC was 0.25 days. Interestingly, 87.9 percent of S&P 500 companies filed their 10-K with the SEC on the same date as the date of the auditor's report.

Source: Drawn from Wharton Research Data Services *Audit Analytics* database.

Alternatively, auditors may learn of facts following the issuance of the financial statements and auditor's report. Obviously, this situation presents additional challenges because the financial statements and auditor's report have already been issued to financial statement users. If these facts would result in either the revision of the auditor's report or the financial statements and individuals continuing to rely on these financial statements, the client should take the following actions:

1. Notify individuals known to be relying on the financial statements or likely to rely on the financial statements that (a) the financial statements should not be relied upon and (b) revised financial statements and a new auditor's report will be issued.
2. Issue revised financial statements as soon as practicable with appropriate disclosure of the matter related to the subsequently discovered facts.

In the event that management refuses to take either of these actions, auditors should notify management, regulatory agencies, or any individuals known to be relying on the financial statements that the auditor's report cannot be relied upon. If auditors determine that the subsequently discovered facts would require revision to the financial statements, the nature of the matter and effect on the financial statements should also be included in the auditor's notification. The nearby Auditing Insight highlights recent examples where the audit report could not be relied upon.

AUDITING INSIGHT   Don't Rely?

- On May 2, 2019, **Kraft Heinz** filed a Form 8-K with the Securities and Exchange Commission indicating that its previously issued financial statements for fiscal 2017 and 2016 (including interim financial statements) should no longer be relied upon because of certain accounting errors and irregularities in those financial statements.
- In January 2020, **Grant Thornton** announced the withdrawal of audit reports for the 2018, 2017, and 2016 year-end for **KEW Media Group.** Grant Thornton indicated the withdrawal was due to "actions" of KEW's former CFO and they could therefore no longer rely on representations made by the CFO to them during the course of the audits.

Sources: *Kraft Heinz Form 8-K,* May 2, 2019. "KEW Media Group Announces Withdrawal of Auditor Reports," *BusinessWire,* January 15, 2020.

The audit time line and actions for subsequent events and subsequently discovered facts follow:

Year-End Date (December 31, 2023)	Date of the Auditor's Report (audit completion date) (February 15, 2024)	Audit Report Release Date (February 17, 2024)
• Perform procedures related to subsequent events • Adjust financial statements or disclose subsequent events	• Perform procedures related to subsequently discovered facts • Adjust financial statements or disclose subsequently discovered facts • Extend date of the auditor's report or dual date auditor's report on financial statements	• Request client to take action to reduce reliance on financial statements and auditor's report and reissue financial statements • If client refuses to take above actions, notify client, regulatory agencies, and users that auditor's report is not to be relied upon

☑ REVIEW CHECKPOINTS

11.21   What is a *subsequent event*?

11.22   What procedures do auditors perform to identify subsequent events?

11.23   Identify the two types of subsequent events. How should information about these events be reflected in the financial statements?

11.24   What are *subsequently discovered facts*?

11.25   What are auditors' responsibilities for subsequently discovered facts if these are identified (a) prior to the audit report release date and (b) following the audit report release date?

11.26   What is the purpose of dual dating the auditor's report?

RESPONSIBILITIES FOLLOWING THE AUDIT REPORT RELEASE DATE

LO 11-6

Identify important activities and communications following the completion of the audit and audit report release date.

Omitted Procedures

Although auditors have no responsibility to continue to review their work after the audit report release date, auditor's reports and audit documentation may be subjected to a PCAOB inspection, external peer review, or the firm's own internal inspection program as part of its system of quality control. Section 104 of Sarbanes–Oxley requires inspections to be conducted annually by the PCAOB (if the firm provides services for more than 100 issuer clients) or every three years (if the firm provides services for 100 or fewer issuer clients). These inspections could reveal situations in which an audit was not performed in accordance with generally accepted auditing standards. In particular, auditors could have failed to perform necessary audit procedures prior to the audit report release date. This situation is referred to as **omitted procedures**.

Professional standards provide guidance for such situations. If (1) the omitted procedures are important in supporting the auditor's opinion and (2) individuals are currently relying on the client's financial statements (and auditor's reports), auditor's should perform the omitted procedure or alternative procedure(s), if practicable. Assuming that the procedures allow auditors to support the previously expressed opinion, no further action is necessary. However, if they do not, auditors should formally withdraw the original opinion, issue a revised opinion, and inform persons currently relying on the financial statements.

Communications with Individuals Charged with Governance

During the engagement, matters can arise that are of such importance that they must be communicated with "individuals charged with governance." **Individuals charged with governance** are the person(s) responsible for overseeing the client's financial reporting process, including the internal control over financial reporting. Although this phrase can include the client's management and full board of directors, for issuers it is typically the audit committee of the board of directors. Audit committees are required for registrants under Sarbanes–Oxley and must be composed of only independent directors. Audit committees are an important element in the governance process because they are directly responsible for the appointment, compensation, and oversight of auditors and the audit examination.

Sections 204 and 404 of Sarbanes–Oxley both address required communications between auditors and the client's audit committee. Professional standards require auditors to communicate *(in writing) all* significant internal control deficiencies and material weaknesses to the client and individuals charged with governance. For issuers, the communication must be made prior to the audit report release date. For nonissuers, it is preferable to provide this communication prior to the audit report release date, but it should be made no later than 60 days following the audit report release date. Although auditors may decide to communicate significant deficiencies and material weaknesses to the client as they are discovered during the audit, if the client has not corrected (or remediated) these deficiencies or weaknesses, they must be communicated again in writing near the end of the audit.

For nonissuers, auditors' communication would acknowledge that the purpose of the audit is to express an opinion on the financial statements, not on internal control over financial reporting; furthermore, the communication would explicitly state that auditors are not expressing an opinion on internal control over financial reporting. For issuers subject to the reporting requirements of Sarbanes–Oxley, this communication would parallel the form and content of the auditor's report on internal control over financial reporting, which expresses an opinion on internal control over financial reporting.

In addition to internal control deficiencies, professional standards require auditors to communicate various other matters to the client. As with internal control communications, auditors ordinarily make these communications with individuals charged with governance after the audit; however, if the matters are particularly significant, they should be communicated during the audit. These communications may be made either orally or in writing (however, because of the important nature of these matters, one would anticipate that they be made in writing).

Auditors should communicate the following information to individuals charged with governance:

- Auditors' responsibility under generally accepted auditing standards.
- An overview of the planned scope and timing of the audit.
- Auditors' judgment about the quality of the client's critical accounting policies, accounting estimates, and financial statement disclosures.
- Any significant difficulties encountered during the audit.
- Any uncorrected misstatements identified during the audit other than those auditors believe to be trivial and a request to correct the misstatements.
- Any disagreements with management.
- Material, corrected misstatements that were brought to the attention of management.
- Representations requested from the client's management.
- Any management consultations with other auditors or any contentious matters about which the auditor consulted outside the engagement team that may be relevant to the oversight of the financial reporting process.
- Any significant issues arising from the audit that were discussed with management.
- The auditor's understanding of the business rationale for significant unusual transactions.
- Other findings or issues that are significant and relevant to individuals charged with governance.

Auditors also should determine that individuals charged with governance have received copies of written communications regarding material issues between auditors and management such as engagement letters, written representations, and reports on deficiencies in internal control over financial reporting. Because of its important role, auditors communicate frequently with the audit committee throughout the engagement. The accompanying Auditing Insight provides some insight into what those communications might look like.

AUDITING INSIGHT \ Audit Committee Communications—What Really Happens?

Academic studies can provide a glimpse of what communications between audit committees and auditors look like. Here's what we have learned so far:

- The most frequent issues discussed in audit committee meetings relate to accounting/auditing issues encountered in the engagement, the audit plan, the results of the audit, and other mandated disclosures (discussed in this section).

- About half of the auditors interviewed by Cohen et. al indicated that audit committees have played an important role in resolving auditor disputes with management.

- Auditors don't use the same "boilerplate" communications with audit committees; they adjust their communication style to fit the audit committee's oversight approach.

- Auditors also adjust their conversation style based on the audit committee's industry and accounting knowledge, the audit committee chair's preferred communication style, and prior interactions with the audit committee.

Source: J. Cohen, G. Krishnamoorthy, and A. Wright, "Corporate Governance in the Post-Sarbanes–Oxley Era: Auditors' Experiences," *Contemporary Accounting Research* (Fall 2010), pp. 751–786. K. Fiolleau, K. Hoang, B. Pomeroy, "Auditors' Communications with Audit Committees: Influence of the Audit Committee's Oversight Approach," *Auditing: A Journal of Practice and Theory,* (May 2019), pp. 125–150.

Management Letter

During the engagement (particularly the study and evaluation of the client's internal control over financial reporting, assessment of the risk of material misstatement, and evaluation of the effectiveness of internal control over financial reporting), auditors note matters that can be made as recommendations to the client. These recommendations may allow the client to improve the efficiency and effectiveness of their operations. Near the end of the audit, these matters are summarized in a letter (commonly referred to as the **management letter**) that is delivered to and discussed with the client. Management letters are not required by generally accepted auditing standards but are considered an important method of adding value to clients beyond that provided by the audit examination. In this spirit, some firms encourage consulting and tax professionals to participate in preparing the management letter.

Management letters are a service provided as a by-product of the audit. The management letter is an excellent opportunity to develop rapport with the client and to make the client aware of other business services offered by the public accounting firm.

Summary of Audit Communications

This text has mentioned many types of formal communications. Because you are learning the final procedures to complete the audit, this is a good place to summarize these various communications. See Exhibit 11.4 for a summary of audit correspondence other than auditor's reports on the financial statements and internal control over financial reporting (discussed in Chapter 12).

EXHIBIT 11.4 Audit Communications

Type	From	To	Timing	Reference	Method
Engagement letter	Auditors	Client	Before engagement	AU-C 210; AS 1301	Written
Acceptance letter (signed copy of engagement letter)	Client	Auditors	Before engagement	AU-C 210; AS 1301	Written
Attorney letter response	Attorney	Auditors	Near date of the auditor's reports	AU-C 501; AS 2505	Written
Written representations	Client	Auditors	Date of the auditor's reports (audit completion date)	AU-C 580; AS 2805	Written
Internal control deficiencies	Auditors	Individuals charged with governance (audit committee)	Prior to audit report release date (for issuers) or within 60 days of audit report release date (for large nonissuers)	AU-C 265; AS 1305	Written
Communications with individuals charged with governance	Auditors	Individuals charged with governance (audit committee)	After audit	AU-C 260; AS 1301	Oral or written
Management letter	Auditors	Client	After audit	None	Oral or written

---

✔ REVIEW CHECKPOINTS

11.27 What steps should auditors take if, after the audit report release date, they discover that an important audit procedure was omitted?

11.28 Identify information that auditors are required to communicate to individuals charged with governance of the client.

11.29 What is a *management letter*? Are management letters required by generally accepted auditing standards?

Summary

This chapter began by identifying four major periods during an audit: (1) prior to the date of the financial statements, (2) between the date of the financial statements and the date of the auditor's report, (3) between the date of the auditor's report and the audit report release date, and (4) following the audit report release date. As various matters are discussed, it is important to determine the time period in which auditors identify issues because this will affect auditors' responsibility for these matters.

Within the context of the four periods, the chapter discussed several aspects of completing an audit. These events include: (1) completing substantive procedures, (2) obtaining responses to attorney letters, (3) obtaining written representations, (4) evaluating the entity's ability to continue as a going concern, (5) summarizing proposed adjustments to the financial statements, (6) reviewing audit documentation, (7) considering the effects of subsequent events and subsequently discovered facts, (8) evaluating omitted audit procedures identified following the audit examination, and (9) providing communications near the end of the audit. The purpose of these procedures is to enable auditors to issue and support opinions on financial statements and internal control over financial reporting.

Key Terms

analytical procedures: Procedures that allow auditors to evaluate financial information by studying relationships among both financial and nonfinancial data. When used near the end of the audit, analytical procedures allow auditors to assess the conclusions reached during the audit and evaluate the overall financial statement presentation, 490

attorney letter: A communication prepared by the client but sent by the auditors to the client's attorneys that details all pending litigation, claims, and assessments against the client and that requests the attorneys to comment on these matters directly to the client's auditors, 493

audit report release date: The date on which auditors allow the client to use their reports in conjunction with the financial statements; also the date on which the client's financial statements are issued, 489

contingency: An existing condition, situation, or set of circumstances involving uncertainty as to possible gain or loss to an enterprise that will ultimately be resolved when one or more future events occur or fail to occur, 492

date of the auditor's report: The date on which auditors have gathered sufficient appropriate evidence on which to base their opinions on the financial statements and internal control over financial reporting; the date that will be used for the auditor's reports on clients' financial statements and internal control over financial reporting, 489

date of the financial statements: The year-end date of the latest period covered by the client's financial statements, 489

dual date: The use of two dates in the auditor's report to limit the responsibility beyond the date of the auditor's report to a specific subsequent event identified in the report, 503

engagement quality review: A review of audit documentation by an additional person (normally, a partner or equivalent with the firm who has not been involved with the audit) to ensure that the quality of the audit work and reporting is consistent with the quality standards of the public accounting firm, 501

individual(s) charged with governance: The person(s) responsible for overseeing the client's financial reporting process, including the internal control over financial reporting; individuals charged with governance may include the client's management and full board of directors, but typically refers to issuers' audit committee of the board of directors, 505

iron curtain method: The process used when evaluating the effect of uncorrected misstatements that considers the aggregate effect of current and prior misstatements in the entity's balance sheet, 499

management letter: A communication that provides a summary of auditors' recommendations resulting from the audit engagement that allows the client to improve the effectiveness and efficiency of its operations, 507

omitted procedures: The inadvertent failure of auditors to perform necessary audit procedures prior to the audit report release date, 505

roll-forward procedure(s): The procedure(s) performed by auditors to extend the conclusions from an interim date to the date of the financial statements, 490

rollover method: The process used when evaluating the effect of uncorrected misstatements that considers only the current-period income effect(s) of the potential adjustment, 499

subsequent events: Events occurring between the date of the financial statements and the date of the auditor's report, 502

subsequently discovered facts: Information that becomes known to auditors after the date of their report that, had it been known at that time, may have caused the auditors to revise their report, 503

unasserted claim: A representation that no formal lawsuit or assertion has been filed or threatened on behalf of others against the audit client but that circumstances such as a catastrophe, accident, or other physical occurrence could result in a suit or assertion being filed in the future, 494

uncorrected misstatement: A misstatement that the auditor identified and accumulated during the audit that has not been corrected (or adjusted) by the client, 498

written representation: A written assertion provided by management to auditors related to the entity's financial statements, the information provided to the auditors, and management's internal control over financial reporting to confirm certain matters and support other evidence obtained during the audit; also referred to as management representation, 495

Multiple-Choice
Questions for
Practice and
Review

 All applicable questions are available with *Connect*

LO 11-1

11.30 Which of the following best describes the role of analytical procedures near the end of the audit engagement?

a. To identify possible deficiencies in the client's internal control over financial reporting.

b. To identify accounts that appear to be misstated with the intention of planning the nature, timing, and extent of other substantive procedures.

c. To gather evidence to support one or more assertion(s) related to the account balance or class of transactions.

d. To provide an overall review of the financial information and assessment of the adequacy of evidence gathered during the audit engagement.

LO 11-3

11.31 A major objective of written representations is to

a. Shift responsibility for financial statements from the management to auditors.

b. Provide a substitute source of audit evidence for substantive procedures that auditors would otherwise perform.

c. Provide management an opportunity to make assertions about the quantity and valuation of the physical inventory.

d. Impress on management its ultimate responsibility for the financial statements and disclosures.

LO 11-2

11.32 Which of these substantive procedures is *not* used to obtain evidence about contingencies?

a. Scanning expense accounts for credit entries.

b. Obtaining a letter from the client's attorney.

c. Reading the minutes of the board of directors' meetings.

d. Examining terms of sale in sales contracts.

LO 11-5

11.33 Subsequent knowledge of which of the following would cause the entity to adjust its December 31 financial statements?

a. Sale of an issue of new stock for $500,000 on January 30.

b. Settlement of a damage lawsuit for a customer's injury sustained February 15 for $10,000.

c. Settlement of litigation in February for $100,000 that had been estimated at $12,000 in the December 31 financial statements.

d. Storm damage of $1 million to the entity's buildings on March 1.

LO 11-5

11.34 J. Griffith audited the financial statements of Mets Magnificent Corporation for the year ended December 31, 2023. She completed gathering sufficient appropriate evidence on January 30 and later learned of a stock split voted by the board of directors on February 5. The financial statements were changed to reflect the split, and she now needs to dual date the report on the entity's financial statements. Which of the following is the proper form?

a. December 31, 2023, except as to Note X, which is dated January 30, 2024.

b. January 30, 2024, except as to Note X, which is dated February 5, 2024.

c. December 31, 2023, except as to Note X, which is dated February 5, 2024.

d. February 5, 2024, except for the date of the auditor's report, for which the date is January 30, 2024.

LO 11-5

11.35 Auditors have a responsibility related to management's disclosure of new information related to subsequent events until

a. The date of the financial statements.

b. The date of the auditor's report.

c. The audit report release date.

d. The following year's date of the financial statements.

LO 11-5 11.36 The auditing standards regarding subsequently discovered facts refer to knowledge obtained after
  a. The date the fieldwork began.
  b. The date of the auditor's report.
  c. The date of the financial statements.
  d. The date interim audit work was complete.

LO 11-6 11.37 Which of the following is *not* required by generally accepted auditing standards?
  a. Written representations
  b. Attorney letter
  c. Management letter
  d. Engagement letter

LO 11-6 11.38 Which of the following is ordinarily performed *last* in the audit examination?
  a. Securing a signed engagement letter from the client.
  b. Performing tests of controls.
  c. Performing a review for subsequent events.
  d. Obtaining signed written representations.

LO 11-1 11.39 Which of the following normally occurs *earliest* in the audit examination?
  a. Discovery of an omitted audit procedure.
  b. Dual dating the auditor's report on the entity's financial statements for subsequent events that exist at the date of the financial statements.
  c. Preparation of the management letter.
  d. Review of audit documentation.

LO 11-5 11.40 Ambrose is auditing the financial statements of Mays (dated December 31, 2023). The date of the auditor's report is February 17, 2024, and the audit report release date is February 20, 2024. For which of the following matters would Ambrose have the *least* responsibility?
  a. The obsolescence of inventory held on December 31, 2023, that was identified on January 20, 2024.
  b. A customer's deteriorating financial condition that was identified on February 19, 2024.
  c. A merger that was announced by Mays and known by Ambrose on February 12, 2024.
  d. A major loss due to a catastrophe that occurred and was known by Ambrose on March 1, 2024.

LO 11-2 11.41 Which of the following statements is *most likely* to be included in an attorney letter?
  a. "Certain representations in this letter are described as being limited to matters that are material."
  b. "If any unasserted claims or assessments are omitted from this disclosure, please provide this information directly to our auditors."
  c. "Our work enabled us to notice some actions that could enhance the profitability of the Company."
  d. "Please furnish to our auditors such explanation, if any, that you consider necessary to supplement the foregoing information."

LO 11-6 11.42 After the audit report release date, auditors determine that an important auditing procedure was omitted. Which of the following initial courses of action is most appropriate?
  a. Perform the omitted procedure or an alternative procedure.
  b. Notify the board of directors and regulatory agencies that are currently relying on auditor's reports.
  c. Determine whether the omitted procedure is important in supporting the auditor's opinion on the entity's financial statements.
  d. Engage another public accounting firm to conduct a quality assurance review.

LO 11-3 11.43 Which of the following statements is *not* true with respect to written representations?
  a. The failure of management to furnish them is a significant scope limitation, resulting in either an adverse opinion or a disclaimer of opinion.

b. They should address management's responsibility for designing internal control to prevent and detect fraud.

c. Auditors use them to corroborate information received during the audit from the client and its employees.

d. They are dated the same date as the auditor's report.

LO 11-3

11.44 Hall accepted an engagement to audit the year 1 financial statements of XYZ Company. XYZ completed the preparation of the year 1 financial statements on February 13, year 2, and its auditors began the fieldwork on February 17, year 2. Hall completed gathering sufficient appropriate evidence on March 24, year 2; Hall's report and XYZ's financial statements were released on March 28, year 2. The written representations normally would be dated

a. February 13, year 2.

b. February 17, year 2.

c. March 24, year 2.

d. March 28, year 2.

(AICPA adapted)

LO 11-2

11.45 What is an auditor's *primary* method to corroborate information on litigation, claims, and assessments?

a. Examining legal invoices sent by the client's attorney.

b. Verifying attorney–client privilege through interviews.

c. Reviewing the response from the client's lawyer to a letter of audit inquiry.

d. Reviewing the written representation letter obtained from management.

(AICPA adapted)

LO 11-5

11.46 Which of the following substantive procedures should auditors ordinarily perform regarding subsequent events?

a. Compare the latest available interim financial statements with the financial statements being audited.

b. Send second requests to the client's customers who failed to respond to initial accounts receivable confirmation requests.

c. Communicate material weaknesses in internal control over financial reporting to the client's audit committee.

d. Review the cutoff bank statements for several months after the date of the financial statements.

(AICPA adapted)

LO 11-5

11.47 Which of the following substantive procedures would auditors most likely perform to obtain evidence about the occurrence of subsequent events?

a. Recompute a sample of large-dollar transactions occurring after the date of the financial statements for arithmetic accuracy.

b. Investigate changes in shareholders' equity occurring after the date of the financial statements.

c. Send confirmations to vendors with whom the client normally does business but for which no balance in accounts payable is noted.

d. Confirm bank accounts established after the date of the financial statements.

(AICPA adapted)

LO 11-2

11.48 The primary reason auditors request responses to attorney letters is to provide auditors

a. The probable outcome of asserted claims and pending or threatened litigation.

b. Corroboration of the information furnished by management about litigation, claims, and assessments.

c. The attorney's opinions of the client's historical experiences in recent similar litigation.

d. A description and evaluation of litigation, claims, and assessments that existed at the date of the financial statements.

(AICPA adapted)

LO 11-2

11.49 The scope of an audit is *not* restricted when an attorney letter limits the response to

    a. Matters to which the attorney has given substantive attention in the form of legal representation.

    b. An evaluation of the likelihood of an unfavorable outcome of the matters disclosed by the entity.

    c. The attorney's opinion of the entity's historical experience in recent similar litigation.

    d. The probable outcome of asserted claims and pending or threatened litigation.

(AICPA adapted)

LO 11-4

11.50 Lee and Kerzman is the auditor for Nance Corporation. During the course of the audit, the audit team noticed that Nance Corporation showed signs of financial distress. In particular, Nance Corporation was at risk for defaulting on several key loans and had therefore begun the process of restructuring their debt. This, among other indicators, led the audit team to have substantial doubt regarding Nance Corporation's ability to continue as a going concern. The next step the team should take is to

    a. Do nothing, as the auditors have no responsibility related to going concern assessments.

    b. Obtain and discuss with management their plan to continue as a going concern and assess the likelihood the plan will be successful.

    c. Issue an unmodified opinion with a separate *Substantial Doubt About the Entity's Ability to Continue as a Going Concern* section discussing Nance Corporation's ability to continue as a going concern.

    d. Resign from the engagement.

LO 11-4

11.51 What does the auditor need to document when there is substantial doubt that a client will continue as a going concern?

    a. The conditions or events that suggest there is a going concern uncertainty.

    b. Management's plan (or lack thereof) to mitigate the conditions and to continue as a going concern.

    c. The auditor's conclusion on whether, after evaluating management's plan, substantial doubt exists regarding the company's ability to continue as a going concern and whether any report modifications are needed.

    d. All of the above.

Exercises, Problems, and Simulations

 All applicable questions are available with *Connect*

LO 11-3

11.52 **Written Representations.** Hart, an assistant accountant with the firm of Better & Best, CPAs, is auditing the financial statements of Tech Consolidated Industries Inc. The firm's audit plan calls for the preparation of written representations.

Required:

    a. In an audit of financial statements, in what circumstances are auditors required to obtain written representations?

    b. What are the major categories of items covered by written representations?

    c. To whom should the representations be addressed and as of what date should they be dated?

    d. Who should sign the representations, and what would be the effect of a refusal to sign them?

    e. In what respects may auditors' other responsibilities be relieved by obtaining written representations?

(AICPA adapted)

LO 11-3

11.53 **Written Representations Omissions.** During the audit of the annual financial statements of Amis Manufacturing Inc., the company's president, Vance Molar, and the engagement partner, Wanda Dweebins, reviewed matters that were supposed to be included in written representations. Amis Manufacturing is a nonissuer. Upon receipt of the following representations, Dweebins contacted Molar to state that they were incomplete.

To John & Wayne, CPAs:

In connection with your examination of the balance sheet of Amis Manufacturing Inc., as of December 31, 2023, and the related statements of income, retained earnings, and cash flows for the year then ended, for the purpose of expressing an opinion on whether the financial statements present fairly the financial position, results of operations, and cash flows of Amis Manufacturing Inc., in conformity with generally accepted accounting principles, we confirm, to the best of our knowledge and belief, the following representations made to you during your audit. There were no

- Plans or intentions that could materially affect the carrying value or classification of assets or liabilities.
- Communications from regulatory agencies concerning noncompliance with, or deficiencies in, financial reporting practices.
- Agreements to repurchase assets previously sold.
- Violations or possible violations of laws or regulations whose effects should be considered for disclosure in the financial statements or as a basis for recording a contingent liability.
- Unasserted claims or assessments that our lawyer has advised are probable of assertion that must be disclosed in accordance with *Accounting Standards Codification (ASC) 450*.
- Capital stock purchase options or agreements or capital stock reserved for options, warrants, conversions, or other requirements.
- Compensating balance or other arrangements involving restrictions on cash balances.

Vance Molar, President

Amis Manufacturing Inc.
March 14, 2024

Required:

Identify the other matters that Molar's representations should specifically confirm.

(AICPA adapted)

LO 11-3

11.54 **Written Representations.** Each of the following statements is a communication from management. Indicate whether the inclusion of each statement in written representations is appropriate. Provide your rationale for any statements whose inclusion in written representations is *not* appropriate.

a. "Certain representations in this letter are described as being limited to matters that are material."

b. "No frauds involving management, employees who have significant roles in internal control over financial reporting, or other frauds that could have a material effect on the financial statements have occurred during the year under audit."

c. "Based on our assessment, we conclude that the Company has maintained an effective internal control over financial reporting as of December 31, 2023."

d. "We have prepared a description and evaluation of certain contingencies for which our attorneys have devoted substantive attention on our behalf in the form of legal representation."

e. "There are no significant deficiencies, including material weaknesses, in the design or operation of internal controls that could adversely affect our ability to record, process, summarize, and report financial data."

f. "Summarized below are important actions taken in response to comments provided by you in the management letter dated March 22, 2024, based on your prior audit."

g. "Our assessment of internal control over financial reporting provides us absolute assurance that no material misstatements will occur and be undetected by our internal control."

h. "We have made available to you all financial records and related data."

LO 11-3

11.55 **Written Representations.** Classify each of the following issues according to whether they will be (1) included in written representations in all audits, (2) included in written representations in audits of issuers (under PCAOB standards), or (3) not included in written representations:

a. Management acknowledgment of its responsibility for the fairness of the financial statements in accordance with U.S. GAAP.

b. A list of pending or threatened litigation, claims, or assessments currently outstanding against the client.

c. A description of recommendations that allow the client to improve the efficiency and effectiveness of its operations.

d. Availability of all financial records and related data.

e. Information related to the presentation and disclosure of items within the financial statements.

f. Disclosure of all significant deficiencies and material weaknesses in internal control over financial reporting.

g. Information concerning fraud involving management and employees who have significant roles in internal control over financial reporting.

h. Auditors' judgment about the quality of the client's accounting principles.

i. Management's conclusion about the effectiveness of its internal control over financial reporting.

j. A statement that the financial statements are prepared according to U.S. GAAP.

LO 11-2

11.56 **Client Request for Attorney Letter.** The firm of Cole & Cole, CPAs, is auditing the financial statements of Consolidated Industries Co. for the year ended December 31, 2023. On March 6, 2024, C. R. Brown, Consolidated's chief financial officer, gave the auditors a draft of an attorney letter for Cole's review before mailing it to J. J. Young, Consolidated's outside counsel. This letter is intended to elicit the attorneys' responses to corroborate information furnished to the auditors by management concerning pending and threatened litigation, claims, assessments, and unasserted claims and assessments.

March 6, 2024

J. J. Young, Attorney at Law
123 Main Street, Anytown, USA

Dear J. J. Young:

In connection with an audit of our financial statements at December 31, 2023, and for the year then ended, management of the Company has prepared, and furnished to our auditors, Cole & Cole, CPAs, a description and evaluation of certain contingencies, including those set forth below, involving matters with respect to which you have been engaged and to which you have devoted substantive attention on behalf of the Company in the form of legal consultation or representation. Your response should include matters that existed at December 31, 2023. Because of the confidentiality of all these matters, your response may be limited.

In November 2023, an action was brought against the Company by an outside salesman alleging breach of contract for sales commissions and asking an accounting with respect to claims for fees and commissions. The causes of action claim damages of $3,000,000, but the Company believes it has meritorious defenses to the claims. The possible exposure of the Company to a successful judgment on behalf of the plaintiff is slight.

In July 2023, an action was brought against the Company by Industrial Manufacturing Company (Industrial) alleging patent infringement and seeking damages of $20,000,000. On October 16, 2020, the U.S. District Court decided that the Company had infringed on seven Industrial patents and awarded damages of $14,000,000. The Company vigorously denies these allegations and has filed an appeal with the U.S. Court of Appeals. The appeal process is expected to take approximately two years, but there is some chance that Industrial may ultimately prevail.

Please furnish to our auditors such explanation, if any, that you consider necessary to supplement this information, including an explanation of those matters as to which your views may differ from those stated, and an identification of the omission of any pending or threatened litigation, claims, and assessments or a statement that the list of such matters is complete. Your response may be quoted or referred to in the financial statements without further correspondence with you.

You also consulted on various other matters considered to be pending or threatened litigation. However, you may not comment on these matters because publicizing them may alert potential plaintiffs to the strengths of their cases. In addition, various other matters probable of assertion that have some chance of an unfavorable outcome, as of December 31, 2023, are presently considered unasserted claims and assessments.

Respectfully,

C. R. Brown
Chief Financial Officer

Required:

Describe the omissions, ambiguities, and inappropriate statements and terminology in Brown's letter. Remember that this is Brown's letter requesting a response to auditors, but it must request responses in the manner most useful to auditors.

(AICPA adapted)

LO 11-2

11.57 Attorney Letters. Faye Jaworski, CPA, is auditing the financial statements of Fulbright Company. As she is nearing the audit completion date, Jaworski realizes that she needs to evaluate whether all material contingencies are properly accounted for and disclosed in Fulbright's financial statements. Because of its size, Fulbright has retained external counsel (Vinson, LLP) to handle its various legal matters.

Required:

a. List some common procedures that Jaworski will perform with respect to Fulbright's litigation, claims, and assessments.

b. What are the responsibilities of Jaworski, Fulbright, and Vinson with respect to litigation, claims, and assessments?

c. Attorney letters are used to provide corroboration of litigation, claims, and assessments against the client. Briefly describe the process through which attorney letters are prepared, sent, and used in the audit examination.

d. What information is normally included in an attorney letter?

LO 11-4

11.58 Uncorrected Misstatements and Performance Materiality. Aaron Rivers, CPA, is auditing the financial statements of Charger Company, a client for the past five years. During past audits of Charger, Rivers identified some immaterial misstatements (most of which relate to isolated matters and do not have common characteristics). A summary of these misstatements follows. (To illustrate, in 2018, the misstatements would have reduced net income by $13,200 if corrected:)

Year	Effect on Net Income	Effect on Assets	Effect on Liabilities	Effect on Equity
2018	($13,200)	($20,000)	($6,800)	($13,200)
2019	5,000	12,000	7,000	5,000
2020	(9,250)	(11,000)	(1,750)	(9,250)
2021	(2,000)	(5,500)	(3,500)	(2,000)
2022	1,000	1,000	0	1,000

During the most recent audit, Rivers concluded that service revenue totaling $11,000 was recognized as of December 31, 2023 and it did not meet the criteria for recognition until 2024. When Rivers discussed this issue with Chris Turner, Charger Company's chief financial officer, Turner asked Rivers about the performance materiality level used in the audit, which was $25,000. Upon learning of this, Turner remarked, "Then there's no need to worry . . . it's not a material amount. Why should we bother with this item?"

Required:

a. How does the misstatement identified in 2023 affect net income, assets, liabilities, and equity in 2023? (Assume a 21 percent tax rate for Charger.)

b. Comment upon Turner's remark to Rivers. Is Turner's reasoning correct?

c. Upon doing some research, Rivers learned of the rollover method and iron curtain method for evaluating the performance materiality of misstatements. Briefly define each of these methods.

d. How would Rivers evaluate the performance materiality of the $11,000 sales cutoff error in 2023 under the *rollover method* and *iron curtain method?*

e. Based on your response to part (d), what adjustments (if any) would Rivers propose to Charger Company's financial statements under the rollover method and iron curtain method?

LO 11-4

11.59 Uncorrected Misstatements and Performance Materiality. During the conduct of an audit, auditors may identify misstatements as a result of the completion of their substantive procedures. An important activity performed in the completion stages of the audit is considering the materiality of misstatements identified during the audit.

Required:

a. What is an *uncorrected misstatement*? What is the auditors' responsibility for uncorrected misstatements during the completion stage of the audit engagement?

Because of an important deadline for submitting the financial statements to lenders for evaluation, Raider did not modify its financial statements for the preceding events despite the fact that they were material. Raider's justification was that because the events occurred after the date of the financial statements, they were not required to be disclosed in the financial statements. Ralph acquiesced to Raider's wishes and did not modify the report on Raider's financial statements.

b. On March 16, 2024, Ralph initially learned of the following events affecting Raider Company, neither of which was disclosed in Raider's financial statements:

(1) Raider Company declared a significant dividend payable to its shareholders. This dividend was declared on March 14, 2024, to be paid to Raider's shareholders of record on May 16, 2024.

(2) Raider Company activated a portion of its line of credit on February 1, 2024, by borrowing $2.5 million. This additional obligation increased Raider Company's long-term liabilities by 10 percent.

c. Reviewing Ralph's audit documentation, it does not appear that any tests were conducted to evaluate the need for impairment of the carrying value of Raider Company's property, plant, and equipment.

Required:

For each of the preceding items, describe what actions Ralph should take after the firm's quality review identified these issues.

LO 11-3, 11-4, 11-5, 11-6

11.69 **Various Completion Matters.** For each of the following independent situations, describe the most appropriate course of action that the auditors should take:

a. Drew Allison is conducting the audit of Anderson Inc. as of December 31, 2023. At the beginning of the evidence gathering, Allison becomes aware that one of Anderson's major customers (Jones) is experiencing significant financial difficulties. Jones normally accounts for 5 percent of Anderson's net sales. After performing the necessary procedures, Allison believes that $2.8 million of Jones's receivable balance will ultimately become uncollectible. Allison further believes this amount is material to Anderson's financial condition and results of operations.

b. Nagan Carmelo is completing the December 31, 2023, audit of Nugget Company. As part of the final procedures, Carmelo has requested representations from Nugget's management regarding their assertion as to the fairness of the financial statements and other important matters addressed by professional standards. Because Nugget's management is attending an analyst briefing in the upcoming week, Carmelo receives these signed representations dated February 6, 2024. Carmelo has a few remaining items to complete, does so, and dates the auditor's report February 9, 2024.

c. Pat Colt completed the December 31, 2023, audit of Manning and issued an unmodified opinion on Manning's financial statements dated March 15, 2024. Colt's opinion was released, along with Manning's financial statements, on March 21, 2024. During a review of Manning's first quarter 10-Q in late April, Colt became aware of the company's settlement with a customer over a product warranty lawsuit; this case had been settled on March 13, 2024. Although Colt had received the necessary letter from Manning's attorneys, the letter arrived prior to the settlement of the case and did not mention this development. After reviewing the information related to the settlement, Colt does not believe that the settlement is material to Manning's financial condition or results of operations and believes the opinion on Manning's financial statements is still supportable.

d. Cameron Alta completed the December 31, 2023, audit of Saxe Company on February 10, 2024. Saxe is planning to release its financial statements, along with Alta's opinion on these financial statements and internal control over financial reporting, on February 17, 2024. On February 12, 2024, a flood in one of Saxe's warehouses located in the Gulf Coast region destroyed more than $10 million of inventory. Although the extent to which this loss is recoverable through Saxe's insurance is uncertain at this time, Alta believes that this loss could have a material impact on Saxe's financial condition and results of operations.

e. During the audit of Glomco, Angel Myron identified a number of misstatements. These misstatements are not material in dollar amount, do not appear to represent any discernable pattern, and do not represent fraudulent activity. As a result, Myron has decided that Glomco's financial statements do not need to be adjusted to reflect the effect of these misstatements.

f. Following the completion of the 2023 audit of Blankenship Corporation and release of the financial statements and auditor's reports, Reese Jill met with the manager to conduct a postmortem on the engagement and identify how changes in Blankenship's operations noted during the most recent audit may affect future audits. During this review, Jill became aware that Blankenship's process for evaluating goodwill related to an acquisition made by Blankenship during the most recent year for potential impairment had not been considered. Jill believes that the omitted procedure is important in supporting the opinion on Blankenship's financial statements and that users continue to rely on the financial statements and the auditor's reports.

LO 11-2

11.70 **Attorney Letter Responses.** Omega Corporation is involved in a lawsuit brought by a competitor for patent infringement. The competitor is asking $14 million actual damages for lost profits and unspecified punitive damages. The lawsuit has been in progress for 15 months, and Omega has worked closely with its outside counsel preparing its defense. Omega recently requested its outside attorneys with the firm of Wolfe & Goodwin to provide information to its auditors.

The managing partner of Wolfe & Goodwin asked four different lawyers who have worked on the case to prepare a concise response to auditors. The auditors received these responses from the lawyers:

1. The action involves unique characteristics in which authoritative legal precedents bearing directly on the plaintiff's claims do not seem to exist. We believe the plaintiff will have serious problems establishing Omega's liability; nevertheless, if the plaintiff is successful, the damage award may be substantial.

2. In our opinion, Omega will be able to defend this action successfully, but, if not, the possible liability to Omega in this proceeding is nominal in amount.

3. We believe the plaintiff's case against Omega is without merit.

4. In our opinion, Omega will be able to assert meritorious defenses and has a reasonable chance of sustaining an adequate defense with a possible outcome of settling the case for less than the damages claimed.

Required:

a. Interpret each of the four responses separately. Decide whether each is (1) adequate to conclude that the likelihood of an adverse outcome is "remote," requiring no disclosure in financial statements or (2) too vague to serve as adequate information for a decision, requiring more information from the lawyers or from management.

b. What response do you think auditors would receive if they asked the plaintiff's counsel about the likely outcome of the lawsuit? Discuss.

LO 11-2

11.71 **Accounting for a Contingency: Attorney Letter Information.** Central City was involved in litigation brought by Mexican American Legal Defense and Educational Fund (MALDEF) over the creation of single-member voting districts (which require candidates to receive only the highest number of votes, even if not a majority) for city council positions. Auditors were working on the financial statements for the year ended December 31, 2023, and had almost completed gathering sufficient appropriate evidence by February 12, 2024.

The court heard final arguments on February 1 and rendered its judgment on February 10. The ruling was in favor of MALDEF and required the creation of certain single-member voting districts. This ruling did not impose a monetary loss on Central City, but the court also ruled that MALDEF would be awarded a judgment of court costs and attorney fees to be paid by Central City.

Local newspaper reports stated that MALDEF would seek a $250,000 recovery from the city. Auditors obtained an attorney letter dated February 15 that stated the following: In my opinion, the court will award some amount for MALDEF's attorney fees. In regard to your inquiry about an amount or range of possible loss, I estimate that such an award could be anywhere from $30,000 to $175,000.

Required:

    a. What weight should be given to the newspaper report of the $250,000 amount that MALDEF might ask? What weight should be given to the attorney's estimate?

    b. How should this subsequent event be reflected in the 2023 financial statements of Central City?

Apollo Shoes

Completing the Audit

You are a recently promoted senior (in charge) auditor for Anderson, Olds, and Watershed and have been assigned to the engagement team of a new audit client, Apollo Shoes Inc. You have been asked to help in performing procedures related to wrapping up the audit. Detailed instructions for performing the wrap-up procedures, as well as working papers, can be found in *Connect*.

CHAPTER 12

Reports on Audited Financial Statements

As discussed in Note 2 to the consolidated financial statements, the ongoing effects of COVID-19 on the Company's operations and global bookings have had, and will continue to have, a significant impact on the Company's financial results and liquidity. Further, subsequent to February 2022, the Company will require additional liquidity to meet ongoing obligations, including debt amortization payments and ship milestone payments that are due in April 2022, in order to maintain minimum liquidity covenant requirements. Management's evaluation of the events and conditions and management's plans to mitigate these matters are also described in Note 2.

Excerpt from PwC's audit report for Norwegian Cruise Lines (dated February 26, 2021)

Professional Standards References

Topic	AU-C/ISA Section	AS Section
Going Concern	570	2415
Audits of Group Financial Statements	600	1205
Reporting on Financial Statements	700	3101
Communicating Key/Critical Audit Matters	701	3101
Modifications to Reports on Financial Statements	705	3105
Emphasis-of-Matter and Other-Matter Paragraphs	706	3101
Consistency	708	2820
Other Information	720	2710
Supplementary Information	725	2701
Required Supplementary Information	730	2705
Special Purpose Frameworks	800	3305
Elements, Accounts, or Items of Financial Statements	805	3305
Compliance with Contractual and Regulatory Requirements	806	3305
Summary Financial Statements	810	3315
Integrated Audit of Internal Control over Financial Reporting	N/A	2201

LEARNING OBJECTIVES

Management has the primary responsibility for the presentation of financial statements in accordance with generally accepted accounting principles (GAAP) or other applicable reporting frameworks. Following the substantive procedures, auditors express an opinion on the fairness of these financial statements, which represent the culmination of the audit examination.

Your objectives are to be able to

LO 12-1 Understand the types of reports that accompany an entity's financial statements and the content of the auditors' standard (unmodified) report.

LO 12-2 Identify situations in which language in the standard (unmodified) report is modified and the type of opinion issued in those situations.

LO 12-3 Identify situations in which auditors add explanatory language to an unmodified opinion.

LO 12-4 Understand the auditors' responsibility for reporting on financial statements presented in comparative form.

LO 12-5 Identify other reporting considerations related to GAAS audits.

LO 12-6 Understand the contents of the auditors' report for the financial statements of issuers (Appendix 12A).

INTRODUCTION

Like many companies in the travel and leisure industry, **Norwegian Cruise Lines** was significantly affected by COVID-19, with its operations being shut down through most of 2020 following the onset of the pandemic. The effect of COVID-19 on Norwegian and one of its competitors (**Carnival Cruise Lines**) can be clearly seen in their financial statements, as follows (all amounts other than liabilities-to-assets in billions):

	Norwegian Cruise Lines		Carnival Cruise Lines	
	2019	2020	2019	2020
Revenues	$6.5	$1.3	$20.8	$5.6
Operating income	$1.2	($3.4)	$3.3	($8.9)
Net income	$0.9	($4.0)	$3.0	($10.2)
Cash flow from operations	$1.8	($2.6)	$5.4	($6.3)
Liabilities-to-assets	0.60	0.76	0.44	0.61

Sources: *Norwegian Cruise Lines Holdings Form 10-K* (filed February 26, 2021); *Carnival Corp Form 10-K* (filed January 26, 2021).

In their audits of Norwegian Cruise Lines and Carnival Cruise Lines, **PwC** concluded that their financial statements were prepared in accordance with generally accepted accounting principles (GAAP). However, because of the effect of COVID-19 on 2020 operations, as well as the potential effect on both companies' future operations, PwC's audit report included an additional paragraph (labeled "Emphasis of Matter") related to COVID-19 (see the introductory quote to this chapter).

EY referenced COVID-19 and its potential negative effect on future operations in its opinion on **AMC Entertainment Holdings'** financial statements. However, even though the significant negative current financial and potential future impacts of COVID-19 were identified by **Wynn Resorts** (audited by EY), **Marriott International** (EY), **Disney** (PwC), and **American Airlines (KPMG)** in their Form 10-Ks, the audit reports for these companies did not reference potential future impacts of COVID-19. In all cases, the audit opinion concluded that these companies' financial statements were presented in accordance with GAAP.

The 'above vignette illustrate the type of information communicated in auditors' reports. While the primary role of the report is to address whether the financial statements are presented in accordance with GAAP, when appropriate the audit report also provides users of financial statements with other information related to the company. In addition, both the PCAOB and AICPA revised their auditors' reports to include disclosure of important issues that involve challenging, subjective, or complex auditor judgment relating to material accounts and disclosures (known as *critical audit matters,* or *key audit matters*). COVID-19 was referenced as a critical audit matter in over 12 percent of all auditors' reports issued in the fiscal year immediately following March 1, 2020 (which coincided with the onset of COVID-19 in the United States).[1]

OVERVIEW OF AUDITORS' REPORTS

LO 12-1

Understand the types of reports that accompany an entity's financial statements and the content of the auditors' standard (unmodified) report.

Because the entity's management is responsible for preparing its financial statements, the auditors' examination (and report on that examination) plays an important role in users' ability to rely on the financial statements when making economic decisions. **Issuers**, or public entities (those entities that offer registered securities for sale to the general public) are required to file certain financial information with the Securities and Exchange Commission (SEC) within 60 to 90 days (depending upon their size) of their fiscal year-end. This information, which includes audited financial statements, footnotes, and other required disclosures related to the financial statements, is filed using Form 10-K.

In contrast, **nonissuers** (or nonpublic entities) are not subject to these filing or audit requirements. However, third-party users may demand audited financial statements as a condition for certain lending or investing activities or for use in monitoring the entity's activities. In addition, regulatory bodies other than the SEC may require audits for governmental and other types of nonissuers.

For both issuers and nonissuers, the auditors' report on financial statements and related disclosures provides (or disclaims) an opinion on whether the entity's financial statements and related disclosures are presented in accordance with GAAP. This opinion is based on the tests of controls and substantive procedures that have been performed during the audit engagement and discussed throughout this text.

In addition to the auditors' report on financial statements and related disclosures, issuers are subject to additional reporting requirements. The Sarbanes-Oxley Act of 2002 and professional standards have mandated two additional types of reports:[2]

1. A report, prepared by the entity's management, on the effectiveness of the entity's internal control over financial reporting.

2. A report, prepared by the auditors, on the effectiveness of the entity's internal control over financial reporting.

The following is a summary of the reports that accompany an entity's financial statements. The focus of this chapter is on the auditors' report on financial statements and related disclosures for nonissuers; auditors' reports on the financial statements for issuers are discussed in Appendix 12A. (While less common, nonissuers may request reports on internal control over financial reporting.)

Type of Entity	Report(s)
Issuer	Mandatory reports on • Effectiveness of internal control over financial reporting (prepared by management) • Effectiveness of internal control over financial reporting (prepared by auditors) • Fairness of financial statements and related disclosures (prepared by auditors)
Nonissuer	Fairness of financial statements and related disclosures based on user demand (prepared by auditors)

[1] *Insights from COVID-19 References in CAMs,* Audit Analytics, March 31, 2021 (online source).
[2] Issuers with an aggregate market value of voting and nonvoting common equity of less than $75 million (known as nonaccelerated filers) are required to have management reports on internal control over financial reporting but not auditor engagements or reports on internal control over financial reporting.

The Standard Report for Nonissuers

The auditors' report on the financial statements expresses an opinion on whether the financial statements present the entity's financial position, results of operations, and cash flows in accordance with GAAP (or other applicable financial reporting framework). The report should be titled *independent auditor's report* (or other suitable title stressing the independence of the auditors). The report is typically addressed to the board of directors and shareholders but may also be addressed to an individual lender, creditor, or investor who requested the audit.

Because the Auditing Standards Board (ASB) prescribes the format and contents of the report for nonissuers, these reports are sometimes referred to as the *Auditing Standards Board* (or *ASB) Report.* See Exhibit 12.1 for an example of a standard (unmodified) report issued for a nonissuer. The report in Exhibit 12.1 is appropriate when no material issues are encountered during the audit and the financial statements are prepared in accordance with GAAP.[3]

All standard (unmodified) reports contain the following major sections:

1. *Opinion.* This section identifies the financial statements and years examined by the audit team and the opinion on the financial statements. The report in Exhibit 12.1 identifies the balance sheet, income statement, statement of changes in shareholders' equity, and statement of cash flows for the year ended December 31, 2023, as the financial statements and years examined. The auditors' opinion is that these financial statements are prepared in accordance with GAAP.

2. *Basis for Opinion.* This section indicates that the audit was conducted according to GAAS, the auditors were independent and met other ethical responsibilities, and that the audit evidence provides a basis for the opinion.

3. *Responsibilities of Management for the Financial Statements.* This section identifies the management's responsibility for both the fairness of the financial statements and the design, implementation, and maintenance of internal control. In addition, this section discloses management's responsibility to evaluate whether substantial doubt exists about the entity's ability to continue as a going concern.

4. *Auditor's Responsibilities for the Audit of the Financial Statements.* This section discusses the audit team's responsibility to obtain reasonable assurance regarding the fairness of the financial statements, identifies several important components of a GAAS audit, and discusses the audit team's responsibility to communicate matters to those charged with governance.

Following the *Auditor's Responsibilities for the Audit of the Financial Statements* section, the auditors' report should:

- Be signed using the firm's name.
- Identify the city and state of the firm's office.
- Be dated using the date when the audit team has obtained sufficient appropriate evidence to support the opinion (the **date of the auditors' report**).

[3]The report shown in Exhibit 12.1 does not include references to other information or supplementary information presented with the financial statements that may be required under professional standards for reporting.

EXHIBIT 12.1   Standard (Unmodified) Report for Nonissuer

Independent Auditor's Report

To the Board of Directors and Shareholders of Dunder-Mifflin, Inc.

Report on the Audit of the Financial Statements

Opinion

We have audited the financial statements of Dunder-Mifflin, Inc., which comprise the balance sheet as of December 31, 2023, and the related statements of income, changes in stockholders' equity, and cash flows for the year then ended, and the related notes to the financial statements.

In our opinion, the accompanying financial statements present fairly, in all material respects, the financial position of Dunder-Mifflin, Inc. as of December 31, 2023, and the results of its operations and its cash flows for the year then ended in accordance with accounting principles generally accepted in the United States of America.

Basis for Opinion

We conducted our audit in accordance with auditing standards generally accepted in the United States of America (GAAS). Our responsibilities under those standards are further described in the Auditor's Responsibilities for the Audit of the Financial Statements section of our report. We are required to be independent of Dunder-Mifflin, Inc. and to meet our other ethical responsibilities, in accordance with the relevant ethical requirements relating to our audit. We believe that the audit evidence we have obtained is sufficient and appropriate to provide a basis for our audit opinion.

Responsibilities of Management for the Financial Statements

Management is responsible for the preparation and fair presentation of the financial statements in accordance with accounting principles generally accepted in the United States of America, and for the design, implementation, and maintenance of internal control relevant to the preparation and fair presentation of financial statements that are free from material misstatement, whether due to fraud or error.

In preparing the financial statements, management is required to evaluate whether there are conditions or events, considered in the aggregate, that raise substantial doubt about Dunder-Mifflin, Inc.'s ability to continue as a going concern for one year following the issuance of the financial statements.

Auditor's Responsibilities for the Audit of the Financial Statements

Our objectives are to obtain reasonable assurance about whether the financial statements as a whole are free from material misstatement, whether due to fraud or error, and to issue an auditor's report that includes our opinion. Reasonable assurance is a high level of assurance but is not absolute assurance and therefore is not a guarantee that an audit conducted in accordance with GAAS will always detect a material misstatement when it exists. The risk of not detecting a material misstatement resulting from fraud is higher than for one resulting from error, as fraud may involve collusion, forgery, intentional omissions, misrepresentations, or the override of internal control. Misstatements are considered material if, individually or in the aggregate, they could reasonably be expected to influence the economic decisions of users made on the basis of these financial statements.

In performing an audit in accordance with GAAS, we

- Exercise professional judgment and maintain professional skepticism throughout the audit.
- Identify and assess the risks of material misstatement of the financial statements, whether due to fraud or error, and design and perform audit procedures responsive to those risks. Such procedures include examining, on a test basis, evidence regarding the amounts and disclosures in the financial statements.
- Obtain an understanding of internal control relevant to the audit in order to design audit procedures that are appropriate in the circumstances, but not for the purpose of expressing an opinion on the effectiveness of Dunder-Mifflin, Inc.'s internal control. Accordingly, no such opinion is expressed.
- Evaluate the appropriateness of accounting policies used and the reasonableness of significant accounting estimates made by management, as well as evaluate the overall presentation of the financial statements.
- Conclude whether, in our judgment, there are conditions or events, considered in the aggregate, that raise substantial doubt about Dunder-Mifflin, Inc.'s ability to continue as a going concern for a reasonable period of time.

We are required to communicate with those charged with governance regarding, among other matters, the planned scope and timing of the audit, significant audit findings, and certain internal control–related matters that we identified during the audit.

Michael Scarn, LLP
Scranton, PA
January 29, 2024

In addition to the above, the audit team may be requested by management to communicate key audit matters in the report. **Key audit matters** are those matters communicated to those charged with governance (such as the audit committee) that are the most significant in the audit and may include areas of higher risk, areas requiring significant audit team and management judgment, or significant transactions or events. If the audit team has been engaged to communicate key audit matters, they would do so in an additional *Key Audit Matters* section in close proximity to the *Opinion* and *Basis for Opinion* sections that would indicate:

- Why the matter was considered to be a key audit matter.
- How the matter was addressed during the audit.

The report shown in Exhibit 12.1 assumes that the financial statements are not presented along with other information (such as financial summaries, financial ratios, or management commentary on the financial statements). If other information is presented along with the financial statements, the auditors' report would include a section addressing the consistency of this information with the financial statements. This matter is discussed later in this chapter.

Types of Opinions

Users of audited financial statements are generally most interested in the *Opinion* section, which contains the conclusions about the financial statements. This conclusion is in the form of an *opinion* on whether the entity's financial statements present its financial condition, the results of operations, and cash flows in accordance with GAAP.

Auditors may issue four types of opinions:

1. An **unmodified opinion** in which the conclusion is that the financial statements present the financial condition, results of operations, and cash flows in accordance with GAAP. The *auditors' standard (unmodified) report* in Exhibit 12.1 is an example of an unmodified opinion; however, unmodified opinions can be issued in forms other than the standard (unmodified) report.

2. A **qualified opinion** in which the conclusion is that, with the exception of one or more nonpervasive issues, the financial statements present the financial condition, results of operations, and cash flows in accordance with GAAP. Qualified opinions use the phrase *except for* in describing the issues that give rise to the qualification. Interestingly, although the term "qualified" normally has a positive connotation, qualified opinions are issued when one or more issues are encountered during the audit.

3. An **adverse opinion**, in which the conclusion is that the financial statements *do not* present the financial condition, results of operations, and cash flows in accordance with GAAP.

4. A **disclaimer of opinion**, in which the auditors do not express an opinion on the fairness of the entity's financial statements.

Professional standards refer to qualified opinions, adverse opinions, and disclaimers of opinion as **modified opinions**.

✔ REVIEW CHECKPOINTS

12.3 To whom is the auditors' report for a nonissuer addressed?

12.4 Identify the four major sections of the auditors' standard (unmodified) report for a nonissuer and the major contents of each section.

12.5 What are *key audit matters*? If the audit team is engaged to communicate key audit matters, what type of communication is provided in their report on the financial statements?

12.6 What are the types of opinions and the conclusion of each type of opinion?

CONDITIONS THAT REQUIRE MODIFICATIONS TO THE AUDITORS' STANDARD (UNMODIFIED) REPORT

LO 12-2
Identify situations in which language in the standard (unmodified) report is modified and the type of opinion issued in those situations.

In some cases, audit teams encounter situations that require them to modify the language in the standard (unmodified) report shown in Exhibit 12.1 as well as the conclusion with respect to the entity's financial statements. These situations include departures from GAAP and scope limitations and are discussed as follows.

Departures from GAAP[4]

Audit examinations may identify transactions that have not been recorded according to GAAP. In most of these situations and assuming that the results are material to the financial statements, entities adjust their financial statements to reflect the proper accounting treatment for the transactions. The process through which audit teams propose adjustments to financial statements for misstatements identified during the audit was discussed in Chapter 11.

An entity's management may decide to present financial statements containing an accounting treatment or disclosure that is not in accordance with GAAP. Situations in which an entity does not follow GAAP in preparing its financial statements are referred to as **departures from GAAP**. Exhibit 12.2 summarizes auditors' reporting options when departures from GAAP are noted.

As with any issue, a departure from GAAP may not be material to the entity's financial statements. Recall the wording of the opinion in the auditors' standard (unmodified) report: "In our opinion, the accompanying financial statements present fairly, *in all material respects. . .*" [emphasis added]. As a result, if a departure from GAAP is immaterial, the audit team would treat the departure as if it did not exist. In this case, they can express an unmodified opinion and issue the standard (unmodified) report.

If the departure is sufficiently material to affect users' decisions that are based on the financial statements but the departure can be compartmentalized, the auditors must *qualify* the opinion. By "compartmentalized," we mean that the departure can be isolated to a particular account group (e.g., accounts receivable not valued at net

EXHIBIT 12.2
GAAP Departures

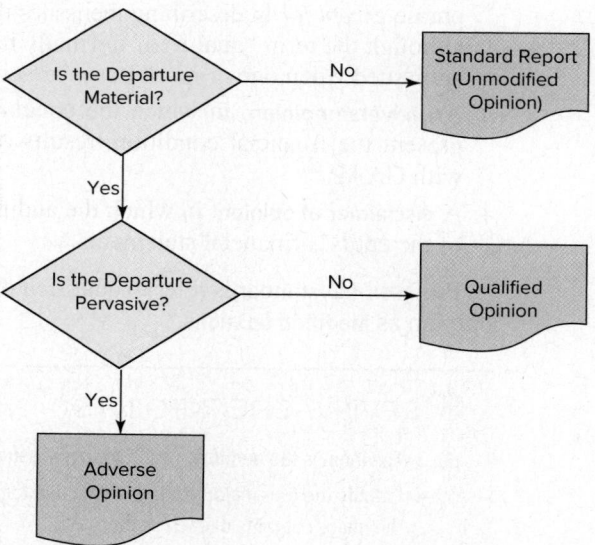

[4]The discussion in this section does not refer to situations in which departures from GAAP are undertaken to prevent the financial statements from being misleading. In such cases, auditors should modify the standard (unmodified) report to describe the departure, its impact, and the reasons why compliance with GAAP would result in misleading financial statements. These cases (referred to as Rule 203 reports) are extremely rare and no guidance is provided in the clarified standards for appropriate report wording.

realizable value) or transactions (e.g., failure to appropriately classify leases) without affecting other accounts to a material extent. In other words, this departure would not be considered *pervasive*. This qualification identifies a particular departure but indicates that the financial statements are otherwise in accordance with GAAP. The nature of the GAAP departure must be explained in the *Basis for Qualified Opinion* section, as shown in Exhibit 12.3.[5]

On the other hand, if the GAAP departure is pervasive, affecting numerous accounts and financial statement relationships, or is material to the point that the financial statements as a whole are misleading, the auditors must issue an adverse opinion. As noted earlier, in an adverse opinion, auditors conclude that the financial statements *do not present fairly* the financial position, results of operations, and cash flows in accordance with GAAP. As with the qualified opinion, the departure(s) and its effects must be disclosed in the report.

The example in Exhibit 12.4 assumes that the same departure in GAAP that served as the focus of the qualified opinion in Exhibit 12.3 reached a level of materiality and pervasiveness to warrant an adverse opinion.

EXHIBIT 12.3
Departure from GAAP Report (Qualified Opinion)

Independent Auditor's Report

To the Board of Directors and Shareholders of Dunder-Mifflin, Inc.

Report on the Audit of the Financial Statements

Qualified **Opinion**

No revisions to first paragraph

In our opinion, *except for the effects of the matter described in the Basis for Qualified Opinion section of our report,* the accompanying financial statements present fairly, in all material respects, the financial position of Dunder-Mifflin, Inc. as of December 31, 2023, and the results of its operations and its cash flows for the year then ended in accordance with accounting principles generally accepted in the United States of America.

Basis for *Qualified* Opinion

As discussed in Note 16, an additional provision in the amount of $30,000,000 for possible uncollectible receivables at December 31, 2022, was charged to operations during the year ended December 31, 2023, which, in our opinion, should have been reflected in the financial statements for 2022. Had this provision been properly recorded in the 2022 financial statements, Dunder-Mifflin, Inc. would have reported net earnings of $700,000 for the year ended December 31, 2023, rather than the net loss of $29,300,000 as reflected in the statements of income, changes in shareholders' equity, and cash flows for that period.

We conducted our audit in accordance with auditing standards . . . We believe that the audit evidence we have obtained is sufficient and appropriate to provide a basis for our *qualified* audit opinion.

Responsibilities of Management for the Financial Statements

No revisions to section

Auditor's Responsibilities for the Audit of the Financial Statements

No revisions to section

Michael Scarn, LLP
Scranton, PA
January 29, 2024

---

[5]For easier reference, all revisions to the auditors' standard (unmodified) report in Exhibit 12.1 are shown in color and italicized in reports presented throughout this chapter.

EXHIBIT 12.4
Departure from GAAP Report (Adverse Opinion)

Independent Auditor's Report

To the Board of Directors and Shareholders of Dunder-Mifflin, Inc.

Report on the Audit of the Financial Statements

Adverse **Opinion**

No revisions to first paragraph

In our opinion, *because of the significance of the matter discussed in the Basis for Adverse Opinion section of our report,* the accompanying financial statements *do not* present fairly *[omit phrase "in all material respects"]* the financial position of Dunder-Mifflin, Inc. as of December 31, 2023, and the results of its operations and its cash flows for the year then ended in accordance with accounting principles generally accepted in the United States of America.

Basis for *Adverse* **Opinion**

As discussed in Note 16, an additional provision in the amount of $30,000,000 for possible uncollectible receivables at December 31, 2022, was charged to operations during the year ended December 31, 2023, which, in our opinion, should have been reflected in the financial statements for 2022. Had this provision been properly recorded in the 2022 financial statements, Dunder-Mifflin, Inc. would have reported net earnings of $700,000 for the year ended December 31, 2023, rather than the net loss of $29,300,000 as reflected in the statements of income, changes in shareholders' equity, and cash flows for that period.

We conducted our audit in accordance with auditing standards . . . We believe that the audit evidence we have obtained is sufficient and appropriate to provide a basis for our *adverse* audit opinion.

Responsibilities of Management for the Financial Statements

No revisions to section

Auditor's Responsibilities for the Audit of the Financial Statements

No revisions to section

Michael Scarn, LLP
Scranton, PA
January 29, 2024

The following summarizes modifications to the auditors' standard (unmodified) report for departures from GAAP (assuming such departures are material). Referring to Exhibits 12.3 and 12.4, notice that both the *Opinion* and *Basis for Opinion* sections include either "Qualified" or "Adverse" to emphasize the type of modified opinion issued.

Section	Qualified Opinion	Adverse Opinion
Opinion	• Title of section is *Qualified Opinion* • Modify second paragraph to note "except for" a specific departure, financial statements are presented according to GAAP	• Title of section is *Adverse Opinion* • Modify second paragraph to note that financial statements are not presented according to GAAP • Omit phrase "in all material respects" from second paragraph
Basis for Opinion	• Title of section is *Basis for Qualified Opinion* • Identify departure from GAAP • Modify phrase "basis for our audit opinion" in last sentence to "basis for our qualified audit opinion"	• Title of section is *Basis for Adverse Opinion* • Identify departure from GAAP • Modify phrase "basis for our audit opinion" in last sentence to "basis for our adverse audit opinion"
Responsibilities of Management for the Financial Statements	No modification	No modification
Auditor's Responsibilities for the Audit of the Financial Statements	No modification	No modification

Audits of Group Financial Statements

Many large entities prepare consolidated financial statements that include more than one component (division, subsidiary, or other segment); these financial statements are referred to as **group financial statements**. In some cases, principal auditors (known as the *group engagement team, lead auditors,* or **group auditors**) perform the audit of a material portion of the consolidated entity's assets, liabilities, revenues, and expenses, and other independent auditors (known as *other auditors* or **component auditors**) may be engaged to audit divisions, subsidiaries, or components that are included in the group financial statements.[6]

Situations such as this may occur if clients have significant remote subsidiaries or if clients have an investment in another entity that is accounted for using the equity method. Because the group engagement partner's signature appears in the report on the financial statements of a consolidated or parent entity, the group auditors must make decisions regarding the use of the work and reports of the component auditor(s).

The group auditors must first obtain information about the independence and professional reputation of the component auditors. If the group auditors are satisfied with these qualities, they must next communicate with the component auditors and decide whether to refer to their work in the group auditors' report. As shown in Exhibit 12.8, the group auditors may decide to make no reference and issue the standard (unmodified) report. In this case, the group auditors assume full responsibility for the component auditors' work.

On the other hand, the group auditors may decide to refer to the work and reports of the component auditors; this is referred to as a **division of responsibility**. Such a reference is not in itself a scope limitation and the report should not be considered to be less reliable than a standard (unmodified) report that does not contain such a reference. The explanation should disclose the extent of the component auditors' work by indicating the percent or amount of assets, revenues, and expenses related to their work.

When the group auditors refer to the component auditors' work, the component auditors are ordinarily not identified by name. In fact, the component auditors may be named in the group auditors' report only by express permission and with publication of their report along with the group auditors' report. Refer to Exhibit 12.8 for a summary of the options

EXHIBIT 12.8
Reporting Options for Audits of Group Financial Statements

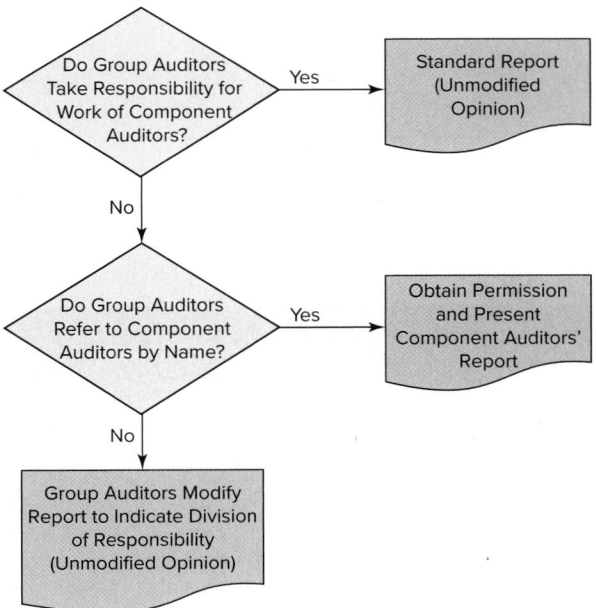

[6] The PCAOB issued a standard that amends existing guidelines related to the supervision, planning, documentation, and engagement quality review by group auditors (referred to by the PCAOB as "lead auditors") of the work of component auditors (referred to as "other auditors"). See *Amendments Relating to the Supervision of Audits Involving Other Auditors* and *Proposed Auditing Standard—Dividing Responsibility for the Audit with Another Accounting Firm,* PCAOB Release No. 2022-002, June 21, 2022.

available to group auditors for reporting when component auditors are involved in the audit of group financial statements.

Exhibit 12.9 is an example of a group auditors' report that expresses an unmodified opinion on financial statements and references the work of component auditors. Note in this report that the group auditors do not identify the "other auditors" by name.

EXHIBIT 12.9
Report on Audit of Group Financial Statements

Independent Auditor's Report

To the Board of Directors and Shareholders of Dunder-Mifflin, Inc.

Report on the Audit of the Financial Statements

Opinion

We have audited the financial statements of Dunder-Mifflin, Inc., which comprise the balance sheet as of December 31, 2023, and the related statements of income, changes in stockholders' equity, and cash flows for the year then ended, and the related notes to the financial statements.

In our opinion, *based on our audit and the report of the other auditors,* the accompanying financial statements present fairly, in all material respects, the financial position of Dunder-Mifflin, Inc. as of December 31, 2023, and the results of its operations and its cash flows for the year then ended in accordance with accounting principles generally accepted in the United States of America.

We did not audit the financial statements of B Company, a wholly-owned subsidiary, which statements reflect total assets constituting 20 percent of total assets at December 31, 2023, and total revenues constituting 18 percent of total revenues for the year then ended. Those statements were audited by other auditors whose report has been furnished to us, and our opinion, insofar as it relates to the amounts included for B Company, is based solely on the report of the other auditors.

Basis for Opinion

No revisions to section

Responsibilities of Management for the Financial Statements

No revisions to section

Auditor's Responsibilities for the Audit of the Financial Statements

No revisions to section

Michael Scarn, LLP
Scranton, PA
January 29, 2024

Beginning in 2017, accounting firms are required to file a disclosure (Form AP) with the PCAOB that discloses the involvement of other firms in audit engagements of issuers. The Auditing Insight "Component Auditors in Practice" illustrates some examples of the use of component auditors in practice.

 AUDITING INSIGHT   Component Auditors in Practice

- EY's 2021 Form AP disclosure on its audit of **Abbott Laboratories** indicated that **Ernst & Young Chartered Accountants** (EY's Dublin, Ireland affiliate firm) provided between 10 percent and 20 percent of the total audit hours and 25 unnamed firms provided between 20 percent and 30 percent of the total audit hours.

- In its 2021 auditors' report on **DuPont de Nemours, Inc., PwC** disclosed that other auditors (Deloitte, whose report was presented along with PwC's report) audited **Dow Chemical Company,** at the time a wholly owned subsidiary of DuPont de Nemours.

- After excluding audits of investment companies and employee benefit plans, U.S. Big Four firms filed over 17,000 Form AP disclosures for the five-year period 2017–2021. Of these, 5,776 (32%) indicted that other firms participated in the audit, with an average of 3.5 participants per audit. 82 reports divided responsibility with component auditors (primarily another Big Four firm for the audits of subsidiaries or equity/partnership investments held by the group auditor's client).

Sources: PCAOB Form AP database (online source); *DuPont de Nemours, Inc. Form 10-K* (filed February 12, 2021).

The Auditing Insight "Academic Research on Group Audits" summarizes academic research that has investigated the impact of using component auditors on various outcomes.

AUDITING INSIGHT | Academic Research on Group Audits

- Docmio et al. found that the group auditors' use of a component auditor had a positive effect on the financial reporting quality for foreign subsidiaries of U.S. multinational companies.

- Hux concluded that nonprofessional investors perceived financial statements as more reliable and the audit team more trustworthy when a component auditor was not used.

- Burke et al. found that component auditor use is associated with higher likelihood of financial restatements, longer audit delays, and higher audit fees, particularly when the component auditors are of lower quality and audits require greater coordination and communication.

Sources: W. M. Docimo, J. L. Gunn, C. Li, and P. N. Michas, "Do Foreign Component Auditors Harm Financial Reporting Quality? A Subsidiary-Level Analysis of Foreign Component Auditor Use?," *Contemporary Accounting Research,* Winter 2021, pp. 3113–3145; C. T. Hux, "How Does Disclosure of Component Auditor Use Affect Nonprofessional Investors' Perceptions and Behavior?," *Auditing: A Journal of Practice & Theory,* February 2021, pp. 35–54; J. J. Burke, R. Hoitash, and U. Hoitash, "The Use and Characteristics of Component Auditors: Implications from U.S. Form AP Filings," *Contemporary Accounting Research,* Winter 2020, pp. 2398–2437.

Shown below is a summary of reporting options for the three situations described in this section (departures from GAAP, scope limitations, and audits of group financial statements). Notice that unmodified opinions are issued for matters that are not material, qualified opinions for matters that are material but less pervasive, and adverse opinions and disclaimers of opinions for matters that are material and more pervasive.

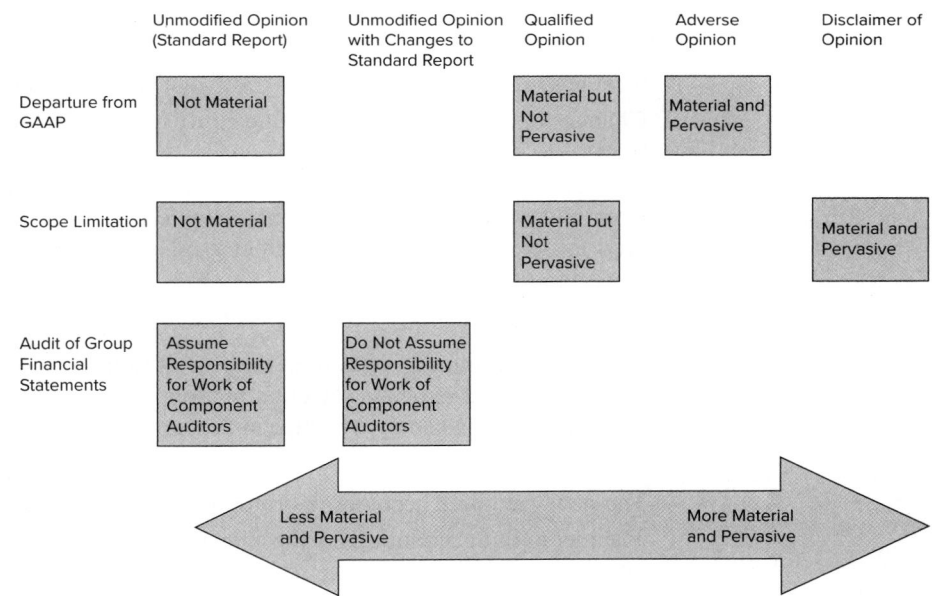

REVIEW CHECKPOINTS

12.14 Define *group auditors* and *component auditors.* What issues are introduced when component auditors examine a division, subsidiary, or segment of group financial statements?

12.15 What options are available to group auditors when component auditors are involved in the examination of group financial statements?

12.16 Is the reference in the auditors' report to work performed by component auditors a scope limitation? Explain.

AUDITORS' REPORTS REFERENCING OTHER MATTERS ENCOUNTERED DURING THE AUDIT

LO 12-3
Identify situations in which auditors add explanatory language to an unmodified opinion.

The preceding section illustrated reporting options for situations in which the language in the auditors' standard (unmodified) report was modified; in many cases, these situations required an opinion other than an unmodified opinion (qualified opinion, adverse opinion, or disclaimer of opinion) to be issued. In other cases, situations encountered during the audit involve adding a paragraph to the standard (unmodified) report shown in Exhibit 12.1 to describe the matter. These paragraphs are labeled as follows:

- Paragraphs that provide information fundamental to users' understanding of the entity's financial statements are known as **emphasis-of-matter paragraphs**.
- Paragraphs that provide information relating to users' understanding of the audit, audit team's responsibility, or auditors' report are known as **other-matter paragraphs**.

Emphasis-of-matter and other-matter paragraphs may be collectively referred to as **explanatory paragraphs**. In most cases, the auditors' reporting responsibility is exception-based reporting, which means that the report will refer only to these matters if an issue is noted during the audit.

Consistency

The concept of *consistency* is based on the importance of permitting users to appropriately compare an entity's financial statements across years. GAAS require that the auditors' report be modified by adding an *emphasis-of-matter paragraph* (following the *Basis for Opinion* section) for the following issues related to consistency:

1. Changes in accounting principles (from one GAAP method to another GAAP method).
2. Changes in the form of the reporting entity (other than that resulting from a transaction or event).
3. Changes in an accounting principle that is not a generally accepted accounting principle to one that is a generally accepted accounting principle (which is considered to be an adjustment to correct a misstatement in previously issued financial statements).
4. Changes in accounting principles inseparable from changes in estimates.

Changes in accounting principles may result from the issuance of new accounting standards or from management's selection of alternatives provided under existing accounting standards. When evaluating a change in accounting principle, audit teams should be satisfied that:

- The newly adopted accounting principle is a generally accepted accounting principle.
- The method of accounting for the change is appropriate.
- Disclosures relating to the change are appropriate.
- The newly adopted principle is preferable to the previously used principle.

If these criteria are not met, the audit team should treat the change in principle as a departure from GAAP and modify the report accordingly.

Recent changes in accounting principles have resulted in additional paragraphs in the audit reports of companies such as **Costco Wholesale, Cisco Systems, Ebay, Nike,** and **Verizon** (lease accounting) and **American Express, Bank of America, Goldman Sachs, Visa,** and **Wells Fargo** (accounting for credit losses). The following is an excerpt from PwC's July 20, 2021, audit report for Nike:[7]

---

[7] *Nike Form 10-K* (filed July 20, 2021).

> **Changes in Accounting Principles**
>
> As discussed in Note 1 to the consolidated financial statements, the Company changed the manner in which it accounts for leases as of June 1, 2019 and the manner in which it accounts for revenue from contracts with customers and the manner in which it accounts for income taxes related to intra-entity transfers other than inventory as of June 1, 2018.

"Going-Concern" Uncertainties

GAAP are based on the *going-concern* principle, which means the entity is expected to continue in operation and meet its obligations as they become due without substantially disposing of its assets outside the ordinary course of business, restructuring its debt, or taking similar actions. Hence, an opinion that financial statements are in accordance with GAAP means that continued existence may be presumed for a "reasonable time" not to exceed one year beyond the date of the financial statements. As noted in Chapter 11, one of the activities performed by audit teams during the completion of the audit is assessing the entity's ability to continue as a going concern for a period not to exceed one year beyond the date the financial statements are issued.

Questions raised about the entity's ability to continue in operation and meet its obligations as they become due are known as **going-concern uncertainties**. The most common report issued when going-concern uncertainties exist is an unmodified opinion with a separate section in the report with the heading *Substantial Doubt About the Entity's Ability to Continue as a Going Concern.* This section would:

- Identify the footnote or other disclosure that references the going-concern issue and management's plans to address the issue.
- Indicate that the opinion on the financial statements is not modified with respect to the going-concern issue.

In highly unusual circumstances involving very severe going-concern uncertainties, auditors may issue a disclaimer of opinion with the auditors' report providing all substantive reasons for the disclaimer.

The following is an excerpted paragraph from Deloitte's 2020 report on **PG&E Corporation's** financial statements:[8]

> **Going Concern**
>
> The accompanying financial statements have been prepared assuming that the Company will continue as a going concern. As discussed in Notes 1 and 14 to the financial statements, the Company suffered material losses as a result of the 2017 Northern California wildfires and the 2018 Camp fire (wildfire-related contingencies are also communicated as a critical audit matter below), which contributed to the Company's decision to voluntarily file for bankruptcy. These circumstances raise substantial doubt about its ability to continue as a going concern. Management's plans in regard to these matters are also described in Notes 1 and 2. The financial statements do not include any adjustments that might result from the outcome of this uncertainty.

These reporting options assume that the entity has properly disclosed matters related to the going-concern uncertainty. If they have not done so, auditors would issue a qualified or adverse opinion on the entity's financial statements, similar to actions taken for other departures from GAAP.

The Auditing Insight "Audit Analytics and Going-Concern Reports" summarizes the incidence and nature of going-concern reports issued in practice.

---

[8]*PG&E Form 10-K* (filed February 18, 2020).

AUDITING INSIGHT — Audit Analytics and Going-Concern Reports

A research report by Audit Analytics covering the time period 2000–2020 revealed the following with respect to going-concern reports.

- The percentage of auditors' reports indicating going-concern uncertainties in 2020 was 17.9 percent, the lowest percentage over the 21-year period covered by this study. The highest percentage was 28.2 percent in 2008, concurrent with the financial crisis.

- The most frequent concerns raised in reports issued in 2020 (percentage of going-concern reports in parentheses) were recurring losses (72%), cash constraints (36%), cash flow concerns (26%), and no or limited operations (21%) (more than one issue was mentioned in some reports).

- In 2020, smaller companies were more likely to receive a going-concern report; the percentage of auditors' reports indicating

going-concern uncertainties were lowest for large accelerated filers (public equity of $700 million or more) (0.4%), followed by accelerated filers (public equity of between $75 million and $700 million) (2.8%), then by smaller companies (31.1%).

- Using the Audit Analytics database, only four going-concern reports have been received by S&P 500 companies since 2012: **American Airlines Group Inc.** (2012), **Enphase Energy** (2016), **NRG Energy Inc.** (2016), and Norwegian Cruise Line Holdings (2019, reissued in 2020 based on the onset of COVID-19 in early 2020).

Source: *Going Concerns: A 21-Year Review,* Audit Analytics, February 2022; Audit Analytics database.

The Auditing Insight "Academic Research on Going-Concern Reports" summarizes the results of academic studies that have examined the factors influencing decisions to issue going-concern reports and the impact of those reports.

AUDITING INSIGHT — Academic Research on Going-Concern Reports

The following academic studies have examined going-concern reports:

- Ettredge et al. found that companies who were able to negotiate reduced fees during the "great recession" of 2007–2009 were less likely to receive a going-concern opinion in 2008; however, this relationship was not observed prior to or following 2008.

- Berglund found that firms failing to issue going-concern reports to companies that subsequently experienced bankruptcy did not suffer any adverse consequences (dismissals, lower audit fees, or lower likelihood of being selected for new engagements).

- Dhaliwal et al. found that financially distressed companies were more likely to receive going-concern reports when they relied more heavily on major customers as a source of revenue.

Sources: M. Ettredge, E. E. Fuerherm, F. Guo, and C. Li, "Client Pressure and Auditor Independence: Evidence From the 'Great Recession' of 2007–2009," *Journal of Accounting and Public Policy,* July 2017, pp. 262–283; N. R. Berglund, "Do Client Bankruptcies Preceded by Clean Audit Opinions Damage Auditor Reputation?," *Contemporary Accounting Research,* Fall 2020, pp. 1914–1951; D. Dhaliwal, P. N. Michas, V. Naiker, and D. Sharma, "Greater Reliance on Major Customers and Auditor Going-Concern Opinions," *Contemporary Accounting Research,* Spring 2020, pp. 160–188.

Other Information Included in Annual Reports

In many cases, audited financial statements include a variety of information that accompanies the financial statements. For example, all annual reports to shareholders and SEC filings contain such sections as a president's letter and management's discussion and analysis (MD&A) of operations. In addition, the financial statements may be accompanied by financial summaries, financial ratios, or other management commentary. Audit teams have an obligation to read the other information and determine whether this information is consistent with the audited financial statements or contains material misstatements.

When other information is presented along with the financial statements, the auditors' report should be modified by including a section (labeled *Other Information* or *Other Information Included in the Annual Report*). This section would include the following information:

- A statement that management is responsible for the other information.
- An indication that the audit team does not express an opinion or any form of assurance on the other information.

- The audit team's responsibility with respect to the other information and to report any material misstatements in the other information.
- A description of any material misstatements of the other information (if applicable).

Supplementary Information

In many cases, companies present supplementary information in addition to the financial statements and footnotes accompanying the financial statements. Accounting standard-setting bodies may require companies to provide supplementary information that is not part of the basic financial statements (often referred to as **required supplementary information**). For example, the FASB requires energy companies to present oil, gas, and other mineral reserve information as supplementary information. Other industries and companies subject to supplementary information reporting requirements include construction, development-stage entities, financial services, and real estate .

Audit teams are required to perform limited procedures (inquiring of management, comparing information for consistency with the financial statements, and obtaining written representations from management) with respect to the required supplementary information. When companies present required supplementary information, auditors are required to expand their report on the financial statements to include an *other-matter paragraph* (with a heading such as "Required Supplementary Information") that identifies the supplementary information, describes any procedures performed with respect to this information, and identifies any issues related to this information. However, the paragraph specifically disclaims an opinion or any form of assurance on the supplementary information.

In addition to required supplementary information, other types of supplementary information may be presented outside the basic financial statements; this information differs in that there is no expressed requirement for presenting it or any authoritative standards for presenting or preparing this information. While no audit requirement exists for this information, audit teams may be engaged to examine and report on supplementary information. The auditors' conclusion will not express an opinion on the supplementary information but will indicate whether it is fairly stated, in all material respects, in relation to the financial statements as a whole. Auditors may report on this information either by adding an *other-matter paragraph* (with a heading such as "Supplementary Information") to their report on the financial statements or by preparing a separate report on the supplementary information. The Auditing Insight "GE and Supplemental Information" provides an example of how KPMG reported on supplemental information provided by **General Electric**.

AUDITING INSIGHT \ GE and Supplemental Information

Accompanying Supplemental Information

The accompanying consolidating information appearing on pages 57, 59, and 61 [of Form 10-K] (the supplemental information) has been subjected to audit procedures performed in conjunction with the audit of the Company's consolidated financial statements. The supplemental information is the responsibility of the Company's management. Our audit procedures included determining whether the supplemental information reconciles to the consolidated financial statements or the underlying accounting and other records, as applicable, and performing procedures to test the completeness and accuracy of the information presented in the supplemental information. In our opinion, the supplemental information is fairly stated, in all material respects, in relation to the consolidated financial statements as a whole.

Source: *General Electric Form 10-K* (filed February 12, 2021).

Other Modifications

Beyond the wording in the standard (unmodified) report, auditors can enrich the information content in their reports by adding one or more paragraphs to emphasize something they believe readers should consider important or useful. Although auditing standards place no official limits on the content of these paragraphs, auditors often use them to describe circumstances that present some business or information risk. Matters that may be emphasized include a warning that a bankruptcy filing may be imminent, a description of the auditee as a subsidiary of a larger entity, the effects of business events on the comparability of financial statements, the interaction of the auditee with related parties, and the effect of events that occur after the date of the financial statements (commonly referred to as *subsequent events*). Some recent examples are shown in the Auditing Insight "Additional Disclosures in Auditors' Reports."

AUDITING INSIGHT · Additional Disclosures in Auditors' Reports

- The fact that PG&E voluntarily filed for reorganization under Chapter 11 of the U.S. Bankruptcy Code (2020 auditors' report) and subsequently emerged from Chapter 11 bankruptcy (2021 auditors' report).

- The existence of significant related-party transactions for **Marathon Oil** (2021 auditors' report).

- The negative impact of COVID-19 on the operations of Carnival Corp, Draft Kings, and Norwegian Cruise Line Holdings (2021 and 2022 auditors' reports).

- The fact that **Federal Home Loan Mortgage Corporation (Freddie Mac)** is under the conservatorship and is dependent upon the continued financial support of the **United States Treasury** and the **Federal Housing Finance Agency** (2022 auditors' report).

Sources: *PG&E Forms 10-K* (filed February 25, 2021, and February 18, 2020); *Marathon Oil Form 10-K* (filed February 23, 2021); *Carnival Corp Form 10-K* (filed January 27, 2022); *Draft Kings Form 10-K/A* (filed May 3, 2021); *Norwegian Cruise Line Holdings Form 10-K* (filed February 26, 2021); *Federal Home Loan Mortgage Corporation Form 10-K* (filed February 10, 2022).

Summary: *Emphasis-of-Matter* and *Other-Matter Paragraphs*

Assuming that the matters discussed in this section are properly accounted for and disclosed by the entity, the auditors' report is modified by adding a paragraph labeled "Emphasis of Matter" or "Other Matter" to the report. (As noted earlier, professional standards provide specific wording for the section for going-concern uncertainties and supplementary information.) It is important to reiterate that the opinion on the financial statements would still be unmodified. Professional standards indicate that the placement of the paragraph depends upon the nature and significance of the information.

An academic study analyzing audit opinions that were issued between 2000 and 2014 with explanatory paragraphs identified the following disclosures (as a percentage of all opinions with explanatory paragraphs; each report could have more than one matter referenced):[9]

- Supplementary information (65 percent).
- Change in accounting principles (49 percent).
- Restatements (3 percent).
- Other matters (2 percent).

✔ REVIEW CHECKPOINTS

12.17 Define *emphasis-of-matter* and *other-matter* paragraphs. What type of information do auditors provide in these paragraphs?

12.18 What types of matters would result in the auditors' report being modified for consistency?

12.19 What are *going-concern uncertainties*? What is the audit team's responsibility for evaluating going-concern uncertainties?

12.20 What are auditors' reporting options when going-concern uncertainties are noted?

12.21 What is the auditors' reporting responsibility for (a) other information accompanying the audited financial statements, (b) required supplementary information, and (c) other supplementary information?

[9]K. Czerney, J. J. Schmidt, and A .M. Thompson, "Do Investors Respond to Explanatory Language Included in Unqualified Audit Reports?" *Contemporary Accounting Research,* Spring 2019, pp. 198–229.

COMPARATIVE FINANCIAL STATEMENTS

LO 12-4

Understand the auditors' responsibility for reporting on financial statements presented in comparative form.

The SEC requires issuers to present balance sheets for two years and statements of income, comprehensive income, changes in shareholders' equity, and cash flows for three years in comparative (side-by-side) format. Financial statement footnotes also contain disclosures in comparative form. Together, these comparative financial statements and footnotes are the subject of the auditors' work and report. Although nonissuers are not subject to similar requirements, users may request that entities provide multiple years of financial statements in comparative form.

The issue introduced when financial statements are presented in comparative form is that users may assume that the audit team has examined all comparative years presented. Therefore, it is important that the auditor's report specifically identify the responsibility assumed for all financial statements presented in comparative form.

Same Auditors, Same Opinions for Comparative Years

When auditors issue a report on the current year financial statements, they are required to update their report on the prior years' financial statements by considering whether the opinions on the prior years' financial statements are still appropriate. The **updated report** is based not only on the prior year audits but also on information that has come to the audit team's attention since then (particularly in the course of the most recent audit). An updated report carries the most recent date of the auditors' report, and the auditors' responsibility for the comparative financial statements now extends to this date.

Recall the standard (unmodified) report shown in Exhibit 12.1. Assume that Dunder-Mifflin, Inc. presented balance sheets, statements of income, changes in shareholders' equity, and cash flows for 2022 and 2023. If Michael Scarn had audited Dunder-Mifflin in all years and concluded that an unmodified opinion was appropriate in all years, a "plural" form of the standard (unmodified) report would be issued that expresses an opinion on the financial condition, results of operations, and cash flows for 2022 and 2023.

An updated report differs from a **reissued report**. When auditors reissue a report, they simply provide additional copies of a previously issued report or grant entities permission to use a previously issued report in another document sometime after its original date. However, auditors do not attempt to update the report or otherwise consider events that have occurred since the date of the original report. The date of a reissued report is the same as that for the original report, indicating a cutoff date for the auditors' responsibility.

Same Auditors, Different Opinions for Comparative Years

Auditors can express different opinions on comparative years' financial statements in the same report. For example, assume that Dunder-Mifflin incorrectly recorded a $30 million provision for uncollectible receivables in the 2022 financial statements instead of in 2021. As a result, the 2022 financial statements were not prepared in accordance with GAAP, so Michael Scarn issued a qualified opinion. However, Scarn concluded that an unmodified opinion was appropriate in 2023. The report shown in Exhibit 12.10 would be appropriate in the circumstances.

Essentially, the report in Exhibit 12.10 combines a qualified opinion on Dunder-Mifflin's financial statements for 2022 with an unmodified opinion on its financial statements for 2023.

Same Auditors with Modification of Previously Issued Opinion

Auditors should modify the opinion expressed on prior years' financial statements if circumstances have changed in the intervening period. For example, consider the departure from GAAP shown in Exhibit 12.10 and discussed in the preceding section. In 2023, if Dunder-Mifflin restated its 2022 financial statements to record the provision in the appropriate year (2021), all years of financial statements would now be in accordance with GAAP. Therefore, an unmodified opinion (standard report) on all three years would now be appropriate.

EXHIBIT 12.10
**Different Opinions
in Comparative Year
Financial Statements**

Independent Auditor's Report

To the Board of Directors and Shareholders of Dunder-Mifflin, Inc.

Report on the Audit of the Financial Statements

Opinion

We have audited the financial statements of Dunder-Mifflin, Inc., which comprise the balance sheet as of December 31, 2023 and 2022 and the related statements of income, changes in stockholders' equity, and cash flows for the years then ended, and the related notes to the financial statements.

In our opinion, *except for the effects on the accompanying 2022 financial statements of incorrectly charging the provision for uncollectible receivables as described in the Basis for Qualified Opinion section of our report,* the financial statements present fairly, in all material respects, the financial position of Dunder-Mifflin, Inc. as of December 31, 2023 and 2022 and the results of its operations and its cash flows for the years then ended in accordance with accounting principles generally accepted in the United States of America.

Basis for Qualified Opinion on 2022 Financial Statements

As discussed in Note 16, an additional provision in the amount of $30,000,000 for possible uncollectible receivables at December 31, 2021 was charged to operations during the year ended December 31, 2022, which, in our opinion, should have been reflected in the financial statements for 2021. Had this provision been properly recorded in the 2021 financial statements, net income and shareholders' equity for 2022 would have been $30,000,000 higher than that reported, as reflected in the balance sheet and statements of income, changes in shareholders' equity, and cash flows for those years.

No modifications to standard paragraph

Responsibilities of Management for the Financial Statements

No modifications to section

Auditor's Responsibilities for the Audit of the Financial Statements

No modifications to section

Michael Scarn, LLP
Scranton, PA
January 29, 2024

One concern with not referring to the previous opinions is that Michael Scarn's updated opinion on the 2022 financial statements is now different from the originally issued opinion. To alert readers to this fact, an explanatory other-matter paragraph such as the following one would be added to the report (following the *Basis for Opinion* section):

Other Matter

In our report dated January 30, 2023, we expressed an opinion that, except for the effects of incorrectly charging the provision for uncollectible receivables, the 2022 financial statements presented the financial position, results of operations, and cash flows in accordance with principles generally accepted in the United States of America because Dunder-Mifflin, Inc. incorrectly recorded a $30,000,000 provision for uncollectible receivables in 2022 rather than in 2021. As described in Note 2, Dunder-Mifflin, Inc. has restated its 2022 financial statements to conform with accounting principles generally accepted in the United States of America. Accordingly, our present opinion on the restated 2022 financial statements, as presented herein, is different from that expressed in our previous report.

Different Auditors in Comparative Years

Assume that Michael Scarn became the auditor of Dunder-Mifflin in 2023 and another (predecessor) firm had examined the 2022 financial statements and issued an unmodified opinion (standard report) on these statements. In this case, Michael Scarn's report should indicate that he audited the 2023 financial statements and expressed an opinion on the 2023 financial statements. However, how should the results of the other firm's audit of the 2022 financial statements be communicated?

One option would be to add an other-matter paragraph (following the *Basis for Opinion* section) that summarizes the predecessor auditors' responsibility and report. An example of this type of paragraph follows. If the predecessor auditors issued an opinion other than the standard (unmodified) opinion, the paragraph should be expanded to provide information about the report modification.

Other Matter

The financial statements of Dunder-Mifflin, Inc. as of December 31, 2022 were audited by other auditors whose report dated February 4, 2023, expressed an unmodified opinion on those statements.

A second option would be for the successor auditor to express an opinion on the current year's financial statements without any reference to the predecessor auditor. The predecessor auditors' report would then be included along with the comparative financial statements. An example of this reporting option is shown in the Auditing Insight "Auditor Change at General Motors."

 AUDITING INSIGHT | Auditor Change at General Motors

In 2018, EY became the auditor for General Motors Company (prior to that time, Deloitte had served as General Motors' auditor since 1918!). The following summarizes the auditors' reports presented with General Motors' financial statements:

	2015	2016	2017	2018	2019	2020
2017	Deloitte	Deloitte	Deloitte			
2018		Deloitte	Deloitte	EY		
2019			Deloitte	EY	EY	
2020				EY	EY	EY

The rows in the matrix represent the fiscal year and the columns represent the years presented in comparative format. For example, in fiscal 2019, EY issued opinions on the General Motors' 2018 and 2019 financial statements and Deloitte's report on the 2017 financial statements was presented (using the original report date).

✅ REVIEW CHECKPOINTS

12.22 What are *comparative financial statements?* What issue is introduced when entities present information in comparative format?

12.23 What is an *updated report?* What is a *reissued report?*

12.24 If auditors wish to express a different opinion on prior years' financial statements in the current report than in a previously issued report, how should their current report be modified?

12.25 What reporting options are available if predecessor auditors examined prior years' financial statements presented in comparative form?

OTHER REPORTING TOPICS

LO 12-5
Identify other reporting considerations related to GAAS audits.

This chapter has focused on auditors' reports issued following an audit conducted under generally accepted auditing standards. In those cases, the auditors' report expressed an opinion as to whether the financial statements and footnotes presented the financial condition, results of operations, and cash flows in accordance with generally accepted accounting principles (GAAP). While this is a fairly common setting for audit engagements, there are instances where auditors may conduct GAAS audit engagements and issue reports in connection with

- Financial statements prepared using a framework other than GAAP.
- Specified elements, accounts, or items of a financial statement.
- Summary financial statements
- Compliance with contractual agreements or regulatory requirements as part of a GAAS audit.
- Engagements in which a disclaimer of opinion must be issued.

Special Purpose Frameworks

As noted throughout this text, issuers (or public entities) are required to prepare financial statements using GAAP or another appropriate financial reporting framework (such as International Financial Reporting Standards, or IFRS). While many nonissuers will also use GAAP, smaller nonissuers often choose to report using **special purpose frameworks**, also known as *other comprehensive bases of accounting,* or *OCBOA.* A special purpose framework in this context refers to a coherent accounting treatment in which substantially all important financial measurements are governed by criteria other than GAAP. Some examples include statements prepared under (1) regulatory agency accounting rules, (2) tax basis accounting, (3) **cash basis accounting** (i.e., no accruals) or **modified cash basis accounting** (i.e., limited accruals such as long-term assets and liabilities or inventory), and (4) some other method required for contractual purposes.

Professional standards warn that special purpose framework financial statements should not use the titles normally associated with GAAP statements (such as balance sheet, statement of financial position, statement of operations, income statement, statement of comprehensive income, and statement of cash flows). Instead, special purpose framework statements should use titles such as statement of assets and liabilities and statement of revenue and expenses, with a designator for the basis used (regulatory, cash, income tax, etc.).

The only difference introduced for auditors in these engagements is that a basis of accounting different from GAAP is used in the preparation of the financial statements. In addition to the normal procedures performed in a GAAS audit, audits of financial statements prepared under special purpose frameworks introduce the following requirements:

- Obtain an understanding of (1) the purpose for which the financial statements are prepared, (2) the intended users, and (3) the steps taken by management to determine that the special purpose framework is acceptable in the circumstances.
- Obtain the agreement of management that it acknowledges and understands its responsibility to include all informative disclosures that are appropriate for the special purpose framework used to prepare the financial statements.
- In the case of special purpose financial statements prepared in accordance with a contractual basis of accounting, obtain an understanding of any significant interpretations of the contract that management made in the preparation of those financial statements and to evaluate whether the financial statements adequately describe such interpretations.

Exhibit 12.11 provides an example of a report on financial statements prepared under the cash basis of accounting. Some of the key differences in this report and the

EXHIBIT 12.11
Report on Financial Statements Prepared Using Special Purpose Framework (Cash Basis)

Independent Auditor's Report

To the Board of Directors and Shareholders of Dunder-Mifflin, Inc.

Opinion

We have audited the financial statements of Dunder-Mifflin, Inc., which comprise the statement of assets and liabilities arising from cash transactions as of December 31, 2023, and the related statement of revenue collected and expenses paid for the year then ended, and the related notes to the financial statements.

In our opinion, the accompanying financial statements present fairly, in all material respects, the assets and liabilities arising from cash transactions of Dunder-Mifflin, Inc. as of December 31, 2023, and its revenue collected and expenses paid during the year then ended in accordance with the cash basis of accounting described in Note 1.

Basis for Opinion

We conducted our audit in accordance with auditing standards generally accepted in the United States of America (GAAS). Our responsibilities under those standards are further described in the Auditor's Responsibilities for the Audit of the Financial Statements section of our report. We are required to be independent of Dunder-Mifflin, Inc., and to meet our other ethical responsibilities, in accordance with the relevant ethical requirements relating to our audit. We believe that the audit evidence we have obtained is sufficient and appropriate to provide a basis for our audit opinion.

Emphasis of Matter—Basis of Accounting

We draw attention to Note 1 of the financial statements, which describes the basis of accounting. The financial statements are prepared on the cash basis of accounting, which is a basis of accounting other than accounting principles generally accepted in the United States of America. Our opinion is not modified with respect to this matter.

Responsibilities of Management for the Financial Statements

Management is responsible for the preparation and fair presentation of the financial statements in accordance with the cash basis of accounting described in Note 1, and for determining that the cash basis of accounting is an acceptable basis for the preparation of the financial statements in the circumstances. Management is also responsible for the design, implementation, and maintenance of internal control relevant to the preparation and fair presentation of financial statements that are free from material misstatement, whether due to fraud or error.

Auditor's Responsibilities for the Audit of the Financial Statements

Our objectives are to obtain reasonable assurance about whether the financial statements as a whole are free from material misstatement, whether due to fraud or error, and to issue an auditor's report that includes our opinion. Reasonable assurance is a high level of assurance but is not absolute assurance and therefore is not a guarantee that an audit conducted in accordance with GAAS will always detect a material misstatement when it exists. The risk of not detecting a material misstatement resulting from fraud is higher than for one resulting from error, as fraud may involve collusion, forgery, intentional omissions, misrepresentations, or the override of internal control. Misstatements are considered material if there is a substantial likelihood that, individually or in the aggregate, they would influence the judgment made by a reasonable user based on the financial statements. In performing an audit in accordance with GAAS, we

- Exercise professional judgment and maintain professional skepticism throughout the audit.
- Identify and assess the risks of material misstatement of the financial statements, whether due to fraud or error, and design and perform audit procedures responsive to those risks. Such procedures include examining, on a test basis, evidence regarding the amounts and disclosures in the financial statements.
- Obtain an understanding of internal control relevant to the audit in order to design audit procedures that are appropriate in the circumstances, but not for the purpose of expressing an opinion on the effectiveness of Dunder-Mifflin's internal control. Accordingly, no such opinion is expressed.

(continued)

EXHIBIT 12.11
(concluded)

• Evaluate the appropriateness of accounting policies used and the reasonableness of significant accounting estimates made by management, as well as evaluate the overall presentation of the financial statements.
• Conclude whether, in our judgment, there are conditions or events, considered in the aggregate, that raise substantial doubt about Dunder-Mifflin's ability to continue as a going concern for a reasonable period of time.

We are required to communicate with those charged with governance regarding, among other matters, the planned scope and timing of the audit, significant audit findings, and certain internal control-related matters that we identified during the audit.

Michael Scarn, LLP
Scranton, PA
January 29, 2024

---

report prepared for financial statements discussed earlier in this chapter include the following:

• The names of the financial statements reflect the special purpose framework (e.g., statement of assets and liabilities arising from cash transactions) and not GAAP (balance sheet).
• The report identifies the special purpose framework and explicitly notes management's responsibility for determining that this framework is acceptable.
• The report expresses the opinion as it relates to the special purpose framework ("in accordance with the cash basis of accounting described in Note 1") and not GAAP.
• An *emphasis-of-matter* paragraph indicates that the financial statements are prepared using a special purpose framework other than GAAP and references disclosures that describe the framework.

Summary Financial Statements

Published financial statements are lengthy and often complex. Entities sometimes have occasion to present the financial statements in considerably less detail (e.g., summary totals of current assets, current liabilities, long-term liabilities, operating income, or other subtotals). Generally, such summary financial statements (sometimes referred to as *condensed financial statements*) are derived directly from the full audited financial statements. However, summary financial statements are not fair presentations of financial position, results of operations, and cash flows in accordance with GAAP.

In some cases, users may engage audit teams to examine and report on summary financial statements. Audit teams can do so only if they have audited the full financial statements. The report on summary financial statements parallels the auditors' report on the financial statements illustrated throughout this chapter and must refer to the auditors' report on the full financial statements, giving the date and the type of opinion expressed. The auditors' conclusion on summary financial statements will not express an opinion on the summary financial statements but will indicate whether the information in the summary financial statements is fairly stated in all material respects in relation to the complete financial statements.

Specified Elements, Accounts, or Items

Either as part of the audit of the complete financial statements or a separate engagement, entities may have a lender or another user request an opinion on a single financial statement (e.g., balance sheet only) or an element, account, or item within the financial statements. The only issue introduced in these situations is that both the scope of the engagement and the auditors' conclusion are limited to the specific element, account, or item within the financial statements. In cases where a complete audit of the financial statements is not undertaken, professional standards note that auditors should determine whether engagements on elements, accounts, or items within the financial statements are practicable.

The auditors' report on a single statement or elements, accounts, or items is very similar to the auditors' standard (unmodified) report on the complete set of financial statements. The identification of the financial information, auditors' opinion, management's responsibility, and auditors' responsibility will be limited to the specific element, account, or item examined (e.g., the accompanying schedule of accounts receivable). However, it is important to note that an opinion can still be expressed with respect to the fairness of the element, account, or item.

If the report is issued in conjunction with an audit of the complete set of financial statements and an adverse opinion or disclaimer of opinion is issued for the financial statements taken as a whole, the auditors may separately report only on an element, account, or item in the financial statements if that report is *not* published with the report containing the adverse or disclaimer of opinion, and the element is not a major portion of the financial statements and is not related to stockholders' equity or net income. Auditors cannot express an unmodified opinion on a single financial statement if they expressed a disclaimer or adverse opinion on the complete set of financial statements. This is intended to ensure that the positive opinion on the element, account, or item does not distract from the adverse opinion or disclaimer of opinion on the financial statements.

Compliance with Contractual Agreements or Regulatory Requirements

Management often must report its compliance with contractual obligations to third parties. For example, entities may have restrictive covenants in loan agreements, and lenders may require a periodic report on whether the entity has complied with these covenants. Contractual agreements could include dividend limitations, loan limitations, mandatory debt-to-equity ratios, or limitations on geographic operations. In addition, companies and governmental agencies must comply with applicable laws and regulations.

Companies subject to these reporting requirements may request auditors to report on compliance based on the procedures performed during the GAAS audit of their financial statements. It is important to note that the audit team does not perform procedures specifically designed to evaluate compliance but is considering whether evidence they gather during the financial statement audit indicates instances of noncompliance. The AICPA refers to these reports on compliance as *by-product reports,* as evaluating and reporting on compliance were not the primary objectives of the audit.

In these cases, the audit team can either issue a separate report on compliance or a combined report that expresses an opinion on the financial statements as well as compliance with contractual agreements or regulatory requirements. These reports should:

- Indicate that a GAAS audit has been conducted.
- Assuming that no instances of noncompliance have been identified, indicate that the audit team is unaware of any instances of noncompliance (any instances of noncompliance should be identified in the report).
- Indicate that the audit was not directed toward identifying noncompliance and additional procedures might have revealed instances of noncompliance.
- Indicate that the communication on compliance is intended solely for the use of certain parties (ordinarily, the management, board of directors, and a specified third party).

In other instances, entities may engage accountants to specifically report on compliance; this is a separate type of attestation engagement and is discussed in Module A.

Disclaimers of Opinion

In addition to the situations described in the previous sections of this chapter, other circumstances may result in auditors issuing disclaimers of opinion. Audit teams may be engaged to conduct an audit but subsequently discover a relationship involving the firm that results in a lack of independence. In other cases, audit teams may consent to the use of the firm's name in some form of communication containing the entity's financial statements or submit to their clients or others (such as third-party users) financial statements they have prepared or assisted in preparing. These situations are referred to as being **associated with financial statements.**

EXHIBIT 12.12
Disclaimer of Opinion on Unaudited Financial Statements

> The accompanying balance sheet of Dunder-Mifflin, Inc. as of December 31, 2023, and the related statements of income, changes in shareholders' equity, and cash flows for the year then ended were not audited by us and, accordingly, we do not express an opinion on them.
>
> *Michael Scarn, LLP*
> Scranton, PA
> January 29, 2024

In these situations, auditors will issue a single paragraph report shown in Exhibit 12.12. Note that this report is not addressed to any specific users, nor does it reference any procedures performed on Dunder-Mifflin's financial statements.

When audit teams are not independent, the report in Exhibit 12.12 would begin with the phrase "We were not independent with respect to Dunder-Mifflin, Inc." The report should not mention any reasons for not being independent because readers may erroneously interpret them as unimportant.

☑ REVIEW CHECKPOINTS

12.26 What is a *special purpose framework?* Provide some examples of special purpose frameworks.

12.27 What is an advantage of preparing financial statements using a special purpose framework?

12.28 What are the major modifications to the auditors' report when a nonissuer uses a special purpose framework to prepare its financial statements?

12.29 Briefly describe the options and information provided by auditors when engaged to report on summary financial statements.

12.30 What are the major modifications to the auditors' report when an opinion is expressed on a specified element, account, or item within the financial statements?

12.31 What are the reporting options when an auditor examines compliance with contractual agreements or regulatory requirements in conjunction with a GAAS audit?

12.32 What type of report should be issued when audit teams are *not* independent with respect to the entity?

Summary

This chapter has discussed a wide range of reporting issues. The array and variety of reports may seem confusing, but several simple rules will enable you to remember the basics of auditors' reports on financial statements. First, begin with the standard (unmodified) report in Exhibit 12.1. Keeping the four sections in mind, remember that the following basic rules apply:

- The *Opinion* section is modified when the responsibility assumed by the audit team changes, an opinion other than an unmodified opinion is issued, a special purpose framework is used by the entity instead of GAAP, or a report is issued on a subset of the full set of financial statements.
- The *Basis for Opinion* section is modified when an opinion other than an unmodified opinion is issued.
- *The Responsibilities of Management for the Financial Statements* section is not modified for any of the issues discussed in this chapter because they are not related to management's responsibility for the financial statements and internal control over financial reporting.
- The *Auditor's Responsibilities for the Audit of Financial Statements* section is modified for matters that affect the audit team's responsibility for the financial statements (material and pervasive scope limitation).
- Additional paragraphs are added to the report when some other matter related to the financial statements or audit is noted.

See Exhibit 12.12 for a comprehensive summary of auditors' reports discussed in this chapter. In reviewing Exhibit 12.12, it is important to note that if any of the issues do not have a material effect on the financial statements, auditors can issue the standard (unmodified) report without any reference to the issue (except for a lack of independence, which is always considered to be material).

While not shown in Exhibit 12.12, recall that auditors may also issue opinions on summary financial statements or compliance with regulatory contractual agreements or regulatory requirements. The related reports for these situations are based on the procedures performed by the audit team in the GAAS audit of the financial statements.

EXHIBIT 12.12   Summary of Reporting Issues

	Significance of Matter		Sections Modified				
	Material	Pervasive	Opinion	Basis for Opinion	Auditor's Responsibilities	Additional Language	Other Comments
Departure from GAAP	Qualified	Adverse	x	x			
Scope limitation	Qualified	Disclaimer	x	x	x		*Auditor's Responsibilities* section only modified for disclaimer
Audit of group financial statements	Unmodified	Unmodified	x				Can issue a standard (unmodified) report if group auditors assume responsibility for component auditors' work
Consistency	Unmodified	Unmodified				x	
Going-concern uncertainty	Unmodified	Disclaimer	x	x		x	*Opinion and Basis for Opinion* sections only modified for disclaimer
Other information	Unmodified	Unmodified				x	Add section titled *Other Information* or *Other Information Included in the Annual Report*
Required supplementary information	Unmodified	Unmodified				x	
Emphasis of a matter	Unmodified	Unmodified				x	
Special purpose frameworks	Unmodified	Unmodified	x			x	• Modify names of financial statements and express opinion as it relates to special purpose framework • Add paragraph referencing special purpose framework
Specified elements, accounts, or items	Unmodified	Unmodified	x		x		Limit opinion and responsibility to item(s) examined
Lack of independence	Disclaimer	Disclaimer					Issue one-paragraph standard disclaimer
Association with unaudited financial statements	Disclaimer	Disclaimer					Issue one-paragraph standard disclaimer

Key Terms

adverse opinion (financial statements): The opinion issued when auditors conclude the financial statements do not present the financial condition, results of operations, and cash flows in accordance with GAAP; adverse opinions are issued for material and pervasive departures from GAAP, 529

associated (association) with financial statements: Situations in which auditors consent to the use of their name in some form of communication containing the entity's financial statements or submit to their clients or others (such as third-party users) financial statements they have prepared or assisted in preparing; auditors should issue a one-paragraph disclaimer when they are associated with (but did not audit) financial statements, 551

cash basis accounting: A special purpose framework in which revenues are recognized when cash is received and expenses are incurred when cash is disbursed, 548

circumstance-imposed scope limitation: A restriction on auditors from gathering sufficient appropriate evidence because of a situation beyond control of both the auditors and client, such as late appointment of the auditors, 533

client-imposed scope limitation: A restriction on auditors from gathering sufficient appropriate evidence because of the client's imposition of limitations on the auditor's application of auditing procedures or the client's deliberate refusal to provide auditors access to evidence, 533

component auditors: The auditors who audit divisions, subsidiaries, or components that are included in the group financial statements (also known as *other auditors*), 537

date of the auditors' report: The date on which auditors have obtained sufficient appropriate evidence to support their opinion, 527

departures from GAAP: Situations in which the entity's financial statements are not prepared in accordance with GAAP; auditors can issue qualified or adverse opinions for material departures from GAAP, 530

disclaimer of opinion (financial statements): A report issued when auditors do not express an opinion on the fairness of the entity's financial statements; disclaimers of opinion are issued for pervasive going-concern uncertainties, pervasive scope limitations, situations in which auditors are associated with (but did not audit) the financial statements, and situations in which the auditors are not independent, 529

division of responsibility: Situation in which other auditors are involved with the examination of a subsidiary, branch, component, or investment that is included in the financial statements audited by principal auditors, 537

emphasis-of-matter paragraphs: Paragraphs added to an auditors' report that provide information fundamental to users' understanding of the financial statements (such as consistency or going-concern uncertainties), 540

explanatory paragraphs: Paragraphs added to an auditors' report that either provide information fundamental to users' understanding of the financial statements (emphasis-of-matter paragraph) or are relevant to users' understanding of the audit, the auditor's responsibility, or auditors' report (other-matter paragraph), 540

going-concern uncertainty: Situation in which questions are raised about an entity's ability to continue operations and meet its obligations as they become due, 541

group auditors: The auditors who perform the audit of a material portion of the assets, liabilities, revenues, and expenses of an entity's group financial statements; also known as *principal auditors* or *lead auditors,* 537

group financial statements: The financial statements of more than one component (division, subsidiary, or other segment), 537

issuers: An entity that offers registered securities, such as stocks and bonds, for sale to the general public (also known as a public entity); issuers are subject to mandatory audit requirements, 526

key audit matters: Matters communicated to those charged with governance that are the most significant in the audit, including areas of higher risk, areas requiring significant judgment, or significant transactions or events, 529

modified cash basis accounting: A special purpose framework that provides limited accruals for items such as fixed assets or inventories and long-term debt, 548

modified opinion: Any opinion other than an unmodified opinion on an entity's financial statements (qualified opinion, adverse opinion, or disclaimer of opinion), 529

nonissuer: An entity that does not offer registered securities, such as stocks and bonds, for sale to the general public (also known as a nonpublic entity); nonissuers are not subject to mandatory audit requirements, 526

other-matter paragraphs: Paragraphs added to the auditors' report that are relevant to users' understanding of the audit, the auditor's responsibility, or the auditors' report, 540

qualified opinion: An opinion issued when the auditors conclude that, with the exception of one or more issue(s), the financial statements present the financial condition, results of operations, and cash flows in accordance with GAAP; qualified opinions can be issued for material (but not pervasive) departures from GAAP and scope limitations, 529

reissued report: A copy of a previously issued report that auditors provide or grant entities permission to use in another document after its original date; the report is not modified to consider events occurring subsequent to the date of the original report, 545

required supplementary information: Information presented along with financial statements and footnotes that is mandated by an accounting standard-setting body, 543

scope limitation: A situation in which the auditors are unable to obtain sufficient appropriate evidence; if material, a scope limitation results in the issuance of either a qualified opinion or disclaimer of opinion, 533

special purpose frameworks: A coherent accounting framework in which substantially all important financial measurements are governed by criteria other than GAAP or IFRS, 548

unmodified opinion: An opinion issued when the auditors conclude that the financial statements present the financial condition, results of operations, and cash flows in accordance with GAAP, 529

updated report: The auditors' report on prior-year financial statements that is based on both the prior-year audit and information that has come to the auditors' attention in the most recent audit, 545

Multiple-Choice Questions for Practice and Review

 All applicable questions are available with *Connect.*

LO 12-1

12.33 In the standard audit report under GAAS, certain conclusions are required to be stated in the report ("explicit") while other conclusions are implied ("implicit"). Which combination that follows correctly describes the auditors' conclusions as explicit or implicit?

	(a)	(b)	(c)	(d)
1. GAAP	Explicit	Explicit	Implicit	Implicit
2. Consistency	Implicit	Explicit	Explicit	Implicit
3. Going concern	Implicit	Implicit	Explicit	Explicit
4. Opinion	Explicit	Explicit	Implicit	Implicit

LO 12-1

12.34 How is the auditors' responsibility for expressing the opinion on financial statements disclosed in the standard (unmodified) report for a nonissuer?

a. Stated explicitly in the *Auditor's Responsibility for the Audit of the Financial Statements* section.

b. Unstated but understood in the *Auditor's Responsibility for the Audit of the Financial Statements* section.

c. Stated explicitly in the *Opinion* section.

d. Stated explicitly in the *Basis for Opinion* section.

LO 12-1

12.35 Which of the following is *not* included in the standard (unmodified) report on the financial statements?

a. An identification of the financial statements that were audited.

b. A general description of an audit.

c. An opinion that the financial statements present financial position in accordance with GAAP.

d. An *emphasis-of-matter paragraph* commenting on the effect of economic conditions on the entity.

LO 12-1

12.36 Which of the following statements is *not* true with respect to the audit examinations and reports for issuers and nonissuers?

a. Audit examinations for nonissuers are based on user demand but for issuers audit examinations are based on legislative requirements.

b. The reports for both issuers and nonissuers express an opinion on the entity's financial statements.

c. Auditors are required to express an opinion on internal control in the audit of nonissuers but not in the audit of issuers.

d. Management is responsible for the fairness of the financial statements for both issuers and nonissuers.

LO 12-2

12.37 The audit team found that the entity has not capitalized a material amount of leases in the financial statements. When considering the materiality of this departure from GAAP, the auditors would choose between which reporting options?

a. Unmodified opinion or disclaimer of opinion.

b. Unmodified opinion or qualified opinion.

c. Unmodified opinion with an emphasis-of-matter paragraph or an adverse opinion.

d. Qualified opinion or adverse opinion.

LO 12-2

12.38 Which of the following situations would *not* ordinarily require auditors to modify the *Opinion* section of the report on the financial statements of a nonissuer?

a. A material departure from GAAP.

b. Reference to the use of a component auditor in the examination of group financial statements.

c. A significant scope limitation.

d. A change from one generally accepted accounting principle to another.

LO 12-2

12.39 In which of the following instances would a qualified opinion be an appropriate option (assuming no other issues have been encountered)?

	Scope Limitation	Audit of Group Financial Statements
a.	Yes	Yes
b.	No	Yes
c.	Yes	No
d.	No	No

LO 12-2

12.40 If audit teams are unable to apply an auditing procedure to an account balance or class of transactions and the impact has a material effect on the audit, the audit team should first

a. Attempt to determine whether alternative auditing procedures are available and can be applied.

b. Withdraw from the engagement and issue a disclaimer of opinion.

c. Assess the significance of the scope limitation on the overall fairness of the financial statements.

d. Notify individuals currently relying on the financial statements that the statements may no longer be relied upon.

LO 12-2

12.41 Which of the following sections of the standard report on the financial statements of a nonissuer would be modified in response to a material departure from GAAP?

	Basis for Opinion	Auditor's Responsibilities
a.	Yes	Yes
b.	Yes	No
c.	No	Yes
d.	No	No

LO 12-2

12.42 When component auditors are involved in the audit of group financial statements, the group auditors may issue a report that

a. Refers to the component auditors, describes the extent of the component auditors' work, and expresses an unmodified opinion.

b. Does not consider or evaluate the component auditors' work but expresses an unmodified opinion in a standard report.

c. Places primary responsibility for the reporting on the component auditors.

d. Names the component auditors, describes their work, and presents only the group auditors' report.

LO 12-2, 12-3

12.43 Under which of the following conditions can a disclaimer of opinion *never* be issued?

a. The entity's going-concern problems are highly material and pervasive.

b. The entity does not allow the audit team access to evidence about important accounts.

c. Members of the audit team own stock in the entity.

d. The audit team has determined that the entity uses the NIFO (next-in, first-out) inventory costing method.

LO 12-3

12.44 The audit team determined that the entity is suffering financial difficulty and its going-concern status is seriously in doubt. Assuming that the entity adequately disclosed this matter in the financial statements, the auditors must choose between which of the following report alternatives?

a. Unmodified opinion with a reference to going-concern or disclaimer of opinion.

b. Standard (unmodified) report or a disclaimer of opinion.

c. Qualified opinion or adverse opinion.

d. Standard (unmodified) report or adverse opinion.

LO 12-3

12.45 Which of these situations would require auditors to include an *emphasis-of-matter paragraph* about consistency to an otherwise unmodified opinion?

a. Entity changed its estimated allowance for uncollectible accounts receivable.

b. Entity corrected a prior mistake in accounting for interest capitalization.

c. Entity sold one of its subsidiaries and consolidated six subsidiaries this year compared to seven last year.

d. Entity changed its inventory costing method from FIFO to LIFO.

LO 12-3

12.46 When auditors wish to issue an unmodified opinion but highlight that the entity changed its method of accounting for software development costs, they would most appropriately identify the change in accounting method in which of the following?

a. The *Opinion* section.

b. The *Basis for Opinion* section.

c. An *emphasis-of-matter paragraph*.

d. An *other-matter paragraph*.

LO 12-3

12.47 Which of the following would *not* be addressed in an *emphasis-of-matter* or *other-matter paragraph*?

a. A change in accounting principles that was accounted for in conformity with GAAP.

b. Information relating to a material acquisition made during the previous year.

c. The financial statement effects of a material departure from generally accepted accounting principles.

d. Procedures performed on supplementary information required by the Financial Accounting Standards Board.

LO 12-4

12.48 R. Wolfe became the new auditor for Royal Corporation, succeeding C. Mason, who audited the financial statements last year. Wolfe needs to report on Royal's comparative financial statements and should disclose in the report an explanation about other auditors having audited the prior year

a. Only if Mason's opinion last year was qualified.

b. To describe the prior audit and the opinion but not name Mason as the predecessor auditor.

c. To describe the audit but not reveal the type of opinion issued by Mason.

d. To describe the audit and the opinion and name Mason as the predecessor auditor.

LO 12-4

12.49 When financial statements are presented in comparative form and another firm audited the prior years' financial statements (but the other firm's report is not presented with the financial statements), the auditors' report on the current year financial statements should

    a. Disclaim an opinion on the prior years' financial statements.

    b. Not refer to the prior years' financial statements.

    c. Refer to any procedures performed by the current auditor to verify the opinion on the prior years' financial statements.

    d. Refer to the report and type of opinion issued by the other firm on the prior years' financial statements.

LO 12-4

12.50 If the opinion issued on prior years' financial statements is no longer appropriate and financial statements are presented in comparative form, the auditors' current report should

    a. Not reference the prior years' financial statements.

    b. Indicate that the opinion on the prior years' financial statements cannot be relied upon.

    c. Reference the type of opinion issued on the prior years' financial statements and indicate that the current opinion on these financial statements differs from that expressed in the prior years.

    d. Express the revised opinion on the prior years' financial statements without referencing the previously issued opinion.

LO 12-4

12.51 When a predecessor auditor has examined comparative financial statements and that report is not presented with the successor auditor's report, the successor auditor should

    a. Assume responsibility for the work of the predecessor auditor and report on all comparative years presented.

    b. Express an opinion on the year(s) examined by the successor auditor without referencing the comparative years examined by the predecessor auditor.

    c. Indicate that comparative year(s) were examined by the predecessor auditor and disclose the type of opinion issued.

    d. Express an opinion on the year(s) examined by the successor auditor and disclaim an opinion on the comparative year(s) examined by the predecessor auditor.

LO 12-4

12.52 If auditors examine all years presented in comparative form, which of the following best describes their responsibility for prior years' financial statements in their current report?

    a. Auditors are not required to address prior years' financial statements in their current report.

    b. Auditors should consider whether information has come to their attention that might affect their previous opinion on the prior years' financial statements.

    c. Auditors should not modify their previous opinion on prior years' financial statements.

    d. Auditors are only required to consider whether new information might affect their previous opinion on prior years' financial statements if a report other than unmodified was issued.

LO 12-5

12.53 Which of the following would *not* be included in an auditors' report on financial statements prepared using a special purpose framework?

    a. A statement that the financial statements are the responsibility of management.

    b. An identification of the financial statements and years examined.

    c. An opinion on the appropriateness of the special purpose framework.

    d. A reference to a footnote or other disclosure discussing the special purpose framework used in preparing the financial statements.

LO 12-5

12.54 Auditors may accept an engagement and express an unmodified opinion on an element, account, or item of the financial statements if they

    a. Perform analytical procedures related to all significant account balances and classes of transactions.

    b. Limit the use of their report to specified users.

    c. Conduct the engagement in accordance with generally accepted auditing standards.

    d. Have expressed an adverse opinion on the full financial statements.

LO 12-5

12.55 Which of the following sections or paragraphs of the auditors' report would be modified if the report expresses an opinion on financial statements prepared using the cash basis of accounting rather than generally accepted accounting principles?

	Opinion Section	Auditor's Responsibility Section
a.	Yes	Yes
b.	Yes	No
c.	No	Yes
d.	No	No

LO 12-5

12.56 Which of the following statements is *not* true regarding an auditors' report on compliance with contractual provisions conducted in conjunction with a GAAS audit?

a. Auditors may issue either a separate report on compliance with contractual provisions or a combined report on compliance included with the report on the financial statements.

b. The auditors' report expresses an opinion on the financial statements and compliance with contractual provisions.

c. The use of the auditors' report is limited.

d. The auditors' report acknowledges that the audit was not conducted with the purpose of obtaining knowledge regarding compliance with contractual provisions.

Exercises and Problems

Mc Graw Hill **connect** All applicable questions are available with *Connect.*

LO 12-2

12.57 **Basic Reports.** The concepts of materiality and pervasiveness are important to audit teams in examinations of financial statements and expressions of opinion on these statements.

Required:

How will materiality influence auditors' reporting decisions in the following circumstances? In your response, consider both the matter's materiality and pervasiveness.

a. The entity prohibits confirmation of accounts receivable, and sufficient and appropriate evidence cannot be obtained using alternative procedures.

b. The entity is a gas and electric utility company that follows the practice of recognizing revenue when it is billed to customers. At the end of the year, amounts earned but not yet billed are not recorded in the accounts or reported in the financial statements.

c. The entity leases buildings for its chain of transmission repair shops, but does not account for these lease obligations in accordance with GAAP.

d. The entity has lost a lawsuit in federal district court. The case is on appeal in an attempt to reduce the amount of damages awarded to the plaintiffs. No loss amount is recorded.

LO 12-2

12.58 **Departures from GAAP.** For each of the following departures from GAAP, indicate the type of opinion that the auditors would issue as well as any modifications that would be made to the standard (unmodified) report in the audit of a nonissuer.

a. A departure that had an immaterial effect on the financial statements.

b. A departure that had a material effect on the financial statements (this effect was not pervasive and affected only one account).

c. A departure that had a material effect on the financial statements and was pervasive (affected a number of accounts on both the balance sheet and income statement).

LO 12-2   12.59   **Scope Limitations.** Situations in which audit teams are unable to obtain sufficient appropriate evidence necessary to support their opinion on the entity's financial statements are referred to as *scope limitations*.

Required:

a.   Distinguish between *client-imposed* scope limitations and *circumstance-imposed* scope limitations. Which of these is generally of more concern to audit teams?

b.   Why do scope limitations impact the auditors' ability to express an opinion on the entity's financial statements?

c.   Assume that a circumstance-imposed scope limitation prevented audit teams from performing procedures they considered to be necessary. How would each of the following factors independently influence the opinion expressed on the entity's financial statements?

1.   The account balances affected by the scope limitation are not material to the entity's financial position, results of operations, or cash flows.

2.   The account balances affected by the scope limitation are material to the entity's financial position, results of operations, and cash flows. However, the audit team is able to perform alternative procedures that provide evidence supporting the accounts affected by the scope limitation.

3.   The account balances affected by the scope limitation are material to the entity's financial position, results of operations, and cash flows. Because of a lack of supporting documentation and key accounting records, the audit team is unable to perform alternative procedures that provide evidence supporting the accounts affected by the scope limitation.

d.   For each of the situations in part (c), briefly describe how the auditors' report on the entity's financial statements would be affected. (Assume the entity is a nonissuer and do *not* rewrite or draft the report that would be issued in each of these circumstances.)

LO 12-2   12.60   **Scope Limitations.** Following are four possible scenarios that reflect scope limitations encountered by J. Bruce, CPA, during the audit of Weaver Inc., a nonissuer. In all cases, assume that the ending balance in inventory is material to Weaver's financial position, results of operations, and cash flows.

•   *Scenario A.* Because of the late appointment to the audit engagement, Bruce is unable to observe Weaver's physical inventory for the year ended December 31, 2023. However, Weaver maintains extensive perpetual inventory records, and Bruce has been able to perform other substantive procedures and is satisfied as to the fairness of the ending inventory balance for December 31, 2023.

•   *Scenario B.* Because of the late appointment to the audit engagement, Bruce is unable to observe Weaver's physical inventory for the year ended December 31, 2023. Because Weaver's accounting records are not complete, Bruce is unable to perform other substantive procedures and is not satisfied as to the fairness of the ending inventory balance for December 31, 2023.

•   *Scenario C.* Because of a direct request by Weaver's management, Bruce did not observe Weaver's physical inventory for the year ended December 31, 2023. However, Weaver maintains extensive perpetual inventory records, and Bruce has been able to perform other substantive procedures and is satisfied as to the fairness of the ending inventory balance for December 31, 2023.

•   *Scenario D.* Because of a direct request by Weaver's management, Bruce did not observe Weaver's physical inventory for the year ended December 31, 2023. Weaver's accounting records are not complete, so Bruce is unable to perform other substantive procedures and is not satisfied as to the fairness of the ending inventory balance for December 31, 2023.

Required:

For each of these scenarios, indicate what reporting option(s) and factors Bruce should consider in deciding which type of opinion to issue in the circumstances. (Do *not* draft Bruce's report on Weaver Inc.'s financial statements for the year ended December 31, 2023.)

LO 12-2

12.61 **Scope Limitations.** D. Brady has been engaged as the auditor of Patriot Company (a nonissuer) and is currently planning the year-end physical inventory counts. Patriot is a retailer that holds significant inventories in its warehouses and stores in six regions across the United States. Because of timing and logistics, Brady is able to observe the physical inventory at only one of Patriot's warehouses, which accounts for 20 percent of Patriot's inventories.

In Brady's professional judgment, the fact that inventories held at only one warehouse can be observed does not provide sufficient evidence with respect to Patriot's inventory balances at the date of the financial statements. Although physical inventory counts could be delayed at the remaining warehouses for Brady to observe the counts, the flow of goods in and out of the warehouses would result in a discrepancy between the inventory quantities on hand at year-end and the inventory quantities on hand at the date of the count.

Required:

a. Assume that Brady observes physical inventory at only the one warehouse and does not perform alternative procedures related to inventories held at the other warehouses. Does this cause a scope limitation? If so, is this a client-imposed or circumstance-imposed scope limitation?

b. What type of opinion would Brady likely issue for the situation in part (a)? How would the wording in the standard (unmodified) report be modified to reflect this opinion?

c. What alternative procedures might be available to Brady with respect to this scope limitation? (*Hint:* You may wish to refer to Chapter 9 to identify alternative procedures for inventory.)

d. Assume that Brady performs one or more of the alternative procedures in part (c) and is able to gather evidence to support the recorded balance in inventory. What type of opinion would Brady issue on Patriot's financial statements (assuming that no other issues were identified in the audit examination)?

LO 12-2

12.62 **Audit of Group Financial Statements.** Lando Corporation is a nonissuer domestic company with two wholly owned subsidiaries. Michaels, CPA, has been engaged to audit the financial statements of the parent company and one of its subsidiaries and to serve as the group auditor. Thomas, CPA, has audited the financial statements of the other subsidiary whose operations are material in relation to the consolidated financial statements.

The work performed by Michaels is sufficient for serving as the group auditor and to report as such on the financial statements. Michaels has not yet decided whether to refer to the part of the audit performed by Thomas.

Required:

a. What responsibilities does Michaels have with respect to Thomas when deciding whether to rely on the work of Thomas?

b. What are the reporting requirements with which Michaels must comply in naming Thomas and referring to the work done by Thomas?

c. What report should be issued if Michaels does not wish to assume responsibility for Thomas's work or refer to Thomas's work?

LO 12-2, 12-3

12.63 **Various Reporting Situations.** Assume that the audit team encountered the following separate situations when deciding on the report to issue for the current year financial statements for a nonissuer.

1. The audit team decided that sufficient appropriate evidence could not be obtained to complete the audit of significant investments the entity held in a foreign entity.

2. The entity failed to account for lease assets and obligations in accordance with GAAP, but provided complete disclosures of these asset and obligations in the notes to the financial statements.

3. The entity is defending a lawsuit on product liability claims. (Customers allege that power saw safety guards were improperly installed.) All facts about the lawsuit are disclosed in the notes to the financial statements, but the audit team believes the entity should record a loss based on a probable settlement mentioned by the entity's attorneys.

4. The entity hired the audit team after taking inventory on December 31. The accounting records and other evidence are not reliable enough to enable the audit team to have sufficient evidence about the proper inventory amount.

5. The FASB requires the energy company to present supplementary oil and gas reserve information outside the basic financial statements. The audit team finds that this information, which is not required as a part of the basic financial statements, has been omitted.

6. The auditors are group auditors of the parent company, but they reviewed the component auditors' work and reputation, and decided not to take responsibility for the work of the component auditors on three subsidiary companies included in the consolidated financial statements. The component auditors' work amounts to 32 percent of the consolidated assets and 39 percent of the consolidated revenues.

7. The entity changed its depreciation method from units of production to straight line, and its audit team believes the straight-line method is the more appropriate method in the circumstances. The change, fully explained in the notes to the financial statements, has a material effect on the year-to-year comparability of the comparative financial statements.

8. Because the entity has experienced significant operating losses and has had to obtain waivers of debt payment requirements from its lenders, the audit team decides that there is substantial doubt that the entity can continue as a going concern. The entity has fully described all problems in a note in the financial statements and the audit team believes that, while material, the uncertainty is not serious enough to warrant a disclaimer of opinion.

Required:

a. What kind of opinion should the auditors express in each separate case?

b. What other modification(s) or addition(s) to the standard (unmodified) report is (are) required for each separate case?

LO 12-2, 12-3, 12-5 12.64 **Various Reporting Situations.** Assume that Stanford CPAs encountered the following issues during its various audit engagements for nonissuers in 2023:

1. Stanford conducted the audit of Luck, a new client, this past year. Last year, Luck was audited by another CPA, who issued an unmodified opinion on its financial statements. Luck is presenting financial statements for 2022 and 2023 in comparative form.

2. One of Stanford's clients is RealCo, a real estate holding company. Assume that RealCo experienced a significant decline in the value of its investment properties during the past year because of a downturn in the economy and has appropriately recognized that decline in market value under GAAP. Stanford wishes to emphasize the decline in the economy and its impact on RealCo's financial position and results of operations for 2023 in its audit report.

3. For the past five years, Stanford has conducted the audits of TechTime, a company that provides technology consulting services, and has always issued unmodified opinions on its financial statements. Based on its 2023 audit, Stanford believes that an unmodified opinion is appropriate; however, Stanford did note that TechTime reported its third consecutive operating loss and has experienced negative cash flows because of the inability of some of its customers to promptly pay for services received.

4. Stanford has assisted Cardinal Inc. with the preparation of its financial statements but has not audited, compiled, or reviewed those financial statements. Cardinal wishes to include these financial statements in a communication that would describe Stanford's involvement in the preparation of the financial statements. Stanford believes that Cardinal's communication is adequate and appropriately describes Stanford's limited role in the preparation of the financial statements.

5. Trees Inc. presents summary financial information along with its financial statements. The summary financial information has been derived from the complete set of financial statements that Stanford has audited (and issued an unmodified opinion on the complete financial statements). A lender has engaged Stanford to evaluate and report on Trees' summary financial information; Stanford believes that the summary financial information is fairly stated in relation to Trees' complete financial statements.

6. Stanford believes that some of the verbiage in Plunkett's Management Discussion & Analysis section is inconsistent with the firm's financial statements. Stanford has concluded that Plunkett's financial statements present its financial position, results of operations, and cash flows in accordance with GAAP and has decided to issue an unmodified opinion on Plunkett's financial statements.

7. Oil Patch is a client in the energy industry that is required to present supplementary oil and gas reserve information. Stanford has performed certain procedures regarding this information and concluded that it is presented in accordance with FASB presentation guidelines and does not appear to depart from GAAP. Based on Stanford's audit, it plans to issue an unmodified opinion on Oil Patch's financial statements.

Required:

How would each of these issues affect Stanford's report on the client's financial statements? (Do *not* draft the report that Stanford would issue in each situation.)

LO 12-2, 12-3, 12-5

12.65 **Various Reporting Situations.** For each of the following situations, indicate the type of opinion(s) that auditors could issue in the audit of a nonissuer (more than one opinion may be appropriate in each circumstance). Unless otherwise noted, assume that no departures from GAAP were identified in the audit engagement. In addition, indicate how the standard (unmodified) report would be modified, if appropriate.

1. The audit team has identified an immaterial departure from GAAP in their examination, but the entity has not adjusted its financial statements for this departure or disclosed this departure in its financial statements or related disclosures.

2. Because they were appointed to the engagement after the date of the financial statements, the audit team has experienced a significant scope limitation and was unable to perform standard auditing procedures used in their engagements. The account(s) affected by this scope limitation were material and pervasive. However, the audit team has been able to completely satisfy themselves as to the fairness of the related account balances and classes of transaction by performing alternative procedures.

3. During the year, the entity changed its method of accounting for inventories from FIFO to LIFO and has disclosed this change in the footnotes to the financial statements and accounted for the change properly. However, the audit team does not agree with the rationale for the change and believes that it was made to report a higher level of earnings.

4. Subsequent to accepting the audit engagement, the audit team determined that they are not independent with respect to the client because of a financial interest in the client held by a newly admitted partner to the audit firm.

5. Evidence gathered during the audit examination and inquiry of the client's management revealed substantial doubt about the client's ability to continue in existence. The audit team believes that the client has appropriately disclosed the going-concern uncertainties in its financial statements and footnotes.

6. The auditors wish to emphasize the company's acquisition of two large subsidiaries during the most recent year.

7. The auditors have engaged component auditors to conduct a portion of the audit but do not wish to assume responsibility for their work. The auditors have not approached the component auditors about presenting their reports with the company's financial statements and do not plan to do so.

8. The client has not recognized a material loss related to a decline in the market value of its investments. Because the audit team believes this decline in value is not temporary, they believe the financial statements do not present the client's financial position and results of operations in accordance with GAAP.

9. The audit team has experienced a significant scope limitation and is unable to satisfy themselves as to the fairness of the affected account balances through alternative procedures.

LO 12-2, 12-3

12.66 **Various Reporting Situations.** For each of the following situations, indicate the type of report that would be required as well as how various paragraphs/sections of the auditors' report would be modified in the audit of a nonissuer. Assume any amount in question is material on an overall basis (but not pervasive) unless otherwise noted.

1. The entity is subject to a going-concern uncertainty and has properly disclosed this uncertainty in its financial statements.

2. The entity has changed from an accounting principle in accordance with GAAP to an accounting principle not in accordance with GAAP.

3. The audit team encounters a material, but not pervasive, scope limitation; this limitation has not been imposed by the client.

4. The entity's financial statements are presented in accordance with GAAP.

5. The entity has changed from one accounting principle in accordance with GAAP to another principle in accordance with GAAP; this change has been properly reported by restating prior years' financial statements.

6. After accepting the engagement, the audit team determines that the firm is not independent.

7. The entity's financial statements contain a material and pervasive departure from GAAP.

8. The group auditors' opinion on group financial statements is based partially on the report of component auditors.

9. The entity presents summary financial statements along with its full set of financial statements.

10. The audit team was unable to observe ending inventories because of late appointment; this represented a material and pervasive limitation on the scope of their examination.

LO 12-2, 12-3 12.67 **Audit Report Deficiencies.** On September 23, 2024, Betsy Ross drafted the following report on Continental Corporation's (a nonissuer) financial statements.

To Whom It May Concern:

Report on the Audit of the Financial Statements

Opinion

We have audited the accompanying financial statements of Continental Corporation, which comprise the balance sheet as of July 31, 2024, and the related statements of income and changes in shareholders' equity for the year then ended, and the related notes to the financial statements.

In our opinion, with the explanation given below and with the exception of some minor errors we consider immaterial, the accompanying financial statements present the financial position of Continental Corporation as of July 31, 2024, and the results of its operations and its cash flows for the year then ended in accordance with pronouncements of the Financial Accounting Standards Board.

Basis for Opinion

In accordance with instructions by Continental's management, we have conducted a complete audit. Our responsibilities under those standards are further described in the Auditor's Responsibilities for the Audit of the Financial Statements section of our report. We are required to be independent of Continental Corporation and to meet our other ethical responsibilities, in accordance with the relevant ethical requirements relating to our audit. We believe that the audit evidence we have obtained is sufficient and appropriate to provide a basis for our audit opinion.

Emphasis of Matter

In many respects, this was an unusual year for Continental Corporation. The weakening of the economy in the early part of the year and the strike of plant employees in the summer led to a decline in sales and net income. After making several tests of the sales records, nothing came to our attention that would indicate sales have not been properly recorded.

Responsibilities of Management for the Financial Statements

Management is responsible for the preparation and fair presentation of the financial statements in accordance with accounting principles generally accepted in the United States of America, and for the design, implementation, and maintenance of internal control relevant to the preparation and fair presentation of financial statements that are free from material misstatement, whether due to fraud or error.

In preparing the financial statements, management is required to evaluate whether there are conditions or events, considered in the aggregate, that raise substantial doubt about Continental Corporation's ability to continue as a going concern for one year following the issuance of the financial statements.

Auditor's Responsibilities for the Audit of the Financial Statements

Reasonable assurance is a high level of assurance but is not absolute assurance and therefore is not a guarantee that an audit conducted in accordance with GAAS will always detect a material misstatement when it exists. The risk of not detecting a material misstatement resulting from fraud is higher than for one resulting from error, as fraud may involve collusion, forgery, intentional omissions, misrepresentations, or the override of internal control. Misstatements are considered material if, individually or in the aggregate, they could reasonably be expected to influence the economic decisions of users made on the basis of these financial statements.

In performing an audit in accordance with GAAS, we:

[Standard report language on professional judgment and skepticism, risks of misstatement, internal control, accounting policies and estimates, and going concern]

We are required to communicate with those charged with governance regarding, among other matters, the planned scope and timing of the audit, significant audit findings, and certain internal control-related matters that we identified during the audit.

Betsy Ross & Co, CPA

Philadelphia, PA
July 31, 2024

Required:

List and explain the deficiencies and omissions in the report prepared by Ross on Continental Company's financial statements. (Assume that Ross was not engaged to communicate key audit matters.)

LO 12-2

12.68 **Audit Report Deficiencies: Adverse Opinion.** The board of directors of Cook Industries Inc. (a nonissuer) engaged Brown & Brown, CPAs, to audit the financial statements for the year ended December 31, 2023.

Independent Auditor's Report

To the President of Cook Industries Inc.:

Report on the Audit of the Financial Statements

Opinion

We have audited the financial statements of Cook Industries, Inc. as of December 31, 2023, and the related notes to the financial statements. We conducted our audit in accordance with auditing standards generally accepted in the United States of America (GAAS). Our responsibilities under those standards are further described in the Auditor's Responsibilities for the Audit of the Financial Statements section of our report. We believe that the audit evidence we have obtained is sufficient and appropriate to provide a basis for our audit opinion.

In our opinion, the accompanying financial statements present fairly, in all material respects, the financial position of Cook Industries Inc. as of December 31, 2023, and the results of its operations and its cash flows for the year then ended in accordance with accounting principles generally accepted in the United States of America.

Basis for Adverse Opinion

As discussed in Note G to the financial statements, the Company carries its property and equipment at appraisal values and provides depreciation on the basis of such values. Furthermore, the Company does not provide for income taxes with respect to differences between financial income and taxable Income arising from the use, for income tax purposes, of the installment method of reporting gross profit from certain types of sales.

Auditor's Responsibilities for the Audit of the Financial Statements

Our objectives are to obtain reasonable assurance about whether the financial statements as a whole are free from material misstatement, whether due to fraud or error, and to issue an auditor's report that includes our opinion. Reasonable assurance is a high level of assurance but is not absolute assurance and therefore is not a guarantee that an audit conducted in accordance with GAAS will always detect a material misstatement when it exists. The risk of not detecting a material misstatement resulting from fraud is higher than for one resulting from error, as fraud may involve collusion, forgery, intentional omissions, misrepresentations, or the override of internal control. Misstatements are considered material if, individually or in the aggregate, they could reasonably be expected to influence the economic decisions of users made on the basis of these financial statements.

In performing an audit in accordance with GAAS, we:

[Standard report language on professional judgment and skepticism, risks of misstatement, internal control, accounting policies and estimates, and going concern]

We are required to communicate with those charged with governance regarding, among other matters, the planned scope and timing of the audit, significant audit findings, and certain internal control-related matters that we identified during the audit.

Brown & Brown, CPAs
Los Angeles, CA
March 14, 2024

(AICPA adapted)

Required:

Identify the deficiencies in the following draft of the report (assume that Brown & Brown were not engaged to communicate key audit matters). Do *not* rewrite the report.

LO 12-4

12.69 **Audit Report Deficiencies: Comparative Reporting.** An assistant drafted the following auditors' report at the completion of the audit of Cramdon Inc. (a nonissuer) on March 5, 2024. The partner in charge of the engagement has decided the opinion on the 2023 financial statements should be modified only with reference to the change in the method of computing the cost of inventory. In 2022, Cramdon used the next-in, first-out (NIFO) method, which is not permissible under GAAP, but in 2023 changed to FIFO and restated the 2022 financial statements. The auditors' report on the 2022 financial statements was prepared by the same firm and dated March 5, 2023.

Independent Auditor's Report

To the Board of Directors of Cramdon Inc.:

Report on the Audit of the Financial Statements

Opinion

We have audited the financial statements of Cramdon, Inc. as of December 31, 2023 and 2022, and the related notes to the financial statements.

In our opinion, based upon the following, the accompanying financial statements present fairly, in all material respects, the financial position of Cramdon Inc. as of December 31, 2023, and the results of operations and cash flows for the year then ended in accordance with accounting principles generally accepted in the United States of America, consistently applied, except for the changes in the method of computing inventory cost as described in Note 7 to the financial statements.

Basis for Opinion

We conducted our audits in accordance with auditing standards generally accepted in the United States of America (GAAS). Our responsibilities under those standards are further described in the Auditor's Responsibilities for the Audit of the Financial Statements section of our report. We are required to be independent of Cramdon Inc. and to meet our other ethical responsibilities, in accordance with the relevant ethical requirements relating to our audits. We believe that the audit evidence we have obtained is sufficient and appropriate to provide a basis for our audit opinions.

As discussed in Note 7 to the financial statements, the company changed its method of accounting for inventory cost from NIFO to FIFO. The 2022 financial statements have been restated to reflect this change in accordance with accounting principles generally accepted in the United States of America. Accordingly, our present opinion on the 2022 financial statements, as presented herein, is different from the opinion we expressed in our previous report.

Responsibilities of Management for the Financial Statements

Management is responsible for the preparation and fair presentation of the financial statements in accordance with accounting principles generally accepted in the United States of America, and for the design, implementation, and maintenance of internal control relevant to the preparation and fair presentation of financial statements that are free from material misstatement, whether due to fraud or error.

In preparing the financial statements, management is required to evaluate whether there are conditions or events, considered in the aggregate, that raise substantial doubt about Cramdon Inc.'s ability to continue as a going concern for one year following the issuance of the financial statements.

Auditor's Responsibilities for the Audit of the Financial Statements

Our objectives are to obtain reasonable assurance about whether the financial statements as a whole are free from material misstatement, whether due to fraud or error, and to issue an auditor's report that includes our opinion. Reasonable assurance is a high level of assurance but is not absolute assurance and therefore is not a guarantee that an audit conducted in accordance with GAAS will always detect a material misstatement when it exists. The risk of not detecting a material misstatement resulting from fraud is higher than for one resulting from error, as fraud may involve collusion, forgery, intentional omissions, misrepresentations, or the override of internal control. Misstatements are considered material if, individually or in the aggregate, they could reasonably be expected to influence the economic decisions of users made on the basis of these financial statements.

In performing an audit in accordance with GAAS, we:

[Standard report language on professional judgment and skepticism, risks of misstatement, internal control, accounting policies and estimates, and going concern]

We are required to communicate with those charged with governance regarding, among other matters, the planned scope and timing of the audit, significant audit findings, and certain internal control-related matters that we identified during the audit.

George Constanza, CPA
New York, NY
March 5, 2024

Required:

Identify the deficiencies and errors in the draft report and write an explanation of the reasons they are errors and deficiencies (assume that the auditors were not engaged to communicate key audit matters). Do *not* rewrite the report.

LO 12-2

12.70 **Audit Report Deficiencies: Audits of Group Financial Statements and Other Operating Matters.** Following is Rex Wolf's report on Bonair Corporation's (a nonissuer) financial statements. Bonair publishes general-purpose financial statements for distribution to owners, creditors, potential investors, and the general public.

Independent Auditor's Report

To the Board of Directors and Shareholders of Bonair Corporation:

Report on the Audit of the Financial Statements

Opinion

We have audited the financial statements of Bonair Corporation, which comprise the balance sheet as of December 31, 2023, and the related statements of income, changes in stockholders' equity, and cash flows for the year then ended, and the related notes to the financial statements.

In our opinion, except for the matter of the report of the component auditors, the accompanying financial statements present fairly, in all material respects, the financial position of Bonair Corporation as of December 31, 2023, and the results of its operations and its cash flows for the year then ended.

We did not examine the financial statements of Caet Company, a wholly owned subsidiary. Those statements were audited by Nero Stout, CPA, whose report has been furnished to us, and our opinion insofar as it relates to the amounts included for Caet Company, is based solely on the report of other auditors.

Basis for Group Financial Statement Opinion

With the exception of the matter discussed above, we conducted our audit in accordance with auditing standards generally accepted in the United States of America (GAAS). Our responsibilities under those standards are further described in the Auditor's Responsibilities for the Audit of the Financial Statements section of our report. We are required to be independent of Bonair Corporation and to meet our other ethical responsibilities, in accordance with the relevant ethical requirements relating to our audit. We believe that the audit evidence we have obtained is sufficient and appropriate to provide a basis for our audit opinion.

Other Matter

As noted in the Opinion section of this report, Nero Stout, CPA, audited the financial statements of Caet Company, a wholly owned subsidiary.

Responsibilities of Management for the Financial Statements

Management is responsible for the preparation and fair presentation of the financial statements in accordance with accounting principles generally accepted in the United States of America, and for the design, implementation, and maintenance of internal control relevant to the preparation and fair presentation of financial statements that are free from material misstatement, whether due to fraud or error.

In preparing the financial statements, management is required to evaluate whether there are conditions or events, considered in the aggregate, that raise substantial doubt about Bonair Corporation's ability to continue as a going concern through December 31, 2024.

`Auditor's Responsibilities for the Audit of the Financial Statements

Our objectives are to obtain reasonable assurance about whether the financial statements as a whole are free from material misstatement, whether due to fraud or error, and to issue an auditor's report that includes our opinion. Reasonable assurance is a high level of assurance but is not absolute assurance and therefore is not a guarantee that an audit conducted in accordance with GAAS will always detect a material misstatement when it exists. The risk of not detecting a material misstatement resulting from fraud is higher than for one resulting from error, as fraud may involve collusion, forgery, intentional omissions, misrepresentations, or the override of internal control. Misstatements are considered material if, individually or in the aggregate, they could reasonably be expected to influence the economic decisions of users made on the basis of these financial statements.

In performing an audit in accordance with GAAS, we:

[Standard report language on professional judgment and skepticism, risks of misstatement, internal control, accounting policies and estimates, and going concern]

We are required to communicate with those charged with governance regarding, among other matters, the planned scope and timing of the audit, significant audit findings, and certain internal control-related matters that we identified during the audit.

Rex Wolf, CPA

Minneapolis, MN
March 5, 2024

Required:

Describe the reporting deficiencies and explain why they are considered deficiencies. Organize your response according to each of the paragraphs or sections in the standard (unmodified) report. (Assume that Wolf was not engaged to communicate key audit matters.)

LO 12-5

12.71 Audit Report Deficiencies: Disclaimer of Opinion. Your partner drafted the following report in the audit of a nonissuer yesterday. You need to describe the reporting deficiencies, explain the reasons for them, and discuss with the partner how the report should be corrected. You have decided to prepare a three-column worksheet showing the deficiencies, reasons, and corrections needed. Your partner's report follows:

> I made my examination in accordance with auditing standards generally accepted in the United States of America. However, I am not independent with respect to Mavis Corporation because my wife owns 5 percent of the company's outstanding common stock. The accompanying balance sheet as of December 31, 2023, and the related statements of income, changes in shareholders' equity, and cash flows for the year then ended were not audited by me. Accordingly, I do not express an opinion on them.

Required:

Prepare the three-column worksheet described.

LO 12-3, 12-4

12.72 Audit Report Deficiencies: Accounting Change and Uncertainty. The following auditors' report was drafted by Quinn Moore, a staff auditor with Tyler & Tyler, CPAs, at the completion of the audit of the financial statements of Park Publishing Company (a nonissuer) for the year ended September 30, 2023. The engagement partner reviewed the audit documentation and properly decided to issue an unmodified opinion. In drafting the report, Moore considered the following:

- During fiscal year 2023, Park changed its depreciation method. The engagement partner concurred with this change in accounting principles and its justification.
- The 2023 financial statements are affected by an uncertainty concerning a lawsuit, the outcome of which cannot presently be estimated. Moore included an emphasis-of-matter paragraph in the report to disclose this uncertainty.
- The financial statements for the year ended September 30, 2022, are to be presented for comparative purposes. Tyler & Tyler previously audited these statements and expressed an unmodified opinion.

Independent Auditor's Report

To the Board of Directors of Park Publishing Company:

Report on the Audit of the Financial Statements

Opinion

We have audited the financial statements of Park Publishing Company, which comprise the balance sheet as of September 30, 2023 and 2022, and the related statements of income, changes in stockholders' equity, and cash flows for the years then ended, and the related notes to the financial statements.

In our opinion, except for the accounting change, with which we concur, the accompanying financial statements present fairly, in all material respects, the financial position of Park Publishing Company as of September 30, 2023, and the results of its operations and its cash flows for the year then ended in accordance with accounting principles generally accepted in the United States of America.

As discussed in Note X to the financial statements, the company changed its method of computing depreciation in fiscal 2023.

Basis for Opinion

We conducted our audits in accordance with auditing standards generally accepted in the United States of America (GAAS). Our responsibilities under those standards are further described in the Auditor's Responsibilities for the Audit of the Financial Statements section of our report. We are required to be independent of Park Publishing Company and to meet our other ethical responsibilities, in accordance with the relevant ethical requirements relating to our audits. We believe that the audit evidence we have obtained is sufficient and appropriate to provide a basis for determining whether any material modifications should be made to the financial statements.

Emphasis of Matter

As discussed in Note Y to the financial statements, the company is a defendant in a lawsuit alleging infringement of certain copyrights. The company has filed a counteraction, and preliminary hearings on both actions are in progress. Accordingly, any provision for liability is subject to adjudication of this matter.

Responsibilities of Management for the Financial Statements

Management is responsible for the preparation and fair presentation of the financial statements and for the design, implementation, and maintenance of internal control relevant to the preparation and fair presentation of financial statements that are free from material misstatement, whether due to fraud or error.

In preparing the financial statements, management is required to evaluate whether there are conditions or events, considered in the aggregate, that raise substantial doubt about Park Publishing Company's ability to continue as a going concern for one year following the issuance of the financial statements.

Auditor's Responsibilities for the Audit of the Financial Statements

Our objectives are to obtain reasonable assurance about whether the financial statements as a whole are fairly presented. Reasonable assurance is a high level of assurance but is not absolute assurance and therefore is not a guarantee that an audit conducted in accordance with GAAS will always detect a material misstatement when it exists. The risk of not detecting a material misstatement resulting from fraud is higher than for one resulting from error, as fraud may involve collusion, forgery, intentional omissions, misrepresentations, or the override of internal control. Misstatements are considered material if, individually or in the aggregate, they could reasonably be expected to influence the economic decisions of users made on the basis of these financial statements.

In performing an audit in accordance with GAAS, we:

[Standard report language on professional judgment and skepticism, risks of misstatement, internal control, accounting policies and estimates, and going concern]

We are required to communicate with those charged with governance regarding, among other matters, the planned scope and timing of the audit, significant audit findings, and certain internal control-related matters that we identified during the audit.

Tyler & Tyler, CPAs
Tacoma, WA
November 5, 2023

Required:

Identify the deficiencies in the auditors' report as drafted by Moore (assume that Tyler & Tyler were not engaged to communicate key audit matters). Group the deficiencies by section or paragraph and in the order in which they appear. Do *not* rewrite the report.

(AICPA adapted)

Preparing Auditors' Reports

Cases 12.73 through 12.79 require you to draft auditors' reports. A Word file (AUDIT REPORT NONISSUER) containing the standard (unmodified) report can be found in *Connect*. This report can be modified (as necessary) for the conditions noted in the following cases. Unless instructed otherwise, assume the following in drafting your reports: (1) your firm, Anderson, Olds, & Watershed (AOW), conducted the audit examination of the identified client; (2) the fiscal year-end is December 31, 2023; (3) the date of the auditors' report is February 10, 2024; (4) your firm was not engaged to identify and communicate key audit matters; and (5) the client is a nonissuer and, therefore, not subject to the auditing and reporting requirements for internal control over financial reporting.

LO 12-3

12.73 **Financial Difficulty: The "Going-Concern" Problem.** Pitts Company has experienced significant financial difficulty. Current liabilities exceed current assets by $1 million, cash has decreased to $10,000, the interest on the long-term debt has not been paid, and a customer has brought a lawsuit against Pitts for $500,000 on a product liability claim. Significant questions concerning the going-concern status of the company exist. The lawsuit and information about the going-concern status have been appropriately described in footnote 3 to the financial statements, along with Pitts' acknowledgment that substantial doubt exists about its ability to continue as a going concern.

Required:

a. Draft AOW's report, assuming that the audit team decides that an unmodified opinion instead of a disclaimer of opinion is appropriate in the circumstances.

b. Draft AOW's report, assuming that the audit team decides the uncertainties are so serious that they do not wish to express an opinion on Pitts' financial statements.

LO 12-5

12.74 **Disagreement with Auditors.** Officers of Richnow Company do not wish to disclose information about a product liability lawsuit filed by a customer seeking $500,000 in damages. They believe the suit is frivolous and without merit. Outside counsel is more cautious. The audit team insists on disclosure. Angered, Richnow's chair of the board threatens to sue AOW if a standard (unmodified) report is not issued within three days.

Required:

Draft AOW's appropriate report under the circumstances.

LO 12-2

12.75 **Late Appointment of the Audit Team.** AOW has completed the audit of the financial statements of Musgrave Company for the year ended December 31, 2023, and is now preparing the report.

AOW has audited Musgrave's financial statements for several years, but this year Musgrave delayed the start of the audit work, so AOW was not present to observe the taking of the physical inventory on December 31, 2023. The inventory balance is $194,000, which represents 39 percent of Musgrave's total assets and 69 percent of its current assets. However, AOW performed alternative procedures including (1) examination of shipping and receiving documents with regard to transactions since the date of the financial statements, (2) extensive review of the inventory count sheets, and (3) discussion of the physical inventory procedures with responsible company personnel. AOW also is satisfied about the propriety of the inventory valuation calculations and the consistency of the valuation method. Musgrave determines year-end inventory quantities solely by means of physical count.

Required:

Draft AOW's report on the balance sheet at the end of the current year and on the statements of operations, changes in shareholders' equity, and cash flows for the year then ended. (*Hint:* Did the alternative procedures produce sufficient appropriate evidence?)

LO 12-2

12.76 **Audits of Group Financial Statements.** AOW is the group auditor for the December 31, 2023, consolidated financial statements of Ferguson Company and subsidiaries. However, component auditors perform the work on certain subsidiaries for the year under audit amounting to 29 percent of total assets and 36 percent of total revenues.

AOW evaluated the independence and professional reputation of the component auditors, as required by professional standards, and they furnished AOW their reports. AOW has decided to rely on their work and to refer to the component auditors in their report. None of the audit work revealed any issues with respect to Ferguson Company or its subsidiaries.

Required:

Draft AOW's report.

LO 12-3

12.77 **Other Information in a Financial Review Section of an Annual Report.** Gustav Humphreys (chair of the board) and Ingrid VanEns (vice president, finance) prepared the draft of the financial review section of the annual report. You are reviewing it for consistency with the audited financial statements. The draft contains the following explanation about income coverage of interest expense:

Last year, operating income before interest and income taxes covered interest expense by a ratio of 6:1. This year, on an incremental basis, the coverage of interest expense increased to a ratio of 6.59:1.

The relevant portion of the audited financial statements showed the following:

	Current Year	Prior Year
Operating income	$400,000	$360,000
Extraordinary gain from realization of tax benefits	100,000	0
Interest expense	(81,250)	(60,000)
Income taxes	(127,500)	(120,000)
Net income	$291,250	$180,000

Required:

a. Determine whether the financial review section statement about coverage of interest is or is not consistent with the audited financial statements. Be able to show your conclusion with calculations.

b. Assume that you find an inconsistency and the officers disagree with your conclusions. Draft the appropriate language you should include in your auditors' report.

LO 12-2

12.78 **Departures from GAAP.** On January 1, Graham Company purchased land (the site of a new building) for $100,000. Soon thereafter, the state highway department announced that a new feeder road would run next to the site. The effect was a dramatic increase in local property values. Comparable land located nearby sold for $700,000 in December of the current year. Graham presents the land at $700,000 in its accounts and, after reduction for implicit taxes at 33 percent, the fixed asset total is $400,000 higher than historical cost with the same amount shown separately in the shareholder equity account Current Value Increment. The valuation is fully disclosed in a footnote to the financial statements with a letter from a certified property appraiser attesting to the $700,000 value.

Required:

a. Draft the appropriate auditors' report, assuming that you believe the departure from GAAP is material but not pervasive enough to cause you to issue an adverse opinion.

b. Draft the appropriate auditors' report, assuming that you believe an adverse opinion is necessary.

LO 12-2, 12-3

12.79 **Reporting on an Accounting Change.** In December of the current year, Williams Company changed its method of accounting for inventory and cost of goods sold from LIFO to FIFO. The account balances shown in the trial balance have already been recalculated and adjusted retroactively as required by GAAP. The accounting change and the financial effects are described in Note 2 in the financial statements.

Required:

a. Assume that you believe the accounting change is justified as required by GAAP. Draft the report appropriate in the circumstances.

b. Assume that you believe the accounting change is not justified and causes the financial statements to be materially misstated. Inventories that would have been reported at $1.5 million (LIFO) are reported at $1.9 million (FIFO); operating income before tax that would have been $130,000 is reported at $530,000. As a result of this change, current assets, total assets, and shareholders' equity have increased by 17 percent, 9 percent, and 14 percent, respectively. Draft the report appropriate in the circumstances.

LO 12-5

12.80 **Reporting on a Special Purpose Framework.** You are issuing a report on the financial statements of Mega Offshore Trust for the year ended December 31, 2023. Mega uses a special purpose framework and prepares two major financial statements: (1) a statement of assets and liabilities arising from cash transactions and (2) a statement of revenue collected and expenses paid. The following footnote from Mega's financial statements describes the basis of accounting used to prepare Mega's financial statements.

Note 2: Financial Statement Presentation

The financial statements have been prepared using the cash basis of accounting, which is a comprehensive basis of accounting other than accounting principles generally accepted in the United States ("U.S. GAAP"). Consequently, inflows or receipts are recognized when received rather than when earned, and expenses or disbursements are recognized when paid rather than when the obligation is incurred. Cash basis accounting excludes accounts such as accounts receivable, prepaid expenses, accounts payable, fixed assets accrued liabilities, and long-term debt.

Required:

Assuming that the financial statements are fairly stated, prepare a draft of the *Opinion* section of the auditors' report along with any necessary explanatory language related to the use of the special purpose framework.

LO 12-5

12.81 **Reporting on a Special Purpose Framework.** Brooklyn Life Insurance Company prepares its financial statements in conformity with a special purpose framework (the accounting practices prescribed and permitted by the Insurance Department of the State of New York). The use of this framework results in financial statements that differ materially from statements prepared in conformity with generally accepted accounting principles. For example, using this framework, agents' first-year commissions are expensed instead of being partially deferred.

The company engaged its auditors, Major and Major Associates, to audit the financial statements and express an opinion on whether they are prepared in accordance with the special purpose framework. Footnote 10 in the statements contains a narrative description and a numerical table explaining the differences between the framework and GAAP accounting. Footnote 10 also reconciles the assets, liabilities, income, expense, and net income determined under the framework to these same subtotals determined under GAAP.

Required:

Write the audit report appropriate in the circumstances. The year-end date is December 31, 2023, and the audit fieldwork was completed on February 20, 2024. Assume that no issues were encountered during the audit and that the financial statements were fairly presented in accordance with the special purpose framework.

LO 12-5

12.82 **Reporting on a Special Purpose Framework.** Indicate (either yes or no) whether each of the following would be included in an auditors' report on financial statements prepared using a special purpose framework.

1. A statement that the engagement was performed under auditing standards related to the special purpose framework.
2. Statements providing a general description of an audit examination.
3. The auditors' opinion on the fairness of the financial statements.
4. A statement indicating that the financial statements were prepared using a special purpose framework as well as identifying footnote or other disclosures providing further information about the special purpose framework.
5. The auditors' opinion on the appropriateness of the special purpose framework for general use.
6. Statements describing management's responsibility for the financial statements.
7. A statement indicating that management is responsible for the selection of the special purpose framework used to prepare the financial statements.
8. The auditors' opinion on the materiality of differences between the financial information prepared using the special purpose framework and that under generally accepted accounting principles.

LO 12-5

12.83 **Reporting on Compliance in Conjunction with an Audit Engagement.** Prescott is conducting the audit of the financial statements of Mueller. In addition to the financial statement audit, various union groups have requested that Mueller provide evidence of compliance with the Fair Labor Standards Act (FLSA) of 1938. When discussing this matter with Prescott, he indicated that he could expand the auditors' report to reference compliance with the FLSA.

Required:

a. Under generally accepted auditing standards, is Prescott permitted to evaluate compliance with FLSA? If so, what procedures beyond those in a financial statement audit should he perform?
b. What are the options available to Prescott for reporting on compliance with the FLSA in conjunction with his audit of the financial statements?
c. What matters should Prescott address with respect to compliance with the FLSA in his report (assume that a separate report on compliance is prepared)? (Do not write the actual report.)

Appendix 12A

LO 12-6
Understand the contents of the auditors' report for the financial statements of issuers.

AUDITORS' REPORTS FOR ISSUERS (PUBLIC ENTITIES)

This chapter focused on auditors' reports for nonissuers. As noted, in addition to the opinion on the entity's financial statements, auditors are also required to express an opinion on the effectiveness of the entity's internal control over financial reporting (ICFR) for larger issuers (known as accelerated filers). An unqualified opinion on the financial statements for issuers (sometimes referred to as the *PCAOB report*) is shown in Exhibit 12A.1.[10]

EXHIBIT 12A.1

Standard PCAOB Report for Issuer

Report of Independent Registered Public Accounting Firm

To the Board of Directors and Shareholders of Dunder-Mifflin, Inc.

Opinion on the Financial Statements

We have audited the accompanying balance sheet of Dunder-Mifflin Inc. as of December 31, 2023 and the related statements of income, comprehensive income, changes in stockholders' equity, and cash flows for the period ended December 31, 2023, and the related notes (collectively referred to as the "financial statements"). In our opinion, the financial statements present fairly, in all material respects, the financial position of Dunder-Mifflin Inc. as of December 31, 2023, and the results of its operations and its cash flows for the period ended December 31, 2023 in conformity with accounting principles generally accepted in the United States of America.

We also have audited, in accordance with the standards of the Public Company Accounting Oversight Board (United States) ("PCAOB"), Dunder-Mifflin's internal control over financial reporting as of December 31, 2023, based on criteria established in *Internal Control—Integrated Framework* issued by the Committee of Sponsoring Organizations of the Treadway Commission and our report dated January 29, 2024 expressed an unqualified opinion thereon.

Basis for Opinion

These financial statements are the responsibility of Dunder-Mifflin Inc.'s management. Our responsibility is to express an opinion on Dunder-Mifflin Inc.'s financial statements based on our audit. We are a public accounting firm registered with the Public Company Accounting Oversight Board (United States) ("PCAOB") and are required to be independent with respect to the Company in accordance with the U.S. federal securities laws and the applicable rules and regulations of the Securities and Exchange Commission and the PCAOB.

We conducted our audit in accordance with the standards of the PCAOB. Those standards require that we plan and perform the audit to obtain reasonable assurance about whether the financial statements are free of material misstatement, whether due to error or fraud. Our audit included performing procedures to assess the risks of material misstatement of the financial statements, whether due to error or fraud, and performing procedures that respond to those risks. Such procedures included examining, on a test basis, evidence regarding the amounts and disclosures in the financial statements. Our audit also included evaluating the accounting principles used and significant estimates made by management, as well as evaluating the overall presentation of the financial statements. We believe that our audit provides a reasonable basis for our opinion.

Critical Audit Matters

The critical audit matter communicated is a matter arising from the current period audit of the financial statements that was communicated or required to be communicated to the audit committee and that: (1) relates to accounts or disclosures that are material to the financial statements and (2) involved our especially challenging, subjective, or complex judgments. The communication of critical audit matters does not alter in any way our opinion on the financial statements, taken as a whole, and we are not, by

---

(continued)

[10]Issuers are required to present two years of comparative balance sheets and three years of comparative statements of income, comprehensive income, changes in stockholders' equity, and cash flows. Thus, a report on a single year (such as that shown in Exhibit 12A.1) would not be appropriate for an issuer. A single year is illustrated to allow comparisons of this report with that for nonissuers (Exhibit 12.1).

EXHIBIT 12A.1
(concluded)

communicating the critical audit matter below, providing separate opinions on the critical audit matter or on the accounts or disclosures to which it relates.

As described in Notes 1 and 8 of the consolidated financial statements, Dunder-Mifflin's consolidated goodwill balance was $110 million at December 31, 2023. The determination of the fair value of reporting units comprising this balance requires management to make significant estimates and assumptions that could have a significant impact on the fair value of the reporting units, the amount of any goodwill impairment charge, or both. We identified the goodwill impairment assessment as a critical audit matter.

The primary procedures we performed to address this critical audit matter included:

- Testing the effectiveness of controls related to management's goodwill impairment tests.
- Testing management's process for determining the fair value of units included in the goodwill balance, including evaluating the reasonableness of management's forecasts of future revenues and operating margins.
- Utilizing a valuation specialist to assist in testing Dunder-Mifflin's discounted cash flow model and certain significant assumptions, including the discount rate.
- Evaluating the reasonableness of Dunder-Mifflin's assumptions based on past performance, third party market data, and consistency with evidence obtained in other areas of the audit.

Michael Scarn, LLP

We have served as Dunder-Mifflin's auditor since 2007
Scranton, PA
January 29, 2024

NOTE: The example in the *Critical Audit Matters* section was drawn from *Critical Audit Matters: Lessons Learned, Questions to Consider, and an Illustrative Example,* Center for Audit Quality, December 2018.

The report shown in Exhibit 12A.1 assumes that the audit team prepares two separate reports: one on the financial statements and one on internal control over financial reporting (ICFR) (professional standards allow either two separate reports or a combined report, as discussed in Module I). The above report contains three major sections:

1. *Opinion on the Financial Statements.* The first paragraph of this section identifies the financial statements and years examined by the audit team and expresses the audit team's opinion on the financial statements. The second paragraph references the audit team's opinion on the ICFR.
2. *Basis for Opinion.* The first paragraph of this section indicates the responsibilities of management, the responsibilities of the audit team, and the fact that the firm is registered with the PCAOB and meets the independence requirements of the SEC and PCAOB. The second paragraph provides a description of the audit and the fact that the audit provides a reasonable basis for the opinion.
3. *Critical Audit Matters.* This section identifies any critical audit matters identified during the audit engagement (see below for additional discussion).

Although the length of the report and format varies from the report for nonissuers shown in Exhibit 12.1, you should see many similarities in the general content and message communicated by the two reports. Some noteworthy differences are

- In describing the standards under which the audit is conducted, the PCAOB report references "standards of the Public Company Accounting Oversight Board (United States)" (because these audits are conducted under PCAOB standards) rather than "auditing standards generally accepted in the United States of America."
- The PCAOB report has a paragraph that references the auditors' report and opinion on ICFR, which is required in the audit of larger issuers (a similar requirement does not exist for the audit of nonissuers).
- The PCAOB report requires the audit team to communicate *critical audit matters* in the report.

- The PCAOB report contains a statement disclosing the year in which the auditor began serving as the company's auditor.

The inclusion of critical audit matters is particularly noteworthy; then-PCAOB Chairman James Doty described this as ". . . the first significant change to the standard form of the auditor's report in more than 70 years."[11] **Critical audit matters** (referred to as key audit matters in other jurisdictions) are those issues communicated or required to be communicated to the audit committee that involve challenging, subjective, or complex audit team judgment relating to material accounts and disclosures. For each critical matter identified, the auditor's report should:

- Describe the considerations that led the audit team to identify the critical audit matter.
- Describe how the critical audit matter was addressed in the audit.
- Refer to the relevant financial statement accounts or disclosures that relate to the critical audit matter.

The Auditing Insight "Critical/Key Audit Matters" summarizes academic research and an analysis of auditors' reports involving critical or key audit matters.

AUDITING INSIGHT Critical/Key Audit Matters

- Sirois et al. found that the identification of an issue as a key audit matter increased the level of attention paid to the related disclosures in lending judgments (credit risk scores, loan approvals, loan amounts, and interest rate premiums).
- Rapley et al. found that nonprofessional investors were less likely to choose to invest in companies whose auditor reports disclosed critical audit matters.
- S&P 500 companies averaged 3.4 critical audit matters (CAMs) in auditors' reports issued for the two-year period 2020–2021. Companies with the largest number of CAMs over this two-year period were **American International Group (AIG)** (10 CAMs), **Cardinal Health** (9 CAMs), **General Electric** (8 CAMs), and **NOV Inc.** (8 CAMs).

- An analysis of CAMs from auditors' reports of S&P 500 companies identified goodwill and intangible assets (14% of all CAMs cited), revenue from customer contracts (11%), business combinations (9%), uncertain tax positions (8%), and contingent liabilities (7%) as the most commonly cited matters since the implementation of this reporting requirement.

Sources: L. P. Sirois, J. Bedard, and P. Bera, "The Informational Value of Key Audit Matters in the Auditor's Report: Evidence from an Eye-Tracking Study," *Accounting Horizons,* June 2018, pp. 141–162; E. T. Rapley, J. C. Robertson, and J. L. Smith, "The Effects of Disclosing Critical Audit Matters and Auditor Tenure on Nonprofessional Investors' Judgments," *Journal of Accounting and Public Policy,* September–October 2021, pp. 1–21; Audit Analytics Database.

Modifications from the Standard Report

As with nonissuers, circumstances may require audit teams to depart from the wording in the standard report. These matters may result in the issuance of *qualified opinions* (for material but less pervasive departures from GAAP and scope limitations), *adverse opinions* (for material and pervasive departures from GAAP), or *disclaimers of opinion* (for material and pervasive scope limitations and significant going-concern matters).[12] Report modifications are handled in a similar manner to those encountered in the audit of nonissuers; some of the more significant modifications are as follows:

- The *Opinion on the Financial Statements* section is modified if an opinion other than unqualified is expressed. The first paragraph of this section should be modified to express the appropriate type of opinion and a separate paragraph should be included to disclose the issue(s) affecting the opinion.
- If a scope limitation is encountered by the audit team, the *Basis for Opinion* section is modified to reference the scope limitation.

---

[11]"PCAOB OKs First Big Change to Audit Report in 70 Years," *CFO.com,* June 1, 2017.

[12]Under Regulation S-X, issuers are not permitted to file false or misleading financial statements with the SEC. As a result, any financial statements filed with a qualified or adverse opinion because of a departure from GAAP would be considered a "deficient" filing by the SEC and would not satisfy its reporting requirements.

- For audits of group financial statements, both the *Opinion on the Financial Statements* section and *Basis for Opinion* section are modified to disclose the involvement of other auditors and report of other auditors.
- If a qualified opinion is expressed, the audit team should consider whether the reason(s) for the qualification are critical audit matter(s). If an adverse opinion or a disclaimer of opinion is expressed, the *Critical Audit Matters* section should not be included in the report.
- A separate explanatory paragraph may be added to an unqualified opinion to provide additional information related to the audit or the client.

Modified examples of auditors' reports corresponding to those presented in Chapter 12 for nonissuers can be found in the *Connect* and are identified in a similar manner and designated with an "I" (e.g., Exhibit 12.3 shows report modifications for nonissuers when a departure from GAAP results in a qualified opinion; the corresponding report for issuers is Exhibit 12.3[I]).

Comparative Financial Statements

The SEC requires issuers to present two years of balance sheets and three years of statements of income, changes in shareholders' equity, and cash flows; as a result, the PCAOB report shown in Exhibit 12A.1 would normally refer to all of the years presented in comparative form in the *Opinion on the Financial Statements* section and refer to multiple years of audits in the *Basis for Opinion* section ("We conducted our audits . . .," "Our audits included . . .," etc.).

As with the reports for nonissuers discussed in Chapter 12, certain circumstances involving comparative reporting may result in report modifications. The following represent additional considerations when comparative financial statements are presented:

- One or more auditors' reports must cover all years presented in comparative format (assuming all years have been audited)
- If the current opinion on a comparative financial statement differs from the opinion originally issued in a previous year, information regarding (1) the nature of the previously issued opinion, (2) reason(s) why the previously issued opinion is no longer appropriate, and (3) the fact that the current opinion differs from the previously issued opinion should be included in a separate paragraph in the *Opinion on the Financial Statements* section
- If predecessor auditors examined comparative years, the current auditors' report should only express an opinion on the financial statements examined by the current auditor. With respect to the comparative years, the current auditor should (1) present the predecessor auditors' report on the comparative years' financial statements or (2) reference the fact that the comparative years' financial statements were audited by a predecessor auditor in the current auditors' report.

✅ REVIEW CHECKPOINTS

12A.1 What are the major contents of the PCAOB report for the audit of the financial statements of issuers?

12A.2 Define *critical audit matters*. What is the audit team's responsibility for reporting critical audit matters?

Key Term

critical audit matters: Matters communicated or required to be communicated to the audit committee that involve challenging, subjective, or complex auditor judgment relating to material accounts and disclosures, 575

Multiple Choice Questions, Exercises and Problems

Mc Graw Hill **connect** All applicable Exercises and Problems are available with *Connect.*

In addition to the following, alternative versions of Chapter 12 multiple-choice questions 12.33–12.56 and exercises and problems 12.57–12.83 applicable to the PCAOB version of the auditors' report on the financial statements of issuers can be found on *Connect.*

LO 12-5

12A.3 **Internet Exercise: Reports on Financial Statements.** One of the great resources for auditors is the SEC's Electronic Data Gathering, Analysis and Retrieval (EDGAR) system database at www.sec.gov. Issuers file SEC-required documents electronically. The SEC makes this information available on its web page.

Required:

Five of the largest companies (in terms of market capitalization) are shown in the following table, along with their ticker symbols. After accessing the EDGAR database, download copies of auditors' reports from the Form 10-K filings and complete the following table (Apple has been done as an example). (*Hint:* Search the 10-K filing by using the key word "independent," as in Report of Independent Registered Public Accounting Firm.) Use the following responses in completing the table.

Report on Financial Statements: Type of Opinion (Unqualified, Qualified, Adverse, Disclaimer) and any additional matters discussed in report

Form of Reports: Combined or Separate

Auditor: Identify Name of Firm

Tenure: Year in which firm began serving as auditor

Company / Date	Report on Financial Statements	Form of Reports	Auditor	Tenure
Apple (AAPL) 10/28/2021	Unqualified opinion	Separate	EY	2009
Microsoft (MSFT) 7/29/2021				
Alphabet (GOOGL) 2/2/2022				
Amazon.com (AMZN) 2/4/2022				
Tesla (TSLA) 2/7/2022				

Other Public Accounting Services

And the Academy Award for best picture..La La Land

> *Warren Beatty and Faye Dunaway, actor and actress known for their roles in Bonnie and Clyde (mistake in announcing the Academy Awards "Best Picture" in 2017 based on information provided by PwC)*

There's a mistake. Moonlight, you guys won best picture

> *Jordan Horowitz, film producer known for the movie La La Land*

Professional Standards References

Topic	AICPA/ISA Reference	PCAOB Reference
Attestation Engagements		
Assertion-Based Examination Engagements	AT-C 205 / ISAE 3000	AT 101
Direct Examination Engagements	AT-C 206 / ISAE 3000	AT 101
Agreed-Upon Procedures Engagements	AT-C 215 / ISAE 4400	AT 201
Prospective Financial Information	AT-C 305 / ISAE 3400	AT 301
Compliance Attestation	AT-C 315	AT 601
Service Organizations	AT-C 320 / ISAE 3402	AS 2601
Broker–Dealer Compliance	N/A	AT 1, AT 2
Accounting and Review Service Engagements		
Preparation of Financial Statements	AR-C 70	N/A
Compilation Engagements	AR-C 80 / ISRE 4410	N/A
Review Engagements	AR-C 90 / ISRE 2400	N/A

*References are as follows: AT-C (*Statements on Standards for Attestation Engagements*), AR-C (*Statements on Standards for Accounting and Review Services*), ISAE (*International Standards on Assurance Engagements*), ISRE (*International Standards for Review Engagements*), and AT (*PCAOB Attestation Standards*).

LEARNING OBJECTIVES

Certified public accountants (CPAs) are trusted professionals with a reputation for objectivity and integrity. The reputation has its foundation in a long history of service to the business community and the general public. Individuals and businesses view their CPAs as trusted business professionals who add value to their businesses and provide valuable guidance concerning difficult business decisions. In this tradition, CPAs and other accountants offer numerous assurance and attestation services on information other than audited financial statements. These services result from consumer demand for assurance by objective experts. This module covers several areas of public accounting practice related to accountants' association with information other than audited historical financial statements.

Your objectives are to be able to

LO A-1   Explain and provide examples of attestation engagements.

LO A-2   Identify attestation engagements other than audits and understand the content of reports on those engagements.

LO A-3   Describe review, compilation, and preparation engagements for historical financial information and prepare appropriate reports given specific factual circumstances.

LO A-4   Explain and provide examples of assurance services engagements.

INTRODUCTION

For more than 80 years, **PwC** has worked behind the scenes at one of Hollywood's premiere events (the Academy Awards) securing the ballots submitted by voters and tabulating the results. Other than a brief reference during the telecast, their work has largely gone unnoticed. This all changed in February 2017 when Brian Cullinan (a PwC partner) handed presenters Warren Beatty and Faye Dunaway the wrong envelope that indicated La La Land had won the Academy Award for best picture (the mistake was corrected before the telecast ended to recognize the actual winner, Moonlight).[1]

While tabulating the results of the Academy Awards seems to be an unusual service for accounting firms, PwC is not alone in providing this type of service. **Deloitte** (Country Music Awards, Heisman Trophy, Grammy Awards), **Grant Thornton** (Tony Awards), and **EY** (Emmy Awards, Golden Globe Awards, Baseball Hall of Fame) also provide services of this nature. These are just a few examples of how accounting firms have expanded their services beyond the traditional audit examination.

To this point in the text, we have focused on one type of engagement performed by CPAs (an audit of the historical financial statements and footnotes accompanying the historical financial statements). However, in practice, CPAs perform a wide range of engagements on both historical financial statements as well as other matters. Three broad types of engagements/services have emerged:

1. **Attestation engagement**: Engagements in which CPAs provide assurance and report on an assertion that is the responsibility of another party (because the financial statements are an assertion of management, an audit is an example of an attestation engagement).

2. **Accounting and review engagement**: Engagements that are less in scope than an audit that are performed by CPAs on historical financial statements.

3. **Assurance engagement**: Engagements performed by CPAs that improve the quality of information for decision makers. Assurance engagements are unique in that these engagements may involve both financial and non financial information.

The following table summarizes these three types of engagements. While accounting and review engagements are currently limited to historical financial information, the type of information that might serve as the focus of an attestation or assurance engagement is almost unlimited and is constantly expanding. Our discussion focuses on the more common types of services provided in practice.

---

[1]"The Accountant: Who Is Brian Cullinan," *The Wall Street Journal*, March 1, 2017, p. A13.

	Attestation Engagement	Accounting and Review Engagement	Assurance Engagement
Levels of service	• Assertion-based examination • Direct examination • Review • Agreed-upon procedures	• Compilation • Review • Preparation	• Varies
Information evaluated/examples	• Historical financial statements/information • Financial forecasts and projections • Compliance • Controls at service organization	• Historical financial statements	• Varies
Conclusion provided	• Opinion • Limited assurance • Findings	• None • Limited assurance	• Opinion • Findings

The Auditing Insight "Assurance on Bayer's Acquisitions" provides a recent example of the broad array of assurance services that may be provided by accountants and others.

AUDITING INSIGHT — Assurance on Bayer's Acquisitions

On the heels of a $63 billion acquisition of **Monsanto** that exposed the company to significant litigation risks related to its Roundup weedkiller product, **Bayer AG** has indicated that it would engage an independent (unnamed) expert to review its policies for evaluating acquisitions, as well as specifically reviewing how it evaluated risks in the acquisition of Monsanto.

Source: "Bayer Toughens Scrutiny of Deals," *The Wall Street Journal*, February 28, 2020, p. B1, B2.

 REVIEW CHECKPOINTS

A.1 Define *attestation, accounting and review,* and *assurance* engagements. Provide some examples of information that are evaluated in each type of engagement.

INTRODUCTION TO ATTESTATION ENGAGEMENTS

LO A-1
Explain and provide examples of attestation engagements.

Although the majority of this textbook is devoted to the audit of financial statements, audit services are really a subset of a larger group of services referred to as *attestation services* or simply *attestation engagements*. An attestation engagement is defined as an engagement in which an accountant is engaged to issue or does issue a report on subject matter that is the responsibility of another party.

While an audit conducted using generally accepted auditing standards (GAAS) focuses on historical financial statements and accompanying footnotes, the subject matter of an attestation engagement may include a wide variety of information, such as:

- Historical or prospective performance or conditions (e.g., backlog data).
- Physical characteristics (e.g., narrative descriptions, square footage of facilities).
- Historical events (e.g., the price of a market basket of goods on a certain date).
- Environmental information (e.g., greenhouse gas emissions, energy consumption).
- Systems and processes (e.g., internal control).
- Behavior (e.g., corporate governance, compliance with laws and regulations, and human resource practices).

A key feature of attestation engagements in the preceding definition is the role of a responsible party. The **responsible party** is the person at the client who is accountable for the information (e.g., the company's controller for financial information). The accountant[2] should obtain written acknowledgment or other evidence of the party's responsibility for the subject matter or the written assertion.

Professional standards identify four types of attestation engagements:

1. In an **assertion-based examination engagement**, accountants evaluate a written assertion of another party by evaluating internal controls, assessing the risk of material misstatement, gathering evidence, and rendering an opinion that represents a high level of assurance. Because the financial statements are a written assertion of management, a financial statement audit is an example of an assertion-based examination.

2. A **direct examination engagement** is similar to an assertion-based examination, with the exception that the practitioner is not evaluating a written assertion but is evaluating the subject matter against specified criteria.

3. A **review engagement** provides only a limited level of assurance. The primary procedures performed in a review engagement are making inquiries of management and performing analytical procedures.

4. In an **agreed-upon procedures engagement**, a specific user (known as an *engaging party*) delineates exactly what procedures it wants accountants to perform. Therefore, the level of assurance provided by such an engagement varies depending on the procedures requested by the engaging party.

 REVIEW CHECKPOINTS

A.2   What is *attestation*? Provide some examples of attestation engagements.

A.3   What is a *responsible party*? Why is it necessary for the accountant to identify one?

A.4   What are the differences among examination, review, and agreed-upon procedures engagements?

A.5   Distinguish between an *assertion-based examination engagement* and a *direct examination engagement*.

ATTESTATION ENGAGEMENTS

LO A-2
Identify attestation engagements other than audits and understand the content of reports on those engagements.

In addition to the scope of these engagements, another issue introduced is the intended use of the accountant's report on these engagements. In some cases, a specific third party engages the accountant or the client is negotiating with a specific third party and the report is only intended for the use of these third parties. In these instances, the accountant's report would be intended for **restricted use** (or *limited use*) by only these parties. Conversely, some information (and the related accountant's report) may be intended for broad dissemination and use (such as in an audit engagement); the accountant's report in these engagements would be available for **general use** and no restriction is placed on the use of the report.

As noted previously, audits (and examination engagements) are only one example of an attestation engagement that may be performed by an accountant. In addition to assertion-based examination and direct examination engagements, accountants may perform engagements of a lesser scope that provide lower levels of assurance.

This section discusses some of the more common attestation engagements performed in practice.

---

[2]Because this module discusses a wide variety of engagements, the word *accountant* is used to refer to practitioners performing nonaudit engagements rather than the word *auditor*, which has been used to this point in the text.

Service Organization Control (SOC) Engagements

Often, a **service organization** processes clients' transactions that are likely to be relevant to the client's internal control over financial reporting. Examples of service organizations include payroll processing companies, computerized information processing service centers, trust departments of banks, insurers that maintain the accounting records for reinsurance transactions, mortgage bankers and savings and loan associations that service loans for owners, and transfer agents that handle the shareholder accounting for mutual and money market investment funds. The fact that management is *outsourcing* some of its noncore functions does not absolve management of its responsibility for internal control over those functions. Management (as well as the audit team) of *user entities* must gain assurance that appropriate controls have been placed in operation and are operating effectively.

The solution to this dilemma is a special purpose report on internal control in which the service organization's auditors (*service auditors*) report on the effectiveness of the service organization's internal control to the user entities (and their auditors, known as *user entity auditors*).

To illustrate, assume that Michael Scarn, LLP, is conducting the audit of Dunder-Mifflin. Dunder-Mifflin has its payroll processed by ADP, a global provider of business outsourcing services. Because important controls over payroll processing are implemented at ADP, Scarn is required to obtain an understanding of the design of these controls and, if Scarn intends to rely on internal control, the operating effectiveness of these controls. In a case such as this, Scarn will obtain this understanding through work performed by and a report provided by ADP's auditor.

The relationship among these parties is shown in the following diagram:

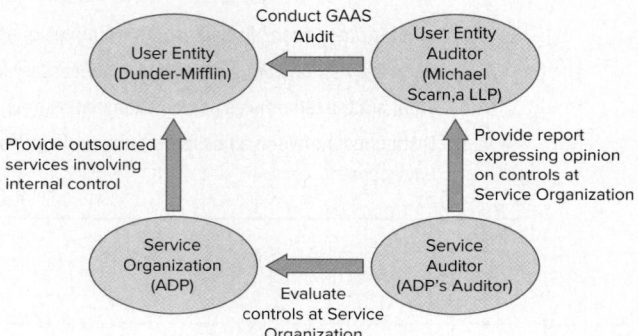

The following section summarizes the types of reports that may be requested by user entity auditors and provided by service auditors.

Design and Operating Effectiveness of Controls (SOC 1, Type 2)

If, as part of a GAAS audit, user entity auditors require assurance on the operating effectiveness of controls in place at a service organization, management of the service organization is required to provide the user entity auditor with a written assertion with respect to:

- The fairness of the presentation of the description of the service organization's system.
- The suitability of the design of controls to achieve the related control objectives.
- The operating effectiveness of the controls.

The service auditors will provide a report to the user entity and user entity auditors that includes the following major components. This report is known as a Service Organization Control (SOC) 1 "Type 2" report (**SOC 1 Type 2 report**) and includes:

- A description of the service organization's assertions regarding internal controls.
- The service auditors' responsibility to express an opinion on the fairness of the presentation of the description of internal control, suitability of the design of controls, and operating effectiveness of the controls.

- A summary of the tests of operating effectiveness of the controls (tests of controls) performed by the service auditor.
- The service auditors' opinion on the fairness of the presentation of the description of internal control, the suitability of design of controls, and operating effectiveness of the controls.
- A restriction on the use of the report to the service organization, user entities of the service organization, and user entity auditors.

Note that the above report provides the service auditors' opinion on both the design of the controls and the operating effectiveness of the controls. Because user entity auditors are required to report on both the financial statements and internal control over financial reporting in the audits of issuers, a Type 2 report would be requested from service auditors as part of an integrated audit (discussed in greater detail in Module I).

Design of Controls (SOC 1, Type 1)

Recall that, in a GAAS audit of a nonissuer, if the audit team chooses not to rely on internal control over financial reporting, they are not required to conduct tests of the operating effectiveness of controls but are required to obtain an understanding of the design of controls. An **SOC 1 Type 1 report** addresses the description of the service organization's system and design of the controls but does not address the operating effectiveness of the controls. Essentially, the report is similar to that for a Type 2 report, with the exception that it specifically indicates that the service auditor did not perform any procedures regarding the operating effectiveness of controls and does not express an opinion on operating effectiveness.

Key Elements of SOC Reports

SOC reports are typically quite lengthy. Excerpted portions of Type 1 and Type 2 reports are shown in Exhibit A.1 to illustrate key differences in the related engagements. For Type 2 reports, the paragraphs related to scope, service auditor's responsibilities, and opinion all reference both the design and operating effectiveness of the service organization's controls. The language in color and italics would not be included in a Type 1 report, which limits the scope, service auditor's responsibilities, and opinion to the design of the service organization's controls.

EXHIBIT A.1
Excerpted Elements from SOC Reports

> *Scope*
> We have examined Payroll Inc.'s description of its payroll processing system entitled "Payroll Inc.'s Description of its Payroll Processing System" for processing user entities' transactions throughout the period January 1, 2023 to December 31, 2023 and the suitability of the *design and operating effectiveness* of the controls included in the description to achieve the related control objectives stated in the description, based on the criteria identified in "Payroll Inc.'s Assertion Regarding Payroll Processing". . .
>
> *Service Auditor's Responsibilities*
> Our responsibility is to express an opinion on the fairness of the presentation of the description and on the suitability of the design *and operating effectiveness* of the controls to achieve the related control objectives stated in the description, based on our examination.
> Our examination was conducted in accordance with attestation standards established by the American Institute of Certified Public Accountants. . . those standards require that we plan and perform the examination to obtain reasonable assurance about whether, in all material respects, based on the criteria in management's assertion, the description is fairly presented and the controls were suitably designed *and operating effectively* to achieve the related control objectives. . .
>
> *Opinion*
> In our opinion, in all material respects, based on the criteria described in Payroll Inc.'s assertion
> a. the description fairly presents the payroll processing system that was designed and implemented throughout the period January 1, 2023 to December 31, 2023.

(continued)

EXHIBIT A.1
(concluded)

> b. the controls related to the control objectives stated in the description were suitably designed to provide reasonable assurance that the control objectives would be achieved if the controls operated effectively throughout the period January 1, 2023 to December 31, 2023. . .
>
> c. *the controls operated effectively to provide reasonable assurance that the control objectives stated in the description were achieved throughout the period January 1, 2023 to December 31, 2023. . .*
>
> **Source:** AT-C 320.A75

The PCAOB Inspection Focus "PCAOB Inspections and Service Organizations" illustrates audit issues that may arise when control activities are applied at a service organization.

While not of sufficient scope to satisfy the requirements of audit engagements, other types of SOC reports (referred to as SOC 2 and SOC 3 reports) are related to Trust Service Engagements and are discussed in a later section of this module.

PCAOB INSPECTION FOCUS | PCAOB Inspections and Service Organizations

The following are examples of deficiencies noted in PCAOB inspection reports related to service organizations:

- The issuer was self-insured for certain liabilities, and it used a service organization to administer the majority of the related claims. The claims data processed by this service organization were used to estimate the issuer's liabilities for unpaid insurance claims. The firm selected for testing a control over the accuracy of these claims data that consisted of claim audits performed by the service organization. The firm obtained the service auditor's report on the operating effectiveness of the service organization's controls but did not identify that the service auditor's testing of this control did not address the accuracy of the claims data.

- The issuer used a service organization to process claims for certain benefits that the issuer provided to its employees. The firm selected

for testing a control that consisted of the issuer's review of the service auditor's report for (1) control deficiencies identified by the service auditor and (2) complementary user controls that the issuer needed to have in place in order to achieve the control objectives described in the service auditor's report. The firm did not evaluate the review procedures that the control owner performed, including the procedures to identify matters for follow up and the procedures to determine whether those matters were appropriately resolved. In addition, the firm did not perform any procedures to evaluate whether the issuer implemented the appropriate complementary user controls as described in the service auditor's report.

Source: *Report on 2018 Inspection of Deloitte, PCAOB, April 28, 2020; Report on 2020 Inspection of KPMG, PCAOB, September 30, 2021.*

✅ REVIEW CHECKPOINTS

A.6 What are the roles of a *user entity auditor* and a *service entity auditor* in an audit of a service organization's controls?

A.7 What is a *service organization*? Why would it engage an auditor to report on its controls?

A.8 Distinguish between an SOC 1 Type 1 and SOC 1 Type 2 report. Which of these reports would most likely be requested by an issuer?

A.9 What role does an SOC report play in an integrated audit of an issuer?

Agreed-Upon Procedures Engagements

Specified parties (including clients or third-party users) sometimes engage accountants to perform specified procedures, known as *agreed-upon procedures.* For example, restaurant managers may ask their accountants to classify and summarize customer comment cards, or a music composer might ask an accountant to verify the mathematics on a royalty report. Such engagements should not be considered audits because the specified procedures are usually not sufficient to be considered as a GAAS audit.

Because professional standards do not dictate a standard scope or minimum level of procedures for agreed-upon procedures engagements, accountants must reach a clear understanding with the client and the report users about the users' needs and the procedures to be performed. For these types of engagements, clearly worded engagement letters specifically delineating the desired procedures to be performed are of utmost importance. The *engaging party* is the entity (either the company itself or a third-party user) who establishes the scope of the agreed-upon procedures engagement.

A report on an agreed-upon procedures engagement is quite different from the standard audit report, with the following major differences:

- The report identifies the specified parties and describes the specific procedures performed by the accountant.
- The report specifically notes that an examination was not performed by the accountant and disclaims an opinion.
- The report provides a summary of findings as a result of performing the agreed-upon procedures.

In some cases, the engaging parties or accountants may wish to restrict the use of the report to specified parties. If so, the report should be expanded to indicate that it is intended solely for the use of the specified parties and should not be used by person(s) other than those parties. The Auditing Insight "Agreed-Upon Procedures and the NCAA" illustrates the procedures the **National Collegiate Athletic Association** (NCAA) requires for member institutions.

 AUDITING INSIGHT   Agreed-Upon Procedures and the NCAA

As part of its financial reporting system, the National Collegiate Athletic Association (NCAA) requires member institutions to submit financial information which has been subjected to an agreed-upon procedures engagement performed by an independent accountant. In its 2021 reporting guidelines, the NCAA identifies the following:

- A minimum of 28 specific agreed-upon procedures for all revenue items comprising at least 4 percent of total revenues (for example, comparing tickets sold to the related revenues and attendance and recalculating totals).

- A minimum of 38 specific agreed-upon procedures for all expense items comprising at least 4 percent of total expenses (for example, selecting a sample of coaches' contracts and comparing and agreeing the terms to salaries, benefits, and bonuses recorded during the period).

- A minimum of 14 specific agreed-upon procedures for other items (for example, agreeing the total fair market value of institutional endowments to supporting documentation).

Source: *2021 Agreed-Upon Procedures,* NCAA, Revised March 10, 2021 (online source).

Prospective Financial Information

Prospective financial information is financial information representing the financial position, results of operations, and cash flows for some period of time in the future. A **financial forecast** is prospective financial information based on *expected* conditions and courses of action. A **financial projection** is prospective financial information based on the occurrence of one or more *hypothetical* events that change the entity's existing business structure (e.g., possible addition of a new distribution center, potential new product line).

In many cases, the entity is negotiating directly with a single user that has requested prospective financial information for use in making economic decisions (e.g., for a bank loan). Both financial projections and financial forecasts can be provided for restricted use because users directly requested the information and are aware of the nature of this information. However, only financial forecasts can be provided for general use because the users may not be familiar with the hypothetical event(s) underlying a financial projection.

Prospective financial statements may take the form of a complete set of financial statements or may be limited to certain minimum items, which include the following:

- Specific income statement components (sales or gross revenues, gross profit or cost of sales, unusual or infrequently occurring items, provision for income taxes, discontinued operations, income from continuing operations, net income and basic and diluted earnings per share).
- Significant changes in financial position.
- A description of the nature of the prospective financial statements, a statement that the assumptions are based on the responsible party's judgment, and a caveat that the expected results might not be achieved.
- Summary of significant assumptions.
- Summary of significant accounting policies.

A presentation of prospective financial information that omits any of the above items is known as a *partial presentation;* partial presentations are only appropriate for specific users with whom the entity is negotiating (*restricted use*).

Exhibit A.2 illustrates an accountants' report on an examination of a financial forecast that will be used by Allied National Bank in considering extending a line of credit. Because the financial forecast is an assertion of management, this would be considered to be an *assertion-based examination engagement.*

EXHIBIT A.2
Accountants' Report on Examination of Financial Forecast

Independent Accountant's Report

To Allied National Bank

We have examined the accompanying forecast of Dunder-Mifflin, Inc. which comprises the forecasted balance sheet as of December 31, 2024 and the related forecasted statements of income, changes in shareholders' equity, and cash flows for the year then ending, based on the guidelines for the presentation of a forecast established by the American Institute of Certified Public Accountants. Dunder-Mifflin's management is responsible for preparing and presenting the forecast in accordance with the guidelines for the presentation of a forecast established by the American Institute of Certified Public Accountants. Our responsibility is to express an opinion on the forecast based on our examination.

Our examination was conducted in accordance with attestation standards established by the American Institute of Certified Public Accountants. Those standards require that we plan and perform the examination to obtain reasonable assurance about whether the forecast is presented in accordance with the guidelines for the presentation of a forecast established by the American Institute of Certified Public Accountants, in all material respects. An examination involves performing procedures to obtain evidence about the forecast. The nature, timing, and extent of the procedures selected depend on our judgment, including an assessment of the risks of material misstatement of the forecast, whether due to fraud or error. We believe that the evidence we obtained is sufficient and appropriate to provide a reasonable basis for our opinion.

In our opinion, the accompanying forecast is presented, in all material respects, in accordance with the guidelines for the presentation of a forecast established by the American Institute of Certified Public Accountants, and the underlying assumptions are suitably supported and provide a reasonable basis for management's forecast.

There will usually be differences between the forecasted and actual results because events and circumstances frequently do not occur as expected, and those differences may be material. We have no responsibility to update this report for events and circumstances occurring after the date of this report.

Michael Scarn, LLP
Scranton, PA
May 1, 2024

Note the following differences in this report compared to that for an audit on historical financial statements:

- Guidelines for the presentation of a forecast established by the AICPA are identified as the appropriate criteria (rather than GAAP).
- Attestation standards are referenced as the basis for the examination, rather than GAAS.
- An opinion is expressed on both the forecast information and the reasonableness of the assumptions as a basis for the forecast.
- The report acknowledges that differences may occur between actual and forecasted results.

For examinations of *financial projections,* the accountants' report will also identify the hypothetical assumption(s) upon which the projection is based and note that the report is not intended to be used by those other than the specified parties.

In addition to examination engagements, accountants may perform *agreed-upon procedures* engagements on prospective financial information. These engagements are lesser in scope than an examination and the reports will be modified to describe the nature of the engagement as well as the level of assurance provided by the accountant. Unlike agreed-upon procedures engagements for historical financial information discussed earlier, the use of reports on engagements to apply agreed-upon procedures to prospective financial information is restricted.

Exhibit A.3 provides a summary of engagements related to prospective financial information.

EXHIBIT A.3
Comparison of Engagements on Prospective Financial Information

	Agreed-Upon Procedures	Examination
Level of assurance	List of findings	Opinion on financial information and assumptions
Use of report	• General or restricted use (forecast) • Restricted use (projection)	• General use (forecast) • Restricted use (projection)

✓ REVIEW CHECKPOINTS

A.10 Why are clearly worded engagement letters so important in agreed-upon procedures engagements?

A.11 What role does an engaging party play in an agreed-upon procedures engagement?

A.12 What are the general contents of an accountants' report on an agreed-upon procedures engagement?

A.13 Distinguish between *financial forecasts* and *financial projections.* Which of these presentations of prospective financial information is appropriate for general use?

A.14 What are the basic contents of the accountants' report on an examination of a financial forecast? What additional information is provided in the report of an examination of a financial projection?

A.15 What levels of assurance are provided in agreed-upon procedures and examination engagements on prospective financial information?

Compliance Attestation

In Chapter 12, we discussed auditor reporting on compliance in conjunction with the audit of the entity's financial statements. In these cases, the auditor's conclusion with respect to compliance will be based on evidence obtained to evaluate the fairness of the entity's financial statements. That is, the auditor's primary objective is not to evaluate and express a conclusion on the entity's compliance *per se.* In other cases, management of entities not subject to the requirements of an audit examination may specifically engage accountants to report on (1) the entity's compliance with laws, regulations, rules, contracts, or grants or (2) the effectiveness of an entity's internal controls that ensure compliance with these requirements.

To conduct an engagement related to compliance, three conditions must be met:

1. Management must accept responsibility for compliance.
2. Compliance or the controls over compliance are capable of evaluation and measurement against reasonable criteria.
3. Sufficient evidence must be available to support management's evaluation.

Two levels of accountant services related to compliance are *examination* engagements and *agreed-upon procedures* engagements. Similar to an audit, in an examination engagement, the accountant is required to test relevant controls over compliance, assess control risk, and obtain sufficient evidence regarding compliance. These procedures allow the accountant to express an *opinion* with respect to compliance.

Assuming then entity is in compliance, the accountant would issue an unqualified opinion that the entity has complied ". . .in all material respects, with *[regulation or contractual obligation]* for the year ended. . . ."

Considerations that may affect the accountants' report on compliance in an examination engagement include the following:

- If the entity is not in full compliance, the accountants report may be modified to (1) disclose a noncompliance event (while still expressing an unqualified opinion), (2) express a qualified opinion for material noncompliance, or (3) express an adverse opinion indicating that the entity is not in compliance.

- In many cases, management will make an assertion about compliance in a written communication (e.g., "the Agency is in full compliance with the Department of Employment Regulation JR-52.") In those cases, the report would be modified to indicate that *management's assertion* related to compliance is being examined and the accountant will express an opinion on *management's assertion* related to compliance.

If an agreed-upon procedures engagement is performed, the report will identify the specific procedures performed and the findings related to those procedures. In addition, because an examination was not performed, the report will disclaim an opinion on compliance.

Broker–Dealer Compliance

In 2010, in response to several high-profile **broker–dealer** collapses, including **Madoff Investment Securities,** the *Dodd–Frank Wall Street Reform and Consumer Protection Act* gave the PCAOB the authority to oversee audits of broker–dealers. The SEC responded in 2011 with Rule 17a-5, which outlines reporting, audit, and notification requirements for broker–dealers. Among other requirements, this rule requires a broker's or dealer's *compliance report* to include the following assertions:

- Internal control over compliance was effective during the most recent fiscal year and at the end of the most recent fiscal year.
- The broker–dealer was in compliance with rules relating to net capital requirements and reserve requirements at the end of the most recent fiscal year.
- The information used to assess compliance with the net capital requirements and reserve requirements rules was derived from the broker–dealer's records.

The PCAOB established professional standards for accountants performing *examination engagements* related to the above assertions. Similar to audit engagements, accountants must (1) test both the design and operating effectiveness of the entity's internal control over compliance, (2) perform sufficient procedures to support the broker–dealer's compliance with the net capital rule and reserve requirement rule, (3) obtain a management representation letter, and (4) express an opinion on the broker–dealer's assertions.

Rule 17a-5 identifies certain provisions that exempt broker–dealers from the SEC's compliance reporting requirements (e.g., if broker–dealers trade on their own behalf and do not hold customer funds). In such cases, broker–dealers must file an *exemption report* containing the following statements/information:

- Provisions under which the broker–dealer claimed an exemption.
- Statement that these provisions were met during the most recent fiscal year or that identifies exceptions from these provisions during the most recent fiscal year.
- If exceptions existed, identification of the exceptions, the nature of the exceptions, and the date(s) on which the exceptions existed.

The exemption report is subject to a *review engagement* under PCAOB professional standards. The SEC concluded that because safeguarding customer assets is so important, some degree of assurance is required. The review standard requires auditors to obtain limited assurance whether conditions exist that would indicate that the broker–dealer should not have claimed an exemption. Procedures performed during a review include identifying the exemption provisions claimed by the broker–dealer, performing various inquiries, reading internal compliance reports, and reading regulatory filings relevant to the exemption provisions.

The Auditing Insight "Broker–Dealer Compliance and PCAOB Sanctions" summarizes a recent sanction levied related to the audit and review engagements for a broker–dealer client.

AUDITING INSIGHT | Broker–Dealer Compliance and PCAOB Sanctions

The following examples of failure to obtain sufficient appropriate evidence were identified in a recent PCAOB sanction related to a sole practitioner's engagements for an unidentified broker–dealer client:

- In an examination engagement on the financial statements, failure to perform any procedures other than obtaining representations from management.
- In an examination engagement on supplemental information, failure to perform any procedures other than obtaining calculations and agreeing them to regulatory reports provided by management.

- In a review engagement related to an exemption report, failure to make inquiries of management and obtain representations from management.

As a result of the above, the practitioner received a censure, two-year prohibition on audit engagements or engagements for broker–dealers, and requirement to complete 50 hours of continuing professional education related to the audits of issuers or broker–dealers.

Source: *In the Matter of Tamba S. Mayah, CPA, and Tamba Seibu Mayah, CPA*, PCAOB Release No. 105-2021-007, PCAOB, September 13, 2021.

Other Attestation Engagements and Summary

In addition to the engagements noted above, professional standards provide accountants with guidance for performing and reporting on engagements related to pro forma financial information, internal control over financial reporting (for nonissuers), and Management's Discussion and Analysis disclosures accompanying the financial statements. While the nature of the subject matter subject to evaluation obviously differs from the engagements discussed above, the general nature of the engagement and the assurance provided by the accountants in these engagements is similar.

Exhibit A.4 summarizes the types of engagements and use of the reports for the attestation engagements discussed in this section. One general conclusion that may be drawn from Exhibit A.4 is that accountants may decide to restrict the use of reports on agreed-upon procedures engagements to the individual(s) who participated in determining the scope of the engagement, while the use of the reports in examination and review engagements is generally not restricted in this manner.

EXHIBIT A.4 Summary of Attestation Engagements and Reports

Subject of Engagement	Type of Engagement	Use of Reports
Service organizations (AT-C 320)	• Examination	• Restricted use (SOC 1 reports)
Historical financial information (AT-C 215)	• Agreed-upon procedures	• General or restricted use
Prospective financial information (AT-C 305)	• Examination • Agreed-upon procedures	• General use (financial forecast/examination) • Resricted use (financial projection/examination) • General or restricted use (agreed-upon procedures)
Compliance (AT-C 315)	• Examination • Agreed-upon procedures	• General use (examination) • General or restricted use (agreed-upon procedures)
Broker-dealer compliance (PCAOB AT 1, AT 2)	• Examination (compliance report) • Review (exemption report)	• General use
Pro forma information (AT-C 310)	• Examination • Review	• General use
Management's Discussion and Analysis (AT-C 395)	• Examination • Review	• General use
Internal control over financial reporting (non issuer) (AU-C 940)	• Examination	• General use

 REVIEW CHECKPOINTS

A.16 What types of engagements may be performed by an accountant in a compliance attestation? What type of assurance is provided in each of these engagements?

A.17 What are the two types of reports (and the related level of accountant assurance) that may be filed by broker–dealers under Rule 17a-5?

ACCOUNTING AND REVIEW SERVICES FOR HISTORICAL FINANCIAL INFORMATION

LO A-3
Describe review, compilation, and preparation engagements for historical financial information and prepare appropriate reports given specific factual circumstances.

As noted throughout this text, issuers are required to have audits (a form of *examination engagement*) on their historical financial statements. However, nonissuers are not required to have audits; in some cases, lenders and other users of their financial statements may request a lower (and less costly) level of assurance than provided by an audit; these services are collectively referred to as accounting and review engagements. The Accounting and Review Services Committee issues *Statements on Standards for Accounting and Review Services (SSARS),* which apply to accountants' engagements on unaudited financial statements of non issuers.

Review Engagements

A review engagement is a service performed by accountants to obtain limited assurance that no material modifications should be made to the financial statements in order for the statements to be in conformity with the applicable reporting framework (usually GAAP). Because some assurance is provided in a review engagement, accountants must be independent in order to perform review services.

After obtaining a written understanding with management about the nature of a review engagement (through an engagement letter), the accountant performs the following procedures during a review of unaudited financial statements:

1. Determining materiality levels and revising these levels as necessary based on information obtained during the review.

2. Obtaining knowledge of the entity's business, accounting principles in the entity's industry, and the entity's organization and operations.
3. Making inquiries of management regarding:
    - Whether the financial statements have been prepared and fairly presented in accordance with the applicable financial reporting framework.
    - Significant transactions and journal entries.
    - Uncorrected misstatements identified during a previous review.
    - Subsequent events.
    - Knowledge of fraud or suspected fraud.
    - Noncompliance with laws and regulations.
    - Related-party transactions.
    - Litigation.
    - The reasonableness of significant estimates.
    - Actions taken at meetings of shareholders, directors, and other important executive committees
    - Material commitments, contractual obligations, or contingencies.
    - Material nonmonetary transactions.
    - The basis for management's assessment of the entity's ability to continue as a going concern
4. Conducting analytical procedures (presumptively mandatory analytical procedures include comparing current amounts and ratios to comparable information for the prior period or to information for the entity's industry).
5. Reconciling the financial statements to the underlying records.
6. Obtaining written representations from management.

While the above does provide some limited audit evidence, a review engagement is far less extensive than an audit (e.g., a review does not require the accountant to obtain an understanding of the entity's internal control). As a result, a review engagement does *not* provide a basis for expressing an opinion on financial statements. Instead, the accountant will provide *limited assurance* through a phrase in the report such as "we are not aware of any material modifications" that are necessary for the financial statements to be in conformity with an appropriate financial reporting framework. In addition, each page of the company's financial statements should be marked "See independent accountants' review report" to clearly indicates to users that an audit engagement was not performed. An example of a review report is provided in Exhibit A.5.
Note the following from Exhibit A.5:

- The first paragraph summarizes the procedures performed in a review engagement, acknowledges that these procedures are less in scope than an audit, and indicates that these procedures do not permit the accountant to express an opinion on the financial statements.
- The *Management's Responsibility for the Financial Statements* and *Accountant's Responsibility* sections are similar in nature to those sections in an auditors' report (modified for the nature of a review engagement).
- The *Accountant's Conclusion* section provides limited assurance on the financial statements.

**EXHIBIT A.5
Example Review
Report**

Independent Accountant's Review Report

To the Board of Directors of Dunder-Mifflin, Inc.

We have reviewed the accompanying financial statements of Dunder-Mifflin, Inc., which comprise the balance sheet as of December 31, 2023, and the related statements of income, changes in stockholders' equity, and cash flows for the year then ended, and the related notes to the financial statements. A review includes primarily applying analytical procedures to management's financial data and making inquiries of company management. A review is substantially less in scope than an audit, the objective of which is the expression of an opinion regarding the financial statements as a whole. Accordingly, we do not express such an opinion.

Management's Responsibility for the Financial Statements

Management is responsible for the preparation and fair presentation of these financial statements in accordance with accounting principles generally accepted in the United States of America; this includes the design, implementation, and maintenance of internal control relevant to the preparation and fair presentation of financial statements that are free from material misstatement whether due to fraud or error.

Accountant's Responsibility

Our responsibility is to conduct the review engagement in accordance with Statements on Standards for Accounting and Review Services promulgated by the Accounting and Review Services Committee of the AICPA. Those standards require us to perform procedures to obtain limited assurance as a basis for reporting whether we are aware of any material modifications that should be made to the financial statements for them to be in accordance with accounting principles generally accepted in the United States of America. We believe that the results of our procedures provide a reasonable basis for our conclusion.

We are required to be independent of Dunder-Mifflin, Inc. and to meet our other ethical responsibilities, in accordance with the relevant ethical requirements related to our review.

Accountant's Conclusion

Based on our review, we are not aware of any material modifications that should be made to the accompanying financial statements in order for them to be in accordance with accounting principles generally accepted in the United States of America.

Scranton, PA
March 1, 2024

Other potential issues (and reporting implications) related to review engagements include:

- Similar to audit reports, if the accountants' review procedures reveal a departure from GAAP (or other appropriate financial reporting framework), the report would provide either a qualified or adverse conclusion and discuss the departure in a separate section (labeled *Basis for Qualified Conclusion or Basis for Adverse Conclusion*) and refer to the departure in the conclusion section (labeled *Qualified Conclusion* or *Adverse Conclusion*).

- Similar to audit reports, accountants may include *emphasis-of-matter* paragraphs and *other-matter* paragraphs in review reports to draw users' attention to certain matters or communicate matters other than those presented or disclosed in the financial statements.

- If the reviewed financial statements are presented in comparative form, the accountants' report should refer to each year presented.

- If a client requests a change in scope of an engagement from an audit to a review, the accountant would normally agree to this change if the reason is because of changes in the needs of the client (a lender indicated a willingness to accept a review rather than an audit) or a misunderstanding about the level of services.

- Accountants may perform review engagements on a single financial statement (e.g., the balance sheet) or specific elements or accounts of a financial statement (e.g., accounts receivable).

The Auditing Insight "Review Engagements and Crowdfunding Success" summarizes recent academic research related to how accountant assurance provided through review engagements affects the success of crowdfunding efforts.

AUDITING INSIGHT Review Engagements and Crowdfunding Success

- Bogdani et al. found that the assurance provided by both audit and review engagements resulted in companies raising a greater amount of funds and attracting more investors compared to assurance provided through management certification.

- Gong et al. found that the assurance provided by review engagements (particularly voluntary reviews as opposed to mandatory reviews) resulted in a higher probability of crowdfunding success and total amount of funds raised.

Source: E. Bodgani, M. Causholli, and W. R. Knechel, "The Role of Assurance in Equity Crowdfunding," *The Accounting Review,* March 2022, pp. 51–76; J. Gong, J. Krishnan, and Y. Liang, "Securities-Based Crowdfunding by Startups: Does Auditor Attestation Matter?," *The Accounting Review,* March 2022, pp. 213–239.

Compilation Engagements

The purpose of a **compilation engagement** is to assist management in presenting financial information that is the representation of management in the form of financial statements—without providing any assurance on the accuracy or completeness of that information. Essentially, you may think of a compilation as assembling a balance sheet, income statement, statement of cash flows, and so on, from account information supplied by the entity's management.

When performing a compilation engagement, the accountant has no responsibility to assess the conformity of the entity's financial statements with GAAP or other financial reporting frameworks. After obtaining an engagement letter from the client, accountants should perform the following procedures:

- Obtain an understanding of the entity's business and applicable accounting principles in the entity's industry.
- Read the financial statements, looking for obvious clerical or accounting errors.
- Follow up on information that is incorrect, incomplete, or otherwise questionable.

Note that accountants are *not* required to conduct tests of the operating effectiveness of control procedures or to perform any other evidence-gathering procedures. Given the very limited procedures performed, accountants do not express an opinion or any form of assurance on the conformity of the financial statements with GAAP. Because no assurance is provided, accountants are *not* required to be independent to perform compilation engagements or issue compilation reports. However, accountants must assess whether they are independent and disclose any lack of independence in their report.

An example report for a compilation engagement is presented in Exhibit A.6. Note that this report specifically indicates that the accountant did not perform any procedures to verify management's information and disclaims an opinion, conclusion, or any form of assurance on the financial statements. In addition to the report, each page of the financial statements should be marked "See accountants' compilation report."

EXHIBIT A.6
Example Compilation Report

> Management is responsible for the accompanying financial statements of Dunder-Mifflin, Inc., which comprise the balance sheet as of December 31, 2023 and the related statements of income, changes in stockholders' equity, and cash flows for the year then ended, and the related notes to the financial statements in accordance with accounting principles generally accepted in the United States of America. We have performed a compilation engagement in accordance with Statements on Standards for Accounting and Review Services promulgated by the Accounting and Review Services Committee of the AICPA. We did not audit or review the financial statements, nor were we required to perform any procedures to verify the accuracy or completeness of the information provided by management. We do not express an opinion, a conclusion, or provide any form of assurance on these financial statements.
>
> *Michael Scarn, LLP*
> Scranton, PA
> March 1, 2024

In addition to the scope of the engagement and level of assurance provided, two significant differences between compilation reports and other reports discussed in this module can be noted:

- Because compilation engagements do not require accountants to be independent, the report is not titled using the word "independent."
- Because no assurance is provided, the report is not addressed to a particular user(s) or group of user(s).

Other potential issues (and reporting implications) related to compilation engagements include:

- Similar to an audit, if the accountants' compilation procedures revealed a departure from GAAP (or other appropriate financial reporting framework), a paragraph should be added to the compilation report describing the departure.
- If the entity decides to omit all footnote disclosures required by GAAP (believing such disclosures are not necessary for their purposes), the accountants' report would note the omission and indicate that the omission of these disclosures might influence users' conclusions.
- If accountants are not independent, their report should specifically state their lack of independence and may provide a general description of the reason for their lack of independence.

Preparation Engagements

In some cases, entities wished to engage accountants to assemble financial statements without performing even the limited procedures in a compilation engagement or issuing a report. In response, the AICPA created an engagement known as a **preparation engagement**. When performing a preparation of financial statements engagement, the accountant should prepare an engagement letter, but they are not required to perform any procedures, evaluate their independence, or issue a report.

Examples of engagements include preparation of:

- Financial statements prior to audit or review by another accountant.
- Financial statements presented alongside the entity's tax return.
- Personal financial statements for presentation alongside a financial plan.
- Individual financial statements with substantially all disclosures omitted.
- Financial statements from information in a general ledger outside of an accounting software system.

The accountant should prepare the financial statements using the client's records and should include a statement on each page of the financial statements indicating that "no assurance is provided." Alternatively, while not a requirement, the accountant could issue a disclaimer of opinion indicating that the financial statements were not subject to an audit, review, or compilation and that no opinion, conclusion or assurance is provided on the financial statements.

EXHIBIT A.7 Summary of Engagements on Historical Financial Information

	Audit	Review	Compilation	Preparation	Agreed-Upon Procedures
Procedures	Audit procedures required by GAAS	Inquiries and analytical procedures	Read financial statements for obvious errors	Assemble financial statements	Procedures requested by specific users
Assurance/ Conclusion	Opinion	Limited assurance	None	None	List of Findings
Independence required?	Yes	Yes	No	No	Yes
Professional Standards	PCAOB *Auditing Standards* (issuers) and ASB *Statements on Auditing Standards* (non issuers)	AICPA *Statements on Standards for Accounting and Review Services* (SSARS)	AICPA *SSARS*	AICPA *SSARS*	AICPA *Statements on Standards for Attestation Engagements*
Use of Report	Not restricted	Not restricted	Not restricted	Not restricted (if disclaimer issued)	May be restricted to specified parties

Summary of Engagements on Historical Financial Information

This section discussed accountant engagements on historical financial statements having a lesser scope than an audit (examination engagement). Exhibit A.7 summarizes the differences between these engagements as well as two other alternatives (audit engagements and agreed-upon procedures engagements). As shown below, these engagements involved a wide range of professional standards (AICPA *Statements on Auditing Standards,* AICPA *Attestation Standards,* AICPA *Statements on Standards for Accounting and Review Services,* and PCAOB *Auditing Standards*) and varying scope of accountant procedures and levels of assurance.

 REVIEW CHECKPOINTS

A.18 Identify and provide a brief overview of the procedures required under the three engagements defined under *SSARS*.

A.19 What are the major content(s) of the accountants' report in a review engagement? A compilation engagement?

A.20 What is *limited assurance*? Why is limited assurance (and not an opinion) provided in a review engagement?

A.21 How does a preparation engagement differ from a compilation engagement?

ASSURANCE SERVICES ENGAGEMENTS

LO A-4
Explain and provide examples of assurance services engagements.

Auditing courses focus on the role of auditors and accountants in the financial reporting process. However, just as providing opinions and assurance on financial information adds reliability to that information, accountants may also add value by providing opinions and assurance on other types of information. This section discusses various areas other than traditional financial reporting in which accountants may provide assurance to add credibility and value to information for decision makers.

Scope of Assurance Services

Assurance engagements are engagements performed by CPAs that improve the quality of information, or its context, for decision makers. A large group of activities can fit within this definition; for example, most of the services discussed to this point in the module meet these criteria. While attestation and audit services are highly structured and intended to be useful for large groups of decision makers (e.g., investors, lenders), assurance services are more customized and intended to be focused on the needs of smaller, targeted groups of decision makers. In this sense, assurance services resemble consulting services. (The vignette at the beginning of this module on PwC's work with the **Academy of Motion Picture Arts and Sciences** is an example.)

Although there are many potential assurance services with more emerging continuously, several have been featured by the AICPA's Assurance Services Executive Committee (ASEC) as having potential to provide value and improve the quality and transparency of information entities provide to their constituents. Currently, the ASEC has created task forces and working groups in the following broad areas:[3]

1. *Continuous assurance and continuous controls monitoring:* These services involve "real-time" assurance and monitoring of controls as transactions are processed by clients.
2. *Audit data standards:* These services relate to enhancing the efficiency and effectiveness of audits by standardizing formats of files and fields commonly requested for audits and other purposes.
3. *Risk assurance and advisory services:* These services relate to advising clients on enterprise risk management processes.
4. *Sustainability assurance and advisory services:* Sustainability [sometimes referred to as *corporate social responsibility* or *environmental, social, and governance (ESG)*] includes an entity's consideration of economic viability, social responsibility, and environmental responsibility in conducting its activities. These activities are becoming increasingly important to shareholders, governmental entities, and other groups of stakeholders and companies are expanding the information provided related to these activities. In conjunction with the increased availability of sustainability information, accountant assurance is valuable in enhancing the reliability and usefulness of this information.

An example of the type of information and assurance that may serve as the focus of a sustainability assurance and advisory services engagement is shown in the Auditing Insight "Phillip Morris's Integrated Report."

AUDITING INSIGHT — Phillip Morris's Integrated Report

In addition to financial highlights, the following is an example of corporate social responsibility highlights provided by **Phillip Morris International** in its 2020 integrated report:

- 12.7 million adult users have stopped smoking and switched to smoke-free products
- 76% of commercial expenditures were related to smoke-free products
- Total workplace incident rate was 0.12 per 200,000 hours worked
- Carbon dioxide equivalent emissions were 18 percent lower in 2020 compared to 2019
- 84% of all smoke-free devices were recycled at Phillip Morris' centralized recycling hubs

PwC SA Lausanne (a Switzerland affiliate of PwC) provided limited assurance on the following:

- Financial information, both total and related to smoke-free products (research and development, shipments, revenues)
- Proportion of factories producing smoke-free products
- Smoke-free products (number of markets, proportion of markets, number of users, number of users who have stopped smoking and switched to smoke-free products)

Source: *Delivering a Smoke-Free Future: Progress Toward a World Without Cigarettes, Integrated Report 2020,* Phillip Morris International, 2020 (online source).

In addition to the above task forces, the ASEC has issued guidance for accountants conducting assurance engagements in the following areas:

- System and Organization Control (SOC) reporting on cybersecurity risk management programs and supply chains
- Information reporting in Extensible Business Reporting Language (XBRL) format
- Blockchains and digital assets
- Use of audit data analytics

[3]AICPA Assurance and Advisory Services website (online source).

The Auditing Insight "Trends in Corporate Responsibility Reporting" highlights the increasing frequency of corporate responsibility reporting (including sustainability reporting), third-party assurance on these reports, and benefit to the companies for providing third-party assurance on these reports.

AUDITING INSIGHT   Trends in Corporate Responsibility Reporting

- The Governance & Accountability Institute reports that 92 percent of the S&P 500 companies and 70 percent of the Russell 1000 companies published sustainability reports in 2020, up from 86 and 60 percent in 2018, respectively.

- A KPMG survey reports that 93% of the Fortune 250 companies (referred to as the G250) and 75% of the 100 largest companies in each of 49 different countries (for a total of 4,900 companies, referred to as the N100) published corporate responsibility reports in 2020. Third-party assurance was provided for 71% and 51% of reports for the G250 and N100, respectively.

- In their sample of audits conducted by Big 4 firms between 2002 to 2017, Dal Maso et al. found 36 percent of the clients issued Corporate Social Responsibility (CSR) reports. The audit assurance provided on these reports is as follows: (1) 7 percent by the same Big 4 firm, (2) 4 percent by another Big 4 firm, (3) 11 percent by another provider, and (4) 14 percent with no assurance. In addition, their findings indicate that clients using the same firm for the financial statement audit and CSR reporting have larger environmental and litigation provisions.

- Hoang and Trotman found that investors' estimates of firm value and information reliability were positively influenced by accountant assurance on CSR information.

- Maroun found that external assurance improved the perceived quality of environmental, social, and governmental disclosures (measured by receipt of an *EY Excellence in Integrated Reporting Award*); this quality was influenced even more significantly when the assurance was provided by a Big Four firm.

Source: *2021 Sustainability Reporting in Focus,* Governance & Accountability Institute (online source); *The Time has Come: The KPMG Survey of Sustainability Reporting 2020,* KPMG, December 2020 (online source); L. Dal Maso, G. J. Lobo, F. Mazzi, and L. Paugam, "Implications of the Joint Provision of CSR Assurance and Financial Audit for Auditors' Assessment of Going-Concern Risk," *Contemporary Accounting Research,* Summer 2020, pp. 1248–1289; H. Hoang and K. T. Trotman, "The Effect of CSR Assurance and Explicit Assessment on Investor Valuation Judgments," *Auditing: A Journal of Practice & Theory,* February 2021, pp. 19–33; W. Maroun, "Does External Assurance Contribute to Higher Quality Integrated Reports?," *Journal of Accounting and Public Policy,* July–August 2019.

Trust Services

Electronic commerce (or e-commerce), the sale of goods and services via the Internet, is exploding. According to the U.S. Census Bureau, U.S. e-commerce revenues represented 13 percent of all retail sales in the third quarter of 2021, up from 8 percent in the same quarter of 2016.[4] Although the growth of e-commerce continues unabated, security issues, both real and perceived, have prevented many potential customers from purchasing goods and services via the Internet. Many customers and business owners distrust the Internet as a medium of conducting business. Indeed, a general lack of security is the top reason nonbuyers give for not purchasing products online and the top concern among current online buyers. Specifically, prospective buyers have expressed concerns about ascertaining whether an e-commerce company is authentic, is trustworthy (the e-tailer will do what it says it will do), and will safeguard buyers' personal information. Customers also want to be reassured that they can get their products, services, and repairs on a timely basis. Despite growing familiarity with doing business on the Internet, these security issues have not diminished for potential customers.

For significant customer–supplier business relationships, company computers are often directly linked through Internet-based virtual private networks. Purchase orders for goods are made and sent via computer, and payment is made automatically through electronic funds transfer directly to the vendors bank. The primary benefit of such a relationship is an increase in the timeliness of the process; transactions that once took several weeks to complete manually (from customer purchase order generation to final payment being deposited to the suppliers bank account) now take only as long as it takes to ship and receive the goods.

[4]United States Census Bureau E-Commerce Sales website (online source).

However, just as Internet customers are wary of purchasing online, business customers are often cautious about entering into such relationships with other businesses.

In response to these concerns, the AICPA and the Canadian Institute of Chartered Accountants (CICA) developed **WebTrust Services** (which are now managed by CPA Canada) to provide assurance to the consumer on the reliability of Internet websites and **SysTrust Services** to focus on a company's systems as a means of increasing the reliability of business-to-business (B-to-B) computer transactions. Because these two services have a common framework to address risks and technological opportunities, the AICPA has adopted the term **trust services** to define a set of professional attestation and advisory services based on a core set of principles and criteria that address the risks and opportunities of IT-enabled systems and privacy programs.

Trust Services comprise a set of professional attestation and advisory services based on a core set of principles and criteria that address the risks and opportunities of IT-enabled systems and privacy programs. Practitioners use the following principles and related criteria in the performance of trust services engagements:[5]

- *Security.* The system is protected against unauthorized access (both physical and logical).
- *Availability.* The system is available for operation and use as committed or agreed.
- *Processing integrity.* System processing is complete, accurate, timely, and authorized.
- *Confidentiality.* Information designated as confidential is protected as committed or agreed.
- *Privacy.* Personal information is collected, used, retained, disclosed, and destroyed in conformity with the commitments in the entity's privacy notice and with criteria set forth in generally accepted privacy principles issued by the AICPA and CICA.

Two common types of reports issued in conjunction with Trust Service engagements are:

1. SOC 2 reports, which provide assurance on the above principles for restricted use (management and/or specified parties).
2. SOC 3 reports, which provide assurance on the above principles for general use.

SOC 2 and SOC 3 are similar in content, with the primary difference being the intended recipients of the reports. As with SOC 1 reports requested in conjunction with the examination of internal control over financial reporting for an issuer, two versions of these reports reflect differences in the scope of the engagement and assurance provided by the accountant. A Type 1 report provides assurance on the effectiveness of design of relevant controls, while a Type 2 report provides assurance on both the effectiveness of design and operations of relevant controls. The controls can be related to individual principles of a combination of principles.

The Auditing Insight "Amazon Trust Services" provides an example of assurances provided in one such situation.

AUDITING INSIGHT · Amazon Trust Services

Amazon Trust Services issues digital certificates that allow the identities of websites, devices, and users to be verified and ensure safe data exchange and transactions among users. In 2020, **BDO** provided assurance on assertions by **Amazon Trust Services** (ATS) that it has

- Disclosed its extended validation code signing (EV CS) practices, including its commitment to provide EV CS certificates in conformity with published guidelines.

- Maintained effective controls to provide reasonable assurance that the integrity of keys and EV CS certificates it manages is established and protected.

Source: *BDO Report on Amazon Trust Services Certification Authority* (online source).

---

[5] *2017 Trust Services Criteria for Security, Availability Processing, Integrity, Confidentiality, and Privacy,* AICPA, 2017 (updated March 2020).

The Future of Assurance Services

While it is difficult to identify specific areas that may emerge, it is safe to say that accountant assurance services will continue to evolve and expand, creating both opportunities and challenges for practitioners. One particular likely area of future expansion is the use of blockchain technologies to conduct transactions and update ledgers without the involvement of intermediaries. A recent whitepaper prepared by the Chartered Professional Accountants of Canada and the AICPA identified the following potential applications of assurance services in this arena:[6]

- Verifying that smart contracts embedded in a blockchain are implemented with the correct business logic.
- Verifying the interface between smart contracts and external data sources that trigger business events.
- Ensuring the effectiveness of controls that protect sensitive information included in a blockchain platform.
- Ensuring the effectiveness of controls over participant access to blockchain platforms.

The Auditing Insight "Assurance Services in the 2020s" illustrates recent examples of the expanding situations in which the reliability added by accountant assurance on information will lead to the continued evolution of assurance services.

AUDITING INSIGHT   Assurance Services in the 2020s

- **ExxonMobil's** shareholders submitted a proposal for consideration at its 2021 annual shareholders' meeting that would require an audited report on how a significant reduction in fossil fuel demand would impact its financial position and underlying assumptions. This proposal received significant support (49.4 percent) from ExxonMobil's shareholders.

- **Intel's** shareholders submitted a proposal to request a third-party audit on whether written policies or unwritten norms at Intel reinforce racism in its company culture. This proposal received only 17 percent support from Intel's shareholders.

- The Securities and Exchange Commission has proposed requirements for publicly traded companies to disclose information about greenhouse-gas emissions and energy consumption from their operations. In addition, companies would be required to report greenhouse-gas emissions of their supply chains and consumers (known as Scope 3 emissions), which would impact most of the companies in the S&P 500. The current proposal would require this information to be "independently certified."

Source: *ExxonMobil Form 8-K/A* (filed June 21, 2021); *Intel Form 8-K* (filed May 16, 2022); "SEC Pushes on Climate Disclosure," *The Wall Street Journal*, March 22, 2022, p. B1, B10; "SEC Climate Proposal Would Expand Auditors' Roles," *Accounting Today*, March 29, 2022.

✅ REVIEW CHECKPOINTS

A.22 What are the four broad areas of assurance services currently being evaluated by the ASEC? Provide a brief summary of each area.

A.23 Why would a company choose to provide a sustainability report and seek independent assurance on its sustainability activities?

A.24 Identify and define the two types of trust services developed by the AICPA and CICA.

---

[6]*Blockchain Technology and Its Potential Impact on the Audit and Assurance Profession,* CPA Canada and AICPA, 2017.

Summary

While the focus in this text has been on audit engagements provided by accounting firms, other forms of services have arisen. This module discussed the following three broad types of engagements:

1. **Attestation engagements:** Engagements in which CPAs provide assurance and report on an assertion that is the responsibility of another party.
2. **Accounting and review engagements:** Engagements performed by CPAs on historical financial statements that are less in scope than an audit.
3. **Assurance engagements:** Engagements performed by CPAs that improve the quality of information for decision makers.

Professional standards provide guidance for a wide range of engagements, which differ in terms of scope as well as the intended level of assurance provided by the accountant, as shown below (an agreed-upon procedures engagement will vary in terms of scope, depending upon the extensiveness of the procedures performed).

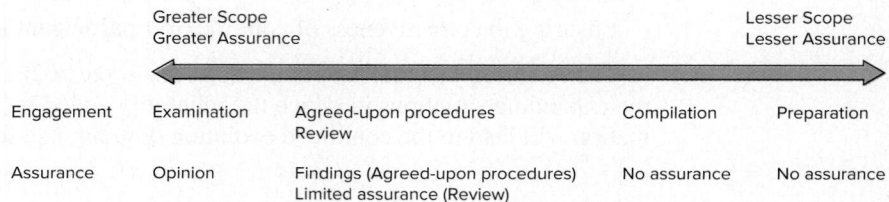

	Greater Scope Greater Assurance			Lesser Scope Lesser Assurance	
Engagement	Examination	Agreed-upon procedures Review		Compilation	Preparation
Assurance	Opinion	Findings (Agreed-upon procedures) Limited assurance (Review)		No assurance	No assurance

Key Terms

accounting and review engagement: Engagements performed by accountants on historical financial statements that are less in scope than an audit, 579

agreed-upon procedures engagement: Engagements in which the accountant performs procedures that are specified by specific user(s), 581

assertion-based examination engagement: Engagements in which a practitioner expresses an opinion with respect to a written assertion that is the responsibility of another party, 581

assurance engagement: Engagements performed by CPAs that improve the quality of information for decision makers, 579

attestation engagement: An engagement in which a practitioner is engaged to issue or does issue a report on an assertion (or assertions) about subject matter that is the responsibility of another party, 579

broker–dealer: An individual or company involved in the business of buying and selling investment securities either for its own account or on behalf of customers, 588

compilation engagement: An engagement in which an accountant performs limited procedures (such as reading the entity's financial statements) in assembling financial information but does not provide any assurance on that information, 593

direct examination engagement: Engagements similar in scope to an assertion-based examination, with the exception that the practitioner is not evaluating a written assertion but is evaluating the subject matter against specified criteria, 581

financial forecast: The prospective financial information reflecting an entity's estimates of what is likely to occur in a future period, 585

financial projection: The prospective financial information reflecting a transaction or event that may occur in the future, 585

general use Situation in which information and accountant reports providing assurance on that information may be provided to users other than those who engaged the accountant or with whom the entity is negotiating, 581

preparation engagement: An engagement in which an accountant assembles financial statements without performing any additional procedures or issuing a report, 594

responsible party: The person or persons, either as individuals or representatives of the entity, responsible for the subject matter of an attestation engagement, 580

restricted use Also known as limited use, a situation in which information and accountant reports providing assurance on that information may only be provided to users who engaged the accountant or with whom the entity is negotiating, 581

review engagement: Engagements in which an accountant performs inquiries and analytical procedures and provides limited assurance about financial information, 581

service organization: An entity that provides services to user entities that are relevant to user entities' internal control over financial reporting, 582

SOC 1 "Type 2" Report: A report on a service organization's internal controls that provides an opinion on both the design and operating effectiveness of internal controls, 582

SOC 1 "Type 1" Report: A report on a service organization's internal controls that provides an opinion on the design of internal controls but not the operating effectiveness of internal controls, 583

sustainability: An entity's consideration of economic viability, social responsibility, and environmental responsibility in conducting its activities, 596

SysTrust Services: An assurance function that evaluates the reliability of business-to-business computer transactions, 598

trust services: A set of professional attestation and advisory functions based on a core set of principles and criteria that addresses the risks and opportunities of IT-enabled systems and privacy programs, 598

WebTrust Services: An assurance function that relates to the reliability of internet websites, 598

Multiple-Choice Questions for Practice and Review

Mc Graw Hill connect   All applicable questions are available with *Connect.*

LO A-2, A-3

A.25 When accountants are *not* independent, which of the following reports can they issue?

    a. Compilation report on historical financial statements.

    b. Standard unmodified audit report on historical financial statements.

    c. Examination report on a financial forecast.

    d. Examination of internal control over financial reporting for an issuer.

LO A-2

A.26 To perform an attestation engagement on prospective financial information, accountants must do all of the following *except*

    a. Obtain knowledge about the entity's business and accounting principles.

    b. Understand the internal controls used in the processes that generated the prospective financial information.

    c. Obtain an understanding of the process through which the prospective financial information was developed.

    d. Evaluate the assumptions used to prepare the prospective financial information.

LO A-2

A.27 Which of the following is *not* correct with respect to a user auditors' request for an SOC 1 report?

    a. An SOC 1 report should be requested in the audit of an issuer.

    b. Type 1 reports would be most appropriate for auditors' reporting requirements for issuers.

    c. The user entity is the entity on whom the audit of the financial statements and internal control over financial reporting is being conducted.

    d. An SOC 1 report may express an opinion on the design and/or operating effectiveness of internal controls.

LO A-2

A.28 Which of the following statements should be included in a practitioners' report on the application of agreed-upon procedures?

    a. A statement that the practitioner performed an examination of prospective financial statements.

    b. A statement of scope limitation that will qualify the practitioners' opinion.

    c. A statement referring to standards established by the AICPA.

    d. A statement of limited assurance based on procedures performed.

(AICPA adapted)

LO A-2   A.29 Which of the following statements would *not* be included in an accountants' report on an examination of a financial forecast?

    a. The examination was conducted in accordance with attestation standards established by the AICPA.

    b. An opinion on the likelihood of achieving the forecasted results.

    c. An acknowledgment that differences may occur between forecasted and actual results.

    d. A statement indicating the accountants have no responsibility to update the report for future events and circumstances.

LO A-2   A.30 In which of the following engagements would general use of the accountants' report be appropriate?

    a. Agreed-upon procedures engagement on a financial forecast.

    b. Examination of financial projection.

    c. Examination of financial forecast.

    d. None of the above.

LO A-2   A.31 Prospective financial information that reflects the results assuming the occurrence of one or more hypothetical events is referred to as a

    a. Financial estimate.

    b. Financial forecast.

    c. Financial projection.

    d. Pro forma financial information.

LO A-2   A.32 An SOC 1 Type 2 report supporting the auditors' report on internal control over financial reporting for an issuer provides assurance with respect to

	Controls placed in operation	Operating effectiveness of controls
a.	Yes	Yes
b.	Yes	No
c.	No	Yes
d.	No	No

LO A-2   A.33 The conclusions provided in an accountants' report on an agreed-upon procedures engagement are in the form of a(n)

    a. Limited assurance.

    b. Summary of findings.

    c. Opinion.

    d. No conclusions are provided in an agreed-upon procedures engagement.

LO A-2   A.34 Which of the following would be included in an accountants' report on an agreed-upon procedures engagement?

	Summary of Findings	Summary of Procedures Performed
a.	Yes	Yes
b.	Yes	No
c.	No	Yes
d.	No	No

LO A-2   A.35 Which of the following would *not* be included in an accountants' report on compliance with laws, regulations, or other matters conducted separately from an audit?

    a. Identification of the law, regulation, or other matter that serves as the basis for the engagement.

    b. A statement that the engagement was conducted in accordance with AICPA standards.

    c. A statement that the accountants' engagement provides a legal determination with respect to compliance.

    d. The accountants' conclusion with respect to compliance.

LO A-2
A.36 Which of the following is *not* a condition that must be met for an engagement to evaluate compliance with laws, regulations, or other matters?

   a. Management must accept responsibility for compliance.

   b. Management's evaluation of compliance is capable of evaluation and is measured against reasonable criteria.

   c. Sufficient evidence is available to support management's evaluation.

   d. Management provides a report attesting to satisfactory compliance.

LO A-3
A.37 Which of the following best describes the scope of audit and compilation engagements compared to a review engagement?

	Audit	Compilation
a.	Lesser than review	Lesser than review
b.	Greater then review	Lesser than review
c.	Lesser than review	Greater than review
d.	Greater than review	Greater than review

LO A-3
A.38 Accountants are permitted to express limited assurance in which of the following reports?

   a. Standard unmodified report on audited financial statements.

   b. Compilation report on unaudited financial statements.

   c. Review report on unaudited financial statements.

   d. Adverse opinion on audited financial statements.

LO A-3
A.39 During a review of a nonissuer's financial statements, accountants are required to make certain inquiries of management. Which of the following inquiries is *not* required by SSARS?

   a. The basis for the preparation of financial statements.

   b. Internal control deficiencies.

   c. Significant transactions occurring near the end of the reporting period.

   d. Material subsequent events.

LO A-3
A.40 Which of the following would *not* ordinarily be included in an accountants' review report on a nonissuer's financial statements?

   a. An indication that a review engagement is substantially less in scope than an audit engagement.

   b. A statement that a review engagement was conducted in accordance with SSARS.

   c. A statement that a review engagement is greater in scope than a compilation.

   d. Limited assurance on the fairness of the financial statements.

LO A-3
A.41 Dale, CPA, was engaged to conduct an audit of the financial statements of AM Company (a nonissuer). After considering the scope and cost of an audit engagement, AM Company has asked Dale to modify the scope of the engagement to a review. Which of the following best describes the professional guidance for this situation?

   a. Dale would be required to issue a disclaimer of opinion on the financial statements because of the limited scope of a review engagement.

   b. Dale would be permitted to modify the scope of the engagement if AM Company's request is based on their lender's willingness to accept a review engagement rather than an audit.

   c. Dale would be permitted to modify the scope of the engagement, regardless of the reason for AM Company's request.

   d. Dale would be precluded from modifying the scope of the engagement under any circumstances.

LO A-3
A.42 In which of the following engagements would an accountant be required to be independent of the client?

	Compilation Engagement	Preparation Engagement
a.	Yes	Yes
b.	Yes	No
c.	No	Yes
d.	No	No

LO A-3

A.43 If a nonissuer prepares financial statements that omit substantially all footnote disclosures required by GAAP, the accountants' compilation report

    a. Is not affected, since no assurance is provided in a compilation engagement.

    b. Should be modified to provide the omitted disclosures.

    c. Should indicate that the disclosures are omitted and that this omission might affect users' conclusions.

    d. Should disclaim an opinion on the financial statements because of a significant scope limitation.

LO A-3

A.44 If an accountant is not independent with respect to a nonissuer and has been requested to conduct a compilation engagement, the accountant should

    a. Decline to accept the engagement because of the lack of independence.

    b. Decline to accept the engagement and conduct a preparation engagement.

    c. Accept the engagement and disclose the lack of independence in the compilation report.

    d. Accept the engagement and express limited assurance on the financial statements because of the lack of independence.

LO A-3

A.45 Which of the following is *not* true with respect to a preparation engagement?

    a. The accountant should obtain an engagement letter from the client.

    b. While not required to be independent, the accountants' communication to third parties should disclose their lack of independence.

    c. The accountants' communication should include a statement on the financial statements such as "no assurance is provided."

    d. The accountant may issue a report disclaiming an opinion or assurance on the financial statements.

LO A-3

A.46 *Statements on Standards for Accounting and Review Services* are applicable to engagements involving

    a. Audited financial statements of issuers.

    b. Unaudited financial statements of issuers.

    c. Unaudited financial statements of nonissuers.

    d. Audited financial statements of nonissuers.

LO A-4

A.47 In providing assurance services to clients, CPAs are building on their reputations for

    a. Knowledge and integrity.

    b. Objectivity and integrity.

    c. Expertise in accounting and financial matters.

    d. Professionalism and trust.

LO A-4

A.48 An assurance service is defined as a service that

    a. Expands auditing services to nonfinancial information.

    b. Reviews unaudited financial information.

    c. Improves the quality of information for decision makers.

    d. Reduces the risk in management decision making.

LO A-4

A.49 B. Harper is shopping online and finds a great pair of running shoes at a really low price. However, he is not familiar with the company and is concerned with the accuracy of the website in presenting the quality of the shoes. Harper may be more willing to place an order with this company if

    a. The website displays the WebTrust seal.

    b. The company provides its annual report and the report of the independent auditors on its website.

    c. The company provides a money-back guarantee.

    d. Only a partial payment is required prior to receiving the product.

Exercises and Problems

All applicable questions are available with *Connect*.

LO A-1

A.50 **Attestation Evaluation.** The local high school experienced performance issues two years ago. Its graduation rates had declined to the bottom 10 percent in the state, college admission rates were low, and graduates had a high unemployment rate. The school board and administration have notified the state Department of Education and the taxpayers in the school district that these problems have been fixed. Graduation rates have increased, a higher percentage of students are continuing with their education, and a higher percentage of graduates are employed. The Department of Education wants an independent attestation to these assertions. It is concerned not only about the performance results claimed by the school board and administration but also about the underlying process and means used to obtain these results.

Required:

What information would you gather and evaluate against benchmark schools to validate the claim of the school board and administration?

LO A-2

A.51 **Prospective Financial Information.** For each of the following statements, indicate whether it is appropriately related to financial forecasts (FF), financial projections (FP), both (B), or neither (N).

1. Financial information is prepared based on expected conditions or courses of action.
2. Accountant may perform an examination engagement.
3. Accountant is required to be independent to conduct engagement.
4. Engagement is conducted under attestation standards.
5. Financial information is prepared based on the occurrence of one or more hypothetical events.
6. Accountants' report indicates that differences between prospective financial information and actual results may occur.
7. Accountant may perform a review engagement.
8. Use of the accountants' report is restricted to specific users.

LO A-2

A.52 **Prospective Financial Information.** TrailBlazer, Inc. is considering the acquisition of Sonic Company and has prepared prospective financial statements under the assumption that financing would be received and the transaction would be approved by their respective boards of directors and would be consummated by March 15, 2024. In order to obtain financing, TrailBlazer has approached Oregon National Bank for a $10 million loan. After reviewing the prospective financial statements, Oregon National Bank has requested having an independent accountant evaluate the prospective financial statements.

Required:

a. Identify and briefly define the two types of prospective financial information.
b. Based on the scenario above, which type of information has been prepared by TrailBlazer?
c. What are the major types of engagements that can be performed on prospective financial information? What type of assurance is provided in each type of engagement?
d. For each type of engagement in (c), indicate whether the following statements or issues would be referenced in an accountants' report on that engagement. (Your responses may be "Yes," "No," or "Possibly.")
   1. The financial statements/information evaluated by the accountant.
   2. The accountants' opinion on the presentation of the prospective financial information.
   3. A description of the nature of the engagement.
   4. A limitation on the use of the accountants' report.
   5. The procedures performed by the accountant on TrailBlazer's internal control over financial reporting.
   6. A notation that differences between prospective financial information and actual results may occur.
   7. An opinion on the achievability of the results reflected in the prospective financial information.

8. A detailed listing of procedures performed by the accountant.

9. The accountants' opinion on the reasonableness of the assumptions used in preparing the prospective financial information.

LO A-2

A.53 **Review of Forecast Assumptions.** Dodd Manufacturing Corporation has engaged you to attest to the reasonableness of the assumptions underlying its forecast of revenues, costs, and net income for the next calendar year, 2024. Four of the assumptions used by Dodd follow:

1. Dodd intends to sell certain real estate and other facilities held by Division B at an after-tax profit of $600,000; the proceeds of this sale will be used to retire outstanding debt.

2. Dodd will call and retire all outstanding 9 percent subordinated debentures (callable at 108). The debentures are expected to require the full call premium given present market interest rates of 8 percent on similar debt. A rise in market interest rates to 9 percent would reduce the loss on bond retirement from the projected $200,000 to $190,000.

3. Current labor contracts expire on September 1, 2024, and the new contract is expected to result in a wage increase of 5.5 percent. Given the forecasted levels of production and sales, after-tax operating earnings would be reduced approximately $50,000 for each percentage point of wage increase in excess of the expected contract settlement.

4. The sales forecast for Division A assumes that the new Portsmouth facility will be complete and operating at 40 percent of capacity on February 1, 2024. It is highly improbable that the facility will be operational before January 2024. Each month's delay would reduce Division A sales by approximately $80,000 and operating earnings by $30,000.

Required:

For each assumption, state the sources of evidence and procedures you would use to determine the reasonableness of that assumption.

LO A-2

A.54 **Service Organization Control Reports.** SA has accepted the engagement as auditor of Love Company (an issuer). Love uses an outside entity (Worknight) to process a significant volume of transactions related to a material account balance. Because SA will need to obtain some assurance as to the operating effectiveness of those controls for both the opinion on the financial statements and the opinion on internal control over financial reporting, they are considering various alternatives, including engaging a service auditor (PM) to test key controls applied at Worknight.

a. Define *user auditor, service auditor, user organization,* and *service organization.* Identify the parties who meet these definitions in this scenario.

b. Identify and define the two major types of Service Organization Controls 1 (SOC 1) reports. What are the major differences in these two types of SOC 1 reports?

c. In this particular instance, which type of SOC 1 report should SA request? Why?

d. Identify the major contents of the SOC 1 report that would be appropriate for SA in this engagement.

LO A-2

A.55 **Service Organization Control Reports.** Service organization control (SOC) reports may be requested by auditors when a service organization processes transactions related to a client's (user organization) internal control over financial reporting.

Required:

For each of the following statements related to Service Organization Control (SOC) reports, indicate whether it is appropriately related to a Type 1 report (T1), Type 2 report (T2), both a Type 1 and Type 2 report (B), or neither a Type 1 or Type 2 report (N).

a. Disclaims an opinion on the fairness of the entity's financial statements.

b. Provides a description of the service organization's internal control over financial reporting.

c. Summarizes tests of operating effectiveness of controls at the service organization.

d. Expresses an opinion on the suitability of design of internal controls over financial reporting.

e. Use of the service auditor's report is restricted to specified parties.

f. Would be requested when client is an issuer.

g. Disclaims an opinion on the operating effectiveness of internal control over financial reporting.

h. Would be requested in the audit of a nonissuer if the audit team has decided to rely on internal control over financial reporting to reduce substantive testing.

LO A-2

A.56 Compliance Reporting. Accountants can report on compliance with laws and regulations either in conjunction with an audit engagement or as a separate engagement.

Required:

a. What is the difference in the objective of reporting on compliance with laws and regulations in conjunction with an audit engagement and reporting as a separate engagement?

b. What are the requirements for conducting an engagement to report on compliance with laws and regulations?

c. What are the two levels of accountant services in an engagement to report on compliance with laws and regulations? What type of procedures are performed and assurances are provided for these levels of service?

LO A-2

A.57 Accounting and Review Services. Henry Horkheimer, MD, is considering expanding his office as a result of adding a new doctor to his family medical practice. Dr. Horkheimer knows that his business is profitable, but he does not produce regular financial statements, nor does he possess the technical knowledge to do so. Although he is financially savvy enough to know that he needs financial statements to obtain financing to expand his business, he is completely unsure as to what services he needs or even what is available. He has asked you for advice.

Required:

Consider Dr. Horkheimer's need for financing and write a memo outlining the pros and cons of four services an accountant could provide: audit, review, compilation, and preparation of financial statements. Conclude your memo with a recommendation for which service you believe would best suit Dr. Horkheimer's needs.

LO A-3

A.58 Errors in an Accountants' Review Report. M. Jordan & E. Stone, CPAs, audited the financial statements of Tech Company, a non issuer, for the year ended December 31, 2022, and expressed an unmodified opinion. For the year ended December 31, 2023, Tech issued comparative financial statements. Jordan & Stone reviewed Tech's 2023 financial statements and B. Kent, an assistant on the engagement, drafted the accountants' review report that follows. Stone, the engagement supervisor, decided not to reissue the prior year audit report but instructed Kent to include a separate paragraph in the current year review report describing the responsibility assumed for the prior year audited financial statements.

Stone reviewed Kent's draft and indicated in the following supervisor's review notes that the draft contained several deficiencies.

Accountants' Review Report—Kent's Draft

We have reviewed and audited the accompanying financial statements of Tech Co, which comprise the balance sheets as of December 31, 2023 and 2022, and the related statements of income, changes in stockholders' equity, and cash flows for the years then ended, and the related notes to the financial statements. These engagements were conducted in accordance with Statements on Standards for Accounting and Review Services promulgated by the Accounting and Review Services Committee of the AICPA and generally accepted auditing standards. A review includes primarily applying analytical procedures to management's financial data and making inquiries of company management. A review is substantially less in scope than an audit, the objective of which is the expression of an opinion regarding the financial statements as a whole.

Management's Responsibility for the Financial Statements
Management is responsible for the preparation and fair presentation of these financial statements; this includes the design, implementation, and maintenance of internal control relevant to the preparation and fair presentation of financial statements that are free from material misstatement whether due to fraud or error.

Accountant's Responsibility
We are required to perform procedures to obtain limited assurance as a basis for reporting whether we are aware of any material modifications that should be made to the financial statements for them to be in accordance with accounting principles generally accepted in the United States of America. We believe that the results of our procedures provide a reasonable basis for our conclusion.

Accountant's Conclusion
Based on our review, we are not aware of any material modifications that should be made to the accompanying financial statements in order for them to be in accordance

with accounting principles generally accepted in the United States of America. Because of the inherent limitations of a review engagement, this report is intended for the information of management and should not be used for any other purpose.

Other Matter

We audited the financial statements for the year ended December 31, 2022, and our report was dated March 2, 2023. We have no responsibility for updating that report for events and circumstances occurring after that date.

Betsy Ross & Co. CPA
Chicago, IL
March 1, 2024

Required:

These supervisor's review notes may or may not be correct. For each item (a)–(m), indicate whether Stone is correct (C) or incorrect (I) in the criticism of Kent's draft.

a. The report should contain no reference to the prior year audited financial statements in the first paragraph.

b. All current year financial statements are not properly identified in the first paragraph.

c. The report should contain no reference to the American Institute of Certified Public Accountants in the first paragraph.

d. The basic procedures performed in a review (analytical procedures and inquiries) should be provided in the *Accountant's Responsibility* section of the report and not the first paragraph.

e. The report should contain no comparison of the scope of a review to an audit in the first paragraph.

f. Limited assurance should be expressed on the current year reviewed financial statements in the first paragraph.

g. The report should contain a statement that no opinion is expressed on the current year financial statements in the first paragraph.

h. The report should contain a reference to "accounting principles generally accepted in the United States of America" in the *Management's Responsibility for the Financial Statements* section.

i. The report should not express a restriction on the use of the accountants' review report in the *Accountant's Conclusion* section.

j. The *Accountant's Responsibility* section should indicate that the accountant is required to be independent of the client.

k. The report should indicate the type of opinion expressed on the prior year audited financial statements in the *other-matter paragraph*.

l. The report should indicate that no auditing procedures were performed after the date of the report on the prior year financial statements in the *other-matter paragraph*.

m. The report should not contain a reference to "updating the prior year auditors' report for events and circumstances occurring after that date" in the *other-matter paragraph*.

(AICPA adapted)

LO A-3

A.59 **Compilation and Review Procedures.** The following numbered items 1–10 state procedures accountants should consider performing in review engagements and compilation engagements on the annual financial statements of nonissuers.

Required:

For each item (taken separately), tell whether the item is required in all review engagements and/or required in all compilation engagements. For each item, give two responses, one regarding review engagements and the other regarding compilation engagements.

1. The accountants should establish an understanding in writing with the entity's management regarding the nature and limitations of the services to be performed.

2. The accountants should make inquiries concerning actions taken at the board of directors' meetings.

3. The accountants, as the entity's successor accountants, should communicate with the predecessor accountants to obtain access to the predecessors' documentation.

4. The accountants should obtain a level of knowledge of the accounting principles and practices of the entity's industry.

5. The accountants should obtain an understanding of the entity's internal control over financial reporting.

6. The accountants should perform analytical procedures designed to identify unusual relationships.

7. The accountants should assess the risk of material misstatement.

8. The accountants should obtain a letter from the entity's attorney to corroborate the information furnished by management concerning litigation.

9. The accountants should obtain written representations from the entity's management.

10. The accountants should study the relationship of the financial statement elements that would be expected to conform to a predictable pattern.

(AICPA adapted)

LO A-3

A.60 Limited Assurance in Review Reports. One portion of the report on a review services engagement is the following: "Based on my review, I am not aware of any material modifications that should be made to the accompanying financial statements in order for them to be in conformity with accounting principles generally accepted in the United States of America [or another framework for financial reporting]."

Required:

a. Does this paragraph represent "limited assurance" provided by the accountants?

b. Why is limited assurance generally prohibited in audit reports?

c. What justification is there for permitting limited assurance in a review engagement on the financial statements of a nonissuer?

(AICPA adapted)

LO A-3

A.61 Prepare a Compilation Report. The Coffin brothers have engaged you to compile their financial schedules from books and records maintained by James Coffin. The brothers own and operate three auto parts stores in Central City. Even though their business is growing, they have not wanted to employ a full-time bookkeeper. James specifies that all he wants is a balance sheet, a statement of operations, and a statement of cash flows. He does not have time to prepare footnotes to accompany the financial statements.

James directed the physical count of inventory on June 30, 2024, and adjusted and closed the books on that date. You find that he actually is a good accountant, having taken some night courses at the community college. The accounts appear to have been maintained in conformity with generally accepted accounting principles. At least you have noticed no obvious errors.

Required:

You are independent with respect to the Coffin brothers and their Coffin Auto Speed Shop business. Prepare a report on your compilation engagement.

LO A-3

A.62 Reporting on Comparative Unaudited Financial Statements. A. Jones, CPA, conducted a review engagement for the Independence Company in 2023. He wants to present comparative financial statements. However, the 2022 statements were compiled by Able and Associates, CPAs, and Able has not agreed to reissue the prior year compilation report. Jones has no indication that any adjustments should be made to either the 2023 or the 2022 financial statements, which are to be presented with all necessary disclosures. However, he does not have time to perform a review of the 2022 financial statements. Jones completed his work on January 15, 2024, for the financial statements dated December 31, 2023.

Required:

Write Jones's review report and include the paragraph describing the report on the 2022 statements. List any assumptions Jones needs to make to write the report.

LO A-2, A-3   A.63 **Various Engagement and Reporting Standards.** Indicate the type of standards [*Statements on Auditing Standards (SAS), Statements on Standards for Attestation Engagements (SSAE), PCAOB Attestation Standards (PCAOB),* and *Statements on Standards for Accounting and Review Services (SSARS)*] that may apply to engagements associated with the following:

1. Historical financial information.
2. Prospective financial information.
3. Compliance with laws and regulations (conducted in conjunction with an audit)
4. Operating effectiveness of internal controls applied at a service organization.
5. Performing agreed-upon procedures on historical financial statements.
6. Matters relating to broker-dealer compliance.
7. Audited financial statements prepared using a special purpose framework.
8. Compliance with laws and regulations for a nonissuer (not conducted in conjunction with a financial statement audit).
9. Engagements lesser in scope than an audit on historical financial information
10. Audits on elements, account or items of a financial statement

LO A-2, A-3   A.64 **Various Engagements on Historical Financial Information.** Indicate which of the engagements performed on historical financial information [examination (E), agreed-upon procedures (AU), review (R), compilation (C), and preparation (P)] are associated with the following statements. (Your responses may be "Yes," "No," or "Possibly.")

1. Accountant prepares an engagement letter with the client to document an understanding of the scope of the engagement.
2. Accountant works with identified users in establishing the scope of the engagement.
3. Accountant performs the engagement in accordance with generally accepted auditing standards.
4. Engagement requires accountant to perform some level of substantive procedures.
5. Engagement allows accountant to express limited assurance on the fairness of the financial statements.
6. Accountant is required to be independent to conduct engagement.
7. Accountant will perform inquiries of management during the engagement.
8. Engagement allows accountant to express an opinion on the fairness of the financial statements.
9. Use of the accountants' report may be restricted to specified users.
10. Accountant obtains an understanding of the client's internal control over financial reporting.

LO A-4   A.65 **Assurance Services.** Davis has a store that sells old baseball cards. To expand the business, he has decided to open an Internet site where potential customers can view the cards and place orders. Davis hires Johnson, who is an expert in constructing websites for small businesses. She explains that even with a quality website and pictures of the merchandise for sale, customers may be reluctant to purchase baseball cards from Davis's website.

Required:

a. Explain the reasons for Johnson's concerns.
b. What steps can Davis and Johnson take to reduce customer's reluctance to make purchases on the Internet?

LO A-4   A.66 **Assurance Services.** Henry's Health Food Store maintains a perpetual inventory on its computer. The sales representative from A-Plus Vitamins has recommended the following to Henry:

- All the files should have password protection.
- A-Plus Vitamins should be given the URL and the password for Henry's inventory file on the computer, which can be accessed from outside.
- A-Plus Vitamins will search the inventory for items that fall below an established reorder point and will automatically ship a set amount of product to Henry's.

Required:

      a. What are the advantages of this arrangement for Henry's? For A-Plus Vitamins?

      b. What concerns might Henry's have in this arrangement?

      c. How might these concerns be addressed?

LO A-4   A.67 **Internet Assignment: Global Reporting.** Go to the GRI website (www.globalreporting.org) and obtain the Consolidated Set of GRI Sustainability Reporting Standards.

Required:

      a. Identify the categories of topic-specific standard disclosures. For each category, identify the subcategories of disclosures.

      b. How can accountants provide assurance for sustainability reporting as a service to their clients?

Professional Ethics

> *To educate a person in mind and not in morals is to educate a menace to society.*
>
> > Theodore Roosevelt, 26th President of the United States (1858–1919)
>
> *Always do right—this will gratify some and astonish the rest.*
>
> > Mark Twain, famous American writer (1835–1910)

Professional Standards References

Topic	AU-C/ISA Section	AS Section
Responsibilities and Functions of the Independent Auditor	200	1001
Independence		1005
Training and Proficiency of the Independent Auditor		1010
Due Professional Care in the Performance of Work		1015
Engagement Quality Review	220	1220
Responsibility Not to Knowingly or Recklessly Contribute to Violations		Rule 3502
Auditor Independence		Rule 3520
Contingent Fees		Rule 3521
Tax Transactions		Rule 3522
Tax Services for Persons in Financial Reporting Oversight Roles		Rule 3523
Audit Committee Preapproval of Certain Tax Services		Rule 3524
Audit Committee Preapproval of Nonaudit Services Related to Internal Control over Financial Reporting		Rule 3525
Communication with Audit Committees Concerning Independence		Rule 3526

Topic	ET Section*
Preface	ET 0.100–0.701
Members in Public Practice	ET 1.000–1.800
Members in Business	ET 2.000–2.400
Other Members	ET 3.000–3.400
AICPA Code of Conduct—Council Resolution Designating Bodies to Promulgate Technical Standards	ET Appendix A
AICPA Code of Conduct—Council Resolution Concerning Form of Organization and Name	ET Appendix B
AICPA Code of Conduct—Revision History Table	ET Appendix C
AICPA Code of Conduct—Mapping Document	ET Appendix D

*ET references represent sections in the AICPA Code of Professional Conduct.

LEARNING OBJECTIVES

As described in Chapter 2, the responsibilities principle identifies three specific responsibilities. Two of the responsibilities—(1) having appropriate competence and capabilities to perform the audit and (2) maintaining professional skepticism and exercising professional judgment throughout the planning and performance of the audit—have been focused on in other chapters of this book. This module focuses on the third responsibility: complying with relevant ethical requirements. In this spirit, this module is designed to teach you about the AICPA Code of Professional Conduct and demonstrate why it is so important to your success as a professional accountant. As you will soon learn, regulation of the profession, including any discipline for violations, depends on the prevailing published codes of ethics and enforcement practices. As a result, we believe this module is essential to your success.

Your objectives are to be able to

LO B-1 Understand what is meant by ethics and the steps that are necessary for making ethical decisions.

LO B-2 Reason through an ethical decision problem using the imperative, utilitarian, and virtue theories of moral philosophy.

LO B-3 Identify the different entities that make ethics rules for CPAs and public accounting firms.

LO B-4 With reference to American Institute of Certified Public Accountants (AICPA), Government Accountability Office (GAO), Public Company Accounting Oversight Board (PCAOB), and Securities and Exchange Commission (SEC) rules, analyze factual situations and decide whether an accountant's conduct does or does not impair independence.

LO B-5 With reference to AICPA rules on topics other than independence, analyze factual situations and decide whether an accountant's conduct does or does not conform to the AICPA Code of Professional Conduct.

LO B-6 Explain the types of penalties that can be imposed on accountants.

INTRODUCTION

Scott London seemed to have it all. One of three sons of a Los Angeles certified public accountant, he followed his father into the accounting business. He graduated in 1984 from California State University, Northridge, and soon landed a job at a firm that later became part of **KPMG.** From an outsider's perspective, London appeared to have an ideal personal life. He and his wife Michele had two children and lived in an expensive home at the end of a cul-de-sac in a Los Angeles suburb known as the gateway to the Santa Monica Mountains. Professionally, as the KPMG partner in charge of the firm's Pacific Southwest Audit practice, he had more than 50 partners and 500 employees reporting to him. After 29 years with the firm, he seemed to be set financially. However, with all this going for him, he plead guilty to passing confidential client information to a golf buddy who then traded stocks based on that information to make more than $1 million in illegal gains. Although the information was initially passed "innocently" in casual conversation on the golf course, London began accepting payments of cash and jewelry in exchange for the tips. Bryan Shaw, the recipient of the information who profited from the illegal trades, cooperated with authorities, including agreeing to wear a wire to gain evidence against his benefactor. In return for the confidential information, London received more than $50,000 in cash and gifts, including a $12,000 Rolex watch; however, the total value of these "gifts" is clearly immaterial given London's estimated salary of greater than $1 million per year.

The sting operation that nabbed London was the result of a joint investigation by the FBI, SEC, and Department of Justice. When first notified of the allegations, KPMG acted immediately and decisively, firing London, who the firm said "violated the firm's rigorous policies and protections, betrayed the trust of clients as well as colleagues, and acted with deliberate disregard for KPMG's long-standing culture of professionalism and integrity."[1] The firm also took legal action against London. Due to independence concerns, the firm resigned as auditor of **Skechers** and **Herbalife,** companies whose audits London oversaw. KPMG also announced that it would reassess its quality control standards, which include employee training, monitoring key employees' personal investments, and a whistleblowing hot line.

In addition to losing his job and being sued by his former employer, London ended up serving 14 months in prison and paying $100,000 in fines. He has openly confessed to his misconduct and has expressed his remorse: "I cannot begin to apologize for my incredibly stupid actions. There is no excuse for my wrongful conduct." However, even in hindsight, London has trouble explaining his behavior: "I felt guilt about it regularly—I can't explain it to be honest with you. . . . I look back at when this started and I can't explain it. . . . I guess [the] best way to describe it is that humans make mistakes."[2]

We may never know the true motives behind his actions, but we do know that London made a conscious decision to betray his employer, his clients, and his profession, and violated a number of rules from the AICPA Code of Professional Conduct in the process. In this module, we discuss the AICPA Code of Professional Conduct and many of the rules that London violated when sharing stock tips on the golf course.

AN ETHICAL DECISION PROCESS

LO B-1
Understand what is meant by ethics and the steps that are necessary for making ethical decisions.

What is ethics? Wheelwright defined **ethics** as "that branch of philosophy which is the systematic study of reflective choice, of the standards of right and wrong by which it is to be guided, and of the goods toward which it may ultimately be directed."[3] In this definition, you can detect three key elements about ethics. First, ethics involves questions requiring reflective choice (*decision problems*). Second, ethics involves guides of right and wrong (*moral principles*). And third, ethics is concerned with the consequences (*good or bad*) of decisions.

What is an ethical problem? A **problem situation** exists when an individual must make a choice among alternative actions and the right choice is not absolutely clear. An *ethical problem situation* may be described as one in which the choice of alternative actions affects the well-being of other persons. Although these are technical definitions of ethical dilemmas, we are often faced with situations in which what we want to do conflicts with what we know is the right course of action. While pure ethicists may argue that these are not "pure" ethical dilemmas, this does not make the decisions any easier to make.

What is **ethical behavior**? You can find three standard philosophical answers to this question: Ethical behavior is that which (1) produces the greatest good, and/or (2) conforms to moral rules and principles, and/or (3) best demonstrates the virtues you value most. The most difficult problem situations arise when two or more rules conflict or when a rule and the criterion of "greatest good" conflict. However, as a professional auditor, you must always conform to the code of ethical behavior that applies to your jurisdiction or face the possibility of being formally sanctioned by the profession.

Why does an individual or group need a code of ethical conduct? A *code* makes explicit some of the criteria for conduct unique to the profession. *Codes of professional ethics* provide guidance in addressing situations that may not be specifically available in general ethics theories. An individual is better able to know what the profession expects when a code exists. From the viewpoint of the organized profession, a *code* is a public

---

[1]Geller, Martinne, and Emily Flitter. "FBI probes trading as KPMG quits Herbalife, Skechers audits." Reuters, April 9, 2013. https://www.reuters.com/article/us-herbalife-auditor/fbi-probes-trading-as-kpmg-quits-herbalife-skechers-audits-idUSBRE9380N920130409.

[2]"Insider Trader Is Identified," *The Wall Street Journal,* April 11, 2013, p. C1.

[3]Philip Wheelwright, *A Critical Introduction to Ethics,* 3rd ed. (Indianapolis, IN: Odyssey Press, 1959).

declaration of principled conduct and a means of facilitating *enforcement* of standards of conduct. Once again, you can see the value of ethical behavior. Remember that accounting is the only business discipline that is considered a profession similar to those of doctors and lawyers. As a student of auditing, you must commit yourself to knowing and understanding the AICPA *Code of Professional Conduct.* Understanding the Code of Professional Conduct will allow you to be better prepared to handle difficult situations like the one posed in the following example of unethical behavior.

A Shocking Example of Unethical Behavior

In a famous experiment conducted by Stanley Milgram (a psychologist at Yale University), subjects were told to ask questions of an individual in another room. If the individual answered incorrectly, the subjects were told to inflict an electric shock as punishment. In reality, no shock was actually administered; however, the subjects believed they were administering one and could hear shouts, cries, and appeals to stop emanating from the next room. The experimenter ordered the subjects to continue to apply the shocks at ever-increasing amounts. Many subjects increased the voltage to intensities labeled as dangerous and continued even after the individual in the next room asked for a doctor. Why do you think the subjects continued to apply shocks? What would you have done in this circumstance? Many have used the Milgram study result as an explanation for how good people often get caught up in wide-reaching accounting frauds, by subordinating their judgments to authority figures.

Making Ethical Decisions

When considering general ethics, your primary goal is to arrive at a personal framework for making ethical decisions. Consequently, an understanding of some of the general principles of ethics can provide background for a detailed consideration of standards for professional conduct.

In the earlier definition of ethics, one of the key elements was *reflective choice.* This involves engaging in an important sequence of events beginning with the recognition of a decision problem. Collection of evidence, in the ethics context, refers to thinking about rules of behavior and outcomes of alternative actions. The process ends with analyzing the situation and taking an action. Ethical decision problems almost always involve projecting yourself into the future to live with your decisions. Professional ethics decisions usually turn on these questions: "What written and unwritten rules govern my behavior?" and "What are the possible consequences of my choices—whom will my decision affect?" *Principles of ethics* can help you think about these two questions in real situations.

A good way to approach ethical decision problems is to think through several steps:

1. Define all facts and circumstances known at the time that you need to make the decision. They are the "who, what, where, when, and how" dimensions of the situation. Identify the actor who needs to decide what to do.
   a. Because ethical decision problems are defined in terms of their effects on people, identify the people involved in the situation or affected by it. These are the "stakeholders"; be careful not to expand the number of stakeholders beyond the bounds of reasonable analysis.
   b. Identify and describe the stakeholders' rights and responsibilities in general and to each other.
2. Specify the actor's major alternative decision actions and their consequences (good, bad, short-run, long-run).
3. The actor must choose among the alternative actions.

Let's apply the preceding ethical framework to the following example of an ethical decision process.

An Example of an Ethical Decision Process

Step 1: Define the Problem Kathy Ellis (the chief financial officer) ordered Jorge Santos (a staff accountant) to "improve" net income in the financial statements to be submitted in a loan application to Spring National Bank by understating the allowance for uncollectible accounts receivable saying, "It's an estimate anyway and we need the loan for a short time to keep from laying off our loyal employees." What should Santos do?

Step 1a: Define the Stakeholders The stakeholders include the direct participants—Ellis, Santos, and Luis Perez (Spring National Bank's loan officer)—and some indirect participants—bank stockholders and loyal employees. Other people may be affected—Santos's mother, citizens who depend on the solvency of the banking system as a whole, taxpayers who may eventually need to bail out the insolvent banking system, and others—but identifying them probably will not improve the analysis.

Step 1b: Define the Responsibilities of the Individuals Ellis and Santos should act with integrity, and Ellis should not pressure Santos to cut corners with financial statements. Perez should make careful loan approval decisions. *Rights:* Santos should not be subject to pressures to cut corners with "improved financial statements." Perez should receive information that is not materially misstated or manipulated. (Some rights of employees and bank stockholders also could be identified.)

Step 2: Determine the Consequences (a) Santos can follow orders and improve the financial statements: Ellis is happy, he keeps his job; Perez gets fooled and approves the loan; the employees keep their jobs; the company may fail; the bank may be unable to collect the loan; the employees are laid off anyway; and Ellis and Santos are prosecuted and convicted of making false statements to a federal institution and go to federal prison. (b) Santos can refuse to "improve" the financial statements: Ellis is not happy; Santos is fired; Ellis prepares the financial statements herself; and so on. (c) Santos persuades Ellis of the potential problems and Perez refuses the loan, and the company must find another way to survive; or Perez approves the loan anyway and the bank takes the risk; or Ellis does not agree, and Santos must again face alternatives (a) and (b) anyway. There is a fourth alternative, (d): Santos could resign. This alternative may seem like an ideal way for Santos to extricate himself from the situation, but the problem facing others in this scenario does not go away.

In addition to weighing the consequences, Santos also should consider general and professional rules. If he is a CPA, some of the relevant professional rules relate to maintaining integrity (AICPA Rule 102), application of accounting standards (AICPA Rule 203), and the prohibition of discreditable acts (AICPA Rule 501). Santos needs to decide whether to follow rules or balance the expected consequences in the particular situation.

Step 3 Choose a Course of Action: As the actor, Santos must choose one of the alternative actions and justify it by presenting a convincing argument for its superiority. He can base the argument on rules, consequences, or a combination of both.

✅ REVIEW CHECKPOINTS

B.1   What roles must a professional accountant be prepared to perform in regard to ethical decision problems?

B.2   When might the rule "Let your conscience be your guide" *not* be a sufficient basis for (a) your personal ethical decisions and (b) your professional ethical decisions?

PHILOSOPHICAL PRINCIPLES IN ETHICS

LO B-2
Reason through an ethical decision problem using the imperative, utilitarian, and virtue theories of moral philosophy.

We could skip a discussion of ethical theories if we were willing to accept a simple rule: "Let your *conscience* be your guide." Such a rule is appealing because it calls on an individual's own judgment, which may be based on wisdom, insight, adherence to custom, or an authoritative code. However, it also might be based on caprice, immaturity, ignorance, stubbornness, or misunderstanding. Often, as in the Milgram experiments, undue pressures might cause us to act in a way that we will later regret. The problem with using conscience as a guide is that it sometimes tells you about a wrong decision *after* you take action!

In a similar manner, reliance on the opinions of others or on the weight of opinions of a particular social group is not always enough. Another person or a group of persons may perpetuate a custom or habit that is wrong. To adhere blindly to custom or to group habits is to abdicate individual responsibility. Titus and Keeton summarized this point succinctly: "Each person capable of making moral decisions is responsible for making his own decisions. The ultimate locus of moral responsibility is in the individual."[4]

[4]H. H. Titus and M. Keeton, *Ethics for Today,* 4th ed. (New York: American Book—Stratford Press, 1966), p. 131.

This does not mean you should not consult with friends, colleagues, or family members when facing a dilemma, but that only *you* have the final responsibility.

There are several philosophies, often referred to as ethical principles, that may be used to guide the ethical decision process. Thus, the function of ethical principles is not to provide a simple and sure rule but to provide some guides for your individual decisions and actions. Of course, as a professional auditor, you are required to follow the code of professional conduct. So, in that sense, professional auditors must always apply the imperative principle first and foremost. However, because many decisions go beyond the code, the principle of utilitarianism and the generalization argument are also considered. Finally, the decision must align with your own character (or virtue).

The Imperative Principle

The *imperative principle* directs a decision maker to act according to the requirements of moral rules and principles. Strict versions of the imperative principle maintain that a decision should be made without trying to predict whether an action will create the greatest balance of good over evil. Rather, ethics in the *imperative* sense is a function of moral rules and principles and as such does not involve a situation-specific calculation of the consequences.[5]

The philosopher Immanuel Kant (1724–1804) was perhaps the foremost advocate of the imperative school. Kant maintained that *reason* and the strict *duty to be consistent* should govern our actions. He believed that individuals should act only as they think everyone should act all of the time. This law of conduct (in moral philosophy) is known as Kant's **categorical imperative**, meaning that it specifies an *unconditional obligation*. One such maxim (rule), for example, is "Lying is wrong."

Suppose you believe that Santos (from our earlier ethical decision process example) should agree with Ellis and do everything she asked for by "improving the financial statements," thus participating in a lie (knowingly misrepresenting the facts about the allowance for uncollectible accounts receivable). The Kantian test of the morality of such a lie is this: Can this maxim be a moral rule that should be followed without exception by all persons who have the opportunity to fool a bank loan officer for a good cause? If Santos refuses to manipulate the financial statements and the loan is refused, the result may be economic hardship and employee layoffs. Kant maintained that motive and duty alone define a moral act, not the consequences of the act. This reasoning places the highest value on the duty to be consistent and a lower value on the consequences, in this case the fate of the employees.

The general objection to the imperative principle is the belief that so-called universal rules always turn out to have exceptions. The general response to this objection is that if the rule is stated properly to include the exceptional cases, the principle is still valid. The problem with this response, however, is that human experience is complicated, and extremely complex universal rules would have to be constructed to try to cover all possible cases.[6]

Most professional codes of ethics have characteristics of the imperative type of theory. As a general matter, professionals are expected to act in a manner in conformity with the rules. As it relates to your work as an audit professional, this principle would lead you to follow the code of professional conduct to the letter of the law. This, of course, is what you must do to avoid being sanctioned by the profession. However, society frequently questions not only conduct itself, but also the rules on which conduct is based. Thus, a dogmatic imperative approach to ethical decisions may not be completely sufficient for the maintenance of professional standards. Society may question the rules, and conflicts among them are always possible. A means of estimating the consequences of alternative actions may be useful. Consider the following example which illustrates a classical ethical conflict.

---

[5]I. Kant, *Foundations of the Metaphysics of Morals,* trans. Lewis W. Beck (Indianapolis, IN: Bobbs-Merrill, 1959; originally published in 1785).

[6]Several rules in the AICPA Code of Professional Conduct are explicitly phrased to provide for exceptions to the general rules, notably Rules 203 and 301. Imperative rules also seem to generate borderline cases, so the AICPA Ethics Division issues interpretations and rulings to explain the applicability of the rules.

A Classical Ethical Conflict

Consolidata Inc. was a tax client of **Alexander Grant & Company, CPAs** (AG). Consolidata prepared payrolls for 38 customers, received the customers' money, and then paid the payrolls. AG learned that Consolidata was in serious financial difficulty and advised the company to inform its customers, but company officials did not do so. When AG learned that the company's officers and directors had resigned, AG telephoned 12 Consolidata customers who were also AG clients, told them of the situation, and advised them not to entrust further payroll funds to Consolidata. The 12 were spared the risk of losing their money when Consolidata went out of business one month later.

Consolidata accused AG of breach of contract for breaking an obligation of confidentiality required by the AICPA Code of Professional Conduct (discussed later in this module). One SEC attorney said she thought AG should have alerted all 38 customers, not just the 12 AG clients. Accountants and SEC officials viewed the situation as a balancing of confidentiality (AICPA rule) against the public interest (Consolidata customers who needed a warning). Ethicists would view this dilemma as a conflict between an imperative principle (client confidentiality) and the principle of utilitarianism (what action benefits the most parties), which is now discussed in detail.

Source: Wagenheim v. Alexander Grant Co., 482 N.E.2d 955, Ohio Court of Appeals, December 15 1983 (Original).

The Principle of Utilitarianism

The *principle of utilitarianism* emphasizes examining the *consequences* of action rather than following some rules. The criterion of producing the greater good is made an explicit part of the decision process. The *principle* is very useful, but be sure to notice that it does not specify the *values* that enable you to determine the good or evil of an action. In **act-utilitarianism**, the center of attention is the *individual act* as it is affected by the specific circumstances of a situation. The general difficulty with act-utilitarianism is that it seems to permit too many exceptions to well-established rules. By focusing attention on individual acts, the long-run effect of setting examples for other people appears to be ignored. If an act-utilitarian decision is to break a moral rule, the decision's success usually depends on everyone else's adherence to the rule, which is highly unlikely in auditing.

Rule-utilitarianism, on the other hand, emphasizes the centrality *of rules for ethical behavior* while still maintaining the criterion of the greatest universal good. This kind of utilitarianism means that decision makers must first determine the rules that will promote the greatest general good for the largest number of people. The initial question is not which *action* has the greatest utility but which *rule*.

The Generalization Argument

The generalization argument may be considered a judicious combination of the imperative and utilitarian principles. Basically, the **generalization argument** considers the consequences of a decision made by similar persons acting under similar circumstances.[7] A more everyday expression of the argument is this question: "What would happen if everyone acted in that certain way?" If the answer to the question is that the consequences would be undesirable, the conclusion, according to the generalization test, is that the way of acting is unethical and should not be done.

In our ethical decision example, Santos's problem as a professional accountant and as an employee arose when Ellis asked him to "improve the financial statements" and he saw the enhancement as a lie. His generalization question may be something like this: "What if all accountants fudged financial statements and fooled loan officers when their companies needed to obtain loans?" Most people will see an easy answer: The result would be undesirable (because it might succeed often and cause considerable losses to banks along with other undesirable personal consequences for the actors in addition to the problem of having broken a rule that requires truth telling). Another kind of conflict subject to the generalization test is illustrated by the decision made by **Equifax** to wait six weeks to notify the public about the largest data breach in history, which is featured in the following Auditing Insight.

[7]M. G. Singer, *Generalization in Ethics* (New York: Atheneum, 1961, 1971), esp. pp. 5, 10–11, 61, 63, 73, 81, 105–122.

AUDITING INSIGHT   The Largest Data Breach in History

The largest data breach in history resulted in the names, addresses, and social security numbers of over 147 million Americans being stolen. The data breach occurred in May 2017 but wasn't discovered by Equifax until July 29, nearly two months later. It took the company another six weeks before notifying the public that names and social security numbers of millions had been stolen. Can you imagine if all CEOs waited so long to notify affected customers about a data breach? The generalization argument would clearly suggest an undesirable outcome.

Interestingly, in the aftermath, the SEC brought charges against former Equifax Chief Information Officer Jun Ying in March of 2018,

for using his knowledge of the breach to sell shares of the company's stock before the breach was made public. By then, Equifax had already fired Ying in October 2017 following his disclosure to executives in September 2017 that he sold his stock, perhaps after thinking about the generalization argument.

Sources: *https://www.cnet.com/news/former-equifax-executivecharged-with-insider-trading/; https://www.secureworldexpo.com/ industry-news/day-by-day-timeline-of-equifax-breach.*

Virtue Ethics

Virtue ethics can be traced not only to the Greek philosophers Aristotle and Plato (his *Republic* discusses the Four Cardinal Virtues: wisdom, justice, fortitude, and temperance), but also to Buddhist ethical tradition. Rather than a focus on following rules or weighing outcomes, virtue ethics emphasizes the role of one's character in the decision-making process. Questions that may be asked include, "What action will help me become my ideal self?" or "What action would I be the proudest of?"

To contrast the different approaches, consider the example of cheating on a class assignment. A utilitarian approach might weigh the potential positive outcome of cheating ("I need to pass this class") against the negatives ones (hurting others' grades, possibly getting caught). Under Kant's categorical imperative approach, cheating is always wrong, no matter what positive outcomes may come from it. Under the Aristotelian virtue ethics approach, one would consider whether cheating was most aligned with the person the student aspired to be.

This brief review of ethical principles provides some important background to the ways that many people approach difficult ethical decision problems. As a professional auditor, you are required to adhere to the prevailing code of conduct in all your duties. However, there will be times in your career when the code does not go far enough. In those situations, it is important to consider the three major approaches to ethical decision making—the categorical imperative's focus on rules, utilitarianism's focus on outcomes, and virtue ethics' focus on character—and apply them to decisions. Deciding how you will behave (i.e., what ethical principle you will follow) *before* you find yourself in an ethical dilemma can prepare you for the kind of pressures the Milgram subjects and our hypothetical Santos experienced and allow you to make decisions of which you will be proud.

 REVIEW CHECKPOINTS

B.3   Assume that you accept the following ethical rule: "Failure to tell the whole truth is wrong." In the textbook illustration about Santos's problem with Ellis's instructions, (a) what would this rule require Santos to do, and (b) why is an unalterable rule such as this classified as an element of imperative ethical theory?

B.4   How do utilitarian ethics differ from imperative ethics?

ETHICAL CODES OF CONDUCT

LO B-3
Identify the different entities that make ethics rules for CPAs and public accounting firms.

Independence, professionalism, and integrity have long been concerns of the auditing profession, but the accounting scandals that occurred at the turn of the century (e.g., **Enron, WorldCom, Waste Management**) and the financial crisis that occurred later that decade brought a renewed focus and emphasis on these issues that remain today.

The PCAOB was created, in part, to help bring a new level of independence and integrity to the profession. In that spirit, the PCAOB has issued a number of rules that apply to auditors of issuers. Furthermore, public accounting firms and CPAs also must follow rules set forth by the SEC and the AICPA Professional Ethics Executive Committee (PEEC). Public accounting firms and CPAs completing multinational audits also must comply with the International Federation of Accountants (IFAC) Code of Ethics for Professional Accountants. If you are an internal auditor, you will be expected to observe the rules of conduct of the Institute of Internal Auditors (IIA). As a management accountant, the standards of ethical conduct for management accountants of the Institute of Management Accountants (IMA) will apply to you. Certified fraud examiners are expected to observe the Association of Certified Fraud Examiners (ACFE) Code of Ethics. And, the consequences are severe for any professional violating their governing code of conduct. Consider the following Auditing Insight which describes an example of a fraud auditor being expelled for committing fraud.

AUDITING INSIGHT · Fraud Auditor Expelled for Committing Fraud

A trial board of the ACFE found that a member had wrongfully represented himself as a *certified internal auditor* when in fact he did not hold the CIA designation. Such conduct is in violation of Article 1.A.4 of the Certified Fraud Examiners Code of Professional Ethics, and the member was summarily expelled from the organization.

L. Jackson Shockey, CFE, CPA, CISA, chairperson of the board of regents, said: "We are saddened that a member has been expelled for such conduct. However, in order to maintain the integrity of the CFE program, the trial board vigorously investigates violations of the Code of Professional Ethics. When appropriate, the board of regents will not hesitate to take necessary action."

Source: *CFE News, Association of Certified Fraud Examiners (online source).*

If you find this "alphabet soup" of ethics rule makers confusing, imagine those CPAs who have to deal with complex and often conflicting rules on a daily basis. As a CPA, you will be expected to observe rules of conduct published in several codes of ethics, depending on your own jurisdiction and service area. And, if you do not, as illustrated in the Auditing Insight above, you can be expelled for fraudulent behavior. In summary, if you join the AICPA and a state society of CPAs and practice before the U.S. Securities and Exchange Commission (SEC) on a multinational audit client, you will be subject to the following:

Source of Rules of Conduct	Applicable to
U.S. Securities and Exchange Commission (SEC)	Persons who practice before the SEC as accountants and auditors for SEC-registered companies
Public Company Accounting Oversight Board (PCAOB)	Registered firms and individuals who perform audits of companies under the jurisdiction of the PCAOB
International Federation of Accountants (IFAC)	Public accounting firms and CPAs performing audits of multinational companies
American Institute of CPAs (AICPA)	AICPA members
Applicable state society of CPAs	Members of a state society of CPAs
Applicable state board of accountancy	Persons licensed by the state to practice accounting

U.S. Securities and Exchange Commission (SEC)

The SEC has federal statutory authority to regulate the public accounting profession for the purposes of (1) protecting the reliability and integrity of the financial statements of public companies and (2) promoting investor confidence in financial statements and the securities markets. The SEC's jurisdiction covers only issuers that are required by federal securities laws to file financial statements audited by independent accountants.

EXHIBIT B.1   Comparison of SEC and AICPA Selected Definitions

	AICPA Definition	SEC Definition
Engagement Team	Professionals participating in the audit or attest engagement, including those who perform reviews. The audit or attest engagement team includes all professionals and contractors who participate in the audit or attest engagement, irrespective of their functional classification (e.g., audit, tax, or management consulting services). The audit or attest engagement team excludes specialists and individuals who perform only routine clerical functions.	All partners, principals, shareholders, and professional employees participating in an audit, review, or attestation engagement of an audit client, including those conducting reviews and all persons who consult with others on the audit engagement team during the audit, review, or attestation engagement regarding technical or industry-specific issues, transactions, or events.
Chain of Command	**Partner:** A proprietor, shareholder, equity or nonequity partner, or any individual who assumes the risks and benefits of firm ownership or who is held out by the firm to be the equivalent of an owner or partner. **Manager:** A professional employee of the firm who has either of the following responsibilities: 1. Continuing responsibility for the overall planning and supervision of engagements for specified clients. 2. Authority to determine that an engagement is complete subject to final partner approval.	All persons who (1) supervise or have direct management responsibility for the audit, (2) evaluate the performance or recommend the compensation of the audit engagement partner, or (3) provide quality control or other oversight of the audit.
Covered Person	The following are considered covered members: 1. An individual on the audit or attest engagement team; 2. An individual in a position to influence the audit or attest engagement; 3. A partner or manager who provides nonattest services to the audit or attest client beginning once he or she provides 10 hours of nonattest services to the audit or attest client within any fiscal year and ending on the later of the date (i) the firm signs the report on the financial statements for the fiscal year during which those services were provided or (ii) he or she no longer expects to provide 10 or more hours of nonattest services to the audit or attest client on a recurring basis; 4. A partner in the office in which the lead audit or attest engagement partner primarily practices in connection with the audit or attest engagement; 5. The firm, including the firm's employee benefit plans; or 6. An entity whose operating, financial, or accounting policies can be controlled (as defined by generally accepted accounting principles [GAAP] for consolidation purposes) by any of the individuals or entities described in (1) through (5) or by two or more such individuals or entities if they act together.	The following partners, principals, shareholders, and employees of an accounting firm are considered covered members: 1. An individual on the audit engagement team, 2. An individual in the chain of command, 3. Any other partner, principal, shareholder, or managerial employee of the firm who has provided 10 or more hours of nonaudit services to the audit client for the period beginning on the date such services are provided and ending on the date the accounting firm signs the report on the financial statements for the fiscal year during which those services are provided, or who expects to provide 10 or more hours of nonaudit services to the audit client on a recurring basis, and 4. Any other partner, principal, or shareholder from an office of the accounting firm in which the lead audit engagement partner primarily practices in connection with the audit. *Authors' Note:* In essence, the "covered members" are the firm's professionals closely connected to the audit engagement and the firm's owners who are located in the office where the lead engagement partner practices. However, the SEC added the category of manager-level professionals and owners who provide nonaudit (tax, consulting) services for the audit client. Therefore, almost everyone who provides services of any type for an audit client must observe the independence rules.
Close Family Member	Parent, sibling, or nondependent child.	Parent, sibling, or nondependent child.
Immediate Family Member	Spouse, spousal equivalent, or dependents (whether or not related).	Person's spouse, spousal equivalent, or dependents.

EXHIBIT B.2   Summary of Independence Rule Interpretations

A covered member cannot
- Have a direct financial interest in a client.
- Have a material indirect financial interest in a client.
- Be a trustee or administrator of an estate that has a direct or material indirect financial interest in a client.
- Have a joint investment with a client that is material to the covered member.
- Have a loan to or from a client, any officer of the client, or any individual owning more than 10 percent of the client (except as specifically described in *Interpretation 101-5*).
- Participate on an attest engagement if she or he was formally employed by the client in a position to influence the audit or acted as an officer, director, promoter, underwriter, or trustee of a pension or profit-sharing trust of the client.

A covered member's immediate family cannot
- Have a direct financial interest in a client.
- Have a material indirect financial interest in a client.
- Have vested retirement benefits at a client.

A covered member's close relatives cannot
- Have a key management level position with a client.
- Have a material financial interest in a client that is known to the covered member.
- Have a financial interest in a client that allows the relative to have significant influence in a client.
- Be in a position to influence the audit.

A partner or a professional employee cannot
- Be associated with a client as a director, officer, employee, promoter, underwriter, voting trustee, or trustee of a pension or profit-sharing trust of the client.

adopted a Conceptual Framework (Exhibit B.3) that CPAs can use when facing a situation that is not explicitly covered in the Code of Conduct.

The Conceptual Framework uses a three-step risk-based approach that involves (1) identifying and evaluating threats to independence, (2) determining whether safeguards eliminate or sufficiently mitigate the identified threats, and (3) determining whether independence is impaired.

Identified threats to independence include the following:

1. *Adverse interest threat.* CPAs acting in opposition to clients (e.g., through litigation).
2. *Undue influence threat.* Attempts to coerce or otherwise influence the CPA member (e.g., significant gifts or threats to replace the auditor over an accounting principles disagreement).

EXHIBIT B.3
AICPA Code of Conduct Conceptual Framework

Source: www.aicpa.org.

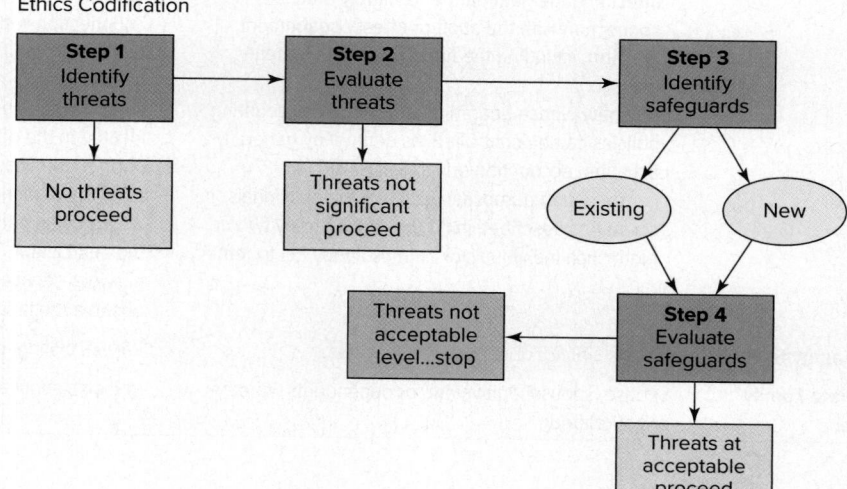

Conceptual Framework
Ethics Codification

3. *Advocacy threat.* CPAs promoting a client's interests or position.

4. *Management participation threat.* CPAs taking on the role of client management or otherwise performing management functions.

5. *Familiarity threat.* CPAs becoming too sympathetic to client interests because of long-standing or close relationships.

6. *Self-interest threat.* CPAs having a financial relationship with a client.

7. *Self-review threat.* CPAs reviewing their own work.

Next we take a closer look at each of these threats to independence.

Adverse Interest and Undue Influence Threats

Conditions can arise when a public accounting firm and a client move into an adversary relationship instead of the cooperative relationship needed in an attest or audit engagement. Public accounting firm independence is considered impaired when the firm is involved in threatened or actual litigation involving an audit. Such cases may be rare, but the AICPA has provided auditors a way out of the difficult audit situation by this rule requiring them to declare "nonindependence" and the ability to give only a disclaimer on financial statements or other information. Essentially, the CPA–client relationship ends and the litigation begins a new relationship.

Occasionally, the public accounting firm may find that it is a defendant in a lawsuit initiated by a third party or parties. Normally, this type of litigation is not considered to adversely impact the independence of the public accounting firm. However, sometimes these lawsuits result in claims from the client's management that existing problems are the result of audit deficiencies or claims from the auditor that deficiencies are the result of fraud or deceit on the part of management. When such cross-claims are threatened or filed, independence may be impaired.

Advocacy and Management Participation Threats

In addition to prohibitions against financial relationships with clients, a covered member is prohibited from acting in the capacity of a manager, employee, promoter, or trustee of a client. Generally, independence is impaired if the public accounting firm even *appears* to investors to be working in the capacity of management at the client. The client management (including its board of directors and audit committee) must understand that they are responsible for establishing and maintaining internal control and directing the internal audit function, if any. The board of directors and/or audit committee (i.e., those charged with governance) must understand their roles and responsibilities with regard to extended audit services including the establishment of guidelines for both management and the public accounting firm to follow in carrying out these responsibilities and monitoring how well the respective responsibilities have been met.

In addition to the guidance discussed in the previous paragraphs, the following additional activities would impair independence:[12]

- Performing ongoing monitoring or control activities.
- Determining which, if any, recommendations for improving internal control should be implemented.
- Reporting to the board of directors or audit committee on behalf of management or the individual responsible for the internal audit function.
- Authorizing, executing, or consummating transactions or otherwise exercising authority on behalf of the client.

---

[12]Although the following information does not prohibit auditors from providing internal audit and a variety of other services, it should be emphasized that the interpretation covers client companies that are public and private. Audits of public companies must comply with the rules of the SEC, the appropriate stock exchange, and the PCAOB. These agencies have rules that prohibit auditors from providing internal audit services to audit clients in most cases and have more stringent requirements regarding extended services.

- Preparing source documents for transactions.
- Having custody of assets.
- Approving or being responsible for the overall internal audit work plan including the determination of the internal audit risk and scope project priorities and the frequency of performance of audit procedures.
- Performing forensic accounting services, litigation support work, or any other service in which it appears that the CPA is taking an advocacy position on the client's behalf. Although performing tax compliance work would not normally impair independence, certain tax work in which an advocacy position is required does (e.g., representing a client in court to resolve a tax dispute).
- Being connected with the client as an employee or in any capacity equivalent to a member of client management (e.g., being listed as an employee in client directories or other client publications, permitting himself or herself to be referred to by title or description as supervising or being in charge of the client's internal audit function, or using the client's letterhead or internal correspondence forms in communications).

Although this list is not all-inclusive, a prohibited activity is one that would force the CPA to act either in the capacity of management or as an advocate for management.

As noted, independence is ordinarily impaired if a CPA serves on an organization's board of directors. However, members can be *honorary* directors of organizations such as charity hospitals, fund drives, symphony orchestra societies, and similar not-for-profit organizations so long as (1) the position is purely honorary, (2) the CPA is identified as an honorary director on letterheads and other literature, (3) the only form of participation is the use of the CPA's name, and (4) the CPA does not vote with the board or participate in management functions. When all of these criteria have been satisfied, the CPA/board member can perform audit and attest services because the appearances of independence will have been preserved. To help think about this issue further, consider the following Auditing Insight which focuses on whether board service impacts auditor independence.

AUDITING INSIGHT   Does Board Service Impact Audit Independence?

For many years, a national public accounting firm encouraged its professionals to become active members of the boards of directors of corporations. The purpose was to provide expertise to businesses in the metropolitan area and to enable the public accounting firm to become well known and well respected. The public accounting firm changed its policy to prohibit such service after it had to refuse the opportunity to obtain some of these corporations as audit clients because of independence concerns. The public accounting firm's audit independence was considered impaired when a member of the firm had served in a director or management capacity during the period covered by the financial statements the corporations wanted the firm to audit. The generalization test was this: If members of the firm serve on the boards of directors of all corporations that may become audit clients, none of these corporations can be accepted as audit clients—a result that is undesirable.

Familiarity Threat

An immediate family member may not hold a position of influence (key position) in an audit client. The close family member's definition comes into play in connection with (1) ownership or control of an audit client or (2) employment with an audit client. An example of (1) is the impairment of the public accounting firm's independence when a close family member of a covered person in the firm owns a material investment in an audit client or is in a position to exert significant influence over an audit client. An example of (2) is the impairment of the public accounting firm's independence when a close family member works in an accounting or financial reporting role at an audit client or was in such a role during any period covered by an audit for which the person in the firm is a covered person. (Neither an immediate family member nor a close family member can work in a capacity such as a member of the board of directors, chief executive officer, president, chief financial officer, chief operating officer, general counsel, chief accounting officer, controller, director of internal audit, director of financial reporting, treasurer, or vice president of marketing.)

Independence problems do not end when owners (partners, shareholders) and professional employees retire, resign, or otherwise leave a public accounting firm. A former owner or professional can cause independence to be impaired if a relationship continues with a client of the former firm. However, the problems are solved and independence is not impaired if (1) the person's retirement benefits are fixed, (2) the person is no longer active in the public accounting firm (sometimes retired owners remain "active"), and (3) the former owner is not held out to be associated with the public accounting firm.

In addition to the preceding considerations, the public accounting firm must ensure that appropriate consideration is given to any increase in risks that may exist due to the former partner's or professional's knowledge of the firm's audit plan and procedures. The firm must consider the following:

- The interaction with the former partner or professional.
- The ability of audit team members to manage the interaction with the former partner or professional employee.
- Modification of the engagement procedures.
- The appropriateness of the review to determine that an appropriate level of skepticism was maintained.

Financial Self-Interest Threat

Any direct financial interest (e.g., ownership of common or preferred stock) is prohibited. This requirement is the strictest one in the code. There are no exceptions; indirect financial interests, on the other hand, are allowed up to the point of materiality (with reference to the member's wealth). This provision permits members to have some limited business transactions with clients so long as they do not reach material proportions. Other provisions define certain specific types of prohibited and allowed indirect financial interests. Immediate family members are subject to the same provisions that prescribe the acceptable actions of the covered person. Like the covered person, an immediate family member may not have a direct financial or material indirect financial interest in a client.

We already understand that a covered member cannot have a financial relationship with a client. However, suppose the client is an investor in another company and the covered member has invested in that company. Has independence been impaired? If the covered member's investment is a direct or materially indirect financial interest in a nonclient investee, independence is considered to be impaired. The reasoning for the basic rule is that the client investor, through its ability to influence a nonclient investee, can increase or decrease the CPA's financial stake in the investee by an amount material to the CPA, and therefore, the CPA may not appear to be independent. If the investment by the client is not material to the nonclient (i.e., there does not appear to be any influence over the investee), then independence is not impaired unless the covered member's investment allows the member to exercise significant influence over the nonclient.

Material cooperative arrangements with clients (i.e., joint participation in a business activity) also impair independence. Examples include joint ventures to develop or market products or to market a package of client and CPA services or one party working to market the products or services of the other.

Most loans to or from audit clients are prohibited: "Independence is considered impaired if a covered member has a loan from a client, officer, director, or any individual owning 10 percent or more of a client." Similarly, independence is impaired if there are unpaid fees or a note receivable arising from unpaid fees from the client outstanding for more than a year. The only loans permitted are "grandfathered loans" and "other permitted loans."

Grandfathered loans are those loans that were obtained either (1) before the independence rules changed (but met the requirements of the Independence Rule in effect at that time) or (2) from a financial institution before it became a client for services requiring independence. These grandfathered loans must at all times be current under all of their terms, and the terms shall not be renegotiated. The specific types of loans that are grandfathered are home mortgages, loans not material to the CPA's net worth, and secured loans for which the collateral value must exceed the balance of the loan at all times.

Other permitted loans include:

- Auto loans and leases collateralized by the automobile.
- Insurance policy loans based on policy surrender value.
- Loans collateralized by cash deposits at the same financial institution.
- Credit card balances and cash advances of $10,000 or less.

Ethics rules do not cover all circumstances in which the appearance of independence might be questioned. It is the member's responsibility to determine whether the personal and business relationships would lead a reasonable person aware of all the relevant facts to conclude that there is an unacceptable threat to the member's and the firm's independence.

Self-Review Threat

Independence is impaired if the public accounting firm performs the bookkeeping or makes accounting or management decisions for a company whose management does not know enough about the financial statements to take primary responsibility for them. The problem in this situation is the appearance of the public accounting firm having both prepared the financial statements or other information and provided the auditors' report or other attestation on its own work. In the final analysis, the management must be able to say, "These are our financial statements (or other information); we made the choices of accounting principles; we take primary responsibility for them." The auditors cannot authorize transactions, control assets, sign checks or reports, prepare source documents, supervise the client's personnel, or serve as the client's registrar, transfer agent, or general counsel.

Other Threats?

Other Independence Rule interpretations include relationships with governmental entities and alternative practice structures. The full list of interpretations, with accompanying detail, can be found on the AICPA's website.[13] As you can see, the detail is substantial, yet you have no choice but to understand the full details of the AICPA independence requirements. Lack of knowledge of the appropriate jurisdiction's ethical requirements is not a defense when facing severe sanctions and penalties.

We have examined a number of threats that have been identified that impair independence. What about those not specifically covered? When those situations arise, the Conceptual Framework guides the CPA to make the best decision to address the threats. Note that the Conceptual Framework is to be used only when specific guidance is not in the Code. It cannot be used to override existing rules or interpretations. Consider the Auditing Insight below where the use of an audit client's product resulted in losing them as a client.

AUDITING INSIGHT   When Using an Audit Client's Product Results in Losing Them as a Client

PricewaterhouseCoopers, LLP (PwC) was the auditor of **Alteryx,** a software company focusing on "self-service data and analytics." Unfortunately for PwC, the firm's use of the software platform and PwC's subsequent promotion of the software to their clients, resulted in their dismissal as the auditor of the company. The reason for their dismissal?

Concern by executives at Alteryx regarding the independence of their auditing firm. As such, in January of 2019, they disclosed in Form 8-K filed with the SEC that they replaced PwC with Deloitte.

Source: Alteryx, Form 8-K, Filed With SEC, January 24, 2019 (online source).

[13]https://www.aicpa.org/content/dam/aicpa/research/standards/codeofconduct/downloadabledocuments/2014december15contentasof2016august31codeofconduct.pdf.

In addition to identifying and considering the significance of each threat, the CPA should identify *safeguards* that might eliminate or reduce the threat to an acceptable level. Safeguards can be client or firm-specific, including policies and procedures in place to prevent ethical problems. Examples include training on the importance of independence, threats of disciplinary action, hotlines to discuss ethical dilemmas, tone at the top, and the use of different offices (or different firms) to perform parts of the engagement.

Lastly, whenever the CPA runs into ethical issues, especially those in which safeguards are identified to eliminate or reduce significant threats, the CPA must document the decisions reached. Failure to do so would be a violation of the Compliance with Standards Rule (discussed later in this module).

SEC and PCAOB Independence Rules

Prior to the issuance of Sarbanes–Oxley in 2002, the SEC accepted most of the independence rules established by the PEEC. However, the SEC became concerned about the public accounting profession's emphasis on consulting fees and the resulting effect on public accounting firm independence. In fact, the SEC issued a comprehensive independence rule in November 2000. The rule is based upon two premises: (1) *independence in fact* is a mental state of objectivity and lack of bias and (2) *independence in appearance* depends on whether a reasonable investor, with knowledge of all relevant facts and circumstances, can conclude that the auditor is not capable of exercising objective and impartial judgment. Hence, an auditor's independence depends on auditors both having the proper mental state and passing the appearance test.

In a preface to the rule, the SEC stated four principles for determining whether a public accounting firm is independent of an audit client, factors the SEC will first consider when making independence determinations in controversial cases. Auditors are *not* independent if they have a relationship that:

1. Creates a mutual or conflicting interest between the public accounting firm and the audit client.
2. Places the public accounting firm in the position of auditing its own work.
3. Results in the public accounting firm personnel acting as management or employees of the audit client.
4. Places the public accounting firm in a position of being an advocate for the audit client.

The SEC independence rules relating to financial relationships are very similar to the AICPA Code of Professional Conduct Rule 101 Interpretations explained earlier. The most significant categories addressed by the SEC rules are in the areas of financial and employment relationships, nonaudit services (e.g., taxation, consulting), and disclosure of fees.

Nonaudit Services

The SEC is very concerned about the fact and appearance of independence when public accounting firms perform consulting services for audit clients. A major issue in the Enron case was that more than half of the fee it paid to Arthur Andersen was for consulting services. This fact exacerbated the concern that auditors would allow a client's improper financial reporting for the sake of preserving lucrative fees from other services. The SEC's concern in this regard is controversial, but the PCAOB has reinforced it. The SEC and PCAOB independence rules prohibit or place restrictions on the following types of *nonaudit* services provided to its own *audit* clients:

- Bookkeeping or other services related to the audit client's accounting records.
- Financial information systems design and implementation.
- Appraisal or valuation services or fairness opinions.
- Actuarial services.
- Internal audit services.

- Management functions, including acting as a director, officer, or employee.
- Human resources.
- Broker–dealer services.
- Legal services.
- Expert services.
- Any service performed for a contingent fee or commission.
- Certain prohibited tax services.

It is important to reinforce that the PCAOB and SEC rules prohibit the above services to be completed by an audit firm for its own audit clients. However, at the present time, audit firms are allowed to complete consulting services for nonaudit clients. Despite this, the SEC has recently questioned whether audit firms should be completing any consulting services as the following Auditing Insight discusses.

AUDITING INSIGHT   Should Audit Firms Complete Any Consulting Services?

In a recent *Wall Street Journal* article, the Securities and Exchange Commission (SEC) says maybe not. The question being asked by the regulator is whether consulting services and any other nonaudit service being offered by an audit firm "undermines their ability to conduct independent reviews of public companies' financials," even if the services are being provided to nonaudit clients.

Simply stated, there are some that believe that audit firms should ONLY focus on performing financial statement audits and by completing other services, they could potentially be distracted in performing their primary duty, which is to protect the capital markets. The SEC's probe makes clear that they believe that the audit firms have an important duty "under federal investor-protection laws" and that "auditors are a shareholder's first line of defense against sloppy or dodgy accounting." Stay tuned!

Source: "Big Four Accounting Firms Come Under Regulator's Scrutiny," *The Wall Street Journal,* March 15, 2022 (online source).

Finally, the PCAOB's Rule 3526 (*Communication with Audit Committees Concerning Independence*) requires public accounting firms to discuss any independence issues with the audit committee (or those charged with governance) *prior* to accepting an initial engagement. This discussion must be documented (usually in the engagement administrative file workpapers).

Disclosures about Fees

The SEC believes that investors who use financial statements and auditors' reports can be enlightened with information about auditors' fee arrangements with clients. Hence, SEC rules require that companies (not auditors) disclose the following in proxy statements delivered to their shareholders:

- Total audit fees paid to the public accounting firm for the annual audit and the reviews of quarterly financial information.
- Total fees paid to the public accounting firm for tax and other advisory work (over and above the audit fees).
- Whether the audit committee or the board of directors considered the public accounting firm's advisory work to be compatible with maintaining the auditor's independence.
- The percentage of the audit hours performed by persons other than the principal auditor's full-time, permanent employees, if greater than 50% of the total audit hours. (This disclosure refers to "leased employees" in an "alternative practice structure" arrangement.)

Other Effects of Sarbanes–Oxley on Auditor Independence

Sarbanes–Oxley required the SEC to modify its position on auditor independence in several ways. Perhaps the most important change in independence arises from the changing role of the audit committee. While auditors must always be vigilant in establishing and monitoring their own independence to ensure that they are in fact independent of their clients, Sarbanes–Oxley has placed the responsibility for the determination of independence in appearance at the door of the audit committee. This is particularly evident by the fact that the audit committee bears the responsibility for determining the scope of services provided by the auditor and reviewing independence issues prior to the appointment of the auditor. The audit committee may do this on a case-by-case basis or may establish a set of policies and procedures that establish acceptable and unacceptable services.

In addition, Sarbanes–Oxley limits the engagement partners and concurring audit partners on an engagement to five-year terms, after which they must rotate off the engagement. Other partners associated with the engagement are limited to seven-year terms with that client. Partners also are deemed as not independent if they receive compensation that is based on selling services to an audit client other than audits, reviews, or attestations. There have been some calls for mandatory rotation of the audit firm on a periodic basis, but as described in the following Auditing Insight, changing auditors is not easy, especially after 110 years!

 AUDITING INSIGHT | Changing Auditors is Not Easy, Especially After 110 Years!

Sounds easy, to change auditors, but when you're as big as GE, such changes never come easy. KPMG has been auditing GE since 1909 but after 35% of shareholders voted to switch auditors, the Company indicated it would begin looking for a new auditor after the 2019 audit was completed. It was not an easy task. While there are many audit firms, a company the size of GE would likely be too large to take on for firms other than the Big 4. Making matters even more difficult, PwC now performs GE's tax work (tax planning, advice, and compliance work) to the tune of $1 billion in yearly revenue. EY provides lobbying services for GE while Deloitte provides nonaudit work and "has business relationships with GE that would be barred" under the SEC's independence rules. So while in theory making a switch to another auditor sounds simple, the reality is that it is anything but. In the end, Deloitte discontinued its nonaudit work being performed for GE and now serves as its auditor, beginning with the 2021 annual report.

Source: "GE to change auditor to Deloitte from KPMG, starting 2021," MarketWatch, June 22, 2020 (online source).

In the past, it was not unusual for a member of an audit team, usually a manager or higher, to leave the public accounting firm to take a financial management position with a client. Under the rules established by Sarbanes–Oxley, a public accounting firm cannot perform an audit of a company in which an individual with financial reporting oversight responsibilities, such as the chief accounting officer or controller, was employed by the company's accounting firm in the preceding one year.

Government Accountability Office (GAO) Independence Requirements

Many state agencies and local municipalities use public accounting firms to perform audits required by government charters, laws, or contractual obligations (usually as part of a grant). During these audits, the public accounting firm is required to follow all GAO standards included in the Government Auditing Standards manual (also called the *Yellow Book;* see Module D). These standards require the auditor to be independent with respect to the government entity. These standards differ from the independence requirements discussed previously in the following ways. Nonaudit services are allowed providing that the audit organization does not perform management functions, make management decisions, or audit its own work. However, the audit organization must employ the following safeguards:

1. Personnel who provide nonaudit services are prohibited from planning, conducting, or reviewing audit work related to the nonaudit services.
2. The audit organization may not reduce the scope or extent of work performed on the audit because a member of the firm performed the nonaudit work. The extent of the audit work may be reduced by an amount consistent with a reduction had the nonaudit work been performed by another public accounting firm.

3. The audit organization must document its reasons that the nonaudit services do not affect the firm's independence.

4. The audit organization must document an understanding with the client regarding the objectives, scope, and work product for the nonaudit service.

5. The audit organization must have established policies and procedures to ensure that effects of nonaudit services on the present and future audits are considered.

6. The audit organization must communicate to the government entity any situation in which the nonaudit service would prohibit it from performing the audit.

7. When subjected to a peer review, the audit organization must identify all nonaudit services provided to the audited entity.

✅ REVIEW CHECKPOINTS

B.7   Yolanda is the executive in charge of the Santa Fe office of Best & Co, an international public accounting firm. She is responsible for the practice in all areas of audit, tax, and consulting, but she does not serve as a field audit partner or a reviewer. Javier is the partner in charge of the Besame Inc. audit (an SEC filing). Is Best & Co independent if (a) Yolanda owns common stock of Besame or (b) her brother owns 10 shares of the common stock of Besame?

B.8   Can audit managers on the audit engagement team, who are also attorneys admitted to the state bar, assist in the defense of a lawsuit against an audit client for product liability defects?

B.9   Why do you think the SEC requires companies to disclose fees paid to independent accounting firms for audit and consulting services? What must be disclosed?

B.10 What do the SEC disclosure rules and PCAOB Rule 3526 have in common with auditors' relations with an audit client's board of directors and its audit committee?

B.11 Given what you have learned about independence, do you believe that there would be a perceived independence problem concerning members of an audit engagement team entertaining employment offers from audit clients? Why or why not?

AICPA RULES OF CONDUCT: INTEGRITY AND OBJECTIVITY, RESPONSIBILITIES TO CLIENTS, AND OTHER RESPONSIBILITIES

LO B-5
With reference to AICPA rules on topics other than independence, analyze factual situations and decide whether an accountant's conduct does or does not conform to the AICPA Code of Professional Conduct.

Now that we have discussed the Independence Rule, we can turn to the other AICPA rules of conduct.

Integrity and Objectivity Rule

> In the performance of any professional service, a member shall maintain objectivity and integrity, shall be free of conflicts of interest, and shall not knowingly misrepresent facts or subordinate his or her judgment to others. (1.100.001 and 2.100.001)

The Integrity and Objectivity Rule applies not only to CPAs in public practice but also to CPAs working in business. (Santos, the staff accountant in the decision process illustration in Ethical Example 2, is a business CPA.) The rule requires integrity and objectivity in all types of professional work—tax practice and consulting practice as well as audit practice for public accountants—and all types of accounting work performed by CPAs employed in corporations, not-for-profit organizations, governments, and individual practices. The rule holds CPAs to the highest of standards of maintaining their integrity and objectivity at all times. The following Auditing Insight illustrates a lack of integrity related to the PCAOB inspection process.

AUDITING INSIGHT Lack of Integrity Related to the PCAOB Inspection Process

KPMG was struggling with an audit deficiency rate of nearly 46% when several partners at the Big 4 audit firm decided to game the system by finding out which of its audits would be inspected by the PCAOB. Those audits would then be re-reviewed by firm personnel and occasionally more audit work was performed. David Middendorf, KPMG's former managing partner for audit quality, along with Jeffery Wada, an inspections leader for the PCAOB, were both found guilty on March 11, 2019, of wire fraud and conspiracy to commit wire fraud as a result of their actions related to the leaked inspections. Four other partners were charged in relation to the matter; three have plead guilty. Of the five

KPMG employees convicted, only one has served jail time. Two partners plead guilty and testified against David Middendorf and received no jail time as a result. A third partner was given a home sentence and ordered to be sent back to his native Australia. Meanwhile, Middendorf and Wada continue to appeal their convictions which remain on hold at this time.

Sources: "Ex-KPMG Partner, Audit Oversight Staffer Found Guilty of Fraud," March 11, 2019, Bloomberg Law (online source); "Ex-KPMG Partner, Inspector Suspended by SEC in Accounting Scandal (1)," January 15, 2020, Bloomberg Law (online); "Ex-KPMG Partner Given Slap on the Wrist From Judge During Cheating Scandal Sentencing," October 13, 2020, Going Concern (online source).

In addition to integrity and objectivity, this rule emphasizes (1) being free from conflicts of interest between CPAs and others, (2) representing facts truthfully in reports and discussions, and (3) not letting other people dictate or influence the CPA's judgment and professional decisions.

Conflicts of interest refer to the need to avoid having business interests in which the accountant's personal financial relationships or the accountant's relationships with other clients might tempt the accountant to fail to serve the best interests of a client or the public. Some examples of conflicts of interest are those in which the CPA:

- Is engaged to perform litigation support services for a plaintiff in a lawsuit filed against a client.
- Recommends that a client makes an investment in a business in which the CPA has a financial interest.
- Performs management consulting for a client and has a financial or managerial interest in a major competitor.

The phrases "shall not knowingly misrepresent facts" and "shall not subordinate his or her judgment to others" emphasize conditions people ordinarily identify with the concepts of integrity and objectivity. Accountants who know about a client's fraudulent tax return, about false journal entries, about material misrepresentations in financial statements, and yet do nothing have violated both the spirit and the letter of the Integrity and Objectivity Rule.

The prohibition of misrepresentations in financial statements applies to the management accountants who prepare companies' statements. Business CPAs should not subordinate their professional judgment to superiors who try to produce materially misleading financial statements and fool their external auditors. They must be candid and not knowingly misrepresent facts or fail to disclose material facts when dealing with their employer's external auditor. They also cannot have conflicts of interest in their jobs and their outside business interests that are not disclosed to their employers and approved. The importance of integrity and objectivity for business CPAs cannot be overemphasized. Too often, CPAs relate the Code of Professional Conduct only to CPAs in public practice. In fact, one of the objectives of the recodification of the AICPA Code of Conduct is to emphasize the importance of business CPAs adhering to ethics rules that relate to them.

The Integrity and Objectivity Rule has two other applications. One concerns serving as a client advocate, which occurs frequently in taxation and rate regulation practice as well as in supporting clients' positions in FASB and SEC proceedings. Client advocacy in support or advancement of client positions is acceptable only so long as the member acts with integrity, maintains objectivity, and does not subordinate judgment to others. (Accountants-as-advocates do not adopt the same attitude as defense attorneys in a courtroom.) The other application is directed specifically to your college professors: They are supposed to maintain integrity and objectivity, be free of conflicts of interest, and not knowingly misrepresent facts to students.

General Standards Rule

A member shall comply with the following standards and with any interpretations thereof by bodies designated by Council:

A. *Professional competence.* Undertake only those professional services that the member or the member's firm can reasonably expect to be completed with professional competence.

B. *Due professional care.* Exercise due care in the performance of professional services.

C. *Planning and supervision.* Adequately plan and supervise the performance of professional services.

D. *Sufficient relevant data.* Obtain sufficient relevant data to afford a reasonable basis for conclusions or recommendations in relation to any professional services performed. (1.300.001 and 2.300.001)

The General Standards Rule is a comprehensive statement of general standards that accountants are expected to observe in all areas of practice. This is the rule that enforces the various series of professional standards. The AICPA Council has authorized the following agencies, boards, and committees to issue enforceable standards under this rule:

- Public Company Accounting Oversight Board (PCAOB).
- Auditing Standards Board.
- Accounting and Review Services Committee.
- Tax Executive Committee.
- Management Consulting Services Executive Committee.

The General Standards Rule effectively prohibits the acceptance of any engagement that the CPA cannot complete in a competent manner. Such engagements may involve audits that require specialized industry knowledge or technical expertise the practitioner does not possess. Practitioners are allowed to accept an engagement if, through education, hiring of additional staff, or contracting with auditors' specialists, the practitioners can obtain the required knowledge *prior to the conclusion* of the engagement. As a result, a practitioner can accept an engagement for which they do not possess knowledge as long as this knowledge can be obtained prior to the conclusion of the engagement. This rule covers all areas of public accounting practice except personal financial planning and business valuation. Of course, a CPA may have to do some research to learn more about a unique problem or technique and may need to engage a colleague as a consultant. As the following Auditing Insight demonstrates, there are a number of factors that can potentially impact competence on an audit engagement. In addition, never forget that an auditor must always be competent.

 AUDITING INSIGHT   An Auditor Must Always Be Competent!

PwC was fined $5.8 million, and two of its partners were also fined individually, for inadequate audit work on British tech company Redcentric PLC. There was a "serious lack of competence in conducting the audit" according to Financial Reporting Council. The Big Four (PwC, EY, KPMG and Deloitte) control "90% of UK audits" for large companies. As such, this latest penalty is causing some in Great Britain to ask whether the big audit firms should restructure their practices.

Source: "PwC's $5.8 mn UK Fine strengthens demand to break up Big Four audit Firms," Hugo Miller, June 13, 2019, business-standard.com (online source).

Compliance with Standards Rule

A member who performs auditing, review, compilation, management consulting, tax, or other professional services shall comply with standards promulgated by bodies designated by Council. (1.310.001 and 2.31.001)

The Compliance with Standards Rule requires adherence to duly promulgated technical standards in all areas of professional service. These areas include the ones cited in the rule: auditing, review and compilation (unaudited financial statements), consulting, tax, or "other" professional services. The "bodies designated by Council" are the Auditing Standards Board, the Accounting and Review Services Committee, the Tax Executive Committee, and the Consulting Services Executive Committee. The practical effect of this rule is to make noncompliance with technical standards (in addition to the general standards) subject to disciplinary proceedings. Therefore, failure to follow auditing standards, accounting and review standards, tax standards, and consulting standards is a violation of the Compliance with Standards Rule.

Accounting Principles Rule

A member shall not (1) express an opinion or state affirmatively that the financial statements or other financial data of any entity are presented in conformity with generally accepted accounting principles or (2) state that he or she is not aware of any material modifications that should be made to such statements or data in order for them to be in conformity with generally accepted accounting principles, if such statements or data contain any departure from an accounting principle promulgated by bodies designated by Council to establish such principles that has a material effect on the statements or data taken as a whole. If, however, the statements or data contain such a departure and the member can demonstrate that due to unusual circumstances the financial statements or data would otherwise have been misleading, the member can comply with the rule by describing the departure, its approximate effects, if practicable, and the reasons why compliance with the principle would result in a misleading statement. (1.320.001 and 2.320.001)

The AICPA Council has designated three rule-making bodies to pronounce accounting principles under the Accounting Principles Rule. The Financial Accounting Standards Board (FASB) is designated to pronounce standards in general, the Governmental Accounting Standards Board (GASB) has the responsibility to pronounce accounting standards for state and local government entities, and the Federal Accounting Standards Advisory Board (FASAB) is charged with respect to statements of federal accounting standards.

The Accounting Principles Rule requires adherence to official pronouncements unless such adherence would be misleading. The consequences of misleading statements to outside decision makers would be financial harm, so presumably the greater good would be realized by explaining a departure and thereby "breaking the rule of officially promulgated accounting principles." Such an instance occurs in very rare situations, and the burden of proving that following pronouncements would be misleading is the responsibility of the auditor.

CPAs in business also can be subject to the Accounting Principles Rule. These accountants produce and certify financial statements and sign written management representation letters for their external auditors. They also present financial statements to regulatory authorities and creditors. Business accountants generally "report" that the company's financial statements conform to GAAP, and this report is taken as an expression of opinion (or negative assurance) of the type governed by the Accounting Principles Rule. The result is that accountants who present financial statements containing any undisclosed departures from official pronouncements face disciplinary action for violating the rule.

Acts Discreditable Rule

A member shall not commit an act discreditable to the profession. (1.400.001, 2.400.001, and 3.400.001)

The Acts Discreditable Rule may be called the *moral clause* of the code, but it is only occasionally the basis for disciplinary action. Penalties normally are invoked automatically under the AICPA bylaws, which provide for expulsion of members found by a court to have committed any fraud, filed false tax returns, been convicted of any criminal offense, or found by the AICPA Trial Board to have been guilty of an act discreditable to the profession. As the following Auditing Insight demonstrates, cheating on professional training exams can be quite costly.

AUDITING INSIGHT · Cheating on Professional Training Exams Can Be Quite Costly

It's never a good idea to cheat. It cost KPMG $50 million in fines to settle with the SEC over charges of cheating on internal training exams and also using "stolen" information to fix audit workpapers for audits that would be examined in the future by the PCAOB. The scope and scale of the cheating on the training exams, however, was extensive. The SEC discovered that both staff and partners shared the answer key and also changed the metric by which an exam would pass or fail. In some cases, the bar was lowered to 25% so that staff could fail 75% of the exam and still earn a passing grade. In the end however, it didn't pay to cheat. Along with the hefty fine, KPMG was also required to "retain an independent consultant to review and assess its ethics and integrity controls."

Source: "KPMG to pay $50M for cheating on PCAOB exams," Michael Cohn, June 17, 2019, Accounting Today (online source).

AICPA interpretations have determined the following to be discreditable acts:

- Withholding a client's books and records and important documentation when the client has requested his or her return.
- Being found guilty by a court or administrative agency as having violated employment antidiscrimination laws, including ones related to sexual and other forms of harassment.
- Failing to follow government audit standards and guides in governmental audits when the client or the government agency expects such standards to be followed.
- Failing to follow the requirements of governmental bodies, commissions, or other regulatory bodies including the PCAOB.
- Soliciting or disclosing CPA Examination questions and answers from the CPA Examination.
- Failing to file tax returns or remit payroll and other taxes collected for others (e.g., employee taxes withheld).
- Making, or permitting others to make, false and misleading entries in records and financial statements.

This last item is specifically applicable to all CPAs, whether in public practice, in business, between jobs, or in retirement. Any management accountant who participates in the production of false and misleading financial statements commits a discreditable act.

Fees and Other Types of Remuneration

Contingent Fees

A member in public practice shall not:

(1) Perform for a contingent fee any professional services for, or receive such a fee from, a client for whom the member or the member's firm performs:
   (a) an audit or review of a financial statement; or
   (b) a compilation of a financial statement when the member expects, or reasonably might expect, that a third party will use the financial statement and the member's compilation report does not disclose a lack of independence; or
   (c) an examination of prospective financial information; or

(2) Prepare an original or amended tax return or claim for a tax refund for a contingent fee for any client. (1.510.001)

Suppose you are a shareholder in New Medical Corporation. You have some concerns about the company's revenue practices, but the fact that New Medical received an unmodified audit opinion reassures you. Now let's assume that you discover that the New Medical contract with its auditor paid the auditor more for an unmodified opinion than a qualified opinion. How might that affect the value you placed on the auditor's report?

A **contingent fee** is a fee established for the performance of any service in an arrangement in which no fee will be charged unless a specific finding or result is attained or the fee otherwise depends on the result of the service. CPAs can charge contingent fees for work such as representing a client in an IRS tax audit and certain other tax matters, achieving goals in a consulting service engagement, or helping a person obtain a bank loan in a financial planning engagement. However, the PCAOB has issued an independence rule that prohibits all contingent fees for audit clients of registered public accounting firms. And, as the following Auditing Insight demonstrates, if a CPA does charge contingent fees to an audit client, the SEC will take action. Simply stated, you just can't do that!

AUDITING INSIGHT   You Just Can't Do That!

The SEC has determined that three Ernst & Young employees violated independence rules when they used contingent fees for billing an audit client for tax services. The violations occurred from 2009–2018 during which time EY was billing Cintas for nonaudit services on a contingent fee basis, clearly in violation of SEC rules. A former employee of Cintas was also charged. All four employees were fined and prohibited from appearing or practicing before the SEC for one to two years. Further, each of the employees was fined for their violations.

Source: SEC, Administrative Proceeding File Nos. 3-20671, 3-20672, 3-20673, and 3-20674 (online source).

CPAs are allowed to receive contingent fees *except* from clients for whom the CPAs perform attest services when users of financial information may be relying on the CPAs' work. The prohibitions in items 1(a), 1(b), and 1(c) all refer to attest engagements in which independence is required. Acceptance of contingent fee arrangements during the period in which the member or the member's firm is engaged to perform any of these attestations or during the period covered by any historical financial statements involved in any of these engagements is considered an impairment of independence.

Contingent fees are also prohibited in connection with the everyday tax practice of preparing original or amended tax returns. This prohibition arose from an interesting conflict between government agencies. The Federal Trade Commission (FTC) wanted to see contingent fees permitted, but the IRS objected on the grounds that such fees might induce accountants and clients to "play the audit lottery"—understate tax improperly in the hope of escaping audit. The IRS asserted that if the AICPA permitted such contingent fees, the IRS would make its own rules prohibiting them. The FTC agreed that the AICPA rule could contain this prohibition.

Commissions and Referral Fees

A. Prohibited Commissions

A member in public practice shall not recommend or refer to a client any product or service for a commission, or recommend or refer any product or service to be supplied by a client for a commission, or receive a commission, when the member or the member's firm also performs for that client:

(a) an audit or review of a financial statement; or

(b) a compilation of a financial statement when the member expects, or reasonably might expect, that a third party will use the financial statement and the member's compilation report does not disclose a lack of independence; or

(c) an examination of prospective financial information.

This prohibition applies during the period in which the member is engaged to perform any of the services listed above and the period covered by any historical financial statements involved in such listed services.

B. **Disclosure of Permitted Commission**

A member in public practice who is not prohibited by this rule from performing services for, or receiving a commission from, and who is paid or expects to be paid a commission, shall disclose that fact to any person or entity to whom the member recommends or refers a product or service to which the commission relates.

C. **Referral Fees**

Any member who accepts a referral fee for recommending or referring any service of a CPA to any person or entity or who pays a referral fee to obtain a client shall disclose such acceptance or payment to the client. (1.520.001)

A **commission** is generally defined as a percentage-based fee charged for professional services in connection with executing a transaction or performing some other business activity. Examples are insurance sales commissions, real estate sales commissions, and securities sales commissions. A CPA can earn commissions except in connection with any client for whom the CPA performs attestation services.

Commissions are an impairment of independence similar to contingent fees. Recall that *contingent fees* are based on attaining a specific finding or result and are prohibited for attestation clients. When involved in an attest engagement with a client, the CPA cannot receive a commission from anyone for (1) referring a product or service to the client or (2) referring to someone else a product or service supplied by the client. It does not matter which party actually pays the commission.

Commissions are permitted provided that the engagement *does not involve attestation* of the types cited in part A of the rule. This permission is tempered by the requirement that the CPA must disclose to clients an arrangement to receive a commission.

Most of the commission fee activity takes place in connection with personal financial planning services. CPAs often recommend insurance and investments to individuals and families. Some critics point out that clients cannot always trust commission agents (e.g., insurance salespersons, securities brokers) to have clients' best interests in mind when the agents' own compensation depends on clients' buying the product that produces commissions.

Referral fees are fees (1) a CPA receives for recommending another CPA's services or (2) a CPA pays to obtain a client. Referral involves the practice of sending business to another CPA and paying other CPAs or outside agencies for drumming up business. Some CPAs have hired services that solicit clients on their behalf, paying a fixed or percentage fee. Many CPAs frown on these arrangements, but they are permitted. However, CPAs must disclose such fees to clients.

Advertising and Other Forms of Solicitation Rule

A member in public practice shall not seek to obtain clients by advertising or other forms of solicitation in a manner that is false, misleading, or deceptive. Solicitation by the use of coercion, overreaching, or harassing conduct is prohibited. (1.600.001)

Advertising consists of messages designed to attract business that are broadcast widely to an undifferentiated audience (e.g., print, radio, television, billboards). Advertising is permitted with only a few limitations. The current rule applies only to CPAs practicing public accounting and relates to their efforts to obtain clients. The guidelines basically prohibit false, misleading, and deceptive messages:

- Advertising may not create false or unjustified expectations of favorable results.
- Advertising may not imply the ability to influence any court, tribunal, regulatory agency, or similar body or official.
- Advertising may not contain a fee estimate when the CPA knows it is likely to be substantially increased unless the client is notified.
- Advertising may not contain any other representation likely to cause a reasonable person to misunderstand or be deceived.

It is hoped that CPAs will carry out only tasteful advertising efforts, and many do not advertising at all. Public practice is generally marked by decorum and a sense of good taste.

However, there are exceptions, and they tend to get much negative attention from other CPAs and the public in general. The danger in bad advertising lies in creating the image of a lack of professionalism, which can backfire in a firm's efforts to build a practice.

Solicitation generally refers to direct contact (e.g., in person, mail, telephone) with a specific potential client. Many CPAs abhor solicitation, and many state boards of accountancy try to prohibit direct, uninvited approaches to prospective clients, especially when the client already has a CPA. Nevertheless, the U.S. Supreme Court has struck down state solicitation prohibitions, declaring them to be an infringement of personal and business rights to free speech and due process.

CPAs sometimes hire marketing firms to obtain clients. The AICPA permits such arrangements but warns that all such "practice development" activity is subject to the Advertising and Other Forms of Solicitation Rule because members cannot do through others, what they are prohibited from doing themselves.

Confidential Client Information Rule

> A member in public practice shall not disclose any confidential information without the specific consent of the client. (1.700.001)

Confidential information is any information that is not available to the public (or in the public domain). As Scott London in this module's opening vignette was well aware, such information should not be disclosed to outside parties unless demanded by a court or an administrative body having subpoena or summons power. *Privileged information* is information that cannot even be demanded by a court. Common-law privilege exists for husband–wife and attorney–client relationships. While physician–patient and priest–penitent relationships have obtained the privilege through state statutes, no accountant–client privilege exists under federal law, and no state-created privilege has been recognized in federal courts. In all recognized privilege relationships, the professional person is obligated to observe the privilege, which can be waived only by the client, patient, or penitent. (These persons are said to be the *holders of the privilege*.)

The rules of privileged and confidential communication are based on the belief that they facilitate a free flow of information between parties to the relationship. The nature of accounting services makes it necessary for the accountant to have access to information about salaries, products, contracts, merger or divestment plans, tax matters, and other information required for the best possible professional work. Managers would be less likely to reveal such information if they could not trust the accountant to keep it confidential. If accountants were to reveal such information, the resulting reduction of the information flow might be undesirable, so no accountant should break the confidentiality rule without a good reason. And as the following Auditing Insight reveals, audit firms have to be aware of the possibility of its audit client's competitors going to great lengths to obtain confidential information.

AUDITING INSIGHT | Audit Client's Competitor Goes To Great Lengths to Obtain Confidential Information

What would you do if a government intelligence agent approached you to assist him in a "top secret" assignment involving national security? Guy Enright, an accountant with **KPMG's Financial Advisory Services Ltd.** in Bermuda, said "yes" to Nick Hamilton, a British intelligence officer, and agreed to deposit confidential audit documents in plastic containers at "dead drop" sites located throughout Bermuda. Unfortunately for Enright, KPMG, and its client, **IPOC International Growth Fund Ltd.** (IPOC), "Nick Hamilton" was in fact Nick Day, a cofounder of **Diligence Inc.**, a Washington-based private intelligence firm that was gathering information for one of IPOC's business competitors.

The setup was quite elaborate. "Hamilton" required Enright to undergo a detailed background check, even producing an official-looking questionnaire with a British government seal at the top, before he could participate on "Project Yucca." The undercover mission came to an abrupt end when someone (still unknown) dropped off a package of Diligence business records and e-mails involving "Project Yucca" at KPMG's Montvale office. After KPMG sued, Diligence ended up paying $1.7 million.

Source: "Spies, Lies & KPMG. An inside look at how the accounting giant was infiltrated by private intelligence firm Diligence," February 26, 2007, Bloomberg Businessweek (online source).

Difficult problems arise over auditors' obligations to "blow the whistle" about clients' shady or illegal practices. For all practical purposes, information is not considered confidential if its disclosure is necessary to prevent financial statements from being misleading. If a client refuses to accept an auditors' report that has been modified because of the inability to obtain sufficient appropriate evidence about a suspected illegal act, failure to account for or disclose properly a material amount connected with an illegal act, or inability to estimate amounts involved in an illegal act, the public accounting firm should withdraw from the engagement and give the reasons in writing to the board of directors. In such an extreme case, the withdrawal amounts to whistleblowing, but the action results from the client's decision not to disclose the information.

Auditors are not, in general, legally *obligated* to blow the whistle on clients. However, circumstances in which auditors are legally *justified* in making disclosures to a regulatory agency or a third party may exist. Such circumstances include when (1) a client has intentionally and without authorization associated or involved a CPA in its misleading conduct (e.g., used the CPA's name on financial statements), (2) a client has distributed misleading draft financial statements prepared by a CPA for internal use only, or (3) a client prepares and distributes in an annual report or prospectus, misleading information for which the CPA has not assumed any responsibility. In addition, the Private Securities Litigation Reform Act of 1995 imposed another reporting requirement in connection with clients' illegal acts (see Module C).

The Confidential Client Information Rule possibly provides accountants with the most difficulties and may be the most violated procedure. First, in its strictest interpretation, the principle of confidentiality applies to the communication of information to anyone who is not involved in the audit except as noted by the rule. Over lunch or after hours, however, you might find auditors discussing the day's work with other members of the firm or company. Second, CPAs should not view the Confidential Client Information Rule as an excuse for inaction when action may be appropriate to right a wrongful act committed or about to be committed by a client. In some cases, auditors' inaction may be viewed as part of a conspiracy or willingness to be an accessory to a wrong. A useful initial course of action is to consult an attorney about possible legal pitfalls of both whistleblowing and silence. Overall, as the following Auditing Insight clearly shows, insider trading is never a good idea.

AUDITING INSIGHT · Insider Trading Is Never a Good Idea

Every audit staff member should know that it is not only unethical but also illegal to use information gleaned from an audit or other "inside" information to purchase shares of stock. However, **EY** staff auditor Nima Hedayati must have skipped training the day those issues were discussed. In 2015, Hedayati used confidential client information to purchase 40 contracts for call options and advised his mother to purchase shares as well. The ill-gotten gains resulted in the junior staff auditor's firing from EY coupled with a settlement with the SEC for over $87,000, including $43,000 of penalties. Hedayati is also suspended from practicing as an accountant before the SEC.

Source: "EY auditor settles with SEC on insider trading charges," Michael Cohn, March 14, 2017, *Accounting Today* (online source).

Accountants can permit other accountants to review confidential audit documentation and other information about clients in connection with arrangements to sell or merge an accounting practice. The AICPA advises accountants to have an agreement among themselves that extends the confidentiality safeguard to the prospective purchasing accountant as it existed with the original accountant.

CPAs also may disclose confidential information without the client's permission to remain in compliance with applicable laws (e.g., responding to a subpoena), as part of an ethics investigation (*of a CPA*), or as part of a peer review or PCAOB investigation of *public accounting firm* practices. The exception related to ethics violations applies only to investigative or disciplinary bodies under the AICPA's jurisdiction, namely the AICPA Professional Ethics Division, the ethics enforcement committees in the various state societies of CPAs, and state boards of accountancy.

While the Confidential Client Information Rule specifically addresses CPAs' responsibilities to clients, CPAs (both in public practice and in business) must also keep their employers' proprietary information confidential. Failure to do so would be a violation of the Acts Discreditable Rule, discussed previously in this module. Before discussing the next rule of conduct, consider the following Auditing Insight which reveals how an online relationship led to insider trading and securities fraud.

AUDITING INSIGHT   Online Relationship Leads To Insider Trading and Securities Fraud

An EY partner was convicted of six counts of securities fraud related to insider trading arising from a relationship that began on an extramarital dating website. The principal witness against the partner was a woman who had befriended him online, and through a guessing game they played from their respective offices, guessed the impending mergers he was working on. She then traded 18 times on the insider information, netting approximately $400,000 on the transactions. Her trading was funded by another man she met on the same website.

Her suspicious trading just before the mergers were announced caused her name to repeatedly appear on SEC watch lists. When confronted, she cut a deal, pleading guilty to 15 counts of securities fraud and agreeing to testify against the EY partner who apparently was unaware of the insider trading scheme and did not make a cent off the trades.

Source: "Insider Affair: An SEC Trial of the Heart," *The Wall Street Journal,* July 28, 2009, p. C1.

Form of Organization and Name Rule

> A member may practice public accounting only in a form of organization permitted by law or regulation whose characteristics conform to resolutions of Council. A member shall not practice public accounting under a firm name that is misleading. Names of one or more past owners may be included in the firm name of a successor organization. A firm may not designate itself as "Member of the American Institute of Certified Public Accountants" unless all of its CPA owners are members of the Institute. (1.800.001)

The Form of Organization and Name Rule allows CPAs to practice public accounting in any form of organization permitted by a state board of accountancy and authorized by law. Organization forms include sole proprietorship, partnership, limited partnership, limited liability partnership (LLP), professional corporation (PC), limited liability corporation (LLC), and ordinary corporation (Inc.). You may have noticed that the large international accounting firms now place LLP after their firm names. Many small accounting firms include PC in their names.

CPAs in public practice cannot use misleading firm names. For example, suppose CPAs Stone and Thompson, who are not in partnership, agree to share expenses for office support, advertising, and continuing education. They cannot put up a sign that states "Stone & Thompson CPAs" because this name suggests a partnership where there is none.

A member who practices public accounting also can participate in the operation of another business organization (e.g., a consulting or tax preparation firm) that offers professional services of the types offered by public accounting firms. If this business is permitted to practice public accounting under state law, the member also is considered to be in the practice of public accounting in it and must observe all rules of conduct. CPAs who work in alternative practice structures occupy an odd position. They can prepare compiled (unaudited) financial statements, which is considered a form of public accounting practice. In such a case, CPA employees of the alternative practice structure (e.g., "PublicCo") must take final responsibility for the accountants' compilation report and must sign it with their own personal names (not the name of PublicCo).

Form of Organization and Name

The characteristics of an accounting organization under the "Form of Organization and Name" rule are as follows:

- A majority (50 percent or more) ownership and voting rights must belong to CPAs.
- Non-CPA owners must be active in the firm, not passive investors.
- A CPA must have ultimate responsibility for the firm's services.
- Non-CPA owners can use titles such as "principal, owner, officer,

member, and shareholder" but cannot hold out to be a CPA.
- Non-CPA owners must abide by the AICPA Code of Professional Conduct.
- Non-CPA owners must hold a bachelor's degree, and after the year 2010, must have 150 semester hours of college education.
- Non-CPA owners must complete the same continuing education requirements as CPAs who are members of the AICPA.
- Non-CPA owners are not eligible to be members of the AICPA.

The last paragraph of the Form of Organization and Name Rule permits a mixed accounting organization consisting of CPA and non-CPA owners to designate itself "Members of the AICPA" if all of the CPA owners are actually AICPA members. However, the AICPA Council limits this privilege of organizational form by expressing certain requirements for ownership and control, especially regarding non-CPAs who have ownership interests in an organization that practices public accounting. The proper characteristics of an accounting organization are detailed above in the feature "Form of Organization and Name."

 REVIEW CHECKPOINTS

B.12 What ethical responsibilities do members of the AICPA have for acts of nonmembers who are under their supervision (e.g., recent college graduates who are not yet CPAs)?

B.13 What rules of conduct apply specifically to members in government and industry?

B.14 What provisions of the AICPA Council Resolution on form of organization place control of accounting services in the hands of CPAs?

B.15 What is the primary difference between commissions and referrals?

CONSEQUENCES OF VIOLATING THE CODE OF PROFESSIONAL CONDUCT

LO B-6
Explain the types of penalties that can be imposed on accountants.

Public accounting firms and responsible professional accountants understand the importance of ethics to the profession and seek to ensure that the organization and all employees are acting in an ethical manner. Unethical behavior by an auditor can have financial implications (e.g., fines, lawsuits) and reputation implications that may be difficult to remedy. Quality control practices and disciplinary proceedings provide the mechanisms of *self-regulation*. **Self-regulation** refers to the quality control reviews and disciplinary actions conducted by fellow CPAs—professional peers.

Self-Regulatory Discipline

Individual persons (not accounting firms) are subject to the rules of conduct of state CPA societies and the AICPA only if they choose to join these organizations. The AICPA and most of the state societies have entered into a Joint Ethics Enforcement Program through which the AICPA can refer complaints against CPAs to state societies or state societies can refer them to the AICPA. Both organizations have ethics committees to hear complaints. They can (1) acquit an accused CPA, (2) find the CPA in violation of rules and issue a letter of required corrective action, or (3) refer serious cases to an AICPA trial board. The letter of required corrective action ordinarily admonishes the CPA and requires specific continuing education courses to bring the CPA up to date in technical areas.

The trial board panel has the power to (1) acquit the CPA, (2) admonish the CPA, (3) suspend the CPA's membership in the state society and the AICPA for up to two years, or (4) expel the CPA from the state society and the AICPA. The AICPA bylaws (not the Code of Professional Conduct) provide for automatic expulsion of CPAs judged to have committed a felony, failed to file their tax returns, or aided in the preparation of a false and fraudulent income tax return. The trial board panels are required to publish the names of the CPAs disciplined in their proceedings.

The expulsion penalty, while severe, does not prevent a CPA from continuing to practice accounting. Membership in the AICPA and state societies, while beneficial, is not required. However, a CPA must have a valid state license in order to practice. Most state boards of accountancy are the agencies that can suspend or revoke the license to practice. As the following Auditing Insight reveals, the AICPA Joint Trial Board most definitely takes action.

AUDITING INSIGHT · The AICPA Joint Trial Board Most Definitely Takes Action

The following is the AICPA's report on cases investigated and their resolutions for 2019 and 2018 cases:

	2019	2018
Total cases at beginning of period (including 118 and 119, respectively, deferred due to pending litigation)	967	997
Cases opened during period	260	517
Cases completed during period	(450)	(547)
Total cases at end of period (including 116 and 118, respectively, deferred due to pending litigation)	777	967
Summary of Disposition of Completed Cases		
Expelled or suspended	113	128
Admonished	34	48
Corrective action required	60	133
No violation/dismissed	82	59
No further action	126	132
Subsequent monitoring completed satisfactorily	25	30
Other	10	17
	450	547

Source: AICPA website (www.aicpa.org)

Public Regulation Discipline

State boards of accountancy are government agencies consisting of CPA and non-CPA office-holders. In most states, the state board of accountancy issues licenses to practice accounting in their jurisdictions. Most state laws require a license to use the designation CPA or certified public accountant and limit the attest (audit) function to license holders only.

State boards have rules of conduct and trial board panels. They can admonish a license holder; perhaps more importantly, most can suspend or revoke the license to practice. Suspension and revocation are severe penalties because a person no longer can use the

CPA title and cannot sign auditors' reports. When candidates have successfully passed the CPA examination and are ready to become CPAs, some state boards administer an ethics examination or require taking an ethics course intended to familiarize new CPAs with the state rules.

The SEC and the PCAOB also conduct public disciplinary actions. Their authority comes from their rules of practice, of which Rule 102(e) provides that the SEC can deny, temporarily or permanently, the privilege of practice before the SEC to any person found to have engaged in unethical or improper professional conduct. When conducting a "Rule 102(e) proceeding," the SEC acts in a quasi-judicial role as an administrative agency. The simple fact is that CPAs have a critically important responsibility to the investing public when completing the financial statement audit and they must do their job in order to honor the public trust, as illustrated in the following Auditing Insight.

AUDITING INSIGHT Do Your Job In Order To Honor The Public Trust

In 2018, three partners from the **Deloitte Mexico** affiliate firm were barred, fined, and censured by the PCAOB. The reason? They failed to do their jobs and then misrepresented to Deloitte U.S. that the work had been performed. The partners did not evaluate the operating effectiveness of certain internal controls over financial reporting (ICFR), nor did they properly evaluate the loan reserves in 2013 and 2014 of a subsidiary of Texas-based EZCORP which was based in Mexico. The result? All three partners are barred from being associated persons of a registered public accounting firm for two years and have been fined in excess of $30,000 each.

Source: "*PCAOB Sanctions Deloitte Mexico Partners for Deficiencies and Misrepresentations in Audit of Mexican Subsidiary,*" October 31, 2018, PCAOBUS.org (online source).

The SEC penalty bars an accountant from signing any documents filed by an SEC-registered company. The penalty effectively stops the accountant's SEC practice. In a few severe cases, such proceedings have resulted in settlements barring not only the individual accountant but also their accounting firm or certain of its practice offices from accepting new SEC clients for a period of time.

The PCAOB's Division of Enforcement and Investigations (DEI) handles disciplinary actions involving accountants (and their firms) who are engaged to audit public companies (also known as "issuers"). The DEI's role is to identify matters (often from tips) for further investigation, conduct an investigation, and recommend disciplinary proceedings (if considered necessary). Common investigations include violations of the PCAOB's *Auditing Standards,* independence violations, and failures to cooperate with inspections/investigations. If violations are found, the DEI makes recommendations for sanctions to the Board. The Board may decide to suspend or permanently bar an accountant from auditing any public companies, suspend or revoke an accounting firm's registration, appoint a monitor to oversee a firm's practice, impose monetary penalties, require additional continuing professional education, or impose other sanctions permitted under PCAOB rules. While accountants (and their firms) most definitely face the possibility of significant penalties and sanctions in the United States for violations, different countries have even more severe penalties, as illustrated in the following Auditing Insight.

AUDITING INSIGHT Different Countries Have Even More Severe Penalties

Different countries have different penalties for accountants caught not honoring the public trust. In China, the *death sentences* for Zhou Limin, the former head of the China Construction Bank, and Liu Yibing, an accountant, were upheld by China's State Supreme Court. The pair was found guilty of stealing more than $60 million by offering fake accounts with high interest rates.

Source: "*Accountant Gets Death Penalty,*" Stephen Taub, December 14, 2002, CFO.com (online source).

☑ REVIEW CHECKPOINTS

B.16 What penalties can be imposed by the AICPA and the state societies on CPAs in their "self-regulation" of ethics code violators?

B.17 What penalties can the SEC and PCAOB impose on CPAs who violate rules of conduct?

Summary

This module begins with philosophers' considerations of moral philosophy, explains the AICPA Code of Professional Conduct as well as the SEC and PCAOB rules related to auditors' independence, provides an overview of the IESBA Code of Ethics, and ends with a review of enforcement actions against those CPAs who choose not to follow the rules. It is important to remember that accounting is the only business discipline that is considered a profession like medicine and the law. As a result, professional ethics for accountants is not simply a matter covered by a few rules in a formal code of professional conduct. Concepts of proper professional conduct permeate all areas of practice. Ethics and accompanying sanctions for ethical failures provide the foundation for public accountants' value in the marketplace.

The spirit of the AICPA Code of Professional Conduct is that, although independence is required for audit and attest services, integrity and objectivity are required in connection with all professional services. In this context, integrity and objectivity are the larger concepts and "independence" is a special condition largely defined by the matters of appearance specified in the interpretations of the Independence Rule. The ethics rules may appear to be restrictive, but they are intended to benefit the public, protect the profession, and allow for sanctions of those CPAs choosing not to comply with the rules. The AICPA Code of Professional Conduct was recently reorganized to address situations faced by accountants in varying business environments; the following graphic illustrates how the different rules affect the varying roles that accountants play, whether in public practice, in business, or in other situations (e.g., between jobs).

Specific rules in the AICPA Code of Professional Conduct may not necessarily be classified under one of the ethics principles. Decisions based on a rule may involve imperative, utilitarian, or personal virtue considerations, or elements of all three. The rules have the form of imperatives because that is the nature of a code. However, elements of utilitarianism and generalization seem to be apparent in the underlying rationale for most of the rules. If this perception is accurate, auditors may use these two principles in difficult decision problems for which adherence to a rule could produce an undesirable result. Your

Applicability of the AICPA Code of Professional Conduct to CPAs

knowledge of philosophical principles in ethics—the imperative, utilitarian, and virtue theories—will help you make decisions about the AICPA, SEC, and PCAOB rules. This structured approach to thoughtful decisions is important not only when you are employed in public accounting but also when you work in government, industry, and education.

Public accountants must be careful in all areas of practice. As an accountant, you must not lose sight of the nonaccountants' perspective. No matter how complex or technical a decision may be, a simplified view of it always tends to cut away the details of special technical issues to get directly to the heart of the matter. A sense of professionalism coupled with sensitivity to the effect of decisions on other people is invaluable in the practice of accounting and auditing. Remember that when you face an ethical dilemma, you are not alone. The AICPA, other professional organizations, and most accounting firms have anonymous hotlines for you to ask questions, and you always have your colleagues, friends, and family members to talk to.

Key Terms

act-utilitarianism: The emphasis on an individual act as it is affected by the specific circumstances of a situation, 618

categorical imperative: Kant's specification of an unconditional obligation to act as one thinks others should act regardless of circumstances, 617

commission: A percentage fee charged for professional services in connection with executing a transaction or performing some other business activity, 640

contingent fee: A type of compensation established for the performance of any service in an arrangement in which no amount will be charged unless a specific finding or result is attained or the fee otherwise depends on the result, 639

covered member: Broadly defined, any individual who might be in a position to compromise the integrity of an audit. In the AICPA Code of Professional Conduct, the term is defined as any individual, among others, who is (1) on the audit engagement team, (2) in a position to influence the audit engagement, (3) a partner or manager of a nonaudit client service team, or (4) a partner from the local office of the public accounting firm, 624

ethical behavior: Ethical behavior is that which (1) produces the greatest good, and/or (2) conforms to moral rules and principles, and/or (3) best demonstrates the virtues you value most. The most difficult problem situations arise when two or more rules conflict or when a rule and the criterion of "greatest good" conflict, 614

ethics: According to Wheelwright, ethics can be thought of as "that branch of philosophy which is the systematic study of reflective choice, of the standards of right and wrong by which it is to be guided, and of the goods toward which it may ultimately be directed, 614

generalization argument: A judicious combination of the imperative and utilitarian principles; to act as one thinks others should act in a similar circumstance, 618

independence: A mental attitude and the appearance that the auditor is not influenced by others in judgments and decisions, 624

independence in appearance: To reflect and possess independence in appearance, the auditor must not have any obligations or interests (in the client, its management, or its owners) that could cause others to believe the auditor is biased with respect to the client, its management, or its owners. Even if the auditor does not have any direct or indirect financial interest or obligation with the client in fact, they must assure that no part of their behavior or actions appear to affect their independence in the opinion of the public, 623

independence in fact: When an auditor possessed independence in fact, this means that the auditor possesses integrity, a character of intellectual honesty and candor; and objectivity, a state of mind of judicial impartiality that recognizes an obligation of fairness to management and owners of a client, creditors, prospective owners or creditors, and other stakeholders, 623

problem situation: A problem situation exists whenever an individual must make a choice among alterative actions and the right choice is not absolutely clear, 614

referral fee: The (1) compensation that a CPA receives for recommending another CPA's services and (2) that a CPA pays to obtain a client; may or may not be based on a percentage of the amount of any transaction, 640

rule-utilitarianism: The emphasis on the centrality of rules for ethical behavior while still maintaining the criterion of the greatest universal good, 618

self-regulation: The quality control reviews and disciplinary actions conducted by fellow CPAs—professional peers, 644

virtue ethics: The focus on the role of one's character in the decision-making process, 619

Multiple-Choice
Questions for
Practice and
Review

 All applicable questions are available with *Connect.*

LO B-2

B.18 Which of the following is not reflective of a standard philosophical answer to the question, "what is ethical behavior" for CPAs to consider in completing their work?

   a. Ethical behavior produces the greatest good.

   b. Ethical behavior conforms to AICPA Code of Conduct.

   c. Ethical behavior conforms to moral rules.

   d. Ethical behavior best demonstrates the virtues you value most.

LO B-1

B.19 Which of the following best defines what is meant by an ethical problem situation?

   a. One where an individual must make a decision with only one clear solution.

   b. One where an individual must make a decision where there is a choice among alternative actions and the right choice is not clear.

   c. One where an individual must make a decision where there is a choice among alternative actions, the right choice is not clear, and the final choice affects the well-being of other persons.

   d. One where an individual must make a decision where there is a choice among alternative actions, the right choice is not clear, and the final choice does not affect the well-being of other persons.

LO B-2

B.20 Which of the following philosophical principles in ethics directs a decision maker to take actions in accordance with the requirements of moral rules and principles?

   a. The Imperative principle.

   b. The principle of Utilitarianism.

   c. The Generalization argument.

   d. Virtue ethics.

LO B-2

B.21 Which of the following philosophical principles in ethics directs a decision maker to take actions in a manner that produces the greatest good?

   a. The Imperative principle.

   b. The principle of Utilitarianism.

   c. The Generalization argument.

   d. Virtue ethics.

LO B-3

B.22 Which of the following is not identified as a principle in the AICPA Code of Professional Conduct?

   a. The public interest.

   b. Risk assessment.

   c. Due care.

   d. Scope and nature of services.

LO B-4

B.23 Auditors are interested in having independence in appearance because

   a. They want to impress the public with their independence in fact.

   b. They want the public at large to have confidence in the profession.

   c. They need to comply with the fundamental principles of GAAS.

   d. Audits should be planned and properly supervised.

LO B-4

B.24 Under Sarbanes–Oxley and PCAOB rules, ensuring that the auditor is independent in appearance is the responsibility of
   a. The public accounting firm.
   b. Senior management.
   c. The audit committee.
   d. The PCAOB.

LO B-2

B.25 If a public accounting firm says it always follows the rule that requires adherence to FASB pronouncements in order to give a standard unmodified auditors' report, it is following a philosophy characterized by
   a. The imperative principle.
   b. The utilitarian principle.
   c. Virtue ethics.
   d. Reliance on members' collective conscience.

LO B-3

B.26 Which of the following agencies issues independence rules for the auditors of public companies?
   a. Financial Accounting Standards Board (FASB).
   b. Government Accountability Office (GAO).
   c. Public Company Accounting Oversight Board (PCAOB).
   d. AICPA Accounting and Review Services Committee (ARSC).

LO B-4

B.27 Audit independence in fact is most clearly lost when
   a. A public accounting firm audits competitor companies in the same industry (e.g., Coca-Cola and Pepsi).
   b. An auditor agrees to the argument made by the client's financial vice president that deferring losses on debt refinancing is in accordance with generally accepted accounting principles.
   c. An audit team fails to discover the client's misleading omission of disclosure about permanent impairment of asset values.
   d. A public accounting firm issues a standard unmodified report, but the reviewing partner fails to notice that the assistant's observation of inventory was woefully incomplete.

LO B-4

B.28 The audit committee's responsibility for auditor independence concerns
   a. Ensuring that partners of the public accounting firm are not stockholders in the company.
   b. Ensuring that nonaudit services provided by the auditor do not impair independence.
   c. Reporting on auditor independence to the PCAOB.
   d. Ensuring that all nonaudit services are provided by auditors who do not perform the financial statement audit.

LO B-5

B.29 AICPA members who work in industry and government must always uphold which *two* of the following AICPA rules of conduct?
   a. The Independence Rule.
   b. The Integrity and Objectivity Rule.
   c. The Confidential Client Information Rule.
   d. The Acts Discreditable Rule.

LO B-4

B.30 A public accounting firm's independence is not impaired when members of the audit engagement team does which of the following for a public company audit client?
   a. Prepares special purchase orders for active plutonium in secure national defense installations.
   b. Completes operational internal audit assignments under the directions of the client's director of internal auditing.
   c. Prepares outsourced internal audit work on the client's financial accounting control monitoring.
   d. Prepares actuarial assumptions used by the client's actuaries for life insurance actuarial liability determination.
   e. All of the above would impair the public accounting firm's independence.

LO B-4

B.31 When a public accounting firm audits FUND-A in a mutual fund complex that has sister funds FUND-B and FUND-C, independence for the audit of FUND-A is *not* impaired when

a. Managerial-level professionals located in the office where the engagement audit partner is located but who are not on the engagement team own shares in FUND-B, which is not an audit client.

b. The wife of the FUND-A audit engagement partner owns shares in FUND-C (an audit client of another of the firm's offices), and these shares are held through the wife's employee benefit plan funded by her employer, the AllSteelFence Company.

c. Both (a) and (b).

d. Neither (a) nor (b).

LO B-4

B.32 Which of the following is considered a close relative (but not an immediate family member) as defined by the AICPA?

a. Spouse

b. Spousal equivalent

c. Parent

d. Uncle

LO B-5

B.33 Which of the following is true if an auditor performs nonaudit services for a government entity?

a. The scope of the audit must be reduced so that the auditor does not audit the area for which the nonaudit work was performed.

b. The auditor is prohibited from providing nonaudit work in areas directly related to the production of accounting information.

c. The senior members of the government entity must document their review of the nonaudit service and indicate why it is appropriate for the auditors to perform this service.

d. The scope of the audit cannot be reduced because the nonaudit work was performed by the public accounting firm.

LO B-4

B.34 Which of the following is true?

a. Members of an audit engagement team cannot speak with audit client officers about matters outside the scope of the audit while the audit engagement is in progress.

b. Audit team members who leave the public accounting firm for employment with audit clients can provide audit efficiencies (next year) because they are very familiar with the firm's audit plans.

c. Audit team partners who leave the public accounting firm for employment with audit clients can retain variable annuity retirement accounts established in the person's former firm retirement plan.

d. The public accounting firm must discuss with the audit client's board or its audit committee the independence implications of the client's having hired the audit engagement team manager as its financial vice president.

LO B-3

B.35 Which of the following "bodies designated by Council" have been authorized to promulgate general standards enforceable under the General Standards Rule of the AICPA Code of Professional Conduct?

a. AICPA Division of Professional Ethics.

b. Financial Accounting Standards Board.

c. Government Accounting Standards Board.

d. Accounting and Review Services Committee.

LO B-5

B.36 Which of the following "bodies designated by Council" have been authorized to promulgate accounting principles enforceable under the Accounting Principles Rule of the AICPA Code of Professional Conduct?

a. Auditing Standards Board.

b. Federal Accounting Standards Advisory Board.

c. Consulting Services Executive Committee.

d. Accounting and Review Services Committee.

LO B-5

B.37 Phil Greb has a thriving practice in which he assists attorneys in preparing litigation dealing with accounting and auditing matters. He is "practicing public accounting" if he

a. Uses his CPA designation on his letterhead and business card.

b. Is in partnership with another CPA.

c. Practices in a professional corporation with other CPAs.

d. Never lets his clients know that he is a CPA.

LO B-5

B.38 The AICPA removed its general prohibition of CPAs taking commissions and contingent fees because

a. CPAs prefer more price competition to less.

b. Commissions and contingent fees enhance audit independence.

c. Nothing is inherently wrong about the form of fees charged to nonaudit clients.

d. Objectivity is not always necessary in accounting and auditing services.

LO B-4

B.39 CPA Kara Rambo is the auditor of Ajax Corporation. Her audit independence will *not* be considered impaired if she

a. Owns $1,000 worth of Ajax stock.

b. Has a husband who owns $1,000 worth of Ajax stock.

c. Has a sister who is the financial vice president of Ajax.

d. Owns $1,000 worth of the stock of Pericles Corporation, which is controlled by Ajax as a result of Ajax's ownership of 40 percent of Pericles' stock, and Pericles contributes 3 percent of its total assets and income in Ajax's financial statements.

LO B-5

B.40 When a client's financial statements contain a material departure from an FASB *Statement on Accounting Standards* and the public accounting firm believes the departure is necessary to ensure that the statements are not misleading,

a. The public accounting firm must qualify the auditors' report for a departure from GAAP.

b. The public accounting firm can explain why the departure is necessary and then give an unmodified opinion paragraph in the auditors' report.

c. The public accounting firm must give an adverse auditors' report.

d. The public accounting firm can give the standard unmodified auditors' report with an unmodified opinion paragraph.

LO B-5

B.41 Which of the following would *not* be considered confidential information obtained in the course of an engagement for which the client's consent would be needed for disclosure?

a. Information about whether a consulting client has paid the CPA's fees on time.

b. The actuarial assumptions used by a tax client in calculating pension expense.

c. Management's strategic plan for next year's labor negotiations.

d. Information about material contingent liabilities relevant for audited financial statements.

LO B-5

B.42 Which of the following would probably *not* be considered an "act discreditable to the profession"?

a. Numerous moving traffic violations.

b. Failing to file the CPA's own tax return.

c. Filing a fraudulent tax return for a client in a severe financial difficulty.

d. Refusing to hire Asian Americans in an accounting practice.

LO B-5

B.43 According to the AICPA Code of Professional Conduct, which of the following acts is generally forbidden to CPAs in public practice?

a. Purchasing bookkeeping software from a high-tech development company and reselling it to tax clients.

b. Being the author of a "TaxAid" newsletter promoted and sold by a publishing company.

c. Having a commission arrangement with an accounting software developer to receive 4 percent of the price of programs recommended and sold to audit clients.

d. Engaging a marketing firm to obtain new financial planning clients for a fixed fee of $1,000 for each successful contact.

firm of Amalgamated Exchange Inc., which is 50 percent owned by the public accounting firm and 50 percent owned by Lynch Merrill Investment Corporation.

i.   The public accounting firm's tax consulting division prepared Section Co.'s export-import tax reports, which involved numerous interpretations of complicated export-import tax law provisions.

LO B-4

B.52   Independence, Integrity, and Objectivity Cases. Read the following cases.

Required:

For each case, state whether the action or situation shows a violation of the AICPA Code of Professional Conduct, explain why if it does, and cite the relevant rule.

a.   CPA Ellen Stout performs the audit of the local symphony society. Because of her good work, she was elected an honorary member of the board of directors.

b.   CPA Darcy Wolfe practices management consulting in the area of computerized information systems under the firm name of Wolfe & Associates. The "associates" are not CPAs, and the firm is not an accounting firm. However, Wolfe shows "CPA" on business cards and uses these credentials when dealing with clients.

c.   CPA Alex Goodwin performs significant day-to-day bookkeeping services for Harper Corporation and supervises the work of the one part-time bookkeeper employed by Hadley Harper. This year, Harper wants to engage CPA Goodwin to perform an audit.

d.   CPA H. Poirot bought a home in 2022 and financed it with a mortgage loan from Farraway Savings and Loan. Farraway was merged into Nearby S&L, and Poirot became the manager in charge of the Nearby audit.

e.   Poirot inherited a large sum of money from old Mr. Giraud in 2023. Poirot sold his house, paid off the loan to Nearby S&L, and purchased a much larger estate. Nearby S&L provided the financing.

f.   Poirot and Mala Lemon (a local real estate broker) formed a partnership to develop apartment buildings. Lemon is a 20 percent owner and managing partner. Poirot and three partners in the accounting firm are limited partners. They own the remaining 80 percent of the partnership but have no voice in everyday management. Lemon obtained permanent real estate financing from Nearby S&L.

g.   Lemon won the lottery and purchased part of the limited partners' interests. She now owns 90 percent of the partnership and remains general partner while the CPAs remain limited partners with 10 percent interest.

h.   CPA Justin Shultz purchased a variable annuity insurance contract that offered the option to choose the companies in which this contract will invest. As directed, the insurance company purchased common stock in one of Shultz's audit clients.

LO B-4

B.53   Independence, Integrity, and Objectivity Cases. Read the following cases.

Required:

For each separate case, state whether the action or situation shows a violation of the AICPA Code of Professional Conduct; if so, explain why and cite the relevant rule or interpretation.

a.   Your client, Contrary Corporation, is very upset over the fact that your audit last year failed to detect an $800,000 inventory overstatement caused by employee theft and falsification of the records. The board discussed the matter and authorized its attorneys to explore the possibility of a lawsuit for damages.

b.   Contrary Corporation filed a lawsuit alleging negligent audit work, seeking $1 million in damages.

c.   In response to the lawsuit by Contrary, you decided to bring litigation against certain officers of the company alleging management fraud and deceit. You are asking for a damage judgment of $500,000.

d.   The Allright Insurance Company paid Contrary Corporation $700,000 under a fidelity bond covering an inventory theft by employees. Allright is suing your public accounting firm for damages on the grounds of negligent performance of the audit, claiming that a proper audit would have uncovered the theft sooner and the amount of loss would have been considerably less.

e.   Your audit client, Science Tech Inc., installed a cost accounting system devised by the consulting services department of your firm. The system failed to account properly for certain product costs (according to management), and the system had to be discontinued. Science Tech management was very dissatisfied and filed a lawsuit demanding return of the $10,000 consulting fee. The audit fee is normally about $50,000, and $10,000 is not an especially large amount for your firm. However, you believe that Science Tech management operated the system improperly. You are willing to do further consulting work at a reduced rate to make the system operate, but you are unwilling to return the entire $10,000 fee.

f. A group of dissident shareholders filed a class-action lawsuit against both you and your client, Amalgamated Inc., for $30 million. They allege there was a conspiracy to present misleading financial statements in connection with a recent merger.

g. CPA Ellis Lisa, a shareholder in the firm of Eden, Benjamin, and Block, P.C. (a professional accounting corporation), owns 25 percent of the common stock of Dove Corporation (not a client of Eden, Benjamin, and Block). This year, Dove purchased a 32 percent interest in Tale Company and is accounting for the investment using the equity method of accounting. The investment amounts to 11 percent of Dove's consolidated net assets. Tale Company has been an audit client of Eden, Benjamin, and Block for 12 years.

h. CPAs Mark and Ben Saliba are the father-and-son partners of Queens, LLP. They have a 12 percent joint private investment in ownership of the voting common stock of Hydra Corporation, which is not an audit client of Queens, LLP. However, the firm's audit client, Howard Company, owns 46 percent of Hydra, and this investment accounts for 20 percent of Howard's assets (using the equity method of accounting).

i. Drew Francie and Madison Brian, CPAs, regularly perform the audit of the First National Bank, and the firm is preparing for the audit of the financial statements for the year ended December 31, 2023.

(1) Two directors of the First National Bank became partners in Francie and Brian, CPAs, on July 1, 2023, resigning their directorship on that date. They will not participate in the audit.

(2) During 2023, the former controller of the First National Bank, now a partner in Francie and Brian, was frequently called on for assistance regarding loan approvals and the bank's minimum checking account policy. In addition, the former controller conducted a computer feasibility study for First National.

j. The Cather Corporation is indebted to a CPA for unpaid fees and has offered to give the CPA unsecured interest-bearing notes. Alternatively, Cather Corporation offered to give the CPA two shares of its common stock, after which 10,002 shares would be outstanding.

k. May Debra is not yet a CPA but is doing quite well in her first employment with a large public accounting firm. She has been on the job two years and has become an "experienced assistant." If she passes the CPA exam this year, she will be promoted to senior accountant. This month, during the audit of Row Lumber Company, Debra told the controller that she is remodeling an old house. The controller likes Debra and had a load of needed materials delivered to the house, billing Debra at a 70 percent discount—a savings over the normal cash discount of about $300. Debra paid the bill and was happy to have the materials that she otherwise could not afford on her meager salary.

l. Groaner Corporation is in financial difficulty. You are about to sign the report on the current audit when your firm's office manager informs you the audit fee for last year has not yet been paid.

m. CPA Aubrey Rowan prepared Goodwin's tax return this year. Last year, Goodwin prepared the return and paid too much income tax because the tax return erroneously contained "income" in the amount of $300,000 from an inheritance received when dear Aunt Martha died. This year, Goodwin sold the inherited property for $500,000. Goodwin argued with Rowan, who agreed to omit the sale of the property and the $200,000 gain this year on the grounds that Goodwin had already overpaid tax last year and this omission would make things even.

n. CPA Sage Watson is employed by Baker Street Company as its chief accountant. Lee Lestrade, also a CPA and the financial vice president of Baker, owns a trucking company that provides shipping services to Baker in a four-state area. The trucking company needs to buy 14 new trailers, and Lestrade authorized a payment to finance the purchase in the amount of $750,000. The related document cited repayment in terms of reduced trucking charges for the next seven years. Lestrade created the journal entry for this arrangement, charging the $750,000 to prepaid expenses. Watson and Lestrade signed the representation letter to Baker's external auditors and stated that Baker had no related-party transactions that were not disclosed to the auditors.

LO B-5

B.54 **Integrity and Objectivity.** Back in 1997, a disagreement arose between **Livent Inc.** and its auditor, Deloitte and Touche (currently Deloitte). Livent, which operated several theaters for live stage production, had sold the naming rights to one of its theaters to **AT&T** for $12.5 million. The agreement was oral, and one of the theaters was under construction. The auditors for Deloitte believed that only a portion of the deal should be included in revenue, but Livent wanted to book the entire $12.5 million. Livent retained Ernst & Young (EY) to provide an opinion on the transaction. EY's report indicated that all $12.5 million could be recorded as revenue. Deloitte hired **Price Waterhouse** (currently **PwC**) to review the transaction. Price Waterhouse agreed with EY and Livent, and Deloitte allowed Livent to book the $12.5 million. In 1998, Livent issued a series of press releases indicating the discovery of significant account irregularities and, later in 1998, declared bankruptcy.

Required:

Comment on the decision to engage EY and Price Waterhouse concerning the $12.5 million transaction. What would your position be on the need for other opinions? What would your position be for the disposition of the transaction?

LO B-5

B.55 **General and Technical Rule Cases.** Read the following cases. For each, state whether the action or situation shows a violation of the AICPA Code of Professional Conduct; if so, explain why and cite the relevant rule.

a. CPA Jerry Cheese became the new auditor for Python Insurance Company. Cheese knew a great deal about insurance accounting but had never conducted an audit of an insurance company. Consequently, Cheese hired CPA Tate Gilliam, who had six years of experience with the State Department of Insurance Audit. Gilliam managed the audit, and Cheese was the partner in charge.

b. CPA Mackenzie Palin practices public accounting and is a director of Comedy Company. Palin's firm performs consulting and tax services for Comedy. Palin prepared unaudited financial statements on Comedy's letterhead and submitted them to First National Bank in support of a loan application. Palin's accounting firm received a fee for this service.

c. CPA Ellery Idle audited the financial statements of Monty Corporation and gave an unmodified report. Monty is not a public company, so the financial statements did not contain the SEC-required reconciliation of deferred income taxes.

d. CPA Gwyn Chapman audited the financial statement of BTV Ltd. These financial statements contain capitalized leases that do not meet FASB criteria for capitalization. They resemble more closely the criteria for operating leases. The effect is material, adding $4 million to assets and $3.5 million to liabilities. However, BTV has a long experience with acquiring such property as its own assets after the "lease" terms end. Chapman and BTV management believe the financial statements should reflect the operating policy of the management instead of the technical requirements of the FASB. Consequently, the auditors' report explains the accounting and gives an unmodified opinion.

LO B-5

B.56 **Responsibilities to Clients' Cases.** Read the following cases. For each case, state whether the action or situation shows a violation or potential for violation of the AICPA Code of Professional Conduct, explain why, and cite the relevant rule.

a. CPA Sal Colt has discovered a way to eliminate most of the boring work of processing routine accounts receivable confirmations by contracting with the Cohen Mail Service. After the auditor has prepared the confirmations, Cohen stuffs them in envelopes, mails them, receives the return replies, opens the replies, and returns them to Colt.

b. Cadentoe Corporation, without consulting Jora Cramer, its CPA, has changed its accounting so that it is not in conformity with GAAP. During the regular audit engagement, Cramer discovers that the statements based on the accounts are so grossly misleading that they might be considered fraudulent. Cramer resigns the engagement after a heated argument. Cramer knows that the statements will be given to Sandy Panzer, a friend at the Last National Bank, and that Panzer is not a very astute reader of complicated financial statements. Two days later, Panzer calls Cramer and asks some general questions about Cadentoe's statements and remarks favorably on the very thing that is misrepresented. Cramer corrects the erroneous analysis and Panzer is very much surprised.

c. A CPA who had reached retirement age arranged to sell the practice to another certified public accountant. Their agreement called for the review of all audit documentation and business correspondence by the accountant purchasing the practice.

d. Martha Jacoby, CPA, withdrew from the audit of Harvard Company after discovering irregularities in Harvard's income tax returns. One week later, Jacoby received a phone call from Jake Henry, CPA, who explained that he had just been retained by Harvard Company to replace her. Henry asked Jacoby why she withdrew from the Harvard engagement, and she told him.

e. CPA Chen Wallace has two audit clients: Willingham Corporation owned by Jayden Willingham and Ward Corporation owned by Bailey Ward. Willingham Corp. sells a large proportion of its products to Ward Corp., which amounts to 60 percent of Ward Corp.'s purchases in most years. Willingham and Ward are also Wallace's tax clients as individuals. This year, while preparing Ward's tax return, Wallace discovered information that suggested Ward Corporation is in a failing financial position. In consideration of the fact that the companies and individuals are mutual clients, Wallace discussed Ward Corporation's financial difficulties with Willingham.

f. Ashley Fiddle, CPA, prepared an uncontested claim for a tax refund on Faddle Corporation's amended tax return. The fee for the service was 30 percent of the amount the IRS rules to be a proper refund. The claim was for $300,000.

g. After Faddle had won a $200,000 refund and Fiddle collected the $60,000 fee, Jordan Faddle, the president, invited Fiddle to be the auditor for Faddle Corporation.

h. Burgess Company engaged CPA Kim Philby to audit Maclean Corporation in connection with a possible initial public offering (IPO) of stock registered with the SEC. Burgess Company established a holding company named Cairncross Inc. and asked Philby to issue an engagement letter addressed to Cairncross stating that Cairncross would receive the auditors' report. Cairncross has no assets, and Philby agreed to charge a fee for the audit of Maclean only if the IPO is successful.

LO B-5

B.57 **Other Responsibilities and Practices Cases.** Read the following cases. For each, state whether the action or situation shows a violation or potential for violation of the AICPA Code of Professional Conduct; if so, explain why, and cite the relevant rule.

a. CPA Ron Stout completed a review of the unaudited financial statements of Wolfe Gifts. Arvida Wolfe was very displeased with the report. An argument ensued, and she told Stout never to darken her door again. Two days later, she telephoned Stout and demanded that he return (1) Wolfe's cash disbursement journal, (2) Stout's documentation schedule of adjusting journal entries, (3) Stout's inventory analysis documentation, and (4) all other documentation prepared by Stout. Wolfe had not yet paid her bill, so Stout replied that state law gave him a lien on all of the records and he would return them as soon as she paid his fee.

b. CPA O'Dell May teaches a CPA review course at the university. He needs problem and question material for students' practice, but the CPA examination questions and answers are no longer published. He pays $5 to students who take the exam for each question they can "remember" after taking the examination.

c. CPA Kelsey Blitz has been invited to conduct a course in effective tax planning for the City Chamber of Commerce. The chamber's president said a brochure would be mailed to members giving the name of Blitz's firm, Blitz's educational background and degrees held, professional society affiliations, and testimonials from participants in the course held last year comparing Blitz's excellent performance with other CPAs who have offered competing courses in the city.

d. CPA Reece Philby is a member of the state bar whose practice is a combination of law and accounting and is heavily involved in estate planning engagements. Philby's letterhead has the following: Member, State Bar of Illinois, and Member, AICPA.

e. The public accounting firm of Burgess & Maclean (B&M) has made a deal with Brit & Company, a firm of management consulting specialists, for mutual business advantage. B&M agreed to recommend Brit to clients who need management consulting services. Brit agreed to recommend B&M to clients who need improvements in their accounting systems. During the year, both firms would keep records of fees obtained by these mutual referrals. At the end of the year, Brit and B&M would settle the net differences based on a referral rate of 5 percent of fees.

f. Jack Robinson and Archie Robertson (both CPAs) are not partners, but they have the same office, the same employees, and a joint bank account and work together on audits. A letterhead they use shows both their names and the description "Members, AICPA."

g. CPA Lou Dewey retired from the two-person firm of Dewey & Cheatham (D&C). One year later, D&C merged practices with Howe & Company to form a regional firm under the name of Dewey, Cheatham, & Howe Company.

LO B-4

B.58 AICPA Independence and Other Services. The Independence Rule of the AICPA Code of Conduct cites several "other services" that do and do not impair audit independence.

Required:

Go to the AICPA website (www.aicpa.org), access the Code of Professional Conduct (ET 1.295) and find whether the following items impair independence (Yes) or do not impair independence (No) when performed for audit clients.

a. Post the client-approved entries to a client's trial balance.

b. Authorize the client's customer credit applications.

c. Use CPA's information-processing facilities to prepare the client's payroll.

d. Use CPA's information-processing facilities to generate checks for the client treasurer's signature.

e. Advise client management about the application or financial effect of provisions in an employee benefit plan contract.

f. Have emergency signature authority to cosign cash disbursement checks in connection with a client's hospital benefit plan.

g. As an investment advisory service, provide analyses of a client's investments in comparison to benchmarks produced by unrelated third parties.

h. Take temporary custody of a client's investment assets each time a purchase is made as a device to reduce cash float expense.

LO B-1

B.59 General Ethics. Is there any moral difference between a disapproved action in which you are caught and the same action that never becomes known to anyone else? Do many persons in business and professional society make a distinction between these two circumstances? If you respond that you do (or do not) perceive a difference while persons in business and professional society do not (or do), how do you explain the differences in attitudes?

LO B-2

B.60 Competition and Audit Proposals. Accounting firms are often asked to present "proposals" to companies' boards of directors. These proposals are comprehensive booklets, accompanied by oral presentations, telling about the firm's personnel, technology, special qualifications, and expertise in the hope of convincing the board to award the work to the firm.

Kourtney Dena has a new job as staff assistant to Selby Michael, chairman of the board of Granof Grain Company. The company has a policy of engaging new auditors every seven years. The board will hear oral proposals from 12 accounting firms. This is the second day of the three-day meeting. Dena's job is to help evaluate the proposals. During the first day of meetings, the proposal presented by Eden, Benjamin, and Block was clearly the best.

At the end of the day, Dena sees Michael's staff chief slip a copy of Eden, Benjamin, and Block's written proposal into an envelope. He then tells Dena to take it to a friend who works for Hunt and Hunt, a public accounting firm scheduled to make its presentation tomorrow, saying, "I told him we'd let him glance at the best proposal." Michael is absent from the meeting and will not return for two hours.

Required:

What should Dena do? What should CPA Hunt do if he receives the Eden, Benjamin, and Block proposal, assuming he has time to modify the Hunt and Hunt proposal before tomorrow's presentation?

LO B-2

B.61 Engagement Timekeeping Records. A time budget is always prepared for audit engagements. Numbers of hours are estimated for various segments of the work, for example, internal control evaluation, cash, inventory, and report review. Audit supervisors expect the work segments to be completed "within budget" and evaluate staff accountants' performance in part on the ability to perform audit work efficiently within budget. Jessica Sara is an audit manager who has worked hard to get promoted. She hopes to become a partner in two or three years. Finishing audits on time is heavily weighted on her performance evaluation. She assigned the cash audit work to Paul Ed, who has worked for the firm for 10 months. Ed hopes to get a promotion and salary raise this year. Twenty hours were budgeted for the cash work. Ed is efficient, but it took 30 hours to finish because the company had added seven new bank accounts. Ed was worried about his performance evaluation, so he recorded 20 hours for the cash work and put the other 10 hours under the internal control evaluation budget.

Required:

What do you think about Ed's resolution of his problem? Was his action a form of lying? What would you think of his action if the internal control evaluation work was presently under budget because it was not yet complete and another assistant was assigned to finish that work segment later?

LO B-2

B.62 **Audit Overtime.** The performance evaluation of all accountants is based in part on their ability to do audit work efficiently and within the time budget planned for the engagement. New staff accountants, in particular, usually have some early difficulty learning speedy work habits, which demand that no time be wasted. Cynthia Elizabeth started work for Julie and Jacob CPAs in September. After attending the staff training school, she was assigned to the Rising Sun Company audit. Her first work assignment was to complete the extensive recalculation of the inventory compilation using the audit test counts and audited unit prices for several hundred inventory items. Her time budget for the work was six hours. She started at 4 P.M. and was not finished when everyone left the office at 6 P.M. Not wanting to stay downtown alone, she took all necessary audit documentation home. She resumed work at 8 P.M. and finished at 3 A.M. The next day, she returned to the CPA offices, put the completed documentation in the file, and recorded six hours in the time budget/actual schedule. Her supervisor was pleased, especially about her diligence in taking the work home.

Required:

a. What do you think about Elizabeth's diligence and her understatement of the time she took to finish the work?

b. What would you think of the case if she had received help at home from her husband Paul?

c. What would you think of the case if she had been unable to finish and had left the work at home for her husband to finish?

LO B-5

B.63 **Conflict of Client's Interests.** Jon Williams, CPA, is in the middle of the real-life soap opera, *Taxing Days of Our Lives.*

The Cast of Characters

Oneway Corporation is Williams's audit and tax client. The three directors are the officers and the only three stockholders, each owning exactly one-third of the shares. President Raul Jack founded the company and is now nearing retirement. As an individual, he is also Williams's tax client. Vice President Jana Jill manages the day-to-day operations. She has been instrumental in increasing the business and its profits. Jill's individual tax work is done by CPA Corin Phil. Treasurer Chris Bill has been a long-term, loyal employee responsible for many innovative financial transactions and reports of great benefit to the business. He is Williams's close personal friend and an individual tax client.

The Conflict

President Jack discussed with CPA Williams the tax consequences to him as an individual of selling his one-third interest in Oneway Corporation to Vice President Jill. Later, meeting with Bill to discuss his individual tax problems, Williams learns that Bill fears that Jack and Jill will make a deal, put him in a minority position, and force him out of the company. Bill says, "Jon, we've been friends a long time. Please keep me informed about Jack's plans, even rumors. My interest in Oneway Corporation represents my life savings and my resources for the kid's college. Remember, you're little Otto's godfather."

Thinking back, Williams realized that Vice President Jill has always been rather hostile. Chances are that Phil would get the Oneway engagement if Jill acquires Jack's shares and controls the corporation. Nevertheless, Bill will probably suffer a great deal if he cannot learn about Jack's plans, and Williams's unwillingness to keep him informed will probably ruin their close friendship.

Later, on a Dark and Stormy Night

Williams ponders the problem. "Oneway Corporation is my client, but a corporation is a fiction—only a form. The stockholders personify the real entity, so they are collectively my clients, and I can transmit information among them as though they were one person. Right? On the other hand, Jack and Bill engage me for individual tax work, and information about one's personal affairs is really no business of the other. What to do? What to do?"

Required:

Give Williams advice about alternative actions, considering the constraints of the AICPA Code of Professional Conduct.

LO B-4

B.64 **AICPA Code of Professional Conduct.** Reread the Module B introduction about Scott London, CPA.

Required:

a. What code violations have occurred in this case?

b. What is the range of penalties that the PCAOB could levy against London? By the California State Board of Accountancy?

c. What do you think is the appropriate penalty?

LO B-6

B.65 **Disciplinary Action.** Go to the PCAOB website (www.pcaobus.org) and find settled disciplinary orders. Review the cases and the penalties indicated for various published cases.

Required:

For the case that you selected, what did the key audit professional do wrong, and what was the penalty assessed by the PCAOB for the wrongdoing?

LO B-6

B.66 **Ethics Case.**[14] Sandy Sally is a sole proprietor CPA who runs a successful practice with five employees. Several years ago, Sally purchased an office building and relocated the practice in about 20 percent of the space and rented out the remaining portion. Things went well for the first few months, but then two of Sally's tenants ran into financial difficulties and had to vacate the building. Sally was unable to quickly find new tenants for the space.

Sally struggled to keep current with the mortgage payments for a few months, but the loss of tenant income combined with the expense of operating a building became a large burden. Cash flow became very tight, and Sally stopped remitting the employee payroll taxes withheld.

The IRS filed a lien for nonpayment of employee payroll taxes, which was published in a local newspaper. A concerned citizen filed an ethics complaint.

Investigation found that, although the company had been delinquent in remitting employee payroll taxes and a federal tax lien had been filed, Sally had brought the tax liabilities into current status and produced evidence that the IRS lien had been released.

Required:

a. What code violation(s) have occurred in this case?

b. What is the range of penalties that could be levied against Sally?

c. What do you think is the appropriate penalty?

---

[14]The following information was obtained from the *Pennsylvania CPA Journal* and is adopted from a case brought before the Pennsylvania Ethics Committee; see R. J. DePasquale and C. Williams, "The CPA's Taxes and the Code of Ethics," *Pennsylvania CPA Journal,* Winter 2004.

MODULE C

Legal Liability

Good people do not need laws to tell them to act responsibly, while bad people will find a way around the laws.

Plato

Professional Standards References

Topic	AU-C/ISA Section	AS Section
Audit Documentation	230	1215
Letters for Underwriters and Certain Other Requesting Parties	920	6101
Filings under the Securities Act of 1933	925	4101

LEARNING OBJECTIVES

Module B on professional ethics dealt mainly with auditors' self-regulation. This module focuses on public regulation enforced by the Securities and Exchange Commission (SEC) and state and federal court systems of the United States. The discussion will help you understand auditors' legal liability for the professional work they perform.

Your objectives are to be able to:

LO C-1 Identify and describe auditors' exposure to lawsuits and loss judgments.

LO C-2 Specify the characteristics of auditors' liability under common law and cite specific case precedents.

LO C-3 Describe auditors' liability to third parties under statutory law.

LO C-4 Specify the civil and criminal liability provisions of the Securities Act of 1933.

LO C-5 Specify the civil and criminal liability provisions of the Securities Exchange Act of 1934.

LO C-6 Understand more current developments that affect auditors' liability to clients and third parties.

INTRODUCTION

PricewaterhouseCoopers (PwC) is one of the largest of the Big Four accounting firms, with revenues of more than $45 billion in 2021.[1] In 2018, a federal judge ruled PwC negligent in the audit of **Colonial Bank**, ordering the firm to pay $625 million to the **Federal Deposit Insurance Corp**. (FDIC) to offset some of the $5 billion the FDIC claims the bank's failure cost them as the insurer.[2]

PwC served as the auditor for Colonial Bank in the early 2000s, up through the collapse and closure of the bank in 2009. The collapse of Colonial Bank was a direct result of the fraud occurring at **Taylor, Bean & Whitaker**.

Taylor, Bean & Whitaker (TBW) was a top mortgage lending firm in the early 2000s; they were the largest privately held mortgage company in the country, employing more than 2,000 people. The problem was that TBW had recorded hundreds of millions of dollars in mortgages that did not exist. Colonial Bank bought many of those nonexistent mortgages from TBW. By 2009, Colonial Bank had purchased and recorded more than $500 million in nonexistent mortgage loans. According to the presiding judge in the 2018 proceedings, PwC was found negligent in part due to their failure to inspect the TBW loan files at Colonial for several years and their failure to inspect the supposed collateral backing of the loans.

In March 2019, the FDIC and PwC reached a settlement where, instead of $625 million, PwC would pay the FDIC $335 million, without admitting auditor negligence. The FDIC agreed to the settlement but noticeably without the support of former FDIC Chair and current board member Martin Gruenberg. According to Mr. Gruenberg, "The settlement announced. . . did not include a written admission of liability by PwC. Given PwC's professional negligence. . . . . I voted against authorizing the settlement without a written admission of liability by PwC."[3]

This is the second settlement PwC has made related to the Colonial Bank collapse. In 2016, the trustee of the TBW Bankruptcy Plan brought suit against PwC, seeking $5.5 billion in damages. Three weeks into the trial, the case was settled for an undisclosed amount.

Legal liability continues to be an important consideration and extremely costly for not just PwC, but for all auditors and accounting firms. Below is just a small sample of some of the larger settlements firms have made:[4]

- **Deloitte & Touche** (Deloitte): Taylor, Bean & Whitaker ($149.5 million in 2018), **Adelphia Communications** ($167.5 million in 2007), **Delphi** ($38 million in 2008), **Fortress Re** ($250 million in 2006), **General Motors** ($26 million in 2008), **Parmalat, SpA** ($159 million in 2007).

[1]*Global Annual Review 2021: The New Equation—Building trust—delivering sustained outcomes,* PricewaterhouseCoopers, 2021. www.pwc.com

[2]"PwC reaches $335 million settlement with FDIC over Taylor, Bean & Whitaker/Colonial Bank audits," *Housing Wire.com,* March 18, 2019, "PwC faces largest ever auditor malpractice damages verdict," *MarketWatch,* April 7, 2018.

[3]"PwC reaches $335 million settlement with FDIC over Taylor, Bean & Whitaker/Colonial Bank audits," *Housing Wire.com,* March 18, 2019; "PwC faces largest ever auditor malpractice damages verdict," *Market Watch.com,* April 7, 2018.

[4]"Deloitte to Be Latest to Settle in Accounting Scandals," *The Wall Street Journal,* April 26, 2005, p. B1; "Deloitte Pays Insurers More than $200 Million," *The Wall Street Journal,* January 6, 2006, p. C3; "Big Accounting Firms Still Pay for Scandals," *The Wall Street Journal,* January 13, 2007, p. B5; "PwC Sets Accord in Tyco Case," *The Wall Street Journal,* July 7–8, 2007, p. A3; "Deloitte to Pay $167.5M in Adelphia Case," *CFO.com,* August 6, 2007; "Deloitte to Pay $38 Million in Delphi Case," *CFO.com,* January 2, 2008; "PwC Zapped in $97.5 Million Settlement," *CFO.com,* October 6, 2008; "GM Reaches Settlement in Securities-Fraud Case," *The Wall Street Journal,* August 9, 2008, p. B5; "Xerox to Pay $670 Million to Settle Securities Suit," *The Wall Street Journal,* March 28, 2008, p. B3; "N.Y. Funds Reach Settlement with Countrywide, KPMG," *The Wall Street Journal* (Online), May 7, 2010;"$91M BDO Seidman Verdict Highlights Malpractice Lawsuits," *South Florida Business Journal,* February 4, 2011; "BDO Seidman Settles New York Lawsuit Over Le-Nature's Loan," *Bloomberg News,* April 5, 2012; "Ex-Parmalat Auditors Settle US Investor Lawsuit," Reuters, November 19, 2009; "Judge OKs $125 Mln New Century Lawsuit Settlement," Reuters, August 10, 2010. "Ernst & Young Settles Lehman Investor Lawsuit for $99 Million," *Accounting Today,* December 2, 2013; "Ernst & Young will pay $10 Million to End N.Y. Lehman Suit," *Housing Wire. com, Reuters, Accounting Today,* April 15, 2015; "PwC Settles MF Global Lawsuit for $65 Million,"*Accounting Today,* April 20, 2015, "Deloitte and Touche to pay $149.5 million in settlement over Taylor, Bean & Whitaker," *HousingWire.com,* February 28, 2018; "PwC to pay $335 million over failed audits of Alabama's Colonial Bank: U.S. regulator," *Reuters,* March 15, 2019. "Malaysia says auditor KPMG to pay $80 million in 1MBD settlement," *Reuters,* September 16, 2021. "Grant Thornton settles with AssetCo for 28m pounds," *Accounting Today UK,* October 6, 2020.

- **EY: Lehman Brothers** ($99 million in 2013), **HealthSouth** ($143 million in 2009), **Bank of New England** ($84 million in 2005), **Cendant** ($335 million in 1999).
- **KPMG: 1Malaysia Development Berhad** ($80.1 million in 2021), **Countrywide** ($24 million in 2010), **New Century** ($44.8 million in 2010), **Xerox** ($80 million in 2008).
- PricewaterhouseCoopers (PwC): **Colonial Bank** ($335 million in 2019), **MF Global** ($65 million in 2015), **American International Group (AIG)** ($97.5 million in 2008), **Tyco** ($225 million in 2007), **Amerco** ($50 million in 2004), **Safety-Kleen** ($48 million in 2005).
- **BDO: Le-Nature's Inc**. ($285 million in 2012), **Grand Court Lifestyles** ($91 million in 2011).
- **Grant Thornton: AssetCo** ($36 million in 2020), Parmalat ($6.5 million in 2009).

Legal issues can be costly in other ways too, as highlighted in the following Auditing Insight.

AUDITING INSIGHT   Not Just a U.S. Issue. . .

Legal ramifications for audit firms is not just an issue in the United States and from the looks of it, there may be a lot more on the line than just a hefty fine.

As a result of high profile accounting scandals in the UK, including the collapse of building contractor **Carillion Plc** and bakery chain **Patisserie Valerie Holdings Ltd,** UK lawmakers are demanding a drastic change in the landscape of the Big 4 accounting firms. In a report issued in early 2019 by the Business, Energy, and Industrial Strategy Committee of the UK Parliament, the committee claims they are "not confident in relying solely on the integrity of auditors to do the right thing in the face of conflicting interest."

Among the many recommendations in the report, the one that will have the biggest and most lasting impact is the recommendation that the Big 4 audit firms make a "full legal separation" of their auditing and consulting work. The Financial Reporting Council, the UK's audit regulator, is enforcing the recommendation, giving the Big 4 until mid-2024 to separate the two. The separation of auditing and consulting will result in significant changes to the business model for the Big 4 firms in the UK.

Sources: "U.K. lawmakers demand breakup of Big Four accounting firms," *Accounting Today.com,* April 3, 2019. "U.K. Regulator Orders Big Four to Separate Audit Practices by 2024," *The Wall Street Journal,* July 6, 2020, www.wsj.com.

THE LEGAL ENVIRONMENT

LO C-1
Identify and describe auditors' exposure to lawsuits and loss judgments.

How does legal liability arise? Consider the following schematic that summarizes the relationship between auditors and two key parties: the client and third-party users. As the graphic shows, auditors owe their clients a responsibility to conduct an audit in accordance with generally accepted auditing standards (GAAS) consistent with the terms in the *engagement letter* that serves as a contract between auditors and their clients.

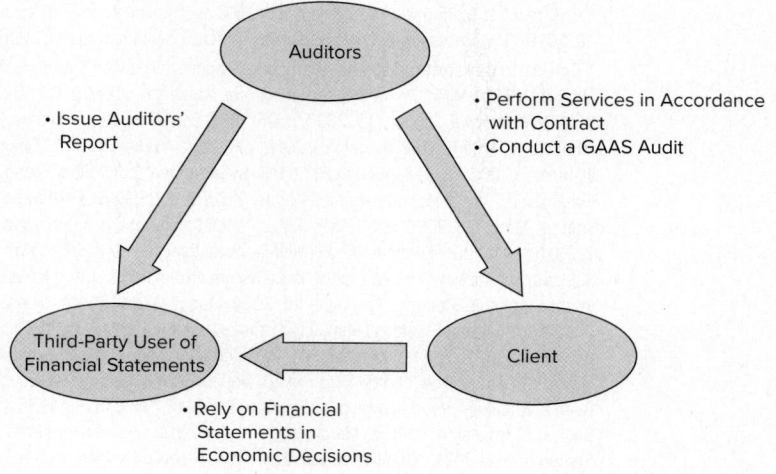

Clients may suffer losses related to these responsibilities for two reasons:

1. A breach of contract between auditors and the client (e.g., auditors' failure to complete the engagement by a specified deadline) may cause economic losses to the client resulting from delays, such as failing to receive funding through loans or investments, issuing its shares through a public offering at a less favorable price, or paying fines or penalties for missed deadlines.

2. Clients may suffer economic losses from acts of fraud or other misappropriation of assets by employees that a GAAS audit *should have identified.*

In either case, whether the client's loss is caused by the breach of contract or failure to exercise the appropriate level of professional care (substandard performance) by auditors, the client may seek legal action.

With respect to third-party users, auditors are responsible for issuing a report based on a GAAS audit that provides reasonable assurance that the financial statements on which these users base their economic decisions (lending decisions and investment decisions) are presented according to generally accepted accounting principles (GAAP). For third-party users, economic losses are either related to the client's inability to repay loans or other obligations or to a decline in the value of the user's investment in the client (in the form of a partnership interest or publicly traded shares of stock). If the user's loss is caused by reliance on financial statements and those financial statements were not presented according to GAAP, users may seek legal action against auditors.

The main defense for auditors is that they followed GAAS and performed their audits with due professional care. In many cases, lawsuits are brought against auditors not because they are necessarily at fault, but in the case of client failure, they are the only party with resources against which recovery can be made (the **"deep pockets" theory**). As Bill Thompson, president of **CPA Mutual Insurance Company of America,** noted, auditors are ". . . the last men standing—and they carry insurance, which, to the attorneys, equals deep pockets."[5]

Many users of auditors' reports expect auditors to detect and report fraud, theft, and illegal acts despite the fact that a GAAS audit cannot be expected to identify all items of this nature. Some financial statement users' expectations are very high; for this reason, an **expectation gap** often exists between the diligence that users expect and the diligence that auditors are able (and required) to provide. For example, in performing an audit on a multibillion-dollar corporation, auditors may choose to exclude testing transactions of $50,000, $100,000, $500,000, or more as immaterial. Certainly, a $1 million error in the financial statements of **Apple Inc.** (2021 revenues of $365.82 billion) would be immaterial to auditors. However, it would be difficult to convince an individual investor with $25,000 of retirement money invested that $1 million is not a significant amount of money. Clearly, many financial statement users believe auditors are looking at most, if not every, transaction; are evaluating each transaction, event, person, and department for fraud; and are certifying that financial statements are accurate. No auditors would, however, accept an engagement for which any of these objectives was required.

When auditors do not meet the expectations of clients or financial statement users, they may be held liable under common law or statutory law, depending on the nature of the action and relationship of the party to the auditors. **Common law** uses legal precedent to identify the fault and responsibility of parties when there is no violation of a written law or statute. When no legal precedent can be found, the judge follows a sense of justice or morality, considering the prevailing customs and moral standards. Common law liability against

[5]"Target: CPAS," *Accounting Today,* July 1, 2011, p. 53.

auditors is available to clients and nonshareholder third parties; the jurisdiction for common law actions is typically a court in the state in which the alleged action occurred.

Statutory law is based on laws passed by legislative bodies and compiled in federal, state, and municipal codes. In a statutory case, the primary basis for a decision is whether the party's actions have violated the law as written in the code. A lawsuit claiming that auditors did not perform the audit in an appropriate manner is a common law action. The primary statutory laws relevant to the audit of financial statements are laws governing the purchase and sale of securities; as a result, auditors' liability under statutory law is primarily to third-party shareholders for securities issued by public entities. The Securities Act of 1933 and Securities and Exchange Act of 1934 (discussed later in this module) provide U.S. district courts with jurisdiction for violations of these acts.

✔ REVIEW CHECKPOINTS

C.1 Identify the general responsibilities auditors owe to clients and third parties.

C.2 Distinguish between *common law* liability and *statutory law* liability. Which parties generally bring suit against auditors under common law and under statutory law liability?

LIABILITY UNDER COMMON LAW

LO C-2
Specify the characteristics of auditors' liability under common law, and cite specific case precedents.

Under common law, lawsuits may be brought against auditors based on the law of contracts or as tort actions for failure to exercise the appropriate level of professional care.

- **Breach of contract** is a claim that accounting or auditing services were not performed in the manner described in the contract. Although auditors may have contractual relationships with third parties, cases involving breach of contract are most frequently brought against auditors by their clients.
- **Tort** actions cover other civil complaints (e.g., fraud, deceit, injury) arising from auditors' failure to exercise the appropriate level of professional care (substandard performance). Clients or users of financial statements can bring tort actions against auditors.

Suits for damages under common law usually result when someone suffers a financial loss after relying on financial statements later found to be materially misstated. The popular press calls such unfortunate events *audit failures*. **Plaintiffs** in legal actions involving auditors (clients or third-party users of financial statements) generally assert all possible causes of action, including breach of contract, tort, deceit, fraud, and whatever else may be relevant to the claim.

Liability to Clients

Clients may bring a lawsuit for breach of contract and other tort actions. The relationship of direct involvement between parties to a contract is known as **privity of contract**. When privity exists, plaintiffs must demonstrate all of the following:

1. They suffered an economic loss.
2. Auditors did not perform in accordance with the terms of the contract (for breach of contract).
3. Auditors failed to exercise the appropriate level of professional care (for tort actions).
4. The breach of contract or failure to exercise the appropriate level of professional care caused the loss.

The first case in the United States involving an auditor and client dispute (*Smith v. London Assurance Corp.*) established auditors' obligation for breach of contract.

Legal Precedent

In addition to breach of contract, auditors may be liable to clients for tort liability. Three levels of substandard performance that may lead to tort liability include (listed from least severe to most severe)

1. **Ordinary negligence**: The unintentional breach of duty owed to another party because of a lack of reasonable care.
2. **Gross negligence**: The breach of duty owed to another party because of a lack of minimal care.
3. **Fraud**: The misrepresentation of facts that the individual knows to be false with the intention to deceive.

Because of the very close relationship between auditors and their clients, auditors have a high level of responsibility to their clients. This responsibility is to conduct an audit in accordance with GAAS; if auditors exhibit *ordinary negligence,* clients will typically prevail in their legal actions against auditors. (Auditors are also liable to their clients for *gross negligence* and *fraud.*)

Auditors' Defenses for Client Claims

Auditors may attempt to mitigate clients' claims by using one of the following three defenses:

1. Auditors exercised the appropriate level of professional care (tort) or performed the engagement in accordance with terms of the contract (breach of contract).
2. The client's economic loss was caused by a factor other than auditors' failure to exercise appropriate levels of professional care or breach of contract (the **causation defense**).
3. Actions on the part of the client were, in part, responsible for the loss (for example, failure of the client to establish effective internal control to prevent embezzlement losses). This is referred to as **contributory negligence** and is available to auditors in certain jurisdictions.

Liability to Third Parties

In the early part of the 20th century, parties other than clients had difficulty succeeding in lawsuits against auditors. Parties not in privity of contract have no cause of action for breach of contract. However, these parties can bring lawsuits against auditors for failure to exercise appropriate levels of professional care (tort action). In these cases, third parties suffer an economic loss because they relied on the audited financial statements and auditors' reports on those statements. Recall that the three levels of failure to exercise the appropriate level of professional care that have emerged through various cases are *ordinary negligence* (lack of reasonable care), *gross negligence* (lack of minimal care), and *fraud* (intention to deceive).

It has been well established that auditors are liable to all third parties for levels of performance representing gross negligence and fraud. However, auditors' liability to various

667

third parties for ordinary negligence has been debated and has changed significantly over time. Furthermore, the extent of liability for ordinary negligence to third parties varies by jurisdiction (state in which the action is brought). As a result, both auditors and third-party users carefully monitor the evolution of auditors' liability to third parties for ordinary negligence through common law precedents. This is particularly important because it is relatively easier for third parties to demonstrate ordinary negligence compared to either gross negligence or fraud.

To bring a suit against auditors under common law, third parties must demonstrate all of the following:

1. They suffered an economic loss (normally, a decline in the value of an investment or failure to be repaid for a loan or other obligation).
2. The auditors failed to exercise the appropriate level of professional care (ordinary negligence, gross negligence, or fraud).
3. The financial statements contained a material misstatement.
4. The loss was caused by reliance on the materially misstated financial statements.

One early and important case involving auditors' liability to third parties is known as *Ultramares*. The *Ultramares Corp. v. Touche* opinion (discussed in detail in the Legal Precedent) expressed the view that, if auditors' failures to exercise the appropriate level of professional care were so great as to constitute gross negligence, grounds might exist for concluding that auditors had engaged in **constructive fraud**, which is characterized by reckless disregard for the truth. The significance of *Ultramares* is that it established an obligation to third parties and others not in privity with auditors for gross negligence and fraud. *Ultramares* has been cited in numerous third-party common law cases against auditors.

Legal Precedent

ULTRAMARES CORP. V. TOUCHE (1931)

In 1924, Touche, Niven & Co. was engaged to audit the 1923 balance sheet of **Fred Stern & Co.**, a rubber importer. Based on the audited balance sheet, **Ultramares Corp.**, a factoring business, made numerous loans to Fred Stern & Co. In January 1925, Fred Stern & Co. went bankrupt and was unable to repay these loans to Ultramares (this represented the economic loss), and Ultramares brought suit against Touche for negligent performance. Although the New York court of appeals denied Ultramares' negligence claim, the court *did not assert that privity of contract was a requirement for third parties to sue auditors*. As a result, this case recognized auditors' potential liability to third parties and the right of third parties to bring suits against auditors.

In part, the court's decision established criteria for auditors' liability to third parties for constructive fraud. To do so, third parties must prove all of the following:

1. There was a misrepresentation of a material fact (usually in the financial statements).
2. The misrepresentation was made consciously or without adequate knowledge to determine whether it was true.

3. There was knowledge (*scienter*) and intent to induce action in reliance on the information.
4. The damaged party justifiably relied on the misrepresentation.
5. There was resulting damage.

The court held that auditors could be liable when they did not have sufficient information (audit evidence) to lead to an opinion. Therefore, the auditors' opinion is deceitful when auditors claim to have knowledge that they do not possess. The court also wrote that when the degree of negligence is gross, it may amount to a constructive fraud, and auditors could be liable to a third-party user.

Case conclusion: Ultramares contributed to the development of common law liability to third parties by establishing that

1. Third parties not in privity with auditors can bring suit against auditors.
2. Auditors may be liable to parties who are not in privity in cases representing constructive fraud (gross negligence) or fraud.
3. Auditors are generally not liable for ordinary negligence to parties who are not in privity.

The *Ultramares* decision was upheld in *State Street Trust Co. v. Ernst,* in which the courts identified auditors' liability to third parties for gross negligence in the following opinion:

[Auditors], however, may be liable to third parties, even where there is lacking deliberate or active fraud.... A representation certified as true to the knowledge of the accountants when knowledge there is none, a reckless misstatement, or an opinion based upon grounds so flimsy, . . . In other words, heedlessness and reckless disregard of consequence may take the place of deliberate intention.[6]

Although the *Ultramares* case opened the door for lawsuits by third parties in which fraud or constructive fraud was present, for many years only parties that had privity of contract (typically, the client) could bring legal action against auditors for ordinary negligence. **Primary beneficiaries** are third parties known by name to the auditors for whose primary benefit the audit or other accounting service is performed (also referred to as *near privity*). In some legal jurisdictions, a beneficiary must be named in the contract; in other jurisdictions, the beneficiary need only be identified to auditors prior to or during the engagement. For example, an accounting firm may be informed that the report is needed for a bank loan application at the First National Bank; in this case, First National Bank is a primary beneficiary because it is known *by name* to auditors. Many cases (e.g., *CIT v. Glover*) indicate that proving ordinary negligence may be sufficient to hold auditors liable for damages to primary beneficiaries. *Credit Alliance v. Arthur Andersen* identified specific criteria that must be met for primary beneficiaries to prevail against auditors for ordinary negligence.

Legal Precedent

CREDIT ALLIANCE V. ARTHUR ANDERSEN (1985)

In this landmark case, **Credit Alliance** (a financial services firm) provided financing for equipment to **L.B. Smith Inc.** In 1978, Credit Alliance advised Smith that any future extensions of credit would require audited financial statements, which Smith subsequently provided for fiscal years 1976 through 1979. In 1980, L.B. Smith filed for bankruptcy and was unable to repay Credit Alliance. (This represented the economic loss.) The New York court of appeals provided a three-pronged test for Credit Alliance's right to sue:

1. Auditors were aware that a particular party intended to rely on the auditors' opinion and financial statements.

2. The third party was specifically identified.
3. Some action by the auditors showed that they had acknowledged the third-party's identification and intent to rely on the opinion and financial statements.

This test has been used as precedent in many cases in determining whether the third party was an intended beneficiary of the auditors' work.

Case conclusion: In many jurisdictions, third parties may bring suit against auditors for ordinary negligence even if they are not in privity of the contract. However, they must meet the three-pronged test established by the New York court of appeals.

In many jurisdictions, auditors also may be liable for ordinary negligence to **foreseen parties**. In these jurisdictions, the *restatement of torts* doctrine specifies that auditors are liable if they are aware that the auditors' opinion and financial statements are to be used by some third party. Auditors need not know the exact identity of the third party but are presumed to owe a duty to persons who could reasonably be expected to rely on the auditors' work. For example, if a client informs auditors that it will be using audited financial statements to obtain financing but does not identify any specific banks, under the doctrine of *restatement of torts,* any bank that uses the audited financial statements in making lending decisions may have legal standing to sue auditors for ordinary negligence. *Rusch Factors v. Levin* concluded that auditors were liable to a lender (**Rusch Factors**) because the auditors were aware that the financial statements were to be shown to potential lenders despite the fact that the auditors were not aware of their actual identity. *Fleet National Bank v. Gloucester Co.* affirmed auditors' obligation to third parties who are foreseen parties but are not known by name to auditors (and, therefore, do not qualify as primary beneficiaries).

[6]*State Street Trust C. v. Ernst,* I278N.Y. 105, 15 N.E. 2d 415 (1938)

Legal Precedent

FLEET NATIONAL BANK V. GLOUCESTER CO. (1994)

Fleet Bank relied on financial statements audited by **Tonneson** when making loans to **Gloucester.** Upon Gloucester's default (the economic loss), Fleet brought suit against Tonneson, alleging that the audited financial statements were the basis for making the loans. Fleet made the following allegations: (1) Tonneson knew about Fleet Bank's loans to Gloucester, (2) Tonneson reviewed the loan agreements between Gloucester and Fleet Bank, (3) Tonneson knew the loan agreements required submission of audited financial statements, and (4) Tonneson believed and expected

Gloucester would provide the audited financial statements to Fleet Bank. The U.S. District Court in Massachusetts found in favor of Fleet, adopting the *restatement of torts* approach.

Case conclusion: Auditors may be liable to third parties for ordinary negligence even if the third party is not named in the engagement contract. If auditors have knowledge that financial statements will be provided to third parties for the purpose of making a decision, in some jurisdictions auditors may be liable to such a third party.

Finally, in other jurisdictions, auditors may be liable to reasonably **foreseeable parties**. These parties (sometimes referred to as *members of an unlimited class)* include creditors, investors, or potential investors whose decisions normally rely on audited financial statements and opinions on those financial statements. If auditors are reasonably able to *foresee* a limited class of potential users (e.g., local banks, regular suppliers) of their reports, liability may be imposed for ordinary negligence. This, however, is an uncertain area, and liability in a particular case depends entirely on the unique facts and circumstances of the case and the jurisdiction of the legal action. This is the most liberal interpretation of the third-party liability and is used in only two states: Mississippi and Wisconsin.[7] *Rosenblum Inc. v. Adler* established auditors' liability for ordinary negligence to individuals who are "reasonably foreseeable."

Legal Precedent

ROSENBLUM INC. V. ADLER (1983)

Giant Stores Corporation acquired the retail catalog showroom business owned by **Rosenblum,** giving stock in exchange for the business. Fifteen months after the acquisition, Giant Stores declared bankruptcy, significantly reducing the value of the shares received by Rosenblum in the acquisition (the economic loss). **Adler** had audited Giant Stores' financial statements and issued unmodified opinions on those financial statements for several prior years. These financial statements were later revealed to be misstated as a result of a fraudulent scheme perpetrated by Giant Stores. Rosenblum subsequently brought suit against the auditor (Adler) to attempt to recover the loss resulting from the decline in the value of the shares.

In finding for Rosenblum on certain motions, the New Jersey Supreme Court held, "Independent auditors have a duty of care to all persons whom the auditor should *reasonably foresee* [emphasis added] as recipients of the statements from the company for proper business purposes, provided

that the recipients rely on those financial statements. . . . It is well recognized that audited financial statements are made for the use of third parties who have no direct relationship with the auditor. . . . Auditors have responsibility not only to the client who pays the fee but also to investors, creditors, and others who rely on the audited financial statements."

Case conclusion: In some jurisdictions, auditors may be liable for ordinary negligence to a large class of users that are reasonably foreseeable but may not be known to the auditor at the time of the audit.

Additional note: Although the opinion in the *Rosenblum* case is an excellent example of a court opinion that extends liability to foreseeable parties, it should be noted that subsequent legislation (1995) in New Jersey has moved that state to a *near privity* standard. However, the *Rosenblum* opinion has been used as precedent in other states. This is an example of how state law can change and how court decisions can provide an impetus to legislatures to enact new law.

It should be noted that these classes of third parties are based on legislation and legal precedents. For example, for primary beneficiaries, auditors know both the name of the party and the intended use of the financial statements; for foreseen parties, auditors know the financial statements will be used by a certain type of third party; for foreseeable parties, auditors *should be* aware that the financial statements *could be used* by third parties.

[7]A. Reinstein, C. J. Pacini, B. P. Green, "Examining the Current Legal Environment Facing the Public Accounting Profession: Recommendations for a Consistent U.S. Policy," *Journal of Accounting, Auditing & Finance,* 2020, pp. 3–25.

For example, if Grand Bank is relying on audited financial statements to decide whether to provide a loan to Prize Company, Grand Bank's classification as a third party could be as follows:

- Grand Bank would be a primary beneficiary if Prize Company informed the auditors that the audited financial statements would be used to obtain a loan from Grand Bank and Grand Bank was identified to the auditors by name.
- Grand Bank would be a foreseen party if Prize Company informed the auditors that the audited financial statements would be used to obtain a loan but did not specify the name of a third party.
- Grand Bank would be a foreseeable party in almost any situation because audited financial statements are commonly used to obtain a loan.

In all jurisdictions, auditors are generally liable for acts of gross negligence and fraud; auditors' liability to third parties for ordinary negligence depends upon the doctrine in effect in the jurisdiction in which auditors practice. Clearly, limiting auditors' liability for acts of ordinary negligence to only primary beneficiaries is most advantageous to auditors, and exposing them to liability for ordinary negligence to foreseeable parties is most disadvantageous to auditors. One study[8] classified various jurisdictions (as of 2017) as follows:

- *Privity or near privity.* Arkansas, Connecticut, Idaho, Illinois, Indiana, Kansas, Louisiana, Maryland, Nebraska, New Jersey, New York, Pennsylvania, Utah, Virginia, Wyoming.
- *Restatement of torts* (foreseen). Alabama, Alaska, Arizona, California, Colorado, Delaware, Florida, Georgia, Hawaii, Iowa, Kentucky, Maine, Massachusetts, Michigan, Minnesota, Missouri, Montana, Nevada, New Hampshire, New Mexico, North Carolina, North Dakota, Ohio, Oklahoma, Oregon, Rhode Island, South Carolina, South Dakota, Tennessee, Texas, Vermont, Washington, West Virginia.
- *Reasonably foreseeable.* Mississippi, Wisconsin.

Auditors' legal liability to third parties as established by these and other cases under common law is summarized in Exhibit C.1.

EXHIBIT C.1   Summary of Auditors' Liability to Third Parties under Common Law

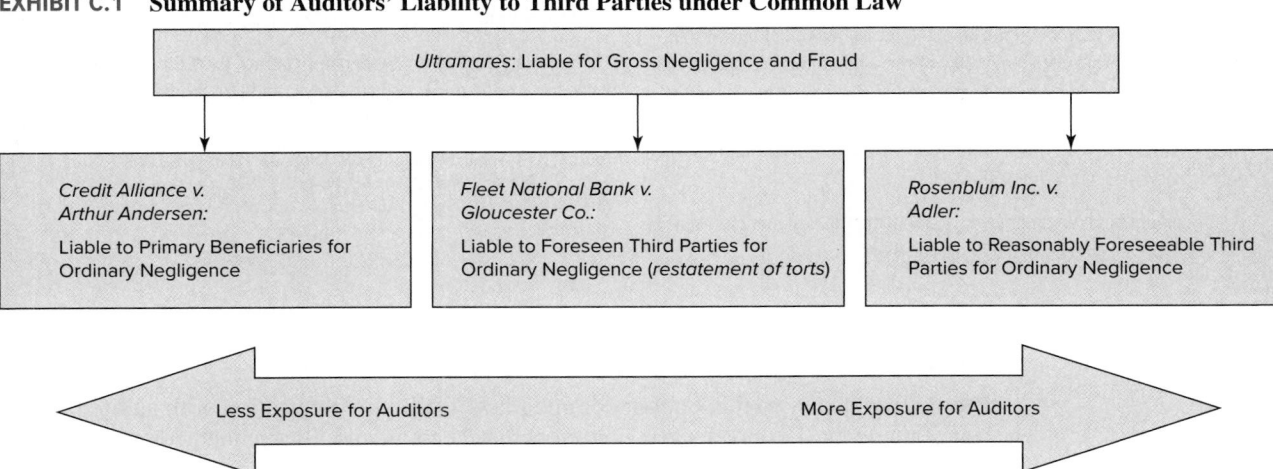

[8]A. Reinstein, C. J. Pacini, B. P. Green, "Examining the Current Legal Environment Facing the Public Accounting Profession: Recommendations for a Consistent U.S. Policy," *Journal of Accounting, Auditing & Finance,* 2020, pp. 3–25.

Auditors' Defenses for Third-Party Claims

Auditors can defend a common law action by presenting arguments and evidence to mitigate third-party plaintiffs' claims and evidence. Assuming that the plaintiff has demonstrated an economic loss and materially misstated financial statements, defenses available to auditors against third parties include the following:

1. The third party did not have appropriate standing to sue in that jurisdiction (for example, bringing suit for ordinary negligence if the appropriate relationship between auditors and third party does not exist). Recall that auditors' liability to third parties for ordinary negligence differs significantly depending on the jurisdiction in which the action is brought.

2. The third party's loss was caused by events other than the financial statements and auditors' examination (causation defense). For example, the failure of an entity (and losses incurred by parties providing capital to that entity) may result from poor business practices and decisions, not misstated financial statements.

3. Auditors' work was performed in accordance with professional standards (e.g., GAAS for audits of financial statements), which is generally interpreted to mean that auditors were not negligent (ordinary negligence).

Note that these are similar to defenses available against clients, except for the unavailability of the contributory negligence defense in cases brought by third parties. The Auditing Insight below discusses how more junior auditors are not immune to legal liability issues and provides some simple proactive measures that can be done to help defend against third-party claims.

AUDITING INSIGHT   Why should you care about legal liability?

As a junior auditor, you might think that legal liability issues are far removed from where you currently are in your career. You couldn't be more wrong. In September 2021, the Financial Reporting Council (FRC), the UK's audit regulator, filed a complaint against **KPMG** and several former employees for their role in the **Carillion PLC** financial statement fraud. For the first time, the FRC named several junior auditors in their complaint. Even though it is the junior auditors that do the majority of the field work during an audit, the engagement partner has ultimate responsibility for the quality of the audit and therefore junior auditors are typically protected from legal liability. But clearly, that is not always the case. So, what can you do as a new auditor to defend yourself and your team from claims or, even better, avoid them altogether? Here are a few things that will help:

- Document, and document well. Inadequate documentation results in a lack of evidence that you did the work.

- Maintain professional skepticism, and don't get too comfortable with your client.

- Avoid the notation "SALY"—same as last year—it might be perceived that you have done nothing.

- Don't leave differences unresolved; investigate them and perform procedures to assure there is not a material error. And don't forget to document it.

Those are just a few things you can do. As a firm, strong client acceptance procedures and carefully crafted engagement letters can help avoid the legal liability issues altogether.

Source: "U.K. Tribunal Against KPGM Raises Questions Over Liability of Junior Auditors," *The Wall Street Journal,* January 30, 2022, www.wsj.com. "Advice from the experts: Defending audit claims," *Journal of Accountancy,* January 1, 2021, (online source).

Liability for Compilation and Review Services

People find it easy to think about common law liability in connection with audited financial statements. Do not forget, however, that accountants also render compilation and review services and are associated with the resultant *unaudited* financial information. Users expect public accountants to perform these services in accordance with professional standards, and courts can impose liability for accounting work found to be substandard. Accountants have been assessed damages for work on such statements, as shown in the *1136 Tenants' Corporation v. Max Rothenberg & Co.* case. In this case, the court concluded that accountants engaged to perform "write-up" (i.e., compilation) work had a duty to inform clients of indicators of fraud that were identified during the engagement.

One significant risk involved with compilation and review engagements is that the client may fail to understand the nature of the service being given. To avoid misunderstandings, accountants should have a discussion and use an engagement letter to explain clearly to the client that a compilation engagement does not involve gathering sufficient appropriate evidence and is lesser in scope than a review engagement. Similarly, a review service should be explained in terms of being less extensive than an audit engagement conducted in accordance with GAAS. Clear understandings at the outset (along with clearly worded engagement letters) can enable accountants and clients to avoid later disagreements. In *Iselin v. Landau* (1992), the court decided that the lack of an opinion on reviewed financial statements precluded the third party (**William Iselin & Company**) from bringing a lawsuit against the auditors (**Mann Judd Landau**) because of losses suffered from the bankruptcy of one of Iselin's customers. (Mann Judd Landau had performed a review engagement on the financial statements of Iselin's customer.)

☑ REVIEW CHECKPOINTS

C.3   For what type of actions can clients bring suit against auditors under common law? What must clients prove prior to bringing suit in each case?

C.4   In terms of tort liability, what level of responsibility do auditors owe clients under common law?

C.5   What must third parties prove in a common law action seeking recovery of damages from auditors?

C.6   What legal theory is derived from the *Ultramares* decision? Can auditors rely on the *Ultramares* decision today?

C.7   Define and explain *privity, primary beneficiary, foreseen party,* and *foreseeable party* in terms of the degree of failure to exercise the appropriate level of professional care on the part of auditors that would trigger the liability.

C.8   What defenses are available to auditors against suits brought by clients under common law? Against suits brought by third parties under common law?

C.9   What additional defenses can accountants use in lawsuits related to compilation and review engagements?

LIABILITY UNDER STATUTORY LAW

LO C-3
Describe auditors' liability to third parties under statutory law.

Auditors can be liable to individuals when they violate a specific law or statute when performing professional services; this is referred to as *statutory liability.* Several federal statutes provide sources of potential liability for auditors, including the Federal False Statements Statute, the Federal Mail Fraud Statute, the Federal Conspiracy Statute, the Securities Act of 1933 (Securities Act), the Securities Exchange Act of 1934 (Securities Exchange Act), and the Sarbanes–Oxley Act. Federal securities regulation in the United States was enacted in the 1930s not only as a reaction to the events of the early years of the Great Depression but also as a culmination of attempts at "blue-sky" regulation by states.[9] The Securities Act and the Securities Exchange Act require registrants to disclose important financial and nonfinancial information required for making informed investment decisions. The securities acts and the SEC operate for the protection of investors and for the facilitation of orderly capital markets. Even so, no federal government agency, including the SEC, rules on the *quality* of investments. The securities acts have been characterized as "truth-in-securities" law. Their

---

[9]The term *blue sky* comes from a state judge's remark during a securities fraud case: "These securities have no more substance than a piece of blue sky."

spirit favors the otherwise uninformed investing public, and caveat vendor—let the seller beware of violations—is applied to the issuer.

As the following graphic shows, auditors are exposed to liability under the Securities Act and the Securities Exchange Act when investors purchase or sell securities ([1] in the graphic). If an economic loss is suffered [2] and if the financial statements contain a material misstatement [3], auditors may be held liable for failure to detect the material misstatement.

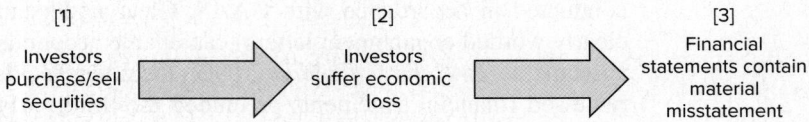

[1]
Investors purchase/sell securities

[2]
Investors suffer economic loss

[3]
Financial statements contain material misstatement

Because of the availability of class action litigation and the wide dissemination and use of financial information filed with the SEC, litigation against auditors under the Securities Act and Securities and Exchange Act is a big concern for auditors. The following sections discuss auditors' liability under these acts in more detail.

☑ REVIEW CHECKPOINT

C.10   How does auditors' liability under statutory law arise?

THE SECURITIES ACT OF 1933 (SECURITIES ACT)

LO C-4
Specify the civil and criminal liability provisions of the Securities Act of 1933.

The Securities Act of 1933 regulates the initial issuance of securities by registrants to the investing public through a market (including **initial public offerings [IPOs]**). The Securities Act provides that no person may lawfully buy, sell, offer to buy, or offer to sell any security by means of interstate commerce unless a **registration statement** is *effective* (a legal term essentially meaning *filed and accepted by the SEC*). A registration statement is a set of documents filed with the SEC prior to the offering of securities. An important component of the registration statement is a **prospectus**, which is a legal document offering securities for sale and includes significant information about the issuing entity, including its historical financial statements and other necessary disclosures. Certain exemptions exist for limited offerings, offerings by small investors, and offerings involving financially sophisticated investors; these exemptions can be found in section 3, section 4, and Regulation D of the Securities Act.

The general point concerning the Securities Act is that, with some minor exceptions, *all* issuances of securities to the public must be registered with the SEC. Importantly for the auditor, the Securities Act requires that the registration statement include financial statements and required disclosures that ". . . shall be certified by an independent public or certified accountant"; this language requires an audit examination. Auditors are required not only to audit the financial statements as of the most recent date of the financial statements but also to ensure that these statements are fairly stated up to the date the registration statement becomes effective, which could possibly be up to one year beyond the date of the financial statements. This audit requirement provides the basis for auditors' liability to investors under the Securities Act.

Section 11: Civil Liability

Section 11 of the Securities Act is of great interest to auditors because of the duties and responsibilities it establishes. This section discusses the principal criteria defining civil liabilities under the statute.

Section 11. Securities Act of 1933

The following excerpts from Section 11 are of particular importance in identifying the responsibilities of auditors under this Act.

Section 11(*a*): . . . any person acquiring such security [in a registered offering] . . . may sue:

- Every person who signed the registration statement.
- Every person who was a director of . . . or partner in, the issuer.
- Every *accountant,* engineer, or appraiser.
- Every underwriter with respect to such security.

Section 11(*b*): Notwithstanding the provisions of subsection (a), no person, other than the issuer, shall be liable as provided therein who shall sustain the burden of proof that . . . as regards any part of the registration statement purporting to be made upon his authority as an expert . . . he had, after reasonable investigation, reasonable grounds to believe . . . that the statements therein were true and that there was no omission to state a material fact.. . .

Although section 11(*a*) notes that a number of parties involved in the registration and sale process might be liable to persons acquiring securities, section 11(*b*) generally limits the liability to the issuers of securities with some exceptions. Because auditors are considered to be the "experts" regarding the fairness of the financial statements and must perform a "reasonable investigation" (an audit in accordance with GAAS), section 11(*b*) is of great importance to auditors. This requirement imposes liability for auditors for acts representing *ordinary negligence.*

Auditors commonly provide assurance to underwriters, who act as intermediaries between the offering entity and investing public by purchasing securities for investment or resale. Auditors provide **comfort letters** to underwriters that address, among other information, the independence of auditors and the fairness of the registrant's financial statements.

Section 11 includes two other very important implications for auditors. First, reviewing the first two words in section 11(*a*), "*any person*" [emphasis added] may bring suit against auditors. Essentially, the Securities Act treats *all* persons as being *reasonably foreseeable* and holds auditors liable to these persons. In addition, section 11 shifts the major burden of proof from the plaintiff (investor) to the auditors; essentially, plaintiffs must prove each of the following:

1. They suffered an economic loss.
2. The financial statements contained a material misstatement.

Recall that under common law liability, plaintiffs had to also allege and prove some level of failure to exercise the appropriate level of professional care and that the loss was caused by reliance on the misstated financial statements. Thus, under the Securities Act, the plaintiff is *not* required to demonstrate that the misstated financial statements caused the loss; the burden of proof regarding professional care rests with auditors. Section 11 has the following major implications for auditors:

- Auditors are liable for ordinary negligence.
- Auditors have potential liability to a large class of parties (investors in securities).
- Auditors (not others) have the burden of proof, in this case, proving that a reasonable investigation under section 11(*b*) was conducted.

The final implication is particularly important because it presumes that auditors are "guilty until proven innocent" and has increased auditors' exposure to investors. However, section 11 was written with the protection of the investing public in mind, not the protection of the expert auditors. The first significant court case under section 11 was *Escott v. BarChris Construction Corporation.*

Legal Precedent

Auditors' Defenses under the Securities Act

Section 11 provides two possible defenses to auditors, assuming that purchasers of securities are able to demonstrate they suffered a loss and the financial statements are materially misstated. Note that these defenses are similar to two defenses available to auditors for actions brought by clients and third parties under common law:

1. The *"due diligence" defense* provides that auditors who can prove they conducted a "reasonable investigation" will not be held liable under the Securities Act. A reasonable investigation can ordinarily be shown by conducting an audit in accordance with GAAS.

2. Under the *causation defense,* if auditors can prove that all or part of the plaintiffs' losses were caused by something other than the materially misstated financial statements included in the registration statement, they are not required to pay all or part of the damages. This defense may create some imaginative "other reasons." In the *BarChris* case, at least one plaintiff had purchased securities *after* the company had gone bankrupt. This claim was settled out of court.

Section 13: Statute of Limitations

Section 13 of the Securities Act requires any suits to be brought within one year after discovery of the materially misstated statement or omission or within three years after the public offering. These limitations restrict auditors' liability exposure to a determinable time span. In many cases, the statute of limitations is a viable defense available to auditors. Although Sarbanes–Oxley generally extended the statute of limitations to within two years of discovery and five years after the action for situations involving fraud, some questions exist as to whether these extended limitations apply to the Securities Act, particularly in cases not involving fraud.

Section 17: Antifraud

Section 17 of the Securities Act is the antifraud section. This section makes it unlawful to "use the mails or instruments of transportation in interstate commerce" in an effort to defraud others. As with section 11, plaintiffs are not required to demonstrate reliance on the fraudulent information or that the fraudulent information resulted in their loss. Therefore, the burden of proof still rests with auditors.

Section 24: Criminal Liability

Section 24 sets forth the criminal penalties imposed by the Securities Act. Criminal penalties are characterized by monetary fines, prison terms, or both. The key words in section 24 are "willful" violation and "willfully" causing materially misstated statements to be filed. Thus, although auditors have civil liability to third parties under section 11 in cases in which ordinary negligence can be demonstrated (failure to conduct a GAAS audit), criminal penalties are possible under the 1933 Securities Act only for instances in which auditors act with knowledge of the materially misstated financial statements (fraud and, perhaps, gross negligence). Section 24 establishes these penalties for fines at $10,000 and imprisonment for up to five years. The *United States v. Benjamin* case is an example of how auditors may be found criminally liable under the Securities Act.

Legal Precedent

UNITED STATES V. BENJAMIN (1964)

The judgment in this case resulted in the conviction of auditors for willingly conspiring by use of interstate commerce to sell unregistered securities and to defraud investors in the sale of securities in violation of section 24 of the Securities Act. The auditors had prepared pro forma balance sheets and claimed that use of the words *pro forma* absolved them of responsibility. The auditors also claimed they did not know their reports would be used in connection with securities sales. The court found otherwise, showing that the auditors did in fact know about the use of their reports and that certain statements about asset values and acquisitions were materially misstated. The court made two significant findings: (1) The willfulness requirements of section 24 may be proved by showing that due diligence would have revealed the materially misstated statements, and (2) use of limiting words such as *pro forma* does not justify showing false ownership of assets in any kind of financial statements.

☑ REVIEW CHECKPOINTS

C.11 What type of transactions are governed by the Securities Act?

C.12 What is a *registration statement*? How does the registration statement introduce potential liability to auditors under the Securities Act?

C.13 How is section 11 of the Securities Act different from the legal environment that exists under common law?

C.14 What must the plaintiff prove in a suit under section 11 of the Securities Act seeking recovery of damages from auditors? What defenses are available to auditors in this situation?

C.15 Describe the *due diligence* and *causation* defenses available to auditors under the Securities Act.

C.16 What liability exposure for auditors is found in the Securities Act in (a) section 17 and (b) section 24?

C.17 According to the *BarChris* decision, how did auditors violate generally accepted auditing standards?

THE SECURITIES EXCHANGE ACT OF 1934 (SECURITIES EXCHANGE ACT)

LO C-5
Specify the civil and criminal liability provisions of the Securities Exchange Act of 1934.

The Securities Exchange Act regulates daily trading of securities and requires most entities whose securities are traded in interstate commerce to register and file pertinent information with the SEC. Entities having total assets of $10 million or more and 500 or more stockholders are required to register under the Securities Exchange Act. The purpose of these size and share criteria is to define securities in which there is a significant public interest. (These criteria are subject to change by the SEC.) For auditors, the most significant aspect of the Securities Exchange Act is the requirement for registrants to file the following reports with the SEC:

- **Form 10-K**, also known as an *annual report,* that is filed annually within 60–90 days (depending on the entity's size) of the date of the entity's financial statements. These reports include financial statements that are audited by independent auditors.

- **Form 10-Q**, which is filed quarterly within 40–45 days of the end of the each of the first three fiscal quarters (again depending on the entity size). The fourth quarter's results are filed within Form 10-K. These reports include financial statements that are reviewed by independent auditors.

- **Form 8-K**, also known as a *current events report,* that is filed periodically upon the occurrence of major events (e.g., earnings releases, major asset sales, acquisitions, and auditor changes). Independent auditors may review these reports or otherwise assist in their preparation.

The form and content of 10-K and 10-Q filings are governed by the SEC through **Regulation S-X** (which covers the annual and interim financial statements) and **Regulation S-K** (which covers other supplementary disclosures). In addition to these two regulations, auditors must be familiar with **Financial Reporting Releases (FRRs)**, which express new rules and policies about disclosure, and **Staff Accounting Bulletins (SABs)**, which provide unofficial, but important, interpretations of Regulations S-X and S-K. Taken together, these four pronouncements provide the authoritative literature for information that must be filed with the SEC.

Section 10 and Rule 10(*b*)-5: Antifraud

Section 10 of the Securities Exchange Act is used against auditors quite frequently. Like section 17 of the Securities Act, section 10 is a general antifraud section that makes it unlawful for persons to use "manipulative" or "deceptive" devices in connection with the purchase or sale of securities. Rule 10(*b*)-5, made by the SEC staff under their authority to create administrative rules related to the statute, is more explicit than section 10 in identifying auditors' specific responsibilities.

Rule 10(*b*)-5. Securities Exchange Act of 1934

Rule 10(*b*)-5. Employment of Manipulative and Deceptive Devices. It shall be unlawful for any person, directly or indirectly, by the use of any means or instrumentality of interstate commerce, or of the mails, or of any facility of any national securities exchange,

1. To employ any device, scheme, or artifice to defraud.
2. To make any untrue statement of material fact or to omit to state

a material fact necessary in order to make the statements made, in the light of the circumstances under which they were made, not misleading.

3. To engage in any act, practice, or course of business that operates or would operate as a fraud or deceit upon any person in connection with the purchase or sale of any security.

An important point about Rule 10(*b*)-5 liability is that plaintiffs must prove **scienter** (a mental state embracing the intent to deceive, manipulate, or defraud) to impose liability under the rule. Mere failure to exercise the appropriate level of professional care is not enough cause for liability. Two cases (*Ernst & Ernst v. Hochfelder* and *Denise L. Nappier et al. v. PricewaterhouseCoopers*) illustrate the need for purchasers and sellers of securities to prove scienter on the part of auditors and confirm the inability for these parties to bring suit against auditors for ordinary negligence. The *Hochfelder* case was also significant in providing exposure for auditors in cases of gross negligence, even in the absence of scienter. These cases are described below.

Legal Precedent

ERNST & ERNST V. HOCHFELDER **(1976)**

In this case, **Hochfelder** represented investors in an escrow account with **First Securities of Chicago;** this account was maintained by Lester Nay (president of First Securities), who diverted funds for his own personal use through a fraudulent scheme that was revealed in a suicide note prepared by Nay. When the escrow accounts proved worthless (the economic loss), the investors (through Hochfelder) brought suit against the auditor (**Ernst & Ernst**), alleging that their negligence prevented them from uncovering the scheme and preventing their losses. Hochfelder specifically disclaimed any allegations of fraud or intentional misconduct on the part of Ernst & Ernst but wanted to sue for liability under section 10(*b*) imposed for ordinary negligence in the auditors' failure to uncover the fraudulent scheme.

The Court reasoned that section 10(*b*) in its reference to "employment of any manipulative and deceptive device" meant that intention to deceive, manipulate, or defraud is necessary to support a private cause of action under section 10(*b*), and failure to exercise the appropriate level of professional care is not sufficient. This decision is considered a landmark for auditors because it relieved them of liability for ordinary negligence under section 10(*b*) of the Securities Exchange Act and its companion SEC Rule 10(*b*)-5.

However, footnote 12 in this opinion noted that "[in] certain areas of the law recklessness is considered to be a form of intentional conduct for purposes of imposing liability for some act. We need not address here the question whether, in some circumstances, reckless behavior is sufficient for civil liability under 10(*b*) and Rule 10(*b*)-5."

Case conclusion: This case established precedent for the plaintiff's need to prove scienter to impose section 10(*b*) liability under the Securities Exchange Act. In addition, the reference to "recklessness" in the footnote to the opinion provides potential exposure to auditors for gross negligence under the Securities Exchange Act.

DENISE L. NAPPIER ET AL. V. PRICEWATERHOUSECOOPERS **(2002)**

Denise L. Nappier (treasurer of the State of Connecticut) successfully brought suit on behalf of shareholders (including **Connecticut Retirement Plans and Trust Funds**) against **Campbell Soup Company** and its directors for losses incurred upon declines in Campbell's stock price (the economic loss). In this suit, Nappier demonstrated that the purchase of these shares was influenced by audited financial statements that were shown to contain material misstatements. The shareholders then attempted to assert an additional claim against Campbell's auditor (**Pricewaterhouse Coopers**), alleging that it violated the provisions of the Securities Exchange Act by being a party to the preparation and certification of fraudulent financial statements.

Case conclusion: The case was dismissed when the shareholders could not prove the allegation that PricewaterhouseCoopers operated with scienter in conducting its audits of Campbell's financial statements.

Recently however, as discussed in the following Auditing Insight, the definition of what is necessary to prove scienter has become even more narrow.

 AUDITING INSIGHT | Has Rule 10(b)-5 lost some of its sting for auditors?

According to a recent academic study, from 1996 through 2016 the number of lawsuits against auditors decreased, the number of dismissals in auditor litigation cases increased, and the settlement payments, both in dollar value and as a percentage of payment by all defendants, decreased. In the study, the authors examine whether the decline in the auditor's liability is at least partially attributable to the Supreme Court case rulings in *Tellabs v. Makor* (2007) and *Janus v. First Derivative* (2011), both of which provide more standardized, and quite possibly more narrow, guidance on what is required to prove scienter under Rule 10(b)-5. Plantiffs must prove scienter on the part of the audit firms to be successful in litigation. By looking at changes in auditor settlements and court rulings on dismissals in the 10 year period, the authors conclude that decision in *Janus v. First Derivative* did indeed reduce liability exposure for auditors.

Source: C. Honigsberg, S. Shivaram, and S. Suraj, "The Changing Landscape of Auditor Litigation," *The Journal of Law and Economics*, May 2020, pp. 367–410.

Section 18: Civil Liability

Section 18 sets forth the pertinent civil liability under the Securities Exchange Act. Under Rule 10(*b*)-5 and section 18, plaintiffs have the same burden of proof as under common law. That is, they must demonstrate that the loss was caused by reliance on the materially misstated financial statements and that the auditors failed to exercise the appropriate level of professional care. Under the Securities Exchange Act, however, plaintiffs must demonstrate scienter on the part of auditors. Thus, plaintiffs must demonstrate all of the following:

1. They suffered an economic loss.
2. The financial statements contained a material misstatement.

3. The loss was caused by reliance on the materially misstated financial statements.
4. Auditors were aware that the financial statements contained a material misstatement. (Recall that, under *Hochfelder,* auditors may be held liable for gross negligence.)

Of note, two key differences in liability under the Securities Exchange Act and Securities Act are that, under the former (1) plaintiffs have the burden of proof and (2) auditors cannot be held liable for ordinary negligence. Clearly, the shift of burden of proof from auditors (in the Securities Act) to plaintiffs (in the Securities Exchange Act) is an important distinction and determinant in plaintiffs' ability to successfully prevail in securities actions.

Section 18 of the Securities Exchange Act establishes a statute of limitations of one year after discovery of the violation of the Act or within three years after the violation of the Act itself; for cases involving fraud, Sarbanes–Oxley extends these dates to two and five years, respectively.

Auditors' Defenses under the Securities Exchange Act

As a defense, auditors can attempt to demonstrate that they acted in "good faith" and had no knowledge of the material misstatement. (Causation is not a defense because it is presumed that the plaintiff has already demonstrated this in bringing suit.) Although this would seem to imply that auditors are liable only for fraudulent actions under the Securities Exchange Act (by demonstrating they had no knowledge of the material misstatement), the *Hochfelder* decision has resulted in some uncertainty as to auditors' liability in the absence of scienter (specifically, for acts that may be considered to represent gross negligence). Importantly, in contrast to the Securities Act, auditors are not liable to shareholders for actions representing ordinary negligence under the Securities Exchange Act.

Section 32: Criminal Liability

Section 32 states the criminal penalties for violation of the Securities Exchange Act. Like that pertaining to section 24 of the Securities Act, the critical test is whether the violator acted "willfully and knowingly." Therefore, to be subject to criminal liability, auditors must be shown to be guilty of fraud. Sarbanes–Oxley markedly increased the criminal penalties for violating the Securities Exchange Act; currently, violators may be fined up to $5 million and imprisoned for up to 20 years. In addition, Sarbanes–Oxley provides that if the "person" was not a natural person (for example, an accounting firm), fines of up to $25 million can be assessed. The *United States v. Natelli* (better known as the "National Student Marketing" case) illustrates potential criminal liability for auditors charged with violations of section 32. It is important to note that this case occurred prior to the increased liability imposed by Sarbanes–Oxley.

Legal Precedent

UNITED STATES V. NATELLI
("NATIONAL STUDENT MARKETING" CASE) (1975)

In this case, two auditors were convicted because of their involvement with materially misstated financial statements included in the proxy statement of **National Student Marketing Corporation.** These financial statements failed to reveal a $1 million write-off of "sales" (about 20 percent of the amount previously reported) and a corresponding large adjustment to National Student Marketing's operating income. The court stated

It is hard to probe the intent of a defendant. . . . When we deal with a defendant who is a professional accountant, it is even harder at times to

distinguish between simple errors of judgment and errors made with sufficient criminal intent to support a conviction, especially when there is no financial gain to the accountant other than his legitimate fee.

Case conclusion: Both the audit partner in charge of the engagement (Anthony Natelli) and his supervisor were fined and received jail sentences of one year each. Although a federal appeals court reversed the supervisor's conviction, it upheld Natelli's conviction because of his apparent motive and action to conceal the effect of some accounting adjustments. Natelli's sentence was eventually reduced to 60 days.

Foreign Corrupt Practices Act (FCPA)

In 1977, Congress passed the FCPA, which

- Made it illegal for corporations or their officers to knowingly bribe foreign officials or participate in bribery schemes involving foreign officials to obtain or retain business.
- Required entities to develop and maintain effective internal controls.

In 1988, the FCPA became codified as an amendment to the Securities Exchange Act. As a result, auditors may be liable for violations of this act if they should have identified these violations during their examination. In 2020, **Goldman Sachs** agreed to pay more than $1 billion to the SEC to settle charges of FCPA violations related to the anti-bribery, books and records, and internal control provisions of the act.[10] More recent settlements related to FCPA violations involve large, well-known companies such as **Walmart,** who agreed in 2019 to pay $144 million to the SEC and $138 to the Department of Justice for violating FCPA provisions for not operating a "sufficient anti-corruption program" for more than 10 years, and **Microsoft,** who agreed to pay $24 million in 2019 for FCPA violations in foreign countries, including Hungary, Thailand, and Saudi Arabia.[11]The following Audit Insight highlights the increased enforcement by the U.S. Department of Justice for FCPA violations.

AUDITING INSIGHT   FCPA Violations: A Big and Costly Deal

The U.S. Department of Justice is continuing to be aggressive in enforcing the FCPA, as evidenced by the following:

- All of the top 10 settlement amounts for FCPA violations have occurred since 2008, with settlement amounts in excess of $300 million for each company.
- Since 2008, DOJ enforcement actions have ranged from a low of 10 (2015) to a high of 35 (2019). There were 21 enforcement actions in 2020 and 11 in 2021.

- Total combined monetary resolutions companies have had to pay related to FCPA violations have varied but generally been increasing, with a peak at over $2.7 billion in 2020.
- From 1978–2017, China led for the most violations per country, with a total 89 violations. Nigeria was second with 75.

Sources: "FCPA Violations: Still a Big Deal in 2018," *Insights: Woodruff Sawyer,* June 12, 2018; "The Top Ten List of Corporate FCPA Settlements," *FCPA Professor,* September 22, 2017; "2021 Year End FCPA Update," Gibson Dunn, January 25, 2022.

✓ REVIEW CHECKPOINTS

C.18 Identify the contents of Form 10-K, Form 10-Q, and Form 8-K. How are auditors involved with the information in these filings?

C.19 What are (a) Regulation S-X, (b) Regulation S-K, (c) Financial Reporting Releases, and (d) Staff Accounting Bulletins?

C.20 Who may bring suit against auditors under the Securities Exchange Act? What must these parties demonstrate in order to bring suit?

C.21 What defenses are available to auditors under the Securities Exchange Act?

C.22 What are the criminal penalties associated with violations of the Securities Exchange Act?

C.23 What is *scienter*? How do the findings in *Ernst & Ernst v. Hochfelder* and *Denise L. Nappier et al. v. PricewaterhouseCoopers* relate to scienter?

C.24 What are the major differences in auditors' liability under the Securities Act of 1933 and the Securities Exchange Act of 1934?

---

[10]*SEC Enforcement Actions: FCPA Cases,"* www.sec.gov
[11]"SEC Enforcement Actions: FCPA Cases," www.sec.gov.

SUMMARY OF AUDITORS' LIABILITY TO CLIENTS AND THIRD PARTIES

Thus far, we have discussed auditors' potential liability to clients and third parties under both common law and statutory law (Securities Act of 1933 and Securities Exchange Act of 1934, respectively). Exhibit C.2 summarizes various elements of this liability, including (1) the level of professional care (performance) owed to various parties by auditors, (2) the burden of proof, and (3) various defenses available to auditors. Most noteworthy in Exhibit C.2 is the fact that plaintiffs have the burden of proving that auditors' failure to exercise the appropriate level of professional care caused the loss ("burden of proof") under common law and the Securities Exchange Act of 1934; however, the burden of proof is with the auditors under the Securities Act of 1933.

EXHIBIT C.2 Summary of Auditors' Liability

Source of Liability	Party(ies) Involved	Plaintiff Proof	Type of Offense	Auditors' Defenses
Common law	Client	• Economic loss • Auditors' breach of contract or failure to exercise the appropriate level of professional care • Loss caused by breach of contract or failure to exercise appropriate level of professional care	• Breach of contract • Ordinary negligence • Gross negligence • Fraud	• No breach of contract or no failure to exercise the appropriate level of professional care • Economic loss caused by other factors (causation) • Clients partially responsible for loss (contributory negligence)
	Third parties	• Economic loss • Auditors' failure to exercise the appropriate level of professional care • Material misstatements in financial statements • Loss caused by reliance on materially misstated financial statements	• Ordinary negligence (depends on jurisdiction and standing of party) • Gross negligence • Fraud	• Lack of appropriate standing (relationship) between third party and auditors • Loss caused by factors other than financial statements and auditors' examination • Work performed in accordance with GAAS or other professional standards
Securities Act of 1933	Purchasers of securities in an initial registration	• Economic loss • Material misstatements in financial statements	• Ordinary negligence • Gross negligence • Fraud	• Due diligence (auditors conducted a GAAS audit) • Loss caused by factors other than financial statements and auditors' examination
Securities Exchange Act of 1934	Purchasers and sellers of securities through subsequent transactions	• Economic loss • Material misstatements in financial statements • Loss caused by reliance on materially misstated financial statements • Auditors were aware of material misstatements and acted with intent (scienter)	• Gross negligence • Fraud	• Auditors acted in good faith • Auditors had no knowledge of material misstatements

EXHIBIT C.3 Significant Cases Affecting Auditors' Liability

Smith v. London Assurance Corp. (1905)	• Established auditors' liability to clients for breach of contract
Ultramares Corp. v. Touche (1931)	• Established rights of third parties not in privity with auditors to bring legal action • Concluded that auditors are generally not liable to third parties not in privity for ordinary negligence but could be liable for gross negligence
Credit Alliance v. Arthur Andersen (1985)	• Established auditors' liability to primary beneficiaries for ordinary negligence
Rusch Factors v. Levin (1968); *Fleet National Bank v. Gloucester Co. (1994)*	• Established auditors' liability to foreseen parties for ordinary negligence *(restatement of torts doctrine)*
Rosenblum Inc. v. Adler (1983)	• Established auditors' liability to foreseeable parties for ordinary negligence
Escott v. BarChris Construction Corp. (1968)	• Confirmed auditor liability for ordinary negligence to investors under the Securities Act • Established importance of auditors' review of subsequent events
Ernst & Ernst v. Hochfelder (1976)	• Confirmed auditors' liability to shareholders under the Securities Exchange Act if scienter is demonstrated • Provided potential exposure to auditors for gross negligence even in the absence of scienter

Exhibit C.3 provides a summary of important cases that have either developed auditor liability (common law) or clarified various provisions of the Securities Acts and Securities Exchange Act.

It is important to note that auditors' liability will continue to evolve over time. In a 2007 case (*Tellabs Inc. v. Makor Issues & Rights Ltd.*), the U.S. Supreme Court held that trial courts must consider all plausible inferences of scienter and that cases should be permitted to proceed only if the possibility of scienter is "cogent and at least as compelling as any opposing inference."[12] Some cases have been dismissed using this standard, but other cases have taken the view that the burden of proof regarding scienter still remains with the defendant. Future cases and rulings will likely provide further clarification as to the relative burden of proof in cases involving accusations of scienter.

Along with the burden of proof, what courts consider scienter will continue to evolve over time as well. In a 2015 case (*Omnicare, Inc. v. Laborers Dist. Council Const. Indus. Pension Fund*), the U.S. Supreme Court ruled that a statement of opinion is not necessarily an untrue statement of fact if the opinion ultimately proves to be incorrect.[13] In 2016, the United States Court of Appeals for the Second Circuit upheld a district court ruling dismissing claims against a Hong-Kong based auditor brought under Section 11 of the Securities Act of 1933, which does not require proof of scienter, and Section 10(b) of the Securities Act of 1934, where proof of scienter is required, in *In re Puda Coal Securities Inc. Litigation.* Both the district and the Second Circuit agreed that audit reports are statements of opinion involving significant judgment and therefore are subject to the standard established in the *Omnicare* case. This ruling provides some defense to auditors against section 10 or section 11 claims based on alleged false statements in audit reports. Regardless of who has the burden of proof, an incorrect audit opinion does not constitute scienter and will likely not be enough for claimants to win against auditors. Instead, there will need to be evidence that the auditors knew statements were false, did not believe their own opinions, and/or omitted material facts in order to assure a victory.[14]

THE CHANGING LANDSCAPE OF AUDITORS' LIABILITY

LO C-6
Understand more current developments that affect auditors' liability to clients and third parties.

The preceding discussion identifies the significant exposure of auditors to legal liability for their actions to various parties. Most people would argue that auditors performing substandard work *should* be held liable for that work, but a number of factors contribute to auditors' exposure to litigation brought by plaintiffs, including

[12]*Tellabs Inc. v. Makor Issues & Rights Ltd.*, 127 S. Ct. 2499 (2007).
[13]*Omnicare, Inc. v. Laborers Dist. Council Constr. Indus. Pension Fund*, 135 S. Ct. 1318 (2015).
[14]"The Second Circuit Clarifies Liability Standard for Audit Opinions," *Practice Points*, June 30, 2016, www.americanbar.org.

- Pressure to hold auditors accountable in light of a number of highly publicized audit failures and the significant losses of billions of dollars to investors as a result.

- Awareness of litigation against auditors as an avenue to recover losses, regardless of the actual reason for and cause of those losses.

- Highly complex accounting standards and difficulty in interpreting and evaluating financial statements prepared under those standards.

- The doctrine of joint and several liability, which may expose auditors to extensive and unreasonable losses when they are only partially at fault.

- The availability of class action suits, which makes it attractive for a small number of individuals to bring suit on behalf of a larger number of others.

The following Auditing Insight discusses additional factors that contribute to auditors' exposure to litigation.

 AUDITING INSIGHT Are CPAs a Target?

In addition to the number of factors listed above that impact auditors' exposure to litigation brought by plaintiffs, the following additional factors have also contributed to the increase in auditor exposure for liability claims:

- A reduced likelihood of judges dismissing charges against auditors.

- The availability of insurance, which makes auditors a desirable target for attorneys for recovery.

- Mergers of smaller firms and larger firms and difficulties during the transition period of these mergers because of the lack of effective risk management practices for smaller firms.

- Clients' increased interest in pursuing professional liability claims to recoup losses during the economic downturn.

Source: "Target CPAs," *Accounting Today,* July 1, 2011, pp. 1, 53.

The auditing profession considers the U.S. tort liability system a crisis of expanding liability exposure in need of reform. Some important reforms that have been implemented in response to these damages are summarized in the remainder of this section. Some of these reforms influence auditors' liability under common law and statutory law described in the preceding sections.

Sarbanes–Oxley

The *U.S. Public Company Reform and Investor Protection Act of 2002,* better known as the *Sarbanes–Oxley Act,* seeks to strengthen corporate accountability and governance of public entities. Although the more publicized aspects of Sarbanes–Oxley affect corporate officers and directors, some of its provisions affect auditors' statutory liability under the securities acts by increasing the penalties for auditors' involvement in financial statement fraud. Many of the aspects of Sarbanes–Oxley that affect auditors' planning, implementation, and reporting processes are discussed in other chapters in this book. Sarbanes–Oxley has impacted auditors' liability as follows:

- Extended the statute of limitations for bringing suit under the Securities Exchange Act to the earlier of (1) two years after the discovery of facts relating to violations of the act or (2) five years following the violation of the act. In addition, as noted earlier, the penalties for securities fraud have been increased to provide for fines of up to $5 million and imprisonment of up to 20 years for violations of the Securities Exchange Act.

- Increased penalties for mail fraud and wire fraud from 5 years to 20 years of imprisonment.

- Addressed the destruction, alteration, or falsification of records in federal investigations and bankruptcies. Firms and individuals found to have altered or destroyed documents with the intent to impede an investigation may be subject to fines and imprisonment for up to 20 years. In addition, under PCAOB standards, accountants performing an audit of a public company must maintain all engagement documentation for a period of seven years. Firms that do not comply with the record-retention provision are subject to fines and imprisonment of individual violators within the firm for up to 10 years.

In addition to the preceding items, Sarbanes–Oxley amended federal sentencing guidelines that increase financial and criminal penalties when securities fraud, obstruction of justice, and criminal fraud exist. This means not only that auditors face a higher liability risk but also that Sarbanes–Oxley may influence the courts in decisions regarding awards in civil cases. These provisions are considered a setback for the accounting profession's sincere desire to reduce auditors' liability.

AUDITING INSIGHT   Whose Responsibility Is It?

In early 2017, PricewaterhouseCoopers (PwC) found itself in the middle of a lawsuit that challenged the line between auditor's responsibility and management's responsibility for financial statements. Former client and now defunct brokerage firm **MF Global** was suing PwC, claiming the audit giant was to blame for the company's bankruptcy. In particular, the lawsuit claimed PwC was negligent in their approval of certain complicated transactions.

It is management that is ultimately responsible for complying with generally accepted accounting principles (GAAP) when determining how to account for complex transactions. PwC's responsibility, according to audit standards, is to obtain reasonable assurance that the financial statements are in accordance with GAAP. This includes evaluating judgments made by management. In this case, MF Global had researched and concluded their method for accounting for the complex transactions in question was in accordance with GAAP. MF Global then asked PwC to review their conclusion. PwC performed their own research and analysis and determined the method MF Global used was in accordance with GAAP.

PwC ended up settling the case for an undisclosed amount in March 2017. According to former Securities and Exchange Commission attorney Jacob Frenkel, "As a settled case, there is zero precedential value. Where there was a risk of extending unreasonably the role of an auditor, the law remains as is, meaning that auditors provide reasonable assurances about financial statements and are not auditors of business judgment."

Source: "All auditors stand to lose if PwC is found responsible for MF Global Collapse," *Forbes.com,* March 17, 2017; "PwC settles with MF Global, Leaving question of auditor liability for a different case," *Forbes.com,* March 23, 2017.

Racketeer Influenced and Corrupt Organizations Act

The Racketeer Influenced and Corrupt Organizations Act (RICO) was enacted to combat organized crime in businesses and other organizations by providing for extended criminal penalties and civil courses of action for various offenses. RICO targeted members of organized crime, but an unintended consequence of this legislation was the exposure of its provisions to auditors, whom attorneys threatened to classify as "racketeers" and impose the threat of penalties for treble (triple) damages under the law. In 1988, **Laventhol & Horwath** (at the time, the seventh-largest accounting firm) became the first firm to lose a jury trial under RICO statutes related to its role in a cattle-breeding venture in which almost 3,000 investors lost more than $20 million. (Laventhol & Horwath subsequently filed for bankruptcy in 1990.)[15]

In 1993, the U.S. Supreme Court (in *Reeves v. Arthur Young*) ruled that auditors are not subject to RICO complaints unless they "actively participate" in the management or operation of a corrupt business. Thus, failure to exercise the appropriate level of professional care (i.e., ordinary negligence) is not sufficient to use the provisions of RICO in a lawsuit against auditors.

---

[15]"Laventhol to Pay $15 Million in Suit," http://articles.philly.com/1988-05-10/business/26262663_1_laventhol-horwath-rico-suits-rico-statute.

Aiding and Abetting

Under the legal doctrine of aiding and abetting, plaintiffs have the ability to include parties in legal actions who were indirectly involved with particular offenses. In the past, shareholders argued that auditors' failure to exercise the appropriate level of professional care exposed them to liability through this legal doctrine. In *Central Bank v. First Interstate Bank* (1994), the U.S. Supreme Court severely limited the extent to which the aiding and abetting doctrine could be used against auditors. In *Stoneridge Investment Partners v. Scientific-Atlanta* (2008), the Supreme Court ruled that investors who suffer losses because of corporate fraud can typically recover losses only from the entity, its officers, and its directors, not from others who are engaged in business with the corporation. Although *Stoneridge* did not directly address involvement of auditors, the court's decision has been viewed as making it more difficult for plaintiffs to recover damages in civil actions from bankers, attorneys, and accountants under the so-called legal theory of scheme liability.[16]

Organization of Accounting Firms as Limited Liability Partnerships

Almost all of the major accounting firms have names that end with the designation LLP (limited liability partnership). Prior to 1990, accounting firms were organized as partnerships. One of the major disadvantages of the partnership form of organization is that the personal assets of all partners within the firm were at risk (i.e., were subject to loss via litigation) for the actions of all others within the firm. In the early 1990s, decisions in New York and Hawaii to permit and recognize limited liability partnerships to practice within their jurisdictions led to accounting firms reorganizing themselves as limited liability partnerships.

A **limited liability partnership** combines the advantages of the traditional partnership form of organization (taxation of partnership income to the partners, limited ownership of partnership interests) with the liability protection afforded to corporations. Specifically, in a limited liability partnership, any claims against the partnership are limited to partnership assets unless an individual partner directly participated in the action giving rise to the claim. It is important to note that the organization of a firm as a limited liability partnership does not affect the firm's legal liability but only the extent to which the individual partners' assets were subject to loss via litigation.

Proportionate Liability

One significant concern for auditors is the doctrine of **joint and several liability**, which allows a successful plaintiff to recover the full amount of a damage award from any defendant found to have failed to exercise the appropriate level of professional care regardless of the relative guilt of this defendant compared to other defendant(s). Stated another way, if both the auditors and the client are found to have been responsible for misstatements in the client's financial statements, plaintiffs can seek recovery from either or both parties. Often in cases of business failures, auditors are the only parties with "deep pockets" of financial resources to pay damages. Thus, when a group of defendants (auditors, management, and client) is found liable for damages, auditors may be required to pay the entire amount even though they may be only partially at fault. In contrast, under **proportionate liability**, a defendant is required to pay a proportionate share of the court's damage award depending on the degree of fault determined by a judge and jury (e.g., 20 percent, 30 percent, but not 100 percent).

Proportionate liability was largely accomplished at the federal level in 1995 with the passage of the *Private Securities Litigation Reform Act.* Civil lawsuits for damages now are governed by these proportionate liability terms:

- The total responsibility for loss is divided among all parties responsible for the loss.
- If other defendant(s) are insolvent, a solvent defendant's liability is extended to 50 percent more than the proportion found at trial. (For example, if an accounting firm is found 20 percent responsible for a loss and the client and its managers are insolvent,

---

[16]"You Can't Sue the Bean Counters," *BusinessWeek*, January 28, 2008, p. 30; "Can Shareholders Sue Third Parties?" *The Wall Street Journal*, October 6–7, 2007, p. A19.

the accounting firm will have to pay 30 percent of the loss but not 100 percent as before.)

- Only the defendants who knowingly committed a violation of securities laws remain jointly and severally liable for all of the plaintiffs' damages. (This is the imposition of penalty for actively participating in an actual fraud.)

The Private Securities Litigation Reform Act includes an exception to these provisions to compensate smaller investors. If plaintiffs have a net worth of less than $200,000 and lost 10 percent or more of the net worth because of auditors' failure to exercise appropriate levels of professional care, auditors remain jointly and severally liable.

AUDITING INSIGHT Liability and Looking Ahead

As of 2019, the current state of auditor liability was "not so bad," according to Michael Young, partner at international law firm **Willkie Farr & Gallagher LLP.** However, he cautioned that when it comes to litigation, auditors need to be thinking 5 to 10 years ahead. Litigation against auditors does not occur soon after the audit's end, but instead many years later. One thing auditors can do to help themselves now: careful and thorough documentation of work done and judgments made. According to Mr. Young, "Five years after the audit, you may be asked to talk about what judgments you made. And you have to

be really, really smart and have a really, really good recollection to be able to recreate from memory the kinds of tough judgment calls that you made. That's where documentation comes in. . . . If you can show that something was a tough judgment call and you considered things on all sides and you came to the best judgment you could, that works. That is really hard to attack."

Sources: "New litigation and regulatory risks," *The CPA Journal,* February 2019, pp. 52–55.

Class-Action Suits

It is not unusual for shareholders or investors who have suffered losses to band together and bring legal action against entities or auditors. In a **class action**, a relatively small number of aggrieved plaintiffs with small individual claims can bring suit for large damages in the name of an extended class. After a bankruptcy, for example, 50 bondholders who lost $40,000 might decide to sue and can do so on behalf of the entire class of bondholders for *all* of their alleged losses (say $40 million). Attorneys typically take these cases on a contingency fee basis (a percentage of the judgment, if any). The size of the claim and the zeal of the attorneys can make the class-action suit a serious matter.

In the past, most class-action lawsuits were adjudicated in state courts, and a great deal of "jurisdiction shopping" was performed to find a court that might be more sympathetic to the plaintiffs. Some of the large corporate failures have resulted in class-action lawsuits that have proven costly for defendants to defend and difficult for them to win. In February 2005, the *Class Action Fairness Act* was signed into law. This act is designed to expand federal jurisdiction over class-action lawsuits and is estimated to result in the movement of 40 percent of class-action lawsuits from various state courts to federal court. Federal courts are preferable venues for defendants in class-action lawsuits because

- Class-action lawsuits come under more scrutiny in federal court compared to state courts.
- Federal courts have more resources at their disposal in managing class-action cases than state courts.
- State courts have been alleged to unfairly discriminate against defendants from other jurisdictions.
- State court verdicts often affect plaintiffs in other jurisdictions (states). A verdict in federal court is regarded as more appropriate when it is applied to multiple jurisdictions.

It is important to note that not all class-action lawsuits will come under federal jurisdiction, and the rules for determining whether a state or federal court has jurisdiction over a case are complex.

In addition to the Class Action Fairness Act, Congress enacted the *Securities Litigation Uniform Standards Act* in 1998. The most significant provision of this legislation requires class-action lawsuits with 50 or more parties to be filed in the federal courts. As noted earlier, federal courts are generally more favorable venues for class-action lawsuits for the defendants (auditors).

The following Auditing Insight provides some interesting facts about the size and number of class action settlements that have occurred in recent years.

AUDITING INSIGHT   How Big Is the Class?

In 2020, the number of class action settlements increased slightly from the previous year, from 74 settlements to 77. The total settlement dollars for 2020 was approximately $4 billion, a substantial increase from the $2 billion of settlement dollars from 2019. The $4 billion figure was due largely to six "mega" settlements (settlements greater equal to or greater than $100 million) ranging from $149 million to $1.2 billion.

Source: *Securities Class Action Settlements—2020 Review and Analysis* (Cornerstone Research, 2021).

Auditors' Liability Caps

A final development in the legal liability arena is related to various measures of limiting (or "capping") auditors' liability to both clients and third parties. In their engagement letters, auditors are attempting to limit their potential liability to clients through careful wording. Firms are doing this in a variety of ways, including requiring some type of alternative dispute resolution. This type of liability cap limits a company's right to sue its auditor by requiring the company to seek arbitration or mediation in the event of a disagreement over the books. Although the effectiveness of this language in limiting auditors' liability has not been legally tested, some opponents of the language contend that restrictions such as this can compromise auditor independence and performance.[17]

Other Developments

Auditor liability continues to change along with the landscape of the auditing profession. In 2009, a U.S. judge denied **Deloitte Touche Tohmatsu**'s motion for a summary judgment that would relieve the firm of any liability for audits of Parmalat conducted by its Italian member firm (**Deloitte & Touche SpA**). This action clearly expands liability for international accounting firms in cases in which the firm itself provides little actual service to the client. Speaking on behalf of the plaintiffs, attorney Stuart Grant noted, "Judge Kaplan has finally made the law reflect reality. These accounting firms sell themselves as worldwide, seamless organizations. Now they are going to be held responsible in the same fashion. In essence, Judge Kaplan has said that the parent can't hide from the misdeeds of its children."[18] In more recent auditor-friendly rulings, the concept of *in pari delicto* has been strengthened as an auditor defense. Basically, this legal concept means that the court should not intercede between two wrongdoers. To put this in context, a corporation whose officers committed fraud cannot later sue the auditors for not catching the fraud; note, however, that innocent shareholders may still proceed with litigation against the auditors.[19]

Regardless of the changing landscape, auditors should be aware of what factors influence litigation. Academic research provides some insight into that question, as discussed further in the following Auditing Insight.

---

[17]"More Companies Are Disclosing Pacts with Auditors on Liability Caps," *The Wall Street Journal,* June 22, 2006, p. C4.

[18]"A Parmalat Ruling May Broaden Liability," *The Wall Street Journal,* January 29, 2009, p. C4; "Judge: OK to Sue Deloitte over Parmalat," *CFO.com,* January 30, 2009.

[19]S. Benson, "Shielding the Auditor from Corporate Fraud Liability," *The CPA Journal,* April, 2012, pp. 58–65.

AUDITING INSIGHT   What Affects Litigation?

Several academic studies have examined factors influencing litigation. The following are some of the things researchers found to have an effect:

- Schmidt concluded that litigation against auditors related to financial statement misstatements is more likely when the misstatement is associated with (1) financial fraud, (2) a regulatory investigation, (3) a large decline in stock price, and (4) a higher number of errors in applying GAAP. In a follow-up study, Schmidt found that the perception that auditors' independence has been impaired by the amount of nonaudit services provided also influences the auditor's decision to settle and increases the amount of the settlement.

- Casterella et al. found that in comparison with smaller firms, larger accounting firms, firms experiencing significant growth, firms with a higher number of claims outstanding against them, and firms that have been investigated or disciplined by a professional oversight body had higher levels of litigation risk.

- Anantharamen et al. examine if, and how, the varying legal liability standards across states influence auditors' reporting decisions, in particular the decision to issue a going-concern modification for distressed companies. They find that auditors are significantly

more likely to issue a going-concern opinion to clients from states where the standard for third-party liability is more expansive and the joint and several liability rule for determining damages among defendants exists.

- Cassell et al. found that auditor litigation risk increases as the number of institutional investors owners increases, as do audit fees.

- Christensen et al. found that for smaller firms (firms subject to PCAOB inspections once every three years), litigation risk increases after the release of a PCAOB inspection report that reveals audit deficiencies.

Sources: J. Schmidt, "Perceived Auditor Independence and Audit Litigation: The Role of Nonaudit Service Fees, *The Accounting Review,* May 2012, pp. 1033–1065; J. R. Casterella, K. L. Jensen, and W. R. Knechel, "Litigation Risk and Audit Firm Characteristics," *Auditing: A Journal of Practice & Theory,* November 2010, pp. 71–82; D. Anantharaman, J. A. Pittman, and N. Wans, "State Liability Regimes within the United States and Auditor Reporting," *The Accounting Review,* November 2016, pp. 1545–1575; C. Cassell, M. Drake, and T. Dyer, "Auditor Litigation Risk and the Number of Institutional Investors," *Auditing: A Journal of Practice & Theory,* August 2018, pp. 71–90. B.E. Christensen, N.G. Lundstrom, and N.J. Newton, "Does the Disclosure of PCAOB Inspection Findings Increase Audit Firms' Litigation Exposure?," *The Accounting Review,* May 2021, pp. 191–219.

 REVIEW CHECKPOINTS

C.25 List some of the major changes in auditors' liability provided by Sarbanes–Oxley.

C.26 What is the difference between *joint and several liability* and *proportionate liability*?

C.27 What major changes did the Private Securities Litigation Reform Act provide? What major changes did the Class Action Fairness Act provide?

C.28 What requirement was enacted in the Securities Litigation Uniform Standards Act that affected class-action lawsuits?

Summary

This module summarizes the potential liability auditors have to clients and third parties who rely on their work. Auditors can be liable under either common law (based on prior legal decisions and precedents) or statutory law (violating a written law). Auditors' liability to clients arises through an economic loss suffered because of failure to perform the engagement in accordance with the contract (breach of contract) or because of auditors' failure to exercise the appropriate level of professional care (tort liability). Because of the close relationship between auditors and clients, auditors owe their clients a very high degree of performance and are liable when they commit ordinary negligence (lack of reasonable care), gross negligence (lack of minimal care), or fraud (knowledge and intent to deceive).

Auditors' liability to third-party investors or creditors under common law arises because of economic decisions made by these parties using audited financial statements. Under common law, auditors are liable to all third-party users for levels of failure to exercise the appropriate level of professional care representing gross negligence or fraud. With respect to ordinary negligence, three separate approaches to liability are for third parties who are primary beneficiaries (*Credit Alliance v. Arthur Andersen*), foreseen third parties (*restatement of torts doctrine, Fleet National Bank v. Gloucester Co.*), or foreseeable third parties (*Rosenblum Inc. v. Adler*). The legal precedent in the jurisdiction in which the action is brought determines auditors' liability to third parties for ordinary negligence.

Under statutory law, the Securities Act of 1933 and the Securities Exchange Act of 1934 dictate liability to investors in securities. These acts differ based on both the burden of proof and the level of failure to exercise the appropriate level of professional care required to bring suit. Under the Securities Act, the burden of proof is on auditors; purchasers of securities may bring suit for ordinary negligence, gross negligence, or fraud. Under the Securities Exchange Act, the burden of proof is on purchasers or sellers of securities, and suit can be brought only for gross negligence or fraud. Clearly, the Securities Act imposes the highest degree of care on auditors and the lowest barriers for plaintiffs to bring suits against auditors.

Although Sarbanes–Oxley has expanded the statute of limitations as well as the penalties to auditors under the Securities Exchange Act, other developments have reduced (or advocate a reduction in) auditors' exposure to legal liability. These developments include the Private Securities Litigation Reform Act, the Class Action Fairness Act, and various calls for limits to auditor liability.

Key Terms

breach of contract: A claim that accounting or auditing services were not performed in the manner described in the contract, 666

causation defense: An argument available to auditors who can show that a plaintiff's economic loss was caused by a factor other than the auditors' failure to exercise the appropriate level of professional care or breach of contract, 667

class action: A situation in which a group of plaintiffs comes together in a legal action against another party, 687

comfort letter: A letter issued by auditors to underwriters of securities that provides an opinion on the fairness of the issuers' financial statements, 675

common law: The liability for injuries that is based on reasons other than violation of a written law or statute. Under common law, legal precedent is used in assessing the degree of responsibility or fault of the parties; auditors have common law liability to clients and nonshareholder third parties, 665

constructive fraud: A failure to provide any care in fulfilling a duty owed to another including a reckless disregard for the truth (similar to gross negligence), 668

contributory negligence: A legal defense theory in which the plaintiff's own failure to perform with the appropriate level of professional care bars recovery from auditors, 667

"deep pockets" theory: The concept that lawsuits may be brought against auditors not because they are necessarily at fault but because they are the only party with resources against which recovery can be made, 665

expectation gap: The difference between the actual work and assurance required by GAAS and the expectation of that work by the general public, 665

Financial Reporting Releases (FRRs): Reports prepared by SEC staff that express new rules and policies about disclosure, 678

foreseeable party: The individuals or organizations whose decisions normally rely on audited financial statements and opinions on those financial statements, 670

foreseen party: A limited class of individuals or organizations that could be reasonably expected to rely on auditors' work, 669

Form 8-K: The "current events" report filed periodically at the occurrence of major events, such as earnings releases, major asset sales, acquisitions, and auditor changes, 678

Form 10-K: The form to use for annual filing of financial statements and related disclosures by public companies with the SEC, 678

Form 10-Q: The form to use for quarterly filing of financial statements and related disclosures by public companies with the SEC, 678

fraud: The misrepresentation of facts that the individual knows to be false with the intention to deceive, 667

gross negligence: The breach of duty owed to another party because of a lack of minimal care (similar to constructive fraud), 667

initial public offering (IPO): The initial issuance of securities by a registrant entity to the investing public through a market that is subject to the provisions of the Securities Act of 1933, 674

joint and several liability: The legal doctrine that when multiple defendants are named, the full amount of a damage award may be collected from any of the defendants named in the lawsuit even though they may be only partially at fault, 686

limited liability partnership: A form of organization adopted by most large accounting firms that combines the advantages of a traditional partnership with the liability protection afforded to corporations, 686

ordinary negligence: The unintentional breach of duty owed to another as a result of a lack of reasonable care, 667

plaintiff: The person or organization that initiates a lawsuit (client or third-party user of financial statements), 666

primary beneficiary: A person known by name to the auditor for whose primary benefit the audit or other accounting service is performed, 669

privity of contract: A situation in which parties have a contractual relationship, 666

proportionate liability: The legal doctrine that payment of a share of the court's damage award be based on the extent (or proportion) of fault exhibited by a convicted defendant, 686

prospectus: A legal document offering securities for sale; includes significant information about the issuing entity, including its historical financial statements and other necessary disclosures, 674

registration statement: A set of documents, including a prospectus, that a company files with the SEC prior to an initial public offering, 674

Regulation S-K: The SEC requirements relating to all business, analytical, and supplementary financial disclosures other than financial statements themselves, 678

Regulation S-X: The SEC accounting requirements for annual and interim financial statements filed under both the Securities Act and the Securities Exchange Act, 678

scienter: A mental state embracing the intent to deceive, manipulate, or defraud prior to committing those actions (e.g., auditors' knowledge of a misstatement in the financial statements and the intentional failure to disclose this misstatement in their report), 678

Staff Accounting Bulletins (SABs): The unofficial but important interpretations of Regulation S-X and Regulation S-K by SEC staff, 678

statutory law: The legal rules affecting liability based on violations of written laws or statutes. Auditors have statutory liability to third-party investors under the securities acts, 666

tort: A civil complaint charging that the action of one person caused injury (personal or financial) to another; such action against auditors is normally initiated by users of financial statements, 666

Multiple-Choice Questions for Practice and Review

 All applicable questions are available with *Connect*

LO C-2

C.29 A lack of reasonable care that may be characterized by the failure of auditors to follow GAAS in the conduct of the audit is known as

    a. Constructive fraud.

    b. Fraud.

    c. Gross negligence.

    d. Ordinary negligence.

LO C-6

C.30 From the auditors' point of view, if financial damages are to be imposed in a civil lawsuit, which of the following is a preferable method of allocation?

    a. Joint and several liability.

    b. Reasonably foreseeable users' approach to privity.

    c. Foreseen third parties' approach to privity.

    d. Proportionate liability.

LO C-1

C.31 Users of financial statements have a different perception concerning the nature of auditors' services than the actual objectives of an audit. This difference is known as

    a. Diverse liability perception.

    b. Reasonable foreseeable third parties.

    c. Insurance hypothesis.

    d. Expectations gap.

LO C-2

C.32 Individuals who believe they relied on misstated financial statements to make a decision and have suffered losses as a result will issue an action known as a

    a. Breach of contract.

    b. Tort.

    c. Securities litigation.

    d. Constructive fraud.

LO C-6

C.33 Assume that auditors lost a civil lawsuit for damages and the court found total losses of $5 million. If the auditors were determined to be 30 percent at fault and were the only solvent defendants, what is the auditors' likely obligation under proportionate liability?

    a. $5,000,000

    b. Zero

    c. $2,250,000

    d. $1,500,000

LO C-6

C.34 Suppose that the auditors in the preceding question participated knowingly in commission of violations of securities laws (with managers and directors of the audit client). What is the auditors' likely obligation?

    a. $5,000,000

    b. Zero

    c. $2,250,000

    d. $1,500,000

LO C-2

C.35 When a client sues an accountant for failure to perform consulting work properly, the accountants' best defense is probably based on the doctrine of

    a. Lack of privity of contract.

    b. Contributory negligence on the part of the client.

    c. Lack of any measurable dollar amount of damages.

    d. No negligence on the part of the consultant.

LO C-2

C.36 When creditors who relied on an entity's audited financial statements suffer monetary losses after a customer (the auditors' client) goes bankrupt, what must the plaintiff creditors in a lawsuit for damages show in a court that follows the doctrine in *Credit Alliance*?

    a. The auditors knew and specifically acknowledged identification of the creditors.

    b. The auditors could reasonably foresee them as beneficiaries of the audit because entities such as this client use financial statements to obtain credit from vendors.

    c. The plaintiffs were foreseen users of the audited financial statements because they were vendors of long standing.

    d. All of the above.

LO C-2   C.37 When accountants agree to perform a compilation or review of unaudited financial statements, the best way to avoid clients' misunderstanding the nature of the work is to describe
it completely in

    a. An engagement letter.

    b. The auditors' opinion.

    c. A report to the clients' board of directors at the close of the engagement.

    d. A management letter to the board of directors' audit committee.

LO C-4   C.38 Entities desiring to issue equity or debt must provide a set of financial statements to any
prospective purchaser. This set of financial statements and other information for prospective
purchasers is known as a

    a. Prospectus.

    b. Review.

    c. Patron's acquisition statement.

    d. Projected audited financial information.

LO C-3   C.39 The Securities Act of 1933 and Securities Exchange Act of 1934 contain

    a. Civil liability provisions applicable to auditors.

    b. Criminal liability provisions applicable to auditors.

    c. Neither *(a)* nor *(b)*.

    d. Both *(a)* and *(b)*.

LO C-2   C.40 Which of the following third parties is known by name to auditors as the audit is conducted?

    a. Foreseeable third party.

    b. Foreseen third party.

    c. General third party.

    d. Primary beneficiary.

LO C-5   C.41 Which of the following would be the auditors' most likely defense in an action brought
under the Securities Exchange Act of 1934?

    a. The investor did not have privity with auditors.

    b. The investor did not suffer a loss based on the materially misstated financial statements.

    c. The auditors acted in good faith and were not aware of the materially misstated financial
statements.

    d. The financial statements were not filed with the Securities and Exchange Commission.

LO C-4   C.42 Which of the following statements regarding auditors' liability under the Securities Act of
1933 is *not* true?

    a. The act relates to the initial issuance of securities to the public, normally through an
initial public offering.

    b. Auditors' liability arises because of audited financial information filed with the SEC.

    c. Third parties must demonstrate that they relied on misstated financial statements that
were examined by auditors.

    d. Auditors may be liable if they are found to have engaged in ordinary negligence.

LO C-5   C.43 Under the Securities Exchange Act of 1934, entities are required to report to the public
about changing auditors on

    a. Form 10-K.

    b. Form 1-SA.

    c. Form 10-Q.

    d. Form 8-K.

LO C-4   C.44 Section 11(*b*) of the Securities Act of 1933 provides that individuals can be sued and may
be liable for investors' losses in connection with a public securities offering under which of
these circumstances?

    a. The chairman of the board of directors performed a reasonable investigation of facts in
connection with preparing the section in the registration statement concerning the specification of the use of the proceeds of the offering.

b. A consulting engineer performed a reasonable investigation and reported in the registration statement on the feasibility of construction of a roadway to be financed with the offering proceeds.

c. The president of the issuing entity had no reason to doubt the report of the consulting engineer, although the president did not perform a separate reasonable investigation of her own.

d. The officers of the issuing entity were relieved that the independent auditors did not make an issue about the excessive valuation of inventory held to support construction in progress.

LO C-5

C.45 In comparison to the burden of proof required of plaintiffs in civil lawsuits against independent auditors under common law, section 10(*b*) of the Securities Exchange Act of 1934

a. Is the same regarding plaintiffs' need to prove damages or losses.

b. Is the same regarding plaintiffs' need to establish privity or a beneficiary relationship with auditors.

c. Does not require that plaintiffs prove their reliance on materially misstated financial statements.

d. Does not require that plaintiffs prove that relying on the materially misstated financial statements caused their losses.

LO C-2

C.46 Which of the following cases provides auditors the broadest exposure for liability to third parties for ordinary negligence under common law?

a. *Credit Alliance v. Arthur Andersen.*

b. *Fleet National Bank v. Gloucester Co.*

c. *Rosenblum Inc. v. Adler.*

d. *Ultramares.*

LO C-4, C-5

C.47 Which of the following is a major difference in auditors' liability under the Securities Act of 1933 and the Securities Exchange Act of 1934?

a. The burden of proving reliance on misstated financial statements and the relationship between these financial statements and the economic loss.

b. The auditors' required degree of professional care.

c. Both of the above.

d. Neither of the above.

LO C-4

C.48 When an entity registers a security offering under the Securities Act of 1933, the law provides an investor

a. An SEC guarantee that the information in the registration statement is true.

b. Insurance against loss from the investment.

c. Financial information examined by independent auditors.

d. Inside information about the entity's trade secrets.

LO C-2

C.49 A group of investors sued Anderson, Olds, and Watershed, CPAs (AOW) for alleged damages suffered when the entity in which they held common stock went bankrupt. To avoid liability under the common law, AOW must demonstrate which of the following?

a. The investors actually suffered a loss.

b. The investors relied on the financial statements audited by AOW.

c. The investors' loss was a direct result of their reliance on the audited financial statements.

d. The audit was conducted in accordance with generally accepted auditing standards and with due professional care.

LO C-5

C.50 The Securities and Exchange Commission document that governs accounting in financial statements filed with the SEC is

a. Regulation D.

b. Form 8-K.

c. Form SB-1.

d. Regulation S-X.

LO C-5   C.51 Which of the following cases upheld the requirement that plaintiffs demonstrate scienter when bringing action under the Securities Exchange Act of 1934?

    a. *Ernst & Ernst v. Hochfelder.*

    b. *Escott v. BarChris Construction Corp.*

    c. *Smith v. London Assurance Corp.*

    d. *Ultramares.*

LO C-5   C.52 A public entity subject to the periodic reporting requirements of the Securities Exchange Act of 1934 must file an annual report with the SEC known as the

    a. Form 10-K.

    b. Form 10-Q.

    c. Form 8-K.

    d. Regulation S-X.

LO C-4   C.53 When investors sue auditors for damages under section 11 of the Securities Act of 1933, they must allege and prove

    a. Scienter on the part of auditors.

    b. The audited financial statements contained a material misstatement.

    c. They relied on the materially misstated financial statements.

    d. Their reliance on the materially misstated financial statements was the direct cause of their loss.

LO C-6   C.54 Which of the following is *not* part of Sarbanes–Oxley?

    a. An increased duty on the part of auditors to identify financial statement fraud.

    b. A requirement that the CEO and CFO certify the financial statements.

    c. Increased penalties for destruction of records in federal investigations.

    d. Increased penalties for mail fraud and criminal violations of the Securities Exchange Act of 1934.

LO C-2   C.55 If a CPA firm is being sued for common law fraud by a third party based upon materially false financial statements, which of the following is the best defense the auditors could assert?

    a. Lack of privity.

    b. Lack of reliance.

    c. A disclaimer contained in the engagement letter.

    d. Contributory negligence on the part of the client.

(AICPA adapted)

LO C-2   C.56 Locke, CPA, was engaged by Hall Inc. to audit Willow Company. Hall purchased Willow after receiving Willow's audited financial statements, which included Locke's unmodified auditors' opinion. Locke was negligent in the performance of the Willow audit engagement; this negligence was caused by failure to perform the engagement in accordance with terms of the engagement letter. As a result of Locke's negligence, Hall suffered damages of $75,000. Hall appears to have grounds to sue Locke for

	Breach of Contract	Negligence
a.	Yes	Yes
b.	Yes	No
c.	No	Yes
d.	No	No

(AICPA adapted)

LO C-4   C.57 An investor seeking to recover stock market losses from a CPA firm associated with an initial offering of securities based on an unmodified opinion on financial statements that accompanied a registration statement must establish that

    a. The audited financial statements contain a false statement or omission of material fact.

    b. The investor relied on the financial statements.

    c. The CPA firm did not act in good faith.

    d. The CPA firm would have discovered the false statement or omission if it had exercised due care in its examination.

(AICPA adapted)

LO C-5

C.58 Donalds & Company, CPAs, audited the financial statements included in the annual report submitted by Markum Securities Inc. to the Securities and Exchange Commission. The audit was improper in several respects. Markum is now insolvent and unable to satisfy the claims of its customers. Customers have instituted legal action against Donalds based on Section 10(*b*) and Rule 10(*b*)-5 of the Securities Exchange Act of 1934. Which of the following is likely to be Donalds' best defense?

    a. The firm did not intentionally certify the false financial statements.

    b. Section 10(*b*) does not apply to the case.

    c. The firm was not in privity of contract with the creditors.

    d. The engagement letter specifically disclaimed any liability to any party that resulted from Markum's fraudulent conduct.

(AICPA adapted)

Problems C.59 and C.60 are based on the following information:

    West & Co., CPAs, rendered an unmodified opinion on the financial statements of Pride Corp., which were included in Pride's registration statement filed with the SEC. Subsequently, Hex purchased 500 shares of Pride's preferred stock as part of a public offering subject to the Securities Act of 1933. Hex has commenced an action against West based on the Securities Act of 1933 for losses resulting from misstatements of facts in the financial statements included in the registration statement.

LO C-4

C.59 Which of the following elements must Hex prove to hold West liable?

    a. West rendered its opinion with knowledge of material misstatements.

    b. West performed the audit negligently.

    c. Hex relied on the financial statements included in the registration statement.

    d. The misstatements were material.

(AICPA adapted)

LO C-4

C.60 Which of the following defenses would be *least* helpful to West in avoiding liability to Hex?

    a. West was not in privity of contract with Hex.

    b. West conducted the audit in accordance with GAAS.

    c. Hex's losses were caused by factors other than the misstatements.

    d. Hex knew of the misstatements when Hex acquired the preferred stock.

(AICPA adapted)

Exercises and Problems

 All applicable questions are available with *Connect*

LO C-2

C.61 **Breach of Contract.** Although large-dollar lawsuits brought by shareholders grab the headlines, auditors are most often sued by the client for breach of contract.

Required:

    a. How can auditors be in breach of contract with a client?

    b. How can a client be in breach of contract with auditors?

    c. What are the best defenses for auditors against breach of contract lawsuits brought by their clients?

LO C-2

C.62 **Liability to Clients.** Thomas, CPA, is a regional firm that provides a variety of services to its clients. The following summarizes some issues that it has encountered with three of its audit clients during the most recent year:

    • Thomas was engaged by Brown Company to conduct an audit of its financial statements. Brown is a nonpublic entity that is seeking financing and is having the audit conducted because of user demand for audited financial statements. Because this was an initial audit, it took Thomas longer to conduct the audit than anticipated. During this time, economic conditions resulted in a general increase in interest rates, and Brown's costs of obtaining financing were higher than it had anticipated.

- Green Stores has been an audit client of Thomas for more than 10 years. Following the most recent audit (which resulted in an unmodified opinion on Green's financial statements), Green Stores learned that its treasurer had been engaged in a significant embezzlement scheme, resulting in Green's losses in excess of $2 million. Throughout Thomas's 10-year relationship with Green Stores, it had issued unmodified opinions on Green's financial statements and had not identified any weaknesses in Green's internal control or other evidence that suggested the existence of this defalcation scheme.

- Fuchsia Inc. has been an audit client of Thomas for the past five years. During the most recent audit, Thomas identified misstatements that understated Fuchsia's liabilities; Thomas believed that these misstatements should be corrected in order to fairly present Fuchsia's financial condition, results of operations, and cash flows in conformity with GAAP. Fuchsia refused to make these misstatements, and Thomas resigned from the engagement. Fuchsia has engaged another auditor, but the delays associated with this change in auditors may result in accelerated payments to Fuchsia's lenders for failure to provide them audited financial statements on a timely basis.

Required:

a. Without specific reference to any of the preceding situations, on what basis/general areas of liability may clients bring suit against auditors?

b. Without specific reference to any of the preceding situations, what facts must clients demonstrate to bring suit against auditors?

c. Without specific reference to any of the preceding situations, what defenses might be available to auditors for suits brought against them by their clients?

d. For each of the preceding situations, identify the potential basis or bases for legal action that might be brought against Thomas.

e. In your opinion, is Thomas likely to be liable to these clients for its actions? What factors should be considered in assessing Thomas' potential liability in these situations?

LO C-2

C.63   **Common Law Responsibility for Errors and Fraud.** Huffman & Whitman (H&W), a large regional accounting firm, was engaged by Ritter Tire Wholesale Company to audit its financial statements for the year ended January 31. H&W had a busy audit engagement schedule from December 31 through April 1 and decided to audit Ritter's purchase vouchers and related cash disbursements on a sample basis. The firm instructed staff members to select a random sample of 130 purchase transactions and gave directions about important deviations, including missing receiving reports. Boyd, the assistant in charge, completed the audit documentation, properly documenting the fact that 13 of the purchases in the sample had been recorded and paid without including the receiving report (required by stated internal control procedures) in the file of supporting documents. Whitman, the partner in direct charge of the audit, showed the findings to Lock, Ritter's chief accountant. Lock appeared surprised but promised that the missing receiving reports would be inserted into the files before the audit was over. Whitman was satisfied, noted in the audit documentation that the problem had been solved, and did not say anything to Huffman about it.

Unfortunately, H&W did not discover the fact that Lock was involved in a fraudulent scheme in which he diverted shipments of tires to a warehouse leased in his name and sent the invoices to Ritter for payment. He then sold the tires for his own profit. Internal auditors discovered the scheme during a study of slow-moving inventory items. Ritter's inventory was overstated by about $500,000 (20 percent), the amount Lock had diverted.

Required:

a. Do you believe H&W has any further audit responsibility with respect to the missing receiving reports? Explain.

b. Do you believe H&W failed to exercise the appropriate level of professional care? Why or why not?

LO C-2

C.64 **Common Law Responsibility for Errors and Fraud.** Herbert McCoy is the president of McCoy Forging Corporation. For the past several years, Donovan & Company, CPAs, has performed the company's compilation and some other accounting and tax work. McCoy decided to have Donovan & Company conduct an audit. He had recently received a disturbing anonymous letter that stated, "Beware; you have a viper in your nest. The money is literally disappearing before your very eyes! Signed: A friend." He told no one about the letter.

McCoy Forging engaged Donovan & Company, CPAs, to render an opinion on the financial statements for the year ended June 30. McCoy told Donovan he wanted to verify that the financial statements were "accurate and proper." He did not mention the anonymous letter. The usual engagement letter providing for an audit in accordance with generally accepted auditing standards (GAAS) was drafted by Donovan & Company and signed by both parties.

The audit was performed in accordance with GAAS. The audit did not reveal a clever defalcation plan. Harper, the assistant treasurer, was siphoning off substantial amounts of McCoy Forging's funds. The defalcations occurred both before and after the audit. Harper's embezzlement was discovered by McCoy's new internal auditor in October after Donovan had delivered the auditors' opinion. Although the scheme was fairly sophisticated, it could have been detected if Donovan & Company had performed additional procedures. McCoy Forging demands reimbursement from Donovan for the entire amount of the embezzlement, some $40,000 of which occurred before the audit and $65,000 after. Donovan has denied any liability and refuses to pay.

Required:

Discuss Donovan's responsibility in this situation. Do you think McCoy Forging could prevail in whole or in part in a lawsuit against Donovan under common law? Explain your conclusions.

(AICPA adapted)

LO C-2

C.65 **Auditors' Liability for Fraud.** Auditors may be liable to third parties for fraud in several ways.

Required:

a. Identify auditors' liability for fraud to third parties.
b. Distinguish between fraud and constructive fraud.
c. What is auditors' liability for constructive fraud to third parties?
d. In your opinion, is auditors' liability to third parties for fraud and constructive fraud appropriate (or "fair")?

LO C-2

C.66 **Common Law Liability Exposure.** An accounting firm was engaged to examine the financial statements of Martin Manufacturing Corporation for the year ending December 31. Martin needed cash to continue its operations and agreed to sell its common stock investment in a subsidiary through a private placement. The buyers insisted that the proceeds be placed in escrow because of the possibility of a major contingent tax liability that could result from a pending government claim against Martin's subsidiary. The payment in escrow was completed in late November. Martin's president told the audit partner that the proceeds from the sale of the subsidiary's common stock, held in escrow, should be shown on the balance sheet as an unrestricted current account receivable. The president held the opinion that the government's claim was groundless and that Martin needed an "uncluttered" balance sheet and a "clean" auditors' opinion to obtain additional working capital from lenders. The audit partner agreed with the president and issued an unmodified opinion on Martin's financial statements, which did not refer to the contingent liability and did not properly describe the escrow arrangement.

The government's claim proved to be valid, and pursuant to the agreement with the buyers, the purchase price of the subsidiary was reduced by $450,000. This adverse development forced Martin into bankruptcy. The accounting firm is being sued for deceit (fraud) by several of Martin's unpaid creditors who extended credit in reliance on the accounting firm's unmodified opinion on Martin's financial statements.

Required:

a. What deceit (fraud) do you believe the creditors are claiming?
b. Is the lack of privity between the accounting firm and the creditors important in this case?
c. Do you believe the accounting firm is liable to the creditors? Explain.

(AICPA adapted)

LO C-2

C.67   **Common Law Liability Exposure.** Risk Capital Limited, a Delaware corporation, was considering the purchase of a substantial investment in Florida Sunshine Corporation, a closely held corporation. Initial discussions with the Florida Sunshine Corporation began late in 2023.

Wilson and Wyatt, Florida Sunshine's auditor, regularly prepared quarterly and annual unaudited financial statements. The most recently prepared financial statements were for the year ended September 30, 2023.

On November 15, 2023, after extensive negotiations, Risk Capital agreed to purchase 100,000 shares of no par, class A capital stock of Florida Sunshine at $12.50 per share. However, Risk Capital insisted on audited statements for 2023. Florida Sunshine engaged Wilson and Wyatt to audit the 2023 financial statements. The contract that was made available to Wilson and Wyatt specifically provided that Risk Capital shall have the right to rescind the purchase of said stock if the audited financial statements of Florida Sunshine show a material adverse change in the financial condition of the corporation.

The audited financial statements furnished to Florida Sunshine by Wilson and Wyatt showed no such material adverse change. Risk Capital relied on the audited statements and purchased the investment in Florida Sunshine. It was subsequently discovered that, as of the date of the financial statements, the audited statements were misstated and that in fact there had been a material adverse change in the corporation's financial condition. Florida Sunshine is insolvent, and Risk Capital will lose virtually its entire investment.

Risk Capital seeks recovery against Wilson and Wyatt.

Required:

Assuming that only ordinary negligence is proved, will Risk Capital prevail

a. Under a privity of contract standard?

b. Under a primary beneficiary standard?

c. Under a foreseen parties standard?

LO C-2

C.68   **Common Law Liability Exposure.** Smith, CPA, is the auditor for Juniper Manufacturing Corporation, a nonpublic entity that has a June 30 fiscal year. Juniper arranged for a substantial bank loan, which depended on the bank receiving audited financial statements showing a debt-to-equity ratio of no more than 2 to 1. The bank's deadline for receiving these financial statements was September 30. On September 25, just before the auditors' opinion was to be issued, Smith received an anonymous letter on Juniper's letterhead indicating that Juniper's five-year lease of a factory building that was classified in the financial statements as an operating lease was in fact a capital lease. The letter stated that Juniper had a secret written agreement with the lessor modifying the lease and creating a capital lease.

Smith confronted the president of Juniper, who admitted that a secret agreement existed but said it was necessary to treat the lease as an operating lease to meet the debt-to-equity ratio requirement of the pending loan and that nobody would ever discover the secret agreement with the lessor. The president said that if Smith did not issue a report by September 30, Juniper would sue Smith for substantial damages that would result from not getting the loan. Under this pressure and because the audit documentation contained a copy of the five-year lease agreement supporting the operating lease treatment, Smith issued the report with an unmodified opinion on September 29. In spite of the fact that it received the loan, Juniper went bankrupt. The bank is suing Smith to recover its losses on the loan, and the lessor is suing Smith to recover uncollected rents.

Required:

Answer the following, setting forth reasons for any conclusions stated.

a. Is Smith liable to the bank?

b. Is Smith liable to the lessor?

c. Was Smith independent?

(AICPA adapted)

LO C-2

C.69   **Common Law Liability to Third Parties.** Flacco, CPA, conducted the audit of Raven Company and issued an unmodified opinion that concluded that the financial statements presented its financial condition, results of operations, and cash flows according to GAAP. As part of the preaudit conference, Flacco was informed by Raven's management that its audited financial statements would be presented to Baltimore National Bank to secure financing for a significant expansion opportunity.

Using these financial statements, as well as Flacco's opinion on those statements, Raven obtained financing from the following parties: (1) Baltimore National Bank, (2) Regional State Bank, and (3) Maryland Equity Partners (a private equity firm). Each of these parties specifically requested audited financial statements and relied on these statements in providing financing to Raven. Six months after obtaining financing, Raven's financial condition worsened, and it declared bankruptcy, forcing Raven to default on its payments to Baltimore National Bank and Regional State Bank. In addition, Maryland Equity Partners' investment in Raven became worthless.

After the bankruptcy, the parties that had provided financing to Raven determined that Raven had intentionally misstated its financial statements by recording fictitious revenues and accounts receivable. These parties decided to file suit against Flacco for failure to identify the fictitious revenues and accounts receivable.

Required:

a. Define the following type of third parties: (1) *primary beneficiary,* (2) *foreseen third parties,* and *(3) foreseeable third parties.*

b. Considering the three types of third parties identified in *(a),* how would you classify (1) Baltimore National Bank, (2) Regional State Bank, and (3) Maryland Equity Partners?

c. Assume that court proceedings concluded that Flacco failed to send confirmations to Raven's customers and simply mathematically verified the summary listing of accounts receivable provided to him by Raven. Which of the parties would be likely to prevail in its claim against Flacco?

LO C-2

C.70 **Common Law Liability to Third Parties.** Madeoff is a small, nonpublic retailer seeking capital for expansion. To obtain necessary capital, Madeoff engaged Allen, CPAs to audit its annual financial statements. In discussing the engagement, Madeoff explicitly informed Allen that the purpose of the audit was to obtain additional financing for expansion into new markets.

Madeoff obtained $3 million from lenders. These lenders included the following:

- First Trust and Bank provided $2 million. When engaging Allen, Madeoff indicated that it would use the audited financial statements and Allen's opinion on these statements to seek financing from First Trust and Bank; also, First Trust and Bank was specifically named in the engagement letter. Prior to committing the capital, First Trust and Bank had reviewed Madeoff's financial statements and, based on the financial condition reflected in its balance sheet, deemed Madeoff to be a qualified loan candidate.

- MoonTrust Bank provided $800,000 of capital to Madeoff. Although not named in the engagement letter or identified to Allen, Madeoff had previous business dealings with MoonTrust and maintained several accounts at MoonTrust. Based primarily on its prior relationships with Madeoff, MoonTrust approved the additional financing to Madeoff prior to receiving the audited financial statements or Allen's report on those financial statements.

- Alice Lay, a local philanthropist, provided $200,000 of capital to Madeoff. Although her decision was primarily motivated by Madeoff's role in the community and its corporate citizenship, she did request and review Madeoff's audited financial statements and Allen's report on those financial statements prior to providing funding. Alice had never entered into a loan agreement of this nature in the past but felt personal ties to Madeoff and was interested in its continued success.

Approximately six months following these loans, Madeoff declared bankruptcy.

Following the bankruptcy, lenders discovered that Allen's audit failed to disclose several material financial statement misstatements that, if corrected, would have presented a less favorable depiction of Madeoff's financial condition, results of operations, and cash flows. These lenders are exploring potential litigation against Allen to recover the funds they provided to Madeoff.

Required:

a. Would these third parties more likely pursue litigation against Madeoff under common law or statutory law?

b. How would each of the lenders likely be classified based on their relationship with Allen and the potential use of Madeoff's financial statements and Allen's report?

c. Assume that Allen's audit did not comply with generally accepted auditing standards but that it did not demonstrate a lack of minimum care or actual knowledge of the misstatements. Given the circumstances noted, how would you assess each of these parties' ability to prevail against Allen in a potential claim?

d. Repeat part *(c)*, assuming that the parties could prove that Allen was aware that Madeoff's financial statements contained a material misstatement.

LO C-2

C.71   Liability in a Review Engagement. Mason & Dilworth (M&D), CPAs, were auditors for Hotshot Company, a closely held corporation owned by 30 residents of the area. Hotshot had previously engaged M&D to perform some compilation and tax work. Bubba Crass, Hotshot's president and holder of 15 percent of the stock, said he needed something more than these services. He told Mason, the partner in charge, that he wanted financial statements for internal use, primarily for management purposes but also to obtain short-term loans from financial institutions. Mason recommended a "review" of the financial statements and did not prepare an engagement letter.

During the review work, Mason had some reservations about the financial statements. Mason told Dilworth at various times he was "uneasy about certain figures and conclusions," but he would "take Crass's word about the validity of certain entries since the review was primarily for internal use in any event and was not an audit."

M&D did not discover a material act of fraud committed by Crass. The fraud would have been detected had Mason not relied so much on the unsupported statements Crass made concerning the validity of the entries about which he had felt so uneasy.

Required:

a. What potential liability might M&D have to Hotshot Company and other stockholders?

b. What potential liability might M&D have to financial institutions that used the financial statements in connection with making loans to Hotshot Company?

(AICPA adapted)

LO C-4, C-5

C.72   Liability under the Securities Acts. Orange is a public entity whose shares are traded on a national exchange. A Public Company Accounting Oversight Board inspection revealed a deficiency in audits conducted by Orange's auditor, LeGrow. LeGrow had failed to perform important auditing procedures; after performing these procedures in response to the inspection, LeGrow identified several material misstatements and requested that Orange restate its financial statements. These restatements had the effect of reducing Orange's reported income and cash flow from operations and increasing its liabilities.

Upon the disclosure of these restatements, Orange's stock price declined more than 40 percent. Angered over this decline, investors are contemplating bringing legal action against LeGrow for failing to detect the misstatements.

Required:

a. Assume that investors are bringing suit under the Securities Act of 1933. What would investors need to demonstrate to bring suit against LeGrow under this act?

b. What is LeGrow's potential liability to investors if LeGrow's audit was characterized as demonstrating (1) ordinary negligence, (2) gross negligence, or (3) fraud?

c. Repeat parts *(a)* and *(b)*, assuming that investors are bringing suit under the Securities Exchange Act of 1934.

d. What are the primary differences in LeGrow's liability to investors under the Securities Act of 1933 and the Securities Exchange Act of 1934?

LO C-4, C-5

C.73   Liability under the Securities Acts. Jones, CPA, audits a number of public companies. During the past year, some deficiencies with respect to audits conducted for two of Jones's clients in the software industry (SoftWare and ExternalDrive) were identified. These deficiencies related to Jones's audit procedures used to evaluate the revenue recognized by these clients. Some pertinent facts in each of these audits are summarized as follows:

- *SoftWare.* In 2023, SoftWare issued securities to investors in an initial public offering with an average offering price of $50 per share. Jones audited the financial statements, which were later determined to have overstated revenues through premature revenue recognition. The net effect on SoftWare's operations was an overstatement of revenue by 25 percent and an overstatement of net income by 63 percent. Following the issuance, the market value of SoftWare's shares declined to $15 per share.

- *ExternalDrive.* ExternalDrive has been a client of Jones for five years and has been publicly traded throughout that entire period. In 2023, ExternalDrive's Form 10-K revealed revenues of $25 million, net income of $8.5 million, and earnings per share of $1.40, all of which exceeded prior years' results and analysts' estimates. ExternalDrive's financial statements were subsequently found to have overstated revenues by $2.25 million, which reduced reported revenues and earnings per share by 11 percent and 24 percent, respectively. Following the revelation of these misstatements, ExternalDrive's stock price declined from $18 per share to $9 per share.

You have been asked to defend Jones in legal actions involving shareholders of both companies and have engaged an auditing expert to evaluate Jones's performance. After reviewing the audit documentation and related professional literature, she concluded that Jones's performance was likely in violation of generally accepted auditing standards; however, it did not rise to the level of being considered "reckless," and it does not appear that Jones was aware of the departures from GAAP. In addition, although unrelated to Jones's audit, she observed that the market price of software companies had declined in a similar manner to that of SoftWare and ExternalDrive because of overall economic conditions.

Required:

a. Which statute would govern Jones's liability to shareholders of SoftWare? ExternalDrive?

b. What would shareholders of SoftWare and ExternalDrive need to demonstrate prior to bringing suit against Jones?

c. Based on the case facts as described, what possible defense(s) would you recommend to Jones in each of these situations?

d. Assume that these two cases went to trial and Jones's performance was deemed to be "reckless" in nature and that Jones possessed scienter. How does this change the likelihood of a favorable outcome for Jones?

LO C-6

C.74 **Class-Action Lawsuits.** In the United States, it has become common to seek recovery of financial losses from other parties, often even if that other party is not at fault. Frequently, this occurs by means of a class-action lawsuit.

Required:

a. What is a class-action lawsuit?

b. What advantages does a class-action lawsuit have for the plaintiffs?

c. What disadvantages does a class-action lawsuit have for the defendant?

d. How has recent legislation affected class-action lawsuits?

e. Perform an Internet search for information regarding class-action lawsuits against auditors. What are the (1) particulars of the lawsuit and (2) auditors' defenses?

LO C-2, C-4

C.75 **Liability under Common Law and the Securities Act of 1933.** Butler Manufacturing Corporation raised capital for a plant expansion by borrowing from a bank and making a stock offering. Butler engaged Weaver, CPA, to audit its December 2023 financial statements. Butler told Weaver that the financial statements would be given to Union Bank and certain other named banks and included in a registration statement for the stock offering.

In performing the audit, Weaver did not confirm accounts receivable and, therefore, failed to discover a material overstatement. Weaver also was aware of a pending class-action product liability lawsuit that was not disclosed in Butler's financial statements. Despite being advised by Butler's legal counsel that the entity's potential liability under the lawsuit would result in material losses, Weaver issued an unmodified opinion on Butler's financial statements.

In May 2024, Union Bank relied on the financial statements and Weaver's opinion to grant Butler a $500,000 loan.

Butler raised additional funds in November 2024 with a $14,000,000 unregistered offering of preferred stock. This offering was sold directly by the entity to 40 nonaccredited private investors during a one-year period.

Shortly after obtaining the Union Bank loan, Butler experienced financial problems but was able to stay in business because of the money raised by the stock offering. Butler lost the product liability suit, resulting in a judgment that the entity could not pay. Butler also defaulted on the Union Bank loan and was involuntarily petitioned into bankruptcy. This caused Union Bank to sustain a loss, and Butler's stockholders' investments became worthless.

Union Bank sued Weaver for failure to provide the appropriate level of professional care and for common law fraud. The stockholders who purchased Butler's stock through the offering sued Weaver, alleging fraud under section 17 of the Securities Act of 1933.

These transactions took place in a jurisdiction providing for auditors' liability for ordinary negligence to known and intended users of financial statements.

Required:

Answer the following questions and give the reasons for your conclusions.

a. Will Union Bank be successful in its suit against Weaver under common law for (1) ordinary negligence and (2) fraud?

b. Will the stockholders who purchased Butler's stock through the offering succeed against Weaver under the antifraud provisions of section 17 of the Securities Act of 1933?

(AICPA adapted)

LO C-4, C-5

C.76 **Liability under the Securities Acts.** One of your firm's clients, Fancy Fashions Inc., is a highly successful, rapidly expanding entity. It is owned predominantly by the Munster family and key corporate officials. Although additional funds would be available on a short-term basis from its bankers, they would represent only a temporary solution of the entity's need for capital to finance its expansion plans. In addition, the interest rates being charged are not appealing. Therefore, Chris Munster, Fancy's chairman of the board, in consultation with the other shareholders, has decided to explore the possibility of raising additional equity capital of approximately $15 million to $16 million. This will be Fancy's first public offering.

At a meeting of Fancy's major shareholders, its attorneys and a member of your firm spoke about the advantages and disadvantages of "going public" and registering a stock offering. One of the shareholders suggested that Regulation D under the Securities Act of 1933 might be a preferable alternative.

Required:

a. Assume that Fancy makes a public offering for $16 million and, as a result, more than 1,000 persons own shares of the entity. Following the public offering, what are the implications with respect to the Securities Exchange Act of 1934? (*Hint:* You can identify the thresholds for being subject to the reporting requirements of the Securities Exchange Act of 1934 through reference to the SEC's website, www.sec.gov.)

b. What federal civil and criminal liabilities under the Securities Act of 1933 could apply in the event that Fancy sells the securities without registration and a registration exemption is not available?

c. Using the SEC's website (www.sec.gov) as a reference, define "accredited investor" and discuss the exemption applicable to offerings made under Regulation D for accredited investors.

(AICPA adapted)

LO C-4

C.77 **Section 11 of Securities Act of 1933: Liability Exposure.** Chriswell Corporation decided to raise additional long-term capital by issuing $20 million of 12 percent subordinated debentures to the public. May, Clark & Company, CPAs, the company's auditors, were engaged to examine the June 30, 2024, financial statements, which were included in the bond registration statement.

May, Clark & Company completed its examination and submitted an unmodified auditors' report dated July 15, 2024. The registration statement was filed and became effective on September 1, 2024. On August 15, one of the partners of May, Clark & Company called on Chriswell Corporation and had lunch with the financial vice president and the controller. He questioned both officials on the company's operations since June 30 and inquired whether there had been any material changes in the company's financial position since that date. Both officers assured him that everything had proceeded normally and that the financial condition of the company had not changed materially.

Unfortunately, the officers' representation was not true. On July 30, a substantial debtor of the company failed to pay the $400,000 due on its account receivable and indicated to Chriswell that it would probably be forced into bankruptcy. This receivable was shown as a collateralized loan on the June 30 financial statements. It was secured by stock of the debtor corporation, which had a value in excess of the loan at the time the financial statements were prepared but was virtually worthless at the effective date of the registration statement. This $400,000 account receivable was material to the financial condition of Chriswell Corporation, and the market price of the subordinated debentures decreased by nearly 50 percent after the foregoing facts were disclosed.

The debenture holders of Chriswell are seeking recovery of their loss against all parties connected with the debenture registration.

Required:

Are May, Clark & Company liable to the Chriswell debenture holders under section 11 of the Securities Act of 1933? Explain. (*Hint:* Review the *BarChris* case in this chapter.)

(AICPA adapted)

LO C-5

C.78 **Rule 10(b)-5 Liability under the Securities Exchange Act of 1934.** Gordon & Groton (G&G), CPAs, were auditors of Bank & Company, a brokerage firm and member of a national stock exchange. G&G examined and reported on the financial statements of Bank, which were filed with the Securities and Exchange Commission.

Several of Bank's customers were swindled by a fraudulent scheme perpetrated by Bank's president, who owned 90 percent of the voting stock of the company. The facts establish that G&G failed to perform the audit with the appropriate level of professional care but neither participated in the fraudulent scheme nor knew of its existence.

The customers are suing G&G under the antifraud provisions of section 10(b) and Rule 10b-5 of the Securities Exchange Act of 1934 for aiding and abetting the president's fraudulent scheme. The customers' suit for fraud is predicated exclusively on G&G's failure to conduct a proper audit, thereby failing to discover the fraudulent scheme.

Required:

Answer the following, setting forth reasons for any conclusions stated.

a. What is the probable outcome of the lawsuit?

b. What might be the result if plaintiffs had sued under common law for ordinary negligence? Explain.

(AICPA adapted)

LO C-5

C.79 **Independence and Securities Exchange Act of 1934.** Anderson, Olds, and Watershed (AOW) have been the independent auditors for Accord Corporation since 1990. Accord is a public entity obligated to file periodic reports under the Securities Exchange Act of 1934.

Beginning in January 2023, the AOW litigation support consulting division performed a special engagement for Accord. The work involved a lawsuit that Accord had filed against Civic Company for patent infringement on microchip manufacturing processes. AOW personnel compiled production statistics—costs and lost profits—under various volume assumptions and then testified in court about the losses to Accord that had resulted from Civic's improper use of patented processes. The amounts at issue were very large, with claims of $50 million for lost profits and a plea for $150 million punitive damages. Accord won a court judgment for a total of $120 million, and Civic has appealed the damage award. The case remained pending throughout 2023 and into 2024. By March 1, 2024, AOW had billed Accord $265,000 for the litigation support work.

In November 2023, AOW started the audit work on Accord's financial statements for the fiscal year ending December 31, 2023. During this work, AOW auditors found that Accord's management and board of directors did not fully disclose the stage of the appeal of the Civic Company case, had improperly deferred a material loss on new product start-up costs as an element of its inventory, and had accrued sales revenue for promotional chip sales that carried an unconditional right of return. As partner in charge of the engagement, D. Ward agreed with the president that the accounting and disclosure were suitable to protect Accord's shareholders from adverse business developments, and he issued a standard unmodified opinion that was included in the entity's 10-K annual report filed with the SEC and dated April 1, 2024.

On April 2, 2024, AOW then billed Accord for the $200,000 audit fee and sent a reminder for payment of the $265,000 consulting fee.

Required:

a. Was AOW independent for the audit of Accord for the fiscal year ended December 31, 2023? Explain.

b. Did Ward and AOW follow generally accepted auditing standards in the audit? Cite any specific standards that might have been violated, and explain your reasoning.

c. Did Ward and AOW violate any section(s) of the Securities Exchange Act of 1934? Explain.

LO C-5

C.80   **Auditors' Liability under Securities Exchange Act of 1934.** Adam, an Illinois resident, was interested in purchasing stock in Joshua Foods Inc. Joshua Foods has corporate headquarters in Fond du Lac, Wisconsin, and is incorporated in Delaware. Adam accessed Joshua Foods' 2023 annual report including the financial statements on its corporate website. Adam also reviewed several analysts' opinions on the Internet, including the opinions provided from his Internet broker, Matthew & Co. ExpressTrade. Adam received the annual report in the mail. Based on the increasing revenues, the $8 million net income indicated on the financial statements, and the other information received from the analysts, Adam purchased $350,000 worth of stock.

Three months later, Joshua Foods announced that over the past three years, the company had included $25 million of fictitious revenue and had capitalized more than $30 million of charges that should have been expensed. These irregularities will result in a restatement of the fiscal 2023 financial statements, resulting in a $1,250,000 loss for fiscal 2023. The press release from the company says that it will likely declare bankruptcy in the next few weeks. In the following two weeks, the value of Adam's holdings in the stock declined to $50,000.

Required:

a. You are Adam's attorney. List the various legal issues and precedents that you will use in trying to recover the losses Adam sustained.

b. You are the attorney for Joshua Foods' auditors. It is apparent that Adam will try to recover losses from your firm. List the defenses you would prepare to protect the auditors from liability.

c. How does Sarbanes–Oxley affect the position of either Adam's attorney or the auditors' attorney? You may find www.soxlaw.com helpful.

MODULE D

Internal Audits, Governmental Audits, and Fraud Examinations

You have a chance to really learn and improve the business. You build relationships with the board and the major business leaders. You can move internal audit to more value-added processes. And it builds your ability to manage people and work with cross-functional teams.

Michael Fung, former CFO, Walmart North American stores division, on his four years spent in internal audit[1]

Professional Standards References

Topic	AU-C/ISA Section	AS Section
Consideration of Fraud in a Financial Statement Audit	240	2401
Consideration of Laws and Regulations	250	2405
Consideration of the Internal Audit Function in a Financial Statement Audit	610	2605
Compliance Auditing Considerations in Audits of Governmental Entities and Recipients of Governmental Financial Assistance	801	6110
		ET/AT Standard[†]
Compliance Attestation		AT-C 315
Independence, Integrity, and Objectivity		ET 101-191
		IIA Standards
International Standards for the Professional Practice of Internal Auditing		IIA 1000–2000 (all)
		Government Audit Standards
Government Auditing Standards (e.g., Yellow Book)		Chapters 1–9 (all)

[†]ET indicates ethics standard.

LEARNING OBJECTIVES

This module further explores other kinds of audit engagements referenced in Chapter 1, specifically, internal audits, governmental audits, and fraud examinations. These fields differ in important respects from financial statement auditing practiced by independent accountants in public accounting.

However, you will find that all fields of auditing share many elements. Fraud examination can be very exciting. It has the aura of detective work—finding things people want to keep hidden. The explanations and examples in this module will help you understand the working environment, objectives, and procedures that characterize internal, governmental, and fraud examination.

[1]*CFO.com,* June 10, 2008.

Your objectives are to be able to

LO D-1   Define *internal auditing,* describe internal audit institutions (e.g., the IIA), describe how internal auditors interact with independent auditors, explain internal auditors' independence problems, and list features of internal audit reports.

LO D-2   Define *governmental auditing,* describe governmental audit institutions (e.g., the GAO), describe the three types of governmental audits, discuss the standards and regulations that govern audits, list features of governmental audit reports, and understand the purpose of the Single Audit Act of 1984 and Amendments of 1996.

LO D-3   Define *fraud examination* and the differences in how external auditors and fraud examiners approach their work. Describe the main objectives of a fraud investigation, how a fraud case is built, and how fraud evidence is handled. Describe the ways CPAs can assist in prosecuting fraud perpetrators.

INTRODUCTION[2]

On March 22, 2018, officials of the city of Atlanta announced that the city had been a victim of a cyberattack. The unleashing of the SamSam ransomware virus on the city's computer system shuts down many of the city's services for several days, with some impacts stretching over several weeks. A month after the attack, water and sewer bills still could not be paid online or over the phone, and business licenses could only be obtained in person. Public Wi-Fi at Atlanta's Hartsfield-Jackson International airport, the busiest airport in the nation, was not available for two weeks. Scheduling for traffic ticket hearings was shut down for almost a month and a significant amount of correspondence related to city council work was lost.

The worst part—the debacle may very well have been avoided had the city acted on the warning of the internal auditor. Months before the attack, the city auditor provided a 41-page audit report indicating that the IT system was susceptible to attacks and that there were no formal processes to manage related risk. Specifically, the report stated that "the large number of severe and critical vulnerabilities identified has existed for so long the organizations responsible have essentially become complacent." The report goes on to note that, "departments tasked with dealing with the vulnerabilities . . . do not have enough time or tools to properly analyze or treat the systems. This situation represents a significant level of preventable risk exposure to the city." Had the city responded in a timely manner to the concerns of the internal auditors, Atlanta may have saved itself from the embarrassment and headaches caused by the attack, along with the $2.7 million spent in contracts with IT consultants and crisis management services to help the city recover.

INTERNAL AUDITS, GOVERNMENTAL AUDITS, AND FRAUD EXAMINATIONS

In today's environment of increased public scrutiny, organizations are asking public accounting firms for more assistance. Public accounting firms are not able to provide internal audit services to their publicly traded audit clients. However, organizations that need assistance with internal audit, investigation, and other related services can turn to public accounting firms that do not serve as their financial statements auditor. One of the main segments in most large public accounting firms is outsourced and co-sourced internal audit services, and this opportunity has led to several business ventures focused primarily on providing internal audit and other nonaudit services to clients. One such

[2]The material in this introduction is based on the following articles, with the quoted material coming from the CBS article: "Atlanta was not prepared to respond to a ransomware attack," *Statescoop.com,* April 24, 2018; "Atlanta was warned about vulnerabilities months before cyberattack, report shows," CBSNews, May 28, 2018.

example is **Protiviti Inc.,** whose business services are described further in the following Auditing Insight.

AUDITING INSIGHT | Taking Care of Business

The following is an excerpt from the Protiviti website:

Protiviti is a global consulting firm that delivers deep expertise, objective insights, a tailored approach and unparalleled collaboration to help leaders confidently face the future. Our consulting solutions span critical business problems in technology, business process, analytics, risk, compliance, transactions and internal audit. We are committed to attracting and developing a diverse workforce of professionals

that share the common value of collaboration. As an organization, we believe that by teaming together, with each other, and our clients, we can see beyond the surface of changes and problems organizations face in this fast changing world to discover opportunities others might miss and face the future with greater confidence.

Source: *https://www.protiviti.com/US-en/about-us*

Many of the tasks and processes that internal auditors and governmental auditors perform are similar to those that financial statement auditors perform. However, services performed by governmental and internal auditors do vary considerably. When internal and governmental auditors perform audits of financial information, the scope of the engagement typically is wider than the scope performed by an external auditor. Internal auditors and governmental auditors often have objectives that go beyond the fair presentation of the financial statements, such as the efficiency of the financial reporting process. Furthermore, governmental and internal auditors often perform audits of monthly financial statements or other internal financial reports to ensure that information for management decisions is reliable. In this module, we explore the services provided by internal auditors and governmental auditors and gain an understanding of the elements that help to define what is meant by a *quality audit*.

Also in this module, we explore services auditors can provide related to fraud and fraud investigations. External auditors, internal auditors, and governmental auditors all have some responsibilities related to the identification of suspected fraud. As discussed in Chapter 4, external auditors are required to assess the risk of material misstatement due to fraud and to design further procedures based off of that assessment in the financial statement audit. Internal auditors are often the ones to discover fraud within organizations. When fraud is suspected or discovered, a fraud examination, with the help of a certified fraud examiner will typically commence. Fraud examinations and other services CPAs can provide with relation to fraud investigations are discussed at the end of the module.

INTERNAL AUDITS

LO D-1

Define *internal auditing,* describe internal audit institutions (e.g., the IIA), describe how internal auditors interact with independent auditors, explain internal auditors' independence problems, and list features of internal audit reports.

Internal Auditing Defined

In the past, *internal auditors* have been defined as auditors working for the organization they were auditing. Internal auditors were employed by an organization such as a bank, hospital, city government, or industrial company. However, in recent years, many professional services firms are providing internal audit services to the business community. Therefore, internal auditors may now be employed by either the organization they are auditing or an independent professional services firm.[3] Many corporations believe that they gain expertise and improve control over audit costs when the internal audit function is outsourced to an external audit firm. Conversely, other companies believe that an in-house internal audit function is better aligned with the company's goals and objectives and auditors gain more experience and expertise with the company's organization and

---

[3]Professional services firms include public accounting firms that offer a variety of auditing, accounting, and consulting services and some consulting firms that do not perform financial statement audit services but do provide other services including internal audit services (examples include Quality Auditing LLC and Protiviti).

business. Currently, we are seeing more firms implementing a co-sourcing strategy in which the company retains an in-house internal audit department augmented by auditors from an outside firm. This strategy allows the company to have a core audit group dedicated to the company with specialized "institutional knowledge" in company policy, procedure, and strategy, yet the company can obtain expertise and audit knowledge from the professional services firm for specific engagements or projects.

The Institute of Internal Auditors (IIA), the organization that sets standards and governs the internal audit profession, defines **internal auditing** and states its objective as follows:

> Internal auditing is an independent, objective, assurance and consulting activity designed to add value and improve an organization's operations. It helps an organization accomplish its objectives by bringing a systematic, disciplined approach to evaluate and improve effectiveness of risk management, control, and governance processes.

Several key elements in this definition warrant further evaluation.

Independence

You may be wondering how in-house internal auditors employed by the company being audited can classify themselves as independent and objective. Although internal auditors employed by the entity under audit cannot be disassociated from their employers in the eyes of the public, they seek organizational and individual independence. Internal auditors achieve independence during the audit process when they are free from direction or constraint by the managers of the business unit under audit. To establish this organizational independence, many internal audit organizations report directly to the audit committees of the board of directors. Such a reporting relationship reduces management's influence over the audit scope and reporting. The other key aspect of independence and objectivity concerns the attitude of the individuals engaged in the audit. An internal auditor must have an impartial, unbiased attitude in performing the audit. In addition, individual auditors must not have any conflicts of interests. Such conflicts may result when the same company employs family members or outside business interests that appear to affect audit judgments.

An element that greatly assists the internal audit department in establishing an independent and objective organization is the **audit charter**. Many departments and organizations have charters, and it is particularly important for the internal audit department to have one. An internal audit charter approved by senior management and the board of directors provides:

- A commitment from management to the establishment of an independent and objective audit organization.
- A definition of the authority and responsibility of the audit department.
- A definition of the scope of the audit department's activities.
- The department's authorization to perform audits, request materials, and gather evidence.
- The performance and reporting requirements for the audit department.

These elements provide an essential foundation for building an independent department. Your university may even have an audit charter, similar to Georgetown University as further highlighted in the following Auditing Insight.

 AUDITING INSIGHT   Accountability at the University Level

An internal audit charter is used to define the purpose, responsibility, and authority for the internal audit function in all types of organizations, including universities. Georgetown University's internal audit charter outlines several important elements of their internal audit function, including its mission, responsibilities, objective, and the independence and objectivity of the internal audit department. According to the charter, the mission of the internal audit function at Georgetown is to "review accounting, financial and other operations to determine for the President and Board of directors that: (1) Assets are safeguarded and their use properly accounted for. (2) Accurate financial and managerial controls exist and function properly. (3) Recommendations are made for improvement in controls. (4) Management plans, policies and procedures are carried out and executed efficiently and effectively." One might interpret the mission of the internal audit function as a way to hold the university accountable.

Source: Georgetown University Internal Audit Department Charter

Add Value and Improve Operations

While internal auditors do often perform work on the company's financial statements, the objective of an internal audit and an external audit are different. As the definition of internal auditing states, internal audits are intended *to add value and improve an organization's operations*. Assuring appropriate financial reporting standards are followed is just one of many ways internal auditors add value. Internal auditors primarily add value to a company by achieving the following four audit objectives:

1. *Recognizing and analyzing industry, business, and operational risks.* Internal auditors use their industry knowledge to recognize and evaluate how changes in the economy, business environment, technology, regulatory environment, and management impact risks. Internal audit will often take a proactive approach to reduce or eliminate the risks identified, therefore adding value to the company.

2. *Improving the effectiveness and efficiency of the operations.* Over a period of a few years, an internal auditor will have evaluated almost every department and almost every aspect of a company's business. This experience makes the auditor a valuable asset to the organization, as the internal auditor may be able to provide insight into which processes work best to improve the effectiveness and efficiency of operations and how they could be implemented in other areas of the company.

3. *Ensuring compliance with management directives.* In fulfilling this objective, internal auditors are concerned with identifying any noncompliance with management directives that (1) increases the risk faced by the company or (2) diminishes the efficiency or effectiveness of the company's operations which might ultimately harm the company's likelihood of meeting its goals and objectives.

4. *Serving as management's representative.* The complexities of managing a large organization often prohibit senior management from visiting locations and departments critical to the success of the organization. Therefore, the reports from the internal audit department may serve as the only critical objective evaluations received by management for certain key areas of the organization.

It should be evident that the four audit objectives discussed here are not mutually exclusive. For example, the evaluation of compliance with company policies and procedures includes elements of reducing risk, evaluating effectiveness and efficiency, and being management's representative.

Internal Audit Standards

The IIA is an international organization that, along with setting and governing standards, also provides continuing education and general rules of conduct for internal auditors as a profession. The IIA issues *International Standards for the Professional Practice of Internal Auditing* (IIA *Standards*). The IIA standards are classified in three major categories:

1. Attribute standards.
2. Performance standards.
3. Implementation standards.

Aptly named, the attribute standards address the *characteristics of internal auditors* (e.g., independence, objectivity) *and organizations* performing internal audit activities. Performance standards relate to *conducting internal audit activities* and provide a *measure of quality* against which the performance of internal audit activities can be measured. The attribute and the performance standards apply to internal audit services in general. Implementation standards, on the other hand, are specific applications of the attribute and performance standards to specific types of engagements (e.g., assurance or consulting engagements).

Internal auditors are expected to comply with the IIA's standards of professional conduct. IIA audit standards are recommended and encouraged, but compliance with them depends on their acceptance, adoption, and implementation by practicing internal auditors. Many internal audit organizations include compliance with IIA standards in their department charters and in their audit reports.

The IIA also issues practice advisories. Because of the diversity of entities serviced by internal auditors, guidance from practice advisories is not mandatory. They suggest "best practices" in internal audit, and internal audit organizations are encouraged to implement those practices that are applicable to the business and industry they serve.

The IIA also administers the certified internal auditor (CIA) program. This certification is a mark of professional achievement that has gained international acceptance. To become a CIA, a candidate must hold a college degree and pass an examination on internal auditing and related subjects. The exam has three parts:

- Part 1—Internal audit basics.
- Part 2—Internal audit practice.
- Part 3—Internal audit knowledge elements.

Candidates also must have two years of audit experience (internal audit or public accounting audit) obtained before or after passing the examination. Holders of master's degrees need only one year of experience. You can sit for the CIA exam prior to completion of your bachelor's degree.

Types of Internal Audit Services

As stated in the definition of internal auditing, the internal audit function "helps an organization accomplish its objectives." To achieve this goal, internal auditors provide a variety of internal audit services including (1) financial audits of financial reports and accounting control systems; (2) compliance audits that ensure conformity with company policies, plans, and procedures and with laws and regulations; (3) operational audits that evaluate the effectiveness and efficiency of business process; (4) governance audits to aid management decision making; and (5) other types of audits specific to the organization.

Financial Audits

Internal auditors usually do not audit quarterly or year-end financial statements in the same manner as external auditors. However, internal auditors may evaluate areas that management believes could be of concern to the external auditors, such as areas that were found to have problems in the prior audit. Such a preliminary evaluation may allow for correction of errors prior to the arrival of the external auditors.

Internal auditors typically perform audits of financial reports for internal use. This type of audit provides managers assurance that the information they are using in the decision-making process is relevant and reliable. Such an assurance function reduces management's risk in making daily operating decisions or in determining appropriate action to address a unique problem. This type of auditing is similar to the auditing described elsewhere in this textbook. As discussed further in Chapter 3, external auditors can, and often do, rely on the work done by internal auditors in this capacity to help reduce the amount of work performed and duplication of efforts.

The following Auditing Insight describes one instance where the internal auditors discovered fraud while performing routine financial auditing procedures.

 AUDITING INSIGHT A Not So Routine Financial Audit

Jim Burton, new to internal audit at **Smith Construction Inc. (SCI),** was performing what was supposed to be the most routine part of internal auditing. He and his supervisor, in accordance with company policy, were evaluating critical general ledger accounts following the departure of a high-level employee, in this case, the company's chief financial officer (CFO), Paul Fournier. Jim was assigned to look over the company's liability accounts.

What Jim discovered, however, was not so routine. He noticed a $30,000 payable made each month to a Boston law firm. After digging, Jim and his supervisor discovered that SCI had not had dealings with the law firm for several years, and that the checks were in fact not being sent to the firm at all. Fournier had accessed the vendor master file and had changed the mailing address to one in Canada. With no formal review of vendor changes, the switch was simple. He then forged invoices from the law firm and submitted them for payment. The checks were mailed to his Canadian address, where he cashed the checks on his own behalf. In total, the former CFO stole $1.1 million from SCI. He was eventually convicted of fraud and sentenced to 18 months in a U.S. federal prison.

Source: "The CFO Check Scam," *Internal Auditor,* June 2018, pp. 18–19.

Compliance Audits

In many functional areas of a business, management's primary concern is compliance with policies, procedures, laws, and regulations—thus, the definition of **compliance audits**. The degree of management's concern for such audits may vary by industry or by functional area. For example, compliance with laws will be of more concern in the banking, insurance, and health care industries as compared with a company in the retail industry. Also, in an audit of the human resources department, the main audit objective may be compliance with policies and procedures designed to ensure conformity with laws regarding fair hiring and proper dismissals of employees.

As the following Auditing Insight highlights, for compliance audits to be useful, management needs to appropriately address any concerns raised during the audits.

AUDITING INSIGHT   Internal Audit Told Them So

Internal auditors at **Kinross Gold,** a Canadian based gold mining company, tried to warn management. In April of 2018, Kinross was hit with charges from the Securities and Exchange Commission (SEC) for not complying with the Foreign Corrupt Practices Act (FCPA)'s books and records and internal control provision. The violations occurred within two African subsidiaries, which Kinross had purchased in 2010. In 2011, the Kinross internal audit department examined the two subsidiaries and found that "the internal accounting controls surrounding vendor selection and disbursement for goods and services . . . were not adequate to meaningfully assess transactions for accuracy or compliance with the FCPA." Despite these warnings, the violations went unfixed for three years which then triggered an SEC investigation. Kinross settled the case by agreeing to pay close to a $1 million fine.

Source: "Ignored Internal Audit Reports Lead to FCPA Violation at Gold Miner," Internal Audit 360°, April 5, 2018.

Operational Audits

Operational auditing refers to auditors' study of business operations for the purpose of making recommendations about the efficient use of resources, effective achievement of business objectives, and compliance with company policies. The goal of operational auditing is to help managers perform their management responsibilities and improve profitability. Internal auditors consider operational auditing as an integral part of internal auditing. The AICPA defines operational auditing performed by independent public accounting firms as a distinct type of consulting service having the goal of helping a client improve the use of its capabilities and resources to achieve its objectives. Therefore public accounting firms could perform operational audits as a consulting service for nonattest clients.

Governance Audits

The definition of internal auditing includes evaluating the *governance process*. Internal auditors do this through the performance of **governance audits.** Governance audits are designed to help provide management with high-quality information for making governance decision. They ensure that senior management receives accurate and timely information concerning management and leadership throughout the organization as well as the proper implementation and execution of company strategy and plans. This function of internal audit is continuing to grow in both scope and importance. When evaluating the governance process, the auditor could report on a wide variety of critical information. It is essential that management understands the risks that the business and industry are facing. It is also imperative that management receives objective, timely feedback concerning corporate strategies and initiatives in order to effectively guide the corporation and fulfill their fiduciary responsibilities.

Other Audits

Internal auditors may perform audits that are specific to the nature of the business they serve.

Quality Control Audits Auditors who work with manufacturing companies may provide **quality control audits** designed specifically to determine whether the product meets the standards established by management. Customer service departments also may be subject to a quality control audit to ensure that customers are being served in the manner prescribed by the company. The auditors are not a substitute for the quality control department, but they can review the work of quality control, quality control reports, and the responses of management to issues raised by quality control.

Environmental Audits Another type of audit performed in some organizations is an **environmental audit.**[4] Many organizations deal with materials that must be handled in manners prescribed by law (e.g., what does Walmart do with those old batteries, tires, and oil?). Auditors can review procedures, record keeping, liability issues, and compliance as they relate to the organization's environmental issues. In addition, auditors can make recommendations for reducing waste (e.g., reusable shipping containers) and making products that are more environmentally friendly (e.g., recyclable packaging materials).

Sustainability Audits In Module A, we discussed sustainability as an assurance service. That is, management may report on sustainability issues such as carbon emissions and instruct the auditors to attest to the validity of the numbers in the report provided. However, as sustainability accounting and reporting gain more acceptance, internal auditors are being asked to provide sustainability service beyond an assurance of numbers. Many organizations need audit assistance in establishing a sustainability program, measurement criteria, reporting standards, and other issues that require the internal auditor's knowledge of the company and sustainability issues.

The IIA includes sustainability under a broad context of corporate social responsibility (CSR). In this context, auditors assist management in areas of:

- Governance.
- Ethics.
- Environment issues.
- Health, safety, and security.
- Human rights and work conditions.

Clearly, we have seen the impact on corporate image and reputation as well as the questioning of the social morality of corporations whose products have been reported as having been manufactured in facilities with substandard conditions. According to the IIA:

> Internal auditors should understand the risks and controls related to CSR objectives. Where appropriate, the CAE [chief audit executive] should plan to audit, facilitate control self-assessments, verify results, and/or consult on the various subjects. Internal auditors should maintain the skills and knowledge necessary to understand and evaluate the governance, risks, and controls of CSR strategies.[5]

Because of the newness of sustainability, many companies have found that this area is best served through outsourced internal audit services. At this time, most large CPA firms have more expertise than some of their clients (especially when they can rely on knowledge transferred from European offices that have been working on sustainability issues for a long period of time). Over time, it is expected that an in-house internal audit department will gain sufficient expertise to service more of the sustainability issues within the company. To that end, as further discussed in the following Auditing Insight, the IIA has recently announced plans to focus on learning and competency opportunities for members around ESG (environmental, social, and governance) reporting issues. ESG is related to CSR, but slightly different in that ESG refers to action and measurable outcome, whereas CSR relates more to the overall value and culture of sustainability within

---

[4]Many organizations are engaged in *sustainability accounting* that includes an environmental component. However, due to the highly technical nature of environmental laws and policy, most organizations that have significant exposure have an environmental audit function.

[5]Institute of Internal Auditors, *Practice Guide, Evaluating Corporate Social Responsibility/Sustainable Development,* p. 1.

AUDITING INSIGHT | The IIA Is Focused on Sustainability

At the kick-off to the IIA's General Audit Management Conference in March 2022, the IIA president and CEO, Anthony Pugliese, highlighted the importance of educating internal auditors on sustainability reporting issues, pointing out that ESG is a topic that is gaining greater urgency.

"It's always been important, but it's become critical because we have 7 billion people living on the same rock and who knows where that's going to go. When you think about all the ESG reporting, there's just more information available, so the more information that's around, the more people want. But really this got started and it really fits our profession well around risk and change."

He further went on to discuss how companies need to utilize technology advances and increased data availability in order to keep up with the demand for ESG information from investors.

"Our access to information has changed. Organizations see it as a growth opportunity. . . People are realizing it truly adds value to the bottom line with net zero and all these terms. ESG does create value."

Based on these remarks, is appears the IIA will make sure internal auditors are in a position to help companies provide that valuable ESG information.

Source: "Internal Auditors Examining Sustainability Issues," *AccountingToday*, March 15, 2022 (www.accountingtoday.com).

an organization[6]. Internal auditors are in a position assist with CSR objectives as well as with ESG reporting for companies.

Information Technology Audits Increasingly, internal auditors perform **information technology (IT) audits**, that is, they examine and evaluate the company's controls within the information technology system to ensure they are operating as expected. With the advances and increased dependency on technology, it is crucial for companies to have both general and automated application IT controls to ensure a safe and secure computing environment and proper recording of transactions. Regular and thorough IT audits help to identify areas of increased risk so that controls can be put in place and help to assure that controls that are in place are working appropriately. A company can choose to hire a third party to perform IT audits, or IT audits may be performed by their own internal staff, either IT auditors that have been employed by the company specifically for that purpose or internal auditors. IT auditing is further discussed in Module H.

Internal Audit Reports

Internal audit reports are nearly not as standardized as external auditors' reports on financial statements. Each report is different because internal auditors need to communicate findings on a variety of assignments and audit objectives. The key criterion for an internal audit report is clear and concise communication of findings and recommendations.

The reporting stage is the internal auditors' opportunity to capture management's undivided attention. To be effective, a report cannot be unduly long, tedious, technical, or laden with minutiae. It must be accurate, concise, clear, and timely. It must speak directly to the risks the auditors evaluated. Most internal audit reports ensure that significant issues are described by five elements:

1. The *condition* the auditor identified.
2. The *criteria* that renders the condition inappropriate.
3. The *cause* of the condition.
4. The *effect* the condition may have on the company.
5. The *recommendation* that may eliminate or mitigate the condition.

Generally, internal auditors meet with the business unit's management team to review the audit report before it is distributed to senior management. This meeting is called the **exit conference**. Its purpose is to inform the business unit's management of the audit results, reach an agreement on the correctness of the findings, and learn of the corrective action that management plans in response. If there are disagreements between the internal

[6]"ESG vs. CRS: Key Distinctions and What Businesses Need to Know" dated 8/9/21, found at https://us.anteagroup.com/news-events/blog/esg-csr-definitions-differences-sustainability

auditors and the business unit's management, auditors may include management's reasons for disagreement in the audit report, in the interest of fair and complete disclosure.

Internal audit reports are sent to the highest level of management in the organization, often including the CEO and the audit committee. Usually the senior manager overseeing a business unit (e.g., the vice president of materials management for distribution centers and purchasing) would receive audit reports and respond to senior management and the audit committee regarding which recommendations will be implemented. The manager also must explain why certain recommendations will not be implemented.

Once senior management agrees with acceptance or rejection of audit recommendations, the business unit is obligated to implement the accepted recommendations. The IIA standards include a requirement for a **follow-up** to ascertain that appropriate action is being taken on accepted recommendations. Only after the follow-up is completed is the audit considered closed.

✅ REVIEW CHECKPOINTS

D.1 How does internal auditing help a company accomplish its objectives?

D.2 How can internal auditors achieve practical independence?

D.3 What four audit objectives do internal auditors try to achieve to add value to a company?

D.4 What are the standards that govern internal auditing?

D.5 What special professional certification is available for internal auditors?

D.6 What auditing services do internal auditors provide?

D.7 Who is responsible for enforcing compliance with laws and regulations in the business?

GOVERNMENTAL AUDITS

LO D-2
Define *governmental auditing*, describe governmental audit institutions (e.g., the GAO), describe the three types of governmental audits, discuss the standards and regulations that govern audits, list features of governmental audit reports, and understand the purpose of the Single Audit Act of 1984 and Amendments of 1996.

Governmental Auditing Defined

Government officials and recipients of federal monies are responsible for carrying out public functions efficiently, economically, effectively, and ethically while achieving desired public objectives.[7] Governmental auditing refers to a variety of services performed in an effort to hold the government accountable and transparent to the public regarding the linking of resources to related program results.

Many federal agencies (e.g., Army, Navy, Department of Transportation) have governmental auditors who are charged with ensuring compliance with agency and department policies and procedures. The accounting, auditing, and investigative agency of the federal government is the Government Accountability Office (GAO). It audits the departments, agencies, and programs of the federal government (even if they are subject to audits by their own internal audit staffs) to determine whether the laws passed by the U.S. Congress are followed and to determine whether programs are being implemented with economy and efficiency and are achieving desired results. The GAO is required to act in a non-partisan fashion in the work they perform, per their website, their job is to provide "timely, fact-based, non-partisan" information to improve government operations and save taxpayer dollars.[8] The U.S. Congress always receives copies of GAO reports.

The U.S. Comptroller General heads the GAO. In one sense, GAO auditors are the highest level of internal auditors for the federal government. State and federal agencies

---

[7]*Government Auditing Standards 2018 Revision,* July 2018, p. 3.
[8]"What GOA Does," March 23, 2022, (www.gao.gov).

and other local government units use the GAO's *generally accepted government auditing standards (GAGAS)* to guide their audits. These standards are published in a book with a yellow cover, referred to as the **Yellow Book**.

Many states also have audit agencies similar to the GAO. They answer to state legislatures and perform the same types of work described here as GAO auditing. In another sense, the GAO and many state agencies are really external auditors with respect to government agencies they audit because they are organizationally independent.

Many government agencies have their own internal auditors and inspectors general. Well-managed local governments also have internal audit departments. For example, most federal agencies (e.g., Department of Defense, Department of the Interior), state agencies (e.g., education, welfare, controller), and local governments (e.g., cities, counties, tax districts) have internal audit staffs. Governmental auditors are charged with looking for projects that do not spend the taxpayers' money wisely. If you were a governmental auditor looking at the project in the following Auditing Insight, would you raise any issues?

 **AUDITING INSIGHT**   A Boozy $5 Million

The National Institute of Health spent $5 million to fund a decade-long study looking at the drinking habits of college students. Guess what they found? College students drink more on game days, and students affiliated with Greek life drink more than their peers. Looks like Hollywood had it right all along.

Source: "18 Outrageous Things Your Taxes Actually Pay For," *Readers Digest,* July 29, 2021 (www.rd.com).

Types of Governmental Audits

The GAO shares with internal auditors many of the same elements of expanded-scope services. The GAO, however, emphasizes the accountability of public officials for the efficient, economical, and effective use of public funds and other resources. The GAO defines and describes *expanded-scope governmental auditing* in terms of three types of governmental audits:

1. Financial statement audits.
2. Attestation engagements.
3. Performance audits.

Financial Statement Audits

Financial statement audits determine whether the financial statements of an audited entity present fairly the financial position, results of operations, and cash flows in conformity with generally accepted accounting principles. In addition, financial audits can have other objectives, including:

- Issuing special reports for specified elements, accounts, or items of a financial statement.
- Reviewing interim financial statements.
- Issuing letters for underwriters.
- Reporting on the processing of transactions by service organizations.
- Auditing compliance with regulations relating to federal award expenditures and other governmental financial assistance.

The GAO performs a financial audit on the consolidated financial statements of the United States government. As you can see in the following Auditing Insight, the results of that audit are different from what you might expect.

AUDITING INSIGHT   The United States Government Is. . .Un-auditable?

For the 2020 fiscal year consolidated financial statement audit of the United States government, the GAO, once again, could not determine whether the financial statements fairly presented the government's finances. While the GAO did not make any new recommendations related to the process for preparing the financial statements, 12 of the 15 recommendations made in prior years to improve control deficiencies remained unaddressed. These 12 deficiencies constituted material weaknesses in internal controls to such an extent that they prevented the GAO from expressing an opinion on the financial statements. In fact, since the GAO first began to audit the accrual-based consolidated financial statements of the United States government in 1997, they have been unable to express an opinion due to ongoing material weaknesses and other limitations.

Source: *Management Report: Continued Improvements Needed in the Processes Used to Prepare the U.S. Consolidated Financial Statements GAO 21-587,* U.S. Government Accountability Office, August 12, 2021.

Attestation Engagements

Attestation engagements involve providing an opinion on a subject matter or an assertion about the subject matter that is the responsibility of another party. The subject matter of an attestation engagement may take many forms, including historical or prospective performance or condition, physical characteristics, historical events, analyses, systems and processes, or behavior. Examples of such engagements include reporting on:

- Internal control over financial reporting or compliance with specified requirements.
- Compliance with requirements of specified laws, regulations, rules, contracts, or grants.
- Management's discussion and analysis presentation.
- Prospective or pro forma financial information.
- The reliability of performance measures.
- The reasonableness and allowability of proposed contract amounts.
- Performance of specified procedures on a subject matter.

Performance Audits

Performance audits provide objective analysis so that management and those charged with governance and oversight can rely on information to improve program performance and operations, reduce costs, facilitate decision making by corrective action, and contribute to public accountability.

Performance audits may be requested by management or a legislative body or may be mandated by the law, grant, or contract under which an agency or company is operating or receiving money. Performance audits provide an objective and systematic examination of evidence of the performance and management of a program against objective criteria. Performance audits provide information to improve program operations and facilitate decision making by those with oversight responsibility. Examples of performance audits include assessing:

- The extent to which legislative, regulatory, or organizational goals and objectives are being achieved.
- The relative ability of alternative approaches to provide better program performance or eliminate factors that inhibit program effectiveness.
- The relative cost and benefits or cost effectiveness of program performance.
- The degree to which, if at all, a program produced the intended results.
- The degree to which, if at all, a program produced unintended effects.
- The extent to which programs duplicate, overlap, or conflict with other related programs.
- The degree to which, if at all, the audited entity is using sound procurement practices.
- The validity and reliability of performance measures or financial information related to the program.

The following Auditing Insight discusses the results of a recent performance audit requested by the Environmental Protection Agency.

AUDITING INSIGHT ▸ The EPA Needs to Help Hazardous Materials Facilities Follow the Rules

In 2022, the GAO issued their findings on an engagement requested by the Environmental Protection Agency (EPA) related to their Risk Management Plan (RMP) rule. The RMP rule requires certain facilities (referred to as RMP facilities) that deal extensively in hazardous materials to develop and implement a risk management program that will detect and prevent, or at the very least, minimize the consequences of an accidental leak. The EPA requested the GAO to review climate change risks at RMP facilities.

The GAO finished their engagement with several recommendations. The recommendations were all aimed towards the EPA and how they need to provide more help to RMPs so they can better meet their risk management goals with respect to climate change. The recommendations included providing more compliance assistance and clarification of compliance requirements to RMPs, improving their criteria for selecting RMPs for inspection and providing inspectors with better evaluation tools, and keeping track of common deficiencies at RMPs with the goal of using that information to help identify areas in need of compliance assistance.

Source: "GAO Concerned by Climate Change Risk Management at Hazardous Chemical Facilities," *Homeland Security Today,* March 1, 2022 (www.hstoday. us); *Chemical Accident Prevention: EPA Should Ensure Regulated Facilities Consider Risks from Climate Change GAO-22-104494,* U.S. Government Accountability Office, February 2022.

Audit Procedures for Performance Audits

The general evidence-gathering procedures used during the audit of financial statements in governmental audits are basically the same as the ones used by external auditors. However, performance audits, which provide assurance on *economy, efficiency,* and *program results,* require special consideration.

Governmental and internal auditors must be as objective as possible when developing conclusions about efficiency, economy, and program results. This objectivity is achieved by (1) finding standards for evaluation, (2) determining the actual results of the program, and (3) comparing the actual results to the standards. Finding standards and deciding on relevant measurements is often very difficult.

An Example of Setting Performance Audit Criteria

Kinerville has instituted a new program in its school system. The program provides a healthy balanced breakfast for underprivileged students in grades K–12. You have been asked to audit the program's effectiveness. In planning this audit, the following issues must be resolved:

First, what is the goal of the program? If you said, "to feed hungry children," you would be only partially correct. The actual goal of school breakfast programs is based on the assumption that children do better in school when they have a good breakfast. Therefore, the main purpose of the program is to improve the educational experience for underprivileged children.

Second, by what standard would you measure success? A comparison to other students in the school who are not in the program? If these students are not "underprivileged," is this a fair measure? Should Kinerville's school district withhold breakfasts from some underprivileged children so there is a comparison group? Is there a moral issue with this type of evaluation? (This is an ethical question that the medical profession wrestles with on a regular basis because in studies of a new medicine, placebos are given to ill patients.) Would a comparison with other schools in other districts be appropriate? Maybe, but the comparison group would have to be carefully selected and matched on many demographic factors.

Third, what is the measure that will be used for comparison? Increased grades? Higher standardized test scores? What are the problems with these measures? Will teachers change their teaching methods and focus exclusively on test preparation? Can there be other reasons for an increase in test scores?

Lastly, how large an improvement is required for the program to be successful?

You may want answers to all of these questions, but real concrete answers do not exist. Most of these issues can be resolved with tests and measures that have some positive aspects and some negative aspects, and the audit team may need to have several measures and make many difficult judgments.

When dealing with standards, measurements, and comparisons, auditors must keep inputs and outputs in perspective. For financial statement audits, evidence about inputs—personnel hours and cost, material quantities and costs, asset investment—is most important in connection with reaching conclusions. For performance audits, output measurements are most important. Management has the responsibility for devising information systems to measure output. Such measurements should correspond to program objectives set forth in laws, regulations, administrative policies, legislative reports, or other such sources. Auditors need to realize that output measurements are usually not expressed in financial terms. Output measurements could include things such as water quality improvement, educational progress, weapons effectiveness, materials-inspection time delays, etc. Auditors also need to recognize that program activity does not necessarily indicate program success, rather success is contingent on the program results, that is, the output.

GAO Government Auditing Standards

The GAO establishes GAGAS (i.e., the Yellow Book) that guide all audits for federal government agencies and facilities and all audits of entities receiving federal funds. Note that these standards must be adhered to even if an accounting firm is engaged to perform one of these audits. (Rule 501 of the AICPA Code of Conduct makes the *failure to follow government standards during a government audit* an act discreditable; see Module B.) In addition, many state and local governments have adopted GAGAS as the audit standards for agencies, municipalities, and government districts (e.g., school districts).

In many areas, GAGAS are similar to the AICPA *Statements on Auditing Standards.* However, GAGAS go beyond the AICPA standards in several respects. Government auditing standards impose additional rules and regulations about handling government funds and accounts.[9] A sample of this literature includes the following:

- Single Audit Act of 1984. This is the federal law that established uniform requirements for audits of federal financial assistance provided to state and local governments (discussed later in the module).
- OMB Uniform Administrative Requirements, Cost Principles, and Audit Requirements for Federal Awards (Uniform Guidance).
- *AICPA Audit and Accounting Guide,* "Audits of State and Local Governments."

Because most governmental programs are created by grants and operate under laws and regulations, GAGAS explicitly require review and testing for compliance with applicable laws and regulations. Governmental auditors must be especially diligent when noncompliance with laws and regulations could result in errors or frauds that could be material to the financial statements.

GAGAS have more elaborate specifications for audit documentation and reporting than GAAS require. The GAO standards require the following written reports in financial statement audits:

1. An audit report on financial statements.
2. A report on the auditee's compliance with applicable laws and regulations, including a report of irregularities, frauds, illegal acts, material noncompliance, and internal control deficiencies.
3. A report on the auditee's internal control and the control risk assessment.

GAGAS also contain an elaborate set of guidelines for reports on performance audits. These audits cover such a wide range of subjects (from food programs to military contracts) that no "standard" report is possible. The details of these standards can be found on the GAO website (www.gao.gov). These GAO standards are good guides for internal

---

[9]Extensive government audit literature can be found at three important websites: (1) the OMB website (www.whitehouse.gov/omb), (2) the AICPA website (www.aicpa.org), and (3) the GAO website (www.gao.gov).

audit reports and for operational audit reports (consulting services engagements) prepared by CPAs in public practice.

GAO Audit Reports

GAGAS have three sets of reporting standards: one for financial audits, one for attestation engagements, and another for performance audits.

Financial audit reports start with an audit report similar to the external auditors' standard report except that the description of the audit in the scope paragraph must include a reference to GAGAS. The report on financial statements contains an opinion regarding conformity with GAAP, just as the reports that independent auditors in public practice give on nongovernmental organizations. In addition, GAGAS require reports on internal control, fraud, illegal acts, violations of provisions of contracts, grant agreements, abuse of government assets, and tests of compliance with laws and regulations as part of the financial reporting requirements.

Governmental auditors, like their public accounting firm counterparts, may be asked to perform attestation engagements. Attestation engagements provide an opinion or conclusion concerning a specific subject or an assertion about a subject matter. It is important when reporting on attestation engagements to clearly specify the subject matter or assertion, the conclusions, and any significant reservations concerning the subject matter or assertion addressed in the report.

Both attestation engagement reports and performance audit reports are completely different from financial audit reports. Like that for internal audit reports, the GAO objective is clear communication for the purpose of making recommendations and improving operations. Hence, the Yellow Book's performance audit reporting standards require timely, well-written communications of findings and recommendations for action. The managers of an audited entity are expected to respond to the report, and this response is usually included in the final version of the report. Unlike internal audit reports, most GAO reports are available to the public and can be requested from the Government Printing Office.

However, performance audits have another side. GAGAS require the reports to relate illegal acts, abuse of public money and property, noncompliance with laws and regulations, and internal control weaknesses. These matters reflect negatively on an organization's management.

Single Audit Act of 1984 and Amendments of 1996

The federal government requires audits of state and local governments that receive federal financial assistance through appropriations, grants, contracts, cooperative agreements, loans, loan guarantees, property, interest subsidies, and insurance. When a state or local government, university, or community organization receives federal financial assistance from several federal agencies, the Single Audit Act of 1984, as amended in 1996, (the Act) requires that organization to obtain a **single audit** on which all of the agencies can rely in many situations.

The Act established an annual audit requirement for all governments, agencies, and nonprofit organizations that expend $750,000 or more of federal funds. A single audit, conducted in accordance with GAGAS, covering financial statements, compliance with laws and regulations, and internal control is required. The Act does not require expanded scope audits of economy, efficiency, or program results. However, federal agencies may require, and pay for, additional audits of economy, efficiency, and program results to monitor the benefits of federal fund expenditures.

The auditors can be from public accounting firms or from state and local agencies provided they meet the GAO independence and proficiency requirements. In a single audit, the auditors are expected to determine and report whether:

1. The financial statements present fairly the financial position and results of operations in accordance with GAAP.

operational auditing: An examination designed to evaluate the processes and procedures of an organization or an area within an organization to ensure the process or area is operating efficiently and effectively, 712

performance audit: An examination designed to ensure that the resources of an organization are being used appropriately and that its objectives are being met, 717

predication: A suspicion that a fraud may have occurred, 724

quality control audit: An examination designed to ensure that an organization is meeting its quality control standards; usually involves determining that personnel responsible for performing quality control are meeting the goals and objectives established and that quality information is being reported to appropriate members of management, 713

single audit: A governmental examination standard that allows an entity to receive one audit of its financial statements, compliance with laws and regulations, and internal control that will be utilized by multiple agencies granting money to the entity, 720

Yellow Book: The common name used to refer to the generally accepted government auditing standards (GAGAS), 716

Multiple-Choice Questions for Practice and Review

 All applicable Exercises and Problems are available with *Connect*

LO D-1

D.21 Which of the following would be considered in determining whether an internal audit department is independent?

   a. The organizational level of the chief audit officer and the objectivity of the audit staff.

   b. A requirement for the auditors to report to the audit committee and for the composition of that committee.

   c. The organizational status of the audit committee and the individual independence of internal auditors in the department.

   d. The nature of the audit charter and the objectivity of the audit staff.

LO D-1

D.22 Which of the following would be considered the most significant problem for internal audit if the chief audit executive reports to the controller?

   a. The controller would amend the audit schedule so more audit time was spent on accounting issues.

   b. The controller may have no training as an internal auditor.

   c. During times when the budget needs to be cut, internal audit would likely be the first to lose funding.

   d. The controller can control the scope of audits and censor audit reports before being sent to management and the audit committee.

LO D-1

D.23 Which of the following is *not* an internal audit objective designed to add value to a purchasing department?

   a. A review of the bidding process indicates that a vendor company may be operating under two different names; therefore, purchasing is not getting the three independent bids required by policy.

   b. The purchasing process is causing unnecessary delays in ordering product.

   c. The purchasing department is not following a new human resource policy requiring a six-month performance review for new employees.

   d. The director of purchasing is new to the organization and has made several decisions regarding vendor approvals with which the auditor does not agree.

LO D-1

D.24 In an internal auditor's report, audit findings would include all of the following *except*

   a. The effect of audit finding on the auditee or the company.

   b. The cause of the audit finding.

   c. The relevance of the audit finding on the audit.

   d. The recommendation to correct the audit finding.

LO D-2

D.25 Governmental auditors' independence and objectivity are enhanced when they report the results of an audit assignment directly to
   a. Managers of the government agency under audit and in which the auditors are employed.
   b. The audit committee of directors of the agency under audit.
   c. Political action committees of which they are members.
   d. The congressional committee that ordered the audit.

LO D-2

D.26 In all audits of governmental units performed according to GAGAS, the most important work is
   a. Compliance auditing.
   b. Obtaining a sufficient understanding of internal control.
   c. Documentation of the audit.
   d. Exit interviews with managers in the governmental unit.

LO D-1

D.27 Which of the following is considered different and more limited in objectives than the others?
   a. Operational auditing.
   b. Performance auditing.
   c. Management auditing.
   d. Financial statement auditing.

LO D-1

D.28 A typical objective of an operational audit is for the auditor to
   a. Determine whether the financial statements fairly present the company's operations.
   b. Evaluate the feasibility of attaining the company's operational objectives.
   c. Make recommendations for achieving company objectives.
   d. Report on the company's relative success in attaining profit maximization.

LO D-2

D.29 A governmental auditor assigned to audit the financial statements of the state highway department would not be considered independent if the auditor
   a. Also held a position as a project manager in the highway department.
   b. Was the state audit official elected in a general statewide election with responsibility to report to the legislature.
   c. Normally works as a state auditor employed in the department of human services.
   d. Was appointed by the state governor with responsibility to report to the legislature.

LO D-2

D.30 Governmental auditing can extend beyond audits of financial statements to include audits of an agency's efficient and economical use of resources and
   a. Constitutionality of laws and regulations governing the agency.
   b. Evaluation of the personal managerial skills shown by the agency's leaders.
   c. Correspondence of the agency's performance with public opinion regarding the social worth of its mission.
   d. Evaluations concerning the agency's achievements of the goals set by the legislature for the agency's activities.

LO D-1

D.31 Which of the following best describes how the detailed audit plan of a financial statement auditor compares with the audit client's comprehensive internal audit plan?
   a. The comprehensive internal audit plan covers areas that an external auditor would normally not review.
   b. The comprehensive internal audit plan is more detailed, although it covers fewer areas than an external audit would normally cover.
   c. The comprehensive internal audit plan is substantially identical to the audit plan used by an external auditor because both review substantially identical areas.
   d. The comprehensive internal audit plan is less detailed and covers fewer areas than an external auditor would normally review.

LO D-1

D.32 Which of the following is usually *not* part of an internal audit department's audit charter?
   a. A commitment from management to ensure the independence of the internal audit department.
   b. A definition of the scope of the audit department's activities.
   c. The organizational structure of the internal audit department.
   d. The reporting requirements of the internal audit department.

LO D-2

D.33 Which of the following would you *not* expect to see in an auditor's report(s) on the financial statements of an independent government agency?

    a. A statement that the audit was conducted in accordance with generally accepted government audit standards.

    b. A report on the agency's compliance with applicable laws and regulations.

    c. Commentary by the agency's managers on the audit findings and recommendations.

    d. A report on the agency's internal controls.

LO D-2

D.34 The federal Single Audit Act of 1984 as amended in 1996 requires auditors to determine and report several things about state and local governments that receive federal funds. Which of the following is *not* normally required to be reported?

    a. An opinion on the fair presentation of the financial statements in accordance with generally accepted accounting principles.

    b. A report on the government's internal control related to federal funds.

    c. The government's performance in meeting goals set in enabling legislation.

    d. A report on the government's compliance with applicable laws and regulations.

LO D-2

D.35 The Government Accountability Office (GAO) describes expanded-scope governmental auditing to include all of the following *except*

    a. Financial statement audits.

    b. Attestation engagements.

    c. Compliance audits.

    d. Performance audits.

LO D-1–D-2

D.36 In government and internal performance auditing, which of the following is the *least* important consideration when performing the fieldwork?

    a. Determining the applicable generally accepted government accounting principles pronounced by the GASB.

    b. Defining problem areas or opportunities for improvement and defining program goals.

    c. Selecting and performing procedures designed to obtain evidence about operational problems and production output.

    d. Evaluating evidence in terms of economy, efficiency, and achievement of program goals.

LO D-2

D.37 Which of the following is the *least* important consideration for a governmental auditor who needs to be objective when auditing and reporting on an agency's achievement of program goals?

    a. Measure the actual output results of agency activities.

    b. Compare the agency's actual output results to quantitative goal standards.

    c. Perform a comprehensive review of management controls.

    d. Determine quantitative standards that describe goals the agency was supposed to achieve.

LO D-2

D.38 Compliance auditing performed under the Single Audit Act of 1984 as amended in 1996 in accordance with GAGAS is necessary for an auditor's

    a. Report on the auditee's internal control, including reportable conditions and material weaknesses.

    b. Opinion on the auditee's observance, or lack thereof, of applicable laws and regulations.

    c. Opinion on the auditee's financial statements.

    d. Report of a supplementary schedule of federal assistance programs and amounts.

LO D-3

D.39 Which *two* of the following characterize the work of fraud examiners?

    a. Analysis of control weaknesses for determination of acceptable fraud risk.

    b. Analysis of control strengths as a basis for planning other audit procedures.

    c. Determination of a materiality amount that represents a significant misstatement of the financial statements.

    d. Consideration of a materiality amount in cumulative terms—that is, becoming large over a number of years.

LO D-3

D.40 When auditing with "fraud awareness," auditors should especially notice and review employee activities under which of these conditions?

a. The company always estimates the inventory but never takes a complete physical count.

b. The petty cash box is always locked in the desk of the custodian.

c. Management has published a company code of ethics and sends frequent communication newsletters about it.

d. The board of directors reviews and approves all investment transactions.

LO D-3

D.41 The *best* way to enact a broad fraud prevention program is to

a. Install airtight control systems of checks and supervision.

b. Name an ethics officer who is responsible for receiving and acting upon fraud tips.

c. Place dedicated hotline telephones on walls around the workplace with direct communication to the company ethics officer.

d. Establish a corporate culture conducive to ethical behavior in the workplace.

LO D-3

D.42 A reason to believe that a fraud has occurred is called

a. Deliberation.

b. Forensics.

c. Predication.

d. Restitution.

LO D-3

D.43 In a fraud examination, original documents must be protected from damage and tampering to

a. Establish motive.

b. Develop documentation for employee dismissal.

c. Protect the chain of custody.

d. Ensure that suspects are unaware of an investigation in progress.

LO D-1

D.44 An environmental audit might include all of following *except*

a. Determining that proper tracking of waste material is being maintained by the organization.

b. Reviewing the liability account established for pending environmental claims against the company.

c. Reviewing the environmental history of another company that the internal auditor's organization is interested in purchasing.

d. All of the above are appropriate issues for an environmental audit.

Exercises and Problems

 All applicable questions are available with *Connect*.

LO D-1, D-2, D-3

D.45 **Identification of Audits and Auditors.** Audits may be characterized as (a) financial statement audits, (b) compliance audits, (c) economy and efficiency audits, and (d) program audits. The work can be done by independent (external) auditors, internal auditors, or governmental auditors (including IRS auditors and federal bank examiners). Following is a list of the purpose or products of various audit engagements. (Students may need to refer to Chapter 1.)

a. Analyze proprietary schools' spending to train students for oversupplied occupations.

b. Determine the fair presentation in conformity with GAAP of an advertising agency's financial statements.

c. Study the Department of Defense's expendable launch vehicle program.

d. Determine costs of municipal garbage pickup services compared to comparable service subcontracted to a private business.

e. Audit tax shelter partnership financing terms.

f. Study a private aircraft manufacturer's test pilot performance in reporting on the results of test flights.

g. Periodically have U.S. comptroller of currency examine a national bank for solvency.

h. Evaluate the promptness of materials inspection in a manufacturer's receiving department.

i. Report on the need for the states to consider reporting requirements for chemical use data.

j. Render a public report on the assumptions and compilation of a revenue forecast by sports stadium/racetrack complex.

Required:

Prepare a three-column schedule showing (1) each of the engagements listed, (2) the type of audit (financial statement, compliance, economy and efficiency, or program), and (3) the kind of auditors you would expect to be involved.

LO D-1

D.46 Organizing a Risk Analysis.   You are the director of internal auditing of a large municipal hospital. You receive monthly financial reports prepared by the accounting department, and your review of them has shown that total accounts receivable from patients has steadily and rapidly increased over the past eight months.

Other information in the reports shows the following conditions:

- The number of available hospital beds has not changed.
- The bed occupancy rate has not changed.
- Hospital billing rates have not changed significantly.
- The hospitalization insurance contracts have not changed since the last modification 12 months ago.

Your internal audit department audited the accounts receivable 10 months ago. The audit documentation file for that assignment contains financial information, a record of the risk analysis, documentation of the study and evaluation of management and internal risk mitigation controls, documentation of the evidence-gathering procedures used to produce evidence about the validity and collectability of the accounts, and a copy of your report, which commented favorably on the controls and collectability of the receivables. However, the current increase in receivables has alerted you to a need for another audit so any existing problem will not get out of hand. You remember news stories last year about the manager of the city water system who got into big trouble because his accounting department double-billed all residential customers for three months.

Required:

You plan to perform a risk analysis to understand the problem if indeed one exists. Write a memo to your senior auditor listing at least eight questions to use to guide and direct the risk analysis. (*Hint:* The questions used last year were organized under these headings: (1) Who does the accounts receivable accounting? (2) What data processing procedures and policies are in effect? and (3) How is the accounts receivable accounting done? This time, you will add a fourth category: (4) What financial or economic events have occurred in the last 10 months?)

(CIA adapted)

LO D-1

D.47 Study and Evaluation of Management Control.   The study and evaluation of management risk control in a governmental or internal audit is not easy. First, auditors must determine the risks and the controls subject to audit. Then they must find a standard by which performance of the control can be evaluated. Next they must specify procedures to obtain the evidence on which an evaluation can be based. Insofar as possible, the standards and related evidence must be quantified.

Students working on this case usually do not have the experience or theoretical background to determine control standards and audit procedures, so the following scenario gives certain information (in italics) that internal auditors would know about or be able to learn on their own. Fulfilling the requirement thus amounts to taking some information from the scenario and learning other things by using accountants' and auditors' common sense.

The Scenario

Ace Corporation ships building materials to more than a thousand wholesale and retail customers in a five-state region. The company's normal credit terms are net/30 days; it offers no cash discounts. Jerry Clark is the chief financial officer and is concerned about risks related to maintaining control over customer credit. In particular, Clark has stated two management control principles for this purpose:

1. Sales are to be billed to customers accurately and promptly. Clark knows that errors will occur but thinks company personnel should be able to hold quantity, unit price, and arithmetic errors down to 3 percent of the sales invoices. Clark considers an invoice error of $1 or less not to matter and believes that prompt billing is important because customers are expected to pay within 30 days. Clark is very strict in thinking that a bill should be sent to the customer one day after shipment and believes the billing department is staffed well enough to be able to handle this workload. *The relevant company records consist of an accounts receivable control account, a subsidiary ledger of customers' accounts in which charges are entered by billing (invoice) date and credits are entered by date of payment receipts, a sales journal that lists invoices in chronological order, and a file of shipping documents cross-referenced by the number on the related sales invoice copy kept on file in numerical order.*

2. Accounts receivable are to be aged and followed up to ensure prompt collection. Clark has told the accounts receivable department to classify all customer accounts in categories of (a) current, (b) 31–59 days overdue, (c) 60–90 days overdue, and (d) more than 90 days overdue. Clark wants this trial balance to be complete and to be transmitted to the credit department within five days after each month-end. In the credit department, prompt follow-up means sending a different (stronger) collection letter to each category, cutting off credit to customers that are more than 60 days past due (putting them on cash basis), and giving the over-90-days accounts to an outside collection agency. These actions are supposed to be taken within five days after receipt of the aged trial balance. *The relevant company records, in addition to the ones listed, consist of the aged trial balance, copies of the letters sent to customers, copies of notices of credit cutoff, copies of correspondence with the outside collection agent, and reports of results—statistics of subsequent collections.*

Required:

Take the role of a senior internal auditor. You are to write a memo to the internal audit staff to inform them about comparison standards for the study and evaluation of these two management control policies. You also need to specify two or three procedures for gathering evidence about performance of the controls. The body of your memo should be structured as follows:

1. Control: Sales are billed to customers accurately and promptly.
    1. Accuracy.
        (1) Policy standard . . .
        (2) Audit procedures . . .
    2. Promptness.
        (1) Policy standard . . .
        (2) Audit procedures . . .
2. Control: Accounts receivable are aged and followed up to ensure prompt collection.
    1. Accounts receivable aging.
        (1) Policy standard . . .
        (2) Audit procedures . . .
    2. Follow-up prompt collection.
        (1) Policy standard . . .
        (2) Audit procedures . . .

LO D-1   D.48   **Quality Control Audit of a University.**   In a quality audit, defining the measurement criteria is often difficult and time consuming. You have been a student at a college or university for several years and should have a basic understanding of its academic operations. You have been engaged to perform a quality audit of your university.

Required:

a. How would you measure quality in a university environment? What departments are responsible for measuring quality?

b. What audit evidence would you look for in performing the quality audit?

LO D-1

D.49   **Internal Audit of Inventory.**   External auditors usually calculate inventory turnover (cost of goods sold for the year divided by average inventory) and use the ratio as a broad indication of inventory age, obsolescence, or overstocking. External auditors are interested in evidence relating to the material accuracy of the financial statements taken as a whole. Internal auditors, on the other hand, calculate turnover by categories and classes of inventory to detect problem areas that might otherwise be overlooked. This kind of detailed analytical audit might point to conditions of buying errors, obsolescence, overstocking, and other matters that could be changed to save money.

The data shown in the following exhibit are for turnover, cost of sales, and inventory investment for a series of four historical years and the current year. In each of the years, the external auditors did not recommend any adjustments to the inventory valuations.

Required:

Calculate the current-year inventory turnover ratios. Interpret the ratio trends and identify what conditions might exist. As an internal auditor, write a memo to the vice president for production explaining your findings, possible causes related to problems, and additional investigation that should be conducted.

Inventory Data

	Inventory				Current-Year Inventory ($000)	
	2020	**2021**	**2022**	**2023**	**Beginning**	**Ending**
Total inventory	2.1	2.0	2.1	2.1	$3,000	$2,917
Materials and parts	4.0	4.1	4.3	4.5	1,365	620
Work-in-process	12.0	12.5	11.5	11.7	623	697
Finished products:						
Computer games	6.0	7.0	10.0	24.0	380	500
Flash drives	8.0	7.2	7.7	8.5	64	300
Semiconductor parts	4.0	3.5	4.5	7.0	80	400
Chargers and cables	3.0	2.5	2.0	1.9	488	400

Additional Information Current Year ($000)

	Transfers	**Sales**	**Cost of Goods Sold**	**Gross Profit**	**Compared to Prior Year**
Materials and parts	$3,970*	NA	NA	NA	
Work-in-process	7,988†	NA	NA	NA	
Computer games	2,320‡	$2,000	$2,200	$<200>	Sales volume declined 60%§
Flash drives	2,236‡	3,000	2,000	1,000	Sales volume increased 35%
Semiconductor parts	2,720‡	4,000	2,400	1,600	Sales volume increased 40%
Chargers and cables	712‡	1,000	800	200	Sales volume declined 3%

NA means not applicable.
*Cost of materials transferred to Work-in-Process.
†Cost of materials, labor, and overhead transferred to Finished Goods.
‡Cost of goods transferred from Work-in-Process to Finished Product Inventories.
§Selling prices also were reduced and the gross margin declined.

LO D-1

D.50   **Internal Auditors in the Fast-Food Industry.**   Internal auditors perform risk-based audits that go beyond the risks of the financial statements. Assume you are on the internal audit staff of **McDonald's.**

Required:

a. Identify the risks in the fast-food industry associated with

   a. Competition.

   b. Customer preference.

   c. The economy.

   d. Technology.

   e. Regulation.

   f. Other risks.

b. Explain how each of the risks you identified could affect McDonald's.

c. Explain how these risks might affect the internal audits performed by the internal audit staff for McDonald's.

LO D-2

D.51 **CPA Involvement in an Expanded-Scope Audit.** A public accounting firm has been engaged to audit a local food distribution program funded by the U.S. Department of Agriculture. The engagement is to encompass both financial and performance audits that constitute the expanded scope of a GAGAS audit and is to be conducted in accordance with the audit standards published by the Government Accountability Office (GAO).

Required:

a. The accountants should perform sufficient audit work to satisfy the financial and compliance element of GAGAS. What is the objective of such audit work? (*Hint:* Go to the Generally Accepted Government Auditing Standards at www.gao.gov.)

b. The accountants should be aware of general and specific kinds of uneconomical or inefficient practices in such a program. What are some examples?

c. What might be some standards and sources of standards for judging program results?

LO D-3

D.52 **Selection of Effective Extended Procedures.** The following lettered items are some "suspicions," and you have been requested to select some effective procedures designed to confirm or repudiate the suspicions.

a. The custodian of the petty cash fund may be removing cash on Friday afternoon to pay for weekend activities.

b. A manager noticed that eight new vendors had been added to the purchasing department's approved list after the assistant purchasing agent was promoted to purchasing manager three weeks ago. The manager suspects all or some of them might be fictitious companies set up by the new purchasing manager.

c. The payroll supervisor may be stealing unclaimed paychecks of people who quit work and do not pick up the last check.

d. Although no customers have complained, cash collections on accounts receivable are down. The counter clerks may have stolen customers' payments.

e. The cashier may have "borrowed" money, covered it by holding each day's deposit until cash from the next day(s)'s collection is enough to make up the shortage from an earlier day, and then send the deposit to the bank.

Required:

Write the suggested procedures for each case in definite terms so another person will know what to do.

LO D-1

D.53 **Internet Exercise: Audit Charters.** Most universities have internal audit departments, and most of them have audit charters that are available on the university website (although you may need to hunt to find it). Go to the website of your college or university and find the internal audit department. Find and print the audit charter or its equivalent. If you are having trouble finding it, call or e-mail the internal audit department and ask whether someone can provide a copy of the audit charter. If your university does not have an internal audit department or does not make its charter available, check the website of one of the larger public universities in your state.

Required:

As described in the audit charter:

a. What are the responsibilities of the internal audit department?

b. What authority does the internal audit department have?

c. To whom does the internal audit department report?

d. When the internal audit department issues a report, who gets it?

e. Are there any items described in the audit charter that you find surprising or interesting?

D.54 **Internet Exercise: Governmental Audit Reports.** Go to the website of the town where you reside and find the Comprehensive Annual Financial Report (CAFR). Find the auditor's report within the CAFR and answer the following questions.

Required:

a. Who audited the financial statements in the CAFR?

b. How does the auditor's report compare to the three-paragraph standard report used when auditing for-profit companies' financial statements?

c. What additional paragraphs were added to the report?

LO D-3

D.55 **Collecting Evidence in a Fraud Examination.** A fraud examiner was called into a business because of a suspicion of fraud. An assistant manager in a bookstore is taking books off the shelf, bringing them to the return book area, completing a customer return form, and pocketing the money. This is done late in the day when few other employees are in the store and are involved in closing activities that occupy them in other areas.

Required:

a. What are the objectives of the fraud examiner in performing a fraud examination?

b. What evidence could the fraud examiner obtain that would help reach the objectives of the audit?

c. How should the fraud examiner handle the evidence obtained?

LO D-2

D.56 **Auditing the Effectiveness of a Loan Program.** The following problem is based on an actual program and situation.

The Office of Economic Opportunity (OEO) designed special programs to have a major impact on unemployment, dependency, and community tensions in urban areas with large concentrations of low-income residents or in rural areas having substantial migration to such urban areas. The purpose of these experimental programs—combining business, community, and personnel development—is to offer poor people an opportunity to become self-supporting through the free enterprise system. The programs are intended to create training and job opportunities, improve the living environment, and encourage development of local entrepreneurial skills.

Assume that the OEO has identified Mayville as a participant in the special impact program. The Mayville program received more than $50 million in federal funds and obtained another $10 million from private foundations.

Problems

Mayville is a three-square-mile section of Mega City with a population of approximately 200,000. This area has serious problems of unemployment and underemployment and inadequate housing.

Mayville's problems are deeply seated and have resisted rapid solution. They stem primarily from the fact that local residents, to a considerable degree, lack the education and training required for the jobs available elsewhere in the city and from the lack of jobs in the area. Unemployment and underemployment, in turn, reduce buying power, which has a depressing effect on the area's economy.

The magnitude of the Mayville problems is indicated by the following data disclosed by the U.S. census:

1. Of the total civilian labor force, 8.9 percent was unemployed compared with unemployment rates of 7.1 percent for Mega City and 6.8 percent for the standard metropolitan statistical area (SMSA).

2. Per capita income was $14,106, compared with $22,720 for Mega City and $29,909 for the SMSA.

3. Families below the poverty level made up 27.8 percent of the population, compared with 12.4 percent in Mega City and 9.2 percent in the SMSA.

4. Families receiving public assistance made up 25.4 percent of the population, compared with 9.6 percent in Mega City and 7.5 percent in the SMSA.

A number of factors aggravate the area's economic problems and make them more difficult to solve. Some of these are

- A reluctance of industry to move into Mega City.
- A net outflow of industry from Mega City.
- High city taxes and a high crime rate.
- A dearth of local residents possessing business managerial experience.

The area's housing problems resulted from the widespread deterioration of existing housing and are, in part, a by-product of below-average income levels resulting from unemployment and underemployment. These problems were aggravated by a shortage of mortgage capital for residential housing associated with a lack of confidence in the area on the part of financial institutions, which, as discussed later, seems to have been somewhat overcome.

Mayville was the target of several special impact programs. Included were programs designed to stimulate private business, to improve housing, to establish community facilities, and to train residents in marketable skills. There were two programs to stimulate private business: a program to loan funds to local businesses and a program to attract outside businesses to the area.

Under the business loan program begun five years ago, the sponsors proposed to create jobs and stimulate business ownership by local residents. At first, investments in local businesses were made only in the form of loans. Later, the sponsors adopted a policy of making equity investments in selected companies to obtain the sponsors' voice in management. Equity investments totaling about $159,000 were made in four companies.

Loans were to be repaid in installments over periods of up to 10 years, usually with a moratorium on repayment for six months or longer. Repayment was to be made in cash or by applying subsidies allowed by the sponsors for providing on-the-job training to unskilled workers. Loans made during the first two years of the program were interest free. Later, the sponsors revised the policy to one of charging below-market interest rates. Rates charged were from 2 to 5 percent. This policy change was made to (1) emphasize to borrowers their obligations to repay the loan and (2) help the sponsors monitor borrowers' progress toward profitability.

Prospective borrowers learned of the loan program through (1) information disseminated at neighborhood centers, (2) advertisements on radio and television and in a local newspaper, and (3) word of mouth. Those who wished to apply for loans were required to complete application forms providing information relating to their education, business and work experience, and personal financial statements and references. The sponsors set up a management assistance division, which employed consultants to supplement its internal marketing assistance efforts and to provide management, accounting, marketing, legal, and other assistance to borrowers.

The sponsors proposed to create at least 1,700 jobs during the first four years of the loan program by making loans to some 73 new and existing businesses.

Required:

Put yourself in the position of the GAO manager in charge of all audits pertaining to the Office of Economic Opportunity. The Mega City field office has been assigned to conduct a detailed review of the special impact program described here. Prepare a memo to the Mega City field office in which you indicate, in as much detail as is possible from the information provided, the specific steps the field office should perform in evaluating the effectiveness of the special impact loan program.

LO D-1

D.57 **Operational Audit: Customer Complaints.** Danny Deck, the director of internal auditing for Rice Department Stores, was working in his office one Thursday when Chris McMurray, president of the company, burst in to tell Deck about a problem. According to McMurray, "Customer complaints about delays in getting credit for merchandise returns are driving Sally Godwin up the wall! She doesn't know what to do because she has no control over the processing of credit memos."

Godwin is the manager in charge of customer relations and tries to keep everybody happy. Upon her recommendation, the company had adopted an advertising motto: "Satisfaction Guaranteed and Prompt Credit When You Change Your Mind." The motto is featured in newspaper ads and on large banners in each store.

Deck performed a preliminary review and found the following:

1. Godwin believes customers will be satisfied if they receive a refund check or notice of credit on account within five working days.

2. The chief accountant described the credit memo processing procedure as follows: When a customer returns merchandise, the sales clerks give a smile, a "returned merchandise receipt," and a promise to send a check or a notice within five days. The store copy of the receipt and the merchandise are sent to the purchasing department, where buyers examine the merchandise for quality or damage to decide whether to put it back on the shelves, return it to the vendor, or hold it for the annual rummage sale. The buyers then prepare a brief report and send it with the returned merchandise receipt to the customer relations department for approval. The buyer's report is filed for reference and the receipt, marked for approval in Godwin's department, is sent to the accounting department. The accounting department sorts the receipts in numerical order, checking the numerical sequence, and files them in preparation for the weekly batch processing of transactions other than sales and cash receipts. When the customer has requested a cash refund, the checks and canceled returned merchandise receipts are approved by the treasurer, who signs and mails the check. When the credit is on a customer's charge account, it is shown on the next monthly statement sent to the customer.

3. The processing in each department takes two or three days.

Required:

a. Analyze the problem. How much time does it take the company to process the merchandise returns?

b. Formulate a recommendation to solve the problem. Write a brief report explaining your recommendation.

LO D-2

D.58 **GAO Auditor Independence.** The GAO reporting standards for performance audits state that each report should include "recommendations for action to correct the problem areas and to improve operations." For example, an audit of the Washington Metropolitan Area Transit Authority found management decision deficiencies affecting some $230 million in federal funds. The GAO auditors recommended that the transit authority could improve its management control over rail car procurement through better enforcement of contract requirements and development of a master plan to test cars.

Suppose the transit authority accepted and implemented specific recommendations made by the GAO auditors.

Required:

Do you believe these events would be enough to impair the independence of the GAO auditors in a subsequent audit of the transit authority? Explain and tell whether it makes any difference to you that the same or different person performs both the first and subsequent audits.

LO D-2

D.59 **Efficiency Standards.** The U.S. Postal Service (USPS) advertises prompt delivery schedules for express mail (overnight delivery) and priority mail (two-to–three-day delivery). The USPS knows various risks that may arise to thwart a timely (as advertised) delivery but believes that systems and controls are in place and operating to mitigate the risks. The USPS advertised that 94 percent of express mail and 87 percent of priority mail was delivered on time from the time the mail was postmarked to the time it reached the destination post office. However, a consulting firm studied the USPS operations and determined that the express mail arrived at the recipients' addresses on time 81 percent of the time (not 94 percent) and the priority mail arrived timely 75 percent of the time (not 87 percent).

Required:

What can account for the difference in these performance statistics between the USPS delivery rates and the consultant's rates? (*Hint:* Think in terms of orientation to customers and standards for measuring performance.)

LO D-3

D.60 **The Perfect Crime.** Consider the following story of a real embezzlement.

The embezzler hired a print shop to print a private stock of Ajax Company checks in the company's numerical sequence. In his job as an accounts payable clerk, he intercepted legitimate checks written by the accounts payable department and signed by the Ajax treasurer and then destroyed them. He substituted the same-numbered check from the private stock, made it payable to himself in the same amount as the legitimate check, and "signed" it with a rubber stamp that looked enough like the Ajax Company treasurer's signature to fool the paying bank. He deposited the money in his own bank account.

The bank statement reconciler (a different person) was able to agree the check numbers and amounts listed in the cleared items in the bank statement to the recorded cash disbursement (check number and amount) and thus did not notice the trick. The embezzler was able to process the vendor's "past due" notice and next month statement with complete documentation, enabling the Ajax treasurer to sign another check the next month paying both the past due balance and current charges. The embezzler was careful to scatter the double-expense payments among numerous accounts (telephone, office supplies, inventory, etc.) so the double-paid expenses did not distort accounts very much. As time passed, the embezzler was able to recommend budget figures that allowed a large enough budget so his double-paid expenses in various categories did not often pop up as large variances from the budget.

Required:

List and explain the ways and means you believe someone might detect this fraud scheme. Think first about the ordinary everyday control procedures. Then think about extensive detection efforts assuming a tip or indication of a possible fraud has been received. Is this a "perfect crime"?

LO D-1

D.61 **Impact of Changing Rules.** Many companies outsource their internal audit function to CPA firms.

Required:

a. What benefits might be gained from having a CPA firm provide its internal audit services?

b. What benefits might be gained from having an in-house internal audit department?

c. What concerns might arise from having a CPA firm provide its internal audit services?

LO D-1, D-3

D.62 **Looking for Evidence of Fraud.** Wen-Li is an internal auditor for Main Electrical Supply in Springfield, Illinois. During her audit, she came across the invoice shown in the following exhibit. The invoice is in almost pristine condition with few marks and no creases. The invoice was properly filed in a vendor folder marked Best Office Supply, which is on the approved vendor list, but the vendor review sheet, which is required to place a vendor on the approved vendor list, is missing from the file.

Three other invoices were in the file:

Vendor Invoice

September 15, 2023

Best Office Supply Company
P.O. Box 1934
Springfield, Illinois 62705

Invoice #0089

Bill to:
Main Electrical Supply
506 Commerce Avenue
Springfield, IL 62707
217-555-2230

Product	Quantity	Price per Unit	Total Cost
Pens	10 boxes	$3.65	$36.50
Copy paper	15 cases	$15.76	$236.40
Toner cartridges	8 units	$22.56	$180.48
Total			$453.38

Payment is due immediately upon receipt

June 14, 2023	Invoice 0076	$238.99
July 17, 2023	Invoice 0081	324.55
August 16, 2023	Invoice 0085	386.82

Required:

    a. Is this a legitimate invoice? What information might lead you to suspect that this invoice may indicate a fraud?

    b. What type(s) of fraud might this indicate?

Attributes Sampling

> *There are five kinds of lies: lies, damned lies, statistics, politicians quoting statistics, and novelists quoting politicians on statistics.*
>
> Stephen K. Tagg, marketing faculty member, University of Strathclyde

Professional Standards References

Topic	AU-C/ ISA Section	PCAOB Reference
Identifying and Assessing the Risks of Material Misstatement	315	2110
Auditors' Responses to Risks of Material Misstatement	330	2301
Audit Sampling	530	2315
Consideration of Internal Control in an Integrated Audit	940	2201

LEARNING OBJECTIVES

Module E provides a comprehensive example of the use of attributes sampling in the audit team's study of internal control.

Your objectives are to be able to:

LO E-1 Identify the objectives of attributes sampling, define *deviation conditions,* and define the population for an attributes sampling application.

LO E-2 Understand how various factors influence the size of an attributes sample and how to determine the sample size for an attributes sampling application.

LO E-3 Identify various methods of selecting an attributes sample.

LO E-4 Evaluate the results of an attributes sampling application by determining the *upper limit rate of deviation.*

LO E-5 Understand how to use *sequential sampling, discovery sampling,* and *nonstatistical sampling* in attributes testing.

INTRODUCTION

During election seasons, the concept of **sampling** (drawing a conclusion about a population by examining a subset, or **sample** from that population) draws significant attention. Pollsters attempt to predict the outcome of elections based on various methods of identifying voter sentiment; however, despite their best efforts, polling is far from an accurate science.

In the 2017 United Kingdom "snap" election, pollsters predicted the Labour party would receive 36 percent of the vote, allowing then prime minister Theresa May to have a majority in Parliament. In a surprising result, the Labour party received 40 percent of the vote, gained 40 seats, and denied Ms. May a majority.[1] Similar surprises occurred in the 2016 U.S. presidential election (in which Donald Trump defeated Hillary Clinton) and in the 2016 Brexit vote (which saw a majority of voters support the withdrawal of the United Kingdom from the European Union). In all three cases, polling leading up to the elections would not have correctly predicted the final outcome.

These results demonstrate the potential disadvantage of using sampling: the decisions based on a sample (voters contacted or whose sentiments were otherwise assessed) may differ from decisions based on the population (the voters who actually participated in the election process). This possibility is referred to as **sampling risk**, and is present whenever sampling is used. Assuming that voters accurately revealed their preferences to pollsters and pollsters accurately recorded these preferences, the major cause of these outcomes is a **nonrepresentative sample**. For example, in the 2016 U.S. presidential election, the reluctance of working-class white voters (who were generally supportive of Trump) to respond to phone calls from pollsters led to an understatement of Trump's level of support among the electorate.[2]

The two primary areas in which sampling is used in the audit examination are

1. Performing tests of controls to determine the operating effectiveness of internal control and assess control risk. In this case, the population of interest is instances in which client personnel were required to perform a control activity. Using sampling in this manner is referred to as **attributes sampling**.

2. Performing substantive tests of details to provide the necessary level of detection risk and evaluate the fairness of an account balance or class of transactions. In this case, the population of interest is transactions or components underlying the account balance. Using sampling in this manner is referred to as **variables sampling**.

To illustrate the use of attributes sampling, assume the audit team is examining accounts receivable and evaluating the effectiveness of internal controls to assess control risk. They would identify key controls that were intended to prevent or detect misstatements and then test the operating effectiveness of those controls. The challenge facing the audit team is that the number of occurrences of these controls is quite large, making it impractical (if not impossible) to evaluate every occurrence. As a result, the audit team may decide to select a sample of these controls and draw a conclusion about the operating effectiveness of these controls based on the results of the sample.

Auditors apply sampling for tests of controls on almost every engagement. The Sarbanes–Oxley Act requires auditors of issuers to test the effectiveness of internal controls. Moreover, auditors of all entities should test the operating effectiveness of controls where control risk is less than the maximum and the audit team is relying on them to reduce substantive procedures. This module focuses on the use of attributes sampling in conducting tests of controls to assess control risk, control the audit team's overall exposure to audit risk, and meet the objectives of the audit.

---

[1]"Democracy's Whipping Boys," *The Economist,* June 17, 2017, pp. 54–56.
[2]"Epic Fail," *The Economist,* November 12, 2016, pp. 29–30.

PLANNING (STEPS 1–3)

LO E-1

Identify the objectives of attributes sampling, define *deviation conditions,* and define the population for an attributes sampling application.

Attributes sampling is used to determine the extent to which some attribute (or characteristic) exists within a population of interest. In tests of controls, that attribute is whether a specific control was properly applied by client personnel and is appropriately functioning to prevent or detect material financial statement misstatements.

The following seven-step procedure serves as the basis for our illustration of attributes sampling:

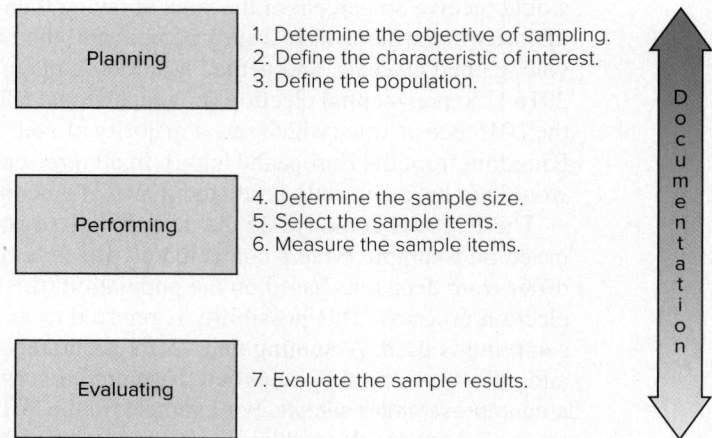

Planning	1. Determine the objective of sampling. 2. Define the characteristic of interest. 3. Define the population.
Performing	4. Determine the sample size. 5. Select the sample items. 6. Measure the sample items.
Evaluating	7. Evaluate the sample results.

Documentation

To illustrate the application of the process, we focus on the audit team's study and evaluation of important controls for the revenue cycle of Dunder-Mifflin, Inc.

Step 1: Determine the Objective of Sampling

The first step in the attributes sampling process is to identify the objective of attributes sampling, which is related to examining key controls corresponding to the management assertions of interest to the audit team. For the examination of Dunder-Mifflin's revenue cycle, the two major assertions of interest are *occurrence* (does the recorded sale represent an actual sale made to a customer?) and *accuracy* (has the sale been recorded at the proper dollar amount?). Once the relevant assertions have been determined, the audit team then specifies one or more controls that, if functioning, allow the client to meet the recording objectives related to these assertions. The following is a summary of the assertions and one relevant control that will be tested.[3]

Assertion	Control
Occurrence	Sales invoices are supported by a valid shipping document.[4]
Accuracy	Sales invoices are initialed or otherwise approved by client personnel as evidence of verification of mathematical accuracy.

Step 2: Define the Characteristic of Interest

Once the specific controls have been identified, the audit team must next define the characteristic of interest; in an attributes sampling context, this is a deviation condition. The word **deviation** (commonly referred to as *exception*) refers to instances in which the client or its personnel do *not* follow prescribed controls; in other words, deviations are instances in which controls *are not functioning as intended.* Defining the deviation conditions at

---

[3]In practice, a greater number of controls would pertain to the occurrence and accuracy assertions. We limit the number of controls examined by the audit team to focus on the application of attributes sampling.

[4]Of course, the possibility exists that the shipping document was fraudulently prepared in an effort to increase sales. However, this possibility is beyond the scope of our discussion of attributes sampling.

the outset is important because deviation conditions provide the audit team evidence regarding the *operating effectiveness* of the client's internal control.

Dunder-Mifflin's control activities indicate sales invoices must be supported by a valid shipping document; therefore, a deviation would be a situation in which a shipping document does not exist to support a sales invoice. For the control activity related to accuracy, a deviation would be the lack of client personnel approval (either manual or electronic) after mathematically verifying the accuracy of each sales invoice. The deviation conditions defined by the audit team are as follows:

Assertion	Control	Example of Deviation
Occurrence	Sales invoices are supported by a valid shipping document.	Instance in which sales invoice is not accompanied by a valid shipping document.
Accuracy	Sales invoices are initialed or otherwise approved by client personnel as evidence of verification of mathematical accuracy.	Lack of authorized employee initials or electronic approval on sales invoice or mathematically incorrect invoice.

A deviation does not necessarily indicate that an error in processing a transaction has occurred. For example, a client employee could have mathematically verified a sales invoice but forgotten to record their initials (or other form of electronic approval) on the sales invoice. In addition, the invoice could be correctly calculated regardless of whether the invoice was verified. However, the failure of client employees to document their performance of key controls represents a deviation from that control activity and should be investigated. Further, the documentation may be initialed, but not by an authorized client employee.

Step 3: Define the Population

The *population* is the set of all items about which a conclusion is desired. In attributes sampling, the population represents all potential occurrences of the control activity of interest. Population definition is important because audit conclusions can be made only about the population from which the sample was selected. For example, consider the following relationships between the sales invoice and shipping document in the revenue cycle:

Have all sales been recorded?

(Completeness)

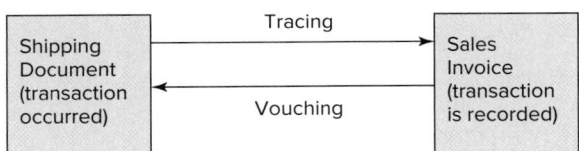

Are all recorded sales valid?

(Occurrence)

Notice that, by defining the population as sales invoices, the audit team is examining only transactions that have been recorded. As a result, this population cannot be used to provide evidence for the *completeness* assertion. However, this population is appropriate if the audit team is interested in verifying that all recorded sales invoices represent valid transactions (as evidenced by the presence of shipping documents), which corresponds to the *occurrence* assertion. As a result, the population should be defined as all sales invoices prepared by Dunder-Mifflin during the period under audit.

When defining the population, the audit team also needs to determine the **physical representation of the population**. The physical representation is the frame of reference that the audit team uses in selecting the sample, also referred to as the *source* of the sample. That is, the audit team will select the sample from the physical representation. While most physical representations would be a computerized or some other electronic form of sales invoices, other possibilities include:

- A journal list of recorded sales invoices.
- Copies of sales invoices contained in a file.

The primary concerns about the physical representation are that it is complete and corresponds with the actual population. If tests of controls are performed at an interim date, the audit team should extend tests from the interim date to the date of the financial statements and ensure that the final population includes all transactions (and possible applications of controls) for the period under audit. This can be done by footing a sales journal and agreeing the total of sales to the general ledger.

Dunder-Mifflin has a computerized list of all sales invoices prepared during the year. It can be sorted by date, customer, or dollar amount. The audit team will use this listing to select the sample.

The first three steps in the sampling process for Dunder-Mifflin are summarized next.

Summary: Steps 1–3 in the Sampling Process for Dunder-Mifflin

Step 1 The audit team's objective in sampling is to evaluate the operating effectiveness of controls related to the occurrence and accuracy assertions.

Step 2 The audit team defined deviation conditions as (a) a sales invoice that is not accompanied by a shipping document (occurrence) and (b) lack of client employee verification on sales invoices or mathematical error on a sales invoice (accuracy).

Step 3 The audit team defined the population as a computerized list of all sales invoices prepared during the year and verified the completeness and accuracy of the listing.

☑ REVIEW CHECKPOINTS

E.1 Define *attributes sampling*. In what stage of the audit would it be used?

E.2 How do the management assertions relate to the objectives of attributes sampling?

E.3 Define *deviation condition*. Why are deviation conditions so important in an attributes sampling application?

E.4 Why is appropriately defining the population of interest so important in an attributes sampling application?

PERFORMING (STEPS 4–6)

LO E-2
Understand how various factors influence the size of an attributes sample and how to determine the sample size for an attributes sampling application.

Step 4: Determine the Sample Size

The *sample size* represents the number of items that the audit team examines within a population of interest. Four main factors influence the sample size in an attributes sampling application:

1. Tolerable rate of deviation.
2. Sampling risk (risk of overreliance, or risk of assessing control risk too low).
3. Expected population deviation rate.
4. Population size.

Intuitively, the audit team would select a larger sample when (1) they require the control activity to be functioning more effectively, (2) the desired level of sampling risk is lower, (3) the expected rate of deviation in the population is higher, and (4) the population is larger. These relationships and the effect of these factors on sample size is discussed in the remainder of this section.

Tolerable Rate of Deviation

Because of human involvement and error, audit teams cannot expect controls to be functioning 100 percent of the time. In evaluating whether controls are functioning effectively, the question does remain about the extent to which deviations are permissible while still allowing the audit team to appropriately rely on the control.

The **tolerable rate of deviation** is the maximum rate of deviations permissible by the audit team without modifying the planned assessed level of control risk. In determining the tolerable rate of deviation, the audit team should consider (1) the planned assessed level of control risk and (2) the degree of assurance desired by the audit evidence in the sample. Generally, if a control is judged to be more important and would result in a more significant reduction in substantive testing, the tolerable rate of deviation should be established at lower levels.

Exhibit E.1 illustrates how the tolerable rate of deviation can be related to control risk assessments. Although control risk is rarely assessed numerically in practice, note that lower levels of control risk are associated with lower tolerable rates of deviation (and vice versa). Using Exhibit E.1, if the audit team established a low acceptable control risk (between 0.10 and 0.30), the corresponding tolerable rate of deviation would range from 3 to 7 percent.[5]

Assume that Dunder-Mifflin's control risk was assessed at a low level (0.30) for the occurrence assertion and a moderate level (0.50) for the accuracy assertion. Using the matrix in Exhibit E.1, the audit team translated these assessments into tolerable rate of deviation of 6 percent and 10 percent for the controls related to the occurrence and accuracy assertions, respectively.

Sampling Risk

Sampling risk is the likelihood that the decision made based on the sample differs from the decision that would have been made had the entire population been examined. There are two types of sampling risks for attributes sampling applications: the **risk of overreliance** and the **risk of underreliance** (sometimes referred to as the *risk of assessing control risk too low* and the *risk of assessing control risk too high,* respectively). Exhibit E.2 summarizes some of the key characteristics of these risks.

EXHIBIT E.1
Effect of Control Risk Assessments on Tolerable Rate of Deviation and Risk of Overreliance

Control Risk (Qualitative)	Control Risk (Quantitative)	Tolerable Rate of Deviation	Risk of Overreliance
Low	0.10–0.30	3%–7%	5%
Moderate	0.40–0.60	6%–12%	5%–10%
Slightly below maximum	0.70–0.90	11%–20%	10%
Maximum	1.00	Not applicable	Not applicable

EXHIBIT E.2
Sampling Risks Associated with Attributes Sampling

Sampling Risk	Sample Results	Actual State of the Population	Loss
Risk of overreliance (risk of assessing control risk too low)	Adjusted sample rate of deviation ≤ Tolerable rate of deviation **Conclusion: Control is functioning effectively**	Population rate of deviation > Tolerable rate of deviation **Conclusion: Control is not functioning effectively**	Effectiveness loss because an insufficient level of substantive procedures will be performed
Risk of underreliance (risk of assessing control risk too high)	Adjusted sample rate of deviation > Tolerable rate of deviation **Conclusion: Control is not functioning effectively**	Population rate of deviation ≤ Tolerable rate of deviation **Conclusion: Control is functioning effectively**	Efficiency loss because additional substantive procedures will be performed

[5]While these rates of deviation may not be acceptable in some situations in practice, they are a statistical necessity to permit the audit team to obtain a reasonable level of assurance through an efficient (smaller) sample size.

Because the risk of overreliance results in the audit team's failure to reduce audit risk to acceptable levels (an effectiveness loss), controlling exposure to this risk is of primary importance. Although the risk of underreliance is also a form of sampling risk, this risk will actually result in the audit team achieving a lower level of audit risk than planned. Therefore, in an attributes sampling plan, the audit team will typically control only the exposure to the risk of *overreliance* in determining the appropriate sample size.

The appropriate risk of overreliance is based on the planned level of control risk; as the audit team wishes to place a greater degree of reliance on internal controls (lower control risk), the risk of overreliance must be controlled to lower levels. Refer to Exhibit E.1 and recall that the audit team has decided to assess control risk at low levels (0.30) for the occurrence assertion and moderate levels (0.50) for the accuracy assertion. Based on the relationships in Exhibit E.1, these assessments of control risk are translated into 5 percent and 10 percent risks of overreliance for the controls related to the occurrence and accuracy assertions, respectively.[6]

In some sampling applications, the risk of overreliance is stated in terms of a *confidence level*, which is *1 – the risk of overreliance*. Thus, the confidence levels for the controls related to the occurrence and accuracy assertions are 95 percent and 90 percent, respectively.

Expected Population Deviation Rate

In practice, audit teams would not ordinarily choose to rely on internal control activities (and conduct tests of controls on those activities) if they expect deviations in the functioning of those activities.[7] However, in determining sample size, audit teams may incorporate some expected level of deviation in the client's internal control activities; this rate is referred to as the **expected population deviation rate**.

How is the expected population deviation rate determined? If the client represents a recurring engagement, the audit team has some knowledge of rate of deviations from prior engagements. These rates might need to be adjusted if changes in the client's controls have occurred since the prior audit, but previous-year rates serve as a reasonable starting point. For example, if the observed rate of deviation from prior audits was 4 percent but the audit team is aware of improvement in controls, the current-year rate of deviation could be estimated at a lower level (say, 3 percent). If, on the other hand, the engagement is a first-year engagement, the audit team might use a small sample (referred to as a *pilot sample*) to estimate the rate of deviations.

Based on their previous experience in examining the operating effectiveness of these controls for Dunder-Mifflin, the audit team assessed the expected population deviation rate at 2 percent and 3.5 percent for the controls related to the occurrence and accuracy assertions, respectively.

Population Size

Common sense probably tells you that samples should be larger for larger populations (a *direct relationship*). Strictly speaking, your common sense is accurate; clearly, the sample size for a population of 10 items would be smaller than for a population of 1,000 items. However, once a population reaches a certain size, any increase has a minimal effect on sample size. As a result, unless the population size is very small (which is not common for most attributes sampling applications), the audit team does not consider population size in determining sample size to a great extent.

To illustrate, the AICPA Audit Guide *Auditing Sampling* provides the following sample sizes for different populations for the same level of the risk of overreliance, expected population deviation rate, and tolerable rate of deviation.

---

[6]Exhibit E.1 reflects the common practice of selecting one of two levels of the risk of overreliance (5 percent and 10 percent).
[7]B. E. Christensen, R.J. Elder, and S.M. Glover, "Behind the Numbers: Insights into Large Audit Firm Sampling Policies," *Accounting Horizons*, March 2015, pp. 61–81.

Attribute Sampling

Planning (Beta Risk Control)	Planning (Beta and Alpha Risk Control)	Sample Evaluation

Population size: [20000]   Number of deviations in sample: [2]

Sample size: [127]   % Desired confidence level: [95.00]

Sample deviation rate: 1.57%   (2 / 127)

1-Sided Upper Limit	2-Sided Lower Limit	2-Sided Upper Limit
4.86	0.19	5.56

Conclusion: For an observed number of 2 deviations in a sample of size 127, you can be 95.00% confident that the population deviation rate is no more than 4.86%. Alternatively, you can be 95.00% confident that the population deviation rate is between 0.19% and 5.56%.

Key elements in this data entry screen include (data input by the audit team are shown in brackets):

- The tab "Sample Evaluation" is used to evaluate the results of the sample after performing tests of controls.
- The audit team enters the "Population size" (number of transactions) (note that IDEA will not accept entries with commas). [20000]
- The audit team enters the "Sample size." [127]
- The audit team enters the "Number of deviations in the sample." [2]
- The audit team enters the "% Desired confidence level," which corresponds to *1 – the risk of overreliance.* [95.00%]

Based on these parameters, IDEA calculates a sample deviation rate of 1.57 percent and a "1-Sided Upper Limit" of 4.86 percent (which corresponds to the ULRD). The "Conclusion" indicates that, at a 95 percent confidence level (5 percent *risk of overreliance*), the population deviation rate is less than or equal to 4.86 percent (the *ULRD*). Since the ULRD is less than the tolerable rate of deviation, the audit team would conclude that the control is functioning correctly and can rely on control risk at planned levels.

Qualitative Evaluation of Deviations

The focus thus far has been on quantitative factors: sample sizes, numbers of deviations, tolerable rate of deviation, and ULRD. Regardless of the results of the attributes sampling application, the audit team should conduct a *qualitative evaluation* of deviations to determine their nature and cause. In some cases, deviations can truly represent an isolated incident on a specific transaction; in others, they can represent something far more serious.

A qualitative evaluation of deviations attempts to answer questions such as these with regard to observed deviations:

- Do deviations represent a pervasive error made consistently on all transactions or an isolated mistake made on a specific transaction?
- Are deviations intentional or unintentional in nature?

- Do deviations represent a misunderstanding of instructions or careless attention to duties?
- Do deviations have implications with regard to the effectiveness of other controls (for example, information technology general controls or other Committee of Sponsoring Organizations of the Treadway Commission, or COSO, components)?

If any deviations appear to be pervasively occurring throughout the sample, to represent intentional actions on the part of client employees, to represent careless attention, or to have implications with respect to other controls, they have additional implications for the audit and should be discussed with the client and its audit committee. In addition, for public entities, these deviations may reflect significant deficiencies or material weaknesses that must be disclosed in the audit team's report on internal control over financial reporting.

Summary: Step 7 in the Sampling Process for Dunder-Mifflin

Step 7 The audit team determined a ULRD of 5.0 percent and 15.4 percent for the controls related to the occurrence and accuracy assertions, respectively. Based on a comparison of the ULRD to the tolerable rate of deviation, the audit team would

- Conclude that the control related to the occurrence assertion is functioning effectively and rely on internal control as planned.
- Conclude that the control related to the accuracy assertion is not functioning effectively and either (1) reduce reliance on internal control or (2) expand the sample to examine a larger number of items.

DOCUMENTING

Exhibit E.5 summarizes the audit documentation related to the Dunder-Mifflin example discussed throughout this module. Note that it includes the following information:

- Parameters used to determine sample size (control risk, risk of overreliance, tolerable rate of deviation, expected population deviation rate).
- Description of method used to select sample.
- Sample items selected.
- Measurement of sample items (identification of deviations).
- ULRD.
- Conclusions with respect to the operation of the occurrence and accuracy controls.

EXHIBIT E.5
Sample Audit Documentation for Dunder-Mifflin Tests of Controls

Invoice #	Occurrence Control	Accurracy Control
1000-011	✓	✓
1000-018	✓	✓
1000-025	✓	x
1000-032	✓	✓
1000-039	✓	✓
*		
*		
1000-888	✓	✓
1000-895	✓	✓
Sample size	127	52
# Deviations	2	4
Upper limit rate of deviation	5.0%	15.4%

NOTES:

Occurrence Control: For selected sales invoice identified valid shipping document

Accuracy Control: For selected sales invoice, verified initials of client employee supporting mathematical verification of invoice

✓ Control operating as planned

x Control not operating as planned

PARAMETERS:

	Occurrence	Accuracy
Control Risk	Low (0.30)	Moderate (0.50)
Risk of overreliance	5.0%	10.0%
Tolerable rate of deviation (TRD)	6.0%	10.0%
Expected population deviation rate	2.0%	3.5%

CONCLUSIONS:

- Rely on occurrence control as planned, since ULRD < TRD
- Reduce reliance on accuracy control, since ULRD > TRD; control risk increased to "slightly less than maximum" (0.80)

 REVIEW CHECKPOINTS

E.19   What is the audit team's decision rule with respect to the relationship between the ULRD and the tolerable rate of deviation?

E.20   What options are available to the audit team if the ULRD is less than or equal to the tolerable rate of deviation?

E.21   What options are available to the audit team if the ULRD is greater than the tolerable rate of deviation?

E.22   What information does the audit team typically document in an attributes sampling application?

OTHER ATTRIBUTES SAMPLING METHODS

LO E-5
Understand how to use *sequential sampling, discovery sampling,* and *nonstatistical sampling* in attributes testing.

Sequential sampling methods provide the audit team the opportunity to draw conclusions using a smaller sample than a traditional fixed sampling plan. It is sometimes called "stop-or-go" sampling because the plan allows the audit team to *stop* after examining a relatively small sample and evaluate the results. If the results are clearly acceptable or clearly unacceptable, the audit team can draw its conclusion; if the results are inconclusive, the audit team can *go* forward and examine additional items.

A significant advantage of sequential sampling methods is that they can allow the audit team to evaluate the operating effectiveness of controls more efficiently. One disadvantage of these methods is that the allowable rate of deviations in the sample is lower than that in a fixed sampling plan (i.e., sequential sampling is more conservative). In addition, the audit team should be careful in continuing to extend the sample using a sequential sampling approach if the preliminary sample evidence does not support the planned level of control risk (in other words, once the audit team has determined that the control is not functioning effectively, there is no reason to expand testing).

Another variation of attributes sampling is **discovery sampling**, a form of attributes sampling that is used when deviations from controls are very critical yet are expected to occur at a relatively low rate. Discovery sampling should be used when a control is extremely important for the audit team's examination or when the audit team suspects the existence of fraud. In this situation, the audit team uses sample sizes from Exhibits EA.1 and EA.2 corresponding to an expected population deviation rate of 0 percent. Then, if even one deviation is discovered, the audit team stops immediately and concludes that the control is not operating effectively.

Nonstatistical sampling methods are permissible under generally accepted auditing standards and differ from the statistical methods discussed in this chapter as follows:

1. The audit team may judgmentally determine the sample size and is not required to quantify the various parameters (although the sample sizes under statistical and nonstatistical methods should be comparable).
2. The audit team may use nonrandom methods in selecting sample items, such as block selection or haphazard selection.
3. The audit team may judgmentally evaluate sample results, based on the sample rate of deviation and tolerable rate of deviation.

A recent survey of the sampling practices of six international accounting firms (including the Big Four) found that the firms either explicitly require the use of statistical methods or ensure that the sample sizes and sampling conclusions reached with nonstatistical methods are comparable to those if statistical methods were used, suggesting that nonstatistical methods are not frequently used in practice.[13]

The PCAOB Inspection Focus "PCAOB Findings for Attributes Sampling" provides examples of deficiencies noted by the PCAOB in its inspections of audits conducted by Big Four firms.

 REVIEW CHECKPOINTS

E.23 What is *sequential sampling*? What are its advantages and disadvantages?

E.24 Define *discovery sampling*. When is it typically used?

E.25 In what steps of a sampling plan would the use of nonstatistical sampling differ from the use of statistical sampling?

E.26 How should an audit team using nonstatistical sampling for attributes testing evaluate the results of the test?

 PCAOB INSPECTION FOCUS | PCAOB Findings for Attributes Sampling

The following excerpts from PCAOB inspection reports of audits conducted by Big Four firms illustrate issues identified in the attributes sampling applications conducted by these firms.

- The firm's testing of certain automated controls using a sample of only one instance of the control's operation was not sufficient because the firm did not test the configuration or programming of these controls, or perform other procedures that would have provided sufficient appropriate audit evidence that these controls were designed and operating effectively.

- The firm selected for testing a manual control that consisted of the review of pricing in all new and modified contracts. The sample that the firm used to test this control was too small to provide sufficient appropriate audit evidence that the control was operating effectively because it limited the sample to one contract modification.

- The issuer's processes related to loans receivable, the [allowance for loan losses], investments, derivatives, and investment and brokerage services income were highly automated. . . The firm tested certain automated and IT-dependent manual controls that used data and reports generated or maintained by these IT systems. The accuracy and completeness of these data and reports depended on effective IT general controls ("ITGCs"). The firm's sampling approach for testing ITGCs was inappropriate because it was based on an unsupported assumption that the population of ITGCs was homogeneous. As a result, the firm's testing of these automated and IT-dependent manual controls over these areas was not sufficient.

Sources: *Report on 2020 Inspection of EY LLP*, PCAOB, September 30, 2021; *Report on 2019 Inspection of EY LLP*, PCAOB, December 17, 2020; *Report on 2018 Inspection of PricewaterhouseCoopers LLP*, PCAOB, April 28, 2020.

---

[13]B.E. Christensen, R.J. Elder, and S.M. Glover, "Behind the Numbers: Insights into Large Audit Firm Sampling Policies," *Accounting Horizons*, March 2015, pp. 61–81.

Summary

This module discusses attributes sampling, which the audit team uses to evaluate the operating effectiveness of internal control activities. When performing attributes sampling, the audit team's primary objective is to assess the extent to which the client's internal control activities are functioning effectively. As with any sampling application, the audit team is exposed to sampling risk (the risk that the decision made based on the sample differs from the decision that would have been made if the entire population had been examined). The audit team controls this sampling risk (referred to as the *risk of overreliance* or the *risk of assessing control risk too low*) in determining the appropriate sample size and evaluating the sample results.

After the sample is selected, the audit team performs tests of controls to determine whether the control is functioning as intended. A sample rate of deviation is determined by dividing the number of deviations by the sample size; this rate is adjusted to control for the acceptable exposure to the risk of overreliance to determine the upper limit rate of deviation (ULRD). The ULRD is a measure that has a 1 – *Risk of overreliance* probability of equaling or exceeding the true rate of deviation in the population.

Once calculated, the ULRD is compared to the tolerable rate of deviation. If the ULRD is less than the tolerable rate of deviation, the audit team can rely on internal control as planned and accept the planned level of control risk. If the ULRD is higher than the tolerable rate of deviation, the audit team can either increase the assessed level of control risk (which will increase the necessary level of substantive procedures) or expand the sample to attempt to provide a ULRD that is lower than the tolerable rate of deviation. Decisions regarding the assessed level of control risk should consider the costs of performing additional tests of controls versus the cost savings from reduced substantive procedures.

Key Terms

allowance for sampling risk: The difference between the upper limit rate of deviation and the sample rate of deviation; "adjusts" the sample rate of deviation to allow the audit team to control the exposure to the risk of overreliance, 755

attributes sampling: A form of sampling used to determine the extent to which some characteristic (attribute) exists within a population of interest; used by the audit team during tests of controls, 743, 744

block selection: A method of choosing sample items in which a series of contiguous (or adjacent) items is chosen from the population, 752

deviation: A condition that refers to instances in which client personnel do not follow prescribed controls and controls are not functioning as intended, 754

discovery sampling: A form of attributes sampling that audit teams use when deviations from controls are very critical but are expected to occur at a relatively low rate, 759

expected population deviation rate: The rate of variations anticipated by the audit team in the client's internal control activities; based on prior experience or a pilot sample, 748

haphazard selection: The method of choosing sample items in an unstructured manner but without any intentional bias, 752

nonrepresentative sample: A sample that differs substantially from the population on one or more key characteristics of interest from which it is drawn, 743

nonstatistical sampling methods: In attributes sampling, methods that do not control the audit team's exposure to the risk of overreliance in determining sample size, selecting sample items, or evaluating sample results, 760

physical representation of the population: An audit team's frame of reference for selecting a sample, 745

random selection: See *unrestricted random selection*, 752

risk of overreliance (risk of assessing control risk too low): The likelihood that the audit team will conclude that the client's controls are functioning effectively when they are not functioning effectively, 747

risk of underreliance (risk of assessing control risk too high): The likelihood that the audit team will conclude that the client's controls are not functioning effectively when they are functioning effectively, 747

sample: A subset of items drawn from a population of interest, 743

sample rate of deviation: The extent of variations found in the audit team's sample; determined by dividing the number of deviations by the sample size, 754

sampling: The process of making a statement about a population of interest based on examining only a subset (or sample) of that population, 743

sampling interval: An interval determined by dividing the recorded amount of the population (account balance) by the sample size, 752

sampling risk: The likelihood that the decision made based on the sample will differ from the decision that would have been made if the entire population had been examined, 743

sequential sampling: A plan in which an initial sample is selected and the audit team (1) draws a final conclusion regarding the effectiveness of the control or (2) selects additional items before drawing a final conclusion regarding the effectiveness of the control; also referred to as *stop-or-go sampling*, 759

systematic random selection (systematic selection): The method of selecting sample items in which a starting point is determined and a fixed number of items are bypassed between selections, 752

systematic selection: See *systematic random selection*, 752

tolerable rate of deviation: The maximum rate of deviation permissible by the audit team without modifying the planned assessed level of control risk, 747

unrestricted random selection (random selection): A method of selecting items in which all items in the population are assigned a number and chosen based on random numbers, 752

upper limit rate of deviation (ULRD): A measure that adjusts the sample rate of deviation for the audit team's acceptable level of sampling risk; the rate of deviation that has a (1 − *Risk of overreliance*) probability of equaling or exceeding the true population rate of deviation, 754

variables sampling: A form of sampling used to examine a population to estimate the amount or value of some characteristic of that population; used by auditors during their substantive procedures, 743

Multiple-Choice Questions for Practice and Review

 All applicable Exercises and Problems are available with *Connect*

LO E-1

E.27 Which of the following major stages of the audit is most closely related to attributes sampling?

    a. Determining preliminary levels of materiality.

    b. Performing tests of controls.

    c. Performing substantive procedures.

    d. Searching for the possible occurrence of subsequent events.

LO E-1

E.28 Which of the following steps in attributes sampling is most closely related to identifying key controls corresponding to the relevant management assertions?

    a. Determine the objective of sampling.

    b. Define the deviation condition.

    c. Define the population.

    d. Determine the sample size.

LO E-2

E.29 Which of the following factors has a *direct* relationship with sample size in an attributes sampling application?

	Tolerable Rate of Deviation	Expected Population Deviation Rate
a.	Yes	Yes
b.	No	Yes
c.	Yes	No
d.	No	No

LO E-2

E.30 Which of the following sampling risks does the audit team control in an attributes sampling application (ROO = risk of overreliance, ROU = risk of underreliance)?

	ROO	ROU
a.	Yes	Yes
b.	No	Yes
c.	Yes	No
d.	No	No

LO E-2

E.31 Why is the audit team more concerned with controlling the exposure to the risk of overreliance than with the risk of underreliance?

a. Only the risk of overreliance results in an incorrect audit decision.

b. The risk of underreliance is not related to the audit team's study and evaluation of internal control.

c. The risk of overreliance can ultimately result in the audit team's failing to reduce audit risk to acceptable levels.

d. The risk of underreliance can be controlled by performing tests of controls during the interim period.

LO E-2

E.32 Which of the following would *not* result in the audit team's selecting a larger sample of controls for examination?

a. A reduction in the risk of overreliance from 10 percent to 5 percent.

b. An increase in the tolerable rate of deviation from 3 percent to 6 percent.

c. An increase in the expected population deviation rate from 2 percent to 4 percent.

d. All of the above would result in a larger sample of controls.

LO E-2

E.33 Baily Cox, an audit manager, judged that the test of controls of the company's 50,000 purchase transactions should be based on a tolerable rate of deviation of 6 percent, a risk of overreliance of 5 percent, and an expected population deviation rate of 3 percent. Using AICPA sample size tables, Cox determined that the appropriate sample size in this situation would be

a. 49.

b. 78.

c. 132.

d. 195.

LO E-2

E.34 Francona Madden, an audit manager, considered the control risk assessments listed in the left column of the following table in evaluating A. Cardinal's internal control over sales transactions. The sample sizes for the substantive procedures of the customer accounts receivable are shown to the right of each control risk. What risk of overreliance (ROO) could be assigned for tests of controls at each control risk level?

Control Risk	Accounts Receivable Sample	ROO
0.20	400	?
0.50	390	?
0.80	350	?
0.90	190	10%

a. From top to bottom: 5 percent, 10 percent, 1 percent.

b. From top to bottom: 10 percent, 1 percent, 5 percent.

c. From top to bottom: 1 percent, 10 percent, 5 percent.

d. From top to bottom: 1 percent, 5 percent, 10 percent.

LO E-4   E.35 Assume that Dylan Lee found two deviations in a sample of 90 transactions. Using AICPA sample evaluation tables, Lee determined that the ULRD at a 5 percent risk of overreliance is

    a. 2.0 percent.

    b. 2.2 percent.

    c. 5.9 percent.

    d. 6.9 percent.

LO E-4   E.36 The interpretation of the ULRD in an attributes sampling application is

    a. The estimated rate of deviation in the population with probability equal to the risk of overreliance that the population deviation rate is higher.

    b. The estimated rate of deviation in the population with probability equal to the risk of overreliance that the actual rate of deviation is lower.

    c. The estimated rate of deviation in the population with certainty that the actual rate of deviation is lower.

    d. The estimated rate of deviation in the population with certainty that the actual rate of deviation is higher.

LO E-4   E.37 If an audit team examined 100 transactions and found one deviation from an important control activity, the audit conclusion could be that control risk can be assessed at the associated control risk level when

    a. The tolerable rate of deviation is 2 percent.

    b. The tolerable rate of deviation is 3 percent.

    c. The tolerable rate of deviation is 4 percent.

    d. More information about decision criteria is available.

LO E-4   E.38 If an audit team calculated a ULRD of 5 percent when the tolerable rate of deviation was 4 percent, both at the same risk of overreliance, control risk should be

    a. Assessed at the level associated with the 4 percent tolerable rate of deviation.

    b. Increased and substantive procedures should be adjusted accordingly.

    c. Assessed at the maximum level (100 percent) because the company's performance failed the test.

    d. Decreased and substantive procedures should be adjusted accordingly.

LO E-1   E.39 In which of the following circumstances would the audit team most likely use attributes sampling?

    a. Selecting customer accounts receivable for confirmation.

    b. Selecting inventory items for verification of physical quantities.

    c. Selecting purchase orders for indication of proper authorization.

    d. Selecting additions to property, plant, and equipment during the year.

LO E-4   E.40 Using AICPA sample evaluation tables, determine the conclusion from a statistical sample of internal controls when a sample of 125 documents indicates five deviations if the tolerable rate of deviation is 5 percent, the expected population deviation rate is 2 percent, and the allowance for sampling risk is 3 percent.

    a. Accept the evidence as support for assessing a low control risk because the tolerable rate of deviation less the allowance for sampling risk is less than the expected population deviation rate.

    b. Use the evidence to assess a higher control risk than planned because the sample rate of deviation plus the allowance for sampling risk exceeds the tolerable rate of deviation.

    c. Use the evidence to assess a higher control risk than planned because the tolerable rate of deviation plus the allowance for sampling risk exceeds the expected population deviation rate.

    d. Accept the evidence as support for assessing a low control risk because the sample rate of deviation plus the allowance for sampling risk exceeds the tolerable rate of deviation.

LO E-4   E.41 An audit team designed a sample that would provide a 10 percent risk of overreliance that not more than 7 percent of sales invoices lacked credit approval. From previous audits, the audit team expected that 3 percent of the sample invoices lacked proper approval. From the

LO E-4

E.70 Sample Results Evaluation.   Kendall Jackson, CPA, is examining the operating effectiveness of the internal control of Town Mo, a large conglomerate in the music industry. As part of the evaluation, Jackson determined a necessary sample size of 93 items (based on a tolerable rate of deviation of 5 percent, an expected population deviation rate of 0.5 percent, and a risk of overreliance of 5 percent). After properly selecting the 93 items, Jackson found no deviations from the prescribed control activities.

Required:

a. Based on Jackson's sample, determine the sample rate of deviation and ULRD. (Because the AICPA sample evaluation tables do not contain a row for a sample size of 93, round down and use a sample size of 90.)

b. Explain the difference between the ULRD and the sample rate of deviation observed in part (a). How does this difference relate to the use of statistical sampling?

c. What would Jackson conclude with respect to the operating effectiveness of Town Mo's internal control?

d. If Jackson found three deviations in the sample, calculate the sample rate of deviation and use AICPA sample evaluation tables to determine the ULRD. What would Jackson conclude with respect to the operating effectiveness of Town Mo's internal control in this case?

e. Using AICPA sample evaluation tables, determine the maximum number of deviations that Jackson could identify without reducing the reliance on Town Mo's internal control.

f. Repeat part (e) using a 10 percent risk of overreliance. What is the explanation for any differences between this number of deviations and that in part (e)?

LO E-1–E-4

E.71 Evaluating a Sampling Application.   Tom Barton, an assistant accountant with a local CPA firm, recently graduated from Other University. He studied statistical sampling for auditing in college and wants to impress his employers with his knowledge of modern auditing methods.

Barton decided to select a random sample of payroll checks for the test of controls using a tolerable rate of deviation of 5 percent and an acceptable risk of overreliance of 5 percent. The senior accountant told Barton that 2 percent of the checks audited last year had one or more errors in the calculation of net pay. He decided to audit 100 random checks. Because supervisory personnel had paychecks with higher amounts than production workers, he selected 60 of the supervisor checks and 40 checks of the others. He was very careful to see that the selections of 60 from the April payroll register and 40 from the August payroll register were random.

The audit of this sample yielded two deviations, exactly the 2 percent rate experienced last year. The first was the deduction of federal income taxes based on two exemptions for a supervisory employee whose W-4 form showed four exemptions. The other was payment to a production employee at a rate for a job classification one grade lower than it should have been. The worker had been promoted the week before, and Barton found that in the next payroll he was paid at the correct (higher) rate.

When he evaluated this evidence, Barton decided that these two findings were really not control deviations at all. The withholding of too much tax did not affect the expense accounts, and the proper rate was paid the production worker as soon as the clerk caught up with the change orders. Barton decided that having found zero deviations in a sample of 100, the ULRD for a 5 percent risk of overreliance was 3 percent, which easily satisfied his predetermined criterion.

The senior accountant was impressed. Last year he had audited 15 checks from each month, and Barton's work represented a significant time savings. The reviewing partner on the audit also was impressed because she had never thought that statistical sampling could be so efficient, and that was the reason she had never studied the method.

Required:
Identify and explain the mistakes made by Barton.

LO E-2

E.72 Comprehensive Attributes Sampling.   Audra Dodge, CPA, is performing an attributes sampling plan for her audit of Truck Company. In her audit of cash disbursements, she has identified preparing a voucher and marking it as "paid" prior to preparing and mailing a check to the vendor as an important control. Dodge defined any voucher that was not marked as "paid" as being a deviation.

In performing her sampling application, she established the following parameters:

Risk of overreliance	5%
Expected population deviation rate	1.5%
Tolerable rate of deviation	4%

Required:

a. Identify what factors Dodge considered in establishing the risk of overreliance, expected population deviation rate, and tolerable rate of deviation.

b. Assume that Dodge wished to place additional reliance on this control. How would that affect the three parameters in part (a)?

c. Based on the original parameters, use AICPA sample size tables to determine the appropriate sample size.

d. If Dodge selected the sample size in part (c) and found four deviations, what is the sample rate of deviation?

e. Using AICPA sample evaluation tables, determine the ULRD. (*Note:* If the sample size cannot be directly located on the sample evaluation table, round down to the next highest sample size.)

f. What would Dodge's conclusion be with respect to the functioning of this control?

LO E-1, E-3, E-5   E.73   **Nonstatistical Attributes Sampling.**   Aubrey Marblehead is conducting tests of controls on the control that quantities on Rock's receiving reports are appropriately verified. In so doing, Marblehead has inquired of Rock's receiving personnel, who said that they place a mark near the quantities verified and sign the receiving report upon delivery. Marblehead has decided to use nonstatistical sampling for this engagement. Based on the importance of this control and the rate of deviation that has been observed in prior audits, Marblehead has established the following parameters.

Risk of overreliance	5%
Expected population deviation rate	2.75%
Tolerable rate of deviation	7%

Based on the parameters established, Marblehead decides to use a sample of 100 receiving reports.

Required:

a. How would Marblehead define a deviation condition?

b. How would Marblehead appropriately define the population? What steps should be taken to ensure that it is complete?

c. If Rock has a computerized list of all receiving reports, what are some options available to Marblehead in selecting specific items for examination? What precautions should be taken before undertaking the selection of items?

d. For each of the following deviations, determine the sample rate of deviation and indicate Marblehead's decision with respect to the functioning of the control.

   1. 2 deviations.

   2. 4 deviations.

   3. 10 deviations.

LO E-1, E-3, E-5   E.74   **Nonstatistical Attributes Sampling.**   Monroe Curtis is auditing the revenue cycle of Kentucky Distilleries and has elected to perform a nonstatistical test of controls. Kentucky Distilleries sells Old Horse Bourbon to wholesale distributors around the country. Because the sale of bourbon is strictly controlled, Curtis does not expect deviations to be present in the system and has assessed control risk as low and selected a sample size of 50 sales. Curtis has defined a deviation as a recorded sale not being supported by a shipping document with a federal tax stamp.

Required:

a. How does nonstatistical sampling differ from statistical sampling?

b. Why would Curtis choose to perform nonstatistical sampling instead of statistical sampling?

    c. How should Curtis select the sample?

    d. What conclusion should Curtis make if one deviation is found?

LO E-1, E-2, E-4

E.75 Comprehensive Attributes Sampling. The firm of Buy and Best, CPAs, is engaged to conduct the audit of Radio Hut, a retailer of electronic and other high-technology products. Because of technological advances in Radio Hut's inventory products, an important risk that it faces is that prices charged by suppliers reflect current industry prices (which tend to fluctuate relatively significantly, particularly as new technologies are introduced and as older technologies are discontinued). The nature of Radio Hut's inventories is such that a small number of suppliers exist and each supplier has a similar pricing structure. This pricing structure is reflected in an electronic industry pricing guide, which is updated on a daily basis.

You are a staff accountant with Buy and Best and have been asked to identify a potential audit approach to address this risk. In the past, your firm has decided to place relatively limited reliance on internal control activities related to Radio Hut's purchasing function and has instead conducted relatively extensive substantive procedures related to its inventories. However, the new partner on the Radio Hut engagement has successfully reduced substantive procedures for the firm's other clients in the retail industry by performing more extensive tests of controls. Because of previous experience in the industry as well as having used this audit approach successfully for other clients, the new partner asks you to evaluate the possibility of using more extensive tests of controls in the audit of Radio Hut.

The following controls are relevant to Radio Hut's processing of vendor invoices:

- Similar to most retailers in the industry, Radio Hut has a highly automated inventory monitoring and control system. Based on anticipated product life, current sales, and existing inventory levels, Radio Hut generates an automatic purchase order when inventory levels reach predetermined thresholds.

- Once a purchase order has been generated, the store manager reviews it prior to transmitting it to the appropriate vendor. This review ensures that the vendor is from an approved list and that the proposed purchase is consistent with the store's objectives and near-term plans (e.g., not purchasing a large number of laptop computers just prior to a major promotion for tablets).

- Upon receipt of the items, warehouse personnel prepare "blind" copies of a receiving report, noting the quantity of each item received.

- Purchasing personnel verify the vendors' invoices by (1) comparing the invoice to a purchase order by referencing the purchase order number on the vendor invoice, (2) comparing quantities on the vendor invoice to quantities from the receiving report prepared by warehouse personnel, (3) comparing prices on the invoice for reasonableness through reference to industry pricing data, and (4) mathematically verifying the accuracy of the invoice.

These controls have been in place for a number of years, and Radio Hut has experienced relatively little turnover in its purchasing and related functions. You did not observe any remediation or major changes with respect to these controls or to Radio Hut's control environment during the past year.

You reviewed the prior audit documentation, which was prepared by another staff accountant who has since left the firm. Based on your review, you prepared the following notes:

- The control activity tested by the staff accountant is the employee verification of the reasonableness of prices on the invoices by placing a checkmark or other notation adjacent to the price on the invoice.

- Using an expected population deviation rate of 1 percent, a tolerable rate of deviation of 7 percent, and a risk of overreliance of 10 percent, the staff accountant selected a sample of 55 invoices.

- Tests of controls revealed three misstatements; based on the sample size of 55 and a risk of overreliance of 10 percent, the ULRD was 11.8 percent. Because this exceeded the tolerable rate of deviation 7 percent, the other staff accountant reduced reliance on the control activity and conducted more extensive substantive procedures.

Required:

a. Comment on the appropriateness of the work done in the prior audit with respect to testing this control activity.

b. Based on the results of tests of controls in the prior year, provide your initial thoughts regarding the viability of increasing your reliance on this control activity in the current audit.

c. How will your decision to increase the reliance on the control activity affect the sample size in the current audit? What specific factors will be affected by this decision?

d. Assume that you have established a risk of overreliance of 5 percent, a tolerable rate of deviation of 6 percent, and an expected population deviation rate of 1 percent. Using AICPA sample size tables, determine the necessary sample size in the current audit. Is this sample size consistent with your expectations compared to that examined in the prior year?

e. Using AICPA sample size tables, determine what factor(s) resulted in the increased sample size from the prior year. Can you determine the extent to which each factor contributed to this increase?

   [Note: Requirements (f)–(h) are unrelated to (a)–(e).]

f. Refer to the AICPA sample evaluation tables. Assuming a sample size of 100 items, how many deviations would be permissible for you to rely on this control activity using a 5 percent risk of overreliance and a 6 percent tolerable rate of deviation?

g. Repeat part (f), assuming that you decided to reduce your reliance on internal control and establish a risk of overreliance of 10 percent.

h. What does a comparison of your results in parts (f) and (g) tell you about the effect of the risk of overreliance on the ULRD?

LO E-1, E-2, E-4   E.76 **General Attributes Sampling.**   You overheard the following dialogue between Joe Ashley (a staff assistant) and Monique Estrada (his supervisor).

Required:

Referring to appropriate professional standards, comment on each of these statements.

a. "It's unfortunate that generally accepted auditing standards don't allow us to use nonstatistical sampling for this control. I just don't feel that the extra time and effort to use statistical sampling are worth the benefits."

b. "I'm not sure what level of control risk we should plan to use. We need to determine the amount of substantive procedures that we will conduct and then assess control risk accordingly."

c. "We really need to be careful to limit our exposure to the risk of overreliance. This risk could result in our failure to perform enough substantive procedures."

d. "Separation of duties is such an important control that we should use statistical sampling to evaluate the extent to which the custody, recording, and approval functions for purchases are performed by different individuals."

e. "Because we're really relying heavily on this control, it's important that it be operating very effectively. That's why I set the tolerable rate of deviation at such a low level."

f. "We found six deviations of the 120 items we examined. That's a 5 percent rate of deviation. Because our tolerable rate of deviation is 8 percent, it looks like we can rely on internal control as planned."

g. "A deviation is a deviation. Some of these problems were honest mistakes, but others looked like client employees intentionally ignored the controls. However, they all have the same effect on the ULRD."

h. "Because our upper limit rate of deviation is lower than the tolerable rate of deviation, we don't have to do anything with the deviations we found."

LO E-1, E-2, E-5   E.77 **Comprehensive Nonstatistical Attributes Sampling.**   Marty Alewine, a newly promoted senior at your firm, has been assigned as in charge of the audit of Doxey Electronics. Doxey has been a client of your firm for years. Controls are considered effective, and statistical attributes sampling to test sales transactions has been used for several years. Last year's audit documentation revealed the following: risk of overreliance, 5 percent; expected population deviation rate, 2 percent; tolerable rate of deviation, 5 percent; sample size, 181; deviations found, three; and ULRD, 4.2 percent. Alewine's conclusion from the documentation is that the controls were accepted as operating effectively.

Deciding to use nonstatistical sampling this year to reduce audit hours, Alewine selected 100 invoices from the December invoice files, reasoning that tests closer to year-end are more effective, by selecting every 10th invoice until 100 invoices had been identified. Two invoices differed in amount from the shipping document, and one invoice could not be located. Alewine decided to accept the controls as effective again this year, reasoning the sample rate of deviation was only 2 percent, which is much less than the tolerable rate of deviation used last year.

Required:

As the manager of the Doxey Electronics audit, you have been reviewing the audit documentation. Prepare a list of reviewer comments to discuss with Alewine.

LO E-5

E.78 **Discovery and Sequential Attributes Sampling.**   Sydney Siebenthaler, the audit manager for Jennifer's Running Shirts Inc., has just returned from a continuing education class on audit sampling and now wants to use discovery sampling or sequential sampling on the Jennifer's audit because the class instructor said that the sample sizes would be significantly smaller. "Talk about a no-brainer!" Siebenthaler exulted.

Jennifer's has good controls, and the audit team has performed tests of controls over the payroll procedures in previous years to reduce substantive tests of payroll accounts to only analytical procedures. In the previous year, the audit team used the following parameters: risk of overreliance, 10 percent; expected population deviation rate, 2 percent; and tolerable rate of deviation, 10 percent, which resulted in a sample size of 38. The auditors increased (rounded) the sample size to 40 items, and one deviation was found. The resulting ULRD rate was 9.4 percent, and the control was accepted as operating effectively.

Required:

a. Define *discovery sampling*.
b. Do you agree that discovery sampling should be used on the audit of Jennifer's?
c. How would discovery sampling be used?
d. Define *sequential sampling*.
e. Do you agree that sequential sampling should be used on the audit of Jennifer's?
f. How would sequential sampling be used?

USING IDEA IN ATTRIBUTES SAMPLING

Exercises E.79, E.80, and E.81 require the use of IDEA in an attributes sampling context. Elm Manufacturing Company (ELM) is a small manufacturer of backpacks located in Rochelle, Illinois. You are testing controls related to the authorization of sales made to customers on account and are interested in ensuring that goods are only shipped to customers following a formal credit approval. You have access to ELM's electronic records in *Connect*. The appropriate file for these exercises is the Sales 2023–4th Q data set.

Detailed information about ELM, instructions for accessing data sets, a data directory for data sets, and a detailed attributes sampling example (with IDEA screenshots) can be found in *Connect*.

NOTE: The Sales 2023–4th Q data set contains a total of 410 transactions; because you are only examining the credit approval for goods that have been shipped, you would only examine orders through No. 17383 (a total of 388 shipments).

LO E-2, E-3, E-4

E.79 **Attributes Sampling with IDEA: Determining Sample Size, Selecting Sample Items, and Evaluating Sample Results.**   Your audit team has established the following parameters for the examination of ELM's control over the authorization of sales:

Population size	388 shipments
Risk of overreliance	10%
Expected population deviation rate	1%
Tolerable rate of deviation	6%

Required:

Using IDEA, perform the following related to ELM's control over credit approvals.

a. Determine the appropriate sample size. Based on the sample size and preceding parameters, how many deviations could be observed without the audit team reducing their reliance on the authorization control?

b. Using systematic random selection, a random start of 23, as well as the sample size in part (a), select sample items from the population. What are the first five transactions that will be selected for examination?

c. After performing your tests of controls, you have identified three deviations in your sample. What is the ULRD? What conclusion would you draw with respect to the functioning of ELM's controls over the authorization of sales?

LO E-2

E.80 Attributes Sampling with IDEA: Determining Sample Size. Your audit team has established the following parameters for the examination of ELM's control over the authorization of sales:

Population size	388 shipments
Risk of overreliance	10%
Expected population deviation rate	1%
Tolerable rate of deviation	6%

Required:

a. Use IDEA to determine the necessary sample size, given the preceding parameters.

Parts (b), (c), and (d) are independent scenarios that affect sample size.

b. Assume the audit team has decided to increase its reliance on this control and reduce control risk related to the authorization of sales on account. Accordingly, it has decided to reduce the risk of overreliance to 5 percent. What is the necessary sample size, holding all other factors constant?

c. Assume that in the past year the audit team noted a greater extent of deviations in the population and decided that an expected population deviation rate of 2 percent would be more appropriate. What is the necessary sample size, holding all other factors constant?

d. Assume that the audit team has decided to reduce its reliance on this control and is willing to increase the tolerable rate of deviation from 6 percent to 8 percent. What is the necessary sample size, holding all other factors constant?

e. How do the results in parts (b), (c), and (d) reflect the relationship between various parameters and sample size?

LO E-4

E.81 Attributes Sampling with IDEA: Evaluating Sample Results. Based on a population size of 388 shipments, a 10 percent desired risk of overreliance, an expected population deviation rate of 1 percent, and a tolerable rate of deviation of 6 percent, the audit team selected a sample of 58 items.

In performing tests of controls, your audit team identified three shipments that were not supported by an approved sales order and concluded that these represent deviations from the control activity.

Required:

a. Use IDEA to determine the ULRD. What would the audit team's conclusion be with respect to the functioning of ELM's control over the authorization of sales transactions?

Part (b) is a set of independent scenarios that affect the evaluation of sample results.

b. For each of the following numbers of deviations, use IDEA to determine the ULRD and provide the audit team's conclusion with respect to the functioning of ELM's control over the authorization of sales transactions.

1. 0 deviations
2. 1 deviation
3. 2 deviations

c. How do the results in part (b) reflect the relationship between the number of deviations and the ULRD?

AICPA Sample Size Tables

EXHIBIT EA.1 **Sample Size Table for 5 Percent Risk of Overreliance (Number of Expected Deviations)**

Expected Population Deviation Rate	Tolerable Rate of Deviation										
	2%	3%	4%	5%	6%	7%	8%	9%	10%	15%	20%
0.00%	149 (0)	99 (0)	74 (0)	59 (0)	49 (0)	42 (0)	36 (0)	32 (0)	29 (0)	19 (0)	14 (0)
0.25	236 (1)	157 (1)	117 (1)	93 (1)	78 (1)	66 (1)	58 (1)	51 (1)	46 (1)	30 (1)	22 (1)
0.50	313 (2)	157 (1)	117 (1)	93 (1)	78 (1)	66 (1)	58 (1)	51 (1)	46 (1)	30 (1)	22 (1)
0.75	386 (3)	208 (2)	117 (1)	93 (1)	78 (1)	66 (1)	58 (1)	51 (1)	46 (1)	30 (1)	22 (1)
1.00	590 (6)	257 (3)	156 (2)	93 (1)	78 (1)	66 (1)	58 (1)	51 (1)	46 (1)	30 (1)	22 (1)
1.25	1,030 (13)	303 (4)	156 (2)	124 (2)	78 (1)	66 (1)	58 (1)	51 (1)	46 (1)	30 (1)	22 (1)
1.50		392 (6)	192 (3)	124 (2)	103 (2)	66 (1)	58 (1)	51 (1)	46 (1)	30 (1)	22 (1)
1.75		562 (10)	227 (4)	153 (3)	103 (2)	88 (2)	77 (2)	51 (1)	46 (1)	30 (1)	22 (1)
2.00		846 (17)	294 (6)	181 (4)	127 (3)	88 (2)	77 (2)	68 (2)	46 (1)	30 (1)	22 (1)
2.25		1,466 (33)	390 (9)	208 (5)	127 (3)	88 (2)	77 (2)	68 (2)	61 (2)	30 (1)	22 (1)
2.50			513 (13)	234 (6)	150 (4)	109 (3)	77 (2)	68 (2)	61 (2)	30 (1)	22 (1)
2.75			722 (20)	286 (8)	173 (5)	109 (3)	95 (3)	68 (2)	61 (2)	30 (1)	22 (1)
3.00			1,098 (33)	361 (11)	195 (6)	129 (4)	95 (3)	84 (3)	61 (2)	30 (1)	22 (1)
3.25			1,936 (63)	458 (15)	238 (8)	148 (5)	112 (4)	84 (3)	61 (2)	30 (1)	22 (1)
3.50				624 (22)	280 (10)	167 (6)	112 (4)	84 (3)	76 (3)	40 (2)	22 (1)
3.75				877 (33)	341 (13)	185 (7)	129 (5)	100 (4)	76 (3)	40 (2)	22 (1)
4.00				1,348 (54)	421 (17)	221 (9)	146 (6)	100 (4)	89 (4)	40 (2)	22 (1)
5.00					1,580 (79)	478 (24)	240 (12)	158 (8)	116 (6)	40 (2)	30 (2)
6.00						1,832 (110)	532 (32)	266 (16)	179 (11)	50 (3)	30 (2)
7.00								585 (41)	298 (21)	68 (5)	37 (3)
8.00									649 (52)	85 (7)	37 (3)
9.00										110 (10)	44 (4)
10.00										150 (15)	50 (5)
12.50										576 (72)	88 (11)
15.00											193 (29)
17.50											720 (126)

Note: This table assumes a large population. Sample sizes of more than 2,000 not shown.

Source: AICPA Audit Guide *Audit Sampling*

EXHIBIT EA.2 **Sample Size Table for 10 Percent Risk of Overreliance (Number of Expected Deviations)**

Expected Population Deviation Rate	Tolerable Rate of Deviation										
	2%	3%	4%	5%	6%	7%	8%	9%	10%	15%	20%
0.00%	114 (0)	76 (0)	57 (0)	45 (0)	38 (0)	32 (0)	28 (0)	25 (0)	22 (0)	15 (0)	11 (0)
0.25	194 (1)	129 (1)	96 (1)	77 (1)	64 (1)	55 (1)	48 (1)	42 (1)	38 (1)	25 (1)	18 (1)
0.50	194 (1)	129 (1)	96 (1)	77 (1)	64 (1)	55 (1)	48 (1)	42 (1)	38 (1)	25 (1)	18 (1)
0.75	265 (2)	129 (1)	96 (1)	77 (1)	64 (1)	55 (1)	48 (1)	42 (1)	38 (1)	25 (1)	18 (1)
1.00	398 (4)	176 (2)	96 (1)	77 (1)	64 (1)	55 (1)	48 (1)	42 (1)	38 (1)	25 (1)	18 (1)
1.25	708 (9)	221 (3)	132 (2)	77 (1)	64 (1)	55 (1)	48 (1)	42 (1)	38 (1)	25 (1)	18 (1)
1.50	1,463 (22)	265 (4)	132 (2)	105 (2)	64 (1)	55 (1)	48 (1)	42 (1)	38 (1)	25 (1)	18 (1)
1.75		390 (7)	166 (3)	105 (2)	88 (2)	55 (1)	48 (1)	42 (1)	38 (1)	25 (1)	18 (1)
2.00		590 (12)	198 (4)	132 (3)	88 (2)	75 (2)	48 (1)	42 (1)	38 (1)	25 (1)	18 (1)
2.25		974 (22)	262 (6)	132 (3)	88 (2)	75 (2)	65 (2)	42 (1)	38 (1)	25 (1)	18 (1)
2.50			353 (9)	158 (4)	110 (3)	75 (2)	65 (2)	58 (2)	38 (1)	25 (1)	18 (1)
2.75			471 (13)	209 (6)	132 (4)	94 (3)	65 (2)	58 (2)	52 (2)	25 (1)	18 (1)
3.00			730 (22)	258 (8)	132 (4)	94 (3)	65 (2)	58 (2)	52 (2)	25 (1)	18 (1)
3.25			1,258 (41)	306 (10)	153 (5)	113 (4)	82 (3)	58 (2)	52 (2)	25 (1)	18 (1)
3.50				400 (14)	194 (7)	113 (4)	82 (3)	73 (3)	52 (2)	25 (1)	18 (1)
3.75				583 (22)	235 (9)	131 (5)	98 (4)	73 (3)	52 (2)	25 (1)	18 (1)
4.00				873 (35)	274 (11)	149 (6)	98 (4)	73 (3)	65 (3)	25 (1)	18 (1)
5.00					1,019 (51)	318 (16)	160 (8)	115 (6)	78 (4)	34 (2)	18 (1)
6.00						1,150 (69)	349 (21)	182 (11)	116 (7)	43 (3)	25 (2)
7.00							1,300 (91)	385 (27)	199 (14)	52 (4)	25 (2)
8.00								1,437 (115)	424 (34)	60 (5)	25 (2)
9.00									1,577 (142)	77 (7)	32 (3)
10.00										100 (10)	38 (4)
12.50										368 (46)	63 (8)
15.00											126 (19)
17.50											457 (80)

Note: This table assumes a large population. Sample sizes of more than 2,000 not shown.

Source: AICPA Audit Guide *Audit Sampling*

Appendix EB

AICPA Sample Evaluation Tables

EXHIBIT EB.1   Sample Evaluation Table for 5 Percent Risk of Overreliance

Sample Size	Actual Number of Deviations Found										
	0	1	2	3	4	5	6	7	8	9	10
20	14.0	21.7	28.3	34.4	40.2	45.6	50.8	55.9	60.7	65.4	69.9
25	11.3	17.7	23.2	28.2	33.0	37.6	42.0	46.3	50.4	54.4	58.4
30	9.6	14.9	19.6	23.9	28.0	31.9	35.8	39.4	43.0	46.6	50.0
35	8.3	12.9	17.0	20.7	24.3	27.8	31.1	34.4	37.5	40.6	43.7
40	7.3	11.4	15.0	18.3	21.5	24.6	27.5	30.4	33.3	36.0	38.8
45	6.5	10.2	13.4	16.4	19.2	22.0	24.7	27.3	29.8	32.4	34.8
50	5.9	9.2	12.1	14.8	17.4	19.9	22.4	24.7	27.1	29.4	31.6
55	5.4	8.4	11.1	13.5	15.9	18.2	20.5	22.6	24.8	26.9	28.9
60	4.9	7.7	10.2	12.5	14.7	16.8	18.8	20.8	22.8	24.8	26.7
65	4.6	7.1	9.4	11.5	13.6	15.5	17.5	19.3	21.2	23.0	24.7
70	4.2	6.6	8.8	10.8	12.7	14.5	16.3	18.0	19.7	21.4	23.1
75	4.0	6.2	8.2	10.1	11.8	13.6	15.2	16.9	18.5	20.1	21.6
80	3.7	5.8	7.7	9.5	11.1	12.7	14.3	15.9	17.4	18.9	20.3
90	3.3	5.2	6.9	8.4	9.9	11.4	12.8	14.2	15.5	16.9	18.2
100	3.0	4.7	6.2	7.6	9.0	10.3	11.5	12.8	14.0	15.2	16.4
125	2.4	3.8	5.0	6.1	7.2	8.3	9.3	10.3	11.3	12.3	13.2
150	2.0	3.2	4.2	5.1	6.0	6.9	7.8	8.6	9.5	10.3	11.1
200	1.5	2.4	3.2	3.9	4.6	5.2	5.8	6.5	7.2	7.8	8.4
300	1.0	1.6	2.1	2.6	3.1	3.5	4.0	4.4	4.8	5.2	5.6
400	0.8	1.2	1.6	2.0	2.3	2.7	3.0	3.3	3.6	3.9	4.3
500	0.6	1.0	1.3	1.6	1.9	2.1	2.4	2.7	2.9	3.2	3.4

Note: This table presents ULRDs as percentages and assumes a large population.

Source: AICPA Audit Guide *Audit Sampling*

EXHIBIT EB.2 Sample Evaluation Table for 10 Percent Risk of Overreliance

Sample Size	Actual Number of Deviations Found										
	0	1	2	3	4	5	6	7	8	9	10
20	10.9	18.1	24.5	30.5	36.1	41.5	46.8	51.9	56.8	61.6	66.2
25	8.8	14.7	20.0	24.9	29.5	34.0	38.4	42.6	46.8	50.8	54.8
30	7.4	12.4	16.8	21.0	24.9	28.8	32.5	36.2	39.7	43.2	46.7
35	6.4	10.7	14.5	18.2	21.6	24.9	28.2	31.4	34.5	37.6	40.6
40	5.6	9.4	12.8	16.0	19.0	22.0	24.9	27.7	30.5	33.2	35.9
45	5.0	8.4	11.4	14.3	17.0	19.7	22.3	24.8	27.3	29.8	32.2
50	4.6	7.6	10.3	12.9	15.4	17.8	20.2	22.5	24.7	27.0	29.2
55	4.2	6.9	9.4	11.8	14.1	16.3	18.4	20.5	22.6	24.6	26.7
60	3.8	6.4	8.7	10.8	12.9	15.0	16.9	18.9	20.8	22.7	24.6
65	3.5	5.9	8.0	10.0	12.0	13.9	15.7	17.5	19.3	21.0	22.8
70	3.3	5.5	7.5	9.3	11.1	12.9	14.6	16.3	18.0	19.6	21.2
75	3.1	5.1	7.0	8.7	10.4	12.1	13.7	15.2	16.8	18.3	19.8
80	2.9	4.8	6.6	8.2	9.8	11.3	12.8	14.3	15.8	17.2	18.7
90	2.6	4.3	5.9	7.3	8.7	10.1	11.5	12.8	14.1	15.4	16.7
100	2.3	3.9	5.3	6.6	7.9	9.1	10.3	11.5	12.7	13.9	15.0
125	1.9	3.1	4.3	5.3	6.3	7.3	8.3	9.3	10.2	11.2	12.1
150	1.6	2.6	3.6	4.4	5.3	6.1	7.0	7.8	8.6	9.4	10.1
200	1.2	2.0	2.7	3.4	4.0	4.6	5.3	5.9	6.5	7.1	7.6
300	0.8	1.3	1.8	2.3	2.7	3.1	3.5	3.9	4.3	4.7	5.1
400	0.6	1.0	1.4	1.7	2.0	2.4	2.7	3.0	3.3	3.6	3.9
500	0.5	0.8	1.1	1.4	1.6	1.9	2.1	2.4	2.6	2.9	3.1

Note: This table presents ULRDs as percentages and assumes a large population.

Source: AICPA Audit Guide *Audit Sampling*

Variables Sampling

> *Facts are stubborn, but statistics are more pliable.*
>
> *Mark Twain, (pseudonym of Samuel L. Clemens), famous American writer 1835–1910*

Professional Standards References

Topic	AU-C/ISA Section	AS Section
Identifying and Assessing the Risks of Material Misstatement	315	2110
Materiality	320	2105
Evaluation of Misstatements	450	2810
Audit Evidence	500	1105
Audit Sampling	530	2315

LEARNING OBJECTIVES

Module F provides a comprehensive example of the use of variables sampling in the audit team's substantive procedures.

Your objectives are to be able to:

LO F-1   Define *variables sampling* and understand when it is used in the audit.

LO F-2   Understand the basic process underlying *probability proportional to size sampling* (PPS) and when to use PPS.

LO F-3   Identify the factors affecting the size of a PPS sample and calculate the sample size for a PPS application.

LO F-4   Evaluate the results for a PPS sample by calculating the projected misstatement, incremental allowance for sampling risk, and basic allowance for sampling risk.

LO F-5   Understand the basic process underlying *classical variables sampling* and the use of classical variables sampling in an audit (Appendix FB).

LO F-6   Understand the use of nonstatistical approaches to variables sampling (Appendix FC).

INTRODUCTION

The need for audit teams to control their exposure to *audit risk* (the risk that a material misstatement occurs, is not prevented or detected by the client's internal control, and is not detected by the audit team's substantive procedures) has been discussed throughout the text. The following provides a general overview of how audit teams control this risk:

1. Establish the desired level of audit risk.
2. Based on the susceptibility of the account balance or class of transactions to misstatement, assess *inherent risk.*
3. Based on the effectiveness of the client's internal controls in preventing or detecting misstatements, assess *control risk.* (The use of *attributes sampling* in performing tests of controls and assessing control risk was discussed in Module E of this text).
4. Using the audit risk model and considering the risks in (1) through (3), determine the *detection risk* (which reflects the nature, timing, and extent of the audit team's substantive tests).[1]

The detection risk determined above dictates the number of transactions or components of the account balance or class of transactions that are examined. As such, this risk is directly related to the audit team's need to select an appropriate sample of transactions or components of the account balance. This module discusses the process through which audit teams select and evaluate samples of transactions and components of the account balance or class of transactions to achieve the necessary level of tests of details risk, control their overall exposure to audit risk, and meet the objectives of the audit.

The PCAOB Inspection Focus "Audit Risk and Sampling" illustrates how the risk of material misstatement (combined levels of inherent risk and control risk) impacts the audit team's sample size.

 ## PCAOB INSPECTION FOCUS — Audit Risk and Sampling

In its inspection of an unnamed audit conducted by Deloitte in 2019, the PCAOB documented the following deficiency in its inspection report:

The firm's sample for testing certain revenue was too small to provide sufficient appropriate audit evidence because, in determining its sample size, the firm inappropriately used a risk of material misstatement that was lower than its assessed risk of material misstatement for this revenue.

In this situation, Deloitte felt that the combined level of inherent risk and control risk would result in the need for less extensive substantive testing (lower sample size)

Source: *Report on 2019 Inspection of Deloitte & Touche LLP, PCAOB, December 17, 2020.*

DEFINITION OF VARIABLES SAMPLING

LO F-1
Define *variables sampling* and understand when it is used in the audit.

Module E illustrated the use of sampling in the audit team's study and evaluation of the client's internal control, or *attributes sampling.* This module focuses on the use of **variables sampling,** which is used to examine a population when the audit team wants to estimate the "true" balance or the misstatement of a particular account or class of transactions. The **true balance** is the amount at which the account should be recorded if no misstatements exist. A *misstatement* is the difference between the true balance and the recorded balance of the account. Variables sampling is used as the audit team performs substantive tests of details.

---

[1]The audit team's substantive tests include both analytical procedures and tests of details. Because of the nature of these tests, sampling will be used in performing tests of details.

The following seven-step procedure serves as the basis for our illustration of variables sampling:

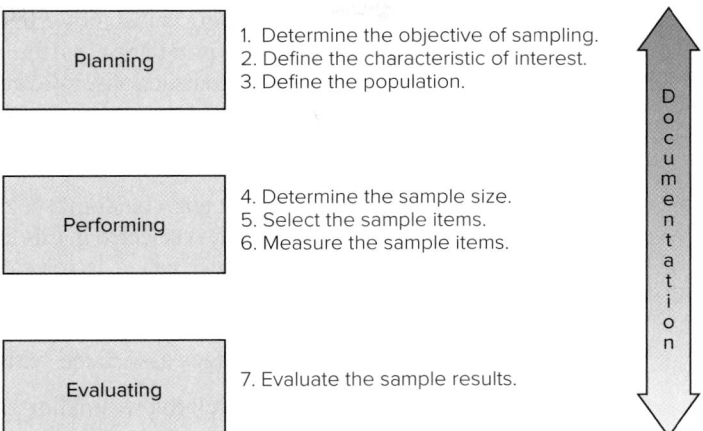

The audit team can use one of two statistical approaches for variables sampling. **Probability proportional to size (PPS) sampling** provides an estimate of the amount of misstatement in the account balance or class of transactions. The distinguishing feature of PPS is that items are selected based on their size (in an audit context, dollar amounts). (Because dollar amounts serve as the size in an audit context, PPS sampling is also referred to as **monetary unit sampling**). **Classical variables sampling** uses the laws of probability and the central limit theorem to estimate either (1) the amount of misstatement in the account balance or class of transactions or (2) the true balance for an account balance or class of transactions. Classical variables sampling is discussed in Appendix FB of this module.

PPS Sampling

Assume that two of Dunder-Mifflin's outstanding accounts receivable are as follows:

- Account 101: $100,000
- Account 102: $10,000

If the population were defined as these two accounts, a random selection technique (or one that did not consider the size of the account) would result in each of these accounts having an equal likelihood of selection. Under PPS sampling, because Account 101 is 10 times larger than Account 102, it would have a higher likelihood of being selected.

Auditors use both PPS and classical variables sampling to determine the fairness of the client's financial statements. When using either of these variables sampling methods, auditors examine transactions or components of clients' account balances or class of transactions. Based on this sample of transactions or components and analytical procedures, auditors then assess the overall fairness of the account balance or class of transactions.

REVIEW CHECKPOINTS

F.1 Define *variables sampling.* In what stage of the audit is variables sampling used?

F.2 What are two statistical approaches available to the audit team for variables sampling?

PPS SAMPLING: PLANNING

LO F-2
Understand the basic process underlying *probability proportional to size sampling* (PPS) and when to use PPS.

PPS (also known as *monetary unit sampling*) is one method of variables sampling the audit team uses in performing substantive testing procedures. The unique feature of PPS is its definition of the population as the number of dollars (or other unit) in an account balance or class of transactions. (Viewed another way, individual dollars within an account balance or class of transactions are identified as sampling units.) Thus, if a client's accounts receivable are recorded at $300,000, the population is defined as 300,000 one-dollar units.

When using PPS, the audit team randomly selects individual dollars from the population for examination. When a dollar is selected in this fashion, the entire "logical unit" (transaction or component of the account balance) is selected for examination. This feature typically makes PPS samples efficient because a small number of transactions or components can be selected for examination yet account for a relatively large dollar amount.

The following are advantages associated with the use of PPS:

- PPS typically results in relatively smaller sample sizes (in terms of the number of transactions or components selected for examination) compared to classical variables sampling.
- PPS samples typically include transactions or components reflecting relatively large dollar amounts.
- PPS is more effective in identifying misstatements in accounts when overstatement is the primary concern (such as revenues and assets).

In contrast, the following are disadvantages associated with the use of PPS:

- PPS provides a more conservative (higher) estimate of misstatement in the account balance or class of transactions compared to classical variables sampling. As a result, PPS is more likely to signal the need for an adjustment in the account balance or class of transactions, which will likely entail performance of additional procedures by the audit team. (While an advantage in terms of effectiveness, this would be a disadvantage in terms of efficiency.)
- PPS is not effective in identifying misstatements in accounts when understatement is the primary concern (such as liabilities and expenses).
- The expansion of an PPS sample is difficult when preliminary results indicate that the account balance or class of transactions is materially misstated.
- PPS requires special considerations for logical units having a zero or negative balance. In some cases, logical units having these characteristics indicate employee fraud.

In summary, PPS is best used when the audit team expects to find few or no misstatements and when overstatement (existence assertion) is of greatest concern. In contrast, when a relatively large number of misstatements is expected or when understatement (completeness assertion) is of greatest concern, PPS is less effective.

To illustrate the steps used in PPS, we provide a comprehensive example of the audit team's examination of Dunder-Mifflin's accounts receivable (represented by a listing of billed but unpaid sales transactions). In this example, we illustrate how the audit team calculates sample size, selects sample items, and evaluates sample results.

Steps 1–3: Planning

Recall that, in the planning stages of PPS, the audit team (1) determines the objective, (2) defines the characteristic of interest, and (3) defines the population. The objective of any variables sampling application is to provide evidence regarding the fairness of the relevant assertions for the account being examined. These assertions determine the type of substantive procedures selected by the auditor for an account balance or class of transactions, which ultimately determines the nature of items selected for examination. In the audit of accounts receivable, the *occurrence* and *accuracy* assertions are of particular importance. To verify these assertions, the audit team will use confirmation procedures and select a sample of "items" for confirmation.

Once the objective of sampling has been determined, the audit team defines the characteristic of interest. In a variables sampling application, the audit team is interested in determining the proper amount at which the items *should be* recorded; this amount is often referred to as the **audited value**, which is simply the dollar amount at which the item would be recorded assuming that no mistakes in judgment or mistakes in the application of generally accepted accounting principles were made. In a PPS application, the characteristic of interest is the difference between the recorded balance and the audited value, or the amount of *misstatement.*

The final step in the planning stage of PPS is to define the population of interest. As noted earlier, one of the most important distinctions of PPS is that the population is defined as all of the *individual dollars* (or other monetary unit) within the account balance or class of transactions. The following summarizes the composition of Dunder-Mifflin's sales transactions.

Planning PPS: Dunder-Mifflin's Sales Transactions

- Total invoices = 900
- Total dollar amount of invoices = $12,563,283 (rounded)
- Number of invoices with zero balance = 4
- Number of invoices with negative balance = 1 ($53, rounded)

Because zero and negative items require special consideration in PPS, the audit team will exclude these transactions from the population to be sampled, resulting in a population of 895 transactions with a recorded balance of $12,563,336.

As a result, PPS defines the population as 12,563,336 individual dollars of sales transactions. Once defined, it is important that the audit team ensure the completeness and accuracy of the population prior to beginning the sampling process. This population is included in the *Sample-Detailed Sales* database in IDEA.

The PCAOB Inspection Focus "Population Definition and Sampling" illustrates the importance of properly defining the population from which a sample is selected.

PCAOB INSPECTION FOCUS — Population Definition and Sampling

In its inspection of an unnamed audit conducted by EY in 2020, the PCAOB documented the following deficiency in its inspection report:

The firm's approach for substantively testing certain revenue . . . was dependent upon the firm's testing of certain data underlying the analysis.

The firm did not sufficiently test this underlying data because it did not select its sample from the data that was used in this analysis.

Source: *Report on 2020 Inspection of EY, PCAOB, September 30, 2021.*

REVIEW CHECKPOINTS

F.3 Define *probability proportional to size sampling (PPS).* What is the unique feature of PPS?

F.4 What are the advantages and disadvantages of using PPS? Under what conditions is it best used?

F.5 How are the substantive procedures performed by the audit team related to the objective of PPS?

F.6 What is the typical characteristic of interest in a PPS application?

PPS SAMPLING: PERFORMING

LO F-3
Identify the factors affecting
the size of a PPS sample and
calculate the sample size for
a PPS application.

Step 4: Determine the Sample Size

The *sample size* represents the number of items that the audit team examines. In variables sampling, these items are transactions or components underlying the account balance or class of transactions being audited. Four main factors influence the sample size in an PPS application:

1. Sampling risk (risk of incorrect acceptance).
2. Tolerable misstatement.
3. Expected misstatement.
4. Population size.

Sampling Risk

Sampling risk occurs when the sample selected by the audit team is not representative of the population from which it is drawn. There are two types of sampling risks for variables sampling applications: the **risk of incorrect acceptance** and the **risk of incorrect rejection**. Refer to Exhibit F.1 for a summary of some of the key characteristics of these risks.

Because the risk of incorrect acceptance results in the audit team issuing an inappropriate opinion on financial statements that are materially misstated, controlling exposure to this risk is of primary importance. As the sample size increases, the likelihood that the sample is representative of the population increases (i.e., sampling risk would be zero if 100 percent of the account were examined). Therefore, sample size varies *inversely* with sampling risk.

The risk of incorrect acceptance is determined using the audit risk model introduced earlier in the text and is based on the auditors' desired exposure to audit risk and assessments of the risk of material misstatement and analytical procedures risk. Module E illustrated how the audit team used attributes sampling to evaluate control risk (a component of the risk of material misstatement). To focus on the application of PPS, assume that the auditors used the audit risk model and determined a necessary level of the risk of incorrect acceptance of 10 percent.

Tolerable Misstatement

The level of **tolerable misstatement** is the maximum amount the account balance or class of transactions can be misstated without the audit team requiring an adjusting entry to prevent a modified opinion. In other words, the audit team members determine in advance the largest misstatement that they will allow (or tolerate) before they conclude that the account balance or class of transactions is materially misstated.

The audit team assesses tolerable misstatement judgmentally after considering the recorded balance as well as the relationship between the account balance or class of transactions with important financial statement subtotals (such as total assets, total revenue, and net income). Auditors normally estimate tolerable misstatement after calculating *performance materiality* for the various account balances and classes of transactions.

EXHIBIT F.1
Sampling Risks Associated with Variables Sampling

Sampling Risk	Sample Results	Unknown State of the Population	Loss
Risk of incorrect acceptance	Estimate of misstatement ≤ Tolerable misstatement **Conclusion: Account is fairly stated**	Actual misstatement > Tolerable misstatement **Conclusion: Account is not fairly stated**	Effectiveness loss because the audit team will make an incorrect conclusion and issue an inappropriate opinion on the financial statements.
Risk of incorrect rejection	Estimate of misstatement > Tolerable misstatement **Conclusion: Account is not fairly stated**	Actual misstatement ≤ Tolerable misstatement **Conclusion: Account is fairly stated**	Efficiency loss because additional transactions or components will be examined.

Logically, as the amount of tolerable misstatement decreases, the necessary sample size increases because auditors need to examine more of the population to ensure that there are not numerous small misstatements that would accumulate to a material amount. Therefore, tolerable misstatement has an *inverse relationship* with sample size.

In the audit of sales transactions, assume that the audit team assessed tolerable misstatement at $628,167 (or 5 percent of the recorded balance of $12,563,336) for Dunder-Mifflin. This is consistent with rules of thumb commonly used in practice, such as assessing performance materiality at between 1 percent and 5 percent of asset balances.

Expected Misstatement

The **expected misstatement** is the amount of misstatement the audit team anticipates in the account balance or class of transactions. The audit team's estimate of expected misstatement is ordinarily based on prior experience with the client—that is, the amount by which misstatements have been identified in specific accounts in prior audits. If the engagement is a first-year engagement, the audit team can estimate the expected misstatement based either on a small preliminary sample (referred to as a *pilot sample*) or on experience with other clients in the same industry. Based on prior audits of Dunder-Mifflin, the audit team estimates an expected misstatement of $188,450 (or 1.5 percent of the recorded balance).

How does expected misstatement affect sample size? It seems reasonable to surmise that, as the expected misstatement increases (particularly in relation to tolerable misstatement), the audit team increases the level of assurance provided by substantive procedures. To do so, the team would examine a larger number of components or transactions (i.e., the necessary sample size increases). Therefore, expected misstatement has a *direct relationship* with sample size.

Population Size

One of the unique characteristics of PPS is that the sampling unit is defined as a dollar in an account balance or class of transactions. Thus, Dunder-Mifflin's sales transactions totaling $12,563,336 are characterized as a population size of 12,563,336 one-dollar items. Logically, as the population size increases, the necessary sample size increases. This represents a *direct relationship* between population size and sample size.

The following summarizes the impact of various factors on sample size in a PPS application:

Factor	Effect on Sample Size
Risk of incorrect acceptance	Lower levels of risk of incorrect acceptance correspond to larger sample sizes
Expected misstatement	Higher levels of expected misstatement correspond to larger sample sizes
Tolerable misstatement	Lower levels of tolerable misstatement correspond to larger sample sizes
Population size	Larger populations correspond to larger sample sizes

Determining Sample Size

To determine the appropriate sample size, the audit team may use formulas or computer software programs that are based on these formulas. Alternatively a table such as that in Appendix FA, which is drawn from the AICPA Audit Guide *Audit Sampling,* can be used. (An excerpt of this table is shown in Exhibit F.2.)

EXHIBIT F.2   PPS Sample Sizes

Risk of Incorrect Acceptance	Ratio of Expected to Tolerable Misstatement	Tolerable Misstatement as a Percentage of Population										
		50%	30%	10%	8%	6%	5%	4%	3%	2%	1%	0.50%
10	—	5	8	24	29	39	47	58	77	116	231	461
10	0.20	7	12	35	43	57	69	86	114	171	341	682
10	0.30	9	15	44	55	73	87	109	145	217	433	866
10	0.40	12	20	58	72	96	115	143	191	286	572	1,144
10	0.50	16	27	80	100	134	160	200	267	400	799	1,597

To use the table, the audit team proceeds as follows:

1. Determine appropriate risk of incorrect acceptance (10%).
2. Calculate the ratio of expected misstatement (1.5%) to tolerable misstatement (5%) [1.5% ÷ 5.0% = 0.30].
3. Using (1) and (2), identify appropriate row from Exhibit F.2.
4. Calculate the ratio of tolerable misstatement to the size of the population (5%).
5. Read the sample size at the intersection of the row in (3) and the column in (4).

Examining Exhibit F.2, a sample size of 87 would be used. In cases where exact values of the rows and columns in (3) and (4), the audit team can either select the more conservative level (resulting in a larger sample size) or interpolate. (An example of interpolation is shown in Appendix FA.)

Using IDEA to Determine Sample Size

Using the *Analysis > Sample > Monetary Unit > Plan* function tab (note that IDEA uses the term Monetary Unit Sampling, which is a form of PPS) provides the following data entry screen:[2]

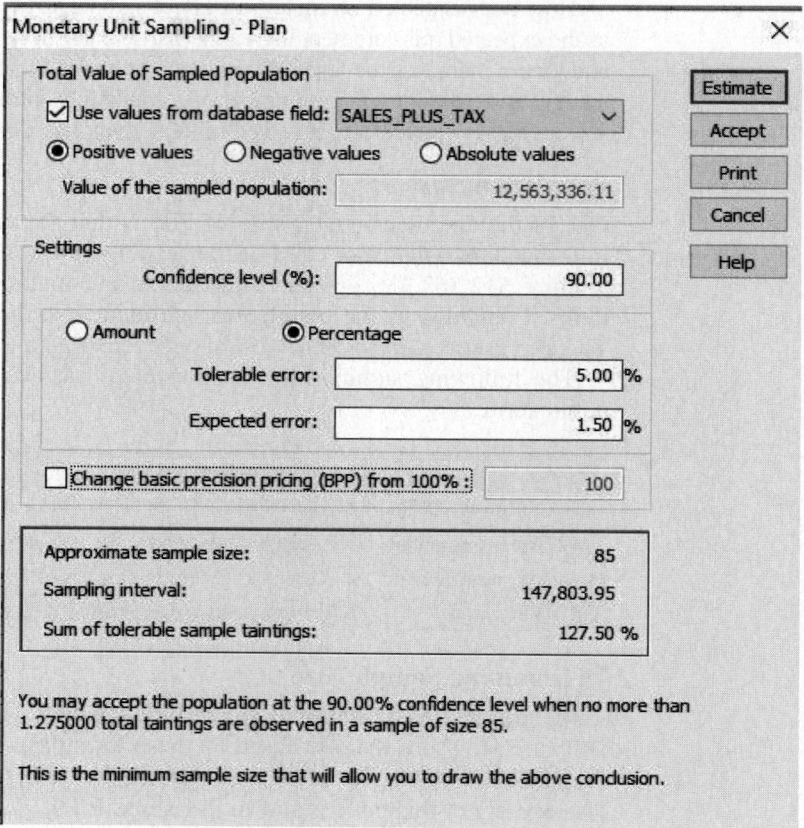

Key elements in this data entry screen include (data input by the audit team are shown in brackets):

- For "Use values from the database field," the audit team would select [SALES_PLUS_TAX] and ensure that the "Positive values" option is checked. (When the appropriate field is identified, IDEA will provide the "Value of the sampled population" of $12,563,336.11.)

[2]More detailed information on the use of IDEA in variables sampling (including additional input and output screens for selecting sample items and entering the audited value of sample items) can be found in *Connect.*

- The audit team enters the "Confidence level (%)," which corresponds to *1 – the risk of incorrect acceptance.* [90.00%]
- The audit team enters the "Tolerable error" [5.00%] and "Expected error" [1.50%]. (Note that these parameters can be entered as either amounts or percentages.)

Based on these parameters, IDEA provides a sample size of 85 items and will calculate the sampling interval by dividing the population size by the sample size ($12,563,336.11 ÷ 85 = $147,803.95).

Note that the sample size differs from that determined through the use of AICPA sampling tables (n = 87). The reason for this difference is that AICPA tables assume a slightly different statistical distribution of the account balances.

The PCAOB Inspection Focus "Tolerable Misstatement and Sample Size" illustrates the effect of tolerable misstatement on the sample size determined by the audit team.

PCAOB INSPECTION FOCUS   Tolerable Misstatement and Sample Size

In its inspection of an unnamed audit conducted by KPMG in 2019, the PCAOB documented the following deficiency in its inspection report:

In determining its sample sizes used to test the acquired commercial loans, the firm did not take into account tolerable misstatement. As a result, the samples that the firm used to test the valuation of these loans were too small to provide sufficient appropriate evidence.

Source: *Report on 2019 Inspection of KPMG, PCAOB, December 17, 2020.*

☑ REVIEW CHECKPOINTS

F.7 What are the two sampling risks associated with variables sampling? What types of losses are associated with each of these risks?

F.8 How does the audit team determine the acceptable level of the risk of incorrect acceptance? What is the relationship between this risk and sample size?

F.9 How does the audit team determine tolerable misstatement? What is the relationship between tolerable misstatement and sample size?

F.10 How does the audit team determine expected misstatement? What is the relationship between expected misstatement and sample size?

F.11 In a PPS application, how is the population size defined? What is the relationship between population size and sample size?

Step 5: Select the Sample Items

When using PPS, the audit team normally selects the sample items using a *systematic random selection* method. When a systematic method is used, the audit team determines a random starting point within the population, which represents the first item selected. The audit team then bypasses a fixed number of items in the population and selects the next item for examination. This process is continued until the number of sampling units equal to the necessary sample size has been selected.

One unique feature of using systematic random selection in PPS is that the sampling unit is defined as *an individual dollar within a population.* However, it is not reasonable for the audit team to examine only a dollar of a component; the entire component should be verified. In this case, the component is the customer's account receivable (which is represented by individual sales transactions); however, it could be an item of inventory or any other component of an account balance or class of transactions.

To select a PPS sample, the audit team calculates a **sampling interval** by dividing the recorded account balance by the necessary sample size. In the examination of accounts receivable, recall that the transactions were recorded at $12,563,336 and that the audit team determined a sample size of 85 items.[3] The sampling interval is $147,804, as follows:

$$\text{Sampling interval} = \frac{\text{Population size (recorded balance)}}{\text{Sample size}}$$

$$= \frac{\$12,563,336}{85}$$

$$= \$147,804$$

Thus, the audit team examines every 147,804th dollar of sales transactions. Recall that the tolerable misstatement for accounts receivable was assessed at $628,167. Because the tolerable misstatement exceeds the sampling interval ($147,804), the audit team examines every transaction that would be material to the financial statements taken as a whole. This is an explicit advantage of PPS because it results in higher dollar components of an account balance or class of transactions having a higher likelihood of selection. In contrast, if the audit team randomly selected 85 of the 895 individual transactions for examination, no guarantee exists that the larger dollar transactions would be selected.

Using a random start of 123,811, Exhibit F.3 illustrates the selection of the first few transactions. (Transactions 1 and 33 would not be selected, but are included to show the first item in the population and the item immediately preceding the first item selected.) These could be selected either manually or using IDEA, if the transactions are maintained in computerized form.

The Ending Dollar column is simply a running total of the transactions (note that the total equals $12,563,336). The Dollar Selected column reflects a random start of 123,811 and a sampling interval of 147,804. Each entry in this column is determined by adding the sampling interval to the preceding entry; this dollar is contained within the associated invoice (e.g., the 271,615th dollar is contained within Invoice 1000040).

If a dollar within a transaction is selected, the component (i.e., entire transaction) is selected for examination. For example, using a random start of 123,811, the audit team would examine the 123,811th dollar of the population. In Exhibit F.3, note that Invoice 1000413 (recorded at $46,504) contains dollars 84,709 through 131,213. Because this transaction contains the 123,811th dollar, the audit team examines the entire transaction.

EXHIBIT F.3
PPS Sample Selection of Sales Transactions

Transaction	Invoice No.	Invoice Amount	Beginning Dollar	Ending Dollar	Dollar Selected
1	1000047	$ 474	$ 0	$ 474	N/A
33	1000384	59	84,650	84,709	N/A
34	1000413	46,504	84,709	131,213	123,811
47	1000040	4,717	271,282	275,999	271,615
59	1000319	108,719	314,782	423,501	419,419
93	1000410	40,807	532,565	573,372	567,223
104	1000594	147,573	595,492	743,065	715,027
107	1000609	290,648	749,074	1,039,722	862,831
107	1000609	290,648	749,074	1,039,722	1,010,635
895	1000896	857	12,562,479	12,563,336	

[3] In this example, we use the sample size of 85 items determined through the IDEA software to illustrate the use of IDEA from the determination of sample size through the evaluation of sample results.

EXHIBIT F.6
Calculation of Incremental Allowance for Sampling Risk for Sales Transactions

Invoice	Projected Misstatement		Incremental Confidence Factor		Incremental Allowance for Sampling Risk
1000762	$29,561	×	(3.89 − 2.31) − 1.00	=	$ 17,145
1000413	14,780	×	(5.33 − 3.89) − 1.00	=	6,503
					$23,648

Basic Allowance for Sampling Risk

Both the projected misstatement and the incremental allowance for sampling risk apply to sampling intervals in which the audit team's substantive procedures revealed a misstatement. However, what about those sampling intervals in which no misstatement was discovered? For example, assume that the audit team evaluated an invoice recorded at $42,821 and found no misstatement. Is it reasonable to conclude that the entire sampling interval of $147,804 represented by that invoice contained no misstatements? To account for this possibility, the audit team calculates a **basic allowance for sampling risk** to provide a statistical measure of the misstatement that could be included in sampling intervals in which the audit team did not detect a misstatement.

Although the philosophy behind the calculation of the basic allowance for sampling risk is somewhat technical, the calculation is relatively straightforward. To calculate the basic allowance for sampling risk, multiply the sampling interval by the confidence factor for the risk of incorrect acceptance. The confidence factor corresponding to zero overstatement errors is selected because these sampling intervals did not contain an overstatement error. The basic allowance for sampling risk is calculated as follows:

$$\text{Basic allowance for sampling risk} = \text{Sampling interval} \times \text{Confidence factor}$$
$$= \$147,804 \times 2.31$$
$$= \$341,427$$

Note that the basic allowance for sampling risk would be calculated in all instances, even when the audit team detected no misstatements.

Upper Limit on Misstatements

The **upper limit on misstatements (ULM)** is the sum of the three components discussed in this subsection: the projected misstatement, the incremental allowance for sampling risk, and the basic allowance for sampling risk. The upper limit on misstatements is the amount that has a (1 − *Risk of incorrect acceptance*) probability of equaling or exceeding the true amount of misstatement in the population. Stated another way, there is a (*risk of incorrect acceptance*) probability that the true amount of misstatement in the population exceeds the upper limit on misstatements.

How do auditors use the upper limit on misstatements? They compare this measure to the amount of tolerable misstatement, as follows:

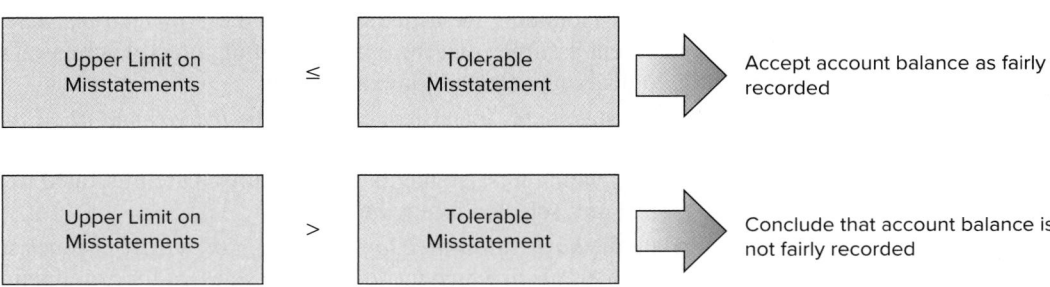

The upper limit on misstatements is calculated as

Projected misstatement	$130,138
Incremental allowance for sampling risk	23,648
Basic allowance for sampling risk	341,427
Upper limit on misstatements	$495,213

Based on the upper limit on misstatements, the audit team would conclude that the true misstatement in accounts receivable has a 90 percent chance (1 − *Risk of incorrect acceptance* of 10 percent) of being less than or equal to $495,213. Conversely, the true misstatement in accounts receivable has a 10 percent chance (risk of incorrect acceptance of 10 percent) of being more than $495,213.

Because the tolerable misstatement for accounts receivable is $628,167, the audit team would accept the account balance as being fairly stated. In so doing, the team has controlled the risk of incorrect acceptance to a level of 10 percent. The audit team ordinarily accumulates the three misstatements actually identified (see Exhibit F.4) and recommends that the client adjust the financial statements to reflect these misstatements. If the client does not make the adjustment, the $93,738 will be included on the score sheet (discussed in Chapter 11) as a "known misstatement." The added allowances of $401,475 ($495,213 − $93,738) are included on the score sheet as a "likely misstatement." The audit team also investigates the causes of all misstatements to ensure they do not represent a lack of controls or a pattern of fraud.

What would have occurred if the upper limit on misstatements had exceeded $628,167? For example, assume that the upper limit on misstatements was calculated as $650,000. In this situation, the audit team would conclude that the true misstatement in the population had a 90% chance of being less than or equal to $650,000, which does not allow them to conclude that the account balance is fairly stated. In this instance, one of two options exists:

1. The audit team could increase the sample size and examine additional items. These additional items would effectively reduce the sampling interval, reducing the projected misstatement, incremental allowance for sampling risk, and basic allowance for sampling risk. If enough additional items are examined and *no additional misstatements are detected,* the recalculated upper limit on misstatements could fall below the tolerable misstatement of $628,167. If so, the audit team could conclude that the financial statements were not materially misstated.

2. The audit team could recommend making an adjustment to the recorded balance of the client's accounts receivable. With an upper limit on misstatements of $650,000, an adjustment of $21,833 would result in a revised upper limit on misstatements of $628,167 ($650,000 − $21,833). This revised upper limit on misstatements allows the audit team to conclude that the account balance is fairly stated at a risk of incorrect acceptance of 10 percent.

Summary: Evaluating Sample Results

The following summarizes the major steps in calculating the upper limit on misstatements and components of the upper limit on misstatements:

1. For all misstatements identified, calculate the *projected misstatement.* The projected misstatement assumes that the entire sampling interval is misstated to the same extent as the logical unit selected for examination.

2. For all misstatements identified, calculate the *incremental allowance for sampling risk.* The incremental allowance for sampling risk considers the possibility that sampling intervals in which misstatements were identified are misstated to a greater extent than the logical unit selected for examination.

3. Calculate the *basic allowance for sampling risk,* which assumes some misstatement in sampling intervals in which the logical unit selected for examination was not misstated.

- The audit team determined an upper limit on misstatements of $495,213, comprised of
  - Projected misstatement of $130, 138
  - Incremental allowance for sampling risk of $23,648
  - Basic allowance for sampling risk of $341,427

- Because the upper limit on misstatements is less than the tolerable misstatement ($628,167), the audit team would accept the account balance as fairly stated.
- The audit team would recommend that Dunder-Mifflin adjust the financial statements for the three misstatements totaling $93,738.

Using IDEA to Evaluate Sample Results

After conducting the appropriate substantive tests, the audit team inputs the audited values into the sample files and uses the *Analysis>Sample>Monetary Unit>Evaluate>* function. The audit team should select the "Stringer Bound" option and, after identifying various parameters and confirming information provided by IDEA, the following output screen would be generated:[6]

MUS - Stringer Bound Evaluation Summary

Confidence Level 90.00

Value of the sampled population excluding high values 4,092,727.92
Total value of high value items   8,470,608.19
Value of the sampled population including high values 12,563,336.11

Results Excluding High Value Items	Overstatements	Understatements
Combined Sample Size	27	27
Number of errors	2	0
Gross most likely error	45,473.97	0.00
Net most likely error	45,473.97	-45,473.97
Total Precision	353,907.77	334,560.99
Gross upper error limit	399,381.74	334,560.99
Net upper error limit	399,381.74	289,087.02
Results for High Value Items		
Number of high value items	3	3
Number of errors	1	0
Value of errors	85,796.50	0.00
Results Including High Value Items		
Total number of items examined	30	30
Number of errors	3	0
Gross most likely error	131,270.47	0.00
Net most likely error	131,270.47	-131,270.47
Gross upper error limit	485,178.24	334,560.99
Net upper error limit	485,178.24	203,290.52

Key elements in the above include

1. The confidence level (90.00%) (corresponding to a *risk of incorrect acceptance* of 10%) and the total value of the population ($12,563,336.11), separated into (a) high value items and (b) items excluding high value items.
2. Under "Results Including High Value Items," a total of 30 items were examined and 3 errors (all overstatement) were identified.
3. The "Gross Most Likely Error" ($131,270.47) corresponds to the *projected misstatement* discussed previously.
4. The "Total Precision" of $353,907.77 represents the sum of the *basic allowance for sampling risk* and the *incremental allowance for sampling risk*.
5. The "Gross Upper Error Limit" of $485,178.24 corresponds to the *Upper limit on misstatements* and is the sum of (3) and (4) above.

[6]Detailed information and a step-by-step walkthrough of this process is provided in *Connect.*

The above values will differ slightly from those determined previously because of the statistical distribution assumed by IDEA.

Because the gross upper error limit ($485,178.24) is less than the tolerable misstatement of $628,167 (5 percent of the recorded balance), the audit team is able to conclude with 90 percent confidence (representing a 10 percent risk of incorrect acceptance) that the account balance is fairly stated.

✅ REVIEW CHECKPOINTS

F.17   Identify the three components of the upper limit on misstatements. How is each component calculated?

F.18   Why are misstatements in logical units that are higher than the sampling interval not projected over the sampling interval?

F.19   What is the *upper limit on misstatements*? What information does it provide the auditor?

F.20   What options are available to the audit team if the upper limit on misstatements exceeds the tolerable misstatement?

OTHER VARIABLES SAMPLING APPROACHES

Our discussion in this module has focused on PPS because of its frequent use in practice. PPS is particularly beneficial when overstatements are of greater concern (such as the audit of assets and revenues), as this method automatically selects items with larger dollar balances for examination. Another statistical sampling approach available to auditors is classical variables sampling. Further discussion of classical variables sampling, as well as a comprehensive example using one type of this sampling approach, is shown in Appendix FB.

Both PPS and classical variables sampling are statistical sampling methods that explicitly control the audit team's exposure to sampling risk in determining sample size, selecting sample items, and evaluating sample results. However, it is important to note that generally accepted auditing standards do not require the use of statistical sampling methods; in many cases, it is easier and more efficient to use **nonstatistical sampling methods**. Nonstatistical sampling methods differ from statistical sampling methods in how the audit team determines sample size, selects sample items, and evaluates sample results. Further discussion of nonstatistical sampling, as well as an example of using nonstatistical sampling, is shown in Appendix FC.

The Auditing Insight "Audit Sampling in Practice" presents the results of a survey that examined the types of variables sampling methods used in practice.

AUDITING INSIGHT   Audit Sampling in Practice

A survey of the sampling practices of six international accounting firms (including the Big Four) revealed the following with respect to variables sampling techniques:

1.   While both PPS and classical variables sampling approaches were used, PPS approaches were used more frequently.

2.   Four of the six firms emphasized the use of statistical sampling methods but permitted the use of nonstatistical methods. Three of these four firms indicated that a larger sample size would be required if a nonstatistical technique was used (essentially imposing a "penalty" for the use of nonstatistical methods).

Source: B.E. Christensen, R.J. Elder, and S.M. Glover, "Behind the Numbers: Insights into Large Audit Firm Sampling Practices," *Accounting Horizons,* March 2015, pp. 61–81.

Documentation in Variables Sampling

The audit team is required to document various information related to the sampling procedure. The information that would be documented depends upon the type of sampling application (PPS, classical variables sampling, or nonstatistical sampling) but generally includes the following:

- Information on the objective of sampling and assertions evaluated; definition of the characteristic of interest; and definition of the population and the sampling unit, including how the audit team verified the completeness and accuracy of the population being sampled (steps 1–3).
- The sampling technique used and definition of a misstatement.
- The method and parameters used to determine sample size, as well as the rationale for these assessments (step 4).
- The sample size determined based on the parameters (step 4).
- Information on the selection of sample items and a list of items selected and examined by the audit team (step 5).
- A description of the substantive procedures performed on each item selected; a list of misstatements (step 6); and the determination of the upper limit on misstatements (PPS), precision interval (classical variables sampling), or estimated audited balance (nonstatistical sampling) (step 7).
- The audit team's conclusion with respect to the fairness of the recorded balance, including qualitative factors considered, and the effect of this conclusion on the financial statement opinion.

By archiving the IDEA program used in their sampling process, the audit team will meet many of these documentation requirements, as noted in Auditing Insight "IDEA and Variables Sampling Documentation."

AUDITING INSIGHT   IDEA and Variables Sampling Documentation

The following steps illustrated previously in this module will document some of they elements of the audit team's variables sampling plan.

- The ***Analysis > Sample > Monetary Unit > Plan*** function tab will require the audit team to input the population from which to sample and parameters used to determine sample size.

- Following input of information related to the population and parameters, the ***Analysis > Sample > Monetary Unit > Plan***

function tab will determine the appropriate sample size and sampling interval.

- The ***Analysis > Sample > Monetary Unit > Extract*** function will document the random start, identify the items selected for examination, and provide a listing of items selected for examination.

- The ***Analysis > Sample > Monetary Unit > Evaluate*** function will determine the upper limit on misstatements based on the results of the audit team's substantive procedures.

The Auditing Insight "'Big Data' and Audit Sampling" illustrates how enhanced technology has changed the approach to audit sampling in practice.

AUDITING INSIGHT   "Big Data" and Audit Sampling

New technologies and the use of "Big Data" have significantly affected the traditional audit engagement. Previously, audit teams were limited to gathering traditional forms of evidence as to the fairness of financial statement account balances (or individual classes of transactions) by performing substantive tests of details on only a sample of items

that comprise the entire population. In effect, under current auditing standards and practice, a significant portion of many audit populations are not subjected to any form of testing or assurance.

In today's environment, the use of new technologies and both qualitative and quantitative data can be used by audit teams to provide

(continued)

AUDITING INSIGHT — *(concluded)*

some level of assurance on an entire audit population. For example, assume that a client's accounts receivable is comprised of more than 150,000 customer accounts and that the audit team has identified a number of factors that can be used to identify components or transactions that have an extremely low likelihood of being misstated. Based on initial screens of all 150,000 accounts, the audit team concludes that all but 100 of these accounts have an extremely low likelihood of being misstated; the audit team then decides to perform substantive tests of detail (e.g., traditional positive confirmation procedures with customers) on each of these 100 accounts.

The audit team's testing could be viewed through one of two perspectives. From a traditional perspective, the audit team has performed substantive tests and obtained assurance on 100 of the 150,000 customer accounts. Alternatively, the use of qualitative and quantitative factors as an initial screen could be viewed as having provided some assurance (albeit a lower level than confirmation) on 149,900 components, with the audit team using confirmations to provide higher levels of assurance on the remaining 100 components. In this latter case, it could be argued that the audit team did not sample, but has examined the entire population.

As the existence and availability of new technologies and the use of Big Data continue to increase, auditing standards setting bodies will face situations such as that described above. These considerations will obviously impact the role and nature of sampling in the audit.

 REVIEW CHECKPOINTS

F.21 Define *classical variables sampling* and *nonstatistical sampling.* Are these methods viable options to monetary unit sampling?

F.22 What information related to variables sampling applications does the audit team typically document?

Summary

This module discusses variables sampling, which the audit team uses in performing substantive procedures. When performing variables sampling, the audit team has the primary objective of determining whether an account balance or class of transactions is fairly stated. As with any sampling application, the audit team is exposed to sampling risk (the risk that the decision made based on the sample differs from the decision that would have been made if the entire population were examined). Using statistical sampling allows the audit team to control this sampling risk (referred to as the *risk of incorrect acceptance*) in determining the appropriate sample size and evaluating the sample results. Two primary statistical types of variables sampling plans are probability proportional to size sampling (PPS) and classical variables sampling. (Of these, PPS is more commonly used in practice.)

When using PPS, the audit team calculates an upper limit on misstatements, which has a (1 – *Risk of incorrect acceptance*) probability of equaling or exceeding the true amount of misstatement in the population. If the upper limit on misstatements is less than or equal to the tolerable misstatement, the audit team would conclude that the account balance is fairly stated; in contrast, if the upper limit on misstatements exceeds the tolerable misstatement, the audit team would either propose an adjustment to the account balance or class of transactions or expand the sample. PPS is unique in defining the sampling unit as an individual dollar in an account balance or class of transactions. As a result, PPS tends to select larger dollar components for examination.

Classical variables sampling uses normal distribution theory and the central limit theorem to provide a range of either the recorded balance of the account balance or class of transactions or the misstatement in the account balance or class of transactions.

Nonstatistical sampling is acceptable under generally accepted auditing standards. Instead of using statistical theory to determine sample size and allowance for sampling risk, auditors rely on their professional judgment in making these decisions.

Key Terms

audited value: The amount at which an account balance or class of transactions should be recorded, assuming no departures from generally accepted accounting principles, 787

basic allowance for sampling risk: A component of the upper limit on misstatements determined by multiplying the sampling interval by the confidence factor corresponding to the appropriate risk of incorrect acceptance; its calculation acknowledges that sampling intervals can contain some level of misstatement despite the fact that the logical unit drawn from that sampling interval was not misstated, 797

block selection: A method of choosing sample items in which a series of contiguous (or adjacent) items is chosen from the population (Appendix FC), 831

classical variables sampling: An approach that uses the laws of probability and the central limit theorem to provide an estimate of either the amount of misstatement or the true balances of an account balance or class of transactions, 785

difference estimation: A classical variables sampling method that bases its calculation of the estimated account balance on differences between audited values and recorded balances of components of the account balance or class of transactions (Appendix FB), 820

expected misstatement: The amount of misstatement the audit team anticipates in the account balance or class of transactions, 789

haphazard selection: The method of choosing sample items in an unstructured manner but without intentional bias (Appendix FC), 831

incremental allowance for sampling risks: A component of the upper limit on misstatements determined by adjusting the projected misstatement for the change in confidence factors resulting from detecting the misstatement; its calculation acknowledges that the sampling interval can be misstated to a greater extent than the logical unit drawn from that sampling interval, 796

individually significant item: An item in the population whose amount exceeds the tolerable misstatement (Appendix FB), 822

logical unit: The component of an account balance or class of transactions containing an individual dollar selected under MUS; can include customer account balances, items of inventory, and accounts payable to specific vendors.

mean-per-unit estimation: A classical variables sampling method that bases its calculation of the estimated balance on the average audited values of components of the account balance or class of transactions (Appendix FB), 820

monetary unit sampling (MUS): A form of PPS sampling in which the population is expressed in some form of monetary unit (such as a dollar). MUS is a form of PPS sampling that is applicable in an audit context, 785

nonstatistical sampling methods: In attributes sampling, methods that do not control the audit team's exposure to the risk of overreliance in determining sample size, selecting sample items, or evaluating sample results, 800

precision interval: The range around the sample estimate that has a likelihood equal to reliability of including the true population value, 821

probability proportional to size (PPS) sampling: A variables sampling method in which the population is viewed as being composed of individual dollars within an account balance or class of transactions; effective in ensuring that large dollar components are selected for examination, 785

projected misstatement: A component of the upper limit on misstatements determined by multiplying the sampling interval by the tainting percentage; its calculation assumes that the entire sampling interval is misstated to the same extent as the logical unit drawn from that sampling interval, 795

ratio estimation: A classical variables sampling method that bases its calculation of the estimated balance on the ratio of audited values to recorded balances of components of the account balance or class of transactions (Appendix FB), 820

risk of incorrect acceptance: The likelihood that the audit team will conclude that the client's account balance is fairly stated when it is materially misstated, 788

risk of incorrect rejection: The likelihood that the audit team will conclude that the client's account balance is materially misstated when it is fairly stated, 788

sampling interval: An interval determined by dividing the recorded amount of the population (account balance) by the sample size, 792

standard deviation: A measure of the variability of the population that is considered when using classical variables sampling (Appendix FB), 823

strata: A subgroup into which a population is divided to reduce sample size; has a smaller standard deviation with respect to the characteristic of interest than the complete population (Appendix FB), 822

stratification: The process of subdividing a population into more homogenous subgroups (or *strata*); reduces the necessary sample size in a classical variables sampling application (Appendix FB), 822

tainting percentage: An amount that represents the proportion by which a logical unit is misstated; determined by dividing the amount of the misstatement by the recorded balance, 794

tolerable misstatement: The maximum amount by which the account balance or class of transactions can be misstated without the audit team concluding that the account balance or class of transactions is materially misstated; based on performance materiality, 788

true balance: The amount at which the client's account balance should be recorded if no misstatements or departures from generally accepted accounting principles exist, 784

upper limit on misstatements (ULM): A measure that adjusts the sample estimate of misstatement for the audit team's acceptable level of sampling risk, 797

variables sampling: A form of sampling used to examine a population to estimate the amount or value of some characteristic of that population; used by auditors during their substantive procedure, 784

Multiple-Choice Questions for Practice and Review

Mc Graw Hill connect® All applicable Exercises and Problems are available with *Connect.*

LO F-1

F.23 Which of the following major stages of the audit is most closely related to variables sampling?

    a. Determining preliminary levels of performance materiality.

    b. Performing tests of controls procedures.

    c. Performing substantive procedures.

    d. Searching for the possible occurrence of subsequent events.

LO F-1

F.24 Which of the following types of variables sampling plans has a tendency to select higher-dollar items for examination?

    a. Difference estimation.

    b. Mean-per-unit estimation.

    c. PPS sampling.

    d. Ratio estimation.

LO F-1

F.25 Variables sampling methods can be used to estimate

	Amount of Misstatement	True Account Balance
a.	Yes	Yes
b.	Yes	No
c.	No	Yes
d.	No	No

LO F-4

F.26 When evaluating the results of a PPS application, the audit team should compare the upper limit on misstatements to the

    a. Expected misstatement.

    b. Incremental allowance for sampling risk.

    c. Projected misstatement.

    d. Tolerable misstatement.

LO F-2

F.27 When making a decision about the dollar amount in an account balance based on a sample, the audit team considers the risk of incorrect acceptance to be more serious than the risk of incorrect rejection because

    a. The incorrect rejection decision impairs the efficiency of the audit.

    b. The audit team will do additional work and discover the misstatement of the incorrect decision.

    c. The incorrect acceptance decision impairs the effectiveness of the audit.

    d. Sufficient appropriate audit evidence will not have been obtained.

LO F-2

F.28 The unique feature of PPS sampling is that

    a. Sampling units are not chosen at random.

    b. A dollar unit selected in a sample is not replaced before the sample selection is completed.

    c. Auditors need not worry about the risk of incorrect acceptance decision.

    d. The population is defined as the number of monetary units in an account balance or class of transactions.

LO F-3

F.29 When determining sample size under PPS sampling, an audit team does *not* need to make a judgment or estimate of

    a. Audit risk.

    b. Tolerable misstatement.

    c. Expected misstatement.

    d. Standard deviation.

LO F-2

F.30 Which of the following statements is *correct* about PPS sampling?

    a. The risk of incorrect acceptance must be specified.

    b. Smaller logical units have a higher probability of selection in the sample than larger units.

    c. Each logical unit in the population has an equally likely chance of being selected in the sample.

    d. The projected misstatement cannot be calculated when one or more misstatements are discovered.

LO F-2

F.31 One of the primary advantages of PPS sampling is the fact that

    a. It is an effective method of sampling for evidence of understatement in asset accounts.

    b. The sample selection automatically achieves high-dollar selection and stratification.

    c. The sample selection provides for including a representative number of small-value components.

    d. Expanding the sample for additional evidence is relatively simple.

LO F-3

F.32 Which of the following would *not* cause the audit team to select a larger sample of items under a PPS sampling application?

    a. A reduction in the risk of incorrect acceptance from 10 percent to 5 percent.

    b. An increase in the tolerable misstatement from $30,000 to $60,000.

    c. An increase in the expected misstatement from $20,000 to $40,000.

    d. All of these would result in selecting a larger sample.

LO F-4

F.33 Assume that an account with a recorded balance of $5,000 has an audited value of $3,000. By using PPS sampling, if the sampling interval is $1,500, the projected misstatement would be

    a. $600.

    b. $900.

    c. $2,000.

    d. $3,000.

LO F-4

F.34 If the _____ is less than the _____, the audit team would conclude that the account balance is fairly stated.

    a. Projected misstatement; tolerable misstatement.

    b. Tolerable misstatement; projected misstatement.

    c. Upper limit on misstatements; tolerable misstatement.

    d. Tolerable misstatement; upper limit on misstatements.

LO F-4

F.35 If the upper limit on misstatements is calculated at $17,800 and the tolerable misstatement is $15,000, what is the minimum amount of adjustment necessary for the audit team to issue an unmodified opinion on the client's financial statements?

    a. $0.

    b. $2,800.

    c. $4,800.

    d. $14,800.

LO F-1

F.36 In which of the following stages of the audit is variables sampling most appropriately used?

a. Establishing the desired audit risk.

b. Assessing the appropriate level of inherent risk.

c. Performing tests of controls to assess control risk.

d. Performing substantive tests of details to achieve the appropriate level of detection risk.

LO F-3

F.37 Which of the following represents the appropriate relationship between the factor and sample size using PPS?

	Tolerable Misstatement	Population Size
a.	Direct	Direct
b.	Direct	Inverse
c.	Inverse	Direct
d.	Inverse	Inverse

LO F-4

F.38 Which of the following components is *not* used in determining the upper limit on misstatements?

a. Basic allowance for sampling risk.

b. Incremental allowance for sampling risk.

c. Projected misstatement.

d. Tolerable misstatement.

LO F-4

F.39 The projected misstatement is determined by multiplying the sampling interval by the

a. Risk of incorrect acceptance.

b. Incremental confidence factor.

c. Confidence factor.

d. Tainting percentage.

LO F-4

F.40 Which of the following steps involved with determining the upper limit on misstatements is ordinarily performed *earliest*?

a. Multiply the sampling interval by the tainting percentage.

b. Determine the audited value of the item and compare it to the recorded balance.

c. Calculate the basic allowance for sampling risk.

d. Calculate the incremental allowance for sampling risk.

LO F-3

F.41 A component of an account balance has a recorded balance of $10,000 and an audited value of $8,000. By using PPS sampling, if the sampling interval is $20,000, the projected misstatement would be

a. $2,000.

b. $4,000.

c. $5,000.

d. $10,000.

LO F-4

F.42 Which of the following statements is *not* true with respect to the calculation of the upper limit on misstatements?

a. The tainting percentage is determined based on the difference between the recorded balance and the audited value.

b. A separate incremental allowance for sampling risk is calculated for each misstatement discovered by the auditor.

c. If no misstatements are detected, the basic allowance for sampling risk equals zero.

d. The projected misstatement is determined by multiplying the sampling interval by the tainting percentage.

LO F-4

F.43 Which of the following does *not* impact the calculation of the basic allowance for sampling risk?

a. An increased misstatement in an account balance or transaction.

b. A lower level of the risk of incorrect acceptance.

c. An increase in the necessary sample size.

d. A reduction in the sampling interval used to select sample items.

Exercises and Problems		

LO F-3

F.44 Sample Selection: PPS Sampling. Emerson Washburn is examining the accounts receivable of Anaheim Company and has decided to use PPS sampling to select a sample of customer accounts for confirmation. Anaheim's accounts receivable totaled $3,500,000 and comprised 3,000 different customer accounts ranging in amount from $200 to $125,000. Based on the characteristics of the population and acceptable risk of incorrect acceptance, tolerable misstatement, and expected misstatement, Washburn determined a sample size of 20 accounts.

Required:

a. Without making any calculations, briefly describe how Washburn would select a sample of customer accounts from the population of accounts receivable.

b. If Washburn selected a random starting point of 172,600, what are the first four dollars that would be selected? How would Washburn proceed to evaluate these items?

c. What would Washburn do if two of the dollars selected are contained within the same customer account?

d. Anaheim maintains its accounts receivable balances in a computerized file that has the following information: (1) customer number, (2) customer name, (3) total account balance, and (4) account status (current versus past due). For each of these elements, comment on any procedures that Washburn should perform before selecting the sample if the population were arranged based on these elements (e.g., arranged numerically by customer number, alphabetically by customer name).

LO F-3

F.45 Sample Selection: PPS Sampling. You have been assigned to select a PPS sample from Whitney Company's detailed inventory records as of September 30. Whitney's controller gave you a list of the 23 different inventory items and their recorded book amounts. The senior accountant told you to select a sample of 10 dollar units and the inventory items that contain them.

ID	Amount	ID	Amount	ID	Amount	ID	Amount
1	$ 1,750	7	$ 1,255	13	$ 937	19	$ 2,577
2	1,492	8	3,761	14	5,938	20	1,126
3	994	9	1,956	15	2,001	21	565
4	629	10	1,393	16	222	22	2,319
5	2,272	11	884	17	1,738	23	1,681
6	1,163	12	729	18	1,228		

Required:

Prepare audit documentation showing a systematic selection of 10 dollar units and the related logical units. Arrange the items in their numerical identification number order and use a random starting point at the 1,210th dollar.

LO F-3

F.46 Sample Size Determination: PPS Sampling. The recorded accounts receivable balance for Warner Company was $500,000.

Required:

For each of the following independent sets of conditions, determine the appropriate sample size for the examination of Warner's accounts receivable in PPS. Based on the differences in your calculations, identify the general relationship between different factors and sample size. (RIA = risk of incorrect acceptance, TM = tolerable misstatement, EM = expected misstatement.)

a. RIA = 5%, TM = $50,000, EM = $10,000

b. RIA = 5%, TM = $50,000, EM = $25,000

c. RIA = 10%, TM = $50,000, EM = $10,000

d. RIA = 10%, TM = $50,000, EM = $25,000

LO F-3

F.47 Sample Size and Sampling Interval Determination: PPS Sampling. Reagan Simmons is conducting the audit of Ace Inc., and is using PPS to select a sample of inventory items for examination. The recorded balance in Ace's inventory account was $1,200,000. In carrying out the sampling plan, Simmons established a risk of incorrect acceptance of 5 percent, a tolerable misstatement of $100,000, and an expected misstatement of $20,000.

Required:

a. What parameters would Simmons consider in determining the sample size for Ace's inventory?

b. How would Simmons identify or establish each of these parameters?

c. Determine the necessary sample size for the audit of Ace's inventory.

d. Based on the sample size determined in part (c), determine the appropriate sampling interval.

e. Briefly describe how Simmons would select the sample from a computerized inventory list that Ace maintains.

LO F-3

F.48 Sample Size and Sampling Interval Determination: PPS Sampling. Casey Paul is considering the use of PPS in examining Stanley's accounts receivable, which were recorded at $300,000. Using the audit risk model, Paul has identified a necessary risk of incorrect acceptance of 10 percent and has established a tolerable misstatement of $25,000 and an expected misstatement of $10,000.

Required:

a. Determine the necessary sample size for the audit of Stanley's accounts receivable.

b. Based on the sample size determined in part (a), what is the appropriate sampling interval?

c. Briefly describe how Paul would select the sample from a computerized customer list that Stanley maintains.

d. How would each of the following changes in Paul's sampling plan impact the sample size and sampling interval? For each change, use the original parameters noted in the problem. (Verify your answer by calculating the sample size associated with each change.)

1. A reduction in the necessary level of the risk of incorrect acceptance to 5 percent.

2. An increase in the expected misstatement to $12,500.

3. A decrease in the tolerable misstatement to $20,000.

LO F-3

F.49 Sample Size and Sampling Interval Determination: PPS Sampling. Blythe Drake is conducting an audit of Newman and is using PPS to select a sample of customer accounts receivable for confirmation. Newman's accounts receivable are recorded at $10,000,000 and comprise 2,000 customer accounts. Drake has established the following parameters for the investigation:

- Risk of incorrect acceptance = 5%.
- Tolerable misstatement = $250,000.
- Expected misstatement = $50,000.

Required:

a. Determine the sample size and sampling interval that Drake used in the audit of Newman's accounts receivable.

b. Based on the calculations in part (a), briefly describe how Drake would select customer accounts from the population of accounts receivable balances for confirmation.

c. Holding all other factors constant, determine the sample size and sampling interval assuming each of the following independent changes in Drake's sampling parameters:

1. Because of improvements in Newman's internal control policies related to accounts receivable processing from previous years, Drake believes that a risk of incorrect acceptance of 10 percent is now acceptable in the current engagement.

2. Because of the closeness of certain ratios to key debt covenants (particularly the current and quick ratios, which are highly influenced by accounts receivable), Drake believes that the tolerable misstatement should be decreased from $250,000 to $125,000.

3. Because of unusual circumstances in the previous year, some misstatements occurred in sales transaction processing that resulted in misstatements in accounts receivable. These misstatements are not anticipated to occur during the upcoming year. As a result, Drake believes that expected misstatement can be decreased from $50,000 to $25,000.

   d. How do the changes noted in part (c) illustrate the relationship between sample size and various factors?

   e. Describe the relationship between the sample size and sampling interval. Provide a brief explanation as to the nature of this relationship.

LO F-3

F.50 **Sample Size Relationships: PPS Sampling.** For each of the following cases, provide the missing information.

Recorded balance	$1,500,000	$190,000	(C)
Sample size	115	(B)	124
Sampling interval	(A)	$ 4,222	$ 18,000

LO F-3

F.51 **Sample Size Relationships: PPS Sampling.** Noel Frehley is examining the accounts receivable of Kiss Company and is considering the use of PPS. Kiss's accounts receivable are recorded at $400,000. Based on the necessary level of risk, Frehley has established a risk of incorrect acceptance of 5 percent. In addition, based on previous audits, Frehley estimates misstatements of $10,000. Finally, based on the overall level of performance materiality, Frehley has established tolerable misstatement at $20,000.

Required:

a. Determine the necessary sample size for Frehley's examination of Kiss Company's accounts receivable.

b. Assume that Frehley was interested in trying to reduce the necessary sample size. What are some options available in this regard?

c. Based on a discussion with the senior manager, Frehley knows that increasing the level of the risk of incorrect acceptance will reduce sample size. For the same level of expected misstatement, tolerable misstatement, and population size, determine the sample size for a risk of incorrect acceptance of 10 percent.

LO F-4

F.52 **Projected Misstatement Calculation: PPS Sampling.** For each of the following independent misstatements, identify the missing value:

	1	2	3	4
Recorded balance	$15,000	$30,000	(e)	$12,000
Audited value	$12,000	(c)	$6,000	(g)
Tainting percentage	(a)	5%	25%	(h)
Sampling interval	$50,000	(d)	$25,000	$48,000
Projected misstatement	(b)	$5,000	(f)	$24,000

LO F-4

F.53 **Upper Limit on Misstatements Calculation: PPS Sampling.** Jordan Thomas is using PPS to examine a client's accounts receivable balance. Using a sample size of 100 items and a sampling interval of $12,300, Thomas identified the following misstatements:

Item	Recorded Balance	Audited Value
1	$15,000	$12,500
2	10,000	4,000
3	3,000	2,000

Required:

a. Calculate the upper limit on misstatements assuming a risk of incorrect acceptance of (1) 5 percent and (2) 10 percent.

b. Based on your calculations in part (a), comment on the relationship between the risk of incorrect acceptance and the upper limit on misstatements.

LO F-4

F.54 **Upper Limit on Misstatements Calculation: PPS Sampling.**   Carson Allister is performing a PPS application in the audit of Bird Company's accounts receivable. Based on the acceptable level of the risk of incorrect acceptance of 5 percent and a tolerable misstatement of $120,000, Allister has calculated a sample size of 75 items and a sampling interval of $25,000. After examining the sample items, the following misstatements were identified:

Item	Recorded Balance	Audited Value
1	$35,000	$28,000
2	10,000	8,000
3	6,000	3,000

Required:

a. Calculate the upper limit on misstatements for Bird Company's accounts receivable.

b. Provide a brief description of the meaning of the upper limit on misstatements calculated in part (a).

c. What would Allister's conclusion be with respect to the fairness of Bird's accounts receivable balance?

LO F-4

F.55 **Upper Limit on Misstatements Calculation: PPS Sampling.**   The auditors mailed positive confirmations on 60 customers' accounts receivable balances. The company's accounts receivable balance comprised 2,356 customer accounts with a total recorded balance of $19,600,000, and the sampling interval was $280,000. The auditors received four positive confirmation returns reporting exceptions. Upon follow-up, they found the following:

- *Account 2333.* Recorded balance $8,345. The account was overstated by $1,669 because the client made an arithmetic mistake recording a credit memo. The company issued only 86 credit memos during the year. The auditors examined all of them for the same arithmetic mistake and found no similar misstatements.

- *Account 363.* Recorded balance $7,460. The account was overstated by $1,865 because the company sold merchandise to a customer with payment due in six months plus interest. The billing clerk made a mistake and recorded the sales price and the unearned interest as the sale and receivable amount. Inquiries revealed that the company always sold on "payment due immediately" terms but had made an exception for this customer. Numerous sales transactions had been audited in the sales control audit work, and none had shown the extended terms allowed to Account 363.

- *Account 1216.* Recorded balance $19,450. The account was overstated by $1,945 because an accounting clerk had deliberately misadded several invoices to create extra charges to a business that competed with his brother's business. The accounting clerk (who was a temporary employee) had forged the initials of the supervisor who normally reviewed invoices for accuracy. The auditors examined all invoices for this and other customers processed by this clerk and found no similar misstatements.

- *Account 2003.* Recorded balance $9,700. The account was overstated by $1,455 because of a fictitious sale submitted by a salesperson, apparently part of an effort to boost third-quarter sales and commissions. The auditors learned that the salesperson was employed from August 20 through October 30 before being dismissed as a result of customer complaints. They examined all other unpaid balances attributed to this salesperson and found no other fictitious sales.

Required:

a. Decide which, if any, of the account misstatements should be considered monetary misstatements and included in the calculation of the upper limit on misstatements using PPS.

b. Calculate the upper limit on misstatements and decide whether the evidence from these misstatements indicates that the accounts receivable balance is or is not materially misstated. (The tolerable misstatement for the accounts receivable was $1,000,000, and the auditors had already decided on a risk of incorrect acceptance of 5 percent.)

c. Are any additional procedures required of the audit team regarding account 1216 or account 2003?

LO F-4

F.56 Upper Limit on Misstatements Calculations: PPS Sampling.   Assume that Parker Fran has calculated a sampling interval for Tide Inc.'s inventory of $10,000 and has conducted an examination of a sample of inventory balances. Fran has identified the following three misstatements:

Item No.	Recorded Balance	Audited Value
X-21	$ 3,000	$ 1,200
Z-24	550	440
AA-02	6,000	1,500

Required:

Calculate the upper limit on misstatements for the following levels of the risk of incorrect acceptance. In general, what relationship do you observe between the risk of incorrect acceptance and the upper limit on misstatements?

a. 5 percent

b. 10 percent

LO F-4

F.57 Upper Limit on Misstatements Calculations: PPS Sampling.   Clyde Billy is conducting the audit of Hoops Inc. and is examining Hoops's inventory balances. Billy plans to select a sample of inventory items for examination and will verify quantities and perform price tests to ascertain that the items are properly recorded according to generally accepted accounting principles.

Item No.	Recorded Balance	Audited Value
10–865	$ 12,600	$ 8,400
20–954	110,000	95,000
30–781	55,000	44,000
40–269	80,000	60,000

Billy determined a sampling interval of $100,000 and, using systematic random selection techniques, has identified the following misstatements:

Required:

a. Using a 5 percent risk of incorrect acceptance, calculate the upper limit on misstatements.

b. Provide a brief description of the meaning of the upper limit on misstatements using the information calculated in part (a).

c. Reperform part (a) using a risk of incorrect acceptance of 10 percent.

d. What relationship do you observe between the acceptable level of the risk of incorrect acceptance and the upper limit on misstatements? Provide a brief explanation about what causes this relationship.

e. Based on the levels of the upper limit on misstatements determined in this example, what are the advantages and disadvantages of establishing lower and higher acceptable levels of the risk of incorrect acceptance?

LO F-1, F-3, F-4

F.58 Comprehensive Problem: PPS Sampling.   Zachary Mayo is a new staff accountant participating in his first audit engagement. He has been assigned to the Foley Company engagement and is examining Foley's accounts receivable. Foley maintains a computerized ledger of its accounts receivable balances, which are recorded at $5,000,000 and comprise 5,560 individual customer accounts.

Mayo established the following parameters for use in this year's audit. In so doing, he relied extensively on parameters established in prior audits:

- Expected misstatement is established at $100,000, which is the average amount of misstatement identified in the past five audits. During the past year, Foley has experienced a great deal of turnover among its sales processing personnel and has made some relatively large sales that present some unusual revenue recognition issues. In addition, accounts receivable have increased by almost 15 percent from the prior year.

- The tolerable misstatement is 10 percent of the ending accounts receivable balance, or $500,000 ($5,000,000 × 0.10). Compared to previous years, Foley's financial condition has slightly deteriorated. Its current and quick ratios, although still above levels necessary to satisfy its debt covenants, have deteriorated.

- The risk of incorrect acceptance is 10 percent, which is the same as that used in the previous year. In evaluating the components of the audit risk model, some of the issues related to the turnover among sales processing personnel as well as the more limited use of analytical procedures during the current audit represent important differences from previous years.

Mayo sent positive confirmations to Foley's customers. His work identified the following differences between audited values and recorded balances:

Customer	Recorded Balance	Audited Value
R. Gerer	$ 15,000	$ 10,000
D. Wings	25,000	20,000
L. Goss	60,000	30,000
K. David	120,000	90,000

Unfortunately, Mayo resigned from the firm shortly after identifying these differences. The only documentation you were able to locate was information related to (1) the levels of expected misstatement, tolerable misstatement, and risk of incorrect acceptance that were used in the Foley audit and (2) the four confirmations returned by customers indicating differences between their records and Foley's recorded balances.

Required:

a. Mayo decided to use PPS primarily because it had been used in previous audits of Foley. Based on the nature of this sampling application and the composition of Foley's accounts receivable, was the use of PPS appropriate?

b. Based on the parameters established by Mayo, determine the sample size and sampling interval he used in the sampling application.

c. Describe the sample selection process used by Mayo. Are you able to replicate or otherwise determine which customer balances he confirmed?

d. Based on the four overstatements identified by Mayo, calculate the upper limit on misstatements. Based on this upper limit on misstatements, what general statement can be made with respect to the extent of misstatement in the account balance?

e. What is your initial decision with respect to the fairness of Foley's accounts receivable balance?

f. Review each of the parameters established by Mayo (expected misstatement, tolerable misstatement, and risk of incorrect acceptance). Do any differences in the current engagement raise questions with respect to the level of these parameters?

g. What are the potential effect(s) of the changes in parameters noted in part (f) on the sampling application?

LO F-3, F-4

F.59 **Comprehensive Problem: PPS Sampling.** Clint Walker was examining the accounts receivable of Country Music Inc. Its accounts receivable were recorded at $1,500,000. Based on past audits, Walker established tolerable misstatement at 10 percent of the recorded account balance and anticipated a very small level of misstatement in Country Music's accounts receivable ($50,000). In his previous assessments of audit risk, risk of material misstatement, and analytical procedures risk, Walker had established a necessary risk of incorrect acceptance of 10 percent.

Required:

a. Calculate the sampling interval and sample size that Walker would use in the audit of Country Music.

b. Reperform the calculations in part (a) if Walker had established a risk of incorrect acceptance of (1) 5 percent and (2) 20 percent. Based on your calculations, describe the relationship between the necessary level of the risk of incorrect acceptance and the sample size and sampling interval.

c. [*Note: Part (c) is unrelated to parts (a) and (b)*.] If Walker had detected the following four overstatements, determine the projected misstatement.

Recorded Balance	Audited Value	Sampling Interval
$ 3,500	$ 1,750	$8,000
1,000	200	8,000
12,000	10,000	8,000
5,000	4,000	8,000

d. Based on the results in part (c) and using a 10 percent risk of incorrect acceptance, calculate the upper limit on misstatements.

e. Reperform the calculation in part (d) using a risk of incorrect acceptance of (1) 5 percent and (2) 20 percent. Based on your calculation, describe the relationship between the necessary level of the risk of incorrect acceptance and the upper limit on misstatements.

f. Using a risk of incorrect acceptance of (1) 5 percent, (2) 10 percent, and (3) 20 percent, determine what Walker's conclusion would be with respect to Country Music's accounts receivable. How do different levels of the risk of incorrect acceptance influence the likelihood of concluding that the account balance is fairly stated?

LO F-3, F-4

F.60 **Comprehensive Problem: PPS Sampling.** Dylan Mays is auditing the accounts receivable of Channel Company. Channel's accounts receivable were recorded at $2,000,000 and comprised more than 1,500 customer accounts. However, Channel's ten largest customers' balances constituted a high percentage of the recorded accounts receivable (over $500,000, or 25 percent). As a result, Mays is considering the use of PPS.

Based on prior audits and other judgments, Mays has established the following parameters:

Risk of incorrect acceptance	5%
Tolerable misstatement	$120,000
Expected misstatement	$ 24,000

Required:

a. Briefly identify what factors Mays should consider in determining sample size and how these factors would be assessed.

b. Calculate the necessary sample size and sampling interval used by Mays in the audit of Channel Company.

c. Given the information in part (b), describe how Mays would select the sample from Channel's computerized accounts receivable ledger.

d. [*Note: Part (d) is unrelated to parts (b) and (c)*.] If Mays detected the following three misstatements, determine the projected misstatement.

Recorded Balance	Audited Value	Sampling Interval
$45,000	$40,000	$13,000
8,000	6,000	13,000
12,000	9,000	13,000

e. Based on the results in part (d) and a 5 percent risk of incorrect acceptance, calculate the upper limit on misstatements.

f. Based on the calculation in part (e), determine what Mays's conclusion would be with respect to Channel Company's accounts receivable.

LO F-2, F-3, F-4

F.61 **Mistakes in a PPS Sampling Application.** Kelsey Mead, CPA, was engaged to audit Jiffy Company's financial statements for the year ended August 31.

For the current year, Mead decided to use PPS to select accounts receivable for confirmavtion because PPS uses each account in the population as a separate sampling unit. Mead expected to discover many overstatements but presumed that the PPS sample size still would be smaller than the corresponding sample size for classical variables sampling.

Mead reasoned that the PPS sample would automatically result in a stratified sample because each account would have an equal chance of being selected for confirmation. Additionally, the selection of negative (credit) balances would be facilitated without special considerations.

Mead computed the sample size using the risk of incorrect acceptance, the total recorded book amount of the receivables, and the number of misstated accounts allowed. Mead divided the total recorded book amount of the receivables by the sample size to determine the sampling interval and then calculated the standard deviation of the dollar amounts of the accounts selected for evaluation of the receivables.

Mead's calculated sample size was 60 and the sampling interval was determined to be $10,000. However, only 58 different accounts were selected because two accounts were so large that the sampling interval caused each of them to be selected twice. Mead proceeded to send confirmation requests to 55 of the 58 customers. Each of the three accounts originally selected for the sample had insignificant recorded balances under $20. Mead ignored these three small accounts and substituted the three largest accounts that had not been selected by the random selection procedure. Each of these accounts had balances in excess of $7,000, so Mead sent confirmation requests to these customers.

The confirmation process revealed two differences. One account with an audited value of $3,000 had been recorded at $4,000. Mead projected this to be a $1,000 misstatement. Another account with an audited value of $2,000 had been recorded at $1,900. Mead did not count the $100 difference because the purpose of the procedure was to detect overstatements.

In evaluating the sample results, Mead decided that the accounts receivable balance was not overstated because the projected misstatement ($1,000) was less than the allowance for sampling risk.

Required:

Describe each incorrect assumption, statement, and inappropriate application of sampling in Mead's procedures.

(AICPA adapted)

LO F-4

F.62 **PPS Sampling.** Georgie Costanza, CPA, is auditing the accounts receivable of Vandalay Industries and is considering the use of PPS techniques. Costanza has a number of questions regarding the use of PPS and has asked you to provide answers to them.

Required:

a. Under generally accepted auditing standards, can Costanza use nonstatistical sampling in the examination of Vandalay accounts receivable?

b. What are the advantages to using statistical sampling in the audit?

c. What are the risks associated with sampling, and to what type of losses do they expose Costanza?

d. How does Costanza establish the appropriate level of the risk of incorrect acceptance?

e. Is Costanza permitted to specify that certain items be examined, or do all items need to be randomly selected?

f. How can Costanza increase the likelihood that the items in the sample are representative of the population?

g. Other than the dollar amount of the misstatements, are any other factors important for Costanza to consider with respect to the misstatements?

Using IDEA in PPS Sampling

Exercises F.63 through F.66 require the use of IDEA in a PPS sampling context.

Elm Manufacturing Company (ELM) is a small manufacturer of back packs located in Rochelle, Illinois. Your audit team is conducting substantive tests of sales made to customers on account and will select a sample of transactions and confirm them with customers. You have access to ELM's electronic records in *Connect*. The appropriate file for these exercises is the Sales 2023–4th Q data set. Detailed information about ELM, instructions for accessing data sets, a data directory for data sets, and a detailed PPS sampling example (with IDEA screenshots) can also be found in *Connect*.

NOTE: The Sales 2023–4th Q data set contains a total of 410 transactions; of these, invoices have been prepared for the first 362 transactions (through Order No. 17357). You should use the INVAMT (which represents the amount of the sale prior to any discount) as the monetary unit from which to sample.

In selecting and evaluating the samples, select the following options:

For extraction type, select "Fixed interval."

For high values handling, select "High values in database."

For evaluation, select "Stringer Bound."

LO F-3

F.63 **PPS Sampling with IDEA: Determining Sample Size.** Assume that your audit team has established the following parameters for the examination of ELM's sales transactions:

Risk of incorrect acceptance	10%
Tolerable misstatement	$311,711 (or 8% of the recorded balance of the transactions)
Expected misstatement	$77,928 (or 2% of the recorded balance of the transactions)

Required:

a. Use IDEA to determine the necessary sample size, given the above parameters.
   Parts (b), (c), and (d) are independent scenarios that affect the sample size in this example.

b. Assume that your audit team has decided to increase their reliance on internal control and permit a corresponding increase in the risk of incorrect acceptance from 10 percent to 15 percent, which maintains overall audit risk at the same level. What is the necessary sample size, holding all other factors constant?

c. Assume that your audit team has decided to reduce the level of tolerable misstatement from $311,711 to $233,783 (or 6 percent of the recorded balance of the transactions). What is the necessary sample size, holding all other factors constant?

d. Assume that based on additional controls implemented by ELM, your audit team has decided to reduce the expected misstatement from $77,928 to $19,482 (0.5 percent of the recorded balance of the transactions). What is the necessary sample size, holding all other factors constant?

e. How do the results in parts (b), (c), and (d) reflect the relationship between various parameters and sample size?

LO F-3

F.64 **PPS Sampling with IDEA: Determining Sample Size and Selecting Sample Items.** Assume that your audit team has established the following parameters for the examination of ELM's sales transactions:

Risk of incorrect acceptance	10%
Tolerable misstatement	$389,638 (or 10% of the recorded balance of the transactions)
Expected misstatement	$58,446 (or 1.5% of the recorded balance of the transactions)

Required:

a. Use IDEA to determine the necessary sample size, given the above parameters.

b. What is the sampling interval? Show how the sampling interval can be arithmetically determined from the sample size and the population size.

c. Assuming a random start of 5,678, use IDEA to extract sample items from the population. List the transactions associated with the sample items selected by your audit team for examination. (Be sure to use "fixed interval extraction" and "high values in database" as options.)

d. Describe how IDEA extracts sample items from the population of sales transactions.

e. Based on the items selected from the population, does it appear that PPS sampling selects larger dollar items for examination? Provide the basis for your answer.

f. Why does the number of transactions extracted in part (c) differ from the sample size? Is this a concern?

LO F-4

F.65 **PPS Sampling with IDEA: Evaluating Sample Results**.

Assume that your audit team has established the following parameters for the examination of ELM's sales transactions:

Risk of incorrect acceptance	10%
Tolerable misstatement	$292,229 (or 7.5% of the recorded balance of the transactions)
Expected misstatement	$38,964 (or 1% of the recorded balance of the transactions)

Based on these parameters and a random start of 46,105, your audit team determined a sample size of 38 items and a corresponding sampling interval of $102,536.42.

The IDEA files for items selected by your audit team are included as Monetary Sample F.65 and High Values F.65 in Connect.

Students should begin a new project for each part of this exercise and copy the IDEA files into the folder related to that project, as IDEA automatically overwrites the file being used with the audited value.

Required:

a. After receiving replies to confirmations, you noted the following discrepancies:

Order No.	Recorded Balance	Audited Value
17025	$ 89,039.21	$ 88,126.24
17302	$ 16,617.54	$ 15,500.00
17020	$144,515.21	$140,967.20

Use IDEA to calculate the upper limit on misstatements. What would your conclusion be with respect to the recorded balance of ELM's sales transactions?

b. [*Note: Part (b) is independent of part (a).*] After receiving replies to confirmations, you noted the following discrepancies:

Order No.	Recorded Balance	Audited Value
17050	$ 23,239.34	$ 20,000.00
17215	$ 79,231.54	$ 71,308.39
17260	$ 7,001.52	$ 5,000.00
17190	$151,469.58	$145,000.00

Use IDEA to calculate the upper limit on misstatements. What would your conclusion be with respect to the recorded balance of ELM's sales transactions?

LO F-3, F-4

F.66 **PPS Sampling with IDEA: Comprehensive Problem.** Assume that your audit team has received the electronic file of sales transactions from ELM and is preparing to use PPS sampling in evaluating the fairness of ELM's sales transactions.

Required:

a. How many transactions are included in ELM's sales transaction file? Using the "Field Statistics" function, what is the recorded balance of the population of sales transactions (INVAMT)?

b. By double-clicking on the INVAMT column of the file, sort the population by dollar amount. Based on the composition of this population, which specific item(s) might your audit team wish to consider separately as it designs its PPS application?

c. Determine the sample size and sampling interval for each of the following combinations of parameters. Based on comparisons among these scenarios, describe the impact of each of these parameters on sample size:

	Confidence (Risk of Incorrect Acceptance)	Tolerable Misstatement	Expected Misstatement
1.	90% (10%)	$350,000	$100,000
2.	90% (10%)	450,000	100,000
3.	90% (10%)	350,000	50,000
4.	85% (15%)	350,000	100,000

d. Using the parameters in Scenario (c)(1) and a random start of $22,053, select a sample from the population of sales transactions. How many transactions were selected (including high value items)?

e. Express your sample in terms of the percentage of the number of transactions and percentage of total dollar value of transactions from the population. Does this appear to give you adequate coverage of the population? (You can use the "Field Statistics" function or export the transactions selected to an Excel file to simplify your calculations.)

For part (f), the IDEA files for items that were selected by the audit team are included as Monetary Sample F.66 and High Values F.66 in Connect. Students may wish to make copies of the data files for this part of the exercise, as IDEA automatically overwrites the file being used with the audited value entered.

f. Assume that the audit team's procedures identified the following misstatements:

Order No.	Recorded Balance	Audited Value
17005	$ 62,812.33	$ 60,000.00
17183	$ 4,676.54	$ 4,529.92
17326	$ 14,725.48	$ 12,000.00
17190	$151,469.58	$ 148,992.56

Use IDEA to calculate the upper limit on misstatements. What would your conclusion be with respect to the recorded balance of ELM's sales transactions?

Appendix FA

AICPA PPS TABLES

EXHIBIT FA.1
PPS Sample Sizes

Risk of Incorrect Acceptance	Ratio of Expected to Tolerable Misstatement	Tolerable Misstatement as a Percentage of Population										
		50%	30%	10%	8%	6%	5%	4%	3%	2%	1%	0.50%
5%	—	6	10	30	38	50	60	75	100	150	300	600
5	0.10	8	13	37	46	62	74	92	123	184	368	736
5	0.20	10	16	47	58	78	93	116	155	232	463	925
5	0.30	12	20	60	75	100	120	150	200	300	600	1,199
5	0.40	17	27	81	102	135	162	203	270	405	809	1,618
5	0.50	24	39	116	145	193	231	289	385	577	1,154	2,308
10	—	5	8	24	29	39	47	58	77	116	231	461
10	0.20	7	12	35	43	57	69	86	114	171	341	682
10	0.30	9	15	44	55	73	87	109	145	217	433	866
10	0.40	12	20	58	72	96	115	143	191	286	572	1,144
10	0.50	16	27	80	100	134	160	200	267	400	799	1,597
15	—	4	7	19	24	32	38	48	64	95	190	380
15	0.20	6	10	28	35	46	55	69	91	137	273	545
15	0.30	7	12	35	43	57	69	86	114	171	341	681
15	0.40	9	15	45	56	74	89	111	148	221	442	883
15	0.50	13	21	61	76	101	121	151	202	302	604	1,208
20	—	4	6	17	21	27	33	41	54	81	161	322
20	0.20	5	8	23	29	38	46	57	76	113	226	451
20	0.30	6	10	28	35	47	56	70	93	139	277	554
20	0.40	8	12	36	45	59	71	89	118	177	354	707
20	0.50	10	16	48	60	80	95	119	159	238	475	949
25	—	3	5	14	18	24	28	35	47	70	139	278
25	0.20	4	7	19	24	32	38	48	64	95	190	380
25	0.30	5	8	23	29	39	46	58	77	115	230	460
25	0.40	6	10	29	37	49	58	73	97	145	289	578
25	0.50	8	13	38	48	64	76	95	127	190	380	760
30	—	3	5	13	16	21	25	31	41	61	121	241
30	0.20	4	6	17	21	27	33	41	54	81	162	323
30	0.40	5	8	24	30	40	48	60	80	120	239	477
30	0.60	9	15	43	54	71	85	107	142	213	425	850
35	—	3	4	11	14	18	21	27	35	53	105	210
35	0.20	3	5	14	18	23	28	35	46	69	138	276
35	0.40	4	7	20	25	34	40	50	67	100	199	397
35	0.60	7	12	34	43	57	68	85	113	169	338	676
50	—	2	3	7	9	12	14	18	24	35	70	139
50	0.20	2	3	9	11	15	18	22	29	44	87	173
50	0.40	3	4	12	15	19	23	29	38	57	114	228
50	0.60	4	6	17	22	29	34	43	57	85	170	340

Source: AICPA Audit Guide *Audit Sampling*

EXHIBIT FA.2
PPS—Confidence
Factors for Sample
Evaluation

Number of Overstatement Misstatements	Risk of Incorrect Acceptance								
	5%	10%	15%	20%	25%	30%	35%	37%	50%
0	3.00	2.31	1.90	1.61	1.39	1.21	1.05	1.00	0.70
1	4.75	3.89	3.38	3.00	2.70	2.44	2.22	2.14	1.68
2	6.30	5.33	4.73	4.28	3.93	3.62	3.35	3.35	2.68
3	7.76	6.69	6.02	5.52	5.11	4.77	4.46	4.35	3.68
4	9.16	8.00	7.27	6.73	6.28	5.90	5.55	5.43	4.68
5	10.52	9.28	8.50	7.91	7.43	7.01	6.64	6.50	5.68
6	11.85	10.54	9.71	9.08	8.56	8.12	7.72	7.57	6.67
7	13.15	11.78	10.90	10.24	9.69	9.21	8.79	8.63	7.67
8	14.44	13.00	12.08	11.38	10.81	10.31	9.85	9.68	8.67
9	15.71	14.21	13.25	12.52	11.92	11.39	10.92	10.74	9.67
10	16.97	15.41	14.42	13.66	13.02	12.47	11.98	11.79	10.67
11	18.21	16.60	15.57	14.78	14.13	13.55	13.04	12.84	11.67
12	19.45	17.79	16.72	15.90	15.22	14.63	14.09	13.89	12.67
13	20.67	18.96	17.86	17.02	16.32	15.70	15.14	14.93	13.67
14	21.89	20.13	19.00	18.13	17.40	16.77	16.20	15.98	14.67
15	23.10	21.30	20.13	19.24	18.49	17.84	17.25	17.02	15.67
16	24.31	22.46	21.26	20.34	19.58	18.90	18.29	18.06	16.67
17	25.50	23.61	22.39	21.44	20.66	19.97	19.34	19.10	17.67
18	26.70	24.76	23.51	22.54	21.74	21.03	20.38	20.14	18.67
19	27.88	25.91	24.63	23.64	22.81	22.09	21.43	21.18	19.67
20	29.07	27.05	25.74	24.73	23.89	23.15	22.47	22.22	20.67

Source: AICPA Audit Guide *Audit Sampling*

INTERPOLATING TABLE VALUES IN DETERMINING SAMPLE SIZE

In the event that the audit team's parameters do not permit exact rows or columns to be identified in Exhibit FA.1, the audit team can either use the most conservative levels (the levels providing the higher sample sizes) or interpolate the values in Exhibit FA.1. To illustrate, assume that the audit team had established the following parameters:

- Risk of incorrect acceptance of 10 percent.
- Tolerable misstatement of 3.33 percent of the population.
- Expected misstatement of 1.32 percent of the population (which provides a ratio of 0.40 of expected misstatement to tolerable misstatement).

While a row corresponding to a ratio of 0.40 of expected misstatement to tolerable misstatement can be identified, a column for a tolerable misstatement of 3.33 percent cannot. Note from Exhibit FA.1 that the sample size for a tolerable misstatement of 3 percent is 191 items and for a tolerable misstatement of 4 percent is 143. One option would be to select the more conservative (higher) sample size of 191. Alternatively, the audit team could interpolate as follows:

1. Calculate the difference in sample size for a 3% tolerable misstatement and a 4% tolerable misstatement (191 − 143 = 48 items).
2. Because the actual tolerable misstatement (3.33 percent) is one-third of the difference between the 3% and 4% levels [(3.33% − 3.00%)/(4.00% − 3.00%)], multiply the difference in (1) by one-third (33% × 48 items = 16 items).
3. Adjust the sample size for the 3 percent tolerable misstatement by the result in step 2 to determine a sample size of 175 items (191 items − 16 items = 175 items). As a quick validation, note that because the tolerable misstatement is closer to 3 percent than 4 percent, the final sample size is closer to that shown for the 3 percent tolerable misstatement than the 4 percent tolerable misstatement.

Appendix FB

LO F-5
Understand the basic process underlying *classical variables sampling* and the use of classical variables sampling in an audit (Appendix FB).

CLASSICAL VARIABLES SAMPLING

Classical variables sampling approaches use normal distribution theory and the central limit theorem to provide an estimated range of either the *recorded balance* of the account balance or class of transactions or the *misstatement* in the account balance or class of transactions. To demonstrate the calculation of estimates under different classical variables sampling approaches, recall the sales transactions in the *Sample-Detailed Sales* database in IDEA. This database included 900 transactions with a recorded total balance of $12,563,283.[7] Also recall that the tolerable misstatement was $628,167. Assume that the audit team performed a classical variables sampling plan with the following parameters:

- Sample size of 500 transactions
- Recorded balance of transactions sampled = $6,900,000
- Audited value of transactions sampled = $6,850,500

Three common approaches to estimating the recorded account balance under classical variables sampling are discussed next.

Mean-per-Unit Estimation

Mean-per-unit estimation assumes that each item (transaction) in the population has an equal recorded balance. After performing the appropriate auditing procedures and determining the total audited value, the audit team determines a mean audited value per item and estimates the recorded balance of the population as follows:

$$\frac{\text{Audited value of sample}}{\text{Number of transactions in sample}} \times \text{Number of transactions in population}$$

$$\frac{\$6,850,500}{500\,\text{transactions}} \times 900\,\text{transactions} = \$12,330,900$$

Ratio Estimation

Ratio estimation assumes that each dollar in the population has an equal percentage of misstatement. After performing the appropriate auditing procedures and determining the total audited value, the audit team estimates the recorded balance of the population under ratio estimation as follows:

$$\frac{\text{Audited value of sample}}{\text{Recorded balance of sample}} \times \text{Recorded balance of population}$$

$$\frac{\$6,850,500}{\$6,900,000} \times \$12,563,283 = \$12,473,155$$

Difference Estimation

Both mean-per-unit estimation and ratio estimation provide estimates of the recorded balance of the accounts; in contrast, difference estimation provides an estimate of the degree of misstatement in the account balance. **Difference estimation** assumes that each transaction has an equal dollar misstatement. After performing the appropriate auditing procedures and determining the total audited value, the audit team estimates the total

---

[7]Recall that the database includes four transactions with zero balances and one with a negative balance. This explains the discrepancy between the recorded balance of $12,563,283 used in this example and the $12,563,336 used in the PPS example, as the zero and negative balances were excluded in the PPS example.

misstatement as follows:

$$\frac{\text{Misstatement in sample}}{\text{Number of transactions in sample}} \times \text{Number of transactions in population}$$

$$\frac{(\$6,900,000 - \$6,850,500)}{500 \text{ transactions}} \times 900 \text{ transactions} = \$89,100 \text{ overstatement}$$

This \$89,100 overstatement implies an audited value of \$12,474,183 (\$12,563,283 − \$89,100).

Evaluating Sample Results

Once the estimated recorded balance or the estimated overstatement are calculated, these approaches use normal distribution theory and the central limit theorem to form an estimate of the range of recorded balances or misstatements that has some specified probability (1 − *Risk of incorrect acceptance*) of including the true account balance or misstatement. Based on this range, as well as the tolerable misstatement, the audit team would draw a conclusion with respect to the fairness of the account balance.

To illustrate, assume that the range of account balances under ratio estimation was determined to be \$11,973,155 to \$12,973,155. (Recall that the estimated account balance was \$12,473,155; this range is known as the **precision interval**.) Based on this range, the maximum amount of misstatement is \$590,128 (\$12,563,283 recorded balance − \$11,973,155 farthest end of the range). If tolerable misstatement was established at \$628,167, the audit team would be willing to accept the account balance as fairly stated, as the maximum misstatement is less than the tolerable misstatement.

✓ REVIEW CHECKPOINTS

FB.1   Define *classical variables sampling*. How does classical variables sampling provide the audit team evidence as to the fairness of an account balance or class of transactions?

FB.2   Briefly describe how *mean-per-unit estimation, ratio estimation,* and *difference estimation* are used to provide an estimate of the recorded account balance or class of transactions.

FB.3   Once the audit team estimates the balance of an account balance or class of transactions using classical variables sampling, how can they evaluate the fairness of that account balance?

COMPREHENSIVE EXAMPLE: MEAN-PER-UNIT ESTIMATION

This appendix briefly illustrates one form of classical variables sampling, *mean-per-unit estimation,* which estimates the total amount of the account or class of transactions by determining an average for each item and multiplying the average by the number of items in the population. As with the PPS example in the module, we illustrate the manual calculations necessary to determine sample size and evaluate sample results.

Steps 1–3: Planning

In the planning stages of classical variables sampling, the audit team (1) determines the objective of sampling, (2) defines the characteristic of interest, and (3) defines the population as in PPS. We continue to use the basic information from the examination of accounts receivable in the *Sample-Detailed Sales* database in IDEA. Recall that this database includes 900 individual transactions totaling \$12,563,283. Also recall that the audit team is interested in evaluating the *existence* and *valuation and allocation* assertions and that the following assessments or judgments have been made prior to selecting individual sales transactions for confirmation:

- Risk of incorrect acceptance = 10%
- Expected misstatement = $188,450
- Tolerable misstatement = $628,167

One issue regarding classical variables sampling is whether certain items should be included in the population to be sampled. For example, the *Sample-Detailed Sales* database includes two transactions that totaled more than $8 million, each of which exceeded the tolerable misstatement. What should the audit team do? Obviously, they would like to examine these transactions separately because they constitute 65 percent of the population's total, and each of these items is an **individually significant item** (i.e., each item exceeds the tolerable misstatement). The audit team would then sample from among the remaining 898 transactions, none of which is individually significant.

When using classical variables sampling, the audit team can reduce the variability of the population and ensure the selection of individually significant items by subdividing the population into different (more homogenous) groups based on size. This process of subdivision known as **stratification** is useful because it permits the audit team to reduce the necessary sample size in a classical variables sampling application by reducing the variability within each stratum. Stratification also allows auditors to give more attention to high-dollar items. In the preceding scenario, the audit team could subdivide the population into two subgroups, or **strata**: the two large-dollar transactions and the remaining 898 transactions.

Step 4: Determine the Sample Size

The formula for calculating sample size using mean-per-unit estimation is

$$n = \left(\frac{N \times [\,\text{R(IR)} + \text{R(IA)}\,] \times \text{SD}}{\text{TM} - \text{EM}} \right)^2$$

where

n	=	Sample size
N	=	Population size (number of transactions)
R(IR)	=	Confidence factor for the risk of incorrect rejection
R(IA)	=	Confidence factor for the risk of incorrect acceptance
SD	=	Standard deviation
TM	=	Tolerable misstatement
EM	=	Expected misstatement

The remainder of this section focuses on the two new factors that are considered in classical variables sampling but not PPS: the risk of incorrect rejection and standard deviation. Discussion of the determination of the remaining factors and their effects on sample size can be found in the section on PPS discussed earlier in this module.

Risk of Incorrect Rejection

Unlike PPS (which considers only the risk of incorrect acceptance), classical variables sampling explicitly considers the risks of both incorrect acceptance and incorrect rejection in determining sample size. The *risk of incorrect rejection* is the probability that the audit team will conclude that the account balance is materially misstated when, in fact, it is fairly stated. As with any sampling risk, lower levels of the risk of incorrect rejection would result in an increase in the necessary sample size. That is, the risk of incorrect rejection has an *inverse relationship* with sample size.

Remember that the risk of incorrect rejection results in an efficiency loss to the audit team because prior to proposing an adjustment to the financial statements, the team ordinarily expands the sample to include additional components or transactions. The key question of interest to the audit team in assessing the level of exposure to the risk of incorrect rejection is related to the *efficiency loss* that this risk causes; that is, what is the cost to the audit team of expanding the sample? In some cases, the audit team can quickly and inexpensively select additional items; if so, it would be more cost efficient to examine a smaller initial sample and subsequently select additional items if necessary. This smaller initial sample would be achieved by assessing a higher level of the risk of incorrect rejection.

In contrast, if the cost of expanding the sample is relatively high, the audit team would be concerned about it and would ordinarily choose to assess a lower level of the risk of incorrect rejection. This lower risk would, in turn, result in an increased initial sample size.

How are sampling risks incorporated in the determination of sample size? Refer to Exhibit FB.1 for a list of confidence factors for various levels of the risk of incorrect rejection and the risk of incorrect acceptance that can be used in classical variables sampling. The determination of these factors is beyond the scope of the text, but they represent various areas of observations that fall within a certain number of standard deviations in a normally distributed population.

After considering the costs of selecting and confirming additional sales transactions, assume that the audit team sets the risk of incorrect rejection at 15 percent. (Recall that the risk of incorrect acceptance has been established at 10 percent.)

Standard Deviation

The **standard deviation** represents the variability of the population being examined; it is the average of the squared differences between each item in the population and the population mean. When the population is more variable (i.e., the items composing the population differ more widely with respect to dollar amount), the standard deviation increases. When the standard deviation of dollar amounts is higher, the audit team has more difficulty in selecting a representative sample. To do so, the team increases the necessary sample size. Thus, the standard deviation has a *direct relationship* with sample size. That is, as the standard deviation increases, the sample size increases.

How can the audit team estimate the standard deviation? In using mean-per-unit estimation, the audit team is interested in knowing the standard deviation of audited values of sales transactions. As with expected misstatement, the audit team can either rely on experience from prior audits or use a small subsample (pilot sample) in the current year. Assume that the sample standard deviation for sales transactions is $3,173. (The standard deviation is easily calculated by using programs such as Microsoft Excel; its calculation is beyond the scope of this text.)

Recall that, if the population is highly variable, the audit team can use stratification to reduce the variability of the population. By examining individually significant items and selecting a sample from a stratum of the population with lower variability, the audit team can reduce the necessary sample size.

EXHIBIT FB.1
Confidence Factors for Different Levels of Sampling Risk in Classical Variables Sampling

Level of Risk (%)	Risk of Incorrect Rejection	Risk of Incorrect Acceptance
1%	2.58	2.33
5	1.96	1.65
10	1.65	1.28
15	1.44	1.04
20	1.28	0.84

Calculating Sample Size

At this point, the sample size can be determined as follows (the sample size is rounded up to be conservative):[8]

$$n = \left(\frac{N \times [R(IR) + R(IA)] \times SD}{TM - EM} \right)^2$$

$$= \left(\frac{900 \times (1.44 + 1.28) \times \$3,173}{\$628,167 - \$188,450} \right)^2$$

$$= 312 \text{ transactions}$$

N (the number of transactions) can be readily determined from the client's records; in this case, accounts receivable include 900 transactions.[9] The factors for R(IR) and R(IA) correspond to a risk of incorrect rejection of 15 percent and risk of incorrect acceptance of 10 percent and are drawn from Exhibit FB.1. Based on previous audits, the audit team estimated that the standard deviation was \$3,173. Tolerable misstatement determined based on the total of the transactions and overall financial statement materiality was established at \$628,167. Finally, the audit team judgmentally established the expected misstatement of \$188,450 based on previous audits. We use the sample size of 312 in the remainder of this example to illustrate classical variables sampling.

Earlier, we noted that stratified sampling can be useful in reducing sample sizes if a great deal of variability exists in the population. By using the preceding formula, if the audit team decided to examine the two individually significant sales transactions and reduce the variability of the remainder of the population from \$3,173 to \$2,202, the sample size for the nonsignificant items would be 150 transactions.[10] Including the two individually significant items, the total sample would be 152. This provides an example of how using stratification can result in a more efficient sample for the auditor.

 REVIEW CHECKPOINTS

FB.4 What is *stratification*? What are the benefits to the audit team of stratifying the sample?

FB.5 What is the *standard deviation*? How does it affect the necessary sample size?

FB.6 Identify differences between the determination of sample size under classical variables sampling and PPS.

Step 5: Select the Sample Items

One of the basic tenets of statistical sampling methods is that each sampling unit has an equal probability of selection. The sample of sales transactions could be selected in either of the following ways:

1. Identify 312 random numbers and select the corresponding transactions for confirmation (unrestricted random selection).

2. Randomly select a starting point (or a number of starting points) in the population and select every *n*th transaction thereafter for confirmation (systematic random selection).

One very important difference between sample selection under classical variables sampling and PPS is the definition of the sampling unit. Classical variables sampling

---

[8]Because the audit team's primary concern is incorrectly accepting a misstated account balance, a variation of this formula can be used that only considers the risk of incorrect acceptance and does not consider the risk of incorrect rejection. Excluding the risk of incorrect rejection from the determination of sample size is justifiable, as the audit team will normally expand the sample when the results indicate that the account balance or class of transactions is materially misstated. In this example, the sample size used by the audit team if the risk of incorrect rejection is not considered would be 69.

[9]In this example, we did not stratify the sample by excluding the two large transactions to focus on the methodology and calculations associated with mean-per-unit estimation. In an actual audit context, these two transactions would undoubtedly be examined and not subject to selection.

[10]The sample size formula would be modified by replacing the 900 sales transactions with 898 and the \$3,173 sample standard deviation with \$2,202.

defines the sampling unit as a logical unit (in this case, a sales transaction). As a result, the audit team will select 312 of the 900 sales transactions for examination. In contrast, PPS defines the sampling unit as an individual dollar of a sales transaction and selects individual dollars for examination. Unlike PPS, classical variables sampling does not ensure that the highest dollar transactions are selected for examination. Under classical variables sampling, a $1 transaction has the same probability of being selected as a $1 million transaction! This characteristic is why the use of stratification to automatically select high dollar items is so important under classical variables sampling, as *individually significant items* can be identified and selected.

Step 6: Measure the Sample Items

Once the sample size has been determined and the sample has been selected, the audit team measures the sample items. In the audit of sales transactions, measuring sample items requires the audit team to determine the audited value of the transaction. This will be done using standard accounts receivable confirmation procedures as well as additional procedures necessary to follow up on any discrepancies revealed by the confirmation procedures.

Assume that the audit team's examination of the 312 customer sales transactions revealed a total audited value of $4,259,736. Therefore, the mean audited value per unit is $13,653 ($4,259,736 ÷ 312). Also assume that the audit team calculated a $2,425 standard deviation of audited values.

Step 7: Evaluate the Sample Results

Evaluating the sample results requires the audit team to determine an overall estimate of the audited value (based on the mean audited value per unit) and construct an interval of sample estimates that controls the exposure to the risk of incorrect acceptance (10 percent) and risk of incorrect rejection (15 percent) to desired levels. This interval is referred to as the *precision interval,* and once it has been constructed, the audit team's decision rule is as follows:

- Accept the account balance as being fairly stated if the difference between the recorded balance and the farthest precision estimate is smaller than or equal to the tolerable misstatement.
- Reject the account balance as being fairly stated if the difference between the recorded balance and the farthest precision estimate is larger than the tolerable misstatement.

The first step in the construction of the precision interval is to determine the overall estimate of the audited value. If the mean audited value of the sample of sales transactions is $13,653, the audit team's best estimate of the audited value of the entire account is determined by multiplying $13,653 by the number of transactions in the population (900), or $12,287,700 ($13,653 × 900 = $12,287,700).

Next, the audit team determines the appropriate level of precision. *Precision* is the numeric distance from the estimated population value in which the true (but unknown) population value may lie with a given probability. The determination of precision allows the audit team to construct a precision interval that controls exposure to sampling risk to acceptable levels.

Recall from the calculation of sample size that the population size is 900 transactions, the confidence factor for the risk of incorrect acceptance is 1.28, and the sample size is 312. Also, after measuring the sample items, recall that the standard deviation of audited values is $2,425. The precision is calculated as $158,156:

$$\text{Precision} = \text{N} \times \text{R(IA)} \times (\text{SD} \div \sqrt{n})$$
$$= 900 \times 1.28 \times (\$2,425 \div \sqrt{312})$$
$$= \$158,156$$

n	=	Sample size
N	=	Population size (number of sales transactions)
R(IA)	=	Confidence factor for the risk of incorrect acceptance
SD	=	Standard deviation (for items selected for examination)

Once the precision has been calculated, the precision interval can be determined by adding and subtracting it from the sample estimate. The relationship between the sample estimate, precision, and the recorded balance is shown as

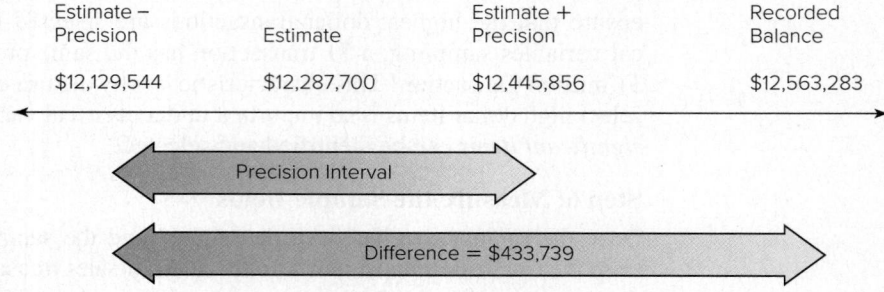

Estimate − Precision	Estimate	Estimate + Precision	Recorded Balance
$12,129,544	$12,287,700	$12,445,856	$12,563,283

Precision Interval

Difference = $433,739

The significance of the precision interval is that it has a (1 − *Risk of incorrect acceptance*) probability of including the true balance; conversely, the true balance has a (*risk of incorrect acceptance*) probability of falling outside the precision interval. The difference between the recorded balance and the farthest end of the precision interval ($12,563,283 − $12,129,544 = $433,739) is compared to the tolerable misstatement ($628,167). In this case, the population can be accepted as being fairly stated and the audit team has limited its exposure to the risk of incorrect acceptance to 10 percent.

PPS VERSUS CLASSICAL VARIABLES SAMPLING

When considering the use of PPS and classical variables sampling, recall that PPS defines the sampling unit as an individual dollar within an account balance or class of transactions. As a result, this method tends to identify large-dollar items for examination, which is the primary benefit associated with the use of PPS. Compared to classical variables sampling, PPS is most appropriate when

1. Overstatements are of greater concern to the audit team (such as the audit of assets and revenues) because PPS automatically selects items with larger recorded balances for examination.
2. It is difficult or impractical to estimate the standard deviation. (While not illustrated in the text, classical variables sampling methods require an estimate of the standard deviation in determining sample size and evaluating sample results.)
3. Zero or few misstatements are anticipated.
4. The population is relatively heterogeneous with respect to the dollar amount of components and a number of relatively large-dollar items exist (i.e., a high level of variability exists).

With respect to this final matter, when using classical variables sampling, the audit team may choose to subdivide the population into more homogenous groups based on size. (This process is known as *stratification* and has been discussed previously.) In particular, any large items (including individually significant items) may be selected for examination, and the audit team would then sample from the remainder of the population. In addition to ensuring that large items are examined, stratification reduces the variability of the remaining population and reduces the necessary sample size.

✓ REVIEW CHECKPOINT

FB.7   How does sample selection under classical variables sampling differ from sample selection under PPS?

FB.8   Define *precision* and the *precision interval.* What factors are used to determine the level of precision?

FB.9   What is the audit team's decision rule when comparing the recorded balance to the precision interval?

FB.10   When selecting a variables sampling approach, when should the audit team use PPS and when should it use classical variables sampling?

**Multiple-Choice
Questions for
Practice and
Review**

   All applicable questions are available with
McGraw-Hill's *Connect® Accounting.*

LO F-5

FB.11 Alice Rathermel audited LoHo Company's inventory using sampling. She examined 120 items from an inventory compilation list and discovered net overstatement of $480. The audited items had a book (recorded) value of $48,000. There were 1,200 inventory items listed, and the total recorded inventory amount was $490,000. What is the projected misstatement using mean-per-unit estimation?

    a. $480.

    b. $14,800.

    c. $10,000.

    d. $480,000.

LO F-5

FB.12 To determine the sample size for a classical variables sampling application, an audit team should consider the tolerable misstatement, risk of incorrect acceptance, risk of incorrect rejection, population size, population variability, and

    a. Expected misstatement in the account.

    b. Overall materiality for the financial statements taken as a whole.

    c. Risk of assessing control risk too low.

    d. Risk of assessing control risk too high.

LO F-5

FB.13 Which of the following courses of action would an audit team most likely follow in planning a sample of cash disbursements if the audit team is aware of several unusually large cash disbursements?

    a. Increase the sample size to reduce the effect of the unusually large disbursements.

    b. Continue to draw new samples until all unusually large disbursements appear in the sample.

    c. Set the tolerable misstatement at a lower level than originally planned.

    d. Stratify the cash disbursements population so that the unusually large disbursements are selected.

                                                        (AICPA adapted)

**Exercises and
Problems**

   All applicable questions are available with
McGraw-Hill's *Connect® Accounting.*

LO F-1, F-5

FB.14 **PPS and Classical Variables Sampling.**

Required:

For each of the following independent situations, indicate the advantages and disadvantages of PPS and classical variables sampling.

    a. You are selecting a sample of customer accounts receivable balances for confirmation. The sample is to be selected from a population of customer accounts receivable, the total of which exceeds $4,000,000. This list comprises 4,000 individual customer accounts that are relatively similar in dollar amount with balances ranging from $800 to $8,000. In past years, you have identified a moderate level of misstatement in the client's accounts receivable, although the level of misstatement was always less than the tolerable misstatement.

    b. You are selecting a sample of accounts payable balances for confirmation with vendors. The population is a list of accounts payable to vendors; at year-end, the total (unaudited) accounts payable balance is $800,000. Amounts owed by the client to 200 separate vendors are included in this balance. Because the client has two major suppliers, a disproportionate amount of this balance ($500,000) is concentrated in these two accounts.

c. You are selecting a sample of customer accounts receivable balances for confirmation. The population is a list of customer accounts receivable; at year-end, the accounts receivable total is $2,500,000. Compared to most of your clients, the number of customer accounts included in this balance is relatively small, and the balances range from $1,000 to $525,000.

LO F-5

FB.15 Sample Size Determination: Classical Variables Sampling. The recorded inventory balance for Faulk Company was $1,000,000 and comprised 2,500 customer accounts.

Required:

For each of the following independent sets of conditions, determine the appropriate sample size for the audit of Faulk's inventory using classical variables sampling (mean-per-unit estimation). Based on the differences in your calculations, identify the general relationship between different factors and sample size. (RIA = risk of incorrect acceptance, RIR = risk of incorrect rejection, TM = tolerable misstatement, EM = expected misstatement, SD = standard deviation.)

a. RIA = 5%, RIR = 5%, TM = $50,000, EM = $20,000, SD = $40
b. RIA = 10%, RIR = 5%, TM = $50,000, EM = $20,000, SD = $40
c. RIA = 10%, RIR = 10%, TM = $50,000, EM = $20,000, SD = $40
d. RIA = 5%, RIR = 5%, TM = $30,000, EM = $20,000, SD = $40
e. RIA = 5%, RIR = 5%, TM = $50,000, EM = $10,000, SD = $40
f. RIA = 5%, RIR = 5%, TM = $50,000, EM = $10,000, SD = $30

LO F-5

FB.16 Sample Size Determination: Classical Variables Sampling. Shannon Solomon, CPA, is auditing the accounts receivable of Warner Company and is using mean-per-unit estimation. Accounts receivable were recorded at $2,000,000 and comprised 1,250 individual customer accounts. Solomon established the following parameters for the audit of accounts receivable:

- Using firm policy, tolerable misstatement for accounts receivable is established at 6 percent of the recorded account balance.
- Based on prior audits of Warner's accounts receivable, the standard deviation of audited values is estimated to be $100.
- Based on prior audits of Warner's accounts receivable, Solomon estimates that accounts receivable will be misstated by 4 percent of the recorded account balance.

Solomon is now establishing the acceptable levels of the risk of incorrect acceptance and the risk of incorrect rejection for the audit of Warner Company's accounts receivable.

Required:

a. What factors should Solomon consider in establishing acceptable levels of the risk of incorrect acceptance and the risk of incorrect rejection?
b. What are the advantages and disadvantages of Solomon's establishing lower levels of the risk of incorrect acceptance and the risk of incorrect rejection?
c. If Solomon establishes levels of the risk of incorrect acceptance and the risk of incorrect rejection of 5 percent, what is the resultant sample size?
d. Determine the sample size for each of the following combinations of risk of incorrect acceptance and risk of incorrect rejection:
   1. Risk of incorrect acceptance of 5 percent, risk of incorrect rejection of 10 percent.
   2. Risk of incorrect acceptance of 10 percent, risk of incorrect rejection of 5 percent.
   3. Risk of incorrect acceptance of 10 percent, risk of incorrect rejection of 10 percent.
e. Based on the sample sizes you calculated in parts (c) and (d), determine how the levels of sampling risks affect sample size.

LO F-5

FB.17 Evaluating Results: Classical Variables Sampling. Kyle Berry is using mean-per-unit estimation in the audit of Leonard's inventory balances. Leonard's inventory is recorded at $240,000 and comprises 1,200 different items. Berry determined a sample size of

120 items and performed the appropriate substantive procedures. Based on this sample, he determined the following:

Average audited value (per item)	$204
Standard deviation of audited values	$ 22

A summary of some additional parameters estimated by Berry follow:

Tolerable misstatement	$17,500
Expected misstatement	$7,500
Risk of incorrect acceptance	5%
Risk of incorrect rejection	10%

Required:

a. What is Berry's estimate of the audited value of Leonard's inventory?

b. Calculate the precision and precision interval for Leonard's inventory. Provide a brief description of the meaning of the precision interval.

c. What is Berry's conclusion with respect to Leonard's inventory balance?

d. Using a risk of incorrect acceptance of (1) 1 percent and (2) 10 percent, calculate the precision and the precision interval for Leonard's inventory.

LO F-5

FB.18 **Evaluating Sample Results: Classical Variables Sampling.** You are auditing Hernandez Inc.'s accounts receivable balance using classical variables sampling. Hernandez's accounts receivable comprised 2,500 customer accounts and were recorded at $3,500,000.

Using a risk of incorrect acceptance and a risk of incorrect rejection of 5 percent, you selected a sample of 200 accounts for examination and confirmed the accounts with the customers. The total recorded balance of these 200 accounts was $1,000,000; based on your confirmations as well as an investigation of differences reported by customers, you determined an audited value of $900,000. Tolerable misstatement was established at $175,000.

Required:

a. What is the sample estimate of Hernandez's accounts receivable balance using mean-per-unit estimation?

b. If you used difference estimation or ratio estimation, how would you expect the sample estimate to be different?

c. In what circumstances should each of the different methods of classical variables estimation be used?

d. If you calculate a sample estimate of $3,000,000 and precision of $750,000, form a precision interval for Hernandez's accounts receivable using mean-per-unit estimation. Briefly describe the meaning of the precision interval as well as your conclusion with respect to Hernandez's accounts receivable balance.

LO F-5

FB.19 **Comprehensive Problem: Classical Variables Sampling.** Jessie Howe is examining Met Company's accounts receivable balance and has decided to use mean-per-unit estimation. Met's accounts receivable were recorded at $650,000 and comprised 2,000 individual customer accounts. Howe established tolerable misstatement at 5 percent of the recorded balance. Based on prior experience with Met, Howe assessed expected misstatement at $22,500 and estimated a standard deviation of the mean audited value of $30.

Required:

a. Using the preceding parameters, identify the appropriate sample size for the following combinations of risk of incorrect acceptance (RIA) and risk of incorrect rejection (RIR):

1. RIA = 1%, RIR = 5%

2. RIA = 1%, RIR = 10%

3. RIA = 5%, RIR = 10%

b. What factors would Howe consider in establishing the risk of incorrect acceptance and the risk of incorrect rejection?

   c. Based on the results in part (a), explain how the risk of incorrect acceptance and the risk of incorrect rejection influence the determination of sample size.

   d. If Howe had determined an audited value of $330 per account and a standard deviation of audited values of $30, determine the precision interval for each of the following combinations of the risk of incorrect acceptance (RIA) and risk of incorrect rejection (RIR). In each of these cases, what is Howe's conclusion with respect to Met's accounts receivable?

     1. RIA = 1%, RIR = 5%.

     2. RIA = 1%, RIR = 10%.

     3. RIA = 5%, RIR = 10%.

LO F-5

FB.20 **Comprehensive Problem: Classical Variables Sampling.** Wade Wallace designed a classical variables sampling application to examine the accounts receivable for Rasheed Inc. After considering several possibilities, Wallace decided to use mean-per-unit estimation. The following parameters are noted through a review of Wallace's audit documentation:

Recorded balance of accounts receivable	$800,000
Number of customer accounts included in accounts receivable balance	2,000
Risk of incorrect acceptance	5%
Risk of incorrect rejection	20%
Tolerable misstatement	$50,000
Expected misstatement	$10,000
Standard deviation of audited value	$52

Required:

   a. Describe how Wallace would establish each of these parameters.

   b. What is the appropriate sample size for this application?

   c. Assume that Wallace is considering an increase in the necessary level of the risk of incorrect acceptance to 10 percent. How would this increase affect the sample size?

   d. Using a 5 percent risk of incorrect acceptance, assume that Wallace determined a $380 average audited value per item and a $50 standard deviation of audited values. Construct the precision interval for Rasheed's accounts receivable.

   e. Based on the precision interval in part (d), provide Wallace's conclusion with respect to Rasheed's accounts receivable.

   f. Repeat parts (d) and (e) assuming that the average audited value per item is $405. Why does Wallace's conclusion differ from that reached in part (e)?

LO F-2, F-5

FB.21 **PPS and Classical Variables Sampling.** Indicate whether each of the following characteristics applies to PPS sampling (PPS), classical variables sampling (CVS), both PPS and CVS (both), or neither PPS nor CVS (neither).

   a. May be used in conjunction with substantive procedures.

   b. Tends to select higher dollar items for examination.

   c. Is more effective in identifying overstatements.

   d. Incorporates assessments of tolerable misstatement in determining sample size.

   e. Incorporates assessments of the population variability in determining sample size.

   f. Controls the audit team's exposure to the risk of incorrect rejection and the risk of incorrect acceptance.

   g. Requires the audit team to project discovered misstatements to the population.

   h. Can expose the audit team to nonsampling risk.

   i. May be used in conjunction with the study and evaluation of internal control.

   j. Is more appropriate for use when a higher number of misstatements is anticipated.

Appendix FC

LO F-6

Understand the use of nonstatistical approaches to variables sampling (Appendix FC).

NONSTATISTICAL SAMPLING

The primary advantage of statistical sampling methods is that they explicitly measure and control the audit team's exposure to sampling risk in determining the sample size and evaluating sample results. However, it is important to note that generally accepted auditing standards do not require the use of statistical sampling methods; in many cases, it is easier and more efficient to use nonstatistical sampling methods.

The primary differences in statistical and nonstatistical sampling methods are as follows:

1. *Determining sample size.* While the AICPA Audit Guide *Audit Sampling* suggests using the PPS table to determine sample size, the audit team members can use their professional judgment in determining the appropriate sample size.

2. *Selecting sample items.* Nonstatistical sampling permits the audit team to use non-probabilistic selection techniques, such as **haphazard selection** (e.g., picking vouchers from a drawer) and **block selection** (e.g., selecting all cash disbursements for a particular month). These methods allow the audit team to use their professional judgment when selecting the sample.

3. *Evaluating sample results.* After estimating the account balance or amount of misstatement and considering the tolerable misstatement, the audit team can judgmentally draw a conclusion about the fairness of the account balance or class of transactions without controlling for exposure to sampling risk. For example, if the recorded balance is $12,563,283, the audit team's estimated account balance is $12,200,000, and tolerable misstatement is $628,167, the team may conclude that the account is fairly stated without further analyses or formal calculation of a range of account balances.

Comprehensive Example: Nonstatistical Sampling

To illustrate the use of nonstatistical sampling, consider the IDEA example introduced in the module. Recall that the population consisted of 900 sales transactions totaling $12,563,283. (This included the five transactions with zero or negative amounts.) Also recall the following parameters that were established by the audit team:

- Risk of incorrect acceptance = 10%
- Expected misstatement = $188,450
- Tolerable misstatement = $628,167

In determining sample size under nonstatistical sampling, *Audit Sampling* notes that the audit team may use tables similar to those for PPS (see Exhibit FA.1). Alternatively, a nonstatistical sample size can be calculated through the use of the following formula:

$$\text{Sample size} = \frac{\text{Recorded balance of population}}{\text{Tolerable misstatement}} \times \text{Confidence factor}$$

The confidence factor incorporates the level of confidence desired through the substantive tests, as expressed in the risk of incorrect acceptance. For a 10 percent risk of incorrect acceptance, the appropriate confidence factor would be 2.3, as shown below (drawn from Table C.2 in *Audit Sampling*):

| | **Risk of Incorrect Acceptance** | | | | | |
	5%	10%	15%	20%	25%	30%
Factor	3.0	2.3	1.9	1.6	1.4	1.2

The appropriate sample size would be 46 transactions, as shown here:

$$\frac{\$12,563,283}{\$628,167} \times 2.3 = 46\,\text{transactions}$$

Assume that this population includes two transactions that exceed the tolerable misstatement and total $8,179,960 (65 percent of the recorded balance of the population). Because nonstatistical sampling does not require the audit team members to use random selection techniques, they would undoubtedly select these two transactions for examination and select 44 transactions from the remainder of the population. Unlike statistical sampling, the audit team can use either *block selection* (select transactions occurring on specific dates) or *haphazard selection* (select items without any conscious bias from the listing of transactions).

While the selection process is not illustrated, assume that the 46 transactions had a total recorded balance of $8,455,139, as follows:

Large items	2	$8,179,960
Other items	44	275,179
Total	46	$8,455,139

After selecting the sample items, the audit team performs the appropriate substantive procedures to determine the audited value of the transaction. In this case, assume that the audited value for these transactions was $8,252,216. Using ratio estimation, the audit team would estimate the account balance as follows:

$$\frac{\text{Audited value of sample}}{\text{Recorded balance of sample}} \times \text{Recorded balance of population}$$

$$\frac{\$8,252,216}{\$8,455,139} \times \$12,563,283 = \$12,261,765$$

Comparing the audited value of the population to the recorded balance of the population reveals an estimated misstatement of $301,518 ($12,563,283 − $12,261,765). Because this is significantly lower than the tolerable misstatement ($628,167), the audit team would likely conclude that the account balance is fairly stated.

✓ REVIEW CHECKPOINTS

FC.1 How does nonstatistical sampling differ from statistical sampling?

FC.2 What factors are considered in determining the sample size in a nonstatistical sampling application?

Exercises and Problems

LO F-6

FC.3   **Evaluating Sample Results: Nonstatistical Sampling.** Finley Gunny is using nonstatistical sampling in the examination of Highway Company's accounts receivable, which were recorded at $350,000. Gunny determined a tolerable misstatement of $15,000 and a sample size of 49 items.

Required:

a. How does Gunny determine sample size using nonstatistical sampling?

b. If the items selected by Gunny had an aggregate recorded balance of $50,000 and an aggregate audited value of $45,000, calculate the estimated audited value.

c. What would Gunny conclude with respect to the fairness of Highway's accounts receivable?

LO F-6

FC.4   **Nonstatistical Sampling.** Marley Brown is planning the substantive procedures for the audit of Longhorn Company's inventory, which had a recorded (unaudited) balance of $6,500,000. In prior audits, Brown used PPS sampling but is now considering the use of nonstatistical sampling. Brown has established a tolerable misstatement of $250,000 and a sample size of 71 items.

Required:

a. Compared to PPS sampling, what are the advantages and disadvantages to Brown's using nonstatistical sampling in this year's audit of Longhorn's inventory?

b. Compare the factors used by Brown in determining sample size under PPS sampling to those that would be used in nonstatistical sampling.

c. Brown is considering increasing the use of analytical procedures in order to reduce the tests of details of the inventory. What factors would she consider in deciding whether to perform more extensive analytical procedures?

d. If the items selected by Brown had an aggregate audited value of $970,000 and an aggregate recorded balance of $1,000,000, what would be the conclusion with respect to the fairness of Longhorn's inventory?

Data and Analytics in Auditing

"Big data is NOT about the data."

> Gary King, Harvard University

"If you torture the data long enough, it will confess."

> Ronald Coase, economist

"Information is the oil of the 21st century, and analytics is the combustion engine."

> Peter Sondergaard, then Head of Research, Gartner Research

Professional Standards References

Topic	AU-C/ISA Section	AS Section
Audit Documentation	230	1215
Consideration of Fraud in a Financial Statement Audit	240	2401
Evaluating Audit Results	240	2810
Audit Planning	300	2101
The Auditor's Responses to the Risks of Material Misstatement	330	2301
Audit Evidence	500	1105
Substantive Analytical Procedures	520	2305
Audit Sampling	530	2315
Auditing Accounting Estimates	540	2501
Auditing Fair Value Measurements and Disclosures	540	2502

LEARNING OBJECTIVES

Today's external financial statement audit environment is rapidly becoming characterized by the availability of significant amounts of data and advanced analytical tools, the increased use of which is being fueled by "smart" information technology applications. As a direct result, audit firms want to hire entry-level professionals who have completed coursework that has exposed them to the use of these data and analytical tools to achieve audit objectives. This module is designed to provide you with such an overview.

As you read and study the content in this module, please realize that you are about to embark on an exciting journey toward understanding how audit teams are increasingly using available data and advanced analytical tools to their full extent to improve the quality and efficiency of the financial statement audit process. Auditing students today have a unique chance to take advantage of significant opportunities that have emerged as a result of the trends that have impacted the current public accounting environment. What an opportunity! As a new auditor, you really can be a change agent on the audit team, right away.

An important example of the use of additional data involves the use by audit teams of more predictive analytical tools that utilize third-party data to supplement their "traditional" analytical procedures. The additional data can help the audit team to refine their expectations and improve the results of preliminary analytical procedures that form initial beliefs about the nature, timing, and extent of audit evidence to be gathered at an audit client. While this type of access to increased volumes of data on the client has the potential to improve audit effectiveness, it also can have an initial negative impact on audit efficiency if audit professionals are unable to efficiently execute such additional procedures. Consider the audit team that is completing an audit of a water theme park with access to weather data. The audit team would rightfully expect that ticket revenues will be inversely correlated with rainfall and would develop a predictable relationship using daily revenue data from the two prior audited years. The audit team would then use this relationship to identify specific days in the current year that do not follow the predicted pattern. For example, what if the audit team identified high revenue recorded by the client on a very rainy day? This type of testing would enable the audit team to focus testing on abnormal and higher risk revenue patterns.

When completing preliminary analytical procedures, the availability of largely all of the client's internal data can allow for more robust trend analysis (i.e., year over year) on a multitude of financial and nonfinancial data. For example, an audit team could conduct a trend analysis of inventory costs over time. Similarly, an audit team could assess the accounts receivable collection periods by region for the audit client. Or, another example would be for an audit team to assess the inventory aging and/or the number of days inventory is in stock on an item-by-item basis. Another common analytical procedure in the revenue cycle is Days Sales Outstanding. We discuss this procedure in the following Data and Analytics in Practice example.

DATA AND ANALYTICS IN PRACTICE   Risk Assessment

ELM MANUFACTURING COMPANY, RISK ASSESSMENT
During the audit of ELM's revenue cycle, the auditors identified the existence and valuation of accounts receivable as an area of risk. The auditors identified Days Sales Outstanding (DSO) as an analytical procedure that would help identify specific risks within the audit. Please read, "ELM Risk Assessment" in *Connect* for more about the process used by the auditors to identify the risks.

Tests of Controls

An audit team now has far more data available to be used for testing the operating effectiveness of internal controls. Recall that after gaining an understanding of internal controls, if the audit team intends to assess control risk as low and rely on a control activity, the team needs to gather evidence to verify that the control activity has been designed and has operated effectively during the entire period of control reliance. In today's auditing environment, it is critical that audit professionals learn how to make the best use of internal client data when designing and completing the tests of controls needed to support the conclusion that a control activity has been designed and has operated effectively during the period of reliance.

Recall from Chapter 5, when auditing an issuer, audit teams are required to test both entity-level controls and transaction-level controls in order to express an opinion on the effectiveness of internal controls over financial reporting. For certain entity-level controls, such as those related to the control environment, it can be difficult for audit teams to identify persuasive evidence that the controls are operating effectively. Nevertheless, teams are still required to test the control environment on each audit of an issuer. And, there are a number of innovative ways to gather evidence to test the control environment. Consider for example, Exhibit G.5 and Exhibit G.6, which are two visualizations that

EXHIBIT G.5
**Visualization to Assess
Control Environment**

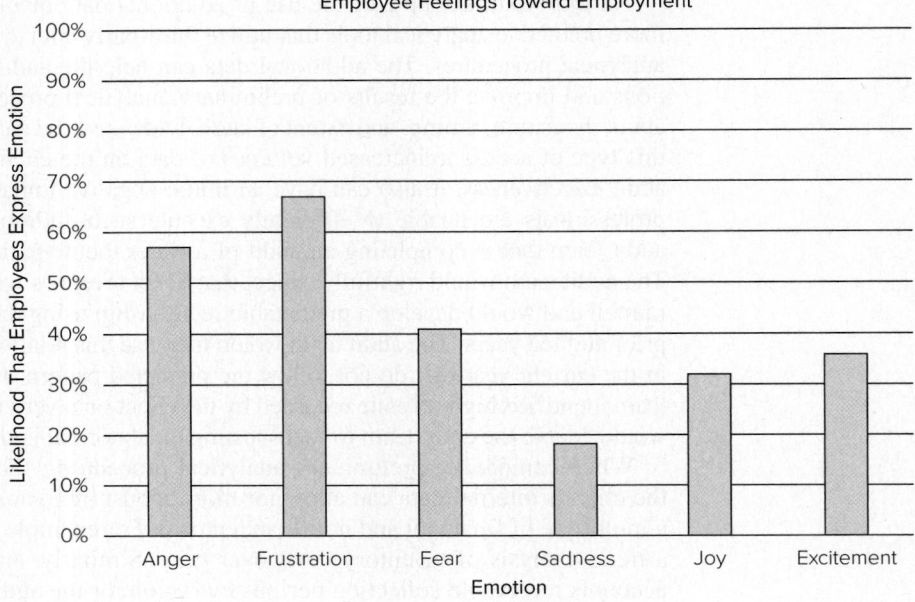

EXHIBIT G.6
**Visualization of
Word Cloud—Employee
Morale**

might be used by audit teams to measure employee morale at the audit client. Measurement of employee morale may help the audit team to reach a final conclusion about the client's control environment.

Of course, the audit team also has to test transaction level controls. Data and analytics (DA) has had a major impact on this type of control testing as well. The professional standards make clear that when designing tests of controls, the auditor needs to consider the means of selecting items for testing. For tests of internal controls, there are two approaches that are commonly used: (1) testing all items in a population; and (2) testing a sample from a population. The decision of which approach to use depends on the nature of the control that is being tested, along with the availability of data. Using audit data analytics (ADA), a control activity that is entirely automated might best be tested by an automated audit procedure that can be efficiently and effectively applied to the entire population of occurrences of that control activity. With ADA, there has been a dramatic increase in the number of tests of controls that are able to be effectively applied to the *entire* population of control occurrences in an efficient manner.

One way to test all items in a population of occurrences for a particular control activity is to use exception testing. Exception testing is designed to identify a violation of a particular control activity through the use of an automated test procedure designed to test all items in a population. Consider an entirely automated control activity that is designed to compare an individual customer's credit limit to the sum of (1) a potential sales transaction; and (2) that customer's outstanding credit balance before approval of that sales transaction. If the control activity operated effectively throughout the year, that customer's outstanding credit balance would not exceed its credit limit. Using data analytics, an auditor can analyze all transaction data from the year to identify instances in which an individual customer's balance exceeded its credit limit (i.e. an exception). Such a testing strategy would not have been possible (at least economically) in previous years. However, due to the emergence of ADA, such testing is now possible.

There are a number of other examples of tests of controls that can be conducted using ADA. For example, audit teams might seek to investigate whether proper approval of purchase transactions over a predetermined threshold was obtained. Or, audit teams could see if any employees at the client had the same address as an approved vendor. Each of these could be tested using the entire population of data with exception testing.

Substantive Analytical Procedures

One of the most exciting opportunities for improved audit testing using ADA relates to substantive analytical procedures. Recall that when conducting substantive testing procedures, audit teams may choose between tests of detail and analytical procedures. Of course, the professional standards point out that an audit team can rely on substantive evidence from either tests of details, analytical procedures, or a combination of both types of tests. The final decision made by the audit team in regards to the types of tests to be used is a matter of professional judgment.

There are a number of examples where ADA can facilitate the performance of substantive analytical procedures. For example, an audit team could use a predictive model of interest expense to gain assurance over the interest expense balance. In addition, an audit team could review the aging of accounts receivable to evaluate the adequacy of the allowance for doubtful accounts. When an audit team chooses among different ways to use ADA to conduct substantive analytical procedures, the professional standards state that more predictable relationships among the data allows the audit team to take much more substantive comfort from the test. Thus, when designing a test, audit teams need to think carefully about predictability when finalizing the audit plan.

One of the most important ways that ADA can be used to improve substantive analytical procedures is when testing the revenue account at an audit client. Let's consider an example of an audit client AbsoluteTech, which has just launched a new product. In such a situation, it can be quite difficult for an audit team to predict revenue from a new product because there is no historical track record. Let's continue with an example of how the audit team might use ADA in an attempt to develop an expectation of recorded revenue. Due to the lack of sales history for a new product, this can be difficult. However, the audit team might consider an analysis of social media posts about the client's new product as compared to its competitors. Consider Exhibit G.7 (found on the next two pages), which illustrates several different visualizations that could be used to help understand customer feelings about the new product.

What could the auditor take away from these visualizations? And, most importantly, how would these observations potentially help in developing an expectation for recorded revenue? Well, based on the first two visualizations, we see that the number of hashtag mentions and daily count of tweets is generally larger than two competitors and generally less than the other two competitors. These visualizations appear to be consistent with the reported weekly sales volume of its new product where weekly sales volume is higher than two competitors and less than the other two competitors.

Based on the next two visualizations, we see that there is a lot of positive sentiment about AbsoluteTech but there is also a fair amount of negative sentiment about AbsoluteTech.

EXHIBIT G.7
Visualizations to Assess the Market's Perception of New Product

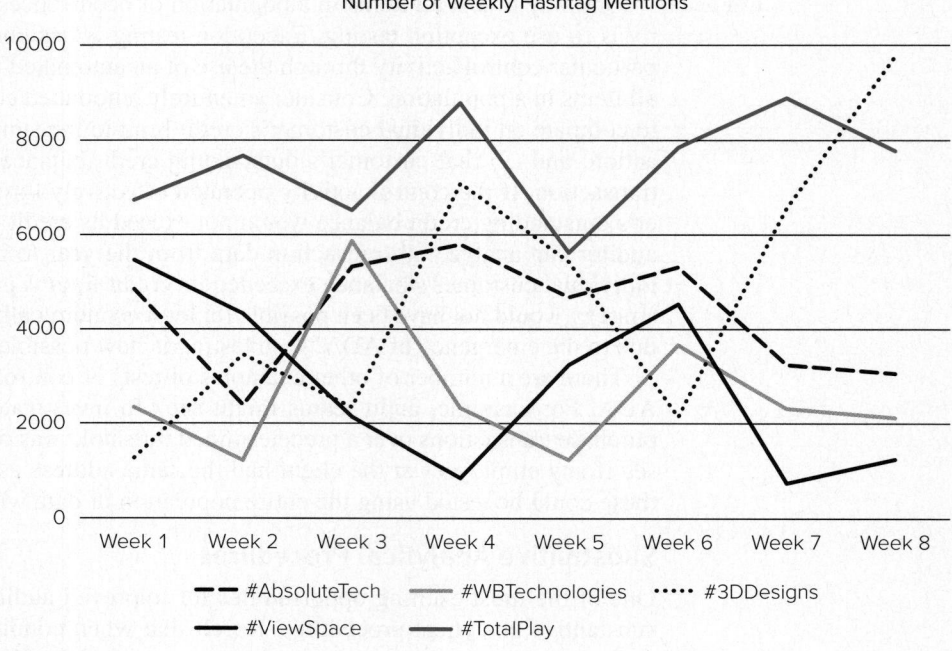

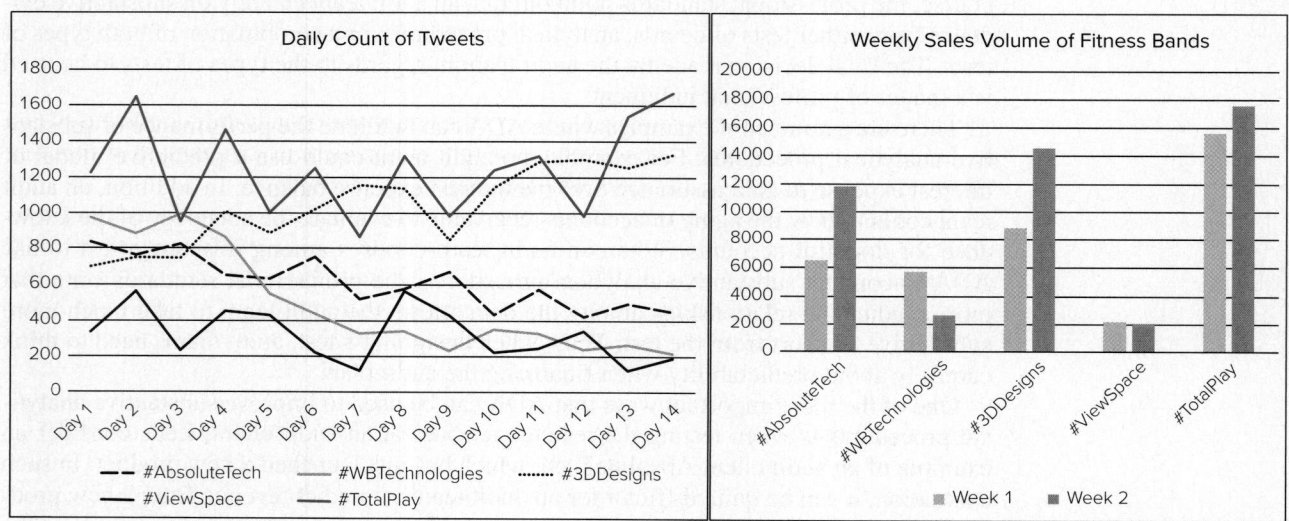

Overall, the visualizations, taken together, reveal a positive impression of the new product which may be helpful when the audit team develops expectations about recorded revenue. Of course, the analyses would likely not be enough to develop a complete expectation of recorded revenue and the audit team would also have to conduct tests of details on recorded revenue.

Tests of Details

ADA also has the potential to assist auditors when completing substantive tests of details. Let's consider a test of details for the revenue account. Assume that the audit team wanted to test the revenue account for understatement (to make sure that the company was not underreporting their taxable income and underpaying their taxes), one way to gather evidence might be to determine the number of new customers secured by the client in the year under audit. If this information was obtained from the sales and marketing

EXHIBIT G.7   Continued

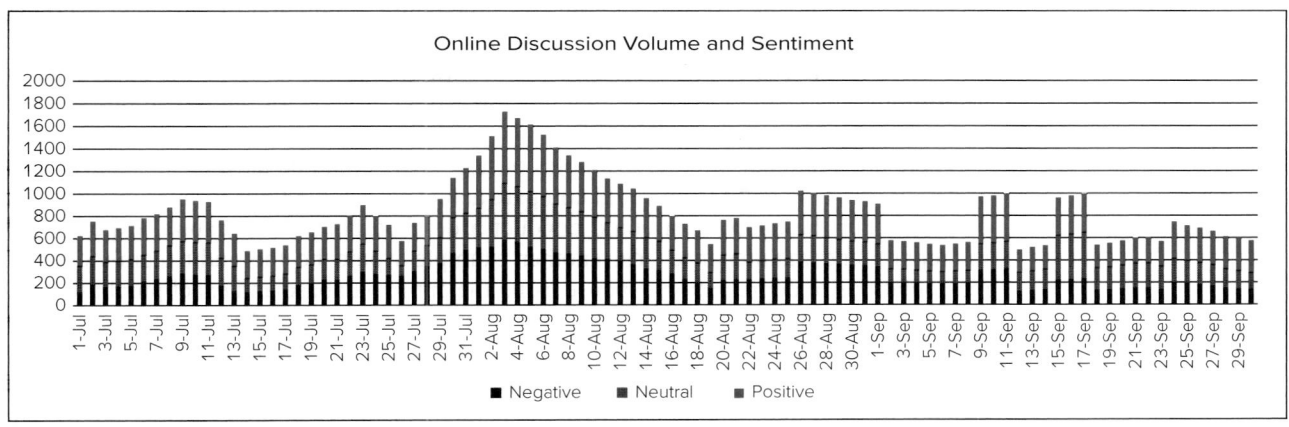

Source	Mentions	Positive	Positive%	Neutral	Neutral%	Negative	Negative%	Net Sentiment
Total	77405	31175	40%	21662	28%	24568	32%	8%
Twitter	59602	23244.72	39%	17284.54	29%	19073	32%	7%
Instagram	9289	4272.756	46%	2229.264	24%	2787	30%	16%
Facebook	5418	2654.992	49%	1517.138	28%	1246	23%	26%
Google+	3096	1083.67	35%	619.24	20%	1393	45%	−10%

department, and the information produced by the entity was tested for completeness and accuracy, it could be traced to the revenue account on the income statement to ensure that all revenue from the new customers was being properly recorded.

There are other issues associated with the application of ADA when completing tests of detail. Consider a situation where a client's accounts receivable comprises 300,000 customer accounts. Additionally, the audit team has identified a number of unique factors that can be used to identify accounts that carry an extremely low likelihood of being materially misstated. For example, some customers had really low account balances and other customers have never been late on a payment due. Based on an initial screening process of all 300,000 accounts, the audit team concludes that all but 50 of these accounts have an extremely low likelihood of being materially misstated, and as a result, the audit team decides to perform substantive tests of details (e.g., positive confirmation procedures with customers) on each of these 50 accounts.

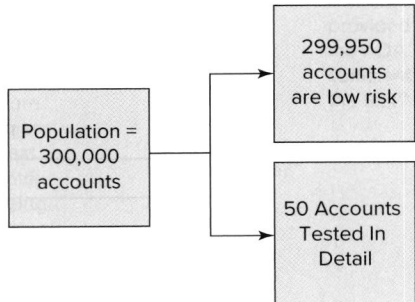

The question becomes whether the audit team still needs to pull a sample from the remaining 299,950 items in the population. Stated differently, how much weight should the audit team give to the audit evidence provided by data analytics? The testing approach could be viewed through one of two perspectives. From a traditional perspective, the audit

and extent of the work that will be completed as part of the ADA. In so doing, the audit team will also need to specify the exact purpose and objectives of the ADA.

According to the AICPA audit guide, as a starting point, the audit team must determine where the ADA is going to be used in the audit process. For example, will it be a risk assessment procedure? A test of control? A substantive test of detail or analytical procedure? Or, will the ADA just be used as a way to help form an overall audit conclusion? Next, the audit team needs to consider how much assurance will be provided by the test. In addition, it is important for the audit team to consider the nature and type of risk of material misstatement and how the evidence provided by the test will help the audit team respond to the identified risk.

Once the purpose and objectives have been identified for the ADA, the audit team must select the techniques and tools to be used to conduct the ADA. In a sense, the audit team must take the time to select the ADA that is best suited for the overall purpose and objective of the audit procedure and the techniques and tools to be used make a big difference. Of course, there are a number of different techniques and tools that can be used by audit professionals. According to the AICPA audit guide, **techniques** can be thought of in terms of the variations in the way in which an ADA might be deployed on an audit. These may include, for example, the way in which data is analyzed in light of a particular audit objective. **Tools** include the software (i.e., IDEA) or features within a particular software tool (i.e., Benford's Law) that are used by the audit team.

Finally, when planning the ADA, the audit team must carefully determine the population of data to be analyzed or tested. When doing so, the completeness and accuracy of the data is chief among the audit team's concerns. Related to completeness and accuracy, the reliability of the client's information system is taken into account to help reach a conclusion about these objectives. This was discussed in detail in Chapter 5 when describing the information and communications component of an internal control system. In practice, auditors consider many factors in planning an ADA, as shown in the following Data and Analytics in Practice example.

 DATA AND ANALYTICS IN PRACTICE   Planning the ADA

ELM MANUFACTURING COMPANY, PLANNING THE ADA
After identifying the specific risks in the audit and what could go wrong (WCGW?), the audit team spent time planning an appropriate analytical procedure to assess the risk within accounts receivable and to identify

specific customer accounts or transactions for testing. Please read, "ELM ADA Planning" in *Connect* to learn more about the considerations and approach taken by the audit team.

Access and Prepare the Data

In the not so distant past, the preparation of large data sets for detailed analysis was almost always performed by the information technology audit professionals on the audit engagement. However, in today's environment, the processing of large data sets has become a fundamental task that often is the responsibility of the most junior staff auditor on the team. As a result, it is critically important for new auditors to know how to "cleanse" and "prepare" a large data set for analysis.

According to the AICPA audit guide, there are two "key issues" that the audit team faces when accessing a client's data. The first is that the audit team needs to gain access to the data in a format (e.g., in an Excel file) that the team can use on the financial statement audit. In addition, at all times, the audit team must make sure that the integrity of the data is properly maintained and that the data is complete and accurate. As mentioned previously, the importance of completeness and accuracy of the data being analyzed cannot be overstated, and as a staff auditor, you must always ensure that is the case when completing an ADA.

In summary, in order to complete an ADA, the client's data set must be provided to the auditor in a format that can be used in the auditor's available tools. Further, while we fully recognize that audit clients may store their data in a variety of different file formats and that generalized audit software tools (such as IDEA) are programmed to be able to import data from a variety of different file formats (e.g., SAP, Excel, PDF), care must still always be taken by the auditor to make sure that the data has been imported in a complete and accurate manner.

In addition, and most importantly, the auditor must always take actions to make sure that the data being tested remains secure and maintains its integrity at all times. Indeed, management is likely to ask questions about the steps being taken by the auditor to guard against possible data breaches and/or violations of confidentiality. In some circumstances, auditors may even need to subject their own information systems to reliability testing by the client. In fact, according to the AICPA audit guide, since audit clients need to be convinced that their data will be protected by the audit team, it is important that audit professionals are aware of management concerns that analyses performed by the audit team may corrupt or even change the data. While audit teams generally work hard to make sure that such corruption does not occur, some entities may still be concerned about data security breaches and the possibility of loss of confidentiality when the audit teams are testing audit client data.

Once the data is accessed from the client, the next step for the audit team is to properly cleanse the data. That is, before an audit team can properly analyze client data, it must be cleansed and prepared for proper use by someone on the team. This process includes working to identify data errors that may exist in the file. For example, some fields that should always contain data may have none; fields that should contain dates may have letters; or there may even be fields that contain data outside preset acceptable values. Beyond searching for errors, an audit team will also have to check the data file for proper formatting, remove all subtotals and make sure no blank columns exist, among many steps that are taken during the data cleansing process. Sometimes, the auditors can encounter significant difficulties in accessing and preparing client data, as discussed in the following Data and Analytics in Practice example.

DATA AND ANALYTICS IN PRACTICE

Data Acquisition and Preparation

ELM DATA ACQUISITION AND PREPARATION

After planning the ADA, ELM's audit team needed to obtain the data necessary to perform the ADA, and prepare it for analysis. Please read,

"ELM ADA Data Acquisition and Preparation" in *Connect* for more information about the difficulties the auditors encountered in acquiring and preparing the client data.

 REVIEW CHECKPOINTS

G.6   According to the AICPA, what are the five steps that need to be conducted when completing ADA?

G.7   When planning the ADA, what is the first step that needs to be taken? Hint: It is the same as with any audit step

G.8   What is meant by "cleansing" and preparing a data set? Why is it important to conducting the ADA?

Consider the Relevance and Reliability of the Data

When performing an ADA, a key step is to determine whether the underlying data being used in the analysis has a connection to the assertion being tested and the ultimate purpose of the audit procedure. Recall that the professional standards clearly elevate the importance of relevance of audit evidence and that does not change when conducting ADA. For example, certain evidence might be logically connected to a particular assertion. It may only be relevant for overstatement testing and not a test of understatement. So, the audit team must evaluate the connection to the assertion and the specific audit procedure being tested.

Yet another consideration that needs to be made by the audit team is whether the data being considered for use is the most relevant data available to the auditor. Stated differently, are there other sets of data that might be more relevant, depending on the existing facts and circumstances, or are there alternative forms of data that could be used?

Audit teams must also evaluate the reliability of any data used in ADA, including the source reliability, the nature and relevance of information available and, most importantly, the internal controls over the preparation of such data. When evaluating the controls over the preparation of the data being used, the audit team is primarily interested in whether the data is complete and accurate. Generally, in order to accomplish this objective at an audit client, the reliability of accounting systems and information technology general controls must be tested prior to using data from a client system.

In a sense, auditor testing of the reliability of a client data set is an example of the auditor testing the client's **information produced by the entity (IPE)**. The concept of IPE is quite broad for purposes of the financial statement audit as IPE can result from any information technology process at the audit client, including any transaction process that is in use.

Let's consider what might be considered IPE that could be used by the audit team when testing the accounts receivable balance. One example that might be particularly useful would be a listing of all the individual customer account balances that make up the total accounts receivable general ledger balance. Such a listing would be a terrific example of IPE resulting from an accounts receivable transaction process which might be used by the audit team to make selections for tests of details (e.g., positive confirmation testing) for the accounts receivable balance. Alternatively, the auditor may request a listing of all sales invoices to enable a test of the existence of accounts receivable.

In this example, before using a listing of all the individual customer account balances as IPE in the audit process as reliable audit evidence, the audit team would need to determine that the IPE is complete and accurate. There are a number of risks that an audit team needs to address before concluding that the report is complete and accurate. Among the risks, the following are most salient and need to be considered by the audit team with respect to the completeness and accuracy of IPE from an IT transaction process:

- The IT process is not processing data in a complete or accurate manner.
- The IT process is not capturing data in a complete or accurate manner.
- The IT process is not categorizing data correctly for output purposes.

The testing process employed by audit teams when addressing these risks is covered in detail in Module H. However, for now, remember that audit teams must make sure to consider the above risks when testing IPE for completeness and accuracy. A discussion of the issues related to completeness and accuracy of client data is included in the following Data and Analytics in Practice example.

 DATA AND ANALYTICS IN PRACTICE — IPE Considerations

ELM IPE CONSIDERATIONS

After acquiring and preparing the client's data, ELM's auditors assessed whether the data were sufficiently relevant and reliable for the purposes of conducting the ADA. Please read, "ELM IPE Considerations" in *Connect* for more information about how the audit team addressed relevance and reliability concerns.

Beyond completeness and accuracy, there are different types of characteristics of the data that also may have a large impact on the reliability of data. For example, the source of the data may be external to the audit client. In general, it is easier to assess the reliability of the data when its source is internal. In addition, the audit team would likely

**EXHIBIT G.10
Characteristics
of Data Affecting
Relevance and
Reliability**

Nature	Financial vs. nonfinancial, historic, time-sensitive, economic
Source	Controlled by accounting department, controlled internally but outside accounting department, external
Format	Numerical, text, fixed fields, unstructured
Timing	Point in time or period of time, rate of change
Extent	Volume and variety of subject matter/sources
Level of Aggregation	Account balance vs. transaction, annual vs. hourly, consolidated vs. segment

consider characteristics such as whether the data is a forward looking estimate or historical data when assessing the reliability of the data being used on the audit. These type of factors would help the audit team to determine the extent of procedures and the type of procedures performed by the team to establish a basis to rely on the IPE for testing purposes. There are a number of characteristics of data that may affect relevance and reliability, as illustrated in Exhibit G.10.

Perform the ADA

The actual performance of the ADA will vary, depending on the ultimate purpose of the ADA. For example, an ADA performed as a risk assessment procedure will be executed differently than an ADA that is being performed as a substantive analytical procedure. This is because the risk assessment procedure would not typically be used to gather substantive evidence about a relevant assertion for a significant account, while the substantive analytical procedure would be used for this purpose. As a result, due professional care must be taken to make sure that the ADA is executed in an appropriate manner, given the situation.

Always remember that the professional standards require audit teams to obtain evidence that is sufficient given the facts and circumstances of the situation. As a result, when gathering evidence using ADA, the audit team must make sure that the evidence gathered is sufficient, given the context. In a substantive testing context, the audit team must make sure that the evidence gathered is enough to persuade the team that the financial statement assertion about a significant account being tested does not contain a material misstatement. Ultimately, this is a matter of professional judgment.

The AICPA audit guide provides an example to illustrate. When an ADA is used for substantive testing which involves an analysis of 100 percent of items in a large population, the audit team may begin the testing process by identifying individual items that represent "outliers" that require some level of audit testing to ensure that the risk of material misstatement is sufficiently low for the population. Sometimes, the items identified using an ADA may, in fact, represent a transaction with a higher level of risk of material misstatement which warrants an audit response. In other cases, items identified using the ADA may not represent a transaction with a higher level of risk of material misstatement (i.e., the items may be what are sometimes called *false positives*). When making the determination of whether the items identified warrant an audit response, an audit team is not required to test all items identified by the ADA, necessarily. Professional judgment is required to make this final determination.

This is a critically important point and one that will vary depending on the purpose of the ADA. It is possible that all that is needed is a clearer definition of the matters that require additional audit work and then applying the ADA again. It is also possible that the identification of "subgroups" within the overall population of items will reveal that certain subgroups are less risky than others, which would lead to a change in the nature, timing, and extent of additional procedures. Finally, it is also possible that the application of a different ADA might more clearly identify those items that represent a risk of material misstatement, control deficiencies, or misstatements. The key for the audit team is to think critically about the design and ultimate execution of the ADA and then consider additional procedures on items that warrant further attention. An example of how an audit team would approach this is discussed in the following Data and Analytics in Practice example.

DATA AND ANALYTICS IN PRACTICE
Days Sales Outstanding (DSO)

ELM DAYS SALES OUTSTANDING (DSO)
Having planned the ADA, acquired and prepared the data, and assessed the relevance and reliability of the data, ELM's auditors were ready to perform the DSO test. The auditors chose an appropriate technology

tool and prepared the analysis in a format that would enable them to evaluate the results and reach audit conclusions. Please read, "ELM DSO Analytic" in *Connect* for more information about how the auditors performed the analytic and some output obtained from the ADA.

Evaluate the Results and Draw Conclusions

Once the audit team has completed the ADA, they must collectively "take a step back" and evaluate the results of each procedure performed and ensure that the evidence needed to address the stated audit objective has been gathered. When complete, the audit team must evaluate the evidence and make sure that everything makes sense, in light of all of the circumstances.

If the objective of the test was not achieved, the audit team should plan and perform different procedures. For example, let's consider a situation where the audit team used ADA as a substantive analytical procedure. If the objective of this test was not achieved, it is likely that the audit team would have to consider a different ADA or perhaps even abandon ADA and conduct a substantive test of detail to reduce the risk of material misstatement to an acceptably low level.

Alternatively, it is possible that the execution of the ADA results in the identification of outliers, matters of audit interest, or notable items. Such items might be duplicate items in a population, missing items in a population, or just identified items with elevated risk as it represents an outlier, and so on. In these types of situations, the audit team would have to gather additional evidence to help reduce the risk of material misstatement to an acceptably low level. The following Data and Analytics in Practice example describes how an auditor might evaluate the output from a risk assessment ADA and identify items for further testing.

DATA AND ANALYTICS IN PRACTICE
Results and Conclusions

ELM DSO RESULTS AND CONCLUSIONS
The ELM audit team next considered the output obtained from the ADA and evaluated whether anything within the DSO identified specific risk areas. The audit team was able to identify specific classes of

transactions that resulted in elevated risk within the audit. Please read, "ELM DSO Results and Conclusions" in *Connect* for a description of the approach taken by the auditors.

Next, in situations where unusual items have been identified, the audit team also has to address the risk of material misstatement for remaining population items. Stated differently, the audit team must consider whether there is a risk of material misstatement in the items not identified as unusual. If there is a risk of material misstatement remaining, additional testing may be required that may include sampling the remaining population and completing tests of details. However, it may be appropriate for the audit team to conclude that no additional risk of material misstatement is present and there is no need to conduct additional testing. Of course, the next step is to document the results of the procedures performed, which will be discussed in the following section.

G.9   Explain what is meant by information produced by the entity (IPE).

G.10 Under what circumstances should the audit team test IPE? What are the key objectives for the audit team's test of IPE?

G.11 Assume that the execution of the ADA results in the identification of outliers, matters of audit interest, or notable items. What is the audit team required to do in these situations?

DOCUMENTATION REQUIREMENTS

LO G-4
Understand the requirements for documentation of audit data analytics.

Like any other audit procedure, when completing an ADA, the professional standards are quite clear about the importance of audit documentation. That is, the professional standards state that the documentation must be prepared in a manner that provides a complete understanding of the purpose of the test, the source of evidential matter, and the final conclusion reached. In addition, the documentation should be organized in a manner that allows for a link between the testing results and issues identified on the audit.

Further, the documentation must show how the procedures performed and evidence gathered relates back to the relevant financial statement assertion about the significant account that is being tested. Importantly, the audit documentation must show that the work was in fact performed. Indeed, there is a high bar outlined by the professional standards for audit documentation. Specifically, the documentation must contain enough information to allow an experienced auditor to understand the nature, timing, extent, and results of the procedures performed, evidence obtained, and conclusions reached. In addition, the documentation must include the name of the auditor performing the work, the date the work was finished, and must include the conclusions reached and significant judgments made.

As it relates specifically to an ADA, the audit team should make sure to document the specific objectives of the procedure, the specific risks of material misstatement that were addressed in the procedure at the financial statement assertion level. The audit team should also include a description of the source of the data and how the auditor determined that it was a complete and accurate set of data. In addition, the audit team should describe the exact nature of the ADA and the tools and/or techniques used to complete the ADA. This description should include the steps that were taken to access the underlying data, including the system accessed and how the data were extracted and transformed. Finally, the documentation must include an evaluation of matters identified as a result of applying the ADA and actions that were taken. The following Data and Analytics in Practice example describes the documentation considerations that are made by auditors in practice.

 DATA AND ANALYTICS IN PRACTICE   Documentation

ELM ADA DOCUMENTATION
Following the completion of the ADA, ELMs audit team worked to ensure that their documentation met professional standards. Although an ADA does not require anything different from any other type of audit

procedure, the auditors needed to consider the specifics of the procedures performed to ensure appropriate documentation. Please read "ELM DSO Documentation" in *Connect* for a detailed discussion and presentation of the audit documentation for the ADA performed by the audit team.

According to the AICPA audit guide, when an audit team generates graphics or visualizations to help provide insights into matters identified by the team, the underlying data is generally not required to be included in the audit documentation. However, while there is no requirement to include the data analyzed, screenshots of graphics generated in performing an ADA may be included in an audit professional's documentation. In such situations, only graphics necessary to support the audit team's work and conclusions should be included. The audit team need not document every matter considered or professional judgment made. Of course, all misstatements identified other than those considered clearly trivial should be documented.

✓ REVIEW CHECKPOINTS

G.12 When performing an ADA, what should the audit team document upon completing of the procedures performed?

COMMON TOOLS USED IN ADA

LO G-5
Identify some of the tools that can be used for performing audit data analytics.

As mentioned earlier in this module, we collectively believe that the very best way to acquire relevant knowledge related to audit data analytics is through the use of the most common tools, which can be broadly categorized as (1) spreadsheet tools such as Excel; (2) generalized audit software such as IDEA and ACL; (3) data preparation and statistical analysis tools like Alteryx, R, SAS, and Python; (4) visualization tools like Tableau and Microsoft Power BI, and (5) robotic process automation tools such as UIPath and Automation Anywhere. Each of these areas is now briefly discussed. In addition, the end of chapter materials provide you with numerous opportunities to use these tools, which are currently used by auditors. It is important to note that the focus of this book is on the standards and the techniques behind ADA. Software and tools are changing constantly, and an auditor must be adaptable. For example, many of the tools mentioned above were hardly used or in existence several years ago. By the time you read this, there may be new tools, and others that are no longer used. Skills in data wrangling and critical thinking are more important than being an expert in any one software program!

When considering spreadsheet tools, Microsoft Excel needs to be considered the ultimate "all-purpose" technological tool. Indeed, electronic spreadsheets such as Microsoft Excel are a "mainstay" in the audit profession. We realize that rapid developments in telecommunications and computing technology have resulted in dramatic changes in the technological capabilities within organizations. Nevertheless, spreadsheets are still widely used to aggregate data from different sources, manipulate such data as required, and ultimately disseminate it to users. In addition, some audit clients continue to maintain their original data in spreadsheets. As a result, audit professionals must possess a high level of spreadsheet skills to be effective and efficient auditors.

There are a wide variety of additional tools that can be helpful to audit teams performing ADA. For example, generalized audit software such as IDEA and ACL are comprehensive and powerful data analysis tools that allow an auditor to efficiently make sense of a client's data. The tools are flexible enough to read data from multiple file formats and allow for straightforward data extraction and analysis. The tools enable the identification of outliers and keep track of each step, which greatly aids audit documentation. In addition, many firms have their own audit specific software that keeps all audit-related work in one standard format and system.

Beyond these tools, audit teams are increasingly employing more advanced data preparation and statistical tools such as Alteryx, R, SAS, and Python. These tools allow for more advanced analytical routines to be performed. Finally, visualization tools like Tableau and Microsoft Power BI provide audit teams with an opportunity to conduct detailed visual analysis of data which allows for greater insight into the underlying data. Such insight provides audit teams with the tools to ask better questions and ultimately improve audit outcomes.

Beyond these tools, some clients and even audit firms are beginning to use robotic process automation, often called RPA, to standardize routine processes. Tools such as UIPath and Automation Anywhere enable an audit team to select, process, and send confirmations with a click of a button after building a standardized process. These tools integrate other technology into one automated process. Tools such as these may allow audit teams to focus on more difficult areas with high levels of professional judgment.

Of course, an entire course could be developed for students of auditing to learn about the full range of tools that are currently available to audit teams. And, while more extensive coverage of these tools is beyond the scope of this textbook, we are hopeful that this overview will help you as you embark on a career in auditing. Before we briefly discuss the next generation of tools for audit professionals, we want to remind you about the importance of professional skepticism.

Professional Skepticism in ADA

When planning an ADA, an auditor must do so with professional skepticism, and must exercise professional judgment while executing an ADA. Indeed, throughout its history, the PCAOB has emphasized the importance of maintaining and then applying an attitude of professional skepticism throughout the audit process. The professional standards explicitly define professional skepticism as having "an attitude that includes a questioning mind and a critical assessment of audit evidence" when making professional judgments.

As a direct result, critical thinking and professional judgment skills have become increasingly important in today's auditing environment. Thus when completing an ADA, an audit professional must exercise skepticism when assessing the completeness and accuracy of client data, when making any type of assumptions while both planning the ADA and evaluating the results, and perhaps most importantly, when fully considering any unusual circumstances that might be revealed as a result of the ADA. Of course, the audit team must carefully document their rationale for each professional judgment made when completing an ADA. In most situations, this rationale must clearly demonstrate that the audit team was skeptical while applying their critical thinking skills in making professional judgments. In fact, unless there is proof in the formal audit documentation that audit teams have considered disconfirming evidence, it is possible, if not likely, that inspection teams from the PCAOB would have questions about whether professional skepticism was properly exercised.

☑ REVIEW CHECKPOINTS

G.13   What are the most common tools used by audit teams when completing an ADA?

G.14   Why is it important for an auditor to be professionally skeptical when completing an ADA?

THE NEXT GENERATION OF AUDITING

The next generation of auditing seeks to take full advantage of emerging technologies in a way that will improve audit quality. The global economy has undergone vast change in the last several years, where an emphasis on big data and advanced analytical tools have created new opportunities for audit professionals. As innovation in technology possesses the capability to add efficiency to the audit process, a strong incentive exists for audit firms to employ new tools and methodologies on a large scale basis, as described in the following Auditing Insight.

AUDITING INSIGHT   The Bots Are Coming, the Bots Are Coming. . . .

RPA. It's short for robotic process automation and it's being used by every Big 4 accounting firm, with smaller firms looking to jump into the water of automation as well. RPA replicates the human tasks associated with redundant processes and has "bots" instead of humans perform them. According to experts in the field, robotics is predicted to automate or eliminate "up to 40 percent of transactional accounting work." What exactly does this mean for accountants? As firms

save hundreds of thousands of hours of process work by using bots, accountants will be used for higher-level thinking and analytics, thus creating new opportunities for the tech-savvy, critical thinkers. A different accounting world is coming, one that will require much more of accountants as bots become more commonplace.

Source: "Robotic Software Sweeping Large Accounting Firms and Clients," StarTribune, April 8, 2017.

External Big Data

Thus far, this module has focused on how audit teams can maximize the usefulness of internal client data. However, spurred primarily by advances in information technology, the global economy has undergone watershed change in the last several years, where an emphasis on Big Data and consequent data analytics continually create new opportunities for the analysis of financial statement balances. At present, while the use of Big Data from external sources in financial statement audits is in its early stages, the audit profession continues to invest significant resources to determine how best to leverage Big Data in the financial statement audit.

If we acknowledge that the future of audits includes the employment of advanced analytical tools surrounding Big Data in a meaningful way, one clear challenge will be to ensure the completeness, accuracy, and reliability of Big Data sources. Nevertheless, the potential appears to be almost unlimited. Consider two examples: for years, internal auditors have used big data to detect insurance and purchasing card fraud based on anomalous payments made; and retailers like **Target** send ads to women that are deemed "likely pregnant" based on specific non–baby-related purchases and perhaps even upset a teenage girl's father by sending advertisements for baby supplies based on her purchases.

It is easy to see how auditors could improve risk assessments and analytical procedure expectations using *external data*. Think about it; **Walmart** found quite easily that a hurricane increased sales of flashlights, water, and even Poptarts by seven times the normal rate. In addition, using **Google's** Profile of Mood States and 10 million tweets, researchers predicted stock price changes three to four days in advance. The potential to improve the analytical procedure expectations are clear because auditors are able to leverage more and better data to develop such expectations.

Artificial Intelligence

While audit data analytics on their own have the potential to dramatically increase audit quality, auditors are also working hard to understand the implications of cognitive technologies, like machine learning and artificial intelligence. For example, **artificial intelligence** is a form of cognitive technology that is capable of learning as it absorbs informational cues in a task setting. At the core, artificial intelligence applications are built from chains of algorithms that enable a software application to acquire the information, process, and even reason through the information in a way that compares to human brain functionality. We believe that cognitive technologies like artificial intelligence have the potential to fundamentally change the nature of the financial statement audit process. Consider the link between Elon Musk and AI featured in the following Auditing Insight.

Neuralink, the 2016 startup funded by Elon Musk, made a splash in July 2019 with the announcement of their goal to implant a device into the brains of people who have spinal injuries and corresponding paralysis. The symbiosis between man and machine was unthinkable a generation ago, and now, a company has been formed with the aim of creating a device to enhance the human brain and connect it with an external device to "form brain-machine interface" (BMI). It sounds futuristic, but Musk hired some of the brightest neuroscientists in the world to explore the idea of a human brain-machine interface and hopes to have human testing in the very near future. One thing we know for sure, artificial intelligence (AI) is here to stay, whether a chip is implanted in the human brain or not. We expect wherever it goes in the future, Musk is likely to Tweet about it!

Sources: "Elon Musk's Neuralink Unveils Plans for Revolutionary Brain Implants," MyTechDecisions, June 30, 2019; "Elon 21-13 Musk's Neuralink Implant Will Merge Humans with AI," dezeen, July 22, 2019.

Distributed Ledger Technology

Introduced in 2009, the original intent of **distributed ledger technology (DLT)** was to assist in the safeguarding of financial transactions for the virtual currency **Bitcoin.** However, the technology behind DLT allows for low-cost tracking and dissemination of information through a network of interconnected peer-to-peer ledger systems sharing identical accounts and balances in real-time. As a result, there is potential to actually eliminate intermediaries in the transaction process. Someday, it is believed that DLT will provide auditors with more efficient and effective methodologies for providing assurance due to greatly improved audit trails, automated audit procedures, and permanent recordkeeping. Of all emerging technologies, DLT is likely to have the most far-reaching impact on future accounting and assurance practices. But, based on the Auditing Insight below, regardless of the emerging technology being contemplated, risk assessment remains critically important to auditors.

As technology is evolving and changing, so are the risks within the auditing framework. Robots, AI, cloud sharing, and blockchain are all emerging technologies with significant risks for the audit profession. So, what are firms doing to address the risks associated with these new technologies? One firm, Ernst & Young (EY) has a "new methodology" called Trust by Design. According to Amy Brachio, partner at EY, "risk now needs to be considered and designed at the inception of new products, services, channels or transformation—to create trust, all risks must be addressed together, at the same time—and critically, ahead of time." The point is, each new technology presents a new area of risk and "if managed poorly, could lead to the erosion of trust." Auditors need to be able to ensure the trustworthiness of new technologies from beginning to end.

Source: "How to Manage the Evolving Risks of Emerging Technology," EY, February 15, 2019.

Most importantly, it is not likely that these emerging technologies will ever eliminate the need for auditors. Rather, there will always be a role for auditors to think critically, be adaptable, get along with the audit client, and exercise good professional judgment.

 REVIEW CHECKPOINTS

G.15 It has been said that the next generation of auditing seeks to take full advantage of emerging technologies in a way that will improve audit quality. Which emerging technology do you believe has the most potential to improve audit quality? Why?

Summary

Audit teams must respond to an environment that is characterized by the availability of Big Data, advanced analytical tools, and related technological advances in a meaningful way. Simply stated, audit clients of different sizes across different industries are all facing changes as the result of advances in information technology, and they fully expect that their audit professionals will follow along.

Of course, the possibility of enhancing audit quality while improving efficiency at the same time provides an even stronger incentive for audit firms to employ new and improved technological processes that take full advantage of relevant data. Indeed, it is not surprising that the audit profession has committed vast resources to determine how best to leverage an abundance of data with advanced analytical tools in today's financial statement audit. Given the importance of data and advanced analytical tools in the audit process, we believe it is essential for students of auditing to embrace this opportunity. As a new audit professional, you can be a change agent, and we encourage you to take full advantage of this unique opportunity.

In this module, audit data analytics (ADA) was defined as "the science and art of discovering and analyzing patterns, identifying anomalies, and extracting other useful information in data underlying or related to the subject matter of an audit through analysis, modeling, and visualization for the purpose of planning or performing the audit." We also discussed how ADA can be used by audit teams in a variety of tasks during the audit process, including risk assessment procedures, tests of control, substantive analytical procedures, and tests of detail.

The module also presented a basic five-step process that is typically employed by audit teams when completing ADAs. According to the AICPA Guide to Audit Data Analytics, the five steps are: (1) plan the ADA; (2) access and prepare the data for purposes of the ADA; (3) consider the relevance and reliability of the data used; (4) perform the ADA; and (5) evaluate the results and conclude as to whether the purpose and specific objectives of performing the ADA have been achieved. Of course, careful workpaper documentation of each step is essential when completing ADA.

Importantly, this module was deliberately focused on how to make the best use of *internal* client data in a manner that provides useful insights to the audit team. Our conversations with practitioners have convinced us that this is the best course of action for new staff auditors to take when preparing for work as an audit professional in today's auditing environment.

Among a host of new skills to learn, it has become clear that staff auditors will need to be able to apply advanced analytical tools in a manner that will identify "anomalies" in an underlying data set. Understanding unusual or atypical items of audit interest in an overall data set is an essential first step towards the use of analytical tools in a financial statement audit process. As we stated repeatedly in this module, to accomplish this step, students are well served by learning how to do so by using the same analytical tools as audit professionals use today. As a result, the end-of-chapter materials for this module feature three tools that are commonly used by auditors, IDEA, Excel, and Tableau.

Overall, it seems clear that the auditing environment world has changed and staff auditors must be prepared to enter an exciting new auditing world. We urge you to embrace and to take full advantage of this unique opportunity. You will not regret your decision!

Key Terms

analytics: Analytics in auditing are deliberate and systematic analyses of data in a manner that is designed to yield insights into the financial statement audit process, 838

artificial intelligence: Artificial intelligence is a form of cognitive technology that is capable of learning as it absorbs informational cues in a task setting. At the core, artificial intelligence applications are built from chains of algorithms that enable a software application to acquire the information, process, and even reason through the information in a way that compares to human brain functionality, 856

big data: Big Data consists of large data sets that are generally unstructured. At times, the data sets are so large that they cannot be processed by traditional analytical tools. Students should consider Big Data to be generated continuously from multiple sources, 835

data: In a financial statement audit context, data implies an elemental level of numbers and/or characters that are used within an audit client's organization. To be useful for decision makers, the data must be thought about within a meaningful context which would allow it to be understood, 837

distributed ledger technology (DLT): Distributed Ledger Technology (DLT) is a distributed network of ledgers that is designed to assist in the safeguarding of financial transactions for the virtual currency. However, the technology behind DLT allows for low-cost tracking and dissemination of information through a network of interconnected peer-to-peer ledger systems sharing identical accounts and balances in real-time, 857

heat map: A heat map is a data visualization that illustrates the magnitude of each risk (low, medium, or high) and the likelihood (low, medium or high) of each risk in a manner that improves understandability, 839

information produced by the entity (IPE): Broadly defined, information provided by the entity is any information that is produced by the company's information systems that is being used by the auditor for substantive testing procedures or used by the audit client to execute a control activity, 850

techniques: An audit data analytic technique should be thought of in terms of the different ways in which an ADA might be used on an audit. These may include, for example, the way in which data is analyzed in light of a particular audit objective, 848

tools: An audit data analytic tool includes the software (i.e., IDEA) or features within a particular software tool (i.e., Benford's Law) that are used by the auditor, 848

word cloud: A word cloud is a data visualization image that comprises words that are used in a specific context. The size of each word in the image reflects the frequency and/or the importance of the word in that context. The image is used by auditors as a way to improve understandability of that context, 836

Multiple-Choice Questions for Practice and Review

All applicable Exercises and Problems are available with *Connect*.

LO G-4

G.16 When documenting an audit data analytic (ADA), an experienced auditor with no prior connection to the engagement should be able to understand all these elements of the ADA **except**

a. Results of procedures performed and evidence obtained.

b. Nature, timing, and extent of procedures performed.

c. The software used in performing the ADA.

d. Conclusions reached and significant judgments made.

LO G-3

G.17 The first step of planning an ADA is

a. Select techniques and tools used for performing the ADA.

b. Document the objective of the ADA.

c. Determine the overall purpose and specific objectives of the ADA.

d. Select the ADA that is best suited for the purpose.

LO G-1

G.18 The automated approach to audit analytics can be delivered through

i.   Ad hoc procedures.

ii. Continuous execution.

iii. Repetitive analysis.

a. i only

b. ii and iii

c. iii only

d. i, ii, and iii

LO G-2   G.19 An auditor imports a client's purchasing cycle transactions for the purposes of testing authorization controls. Which of the following is true regarding the implementation of this audit data analytic?

    a. The use of statistical sampling in the performance of the ADA increases the auditor's confidence.

    b. The use of ADA for purchasing transactions often significantly increases audit risk relative to traditional auditing procedures.

    c. A disadvantage of implementation is the increased costs associated with ADA.

    d. Testing can be more efficiently conducted across 100% of transactions.

LO G-4   G.20 Which of the following is correct regarding including client data in audit documentation for an issuer?

    a. Auditors are required to retain their client's data in documentation for seven years.

    b. Auditors should always include client data in their documentation to enable an experienced auditor with no prior connection to the engagement to replicate testing.

    c. Client data should never be included in documentation.

    d. There is no specific requirement to include client data in auditing documentation.

LO G-2   G.21 All of the following procedures are common uses of audit data analytics in risk assessment procedures **except**

    a. Analyzing trends in inventory costs.

    b. Identifying sales that did not follow the typical three-way match control in the revenue cycle.

    c. Comparing cash collections to sales invoices and discounts in the revenue cycle.

    d. Calculating accounts receivable collection periods by region.

LO G-2   G.22 When identifying and assessing inherent risk through the use of audit data analytics, what type of analytic would an auditor most likely perform first?

    a. Detail analysis of specific sales transactions.

    b. Dimension analysis of sales transactions by region.

    c. Trend analysis of sales by month.

    d. Comparison of sales revenue to prior period and expectations.

LO G-3   G.23 Which of the following is not a typical problem found by auditors when cleansing client data for the purposes of performing an ADA?

    a. Some fields may be empty and thus cause errors during analysis.

    b. Some fields may not be sorted in numerical order and require sorting for identification of outliers.

    c. Some date fields may contain letters or be in the wrong format.

    d. Some fields may have country-specific differences such as currency.

LO G-2   G.24 Which of the following is a common use of ADA in performing tests of controls?

    a. The auditor performs an aging of accounts receivable.

    b. The auditor conducts a trend analysis on inventory costs.

    c. The auditor runs a predictive model of interest expense.

    d. The auditor performs journal entry exception testing for employee entry amount limits.

LO G-3   G.25 Select the proper order in performing ADA:

    i. Evaluate the results and conclude on whether the purpose and specific objectives of performing the ADA have been achieved.

    ii. Consider the relevance and reliability of the data used.

    iii. Plan the ADA.

    iv. Perform the ADA.

    v. Access and prepare the data for purposes of the ADA

        a. v, iii, ii, iv, i

        b. ii, iii, v, iv, i

        c. ii, v, iii, iv, i

        d. iii, v, ii, iv, i

LO G-3

G.26 Which of the following would occur during the planning stage of ADA?

    a. Auditor must determine the nature, timing, and extent of the work to be performed in the ADA.

    b. Auditor can conclude that no additional risk of material misstatement is present in population items.

    c. Auditors may need to subject client systems to reliability testing.

    d. Auditor must consider whether the data has a logical connection to the purpose of the audit procedure.

LO G-4

G.27 For documentation of an ADA to be considered sufficient, all the following should be recorded except?

    a. Who reviewed work performed within the output of the ADA.

    b. Who performed the work and created the output of the ADA.

    c. The process used to produce the data examined.

    d. Identifying characteristics of specific items or matters tested.

LO G-3

G.28 In determining the reliability of the data to be used by the audit team, an auditor discovers the data is controlled internally by the accounting department. Which of the following is the most likely step the auditor would take after learning of this information?

    a. The auditor should rely on the data and continue to perform the ADA.

    b. The auditor should consider obtaining information from a more reliable source before continuing with the ADA.

    c. The auditor should ask management if the information can be relied upon.

    d. The auditor should not rely on the data and perform a different procedure to obtain sufficient, appropriate audit evidence.

LO G-2

G.29 Analysis of accounts receivable collection periods by region is most likely a part of which of the following types of ADA?

    a. Risk assessment procedures.

    b. Tests of controls.

    c. Substantive analytical procedures.

    d. Tests of details.

LO G-3

G.30 To determine the reliability of data, the auditor may consider all but which of the following?

    a. The process used to produce the data.

    b. The nature and source of the data.

    c. The extent of other audit procedures.

    d. Whether the auditor's system has been subject to reliability testing.

LO G-2

G.31 When auditing a client in the merchandising business, an auditor became concerned that the client was recording fraudulent credit sales. Which of the following procedures would have most likely alerted them to this potential fraud?

    a. Observing the credit sales figure on the income statement.

    b. Recalculating depreciation on fixed assets.

    c. Analyzing cash receipts as a percentage of sales by month.

    d. Analyzing gross profit percentage by class of revenue.

LO G-1

G.32 Certain characteristics of data may affect the relevance and reliability of the data used in the ADA. The level of aggregation is one of these characteristics. Which of the following does not illustrate differing levels of aggregation?

    a. Number of annual transactions compared to the number of weekly transactions.

    b. A consolidated statement compared to a single segment of a statement.

    c. A total account balance compared to a single transaction within that balance.

    d. All of the above illustrate differing levels of aggregation.

LO G-5

G.33 An auditor is considering choosing an ADA tool for performing a risk assessment procedure. Which of the following best describes the requirements in the auditing standards?

    a. The AICPA Guide to Audit Data Analytics lists the technology tools which are allowed for audits of nonissuers.

b. The auditing standards prohibit the use of artificial intelligence in risk assessment.

c. The ASB and PCAOB standards provide an uniformly agreed upon and updated listing of allowable tools for audits of issuers.

d. The auditing standards do not specifically address the tools auditors may use in performing the audit.

LO G-3

G.34 When performing an ADA, which of the following best describes an appropriate sequence used by an auditor for risk assessment purposes?

a. An auditor develops an audit plan after evaluating the results of the risk assessment ADA.

b. An auditor evaluates the results of a data analytic chosen based off of the audit plan.

c. An auditor cleanses the client's data after modeling the ADA required by the audit plan.

d. The auditor models an ADA based on the evaluation of the audit plan.

LO G-5

G.35 An auditor is considering the appropriate software to perform an ADA for a substantive analytical procedure. Which of the following types of software is the auditor most likely to use?

a. Data visualization software.

b. Data cleansing software.

c. Robotic process automation software.

d. The auditor may use any of the above depending on the purposes of the ADA.

Exercises and Problems

 All applicable questions are available with *Connect.*

LO G-6, LO G-7, LO G-8

Applying Data and Analytics to the Revenue Cycle-College Football Ticket Sales Revenue

Exercises G.36–G.41 require the use of Excel, Tableau, or other software in the revenue cycle audit. This case is loosely based on Florida State University (FSU) football ticket revenues. Many of the facts and all of the transaction-level data are fictitious, however. You have access to five Excel databases obtained from your client for use in auditing football ticket revenue for the 2023 football season. Detailed information about the client and data dictionaries, along with the required data sets, can be found in *Connect.*

LO G-6

G.36 **Information Produced by the Entity.** Performance of an analytical procedure requires use of information produced by the entity being audited (IPE).

Required:

a. Whenever an auditor uses IPE in an audit procedure, the auditor must ensure that the information is reliable. According to auditing standards, when using IPE as audit evidence, what procedures should the auditor evaluate to determine whether the information is sufficient and appropriate for purposes of the audit?

b. Which of the following information from the case would be considered IPE and why?

Information	Yes/No and why?
Schedule of unsold tickets	
Bank statement listing cash deposits	
Listing of football games played	
Recorded ticket sales obtained directly from general ledger	
Average number of complimentary tickets provided (client's calculation)	

LO G-6, LO G-7

G.37 **Cleansing Client Data** The client has provided you with the following data files:

i. Unsold tickets by game

ii. Season ticket sales revenue

      iii. Champion's Club ticket revenue

      iv. Single game ticket sales, by game

      v. Issued tickets, by game

Required:

When using information for the purposes of performing analytical procedures, data must be cleansed prior to use. Consider the following common issues found in cleansing data and provide documentation of the number of instances of the following. You may also provide documentation of any other data anomalies you find. Remember that some data tables must be used in combination to provide a complete picture of the client's revenue data.

a. Duplicate listings

b. Missing items from a sequence

c. Dates outside of appropriate range

d. Characters in a numeric column

e. Apparent issues with data truncation (either missing rows, or limited characters in a column)

LO G-6, LO G-7, LO G-8

G.38 **Performing an Analytical Procedure Using Client Estimates.** Your client has provided you with the following information which they have calculated based on the underlying accounting information:

Season tickets sold (excluding Champion's Club)	28,630
Champions Club seats sold	3,404
Student tickets provided, per game	16,000
Average number of complimentary tickets provided	1,400
Average season ticket price	$330

For the purposes of performing the following procedure, you may assume that you have tested the underlying transaction-level data produced by the entity (IPE) and it is sufficiently reliable. Assume that performance materiality has been set at $230,000 for the purpose of this analytical procedure.

Required:

Prepare and appropriately document an estimate of football ticket revenue using only the summary estimates provided above by the client, as well as the client's summarized single game total tickets issued summary. Use this calculation to test the reported sales revenue of $26,726,864 and answer the following questions:

a. What is your best estimate of 2023 football ticket revenue using the client's average ticket sales and prices provided in the case? Do not use the actual data for this calculation.

b. Based on the performance materiality set, does 2023 football ticket revenue appear to be fairly stated? Why or why not?

c. At what level would you assess the risk of material misstatement related to 2023 football ticket revenue after the performance of your analytical procedure (low, moderate, high)?

d. What additional procedures would you recommend performing related to your audit of football ticket revenue?

LO G-6, LO G-7, LO G-8

G.39 **Testing the Client's Estimates with Underlying Data.** The client provided you with certain calculations based on the underlying transaction level data. Are the following calculations provided by the client sufficiently accurate for the purposes of the analytical procedure based on the underlying transaction level data? Provide documentation of your work to support your conclusion.

a.	Season Ticket Sales	28,630
b.	Champions Club seats sold	3,404
c.	Average number of complimentary tickets provided	1,400
d.	Average season ticket price	$330

LO G-6, LO G-7

G.40 Conducting Additional Risk Assessment Procedures. Regardless of your conclusions reached in the questions above, perform some exploratory risk analysis on the data provided. Identify any areas where you believe there may be elevated risk after performing your procedures and identify any specific accounts and assertions that may be affected. You may classify and break down the data in any way you deem appropriate for the purposes of risk assessment. Be sure to provide proper documentation of your work.

Required:

a. Does the listing of unissued tickets appear to be complete and accurate?

b. Do you notice any unusual variations in the ratio of online vs. window ticket sales?

c. Do you identify any unusual variations in the number of complimentary tickets issued?

d. Do the patterns of timing of internet ticket sales appear reasonable?

e. Does the pricing of individual game and season tickets appear to be consistent with stated prices?

LO G-8

G.41 Considering the Adequacy of Data Provided by the Client. The schedules provided by the client for this analytical procedure lack many details that might be helpful to an auditor. Consider the columns provided by the client. What other information would you expect an auditor to want for the purposes of analyzing the reasonableness of the data provided by the client and performing follow-up procedures?

Applying Data and Analytics to the Revenue Cycle—Billy's Big Box, Inc. Sales Returns and Allowances

Exercises G.42–G.46 require the use of IDEA or Excel for performing tests on the adequacy of sales returns and allowances for Billy's Big Box, Inc. (BBB) BBB is a regional discount retailer that operates large discount stores in the southeastern United States. They compete directly in their markets with other "big box" stores. One hallmark of BBB is their generous return policy which allows customers to return any item at any time within 90 days for a full refund. Additional information about BBB and the required databases, along with data dictionaries, are available in *Connect*.

Use the data and information from *Connect* to answer questions G.39–G.43 below

LO G-6, LO G-7

G.42 Summarizing Client Data In accessing and cleansing client data, the auditor must consider the completeness and accuracy of the information produced by the entity, as well as the appropriateness of the data for the purposes of the audit. This often involves summarizing the data and reconciling differences with reported client balances.

Required:

a. What are the total sales included in the **Product Sales Summary** database?

b. What are the total dollar amount of returns in the **Product Returns Summary** database?

LO G-6

G.43 Identifying Issues in Data Cleansing In assessing the cleanliness of the data for the purposes of performing audit data analytics, are any of the following issues present in the database?

Data Cleansing Issue	Number of instances
a. Characters in monetary or numeric fields	
b. Negative dollar amounts	
c. Characters in PRODCAT category	
d. Duplicate or missing months or categories	

LO G-6, LO G-7

G.44 Obtaining an Understanding of Client Data To obtain a better understanding of the data, complete the table below:

Question	Answer
a. Which product category (PRODCAT) had the highest dollar amount of sales?	
b. Which store (STOREID) had the highest dollar amount of returns during the month of February, 2024?	
c. Which product category (PRODCAT) had the highest percentage of returns relative to sales for the three-month subsequent period presented?	
d. Which store (STOREID) had the highest percentage of returns relative to sales for the three-month subsequent period presented?	

LO G-6, LO G-7

G.45 **Estimating Sales Returns and Allowances** Your firm has decided to try two approaches to estimating a valuation allowance for sales returns.

Required:

a. Your firm decides to estimate that 10% of all sales will eventually be returned. Using the data provided and the monthly returns information above, estimate the allowance for sales returns as of 1/31/2024.

b. Your firm decides to use the return percentage information acquired from the auditor specialist. Using the data provided and the monthly returns information above, estimate the allowance for sales returns as of 1/31/2024.

LO G-6, LO G-7, LO G-8

G.46 **Reaching an Audit Conclusion** Based solely on your analysis in G.42, select the most appropriate conclusion.

a. Based on both analyses, allowance for sales returns appears to be materially understated as of 1/31/2024.

b. Based on both analyses, allowance for sales returns appears to be materially overstated as of 1/31/2024.

c. Based on both analyses, allowance for sales returns appears to be fairly stated in all material respects.

d. Based on one analysis, allowance for sales returns appears to be materially misstated but appears appropriate based on the other.

Applying Data and Analytics to the Purchasing Cycle—Mini-Bullseye Discount, Inc. PCards

Exercises G.47–G.51 require the use of Excel or IDEA for analyzing employee expenditures using purchasing cards (PCards). Mini-Bullseye Discount (MBD) is a medium-size national retailer with thousands of stores across the United States. MBD sells all types of products, ranging from groceries to pet foods and automotive supplies. Many of MBD's corporate employees are required as part of their jobs to travel, as well as purchase items on behalf of the company when they are out on jobs. To help with the processing of employee purchases, corporate-level employees are assigned a sequentially numbered purchasing card. Each purchasing card has both an authorized transaction limit, which is set based on the typical expenditures made by the employee, and single transaction limit. Employees are told what their limits are and they know the company policies, but the issuing bank is unable to limit individual transactions beyond a maximum balance placed on the card, which is set to the authorized total annual purchase limit for an employee. Management monitors the use of the cards regularly and follows up on any unusual expenses found.

More information, data dictionaries, and required data are available on *Connect*.

LO G-6, LO G-7

G.47 **Assessing completeness and accuracy of IPE** In accessing and cleansing client data, the auditor must consider the completeness and accuracy of the information produced by the entity, as well as the appropriateness of the data for the purposes of the audit.

Required:

a. What are the total expenses included in the **Employee Card Expenses 2023** database?

b. This total does not match what was reported by the client in the information provided within *Connect*. Which of the following reasons explain the differences?

Reason for Difference	Number of Instances	Total Dollar Amount (positive number)
a. Some expenditures from before fiscal 2023 are included in the database		
b. Some expenditures from after 2023 are included in the database		
c. Some nonemployee expenses are included in the database		

LO G-6

G.48 **Data Cleansing** In assessing the cleanliness of the data, are any of the following issues present in the database?

Data Cleansing Issue	Number of instances
a. Characters in dollar amount fields	
b. Negative expenditures	
c. Missing EXPID	
d. Duplicate EXPID	

LO G-6, LO G-7

G.49 **Obtaining an Understanding of Client Data** To obtain a better understanding of the data, complete the table below:

Question	Answer
a. Which employee (EMPID) had the highest quantity of p-card expenditures during the year?	
b. Which employee (EMPID) had the highest dollar amount of p-card expenditures during the year?	
c. Which category of expenditures (EXPCAT) had the highest quantity of p-card expenditures during the year?	
d. Which category of expenditures (EXPCAT) had the highest dollar amount of p-card expenditures during the year?	

LO G-6, LO G-7

G.50 **Exceptions testing in Purchasing Transactions** This step requires you to complete some exceptions testing for the Employee p-card expenditures for the year ended 12/31/2023.

Required:

a. How many unique employees exceeded their annual authorized transaction limit (AUTHLIMIT)?

b. How many unique employees exceeded their individual transaction limit at least once (TRANLIMIT)?

c. How many total expenditures were above the CATLIMIT authorized for the transaction category?

d. How many employees made purchases with p-cards after their termination date (TERMDATE)?

e. How many employees made purchases with p-cards before the ISSUEDATE?

LO G-8

G.51 **Writing an Audit Documentation Memo** Based on your above analysis, please write a memo for the audit file outlining any employees or categories of expenses that you believe deserve special attention in the audit. You may assume for the purposes of this memo that the client believes that any misuse of p-cards is considered material.

Audits of Plant, Property, and Equipment—ELM Manufacturing Company

Exercises G.52–G56 require the use of IDEA or Excel for analyzing property, plant, and equipment. Elm Manufacturing Company (ELM) is a small manufacturer of back packs located in Rochelle, Illinois. ELM has three buildings, all on one property. First, they own a manufacturing plant, where all the backpacks are manufactured and product repairs are made. All raw materials are also stored at the manufacturing plant. Second, they own a warehouse where all finished goods are stored and products are shipped to customers. Finally, they own a small office building where they conduct their operations, including processing of orders, purchases, as well as all managerial activities. The company also provides company cars to several employees and has the expected manufacturing equipment, furniture and fixtures.

Additional relevant information related to property, plant, and equipment for ELM, including depreciation policies, data dictionaries, and required data are available in *Connect*.

LO G-6, LO G-7

G.52 **Assessing the Completeness and Accuracy of IPE** In assessing the completeness and accuracy of the information prepared by the entity, consider the following:

a. Does depreciation expense as reported by the client agree with the total depreciation expense on the client's worksheet?

b. Are the numerical sequences in the fixed asset register complete? If no, how many assets are missing?

c. Are there any duplicate asset numbers listed in the fixed asset register or on the depreciation schedule? If yes, how many?

LO G-6

G.53 **Data Cleansing** Prior to analyzing the reasonableness of the client's property and equipment accounts, please consider whether any of the following potential issues with the **Fixed Asset Register** database exist. If no instances exist, please answer 0.

Issue	Number of Instances
a. Useful lives different from company policy	
b. Negative net asset values	
c. Characters in numeric columns	
d. Salvage values greater than posted policy	
e. Manufacturing equipment purchased by nonmanufacturing location	

LO G-6, LO G-7

G.54 **Assessing Risk in Property and Equipment Additions** Consider the amount of property additions during the fiscal year.

Required:

a. What were the total number of property additions by asset class during the year ended 3/31/2023 for the following classes of assets?

Asset Class	# of new additions	Total Cost
Furniture and fixtures		
Manufacturing equipment		
Computer hardware		

b. What were the total number of property additions by location during the year ended 3/31/2023?

Location	# of new additions	Total Cost
1		
2		
3		

c. How would the above information help the auditor in planning tests of additions to property and equipment?

LO G-6, LO G-7

G.55 **Testing Estimates of Depreciation Expense** Reperform the company's calculation of depreciation expense for the current year using the information in the **fixed asset register.**

Required:

a. What is the total amount of depreciation expense calculated in your reperformance?

b. Are there any assets that should have had depreciation expense during the current year that are not included in the client's depreciation schedule? How many?

c. Is the difference between your reperformance of the depreciation expense and the client's recorded depreciation expense considered a material difference? Why or why not?

LO G-8

G.56 **Assessing the Adequacy of Audit Evidence** Do you believe that you have sufficient appropriate evidence to conclude that depreciation expense and fixed assets are fairly stated in all material respects? What are the next steps you would take in performing your tests of fixed assets and depreciation expense?

Assessing Valuation of Inventory—Granny's Farmer Store Exercises G.57–G.61 require the use of IDEA or Excel for analyzing the inventory obsolescence reserve for a client. Granny's Farmer Store (GFS) is a smaller chain of 10 sustainable farming produce stores that operates in three west-coast states, but mostly in California. The company first opened in 2007 and has built up a strong customer base. The store prides itself on local sourcing and carrying organic products. However, one of the biggest issues for GFS is the obsolescence of their produce items, particularly because of their insistence on organic production and lack of preservatives. Because nearly all of the company's inventory can spoil, accurate valuation of inventory at year-end is a tremendously difficult audit issue.

Additional information about GFS, including data dictionaries and required data is available in *Connect*.

LO G-6, LO G-7

G.57 Evaluating the Completeness and Accuracy of IPE In accessing client data, the auditor must consider the completeness and accuracy of the information produced by the entity, as well as the appropriateness of the data for the purposes of the audit.

Required:

a. What is the total gross inventory included in the **Inventory** database?

b. This total does not match what was reported by the client above. Which of the following reasons explain the differences?

Reason for Difference	Number of Instances	Total Dollar Amount (positive number)
i. Some purchases from after fiscal 2023 are included in the database		
ii. Some purchases from before 2023 are included in the database		

LO G-6

G.58 Cleansing Client Data In assessing the cleanliness of the data, are any of the following issues present in the database?

Data Cleansing Issue	Number of instances
a. Characters in dollar amount fields	
b. Negative unit costs	
c. Characters in INVCAT category	
d. Duplicate PURCHID	

LO G-6, LO G-7

G.59 Summarizing Client Data

a. To obtain a better understanding of the data, complete the table below:

Question	Answer
i. Which inventory category (INVCAT) had the highest quantity of inventory in stock as of the end of the year?	
ii. Which inventory category (INVCAT) had the highest dollar amount of inventory in stock as of the end of the year?	
iii. Which store (STOREID) had the highest quantity of inventory in stock as of the end of the year?	
iv. Which store (STOREID) had the highest dollar amount of inventory in stock as of the end of the year?	

b. How would the above information help the auditor in planning the audit of GFS's inventory?

LO G-6, LO G-7

G.60 Auditing Client's Estimates Recalculate the Inventory Valuation Allowance using the **Inventory** and **Inventory Obsolescence Percentages** databases. (Hint: You may want to do this with a new column for each item in the Inventory database.)

Required:

a. What is your calculated Inventory Valuation Allowance?

b. Is the difference between your Inventory Valuation Allowance and the client's materially different?

c. Which store (STOREID) has the highest calculated inventory valuation allowance as a percentage of its inventory?

d. Which Inventory Category (INVCAT) has the highest calculated inventory valuation allowance as a percentage of gross inventory for that category?

e. Are there any instances of the following in the client's data and how could this effect the valuation allowance?

Issue	Number of Instances	Potential Effect on Valuation Allowance
i. There are inventory categories (INVCAT) with changes to valuation percentages after testing by your team		
ii. STOREID 8 has many categories of inventory out of stock		

LO G-7, LO G-8

G.61 Documenting Audit Findings in an Audit Memo

Based on your above analysis, please write a memo for the audit file outlining any issues that you believe deserve special attention in the audit.

Auditing Warranty Reserves—ELM Manufacturing Company

Exercises G.62–G.66 require the use of IDEA or Excel. Elm Manufacturing Company (ELM) is a small manufacturer of backpacks located in Rochelle, Illinois. They make three different types of backpacks. To increase sales and improve customer satisfaction, ELM provides a full two-year warranty on all their products.

Additional information about ELM's warranty and accounting policies, as well as data dictionaries and all required data, is available in *Connect*.

LO G-6, LO G-7

G.62 Assessing the Completeness and Accuracy of Client Information In assessing the completeness and accuracy of the information prepared by the entity, consider the following.

Required:

a. Is warranty expense of $156,475 calculated accurately based on the information provided and the client's warranty policy?

b. Are the Warranty Costs in the reconciliation provided by the client mathematically accurate based on the Warranty Claim 2023 database?

c. The final CLAIMNO filed during the year ended 3/31/22 was 36,454. Based on the client's policy and use of sequential claim numbers, do all claims appear to be present during the current year? If no, how many claim numbers are missing?

d. Are there any duplicate CLAIMNO recorded during the year?

LO G-6

G.63 Cleansing Client Data Prior to analyzing the reasonableness of the client's warranty expense and accrued liability, please consider whether any of the following potential issues with the **Warranty Claim 2023** database exist. If no instances exist, please answer 0.

Issue	Number of Instances
a. Dates outside the fiscal year	
b. Claims filed after warranty period ended	
c. Repairs made for greater than replacement cost	
d. Incorrect shipping costs	
e. Improperly authorized claims	

LO G-6, LO G-7

G.64 Summarizing Client Warranty Claims Data Consider the reasonableness of the warranty expense and warranty liability. In reaching your conclusions, consider the following:

a. How many warranty claims were filed for each product and what was the total amount of the claims?

PRODNO	# of claims filed	Total Cost (including Freight)
i. SP001		
ii. HB005		
iii. CB008		

b. Does this match your expectations? Why or why not?

   i. Yes, the number of claims are materially the same for all products.

   ii. Yes, there are more claims for the most complex product.

   iii. Yes, the highest total cost is for the most complex product.

   iv. No, the client claimed all products have similar numbers of claims filed.

c. How many customers filed more than one warranty claim during the year?

d. Which CLAIMCUSTNO filed the most warranty claims during the year? How many claims?

e. What were the total number and dollar amount of claims filed by quarter?

Quarter	Number of Claims	$ Amount of Claims
i. 1st (4/1-6/30/22)		
ii. 2nd (7/1-9/30/22)		
iii. 3rd (10/1-12/31/22)		
iv. 4th (1/1-3/31/23)		

LO G-6, LO G-7

G.65 **Assessing Risk Factors in Client Estimates** Identify risk factors related to ELM's warranty expense and accrued warranty liability. Select any risk factors from the list that you believe are present.

Risk Factor	Present?
a. Product CB008 is high risk because of the large dollar amount of warranty cost.	
b. Product HB005 is high risk because of the high percentage of warranty claims.	
c. Based on the rates of claims during the year, warranty liability appears to be materially understated.	
d. Based on the rates of claims during the 3rd quarter, warranty expense percentage may be understated.	
e. Missing warranty CLAIMNOs indicate potential risk related to the existence assertion of warranty expense.	

LO G-6, LO G-7, LO G-8

G.66 **Reaching and Documenting Audit Conclusions**

a. Based on your analysis conducted above, what percentage would you recommend the client use for warranty reserve as a percentage of sales for the subsequent fiscal year?

b. Write a memo documenting your conclusions from your tests of ELM's warranty expense and liability. Propose an audit adjustment if necessary.

Revenue Cycle Risk Assessment—Urgent Medical Device, Inc. Exercises G.67–G.72 require the use of IDEA or Excel and the Urgent Medical Device, Inc. (Urgent) case from KPMG University. Your professor will provide you access to the Urgent case from https:// www.kpmguniversityconnection.com/.

LO G-6, LO G-7

G.67 **Assessing Fraud Risk** According to the professional auditing standards, an audit team should ordinarily presume that revenue recognition is a fraud risk.

Required:

a. Based on your understanding of fraud risk assessment and the case information, identify at least three specific fraud risk factors related to Urgent. Classify these risks in terms of What Could Go Wrong (WCGW) with each of the significant accounts and relevant assertions identified for Urgent's revenue and accounts receivable cycle.

b. What do you believe is the most significant risk related to the revenue account for Urgent?

c. What special audit considerations would you propose in response to the significant risk you identified above? In your response, consider how you would change your approach to the nature, timing, and extent of evidence in response to the identified risk.

LO G-6, LO G-7

G.68 **Assessing Completeness and Accuracy of Client Data** Based on the tests of controls and other Information Technology General Controls (ITGC) testing, your firm has concluded that the data files supplied to you for your procedures are complete and accurate. The conclusion was based on tests of controls over data input risks, including all relevant data elements (e.g., invoice date), data integrity risks, and the relevant automated application controls. However, it is also important to confirm that the data, once imported into IDEA or Tableau, was transferred into the technology tool in a complete and accurate manner prior to working with the data within the technology tool. Import all supplied data into IDEA and then reconcile the data with the supplied trial balance and check figures from the case. Simply stated, you must check that the data has been transferred in a complete and accurate manner at each step in the process. Thus, you must to ensure that you are working with the set of transactions and balances that the client used to calculate sales revenue and accounts receivable.

Required:

a. What are the total number of valid sales that comprise the $84,867,855 sales revenue shown on the trial balance as of 12/31/2017?

b. What are the total number of unpaid invoices that comprise the $11,988,886 gross accounts receivable balance shown on the trial balance as of 12/31/2017? Assume that Urgent has no outstanding accounts receivable from 2016.

LO G-6, LO G-7

G.69 **Assessing Risk with Visualizations** Data visualization tools such as Tableau can be used to help audit teams identify items or specific areas of higher risk within an entire population. Your data and analytics center has provided you with a set of Tableau visualizations to consider during your substantive testing procedures:

   i. Three-way match of SalesOrderID, InvoiceID, and ShipID based solely on SalesOrders database

   ii. Sales by territory

   iii. Sales by distributor

   iv. Sales by quarter

   v. Sales by territory by quarter

   vi. Product sales by territory

   vii. Fourth quarter sales by territory

   viii. Sales vs. sales goals for fourth quarter by territory

   ix. Sales by quarter by territory vs. fourth quarter sales goals

Required:

a. Using the data visualizations provided in Tableau, compose a memo to be included in the audit documentation file that identifies any pattern in the data that you believe may be indicative of specific audit risks. In your memo, be sure to link the identified risks to the appropriate significant account and relevant assertions.

b. Based on the analysis completed above, what further testing, if any, needs to be performed over the identified risks and the remaining population? Stated differently, do any further tests need to be performed or does the three-way match visualization, combined with your tests of controls and additional visualizations, provide you with sufficient appropriate evidence to conclude about the occurrence of revenue at Urgent?

LO G-6, LO G-7

G.70 **Assessing Risk through Data Analysis** Technology tools like IDEA can also be used to help audit teams identify items with potentially higher risks within an entire population of items in an efficient and effective manner.

Required:

a. The SalesOrder database was used to produce a Tableau visualization of three-way match in the revenue cycle as described in the previous requirement. Using IDEA, verify the accuracy of the SalesOrder database by creating a three-way match on your own using the SalesOrder, Shipments, and CustomerInvoices databases. Are your conclusions the same? If so, how does this increase your assurance about the accuracy of the SalesOrder database? If not, why not? Did you identify any specific transaction that you believe should be considered higher risk for the audit?

b. Analyze the sales revenue file using IDEA to determine whether any sales were made to distributors without an established credit limit. Are there any exceptions? If there are exceptions, what further testing would you perform on these exceptions?

c. Analyze the accounts receivable and related credit authorization limits using IDEA to determine whether any customers have account balances as of 12/31/17 that exceed their existing credit limit. Are there any exceptions to the credit limit control as of 12/31/17? Do you notice any pattern in the exceptions? What further testing would you perform on these exceptions?

d. For some time, Urgent has based its allowance for doubtful accounts on an aging analysis and the results have been historically accurate. Below, you have been provided with the client's list of customer balances in excess of 90 days. These are the accounts that the client will consider when calculating the allowance for doubtful accounts as of 12/31/2017. Perform an aging analysis using IDEA to assess the completeness and accuracy of Urgent's list of customer balances in excess of 90 days.

Urgent Medical Devices		
Analysis of >90 Day Delinquent Accounts Receivable As of December 31, 2017		
SalesOrderID	InvoiceDate	TotalDue
3236	7/4/2017	$56,251.34
3241	7/9/2017	73,450.67
3422	9/5/2017	73,450.67
3466	9/21/2017	59,932.09
3490	9/21/2017	54,851.15
		$317,935.92

i. Based on your analysis, does the client's listing agree with your analysis completed in IDEA?

ii. Do you have any concern with the client's process for identifying the total amount of significantly delinquent accounts? You may think broadly, beyond mechanical accuracy, in considering the sufficiency of their process for identification of delinquent accounts.

iii. According to Urgent's unaudited trial balance, the balance for allowance for doubtful accounts is $310,000. Does the test performed above provide sufficient appropriate evidence to support a conclusion on the valuation of accounts receivable? If not, what additional testing would you recommend to reach an audit conclusion for this relevant assertion?

LO G-6, LO G-7

G.71 **Performing Exploratory Risk Assessment** Based on your risk analysis and findings in requirements G.64–G.67, perform additional analyses using IDEA to identify specific transactions, territories, or distributors that may require additional substantive testing. Be creative when doing so. For example, consider patterns in the data provided that might indicate management override of a control activity. Focus your additional analytics on those areas. Prepare a listing of specific findings from your additional analytics that you believe warrant additional testing.

LO G-8

G.72 **Reaching Overall Conclusions** In order to conclude on whether the risk of material misstatement has been reduced to an acceptably low level for the relevant assertions identified, you need to consider, on an overall basis, whether the results of your procedures provide sufficient appropriate evidence. Based on the evidence that you have considered, can you reach a conclusion for the relevant assertions identified? Why or why not?

Information Technology Auditing

Advancements in technology continue to affect the nature, timing, and preparation of financial information, including preparers' controls around financial information, and the planning and performance of audits.

PCAOB Data and Technology Project Update, May 2021

To err is human, but to really foul things up you need a computer.

Attributed to Paul R. Ehrlich, American biologist, author, and technology commentator

Professional Standards References

Topic	AU-C/ISA Section	AS Section
Consideration of Internal Control in an Integrated Audit		2201
Identifying and Assessing the Risks of Material Misstatement	315	2110
Auditors' Responses to Risks of Material Misstatement	330	2301
Reporting on Controls at a Service Organization (Attestation Standard)	AT-C 320	2601

LEARNING OBJECTIVES

Given its extensive use by clients, audit teams must consider a client's information technology (IT) systems during *all* stages of the audit engagement. In addition, a major trend in auditing practice is the use of increasingly powerful data analytic tools that are able to take advantage of the growing amounts of internal client data now available to auditors.

This data can take many forms and come from different places at the client, and thus for it to be useful, the auditor must test the client's information technology systems in great detail. Simply stated, the client's technological infrastructure and computing environment must be safe and secure for an auditor to rely on the information produced by the entity.

As a direct result, public accounting firms hire entry-level audit professionals who have completed coursework that has exposed them to how auditors test a client's technological systems. Critical issues for auditing students to learn include how to test general controls and application controls, and how to carefully document this work at an audit client. Staff audit professionals in today's environment need to learn how to make the best use of internal client data, which includes validating the completeness and accuracy of such data.

Students today have a chance to take advantage of significant opportunities that have emerged as a result of the increased importance of information technology in the financial statement auditing process. We encourage you to do so.

The focus of this module is on the audit team's examination of the client's accounting information system and its related computer controls. The module is subdivided into three parts. The first part reviews the basic elements of an accounting information system and the related controls. The second part describes the procedures that audit teams perform to test the operating effectiveness of the client's IT controls. The module concludes with a discussion of computer fraud and the controls that can be used to prevent it.

Your objectives are to be able to:

LO H-1 Understand the steps that are taken to determine whether an audit team can rely on IT controls.

LO H-2 Provide examples of general controls and understand how these controls relate to transaction processing in an accounting information system.

LO H-3 Provide examples of automated application controls and understand how these controls relate to transaction processing in an accounting information system.

LO H-4 Describe how the audit team assesses control risk in an IT environment.

LO H-5 Identify how audit teams perform tests of controls in an IT environment.

LO H-6 Describe the characteristics and control issues associated with end-user and other computing environments.

LO H-7 Define and describe computer fraud and the controls that can be used to prevent it.

INTRODUCTION

In today's financial statement audit environment, it is absolutely essential for staff auditors to understand the effect of a client's use of information technology on the financial reporting process. The simple fact is that the use of information technology is pervasive for largely all types of organizations and there are a multitude of ways that errors can occur that can impact an audit client. Consider the awarding of scholarships to accepted students at colleges and universities. Digital processing of college admissions has created some real issues for prospective students and administrators alike, as thousands of incorrect acceptances and scholarship notifications go out every year.

In January 2022, **Oakland University** in Michigan sent emails to 5,500 students indicating that they were the recipient of the university's highest scholarship award of $12,000 per year.[1] The trouble was that none of the students met the scholarship requirements for that prestigious award. The mistake was attributed to incorrect digital processing. That same month, **Central Michigan University** notified 58 students that they had received a full-ride scholarship (tuition plus room and board) as they were testing a new computerized messaging system. Fortunately for those 58 students, the university provided an apology with a full tuition scholarship, a costly mistake by the university that occurred as a result of information technology (IT).[2]

This problem is not a new one. In 2009, the **University of California at San Diego** sent email acceptances to 28,000 students, all incorrect. In 2016, **Tulane University** sent 130 acceptances to students incorrectly. But one of the largest errors occurred in April 2021, when the **University of Kentucky** sent an email to 500,000 students for acceptance to a program that typically accepts three dozen students a year; the university fortunately corrected the mistake within 24 hours, but the damage was done. The simple fact is that human error combined with digital processing can make this type of situation ripe for large-scale errors to occur.[3]

Of course, the nature of computing environments that staff auditors will encounter varies significantly. And, these type of IT related errors *may or may not* impact the financial statement audit process. Nevertheless, the use of technology is pervasive in audit clients of all sizes across all industries, and accounting processes are largely

[1] "Colleges Send Mistaken Acceptance Every Year. Why Does This Keep Happening?" *Chronicle of Higher Education*, February 3, 2022 (online source).

[2] "School offers full tuition to 58 students after a scholarship award message error," *The Associated Press - NPR* January 27, 2022 (online source).

[3] "University of Kentucky Mistakenly Sends 500,000 Acceptances," *The Associated Press - Huffpost* April 8, 2021 (online source).

automated across the board. As a result, when gaining an understanding of the client's internal control system, the auditor must identify each of the **information technology dependencies** within each aspect of the financial reporting process. This process includes answering questions such as, what is the nature of the information produced by the entity's systems that are necessary in the financial reporting process? And, what must the auditor do to validate the completeness and accuracy of this information? In this module, we more thoroughly identify the elements of an accounting information system and the controls that operate within these systems.

Automated Transaction Processing

To identify considerations that emerge when the client uses information technology, Exhibit H.1 illustrates the automated processing of sales transactions. As part of its *walk-through,* audit teams would typically identify the sequence of activities, files, documents, and controls for sales transactions, shown in Exhibit H.1, from origination through recording in the financial statements during the study and evaluation of internal control. The process is as follows:

1. A *customer order* for products or services is received. Typically, orders are received electronically and the information is entered by the customer and automatically included in a *customer order transaction file.* However, if the order is still received via mail or even telephone, client personnel would have to enter the relevant information (customer name/number, items requested, and quantities requested) into the *customer order transaction file.*

2. The customer order transaction file is then submitted for *automated processing.* At this point, the system accesses the *customer master file* using the customer name/number to ensure that the sale is made to an approved customer and that his or her credit limit has not been exceeded. If the order is received from a new customer, the transaction would be identified as requiring a credit check prior to further processing. The program then accesses the *inventory master file* to verify that the desired item(s) are available and identifies the current inventory prices. The dual arrows between the two master files and the automated processing symbol indicate that these files are accessed by the computerized system and are also updated after processing to reflect the customer order.

3. The computerized system then processes the order and, using the price from the inventory master file and quantity from the customer order, prepares a *shipping document* and *sales invoice* and updates the *sales transaction file.*

The processing shown in Exhibit H.1 is similar to the sequence of events when you place an order for a product online. When accessing the vendor's website, you are requested to enter various types of information (name, address, and credit card information) into a file that is analogous to the customer order transaction file. If you have not

EXHIBIT H.1
Automated Processing
of Sales Transactions

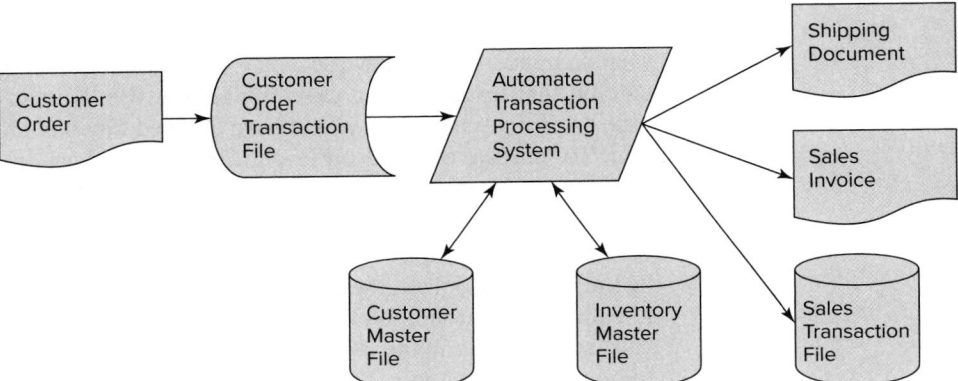

previously ordered from that vendor, you are given an option to "save" your information in a customer profile (similar to the customer master file) for future use. If you are a continuing customer, you are usually given the option to bypass the entry of this information if it has been saved in your customer profile. However, and most importantly, because you are required to enter a valid credit card prior to making a purchase, there is no need for a credit check in this environment.

The vendor's system then accesses an inventory master file and can instantaneously inform you whether the items you have ordered are in stock. In addition, the program determines the current price of the items and provides you with an electronic sales invoice that you are required to review prior to the final processing of the sale.

The following matters are introduced in information technology environments such as that shown in Exhibit H.1 and need to be considered by the audit team:

1. *The existence of systematic rather than random processing errors.* In a manual processing system, random errors occur because humans are processing transactions and humans make random mistakes. In contrast, automated processing systems handle all transactions in an identical manner. As a result, if an accounting information system processes a transaction erroneously (either because of an unintentional programming error or a planned error intended to perpetrate fraud), all transactions are affected in the same manner. As a result, although audit teams do not need to be concerned about random errors in an IT environment, they need to evaluate the accuracy of processing in these environments because of the systematic processing errors that can occur.

2. *The lack of an audit trail.* An **audit trail** is a chain of evidence provided through coding, cross-references, and documentation connecting account balances and other summary results with the original transaction source documents. In an IT environment, data are often entered directly into the system and processing is completed electronically. As a result, in many situations, the only hard copy is the final result of processing, or output. This leaves the audit team in the position of not having the ability to view a paper trail (audit trail) of the processing of transactions. Although not discussed in this text, the use of techniques embedded in client computer programs can allow audit teams to electronically view the various stages of transaction processing that would not otherwise be possible because of the lack of hard-copy documentary evidence.

3. *The possibility of inappropriate access to computer files and programs.* The use of information technology introduces the possibility that inappropriate access to computer files and programs can occur, both on- and off-site. This possibility requires clients to implement strong password controls and firewalls for access as well as to periodically monitor what files and programs have been accessed and by whom.

4. *The reduced human involvement in the processing of transactions.* The use of information technology reduces human involvement in the processing of transactions. For example, a computer program will perform the credit check that would have been performed by humans in a manual processing system. In addition, when using a manual system, humans would have accepted the customer order, prepared a sales invoice, and entered that invoice into a sales transaction file. Human involvement in the various aspects of the transaction would have allowed obvious processing errors to be identified. To mitigate the reduced level of human involvement in IT environments, clients implement controls to verify the accuracy of processing and the reasonableness of its output.

5. *The possibility of input errors.* Although most transactions processed are likely input by the customer online, the possibility still does exist that client personnel would have to enter information into electronic format, which introduces the possibility of errors. As discussed later in this module, clients implement various controls that are designed to prevent or detect this type of input errors made by their own employees.

Restricting access in this manner serves as an important component of separation of duties related to the authorization to execute transactions, recording of transactions, and custody of the related assets.

Once established, employee access should be restricted based on passwords. Important characteristics of passwords are that they should be of sufficient length (number of characters); include letters, numbers, and (in some instances) symbols; and be modified periodically (every six months is common). Establishing passwords in this manner reduces the likelihood of an employee's password being hacked (or guessed) by others. A study showed that a password with six lowercase alphabetic characters could be hacked through computer-generated algorithms in 10 minutes while a password with nine characters (including lowercase, uppercase, numbers, and symbols) would take 44,530 *years* to hack.[4]

In addition to passwords, physical security controls over terminals and input devices (such as locked doors and the use of badges or swipe cards to access certain locations) are used. However, with the increasing ability of employees to access systems remotely (i.e., offsite), physical security controls are becoming less effective in restricting access to programs and data. As the following Auditing Insight illustrates, you always need to make sure that your password is strong!

AUDITING INSIGHT \ Make Sure Your Password Is Strong!

Perhaps the most important control activity regarding access to IT systems is to make sure that your passwords are strong enough to withstand a cybercriminal's guess. You can be sure that the IT professionals at **HSBC**, a global banking giant are reminding their professionals about the importance of strong passwords and changing your password regularly.

In October 2018, HSBC disclosed that the company's networks had been breached and that the hackers were able to access bank customer's personal data including names, addresses, account types, account balances, transaction history, and statements. How did it happen? Security experts believe it was through a "brute-force method used to guess at passwords." The breach clearly shows how important it is for employees to actively manage and regularly change their passwords.

Source: "HSBC Data Breach Shows Failure to Protect Passwords & Access Controls," *Security Now.Com,* November 8, 2018 (online source).

Other common controls to restrict access to programs and data include

- Establishing time limits when user sessions automatically time out after a predetermined period of time (*automatic terminal logoff*).
- Periodically reviewing and confirming the access rights granted to employees.
- Ensuring that modifications in the level of access permitted to individual users have been properly authorized and are consistent with changes in these individuals' job responsibilities.
- Ensuring that access to programs and data is removed for recently terminated employees on a timely basis.
- Monitoring of user activity to ensure that only authorized users are accessing programs and data.
- Promptly reporting and communicating observed security breaches.

Program Change Controls

Program change controls are implemented by the entity to provide reasonable assurance that requests for modifications to existing programs (1) are properly authorized, conducted in accordance with entity policies, and support the entity's financial reporting requirements; (2) involve appropriate users in the program modification process; (3) are tested and validated prior to being placed into operation; and (4) have been appropriately

---

[4]"Say Goodbye to All Those Passwords," *Bloomberg Businessweek,* January 31, 2011, p. 36.

documented. It is also important that the entity prepare appropriate documentation with respect to the program modifications. This is most definitely an area of PCAOB Inspection Focus, as we now illustrate.

PCAOB INSPECTION FOCUS

The PCAOB is required to perform detailed inspections of the audit process employed by each firm auditing issuers. A formal inspection report is issued by the PCAOB for each firm inspected. In a recent inspection report, the PCAOB highlighted the importance of testing program change controls:

- If the audit client has made any changes to programs or applications within an IT environment, the audit team must test the operating effectiveness of program change controls.
- On this audit engagement, the audit client used "various change management processes . . . including multiple tools to manage and migrate changes into the production environments."
- However, the audit firm made the assumption that the population of program change control activities was homogeneous when

taking a sample. As a result, the "firm's sampling approach for testing ITGCs related to change management and segregation of duties was inappropriate."

- In addition, the audit firm did not "test any controls over, the accuracy and completeness of the system generated reports that it used to select its sample for testing controls over change management."

As a result, the PCAOB identified each of these items as deficiencies in their inspection report.

Source: *Report on 2019 Inspection of Ernst & Young, LLP*, PCAOB, December 17, 2020.

In addition, two other important controls for program changes relate to "emergency" change requests and the migration of new programs into operations. In some cases, modifications to existing programs need to occur outside of the normal process. If so, it is important that:

1. Appropriate documentation exists to support the emergency nature of the program modifications.
2. These modifications should be subject to standard approval procedures after they have been made.
3. When programs have been modified, they should be migrated (or moved) into operation only by appropriate individuals.

Computer Operations Controls

Computer operations controls are concerned with providing reasonable assurance that (1) the processing of transactions through the IT environment is occurring in accordance with the entity's objectives; (2) processing failures are resolved on a timely basis and do not affect or unnecessarily delay the processing of other transactions within the batch; and (3) actions are taken to facilitate proper storage of data and files, backup and recovery when the need arises.

A summary of important roles performed in an IT environment follows:

- *Hardware Engineers* are typically responsible for a wide range of activities including repairing hardware and servers, required network maintenance and system upgrades, including software upgrades in certain environments.
- *Help Desk Assistants* are typically responsible for answering the questions that occur on a day-in, day-out basis in an organization. In many environments, these analysts can be quite helpful in identifying required system upgrades based on the nature and volume of queries received.
- *Network Administrators* are typically responsible for the design of an organization's network in the most efficient and effective manner to support the organization's strategic objectives. They can also be involved in the development of the network in certain environments.

- *IT Liaisons* are typically responsible for linking the IT environment with the various business processes in the entity. The overarching goal for an IT liaison is to facilitate the operation of each business process of the entity through the use of technology. In a sense these liaisons need to speak the language of the business processes and the language of IT to be effective.
- *Project Managers* are typically responsible for getting projects completed within the IT environment. In most environments, project managers need to connect the right people from across the organization to get the job done.
- Finally, the *Chief Technology Officer* is the executive for the IT environment within an organization. In some environments, the title is *Chief Information Officer*. This executive generally reports directly to the CEO and is responsible for ensuring that the IT environment is operating in an effective and efficient manner.

Overall, the entity's system should ensure that any processing failures are resolved on a timely basis and do not delay the processing of other transactions. Typically, this would identify and document (through an exception report or file) transactions for which processing failures occur with timely follow-up and resolution of the processing of these transactions.

Finally, computer operations controls are implemented for files and data used in processing. The three major objectives of these operations controls are:

1. *The files used in automated processing are appropriate.* This is accomplished through the use of external labels on portable files and the use of header and trailer labels on internal records.

2. *The files are appropriately secured and protected from loss.* This is often accomplished by entities through a cloud storage provider. Cloud storage vendors routinely provide data storage on an as needed basis via the Internet. While this does eliminate the need for entities to buy and then manage their own data storage infrastructure, they still must ensure that their files are appropriately secured and protected from loss.

3. *Files can be reconstructed from earlier versions of information used in processing.* This is accomplished by creating and implementing policies for retaining prior versions of files for specified periods of time.

Program Development Controls

The objectives of **program development controls** are to provide reasonable assurance that (1) acquisition or development of computer programs and software is properly authorized, is conducted in accordance with entity policies, and supports the entity's financial reporting requirements; (2) appropriate users participate in the software acquisition or program development process; (3) programs and software are tested and validated prior to being placed into operation; and (4) all software and programs have appropriate documentation.

An important program development control is the entity's use of the **systems development life cycle (SDLC)** process to plan, develop, and implement new accounting information systems (or databases). The SDLC begins with the identification of system requirements. In other words, what does the entity need the system to do? The feasibility analysis stage examines whether the entity should purchase the system "off the shelf" (i.e., from a commercial vendor), develop the system internally, or modify an off-the-shelf system for internal use. The answer depends on the entity's resources and expertise.

Once a decision has been made that a new system is feasible, system specifications are developed. Programmers next write programs to accomplish those specifications and then design procedures. When converting from the old system to the new one, training employees to use the new system is critical. Upon successful implementation, the system must continue to be monitored to ensure that problems do not arise.

Effective SDLC controls ensure that the entity:

- Follows established policies and procedures for acquiring or developing software or programs.
- Involves users in the design of programs, selection of prepackaged software and programs, and testing of programs.
- Tests and validates new programs and develops proper implementation and "back out" plans (plans to cancel the results of processing in the event of an error or program failure) prior to placing the programs into operation.
- Periodically reviews policies and procedures for acquiring and developing software or programs for continued appropriateness and modifying these policies and procedures as necessary.

In addition to the use of the SDLC, it is important that appropriate documentation exist for each of the entity's programs. *Documentation* describes the system and its controls and is the means of communicating the essential elements of the accounting information system to both current and potential users. In evaluating controls over documentation, audit teams review the documentation to (1) gain an understanding of the system and determine whether the documentation is adequate to support the proper use of the programs and (2) determine whether client personnel follow standards. Of utmost importance is whether the client has established systems development and documentation standards. Unless written standards exist, determining whether the program development controls and the documentation are adequate is difficult.

The accompanying Auditing Insight "The Problems with New Systems," illustrates the problems that can occur with the implementation of a new system.

AUDITING INSIGHT — The Problems with New Systems

National Grid spent almost $1 billion to replace old **Oracle** software with new **SAP** software. The project was already three years in the making by the time they were to go live in November of 2012. They were already behind schedule with their upgrade and went live in spite of millions of customers without power due to Hurricane Sandy.

So what could possibly go wrong? Nearly everything. The new system was so flawed that unions sued the company. Why? Employees received incorrect paychecks; some were overpaid while others were grossly underpaid. Nearly 15,000 vendor invoices couldn't be processed and the company's financial reporting system collapsed.

Sources: "A Troubled Project To Replace Oracle With SAP Software Could Cost A New York Gas Utility Nearly $1 Billion," Insider, Oct 6, 2014 (online source); "16 famous ERP disasters, dustups and disappointments," CIO, March 20, 2020 (online source).

Summary

Given the pervasive role of general controls to the overall effectiveness of IT control activities at the transaction level, audit teams *must* test general controls each year. However, it is important to note that auditors are not required to test each and every general IT control at each audit client. Rather, once the auditor has determined the key internal control activities that are being relied upon to mitigate the risk of misstatement for each relevant assertion identified in the planning process, the auditor must only test the specific general control activities that support the effective operation of the key internal control activity that is being relied upon. Consider the example in Exhibit H.2

As you can see, the key internal control activity is the establishment of credit limits in the IT system which is designed to mitigate the risk of material misstatement that the

**EXHIBIT H.2
Testing General IT
Controls**

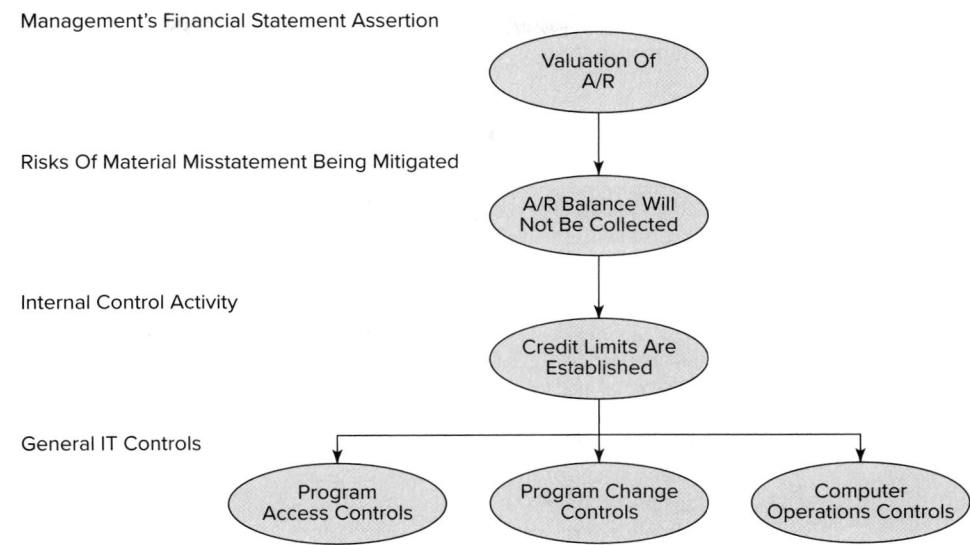

Management's Financial Statement Assertion

Risks Of Material Misstatement Being Mitigated

Internal Control Activity

General IT Controls

accounts receivable balance will be overstated and not be collectible which supports the valuation assertion. In this situation, the auditor determined that there are three specific general controls that support the effective operation of the credit limit control. As a result, these controls would need to be tested. In summary, the auditor has to carefully identify each of the general control activities that support the effective operation of the key internal control activities that are being relied upon by the auditor and then test those general control activities.

As discussed in detail in Module G, one final and very important consideration made by the audit team when evaluating the effectiveness of general controls relates to the use of information produced by the entity during the audit, including **system-generated reports** used by the client to execute its internal control activities and produce its financial statements. Professional standards are clear that an audit team cannot merely rely on information produced by the entity's accounting information system without testing general controls with a particular emphasis on the controls that have been designed to ensure that the information is complete and accurate. Without testing of the relevant general controls, the auditor would have to test the completeness and accuracy of each system-generated report using substantive testing procedures, which would generally take far more time to complete. Indeed, it is useful to consider that from a broad perspective, general control activities primarily support the accuracy and occurrence assertions, as shown here:

Assertion	Explanation	Examples
Accuracy	Ensuring the accuracy of data and testing computer programs prior to implementation increases the probability that transactions are processed properly	• Program development controls • Program change controls • Computer operations controls
Occurrence	Restricting inappropriate access to programs and data reduces the probability that fictitious transactions are entered into the system and processed	• Computer operations controls (particularly separation of duties) • Access to programs and data controls

Exhibit H.3 summarizes the general controls in each of the areas of a client's IT environment.

EXHIBIT H.3   General Controls: Category, Examples, and Objectives

Category	Examples	Objective(s)
Program development	• Use of systems development life cycle (SDLC) for authorization, user involvement, and testing and validation of new programs • Appropriate documentation for new programs	• Programs developed and software acquired by the entity are consistent with the entity's objectives
Program change	• Use of systems development life cycle (SDLC) for authorization, user involvement, and testing and validation of modifications to existing programs • Appropriate documentation to support "emergency" changes to existing programs • Implementation of program changes performed by appropriate personnel • Appropriate documentation for modifications to existing programs	• Modifications to existing programs are authorized and are consistent with the entity's objectives
Computer operations	• Procedures for resolving transaction processing failures • Use of external and header and trailer labels to identify files and programs • Storage of files in a well-secured technological infrastructure (likely cloud based) • Policies to allow for recovery (and or reconstruction) of files from previous versions	• Transactions are processed in accordance with the entity's objectives • Appropriate files and records are used in processing transactions • Files are appropriately secured (likely on the cloud) and protected from loss • Files can be recovered from previous versions if necessary
Access to programs and data	• Use of passwords and appropriate types of passwords • Physical security over terminals and input devices • Use of time limits and automatic terminal logoff functionality • Periodic review of user access rights • Removal of access rights for terminated employees on a timely basis • Monitoring of activity and immediate communication of any security breaches	• Access to programs and data is restricted to authorized users

---

✓ REVIEW CHECKPOINTS

H.7   List the four major categories of general controls, and identify the objectives of each.

H.8   What is the SDLC? What type of controls does the use of the SDLC include with respect to program development and changes?

H.9   Describe the duties of hardware engineers, help desk analysts, network administrators, IT liaisons, project managers, and the chief technology officer.

H.10 Identify and provide examples of controls related to the use of files and data.

H.11 Why are general controls so important in the audit team's evaluation of internal control and assessment of control risk and risk of material misstatement?

AUTOMATED APPLICATION CONTROLS

LO H-3

Provide examples of automated application controls and understand how these controls relate to transaction processing in an accounting information system.

Automated application controls are those applied to specific business activities within an accounting information system to mitigate the risk of material misstatement for relevant assertions about significant accounts and ultimately to achieve financial reporting objectives. Thus, automated application controls are specific to each cycle (e.g., revenue and collection, acquisition and expenditure) and refer to a client's activities designed to ensure the proper recording of transactions and to prevent or detect errors and frauds for transactions within these cycles. Because automated application controls are related to specific transactions, audit teams rely extensively on the effectiveness of these controls to mitigate the risk of material misstatement at the assertion level for account balances or classes of transactions. Most importantly, in many circumstances, the automated application control *is* the internal control activity that is being relied upon by the auditor to mitigate the risk of material misstatement on the audit.

There are many different types of automated application controls. In general, automated application controls are organized under three categories: input controls, processing controls, and output controls.

Input Controls

Input controls are designed to provide reasonable assurance that data received for processing by the computer system have been properly authorized and accurately entered or converted for processing. Data is input in a number of different ways, including via online sources. Nevertheless, human data entry still does occur in an organization and these controls provide the opportunity for entity personnel to correct and resubmit data initially rejected as erroneous. The following controls are particularly important:

- *Data entry and formatting controls.* These controls are related to the design of the data entry interface to provide a familiar and consistent format and reduce the frequency of input errors by personnel. Two such design features are the use of *drop-down menus* (which allow users to select from among a limited number of alternative choices rather than inputting data) and *standardized formats and screens* (which increase user familiarity with various fields and reduce the likelihood that data are inadvertently input in an incorrect field). For example, consider the likelihood of errors when data are input as a string of numeric and alphanumeric characters as opposed to a form in which users can use a tab key to move between fields. A third important design feature is the ability of personnel to review input prior to submitting it for processing within the system (known as *online editing and sight verification*).

- *Authorization and approval controls.* Only properly authorized and approved input should be accepted for processing. In an IT environment, some authorizations (e.g., automatic creation of a purchase order when an inventory item reaches a predetermined reorder point) can be computer controlled or accomplished by utilizing a *digitized signature,* an approved encrypted password that releases a transaction by assigning a special code to it.

- *Check digits.* Numbers are often used in accounting information systems in lieu of customer names, vendor names, and so forth. A *check digit* is an extra number tagged onto the end of a basic identification number such as an employee number or account number. When the identification number is entered (along with the check digit), the computer program calculates the correct check digit and compares it to the one on the input data. When the digits do not match, an error message is indicated on the device or printed out on an input error report. Check digits are used to detect coding errors or keying errors such as the transposition of digits (e.g., coding 387 as 837).

- *Record counts.* The known number of records entered can be compared to the count of records produced by the data-conversion device (e.g., the number of sales transactions or count of records). Differences between the manual counts of transactions and the number of transactions processed indicate that transactions may not have been input (if the manual count exceeds the processed count) or may have been input more than once (if the processed count exceeds the manual count).

- *Batch totals.* Used the same way as record counts, the batch total is the sum of some important and numerically meaningful quantity or amount (e.g., the total sales dollars in a batch of invoices). These totals allow input errors to be detected prior to submission for processing and ensure that all transactions are entered once and only once.

- *Hash totals.* These are similar to batch totals except that the hash total is not meaningful for accounting records (e.g., the sum of all the invoice numbers). Like batch totals, these totals allow input errors to be detected prior to submission for processing and ensure that all transactions are entered once and only once.

- *Valid character tests.* These input controls are used to check input data fields to determine whether they contain numbers when they are supposed to have numbers or alphabetic characters when they are supposed to have alphabetic characters.

- *Valid sign tests.* Similar to valid character tests, signed data fields are checked for appropriate positive or negative signs.

- *Missing data tests.* These input controls evaluate data fields to verify whether any are blank when they must contain data for the record entry to be correct.

- *Sequence tests.* Normally applied to evaluate the input data for numerical sequence of documents when sequence is important for processing, this validation routine also can check for missing documents in a prenumbered series.

- *Limit and reasonableness tests.* Also a processing control (see discussion below), these automated controls are used to determine whether data values exceed or fall below some predetermined limit. For example, a payroll application can have a limit test to flag or reject any weekly payroll time record of 50 or more hours.

- *Error correction and resubmission procedures.* These policies and procedures ensure identification of input errors on a timely basis and correction and resubmission by appropriate personnel for processing.

In thinking about input controls, you likely experience many examples of these when placing orders for merchandise online. If you enter a credit card number in an incorrect format (with or without dashes), enter quantities exceeding some reasonable amount, or inadvertently omit a field, you will be prompted that an error exists and encouraged to correct that error and resubmit your order. After all, the retailer most certainly does not want to lose your sale!

Processing Controls

Processing controls are designed to provide reasonable assurance that data processing has been performed accurately without any omission or duplicate processing of transactions. Many processing controls are similar in nature to input controls, but they are used in the processing phases rather than at the time input is verified. The most fundamental (yet important) processing control a client can implement is periodically testing and evaluating the processing accuracy of its programs. Other important processing controls include the following:

- *File and operator controls.* Controls need to be in place to ensure that proper files are used in applications. In addition, the systems software should produce a log that records time and use statistics for specific computer applications; supervisory personnel should review this log on a periodic basis.

- *Run-to-run totals.* Movement of data from one department to another or one processing program to another should be controlled. One useful control is the *run-to-run* total that refers to sequential processing operations (or runs) on the same data. These totals can be record counts, batch totals, and/or hash totals obtained at the end of one processing run. The totals are distributed to the next run and compared to corresponding totals produced at the end of the second run.

- *Control total reports.* **Control totals** (record counts, batch totals, hash totals, and run-to-run totals) should be calculated during processing operations and summarized in a report. Entity personnel (normally, the control group) should have the responsibility for comparing and/or reconciling these totals to input totals or totals from earlier processing runs.
- *Limit and reasonableness tests.* These should be programmed to ensure that illogical conditions do not occur (e.g., depreciating an asset below zero or calculating a negative inventory quantity). These conditions and others that are considered important should generate error reports for supervisor review.
- *Error correction and resubmission procedures.* Although previously mentioned as an input control, controls related to the identification of errors or unusual conditions encountered in processing transactions on a timely basis and correction and resubmission for processing should also be implemented by entities as transactions are processed.

Output Controls

Output controls represent the final check on the accuracy of the results of automated transaction processing. Output controls are concerned with detecting errors rather than preventing errors (as was the focus with input and processing controls). These controls also should be designed to provide reasonable assurance that only authorized persons receive output (or other types of reports generated by the accounting information system) or have access to files produced by the system. Typical output controls are the following:

- *Control total reports.* Control totals produced as output should be compared and/or reconciled to input and run-to-run control totals produced during transaction processing. An independent data control group should be responsible for reviewing output control totals and investigating differences.
- *Master file changes.* During automated transaction processing, permanent information stored in master files is often updated or modified; these files should be viewed as outputs of the automated processing. Any changes should be properly authorized by the entity and reported in detail to the user department from which the request for change originated because an error can be pervasive.
- *Output distribution.* Systems' output (whether electronic or hard copy) should be distributed only to persons authorized to receive the output. A distribution list should be maintained and used to deliver report copies. The number of copies produced should be restricted to the number needed to prevent unauthorized use.

Finally, perhaps the most common output control involves the manual review of routine computer outputs for reasonableness. An individual that is knowledgeable about the nature of the transactions and processing should perform an overall review of each relevant output for reasonableness within their area of control. This allows systematic errors that might otherwise go undetected to be identified (e.g., an employee being paid 10 times his or her normal salary).

Summary

A summary of the automated application controls discussed in the preceding section is found in Exhibit H.4. Note that some of these controls (record counts, batch totals, hash totals, and limit and reasonableness tests) may be used as both input controls and processing controls. Also note that the columns of Exhibit H.4 correspond to the following management assertions:

- Completeness: All transactions are entered.
- Occurrence: Transactions are entered only once.
- Accuracy: Input and processing of all transactions and data is accurate.

EXHIBIT H.4　Automated Application Controls

	Input of Individual Transactions and Data Is Accurate (Accuracy)	All Transactions Are Entered (Completeness)	Transactions Are Entered Only Once (Occurrence)	Processing of Transactions Is Accurate (Accuracy)	Other
Data entry and formatting	X		X		Ensures that input is approved and authorized
Check digits	X				
Record counts		X	X		
Batch totals	X	X	X	X	
Hash totals	X	X	X	X	
Valid character tests	X				
Valid sign tests	X				
Missing data tests	X				
Sequence tests		X			
Limit and reasonableness tests	X			X	
Error correction and resubmission	X			X	
Periodically testing and evaluating processing accuracy of programs				X	
File and operator controls				X	Ensures that appropriate files are used in applications
Run-to-run totals				X	
Control total reports				X	
Review of output for reasonableness				X	
Master file changes				X	Ensures that changes to master file data are authorized
Output distribution					Ensures output is distributed only to authorized users

Before moving on to the next section, let's take a step back and reinforce the differences between general controls and automated application controls. To better differentiate these two types of controls, think of an iPhone or another type of smartphone. A number of general controls "surround" the smartphone environment, such as requiring a password (system access control) to unlock the phone. For operating system program changes, you must download any upgrades from an approved "App Store" distribution channel. With respect to program development, all apps must be approved by Apple before releasing them to iPhone users. Another general control protecting your iPhone is the iCloud that backs up all of your critical data to an off-site location should your iPhone be lost or stolen.

There are also often controls within each app (application controls), such as password requirements to access many apps (such as Facebook). Error messages appear if you input the wrong password or enter otherwise incorrect data. Other app controls include requesting user permission when accessing Google Maps from ridesharing apps (such as Uber or Lyft). Hopefully, this smartphone analogy makes the differences between general and application controls clearer and easier to understand.

ASSESSING CONTROL RISK IN AN IT ENVIRONMENT

LO H-4

Describe how the audit team assesses control risk in an IT environment.

In the previous section of this module, we focused on the steps that need to be taken before an auditor could consider relying on IT controls. Before moving forward to a discussion of how auditors test such controls, it is important to take a step back and consider the assessment of control risk in an IT environment.

The assessment process that needs to be undertaken for IT controls is essentially the same as would be taken for manual controls. Specifically, the assessment generally begins with a walkthrough of the process that supports financial reporting for any significant account or disclosure identified during planning. Recall from Chapter 5 that during the walkthrough, auditors seek to understand the system of internal control. Once they have obtained a basic understanding of internal control, they then *form an assessment of control risk,* which involves the following major steps:

1. Identify the types of misstatements that can occur in significant accounting applications.
2. Identify the points in the flow of transactions where specific types of misstatements could occur.
3. Identify specific control procedures (such as the automated application controls described in the preceding section) designed to prevent or detect these misstatements.
4. Evaluate the design of control procedures to determine whether the design suggests a low control risk and whether tests of controls might be cost effective.

These four steps parallel those in a manual processing environment. In addition to the type of controls that the audit team considers (general controls and automated application controls), one important difference in assessing control risk in an IT environment is identifying the points in the flow of transactions where misstatements could occur (step 2) because many additional steps and sources of potential misstatement are introduced. These sources can be classified as shown in Exhibit H.5.

Once the audit team has identified the points where a misstatement could occur, it focuses on specific control procedures implemented by the client to prevent or detect such misstatements. For example, one possible misstatement could involve preparing invoices (and billing customers) using incorrect prices because an inappropriate inventory price file is used in processing transactions. In this case, one control procedure might be as follows:

Source of Misstatement		Control Procedure
Use of inappropriate inventory price file to prepare invoices	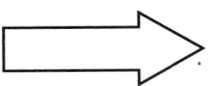	The billing program should identify the most current version of the inventory price file

EXHIBIT H.5
Points of Potential Misstatement in an IT Environment

Potential Source of Misstatement	Control(s)
1. Preparing and converting data to machine-readable form	Various input controls
2. Accessing files and programs during computer processing	Computer operations controls related to file identification (external labels and header and trailer labels)
3. Transferring data between computer programs and applications	Processing controls (run-to-run totals, control totals)
4. Updating master file information following processing	Output controls (related to master file changes)
5. Processing transactions by computer programs	Processing controls and output controls
6. Correcting and resubmitting errors at input or during processing	Error correction and resubmission procedures

You may recall from Chapter 5 that the audit team's study and evaluation of internal control consists of three distinct phases. Applied to the present conversation, at this point in the process, the audit team has obtained an understanding of internal control, including the general controls and automated application controls implemented by the client for the automated processing of transactions (i.e., phase 1). In addition, the audit team has formed a preliminary assessment of control risk based on considering the general controls and automated application controls implemented by the client for the computerized processing of transactions (i.e., phase 2).

The next step in the audit team's evaluation of internal control is to test the operating effectiveness of the identified controls (i.e., phase 3). Because automated controls operate in the same manner for similar transactions, it is only necessary to test each control once to determine effectiveness. The following illustrates three important controls that would mitigate the risk of material misstatement for the accuracy assertion for sales transactions along with how the audit team would test these controls in a manual processing environment and the implications for testing these controls in an IT environment:

Control	Manual Test of Controls	Implication for Testing in an IT Environment
Credit sales are approved by the credit department	Examine invoice for evidence of credit approval	If authorized customer file is updated and accurate, audit team can examine input controls to ensure that only authorized customer numbers are accepted for processing
Quantities shipped to customers are compared to quantities invoiced	Compare quantities shipped from shipping documents to quantities on sales invoices or examine evidence of client comparison of quantities	If sales invoice processing program uses input from computerized shipping document transaction file, audit teams can ensure that quantities are appropriately accepted from shipping document transaction file
Mathematical accuracy of invoices is checked by client personnel	Recalculate mathematical accuracy of invoices or examine evidence of client verification of mathematical accuracy	If calculations are made by the sales invoice processing program, audit teams can verify the (1) operating effectiveness of limits and reasonableness tests and (2) accuracy of the invoice processing program

The process of testing the operating effectiveness of controls in a computerized processing environment is discussed in the next section.

TESTING CONTROLS IN AN IT ENVIRONMENT

LO H-5
Identify how audit teams perform tests of controls in an IT environment.

Clearly, the audit client's IT environment, which is used to process its accounting transactions, will have a significant impact on the financial reporting process and will influence the procedures and techniques used to accomplish the organization's financial reporting goals and objectives. As a result, when evaluating the tests of controls that need to be conducted within an IT environment, the audit team needs to consider characteristics such as the following:

- *Possibility of temporary transaction trails.* Some computerized systems are designed so that a complete transaction trail, useful for audit purposes (i.e., an audit trail), could exist only for a short time or only in a computer-readable form. The loss of hard copy documents and reports and the temporary nature of the audit trail might require the audit team to alter both the timing and the nature of audit procedures.

- *Uniform processing of transactions.* Computerized processing of transactions means that the same processing instructions are applied to similar transactions. Consequently, computerized processing virtually eliminates the occurrence of random errors. As a result, programming errors (or other similar systematic errors in either the computer hardware or software) will result in all similar transactions being processed incorrectly when those transactions are processed under the same conditions.

- *Potential for errors and frauds.* The potential for individuals to gain unauthorized access to or alter data without visible evidence can definitely occur in computerized information systems. In fact, some believe that less human involvement in handling transactions processed by computers may even reduce the potential for observing errors and frauds. As a result, processing errors or fraud can remain undetected for long periods of time.

- *Potential for increased management supervision.* Computerized information systems offer management a wide variety of analytical tools to review and supervise the company's operations. The availability of these additional controls can enhance the entire system of internal control and, therefore, reduce control risk. For example, management review controls, discussed in detail in Module I, can be very helpful in reducing the risk of material misstatement.

- *Initiation or subsequent execution of transactions by computer.* With automatic transaction initiation, many transactions are initiated or executed automatically by a computerized system, without human review. Computer-initiated transactions include the generation of invoices, checks, shipping orders, and purchase orders. Without a human-readable document indicating the transaction event, the correctness of automatic transactions can be difficult to judge. In addition, management's authorization of transactions can be implicit in its acceptance of the design of the information system. Control procedures must be designed into the system to ensure the genuineness and reasonableness of automatic transactions and to prevent or detect erroneous transactions.

- *Use of cloud computing applications.* With cloud computing, an audit client may be accessing certain software applications and data contained in the "cloud" via the

Internet with its laptop, tablet, smartphone, or other computing device. By accessing software applications and data in this manner, a client may save substantial computing costs because it need not purchase its own software site licenses and/or data storage hardware. However, this decision is not without risk because data security, service interruptions, and data migration issues can occur. Control procedures must be designed to ensure the completeness and accuracy of the informational flows to and from the cloud and so that data security within the cloud is ensured.

With this important background information, it is now time to consider exactly how an audit team would test entirely automated controls within an IT environment. Recall that when auditing in an IT environment, it is necessary for audit teams to evaluate the operating effectiveness of controls that are relied upon in the computerized processing of transactions. Recall from Chapter 5 that the four methods of testing the operating effectiveness of controls: (1) inquiry, (2) observation, (3) inspection of documentation, and (4) reperformance. Refer to Exhibits H.6 (for general controls) and H.7 (for automated application controls) for examples of how audit teams can use these methods to test the operating effectiveness of both categories of automated controls.

You will note that many of the methods used to test general controls and automated application controls in Exhibits H.6 and H.7 are similar to tests of controls in a manual processing environment; these tests are necessary because of potential sources of misstatement that are introduced when computerized processing is undertaken.

EXHIBIT H.6
Methods of Testing General Controls

Type of Control	Method of Testing
Program development	• Inspect documentation related to the development of programs
Program change	• Inspect documentation related to proper authorization for program changes and implementation of those changes
Computer operations	• Inspect documentary evidence regarding the use of backup and file reconstruction techniques
Access to programs and data	• Inspect documentary evidence related to authorization for accessing programs and data • Observe the use of passwords required to access programs and data

EXHIBIT H.7
Methods of Testing Automated Application Controls

Type of Control	Method of Testing
Input	• Inquire, observe, or inspect documentary evidence regarding the use of various input controls (check digits, batch totals, hash totals, etc.) • Inspect documentary evidence related to the resolution of errors identified by input controls
Processing	• Inquire, observe, or inspect documentary evidence that the client periodically tests programs for processing accuracy • Through reperformance, test the client's programs for processing accuracy • Inquire, observe, or inspect documentary evidence regarding the use of various processing controls (file and operator controls, run-to-run totals, etc.) • Inspect documentary evidence related to the resolution of errors or unusual conditions identified during processing
Output	• Inquire, observe, or inspect documentary evidence that the client reviews output for reasonableness • Inspect documentary evidence related to the use of control total reports and reconciliation of those reports to input and run-to-run totals • Inspect documentary evidence related to authorization for changes in master file information • Observe, inquire, or inspect documentary evidence related to limited distribution of output to identified users

Of course, audit teams should also evaluate how the client's programs actually process data as part of their tests of controls. Since this processing occurs at the transaction level, the audit team commonly uses a type of reperformance testing in order to evaluate the transaction level data processing. The approach is referred to as the **test data approach**. In order to employ this approach, the auditor creates a set of data which is designed to simulate a series of transactions which contain known errors. The audit team then processes the test data set through the client's IT system under their control in a manner that mirrors how real data would be processed by the client's IT system. In constructing the test data set, the auditor must do so in a manner that will allow the audit team to determine whether the client's control activity is operating effectively within the IT system.

For example, the audit team can evaluate the operating effectiveness of a client's input control activity by creating test data transactions that contain known error conditions (e.g., using an invalid account number in a sales transaction or using the exact same document number in two different transactions). Another example of the test data approach is often referred to as a *test of one*. The reason that it is called a test of one is because the audit team need only test each attribute of a particular control activity once to have enough evidence to conclude that the control is operating effectively. More specifically, because a client's IT system processes transactions in the same manner every time, once the audit team is satisfied based on testing performed that an automated internal control activity operates effectively, there is no need to test the control activity again.

Consider a test of operating effectiveness for an automated three-way match control that is a key control activity in an audit client's purchasing process. Recall from Chapter 8, the three-way match control activity is designed to make sure that before a payment is made to a vendor, a purchase order (indicating the purchase was authorized) is matched to an appropriate receiving report from the warehouse (indicating that the client received the merchandise), which is matched to an invoice from the vendor (indicating the amount to be paid). Once these three documents are matched, a payment can be made to the vendor.

In today's audit environment, this control activity is commonly executed in an entirely automated manner. More specifically, the audit client's IT system would match the details of an automated purchase order, an automated receiving report, and an electronic vendor invoice. If the three "documents" match, the vendor payment would be approved. However, if there was a missing document or one of the documents did not match, the transaction would be listed on an exception report that would have to be followed up on by an employee at the client before the vendor payment would be approved.

Exhibit H.8 illustrates how the automated component of the control could be tested with a test data approach. To do so, the audit team would have to create a test data set that included one transaction file where the purchase order, receiving report, and vendor invoice all matched; one transaction file where the purchase order was missing or incorrect; one transaction file where the receiving report was missing or incorrect; and one transaction file where the vendor invoice was missing or incorrect. Once the test data set was created, the audit team would then process the data through the client's system and observe that the first transaction file was in fact approved for payment, while the other three transactions would be listed on the exception report.

EXHIBIT H.8
Test Data Approach—
Test of One

The Test Data Approach Purchasing Cycle—3 Way Match					
		1	2	3	4
3-Way Match	Purchase Order	✓	Missing/Incorrect	✓	✓
	Receiving Report	✓	✓	Missing/Incorrect	✓
	Vendor Invoice	✓	✓	✓	Missing/Incorrect
Exception Report	Was the Exception Included in Exception Report?	No	Yes	Yes	Yes

☑ REVIEW CHECKPOINTS

H.21 What are test data, and how are they used to test a client's automated controls?

H.22 What are the four types of audit procedures that are used by audit teams to test the operating effectiveness of controls?

END-USER COMPUTING AND OTHER ENVIRONMENTS

LO H-6
Describe the characteristics and control issues associated with end-user and other computing environments.

As the storage and computation capacities of personal computers, laptops, tablets, and other portable computing devices have increased dramatically in recent years, more and more of the day-to-day program development activities have become the responsibility of those individuals (end users) who use the programs in the entity's daily operations. Because of their proliferation, personal computing devices cannot be neglected in the assessment of control risk (and risk of material misstatement). These environments range from commonly available software applications and spreadsheets to sophisticated programs tailored to a specific company's needs.

End-user computing environments introduce the following control issues that audit teams must consider:

1. *Lack of separation of duties.* Within the accounting function, individuals may be in a position to initiate and authorize source documents, enter data, operate the computer, and distribute output reports. Within the computer function, small entities may fail to separate the functions of programming and operations. This lack of separation of duties often occurs because of a lack of resources, not the entity's indifference with respect to internal control.

2. *Lack of physical security.* Computers and files often are located in end-user departments, not in a separate, secured area. As a result, access to computer terminals as well as programs and data files (which may be stored on universal serial bus (USB) drives and other portable storage devices) may not be properly restricted.

3. *Lack of program documentation and testing.* Because users often modify or adapt existing programs for their own use, end-user computing environments are often characterized by a lack of appropriate program documentation and testing.

4. *Limited computer knowledge.* The extensive reliance on packaged software and utility programs in end-user environments may result in personnel having limited computer knowledge.

It should be noted that the use of spreadsheets is common in the financial reporting process. As a result, it is important that entities have controls related to this use. As the following Auditing Insight "Be Careful with Spreadsheets" illustrates, one most always be cautious.

 **AUDITING INSIGHT** Be Careful with Spreadsheets

One important consideration in an end-user computing environment is the ability to protect access to data in spreadsheets and other financial databases, especially when multiple users share these spreadsheets. A recent academic article suggests that spreadsheet errors remain quite common with even some of the largest companies being victimized by spreadsheet errors. Among the companies referenced include **Eastman Kodak Company, Barclays PLC, J.P. Morgan & Co.** and even the **London Olympic Organizing Committee.** The article points out that in "most cases, a careful review of the spreadsheets would have detected the errors and avoided these massive losses." Among a host of recommendations, the authors emphasize the importance of carefully evaluating "spreadsheet processes" while also assessing "the risk of spreadsheet errors" and testing "spreadsheet controls."

Source: P. Bagley, B. Barnes, and N. Harp. "Evaluating Risk and Processing Integrity Controls over Spreadsheets: An Educational Case," *Issues in Accounting Education*, Vol. 34, No. 3, August 2019, pp. 21–40.

End-User Computing Control Considerations

Most of the control issues noted in the previous section result from the lack of separation of duties and automated controls. It follows that most of the audit team's control considerations and techniques are designed to overcome these deficiencies. Audit teams should consider the entire control system, including manual controls, and look for compensating control strengths that could offset apparent weaknesses. This section discusses four such types of controls: computer operations controls, data entry controls, processing controls, and systems development and modification controls.

Computer Operations Controls

An end-user computing environment is similar to the one-person bookkeeping department because a small number of individuals perform the systems analysis, systems design, and programming operations. The main controls involve limiting the concentration of functions (to the extent possible) and establishing the proper supervision over individuals performing these functions.

With respect to separation of duties, important compensating controls that increase the likelihood of accurate processing include (1) comparison of manual control totals with totals from computer output and (2) careful inspection of output for accuracy. In addition, some of the following operations controls may be useful in this regard:

- Joint operation of computerized processing by two or more individuals.
- Rotation of assigned duties among individuals.
- Comparisons of computer use time to averages or norms and investigation of excess usage.
- Proper supervision of computer operations.
- Required vacations for all individuals.

Data Entry Controls

In end-user computing environments, the most important controls are those over online data entry (accounting transactions). Some of these controls include

- *Restrictions on access to input devices.* Common controls used to restrict access to input devices include (1) locking terminals; (2) requiring the use of passwords to access files, initiate changes, and access programs; and (3) using automatic terminal logoff which will terminate the link between the computer and the system after a specified period of time.
- *Standard screens and computer prompting.* Computers can be programmed to produce a standard screen format when a particular function is accessed. The operator must complete all blanks as prompted by the computer, thus ensuring that complete transactions are entered before they are submitted for processing.
- *Online editing and sight verification.* The input edit and validation controls discussed previously can be programmed to occur at the time of input. In some installations, the data on the screen are not released until they have been sight verified and the operator signals the computer to accept the entire screen. This control allows input errors to be detected prior to submission of the related data for processing.

Given the extensive use of laptop computers and other personal computing devices, an additional control consideration is to pay careful attention to the safety and security of your own personal computing devices. And, as illustrated in the following Auditing Insight, "Do Not Leave Your Laptop in the Car," you must always be careful when traveling with your personal computing devices.

The extensive use of laptop computers and other personal computing devices introduces issues because of the potential for theft and the loss of significant data if the machine itself is stolen or lost. Some recent examples of significant data losses include

- **Truman Medical Centers** suffered a data break involving more than 114,000 patients due to a laptop theft from an employee's car.
- **Health Share of Oregon** lost control of more than 650,000 of its members' personal information including names, phone numbers, dates of birth, and Social Security numbers due to a stolen laptop computer.

- **Coplin Health Systems** had to notify 43,000 of its patients about the theft of a laptop which potentially compromised patient names, Social Security numbers, and medical data that were not encrypted.

Sources: "Data of 43,000 patients breached after theft of unencrypted laptop," *Health Care IT News* January 12, 2018 (online source); "New Healthcare Breach Blamed On Stolen Laptop," *IT Solutions of Southern Florida* February 11, 2020 (online source); "A Stolen Laptop Contained Data For More Than 114,000 Patients At Truman Medical Centers," *Kansas City Business Journal,* December 18, 2019 (online source).

Processing Controls

Important controls to ensure the appropriate processing of data include the following:

- *Transaction logs.* Transaction entry through the terminal should be captured automatically in a computerized log. The transaction logs (for each terminal or each class of terminals) should be summarized into the equivalent of batch totals (record counts, batch totals, or hash totals).
- *Control totals.* Master files should contain records that accumulate the number of records and batch totals. The update processing should automatically change these control records.
- *Data comparisons.* The summary of daily transactions and the master file control totals from the computer should be compared to manual control totals maintained by the accounting department.
- *Audit trail.* The transaction logs and periodic dumps of master files should provide an audit trail and means for recovery. In addition, nearly all computer installations have systems software that can provide a log of all files accessed and all jobs processed.

Systems Development and Modification Controls

In our discussion of general controls, we discussed the importance of program development and program change controls. In end-user computing environments, many application programs are purchased from computer manufacturers or software vendors not completely familiar with online control techniques. Purchased programs should be reviewed carefully and tested before implementation. It is particularly important that end users evaluate whether these programs meet their processing needs. The client should carefully test those programs developed internally within the client (as well as subsequent modifications to them). In addition, because end users may create these programs, it is important that adequate documentation exists to allow others to use the program and make subsequent modifications.

Service Organizations

Because of a relative lack of expertise and a cost–benefit analysis, organizations (referred to as a *user entity*) may outsource specialized data processing to other organizations (referred to as *service organizations*). In such cases, specialized transactions (payroll is a common example) are processed in an IT environment that is remotely located from the user entity's premises. The proliferation of "cloud computing" and growing use of these services is likely to increase the extent to which data and transactions are processed at locations other than the client's premises. Given this trend, the various IT controls discussed throughout this module are often not able to be tested directly by the user entity's audit team. As a result, the audit team must gain comfort about the operating effectiveness of these controls in a different manner.

In cases such as this, the user entity's auditors most commonly obtain a report from the service organization's auditors (i.e., an service organization control (SOC) report). It is important to note that the user entity's auditors must still evaluate controls that are related to the service organization's computerized processing of transactions. However, this evaluation considers the procedures performed and results obtained by the service organization's auditors. These type of arrangements and the reports on controls over processing at service organizations are discussed in both Module A and Module I.

☑ REVIEW CHECKPOINTS

H.23 Which important duties are generally *not* separated in end-user computing environments?

H.24 What are the major control issues in end-user computing environments?

H.25 What control procedures can be used to achieve control over computer operations in an end-user computing environment? What control procedures can be used to achieve control over computerized processing in an end-user computing environment?

COMPUTER ABUSE AND COMPUTER FRAUD

LO H-7
Define and describe computer fraud and the controls that can be used to prevent it.

As technology has advanced, so has the ease and speed with which fraud can be perpetrated. Just as criminals use the Internet to commit "cybercrimes" in many forms (such as introducing computer viruses, hacking, committing cybertheft, spamming, phishing, creating evil twins, and performing credit scams and Ponzi schemes), corporate wrongdoers use computers to perform their schemes. Computer experts generally agree that an ingenious programmer can commit theft or misappropriation of assets that is difficult, if not impossible, to detect. Even the use of technology as simple as a spreadsheet can provide fraudsters with an avenue to commit fraud. The accompanying Auditing Insight "Billions of Dollars of Losses," information about the characteristics of computer fraud that can often lead to substantial financial losses.

 AUDITING INSIGHT | Billions of Dollars of Losses

Can an email scam really cost a company billions of dollars? That is exactly what the FBI asked in 2018 when tallying business losses from a scam known as business email compromise (BEC). In fact, as of mid-2018, the estimated global losses to BEC were $12.5 billion with nearly 79,000 companies reporting losses since the FBI began tracking the scam back in 2013.

While there are a number of schemes, the scam most frequently targets finance departments at large companies. Typically, a staff member receives an urgent email, supposedly from the CEO or CFO of the company. The email is usually received when the executive is out of town and will often ask the staff member to wire transfer an amount for a special project or special payment to a vendor. In most cases, the forgeries used by criminals are perfectly aligned with the company's policies and procedures and invoice templates.

What can be done? Well, at the core, the scam involves someone impersonating an authority figure so it is important that finance department staff be diligent in making sure it is a legitimate request. It may not be easy, but failure to do so can cost your company billions!

Source: "Finance Faces Off With Business Email Compromise," *Financial Management,* June 3, 2019 (online source).

Computer fraud is a matter of concern for entities, investors, and audit teams. Experts in the field have coined two definitions related to computer chicanery: *Computer abuse* is the broad definition, but *computer fraud* is probably the term used more often. Both terms involve the use of information technology by a perpetrator to achieve a gain at the expense of a victim.

Computer abuse and fraud include such diverse acts as intentional damage to or destruction of a computer and the use of the computer to assist in a fraud. Perpetrators of the financial fraud at the **Equity Funding Corporation of America** used a computer to print thousands of fictitious records and documents that otherwise would have occupied the time of hundreds of clerks. Still other incidents involving **LinkedIn, Target, Home Depot, Sony Corp. Hilton Hotels, Tesco Bank, and Chipotle** illustrate that, despite significant efforts that have been enacted to prevent cyberattacks, these incidents continue to be a significant threat to businesses and their customers' information.[5] Not surprisingly, as discussed in the following Auditing Insight "Disclosure of Cybersecurity Risks: An Opportunity for CPAs," given the extent and potential magnitude of cyberattacks, the SEC wants issuers to disclose their cybersecurity risks, which of course provides an opportunity for CPAs.

AUDITING INSIGHT · Disclosure of Cybersecurity Risks: An Opportunity for CPAs

It has become clear that cybersecurity risks are significant to investors. As a result, the SEC does require issuers to disclose their risks related to cybersecurity. Since these firms routinely rely on technology to interact with their clients and to conduct normal business operations, "cybersecurity presents ongoing risks and threats to our capital markets and to companies operating in all industries, including public companies regulated" by the SEC.

While the SEC fully recognizes that incidents related to cybersecurity can result from simple mistakes or deliberate attacks, either way, the risks to business operations and company reputation can be substantial. For issuers that are attacked, significant costs can occur including repair of the systems that were attacked, costs of remediation to customers, additional hiring and consulting costs. Given the potential impact to issuers, the SEC believes "that it is critical that public companies take all required actions to inform investors about material cybersecurity risks and incidents in a timely fashion."

Always trying to help their clients achieve their strategic business objectives, CPAs are working hard to respond to this market opportunity. In fact, the AICPA has issued a "cybersecurity reporting framework" which is specifically designed to help clients better describe their risk management program related to cybersecurity and to help CPAs evaluate the internal control activities that their clients have put in place within their programs. In addition, CPAs are well positioned to help their clients recover from cyberattacks if they do occur. For example, CPAs can assist their clients in developing a proactive business continuity plan that is designed to help companies avoid the most negative consequences that can occur if they are in fact victimized by a cyberattack.

Sources: *Commission Statement and Guidance on Public Company Cybersecurity Disclosures,* SEC: 17 CFR Parts 229 and 249; Release Nos. 33-10459; 34-82746. February 26, 2018; "Cybersecurity: A New Engagement Opportunity," *The Journal of Accountancy,* October 2017 (online source); "Helping Clients Build a Cyberattack Recovery Plan," *The Journal of Accountancy,* December 2021 (online source).

Overall, computer financial frauds range from the crude to the complex, and they hit financial institutions with alarming frequency. Moreover, computer financial frauds are frustratingly difficult for auditors to detect in the ordinary course of business. Nevertheless, and not surprisingly, clients are very interested in how to best protect themselves from these type of crimes, which is a topic discussed in the next section.

Preventive, Detective, and Damage-Limiting Controls

Entities can implement control procedures designed to prevent and detect computer frauds and to limit the extent of damage from them. Prevention controls keep errors and frauds from entering the system. Detection controls are designed to discover frauds should they get past the prevention controls. Damage-limiting controls are designed to limit the damage if a fraud does occur. For example, transaction limit amounts restrict the amount of an individual fraudulent transaction to a preset tolerable amount. Some example prevention, detection, and damage limitation controls are presented in Exhibit H.9.

As shown in Exhibit H.9, controls can be classified across three different levels: (1) administrative, (2) physical, and (3) technical. The *administrative level* refers to general controls that affect the management of an entity's computer resources. These controls

[5]"Hacked: A Special Report" *Fortune,* July 1, 2017.

EXHIBIT H.9
Protecting the Computer from Fraud (Selected Controls)

	Objective of Control		
	Prevention	**Detection**	**Damage Limiting**
Administrative Controls			
Security checks on personnel	X		
Separation of duties	X		
Access and execution log records (properly reviewed)		X	
Program testing after modification		X	
Rotation of computer duties		X	X
Transaction limit amounts			X
Physical Controls			
Inconspicuous location	X		
Controlled access	X		
Computer room guard (after hours)	X		
Computer room entry log record	X	X	
Preprinted limits on documents (e.g., checks)			X
Data backup storage			X
Technical Controls			
Data encryption	X		
Access control software and passwords	X		
Transaction logging reports		X	
Control totals (batch and hash totals)	X	X	
Program source comparisons (of versions of programs)		X	
Range checks on permitted transaction amounts			X
Reasonableness checks on permitted transaction amounts			X

are similar in nature to the entity's control environment and relate to the individuals employed by the entity and limitations on the nature and scope of activities they perform.

The *physical controls* affect the computer equipment and related documents. The "inconspicuous location" control simply refers to placing computing devices out of the way of casual traffic. Of course, the equipment used daily must be available in employees' workplaces, but access must be controlled to prevent unauthorized persons from simply sitting down and invading the system and its data files.

Technical controls include some matters of electronic wizardry. Data encryption techniques convert information to scrambled form or code so that it looks like garbled nonsense when transmitted or retrieved from a file. In recent years, industrial spying has increased. Businesses should assume that public and private intelligence services intercept and analyze data submitted by wire and airwaves (e.g., satellite transmission) for the purpose of commercial advantage. Elaborate password software is necessary to thwart unscrupulous industrial spies who try to break into an entity's computerized processing system. (Hackers have been known to program telephones to call random numbers to find a computerized processing system and then try millions of random passwords to try to get in!) *Programmed range and reasonableness checks* refer to computer monitoring of transaction processing to try to detect potentially erroneous or fraudulent transactions. These are the equivalent of the low-tech imprint you may have seen on some negotiable checks (e.g., "Not negotiable if over $500").

Computer Forensics

Computer forensics is one of the fastest growing areas of fraud investigation. The **Federal Bureau of Investigation** (FBI) defines computer forensics as "the science of acquiring, preserving, retrieving, and presenting data that have been processed electronically and stored on computer media." In other words, when computer hard drives are used as storage media, evidence can be retrieved even when the data have been deleted. Computer forensics has proven useful in tracking terrorists, prosecuting child pornographers, and in murder investigations. The FBI has also used computer forensics to successfully identify the creators of several widespread computer viruses.

While computer forensics relates to cybersecurity, it is quite different in its objective. Specifically, cybersecurity is focused on prevention by helping to protect an entity's technological infrastructure from a cyberattack. This is contrasted with a computer forensics team who would be called upon to detect the individual or group that was responsible for a cyberattack when it has already occurred. Given the extent of cybercrime, there are substantial employment opportunities within these areas for interested students.

☑ REVIEW CHECKPOINTS

H.26 Identify physical controls, technical controls, and administrative controls that protect computerized processing systems from fraud.

H.27 What is computer forensics? How can it be used in fraud investigation?

Summary

When completing the financial statement audit, it is absolutely essential for staff auditors to gain an understanding for how a client is using information technology in their financial reporting process. When gaining an understanding, the auditor must identify each of the information technology dependencies within each aspect of the financial reporting process. This process includes answering questions like, what is the nature of the information produced by the entity's systems that are necessary in the financial reporting process? And, what must the auditor do to validate the completeness and accuracy of this information?

In this module, we described how audit teams consider the IT controls that have been implemented by the client as part of their internal control system. We then discussed how audit teams test the operating effectiveness of such IT controls. These steps are an integral part of the audit team's overall assessment of control risk and the corresponding risk of material misstatement for each relevant assertion related to each significant account. Ultimately, this risk assessment will affect the nature, timing, and extent of the audit team's substantive procedures.

Two primary types of IT controls exist. General controls apply to all application systems and have a pervasive effect on the client's IT system. Major categories of these controls include program development controls, program change controls, computer operations controls, and access to programs and data controls. Automated application controls are implemented with respect to the automated transaction processing of specific types of transactions and include input controls, processing controls, and output controls.

The ultimate goal of the tests of IT controls is to reach a conclusion about the operating effectiveness of the IT control procedures in the computing environment. This conclusion allows audit teams to assess control risk (and risk of material misstatement) and determine the nature, timing, and extent of other substantive procedures for auditing the relevant assertions about the significant accounts. This control risk assessment decision is particularly crucial in an IT environment because subsequent work can be performed by auditors using information produced by the entity when the auditor has gained comfort over the IT system.

Not all businesses use large-scale systems, so this module included an end-user environment orientation to information processing systems. Audit teams must be aware of the typical control problems associated with such installations as well as concerns when end users develop their own applications. This module concludes with a section on computer fraud and computer forensics. Although computer financial frauds range from the crude to the complex, they are frustratingly difficult to detect in the ordinary course of business. Computer forensics provides a tool to help audit teams in their efforts to detect computer fraud and abuse.

Key Terms

access to programs and data controls: A type of general control that provides reasonable assurance that access to programs and data is granted only to authorized users, 880

audit trail: The chain of evidence provided through coding, cross-references, and documentation connecting account balances and other summary results with the original transaction source documents, 876

automated application controls: Controls applied to specific business activities within a computerized processing system to address management assertions regarding the financial statements; major categories are input controls, processing controls, and output controls, 879

computer forensics: The science of acquiring, preserving, retrieving, and presenting data that have been processed electronically and stored on computer media, 902

computer operations controls: A type of general control that provides reasonable assurance that (1) the processing of transactions through the computerized processing system is in accordance with the entity's objectives, (2) processing failures are resolved on a timely basis and do not affect or unnecessarily delay the processing of other transactions within the batch, and (3) actions are taken to facilitate the backup and recovery of important data when the need arises, 882

control total: Totals that are determined prior to data input and compared to totals that are generated following input; ensure that all entries were made, no entries were inadvertently made more than once, and entries were accurately made, 889

general controls: Controls that apply to all application systems and help ensure their continued proper operations. Major categories of general controls are program development controls, program change controls, computer operations controls, and access to programs and data controls, 879

information technology (IT) dependencies: Refers to the extent that a key control activity is dependent on the IT system for its effective operation. For each key control activity identified by the auditor, its dependency on the IT system must be carefully determined in order to properly test its operating effectiveness, 875

input control: A type of automated application control designed to provide reasonable assurance that data received for processing by the computer department have been properly authorized and accurately entered or converted for processing, 887

output control: A type of automated application control that is concerned with detecting errors following processing and providing reasonable assurance that only authorized persons receive output or have access to files produced by the system, 889

processing control: A type of automated application control designed to provide reasonable assurance that data processing has been performed accurately without any omission or duplicate processing of transactions, 888

program change control: A type of general control implemented to provide reasonable assurance that requests for modifications to existing programs (1) are properly authorized, conducted in accordance with entity policies, and support the entity's financial reporting requirements; (2) involve appropriate users in the program modification process; (3) are tested and validated prior to being placed into operation; and (4) have been appropriately documented, 881

program development control: A type of general control implemented to provide reasonable assurance that (1) acquisition or development of computer programs and software is properly authorized, is conducted in accordance with entity policies, and supports the entity's financial reporting requirements; (2) appropriate users participate in the software acquisition or program development process; (3) programs and software are tested and validated prior to being placed into operation; and (4) all software and programs have appropriate documentation, 883

systems development life cycle (SDLC): Process used to plan, develop, and implement new computerized processing systems, 883

system-generated reports: Any report that is generated by the audit client's information system that is used to execute its internal control procedures or produce its financial statements. It is important to test that each system-generated report is complete and accurate if it is being used for either of these purposes, 885

test data approach: When using the test data approach, auditors will create a set of test data which will be processed by the client's computer programs under the auditor's control. The data is created based on the objective of the control in a manner that allows the auditor to test whether the control activity is operating effectively. The auditor always maintains control over the processing of the test data, 895

Multiple-Choice Questions for Practice and Review

Mc Graw Hill Connect All applicable Exercises and Problems are available with *Connect*.

LO H-2

H.28 In which of the following circumstances would an auditor expect to find that an entity had implemented automated controls to reduce risks of misstatement?

    a. When errors are difficult to predict.

    b. When misstatements are difficult to define.

    c. When large, unusual, or nonrecurring transactions require judgment.

    d. When transactions are high volume and recurring.

(AICPA adapted)

LO H-3

H.29 An example of a program in which the audit team would be most interested in testing automated application controls is a(n)

    a. Payroll processing program.

    b. Operating system program.

    c. Data management system software.

    d. Utility program.

LO H-3

H.30 Which of the following is not an example of an input control?

    a. Valid sign tests.

    b. Hash totals.

    c. Run to run totals.

    d. Check digits.

LO H-1

H.31 Which of the following is true with respect to fraud risk factors in an IT environment?

    a. Employees in an IT environment are highly skilled.

    b. Audit teams cannot evaluate the accounting information system during the year.

    c. Higher dollar amounts are involved in an IT environment.

    d. Employees have increased access to information systems and computer resources in an IT environment.

LO H-2

H.32 Controls used in the management of a computer center to minimize the possibility of using an incorrect file or program are

    a. Control totals.

    b. Record counts.

    c. Limit checks.

    d. External labels.

LO H-4

H.33 The difference between assessing control risk for IT control activities versus assessing control risk for manual control activities is best described as follows:

    a. In a manual environment it is important for the auditor to gain an understanding of the internal control activity before assessing control risk.

b. In an IT environment, it is not important to gain an understanding of the internal control activity before assessing control risk.

c. In an IT environment, it is likely that control risk will be assessed as low on largely all audit engagements.

d. The assessment process that needs to be undertaken for IT controls is essentially the same as would be taken for manual controls.

LO H-1

H.34 The client's computerized exception reporting system helps audit teams conduct a more efficient audit because it

a. Condenses data significantly.

b. Highlights abnormal conditions.

c. Decreases the necessary level of tests of computer controls.

d. Is an efficient computer input control.

LO H-5

H.35 Audit teams use the test data method to gain certain assurances with respect to

a. Input data.

b. Machine capacity.

c. Control procedures contained within the program.

d. General controls.

LO H-5

H.36 When using test data, why are audit teams required to prepare only one transaction to test each IT control?

a. The speed and efficiency of the computer results in reduced sample sizes.

b. The risk of misstatement is typically lower in an IT environment.

c. Audit teams generally perform more extensive substantive testing in an IT environment, resulting in less need to test processing controls.

d. In an IT environment, each transaction is handled in an identical manner.

LO H-5

H.37 Audit teams can obtain evidence of the proper functioning of password access control to a accounting information system by

a. Writing a computer program that simulates the logic of an effective password control system.

b. Selecting a random sample of the client's completed transactions to check the existence of proper authorization.

c. Attempting to sign on to the accounting information system with a false password.

d. Obtaining representations from the client's computer personnel that the password control prevents unauthorized entry.

LO H-5

H.38 When processing controls within the IT environment may not leave visible evidence that could be inspected by audit teams, the teams should

a. Make corroborative inquiries.

b. Observe the separation of duties of personnel.

c. Review transactions submitted for processing and compare them to related output.

d. Review the run manual.

LO H-5

H.39 Which of the following statements most likely represents a control consideration for an entity that performs its accounting using mobile computing devices?

a. It is usually difficult to detect arithmetic errors.

b. Unauthorized persons find it easy to access the computer and alter the data files.

c. Transactions are coded for account classifications before they are processed on the computer.

d. Random errors in report printing are rare in packaged software systems.

LO H-5

H.40 A customer intended to order 100 units of product Z96014 but incorrectly ordered product Z96015, which is not an actual product. Which of the following controls most likely would detect this error?

a. Check digit verification.

b. Record count.

c. Hash total.

d. Redundant data check.

LO H-6

H.41 Which of the following automated application controls would offer reasonable assurance that inventory data were completely and accurately entered?

    a. Sequence checking.

    b. Batch totals.

    c. Limit tests.

    d. Check digits.

LO H-7

H.42 Entities often implement control activities designed to prevent, detect, and limit the damage related to computer frauds. Which of the following control activities is an example of a prevention type control?

    a. Program testing controls after modification.

    b. Transaction limit controls.

    c. Controlled access type controls.

    d. Transaction log controls.

Exercises and Problems

 All applicable Exercises and Problems are available with *Connect*.

LO H-5

H.43 **Auditing Automated Controls.** You are auditing payroll for Alexander Inc., which uses computerized processing for its payroll transactions; the various steps in Alexander's system follow:

- As employees provide services, they enter the number of hours worked on time sheets that their supervisor approves at the conclusion of the pay period. Time sheets have an identifying field that indicates whether the employee is an hourly (H) or a salaried (S) employee.

- The following data are entered into the input file: (1) employee number, (2) number of hours worked, and (3) employee status (hourly versus salaried).

- For hourly employees, the number of hours worked is multiplied by the wage rate (obtained from the employee master file) to calculate gross pay. For salaried employees, the employee's salary rate is obtained from the employee master file.

- When gross pay has been determined, deductions are automatically calculated using information from the employee master file and standard deduction tables (for federal tax withholdings, FICA withholdings, and Medicare withholdings).

- Net pay is calculated by subtracting deductions from gross pay.

Required

    a. What are the primary sources of error that can occur in the accounting information system just described?

    b. How would you examine Alexander's payroll? What key controls would you evaluate?

LO H-2, H-5

H.44 **Tests of Controls: General Controls.** The audit team of Packer Company identified the following general controls in obtaining its overall understanding of Packer's internal control over the automated processing of transactions:

1. Packer has routine maintenance on its computer equipment and related technology scheduled and performed every six months.

2. Packer has formal, written systems development and documentation standards for the implementation of new programs.

3. Prior to implementing modifications to its existing programs, Packer tests and validates the program changes to ensure accurate processing.

4. Packer has automatic terminal logoff functionality on all of their personal computers.

5. Packer's computer files are protected from loss through frequent backups and storage at an off-site location.

6. Access to computer files and programs is protected through the use of passwords.

7. On a monthly basis, Packer reviews any revisions in the access rights of its employees to ensure consistency between their new job responsibilities and files and programs they may access.

Required:

Consider the four methods of testing the operating effectiveness of controls (inquiry, observation, document examination, and reperformance). For each of the preceding controls, provide an example of how Packer's audit team might choose to test the operating effectiveness of the control using the four methods of test of controls (e.g., how would the audit team use inquiry, observation, document examination, and reperformance to test control #1, routine maintenance on computer equipment and related technology?). [*Note:* Not all types of tests of controls are appropriate for testing all of the controls.]

LO H-3, H-5

H.45 **Tests of Controls: Input Controls.**   Knight Company is a medium-size manufacturing entity that uses an automated transaction system to process its customer orders. Orders are collected and processed on a daily basis in batches. In its processing of customer orders, Knight requires input of the following information into a daily customer order file (# represents a numeric field; A represents an alphabetic field):

- Customer number (###).
- Item number (AA###).
- Quantities (####).

After this information has been entered, the computer program accesses the valid customer master file to ensure that the sale is to an authorized customer and does not exceed that customer's credit limit. The program then accesses the inventory master file, verifies that the appropriate quantities are on hand, and identifies the most current price. The program then prepares an invoice by multiplying the quantities the customer ordered by the appropriate price and generates a total amount for the sale.

To prevent and detect errors during the input process, Knight has established the following controls:

1. Data entry personnel must enter a valid password to access the data entry program.
2. A check digit is appended to the customer number as a fourth digit.
3. The following control totals are manually determined prior to input and then compared to a total generated by the computer program: (a) number of records entered, (b) sum of customer numbers, and (c) sum of quantities.
4. The program rejects a customer number or inventory quantity containing an alphabetic character and any entry for item numbers having an inappropriate character in the given field. Data entry personnel are prompted to reenter the information upon rejection of the original entry.
5. Any quantities ordered in excess of 9,999 are highly unusual and require special authorization by Knight's management. Any such entries are rejected and written to a rejected order file for follow-up and authorization.
6. If data entry is attempted for a customer whose number is not in the customer master file (either a new customer or an erroneous entry for an existing customer), the transaction is rejected and written to a rejected order file. Depending on the reason for the invalid customer number, a credit check is conducted (if an order from a new customer) or the entry is corrected (if an erroneous entry of the customer number).

Required:

Consider the four methods of testing the operating effectiveness of controls (inquiry, observation, document examination, and reperformance). For each of the preceding controls, provide an example of how Knight's audit team might choose to test the operating effectiveness of the control using the four methods of test of controls (e.g., how would the audit team use inquiry, observation, document examination, and reperformance to test control #1, use of valid passwords?). [*Note:* Not all types of tests of controls are appropriate for testing all of the controls.]

LO H-2, H-5

H.46 **Tests of Controls: Processing and Output Controls.**   Mark Company's audit team is evaluating the controls that Mark has implemented over the automated processing of payroll transactions. During the understanding and assessment stages of the audit, the following processing and output controls have been identified as being important in this processing:

1. To detect unauthorized access to payroll programs and processing, a system log is generated and reviewed on a weekly basis. This log identifies the programs that have been accessed during the past week, the individual(s) who have accessed those programs, and the time(s) during which the programs have been accessed. This log is reviewed, and any unexpected or unauthorized access is investigated immediately.

2. Control totals are determined prior to the input of data and compared to computer-generated totals following transaction processing.

3. Any gross pay calculations in excess of $25,000 per month are identified and written to a rejected transaction file for separate investigation because Mark's highest paid employee whose salary is processed through the system earns $300,000 per year.

4. The system generates a report of any errors or unusual situations identified during transaction processing. This report is reviewed and any items are resolved in a timely manner, and the resolution is documented by notations made on the report.

5. Any changes to employee master file information since the last payroll period are evaluated to ensure that they have been properly authorized by the appropriate personnel.

6. The output is reviewed for reasonableness prior to distribution to users.

Required:

Consider the four methods of testing the operating effectiveness of controls (inquiry, observation, document examination, and reperformance). For each of the preceding controls, provide an example of how Mark's audit team might choose to test the operating effectiveness of the control using the four methods of test of controls (e.g., how would the audit team use inquiry, observation, document examination, and reperformance to test control #1, the generation and review of the system log?). [*Note:* Not all types of tests of controls will be appropriate for testing all of the controls.]

LO H-3

H.47 Computer Internal Control Questionnaire Evaluation.   Assume that, when conducting procedures to obtain an understanding of Denton Seed Company's internal controls, you checked "No" to the following internal control questionnaire items:

- Does access to online files require specific passwords to be entered to identify and validate the terminal user?

- Does the user establish control totals prior to submitting data for processing? (Order entry application subsystem.)

- Are input control totals reconciled to output control totals? (Order entry application subsystem.)

Required:

Describe the errors and frauds that could occur because of the weaknesses indicated by the lack of IT controls.

LO H-2

H.48 Separation of Duties and General Control Procedures.   You are engaged to examine the financial statements of Horizon Incorporated, which has its own computer installation. During the preliminary understanding phase of your study of Horizon's internal control, you found that Horizon lacked proper separation of the programming and operating functions. As a result, you intensified the evaluation of the internal control surrounding the computer and concluded that the existing compensating general controls provided reasonable assurance that the objectives of internal control were being met.

Required:

a. In a properly functioning IT environment, how is the separation of the programming and operating functions achieved?

b. What are the compensating general controls that you most likely found?

(AICPA adapted)

LO H-2, H-3, H-7

H.49 Computer Frauds and Missing Control Procedures.   The following are brief stories of actual employee thefts and embezzlements perpetrated in an IT environment.

Required:

What type of control procedure that might have prevented or detected the fraud was missing or inoperative?

a. An accounts payable terminal operator at a subsidiary entity fabricated false invoices from a fictitious vendor and entered them in the parent entity's central accounts payable/cash disbursement system. Five checks totaling $155,000 were issued to the "vendor."

b. A bank provided custodial and record-keeping services for several mutual funds. A proof-and-control department employee substituted his own name and account number for those of the actual purchasers of some shares. He used the accounting information system to conceal and shift balances from his name and account to names and accounts of the actual investors when he needed to avoid detection because of missing amounts in the investors' accounts.

c. The university's accounting information system was illegally hacked. Vandals changed many students' first name to Susan, student telephone numbers were changed to the number of the university president, grade point averages were modified, and some academic files were completely deleted.

d. A computer operator at a state-run horse race betting agency set the computer clock back three minutes. After the race was completed, he quickly telephoned bets to his girlfriend, an input clerk at the agency, gave her the winning horse and the bet amount, and won every time!

H.50 **General Controls.**   Indicate the benefits of each of the following examples of general controls.

a. The access rights granted to employees allow for appropriate segregation of duties in the accounts payable application.

b. The company schedules regular maintenance on its computer hardware.

c. The company involves users in its design of programs and selection of prepackaged software and programs.

d. New programs are tested and validated prior to being implemented.

e. Documentation is required prior to modifying existing programs using "emergency" change orders.

f. Appropriate authorization is required from the Board of Directors for any new technological platform.

g. Appropriate backup and data retention policies are implemented.

h. The access rights granted to employees are periodically reviewed and evaluated, giving consideration to known changes resulting from promotions and transfers within the company.

LO H-2

H.51 **General Controls.**   For each of the following examples of general controls, classify the control based on appropriate category (program development controls, program change controls, computer operations controls, and access to programs and data controls). In addition, for each, provide the objective of the control and one example of how audit teams might test the operating effectiveness of the control.

a. The entity requires the use of passwords and requires these passwords to be modified every three months.

b. Proper documentation exists for "emergency" change requests for programs.

c. Important files, programs, and documentation are backed up and stored in a safe, offsite location.

d. The entity involves users in the design of programs and selection of prepackaged software.

e. The entity resolves failures for transactions processed in a real-time environment on a timely basis.

f. All program development activities are consistent with the entity's needs and objectives.

g. All modifications to existing programs are properly documented.

h. Proper documentation is required for all new computer programs purchased.

i. The entity monitors which individuals access various programs and cross-checks this use against an authorized user listing.

LO H-3

H.52 **Automated Application Controls: Input Controls.**   In its automated processing system over payroll transactions, Brady Company enters the following data from its employees' attendance records (# corresponds to a numeric field; *A* corresponds to an alphabetic field):

• Employee number (###-##-####, the employees' Social Security number).

5. Once the entire batch of records has been accepted for processing, the computer program accesses the payroll master file data. Gross salary is then calculated as follows:

(a) Gross salary for hourly wage employees is determined by multiplying the number of hours worked from the transaction file by the wage rate contained in that employee's master file record.

(b) Gross salary for salaried employees is determined directly from the employee's master file record.

6. After the calculation of gross salary, information from the employee's payroll master file data as well as federal income tax and FICA withholding tables is used to calculate deductions from that employee's pay.

7. A payroll register is generated, distributed, and reviewed for reasonableness and obvious processing errors.

8. Following the review of the payroll register, funds are transferred into the account designated by the employee (for those employees who have authorized electronic transfer of funds) or paychecks are prepared and held for employees (for employees who have not authorized electronic transfer of funds).

Required:

For each of the preceding steps in Merriman's payroll processing, identify appropriate controls that the company has either implemented or should implement to ensure the authorized and accurate processing of payroll transactions.

LO H-3

H.56 Flowchart Control Points. Each number in the following flowchart identifies a control point in the computerized payroll processing system. List the control points and, for each point, describe the type of internal control procedure that should be implemented.

Flowchart Control Points

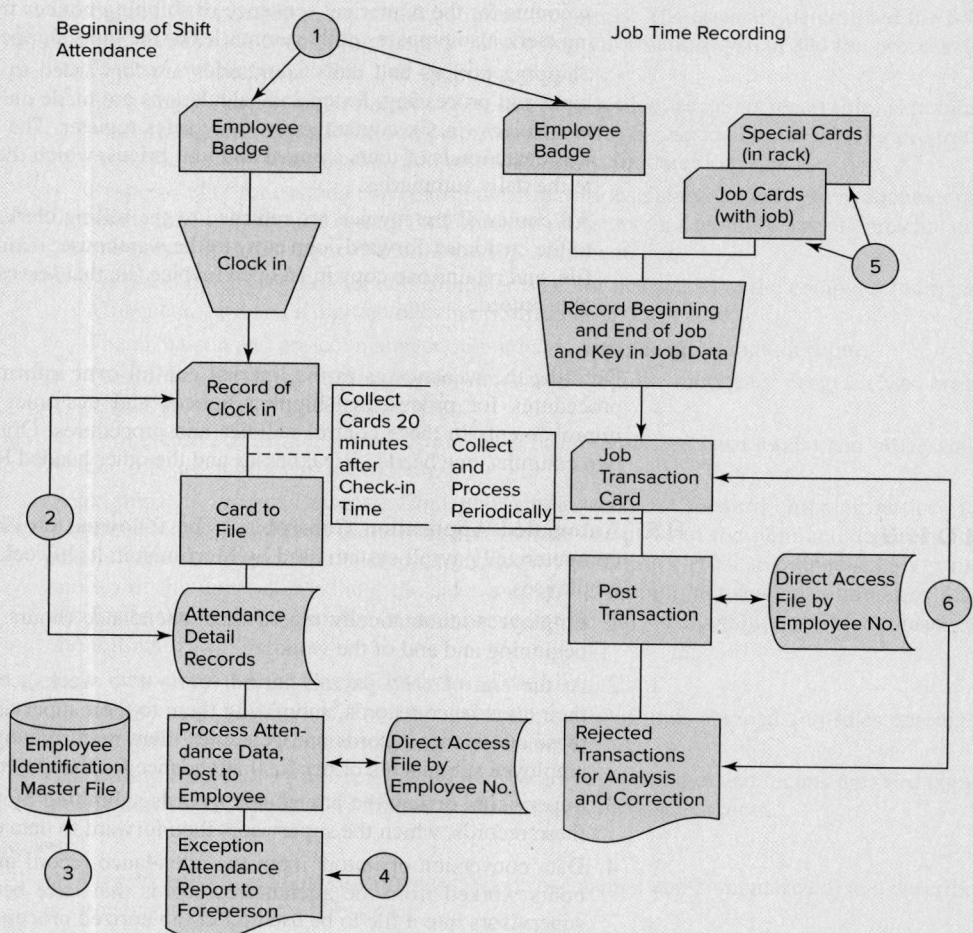

LO H-6

H.57 Internal Control Considerations in End-User Computing Environments. Because of the use of personal computers by many businesses, audit teams must know about the potential internal control weaknesses inherent in such an environment. This knowledge is crucial if audit teams are to make a proper assessment of the related control risk and to plan an effective and efficient audit approach.

Required:

In the following case study, assume that you are participating in the audit of Chicago Appliance Company and that the background information was obtained during the planning phase of the engagement. You have been asked to (a) consider the potential internal control weaknesses that exist in this end-user application and (b) assess how those internal control weaknesses could alter the audit plan for the current year.

Background Information

Chicago Appliance is a wholesale distributor of electric appliances. Its sales in each of the last two years have been approximately $40 million. All accounting applications are handled at Chicago's corporate office.

Automated processing operations have historically centered on an onsite mainframe computer. The computer applications include accounts payable and cash disbursements, payroll, inventory, and general ledger. Accounts receivable and fixed asset records have been prepared manually in the past. Internal controls in all areas have been considered strong in the last few years.

During the past year, financial management decided to automate the processing of sales, accounts receivable, and fixed asset transactions and accounting. Management also concluded that purchasing personal computers (PCs) and related available software was more cost effective than increasing the mainframe computer capacity and hiring a second computer operator. The controller and accounting clerks have been encouraged to find additional uses for the PCs and to "experiment" with them when they are not too busy.

The accounts receivable clerk is enthusiastic about the PCs, but the fixed-asset clerk seems somewhat apprehensive about them because he has limited prior experience with computers. The accounts receivable clerk explained that the controller had purchased a "very easy-to-use" accounts receivable software application program for the PC, which enables her to input the daily information regarding billings and receipts quickly and easily. The controller has added some personally developed programs to the software to give it better report-writing features.

During a recent demonstration, the accounts receivable clerk explained that the program required her to input only the customer's name and invoice amount in the case of billings or the customer's name and check amount in the case of receipts. The computer then automatically updates the respective customer's account balance. At the end of every month, the clerk prints and reconciles the accounts receivable trial balance to the general ledger balance and the controller reviews the reconciliation.

The fixed asset program also was purchased from an outside vendor. The controller indicated that the software package had just recently been put on the market and that it was programmed to compute tax depreciation based on recent changes in the federal tax laws. The controller also stated that, because of the fixed asset clerk's reluctance to use the computer, information from the manual fixed asset records had been input. The controller indicated, however, that the fixed asset clerk would be responsible for the future processing related to the fixed asset files and for generating the month-end and year-end reports used to prepare the related accounting entries.

All the various accounts receivable and fixed asset files are adequately labeled as to the type of program or data file. They are arranged in an organized manner near the PC.

(Adapted from a case contributed by PwC to *The Auditor's Report.*)

MODULE I

The Audit of Internal Control For Issuers

> *The management of all publicly-held companies are required to assess the effectiveness of their internal controls over financial reporting.*
>
> Section 404 (a) of the Sarbanes-Oxley Act of 2002

> *Whenever the amount of outstanding stock held by public investors is greater than $75 million, the auditors of all publicly-held companies are required to attest to, and report on, management's assessment of its internal controls over financial reporting.*
>
> Section 404 (b) of the Sarbanes-Oxley Act of 2002;
> The Dodd-Frank Wall Street Reform Consumer Protection Act

Professional Standards References

Topic[1]	AS Section
General Principles and Responsibilities of the Independent Auditor	1001, 1005, 1010, 1015
Audit Documentation	1215
Consideration of Fraud in a Financial Statement Audit	2401
Communications with Audit Committees	1301
Communications about Control Deficiencies in an Audit of Financial Statements	1305
An Audit of Internal Control over Financial Reporting that is Integrated with an Audit of Financial Statements	2201
Reporting on Whether a Previously Reported Material Weakness Continues to Exist	6115
Audit Planning	2101
Identifying and Assessing Risks of Material Misstatement	2110
Consideration of Materiality in Planning and Performing an Audit	2105
The Auditors' Responses to the Risks of Material Misstatement	2301
Audit Evidence	1105
Consideration of the Internal Audit Function	2605
Compliance Auditing Considerations in Audits of Recipients of Governmental Financial Assistance	6110

[1]Only PCAOB standards apply for the audit of internal control for issuers.

LEARNING OBJECTIVES

The Sarbanes-Oxley Act of 2002 was passed as a direct response to a large number of material financial statement frauds that occurred in the U.S. capital markets, including Enron, WorldCom, Waste Management and Global Crossing, among many others. According to Section 404 of Sarbanes-Oxley, the management team of each issuer must first assess the effectiveness of its own internal control system over financial reporting. Next, the issuer's independent financial statement auditors must render an opinion on the design and effectiveness of the internal control system over financial reporting. It is fair to say that prior to Sarbanes-Oxley, internal control systems have never before faced so much scrutiny by so many professionals!

Remember from Chapter 5 that an important objective of the internal control system is to help ensure that the financial statement information being presented by an entity is credible and can be relied upon. Simply stated, if the internal control system is designed to produce reliable financial statements and is operating effectively, then the output of the system *should be* reliable financial statement information. This logic is the very basis for why Sarbanes-Oxley required an internal control audit to be conducted.

Given this requirement, the evaluation of an entity's internal control system is a critical objective of the financial statement audit process completed for issuers with more than $75 million of outstanding stock held by public investors. In fact, for these entities, two separate opinions must be expressed, one on the effectiveness of the internal control system and one on the reliability of the financial statements. To achieve efficiencies when auditing these entities, audit teams conduct an integrated audit process which is designed to provide evidence to support both opinions. In this module, we present an overview of the steps that need to be taken to complete the audit of the internal control systems.

Your objectives are to be able to:

LO I-1   Define and describe what is meant by *internal control effectiveness* in the context of an audit of internal control over financial reporting at an issuer.

LO I-2   Describe the responsibilities for auditors in an audit of internal control over financial reporting for issuers required by Sarbanes-Oxley and the PCAOB.

LO I-3   Define and describe the five basic components of internal control that serve as the benchmark for internal control effectiveness followed by audit teams.

LO I-4   Explain the process the audit team uses to plan and perform the audit of internal control over financial reporting.

LO I-5   Explain the process the audit team uses to evaluate identified deficiencies and determine whether a significant deficiency or material weakness exists in an audit of internal control over financial reporting at an issuer.

LO I-6   Explain the communication of internal control deficiencies to those charged with governance, such as the audit committee and other key management personnel.

LO I-7   Understand auditors' reporting responsibility for the audit of internal control over financial reporting for issuers.

INTRODUCTION

You may recall from Chapter 5 that in the early part of 2019, the SEC issued "cease and desist" orders against four issuers: **Lifeway Foods Inc., Digital Turbine Inc., CytoDyn Inc.,** and **Grupo Simec S.A.B de C.V.** One commonality shared by these entities is that they each had material weaknesses in their system of internal controls over financial reporting. But the entities also had something else in common—they had all made the decision to not correct these material weaknesses in a timely manner which led the SEC to finally take the "cease and desist" action against each entity.[2] Of course, one question that comes to mind is why an upper management team would want to allow these weaknesses to persist for up to ten years in one situation. And yet another question is why an external audit firm would allow this to happen for so long. How is this possible?

[2]"SEC Charges Four Public Companies With Longstanding ICFR Failures." Securities and Exchange Commission. January 29, 2019 (online source).

In recent years, there has been escalating conversation surrounding the substantial cost to **issuers** of implementing Sarbanes-Oxley. Corporate managers, in particular, have expressed a great deal of frustration with onerous compliance costs associated with Section 404, particularly since they have yet to see what they would consider to be commensurate returns on their investments in their internal control systems over financial reporting. One common complaint among corporate managers is that the internal control audit places too much emphasis on routine accounting entries, but the intense focus on controls also has benefits.

Therefore, the larger question may be, do the benefits of Sarbanes-Oxley Section 404 outweigh its costs? The answer to this question probably depends on one's perspective and time horizon. The two primary objectives of Congress and the Securities and Exchange Commission (SEC) are to protect investors and maintain the integrity of the securities markets. In this light, proponents believe that Sarbanes-Oxley has imposed necessary control and oversight mechanisms that will ultimately enhance audit quality, increase the likelihood of auditors detecting fraud, and improve the accuracy and reliability of financial statements. Accordingly, we propose that its long-run benefits to investors and the securities markets do indeed outweigh the costs.

However, we also want you to reach your own conclusions related to these matters. Thus, in this module, we will describe the steps and complexities involved in the audit of internal control over financial reporting. In so doing, we are hoping to provide you with the knowledge necessary for you to judge for yourselves.

LAWS, REGULATIONS & STANDARDS

LO I-1

Define and describe what is meant by *internal control effectiveness* in the context of an audit of internal control over financial reporting at an issuer.

The Securities and Exchange Act of 1934 was the first law that required issuers to maintain a system of internal controls for the accounting system. In addition, Section 404 (a) of the Sarbanes-Oxley Act of 2002 requires the management team of issuers to assess the effectiveness of its own system of **internal control over financial reporting** and Section 404 (b) requires an independent CPA firm to assess the effectiveness on its own and then attest to the effectiveness of the system of internal control over financial reporting. By holding both management and the auditor responsible for evaluating this effectiveness, Sarbanes-Oxley has imposed two separate layers of oversight that have been designed to improve the accuracy and reliability of the financial statements reported by each issuer.

Effectiveness of Internal Control

If you recall from Chapter 5, Sarbanes-Oxley defines internal control in a manner that is consistent with the Committee of Sponsoring Organization's (COSO) widely accepted definition.[3] However, the Sarbanes-Oxley definition focuses on the system of internal control over financial reporting and notes that control policies and procedures should allow:

- Records to be maintained in reasonable detail to accurately reflect transactions.
- Transactions to be recorded to permit financial statements to be prepared in accordance with GAAP.
- Transactions to be executed in accordance with authorization from the entity's management.
- Unauthorized acquisition, use, or disposition of the entity's assets to be prevented or detected on a timely basis.

When completing the assessment of the system of internal control over financial reporting, COSO is responsible for defining what is meant by internal control effectiveness. Recall that COSO publishes an integrated framework which is used by management teams and auditors as the benchmark to assess internal control effectiveness. The COSO framework defines internal control as "a process, effected by an entity's board of directors, management and other personnel, designed to provide reasonable assurance regarding the achievement of

[3]U.S. Congress, Sarbanes-Oxley Act of 2002, Pub. L. No. 107-204, 116 Stat. 745 (2002).

objectives in the following three categories: 1) reliability of financial reporting; 2) effectiveness and efficiency of operations; 3) compliance with applicable laws and regulations."[4] For purposes of Section 404 of Sarbanes-Oxley, the only relevant category is the *financial reporting category,* which is focused on the internal control objectives that are necessary to produce reliable financial reports, safeguard the entity's assets and prevent and detect fraud.

Importantly, both management and the auditors rely on the COSO framework's definition when fulfilling their responsibility relating to internal control. It should be noted by students of auditing that the use of the COSO framework as the benchmark to determine internal control effectiveness raises the bar quite high for both management and the auditors in order to ensure that internal is functioning well. In fact, when Sarbanes-Oxley was passed, the requirement to audit internal control over financial reporting was included to improve the external financial reporting process at public companies. The following Auditing Insight "The Cost and Benefits of Section 404," provides an overview of an academic research study that seeks to better understand this issue.

AUDITING INSIGHT   The Cost and Benefits of Section 404

Since the passage of Sarbanes-Oxley, much debate has taken place about the costs and benefits on Section 404b, the provision that requires auditors to opine on the internal control effectiveness of their clients.

A recent academic study focuses on this aspect of the law by attempting to measure the benefits and the costs associated with exempting small issuers from this section of the law.

In their study, the authors report a benefit of exemption as "an aggregate $388 million in audit fee savings from 2007–2014." The costs

"stem from internal control misreporting: an aggregate $719 million of lower operating performance due to non-remediation and a $935 million delay in aggregate market value decline due to the failure to disclose ineffective internal controls."

Source: W. Ge., S. Koester, and S. McVay, "Benefits and costs of Sabanes-Oxley Section 404(b) exemption: Evidence from small firms' internal control disclosures." *Journal of Accounting and Economics,* 63, pp. 358–384.

Management's Responsibility

You may remember from Chapter 11 that Section 302 of the Sarbanes-Oxley Act stipulates criminal penalties for both CEOs and CFOs if they issue materially misleading financial statements. A clear intention of this section of the act is to make sure that the upper management team takes full responsibility for establishing and maintaining a system of internal control. Simply stated, the threat of criminal penalties is usually enough to make sure that management takes their responsibility for internal control effectiveness seriously.

Management is also responsible for maintaining documentation that is sufficient to provide evidence that the system of internal control has been designed and is operating effectively. For example, such documentation needs to provide evidence regarding how important internal control decisions were considered, and ultimately how the final decisions were reached for key professional judgments. Finally, the documentation must be robust enough to allow auditors to gain an understanding of the internal control system and ultimately conduct an audit of the effectiveness of the internal control system.

In addition to requiring that the CEO and CFO certify the entity's financial statements and disclosures under Section 302, Sarbanes-Oxley requires management to assess and report on the entity's internal control over financial reporting in Section 404. Specifically, the entity's annual report must include the following:

- A statement that management is responsible for establishing and maintaining adequate internal control over financial reporting.
- A statement identifying the framework (e.g., the COSO framework) that management uses as a benchmark for evaluating the effectiveness of the entity's internal control.
- A statement providing management's assessment of the effectiveness of the entity's internal control.

[4]COSO, "Internal Contro–Integrated Framework Executive Summary," May 2013, New York: AICPA.

EXHIBIT I.1
Excerpts from Stanley Black & Decker Management Report on Internal Control over Financial Reporting

The management of Stanley Black & Decker, Inc. is responsible for establishing and maintaining adequate internal control over financial reporting. Internal control over financial reporting is a process designed to provide reasonable assurance regarding the reliability of financial reporting and the preparation of financial statements for external reporting purposes in accordance with accounting principles generally accepted in the United States of America. Because of its inherent limitations, internal control over financial reporting may not prevent or detect misstatements.

During the fourth quarter of 2021, the Company acquired the remaining 80 percent ownership stake in **MTD Holdings Inc.** ("MTD") and **Excel Industries** ("Excel") for approximately $1.5 billion and $374 million, respectively. Since Stanley Black & Decker, Inc. has not yet fully incorporated the internal controls and procedures of MTD and Excel into Stanley Black & Decker, Inc.'s internal control over financial reporting, management excluded these businesses from its assessment of the effectiveness of internal control over financial reporting as of January 1, 2022. MTD accounted for 5% of Stanley Black & Decker, Inc.'s total assets as of January 1, 2022 and 1% of Stanley Black & Decker, Inc.'s net sales for the year then ended. Excel accounted for less than 1% of Stanley Black & Decker, Inc.'s total assets as of January 1, 2022 and less than 1% of Stanley Black & Decker, Inc.'s net sales for the year then ended.

Management has assessed the effectiveness of Stanley Black & Decker, Inc.'s internal control over financial reporting as of January 1, 2022. In making its assessment, management has utilized the criteria set forth by the Committee of Sponsoring Organizations (COSO) of the Treadway Commission in Internal Control — Integrated Framework (2013 Framework). Management concluded that based on its assessment, and the existence of material weaknesses related to the accounting for equity units issued in May 2017 and November 2019, Stanley Black & Decker, Inc.'s internal control over financial reporting was not effective as of January 1, 2022. **Ernst & Young LLP,** Registered Public Accounting Firm included in this annual report, has issued an attestation report on the registrant's internal control over financial reporting.

Source: *Stanley Black & Decker Form 10-K* (filed February 22, 2022).

Under Section 302, management must also disclose any material weaknesses in internal control. If any material weaknesses exist, management cannot conclude that the entity's internal control over financial reporting is effective. See Exhibit I.1 above for excerpts from the **Stanley Black & Decker** management report on internal control over financial reporting, which identified a material weakness in its system of internal control. This report was issued in February, 2022.

Auditors' Responsibilities

Under Section 404 (b) of Sarbanes-Oxley, an audit of internal control over financial reporting is required to be completed by the independent auditor. When doing so, the audit of internal controls is integrated with the financial statement audit and must not be performed as a separate engagement. Under Sarbanes-Oxley, the PCAOB is responsible for issuing the professional standards that guide the work that the external audit team of an issuer must perform to comply with section 404 (b) of Sarbanes-Oxley. The audit team must plan and perform the audit to obtain *reasonable assurance* about whether the entity maintained effective internal controls over financial reporting. The overall focus in the professional standards is to determine whether a *material weakness* exists at the *end of the year* being reported on. If a material weakness does exist, the entity's internal control over financial reporting cannot be considered effective and the auditor is required to issue an **adverse opinion on internal control over financial reporting.** The remainder of this module is focused on the procedures that are performed by auditors when completing the audit of internal controls over financial reporting. But, before moving forward, Exhibit I.2 contains excerpts from the **Deloitte & Touche, LLP** Opinion on Internal Control over Financial Reporting for **Fannie Mae,** which identified a material weakness in its system of internal control. This report was issued on February 15, 2022.

EXHIBIT I.2
Excerpts from Deloitte & Touche's Opinion on Internal Control over Financial Reporting for Fannie Mae

To Fannie Mae:

Opinion on Internal Control over Financial Reporting

We have audited the internal control over financial reporting of Fannie Mae and consolidated entities (in conservatorship) (the "Company") as of December 31, 2021, based on criteria established in Internal Control – Integrated Framework (2013) issued by the Committee of Sponsoring Organizations of the Treadway Commission (COSO). In our opinion, because of the effect of the material weakness identified below on the achievement of the objectives of the control criteria, the Company has not maintained effective internal control over financial reporting as of December 31, 2021, based on the criteria established in Internal Control – Integrated Framework (2013) issued by COSO.

We have also audited, in accordance with the standards of the Public Company Accounting Oversight Board (United States) (PCAOB), the consolidated financial statements as of and for the year ended December 31, 2021, of the Company and our report dated February 15, 2022, expressed an unqualified opinion on those financial statements . . . .

Basis for Opinion

The Company's management is responsible for maintaining effective internal control over financial reporting and for its assessment of the effectiveness of internal control over financial reporting, included in the accompanying Management's Report on Internal Control over Financial Reporting. Our responsibility is to express an opinion on the Company's internal control over financial reporting based on our audit.

We conducted our audit in accordance with the standards of the PCAOB. Those standards require that we plan and perform the audit to obtain reasonable assurance about whether effective internal control over financial reporting was maintained in all material respects. Our audit included obtaining an understanding of internal control over financial reporting, assessing the risk that a material weakness exists, testing and evaluating the design and operating effectiveness of internal control based on the assessed risk, and performing such other procedures as we considered necessary in the circumstances. We believe that our audit provides a reasonable basis for our opinion.

Definition and Limitations of Internal Control over Financial Reporting

A company's internal control over financial reporting is a process designed to provide reasonable assurance regarding the reliability of financial reporting and the preparation of financial statements for external purposes in accordance with generally accepted accounting principles. A company's internal control over financial reporting includes those policies and procedures that (1) pertain to the maintenance of records that, in reasonable detail, accurately and fairly reflect the transactions and dispositions of the assets of the company; (2) provide reasonable assurance that transactions are recorded as necessary to permit preparation of financial statements in accordance with generally accepted accounting principles, and that receipts and expenditures of the company are being made only in accordance with authorizations of management and directors of the company; and (3) provide reasonable assurance regarding prevention or timely detection of unauthorized acquisition, use, or disposition of the company's assets that could have a material effect on the financial statements.

Material Weakness

A material weakness is a deficiency, or a combination of deficiencies, in internal control over financial reporting, such that there is a reasonable possibility that a material misstatement of the company's annual or interim financial statements will not be prevented or detected on a timely basis. The following material weakness has been identified and included in management's assessment:

- Disclosure Controls and Procedures – The Company's disclosure controls and procedures did not adequately ensure the accumulation and communication to management of information known to the Federal Housing Finance Agency (as conservator) that is needed to meet their disclosure obligations under the federal securities laws as they relate to financial reporting.

- This material weakness was considered in determining the nature, timing, and extent of audit tests applied in our audit of the consolidated financial statements as of and for the year ended December 31, 2021, of the Company and this report does not affect our report on such financial statements.

Deloitte & Touche LLP
McLean, Virginia
February 15, 2022

Source: *Fannie Mae Form 10-K* (filed February 15, 2022).

I.1 Briefly describe the purpose of the COSO framework of internal control effectiveness in the audit of internal control over financial reporting.

I.2 What are the four areas that an internal control system should allow for under the Sarbanes-Oxley Act of 2002?

I.3 What is management's responsibility for reporting on their own internal control over financial reporting?

I.4 What is the auditor's responsibility for their audit client's internal control over financial reporting.

THE AUDIT OF INTERNAL CONTROL OVER FINANCIAL REPORTING

LO I-2
Describe the responsibilities for auditors in an audit of internal control over financial reporting for issuers required by Sarbanes-Oxley and the PCAOB.

As previously stated, under Section 404 (b) of the Sarbanes-Oxley Act, an audit of the internal control system over financial reporting is required to be completed by an independent auditor. The professional standards require that the audit of internal controls over financial reporting be integrated with the financial statement audit and thus cannot be performed as a separate engagement. PCAOB Auditing Standard No. 2201 (AS 2201) details the work that the external audit team of an issuer must perform to complete an **integrated audit** that complies with Sarbanes-Oxley. As you will soon realize, the audit procedures that are required to be completed on internal control in an integrated audit are far more extensive than those in a financial statement audit for a *nonissuer* that you learned about in Chapter 5.

You may recall from Chapter 5 that when auditing a nonissuer, the audit team is required to obtain an understanding of internal controls (and document that understanding) primarily to determine the nature, timing, and extent of further substantive audit procedures to be performed. If the audit team plans to rely on the internal control system to reduce substantive procedures, they must test the controls for operating effectiveness. However, if they do not plan to rely on controls, tests of operating effectiveness are not required. In an integrated audit, tests of operating effectiveness of controls are required.

Another important difference between an audit of internal control over financial reporting on an issuer and the evaluation of internal control on a financial statement audits for a nonissuer is that the audit of internal control is conducted *as of the end of the fiscal year,* whereas, for audits of nonissuers, the audit team must understand and evaluate internal control for the *entire period* to determine its effect on the nature, timing, and extent of further substantive audit procedures. The key differences between the two types of audits are summarized in the following table.

	Audit of Internal Control Over Financial Reporting For An Issuer (following AS 2201)	Evaluation of Internal Control On A Financial Statement Audit For A Nonissuer
Scope	Test each relevant control activity each year	Test relevant control activities only if relying on them
Reporting	Opinion on the effectiveness of internal control	No opinion is issued on the effectiveness of internal control
Timing	Evaluate effectiveness of internal control as of the fiscal year-end date	Evaluate effectiveness of internal control throughout the fiscal year when determining reliance

The auditor's overarching objective when completing the audit of internal control over financial reporting is to express an opinion on the system's effectiveness. Recall from Chapter 5 that to achieve this goal, the COSO framework defines five interrelated components of a well-functioning internal control system. They are (1) control environment, (2) risk assessment, (3) control activities, (4) monitoring, and (5) information and communication. As you will now see, the COSO framework provides an all important benchmark for audit teams to consider as they plan and perform the audit of internal control over financial reporting.

Components of Internal Control over Financial Reporting

LO I-3
Define and describe the five basic components of internal control that serve as the benchmark for internal control effectiveness followed by audit teams.

To help facilitate the evaluation of internal control effectiveness, the COSO framework identifies 17 principles across the five components of internal control over financial reporting. These principles are designed to provide clarity in determining what is meant by internal control effectiveness for each component (i.e., is it present and functioning) and are used by auditors to help evaluate whether the internal control system is indeed designed and operating effectively. These principles are now used to help illustrate each of the five components in detail.

Control Environment

The control environment sets the tone of the organization. It is the foundation for all other components of internal control. It provides discipline and structure to all participants and stakeholders. Control environment factors include the integrity, ethical values, and competence of the entity's people. For purposes of evaluating an entity's control environment, the COSO framework establishes five principles which, if applied properly, should result in an effective control environment component. The five principles of the control environment component are listed in Exhibit I.3.

EXHIBIT I.3
Five Principles of the Control Environment

Principles of Control Environment as per the COSO Framework
1. The organization demonstrates a commitment to integrity and ethical values.
2. The board of directors demonstrates independence from management and exercises oversight of the development and performance of internal control.
3. Management establishes, with board oversight, structures, reporting lines, and appropriate authorities and responsibilities in the pursuit of objectives.
4. The organization demonstrates a commitment to attract, develop, and retain competent individuals in alignment with objectives.
5. The organization holds individuals accountable for their internal control responsibilities in the pursuit of objectives.

Risk Assessment

An effective internal control system will include a risk assessment process where management takes the steps necessary to identify risks, estimate their significance and likelihood, and consider how to manage the risks. In particular, the audit team must understand whether management is specifying the risks of material misstatement in financial reporting and then managing those risks, especially due to fraud. Regardless of the size of the entity, the COSO framework establishes four principles that, if applied properly, should result in an effective risk assessment component when evaluating the system of internal control. The four principles of the risk assessment component are listed in Exhibit I.4.

EXHIBIT I.4
Four Principles of the Risk Assessment

Principles of Risk Assessment as per COSO Framework
1. The organization specifies objectives with sufficient clarity to enable the identification and assessment of risks relating to objectives.
2. The organization identifies risks to the achievement of its objectives across the entity and analyzes the risks as a basis for determining how the risks should be managed.
3. The organization considers the potential for fraud in assessing risks to the achievement of objectives.
4. The organization identifies and assesses changes that could significantly impact the system of internal control.

Control Activities

Internal **control activities** are specific actions that an entity's management team and employees take to help ensure that management's directives are carried out. The professional standards require that the audit team gain an understanding of whether management has implemented control activities that are sufficient to address the risks of material misstatement for each relevant assertion related to each significant account or disclosure. The COSO framework establishes three principles that, if applied properly, should result in an effective evaluation of the control activities component. The three principles of the control activities component are listed in Exhibit I.5.

EXHIBIT I.5
Three Principles of the Control Activities

Principles of Control Activities as per COSO Framework
1. The organization selects and develops control activities that contribute to the mitigation of risks to the achievement of objectives to acceptable levels.
2. The organization selects and develops general control activities over technology to support the achievement of objectives.
3. The organization deploys control activities through policies that establish what is expected and procedures that put policies into action.

Information and Communication

The information and communication component recognizes that the system of internal control over financial reporting is dependent on high quality information for its effective operation. For example, it is absolutely essential that the information produced by the company's information system is complete and accurate, among other considerations. The COSO framework three establishes principles that, if applied properly, should result in an effective evaluation of the information and communication component. The three principles of the information and communication component are listed in Exhibit I.6.

EXHIBIT I.6
Three Principles of Information and Communication

Principles of Information and Communication as per COSO Framework
1. The organization obtains or generates and uses relevant quality information to support the functioning of internal control.
2. The organization internally communicates information, including objectives and responsibilities for internal control, necessary to support the functioning of internal control.
3. The organization communicates with external parties regarding matters affecting the functioning of internal control.

Monitoring

The importance of separate monitoring of its internal control systems. In so doing, the entity is in a position to consider changes in its operating environment that will result in continuous improvement. Effective monitoring involves regular evaluation of internal controls, preferably by an independent group such as internal auditing. Of course, the size of the entity will have an impact on how monitoring will occur. But regardless of the entity's size, the COSO framework establishes two principles that, if applied properly, should result in an effective evaluation of the monitoring component. The two principles of the monitoring component are listed in Exhibit I.7.

EXHIBIT I.7
Two Principles of
Monitoring Activities

Principles of Monitoring Activities as per COSO Framework
1. The organization selects, develops, and performs ongoing and/or separate evaluations to ascertain whether the components of internal control are present and functioning.
2. The organization evaluates and communicates internal control deficiencies in a timely manner to those parties responsible for taking corrective action, including senior management and the board of directors, as appropriate.

☑ REVIEW CHECKPOINTS

I.5   What are the differences between an audit of internal control over financial reporting on an issuer and an evaluation of internal control on a financial statement audit for a nonissuer?

I.6   How does an audit team evaluate the effectiveness of internal control over financial reporting?

I.7   How would an audit team best evaluate whether the control environment is effective at an issuer?

I.8   How would an audit team best evaluate where risk assessment is effective at an issuer?

I.9   How would an audit team best evaluate where the control activities are effective at an issuer?

I.10   How would an audit team best evaluate whether the information and communication component is effective at an issuer?

I.11   How would an audit team best evaluate whether the monitoring of internal controls is effective at an issuer?

PERFORMING THE AUDIT

LO I-4
Explain the process the audit team uses to plan and perform the audit of internal control over financial reporting.

When performing the audit of internal control over financial reporting, the audit team must always remember that the overarching objective of the audit is to express an opinion on the effectiveness of internal control over financial reporting. As described in the previous section, the audit team uses the COSO framework as a benchmark to evaluate this effectiveness. For practical purposes, the 17 principles (across the five components) illustrated in the previous section are designed to provide clarity in determining what is meant by internal control effectiveness for each component (i.e., is it present and functioning). As a result, they are routinely used by auditors in their evaluation. As we now move to the steps taken when planning the internal control audit, it is also important to point out that the five components *do not* operate independently of each other. Rather, they should be considered as working in an integrated manner to support the overall effectiveness of the internal control system.

Audit Planning

The first step in the audit process is to complete the audit plan. When doing so, the auditor must plan the audit in a manner that allows the audit team to obtain sufficient and appropriate evidence about whether internal control over financial reporting is effective in producing reliable financial statements.

To do so, the audit team must plan the audit in part to determine whether a material weakness exists in the system of internal control over financial reporting as of the fiscal year-end date. In addition, since the audit process is required to be *integrated* with the financial statement audit process, the planning of the internal control audit should reflect that there are ultimately two objectives in mind: (1) to obtain the evidence needed to support a separate opinion on internal control over financial reporting and (2) to obtain the evidence needed to support the internal control evaluation that has been made in conducting the audit of the entity's financial statements.

When completing the plan, the audit team must consider the risk that a material weakness exists when determining how much audit attention is needed in a particular area of the internal control system. The professional standards make clear that there is a direct relationship between the risk of a material weakness existing in the system and the amount of audit testing that should be completed. Thus, when determining the scope of testing, the audit team should focus their audit testing in the areas that represent the greatest risk for the existence of a material weakness.

In that spirit, the determination of significant accounts and disclosures is generally the first step when scoping the integrated audit. The audit team must evaluate controls for all *relevant assertions* related to each *significant account or disclosure*. Thus, significant accounts, disclosures, and assertions must be identified. To do so, the professional standards advocate using a top-down approach as a way to focus the audit team's attention on the threats to the integrity of the external financial reporting process. The audit team's first step in gaining an understanding of the client's internal control system should focus on entity-level controls (ELCs) because they can have a pervasive impact on control activities at the process, transaction, or application level. The team next moves down to the significant accounts and disclosures and their *relevant* assertions. By relevant, we mean that the assertion has a reasonable possibility of containing a material misstatement. The audit team is required to understand the internal control process over financial reporting. This aspect of the standard emphasizes performing a *walkthrough* of the internal control process by the audit team members. The top-down approach recommended by the professional standards is illustrated in Exhibit I.8.

EXHIBIT I.8
Top-Down Process

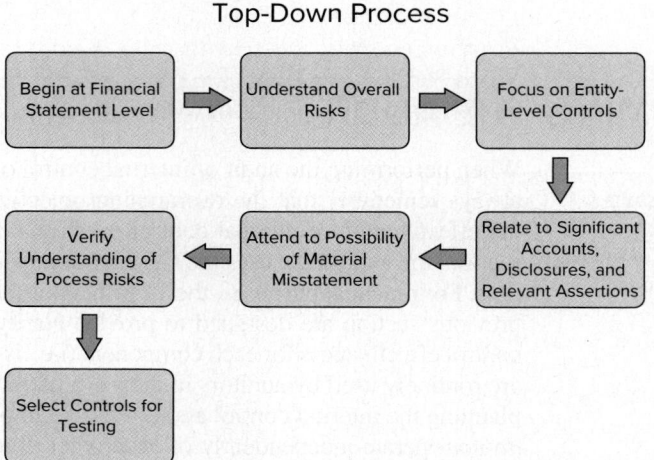

Top-Down Process

Interestingly, a difficult decision faced by the audit team when auditing internal controls over financial reporting for a global organization is the determination of which locations are significant, which would then need to be visited as part of the audit. Each location is evaluated based on size, risks, and whether risks are mitigated by entity-level controls. Overall, the key to determining whether an account, location, or assertion is significant (and included as part of the scope of the audit) is whether there is more than a remote possibility that a material misstatement could be associated with it. Just as *control risk* is used to determine the nature, timing, and extent of further audit procedures in the financial statement audit, *inherent risk* is used to determine the nature, timing, and extent of tests of controls in the audit of internal control over financial reporting.

Testing Design and Operating Effectiveness

Recall that as part of the top-down approach, the audit team must identify all significant accounts and disclosures. Next, for each significant account and disclosure, the audit team must identify all of the relevant assertions. If there is a reasonable possibility that a material misstatement could occur for an assertion about a significant account or disclosure, the assertion is deemed relevant for the internal control audit. The evaluation and testing of controls for each relevant assertion must be performed on an annual basis. As a result, after an understanding of the internal control system is gained by the audit team through inquiry, document examination, and observation, an evaluation must be made to determine whether the control activities that have been put in place by management would prevent or detect a material misstatement for each relevant assertion identified. Specifically, the audit team must determine if the controls have been *designed* effectively.

There are two steps in this process. The first is to determine whether controls have been put in place for each relevant assertion about each significant account. Stated differently, if an assertion has been evaluated as relevant, this implies that there is a reasonable possibility that a material misstatement could occur. Thus, there should be a control in place to mitigate this possibility. Next, if the control has been put in place, the auditor must determine whether it has been designed to mitigate the risk of material misstatement for the relevant assertion supported.

Once the evaluation of internal control design has been completed, the tests of *operating effectiveness* need to be completed. Tests of operating effectiveness are essentially the same as the tests of controls discussed in detail in Chapter 5. That is, a sample of transactions is examined using inquiry, observation, document examination, and reperformance. The more risk associated with a control, the more persuasive evidence is required for testing. Importantly, there is no need to test the operating effectiveness of controls if the internal control system design is not considered effective and a deficiency has already been noted. Only the control activities that are identified as mitigating the risk of material misstatement for each relevant assertion need to be tested by the audit team. However, if the control activity has been identified by the audit team as mitigating the risk of material misstatement for a relevant assertion about a significant account, it must be tested as part of the internal control audit each year. The following PCAOB Inspection Focus provides an example of an audit firm with a finding related to the testing of internal controls.

 PCAOB INSPECTION FOCUS

The PCAOB is required to perform detailed inspections of the audit process employed by each firm auditing issuers, and an inspection report is issued by the PCAOB after each inspection. If an inspection outcome warrants it, the PCAOB will even bring an "action" against an audit firm, as illustrated in the following example which highlights the importance of evaluating both internal control design and operating effectiveness:

- While the information technology (IT) auditors did make inquiries and examined documents related to the issuer's information technology general controls (ITGCs), they did not perform the procedures necessary to determine if the controls that were identified, if operating effectively, would "prevent or detect errors or fraud that could result in material misstatements." Thus, the auditors did not properly evaluate the design of the internal controls.

- In addition, the audit documentation did not include evidence that the IT auditors tested the operating effectiveness of the ITGCs. Since, the auditors did not test the "operating effectiveness of the ITGCs" the audit team "lacked the foundation for its reliance on those controls for other audit procedures" completed during the audit.

Source: *In the Matter of PKF O'Connor Davies LLP.,* Release No. 105-2022-001, *PCAOB,* January, 2022.

Recall from earlier in this chapter that management must reach their own conclusion about the effectiveness of the internal control system over financial reporting before the audit team completes their work. Therefore, there is a significant amount of internal control testing that will likely have already been completed by the internal audit department, client personnel, and sometimes even outside consultants which allowed management to reach their own conclusion about the effectiveness of the internal control system. As a result, the professional standards do encourage the audit team to use this work completed by others (e.g., internal audit) as long as they evaluate the *competence* and *objectivity* of the testers completing the work and perform independent tests of the work completed on their own. For efficiency purposes, the audit team is encouraged to take full advantage of the work completed by management, as allowed by the professional standards.

Finally, when gaining an understanding of the internal control system over financial reporting, the audit team may discover that certain areas of the system have been outsourced to a third-party service provider. For example, payroll accounting and related tax reporting is routinely outsourced to a payroll service provider (e.g., **ADP, Paychex**). In these types of situations, the design and operating effectiveness of internal controls related to the area that has been outsourced would be the responsibility of the service provider, and not the entity being audited. However, this does not mean that the audit team can ignore this area when completing the audit of internal control over financial reporting. Rather, the professional standards provide three options that audit teams can choose from when determining whether such controls are effective. They can: 1) test the user organization's controls over the service organization's activities; 2) request an SOC 1 Type 2 report; or 3) perform tests of controls at the service organization. In reality, audit teams routinely request a report on the service organization's controls to fulfill this requirement (i.e., an SOC report). SOC reporting was discussed in detail in Module A. However, for purposes of the audit of internal control over financial reporting, the audit team will have to request an SOC 1 report.

An SOC 1 report is one that is issued by an independent auditor primarily for purposes of the audit of internal controls over financial reporting. The controls that are included in scope and covered by an SOC 1 report are those controls that are likely to be relevant for the clients of the service organization. There are two types of SOC 1 reports (i.e., Type 1 and Type 2). Both reports include a description of the internal control system and an opinion on the suitability of the internal control design. However, only the Type 2 report describes the tests of operating effectiveness completed and provides an opinion on the effectiveness of such internal control testing. Thus, for internal control activities that are designed to mitigate the risk of material misstatement for each of the relevant assertions that were identified during the planning stage, the audit team is required to obtain and evaluate the Type 2 version of the SOC 1 report as part of the audit of internal control over financial reporting.

☑ REVIEW CHECKPOINTS

I.12 In an integrated audit, what are the two objectives that need to be considered when planning the internal control audit?

I.13 When completing the audit of internal control over financial reporting, the professional standards advocate using a top-down approach as a way to focus the audit team's attention on the threats to the integrity of the financial reporting process. What is meant by a top-down approach?

I.14 Explain how a test of operating effectiveness should be conducted when auditing the internal controls over financial reporting.

I.15 What is an SOC 1 report? What is the difference between a Type 1 and a Type 2 version of an SOC 1 report?

EVALUATING IDENTIFIED DEFICIENCIES

LO I-5
Explain the process the audit team uses to evaluate identified deficiencies and determine whether a significant deficiency or material weakness exists in an audit of internal control over financial reporting at an issuer.

Once the tests of design effectiveness and operating effectiveness of the internal controls have been completed, the audit team must then determine the significance of any identified deficiency discovered during testing. An **internal control deficiency**—whether resulting from a design or an operating deficiency—exists when either the design or the operation of the control under consideration does not allow the entity's management or employees to detect or prevent misstatements in a timely fashion. A *design deficiency* is a problem relating to either a necessary control that is missing, or an existing control that is so poorly designed that it fails to satisfy the control's objective. An *operating deficiency,* on the other hand, occurs when a properly designed control is either ignored or inappropriately applied (possibly because employees are poorly trained). More serious internal control deficiencies can be categorized into one of two groups—material weaknesses or significant deficiencies—depending on their severity.

Severity of Deficiency

A **material weakness** in internal control is defined as a deficiency, or combination of deficiencies, that results in a *reasonable possibility* that a *material misstatement* would not be prevented or detected on a timely basis. The following circumstances should be regarded as strong indicators that a material weakness exists:

- Restatement of previously issued financial statements to reflect the correction of a material misstatement.
- Evidence of material misstatements (identified by the audit team) that were not prevented or detected by the client's internal controls.
- Ineffective oversight of the financial reporting process by the entity's audit committee.
- Indication of fraud (either material or immaterial) by senior management.

A **significant deficiency** is a deficiency or a combination of deficiencies in internal control that is less severe than a material weakness yet important enough to merit attention by those charged with governance. The primary difference between a significant deficiency and a material weakness involves the *magnitude* of the potential misstatement that could occur and would not be detected on a timely basis. As the potential misstatement reaches overall materiality, an auditor may conclude that a material weakness exists. The final determination is always a matter of professional judgment.

Since the primary difference between a significant deficiency and a material weakness relates to the magnitude of the misstatement that could occur as a result of the control deficiency, the audit team must take great care in projecting the potential misstatement and then comparing that amount to the overall materiality. As a result, an important factor that audit teams must consider for each control deficiency identified is the volume of transaction activity related to the identified deficiency. This is a key point because the audit team has to not only consider the magnitude of any error observed in the financial statements as a result of the control deficiency but also the possibility that the error could be even larger. Of course, the audit team must also consider any compensating controls that might exist.

Compensating Controls

When determining the significance of identified deficiencies, the audit team must consider the effect of any compensating controls that may exist at the entity. A compensating control is a control activity that is relied upon because a different control is missing, has not been designed properly, or is not operating effectively. Usually, the compensating control is detective in nature and serves to mitigate the risk of material misstatement that exists due to the identified deficiency. When the audit team is forming a conclusion about whether an identified control deficiency is either a significant deficiency or a material weakness, they should evaluate the impact of any compensating controls that might exist. If the audit team determines that the compensating control would mitigate the risk of material misstatement related to the identified control deficiency, the team must test the operating effectiveness of the compensating control. As shown in the following PCAOB Inspection Focus, failure to do so can lead to an inspection finding.

PCAOB INSPECTION FOCUS

The PCAOB is required to perform detailed inspections of the audit process employed by each firm auditing issuers. A formal inspection report is issued by the PCAOB for each firm inspected. The following inspection finding relates to an audit firm's failure to test a compensating control that was identified by the client related to an identified control deficiency:

- The audit client used a number of different service organizations to host information technology systems that were used to record revenue transactions in the financial statements.

- Since the audit client had outsourced their internal controls related to these revenue transactions, personnel from the audit client were required to evaluate SOC 1 reports for different service organizations to make sure that the internal controls were operating effectively.

- As part of their internal control audit, the audit team properly identified an internal control deficiency because the audit client did not properly evaluate the SOC 1 reports.

- Although the audit team "identified and tested three compensating controls that it believed would mitigate this deficiency," the PCAOB found that the team "did not sufficiently evaluate the effect of these controls" in helping to mitigate the risk of material misstatement related to the revenue account

Source: *Report on 2020 Inspection of RSM US, LLP*, PCAOB, December 16, 2021.

In many situations, a management review control serves as the compensating control. The concept of management review controls was described in Chapter 5 but for purposes of this discussion let's consider an example of such a control that was put in place by the management team to monitor the results of their operations. Specifically, if a CFO completes comparisons of actual income statement results to budgeted results each and every month and does so in a very detailed manner, this is a control that might compensate for a specific transaction level control activity that is not operating effectively. However, for such a control to be considered effective, the audit team would have to see evidence that the CFO really did compare the budgeted income statement figures to the recorded figures and then took the action needed to follow up and investigate any differences that were above a predetermined monetary threshold. Only then would the compensating control be considered effective in mitigating the risk of material misstatement.

In practice, when the audit team evaluates whether an identified control deficiency is either a significant deficiency or a material weakness, it has become routine for an entity's management team to claim that they have a compensating control in place that mitigates the risk of material misstatement related to that identified deficiency. Remember that a significant deficiency or material weakness reflects poorly on the entity's management team and as a result, the audit team's professional judgment is quite consequential as management would like to avoid these outcomes. Thus, when auditors evaluate the effectiveness of a management review control which is serving as a compensating control, the audit team can expect to face resistance from the client if they conclude that it is not operating effectively. As the following Auditing Insight "Management Will Do Anything to Avoid a Material Weakness" clearly shows, these type of conversations between an audit team and its client can be difficult.

AUDITING INSIGHT   Management Will Do Anything to Avoid a Material Weakness

In a recently published academic study, which featured observations from a sample of 20 partners with experience completing audits of internal control over financial reporting, the authors highlighted the difficulties faced by auditors when considering whether an identified deficiency should be classified as either a significant deficiency or material weakness. In fact, the evidence suggests that conversations can become quite "contentious when a material weakness" is assessed by the audit team and, in particular, that "managers have difficulty accepting that material weaknesses can exist without a detected error." In general, the authors report that client managers' immediate reaction to a control deficiency is to deny that it is significant, and routinely claims that compensating controls such as a "management review control" would have caught any material error that might have occurred as a result of the identified control deficiency.

Source: J.R. Cohen, J.R. Joe, J.C. Thibodeau, G.M. Trompeter, "Audit Partners' Judgments and Challenges in the Audits of Internal Control over Financial Reporting." *Auditing: A Journal of Practice & Theory,* November 2020, pp. 57-85.

Communicating the Results of the Audit

LO I-6

Explain the communication of internal control deficiencies to those charged with governance, such as the audit committee and other key management personnel.

When the audit team completes the audit of internal control over financial reporting, they must issue their opinion on the effectiveness of the system of internal controls and communicate the results of the audit. As previously discussed, they do so by evaluating evidence obtained from all sources, including the team's evaluation of the design of controls, tests of operating effectiveness of controls, identified deficiencies, and most importantly, any significant deficiencies and material weaknesses. Audit teams then form an opinion on the effectiveness of internal control over financial reporting. According to the professional standards, audit teams can issue one of three types of opinions on internal controls:

1. **Unqualified opinion on internal control over financial reporting.** No material weaknesses exist in the internal control system.
2. **Disclaimer of opinion on internal control over financial reporting.** The audit team cannot perform all of the procedures considered necessary for some reason and is therefore unable to determine whether material weaknesses exist.
3. **Adverse opinion on internal control over financial reporting.** One or more material weaknesses exist in the internal control system.

Note that because the opinion on internal controls is as of the end of the fiscal year, the entity may be able to correct or remediate deficiencies or weaknesses after they have been detected. However, the audit team must have sufficient time to test the design effectiveness and operating effectiveness of the remediated control before being in a position to issue an unqualified opinion.

In addition to expressing an opinion on the effectiveness of the entity's internal control over financial reporting, the audit team also should evaluate the completeness and presentation of **management's annual report on internal control over financial reporting.** Among other factors, the audit team also must obtain written representations from management that explicitly acknowledge:

- It is responsible for effective internal control over financial reporting.
- It has evaluated the effectiveness of the internal control over financial reporting.
- It has disclosed all internal control deficiencies and frauds to the audit team.

Communicating Significant Deficiencies and Material Weakness

The professional standards require that the audit team communicate significant deficiencies and material weaknesses in internal control that are discovered during the performance of the audit. Auditors' communications of significant deficiencies and material weaknesses are intended to help management carry out its responsibilities for the monitoring of the internal control system.

For issuers, the auditors' report must be in writing and presented to those in charge of governance (usually the audit committee) before their report on internal control over financial reporting is issued to the public. The report is to be addressed to management, the board of directors, or the audit committee. See Exhibit I.9 for an illustration of such a report. In addition, all deficiencies noted must be communicated in writing to management.

If the audit team members do not identify any significant deficiencies, they should not issue a report stating that "no significant deficiencies were noted during the audit." Doing so might be misleading because an integrated audit is not designed to detect all significant deficiencies. A manager receiving such a report could conclude (incorrectly) that the audit team is stating positively that the entity has no internal control issues at the entity.

Audit teams often issue another type of report to management called a *management letter.* This letter may contain commentary and suggestions on a variety of matters in addition to internal control matters. Examples include issues identified during the audit related to operational and administrative efficiency, business strategy, and profit-making possibilities. Auditing standards do not require management letters, but they represent a type of value-added management advice rendered as part of an integrated audit.

EXHIBIT I.9
Internal Control Letter

Michael Scarn, LLP
Scranton, PA

March 7, 2024

Board of Directors
Dunder-Mifflin Inc.

In planning and performing our audit of the financial statements of Dunder-Mifflin Inc. for the year ended December 31, 2023, we considered its internal control in order to determine our audit procedures for the purpose of expressing our opinion on the financial statements as well as the effectiveness of the company's internal control over financial reporting. Our consideration of internal control would not necessarily disclose all deficiencies in internal control that might be significant deficiencies. However, we noted a certain matter involving the internal control and its operation that we consider to be a significant deficiency under standards established by the Public Company Accounting Oversight Board. A significant deficiency is a deficiency, or a combination of deficiencies, in internal control that is less severe than a material weakness, yet important enough to merit attention by those charged with governance.

The matter noted is that shipping personnel have both transaction initiation and alteration authority as well as custody of inventory assets. If invoice/shipping copy documents are altered to show a shipment of smaller quantities than actually shipped, customers or accomplices can receive your products without charge. The sales revenue and accounts receivable could be understated, and the inventory could be overstated. This deficiency caused us to spend additional time auditing your inventory quantities.

A material weakness in internal control is defined as a deficiency, or combination of deficiencies, that results in a reasonable possibility that a material misstatement would not be prevented or detected on a timely basis. We do not believe that the significant deficiency described above is a material weakness.

This report is intended solely for the information and use of the board of directors and its audit committee, and is not intended to be, and should not be, used by anyone other than these specified parties.

Respectfully yours,

Michael Scarn, LLP

✔ REVIEW CHECKPOINTS

I.16   What are (a) an *internal control deficiency,* (b) a *significant deficiency,* and (c) a *material weakness*?

I.17   Define what is meant by a *compensating control*. Describe why a management review control is a good example of a compensating control.

I.18   According to the professional standards, audit teams can issue one of three types of opinions on internal controls. Identify the three types of opinions and provide a brief discussion of each.

I.19   What reports (other than auditors' report) on internal control do audit teams give to an entity's management, board of directors, or audit committee?

AUDIT REPORTING

LO I-7
Understand auditors' reporting responsibility for the audit of internal control over financial reporting for issuers.

The next step in the process is reporting on internal control over financial reporting. For the auditors' report on internal control, two options are available. One option is to have two separate reports: one on the fairness of the entity's financial statements (presented earlier in Chapter 12) and a separate report on internal control over financial reporting. Each report would be separately titled, dated (although using the same date), and signed. The auditors' separate report on internal control is discussed in detail in the next section. The second option is to prepare a *combined report* that expresses one opinion on the financial statements and a second on the effectiveness of internal control over financial reporting. The auditors' separate report is now discussed.

Auditors' Separate Report on Internal Control Over Financial Reporting

Under professional standards, the audit team must plan and perform the audit to express an opinion on the effectiveness of internal control over financial reporting (ICFR).[5] Essentially, this requires the audit team to plan and perform the audit to provide reasonable assurance about whether the entity maintained effective ICFR as of year end. In making this determination, and as discussed previously, three levels of internal control deficiencies have been identified (from least to most significant):

1. An internal control deficiency is a situation in which the design or operation of the control does not allow the entity's management or employees to detect or prevent misstatements in a timely fashion.

2. A significant deficiency is a deficiency or combination of deficiencies less severe than a material weakness but important enough to merit attention to those charged with governance.

3. A material weakness is a deficiency, or combination of deficiencies, that results in a *reasonable possibility* that a *material misstatement* would not be prevented or detected on a timely basis.

Recall that in evaluating the effectiveness of the entity's ICFR, the audit team focuses on whether a *material weakness* in ICFR exists at the *end of the year* being reported on. If a material weakness exists, the entity's ICFR cannot be considered effective. Also remember that the professional standards require that the audit of ICFR be integrated with the financial statement audit and not performed as a separate engagement which is why many entities are given a combined **integrated report**. In this module, we now provide an example of a report on ICFR, assuming that separate reports are prepared on the financial statements and ICFR and that no material weaknesses in ICFR were identified (see Exhibit I.10 on the next page).

When reviewing the separate report, you will notice that the major components of this report include the following three sections:

1. The auditors' opinion on ICFR, along with a reference to the auditors' opinion and report on the financial statements (*Opinion on Internal Control Over Financial Reporting* section)

2. Management's and the audit team's responsibility for ICFR (*Basis for Opinion* section)

3. A definition of ICFR and the inherent limitations of ICFR (*Definition and Limitation of Internal Control Over Financial Reporting* section)

Modifications to the Standard Report

The report in Exhibit I.10 is an unqualified opinion on ICFR. This type of opinion would be appropriate when no material weaknesses in internal control were identified and no significant restriction was placed on the scope of the engagement. When a material weakness in ICFR is identified, the auditors' report would express an *adverse opinion* on ICFR which would include a section (normally titled *Material Weakness* or *Material Weaknesses)* that:

- Defines a material weakness.
- Lists specific material weakness(es) identified during the audit as well as any material weakness(es) identified in management's assessment of ICFR (if the material weakness(es) are not included in management's assessment, the auditors' report should so indicate).
- Indicates that the material weakness(es) were considered in determining the nature, timing, and extent of audit tests and that the report on ICFR does not affect the opinion on the financial statements.

---

[5]This requirement applies only to accelerated filers (issuers with an aggregate market value of voting and non-voting common equity of $75 million or greater). Non accelerated filers (issuers with an aggregate market value of voting and non-voting common equity of less than $75 million) are required to have management reports on ICFR but not auditor engagements or reports on ICFR.

EXHIBIT I.10
Report on ICFR for Issuer (Separate Report)

Report of Independent Registered Public Accounting Firm

To the Board of Directors and Shareholders of Dunder-Mifflin, Inc.

Opinion on Internal Control over Financial Reporting

We have audited Dunder-Mifflin, Inc.'s internal control over financial reporting as of December 31, 2023, based on criteria established in Internal Control-Integrated Framework issued by the Committee of Sponsoring Organizations of the Treadway Commission (the COSO criteria). In our opinion, Dunder-Mifflin, Inc. maintained, in all material respects, effective internal control over financial reporting as of December 31, 2023, based on the COSO criteria.

We also have audited, in accordance with the standards of the Public Company Accounting Oversight Board (United States) (PCAOB), the 2023 consolidated financial statements of the Company and our report dated January 29, 2024, expressed an unqualified opinion thereon.

Basis for Opinion

The Company's management is responsible for maintaining effective internal control over financial reporting and for its assessment of the effectiveness of internal control over financial reporting included in the accompanying Management's Report on Internal Control over Financial Reporting. Our responsibility is to express an opinion on the Company's internal control over financial reporting based on our audit. We are a public accounting firm registered with the PCAOB and are required to be independent with respect to the Company in accordance with the U.S. federal securities laws and the applicable rules and regulations of the Securities and Exchange Commission and the PCAOB.

We conducted our audit in accordance with the standards of the PCAOB. Those standards require that we plan and perform the audit to obtain reasonable assurance about whether effective internal control over financial reporting was maintained in all material respects.

Our audit included obtaining an understanding of internal control over financial reporting, assessing the risk that a material weakness exists, testing and evaluating the design and operating effectiveness of internal control based on the assessed risk, and performing such other procedures as we considered necessary in the circumstances. We believe that our audit provides a reasonable basis for our opinion.

Definition and Limitations of Internal Control over Financial Reporting

A company's internal control over financial reporting is a process designed to provide reasonable assurance regarding the reliability of financial reporting and the preparation of financial statements for external purposes in accordance with generally accepted accounting principles. A company's internal control over financial reporting includes those policies and procedures that (1) pertain to the maintenance of records that, in reasonable detail, accurately and fairly reflect the transactions and dispositions of the assets of the company; (2) provide reasonable assurance that transactions are recorded as necessary to permit preparation of financial statements in accordance with generally accepted accounting principles, and that receipts and expenditures of the company are being made only in accordance with authorizations of management and directors of the company; and (3) provide reasonable assurance regarding prevention or timely detection of unauthorized acquisition, use, or disposition of the company's assets that could have a material effect on the financial statements.

Because of its inherent limitations, internal control over financial reporting may not prevent or detect misstatements. Also, projections of any evaluation of effectiveness to future periods are subject to the risk that controls may become inadequate because of changes in conditions, or that the degree of compliance with the policies or procedures may deteriorate.

Michael Scarn, LLP
Scranton, PA
January 29, 2024

- Expresses an opinion that the entity *has not* maintained effective ICFR.

In situations where a scope limitation is encountered, the auditors' report would express a *disclaimer of opinion* on ICFR. This report would include

- A statement that the audit team does not express an opinion on ICFR.
- A paragraph describing the scope limitation (if the audit team has performed some limited procedures that enable them to conclude that a material weakness exists, the

report should define a material weakness and provide a description of any material weakness(es) identified).

Finally, in the audit of group financial statements, when other auditors examine the financial statements of a subsidiary or significant component of a consolidated issuer, they examine the ICFR. In these cases, the group auditor's report on ICFR would be modified to refer to the report of the component auditors and note that the opinion on ICFR is based, in part, on the report of the component auditors. Assuming no material weaknesses are identified or scope limitation is encountered, an unqualified opinion would be issued on ICFR.

Provisions for Nonaccelerated Filers

Issuers with an aggregate market value of voting and nonvoting common equity of less than $75 million are known as nonaccelerated filers. Nonaccelerated filers are required to have management reports on ICFR but are not required to have auditor engagements or reports on the effectiveness of ICFR. In these cases, the reports (either separate reports or integrated reports) should be modified to indicate that (1) the entity is not required to have an audit of its ICFR and (2) the auditor does not express an opinion on ICFR.

The Auditing Insight "Reporting on ICFR" summarizes current and historical information related to auditors' reports on ICFR.

 AUDITING INSIGHT   Reporting on ICFR

- Using the Audit Analytics database, from 2016–2020, 1.5% of all opinions on ICFR for S&P 500 companies were adverse opinions; the average number of material weaknesses cited was 1.8, with **CBRE Group** having the greatest number in any year (5 in both 2019 and 2020).

- Using this same database, companies receiving multiple adverse opinions during this period include **Newell Brands** (3 years), **Autodesk** (2 years), **Bio-Techne** (2 years), CBRE Group (2 years), **FirstEnergy Corp** (2 years), **Kraft Heinz** (2 years), and **Marriott International** (2 years).

- The Securities and Exchange Commission imposed a cease-and-desist order against **Lifeway Foods, Inc.** (an Illinois-based dairy food producer). In their order, the SEC noted that Lifeway disclosed material weaknesses in ICFR from 2007–2016, did not

complete its ICFR assessment in 2013 and 2014, and announced three financial statement restatements since 2012.

- Since the inception of auditor reporting on ICFR in 2004, the percentage of adverse opinions ranged from 16.2% (in 2004) to 3.6% (in 2010), with a level of 4.6% in 2020. The five most commonly cited issues in 2020 were (in order from highest) (1) material and/or numerous year-end adjustments; (2) inadequate accounting personnel resources; (3) inadequate information technology controls; (4) inadequate disclosure controls; and (5) lack of segregation of duties.

Sources: Audit Analytics database; *In the Matter of Lifeway Foods, Inc.,* Accounting and Auditing Release No. 4016, Securities and Exchange Commission, January 29, 2019; *SOX 404 Disclosures: A Seventeen-Year Review,* Audit Analytics, October 2021.

✅ REVIEW CHECKPOINTS

I.20   Consider an internal control deficiency, significant deficiency, and material weakness within the context of an internal control audit. Which of these is reported by auditors in their report on internal control over financial reporting?

I.21   What alternatives are available to auditors for reporting on the financial statements and internal control over financial reporting?

I.22   What are the major contents of the auditors' report on internal control over financial reporting (assume a separate report is prepared on ICFR)?

I.23   What situations may result in modifying the report on internal control over financial reporting? What type of opinion would be expressed in these situations?

Summary

Section 404 of the Sarbanes-Oxley Act of 2002 requires the management team of each issuer to assess the effectiveness of its own internal control system over financial reporting each year. The issuer's independent financial statement auditors then must render an opinion on the effectiveness of the internal control system over financial reporting. As stated earlier in this chapter, internal control systems have never before faced so much scrutiny by so many professionals!

Given this requirement, the evaluation of an entity's internal control system is a critical objective of the financial statement audit process completed for issuers. In fact, due to Section 404, two separate opinions are expressed by the independent auditor, one on the effectiveness of the internal control system and one on the reliability of the financial statements. To achieve efficiencies when auditing issuers, audit teams conduct an *integrated* audit process which is designed to provide evidence to support both opinions while conducting the audit process. In this module, we presented an overview of the steps that need to be taken to complete the audit of the internal control systems at issuers.

Audit teams use the COSO framework as the benchmark to evaluate internal control effectiveness during the audit of internal control over financial reporting. That is, if an internal control system is effective, an issuer's control environment, risk assessment, information and communication system, control activities, and monitoring of the control system (i.e., the five components of the COSO framework) will all be operating effectively.

When planning the audit, the audit team must do so in a manner that allows the audit team to obtain sufficient and appropriate evidence about whether the internal control system is effective in producing reliable financial statements. In effect, the audit team completes the audit to determine whether a material weakness exists in the system of internal control as of the fiscal year end date.

To perform the audit, the audit team will first gain an understanding of internal controls through inquiry, document examination, and observation. This understanding is completed using a top-down approach that first identifies the significant accounts and disclosures. For each significant account and disclosure, the audit team then identifies the relevant assertions. Once the relevant assertions have been identified, the audit team must determine if the internal control system has been designed to prevent or detect material misstatements.

The internal control design evaluation includes an assessment of whether the internal control activities that have been put in place would mitigate the risk of material misstatement, if operating effectively, for each relevant assertion about each significant account and disclosure. Once the evaluation of internal control design has been completed, the tests of *operating effectiveness* need to be completed. These tests must be completed for each control activity that is being relied upon to mitigate the risk of material misstatement for each relevant assertion.

Once the tests of design effectiveness and operating effectiveness of the internal controls have been completed, the audit team must then determine the significance of any control deficiency (either design or operating effectiveness) that was discovered during audit testing. A material weakness in internal control is defined as a deficiency, or combination of deficiencies, that results in a reasonable possibility that a material misstatement would not be prevented or detected on a timely basis. A significant deficiency is a deficiency or a combination of deficiencies in internal control that is less severe than a material weakness yet important enough to merit attention by those charged with governance. Both material weaknesses and significant deficiencies need to be communicated to those charged with governance (e.g., the audit committee) at the issuer.

Finally, when the audit of internal control over financial reporting is complete, the audit team must issue an audit report. An unqualified report means that there were no material weaknesses identified on the audit. If a material weakness does exist, then the audit team must issue an adverse report.

Key Terms

adverse opinion on internal control over financial reporting: The opinion issued when the company has a material weakness and has not maintained an effective internal control over financial reporting, 918

auditors' report on internal control over financial reporting: A report required by the Sarbanes-Oxley Act that provides an opinion on the effectiveness of the entity's internal control over financial reporting, 930

internal control activities: The specific actions taken by a client's management and employees to help ensure that management directives are carried out, 921

disclaimer of opinion on internal control over financial reporting: A report issued when auditors do not express an opinion on internal control over financial reporting. Disclaimers of opinion are issued for situations in which auditors' are associated with (but did not audit) the internal control over financial reporting, 929

integrated audit: The term used to describe an audit process that is designed to provide an opinion on both the financial statements and the internal control system of an entity, 920

integrated report: A single report issued by auditors expressing their opinion on the fairness of the financial statements and effectiveness of internal control over financial reporting, 931

internal control over financial reporting Policies and procedures implemented by an entity to prevent or detect material accounting frauds or errors and provide for their correction on a timely basis, 916

internal control deficiency: A condition that exists when the design or operation of a control does not allow the entity's management or employees to detect or prevent misstatements in a timely fashion, 926

issuer: An entity that offers registered securities, such as stocks and bonds, for sale to the general public (also known as a public entity). Issuers are subject to mandatory audit requirements for the financial statements and internal control over financial reporting, 916

management's annual report on internal control over financial reporting: A report required by the Sarbanes-Oxley Act that states that management is responsible for establishing and maintaining adequate internal control over financial reporting, identifies the framework management uses to evaluate the effectiveness of the entity's internal control, and provides management's assessment of the effectiveness of the entity's internal control, 929

material weakness: A deficiency or combination of deficiencies that results in a reasonable possibility that a material misstatement would not be prevented or detected on a timely basis, 927

operating effectiveness: Description of a condition expressing whether a control is operating as designed and whether the person performing the control possesses the necessary authority and qualifications to perform the control effectively, 919

significant deficiency: A deficiency or a combination of deficiencies in internal control that is less severe than a material weakness yet important enough to merit attention by those charged with governance, 927

unqualified opinion on internal control over financial reporting: An unqualified opinion on internal control over financial reporting is given when the audit team has completed the audit of internal control over financial reporting based on criteria established in the COSO framework and they conclude that the audit client has maintained, in all material respects, effective internal control over financial reporting, 929

Multiple-Choice Questions for Practice and Review

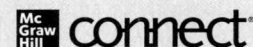 All applicable Exercises and Problems are available with *Connect*.

LO I-3

I.24   The most important foundational component of an entity's internal control system is

    a. Effectiveness and efficiency of operations.

    b. The control environment.

    c. Reliability of financial reporting.

    d. Compliance with applicable laws and regulations.

LO I-4

I.25 According to the PCAOB, during the audit of internal controls for an issuer, the ultimate objective of testing the design effectiveness of internal controls is to
   a. Determine whether the company's controls are processing company data effectively.
   b. Determine that the company's controls will satisfy the company's control objectives and can effectively prevent or detect errors or fraud that could result in material misstatements, if they operate as prescribed.
   c. Determine that the company's employees are processing the controls according to the policy and procedures manuals at the company.
   d. None of the above.

LO I-4

I.26 To test the operating effectiveness of a control, an audit team might use a combination of each of the following tests *except* for
   a. Inquiry of client personnel.
   b. Observation of company operations.
   c. Confirmation of balances.
   d. Inspection of documentation.

LO I-4

I.27 When *planning* the audit of internal controls for an issuer, the audit team should
   a. Identify significant accounts, locations, and relevant assertions.
   b. Conduct a walkthrough of the internal control process.
   c. Make inquiries of employees regarding the existence of control activities.
   d. Reperform control activities performed by client employees to determine their effectiveness.

LO I-5

I.28 A material weakness is a situation in which
   a. It is probable that an immaterial financial statement misstatement would not be prevented or detected on a timely basis.
   b. There is a remote likelihood that a material misstatement would be detected on a timely basis.
   c. It is reasonably possible that a material misstatement would not be detected on a timely basis.
   d. It is reasonably possible that an immaterial misstatement would not be detected on a timely basis.

LO I-5

I.29 When completing the audit of internal controls for an issuer, the severity of an internal control deficiency depends on
   a. Whether there is a reasonable possibility that the company's controls will fail to prevent or detect a misstatement of an account balance or disclosure.
   b. Whether a misstatement has actually occurred as a result of the deficiency.
   c. The magnitude of the potential misstatement resulting from the deficiency or the deficiencies.
   d. Both *(a)* and *(c)* are correct.
   e. All of the above are correct.

LO I-2

I.30 When completing the audit of internal controls for an issuer, the PCAOB requires the audit team to audit internal controls over
   a. Operations.
   b. Compliance with regulations.
   c. Financial reporting.
   d. All of the above.

LO I-2

I.31 When completing the audit of internal controls for an issuer, AS 2201 requires auditors to report on

Management's Report on Internal Control	An Audit of Internal Control
a. No	No
b. Yes	No
c. No	Yes
d. Yes	Yes

LO I-4   I.32   When completing the audit of internal controls for an issuer, AS 2201 requires auditors to test
    a. Operating effectiveness only.
    b. Design effectiveness only.
    c. Both operating and design effectiveness.
    d. Neither operating nor design effectiveness

LO I-5   I.33   Which of the following would probably *not* be considered an indication of a material weakness?
    a. Evidence of a material misstatement.
    b. Ineffective oversight by the audit committee.
    c. Immaterial fraud committed by senior management.
    d. Overproduction by the manufacturing plant.

LO I-7   I.34   Which report would *not* be appropriate for a public accounting firm to provide on financial reporting controls?
    a. Unqualified—no material weaknesses found.
    b. Disclaimer of opinion—unable to perform all necessary procedures.
    c. Disclaimer of opinion—significant deficiencies exist.
    d. Adverse—material weaknesses exist.

LO I-7   I.35   If the auditors encounter a significant scope limitation in evaluating an issuer's internal control over financial reporting, which of the following types of opinions on the effectiveness of the company's internal control over financial reporting would be appropriate?
    a. Unqualified opinion or adverse opinion.
    b. Qualified opinion or adverse opinion.
    c. Unqualified opinion or disclaimer of opinion.
    d. Disclaimer of opinion.

LO I-4   I.36   When testing a control activity's operating effectiveness, procedures the auditor performs to test operating effectiveness would likely include
    a. Inquiry of appropriate personnel.
    b. Reading over the company's code of conduct.
    c. Reperformance of the control activity.
    d. Both *(a)* and *(c)* are correct.

LO I-4   I.37   Matters that could affect the necessary extent of testing for a control activity as it related to the degree of auditor reliance on a control activity would *not* include the following:
    a. The frequency of the performance of the control by the company during the period being audited.
    b. The length of time that the auditor is planning to rely on the operating efficiency of the control activity.
    c. The expected rate of deviation for a control activity.
    d. The relevance and reliability of the audit evidence to be obtained to test the operating effectiveness of a control activity.

LO I-5   I.38   Once the auditor detects an internal control deficiency, which of the following steps must they take first?
    a. Perform tests of other controls related to the same assertion as the control deemed ineffective.
    b. Evaluate the severity of the deficiency on the auditor's control risk assessment for that assertion.
    c. Modify the planned substantive procedures as a result of the deficiency.
    d. Test the deficient control, assuming a maximum level of risk.

LO I-5   I-39   An internal control deficiency in ICFR is a situation in which
    a. It is probable that an immaterial financial statement misstatement would not be detected on a timely basis.
    b. There is a remote likelihood that a material misstatement would be detected on a timely basis.

    c. It is reasonably possible that a material misstatement would not be detected on a timely basis.

    d. It is reasonably possible that an immaterial misstatement would not be detected on a timely basis.

    e. None of the above answers is correct.

LO I-7   **I-40** Which report would be appropriate for a public accounting firm to provide on the ICFR for issuers?

    a. Unqualified— only one material weaknesses in ICFR found.

    b. Disclaimer of opinion—unable to perform all necessary procedures.

    c. Disclaimer of opinion—multiple internal control deficiencies in ICFR exist.

    d. Adverse—significant deficiencies in ICFR exist.

LO I-7   **I-41** Which of the following statements is *not* true with respect to the auditors' report on ICFR?

    a. The report will be dated as of the date of the financial statements.

    b. The report will express an opinion on the effectiveness of ICFR.

    c. The auditor will issue an adverse opinion if one or more material weaknesses in ICFR exist.

    d. The report may be presented with the report on the entity's financial statements as a combined report.

                                                      (AICPA adapted)

LO I-7   **I-42** Which of the following is *not* an element or statement included in the *Basis for Opinion* Section of a standard (unmodified) report on the internal control over financial reporting of an issuer?

    a. The responsibilities of the audit team and management in the financial reporting process.

    b. A broad overview of procedures performed during the audit.

    c. The requirement for audit teams to be independent with respect to the issuer.

    d. The tenure of the auditor.

    I-43 If the auditors decide to present separate reports on the entity's financial statements and ICFR in the audit of an issuer, which of the following should be modified to refer to the other report?

	Report on Financial Statements	Report on ICFR
a.	Yes	Yes
b.	Yes	No
c.	No	Yes
d.	No	No

LO I-7   **I-44** Which of the following information would be included in the *Basis for Opinion* section of the auditors' report on ICFR if the report is presented separately from the auditors' report on the entity's financial statements of an issuer?

    a. The fact that the auditors conducted an audit of the entity's financial statements.

    b. The definition of a material weakness in ICFR.

    c. Statements identifying the responsibility of the auditors and management for ICFR.

    d. A reference to the auditors' report and opinion on the entity's financial statements.

LO I-5   **I-45** On the audit of an issuer, if an audit team completes a test of controls on a control activity that is designed to mitigate the risk of material misstatement for a relevant assertion, concludes that the control activity is not effective and that there is a control deficiency, what should the auditor do next?

    a. Discuss the finding with the client and ask if a compensating control exists.

    b. Issue an adverse report on the internal control over financial reporting.

    c. Document the results of tests of controls and complete additional substantive testing procedures.

    d. None of the above answers is correct.

LO I-4   I-46   On the audit of an issuer, if an audit team determines that a control activity that is designed to mitigate the risk of material misstatement for a relevant assertion about a significant account has been outsourced to a service organization, the audit team must:

     a. Obtain an SOC 3 report that includes the control activities identified.

     b. Obtain an SOC 1, Type 2 report that includes the control activities identified.

     c. Obtain an SOC 2, Type 1 report that includes the control activities identified.

     d. Obtain an SOC 1, Type 1 report that includes the control activities identified.

LO I-1   I-47   When auditing the internal control system of an issuer as required by the Sarbanes-Oxley Act of 2002, which of the following objectives of the internal control system is the most important to auditors?

     a. Compliance with laws and regulations.

     b. Reliable financial reporting.

     c. Effectiveness and efficiency of operations.

     d. All of the above reponses are objectives that are important to auditors.

LO I-1   I-48   Sarbanes-Oxley requires management to assess and report on the entity's internal control over financial reporting in Section 404. Specifically, management's report on ICFR must include the following:

     a. A statement that management is responsible for establishing and maintaining adequate internal control over financial reporting.

     b. A statement identifying the framework (e.g., the COSO framework) that management uses as a benchmark for evaluating the effectiveness of the entity's internal control.

     c. A statement providing management's assessment of the effectiveness of the entity's internal control.

     d. All of the above must be included in the annual report.

     e. None of the above must be included in the annual report.

LO I-2   I-49   Which of the following items are unique to an audit of internal control over financial reporting of an issuer as required by Sabanes-Oxley and guided by AS 2201 issued by the PCAOB:

     a. The auditor must test each relevant control activity each year.

     b. The auditor must evaluate the effectiveness of internal control throughout the entire year.

     c. The auditor must conclude that there is a material weakness in internal control on each audit.

     d. None of the above answers are correct.

LO I-3   I-50   Which of the following is not a component of a well-functioning internal control system according to the COSO framework?

     a. Risk assessment.

     b. Segregation of duties.

     c. Information and communication.

     d. Monitoring of controls.

LO I-3   I-51   Which of the following is not a principle of the control environment, according to the COSO framework?

     a. The organization demonstrates a commitment to integrity and ethical values.

     b. The organization holds individuals accountable for their internal control responsibilities in the pursuit of objectives.

     c. The organization identifies and assesses changes that could significantly impact the system of internal control.

     d. The organization demonstrates a commitment to attract, develop, and retain competent individuals in alignment with objectives.

     e. None of the above answers are correct since all of the above answers are principles.

LO I-3   I-52   Which of the following is not a principle of risk assessment, according to the COSO framework?

     a. The organization specifies objectives with sufficient clarity to enable the identification and assessment of risks relating to objectives.

     b. The organization identifies and assesses changes that could significantly impact the system of internal control.

c. The organization identifies risks to the achievement of its objectives across the entity and analyzes the risks as a basis for determining how the risks should be managed.

d. The organization considers the potential for fraud in assessing risks to the achievement of objectives.

e. None of the above answers are correct since all of the above answers are principles.

LO I-3

I-53 Which of the following is not a principle of control activities, according to the COSO framework?

a. The organization evaluates and communicates internal control deficiencies in a timely manner to those parties responsible for taking corrective action, including senior management and the board of directors, as appropriate.

b. The organization selects and develops control activities that contribute to the mitigation of risks to the achievement of objectives to acceptable levels.

c. The organization selects and develops general control activities over technology to support the achievement of objectives.

d. The organization deploys control activities through policies that establish what is expected and procedures that put policies into action.

e. None of the above answers are correct since all of the above answers are principles.

LO I-3

I-54 Which of the following is not a principle of information and communication, according to the COSO framework?

a. The organization obtains or generates and uses relevant quality information to support the functioning of internal control.

b. The organization selects, develops, and performs ongoing and/or separate evaluations to ascertain whether the components of internal control are present and functioning.

c. The organization internally communicates information, including objectives and responsibilities for internal control, necessary to support the functioning of internal control.

d. The organization obtains or generates and uses relevant quality information to support the functioning of internal control.

e. None of the above answers are correct since all of the above answers are principles.

LO I-4

I-55 When an audit team completes an audit of internal control over financial reporting at an issuer, they are required to test

a. Internal control design for each relevant assertion related to each significant account and disclosure.

b. Internal control operating effectiveness for each control identified that mitigates the risk of material misstatement for each relevant assertion related to each significant account and disclosure.

c. They are not required to test the internal control operating effectiveness for each control identified that mitigates the risk of material misstatement for each relevant assertion related to each significant account and disclosure.

d. Both (a) and (b) are correct.

LO I-4

I-56 The focus of a Type 2 SOC 1 report is on the:

a. Control environment at a service provider.

b. Suitability of the internal control design only.

c. Monitoring of controls at a service provider

d. Operating effectiveness and the internal control design at a service provider.

Exercises, Problems, and Simulations

Mc Graw Hill connect   All applicable Exercises and Problems are available with *Connect*.

LO I-2

I.57   **Impact of Sarbanes-Oxley Act.**   Your long-time client, Central Office Supply, has been rapidly expanding, and the board of directors is considering taking the company public. CEO Terry Puckett has heard that costs of operating a public company have increased significantly as a result of the Sarbanes-Oxley Act. Puckett is particularly concerned with reports that audit fees have doubled because of internal control provisions of the act and PCAOB *Auditing Standard No. 2201*. Puckett has asked you to explain the possible effects on the audit of complying with the requirements of Sarbanes-Oxley.

Required:

Draft a letter to Puckett outlining the changes in the company's responsibilities for internal control and changes in the audit due to Sarbanes-Oxley and PCAOB *Auditing Standard No. 2201*.

LO I-4

I.58   **Internal Control Design Effectiveness.**   When evaluating internal control design effectiveness during the internal control over financial reporting, the audit team must determine whether controls have been put in place for each relevant assertion about each significant account. For each relevant assertion, the audit team must determine the points in the process where a misstatement might occur and then determine if a control activity has been put in place to mitigate the risk of material misstatement for each relevant assertion. For each of the possible misstatements identified below, please select the appropriate financial statement assertion:

Possible Misstatement/Risk

a. Revenue is overstated because the controller created fraudulent invoices and recorded them.

b. Revenue is understated because the accountant closed the sales cycle a week early to go on vacation.

c. Accounts Receivable is overstated because the accounts receivable clerk forgot to apply available discounts.

d. Accounts Receivable is overstated because sales are falsified.

e. Travel expense is overstated because the sales force charged personal expenses on their corporate credit card.

f. Accounts Payable is understated because the office manager lost an invoice for supplies received so it was never recorded.

g. The cash balance is understated because funds held in Japan were converted to $USD at the wrong rate.

h. Cash is overstated because the Treasurer is stealing from the company.

i. Inventory is overstated because it is held on consignment but included in the inventory balance.

j. The cost of goods sold is understated because time sheets have not been submitted for each job.

k. Long Term Debt is overstated due to misclassification by management.

LO I-4

I.59   **Internal Control Operating Effectiveness.** When evaluating internal control operating effectiveness during the internal control over financial statement audit, the audit team must determine whether the controls that have been put in place for each relevant assertion are operating effectively. To do so, the auditor must perform tests of the control activities that have been designed to mitigate the risk of material misstatement for each relevant assertion. For each test of control identified below, please select the appropriate financial statement assertion that would be tested by the procedure (i.e., Existence or Occurrence, Completeness, Valuation, Rights and Obligations, Presentation and Disclosure).

a. Vouch the cost of labor to the actual time sheets for employees authorized by management.

b. Trace a sample of employees in the personnel file to the payroll register.

c. Scan shipping documents for numerical sequence and trace shipments into the daily sales recorded in the general ledger.

d. Trace shipping date on selected shipping documents to actual sales invoice date and check FOB shipping terms.

e. Vouch sales made in sales journal to invoices, shipping documents and customer purchase orders.

f. Inspect documentation for evidential matter that management evaluated the collectability of receivables on a regular basis.

g. Vouch a sample of recorded payables to vendor invoice, purchase order and receiving report.

h. Observe locked inventory areas and functioning cameras in warehouse.

i. Inspect documentation for evidential matter that management evaluated current market prices for inventory.

j. Inspect documentation of procedures for consigned inventory and observe use of separate account numbers.

LO I-3

I.60 Internal Control Components of the COSO Framework. The audit team's overarching objective when auditing the system of internal control over financial reporting is to express an opinion on the system's effectiveness. To achieve this goal, the COSO framework defines five interrelated components of a well-functioning internal control system. They are (1) control environment, (2) risk assessment, (3) control activities, (4) monitoring, and (5) information and communication. For each of the controls identified below for Jackman Ridge, please select the most appropriate component from the COSO framework:

a. Jackman Ridge has a code of conduct that must be read by each employee.

b. Jackman Ridge has a management committee that develops control activities that help to mitigate the risk of material misstatement.

c. Jackman Ridge identifies risks and then carefully analyzes such risks as a basis for determining how the risks should be managed.

d. Jackman Ridge works hard to provide information needed to support the proper functioning of internal control.

e. Jackman Ridge has a management team that carefully established an organizational chart with proper oversight, structures, and reporting lines.

f. Jackman Ridge performs quarterly evaluations to determine whether the components of internal control are present and functioning properly.

g. Jackman Ridge assesses its external competitive market to determine if they should make any changes to their established procedures.

h. The CFO at Jackman Ridge receives an aged trial balance in a timely manner each month for his review of the allowance for doubtful accounts.

i. Jackman Ridge is well known in the industry for holding its employees accountable for their internal control responsibilities.

LO I-3

I.61 Internal Control Components of the COSO Framework. The audit team's overarching objective when auditing the system of internal control over financial reporting is to express an opinion on the system's effectiveness. To achieve this goal, the COSO framework defines five interrelated components of a well-functioning internal control system. They are (1) control environment, (2) risk assessment, (3) control activities, (4) monitoring, and (5) information and communication. For each of the controls identified below for Taft Energy, please select the most appropriate component from the COSO framework:

Control

a. Taft Energy specifies goals and objectives with enough clarity to enable the proper assessment of risks related to the objectives.

b. Taft Energy is committed to attracting competent employees and retaining such employees to achieve objectives.

c. Taft Energy has a track record of using complete and accurate information in their internal control system.

d. Taft Energy has a robust set of general computer controls which allow for a safe and secure computing environment.

e. Taft Energy has an active internal audit department that continually evaluates the proper functioning of key internal control activities.

    f. The CFO at Taft Energy reviews business risks regularly and considers their potential impact on the financial statements.

    g. The Board of Directors at Taft Energy are independent of the management team and regularly ask about the performance of internal controls.

    h. The CFO at Taft Energy receives timely and relevant information to facilitate his review of the monthly budget to actual profit and loss statement.

    i. Taft Energy routinely considers the possibility of fraud in its financial statements and operations. Management identifies the factors and establishes plans to mitigate the possibility.

LO I-5

I.62 **Evaluating Internal Control Deficiencies.** Oldtown is a publicly traded real estate investment firm based in the Northeast. Incorporated 20 years ago, Oldtown's primary business is buying, developing, selling, and renting commercial real estate. Oldtown has been your firm's audit client for approximately 11 years, and this is the second year that you have been assigned to the engagement with overall responsibility for the internal control audit over financial reporting and the financial statement audit (i.e., the integrated audit).

During the tests of internal controls over financial reporting, your team found a control deficiency related to the valuation of Oldtown's rental properties. Specifically, your team determined that the analyst responsible for performing the valuations had applied the incorrect interest rate in the discounted cash flow analyses that was used to value the rental properties. This error was not detected by the client and resulted in an overstatement of the property asset account in the year-end financial statements of $7.5 million. It is likely that any misstatement greater than this would have been detected by their compensating control, a monthly budget to actual analysis.

The management team of Oldtown believes that these errors would have been caught before the financial statements were filed with the SEC. There were no other control deficiencies noted in the internal control audit.

Required:

    a. Assume that overall materiality was $250 million for Oldtown, do you believe that Oldtown has a deficiency, a significant deficiency, or a material weakness? Please justify your answer.

    b. Assume that overall materiality was $10 million for Oldtown, do you believe that Oldtown has a deficiency, a significant deficiency, or a material weakness? Please justify your answer.

    c. Assume that overall materiality was $5 million for Oldtown, do you believe that Oldtown has a deficiency, a significant deficiency, or a material weakness? Please justify your answer.

LO I-5

I.63 **Evaluating Internal Control Deficiencies.** Flex is a publicly traded manufacturing company based in Sarasota, Florida, where it manufactures high-tech surveillance and security equipment. Flex's products are primarily used by the other businesses but, there is a growing demand for household use. Incorporated 45 years ago, Flex has been your firm's audit client for approximately 20 years, and this is the first year that you have been assigned to the engagement with overall responsibility for the internal control audit over financial reporting and the financial statement audit (i.e., the integrated audit).

In October of the year being audited, Flex installed a new cloud-based inventory system. Simply stated, the previous system could not handle the expansion of the business into the household market. Flex's internal IT department was responsible for the implementation of the new system. However, during the tests of internal controls over financial reporting, your team found a control deficiency related to the valuation of Flex's inventory. Specifically, your team determined that the new system was not properly including inventory from their warehouse locations on the west coast. This error was not detected by the client and resulted in an understatement of the inventory account in the year-end financial statements of $190 million. It is likely that any misstatement greater than this would have been detected by their compensating control, a monthly budget to actual analysis.

The management team of Flex believes that these errors would have been caught before the financial statements were filed with the SEC. There were no other control deficiencies noted in the internal control audit.

Required:

   a. Assume that overall materiality was $500 million for Flex, do you believe that Flex has a deficiency, a significant deficiency, or a material weakness? Please justify your answer.

   b. Assume that overall materiality was $200 million for Flex, do you believe that Flex has a deficiency, a significant deficiency, or a material weakness? Please justify your answer.

   c. Assume that overall materiality was $50 million for Flex, do you believe that Flex has a deficiency, a significant deficiency, or a material weakness? Please justify your answer.

LO I-7

I.64 **Internet Exercise: Reports on Financial Statements.** One of the great resources for auditors is the SEC's Electronic Data Gathering, Analysis and Retrieval (EDGAR) system database at www.sec.gov. Issuers file SEC-required documents electronically. The SEC makes this information available on its web page.

Required:

Five of the largest companies (in terms of market capitalization) are shown in the following table, along with their ticker symbols. After accessing the EDGAR database, download copies of auditors' reports from the Form 10-K filings and complete the following table (Apple has been done as an example). (*Hint:* Search the 10-K filing by using the key word "independent," as in Report of Independent Registered Public Accounting Firm.) Use the following responses in completing the table.

   Report on Financial Statements: Type of Opinion (Unqualified, Qualified, Adverse, Disclaimer) and any additional matters discussed in report

   Report on ICFR: Type of Opinion (Unqualified, Adverse, Disclaimer) and any additional matters discussed in report

   Form of Reports: Combined or Separate

   Auditor: Identify Name of Firm

   Tenure: Year in which firm began serving as auditor

Company / Date	Report on Financial Statements	Report on ICFR	Form of Reports	Auditor	Tenure
Apple (AAPL) 10/28/2021	Unqualified opinion	Unqualified opinion	Separate	EY	2009
Microsoft (MSFT)					
Alphabet (GOOGL)					
Amazon.com (AMZN)					
Tesla (TSLA)					

LO I-7

I.65 **Reports on Internal Control over Financial Reporting (Report Modifications).** For each of the following situations, describe how the auditors' report on internal control over financial reporting would be modified from the standard, unqualified report. Do *not* write the actual reports.

   a. The audit team has identified a material weakness in the processing of sales transactions. This weakness has been disclosed by management in its report.

   b. Due to the COVID-19 pandemic, the audit team was unable to test the design and operating effectiveness of the controls at any of the client's warehouses. with respect to the entity's internal control over financial reporting.

   c. Component auditors have audited a significant component of the group financial statements, including internal control over financial reporting relating to that component. They did not find a material weakness in ICFR, and the group auditor believes the component auditor's work can be relied on.

   d. The audit team believes that the entity's management has not adequately disclosed a material weakness in ICFR.

LO I-7

I.66 **Reports on Internal Control over Financial Reporting (Identify Report Deficiencies).** Sorrell, CPA, is auditing the financial statements of Van Dyke as of December 31, 2023. Sorrell's substantive procedures and other tests indicated that Van Dyke's financial statements were prepared in accordance with generally accepted accounting principles and, accordingly, Sorrell's report (dated February 7, 2024) expressed an unqualified opinion on those financial statements. Because Van Dyke's securities are registered with the Securities and Exchange Commission, Sorrell, CPA will examine and report on Van Dyke's ICFR. During its assessment of internal control over financial reporting, Van Dyke's management identified material weaknesses in ICFR related to (1) the method of accounting for sales commissions and (2) separation of duties related to purchase transactions. Sorrell was able to gather sufficient evidence and did not encounter limitations with respect to the evaluation of Van Dyke's internal control over financial reporting. Sorrell prepared the following draft report on (see Exhibit I.66A) Van Dyke's internal control over financial reporting.

EXHIBIT I.66A
Report of Independent Registered Public Accounting Firm

To the Board of Directors and Shareholders of Van Dyke:

Opinion on Internal Control Over Financial Reporting

We have audited the accompanying Management's Report on Internal Control over Financial Reporting, that Van Dyke has not maintained effective internal control over financial reporting as of December 31, 2023, based on criteria established in Internal Control—Integrated Framework issued by the Committee of Sponsoring Organizations of the Treadway Commission (COSO criteria). In our opinion, because of the effect of the material weaknesses described in the Material Weakness Section of our report on the achievement of the objectives of the control criteria, Van Dyke has not maintained, in all material respects, effective internal control over financial reporting as of December 31, 2023, based on the COSO criteria.

We have also audited, in accordance with the standards of the Public Company Accounting Oversight Board (United States), Van Dyke's 2023 consolidated financial statements.

Basis for Opinion

Van Dyke's management is responsible for assessing the effectiveness of internal control over financial reporting included in the accompanying Management's Report on Internal Control over Financial Reporting. We are a public accounting firm registered with the PCAOB and are required to be independent with respect to Van Dyke in accordance with the U.S. federal securities laws and the applicable rules and regulations of the Securities and Exchange Commission and the PCAOB.

We conducted our audits in accordance with the standards of the Public Company Accounting Oversight Board (United States). Those standards require that we plan and perform the audit to obtain reasonable assurance about whether effective internal control over financial reporting was maintained in all material respects.

Our audit included obtaining an understanding of internal control over financial reporting, assessing the risk that a material weakness exists, testing and evaluating the design and operating effectiveness of internal control based on the assessed risk, and performing such other procedures as we considered necessary in the circumstances.

Definition and Limitations of Internal Control Over Financial Reporting

A company's internal control over financial reporting is a process designed to provide reasonable assurance regarding the reliability of financial reporting and the preparation of financial statements for external purposes in accordance with generally accepted accounting principles. A company's internal control over financial reporting includes those policies and procedures that (1) pertain to the maintenance of records that, in reasonable detail, accurately and fairly reflect the transactions and dispositions of the assets of the company; (2) provide reasonable assurance that transactions are recorded as necessary to permit preparation of financial statements in accordance with generally accepted accounting principles and that receipts and expenditures of the company are being made only in accordance with authorizations of management and directors of the company; and (3) provide reasonable assurance regarding prevention or timely detection of unauthorized acquisition, use, or disposition of the company's assets that could have a material effect on the financial statements.

Material Weakness

Two material weaknesses identified and included in Management's Report on Internal Control Over Financial Reporting were related to the design and operation of internal controls over the accounting for sales commissions and separation of duties related to purchases of inventory. Given the nature of the transactions and processes involved and the potential for a misstatement to occur as a result of the internal control deficiencies existing on December 31, 2023, we have concluded that there is more than a remote likelihood that a material misstatement in the annual or interim financial statements would not have been prevented or detected by internal controls.

These material weaknesses were considered in determining the nature, timing, and extent of audit tests applied in our audit of the 2023 financial statements.

In addition to the material weaknesses noted above, we identified several deficiencies in internal control over financial reporting that we deemed to be less significant than a material weakness. These deficiencies have been separately communicated to Van Dyke's management.

Seattle, WA
December 31, 2023

Required:

Identify the deficiencies in the audit report drafted by Sorrell. Group the deficiencies by paragraph and in the order in which they appear. Do not rewrite the report. Cite the relevant sections from the professional standards.

LO I-7

I.67　**Consider the following scenario**　Your client, Adams Company is a large publicly traded national financing company that has been in business for over 15 years. The client has 37 subsidiary companies operating in more than 25 different states throughout the U.S. Adams began operations in the Phoenix area and grew primarily through acquisitions of smaller financing companies. Importantly, all subsidiaries are required to adopt common operations, procedures, accounting systems and internal controls. Company policy provides that, at the entity level, the corporate-level assistant controller receives a monthly profitability report from each of the entity's 37 subsidiary companies, and then compares each report to the year-to-date budget. If these numbers vary by more than 25%, the assistant controller will require the local management to reconcile the observed difference and then provide a detailed explanation for the difference, including persuasive documentary evidence to substantiate their explanation.

Required:

a. What is the definition of a compensating control?

b. Would the management review control described above (which compares actual profitability to budgeted profitability) be an example of a compensating control? Why or why not?

c. If there was an identified control deficiency related to recorded revenue at four different subsidiaries, do you believe that this actual to budgeted profitability control would catch the material misstatement? Why or why not?

LO I-7

I.68　**Consider the following scenario** Your audit client, Wilson Company is a large publicly traded retail company that has been in business for over 25 years. The client has 135 retail locations operating in 17 different states throughout the United States. While conducting tests of internal controls over financial reporting at a sample of Wilson's retail locations for merchandise returns, your audit team found that although Wilson had controls to properly record the customer refund in the general ledger, they did not have effective controls in place to ensure that the merchandise returned was properly recorded as inventory in the general ledger at certain locations. Specifically, at 6 of the 13 locations selected for testing, the retail location had not implemented controls to ensure that the merchandise returned was recorded as inventory. In each situation, the lack of controls was attributed to a failure by the retail location's manager to enforce the proper policies and procedures. Your audit team determined that the financial statement exposure from this identified control deficiency approximates $380,000. Overall materiality for the Wilson company audit is $700,000. When your team approached management about the deficiency, Wilson's management believes that their internal audit department presents a strong compensating control because they conduct a detailed audit of a sample of retail locations each year, and as a result, the internal auditors would have likely detected this weakness and corrected the error.

Required:

a. What is the definition of a significant deficiency?

b. What is the definition of a material weakness?

c. Do you believe that Wilson Company has a deficiency, a significant deficiency or a material weakness? Please justify your answer.

Apollo Shoes　　Auditor's Report on the Financial Statements and Internal Controls Over Financial Reporting

You are a recently promoted senior (in charge) auditor for Anderson, Olds, and Watershed and have been assigned to the engagement team of a new audit client, Apollo Shoes Inc. You have been asked to assist in developing the report on the financial statements and internal control over financial reporting (Apollo Shoes is an issuer and subject to PCAOB reporting standards). Detailed instructions, as well as any information that may be impact the auditor's report, can be found in *Connect*.

Index